Ch

& Easter Island

a Lonely Planet travel survival kit

Wayne Bernhardson

Chile & Easter Island

4th edition

Published by
Lonely Planet Publications
Head Office: PO Box 617, Hawthorn, Vic 3122, Australia
Branches: 155 Filbert St, Suite 251, Oakland, CA 94607, USA
                10 Barley Mow Passage, Chiswick, London W4 4PH, UK
                71 bis rue du Cardinal Lemoine, 75005 Paris, France

Printed by
SNP Printing Pte Ltd., Singapore

Photographs by
Wayne Bernhardson   Ted Stevens
Helen Hughes   Michael Sullivan

Front cover: Volcán Corcovado, Galen Rowell
Title page: illustration of an Araucaria tree, Mark Butler

Published
May 1997

Although the author and publisher have tried to make the information as accurate as possible, they accept no responsibility for any loss, injury or inconvenience sustained by any person using this book.

National Library of Australia Cataloguing in Publication Data

Bernhardson, Wayne.
   Chile & Easter Island.

   4th ed.
   Includes index.
   ISBN 0 86442 421 3.

   1. Chile – Guidebooks. 2. Easter Islands - Guidebooks.
   I. Title. (Series: Lonely Planet travel survival kit).

918.30465

Wayne Bernhardson

Born in Fargo, North Dakota, Wayne Bernhardson grew up in Tacoma, Washington, and earned a PhD in geography at the University of California, Berkeley. He has traveled widely in Latin America, and has lived for extended periods in Chile, Argentina and the Falkland (Malvinas) Islands. His other LP credits include *South America on a shoestring*, *Argentina, Uruguay & Paraguay*, *Baja California* and *Rocky Mountain States*. Wayne resides in Oakland, California, with his Alaskan malamute Gardel.

From the Author

Many longtime friends, other individuals and institutions in Chile and elsewhere were exceptionally helpful and hospitable in the process of pulling this all together. My apologies to anyone I've omitted in the last-minute crush.

Many contributors are or were Santiago residents, including Hernán Torres Santibañez (now of Arlington, Virginia), Martín Montalva Paredes of the Universidad de Santiago, Víctor Maldonado and Marisa Blásquez, Eduardo Nuñez Araya of Conaf, Nicole Mintz of Fundación Lahuen, Steve Anderson of Chip News, Alfredo Goecke Sáez of the Corporación de Promoción Turística, Ana María Morales Ferraro of Sernatur, Juan Alarcón Rojas for customs assistance, Elaine Pilz (now of Antofagasta), Thøger Michelsen (now of Nørager, Denmark), David Roberts of the *News Review*, political officer Carlos García Buria of the US Embassy and his predecessor Jack Deasy, Helen Hughes, Derek Mossman of Viajes Apolo, Micole Zarb, Hugo Moreira of Evasión, Yerko Ivelic K of Cascada Expediciones, and José Agustín Olavarría and Claudia Blancaire Rosas of Navimag.

In the Norte Grande, thanks to Sernatur officials Julio Arenas Coloma of Arica, Mario Marroquín Silva of Iquique and Jessica Díaz Castillo, Alberto Bordeu Schwarze of Conaf Arica, and my longtime friends in Parque Nacional Lauca, especially Hernán Rojas Reyes and Germán Blanco. It was also a great pleasure to renew my acquaintance with Conaf's Alejandro Santoro Vargas in Antofagasta. Martin Beeris of Cosmo Andino in San Pedro de Atacama was generous with his time in discussing this rapidly changing area, as was Ana Carmen Mamani Rodríguez of the Municipalidad.

In the Norte Chico, valuable assistance came from Ray Bienert of the US Peace Corps in La Serena, Ted Stevens (formerly of Caldera, now of La Serena), Rodrigo Sugg Pierry of La Serena, Davíd González of CTIO, Alicia Díaz Fraile of Sernatur La Serena, Washington Hernández and Lelia Manterola Cortés of Sernatur Copiapó, and Fernando Bascuñán of Conaf in Copiapó.

Contributors in the Chilean heartland included the exceptionally helpful municipal offices in Viña del Mar and Valparaíso, Antonio Suzarte of Viña del Mar, Doris Sandoval Gutiérrez of Sernatur in Chillán, and Nelson Oyarzo of Sernatur in Concepción.

In the southern lakes region, thanks to the entire staff of ¡Ecole! in Pucón for a great New Year's weekend; special mention to Rick Klein. Félix Ledesma and Eugenio Ruiz of Conaf were especially helpful in updating the entry on Parque Nacional Conguillío. Luis Canales Leyton of Puerto Varas helped improve the coverage of his hometown and its surroundings, as did Gladys Abarzúa of Sernatur Temuco.

In Puerto Montt, special mention goes to Adrian Turner of Travellers, Carolina Morgado E of the Fundación Educación Ciencia y Ecología, and Nancy Vera Leiva of Sernatur. Ramón G Cabrera Ascensio's counsel on customs was a lifesaver. Lili Sheeline, of the US Peace Corps in Parque Nacional Chiloé, was a wonderful host in Cucao.

In Chilean Patagonia, Sernatur officials Gonzalo Sáinz of Punta Arenas, Miguel Angel Muñoz R of Puerto Natales, Gabriela Neira Morales of Coihaique were all most helpful. British consul John C Rees of Punta Arenas helped locate Steve Beldham. Thanks also to Alessandro Marzolo of Aerovías DAP for up-to-date flight information.

On the Argentine side of Tierra del Fuego, Julio César Lovece and the staff of Ushuaia's Dirección de Turismo have done an outstanding job of keeping in touch.

Cherilyn King and Natalie Smith of the Falkland Islands Tourist Board were most helpful in keeping that information current, as was US representative Leo Lebon of Berkeley. Sally Poncet of Beaver Island, Ian and María Strange of Stanley, Gabriel Ceballos and Claudette Anderson of Stanley, and Graham Bound, Janet Robertson and Steve Beldham also made helpful contributions.

In California, special mention goes to Buddy Lander of LanChile in Los Angeles, and all the LP staff in Oakland but especially Caroline Liou. Paul Arundale of Leeds, England, made cycling suggestions no less useful than those he made for Argentina the year before.

In Australia, continuing thanks to Tony and Maureen Wheeler.

From the Publisher

This book was edited in LP's US office by Laini Taylor. Carolyn Hubbard, Don Gates, Sacha Pearson and Leigh Anne Jones shared the proofreading, and Cyndy Johnsen created the maps with help from Alex Guilbert and Scott Noren. Cyndy also managed layout and design, and Hugh D'Andrade, Hayden Foell, Scott Summers and Mark Butler drew the pictures. All this transpired before the watchful eyes of Caroline Liou and Scott Summers.

This Book

The first two editions of *Chile & Easter Island* were written by Alan Samalgalski. The third edition was researched again from scratch, rewritten and considerably expanded by Wayne Bernhardson.

Wayne updated and expanded this fourth edition on the basis of nearly five months' field time, but many independent travelers and Chilean nationals also contributed to an improved book with their correspondence. A complete list of their names appears on page 545.

Warning & Request

Things change – prices go up, schedules change, good places go bad and bad places go bankrupt – nothing stays the same. So if you find things better or worse, recently opened or long since closed, please write and help make the next edition better.

Your letters will be used to help update future editions and, where possible, important changes will also be included in a Stop Press section in reprints.

We greatly appreciate all information that is sent to us by travelers. Back at Lonely Planet we employ a hard-working readers' letters team to sort through the many letters we receive. The best ones will be rewarded with a free copy of the next edition or another Lonely Planet guide if you prefer. We give away lots of books, but, unfortunately, not every letter/postcard receives one.

Contents

INTRODUCTION **11**

FACTS ABOUT CHILE **13**
History 13
Geography & Climate 23
Ecology & Environment 27
Flora & Fauna 28
Government & Politics 34
Economy 37
Population & People 39
Education 39
Arts 40
Society & Conduct 43
Religion 43

FACTS FOR THE VISITOR **45**
Planning 45
Suggested Itineraries 46
Highlights 46
Tourist Offices 47
Visas & Documents 47
Embassies & Consulates 48
Customs 50
Money 50
Post & Communications 52
Addresses 54
Books 55
Newspapers & Magazines 58
Radio & TV 58
Photography & Video 58
Time 59
Electricity 59
Weights & Measures 59
Laundry 59
Health 59
Courses 62
Toilets 62
Women Travelers 63
Gay & Lesbian Travelers 63
Disabled Travelers 63
Senior Travelers 64
Travel with Children 64
Useful Organizations 64
Dangers & Annoyances 65
Legal Matters 66
Business Hours 66
Holidays & Special Events . . . 66
Activities 67
Courses 69
Work 69
Accommodations 70
Food 72
Drinks 74
Entertainment 76
Spectator Sports 77
Things to Buy 77

GETTING THERE & AWAY **78**
Air 78
Land 86
Leaving Chile 90
Tours 90
Warning 91

GETTING AROUND **93**
Air 93
Bus 94
Train 94
Car 95
Bicycle 97
Hitching 98
Ferry 98
Local Transport 99
Tours 100

SANTIAGO **101**
History 101
Orientation 103
Information 105
Walking Tour 111
Things to See 115
Language Courses 123
Organized Tours 124
Special Events 124
Places to Stay 124
Places to Eat 127
Entertainment 131
Spectator Sports 133
Things to Buy 133
Getting There & Away 134
Getting Around 138
Around Santiago **140**
Templo Votivo de Maipú . . . 140
Pomaire 141
Wineries 142
Cajón del Maipo 142
Ski Resorts 144

MIDDLE CHILE **146**
Valparaíso & the
Central Coast **146**
Valparaíso 146
Around Valparaíso 157
Viña del Mar 158
Around Viña del Mar 166
Parque Nacional
La Campana 167
Los Andes 169
Southern Heartland **170**
Rancagua 170
Around Rancagua 173
Curicó 174
Around Curicó 176
Area de Protección
Radal Siete Tazas 178
Talca 178
Around Talca 182
Parque Nacional
Gil de Vilches 182
Chillán 183
Around Chillán 188
Concepción 188
Around Concepción 195
Los Angeles 197
Around Los Angeles 201
Parque Nacional
Laguna del Laja 202
Angol 204
Parque Nacional
Nahuelbuta 205

NORTE GRANDE 207

Arica 209
Around Arica. 219
Putre 220
Parque Nacional Lauca 222
Reserva Nacional
Las Vicuñas. 226
Monumento Natural
Salar de Surire. 226
Pisagua 226
Iquique. 227
Around Iquique 236

Mamiña 239
Reserva Nacional
Pampa del Tamarugal 240
Antofagasta Region 241
Antofagasta 242
Around Antofagasta 249
Tocopilla 251
Taltal 252
Around Taltal 253
Calama. 253
Chuquicamata 258

Around Calama
& Chuquicamata 260
San Pedro de Atacama. 261
Around San Pedro
de Atacama 265
Reserva Nacional
Los Flamencos. 266
El Tatio Geysers 267
Toconao. 267

NORTE CHICO 268

History. 268
Copiapó. 270
Around Copiapó 275
Caldera &
Bahía Inglesa. 276
Around Caldera 278
Chañaral 279

Parque Nacional
Pan de Azúcar 280
Vallenar. 281
Around Vallenar 283
La Serena. 283
Around La Serena 290
Vicuña 291

Around Vicuña 294
Ovalle 295
Around Ovalle. 297
Parque Nacional
Fray Jorge 298
Los Vilos. 299
Pichidangui 301

LA ARAUCANIA & LOS LAGOS 302

History. 302
Temuco 306
Around Temuco. 313
Parque Nacional Tolhuaca . . 313
Parque Nacional
Conguillío 314
Curacautín 317
Around Curacautín 317
Melipeuco 317
Villarrica 317
Pucón. 322
Around Pucón 327
Parque Nacional
Huerquehue 328

Parque Nacional Villarrica . . 329
Lican Ray 330
Coñaripe 332
Panguipulli 332
Choshuenco. 333
Valdivia. 334
Around Valdivia 340
Futrono 340
Llifén 341
Río Bueno 341
Lago Ranco 341
Osorno. 342
Around Osorno. 347
Parque Nacional Puyehue . . . 348

Puerto Octay 351
Las Cascadas. 352
Frutillar 352
Puerto Varas 355
Ensenada 359
Parque Nacional
Vicente Pérez Rosales. 360
Puerto Montt 363
Around Puerto Montt 373
Parque Nacional
Alerce Andino. 374
Hornopirén 375

CHILOE 376

Ancud 378
Dalcahue 382
Castro 383

Achao 388
Around Achao 389
Chonchi 389

Parque Nacional Chiloé. 390
Quellón 393

AISEN & THE CAMINO AUSTRAL 395

Coihaique 399
Reserva Nacional
Coihaique 406
Monumento Natural
Dos Lagunas 406
Parque Nacional
Río Simpson 407
Puerto Chacabuco 407
Parque Nacional
Laguna San Rafael 408
Northern Aisén 410
Villa Amengual 410

Puerto Cisnes. 410
Parque Nacional Queulat. . . . 410
Puerto Puyuhuapi 411
Around Puerto Puyuhuapi . . . 412
La Junta 412
Lago Yelcho 412
Futaleufú 412
Palena 413
Chaitén 413
Around Chaitén 415
Caleta Gonzalo 415
Southern Aisén. 416

Puerto Ingeniero Ibáñez 417
Reserva Nacional
Cerro Castillo 418
Puerto Río Tranquilo. 418
Puerto Guadal 418
Chile Chico 419
Puerto Bertrand 420
Cochrane 420
Caleta Tortel 421
Puerto Yungay. 421

MAGALLANES & TIERRA DEL FUEGO 422

Magallanes 422
Punta Arenas 422
Around Punta Arenas 433
Parque Nacional
Pali Aike 435
Puerto Natales 435
Around Puerto Natales 439
Parque Nacional
Bernardo O'Higgins 440

Parque Nacional
Torres del Paine 440
El Calafate (Argentina) 446
Parque Nacional
Los Glaciares (Argentina) . . . 450
Fitzroy Range (Argentina) . . 452
Tierra del Fuego 454
Porvenir 456
Cerro Sombrero 458

Lago Blanco 458
Puerto Williams 459
Río Grande (Argentina) 459
Around Río Grande 461
Ushuaia (Argentina) 462
Around Ushuaia 469
Parque Nacional
Tierra del Fuego 469

ARCHIPIÉLAGO JUAN FERNANDEZ 472

History 472
Geography & Climate 474
Flora 476
Fauna 476

Books 477
Getting There & Away 477
Getting Around 477
San Juan Bautista 478

Parque Nacional
Juan Fernández 480

EASTER ISLAND (RAPA NUI) 482

History 482
Geography 491
Flora & Fauna 492
Climate 492

Rapa Nui Stonework 492
Books 496
Maps 498
Getting There & Away 498

Getting Around 498
Hanga Roa 500
Parque Nacional
Rapa Nui 505

FALKLAND ISLANDS (ISLAS MALVINAS) 512

Facts about the Islands 512
Facts for the Visitor 515

Getting There & Away 518
Stanley 519

Around Stanley 521
Camp 522

APPENDICES 526

Climate Charts 526
Online Services 527

Spanish Phrasebook 528
Glossary 533

INDEX 539

Maps 539
Text 539

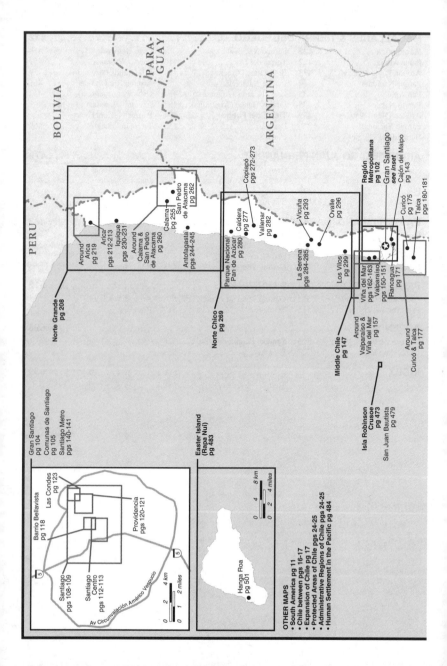

PERU

BOLIVIA

PARA-
GUAY

ARGENTINA

**Norte Grande
pg 208**

Around
Arica
pg 219

Arica
pgs 212-213

Iquique
pgs 230-231

Around
Calama &
San Pedro
de Atacama
pg 260

Calama
pg 255

San Pedro
de Atacama
Lpg 262

Antofagasta
pgs 244-245

**Norte Chico
pg 269**

Parque Nacional
Pan de Azúcar
pg 280

Copiapó
pgs 272-273

Caldera
pg 277

Vallenar
pg 282

Vicuña
pg 293

Ovalle
pg 296

La Serena
pgs 284-285

Los Vilos
pg 299

**Middle Chile
pg 147**

Around
Valparaíso &
Viña del Mar
pg 157

Viña del Mar
pgs 162-163

Valparaíso
pgs 150-151

Rancagua
pg 171

Around
Curicó & Talca
pg 177

**Región
Metropolitana
pg 102**

Gran Santiago
see inset

Cajón del Maipo
pg 143

Curicó
pg 175

Talca
pgs 180-181

Gran Santiago
pg 104

Comunas de Santiago
pg 105

Santiago Metro
pgs 140-141

Barrio Bellavista
pg 118

Las Condes
pg 123

Providencia
pgs 120-121

Santiago
pgs 108-109

Santiago
Centro
pgs 112-113

Av Circunvalación Américo Vespucio

0   2   4 km
0   1   2 miles

**Easter Island
(Rapa Nui)
pg 483**

Hanga Roa
pg 501

0   4   8 km
0   2   4 miles

**Isla Robinson
Crusoe
pg 473**

San Juan Bautista
pg 479

OTHER MAPS
• South America pg 11
• Chile between pgs 16-17
• Expansion of Chile pg 17
• Protected Areas of Chile pgs 24-25
• Administrative Regions of Chile pgs 24-25
• Human Settlement in the Pacific pg 484

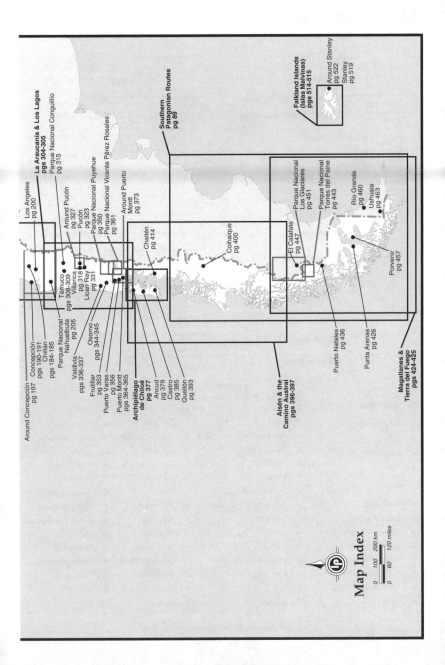

Map Index

Around Concepción pg 197

Los Angeles pg 200

Concepción pgs 190–191

Chillán pgs 184–185

Parque Nacional Nahuelbuta pg 205

Temuco pgs 308–309

Valdivia pgs 336–337

Frutillar pg 353

Osorno pgs 344–345

Puerto Varas pg 356

Puerto Montt pgs 364–365

Archipiélago de Chiloé pg 377

Ancud pg 379

Castro pg 385

Quellón pg 393

La Araucanía & Los Lagos pgs 304–305

Parque Nacional Conguillío pg 315

Around Pucón pg 327

Pucón pg 323

Villarrica pg 318

Lican Ray pg 331

Parque Nacional Puyehue pg 350

Parque Nacional Vicente Pérez Rosales pg 361

Around Puerto Montt pg 373

Chaitén pg 414

Southern Patagonian Routes pg 89

Coihaique pg 400

Aisén & the Camino Austral pgs 396–397

Parque Nacional Los Glaciares pg 451

Parque Nacional Torres del Paine pg 443

El Calafate pg 447

Puerto Natales pg 436

Punta Arenas pg 426

Río Grande pg 460

Ushuaia pg 463

Porvenir pg 457

Magallanes & Tierra del Fuego pgs 424–425

Falkland Islands (Islas Malvinas) pgs 514–515

Around Stanley pg 522

Stanley pg 519

0   100   200 km
0   60   120 miles

Map Legend

BOUNDARIES

- - ·- - ·- - ·- - ·- International Boundary

- - ··- - ··- - ··- - Región/Provincial Boundary

AREA FEATURES

Park

NATIONAL PARK   National Park

National/State Forest

Reservation

HYDROGRAPHIC FEATURES

Water

Coastline

Beach

River, Waterfall

Swamp, Spring

ROUTES

Freeway

Primary Road

Secondary Road

Tertiary Road

Unpaved Road

Trail

Ferry Route

Railway, Train Station

Mass Transit Line & Station

ROUTE SHIELDS

(5) Ruta Nacional	(115) Highway	Chile
(RN 12) Ruta Nacional	(RP 65) Ruta Provincial	Argentina
(1) Red Fundamental	(701) Red Complementaria	Bolivia
(1) Carreteras Sistema Nacional	(113) Carreteras Sistema Departmental	Peru

SYMBOLS

✪ **NATIONAL CAPITAL**	✈ Airfield	⛽ Gas Station	)(Pass
◉ **Región Capital**	✗ Airport	⸸ Golf Course	⼌ Picnic Area
● **City**	∴ Archaeological Site, Ruins	✪ Hospital, Clinic	★ Police Station
● City, Small	◉ Bank, ATM	❶ Information	▭ Pool
● Town	✕ Battlefield	⚲ Lighthouse	✉ Post Office
	⟲ Beach	☀ Lookout	⤳ Shipwreck
	✦⟀ Border Crossing	⎰ Moai	❖ Shopping Mall
▪ Hotel, B&B	⬤ Bus Station, Bus Stop	▲ Monument	⚔ Skiing, Downhill
⛺ Campground	⊟ Cathedral	▲ Mountain	⚵ Skiing, Cross-country
⌂ Hostel	⌒ Cave	🏛 Museum	🏛 Stately Home
⌸ RV Park	✝ Church	✔ Music, Live	☎ Telephone
⌂ Shelter, Refugio	◒ Embassy, Consulate	← One-Way Street	▣ Tomb, Mausoleum
▾ Restaurant	⟯ Foot Bridge	△ Observatory	⚑ Trailhead
⛴ Bar (Place to Drink)	🏛 Fort	▲ Park	⚘ Winery
⚎ Cafe	⁂ Garden	℗ Parking	🐾 Zoo

Note: Not all symbols displayed above appear in this book.

Introduction

On South America's Pacific coast, stretching from the tropics nearly to the Antarctic, Chile is a string bean country rarely wider than 180 km (111 miles). For nearly all its length, the imposing Andes mountains isolate it from Bolivia and Argentina, but it also shares a short border with Peru in the Atacama desert. Its 4300-km (2666-mile) coastline features a great variety of environments: the nearly waterless Atacama, the Mediterranean central valley, a mountainous but temperate lakes district, and Patagonia's spectacular alpine glaciers and fjords, where national parks like Torres del Paine and Queulat offer some of the world's finest trekking and fishing. Even from popular Pacific beaches, the massive Andean crest is almost always within sight; surfing and skiing on the same day is not beyond possibility.

For nearly two decades, Chile was an international pariah because of the bloody 1973 coup that took the life of Socialist Salvador Allende, the constitutional president, and resulted in his replacement by military dictator General Augusto Pinochet. Since Pinochet's rejection by Chilean voters in a referendum and the return to constitutional government in 1989, the country has become an increasingly popular destination. General Pinochet's regime was a remarkably durable anomaly in Chilean history, where military intervention has been the exception rather than the rule since the country's independence from Spain in the early 19th century.

Chile is a mestizo country, of mixed European and indigenous extraction, and the indigenous tradition is still visible and viable in several parts of the country. In the

desert north, once part of the Inca empire, are important archaeological sites. Aymara Indians still farm the valleys and terraces of the Andean foothills and tend flocks of llamas and alpacas on the high plains of the altiplano.

South of the Chilean heartland in the central valley, hundreds of thousands of Mapuche Indians inhabit communities whose symbolic status in Chilean life exceeds their political and economic significance. Nearly into the 20th century, the Mapuche maintained an effective and heroic resistance to the southward advance of Chilean rule, earning a grudging respect from the expansionist Chilean state. Cities like Temuco and Osorno are proud of their indigenous heritage.

For visitors with a taste for the exotic or romantic, Chile has two unique insular possessions. Distant Easter Island (Rapa Nui), with its giant stylized statues, has long attracted explorers, adventurers, anthropologists and archaeologists. Tourist access is better than ever, and its Polynesian hospitality is an unexpected bonus. Nearer the mainland, the Juan Fernández archipelago was the refuge of marooned Scotsman Alexander Selkirk, whose solitary experiences inspired Daniel Defoe's classic novel *Robinson Crusoe*. It is also a national park, as its many endemic plant species have made it a World Biosphere Reserve.

Chile's people are remarkably friendly and hospitable to foreigners. No longer a place to avoid because of its turbulent recent history, the country is drawing increasing numbers of travelers whose itineraries once included only Peru, Bolivia and Argentina. Its tremendous geographic diversity and surprising cultural variety have made it an important destination in its own right.

Facts about Chile

HISTORY
Indigenous Cultures

When Europeans first arrived in present-day Chile in the 16th century, they encountered a variety of native peoples whose customs and economies differed greatly. While politically subject to the Incas, most cultures in the region predated the lords of Cuzco by centuries or even millennia. In the canyons of the desert north, sedentary Aymara farmers cultivated maize in transverse valleys irrigated by the rivers which descended from the Andes; at higher elevations, they grew potatoes and tended flocks of llamas and alpacas. To the south, beyond the Río Loa, Atacameño peoples practiced a similar livelihood, while Chango fisherfolk occupied coastal areas from Arica almost to the Río Choapa, south of present-day La Serena. Diaguita Indians inhabited the interior of this latter region, which comprises the drainages of the Copiapó, Huasco and Elqui Rivers.

Inca rule barely touched the central valley and the forests of the south, where Araucanian (Picunche and Mapuche) Indians fiercely resisted incursions from the north. The Picunche lived in permanent agricultural settlements, while the Mapuche, who practiced shifting cultivation, were more mobile and much more difficult for the Incas, and later the Spaniards, to subdue. Several groups closely related to the Mapuche – the Pehuenche, Huilliche and Puelche – lived in the southern lakes region, while Cunco Indians fished and farmed on the island of Chiloé and along the shores of the gulfs of Reloncaví and Ancud. Not until the late 19th century did the descendants of Europeans establish a permanent presence beyond the Río Biobío.

South of the Chilean mainland, numerous small populations of Indians subsisted through hunting and fishing – the Chono, Qawashqar (Alacalufe), Yamaná (Yahgan), Tehuelche and Ona (Selknam). These isolated archipelagic peoples long avoided contact with Europeans, but are now extinct or nearly so.

The Spanish Invasion

In 1494, the papal Treaty of Tordesillas ratified the Spanish-Portuguese division of the Americas, granting all territory west of Brazil to Spain, which rapidly consolidated its formal authority and, by the mid-16th century, controlled most of an area extending from Florida and Mexico to central Chile. In the same period, they founded most of South America's important cities, including Lima, Santiago, Asunción and La Paz.

Spain's successful invasion of the Americas was accomplished by groups of adventurers, lowlifes and soldiers-of-fortune against whom the colonists of Australia's Botany Bay penal colony look like exemplary citizens – Diego de Almagro, one of the early explorers of Chile and northern Argentina, originally arrived in Panama after fleeing a Spanish murder charge. Few in number (Francisco Pizarro took Peru with only 180 men), the conquerors were determined and ruthless, exploiting factionalism among Indian groups and frightening native peoples with their horses, vicious dogs and firearms, but their greatest ally was infectious disease to which native American peoples lacked immunity.

Before Pizarro's assassination in 1541, he assigned the task of conquering Chile to Pedro de Valdivia. After some difficulty in recruitment (Almagro's earlier expedition had suffered terribly, especially in its winter crossing from Argentina of the bitterly cold and nearly waterless Puna de Atacama), Valdivia's expedition left Peru in 1540, crossed the desert and reached Chile's fertile Mapocho valley in 1541, subduing local Indians and founding the city of Santiago on February 12. Only six

Pedro de Valdivia

months later, the Indians counterattacked, destroyed the city and nearly wiped out the settlers' supplies. The Spaniards held out and six years later their numbers had grown to nearly 500 with assistance and reinforcements from Peru. Meanwhile, they founded settlements at La Serena and Valparaíso, but Valdivia also worked southward, founding Concepción, Valdivia and Villarrica. Despite his death at the battle of Tucapel in 1553, at the hands of Mapuche forces led by the famous *caciques* (chiefs) Caupolicán and Lautaro, Valdivia had laid the groundwork for a new society.

Colonial Society

Ironically, throughout the Americas, the structure of indigenous societies more strongly influenced the economic and political structure of early colonial life than the directives of European authorities. The Spaniards' primary goal was the acquisition of gold and silver, and they ruthlessly appropriated precious metals through outright robbery when possible, and by other no less brutal means when necessary. El Dorado, the legendary city of gold, proved elusive, but the Spaniards soon realized the true wealth of the New World consisted of the surprisingly large Indian populations of Mexico, Peru and other lands.

Disdaining physical labor themselves, the Spaniards exploited the indigenous populations of the New World through mechanisms like the *encomienda*, best translated as 'entrustment,' by which the Crown granted an individual Spaniard *(encomendero)* rights to Indian labor and tribute in a particular village or area. Institutions such as the Catholic Church also held encomiendas. In theory, Spanish legislation required the encomendero to reciprocate with instruction in the Spanish language and the Catholic religion, but in practice imperial administration was inadequate to ensure compliance and avoid the worst abuses. Spanish overseers worked Indians mercilessly in the mines as well as extracting the maximum in agricultural produce.

In the most densely populated parts of the Americas, some encomenderos became extraordinarily wealthy, but the encomienda system failed when Indian populations declined rapidly, not so much from overwork and physical punishment as from epidemic disease. Isolated for at least 10,000 years from Old World diseases, the Indians could not withstand the onslaught of smallpox, influenza, typhus and other such killers – in some parts of the New World, these diseases reduced the native population by more than 95%.

In Chile, the encomienda was most important in the irrigated valleys of the desert north (then part of Peru), where the population was large and sedentary – the most highly organized Indian peoples were the easiest to subdue and control, since they were accustomed to similar forms of exploitation. In hierarchical states like the Inca empire, the Spaniards easily replaced established local authority.

In central Chile, the Spaniards also established dominance, but the semi-sedentary and nomadic peoples of the south mounted vigorous resistance, and even into the late 19th century the area was unsafe for white settlers. Crossing the Andes, the

Mapuche had tamed feral horses which had multiplied rapidly on the fine pastures of the Argentine pampas; they soon became expert riders, aiding their mobility and ability to strike.

Even where Spanish supremacy went unchallenged, Indians outnumbered Spaniards. Since few women accompanied the early settlers, Spanish men, especially of the lower classes, had both formal and informal relationships with Indian women; the resulting children, of mixed Spanish and Indian parentage, were known as *mestizos* and soon outnumbered the Indian population as many natives died through epidemics, forced labor abuses and warfare. As the Indian population declined, encomiendas became nearly worthless, and Spaniards sought new economic alternatives.

Rise of the Latifundio

In Chile, unlike many other parts of Spanish America, the encomienda became highly correlated with land ownership; despite the Crown's disapproval, Chile was too remote for adequate imperial oversight. Valdivia had rewarded his followers with enormous grants, some valleys stretching from the Andes to the Pacific. More than anywhere else in the Americas, the system of control resembled the great feudal estates of Valdivia's homeland of Extremadura in Spain. Such estates *(latifundios)*, many intact as late as the 1960s, became an enduring feature of Chilean agriculture and the dominant force in Chilean society.

As the encomienda system declined, Chile's neo-aristocracy had to look elsewhere for its labor force. The country's growing mestizo population, systematically excluded from land ownership, provided the solution. Landless and 'vagrant,' these ostensible 'Spaniards' soon attached themselves as *inquilinos* (tenant farmers) to the large rural estates, which evolved from livestock *estancias* into agricultural *haciendas* or, as they became more commonly known in Chile, *fundos*.

In becoming inquilinos, laborers and their families became personally dependent on the *hacendado* (master) in exchange for certain rights. Paying little or no rent, they could occupy a shack on the estate, graze livestock on its more remote sections, and cultivate a patch of land for household use. In return, they provided labor during annual *rodeos* (cattle roundups) and watched out for their master's interests. American geographer George McCutcheon McBride found this relationship of 'man and master' endured well into the 20th century and permeated all aspects of Chilean society:

There was a landholding aristocracy, well educated, far-traveled, highly cultured, in full control of the national life; and, quite apart from them, a lower class, often spoken of with mixed disdain and affection as the *rotos* (ragged ones), constituting the fixed tenantry of the rural estates. This distinction, clearly an agrarian one in its origin, was carried into the social structure of the entire people. It gave its cast to the nation.

Other groups gave their cast to the nation as well. Even though the large estates remained intact, they did not always remain in the same hands. Later immigrants, especially Basques, became a major influence from the late 17th century to the end of the colonial era. Surnames like Eyzaguirre, Urrutia and Larraín became prominent in Chilean commerce and those families purchased many landed estates, as well as those confiscated from the expelled Jesuits and offered at public auction. Adopting the pseudo-aristocratic values of the early landed gentry, Basque families have remained important in Chilean politics, society and business.

In colonial times, mining and business brought greater wealth than land. Only after political independence, having broken the mercantile links with imperial Spain, did Chile's agricultural economy begin to flourish.

The Independence Movements

Within a few decades of Columbus's Caribbean landing, Spain possessed an empire twice the size of Europe, stretching from California to Cape Horn. Yet the empire disintegrated rapidly in less than two decades; by the late 1820s, only Puerto Rico and Cuba remained in Spanish hands.

Many factors contributed to the rise of Latin American independence movements. One was the emergence of the *criollo* (creole) class, American-born Spaniards, who soon distinguished themselves from the Iberians. In every Latin American country, the development of a definable American identity increased the desire for self-government.

Of equal importance, influential criollo merchants resented Spain's rigid mercantile trade system. To facilitate tax collection, Madrid decreed that all trade to the mother country must pass overland through Panama to the Caribbean and Havana, rather than directly by ship from the port of Valparaíso. This extraordinarily cumbersome system hampered the commerce of Chile and other colonies, and eventually cost Spain its empire.

Spain's own stagnant economy could not provide the manufactured goods which the American colonies demanded. Spain also had to contend with interloping European countries, as Britain, Holland and France all acquired minor bases in the Caribbean and elsewhere in the New World. By the late 18th century the British had obtained trade concessions from Spain and were surreptitiously encouraging criollo political aspirations.

Several other factors contributed, directly and indirectly, to the independence drive which began between 1808 and 1810: the successful North American rebellion against England, the overthrow of the French monarchy, Napoleon's invasion of Spain (which disrupted communications between Spain and America and allowed the colonies a period of temporary autonomy), and European intellectual trends. The fact that colonial armies consisted mainly of criollos and mestizos, rather than troops from Spain, made it much easier to challenge Spanish authority.

The Revolutionary Wars

During colonial times, the formal jurisdiction of the Audiencia de Chile stretched roughly from present-day Chañaral in the north to Puerto Aisén in the south, and also encompassed the trans-Andean Cuyo region of modern Argentina, comprising the provinces of Mendoza, San Juan and San Luis. The Audiencia was an administrative subdivision of the much larger Viceroyalty of Peru, the capital of which, Lima, was South America's most important city. But Chile was distant from Lima, and developed in near isolation from Peru, with a very distinct identity from its northern neighbor.

Independence movements throughout South America united to expel Spain from the continent by the 1820s. From Venezuela, a criollo army under Simón Bolívar fought its way across the Andes to the Pacific and then south towards Peru. José de San Martín's Ejército de los Andes (Army of the Andes) – nearly a third of them liberated slaves – marched over the cordillera from Argentina into Chile, occupied Santiago and sailed north to Lima.

San Martín's army also included numerous Chileans who had fled the reimposition of Spanish colonial rule after the Napoleonic Wars. The Argentine general appointed Bernardo O'Higgins second-in-command of his forces. O'Higgins, the illegitimate son of an Irishman who had served the Spaniards as Viceroy of Peru, became Supreme Director of the new Chilean republic. San Martín helped drive Spain from Peru, transporting his army in ships either seized from the Spaniards or purchased from Britons or North Americans. British and North American merchants also financed the purchase of arms and ammunition, knowing that expulsion of the Spaniards would create new commercial opportunities. Scotsman Thomas Cochrane, a colorful former Royal Navy officer, founded and commanded Chile's navy.

The Early Republic

Spanish administrative divisions provided the framework for the political geography of the new South American republics. At independence, Chile was but a fraction of its present size, consisting of the *intendencias*

WAYNE BERNHARDSON
Parque Nacional Torres del Paine

HELEN HUGHES
Young Pehuenche woman with Araucaria nuts

HELEN HUGHES
'La Portada' natural arch, symbol of Region II, near Antofagasta

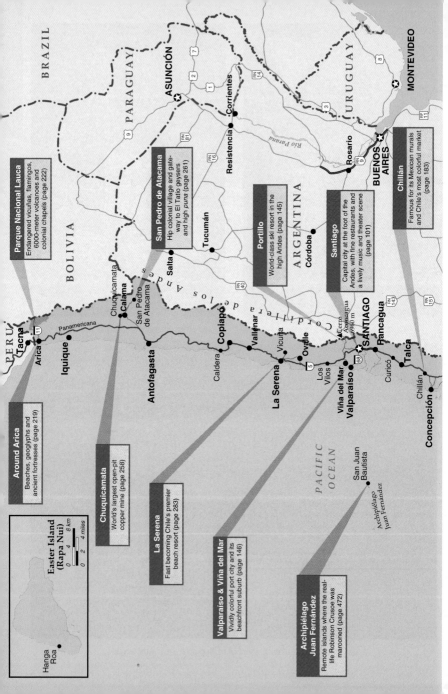

Around Arica
Beaches, geoglyphs and ancient fortresses (page 219)

Parque Nacional Lauca
Endangered vicuñas, flamingos, 6000-meter volcanoes and colonial chapels (page 222)

San Pedro de Atacama
Hip colonial village and gateway to El Tatio geysers and high *puna* (page 261)

Chuquicamata
World's largest open-pit copper mine (page 258)

La Serena
Fast becoming Chile's premier beach resort (page 283)

Portillo
World-class ski resort in the high Andes (page 145)

Valparaíso & Viña del Mar
Vividly colorful port city and its beachfront suburb (page 146)

Santiago
Capital city at the foot of the Andes, with fine restaurants and a lively music and theater scene (page 101)

Chillán
Famous for its Mexican murals and Chile's most colorful market (page 183)

Archipiélago Juan Fernández
Remote islands where the real-life Robinson Crusoe was marooned (page 472)

Easter Island (Rapa Nui)
0   2   4 miles
0   4   8 km

Hanga Roa

BRAZIL

PARAGUAY

ASUNCIÓN

Corrientes

Resistencia

Rosario

URUGUAY

MONTEVIDEO

BUENOS AIRES

Río Paraná

BOLIVIA

Chuquicamata
Calama
San Pedro de Atacama
Salta

ARGENTINA

Tucumán

Córdoba

Cordillera de los Andes

PERU
Tacna
Arica

Iquique

Panamericana

Antofagasta

Caldera
Copiapó
Vallenar
Vicuña
La Serena
Ovalle
Los Vilos

Cerro Aconcagua 6960 m

SANTIAGO

Viña del Mar
Valparaíso

Rancagua

Curicó
Talca

Chillán

Concepción

PACIFIC OCEAN

San Juan Bautista

Archipiélago Juan Fernández

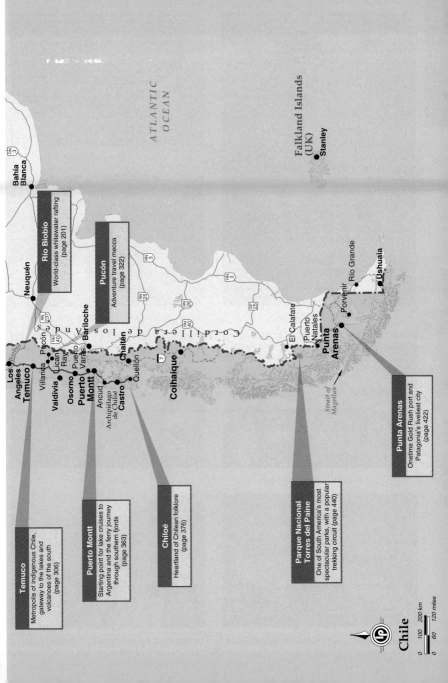

ATLANTIC OCEAN

Falkland Islands (UK)
• Stanley

Río Biobío
World-class whitewater rafting (page 201)

Pucón
Adventure travel mecca (page 322)

Bahía Blanca

Neuquén

Los Angeles
Temuco
Villarica
Licán Ray
Pucón
Valdivia
Osorno
Puerto Varas
Puerto Montt
Ancud
Archipiélago de Chiloé
Castro
Quellón
Chaitén

Bariloche

Cordillera de los Andes

Coihaique

El Calafate
Puerto Natales

Strait of Magellan

Porvenir
Punta Arenas
Río Grande
Ushuaia

Temuco
Metropolis of indigenous Chile, gateway to the lakes and volcanoes of the south (page 306)

Puerto Montt
Starting point for lake cruises to Argentina and the ferry journey through southern fjords (page 363)

Chiloé
Heartland of Chilean folklore (page 376)

Parque Nacional Torres del Paine
One of South America's most spectacular parks, with a popular trekking circuit (page 440)

Punta Arenas
Onetime Gold Rush port and Patagonia's liveliest city (page 422)

0   100   200 km
0   60   120 miles

Chile

Mapuche woman in Cañete

Patricio

Aymara couple, Parinacota, PN Lauca

Upper-class huasos, Santiago

Patriotic Chileans

Aymara boy, Chucuyo, Parque Nacional Lauca

Mapuche women in their traditional dress

(administrative units of the Spanish Empire) of Santiago and Concepción, sharing ambiguous boundaries with Bolivia in the north, Argentina to the east, and the hostile Mapuche nation south of the Río Biobío. Chile lost the important trans-Andean region of Cuyo to the Provincias Unidas del Río de la Plata (United Provinces of the River Plate), forerunner of modern Argentina.

Although other Latin American countries emerged from the wars in severe economic difficulties, Chile quickly achieved a degree of political stability, which permitted rapid development of agriculture, mining, industry and commerce. Regional quarrels were far less serious and violent than they were, for example, in Argentina. Despite social and economic cleavages, the population was relatively homogeneous and less afflicted by racial problems than most other Latin American states. The country was well situated to take advantage of international economic trends, as the port of Valparaíso became an important outlet for Chilean wheat, which satisfied the unprecedented demand of the California Gold Rush.

O'Higgins dominated Chilean politics for five years after formal independence in 1818, enacting political, social, religious and educational reforms, but the landowning elite that first supported him soon objected to increased taxes, abolition of titles and limitations on the inheritance of landed estates. Pressured by military forces allied with the aristocracy, he resigned in 1823 and went into exile in Peru. He died there in 1842, never having returned to his homeland.

Apart from deposing the Spaniards, political independence did not alter the structure of Chilean society, which was dominated by large landowners. The embodiment of landowning interests was Diego Portales, a businessman who, as Interior Minister, was the country's de facto dictator until his execution after an uprising in 1837. His custom-drawn constitution centralized power in Santiago, and established Roman Catholicism as the state religion. It also limited suffrage to literate and propertied adult males, and established indirect elections for the presidency and the Senate; only the lower Chamber of Deputies was chosen directly by voters. Portales' constitution lasted, with some changes, until 1925.

Territorial Expansion

At independence, Chile was a small, compact country whose northern limit was the southern border of the present-day region of Antofagasta, and whose southern limit was the Río Biobío. From the

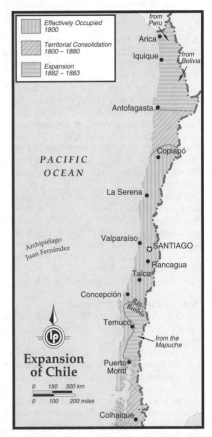

Expansion of Chile

mid-19th century, railroad construction began to revolutionize internal transport. Military triumphs over Peru and Bolivia in the War of the Pacific (1879-1883) and treaties with the Mapuche Indians (from 1881) incorporated the nitrate-rich Atacama and temperate southern territories under Chilean authority. At the same time, however, Chile had to abandon its claims to most of enormous, sparsely populated Patagonia to Argentina.

Santiago's intervention in the Atacama, ostensibly to protect the interests of Chilean nationals laboring in the nitrate fields, proved a bonanza. Just as guano financed Peruvian independence, so nitrates brought prosperity to Chile, or at least to certain sectors of Chilean society. British, North American and German investors supplied most of the capital.

Ever since the California Gold Rush, Valparaíso had been the first Pacific port-of-call on the Cape Horn route between Europe and North America. Soon the nitrate ports of Antofagasta and Iquique also became important in international commerce, until the opening of the Panama Canal nearly eliminated traffic around the Horn, and the development of petroleum-based fertilizers made mineral nitrates obsolete.

Chile also sought a broader Pacific presence, and Chilean vessels sailed to Australia, Asia and Polynesia. Extremists even advocated annexation of the Philippines, still under Spanish control at the time. Chile's only imperial possession, however, was tiny, remote Easter Island (Isla de Pascua or Rapa Nui), annexed in 1888.

Reforms under Balmaceda
Chile emerged from the War of the Pacific considerably enriched by the Atacama's nitrates and, later, copper. Mining expansion created a new working class, as well as a class of nouveaux riches, both of whom challenged the political power of the landowning oligarchy.

The first political figure to tackle the dilemma of Chile's maldistributed wealth and power was President José Manuel Balmaceda, elected in 1886. Balmaceda's administration undertook major public works projects, expanding the rail network and building new roads, bridges and docks, extending telegraph lines and postal services, and improving hospitals and schools.

Balmaceda's policies met resistance from a conservative Congress, which in 1890 rejected his budget, voted to depose him, and appointed Naval Commander Jorge Montt to head a provisional government. More than 10,000 Chileans died in the ensuing civil war, in which Montt's navy controlled the country's ports and eventually defeated the government despite army support for Balmaceda. After several months' asylum in the Argentine embassy, Balmaceda shot himself to death.

Although weakening the presidential system, Balmaceda's immediate successors continued many of his public works projects and also opened Congress to popular rather than indirect elections. Major reform, though, waited until after WWII.

The 20th Century
Despite economic hardship due to a declining nitrate industry, the election of President Arturo Alessandri Palma was a hopeful sign for the Chilean working class. To reduce the power of the landed oligarchy, he proposed greater political autonomy for the provinces, and land and income taxes to finance social benefits to improve working conditions, public health, education and welfare. Congressional conservatives obstructed these reforms, though, and army opposition forced Alessandri's resignation in 1924.

For several years, the dictatorial General Carlos Ibáñez del Campo occupied the presidency and other positions of power, but misguided or miscarried economic policies (exacerbated by global depression) led to widespread opposition, forcing him into Argentine exile in 1931.

After Ibáñez's ouster, Chilean political parties realigned. Several leftist groups briefly imposed a 'Socialist Republic' and merged to form the Socialist Party. Splits between Stalinists and Trotskyites divided the Communist Party, while splinter groups from existing radical and reformist parties created a bewildering mix of new political organizations. For most of the 1930s and 1940s the democratic left dominated politics, and government intervention in the economy through Corfo, the state development corporation, became increasingly important.

Meanwhile, the US role in the Chilean economy also grew steadily, since German investment had declined after WWI and the invention of synthetic nitrates undercut British economic influence. In the first two decades of the 20th century, North American companies had gained control of the copper mines, now the cornerstone of the Chilean economy. WWII augmented the demand for Chilean copper, promoting economic growth even as Chile remained neutral in the conflict.

The Politics of Land Reform

In the 1920s as much as 75% of Chile's rural population still depended on haciendas that controlled 80% of the country's prime agricultural land. Inquilinos remained at the mercy of landowners for access to land, housing and subsistence. Their votes belonged to landowners, who used them to influence Congress and maintain the existing system of land tenure.

To some degree, the Alessandri government avoided antagonizing the landed elite, partly because urban leftists pressed for lower food prices and restrictions on exports of agricultural produce. Controls kept food prices artificially low, pleasing urban consumers but also satisfying landowners who could maintain control over their land and workers, and thus their influence.

As protected industry expanded and the government promoted public works, employment increased and the lot of urban workers improved. That of rural workers, however, deteriorated rapidly; real wages fell, forcing day laborers to the cities in search of work. Inquilinos suffered reduced land allotments, supplies of seed, fertilizer and other assistance, as well as rights to graze animals, and had to supply

the landowner more labor. Given abundant labor, haciendas had little incentive to modernize and production stagnated, a situation that changed little until the 1960s.

In 1952, former dictator General Carlos Ibáñez del Campo won the presidency as an authoritarian but 'apolitical' candidate, largely because of widespread disenchantment with predecessor Gabriel González Videla and political parties in general. Surprisingly, Ibáñez tried to curtail the political power of landowners by reducing their control over the votes of their tenants and laborers; he also revoked an earlier law banning the Communist Party, but his government faltered in the face of high inflation and partisan politicking.

In 1958, Socialist Salvador Allende headed a new leftist coalition known as FRAP (Frente de Acción Popular, Popular Action Front), while Jorge Alessandri, son of Arturo Alessandri, represented a coalition between the conservative and liberal parties. Eduardo Frei Montalva represented the recently formed Democracia Cristiana (Christian Democrats), a reformist party whose goals resembled FRAP's but whose philosophical basis was Catholic humanism.

Alessandri won the election with less than 32% of the vote, while Allende managed 29% and Frei 21%, the best showing ever by a Christian Democrat. An opposition Congress forced Alessandri to accept modest land reform legislation, beginning a decade's battle with the haciendas. Alessandri's term saw little concrete progress in this matter, but the new laws provided a legal basis for expropriation of large estates.

The Christian Democratic Period

The 1964 presidential election was a choice between Allende and Frei, who also drew support from conservative groups who detested the leftist physician. During the campaign, both FRAP and the Christian Democrats promised agrarian reform, supported rural unionization and promised an end to the hacienda system. Frei won with 56% as Allende, undermined by leftist factionalism, polled only 39%.

Genuinely committed to social transformation, the Christian Democrats attempted to control inflation, improve the balance of payments, implement agrarian reform, and improve public health, education and social services. Their policies, however, threatened both the traditional elite's privileges and the radical left's working class support. Fearful of losing their influence, the FRAP coalition urged faster and more radical action. According to Chilean analyst César Caviedes, the 1964 election marked a shift from personalism to ideology in Chilean politics.

The Christian Democrats had other difficulties. In the last years of Jorge Alessandri's presidency, the economy had declined and limited opportunities in the countryside drove the dispossessed to the cities, where spontaneous squatter settlements or *callampas* ('mushrooms') seemed to spring up overnight. As the Christian Democrats inherited these problems, one common response was to attack the visible export sector, dominated by US interests; Frei advocated 'Chileanization' of the copper industry (getting rid of foreign investors in favor of Chileans), while Allende and his backers supported 'nationalization' (placing the industry under state control).

The Christian Democrats also faced challenges from violent groups like the MIR (Movimiento de Izquierda Revolucionario, Leftist Revolutionary Movement), which had begun among upper-middle-class students in Concepción, a southern university town and important industrial center. MIR's activism appealed to coal miners, textile workers and other urban laborers who formed the allied Frente de Trabajadores Revolucionarios (Revolutionary Workers Front); it also agitated among peasants who longed for land reform. Other leftist groups also supported strikes and land seizures by Mapuche Indians and rural laborers.

Too slow to appease leftists, Frei's reforms were too rapid for the conservative National Party and even for some Christian Democrats. Despite improved living conditions for many rural workers and impressive gains in education and public health, increasing inflation, dependence on foreign markets and capital, and inequitable distribution of wealth continued to plague the country. The Christian Democrats could not satisfy rising expectations in an increasingly militant and polarized society.

Allende's Rise to Power

As the presidential election approached in 1970, the new leftist coalition UP (Unidad Popular, Popular Unity), chose Allende as its candidate. The UP's radical program included nationalization of mines, banks and insurance companies, plus expropriation and redistribution of large landholdings.

The other major candidates were Christian Democrat Radomiro Tomic (too left-wing for conservatives) and aged Jorge Alessandri, standing for the National Party. In one of Chile's closest elections ever, Allende won a plurality of 36%, while Alessandri drew 35% and Tomic 28%. Under the constitution, if no candidate

Salvador Allende

obtained an absolute majority, Congress had to confirm the result and could in theory choose the runner-up, although by custom it had never done so. Since no party had a congressional majority, the Christian Democrats pressured Allende for constitutional guarantees to preserve the democratic process, in return for their support. After agreeing to these guarantees, Allende assumed the presidency in October 1970.

Allende's own multi-party coalition of Socialists, Communists and Radicals disagreed on the new government's objectives. Lacking any real electoral mandate, he faced an opposition Congress and a suspicious US government, under President Nixon and Secretary of State Henry Kissinger, and right-wing extremists even advocated his overthrow by violent means.

Allende's economic program, accomplished by evading rather than confronting Congress, included state takeover of many private enterprises and massive income redistribution. By increasing government spending, the new president expected to stimulate demand and encourage private enterprise to increase production and reduce unemployment, to bring the country out of recession. This worked briefly, but apprehensive businessmen and landowners, worried over expropriation and nationalization, sold off stock and disposed of farm machinery and livestock. Industrial production nose-dived, leading to shortages, hyperinflation, and black marketeering.

Peasants, frustrated with an agrarian reform which favored collectives of inquilinos over sharecroppers and *afuerinos* (outside laborers), seized land, and agricultural production fell. The government had to use scarce foreign currency to import food.

Chilean politics grew increasingly polarized and confrontational, as many of Allende's supporters resented his indirect approach to transformation of the state and its economy. MIR intensified its guerrilla activities, while stories circulated about the creation of armed communist organizations in Santiago's factories.

Expropriation of US-controlled copper mines and other enterprises, plus conspicuously friendly relations with Cuba, provoked US hostility. Later hearings in the US Congress indicated that Nixon and Kissinger actively undercut Allende by discouraging credit from international finance organizations and providing both financial and moral support to his opponents. Until the late 1980s, except during the Carter administration, the US maintained friendly relations with the Chilean military.

Faced with such difficulties, the government tried to forestall conflict by proposing clearly defined limits on nationalization. Unfortunately, neither extreme leftists, who believed that only force could achieve socialism, nor their rightist counterparts who believed only force could prevent it, was open to compromise.

The Rightist Backlash

In late 1972, independent truckers led a widespread strike by an alliance of shopkeepers, professionals, bank clerks, rightwing students, and even some urban and rural laborers. Demanding that the government abandon plans for a state-owned trucking enterprise and supported by both the Christian Democrats and the National Party, the strike threatened the government's viability.

As the government's authority crumbled, a desperate Allende invited army commander General Carlos Prats to occupy the critical post of Interior Minister, and also included an admiral and an air force general in his cabinet. Despite the economic crisis, results of the March 1973 congressional elections demonstrated that Allende's support had actually increased since 1970 – but the unified opposition's strengthened control of Congress underscored the polarization of Chilean politics. In June 1973 there was an unsuccessful military coup.

The next month truckers and other rightists once again went on strike, supported by the entire opposition. Having lost military support, General Prats resigned, to be replaced by the relatively obscure General

Augusto Pinochet Ugarte, whom both Prats and Allende thought loyal to constitutional government. On September 11, 1973, Pinochet unleashed a brutal *golpe de estado* (coup) which overthrew the UP government and resulted in Allende's death (an apparent suicide) and the death of thousands of his supporters.

Police and the military apprehended thousands of leftists, suspected leftists and sympathizers. Many were herded into Santiago's National Stadium, where they suffered beatings, torture and even execution. Estimates of deaths range from as few as 2500 to as many as 80,000, though the former is probably much closer to the truth. Hundreds of thousands went into exile.

The military argued that force was necessary to remove Allende because his government had fomented political and economic chaos and he was himself planning to overthrow the constitutional order by force. Certainly inept policies brought about this 'economic chaos,' but reactionary sectors, encouraged and abetted from abroad, exacerbated scarcities, producing a black market which further undercut the government. Allende's record of persistently standing for election and his pledge to the opposition implied commitment to the democratic process, but his inability or unwillingness to control other groups to his left terrified the middle class as well as the oligarchy. His last words, part of a radio address just before the attacks on the government palace La Moneda, expressed his ideals but underlined his failure:

My words are not spoken in bitterness, but in disappointment. They will be a moral judgment on those who have betrayed the oath they took as soldiers of Chile . . . They have the might and they can enslave us, but they cannot halt the world's social processes, not with crimes, nor with guns . . . May you go forward in the knowledge that, sooner rather than later, the great avenues will open once again, along which free citizens will march in order to build a better society. Long live Chile! Long live the people! Long live the workers! These are my last words, and I am sure that this sacrifice will constitute a moral lesson which will punish cowardice, perfidy and treason.

The Military Dictatorship

Many opposition leaders, some of whom had encouraged the coup, expected a quick return to civilian government, but General Pinochet had other ideas. From 1973 to 1989, he headed a durable junta that dissolved Congress, banned leftist parties and suspended all others, prohibited nearly all political activity, and ruled by decree. Assuming the presidency in 1974, Pinochet sought to remake completely the country's political and economic culture through repression, torture and murder. Detainees came from all sectors of society, from peasants to professionals.

The CNI (Centro Nacional de Informaciones, National Information Center) and its predecessor DINA (Directoria de Inteligencia Nacional, National Intelligence Directorate) were the most notorious practitioners of state terrorism. International assassinations were not unusual – a car bomb killed General Prats in Buenos Aires a year after the coup, while Christian Democrat leader Bernardo Leighton barely survived a shooting in Rome in 1975. Perhaps the most notorious case was the 1976 murder of Allende's foreign minister Orlando Letelier by a car bomb, in Washington, DC.

By 1977 even air force General Gustavo Leigh, a member of the junta, thought the campaign against 'subversion' so successful that he proposed a return to civilian rule, but Pinochet forced Leigh's resignation, ensuring the army's dominance and perpetuating himself in power. By 1980, Pinochet felt confident enough to submit a new, customized constitution to the electorate and wager his own political future on it. In a plebiscite with very narrow options, about two-thirds of the voters approved the constitution and ratified Pinochet's presidency until 1989, though many voters abstained in protest.

Return to Democracy

Political parties began to function openly again in 1987. In late 1988, Pinochet held another plebiscite in an attempt to extend his presidency until 1997, but this time voters rejected him. In multi-party elections that took place in 1989, Christian Democrat Patricio Aylwin, compromise candidate of a coalition of opposition parties known as the Concertación para la Democracia, defeated Pinochet protégé Hernán Büchi, a conservative economist and candidate of Renovación Nacional.

Consolidating the return to democracy, Aylwin's relatively uneventful four-year term expired in 1994; in late 1993, Chileans elected Eduardo Frei Ruiz-Tagle, son of the late president Eduardo Frei Montalva, to a six-year term. For more details on current Chilean politics, see the Government entry below.

GEOGRAPHY & CLIMATE
Few countries of Chile's size – slightly larger than Texas at about 800,000 sq km (496,000 sq miles) – can boast such a formidable variety of landscapes; rocky Andean peaks, snow-capped volcanoes, broad river valleys and deep canyons, waterless deserts, icy fjords, deep blue glaciers, turquoise lakes, sandy beaches and precipitous headlands. It owes this diversity – a 'crazy geography' or 'geographical extravaganza' in the words of Chilean writer Benjamín Subercaseaux – to extremes of latitude and altitude: not counting Antarctic claims, Chilean territory extends some 4300 km (2666 miles) north to south between the Andes and the Pacific Ocean, equivalent to the distance from Havana to Hudson Bay; on average less than 200 km (124 miles) wide from east to west, it rises from sea level to more than 6000 meters (19,680 feet). Describing these geographical contrasts, British diplomat James Bryce observed that 'the difference is as great as that between the verdure of Ireland and the sterility of the Sahara.'

Chile's present boundaries are the result of conquest and expansion, first by Spain and later by the republic itself. Only at the end of the 19th century did Chile reach its present extent, from the city of Arica in the northern Atacama desert to the archipelago of Tierra del Fuego in the south. Chile also possesses the Pacific islands of Easter Island (Isla de Pascua, or Rapa Nui in the local Polynesian language) and the Juan Fernández archipelago. The country's Antarctic claims overlap those of Argentina and Britain.

Administrative Regions
For administrative purposes, Chile consists of 13 regions. Except for the Metropolitan Region of Santiago, they are numbered ordinally from north to south, but normally written in Roman numerals. Chileans usually abbreviate the longer formal names, such as O'Higgins and Aisén. See the Administrative Regions of Chile map.

Geographical Regions
Chile's customary, rather than formal, regional divisions reflect ecological zonation and human economy rather than arbitrary political boundaries. Generally, the structure of this book reflects the following geographical regions.

Norte Grande The regions of Tarapacá and Antofagasta together comprise the Norte Grande (Great North), running from the Peruvian border to the province of Chañaral and dominated by the Atacama desert. Transverse river valleys, subterranean water sources and springs, and diversions of distant streams sustain cities such as Arica, Iquique and Antofagasta, which occupy narrow coastal plains. These sources also irrigate the limited but productive farmland even though, in the entire Norte Grande, only the Río Loa regularly reaches the sea, and some weather stations have *never* recorded rainfall. Since the colonial era, mining of silver, nitrates and copper has been the principal economic activity, although irrigated agriculture and native livestock herding are locally significant.

Despite its aridity and tropical latitude, the Atacama is a remarkably temperate desert, moderated by the cool, north-flowing Peru (Humboldt) Current that parallels the coast. High humidity produces an extensive cloud cover and even thick fogs known as *camanchaca*, which condense on

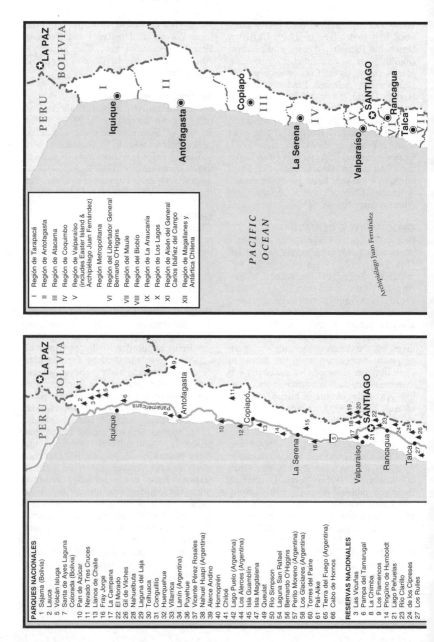

PARQUES NACIONALES

1   Sajama (Bolivia)
2   Lauca
5   Volcán Isluga
7   Santa de Ayes Laguna
     Colorada (Bolivia)
10 Pan de Azúcar
11 Nevado Tres Cruces
13 Llanos de Challe
16 Fray Jorge
17 La Campana
22 El Morado
26 Gil de Vilches
28 Nahuelbuta
29 Laguna del Laja
30 Tolhuaca
31 Conguillío
32 Huerquehue
33 Villarrica
34 Lanín (Argentina)
36 Puyehue
37 Vicente Pérez Rosales
38 Nahuel Huapi (Argentina)
39 Alerce Andino
40 Hornopirén
41 Chiloé
42 Lago Puelo (Argentina)
44 Los Alerces (Argentina)
45 Isla Guamblín
47 Isla Magdalena
49 Queulat
50 Río Simpson
54 Laguna San Rafael
56 Bernardo O'Higgins
57 Perito Moreno (Argentina)
58 Los Glaciares (Argentina)
60 Torres del Paine
61 Pali-Aike
65 Tierra del Fuego (Argentina)
66 Cabo de Hornos

RESERVAS NACIONALES

3   Las Vicuñas
6   Pampa del Tamarugal
8   La Chimba
9   Los Flamencos
14 Pingüino de Humboldt
21 Lago Peñuelas
23 Río Clarillo
24 de los Cipreses
27 Los Ruiles

Región de Tarapacá
I
Región de Antofagasta
II
Región de Atacama
III
Región de Coquimbo
IV
Región de Valparaíso
V
(includes Easter Island &
Archipiélago Juan Fernández)
Región Metropolitana
Región del Libertador General
VI
Bernardo O'Higgins
Región del Maule
VII
Región del Biobío
VIII
Región de La Araucanía
IX
Región de Los Lagos
X
Región de Aisén del General
XI
Carlos Ibáñez del Campo
Región de Magallanes y
XII
Antártica Chilena

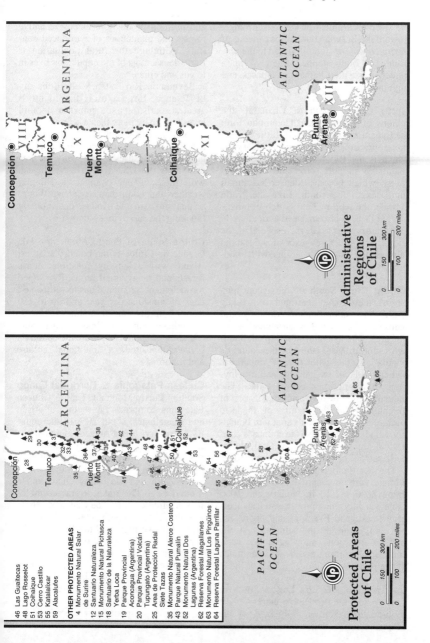

46 Las Guaitecas
48 Lago Rosselot
51 Coihaique
53 Cerro Castillo
55 Katalalixar
59 Alacalufes

OTHER PROTECTED AREAS
4   Monumento Natural Salar
    de Surire
12 Santuario Naturaleza
15 Monumento Natural Pichasca
18 Santuario de la Naturaleza
    Yerba Loca
19 Parque Provincial
    Aconcagua (Argentina)
20 Parque Provincial Volcán
    Tupungato (Argentina)
25 Area de Protección Radal
    Siete Tazas
35 Monumento Natural Alerce Costero
43 Parque Natural Pumalín
52 Monumento Natural Dos
    Lagunas (Argentina)
62 Reserva Forestal Magallanes
63 Monumento Natural Los Pingüinos
64 Reserva Forestal Laguna Parrillar

Protected Areas of Chile

Administrative Regions of Chile

the steep escarpment of the coastal range. Toward the Bolivian border, the canyons of the *precordillera* (foothills) lead to the *altiplano* or high steppe, where Aymara herders graze their llamas and alpacas, and high mountain passes.

Norte Chico South of Chañaral, the regions of Atacama and Coquimbo form the transitional Norte Chico (Little North), the approximate southern boundary of which is the Río Aconcagua. The desert relents to support scrub and occasional forest, which becomes denser as rainfall increases to the south. Like the Norte Grande, the Norte Chico is rich in minerals, but there is also irrigated agriculture in the major river valleys, especially the Elqui. In those rare years of substantial rainfall, the landscape erupts with wildflowers.

Middle Chile South of the Aconcagua begins the fertile heartland of Middle Chile. The intermontane Valle Central (central valley) extends through most of this area, which contains the capital, Santiago (with at least a third of the country's population), the major port of Valparaíso, and the bulk of its industry and employment, plus important copper mines. The industrial city of Concepción and its port of Talcahuano, at the mouth of the Río Biobío, mark the region's southern boundary. Middle Chile is also the country's chief agricultural zone and, in total, holds perhaps 75% of the country's population.

The heartland enjoys a Mediterranean climate, with maximum temperatures averaging 28°C (82°F) in January and 10°C (50°F) in July; the rainy season lasts from May to August. Evenings and nights can be cool, even during summer. At the highest elevations, snow lasts into early summer, permitting excellent skiing much of the year.

La Araucanía & Los Lagos South of Concepción, the Río Biobío marks Chile's 19th-century frontier, homeland of the Mapuche Indians and now an area of cereal and pastoral production, extensive native forests and plantations of introduced conifers. Although the rural population is fairly dense, most of the population lives in towns and cities.

Beyond the Río Toltén, south of the city of Temuco, Los Lagos is the country's greatest tourist area, its numerous foothill lakes framed by more than a score of snow-capped volcanoes, many of them still active. Fishing, agriculture and timber are also major industries. Climatically, the area resembles the USA's Pacific Northwest, with pleasant but changeable summer weather and cool, damp winters. Winter brings snow to the Andes, occasionally blocking the passes to Argentina.

Chiloé South of Puerto Montt, the Isla Grande de Chiloé is the country's largest island, with a lengthy coastline, dense forests and many small farms. Renowned for inclement weather, it has fewer than 60 days of sunshine per year and up to 150 days of storms, but in summer it can be magnificent. The Isla Grande and its surrounding offshore islands are the country's greatest repository of 'traditional' culture and folklore.

Chilean Patagonia & Tierra del Fuego South of Puerto Montt and Chiloé, Chilean Patagonia comprises the regions of Aisén and Magallanes, about 30% of the country's territory. It is a rugged, mountainous area, battered by westerly winds and storms which drop enormous amounts of snow and rain on the seaward slopes of the Andes, although the balmy microclimate around Lago General Carrera resembles that of Middle Chile. The Campo de Hielo Sur, the southern continental ice field, separates the two regions; Magallanes and its capital of Punta Arenas, on the Straits of Magellan, are more easily accessible from Argentine Patagonia than from the Chilean mainland. Before the opening of the Panama Canal in 1914, Punta Arenas was a major port of call for international shipping, but its prosperity now depends on oil, gas, fishing and wool.

Across the straits lies the Isla Grande de Tierra del Fuego, divided between Chile and Argentina, where oil extraction and wool are the main industries. Chile's settled southern extreme is Isla Navarino, separated from Tierra del Fuego by the Beagle Channel; smaller land masses to the south include the Wollaston Islands, with their famous Cape Horn, and the Diego Ramírez archipelago.

In Magallanes and Tierra del Fuego, temperatures drop to a summer average of just 11°C (52°F), and to a winter average of about 4°C (39°F). Dampness and wind chill can make the ambient temperature feel even lower. The weather is highly changeable, even though the nearly incessant winds moderate in the winter. The best time to visit is the southern summer (December to February), when very long days permit outdoor activities despite the unpredictable weather.

The Andes Like the Pacific Ocean, the Andes mountains run the length of the country. In the far north, near the Bolivian border, they include a number of symmetrical volcanoes more than 6000 meters high, while east of Santiago they present an imposing wall of sedimentary and volcanic peaks. Between Copiapó and the Biobío, the range comprises nearly half the country's width, with some of South America's highest peaks. Despite numerous passes, transport and communications are difficult, and have isolated Chile from the rest of South America for most of its history. South of the Biobío, lower in altitude, the Andes are a less formidable barrier except where seasonal snowfields and permanent glaciers obstruct passage between east and west.

Despite their scenic grandeur, the seismically unstable Andes are a major hazard throughout Chile. Many of the country's major cities (including Santiago, Valparaíso, La Serena and Valdivia) have suffered earthquake damage or destruction, and volcanic eruptions are a potential menace in other areas.

ECOLOGY & ENVIRONMENT

The Chilean public's growing awareness of environmental issues often seems at odds with the present government's single-minded commitment to economic growth, which has led to dubious development projects like a series of hydroelectric dams on the Río Biobío and a proposed large-scale effort to harvest native beech forest in one of the most remote parts of Tierra del Fuego. In 1995-96, however, French nuclear tests in the Pacific caused so much ill feeling within Chile that the government felt obliged to lodge formal protests with the French government.

For most Chileans, the single most palpable environmental issue is the cloud of smog that so often hangs over the city of Santiago, which, like Los Angeles, sits in a basin between two mountain ranges and has a virtually identical climate. Efforts to reduce air pollution, which on some days is so severe that school children may not take physical education and older citizens are advised not to leave home, stems from the growing number of private automobiles, the presence of diesel buses and the concentration of polluting industries. While some efforts have been made to improve the quality of public transport vehicles, the government seems more willing to promote automobile ownership through construction of new roads and highways than to restrict vehicular congestion in the crowded central city, or to shut down industrial polluters.

From Region VIII south, the felling of native forest and its replacement by plantations of fast-growing exotics like eucalyptus and Monterey (radiata) pine has attracted international attention. Native forests of Araucaria (monkey-puzzle trees) and alerce (a long-lived conifer resembling the redwood) have declined precipitously over the past decades; the alerce, in particular, has been vulnerable to clandestine cutting. Throughout the south, the burgeoning salmon farming industry has drawn criticism for polluting both fresh and salt water areas.

Another issue is the ever more intensive use of agricultural chemicals and pesticides

Endangered Species

The Convention on International Trade in Endangered Species of Wild Fauna and Flora (CITES) is a diplomatic agreement regulating trade in biotic resources, including plants and animals, which are either in immediate danger of extinction, or else threatened or declining so rapidly that they may soon be in danger of extinction. Regulations are complex, but in general such species are either protected from commercial or noncommercial exploitation or subject to severe restrictions. In many instances, all commerce is prohibited in a given species; in most others, the export of plants and animals in a given country is prohibited without express authorization from that country's government.

Under CITES, most species are assigned either to Appendix I (endangered, under immediate threat of extinction without remedial action) or Appendix II (threatened, perhaps

Appendix I

Flora
Alerce (Chilean false larch)
   (*Fitzroya cupressoides*)
Mammals
Andean cat (*Felis jacobita*)
Beaked whales
   (*Berardius* or *Mesoplodon* spp*}
Blue whale (*Balaenoptera musculus*)
Bottlenosed whales (*Hyperodon* spp)
Fin whale (*Balaenoptera physalus*)
Giant armadillo (*Priodontes maximus*)
Humpback whale
   (*Megaptera novaeangliae*)
Jaguarundi (*Felis yagouarundi*)
Long-tailed otter (*Lutra platensis*)
Marine otter (*Lutra felina*)
Minke whale
   (*Balaenoptera acutorostrata*)

North Andean huemul
   (*Hippocamelus antisensis*)
Pink fairy armadillo (*Clamyphorus truncatus*)
Pudú (*Pudu pudu*)
Pygmy right whale (*Caperea marginata*)
Sei whale (*Balaenoptera borealis*)
South Andean huemul (*Hippocamelus bisulcus*)
Southern right whale (*Eubalaena australis}
Southern river otter (*Lutra provocax*)
Sperm whale (*Physeter catodon*)
Vicuña (*Vicugna vicugna***)

Birds
Andean condor (*Vultur gryphus*)
Black-fronted piping-guan (*Pipile jacutinga*)
Darwin's rhea (*Pterocnemia pennata pennata*)
Eskimo curlew (*Numenius borealis*)
Humboldt penguin (*Spheniscus humboldtii*)
Lesser rhea (*Pterocnemia pennata*)
Solitary tinamou (*Tinamus solitarius*)

to promote Chile's flourishing fruit exports, which take advantage of the southern summer to furnish the Northern Hemisphere with fresh produce. A related matter is agricultural water usage in drought-prone Middle Chile and, even more acutely, in the Norte Chico. Water contamination and air pollution by the mining industry are major concerns throughout the country.

The growing hole in the ozone layer over Antarctica, due to global atmospheric aerosols, has become such a major concern that medical authorities recommend protective clothing and heavy sun block to avoid cancer-causing ultraviolet radiation, especially in Patagonia. Some observant travelers may conclude that the greatest domestic source of this pollution is hair spray.

FLORA & FAUNA

Chile's northern deserts and high-altitude steppes, soaring mountains, alpine and sub-Antarctic forests and extensive coastline all support distinctive flora and fauna which will be unfamiliar to most visitors, or at least those from the Northern Hemisphere. To protect these environments, Chile's Corporación Nacional Forestal (Conaf) administers an extensive system of national parks and reserves, the more accessible of which are briefly described below. More detailed descriptions can be found in individual chapters. A handful of reserves are not part of the Conaf system; these are mentioned in the appropriate chapter.

Jürgen Rottmann's bilingual *Bosques de Chile/Chile's Woodlands* (Unisys, 1988), published in cooperation with the World regionally endangered); some recovering species have been reassigned from Appendix I to Appendix II. Appendix III listings cover species that require close monitoring to determine their degree of vulnerability to extinction.

Travelers should take special care not to hunt, purchase or collect the following species of plants and animals found in Chile, Argentina and the Falkland Islands, nor should they purchase products made from these plants and animals. The list below is partial, and travelers should consult their own country's customs service before attempting to import any such products. Note that US customs no longer permits the importation of birds even with CITES permits from the appropriate country, and that the US Marine Mammal Protection Act prohibits the importation of any marine mammal products whatsoever.

Appendix II

Flora
Cacti (all species not on Appendix I)
Mammals
Argentine gray fox (*Dusicyon griseus*)
Guanaco (*Lamo guanicoe*)
Juan Fernández fur seal
   (*Arctocephalus philippi*)
Mountain lion (*Felis concolor*)
Southern elephant seal
   (*Mirounga leonina*)
Southern fur seal (*Arctocephalus australis*)
Birds
Andean flamingo
   (*Phoenicoparrus andinus*)
Black-necked swan
   (*Cygnus melanocoryphus*)
Caracaras (*Falconidae,* all species in family
   except those on Appendix I)

Chilean flamingo
   (*Phoenicopterus ruber chilensis*)
Coscoroba swan
   (*Coscoroba coscoroba*)
James flamingo
   (*Phoenicoparrus jamesi*)
Greater rhea
   (*Rhea americana albescens*)
Patagonian conure
   (*Cyanoliseus patagonus byroni*)
Peregrine falcon (*Falco peregrinus*)

*All cetaceans (whales and porpoises) not on Appendix I are on Appendix II, but not all are listed individually here.

**In some areas, specifically Parque Nacional Lauca, the vicuña is on Appendix II rather than Appendix I, permitting the export of cloth only.

Wide Fund for Nature (WWF), is a well-illustrated generalist's introduction to the country's forests and their fauna, despite its superficial 'Smokey the Bear' approach to fire ecology.

Flora

Thanks to its latitudinal extent and great altitudinal range, Chile has an extraordinary variety of plants. The northern coastal deserts are virtually devoid of vegetation except in the river valleys. The cacti at slightly higher elevations give way to the patchy grasslands of the very high altiplano, where there are also scrub forests of queñoa (*Polylepis tarapacana*).

From the Norte Chico through most of Middle Chile, the native flora consist mostly of shrubs whose sclerophyllous

(glossy) leaves help conserve water during the long summer dry season. At some higher elevations in the coastal ranges there are forests of southern beech (*Nothofagus* spp), but the native Chilean palm is in decline. Farther south, beyond the Biobío, the distinctive Araucaria (monkey-puzzle tree) is related to the Northern Hemisphere pines. At the southern end of the lakes region, the alerce (*Fitzroya cupressoides*), belonging to the cypress family, is a long-lived conifer which has become the focus of international conservation efforts.

In the far south of Aisén and Magallanes, verdant upland forests consist of several species of the widespread genus *Nothofagus*. On the eastern plains of Magallanes and Tierra del Fuego, decreased rainfall supports extensive grasslands.

Chile's major Pacific island possessions, Easter Island (Rapa Nui) and the Juan Fernández archipelago, are a special case. The latter, in particular, is a major storehouse of biological diversity that has been named a UNESCO World Biosphere Reserve.

Specialists interested in Middle Chile's Mediterranean environments and their comparison with similar settings elsewhere in the world, should consult Mary Kalin Arroyo's edited collection *Ecology & Biology of Mediterranean Ecosystems in Chile, California and Australia* in *Ecological Studies* No 108, (Springer Verlag, 1995). Another interesting book, despite its shallow approach to socioeconomic issues in the Norte Chico, is Conrad Bahre's *Destruction of the Natural Vegetation of North Central Chile* (University of California Press, 1978).

Fauna

Chile's fauna is as varied as its flora, even though it's less conspicuously abundant. Notable mammals include the widespread (though not common) puma; the camel-like guanaco (in both the desert north and Patagonia) and its close relative the vicuña (only in the high steppes of the altiplano); the huemul or Chilean deer (with separate subspecies in the Norte Grande and in Patagonia); the vizcacha (a wild relative of the chinchilla); the rare and diminutive (almost miniature) deer known as the pudú; and several species of foxes. Though more often associated with Peru or Bolivia, the domestic llama and alpaca are abundant in the northern highlands.

Chile's long coastline features many marine mammals, including sea lions, otters and fur seals, along with the finfish and shellfish that have made the fisheries sector one of the world's most important. The food entry in the Facts for the Visitor chapter provides detailed information on the role of seafood in the Chilean diet.

Most foreign visitors will find the country's bird life more easily accessible and very different from that of the Northern Hemisphere. The legendary Andean condor is widespread though not numerous, while the ostrich-like rhea (called ñandú in Spanish) inhabits both the far north and the far south. Parque Nacional Lauca, a world biosphere reserve in the northern altiplano, contains a variety of bird life from Andean gulls and giant coots to three species of flamingos, thanks in large part to the habitat of extensive high-altitude wetlands. The extensive shoreline is home to many species, including penguins, while Patagonian reserves like Parque Nacional Torres del Paine provide particularly rich concentrations of bird life.

Visitors interested in birds should look for Mark Pearman's *The Essential Guide to Birding in Chile* (1995), Nigel Wheatley's *Where to Watch Birds in South America* (Princeton, 1995), or Braulio Araya and Sharon Chester's *The Birds of Chile: a Field Guide* (Wandering Albatross, 1993). Those competent in Spanish should look for the *Guía de Campo de las Aves de Chile* (Editorial Universitaria, Santiago, 1986) by Araya and Guillermo Millie H.

National Parks

Since the establishment of Parque Nacional Vicente Pérez Rosales in the mid-1920s, Chile's national parks have become a major international attraction. As part of its 'Sistema Nacional de Areas Silvestres Protegidas del Estado' (Snaspe, or National System of State-Protected Wild Areas), the government has created many other parks and reserves, administered by Conaf, mostly but not exclusively in the Andean range.

Before leaving Santiago, travelers should visit the central Conaf office (☎ (02) 6711850) at Avenida Bulnes 259, Departamento 206, for maps and brochures which may be in short supply in the parks themselves. Regional Conaf offices, listed in the appropriate city entries, will sometimes assist in transportation to more isolated areas.

Chilean protected areas are of five main types: *parques nacionales* (national parks), *reservas nacionales* (national reserves), *monumentos naturales* (natural monuments), *áreas de protección turística* (tourist protection areas), and *santuarios de la naturaleza* (nature sanctuaries).

National parks are generally extensive areas with a variety of natural ecosystems, while national reserves are areas open to economic exploitation on a sustainable basis, and may include some relatively pristine areas. Natural monuments are smaller but more strictly protected, usually with a single outstanding natural feature. Tourist protection areas are usually private lands where management practices limit economic exploitation in the interest of scenic resources, while nature sanctuaries are primarily intended for research.

Along with Sernatur, the national tourist service, Conaf publishes the very useful and inexpensive paperback *Juventud, Turismo y Naturaleza: Guía Práctica para el Visitante de Areas Silvestres Protegidas*, which includes a great deal of up-to-date information on Chilean parks, including access by public transport. Another worthwhile book is the beautifully illustrated but expensive *Chile: Sus Parques Nacionales y Otras Areas Protegidas* (Incafo, Madrid, 1982). For English speakers, William C Leitch's eloquent survey of *South America's National Parks* (The Mountaineers, Seattle, 1990) contains a valuable chapter on the history and natural history of half a dozen of Chile's most popular parks.

Parque Nacional Lauca In the northern region of Tarapacá, east of the city of Arica, this 138,000-hectare (532-sq-mile) park offers extraordinary natural attractions, including active and dormant volcanoes, clear blue lakes with abundant bird life, and extensive steppes that support flourishing populations of the endangered vicuña, a wild relative of the llama and alpaca. Living in tiny villages with picturesque colonial churches, Aymara Indian shepherds graze their animals on the same pastures.

Adjacent to the park are two other protected areas which are less accessible, the Reserva Nacional Las Vicuñas and Monumento Natural Salar de Surire. The latter features huge nesting colonies of flamingos.

Parque Nacional Volcán Isluga Rarely visited and relatively inaccessible, this 175,000-hectare (675-sq-mile) unit in the altiplano of Iquique bears many similarities to Lauca, but its cultural resources may be even more impressive.

Reserva Nacional Los Flamencos Comprising seven scattered sectors in and around San Pedro de Atacama, this 74,000-hectare (285-sq-mile) reserve protects a variety of salt lakes and high-altitude lagoons with several species of flamingos, as well as eerie desert landforms and hot springs.

Monumento Natural La Portada Symbol of Antofagasta, this offshore stack and its immediate surroundings are a popular day trip for residents of Region II.

Parque Nacional Pan de Azúcar Set in the coastal desert of the regions of Antofagasta and Atacama, near the small port of Chañaral, this 44,000-hectare (170-sq-mile) park features a stark but beautiful shoreline, and unique flora that draw moisture from the coastal fog. Among the fauna are pelicans, penguins, otters and sea lions.

Parque Nacional Nevado de Tres Cruces East of Copiapó, in the high Andes along the Argentine border, this 62,000-hectare (239-sq-mile) unit is destined to attract more travelers in coming years. Its outstanding feature is not its 6330-meter (20,762-foot) namesake peak, but the even more prominent 6893-meter (22,609-foot) Ojos del Salado, a prime climber's destination once thought higher than Aconcagua.

Parque Nacional Llanos de Challe On the coastal plain of the Norte Chico, north of the port of Huasco, the 45,000-hectare (174-sq-mile) Llanos are the best site to view the spectacular 'flowering of the desert' after one of the region's rare heavy rains.

Reserva Nacional Pingüino de Humboldt On the border of Regions III and IV, this 859-hectare (3½-sq-mile) reserve consists of several offshore islands with breeding populations of Humboldt's penguin. Access is difficult, but camping is possible.

Parque Nacional Bosque Fray Jorge In Region IV, 75 km (46 miles) from the city of Ovalle, 10,000-hectare (39-sq-mile) Fray Jorge is an ecological island of humid forest usually found several hundred km to the south. Like Pan de Azúcar, its vegetation depends on coastal fog.

Monumento Natural Pichasca In Region IV, midway between Vicuña and Ovalle, this 128-hectare (316-acre) monument's main attraction is its petrified forest.

Parque Nacional La Campana Easily accessible both from Santiago and Valparaíso/Viña del Mar, this 8000-hectare (31-sq-mile) park is a good choice at any time of year for a short trek through tranquil forests of native oaks and palms.

Santuario de la Naturaleza Yerba Loca In the Andean foothills of the Santiago suburb of Lo Barnechea, 39,000-hectare (150-sq-mile) Yerba Loca is a popular weekend destination for residents of the capital. It is an excellent place to view Middle Chile's diverse Mediterranean vegetation.

Reserva Nacional Río Clarillo Only 45 km (28 miles) from Santiago and suitable for a day trip, this 10,000-hectare (39-sq-mile) reserve offers a variety of Andean ecosystems.

Parque Nacional El Morado This easily accessible 3000-hectare (740-acre) mountain park featuring the Morales Glacier, source of the Río Morado, is only 93 km (58 miles) from Santiago.

Parque Nacional Archipiélago de Juan Fernández Consisting of three islands several hundred km west of Valparaíso, this 9100-hectare (35-sq-mile) unit is one of Chile's hidden ecological treasures,

with spectacular scenery and a great variety of endemic plant species. It is best known as the site of exile for Scottish mariner Alexander Selkirk, immortalized as Robinson Crusoe in Daniel Defoe's novel.

Parque Nacional Rapa Nui Rapa Nui is the proper Polynesian name for 6600-hectare (25-sq-mile) Easter Island, with its huge, enigmatic stone statues, 3700 km (2249 miles) west of Valparaíso. Despite its isolation, distance from the continent, and the expense of getting there, it remains a popular tourist destination.

Reserva Nacional Río de los Cipreses The Andes east of Rancagua are best known for the massive El Teniente copper mine, but this 37,000-hectare (143-sq-mile) reserve is a also recreational resource.

Area de Protección Radal Siete Tazas A virtual staircase of falls and pools along the Río Claro is the major attraction of this 7700-hectare (30-sq-mile) zone in the precordillera of Talca.

Parque Nacional Vilches Recently upgraded to national park status, with excellent access from Talca, 17,000-hectare (66-sq-mile) Vilches is one of central Chile's natural highlights. In addition to spectacular views of the Andean divide, its many hiking trails include a loop trek to Radal Siete Tazas.

Parque Nacional Laguna del Laja In the Andean foothills of Region VIII, this 12,000-hectare (46-sq-mile) park offers waterfalls, lakes, volcanoes and bird life, with numerous trails suitable for hiking.

Parque Nacional Nahuelbuta In the high coastal range of Region IX, Nahuelbuta's 7000 hectares (27 sq miles) preserve the largest remaining Araucaria forests in the area.

Monumento Natural Contulmo This 82-hectare (202-acre) roadside forest corridor west of Angol, on the highway to Concepción, is a highly recommended stopover.

Monumento Natural Cerro Ñielol
Dedicated for its concentration of the copihue, the national flower, the most urban of Chile's national parks consists of 90 hectares (222 acres), barely a half-hour's walk from downtown Temuco.

Parque Nacional Tolhuaca At the end of a narrow mountain road in Region IX, east of the town of Victoria and north of Curacautín, 6400-hectare (25-acre) Tolhuaca is a remote forested getaway in the headwaters of the Río Malleco. The southern approach from Curacautín is very difficult for vehicles beyond Termas de Tolhuaca, but it's short enough for hikers and mountain bikers.

Parque Nacional Conguillío In the Andean portion of the Araucanía, 80 km (50 miles) from Temuco, 61,000-hectare (235-sq-mile) Conguillío features mixed forests of Araucaria, cypress and southern beech surrounding the active, snow-capped Volcán Llaima.

Parque Nacional Huerquehue Small but scenic, 12,500-hectare (48-sq-mile) Huerquehue has excellent hiking trails with outstanding views of nearby Parque Nacional Villarrica (see below). It is 120 km (74 miles) from Temuco.

Parque Nacional Villarrica One of the gems of the lakes region, Volcán Villarrica's smoking, symmetrical cone overlooks the lake and town of the same name. Its 61,000 hectares (235 sq miles) make a popular destination for trekkers and climbers.

Parque Nacional Puyehue One of the country's most-visited parks, 107,000-hectare (413-sq-mile) Puyehue is only 80 km (50 miles) from the city of Osorno, but still offers scenery and solitude to dedicated visitors. There is outstanding hiking and hidden hot springs near Volcán Puyehue, which erupted in 1960 to form a striking volcanic desert as yet colonized by only a few hardy plants.

Parque Nacional Vicente Pérez Rosales Founded in 1926, this is Chile's oldest national park, named for a Chilean explorer, politician and writer who helped found the city of Puerto Montt. Its 254,000 hectares (980 sq miles) include the spectacular Lago Todos Los Santos, which provides a scenic alternative route to Bariloche, Argentina, via Argentina's Parque Nacional Nahuel Huapi.

Parque Nacional Alerce Andino Just 50 km (31 miles) from Puerto Montt, this 40,000-hectare (154-sq-mile) park preserves large tracts of the last remaining alerce trees, resembling the giant redwoods of California.

Parque Nacional Hornopirén Largely undeveloped, 48,000-hectare (185-sq-mile) Hornopirén rewards determined hikers in search of verdant rainforest. It's near its namesake village, the last mainland ferry port southbound on the Camino Austral.

Parque Nacional Chiloé On the remote western shore of Chile's misty southern island, this 43,000-hectare (165-sq-mile) park features excellent hiking trails across sweeping dunes and broad sandy beaches, along blue lagoons and through the forbidding forests which fostered the island's colorful and enigmatic folklore.

Parque Nacional Queulat An increasingly popular destination since the opening of the Camino Austral between Puerto Montt and Cochrane, Queulat consists of 154,000 hectares (594 sq miles) of truly wild evergreen forest, mountains and glaciers, 150 km (93 miles) north of Coihaique and 200 km (124 miles) south of Chaitén.

Reserva Nacional Coihaique Despite its proximity to the city of Coihaique, less than an hour's walk away, this 2150-hectare (15-sq-mile) reserve is surprisingly wild and attractive, with exceptional views of the surrounding area and good opportunities for camping and hiking.

Parque Nacional Río Simpson Though it may be downgraded from national park status, this 41,000-hectare (158-sq-mile) unit, which straddles the highway between Coihaique and Puerto Aisén, is a pleasant and accessible destination with verdant forests, waterfalls and a spectacular canyon.

Reserva Nacional Cerro Castillo Wild, high and remote, this 180,000-hectare (695-sq-mile) reserve south of Coihaique is increasingly popular with hikers who take advantage of its two convenient access points along the Camino Austral.

Parque Nacional Laguna San Rafael Glaciers reach the sea at one of Chile's most impressive parks, part of the Campo de Hielo Norte (northern Patagonian ice field) and accessible only by air or sea, 200 km (124 miles) south of Puerto Chacabuco. Its nearly 1.8 million hectares (6947 sq miles) deserve a visit, but it is either expensive or time-consuming to do so.

Parque Nacional Bernardo O'Higgins Largely inaccessible except at a few points, this massive 3½-million-hectare (13,508-sq-mile) park straddles the Patagonian ice fields in Regions XI and XII.

Parque Nacional Torres del Paine Of all Chile's parks, Torres del Paine is the showpiece, a world biosphere reserve with all the diverse scenery of Alaska in only 181,000 hectares (698 sq miles), and a wealth of wildlife, including the Patagonian guanaco, a wild relative of the Andean llama. It is 150 km (93 miles) from Puerto Natales and 400 km (248 miles) from Punta Arenas, in Region XII.

Monumento Natural Cueva del Milodón Only 16 km (10 miles) from Punta Arenas, this area (only 150 hectares, or 370 acres) contains the cave where pioneers found remains of the milodon, a huge Pleistocene ground sloth.

Reserva Nacional Magallanes Just seven km west of Punta Arenas, this hilly forest reserve consists of 13,500 hectares (52 sq miles) of southern beech and Magellanic steppe, plus a small ski area.

Monumento Natural Los Pingüinos Accessible only by boat from Punta Arenas, this small offshore reserve consists of two islands in the Strait of Magellan, honeycombed with burrowing Magellanic penguins and other seabirds.

Parque Nacional Pali Aike Near the Argentine border, on the eastern mainland of Region XII, 5000-hectare (19-sq-mile) Pali Aike is one of southern South America's major sites for the study of early human habitation. It also supports a notable variety of Patagonian wildlife.

GOVERNMENT & POLITICS
Chile's constitution, ratified by the electorate in a controversial plebiscite in 1980, is a custom document which was largely the work of Pinochet supporter Jaime Guzmán, then a conservative law professor and later a senator, assassinated by leftists in 1990. It provides for a popularly elected president and a bicameral congress, with a 46-member Senado (Senate) and a 120-member Cámara de Diputados (Chamber of Deputies); eight senators are 'institutional,' appointed by the President (in this case, General Pinochet) and not subject to popular vote. Although the President continues to reside in Santiago and work at the Palacio de la Moneda there, the congress now meets in Valparaíso.

Administratively, the country consists of a Metropolitan Region, including the capital of Santiago and its surroundings, plus a dozen more distinct regions, one of which includes the Chilean Antarctic (where territorial claims are on hold by international agreement). The regions, in turn, are subdivided into provinces, which are further subdivided into *comunas*, the units of local government. Traditionally, Chilean politics is highly centralized, with nearly all decisions of importance made in Santiago.

Political Parties & Trade Unions

Since 1987, conventional political parties have operated legally, and the armed resistance that continued into the early years of the constitutional transition has all but ceased. Many prominent exiles have returned to Chile and the trade union movement, generally allied with center-left parties, also operates freely, but the latter's influence is greatly diminished by discriminatory legislation passed during the Pinochet dictatorship. Only about 22% of Chile's 3.5-million-person workforce belongs to unions, whose principal representative is the Central Unitaria de Trabajadores (CUT, Central Union of Workers).

The range and variation of political parties and their incessant transformations make it very difficult for any but the most experienced observer to follow Chilean electoral politics. In the 1989 elections, 17 parties with little in common except their opposition to Pinochet formed an unlikely coalition known as the Concertación para la Democracia, choosing Christian Democrat Patricio Aylwin as a compromise candidate for the presidency. Aylwin easily defeated Pinochet's reluctant protégé Hernán Büchi, who stood for Renovación Nacional (RN, a direct descendant of the conservative National Party), and independent businessman Francisco Errázuriz, a right-wing populist. The right-wing Unión Democrática Independiente (UDI), founded by the late Senator Guzmán, maintains a shaky alliance with the more moderate RN.

In the 1993 presidential elections, the Concertación easily elected Christian Democrat Eduardo Frei Ruiz-Tagle over RN candidate Arturo Alessandri for a six-year term, but as the 1999 election approaches there is increasing internal disagreement over presidential politics. Socialist Ricardo Lagos, currently Frei's public works minister, is a popular nationwide figure, but many Christian Democrats argue that, as the Concertación's largest party, the nominee should be one of theirs. The likeliest conservative candidate is RN's highly regarded and relatively moderate Andrés Allamand.

President Frei's efforts at reforming the constitution to eliminate the institutional Senators failed, despite Allamand's cooperation, when the recalcitrant UDI and the most conservative RN senators failed to go along. The proposed reform, incidentally, would have prevented Frei (or any other president) from choosing replacements for Pinochet appointees whose terms have expired.

The Military

Prussian officer Emilio Körner, contracted to reform the Chilean officer training academy in the late 19th century, is responsible for the army's organization. As head of its general staff from 1891 to 1910, he introduced German instructors, uniforms, discipline and modern equipment. Even today, Chilean soldiers in parade dress bear a disconcerting resemblance to jackbooted German troops of the 1930s and 1940s.

Although the Pinochet regime is often seen as an aberration and the army as apolitical, Chile has suffered four civil wars, 10 successful coups, and many uprisings and mutinies since independence from Spain. Military service is obligatory (though not universal) for males, but there is growing sentiment for eliminating conscription.

Despite the return to civilian rule, the military retain considerable power and the constitution institutionalizes this, at least in the short term – Pinochet's senate appointees, with help from elected conservatives, can block reform, and he himself will take a senate seat upon retirement from the army in 1997. All the services enjoy great autonomy, as the civilian president lacks authority to discipline their chiefs or even junior officers. Unlike neighboring Argentina, where ignominious defeat in the Falklands war of 1982 undercut military privilege, the triumphant Chilean military are nearly unrepentant about human rights abuses under their dictatorship. Only General Máximo Venegas of the FACh (Chile's air force, the most reluctant participant in the 1973 coup) has shown any contrition, saying his branch of the armed forces asks forgiveness 'if wrong deeds were committed.'

Pinochet (born 1915) remains a force in Chilean politics, but his age and declining health have reduced his influence. The influence of the military will remain strong, however, as the civilian president can only choose Pinochet's replacement as commander-in-chief from a list provided by the military themselves. In addition, the heads of the armed services comprise a Consejo de Seguridad Nacional (National Security Council) that, in case of state emergencies, can suspend the constitution and impose martial law.

According to the British-based International Institute for Strategic Studies (IISS), Chile has 93,000 professional military personnel, plus another 30,000 conscripts in uniform. All the services are highly disciplined, cohesive and far more loyal to their commanders than to the civilian head of state, but civilians have sometimes exploited inter-service rivalries, especially between the older army and navy and the newer air force. In 1994 Chile devoted 3.5% of its GDP to military spending (the highest percentage of any Latin American country), and the forces are insulated from budgetary responsibility in part by a legal provision which guarantees them 10% of the profits from state copper sales, about US$400 million annually in hard currency, for arms purchases. By law, the military budget cannot fall below 1989 levels, nor can it go down in real terms.

Geopolitics

One of the mainstays of military ideology and influence is the idea of geopolitics, a 19th-century European doctrine first elaborated by German geographer Friedrich Ratzel and later exaggerated in National Socialist (Nazi) ideology in the 1930s. According to this world view, the state resembles a biological organism which must grow (expand) or die. This means that the state must effectively occupy the territories which it claims, in which process it comes into conflict with other states. Historically, this has been the justification for Chilean expansion into Tarapacá and the Pacific islands, as well as Antarctica.

Other South American countries, particularly Argentina and Brazil, share this perspective. General Pinochet has even written a textbook entitled *Geopolítica*, while his Argentine and Brazilian counterparts expound on topics such as the 'Fifth Column' of Chilean immigrants in Patagonia (largely humble and illiterate sheep shearers from the economically depressed island of Chiloé) or the justification of territorial claims in the Antarctic in accordance with each country's longitudinal 'frontage' on the icebound continent. Chile has gone so far as to establish a 'permanent' settlement of families in Antarctica, with formal state services such as banking and housing. The tenets of geopolitics are most popular among, but not restricted to, the military. At the same time, the country has settled nearly all of its long-standing border disputes with neighboring Argentina.

Among the last geopolitical disputes between Argentina and Chile are the Laguna del Desierto on the border between the regions of Aisén and Magallanes, recently settled in Argentina's favor, and the still unsettled Campo de Hielo Sur, the southern Patagonian ice field. When Chile submitted to arbitration at Laguna del Desierto, it expected to gain something and was shocked when arbitrators awarded the entire disputed area to Argentina. After going through an appeal process to save face, the Chilean government has also had to endure exaggerated criticism from right-wing parties over a proposed settlement in the Campo de Hielo Sur. The Chilean air force, for its part, quickly built an airfield and training base directly on the ice.

Human Rights

Despite the military's self-serving amnesty laws, human rights issues have not gone away. Former DINA chief Manuel Contreras and his deputy Pedro Espinosa have gone to prison for their roles in the Letelier case, though critics consider their incarceration in a custom-built facility near Santiago only a slap on the wrist (some defenders of Contreras and Espinosa consider them scapegoats for the rest of the military). It is worth mentioning that General Contreras inhabits a 'cell' with custom furniture, a large personal library, outside phone lines and an Internet connection, plus his own cook, waiter and full-time nurse.

A greater worry for the former military rulers is the Buenos Aires trial of ex-DINA agent Enrique Arancibia Clavel for the assassination of General Prats, since it could reveal details of covert operations outside the shield of military courts and hand-picked judges. At the same time, the government of Uruguay has been investigating the mysterious death of Eugenio Berríos, a former Chilean intelligence agent who disappeared in 1992 after seeking police protection in that country against his former DINA colleagues.

In addition, while the government of Spain has dropped its demand for extradition and prosecution of the killers of Carmelo Soria (a Spanish diplomat working under United Nations auspices in 1978) because Chile's Supreme Court invoked the amnesty law, Soria's family continues to pursue the case in Spanish and international courts.

ECONOMY

When Pinochet's junta seized power, it had no strategy beyond an urge to eradicate leftist influence and stabilize the economy. Its pledge to reduce inflation and return confiscated property appealed to conservatives and professionals opposed to Allende, but it soon adopted a more radical economic program.

Pinochet appointed civilian economists, disciples of the economics department at the University of Chicago, to direct government policy. To encourage commerce, the so-called 'Chicago Boys' favored measures that slashed government expenditures and eliminated regulatory functions, eliminated price controls, reduced tariffs in the interests of free trade, and sold most state-owned industries to private entrepreneurs, while new financial codes encouraged foreign investment. Codelco (Corporación del Cobre, the national copper company) remained under state ownership, but the government compensated North American mining companies for their losses. State-owned banks froze interest rates for savings, but private banks raised them, causing a flow of personal savings into private institutions.

For some years, inflation remained high despite shrinking domestic demand and declining imports. Industrial production also declined and some inefficient industries disappeared, although growth of 'non-traditional' exports, such as off-season temperate fruits to Europe and North America, helped compensate for falling copper prices. Despite falling wages unemployment reached nearly 20% by early 1976.

In some callampas, where unemployment reached as high as 80% or more, only church-organized soup kitchens prevented starvation. The government's response was the PEM (Programa de Empleo Mínimo, Minimum Employment Program), which paid a token monthly salary to individuals who swept streets or performed other minor public works duties.

As private owners acquired former state banks, interest rates escaped government controls and subsequently soared. Firms borrowing money to avoid bankruptcy fell into debt to private banks and finance companies. Not surprisingly, financiers – some of them Chicago Boys using foreign loan money – obtained failed enterprises at little cost and developed their own personal business empires.

When inflation finally fell, real wages and salaries rose only slowly, increasing consumer demand for goods and services. Since local industry could not satisfy this demand, duty-free zones in the northern city of Iquique and the southern city of Punta

Arenas fueled an import boom, but Chile continued to rely on the export of primary products such as minerals, timber, fruit and seafood in order to earn foreign exchange.

In the early 1980s, global recession reduced the price of copper and other mineral exports, but Chile's international debt (almost all of it created by foreign loans to private banks and firms) increased. By the end of 1981, loan repayments were consuming 75% of export earnings. Interest rates climbed, bankruptcies increased and unemployment soared.

In 1982 the government sought to promote exports by devaluing the peso and further reducing wages, but inflation soon wiped out any benefits for exporters. Rising local and global interest rates exacerbated the banks' debt problems. Allowed to float, the peso plummeted by 40% against the US dollar and, with the Chicago Boys' policies in shambles, the junta backtracked and bailed out key private banks and finance houses in early 1983.

In recent years, the Chilean economy has improved greatly on a macro scale, enjoying a decade of uninterrupted growth at rates of 6% or higher, and some Chileans like to compare their country with advancing industrial powers like South Korea. Chile has been able to maintain its external debt payments, and inflation is historically low at about 8% annually. Exports increased more than 10% in 1995, constituting nearly 25% of the US$66.7 billion GDP, and growth for 1996 was projected at 7.4%, the highest rate in all of Latin America and the Caribbean.

But the elite have benefited more from economic growth than the poor, and unemployment remains distressingly high, with countless city dwellers earning a precarious subsistence as street vendors of ice cream, candy, cigarettes and other cheap goods like audio cassettes. The minimum wage is about US$146 per month (although the government proposed legislation to increase this by about 11% in 1996), and the gap between rich and poor is widening.

While both the Aylwin and Frei administrations have displayed a more sympathetic attitude toward the plight of the poor and dispossessed, they have largely continued the junta's macroeconomic policies despite some increases in social spending. The inequalities of wealth now resemble the inequalities of land distribution in earlier times. According to a recent report by the United Nations' Santiago-based Economic Commission for Latin America and the Caribbean (Cepal), the wealthiest 10% of Chileans receives more than 40% of the national income, while the poorest 40% earns just 13%. While these figures were among the worst in the region, Cepal also reported that the number of Chileans living in poverty fell from nearly 40% in 1987 to less than 25% in 1995.

At the same time, since the return to representative government, there has been an influx of foreign capital from companies that were clearly reluctant to invest in the dictatorship, and there is hope that vigorous economic growth will reduce poverty. Since 1987, Chile has enjoyed an increasing trade surplus; its most important trading partners are the USA, Japan, Germany, Brazil and Argentina.

The export economy is now more diverse and less vulnerable to fluctuations in international markets; the mining sector, for instance, no longer relies exclusively on copper, but also produces less traditional commodities like lithium. Disruptions in the copper industry still have a serious impact on the economy, though, as the satirical *Annals of Improbable Research* noted in granting the 'Ig Nobel Prize' in Economics to former Codelco official Juan Pablo Dávila:

tireless trader of financial futures . . . for instructing his computer to 'buy' when he meant 'sell,' and subsequently attempting to recoup his losses by making increasingly unprofitable trades that ultimately lost .5% of Chile's gross national product. Dávila's relentless achievement inspired his countrymen to coin a new verb *davilar*, meaning 'to botch things up royally.'

Nevertheless, export items like fresh fruit have also increased and diversified, after a brief glitch in 1989 when a handful of Chilean table grapes in Philadelphia were found to be poisoned with cyanide, leading to a suspension of US fruit imports from Chile. This angered all sectors of Chilean society and continues to irritate Chilean producers, but the industry has largely recovered.

International travel and tourism are flourishing – in 1995, 1.5 million foreign visitors spent US$850 million in Chile, constituting about 4% of the GDP and 7% of total export income. Forest products are a rapidly growing but increasingly controversial sector, given the country's declining native forests, the apparent unsustainability of the present level of exports, and dubious reforestation programs of fast-growing exotic species like Monterey pine and eucalyptus.

POPULATION & PEOPLE

Chile's population of about 14.2 million is unevenly distributed. Nearly a third, about 4.3 million, reside in Gran Santiago, which includes the capital and its immediate suburbs; this includes 70% of all Chileans between the ages of 15 and 24. No other city is larger than about 308,000. Moreover, almost 75% live in the Chilean heartland (including the conurbations of Valparaíso/Viña del Mar and Concepción/Talcahuano), which comprises only 20% of the country's total land area. More than 80% of Chileans live in cities or towns, but south of the Río Biobío, there is still a dense rural population.

In the desert north, nearly everyone lives in the large coastal cities of Arica, Iquique, Antofagasta, La Serena and Coquimbo, although the mining centers of Calama/Chuquicamata, El Salvador and Copiapó are relatively large as well. South of Santiago, the most important cities are Rancagua, the Concepción/Talcahuano, Valdivia, Osorno and Puerto Montt. Beyond Puerto Montt, where the fractured landscape complicates communications, the only notable towns are Coihaique, in Region XI, and Punta Arenas in Region XII.

Most Chileans are mestizos, although many can still claim purely European descent. In much of the country, social class is still a greater issue than race – working-class people and others resentfully call the country's elite *momios* (mummies) because, to paraphrase the words of film director Miguel Littín, they are so resistant to change that they might as well be embalmed. In the southern region of La Araucanía, there is a large, visible and increasingly militant Mapuche Indian population, mostly in and around the city of Temuco. Above the once-densely peopled river valleys of the desert north, Aymara and Atacameño peoples farm the terraces of the precordillera and pasture their llamas and alpacas in the altiplano.

Chile did not experience the massive 19th- and 20th-century European immigration which neighboring Argentina did – at the end of the 19th century, only a small percentage of Chileans were foreign-born. After the European upheavals of 1848, many Germans settled near present-day Valdivia, Osorno and Puerto Montt in southern Chile, where use of the German language is still vigorous, if not widespread. Other immigrant groups included the French, Italians, Yugoslavs (particularly in Magallanes and Tierra del Fuego), European Jews and Palestinians.

European immigration did not alter the structure of Chilean society, but added non-Spanish elements to the middle and upper classes. The established aristocracy (the original landed gentry), of mostly Spanish Basque origin, welcomed wealthy immigrants with British, French or German surnames like Edwards, Subercaseaux and Gildemeister. Despite their small numbers, European immigrants became economically powerful, controlling rural estates and commercial, financial and industrial institutions.

EDUCATION

Chile's 94% literacy rate is one of Latin America's highest. From the age of five to 12, education is free and compulsory, although school attendance is low in some rural areas.

Universities are traditionally free and open, but after the 1973 coup the military government installed its own rectors throughout the country; its sweeping university reform of the 1980s reduced state funding, raised student fees, and downgraded or eliminated ostensibly 'subversive' careers such as sociology and psychology. The Universidad de Chile was a particular target because of its reputation for aggressive dissent, and is undergoing further downsizing under the Frei administration.

Like other Latin American countries, Chile suffers from a glut of lawyers and other professionals, and a shortage of trained people in engineering and other more practical fields. The military reform of higher education made it easy to open private 'universities,' but most of these are glorified trade schools with part-time faculty, limited curriculum and dubious standards.

ARTS

Although derivative of European precedents in many ways, Chilean art, literature and music have been influential beyond the

The Paths of Mistral & Neruda

Gabriela Mistral and Pablo Neruda have opened a window on Chile and Latin America through their poetry, but their biographies are no less revealing. In some ways, no two individuals could be more different than these two Nobel Prize winners, but the parallels and divergences in their lives disclose both unifying and contrasting aspects of Chilean life and culture.

They were contemporaries, but of different generations; Mistral was born in 1889, Neruda in 1904. Both belonged to the provinces: Mistral to the remote Elqui valley of the Norte Chico, Neruda to the southern city of Temuco, though his birthplace was Parral, in the heartland province of Maule, and he lived in Santiago, Valparaíso and in a small beach community at Isla Negra. Both poets used pseudonyms: Gabriela Mistral's given name was Lucila Godoy Alcayaga, while Pablo Neruda's was Neftalí Ricardo Reyes Basoalto. Both adopted their aliases out of timidity: the young rural schoolmistress Lucila Godoy sat in the audience at Santiago's Teatro Municipal while a surrogate received a prize for her 'Sonnets on Death,' in memory of a young suitor who had committed suicide; Neftalí Reyes feared the ridicule of his working-class family.

Both enjoyed literary success at a young age. The government rewarded both with diplomatic posts which subsidized their creative writing; in consequence, both traveled extensively and became celebrities outside their own country and the South American continent, which hadn't produced a Nobel Prize winner in literature until Mistral's award in 1945. In 1971, Neruda became the third Latin American writer to receive the Swedish Academy's prize (Guatemalan novelist Miguel Angel Asturias was the second, in 1967).

Despite these similarities, they were very different in other respects. After the death of her beloved, Mistral never married and devoted her life to children and their education at schools from La Serena to Punta Arenas – when she taught in Temuco, the young Neruda and his friends worshipped her. She even traveled abroad to reform the Mexican system of public instruction. She lived austerely, but her stern features masked the sensitivity of a woman whose poetry was compassionate and mystical. Though friendly with political figures, most notably President Pedro Aguirre Cerda, her politics were not a matter of public controversy.

Neruda, by contrast, became a flamboyant figure whose private life was public knowledge, who built eccentric houses and filled them with outlandish objects, and whose politics more than once landed him in trouble. Unlike the somber Mistral, his face was usually smiling, often pensive, but never grim. While consul in Java in the 1930s, he married a Dutch woman, left her for Delia del Carril (a decade older than himself) a few years later, and after nearly 20 years left Delia for the much younger Matilde Urrutia, for whom he built and named La Chascona, his Santiago house at the foot of Cerro San Cristóbal.

Neruda's houses, including his beachfront favorite at Isla Negra and La Sebastiana in country's borders. Many Chilean intellectuals have been educated in European capitals, particularly Paris. In the 19th and early-20th centuries Santiago self-consciously emulated European – especially French – cultural trends in art, music and architecture. There are many art museums and galleries.

Literature

Pablo Neruda and Gabriela Mistral, both Nobel Prize-winning poets, are major figures in Chilean, Latin American and world literature. Much of their work is available in English translation, such as Neruda's *The Heights of Macchu Picchu, Canto General, Passions and Impressions,* and his rambling, selective but still readable *Memoirs* (Farrar, Strauss & Giroux, New York, 1977). For an interestingly conceived view of Neruda and his work, see Luis Poirot's *Pablo Neruda, Absence and Presence* (Norton, New York, 1990), a collection of outstanding black & white photos with accompanying text from Neruda, friends and admirers (both Chilean and foreign). Especially poignant are the photos of Neruda's houses in Santiago,

Valparaíso, were material expressions of his personality, improvised with eclectic assemblies of objects amassed on his travels and at his diplomatic posts – entire rooms are filled with shells, bowsprit figureheads, ships-in-bottles, and of course books, all of which delighted him and his guests and now draw thousands of visitors. The houses themselves break all the rules of standard architecture and, for that reason, intrigue the visitor as much as they pleased the owner. In his autobiography, he wrote that 'I have . . . built my house like a toy house and I play in it from morning till night.'

After Franco's rebels defeated the Spanish Republic, the Chilean diplomat devoted his energies to helping refugees escape the dictator's revenge. In Spain he had made a personal commitment to the Communist party, although he did not enroll officially until his return to Chile, where he was elected Senator for Tarapacá and Antofagasta, the mining provinces of the Norte Grande. After managing Gabriel González Videla's successful presidential campaign of 1946, he fell afoul of the president's caprice and went into hiding and then exile in Argentina, escaping by foot and horseback across the southern Andes to Argentina.

After González Videla left office, Neruda returned to Chile and continued his political activities without reducing his prolific output of poetry. In 1969 he was the Communist candidate for the presidency, but resigned in support of Salvador Allende's candidacy and later became Allende's ambassador to France. He received the Nobel Prize during his tenure in France, but died less than a fortnight after the military coup of 1973.

For all his wealth, Neruda never forgot his modest origins nor abandoned his political convictions, and did not consider his privileged lifestyle incompatible with his leftist beliefs – lacking heirs, he left everything to the Chilean people through a foundation.

Mistral's reflective and mystical verse was uncontroversial, but Neruda's poetry could be committed and combative and, although no government could suppress literature which could be found in almost every household that could spare a penny to buy it, General Pinochet's military regime did its best to erase his memory. After Neruda's death, his houses were vandalized with police and military complicity, but his widow Matilde and dedicated volunteers persisted to establish the Fundación Neruda in spite of legal and extralegal obstacles. It now administers the estate and has successfully restored all three houses, now open to the public. Both Chileans and foreigners flock to them and, with a very few truly extreme exceptions, even those who disagreed with his politics enjoy and respect his work.

Gabriela Mistral, meanwhile, remains a modest but reassuring presence in Chilean life and literature. Every day, thousands of Santiago's citizens pass the mural of Gabriela and her 'children' on the Alameda, at the base of Cerro Santa Lucía, while many more pay her homage at the museum bearing her name in the village of Vicuña, in her native Elqui valley. Though she died in New York, she is buried in her natal hamlet of Montegrande. ∎

Valparaíso and Isla Negra after their vandalization by the military.

US poet Langston Hughes translated some of Gabriela Mistral's work in *Selected Poems of Gabriela Mistral* (Indiana University Press, 1957), while a different book with the same title was published by the Library of Congress and Johns Hopkins Press in 1971. For an interpretation of her work, try Margot Arce de Vásquez's *Gabriela Mistral, the Poet and Her Work* (New York University Press, 1964).

Important contemporary poets include Nicanor Parra, who has drawn Nobel Prize attention, and Jorge Teillier, whose work has been translated and analyzed by Carolyne Wright in *In Order to Talk with the Dead* (University of Texas, 1993).

With novels in the 'magical realism' tradition of Latin American fiction, Isabel Allende (niece of the late President Salvador Allende) has become a popular writer overseas as well as in Chile. Among her works are *House of the Spirits*, *Of Love and Shadows* and *Eva Luna*.

Chile's best contemporary novelist, José Donoso, passed away in late 1996. His *Curfew* (Weidenfield & Nicholson, New York, 1988) offers a portrait of life under the dictatorship through the eyes of a returned exile. Antonio Skármeta's *I Dreamt the Snow was Burning* (Reader's International, London, 1985) is a novel of the early post-coup years, but Skármeta has become more famous for his novel *Burning Patience* (Pantheon, 1987), adapted into the award-winning Italian film *Il Postino* (The Postman).

Recently translated into English, Luis Sepúlveda's misleadingly titled novella *The Old Man Who Read Love Stories* (Harcourt Brace, New York, 1993) is a fictional account of life and society on the Amazonian frontier of Ecuador.

Marco Antonio de la Parra's *The Secret Holy War of Santiago de Chile* (Interlink Books, New York, 1994) is a surrealistic novel of contemporary Chile, with numerous geographical and cultural references which anyone who has visited the capital will find fascinating and challenging.

Music

Probably the best-known manifestation of Chilean popular culture is *La Nueva Canción Chilena* (New Chilean Song Movement), whose practitioners wedded the country's folkloric heritage to the political passions of the late 1960s and early 1970s. Its most legendary figure is Violeta Parra, best known for her enduring theme *Gracias a la Vida* (Thanks to Life), but her children Isabel and Angel, also performers, established the first of many *peñas* (musical and cultural centers) in Santiago in the mid-1960s. Individual performers such as Victor Jara, brutally executed during the 1973 coup, and groups like Quilapayún and Inti-Illimani acquired international reputations for both their music and their political commitment.

Many Chilean folk musicians, exiled during the Pinochet dictatorship, performed regularly in Europe, North America and Australia, and their recordings are available both in Chile and overseas.

Film

Until the coup of 1973, Chilean cinema was among the most experimental in Latin America. Director Alejandro Jodorowsky's surrealistic *El Topo* (The Mole), an underground success overseas, included a performance by the San Francisco-area band Country Joe and the Fish. Exiled director Miguel Littín's *Alsino & the Condor*, nominated for an Academy Award as Best Foreign Film in 1983, is readily available on video.

Director Gustavo Graef-Marino's *Johnny 100 Pesos*, based on a true story about a group of thieves who become trapped in a Santiago highrise, made a favorable impression at 1994's Sundance Film Festival, leading to work-in-progress with Francis Ford Coppola's American Zoetrope studio.

There are also a number of foreign films about Chile. Costa-Gavras' 1982 film *Missing*, available on video, was based on Thomas Hauser's book *The Execution of Charles Horman: An American Sacrifice*. Ben Kingsley and Sigourney Weaver starred in the English-language adaptation of Ariel Dorfman's play *Death and the Maiden*, now available on video. Antonio Skármeta's novel *Burning Patience* was the template for the award-winning Italian film *Il Postino* (The Postman), a fictional exploration of Pablo Neruda and his counsel to a shy but love-struck mail carrier.

Theater

Even in the provinces, live theater is an important medium of expression. While traditional venues like Santiago's Teatro Municipal operated more or less normally during the Pinochet dictatorship, the end of military government has meant a major burst of growth in central neighborhoods like Barrio Bellavista and even suburban comunas like Ñuñoa. Look for small experimental companies like La Tropa, a three-person outfit that plays public parks like Plaza Ñuñoa.

One of Chile's best-known playwrights is Ariel Dorfman, whose *Death and the Maiden* explored issues of brutality and reconciliation in the post-military years; it also became an English-language film. Of a younger generation, Marco Antonio de la Parra remained in Santiago during the Pinochet years, despite censorship of such works as *Lo Crudo, lo Cocido y lo Podrido* (The Raw, the Cooked and the Rotten). Many of his plays have been performed in Europe and North America.

Painting & Sculpture

Chile has many art museums but, with a handful of exceptions, their focus is historical rather than contemporary, and the work is unexceptional. Venues like Santiago's Palacio de Bellas Artes tend to focus on traveling international exhibitions, but places like Providencia's Parque de las Esculturas (an open-air museum along the Río Mapocho), Valparaíso's Museo de Bellas Artes (featuring 19th-century Chilean landscapes by English painter Thomas Somerscales and a handful of subtly political contemporary works), and Castro's Museo de Arte Moderno de Chiloé are worth a visit. Public murals, inspired by

the Mexican muralists who left a visible legacy in Chillán and Concepción, deserve a look.

Among Chile's notable contemporary artists are Máximo Pincheira, whose grim works deal with the anxieties of life under the dictatorship, and María José Romero (daughter of painter Carmen Aldunate), whose self-described 'frivolous' oils deal more with personal than political issues.

SOCIETY & CONDUCT

English-speaking visitors will find Chile, like Argentina, more accessible than other Latin American countries because of its superficial resemblance to their own societies. Foreign travelers are less conspicuous than in countries like Peru and Bolivia, which have large indigenous populations, and can more easily integrate themselves into everyday life. Chileans are exceptionally hospitable and often invite foreigners to visit their homes and participate in daily activities, but may also be very reserved at times.

Travelers should be circumspect in their behavior around indigenous peoples, especially in areas like the altiplano of Arica, around San Pedro de Atacama, and in the Mapuche south. Aggressive picture-taking and rowdiness may be particularly offensive.

RELIGION

Traditionally about 90% of Chileans are Roman Catholic, but evangelical Protestantism is rapidly gaining converts. There are also Lutherans, Jews, Presbyterians, Mormons and Pentecostals. The proselytizing Mormons have caused great controversy, and their churches have been the target of numerous bombings by leftist groups.

Catholicism has provided Chile some of its most compelling cultural monuments – the colonial adobe churches of the Norte Grande, Santiago's Catedral Metropolitana and colonial Iglesia San Francisco, and the modest but dignified shingled chapels of Chiloé. Countless roadside shrines, some of which are extraordinary manifestations of folk art, also testify to the pervasiveness of religion in Chilean society.

Like Chilean political parties, the Church has many factions, but its Vicaria de la Solidaridad compiled such an outstanding human rights record during the dictatorship that it became the major object of the general's vitriolic scorn in his four-volume autobiography. At great risk to themselves, Chilean priests frequently worked in the shantytowns of Santiago and other large cities. Such activism has continued in today's more lenient political climate.

On the other hand, the Church's attitude toward other social issues is starkly reactionary. Its continued resistance to divorce has contributed to the fact that Chile is the world's only democracy without a divorce law, though annulments are not unusual for those who can pay for the legal maneuvering, and the government has found it difficult to institute important sex education programs against ecclesiastical opposition.

Facts for the Visitor

PLANNING
When to Go

For residents of the Northern Hemisphere, Chile offers the inviting prospect of enjoying two summers in the same year, but the country's geographical variety can make a visit rewarding in any season. Santiago and Middle Chile are best in the verdant spring (September through November) or during the fall harvest (late February into April), while popular natural attractions like Parque Nacional Torres del Paine in Magallanes and the lakes region are best in summer (December through March). Conversely, Chilean ski resorts draw many foreigners during the northern summer (June through August).

The Atacama desert is temperate and attractive at any time of year, although nights can be very cold at higher altitudes. In the northern altiplano, the rainy season is the summer months, but this usually means only a brief afternoon thunderstorm. Still, the dry spring months are probably best for explorations off the main highways.

Easter Island is cooler, slightly cheaper and much less crowded outside the summer months. The same is true of the Juan Fernández archipelago, which can be inaccessible if winter rains erode the dirt airstrip; March is an ideal time for a visit.

Maps

Lonely Planet's new *Chile Travel Atlas* maps the entire country in full color at a scale of 1:1,000,000. For members of the American Automobile Association (AAA) and its affiliates, there is a general South American road map that is adequate for initial planning.

The late Australian cartographer Kevin Healey's vivid two-sheet *Contemporary Reference Map of South America* (1:5,000,000) is packed with information but not really suitable for a trip. Even more detailed are his 1:4,000,000 maps, which cover the continent in three sheets. His latest is an excellent 1:30,000 map of Easter Island. All these maps are distributed in North America by ITM, Box 2290, Vancouver, BC V6B 3W5, Canada, and in the UK by Bradt Publications, 41 Nortoft Road, Chalfont St Peter, Bucks SL90LA.

Several useful maps of Chile are available from kiosks and street vendors in the main towns and cities. Atlas de Chile's *Plano de Santiago y Mini Atlas Caminero de Chile 1995* combines an indexed plan of the capital (1:25,000) with a respectable highway map (1:2,000,000). Inupal's *Gran Mapa Caminero de Chile* provides comparable highway coverage but lacks city maps. Esso's inexpensive *Planos* has detailed, indexed street maps of Santiago, Antofagasta, Valparaíso, Viña del Mar, Concepción and Talcahuano; it's available at most Esso stations.

The Instituto Geográfico Militar's *Guía Caminera* (1992) is a reasonably good highway map in a convenient ring-binder format, with scales ranging from 1:500,000 to 1:1,500,000; it also includes several city maps at varying scales. The IGM's *Plano Guía del Gran Santiago* (1989) is the local equivalent of *London A-Z*, at a scale of 1:20,000, but the binding is flimsy and it may have gone out of print.

The IGM's 1:50,000 topographic series is valuable for trekkers, although maps of some sensitive border areas (where most national parks are) may not be available. Individual maps cost about US$15 each in Santiago, where the IGM (☎ (02) 6968221) is at Dieciocho 369, just south of the Alameda. It's open Monday 9 am to 5.30 pm, Tuesday through Friday 9 am to 5.50 pm.

The popular Turistel guidebook series (see Guidebooks, later in this chapter) contains detailed highway maps and excellent plans of Chilean cities and towns, but lacks scales. Juan Luis Matassi Producciones

(☎ (02) 2251365), Casilla 16872, Correo 9, Santiago, publishes reasonably priced specialized maps for tourist areas like San Pedro de Atacama/Antofagasta and Torres del Paine/Magallanes at scales ranging from 1:50,000 to 1:500,000.

Some of these maps may be available at specialist bookshops like Stanford's in London, or in the map rooms of major university libraries. In most major cities, the Automóvil Club de Chile (Acchi) has an office that sells maps, although not all of them are equally well stocked. If you belong to an auto club at home, ask for a discount.

What to Bring

Chile is a mostly temperate, mid-latitude country, and seasonally appropriate clothing for North America or Europe will be equally suitable here. In the desert north, lightweight cottons are a good idea, but at the higher elevations of the Andes and in Patagonia you should carry warm clothing even in summer. From Temuco south, rain is possible at any time of the year, and a small light umbrella is useful in the city (but not in the gales of Magallanes, where heavier rain gear is desirable). In winter, budget hotels in the south may not provide sufficient blankets, so a warm sleeping bag is a good idea even if you're not camping.

There is no prejudice against backpackers and, during the summer, many young Chileans visit remote parts of the country on a shoestring budget themselves. The selection and quality of outdoor equipment are improving, but prices are still relatively high compared to North America or Europe, so it's better to bring camping gear from home.

Personal preference largely determines the best way to carry your baggage. A large zip-up bag or duffel with a wide shoulder strap is convenient for buses, trains and planes but is awkward to carry for long distances, while a backpack is most convenient if you expect to do a lot of walking. Internal frame packs, with a cover that protects the straps from getting snagged in storage on buses or planes, can be a good compromise.

Don't overlook small essentials like a Swiss Army knife, needle and cotton, a small pair of scissors, contraceptives, sunglasses and swimming gear. Basic supplies like toothbrushes and toothpaste, shaving cream, shampoo and tampons are readily available, except in very small, remote places. Visitors staying in budget hotels and traveling on buses or trains will find a good pair of earplugs useful. It's also a good idea to carry toilet paper at all times, since many if not most Chilean bathrooms lack it.

Travelers interested in wildlife, particularly birds, should not forget a pair of binoculars.

SUGGESTED ITINERARIES

Depending on the length of your trip, Chile offers many possible itineraries. A week's trip could include a stay in Santiago and excursions in the vicinity, especially during ski season, or a whirlwind trip to the desert north, taking in sights like Parque Nacional Lauca, or south, to Patagonian attractions like Torres del Paine. A two-week trip might take in both, or the southern lakes region and a four-day cruise through the Chilean fjords to Puerto Natales to get to Torres del Paine, or a side trip to Easter Island (Rapa Nui).

With more time, say a month, it's possible to do all of the above, though the long distances to be covered make some flights desirable or even essential. With more time, two months or more, it's possible to make an intimate acquaintance with Chile by traveling overland, stopping at many points of interest. The fact that nearly everything is on or near one or two major highways, with frequent and comfortable bus service, makes it easy to organize a trip.

HIGHLIGHTS

For most visitors, Chile's principal appeal will be natural attractions like the soaring volcanoes of the Andes and the southern lakes, the wild alpine scenery of Parque Nacional Torres del Paine and Laguna San Rafael, and the stark deserts of the Norte Grande, with their unique wildlife and the

Tatio geysers. Chile's long coastline offers both spectacular scenery and conventional tourist activities.

There are many appealing cultural elements: the indigenous peoples of the Norte Grande and the Araucanian south; the archaeological remains and colonial Andean churches of the Norte Grande; the enigmatic monuments of Easter Island; the vineyards of Middle Chile; the urban delights of Santiago; and the striking vernacular architecture of Valparaíso and the archipelago of Chiloé.

For a fuller listing, with capsule descriptions, consult the country highlights map.

TOURIST OFFICES
Local Tourist Offices
Every regional capital and some other cities have a local representative of Sernatur, the national tourist service, while many municipalities have their own tourist office, usually on the main plaza or at the bus terminal. In some areas, these offices may be open during the summer only.

Tourist Offices Abroad
Chilean embassies and consulates in major cities usually have a tourist representative in their delegation (see embassies and consulates listings, next page). Try also representatives of LanChile, Chile's only intercontinental airline, for tourist information.

VISAS & DOCUMENTS
Passport
Except for nationals of Argentina, Brazil, Uruguay and Paraguay, who need only their national identity cards, passports are obligatory. Citizens of Canada, the UK, the USA, Australia and most Western European countries need passports only, but Luxemburgers and New Zealanders also need advance visas. Other nationalities needing advance visas include Koreans, Poles, Indians, Thais, Jamaicans and Russians.

Note that the Chilean government now collects a US$20 processing fee from arriving US citizens in response to the US government's imposition of a similar fee on Chilean

citizens applying for US visas; this one-time payment is valid for the life of the passport.

It is advisable to carry your passport – though the military are keeping a low public profile under the present civilian government, the Carabineros (national police) can still demand identification at any moment. In general, Chileans are very document oriented, and a passport is essential for cashing travelers' checks, checking into a hotel and performing many other routine activities.

Visas
New Zealanders and citizens of a few other countries do need to obtain a visa in advance and should not arrive at the border without one, or they may be sent back to the nearest Chilean consulate. On arrival, visitors receive a tourist card and entry stamp that allow a stay of up to 90 days but are renewable for an additional 90.

Visa Extensions To renew an expiring tourist card, visit the Departamento de Extranjería (☎ (02) 6725320), Moneda 1342 in Santiago, between 9 am and 1.30 pm, or in other cities. However, since this now costs about US$100, many visitors prefer a quick dash across the Argentine border. Even the quickest trip to Mendoza and back won't cost much less than that, but it's probably more interesting than standing in lines for several days.

Do not lose your tourist card, which Chilean border authorities take very seriously; for a replacement, visit the Policía Internacional (☎ (02) 7372443) at General Borgoño 1052 in the Santiago comuna of Independencia, near the old Mapocho station, from 8.30 am to 12.30 pm or 3 to 7 pm. One reader reports that, with the help of airline staff, a card can be replaced more quickly at the international airport.

Re-Entry Visas If staying longer than six months, it's simplest to make a brief visit to Argentina, Peru or Bolivia, then return and start your six months all over again. There is no formal obstacle to doing so, although border officials sometimes

CHILEAN EMBASSIES ABROAD

Chile has diplomatic representation in most parts of the world; those listed are the ones most likely to be useful to intending visitors. In some places there is a tourist information section with a separate address.

Argentina
San Martín 439, 9th floor
Buenos Aires
(☎ 394-6582)

Australia
10 Culgoa Circuit, O'Malley
ACT 2606
(☎ 286-2430)

Bolivia
Avenida H Siles 5843
Barrio Obrajes, La Paz
(☎ 785275)

Brazil
Praia do Flamengo 382
No 401, Flamengo
Rio de Janeiro
(☎ 552-5349)

Avenida Paulista 1009, 10th floor, São Paulo (☎ 284-2044)

Canada
151 Slater St, Suite 605
Ottawa, Ontario K1P 6L2
(☎ 613-235-4402)

Tourist Information:
56 Sparks St, Suite 801
Ottawa, Ontario K1P 5I4
(☎ 613-235-4402)

Consulates:
170 Bloor St West
Suite 800
Toronto, Ontario M5S 1T9
(☎ 416-924-0106)

1010 Sherbrooke St West
Suite 710
Montréal, Québec H3A 2R7
(☎ 514-499-8964)

New Zealand
7th floor, Robert Jones House
1-3 Welleston St, Wellington
(☎ 725180)

Paraguay
Guido Spano 1687
Asunción
(☎ 600671)

Peru
Javier Prado Oeste 790
San Isidro, Lima
(☎ 440-7965)

UK
12 Devonshire St, London
W1N 2DS
(☎ 0171-580-1023)

Uruguay
Andes 1365, 1st floor
Montevideo (☎ 98-2223)

USA
1736 Massachusetts Ave NW
Washington, DC 20036
(☎ 202-785-3159)

Tourist Information: 1732
Massachusetts Ave NW
Washington, DC 20036
(☎ 202-785-1746)

Consulates:
866 United Nations Plaza
Suite 302
New York, NY 10017
(☎ 212-980-3366)

79 Milk St, Suite 600
Boston, MA 02109
(☎ 617-426-1678)

Public Ledger Building
Suites 444-46, 6th &
Chestnut Sts
Philadelphia, PA 19142
(☎ 215-829-9520)

1110 Brickell Ave, Suite 616
Miami, FL 33131
(☎ 305-373-8623)

American Airlines Building
Suite 800, 1509 López
Landrón, Santurce, San Juan
PR 00911
(☎ 809-725-6365)

875 N Michigan Ave
Suite 3352, Chicago, IL 60611
(☎ 312-654-8780)

1360 Post Oak Blvd
Suite 2330
Houston, TX 77056
(☎ 713-621-5853)

130 S 500 E 510
Salt Lake City, UT 84102
(☎ 801-531-1292)

870 Market St, Suite 1062
San Francisco, CA 94105
(☎ 415-982-7662)

1900 Avenue of the Stars
Suite 1250
Los Angeles, CA 90067
(☎ 310-785-0047)

550 West C St, Suite 1820
San Diego, CA 92101
(☎ 619-222-0080)

1860 Ala Moana Blvd
No 1900, Honolulu, HI 96815
(☎ 808-949-2850)

question returnees from Mendoza, Argentina, to determine whether they are working illegally in Chile.

Onward Tickets

Theoretically, Chile requires a return or onward ticket for arriving travelers, and some airlines may ask for evidence of an onward ticket if the date of your return ticket is beyond the initial 90-day tourist-card limit. However, the author has crossed various Chilean border posts, including international airports, dozens of times over many years without ever having been asked for an onward ticket.

Travel Insurance

In addition to health insurance (see under Health, in this chapter), a policy that protects baggage and valuables like cameras and camcorders is a good idea. Keep your insurance records separate from your other possessions in case you have to make a claim.

FOREIGN EMBASSIES & CONSULATES IN CHILE

All major European and South American countries, and many others as well, have embassies in Santiago. The neighboring countries of Argentina, Bolivia and Peru have consulates in a number of other cities; their addresses appear in the entries on those places. The telephone area code for the following numbers is 02.

Argentina
Vicuña Mackenna 41
(☎ 2228977)

Australia
Gertrudis Echeñique 420
Las Condes
(☎ 2285065)

Austria
Barros Errázuriz 1968
3rd floor, Providencia
(☎ 2234774)

Belgium
Providencia 2653
Oficina 1104, Providencia
(☎ 2321071)

Bolivia
Avenida Santa María 2796
(☎ 2328180)

Brazil
MacIver 225, 15th floor
(☎ 6398867)

Canada
Ahumada 11, 10th floor
(☎ 6962256)

Denmark
Jacques Cazotte 5531
Vitacura
(☎ 2185949)

Finland
Avenida 11 de Septiembre
1480, Oficina 73
Providencia
(☎ 2360107)

France
Condell 65, Providencia
(☎ 2251030)

Germany
Agustinas 785, 7th floor
(☎ 6335031)

Israel
San Sebastián 2812, 5th floor
Las Condes
(☎ 2461570)

Italy
Román Díaz 1270
Providencia
(☎ 2259212)

Japan
Ricardo Lyon 520, Providencia
(☎ 2321807)

Mexico
Félix de Amesti 128
Las Condes
(☎ 2066132)

Netherlands
Las Violetas 2368, Providencia
(☎ 2236934)

New Zealand
Isidora Goyenechea 3516
Las Condes
(☎ 2314204)

Norway
San Sebastián 2839
Oficina 509, Las Condes
(☎ 2342888)

Paraguay
Huérfanos 886, Oficina 514
(☎ 6394640)

Peru
Avenida Andrés Bello 1751
Providencia
(☎ 2354600)

Spain
Providencia 1979, 4th floor
Providencia
(☎ 2040239)

Sweden
Avenida 11 de Septiembre
2353, 4th floor
(☎ 2312733)

Switzerland
Providencia 2653
Oficina 1602
(☎ 2322693)

UK
Avenida El Bosque Norte
0125, 3rd floor, Las Condes
(☎ 2313737)

Uruguay
Pedro de Valdivia 711
Providencia
(☎ 2238398)

USA
Avenida Costanera 2800
Las Condes
(☎ 2322600)

Driver's License & Permits

Driver's License Foreigners resident in Chile may obtain a Chilean driver's license through the municipality in which they live.

International Driving Permit Motorists need an International Driving Permit to complement their national or state licenses, but highway checkpoints are no longer the danger or nuisance they were under the military regime. Carabineros at check-points or on the highways are generally firm but polite and fair, with a much higher reputation for personal integrity than most Latin American police. *Never* attempt to bribe them.

Vehicle Documents For information on purchasing and registering a car in Chile, see the Getting Around chapter. Permits for temporarily imported tourist vehicles may now be extended beyond the initial 90-day period, but not all customs officials are aware of this; it may be easier to cross the border into Argentina and return with new paperwork.

Hostel Card

Chile has a small but growing network of official hostels and affiliates throughout the country. For information, contact the Asociación Chilena de Albergues Turísticos Juveniles (☎ /fax (02) 2333220), the local affiliate of Hostelling International, at Avenida Providencia 2594, Oficina 420, in Providencia (Metro: Tobalaba) in Santiago. Hostel cards can also be purchased at the Santiago hostel, Cienfuegos 151.

Student & Youth Cards

The Instituto Nacional de la Juventud (INJ; ☎ (02) 6323646), Alameda 341 in Santiago (Metro: Universidad Católica) issues an inexpensive *tarjeta joven* (youth card) that entitles the holder to discounts on many travel services, including some airline fares and admission to national parks. It may, however, only be available to Chilean nationals and permanent residents.

International Health Card

Chile does not require an International Health Certificate, but it may be a good idea if you are visiting other South American countries, especially in the tropics. It is advisable to have a medical checkup before your trip.

CUSTOMS

There are no restrictions on import and export of local and foreign currency. Duty-free allowances include 400 cigarettes or 50 cigars or 500 grams of tobacco, 2½ liters of alcoholic beverages, and perfume for personal use. Though Chilean officials generally defer to foreign visitors, travelers crossing the border frequently and carrying electronic equipment like camcorders or laptop computers should carry a typed list of these items, with serial numbers, stamped by authorities.

Inspections are usually routine, although some travelers have had to put up with more thorough examinations because of recent drug smuggling from Peru and Bolivia. Travelers from Regions I (Tarapacá) and XII (Magallanes), both of which enjoy *zona franca* (duty-free) status, are subject to internal customs inspections when leaving those regions.

At international borders, officials of the SAG (Servicio Agrícola-Ganadero – Agriculture & Livestock Service) rigorously check luggage for fruit, the entry of which is strictly controlled to prevent the spread of diseases and pests that might threaten Chile's booming fruit exports. Since Chile has officially eliminated the Mediterranean fruit fly, SAG no longer maintains checkpoints along north-south routes in the Atacama desert.

Photographers should note that at major international border crossings like Los Libertadores (the crossing from Mendoza, Argentina) and Pajaritos (the crossing from Bariloche, Argentina), Chilean customs officials put baggage through x-ray machines; do not leave your film in your luggage.

MONEY
Costs

Revaluation of the Chilean peso and tourist sector inflation have increased travel costs substantially in the past few years, so that Chile is no longer inexpensive. It is still possible to travel on a budget, since modest lodging, food and transport are still more economical than in Europe, North America or even Argentina.

Allow a minimum of US$25 per day for food and lodging, but if you purchase your food at markets or eat at modest restaurants you may be able to get by more cheaply.

Cash

Cash dollars may be exchanged at banks, cambios, hotels and some travel agencies, and often in shops or on the street. At present, cash dollars earn a slightly better rate of exchange than travelers' checks and are not subject to commissions, which, however, are usually modest.

Travelers' Checks

Travelers' checks are unquestionably safer than cash, but in smaller towns and out-of-the-way locations, it can be difficult to find a bank that will change them, so carrying some cash dollars is a good idea. Some travelers have reported that lost Thomas Cook checks will not be replaced unless you notify the Santiago office of the loss within 24 hours; contact the local representative Turismo Tajamar (☎ (02) 2315112), Orrego Luco 023, Providencia, or phone collect to the office in the USA (☎ 609-987-7300).

If you have travelers' checks in US dollars, it may be better to convert them to cash and then change the cash for pesos. This is more problematic than it once was, but the American Express Bank and a few other places in Santiago will still do it.

ATMs

Automated teller machines affiliated with the Plus and Cirrus systems make it easy to get withdrawals or cash advances in major Chilean cities, but Banco del Estado's ATMs in smaller towns are incompatible with foreign ATM or credit cards.

Credit Cards

Credit cards, particularly those that allow cash advances or travelers' check purchases (American Express, Visa and MasterCard), can be very useful. Revaluation of local currency can make your bill higher than anticipated, so be aware of fluctuations in the rate. Credit cards are also useful if you must show 'sufficient funds' before entering another South American country, or in an emergency.

International Transfers

To receive money from abroad, have your home bank send a draft. Money transferred by cable should arrive in a few days; Chilean banks will give you your money in US dollars on request.

Currency

The unit of currency is the peso (Ch$). Bank notes come in denominations of 500, 1000, 5000 and 10,000 pesos, with a new 2000 peso bill entering circulation. Coin values are 1, 5, 10, 50 and 100 pesos, although one-peso coins are rare. Copper-colored coins have replaced light-weight aluminum coins, which are no longer legal tender. In small villages, it can be difficult to change bills larger than Ch$1000.

There is no restriction on export or import of local currency, but demand for pesos is minimal outside Chile, except in a few border towns and capitals.

Currency Exchange

US dollars are by far the preferred foreign currency, although Argentine pesos can be readily exchanged in Santiago, at border crossings and in tourist centers like Viña del Mar and the southern lakes region. If arriving from Argentina, it is probably better to change surplus Argentine currency directly into Chilean pesos rather than into dollars.

Commissions are insignificant except on travelers' checks in some areas, most notably Easter Island.

Exchange rates are generally better in Santiago than in the regions. Generally, only Santiago will have a ready market for European currencies, although the German mark may find purchasers in the southern lakes region. The following exchange rates, current as of late 1996, provide an idea of relative values:

Argentina	Arg$1	=	Ch$400
Australia	A$1	=	Ch$290
Canada	Can$1	=	Ch$290
France	FF1	=	Ch$77
Germany	DM1	=	Ch$275
UK	UK£1	=	Ch$642
USA	US$1	=	Ch$410

Exchange rates were very stable during the period of research, ranging from about Ch$400 to Ch$420 per US dollar. For the most up-to-date information, see *Estrategia* (Chile's equivalent of the *Wall Street Journal* or *Financial Times*) or the financial pages of *El Mercurio*.

Carrying Money

Chile is not a high-crime country, but pick-pocketing is not unknown and travelers should not carry large amounts of money in vulnerable spots like the back pocket. Both money belts and leg pouches are very secure means of carrying cash and other important monetary documents, like travelers' checks.

Black Market

Chile has no black market at present, though some businesses may give an especially favorable exchange rate for purchases in cash dollars. There is nothing illegal about this.

Tipping & Bargaining

In restaurants, it is customary to tip about 10% of the bill. In general, waiters and waitresses are poorly paid, so if you can afford to eat out you can afford to tip. Even a small *propina* will be appreciated. Taxi drivers do not require tips, although you may round off the fare for convenience.

Usually only purchases from handicrafts markets will be subject to bargaining. Hotel prices are generally fixed and prominently displayed, but in the off-season or a slow summer, haggling may be possible; for long-term stays it is definitely possible.

On occasion, long-distance bus or *taxi colectivo* (shared taxi) fares are open to negotiation, especially those between Santiago and Mendoza, Argentina.

Taxes & Refunds

At many mid-range and top-end hotels, payment in US dollars (either cash or credit) legally sidesteps the crippling 18% IVA *(impuesto de valor agregado*, the value-added tax). If there is any question as to whether IVA is included in the rates, clarify before paying.

POST & COMMUNICATIONS

Correos de Chile's postal services are reasonably dependable but sometimes rather slow. Over the past decade, telephone infrastructure has gone from the Paleolithic to the postmodern and is probably the best on the continent. Telegraph, telex and fax services are of equally high quality.

Postal Rates

Within Chile, an ordinary letter costs about US$0.20. An airmail letter costs about US$0.65 to North America and US$0.75 to other foreign destinations, while aerograms cost US$0.60 anywhere. Postcards are slightly cheaper.

Sending Mail

Chilean post offices are open weekdays 9 am to 6 pm and Saturdays 9 am to noon. Send essential overseas mail *certificado* (registered) to ensure its arrival. Mail that appears to contain money is unlikely to arrive at its final destination.

Sending parcels is straightforward, although a customs official may have to inspect your package before a postal clerk will accept it. Vendors in or near the post office will wrap parcels upon request.

Courier Services International courier services are readily available in Santiago, less so outside the capital.

Receiving Mail

You can receive mail via *lista de correos* or poste restante (equivalent to general delivery) at any Chilean post office. Santiago's American Express office offers mail services to its clients, while some consulates will also hold correspondence for their citizens. To collect mail from a post office (or from AmEx or an embassy), you need your passport as proof of identity. Instruct your correspondents to address letters clearly and to indicate a date until which the post office should hold them; otherwise, they may be returned or destroyed. There is usually a small charge, about US$0.25, per item.

Chilean post offices literally maintain separate lists of correspondence for men and women, so check both if your correspondent has not addressed the letter 'Señor,' 'Señora' or 'Señorita.' If expected correspondence does not arrive, ask the clerk to check under every possible combination of your initials, even 'M' (for Mr, Ms etc). There may be particular confusion if correspondents use your middle name, since Chileans use both paternal and maternal surnames for identification, with the former listed first. Thus a letter to 'Augusto Pinochet Ugarte' will be found under the listing for 'P' rather than 'U,' while a letter to North American 'Ronald Wilson Reagan' may be found under 'W' even though 'Reagan' is the proper surname.

Telephone

Chile's country code is ☎ 56. All telephone numbers in Santiago and the Metropolitan Region have seven digits; all other telephone numbers have six digits except for certain toll-free and emergency numbers, and cellular telephones throughout the country, which have seven digits prefixed by 09.

Despite occasional glitches due to rapid technological change, Chilean telephone services are among the best and cheapest in the world. The former state telephone monopoly Entel, the Compañía de Teléfonos de Chile (CTC) and several other carriers offer domestic and international long-distance services throughout most of the country. In the Regions X and XI, Telefónica del Sur provides most long-distance service.

Local calls from public phones cost Ch$100 (about US$0.25) for five minutes,

but outside peak hours (8 am to 8 pm weekdays, 8 am to 2 pm Saturdays) they cost only Ch$50. A liquid-crystal readout indicates the remaining credit on your call; when it reaches zero, insert another coin unless you plan to finish soon. Public phones do not make change, but if there is at least Ch$50 credit remaining you may make another call by pressing a button rather than inserting another coin.

Some CTC phones accept only coins, others only magnetic phone cards and still others accept both. *Cobro revertido* (reverse-charge or collect) calls overseas are simple, as are credit card calls. Only a handful of phones have direct fiber-optic connections to operators in North America and Europe.

CTC magnetic phone cards are available in values of Ch$3000 to Ch$5000, valid in most but not all CTC phones. Entel's 'Entel Ticket' has a similar appearance but has an individual number instead of a magnetic strip. The user dials ☎ 800-800-123, then 2, then the ticket number; at this point, a computer voice states the remaining peso amount and, after you dial the number, tells you the time that amount will permit you to speak.

Because of the so-called multi-carrier system, whereby a number of companies compete for long-distance services, charges for both foreign and domestic calls can be astonishingly cheap, but the system is

---

Carrier Codes

Both Entel and CTC have access codes to overseas operators, though it is often cheaper to pay for the calls in Chile (the opposite is true in neighboring Argentina and most other Latin American countries). The following are local carrier codes, with approximate international prices per minute in US dollars, for peak (and off-peak, when appropriate) hours. Dial the code + 182. If it's a CTC or Entel public phone, you don't need to dial the carrier code.

Carrier	USA	Canada	England	Australia
Entel (123)	1.15/0.90	2.05	2.23	2.23
CTC (188)	1.41/0.95	1.91/1.45	2.21/1.91	2.35/2.15
Chilesat (171)	1.15/0.90	2.12/1.76	2.12/1.62	2.21/2.12
BellSouth (181)	1.15/0.90	1.85/1.56	12.15/1.85	2.21/1.91
VTR (120)	1.15/0.90	2.05/1.45	2.151.65	2.23
Iusatel (155)	0.75	1.91/1.32	1.77/1.18	1.77/1.18
Carrier (121)	1.45/0.95	2.12/1.65	2.26/1.77	2.26/1.77

complicated. Most Entel and CTC offices close by 10 pm. To make a collect call, dial the number of the carrier, then 182 for an operator.

Entel international codes appear below; for countries that are not on this list, phone ☎ 800-200-800.

Australia	☎ 123-003-611
Austria	☎ 123-003-431
Belgium	☎ 123-003-321
Canada	☎ 123-003-018
Denmark	☎ 123-003-451
France	☎ 123-003-331
Germany	☎ 123-003-491
Israel	☎ 123-003-9721
Italy	☎ 123-003-391
Japan	☎ 123-003-811
Netherlands	☎ 123-003-311
New Zealand	☎ 123-003-641
Spain	☎ 123-003-341
Sweden	☎ 123-003-461
Switzerland	☎ 123-003-411
UK (BT)	☎ 123-003-441
USA (AT&T)	☎ 800-800-311

CTC codes appear below; for other countries, contact CTC at ☎ 800-200-300.

Spain	☎ 800-207-334
USA (AT&T)	☎ 800-800-288
USA (MCI)	☎ 800-207-300

When calling or answering the telephone, the proper salutation is *aló* or *hola* (hello). Exchange pleasantries before getting to the point of your conversation.

Cellular Communications

Cellular telephones have become very common in Chile, thanks to companies like BellSouth, which rent them for about US$50 per month, plus additional charges beyond a certain amount of usage. Services often include voicemail, call waiting and three-way calling.

Cell phones throughout the country have seven digits, even in areas where conventional telephones have six; when calling a cell phone, dial the prefix 09 first.

Fax, Telegraph & Email

Entel, CTC, Telex-Chile and VTR offer telex, telegraph and fax services. Like others telecommunications services in Chile, prices are very reasonable.

While it's becoming more common for Chilean businesses and individuals to have email, easy public access is unusual. Try the telephone carrier Chilesat or, in Santiago, the Internet services at Mall Panorámico. Unless you have your own phone line, it will be difficult to get Internet access, but the following places will provide information.

CTC	☎ 800-200-300
Entel	info@entelchile.net
Chilesat	info@chilepac.net

For email addresses and websites for businesses and attractions listed in this book, see the Online Services appendix in the back of the book.

ADDRESSES

In Chilean cities and towns, names of streets, plazas and other features are often very long and elaborate, such as Calle Cardenal José Maria Caro or Avenida Libertador General Bernardo O'Higgins. Long names are often shortened on maps, in writing or in speech, so the former might appear on a map as JM Caro, or just Caro, while the latter might appear as Avenida Gral O'Higgins, Avenida B O'Higgins or just O'Higgins. The word *calle* (street) is usually omitted on maps.

Some addresses include the expression *local* (locale) followed by a number, for example Cochrane 56, Local 5. 'Local' means it's one of several offices at the same street address.

Some street numbers begin with a zero, eg Avenida Bosque Norte 084. This confusing practice usually happens when an older street is extended in the opposite direction, beyond the original number 1. If, for example, street numbers are increasing from north to south, El Bosque Norte 084 will be north of El Bosque 84, which will be north of El Bosque 184.

The abbreviation 's/n' following a street address stands for *sin número* (without number), and indicates that the address has no specific street number.

BOOKS
See the Arts section of the Facts about Chile chapter for Chilean literature.

Lonely Planet
Other guidebooks can supplement or complement this one, especially if you are visiting countries other than Chile. As well as this book, Lonely Planet's *Travel Survival Kit* series includes the following titles: *Argentina, Uruguay & Paraguay; Ecuador & the Galápagos Islands; Bolivia; Peru; Colombia*; and *Brazil*. Budget travelers covering a large part of the continent should look for LP's *South America on a Shoestring*.

If you're interested in trekking, LP's *Trekking in the Patagonian Andes* has detailed descriptions and maps of extensive walks in Chilean national parks and reserves, plus others across the border in Argentina. LP's *Latin American Spanish Phrasebook* is helpful for those without a good grasp of the language.

Guidebooks
The 3rd edition of Bradt Publications' *Backpacking in Chile and Argentina* has information about hiking and camping in the Southern Cone countries; the US publisher is Globe Pequot.

Since the 1920s, Trade & Travel Publications' *The South American Handbook*, now edited by Ben Box, has been the standard guide to the continent.

For Chile's national parks, do not miss William Leitch's beautifully written but also selective *South America's National Parks* (The Mountaineers, Seattle, 1990), which is superb on environment and natural history but much weaker on practical aspects of South American travel. Rumors persist of a new edition of Rae Natalie Prosser de Goodall's bilingual guidebook *Tierra del Fuego*, published in Argentina.

One of the most useful sources of information is the Turistel guide series, published by the Compañía de Teléfonos de Chile, which is annually updated and reasonably priced and is now available in English translation. The Spanish version has separate volumes on the north, center and south of the country, plus an additional volume on camping and campgrounds which has more detailed maps of some important areas. The English version combines all three main guides in a single volume and is less frequently updated.

Oriented toward motorists, Turistel guides provide excellent highway and city maps (the latter beautifully drawn, despite frequent minor errors) and thorough background information, but they rarely cover budget accommodations. Their biggest drawback, though, is the flimsy paper binding that makes them unusable after one season – handle with care.

Travel Literature
Chile has inspired some excellent travel writing. Although Bruce Chatwin's *In Patagonia* (Summit Books, New York, 1977) deals more with Argentina than with Chile, it is one of the most informed syntheses of life and landscape about any part of South America. His collection *What Am I Doing Here?* (Penguin, New York, 1989) contains a beautiful essay on Chiloé Island.

Sara Wheeler's recent *Travels in a Thin Country* (Little Brown & Co, New York, 1996) has drawn favorable commentary but has become hard to find. Luis Sepúlveda's *Full Circle: a South American Journey* (Lonely Planet, 1996) is a hybrid work that combines the political insights of an exile on his own country with travel observations that border on fiction (the author is a novelist as well as a journalist).

Don't overlook works of greater antiquity. Charles Darwin's *Voyage of the Beagle*, available in many editions, is as fresh as yesterday. His accounts of Chiloé and other parts of the Chilean landscape are truly memorable, and a lightweight paperback copy is a perfect companion for any trip to Chile.

There is a voluminous literature on Rapa Nui, spanning the 250 years since Europeans first landed on the island. See the Easter Island chapter for more details.

History

For an account of early European exploration of Chile and other parts of South America, see JH Parry's *The Discovery of South America* (Paul Elek, London, 1979). Another good source is Edward J Goodman's *The Explorers of South America* (University of Oklahoma, 1992).

Although it does not focus specifically on Chile, James Lockhart and Stuart Schwartz's *Early Latin America* (Cambridge, 1983) makes an original, persuasive argument that the structures of native societies like the Mapuche were more important than Spanish domination in the cultural transitions of the colonial period. Uruguayan journalist-historian Eduardo Galeano presents a bitter indictment of European invasion and its consequences in *The Open Veins of Latin America, Five Centuries of the Pillage of a Continent* (Monthly Review Press, New York, 1973). Do not miss Alfred Crosby's fascinating account of southern South America's ecological transformations in comparison with other mid-latitude lands settled by Europeans in *Ecological Imperialism: the Biological Expansion of Europe, 900-1900* (Cambridge, 1986).

On the South American wars of independence, the standard work is John Lynch's *The Spanish-American Revolutions 1808-1826* (WW Norton, New York, 1973). Richard W Slatta's comparison of Argentine gauchos and Chilean huasos with stockmen of other countries in the beautifully illustrated *Cowboys of the Americas* (Yale, 1990) is well worth a look.

Allende & the Unidad Popular

Publishing on the Allende years is a minor industry in its own right, and, as in the 1970s, it's still hard to find a middle ground. Try *Allende's Chile* (International Publishers, New York, 1977) by Edward Boorstein, a US economist who worked for the UP government. A more recent and wide-ranging attempt to explain the UP's failure is Edy Kaufman's *Crisis in Allende's Chile: New Perspectives* (Praeger, 1988).

For a first-hand account of the countryside during these years, read Kyle Steenland's *Agrarian Reform under Allende: Peasant Revolt in the South* (University of New Mexico, 1977), based on research in Cautín province from 1972 to 1973.

For a Marxist analysis of US involvement in the campaign against Allende, try *The United States & Chile: Imperialism & the Overthrow of the Allende Government* (Monthly Review Press, New York, 1975) by James Petras and Morris Morley. For a more thorough historical perspective, see Robert J Alexander's *The Tragedy of Chile* (Greenwood Press, 1978). Nathaniel Davis, former US ambassador to Chile, relates his side of the story in *The Last Two Years of Salvador Allende* (Cornell University Press, 1985).

For a more conservative view, tempered by its critical assessment of extremism among right-wing elements, see Alistair Horne's *A Small Earthquake in Chile* (Papermac, London, 1990; first published 1972). Sergio Bitar, a member of Allende's cabinet, provides systematic analysis of the UP's achievements and failures in *Chile, Experiment in Democracy* (Institute for the Study of Human Issues, Philadelphia, 1986).

Joan Jara, the English wife of murdered folk singer Victor Jara, has written a personal account of life during the 1960s and 1970s in *Victor: An Unfinished Song* (Jonathan Cape, London, 1983). The death of a politically involved US citizen in the 1973 coup was the subject of Thomas Hauser's book *The Execution of Charles Horman: An American Sacrifice* (Harcourt Brace Jovanovich, New York, 1978), which implicated US officials and was the basis of the film *Missing*.

The assassination of Orlando Letelier, a career diplomat and foreign minister under Allende, has been the subject of several books, including John Dinges and Saul

Landau's *Assassination on Embassy Row* (Pantheon, New York, 1980) and Taylor Branch and Eugene Popper's *Labyrinth* (Penguin, New York, 1983).

The Military Dictatorship

Chile: The Pinochet Decade by Phil O'Brien and Jackie Roddick (Latin America Bureau, 1983) covers the junta's early years, concentrating on the economic measures of the 'Chicago Boys.' Pinochet himself has offered the autobiographical *Camino Recorrido: Memorias de Un Soldado* in four volumes (Instituto Geográfico Militar, Santiago, 1990, 1991; Geniart, Santiago, 1993, 1994). As a counterpoint, consult Genaro Arriagada's *Pinochet: the Politics of Power* (Unwin Hyman, Boston, 1988), a critical account by a Christian Democrat intellectual who details the evolution of the military regime from a collegial junta to a personalistic but institutionalized dictatorship.

A riveting account of an exile's secret return is the famous Colombian writer Gabriel García Márquez's *Clandestine in Chile* (Henry Holt, New York, 1987), which tells the story of filmmaker Miguel Littín's secret working visit to Chile in 1985. Argentine writer Jacobo Timerman, famous for criticism of his country's military dictatorship of the late 1970s, has also written *Chile: Death in the South* (Knopf, New York, 1987).

Contemporary Chilean Politics

An outstanding, non-polemical explanation of the complexities of 20th-century Chilean politics is *The Politics of Chile: a Sociogeographical Assessment* by César Caviedes (Westview Press, 1979). For an account of the Pinochet years and their aftermath that eschews partisan rhetoric and focuses on the complexities of political events over two decades, see Pamela Constable and Arturo Valenzuela's *A Nation of Enemies* (WW Norton, New York, 1991).

The Military, Politics & Geopolitics

One standard overview of the military in Latin America is John J Johnson's *The Military & Society in Latin America* (Stanford, 1964). For analysis of geopolitics in Chile, see *Geopolitics of the Southern Cone & Antarctica*, edited by Philip Kelly and Jack Child (Lynne Rienner, 1988). A more general account, dealing with Argentina, Brazil and Paraguay, as well, is César Caviedes' *The Southern Cone: Realities of the Authoritarian State* (Rowman & Allenheld, 1984).

Geography & Natural History

Several readable texts integrate Latin American history with geography. Try Arthur Morris' *South America* (Hodder & Stoughton, 1979), the detailed chapter on Chile in Harold Blakemore and Clifford Smith's collection *Latin America* (Methuen, 1983) and *The Cambridge Encyclopedia of Latin America* (1985), which is rather broader in conception.

General

One widely available book on Chile from the Spanish conquest to the late 1970s is Brian Loveman's rather glib *Chile: The Legacy of Hispanic Capitalism* (Oxford, 1979), which, despite its polemical and condescending tone, presents a common point of view. A better choice, though more restricted in its coverage, is the collection *Chile Since Independence* (Cambridge, 1993), edited by Leslie Bethell.

With a narrower focus, based on painstaking archival research, Arnold Bauer's *Chilean Rural Society from the Spanish Conquest to 1930* (Cambridge, 1975) traces the evolution the Chilean countryside. Though dated in many ways, George McCutcheon McBride's *Chile: Land and Society* (American Geographical Society, 1936) is a vivid portrait of life on the latifundio, which changed little until the late 1960s.

Chile's turn-of-the-century development, based on the nitrate boom, is the subject of many books. Two of the best in English are Thomas F O'Brien's *The Nitrate Industry and Chile's Crucial Transition* (New York University Press, 1982) and Michael Monteón's *Chile in the Nitrate Era* (University of Wisconsin, 1982). German writer

Theodor Plivier's *Revolt on the Pampas* (Michael Joseph, London, 1937) is a hard-to-find fictional account of uprisings in the nitrate enterprises.

NEWSPAPERS & MAGAZINES

Still recovering from the repression of the Pinochet years, the quality of Chilean journalism is rapidly improving. Santiago is the country's media center, but the country's most venerable daily is *El Mercurio de Valparaíso*, founded in 1827.

El Mercurio, Santiago's oldest and most prestigious daily, follows a conservative editorial policy but has a diverse letters section and excellent cultural coverage. Its parent corporation also owns the sleazy tabloids *La Segunda* and *Ultimas Noticias*, which sensationalize crime and radical political dissent (which they seem to consider synonymous).

The Christian Democratic tabloid *La Epoca*, born during the 'No' campaign against Pinochet's continuance in office, is probably the most complete alternative news source, while *La Nación* is the official government daily. *Estrategia* is the daily voice of Chile's financial community and the best source on trends in the exchange rate.

The radical press has not fared well because of difficulties in attracting advertising. *El Siglo*, voice of the Communist party, has become a monthly rather than a weekly because of financial difficulties; the other major leftist paper is the uncompromising fortnightly *Punto Final*.

Since its beginning in late 1991, Santiago's English-language *News Review* has gone from weekly to twice-weekly (Wednesday and Saturday); the Saturday edition includes Britain's *Guardian Weekly*. It's still hard to find outside the capital, but try upscale hotels in the regions. The *News Review's* German-language counterpart is *El Cóndor*, now in its 56th year.

Of great interest to commercial visitors, *The South Pacific Mail* reports on economic trends in Chile and South America. It's available by subscription only.

The weekday English-language digest of the Chilean press, *Chip News* (☎ (02) 7775376, fax 7352267), Casilla 53331, Correo Central, Santiago, is available by fax or email subscription.

The following Chilean news sources have addresses on the World Wide Web.

Chip News
    http://www.chip.cl
Estrategia
    http://www.reuna.cl/estrategia
El Mercurio (Santiago)
    http://hermes.mercurio.cl/
La Epoca
    http://www.reuna.cl/laepoca/

RADIO & TV

In recent years, the end of government monopoly in the electronic media has opened the airwaves to a greater variety of programming than in the past. Broadcasting is far less regulated than before and there are many stations on both AM and FM bands. TV stations include the government-owned Televisión Nacional (TVN) and the Universidad Católica's Channel 13, plus several private stations. International cable service is widely available and is common even in many hospedajes and residenciales.

Chile's most famous television personality is Mario Kreuzberger, popularly known as 'Don Francisco,' host of the weekly variety program *Sábado Gigante*, also seen on Spanish-language TV stations in the USA. The portly, multi-lingual Don Francisco, whose smiling visage endorses various products on billboards throughout the country, also hosts the annual *Teletón* to raise money for disabled children. He conspicuously absents himself when military donors appear on the Teletón.

PHOTOGRAPHY & VIDEO

The latest in consumer electronics is available in Chile at much lower prices than in neighboring countries, especially at the free zones in Iquique (Region I) and Punta Arenas (Region XII), which are good places to replace a lost or stolen camera. Color slide film can also be purchased cheaply at Iquique but is harder to find in

Punta Arenas. Developing color prints is fairly inexpensive; slides are much more costly, especially with frames.

At high altitudes, especially in northern Chile, the bright tropical sun can wash out photographs; a polarizing filter is virtually essential. Photographers should be particularly circumspect about photographing indigenous peoples, who often resent the intrusion. When in doubt, don't do it.

At major international border crossings like Los Libertadores (from Mendoza, Argentina) and Pajaritos (from Bariloche, Argentina), Chilean customs officials put baggage through x-ray machines; do not leave your film in your luggage.

TIME

For most of the year, Chile is four hours behind GMT, but from mid-December to mid-March the country observes daylight savings time (summer time); because of its great latitudinal range, this means that summer sunrise in the desert tropics of Arica, where day and night are roughly equal throughout the year, occurs after 8 am. Easter Island (Rapa Nui) is two hours behind the mainland.

ELECTRICITY

Electric current operates on 220 volts, 50 cycles. In Santiago, numerous electrical supply stores on Calle San Pablo, west of the Puente pedestrian mall, sell transformers for appliances.

WEIGHTS & MEASURES

The metric system is used throughout the country, but for weight the traditional *quintal* of 46 kilos is still common. For motorists, it's very common to find tire pressure measured in pounds per square inch, and the Chilean military often uses feet as a standard measure, for instance for airport elevations.

LAUNDRY

In recent years, self-service laundrettes have become more common in both Santiago and other cities, but it is only slightly more expensive to leave your clothes and pick them up later. Most inexpensive hotels will have a place where you can wash your own clothes and hang them to dry. In some places, maid service will be reasonable, but agree on charges in advance.

HEALTH

In general, Chile presents few serious health hazards, though there were localized outbreaks of cholera after the major 1991 epidemic in Peru. The Ministry of Health prohibited restaurants from serving *raw* vegetables that grow in the ground (such as lettuce, cabbage, celery, cauliflower, beets and carrots) and raw seafood in the form of *ceviche*, which is also suspect (ceviche must now be made with seafood which is cooked and then cooled). Santiago's drinking water is adequately treated and the author has drunk tap water in most other parts of the country without problems, but if you have any doubts, stay with bottled mineral waters.

US residents can call the Centers for Disease Control's International Traveler's Hotline (☎ 404-332-4559), where, by punching in the country's phone code (56 for Chile), you can get recorded information on vaccinations, food and water and current health problems. They also have a fax-back service.

Travelers who wear glasses should bring an extra pair and their prescription. Losing your glasses can be a real nuisance, although in many places you can get new spectacles made up quickly, cheaply and competently.

If you require a particular medication, take an adequate supply and a copy of the prescription, with the generic rather than the brand name.

Health Care Books

For basic health information when traveling, a good source is Dr Richard Dawood's *Travellers' Health: How to Stay Healthy Abroad* (Oxford, 1989). Bradt & Pilkington's *Backpacking in Chile and Argentina* (see Travel Guides, above) has a good section on hazards of hiking and camping in the region. Other possibilities include *The Traveller's Health Guide* by Dr Anthony Turner (Roger Lascelles, London, 1979), *Staying Healthy in Asia, Africa & Latin America* (Moon Publications) and *Where There is No Doctor* by David Werner (Hesperian Foundation).

For children's health problems, see Maureen Wheeler's *Travel with Children* (Lonely Planet, 1995).

Predeparture Preparations

Vaccinations Chile requires no vaccinations for entry from any country, but visitors to nearby tropical countries should consider prophylaxis against typhoid, malaria and other diseases. Typhoid, polio, tetanus and hepatitis immunization are also recommended. All vaccinations should be recorded on an International Health Certificate, available from your physician or health department.

Typhoid protection lasts three years and is useful if traveling in rural areas. You may suffer side effects such as pain at the point of injection site, fever, headache and general discomfort.

A complete series of oral polio vaccines is essential if you haven't had them before. Tetanus and diphtheria boosters are necessary every 10 years and are highly recommended.

Injections of gamma globulin, not a vaccine but a ready-made antibody, provide some protection against infectious hepatitis (hepatitis A).

Malaria does not exist in Chile, but if you are coming from a malarial zone, you should continue to take anti-malarial drugs for a further six weeks.

Health Insurance Relatively small costs can pay great benefits if you get sick. Look for a policy which will pay return travel costs and reimburse you for lost air tickets and other fixed expenses; such policies often cover losses from theft as well. The international travel policies handled by STA or other budget travel organizations are usually a good value.

Medical Kit All standard medications are available in well-stocked pharmacies. Many common prescription drugs can be purchased legally over the counter in Chile. Possible medical supplies include:

- Aspirin or Panadol – for pain or fever
- Antihistamine (such as Benadryl) – useful as a decongestant for colds, allergies, to ease the itch from insect bites or stings or to help prevent motion sickness
- Antibiotics – useful if you're traveling well off the beaten track, but they must be prescribed and you should carry the prescription with you
- Kaolin preparation (Pepto-Bismol), Imodium or Lomotil – for stomach upsets
- Rehydration mixture – for treatment of severe diarrhea; this is particularly important if traveling with children
- Antiseptic, mercurochrome and antibiotic powder or similar 'dry' spray – for cuts and grazes
- Calamine lotion – to ease irritation from bites or stings
- Bandages and band-aids – for minor injuries
- Scissors, tweezers and a thermometer – mercury thermometers are prohibited by airlines
- Insect repellent, sunblock, suntan lotion, lip balm and water-purification tablets

Food & Water

Most North Americans, Europeans and Australians will find Chilean food is generally easy on the stomach, but the great variety of shellfish may take some adaptation. Since the cholera scare has subsided, salad greens and other fresh, unpeeled vegetables are safe to eat, but raw shellfish is not advisable. The water supply of Santiago and most other cities is safe, with little danger of dysentery or similar ailments, but take precautions in rural areas, where latrines may be close to wells and untreated water may be taken from rivers or irrigation ditches. Water in the Atacama desert and its cities has a strong mineral content. Easter Island's water has a similar reputation, but the author found it both safe and tasty.

Geographical & Climatic Considerations

Altitude Sickness From the passes between Chile and the Argentine city of Mendoza northwards to the Bolivian border, altitude sickness *(apunamiento* or *soroche)* represents a potential health hazard. In the thinner atmosphere above 3000 meters or even lower in some cases, lack of oxygen causes many individuals to suffer headaches, nausea, shortness of breath, physical weakness and other symptoms which can lead to very serious consequences, especially if combined with heat exhaustion, sunburn or hypothermia. Most people recover within a few hours or days, as their body produces more red blood cells to absorb oxygen, but if the symptoms persist it is imperative to descend to lower elevations. For mild cases, everyday painkillers such as aspirin or *chachacoma*, a tea made from the leaves of a common Andean shrub, will relieve symptoms until your body adapts. In the northern Chilean Andes, coca leaves are a common remedy, but authorities frown upon their usage even by native peoples, who consume them surreptitiously. Avoid smoking, drinking alcohol, eating heavily or exercising strenuously.

Heat Exhaustion & Sunburn Although Chile is mostly a temperate country, its northern zones lie within the Tropic of Capricorn and the sun's nearly direct rays can be devastating, especially at high altitude. In the desert, summer temperatures are usually not oppressive, but dehydration can still be a very serious problem. Drink plenty of liquids and keep your body well covered with light cotton clothing. Wear a hat that shades your head and neck. Damage to the ozone layer has increased the level of ultraviolet radiation in southern South America, so protection from the sun is especially important – use an effective sun screen on exposed parts of your body and good quality sunglasses. Sweating can also lead to a loss of salt, so adding some salt to your food can be a

good idea. Salt tablets should only be taken to treat heat exhaustion caused by salt deficiency.

Hypothermia Hypothermia occurs when the body loses heat faster than it can produce it, and the core temperature of the body falls. At high altitudes and in Patagonia, changeable weather can leave you vulnerable to exposure: after dark, temperatures can drop from balmy to below freezing, while a sudden soaking and high winds can lower your body temperature so rapidly that you may not survive. Disorientation, dizziness, slurred speech, stumbling, shivering, numb skin and physical exhaustion are all symptoms of hypothermia and are indications that you should seek warmth, shelter and food. Avoid traveling alone; partners are less likely to fall victim to hypothermia.

Always be prepared for cold, wet or windy conditions, even if you're just out walking or hitching. Wear woolen clothing or synthetics that retain warmth when wet. Carry high-energy, easily digestible snacks such as chocolate or dried fruit, both of which are readily available in Chile. If bad weather is approaching, seek shelter before you are caught outside.

Diarrhea & Dysentery

Although Chilean public health standards are reasonably high, stomach problems can arise from dietary changes – they don't necessarily mean you've caught something. Introduce yourself gradually to exotic and/or highly spiced foods (the latter not very common in Chile).

Avoid rushing to the pharmacy and gulping antibiotics at the first signs of trouble. The best thing to do is to rest, avoid eating solids and drink plenty of liquids (tea or herbal solutions, without sugar or milk). Many cafés in Chile serve excellent chamomile tea *(agua de manzanilla)* or other herbal teas; otherwise, try mineral water *(agua mineral)*. As you recover, keep to simple foods like yoghurt, lemon juice and boiled vegetables.

Ordinary 'traveler's diarrhea' rarely lasts more than a few days, so if it lasts more than a week you must get treatment, move on to antibiotics or see a doctor. Lomotil or Imodium can relieve the symptoms but do not actually cure the cause of the problem. For children, Imodium is preferable, but do not use such drugs if you have a high fever or are severely dehydrated.

After a severe bout of diarrhea or dysentery, you will probably be dehydrated, with painful cramps. Relieve these with fruit juices or tea, with a tiny bit of dissolved salt. Antibiotics can help treat severe diarrhea, especially if accompanied by nausea, vomiting, stomach cramps or mild fever.

Sexually Transmitted Diseases
Sexual contact with an infected partner spreads these diseases. While abstinence is the only certain preventative, condoms are also effective. Gonorrhea and syphilis are the most common of these diseases; sores, blisters or rashes around the genitals and discharge or pain when urinating are common symptoms. Symptoms may be less obvious or even absent in women. The symptoms of syphilis eventually disappear completely, but the disease can cause severe problems in later years. Both gonorrhea and syphilis can be treated effectively with antibiotics.

There are numerous other sexually transmitted diseases, and effective treatment is available for most. However, there is no cure for herpes, and there is also currently no cure for AIDS.

HIV/AIDS
AIDS (Acquired Immune Deficiency Syndrome) is most commonly transmitted by unsafe sexual activity. Apart from abstinence, avoiding such activity and using condoms are the most effective preventatives. As of mid-1996, Chile had about 1500 registered cases of AIDS and another 2200 of HIV (the Human Immunodeficiency Virus). The port city of Valparaíso has the highest rate of infection.

AIDS can also be spread by dirty needles (vaccinations, acupuncture and tattooing are potentially as dangerous as intravenous

drug use if the equipment is not clean) or through infected blood transfusions. If you need an injection or a blood test (obligatory if you are a driver involved in an auto accident), purchase a new syringe from a pharmacy and ask the doctor or nurse to use it.

Fear of HIV infection should never preclude treatment for serious medical conditions. Although there may be a risk of infection, it is very small indeed. A good resource for help and information is the US Centers for Disease Control AIDS hotline (☎ 800-343-2347).

Women's Health
Gynecological Problems Poor diet, lowered resistance due to the use of antibiotics for stomach upsets and even contraceptive pills can lead to vaginal infections when traveling in hot climates. Yeast infections, characterized by rash, itch and discharge, can be treated with a vinegar or even lemon juice douche or with yoghurt. Nystatin suppositories are the usual medical prescription. Trichomonas is a more serious infection with a discharge and a burning sensation when urinating. Male sexual partners must also be treated; if a vinegar-water douche is not effective, seek medical attention. Flagyl is the prescribed drug.

Pregnancy Most miscarriages occur during the first three months of pregnancy, so this is the riskiest time to travel. The last three months should also be spent within reasonable distance of good medical care. Pregnant women should avoid all unnecessary medication, but vaccinations and malarial prophylactics should still be taken where possible. Take additional care to prevent illness and pay particular attention to diet and nutrition.

TOILETS
Ordinary toilet paper does not readily disintegrate in Chilean sewers, so most bathrooms have a basket where you discard what you have used. Cheaper accommodations and public toilets rarely provide toilet paper, so carry your own wherever you go.

WOMEN TRAVELERS
Attitudes toward Women
Chilean men are very *machista* (chauvinist) but rarely violent in public behavior towards women. The main nuisances are unwelcome attention and vulgar language, generally in the presence of other males, which usually emphasizes feminine physical attributes. If you respond aggressively ('Are you talking to me?'), you will probably put the aggressor to shame.

Single women checking in at low-budget hotels, both in Santiago and elsewhere, may find themselves objects of curiosity or suspicion, since prostitutes often frequent such places. If you otherwise like the place, ignore this and it should disappear. Outside the larger cities, women traveling alone are objects of curiosity, since Chilean women generally do not travel alone. You should interpret questions as to whether you are running away from parents or husband as expressions of concern.

Some foreign women living in Chile have complained that they find it difficult to make female friends, since some Chilean women view them as competitors for Chilean men. This sometimes contributes to a sense of social isolation.

Scandinavian women (or women who look Scandinavian) may find that some Chilean men associate them with liberal attitudes toward sex and pornography.

Safety Precautions
For women traveling alone, Chile is probably safer than most other Latin American countries, although you should not be complacent. Unwelcome physical contact, particularly on crowded buses or trains, is not unusual, but if you're physically confident, a slap or a well aimed elbow should discourage any further incident. If not, try a scream – another very effective measure.

If you hitchhike, exercise caution and especially avoid getting into a vehicle with more than one man. Though hitching is never completely safe, it is much safer in pairs.

GAY & LESBIAN TRAVELERS
While Chile is a strongly Catholic country and homosexuality or even talk of it is taboo to many, there are enclaves of tolerance, most notably in Santiago. Since Chilean males in general are more physically demonstrative than their counterparts in Europe or North America, behaviors like a vigorous embrace will seem innocuous even to some who dislike homosexuals. Likewise, lesbians walking hand-in-hand will attract little attention, since Chilean women frequently do so, but this would be very indiscreet behavior for males.

After unwarranted raids on gay bars in Santiago in early 1996, homosexual rights advocates managed to get the Policía de Investigaciones to destroy video tapes of the raids, which had resulted in arrests but no charges, and to pledge not to repeat the incidents. Openly gay activist Rolando Jiménez has declared himself a candidate for the Santiago city council for the left-of-center Partido Para la Democracia (PPD), one of the members of the ruling Concertación coalition.

Chile's only gay rights organization is the Movimiento Liberación Homosexual (Movilh; ☎ (02) 6324309), Santa Rosa 170-A in Santiago. Its mailing address is Casilla 52834, Correo Central, Santiago.

DISABLED TRAVELERS
Travelers with disabilities will find Chile difficult at times; the wheelchair-bound in particular will find the narrow sidewalks, which are frequently in disrepair, difficult to negotiate. Crossing streets can also be a problem, though most Chilean drivers are courteous toward individuals with obvious handicaps.

According to the 1992 census, 288,000 Chileans claimed some sort of disability, but the Fondo Nacional del Descapacitado Fondis, National Fund for the Handicapped) believes the figure is at least four times higher. Law now requires new public buildings to provide disabled access, but public transport access remains very poor – even Santiago's newest Metro line, under construction as of writing, does not provide disabled access.

Santiago's Tixi Service (☎ 800-223097 toll-free) caters specifically to disabled individuals, with hydraulic elevators to accommodate wheelchairs.

SENIOR TRAVELERS

Senior travelers should encounter no particular difficulties traveling in Chile, where older citizens typically enjoy a great deal of respect. On crowded buses, for instance, most Chileans will readily offer their seat to an older person.

TRAVEL WITH CHILDREN

Chile is extremely child-friendly in terms of safety, health, people's attitudes and family-oriented activities. For small children, a folding stroller is a good idea, especially where there is a chance of getting lost in crowds. People are also very helpful on public transport; often someone will give up a seat for parent and child, but if that does not happen, an older person may offer to put the child on his or her lap.

In terms of food and health, there are no special concerns in most of the country, but bottled water may be a good idea for delicate stomachs. Most restaurants offer a wide variety of dishes suitable for children (vegetables, pasta, meat, chicken, fish), and Chilean cuisine is generally bland despite the occasional hot sauce. Portions are abundant enough that smaller children probably will not need a separate meals, and there is usually no problem in securing additional cutlery.

In general, public toilets are poorly maintained; always carry toilet paper, which is almost nonexistent in them. While a woman may take a young boy into the ladies' rooms, it would be socially unacceptable for a man to take a girl into the men's room.

Unless you are traveling by plane, remember that distances are long and trips seem never-ending, so bring a comfortable blanket and enough toys and games to amuse your child. Santiago and most other cities have large public parks with playgrounds, so it's easy for children to make international friendships. There are also many activities specifically for children; consult newspapers like *El Mercurio* or *La Epoca* for listings.

For general information on the subject, look for Lonely Planet's *Travel with Children* (1995) by Maureen Wheeler.

USEFUL ORGANIZATIONS

Travelers interested in environmental conservation may wish to contact Codeff (Comité Pro Defensa de la Fauna y Flora (☎ (02) 2510287/0433, fax 2510262), Avenida Francisco Bilbao 691, Providencia, Santiago. Other organizations with environmental interests include Ancient Forests International (☎/fax 707-923-3015), Box 1850, Redway, California 95560, USA; Defensores del Bosque Chileno (☎ (02) 7374280, fax 7775065), Antonia López de Bello 024, Providencia; and Fundación Lahuen (☎ (02) 2342617) at Orrego Luco 054, Providencia.

The Chilean branch of Greenpeace (☎ (02) 7378140, fax 7773203) is at Loreto 20 in Recoleta, Santiago.

The Sociedad Mapuche Lonko Kilápan (☎ (045) 213134), Aldunate 12, Temuco, promotes environmentally sustainable development among Chile's native peoples. It is presently assisting the Pehuenche of Quepula-Ralco, in the upper Biobío, with respect to development issues in the face of the Chilean government's hydroelectric plans for the river basin.

German visitors, business people or intending residents may wish to contact the Deutsch-Chilenischer Bund, Avenida Vitacura 5875, Vitacura, which publishes the useful guide *Chile: Ein Land zum Leben, Arbeiten und Investieren* (1994).

The Instituto Nacional de la Juventud (INJ; ☎ (02) 6323646), Alameda 341 in Santiago, issues the *Tarjeta Joven*, which entitles Chilean (and foreign) students of a certain age to discounts on many services throughout the country.

DANGERS & ANNOYANCES

Chile is much less hazardous than most other Latin American countries and many other parts of the world, but certain precautions will reduce risks and make your trip more enjoyable.

Personal Security & Theft

Although street crime appears to be increasing, personal security problems are minor compared with many other South American countries. Truly violent crime is rare in Santiago; both men or women can travel in most parts of the city at any time of day or night without excessive apprehension. Valparaíso has an unfortunate reputation for robberies in some of its southern neighborhoods. Summer is the crime season in beach resorts like Viña del Mar, Reñaca and La Serena, though these are by no means violent places – be alert for pickpockets and avoid leaving valuables on the beach while you go for a swim.

Take precautions against petty theft, such as purse snatching. Be especially wary of calculated distractions, such as someone tapping you on the shoulder or spilling something on you, since these 'accidents' are often part of a team effort to relieve you of your backpack or other valuables. Grip your bag or purse firmly, carry your wallet in a front pocket and avoid conspicuous displays of expensive jewelry. Valuables like passports and air tickets can be conveniently carried in a light jacket or vest with one or two zip-up or button-up pockets. Money belts and neck pouches are common alternatives, though some travelers find them uncomfortable; an elastic leg pouch is less cumbersome, but can get very sweaty in hot weather.

Baggage insurance is a good idea. Since many budget hotels have only token locks or none at all, do not leave valuables like cash or cameras in your hotel room (such hotels often have secure left-luggage areas). Top-end hotels often have secure strongboxes in each room.

Unauthorized political demonstrations still take place and can be very disputatious; the police will sometimes use tear gas or truck-mounted water cannons – known as *guanacos* after the spitting wild New World camels – to break them up. The single most contentious site in Chile may be Providencia's Avenida 11 de Septiembre, named by the dictatorship after the date of the coup that overthrew the Allende government; on every anniversary of the coup, truculent demonstrators demand that the street be renamed.

The Police & Military

Chile's Carabineros, much less known for corruption than other South American police, behave professionally and politely in ordinary circumstances, but there have been recent credible reports of mistreatment of foreign travelers, especially in Santiago. The United Nations Commission on Human Rights has identified nearly 50 cases of torture (defined as psychological abuse and unnecessary violence) in police interrogations (not of foreigners) over the last few years, and in early 1996 the force expelled nearly 250 officers for disciplinary reasons. Carabineros can demand identification at any time, so you should carry your passport. Throughout the country, the toll-free emergency telephone number for Carabineros is ☎ 133.

The military still take themselves very seriously, even under civilian government, so avoid photographing military installations. In the event of a national emergency, the military-dominated Consejo de Seguridad Nacional (National Security Council) may impose martial law, suspending all civil rights, so make sure someone knows your whereabouts and contact your embassy or consulate for advice.

Natural Hazards

The Pacific coast of South America is part of the 'ring of fire' that stretches from Asia to Alaska to Tierra del Fuego. Volcanic eruptions are not unusual; in 1991, for example, the explosion of Aisén's Volcán Hudson buried Chile Chico and Los

Antiguos, Argentina, knee-deep in ash. Earthquakes are common.

Volcanic activity is unlikely to pose any immediate threat to travelers, since volcanoes usually give some notice before a big eruption. A few popular resorts are especially vulnerable, particularly the town of Pucón at the base of Volcán Villarrica.

Earthquakes are another matter, since they occur without warning. Local construction often does not meet seismic safety standards – adobe buildings are especially vulnerable. Travelers in budget accommodations should make contingency plans for safety, including evacuation, before falling asleep at night.

Recreational Hazards

Many of Chile's finest beach areas have dangerous offshore rip currents, so ask before entering the water and be sure someone on shore knows your whereabouts. Some beaches, such as Iquique's Playa Brava, are unsafe under any conditions.

In wilderness areas such as Parque Nacional Torres del Paine, accidents have become common enough that authorities no longer permit solo trekking.

LEGAL MATTERS

If you are involved in any automobile accident, your license will be confiscated until the case is resolved, although local officials will usually issue a temporary driving permit within a few days. A blood alcohol test is obligatory; purchase a sterile syringe at the hospital or clinic pharmacy when the Carabineros take you there. After this you will be taken to the police station to make a statement and then, under most circumstances, released. Ordinarily you cannot leave Chile until the matter is resolved; consult your consulate, insurance carrier and a lawyer.

The Carabineros do not harass drivers for minor equipment violations (unlike the police in neighboring Argentina). You should *never* attempt to bribe the Carabineros, whose reputation for institutional integrity is very high.

BUSINESS HOURS

Traditionally, business hours in Chile commence by 9 am, but shops close about 1 pm for three or even four hours, when people often return home for lunch and a brief siesta. After the siesta, shops reopen until 8 or 9 pm. In Santiago, government offices and many businesses have adopted a more conventional 9 am to 6 pm schedule. Banks and government offices are often open to the public only in the mornings.

HOLIDAYS & SPECIAL EVENTS

Throughout the year but especially in summer, Chileans from Arica to Punta Arenas celebrate a variety of local and national cultural festivals. Other than religious holidays like Easter and Christmas, the most significant are mid-September's Fiestas Patrias, but many localities have their own favorites. For listings, see individual city entries.

There are numerous national holidays, on which government offices and businesses are closed. There is some pressure to reduce these or to eliminate so-called 'sandwich holidays,' which many Chileans take between an actual holiday and the weekend, by moving some of them to the nearest Monday.

January 1
    Año Nuevo (New Year)
March/April
    Semana Santa (Holy Week, the week before Easter)
May 1
    Día del Trabajo (Labor Day)
May 21
    Glorias Navales (commemorating the naval Battle of Iquique)
May 30
    Corpus Christi
June 29
    Día de San Pedro y San Pablo (St Peter & St Paul's Day)
August 15
    Asunción de la Virgen (Assumption)
September 11
    Pronunciamiento Militar de 1973 (Military Coup of 1973)

September 18
Día de la Independencia Nacional
(National Independence Day)
September 19
Día del Ejército (Armed Forces Day)
October 12
Día de la Raza (Columbus Day)
November 1
Todo los Santos (All Saints' Day)
December 8
Inmaculada Concepción
(Immaculate Conception)
December 25
Navidad (Christmas Day)

ACTIVITIES

Chileans are very fond of a variety of sports, both as participants and spectators, but the most popular is soccer. In the callampas, children will clear a vacant lot, mark the goal with stones and make a ball of old rags and socks to pursue their pastime. Even in exclusive country clubs the sport is popular.

In the summer, the beach is the most popular vacation spot. Paddle-ball, a game like tennis, has gained major popularity – courts have sprung up around the country, and many people play on the beach.

Other popular sports include tennis, basketball, volleyball and cycling. Other outdoor activities such as canoeing, climbing, kayaking, trekking, windsurfing and hang-gliding are gaining popularity. Rivers like the Maipo, Claro and Biobío are increasingly popular for whitewater rafting and kayaking, although hydroelectric development seriously threatens the Biobío. Chile has an increasing number of Santiago-based agencies specializing in adventure travel; many of these also maintain summer offices in the lakes region or elsewhere in the country. Santiago's telephone area code is 02.

Adventure Expedition
Las Tranqueras 62
Las Condes
(☎ 2012951)
Altué Expediciones
Encomenderos 83, Las Condes
(☎ 2321103, fax 2336799)

Cascada Expediciones
Orrego Luco 054, 2nd floor, Providencia
(☎ 2342274, fax 2339768)
Evasión
Santa Beatriz 84-A, Providencia
(☎ /fax 2361325)
Grado Diez
Las Urbinas 56, Providencia
(☎ 2344130)
Kipaventur
Manuel Montt 50, Local 20
(☎ 2361715, fax 2351874)
Mountain Service
Ebro 2801, Las Condes
(☎ 2429723)
Pared Sur
Juan Estéban Montero 5497
Las Condes
(☎ 2073525/3160)
Tranco Expediciones
Avenida Padre Hurtado Central 751
Las Condes
(☎ /fax 2299631)

Cycling & Mountain Biking

Cycling is increasingly popular, both as a recreational activity and as a way to get around the country. Because even some paved roads suffer from potholes and frequent construction, a mountain bike with wide tires is the best choice; on unpaved highways like the Camino Austral, it is utterly essential. Travel agencies like Santiago's Pared Sur, in Las Condes, organize weekend or longer mountain bike trips.

Skiing

Skiing, though increasingly expensive, can be world-class. The most internationally renowned resort is Portillo, the site of several downhill speed records, northeast of Santiago near the Argentine border crossing to Mendoza. Other major resorts are within an hour of the capital, at La Parva, El Colorado and Valle Nevado; east of Chillán at Termas de Chillán; in Parque Nacional Villarrica near the resort town of Pucón; and at Antillanca in Parque Nacional Puyehue, east of Osorno. There are a handful of lesser ski resorts in the Aisén region near Coihaique and near Punta Arenas.

Prospective skiers may wish to consult Chris Lizza's *South America Ski Guide* (1992), published by Bradt Publications in the UK and by Hunter Publications in the USA, which contains substantial chapters on both Chile and Argentina.

Hiking & Trekking

More participants probably enjoy hiking and trekking than any other single activity, thanks to Chile's numerous national parks, most of which have decent and sometimes very good trail networks. International showpieces like Torres del Paine get the most attention, but there are excellent alternatives only a short bus ride from major cities, like Parque Nacional El Morado near Santiago and Parque Nacional La Campana near Viña del Mar. See Clem Lindenmayer's *Trekking in the Patagonian Andes* (Lonely Planet, 1997) for information on extended treks in southern Chile and Argentina.

Hikers and trekkers visiting the Southern Hemisphere for the first time should look for a compensated needle compass like the Recta DP 10; Northern Hemisphere compasses are deceptive as an indicator of direction in far southern latitudes.

Andescape (☎ /fax (02) 2355225), Santa Beatriz 84-A in Providencia, Santiago, operates moderately priced trekking lodges in Parque Nacional Torres del Paine. Their Puerto Natales address (☎ (061) 412592) is Pedro Montt 308.

Mountaineering

Chile has great mountaineering country, ranging from the Pallachatas volcanoes of the northern altiplano to Ojos del Salado east of Copiapó, the numerous volcanic cones of Araucanía and Los Lagos, and the international magnet of Torres del Paine. Climbers should be aware of bureaucratic obstacles, however, most notably Conaf's US$800 fee for climbing in Parque Nacional Torres del Paine. It is also advisable to check in with Conaf and/or the local Carabineros office before starting a climb.

Climbers intending to scale border peaks like the Pallachatas or Ojos del Salado must have permission from Chile's Dirección de Fronteras y Límites (Difrol; ☎ (02) 6714110, fax 6971909, 6722536) at Bandera 52, 4th floor, in Santiago. For other information on climbing and help with the bureaucracy, contact the Federación de Andinismo (☎ (02) 2220888) at Almirante Simpson 77, Providencia, Santiago.

Surfing

Chile's extensive coastline offers plenty of possibilities for surfers, but only at Arica is the water comfortably warm, so wet suits are imperative. Rough surf and rip currents make some areas very inadvisable, and it's best not to surf alone.

Many of the best surfing areas are in or near Arica, Iquique and Antofagasta in the Norte Grande; the paving of coastal Ruta 1 has opened this area to surfers, but has also brought mountains of trash from careless campers. Pichilemu, in Region V, is another popular area.

For detailed information on surfing in Chile, contact Surfer Publications (☎ 714-496-5922, fax 496-7849), PO Box 1028, Dana Point, California 92629, USA. Its monthly *Surf Report* includes issues on Region I (Volume 10, No 5, May 1989; revised in Volume 16, No 6, June 1995); Regions II, III and IV (Volume 10, No 6, October 1989); and Regions V and VI (Volume 14, No 8, August 1993).

Whitewater Rafting & Kayaking

Whitewater enthusiasts agree that Chile's rivers are world-class for both rafting and kayaking, with plenty of Class V challenges on the Biobío, Futaleufú and others in the southern lakes and Aisén. There are respectable whitewater experiences even in the suburbs of Santiago, though, in the Cajón del Maipo, organized by agencies like Tranco Expediciones and Altué Expediciones. Sea kayaking is becoming increasingly popular in and around the sheltered archipelagic waters of Chiloé.

For more information on rafting and kayaking, see the Tours entry in the Getting There & Away chapter.

Diving
Chile is not known for diving or snorkeling, since even the tropical segments of its long coastline experience cold currents. The best places for diving are its Pacific island possessions, the Juan Fernández archipelago and Easter Island (Rapa Nui), but even then it's unlikely anyone would come to Chile just for the diving.

Paragliding
Paragliding is in its very early stages in Chile, but there are ideal conditions in and near the city of Iquique, in the Norte Grande, where a recent French immigrant has opened a paragliding school; see the Iquique entry for information.

COURSES
Language
Santiago is the main center for language courses, but there are also possibilities in Iquique, Pucón, Coihaique and Puerto Natales. See the respective city entries for more details.

Wine
Santiago's Escuela de Vino (☎ (02) 2073520, fax 2070581), Avenida Vitacura 3446 in Vitacura, offers introductory, middle and advanced wine courses, consisting of four to seven two-hour sessions each, with instruction by Chilean vintners, enologists and university professors.

Classes take place Monday through Thursday, monthly between March and December in Spanish only, but the students are international. The cost is about US$100, and there are about 20 students per class.

Outdoor Skills
With Chilean headquarters at Coihaique, the National Outdoor Leadership School (NOLS; ☎ 307-332-6973; fax 332-1220, see the Online Services appendix), 288 Main St, Lander, Wyoming 82520, USA, offers a 'Semester in Patagonia' program, emphasizing wilderness skills and natural history courses, with university credit available.

WORK
It is increasingly difficult to obtain residence and work permits. Consequently, many foreigners do not bother to do so, but the most reputable employers will insist on the proper visa. If you need one, go to the Departamento de Extranjería (☎ (02) 6725320), Moneda 1342, Santiago. Business hours are from 9 am to 1.30 pm.

Teaching English
It is not unusual for visiting travelers to work as English-language instructors in Santiago. Wages are fairly good on a per-hour basis, but full-time employment is hard to come by without a commitment to stay for some time.

Volunteer Work
Options for volunteer work are worth exploring, especially with social and environmental organizations. Two good sources to consult are the comprehensive annual *Directorio de Instituciones de Chile* (popularly known as the 'Guía Silber' after its publisher Silber Editores), a directory of political, labor, church, cultural and other institutions both official and nongovernmental; and the annual *Directorio de Organizaciones Miembros* published by Renace (Red Nacional de Acción Ecológica), a loosely affiliated network of environmental organizations throughout the country.

Bar Work
The best options for bar work are in Santiago, especially in the numerous pubs along Avenida Suecia and General Holley (Metro: Los Leones), and in seasonally popular resorts like Pucón. Wages, however, are much lower than they would be in Europe or North America.

Street Performers
Street musicians and theater performers are a staple of Chilean life, so the competition is stiff and, without some unique skill, foreign visitors are unlikely to attract enough attention to earn a living. In some cases, the police can be a nuisance.

ACCOMMODATIONS

Chile's broad spectrum of accommodations ranges from hostels and campgrounds to five-star luxury hotels. Where you stay will depend on your budget and your standards, where you are, and how hard you look, but you should be able to find something reasonable. You may also find yourself invited into Chilean homes and generally should not hesitate to accept.

Reservations

Nearly all hotels, even the cheapest, have telephones and many have fax machines, so it's easy to make reservations. While it's usually unnecessary, if you're arriving at an awkward hour or during the peak summer season or a holiday weekend, reservations can be a good idea.

Camping & Refugios

Sernatur's Santiago headquarters has a free pamphlet called *Camping* that lists campgrounds throughout Chile and gives details of their facilities. The sites are usually in wooded areas and have excellent facilities – hot showers, toilets and laundry, fire pits for cooking, restaurants or snack bars, grocery stores. Some even have swimming pools or lake access. The Compañía de Teléfonos de Chile publishes an annually updated Turistel camping guide with very detailed information and excellent maps – for some tourist areas, the maps are better than those in the regular Turistel guide. For an excellent practical guide to visiting and camping in Chilean parks, obtain the paperback guidebook *Juventud, Turismo y Naturaleza* from Sernatur or Conaf.

Chilean campgrounds are not the bargain they once were, since most sites charge a five-person minimum; this means that for singles or couples they can be more expensive than basic *hospedajes* or *residenciales* (see below). This is true both at private campgrounds and in national parks where concessionaires control the franchise. In some remote parts of Chile, there is free camping, but drinkable water and sanitary facilities are often lacking.

For comfort, invest in a good, dome-style tent with rainfly before coming to South America, where camping equipment is more expensive. With a good tent, a three-season sleeping bag should be adequate for almost any weather conditions. A campstove which can burn a variety of fuels is a good idea, since white gas *(bencina blanca)* is expensive and available only at chemical supply shops or hardware stores. Firewood is a limited and often expensive resource, which, in any event, smudges your pots and pans. Bring or buy mosquito repellent, since many campsites are near rivers or lakes.

There are also *refugios*, which are rustic – sometimes *very* rustic – shelters for hikers and trekkers in the national parks. The more rustic of these are free or very cheap, but some newer ones are very comfortable commercial enterprises that charge plenty for the privilege.

Travelers with their own vehicles will find that many *servicentros* along Ruta 5, the Panamericana, have spacious lots suitable for parking and sleeping, if the maneuvers of 18-wheelers don't disturb your sleep. In addition to clean toilet facilities, most of these places offer hot showers for less than US$1.

Long-Term Rentals

If you're staying in a place for an extended period, house and apartment rentals can save money. In Santiago, check listings in Sunday's *El Mercurio* or in the weekly classified paper *El Rastro*. In resorts like Viña del Mar, La Serena or Villarrica, you can lodge several people for the price of one by renting an apartment and cooking your own meals. In towns like Valdivia and La Serena, people line the highway approaches in summer to offer houses and apartments. You can also check the tourist office or local papers.

Casas de Familia

In summer, especially from Temuco south, families often rent rooms to visitors. A *casa de familia* can be an excellent bargain, with access to cooking and laundry facilities, hot showers and Chilean hospitality. Tourist offices often maintain lists of such accommodations.

A Santiago organization that arranges accommodations with local families is Amigos de Todo El Mundo (☎ (02) 6726525), Avenida Bulnes 285, Departamento 201; the postal address is Casilla 52861, Correo Central, Santiago. Rates are around US$16 per person.

Hostels

Chile has two kinds of youth hostels. The first is the growing but limited number affiliated with Hostelling International (HI), whose central office is the Asociación Chilena de Albergues Turísticos Juveniles, Avenida Providencia 2594, Oficina 420, Santiago (☎ (02) 2332555). A hostel card, valid worldwide, costs about US$15.

HI has its own custom-built facility in Santiago, but elsewhere its affiliates are usually better budget hotels that have set aside a few beds or rooms for hostelers. In addition to Santiago, there are currently hostel facilities in Calama, Viña del Mar, Temuco, Valdivia, Puerto Montt and Punta Arenas.

The second system is coordinated by the Dirección General de Deportes y Recreación (Digeder; ☎ (02) 2238009), Fidel Oteíza 1956 in Providencia, whose *albergues juveniles* cater mainly to school children and students on holiday and occupy temporary sites at sports stadiums, campgrounds, schools or churches. Usually open in January and February only, they charge only a few dollars per night for a dormitory bed, making them just about the cheapest accommodations in Chile. Since these hostel sites often change from year to year, it is very useful to have the most current listing, but local tourist offices will often refer you to them.

Hospedajes, Pensiones & Residenciales

These offer very reasonable accommodations, but the differences among them are sometimes ill-defined – all may be called hotels. Room and furnishings are modest,

usually including beds with clean sheets and blankets, but never hesitate to ask to see a room. A few have private baths, but more commonly you will share toilet and shower facilities with other guests. Since they don't waste hot water, you will usually have to ask them to turn on the *calefón* (hot water heater) before taking a shower.

An *hospedaje* is usually a large family home that has a few extra bedrooms for guests (the bath is shared). Some are not permanent businesses but temporary expedients in times of economic distress. Similarly, a *pensión* offers short-term accommodations in a family home, but may also have permanent lodgers. Meals are sometimes available.

Residenciales, which are permanent businesses but sometimes only seasonal, more commonly figure in tourist office lists. In general, they occupy buildings designed for short-stay accommodations, although some cater to clients who intend only *very* short stays – say two hours or so. Prostitutes sometimes frequent them, but so do young couples with no other indoor alternative for their passion. Except for a little noise, such activities should not deter you, even if you have children.

Several travelers have complained of fleas at bottom-end hotels throughout Chile and recommend carrying some sort of bug bomb or insect repellent. The author has had no such problems, but may be less sensitive than some of his correspondents.

Hotels & Motels

Hotels vary from one-star austerity to five-star luxury, but correlation between these categories and their standards is less than perfect – many one-star places are better value than their three- and four-star brethren. In general, hotels provide a room with attached private bath, often a telephone and sometimes *música funcional* (elevator Muzak) or a TV. Normally they will have a restaurant; breakfast may be included in the price. Upper-middle to top-end places have room service and laundry service, international cable TV, swimming pools, bars, shopping galleries and other luxuries; these are most common in the major cities and resorts.

In some areas, motels are what North Americans and Europeans expect, a rural or suburban roadside accommodations with convenient parking. However, the term *motel* can also be a euphemism for places catering almost exclusively to unmarried couples (or couples married to others) with no other alternative for privacy. The external decor usually makes it obvious what sort of place a given establishment is. Within cities, their counterpart is known as an *hotel parejero*.

FOOD

From the tropics to the pole, Chile's varied cuisine features seafood, beef, fresh fruit and vegetables. Upwelling of the waters from the Pacific Ocean's cool Humboldt Current sustains a cornucopia of fish and shellfish for Chilean kitchens, while the fields, orchards and pastures of Middle Chile fill the table with superb produce.

Places to Eat

Chilean restaurants range from hole-in-the-wall snack bars to sumptuous international venues. Most Chilean cities feature a central market with many small, cheap restaurants, usually known as *cocinerías* or *comedores*, of surprisingly high quality. Nearly every sizable town also has a *casino de bomberos* (fire station restaurant) with excellent and inexpensive meals.

There are several categories of eating establishments. Bars serve snacks and both alcoholic and non-alcoholic drinks, while *fuentes de soda* are similar but do serve alcohol. Snack bars sell fast food. *Cafeterías* serve modest meals; *hosterías* are more elaborate and usually located outside the main cities. A *salón de té* is not quite literally a teahouse but is a bit more upscale than a cafetería. Full-fledged *restaurantes* are distinguished by quality and service. Distinctions are less than exact, and the term 'restaurante' can be applied to every category of establishment. Almost all serve alcoholic and non-alcoholic drinks.

Except in strictly family establishments, it is customary – and expected – to leave a 10% tip. The menu is *la carta*; the bill is *la cuenta*.

Snacks

Cheap and available almost everywhere, one of the world's finest snacks is the *empanada*, a tasty turnover with vegetables, hard-boiled egg, olive, beef, chicken, ham and cheese or other filling. The most common fillings you'll find, however, are *pino* (ground beef) and *queso* (cheese). Empanadas *al horno* (baked) are lighter than empanadas *fritas* (fried). Travelers arriving from Argentina will find the Chilean empanada larger and more filling than its Argentine counterpart, so don't order a dozen for lunch or your bus trip.

Humitas are corn tamales, frequently wrapped in corn husks and steamed; when served in this manner they are *humitas en chala* – a very popular and tasty snack. There are numerous breads, including *chapalele*, made with potatoes and flour and boiled; *milcao*, another type of potato bread; and *sopaipa*, recognizable by its dark brown exterior, which is made from wheat flour and fruit, but not baked. *Pebre* is a tasty condiment of chopped tomatoes, onion, garlic, chile peppers, cilantro and parsley.

Sandwiches are popular snacks throughout the day. Among sandwich fillings, *churrasco* (steak), *jamón* (ham) and queso are most widely available. Cold ham and cheese make an *aliado*, while a sandwich with ham and melted cheese constitutes a *Barros Jarpa*, after a Chilean painter known for consuming them in large quantities. A steak sandwich with melted cheese is a *Barros Luco*, the favorite of former President Ramón Barros Luco (1910-1915). Beefsteak with tomato and other vegetables is a *chacarero*.

Chile's cheapest fast food is the *completo*, a hot dog with absolutely everything (including a massive cholesterol infusion).

Breakfast

Breakfast *(desayuno)* usually comprises toast *(pan tostado)* with butter *(mantequilla)* or jam *(mermelada)* and tea *(té)*; eggs or sandwiches are also common. *Huevos fritos* are fried eggs, usually served in a *paila* (small frying pan). *Huevos revueltos* are scrambled, *huevos pasados* are boiled, and *huevos a la copa* are poached. *Bien cocidos* means well cooked and *duros* are hard-boiled.

Main Dishes

Many places offer a cheap set meal *(comida corrida* or *almuerzo del día)* for lunch *(almuerzo* or *colación)* and, less often, for dinner *(cena)*. Some of the most common dishes are listed below, but there are many other possibilities. Do not hesitate to ask waiters for an explanation of any dish.

Lunch can be the biggest meal of the day. Set menus tend to be almost identical at cheaper restaurants, generally consisting of *cazuela*, a stew of potato or maize with a piece of beef or chicken, a main course of rice with chicken or meat, and a simple dessert. Soup is *caldo* or *sopa*. *Porotos* (beans) are a common budget entree, but there are more elaborate versions with a variety of vegetables and condiments. One of Chile's most delicious and filling traditional dishes is *pastel de choclo*, a maize casserole filled with vegetables, chicken and beef, but this may be available only during the summer maize harvest.

The biggest standard meal in Chile is *lomo a lo pobre*, an enormous slab of beef topped with two fried eggs and buried in French fries. This is not a low-cal snack, and you may wish to monitor your cholesterol level before and after eating. *Ajiaco* is a spiced beef stew which, traditionally, uses a variety of leftovers.

Beef, in a variety of cuts and styles of preparation, is the most popular main course at *parrillas* – restaurants which grill everything from steak to sausages over charcoal. The *parrillada* proper is an assortment of steak and other cuts which will appall vegetarians and heart specialists. A traditional parrillada will include offal like *chunchules* (small intestines), *tripa gorda* (large intestine), *ubre* (udder), *riñones* (kidneys) and *morcilla* (blood sausage). A token green salad *(ensalada)* will usually accompany the meal.

Many restaurants of all kinds offer *pollo con papas fritas* (chicken with fries) and *pollo con arroz* (chicken with rice).

Seafood

What really distinguishes Chilean cuisine is its varied seafood, among the world's best. Popular seafood dishes include the delicious *sopa de mariscos*, or *cazuela de mariscos*, which is more of a shellfish stew. *Paila marina* is a fish and shellfish chowder, while *sopa de pescado* is a fish soup. Try *chupe de cóngrio* (conger eel stew) or, if available, *chupe de locos* (abalone stew), both cooked in a thick sauce of butter, bread crumbs, cheese and spices. Locos may be in *veda* (quarantine) because of over-exploitation.

Do not overlook the market restaurants in cities like Iquique, Concepción, Temuco and Puerto Montt. Some dishes, like *erizos* (sea urchins) are acquired tastes, but they will rarely upset your stomach. Do insist on all shellfish being thoroughly cooked, which is obligatory since the cholera scare of 1991-92; even the traditional *ceviche* (marinated raw fish or shellfish) must now be cooked, although it is still served cold.

In southern Chile and especially on Chiloé, one of the typical specialties is *curanto*, a hearty stew of fish, shellfish, chicken, pork, lamb, beef and potato. Curanto is eaten with chapalele or milcao (potato breads).

A few seafood terms worth knowing are:

fish	*pescado*
shrimp	*camarones*
prawns	*camarones grandes*
crab	*cangrejo* or *jaiva*
king crab	*centolla*
mussels	*cholgas*
oysters	*ostras*
scallops	*ostiones*
shellfish	*mariscos*
clams	*almejas*
giant barnacle	*picoroco*
razor clams	*machas*
sea urchins	*erizos*
squid	*calamares*
octopus	*pulpo*

Many basic restaurants prepare their fish by frying in heavy oil, which besides its dietary shortcomings also destroys the flavor; on request, however, most will prepare fish *al vapor* (steamed) or *a la plancha* (grilled).

Desserts

Dessert *(postre)* is commonly fresh fruit or *helado* (ice cream). The latter has improved greatly over the past several years, at least at those ice creameries featuring *elaboración artesanal* (small-scale rather than industrial production). Also try *arroz con leche* (rice pudding), *flan* (egg custard) and *tortas* (cakes). In the southern lakes region, Chileans of German descent bake exquisite *kuchen* (pastries) filled with local fruit – the author considers Chile's raspberries the tastiest in the world.

Ethnic Food

Santiago has a large and increasing selection of 'ethnic' restaurants. French, Italian, Spanish, German and Chinese are the most common, but Brazilian, Mexican, Middle Eastern and other national cuisines are also available. Another good place to look for restaurants is the Santiago entry in the Turistel Centro guide book.

In northern coastal cities like Arica and Iquique, there are many Chinese restaurants. These *chifas* are generally cheap, a good value and a pleasant change.

Vegetarian Dishes

While most Chileans are carnivores, vegetarianism is no longer the mark of an eccentric. Santiago has some excellent vegetarian fare, but, other than in strictly vegetarian restaurants, you may have to make a special request. If presented with meat that you don't want, it may help to claim allergy *(alergia)*.

Every town has a market with a wide variety of fruit and vegetables – produce from the Chilean heartland reaches the limits of the republic and overseas. Remember that agricultural regulations forbid importing fruit from foreign countries, including neighboring Argentina.

Fast Food

Fast-food restaurants are mostly inferior clones of Kentucky Fried Chicken or McDonalds, although these foreign franchises are increasingly common. Except at better Italian restaurants, pizzas are generally small, greasy and inferior. The nationwide Dino's chain offers passable standard fare.

DRINKS
Non-Alcoholic Drinks

Soft Drinks & Water Chileans guzzle prodigious amounts of soft drinks, from the ubiquitous Coca Cola to Seven-Up, Sprite and sugary local brands such as Bilz. Mineral water, both carbonated *(con gas)* and plain *(sin gas)*, is widely available, but tap water is potable almost everywhere. The most popular mineral waters are Cachantún and Chusmiza, but others are equally good.

Fruit Juices & Licuados *Jugos* (juices) are varied and excellent. Besides the common *naranja* (orange), *toronja* (grapefruit), *limón* (lemon), *damasco* (apricot) and *piña* (pineapple), *mora* (blackberry), *maracuyá* (passion fruit) and *sandía* (watermelon) are also available. Distinctively Chilean, *mote con huesillo* is a peach nectar with barley kernels, sold by countless street vendors but closely monitored for hygiene.

Licuados are milk-blended fruit drinks, but on request can be made with water. Common flavors are *banana*, *durazno* (peach) and *pera* (pear). Unless you like your drinks *very* sweet, ask them to hold the sugar ('sin azúcar, por favor').

Coffee & Tea While the situation is improving, Chilean coffee will dismay serious caffeine addicts. Except in upscale restaurants and specialized coffee bars like Café Haití and Café Caribe, which serve espresso, semi-soluble Nescafé is the norm. *Café con leche* is literally milk with coffee – a teaspoonful of coffee dissolved in hot milk. *Café solo* or *café negro* is coffee with hot water alone.

Likewise, *té con leche* is a teabag submerged in warm milk. Tea is normally served black, with at least three packets of sugar. If you prefer just a touch of milk, a habit which most Chileans find bizarre, it is easier to ask for *un poquito de leche* later rather than try to explain your eccentric habits in advance.

Yerba mate, or 'Paraguayan tea,' is consumed much more widely in the River Plate countries than in Chile, but some Chilean supermarkets do carry it. Chileans consume herbal teas *(aguas)* such as *manzanilla* (chamomile), *rosa mosqueta* and *boldo* in considerable quantities.

Alcoholic Drinks
Wines & Wine Regions By consensus, Chilean wines are South America's best and rate among the finest in the world; reds *(tintos)* and whites *(blancos)* are both excellent. The country's commercial wine-growing districts stretch from the Copiapó valley of the Norte Chico's Region III (Atacama) to the drainage of the Río Biobío in Region VIII.

From north to south, rainfall increases and irrigation decreases. In the Copiapó area, known as the *zona pisquera*, irrigated vineyards produce grapes with high sugar content which is made into *pisco* (grape brandy). From the drainage of the Río Aconcagua to the Río Maule, there is a middle zone with a Mediterranean climate in which irrigation is still crucial. Reduced irrigation takes place in the more humid conditions south of the Maule. The Biobío drainage receives sufficient rainfall to make irrigation unnecessary, but that same weather makes the harvest unsuitable for finer wines.

Chile's variety of growing conditions, made even more complex by Chile's abrupt topography, produces a considerable variety of wines. While Atacama wineries specialize in the brandy-like pisco and the tasty dessert wine known as *pajarete*, they also produce small quantities of whites and sparkling wines. Middle Chile's *zona de regadío* produces the country's best-known wines, mostly Cabernet Sauvignon and

other reds planted under French tutelage in the 19th century. Acreages planted to whites like Chardonnay and Riesling are increasing. Many major wineries in this zone lack sufficient acreage to produce the quantity they require and buy quality grapes on contract. Major labels include Concha y Toro (and its subsidiary Santa Emiliana), Undurraga, Cousiño Macul, Errázuriz Panquehue, Ochagavía, Santa Rita, Santa Carolina, San Pedro Canepa, Manquehue, Tarapacá and Carmen. Several of these wineries are open to the public.

To the south, in the transitional zone of the Maule, reds give way to whites like Sauvignon Blanc and Sémillon. Curicó and Talca are the centers of production for brands like Miguel Torres and Viña San Pedro, whose wineries also welcome visitors. Like the zone around Copiapó, the Biobío drainage is a peripheral, pioneer zone for wine grapes, with relatively small yields of common reds and whites which are mostly blended and used for jug wines. Further south, in the Araucanía, there are scattered vineyards, but commercial production is precarious indeed.

Wine aficionados who plan a trip to South America should look at Harm de Blij's *Wine Regions of the Southern Hemisphere* (Rowman & Allenheld, Totora, New Jersey, 1985), which contains excellent chapters on the Chilean, Argentine and Brazilian wine industries. A locally published wine guide is the 2nd edition of Fred Purdy's *The Gringo's Guide to Chilean Wine*.

Other Alcoholic Drinks Chile's table wines should satisfy most visitors' alcoholic thirst, but don't refrain from trying the tasty but powerful pisco, often served in the form of a pisco sour, with lemon juice, egg white and powdered sugar. It may also be served with ginger ale *(chilcano)* or vermouth *(capitán)*.

Escudo is the best bottled beer and Cristal the most popular, but Becker has recently gained popularity. Bars and restaurants commonly sell draft beer (known as *chopp* and pronounced 'shop'), which is cheaper than bottled beer *(cerveza)* and often better.

Gol is a translucent alcoholic mixture of butter, sugar and milk, left to ferment for a fortnight. It's drunk in the south, but not readily available in restaurants. *Guinda* is a cherry-like fruit which is the basis of *guindado*, a fermented alcoholic drink with brandy, cinnamon, and clove. A popular holiday drink is the powerful but deceptively sweet *cola de mono* ('tail of the monkey'), which consists of aguardiente (cane alcohol), coffee, clove and vanilla.

ENTERTAINMENT
Cinemas
Traditionally Chileans flock to the cinema, although outside Santiago the video revolution has meant the closure of many theaters that were once the only show in town. Still, in the capital and larger cities like Valparaíso and Viña del Mar, major theaters offer the latest films from Europe, the USA and Latin America. Prices have risen in recent years, but many cinemas offer substantial mid-week discounts.

Repertory houses, cultural centers and universities provide a chance to see classics or less commercial films you may have missed. Films are usually shown in the original language, with Spanish subtitles, but animated features and children's films are invariably dubbed.

Dance Clubs
Santiago has an array of discotheques, mostly in the Bellavista neighborhood north of the Río Mapocho and in the area around Avenida Suecia and General Holley in Providencia. Many but not all of these are sterile, expensive techno-pop venues. Beach resorts like Viña del Mar, Reñaca, Concón and La Serena also have numerous dance clubs.

Nightclubs
In cities like Santiago and Viña del Mar, Chilean nightclubs tend to be tacky affairs, where traditional music and dances are sanitized and presented in glitzy but costly settings for foreign visitors. In ports like Valparaíso and Iquique, they can be disreputable *boites*, frequented by prostitutes and sailors.

Theater
Both in Santiago and the provinces, live theater is well attended and of high quality, from the classics and serious drama to burlesque. In the southern lakes region, many towns offer summer theater presentations in their annual cultural festivals.

Classical Music
Santiago's most prestigious music venues, like the Teatro Municipal and the Teatro de la Universidad de Chile, are the main sites for classical concerts. See the Santiago chapter for details.

Rock
Chile's best known rock groups, like La Ley, play at stadium venues, though only visiting acts like the Rolling Stones can fill the massive Estadio Nacional in the Santiago suburb of Ñuñoa. There's a flourishing, credible rock and blues scene in the less flashy venues of Bellavista and a few other areas.

Jazz
Live jazz is not widespread in Chile, but the quality is often very good. The Santiago venue La Calle del Delfín Verde, on Avenida Suecia, is a much more serious

music venue than the pop- and rock-oriented bars in the area and is highly recommended.

Folk/Traditional Music
Peñas are nightclubs whose performers offer unapologetically political material based on folk themes. The famous *Nueva Canción Chilena* (New Chilean Song Movement) had its origins in the peñas of the 1960s, and many Chilean performers exiled after the military coup of 1973 kept the flame alive in similar venues in their adopted countries.

In the archipelago of Chiloé, folk groups often present music and dance resembling those of the Appalachian region of the eastern USA. These expansive family-oriented groups usually include a bevy of female singers, dancers of both sexes, at least three guitarists, accordions and percussion instruments. Summer folk festivals are the best place to see them.

Pubs/Bars
Pubs and bars are often proving grounds for young bands on the way up, but are also prone to derivative entertainment like Beatles tribute bands and Neil Diamond impersonators. Every once in a while, though, you'll stumble onto something really worthwhile.

SPECTATOR SPORTS
By far the most popular spectator sport is soccer, whose British origins are apparent in the names of teams like Santiago Morning and Everton. The professional season begins in March and ends in November, though the playoffs run almost until Christmas.

The most popular teams are Colo Colo (named for the legendary Mapuche cacique), Universidad de Chile and the more elitist Universidad Católica. Followers of Colo Colo are popularly known as *garras blancas* (the white claws), while those of the Universidad de Chile are called *los de abajo* (the underdogs).

Other popular spectator sports include tennis, boxing, horse racing and basketball. Internationally, the best known Chilean athletes are soccer player Iván Zamorano, a star with Spain's Real Madrid and Italy's Inter Milan, and highly-ranked tennis player Marcelo (Chino) Ríos.

THINGS TO BUY
In artisans' *ferias*, found throughout the country, it is often difficult to choose among a variety of quality handicrafts. There are especially good choices in Santiago's Barrio Bellavista and the suburban comuna of Las Condes, Viña del Mar, Valdivia the Puerto Montt suburb of Angelmó, and the village of Dalcahue, near Castro on the island of Chiloé. Copper and leather goods are excellent choices, while woolens from the Andean north resemble those from Peru or Bolivia.

In the Araucanía, Mapuche artisans produce a wide variety of quality ceramics, basketry, silverwork and weavings (some travelers will find parallels with the Navajo of North America) and carvings. These are widely available in popular tourist destinations like Temuco, Villarrica and Pucón.

Getting There & Away

Chile has direct overseas air connections from North America, the UK, Europe and Australia/New Zealand. The trans-Pacific route from Australia via Tahiti, though expensive, permits a stopover on Easter Island (Rapa Nui).

Another alternative is to fly to a neighboring country like Argentina, Bolivia or Peru, and continue to Chile by air or land. One-way international tickets within South America are usually very expensive but a few, such as the Arica-La Paz route, are fairly reasonable in comparison with slow and difficult overland travel. International flights within South America tend to be costly unless purchased as part of intercontinental travel, but there are real bargain roundtrip fares between Buenos Aires and Santiago.

AIR
Airports & Airlines
Most long-distance flights to Chile arrive at Santiago, landing at Aeropuerto Internacional Arturo Merino Benítez in the suburb of Pudahuel. There are also flights from neighboring countries to regional airports like Arica, Iquique, Temuco, Puerto Montt and Punta Arenas.

LanChile is the national carrier, with the most extensive system of connecting internal routes, but many other reputable airlines also serve Santiago. There is a complete list in the Santiago chapter.

Baggage & Other Restrictions
On most domestic and international flights you are limited to two checked bags, or three if you don't have a carry-on. There could be a charge if you bring more or if the size of the bags exceeds the airline's limits. It's best to check with the individual airline if you are worried about this. On some international flights the luggage allowance is based on weight, not numbers; again, check with the airline.

If your luggage is delayed upon arrival (which is rare), some airlines will give a cash advance to purchase necessities. If sporting equipment is misplaced, the airline may pay for rentals. Should the luggage be lost, it is important to submit a claim. The airline doesn't have to pay the full amount of the claim; rather, they can estimate the value of your lost items. It may take them anywhere from six weeks to three months to process the claim and pay.

Smoking Flights to and from Chile have smoking and non-smoking sections; within Chile, all flights are smoke-free except those to Easter Island, which have both smoking and non-smoking sections.

Illegal Items Items that are illegal to take on a plane, either in checked or carry-on baggage, include aerosols of polishes, waxes and so on; tear gas and pepper spray; camp stoves with fuel; and divers' tanks that are full. Matches should not be checked.

Travelers with Special Needs
If you have special needs of any sort – vegetarianism or other dietary restrictions, a broken a leg, dependence on a wheelchair, responsibility for a baby, fear of flying – let the airline know as soon as possible so that they can make arrangements accordingly. You should remind them when you reconfirm your booking (at least 72 hours before departure) and again when you check in at the airport. It may also be worth ringing round the airlines before making your booking to find out how they can handle your particular needs.

Airports and airlines can be surprisingly helpful, but need advance warning. Most international airports provide escorts from check-in desk to plane where needed, and there should be ramps, lifts, accessible toilets and accessible phones. Aircraft toilets, on the other hand, are likely to present a problem; discuss this with the airline at an early stage and, if necessary, with their doctor.

Guide dogs for the blind will often have to travel in a specially pressurized baggage compartment with other animals, away from their owner; though smaller guide dogs may be admitted to the cabin. All guide dogs are subject to the same quarantine laws (six months in isolation, etc) as any other animal when entering or returning to countries currently free of rabies such as the UK or Australia.

Deaf travelers can ask for airport and in-flight announcements to be written down for them.

Children under two years old travel for 10% of the standard fare (free on some airlines) as long as they don't occupy a seat, although they get no baggage allowance. 'Skycots' should be provided by the airline if requested in advance; these will take a child weighing up to about 10 kg (22 pounds). Children between two and 12 years old can usually occupy a seat for half fare and do get a baggage allowance. Push chairs can often be taken as hand luggage.

Buying Tickets

From almost everywhere, South America is a relatively expensive destination, but discount fares can reduce the bite considerably. One alternative to a straightforward roundtrip is a Round-the-World ticket. If possible, take advantage of seasonal discounts and try to avoid peak times such as Christmas, New Year's or Easter. Advance purchase for a given period of time, usually two to six months, will normally provide the best, but not necessarily most flexible, deal.

The plane ticket will probably be the single most expensive item in your budget, and buying it can be intimidating. It is always worth putting aside a few hours to research the current state of the market. Start shopping for a ticket early – some of the cheapest tickets must be purchased months in advance, and some popular flights sell out early. Talk to other recent travelers – they just might be able to stop

you from making some of the same old mistakes. Look at the ads in newspapers and magazines, consult reference books, and watch for special offers.

Airlines can supply information on routes and timetables, but they do not supply the cheapest tickets except during fare wars and the competitive low season. Travel agents are usually a better source of bargains. Whether you go directly through an airline or use an agent, always ask the representative to clarify the fare, the route, the duration of the journey, and any restrictions on the ticket.

Most major airlines have ticket 'consolidators' who offer substantial discounts on fares to Latin America, but things change so rapidly that even newspaper listings can be quickly out of date. Among the best sources of information are the Sunday travel pages of major dailies like *The New York Times*, the *Los Angeles Times* or the *San Francisco Examiner*. If you're in a university town, look for bargains in the campus newspaper, such as the *Daily Californian* in Berkeley. There will usually be a listing for the local affiliate of the Council on International Travel Exchange (CIEE, or Council Travel), or the Student Travel Network (STA); you needn't be a student to take advantage of their services – see regional sections, below, for discount travel agencies and bucket shops.

Similar listings are available in the travel sections of the magazines like *Time Out* and *TNT* in the UK, or the Saturday editions of newspapers like the *Sydney Morning Herald* and *The Age* in Australia. Ads in these publications offer cheap fares, but don't be surprised if they happen to be sold out when you contact the agents: they're usually low-season fares on obscure airlines with conditions attached.

Cheap tickets are available in two distinct categories: official and consolidator. Official ones have a variety of names including advance-purchase fares, budget fares, Apex, and super-Apex. Consolidator tickets are simply discounted tickets that the airlines release through selected travel agents (not through airline offices). The

Ticket Options

There are several types of discount tickets to South America. The main ones are:

Apex Advance purchase excursion (Apex) tickets must be bought well before departure, but they can be a good deal if you know exactly where you will be going and how long you will be staying. Usually only available on a roundtrip basis, with a 14- or 21-day advance purchase requirement, these have minimum- and maximum-stay requirements (usually 14 and 180 days respectively), allow no stopovers and stipulate cancellation charges.

Courier Flights This relatively new system, which businesses use to ensure the arrival of urgent freight without excessive customs hassles, can mean phenomenal bargains for travelers who can tolerate fairly strict requirements, such as short turnaround time – some tickets are valid for only a week or so, others for a month, but rarely any longer. In effect, the courier company ships business freight as your baggage, so that you can usually take only carry-on luggage, but you may pay as little as US$480 for a ticket from New York to Buenos Aires and back.

Discounted Tickets There are two types of discounted fares – officially discounted (see Promotional Fares) and unofficially discounted. The lowest prices often impose limitations such as flying with unpopular airlines, inconvenient schedules or unpleasant routes and connections. A discounted ticket can save you other things than money – you may be able to pay Apex prices without the associated Apex advance booking and other requirements. Discounted tickets only exist where there is fierce competition.

Economy Class Valid for 12 months, economy-class (Y) tickets have the greatest flexibility within their time period. However, if you try to extend beyond a year, you'll have to pay the difference of any price increase in the interim period.

Excursion Fares Priced midway between Apex and full economy fare, these have no advance booking requirements but may require a minimum stay. Their advantage over advance purchase is that you can change bookings and/or stopovers without surcharge.

Full Fares Airlines traditionally offer first-class (coded F), business-class (coded J) and economy-class (coded Y) tickets. These days there are so many promotional and discounted fares available from the regular economy class that few passengers pay full economy fare.

MCO 'Miscellaneous charges orders' (MCOs) are open vouchers for a fixed US dollar amount, which can be exchanged for a ticket on any IATA (International Air Transport Association) airline. In countries that require an onward ticket as a condition for entry, such as Panama or Colombia, this will usually satisfy immigration authorities. In a pinch, you can turn it into cash at the local offices of the airline from which you purchased it.

Point-to-Point This discount ticket is available on some routes in roundtrip for waiving stopover rights, but some airlines have entirely eliminated stopovers.

Promotional Fares These are officially discounted fares like Apex fares that are available from travel agents or direct from the airline.

RTW Some excellent bargains are possible on 'Round-the-World' tickets, sometimes for less than the cost of a roundtrip excursion fare. You must travel round the world in one direction and cannot backtrack; you are usually allowed five to seven stopovers.

Standby A discounted ticket with which you can fly only if there is a seat free at the last moment. Standby fares are usually only available on domestic routes. ■

cheapest tickets are often non-refundable and require an extra fee for changing your flight. Many insurance policies will cover this loss if you have to change your flight for emergency reasons. Roundtrip (return) tickets usually work out much cheaper than two one-way fares – often *much* cheaper.

See the sidebar on the types of tickets you can purchase. Discounts on such fares are often available from travel agents, but usually not in Latin America, where discount ticketing is unusual. Standby can be a cheap way of getting from Europe to the US, but there are no such flights to Chile or other parts of South America. Foreigners in Chile may pay for international air tickets in local currency, but the disappearance of differential exchange rates has eliminated any incentive to do so.

One of the cheapest means of getting to South America is via courier flights, in which travelers trade all or part of their baggage allowance for a highly discounted fare and agree to accompany business equipment or documents. The major drawbacks to this, in addition to baggage being limited to carry-on items, are the relatively short travel period and the very limited number of gateway airports in Europe and North America.

You may decide to pay more than the rock-bottom fare by opting for the safety of a better-known travel agent. Established firms like STA Travel, which has offices worldwide, Council Travel in the USA, and Travel CUTS in Canada are viable alternatives, offering good prices to most destinations.

Once you have your ticket, write down its number, together with the flight numbers and other details, and keep the information somewhere separate. If the ticket is lost or stolen, this will help you get a replacement. Remember to buy travel insurance as early as possible.

Note: Use the fares quoted in this book as a guide only. They are approximate and based on the rates advertised by travel agents and airlines at press time. Quoted airfares do not necessarily constitute a recommendation for the carrier.

Round-the-World Tickets Round-the-World (RTW) tickets have become very popular in the last few years. They are often real bargains and can work out to be no more expensive or even cheaper than an ordinary roundtrip ticket. Prices start at about UK£850, A$1800 or US$1300.

The official airline RTW tickets are usually put together by a combination of two airlines, and permit you to fly anywhere on their routes so long as you do not backtrack. Other restrictions are that you must usually book the first segment in advance, and cancellation penalties apply. There may be restrictions on the number of stops permitted, and tickets are usually valid from 90 days up to a year. An alternative type of RTW ticket is one put together by a travel agent using a combination of discounted tickets.

Although most airlines restrict the number of segments that can be flown within the USA and Canada to four, and some airlines black out heavily traveled routes like Honolulu to Tokyo, stopovers are otherwise generally unlimited. In most cases a 14-day advance purchase is required. After the ticket is purchased, dates can be changed without penalty and tickets can be rewritten to add or delete stops for US$50 each.

The majority of RTW tickets restrict you to just two airlines. For instance, Qantas flies in conjunction with Delta, Northwest, Canadian Airlines, Air France and KLM. Qantas RTW tickets, with any of the aforementioned partner airlines, cost US$3247 or A$3099.

For travelers starting in Australia, one possibility is the combined ticket offered by Qantas and Aerolíneas Argentinas. Beginning from Sydney, you can stop in New Zealand, Buenos Aires (with a side trip to Santiago included), London, Paris, Bahrain, Singapore and other cities, although you must arrange the itinerary in advance. It does not, unfortunately, permit North American stopovers, but similar fares are available in the USA and Canada. The price for the Aerolíneas-Qantas ticket is A$3000 in Sydney.

Other similar combinations are available through Aerolíneas and Air New Zealand, British Airways, Cathay Pacific, KLM, Singapore Airlines and Thai Airways International. The Aerolíneas-British Airways ticket (A$2250) allows one side trip in South America and another in Europe for A$2250. British Airways and Qantas offer a RTW ticket called the Global Explorer that allows you to combine routes on both airlines to a total of 28,000 miles for US$2999 or A$3099.

Canadian Airlines offers numerous RTW combinations, such as one with Philippine Airlines for C$2790 that could include Manila, Dubai, Pakistan and Europe; another with KLM that could include Cairo, Bombay, Delhi and Amsterdam for C$3149; and a third with South African Airways that could include Australia and Africa for C$3499.

Circle Pacific Tickets Similar in conception to RTW tickets, the 'Circle Pacific' fare including Tahiti may permit a cheap stopover on Easter Island. In conjunction with Aerolíneas Argentinas, Singapore Airlines' Circle Pacific ticket goes for US$2899 and can take in Australia, New Zealand, Japan, San Francisco, Los Angeles and many other Pacific destinations.

The USA

From the USA, the principal gateways to South America are Miami, New York and Los Angeles. Airlines which serve Santiago from the USA include LanChile, Aerolíneas Argentinas (via Buenos Aires), Aeroperú, American, Avianca (via Bogotá and Buenos Aires), Líneas Aéreas de Costa Rica (Lacsa), Lloyd Aéreo Boliviano (LAB), Northwest, Saeta, United, Varig and Vasp (via Brazil) and Viasa.

Líneas Aéreas Paraguayas (Lapsa or Air Paraguay) is traditionally a budget carrier via Miami, but its acquisition by the Ecuadorian airline Saeta may alter this focus; US domestic carriers usually make the connection with Miami. Lapsa (☎ 800-795-2772 toll-free in the USA and Canada) also sells passes valid for travel to other South American countries in conjunction with international flights to its Asunción hub.

Aeroperú's (☎ 800-777-7717 toll-free in North America) Sudameripass includes a roundtrip flight from the US to Lima, and six coupons for flights within the continent to any of the following cities: Caracas, Bogotá, Quito, Guayaquil, La Paz, Santiago, São Paulo, Rio de Janeiro, Asunción and Buenos Aires. Valid for 45 days, low-season tickets cost US$1099 from Miami, Mexico City or Cancún, US$1299 from Los Angeles. Additional international coupons cost US$100 apiece, while internal coupons for Peruvian flights cost US$40 apiece. High-season tickets, from July 1 to August 1 and December 15 to January 15, cost US$200 more.

One alternative to landing in Santiago is to fly to Lima (Peru) and on to the Peruvian border city of Tacna, or to Arica (in northern Chile) – Lloyd Aéreo Boliviano flies from Miami to Arica, but the routing is rather convoluted via Manaus (Brazil), Santa Cruz de la Sierra and La Paz. For visitors to the Atacama Desert, this would save a long trip north from Santiago. The quoted fare is US$879, departing Mondays and Wednesdays only.

Council Travel Council Travel (☎ 800-226-8624) has agencies in the following US cities:

Berkeley, CA
   2486 Channing Way
   (☎ 510-848-8604)
Boston, MA
   Suite 201, 729 Boylston St
   (☎ 617-266-1926)
La Jolla, CA
   UCSD Student Center, B-023
   (☎ 619-452-0630)
Los Angeles, CA
   10904 Lindbrook Drive
   (☎ 213-208-3551)
New York, NY
   205 E 42nd St, ground floor
   (☎ 212-822-2700)
Pacific Beach, CA
   943 Garnett Ave
   (☎ 619-270-6401)

San Francisco, CA
   530 Bush St
   (☎ 415-421-3473)
Seattle, WA
   1314 NE 43rd St, Suite 210
   (☎ 206-632-2448)

Student Travel Network Student Travel Network (STA; ☎ 800-777-0112) has offices in the following US cities:

Boston, MA
   297 Newbury St
   (☎ 617-266-6014)
Chicago, IL
   429 S Dearborn St
   (☎ 312-786-9050)
Los Angeles, CA
   7202 Melrose Ave
   (☎ 213-934-8722)
New York, NY
   10 Downing St
   (☎ 212-627-3111)
Philadelphia, PA
   3730 Walnut St
   (☎ 215-382-2928)
San Francisco, CA
   51 Grant Ave
   (☎ 415-391-8407)
Seattle, WA
   4341 University Way NE
   (☎ 206-633-5000)
Washington, DC
   2401 Pennsylvania Ave, Suite G
   (☎ 202-887-0912)

Courier Flights In the USA, New York and Miami are the only choices for courier flights to South America. For the widest selection of destinations, try Now Voyager (☎ 212-431-1616, fax 334-5253), 74 Varick St, Suite 307, New York, NY 10013, Air Facility (☎ 718-712-0630) or Travel Courier (☎ 718-738-9000) in New York; Linehaul Services (☎ 305-477-0651) in Miami; or Discount Travel International in Miami (☎ 305-538-1616) and New York (☎ 212-362-3636, fax 362-3236), 169 W 81st St, New York, NY 10024.

For the latest information on courier and other budget fares, send US$5 for a newsletter or US$25 for a year's subscription to Travel Unlimited, PO Box 1058,

Allston, MA 02134. Another source of information is the *Air Courier Bulletin* of the International Association of Air Travel Couriers (☎ 407-582-8320), 8 South J St, PO Box 1349, Lake Worth, FL 33460, whose US$35 annual membership includes the alternate monthly newsletter *Shoestring Traveler* (not related to Lonely Planet).

Canada
LanChile no longer has direct service to Canada, but there are good connections via New York, Miami and Los Angeles. Canadian Airlines International flies three times weekly via São Paulo (stopovers permitted), with a Varig connection to Santiago (C$1200), while Aerolíneas Argentinas flies from Toronto and Montreal to Buenos Aires, with connections to Santiago.

Travel Cuts, the Canadian student travel service, has offices across the country; it is not necessary to be a student to use their services. Contact them at 171 College St, Toronto, Ontario M5T 1P7 (☎ 416-977-3703, fax 977-4796).

The UK & Europe
It is no longer necessarily cheaper to fly through New York or Miami than to go directly to South America from Europe. LanChile has the only nonstop service, from Madrid and Frankfurt, but other airlines have direct flights to Santiago via Buenos Aires, Rio de Janeiro and São Paulo from major European cities like Paris, Rome, Zurich, London, Frankfurt, Copenhagen and Amsterdam.

So-called 'bucket shops' in London can provide the best deals. Check out newspapers and magazines like the Saturday *Independent* and *Time Out* for suggestions. Advertised fares from London to Santiago start around £575 roundtrip.

If traveling from the UK, you will probably find that the cheapest flights are advertised by obscure bucket shops whose names haven't yet reached the telephone directory. Many such firms are honest and solvent, but there are a few rogues who will take the money and run, reopening elsewhere a month or two later under a different name. If you're suspicious about a firm, don't give them all the money at once – leave a deposit of 20% or so and pay the balance on receiving the ticket. If they insist on cash in advance, go elsewhere. And once you have the ticket, call the airline to confirm that you are booked on the flight.

Since bucket shops come and go, it's worth inquiring about their affiliation with the Association of British Travel Agents (ABTA), which will guarantee a refund or alternative if the agent goes out of business. The following are reputable London bucket shops:

Campus Travel
    52 Grosvenor Gardens, London SW1
    (☎ 0171-730-3402)
Journey Latin America
    14-16 Devonshire Rd, Chiswick
    London W4 2HD
    (☎ 0181-747-3108)
Passage to South America
    13 Shepards Bush Rd, London, W6 7LP
    (☎ 0171-602-9889)
STA Travel
    86 Old Brompton Rd, London SW7
    (☎ 0171-937-9962)
    117 Euston Rd, London NW1
    (☎ 0171-361-6123)
South American Experience
    47 Causton St, London SW1
    (☎ 0171-976-5511)
Trailfinders
    194 Kensington High St, London W8
    (☎ 0171-938-3939)
    42-50 Earls Court Rd
    London W8 6EJ
    (☎ 0171-938-3366)

In Berlin, check out the magazine *Zitty* for bargain fare advertisements. Throughout Western Europe and the UK you can find agencies that provide bargain fares. Here are some possibilities:

France
    Council Travel, 31 rue Saint Augustine,
    Paris 2ème
    (☎ 01.42.66.20.87)
    Council Travel, rue des Pyramides, Paris
    1er (☎ 01.44.55.55.65)

Germany
    Alternativ Tours
    Wilmersdorferstrasse 94, Berlin
    (☎ (030) 881-2089)
    SRID Reisen, Bergerstrasse 1178, Frankfurt
    (☎ (069) 43-01-91)
    SRS Studentenreise Service
    Marienstrasse 23, Berlin
    (☎ (030) 281-5033)
Ireland
    USIT Travel Office, 19 Aston Quay, Dublin
    (☎ (01) 679-8833)
Italy
    CTS, Via Genova 16, Rome
    (☎ (06) 46 791)
Netherlands
    NBBS, Rokin 38, Amsterdam
    (☎ (020) 642-0989)
    Malibu Travel, Damrak 30, Amsterdam
    (☎ 020) 623-6814)
Spain
    TIVE, Calle José Ortega y Gasset, Madrid
    (☎ (91) 401-1300)
Switzerland
    SSR, Leonhardstrasse 5 & 10, Zürich
    (☎ (01) 261-2956)

Courier Flights British Airways has recently instigated courier service in conjunction with Polo Express. They cover about 40 destinations and give couriers a full luggage allowance. You must dress 'smartly' (ie, no jeans) and be over 18 years of age. You can book up to three months in advance; call ☎ 0181-564-7009, Monday to Friday 9 am to 5 pm. As of press time they were not offering flights to Santiago, but could get you as close as Buenos Aires, for £320 from London.

Australia & New Zealand
South America is one of the most expensive places to fly to or from Australia. It can be cheaper to get a roundtrip flight to Los Angeles or Miami and buy a roundtrip ticket to South America from there, but this will mean a few extra days of flying time and a few more days in the USA, which will consume any savings on the air fare – it's only worth it if you want to visit the USA anyway.

Two routes are more direct to Chile, and don't require flying via the USA. The first is via Tahiti with Qantas or the French airline UTA, connecting with a LanChile flight to Santiago with a possible stopover in Easter Island. A ticket for this route from Sydney or Melbourne, good for up to six months, will cost around US$1920 roundtrip, US$1736 one way. The other possibility is to fly Qantas or Air New Zealand to Auckland, connecting with the Aerolíneas Argentinas trans-Antarctica flight to Buenos Aires and then a short hop across the Andes to Santiago. The flight from Sydney to Buenos Aires, which also stops in Río Gallegos for easy connections to Chilean Patagonia and Tierra del Fuego, costs from around A$2455 roundtrip, including an onward connection to another South American city.

Several travel agencies offer cheap air tickets from Australia. STA Travel, which does not require its clients to prove student status, has offices in all capital cities. Their main toll free number for all ticket sales is ☎ 800-637-444.

Adelaide
    Level 4, The Arcade, Union House
    Adelaide University
    (☎ 08-223-6620, 223-6244, fax 224-0664)
Brisbane
    Shop 25 & 26, Brisbane Arcade
    111-117 Adelaide St, Brisbane 4000
    (☎ 221-3722, fax 229-8435)
Canberra
    Arts Centre, GPO Box 4, ANU
    Canberra 0200
    (☎ 06-247-0800, fax 247-9786)
Darwin
    Shop T17, Smith St Mall, Darwin, NT 0800
Hobart
    Ground Floor, Union Building
    University of Tasmania, Hobart 7005
    (☎ 002-243-496, fax 243-738)
Melbourne
    224 Faraday St, Carlton 3053
    (☎ 03-9347-6911)
Perth
    1st Floor, New Guild Building
    University of West Australia, Crawley 6009
    (☎ 09-380-2302, fax 380-1010)
Sydney
    1st Floor, 732 Harris St, Ultimo 2007
    (☎ 02-9212-1255, fax 9281-4183)

Asia & Africa

Carriers serving Santiago from Asia, usually via North America, include All Nippon Airways (with LanChile) via Los Angeles, Vasp (via Brazil) and Varig (via Brazil).

Malaysia Airlines (with LanChile) connects Santiago with Kuala Lumpur via Buenos Aires, Johannesburg and Capetown, while South African Airways (with British Airways) flies from Santiago to Johannesburg via Buenos Aires, São Paulo and Rio de Janeiro.

Neighboring Countries

Peru Aeroperú and LanChile have daily flights from Lima to Santiago for US$330 one way; Lacsa flies less frequently. Several Peruvian domestic airlines have numerous flights from Lima to the southern Peruvian city of Tacna, only 50 km from the Chilean border city of Arica, for US$108 one way.

National Airlines flies from Santiago to Arequipa via Arica.

Bolivia Lloyd Aéreo Boliviano (LAB) has twice-weekly flights between Santiago and La Paz for US$215 one way. LanChile also flies this route. LanChile and LAB also connect La Paz with Arica for US$92 one way.

National Airlines primarily does domestic routes, but also flies to Asunción, Paraguay (US$266 one way) to Santiago via Iquique; from Iquique, the fare to Asunción is US$184.

Argentina Many airlines fly between Santiago and Buenos Aires for about US$240 one way, but European airlines that pick up and discharge most of their passengers in Buenos Aires try to fill empty seats by selling US$150 roundtrips between the Argentine and Chilean capitals – not much more than the bus fare. Even throwing away the roundtrip portion, one-way air passengers still come out ahead.

There are also LanChile, National Airlines and Aerolíneas Argentinas flights from Santiago to Mendoza (US$96) and to Córdoba. TAN, the regional carrier of Argentina's Neuquén province, connects the city of Neuquén with Temuco (US$70). There are Aerolíneas flights between Iquique and Jujuy, Argentina in summer only; past flights have connected Salta and Antofagasta.

In southern Patagonia, there are flights from Punta Arenas, Chile, to the Argentine cities of Río Gallegos, Río Grande and Ushuaia.

Mexico & Central America LanChile flights from the West Coast of the US sometimes stop in Mexico City. The Costa Rican airline Lacsa's flights from both the East and West Coasts may make stops in Mexico City, Guatemala City, San Salvador, and Managua before San José, where it's necessary to change planes to continue via Panama and Lima before finishing in Santiago.

LAND

Chile has a handful of border crossings with Peru and Bolivia, and many with Argentina, not all of which are served by public transportation. Between 1996 and 2001, the Ministerio de Obras Públicas (MOP, Public Works Ministry) plans to spend US$156 million in improving crossings to Argentina to facilitate contact with the Mercosur free-trade zone.

Photographers should note that at major land borders, such as Los Libertadores complex between Santiago and Mendoza, and the Pajaritos crossing between Osorno and Bariloche, Chilean customs officials x-ray arriving baggage.

Peru

Tacna to Arica is the only overland crossing between Peru and Chile. There is a choice of bus, taxi or train. For details, see the Arica entry in the Norte Grande chapter.

Bolivia

Road and rail connections exist between Bolivia and Chile, but neither is fast or especially comfortable. A weekly *ferrobus*, a sort of bus on rails, goes from Arica to La Paz. Buses, via Visviri or Tambo Quemado (a route now paved all the way to La Paz), are more frequent and cheaper; for details, see the Arica entry in the Norte Grande chapter. There are also buses from Iquique to the border post of Colchane and on to Oruro and La Paz.

A weekly rail service, as well as the occasional bus, links Calama to the border village of Ollagüe, with connections to Oruro and La Paz; from Calama there are easy bus connections to the coastal city of Antofagasta, the former Chilean rail terminus, and to many other destinations in Chile. For details, see the Calama entry in the Norte Grande chapter.

It is possible to travel from Uyuni, Bolivia to San Pedro de Atacama via the Portezuelo del Cajón, near the juncture of the Chilean, Bolivian and Argentine borders, but no regularly scheduled public transport exists in this area. See the San Pedro de Atacama entry for details.

Argentina

Except in Patagonia, every land crossing to Argentina involves crossing the Andes. There is public transportation on only a few of these crossings, and some passes are closed in winter.

Calama to Jujuy & Salta Usually open December to March only, the 4079-meter (13,346-foot) Paso de Lago Sico has superseded the higher Paso de Huaytiquina, but the crossing via the more northerly Paso de Jama to Jujuy also gets traffic, depending on weather conditions. Tramaca and Géminis buses make weekly crossings in summer, with connections from Arica, Iquique and Antofagasta, but bookings are heavy and reservations essential. Automobile traffic is almost nil, so forget about hitching.

There is an occasional Argentine passenger train from Salta to the border at Socompa, but only freight service beyond, although the very uncomfortable Chilean train will sometimes carry passengers to the abandoned station of Augusta Victoria (where it's possible to hitch to Antofagasta), or to Baquedano on Ruta 5 (the Panamericana), where it's easy to catch a bus. See the entries on Antofagasta and Baquedano for details.

Copiapó to Catamarca & La Rioja There is no public transport over the 4726-meter (15,501-foot) Paso de San Francisco, but this recently improved route is seeing an increasing amount of auto traffic.

La Serena to San Juan Dynamited by the Argentine military during the Beagle Channel dispute of 1978-79, the 4779-meter (15,675-foot) Paso del Agua Negra is open for automobile traffic, but the road is rough and bus services continue to use Los Libertadores crossing west of Mendoza.

Santiago to Mendoza & Buenos Aires Many bus companies service this most popular of crossing points between the two countries, along Ruta 60 through the Los Libertadores tunnel. Taxi colectivos are faster, more comfortable and only slighlty more expensive. Winter snow sometimes closes the route, but never for long.

Visiting Argentina

Even travelers who don't plan to spend a lot of time in Argentina may want to pay some brief visits, either making one of the crossings through the lakes region or in order to reach far southern Chile, which has no road connections except through Argentine Patagonia. For full details, see Lonely Planet's *Argentina, Uruguay & Paraguay – a travel survival kit.*

Visas Nationals of the USA, Canada and most Western European countries do not require visas, but Australians and New Zealanders, who do need them, must submit their passports with a payment of US$30. Argentina's Santiago consulate is particularly efficient, and ordinarily the visa will be ready the following day.

Customs On entering Argentina, customs officers will probably only check your bags for fresh fruit. Officials generally defer to foreign visitors, but if you cross the border frequently and carry electronic equipment such as cameras or a laptop computer, it's helpful to have a typed list with serial numbers stamped by authorities.

Money In recent years, Argentina has controlled inflation with very strict fiscal measures, including a fixed exchange rate placing the peso at par with the US dollar. Outside large cities, changing travelers' checks may be difficult or impossible without paying a very high commission, so carry a supply of cash dollars. Since the 'dollarization' of the Argentine economy, many merchants readily accept US dollars in lieu of Argentine pesos, thus avoiding many currency dilemmas – but expect to receive your change in pesos. Many Argentina ATMs conveniently dispense both pesos and cash dollars.

Health Argentina requires no vaccinations for visitors entering from any country and, in general, the country presents few serious health hazards, especially in Patagonia.

Getting Around In Argentine Patagonia, distances are immense, roads can be very bad, and some travelers find the desert monotonous, so the occasional flight is sometimes a welcome relief. Argentina's two major airlines, Austral and Aerolíneas Argentinas, have extensive networks in southern Patagonia and Tierra del Fuego, but their fares are much higher than competitors like LAPA, LADE and Kaikén Líneas Aéreas. In some cases, fares may be less than the bus fare for the same route, but demand is high, especially in summer; try the airport if LADE staff insist that flights are completely booked.

Argentine buses, resembling those in Chile, are modern, comfortable and fast. Most large towns have a central bus terminal, though some companies operate from their own private offices. In some more remote and less populated areas, buses are few or even non-existent, so be patient. There are no passenger railways in southern Patagonia.

Hitching is relatively easy in Argentina, but traffic in Patagonia and Tierra del Fuego is sparse and there may be long waits between lifts. ■

Talca to Malargüe & San Rafael Occasional buses now cross the 2553-meter (8373-foot) Paso Pehuenche, southeast of Talca. A route may open from Curicó over the 2938-meter (9636-foot) Paso del Planchón, also to San Rafael.

Southern Mainland Routes There are a number of scenic crossings from Temuco south to Puerto Montt, some involving bus-boat shuttles. These are very popular in summer, so make advance bookings whenever possible.

Temuco to Zapala & Neuquén
    This route crosses the Andes over the 1884-meter (6179-foot) Paso de Pino Hachado, directly east of Temuco via Curacautín and Lonquimay, along the upper Río Biobío. A slightly more southerly alternative uses the 1298-meter (4257-foot) Paso de Icalma. Both have occasional bus traffic in summer.
Temuco to San Martín de los Andes
    The most popular route from Temuco passes Lago Villarrica, Pucón and Curarrehue en route to the Paso de Mamuil Malal (known to Argentines as Paso Tromen). On the Argentine side, the road skirts the northern slopes of Volcán Lanín. There is regular summer bus service, but the pass is closed in winter.
Valdivia to San Martín de los Andes
    This route starts with a bus from Valdivia to Panguipulli, Choshuenco and Puerto Fuy, followed by a ferry across Lago Pirehueico to the village of Pirehueico. From Pirehueico a local bus goes to Argentine customs at 659-meter (2161-foot) Paso Huahum, where there is a bus to San Martín.
Osorno to Bariloche via Paso Puyehue
    This crossing, commonly known as Pajaritos, is the quickest land route in the southern lakes region, passing through Parque Nacional Puyehue on the Chilean side and Parque Nacional Nahuel Huapi on the Argentine side.
Puerto Montt/Puerto Varas to Bariloche
    Very popular in summer but open all year, this bus-ferry combination via Parque Nacional Vicente Pérez Rosales starts in Puerto Montt or Puerto Varas and goes from Petrohué, at the west end of Lago Todos Los Santos, by ferry to Peulla, where a bus crosses 1022-meter (3352-foot) Paso de Pérez Rosales to Argentine immigration at Puerto Frías. After crossing Lago Frías by launch, there is a short bus hop to Puerto

Blest on Lago Nahuel Huapi and another ferry to Puerto Pañuelo (Llao Llao). From Llao Llao, there is frequent bus service to Bariloche.

Southern Patagonian Routes Since the opening of the Camino Austral (Southern Highway) south of Puerto Montt, it has become more common to cross between Chile and Argentina in this area. There are also several crossing points in extreme southern Patagonia and Tierra del Fuego. See also the Routes through Southern Argentina sidebar in the Aisén & the Camino Austral chapter.

Puerto Ramírez to Esquel
    There are two options here. From the village of Villa Santa Lucía, on the Camino Austral, there is a good lateral road which forks at Puerto Ramírez, at the southeastern end of Lago Yelcho. The north fork goes to Futaleufú, where a bridge crosses the river to the Argentine side where you can catch colectivos to Esquel. The south fork goes to Palena and Argentine customs at Carrenleufú, where there is bus service to Corcovado, Trevelin and Esquel.
Puerto Cisnes to José de San Martín
    At Villa Amengual, a lateral off the Camino Austral climbs the valley of the Río Cisnes to Paso de Río Frías and the Argentine province of Chubut, but there is no public transport.
Coihaique to Comodoro Rivadavia
    There are several buses per week, often heavily booked, from Coihaique to Comodoro Rivadavia via Río Mayo. For private vehicles, there is an alternative route via Balmaceda to Perito Moreno via the 502-meter (1646-foot) Paso Huemules or the slightly more southerly El Portezuelo, which has occasional bus service to Chile Chico via Los Antiguos.
Puerto Ingeniero Ibáñez to Perito Moreno
    This route follows the north shore of Lago General Carrera (Lago Buenos Aires on the Argentine side). There is no public transport, but since all vehicles must pass through the Carabineros post on the lakefront in Puerto Ibáñez, patient waiting may yield a lift.
Chile Chico to Los Antiguos
    From Puerto Ibáñez, take the ferry to Chile Chico on the southern shore of Lago Carrera and a bus to Los Antiguos, which has connections to the Patagonian coastal town of Caleta

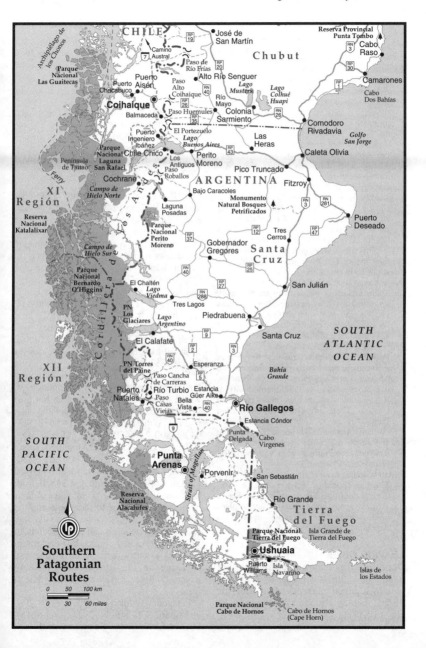

Southern
Patagonian
Routes

Olivia. There is also a narrow mountain road to Chile Chico from Cruce El Maitén at the southwestern end of Lago General Carrera, with infrequent bus services.

Cochrane to Bajo Caracoles
Perhaps the most desolate crossing in the Aisén region, 647-meter (2122-foot) Paso Roballos links the hamlet of Cochrane with a flyspeck outpost in Argentina's Santa Cruz province.

Puerto Natales to Río Turbio & El Calafate
Frequent buses connect Puerto Natales to the Argentine coal town of Río Turbio, where many Chileans work; from Río Turbio there are further connections to Río Gallegos and El Calafate. At least twice weekly in summer there are buses from Chile's Parque Nacional Torres del Paine and Puerto Natales to El Calafate, the gateway to Argentina's Parque Nacional Los Glaciares, via Paso Cancha de Carreras. Improvements on Argentine RN 40 have cut the time on this route nearly in half, from about 10 to six hours.

Punta Arenas to Río Gallegos
There are many buses daily on the much improved highway between Punta Arenas and Río Gallegos, but it's still a six-hour trip because of slow customs checks. There are also occasional flights.

Punta Arenas to Tierra del Fuego
From Punta Arenas, a three-hour ferry trip or a 10-minute flight takes you to Porvenir, on Chilean Tierra del Fuego, where there are two buses weekly to the Argentine city of Río Grande, which has connections to Ushuaia. There are also direct buses from Punta Arenas to Ushuaia via the more northerly, frequent and shorter ferry crossing at Primera Angostura. Regular air services now connect Punta Arenas with both Río Grande and Ushuaia.

Puerto Williams to Ushuaia
There is sporadic, undependable and frequently interrupted ferry service from Puerto Williams, on Isla Navarino (reached by plane or boat from Punta Arenas) opposite the Argentine city of Ushuaia.

LEAVING CHILE

Departure Tax Chilean departure tax for international flights is US$18 or its equivalent in national currency. For domestic flights, there is a modest departure tax of about US$7.

Note that *arriving* US passengers pay a one-time tax of US$20, valid for the life of the passport. Chilean authorities imposed this fee after US officials introduced a US$20 visa application fee for Chilean nationals.

TOURS

Increasingly, both Chilean and foreign companies have become involved in nature-oriented tourism (popularly, but not always accurately, known as *turismo ecológico* or *turismo aventura)*. More conventional tours are also available.

The USA Festival Tours (☎ 407-850-0680, 800-225-0117, fax 240-1480), 737 W Oak Ridge Rd, Orlando, FL 32809, offers a wide variety of trips to Chile, including ski weeks at Portillo and Valle Nevado, four-day excursions to Easter Island, and visits to Laguna San Rafael, Chilean and Argentine Patagonia, Isla Grande de Tierra del Fuego and Antarctica.

For travelers of at least 55 years of age, Elderhostel (☎ 617-426-8056), 76 Federal Street, Boston, MA 02110, operates two-week heartland tours taking in Valparaíso, Viña del Mar, Santiago and Los Andes for about US$3000.

Well-established North American adventure companies operating Patagonian trips, which usually begin in Argentina but take in substantial parts of Chilean Patagonia, include Wilderness Travel (☎ 510-548-0420, 800-247-6700), 801 Allston Way, Berkeley, CA 94710 and Mountain Travel Sobek (☎ 510-527-8100, 800-227-2384, see the Online Services appendix), 6420 Fairmount Ave, El Cerrito, CA 94530. Both have lavishly illustrated catalogues of their numerous excursions to Patagonia and the Andean lakes, which range from easy day hikes, staying at hotels and campgrounds, to strenuous treks and climbs, bivouacking in the back country, whitewater rafting and kayaking on the Biobío and Futaleufú Rivers, and sea kayaking in the Chilean fjords.

Patagonia Wildland Adventures (☎ 206-365-0686, 800-345-4453, fax 363-6615), 3516 NE 155th St, Seattle, WA 98155, arranges 10-day itineraries through local guides and outfitters for as few as two persons for US$1295 per person (land cost). Another possibility is Lost World Adventures (☎ 404-971-8586, 800-999-0558, fax 977-3095). For visitors with limited time, especially in areas like Patagonia where logistics can be difficult, such trips may be ideal.

Natural Habitat Adventures (☎ 303-449-3711, 800-543-8917, fax 449-3712), 2945 Center Green Court, Boulder, CO 80301, runs tours to the Falkland Islands, South Georgia and Antarctica via Santiago or Ushuaia (Argentina). Prices for these trips, which last from 10 to 27 days, range from US$4275 to US$11,990, usually including air transportation.

Nature Expeditions International (☎ 800-869-0639, see the Online Services appendix), 474 Willamette St, Eugene, OR 97401, offers a variety of Chilean tours, combining the lakes region with Easter Island in a 17-day excursion (US$2900), and Chilean Patagonia and Antarctica on a 21-day cruise (US$6900). One of their 19-day Pacific island cruises starts at Easter Island and visits unusual destinations like Pitcairn and the Gambier Islands before ending in Tahiti; prices start around US$5200, air fares not included.

Kayaker Chris Spelius, a former Olympian, runs whitewater trips on the Biobío, Fuy and Futaleufú Rivers through his Expediciones Chile (☎ /fax 704-488-9082), 333 Earl's Road, Bryson, NC 28713. Class IV and V whitewater trips run from December through February, last one to three weeks, and cost from US$1800 to US$2950. Trip videos, including material on the environmental crisis facing Chilean rivers, are available through the above address.

For bicycle tours of southern mainland Chile, contact Backroads (☎ 510-527-1555, fax 527-1444), 1516 5th Street, Berkeley, CA 94710.

Rocky Mountain Adventures (☎ 800-858-6808), PO Box 1989, Fort Collins, CO 80522, arranges 10-day tours of Chile's Futaleufú area which stress hiking,

horseback riding, rafting, kayaking and fly-fishing for around US$1500 (not including airfare).

The UK & Europe Journey Latin America (see under Air; The UK & Europe, above) runs three-week tours of Chile from north to south for about £1650, and 16-day tours taking in both Chilean and Argentine Patagonia for £1566. Passage to South America (see under Air; The UK & Europe, above) arranges 20-day Patagonian trips for £3670, but also arranges tailor-made itineraries, as does Cox and Kings (☎ 0171-834-7472). Explore Worldwide (☎ 0252-344161), 1 Frederick St, Aldershot, Hants GU11 1LQ, Melia Travel (☎ 0181-491-3881), 12 Dover St, London W1X 4NS, and Exodus (☎ 0181-675-5550) are also Latin American specialists.

In Germany, Argentoura Travel (☎ /fax (089) 673-3072), Gustav-Heinemann-Ring 42, 81739 München, operates very comfortable backroads excursions in Patagonia (in summer) and the Atacama desert (in winter) in their custom-designed 'Traction Mobil.' Based in Bariloche (Argentina), the Traction Mobil is also available for charter, and owners Frank and Heike Neumann speak excellent English as well. Their Patagonian representative is Cumbres Patagónicos (☎ /fax (0944) 23831), Villegas 222, San Carlos de Bariloche, Río Negro, Argentina.

Australia In Australia, try World Expeditions, which has two offices: 441 Kent St, Sydney, NSW 2000 (☎ 02-264-3366) and 1/393 Little Bourke St, Melbourne, Victoria 3000 (☎ 03-9670-8400, 800-803-688). Peregrine Bird Tours (☎ 03-9727-3343), 2 Drysdale Place, Mooroolbark, Victoria 3138, also sometimes schedules Patagonian trips. The unaffiliated Peregrine Adventures (☎ 03-9663-8611), 258 Lonsdale St, Melbourne, Victoria 3000, is another possibility.

WARNING
The information in this chapter is particularly vulnerable to change: Prices for

international travel are volatile, routes are introduced and canceled, schedules change, special deals come and go, and rules and visa requirements are amended. Airlines and governments seem to take perverse pleasure in making price structures and regulations as complex as possible. You should check directly with the airline or a travel agent to make sure you understand how a fare (and ticket you may buy) works. In addition, the travel industry is highly competitive, and there are many lurks and perks.

The upshot of this is that you should get opinions, quotes and advice from as many airlines and travel agents as possible before you part with your cash. The details given in the chapter should be regarded as pointers, and are not a substitute for your own careful, up-to-date research.

Getting Around

Travel within Chile is generally easy. The fast, punctual and comfortable buses on the main highways are preferable to railways, which have been neglected since the early 1970s. Flights are reasonably priced, with occasional bargain discounts, and there are several interesting and scenic passenger ferries.

AIR

Because of Chile's latitudinal extension, you may want to avoid tiresome and time-consuming backtracking by taking an occasional flight. For instance, you can travel overland through Chilean and Argentine Patagonia to Tierra del Fuego, then fly from Punta Arenas to Puerto Montt or Santiago. The return flight should be no more expensive than a combination of bus fares and accommodation.

Airports

Most cities have domestic airports with commercial air service, except for some larger cities near Santiago and towns near other major cities. Santiago's Aeropuerto Internacional Arturo Merino Benítez has a separate domestic terminal; the other major domestic airports are in Arica, Iquique, Calama, Copiapó, La Serena, Temuco, Valdivia, Puerto Montt, Coihaique and Punta Arenas. An increasing number of smaller towns have air taxi service.

Domestic Airlines

Two major airlines, LanChile and Ladeco, offer domestic services, but one-time upstart National Airlines is now well-established.

All three major airlines have computerized booking services, so you can book domestic and international flights from their offices anywhere in the country or overseas. Both also publish detailed timetables to which they adhere closely. A list of central airline offices appears in the Santiago chapter, with regional offices in each city entry. Telephone reservations are also simple.

Minor regional airlines include DAP, which connects Santiago with Punta Arenas, Tierra del Fuego, Antarctica and the Falkland Islands; and Alta, which serves many lesser destinations overlooked by the larger companies. Lassa and Líneas Aéreas Robinson Crusoe both operate air taxis to the Juan Fernández Islands, while several air taxi companies connect isolated settlements in the Aisén region, south of Puerto Montt. At press time there were rumors of a new airline called Avant, which was to be undercutting the prices of the other domestic airlines, but no further information was available.

Smoking is prohibited on all domestic flights, except LanChile's Easter Island (Rapa Nui) service, which has a choice of smoking or non-smoking.

Fares For fare information, see the individual cities' Getting There & Away headings. On most flights, a certain number of discount seats are available and, if your travel schedule is flexible, you may be able to take advantage of these. Usually discount ticket purchases must be made at least three days in advance.

Frequent Flyer Credit LanChile is a frequent flyer partner of Continental, while National has a similar agreement with United. Do not be surprised, however, if credits for Chilean international and domestic flights fail to show up on your quarterly statements – save both tickets and boarding passes to corroborate your flights when you return home.

Air Passes

For US$300, LanChile and Ladeco each offers a 21-day 'Visit Chile Pass' that allows flights to and from selected airports either north or south of Santiago; for US$550, it includes airports both north and south. Destinations include Arica, Iquique, Calama, Antofagasta, Copiapó, Concepción, Puerto Montt and Punta Arenas. For US$1080, the basic air pass can include Easter Island – a minor saving as the usual fare to Easter Island from Santiago is US$812 roundtrip. For US$1290 it includes areas both north and south of Santiago, as well as Easter Island, but this might also mean spending most of your trip in airports.

Passes, which must be purchased outside Chile, are available only to foreigners and nonresidents of Chile. The maximum validity is 21 days, but there is no minimum restriction. Intermediate stops can be omitted. Travelers using LanChile for their international flights can obtain a better rate of about US$600 to and from Easter Island. If time is not a factor, it is sometimes possible to arrange flights for less than the Visit Chile Pass.

Ladeco's similarly priced passes permit the usage of LanChile to Easter Island, and also allows stopovers at Balmaceda/Coihaique, an area of considerable interest to travelers.

BUS

Major highways and some others are paved, except for the Camino Austral south of Puerto Montt, but many secondary roads are gravel or dirt. Buses on the main roads are comfortable, some are luxurious, and nearly all are well maintained, fast and punctual. They generally have toilet facilities and often serve coffee, tea and even meals on board; if not, they make regular stops. By European or North American standards, fares are a bargain.

Most Chilean cities have a central bus terminal, but in some the companies have separate offices, usually within a few blocks of each other. Terminals are well organized, with destinations, schedules and fares prominently displayed.

Classes

Long-distance buses now employ a bewildering variety of terms to describe their seating arrangements – about the only one common to all is *Pullman*, which means 44 ordinary reclining seats, two on each side of the aisle. *Executivo* and *semi-cama* usually mean 32 seats, providing extra leg room and calf-rests, while *salón cama* sleepers seat only 24 passengers, with only three seats per row and additional leg room. If you have any doubt about the type of service offered, ask for a seat diagram – obviously, seat No 44 is not going to provide the same amenities that No 24 would on a bus with fewer seats.

Normally departing at night, these premium bus services cost upwards of 50% more than ordinary buses, but on long hauls like Arica to Santiago, they merit consideration. Regular buses are also comfortable enough for most purposes, however. Smoking is now prohibited on buses throughout the country.

On back roads, which include about 70,000 km of gravel or dirt roads, transport is slower and buses are less frequent, older and more basic. These *micros*, which sometimes lack reclining seats, may be packed with peasants and their produce.

Reservations & Fares

Except during holiday season (Christmas, January and February, Easter and mid-September's patriotic holidays), it is rarely necessary to book a seat more than a few hours in advance. On very long trips, like Arica to Santiago, or rural routes with limited services (along the Camino Austral, for example), advance booking is a good idea.

Fares differ from one company to the next, and promotions *(ofertas)* can reduce normal fares by half. Ask for student reductions, which can reduce fares by 25%, or even try bargaining if the bus is soon to leave and appears to have empty seats. Fares between important destinations are listed throughout this book.

TRAIN

Trains can be worthwhile on a long haul, but for most trips buses are more frequent and convenient. Southbound trains from Santiago pass through Talca and Chillán to Temuco all year; in summer only, they continue to Puerto Varas via Osorno and other intermediate points. A spur that leaves the main longitudinal line at Chillán provides direct service from Santiago to Concepción.

With the exception of the Arica-La Paz and Calama-La Paz lines between Chile and Bolivia, there are no long-distance passenger services north of Santiago. It is difficult but not impossible to travel by freight from Baquedano (on the Panamericana northeast of Antofagasta) to the border town of Socompa, and on to Salta in Argentina.

Classes & Fares

Trains have three classes: *economía*, *salón* and *cama*. Cama refers to 'sleeper' class, which has upper and lower bunks; the latter are more expensive. On long overnight journeys, the charming between-the-wars sleepers may be worth consideration, but travelers have remarked that decades of heavy use have left the bunks much less comfortable than they once were.

Typical one-way fares for the three classes are listed below, in US dollars; a roundtrip fare is slightly cheaper than two singles. The approximate length of the journey from Santiago appears after the destination.

Reservations

All trains from Santiago depart from the Estación Central (☎ (02) 6895199), Alameda 3322 (Metro: Estación Central), which is open daily from 7 am to 11 pm. Tickets are also available at the Venta de Pasajes (ticket office) in the Galería

Libertador (☎ (02) 6322801), Alameda 853, Local 21. It's open weekdays from 8.30 am to 7 pm, and Saturday from 9 am to 1 pm. Another office of EFE (☎ (02) 2282983) is at the Escuela Militar Metro station.

CAR

Even though Chile's public transport system is very extensive, many interesting areas are easily accessible only by motor vehicle. Off the main highways, where buses may be few or nonexistent, it's not easy to stop where you want and then continue by public transport.

Operating a car in Chile is cheaper than in Europe but dearer than in the USA. The price of *bencina* (gasoline) is about US$0.55 per liter, that of *gas-oil* (diesel fuel) somewhat cheaper. There is a minimal price difference between 97-octane *super* and lower grades like 81-octane *común*. Unleaded gasoline is readily available throughout the country.

Advantages of driving include freedom from timetables, the ability to stay wherever you like (particularly if you have camping equipment), the opportunity to get off the beaten track, and the flexibility to stop whenever you see something interesting. In some areas – like the Atacama desert, the Camino Austral or Easter Island – a car is definitely the best way to get around. Security problems are minor, but always lock your vehicle and leave valuables out of sight. Note that, because of smog problems, there are frequent restrictions on private vehicle use in Santiago and the surrounding region; usually these are organized according to the terminal digit of the license plate of the car.

Trains: how long and how much?

Destination	time/hours	Economía	Salón	Cama, upper/lower
Concepción	9	$14	$17	$23/31
Temuco	13	$17	$21	$28/39
Osorno	18½	$21	$25	$32/42

Motorists should be aware that, while customs regulations that once stipulated that the 90-day import permit for foreign vehicles could not be extended (unlike tourist cards), that is no longer the case. Not all customs officials are aware of this, however, and it may be easier to leave the country and return.

The Automóvil Club Chileno (Acchi) has offices in most major Chilean cities, provides useful information, sells maps and rents cars. It also offers member services and grants discounts to members of its foreign counterparts, such as the American Automobile Association (AAA) in the USA or the Automobile Association (AA) in the UK. Acchi's central office (☎ (02) 2125702) is at Avenida Vitacura 8620, Vitacura, Santiago, while its tourism and member services office (☎ (02) 2253790) is at Fidel Oteíza 1960. Membership includes free towing and other road-side services within 25 km of an Automóvil Club office.

Rental

Major international rental agencies like Hertz, Avis and Budget have offices in Santiago, and in major cities and other tourist areas. The Automóvil Club also rents cars at some of its offices. To rent a car, you must have a valid driver's license, be at least 25 years of age, and present either a credit card such as MasterCard or Visa, or a large cash deposit.

Even at smaller agencies, basic rental charges are now very high, the cheapest and smallest vehicles going for about US$50 to US$65 per day with 150 to 200 km included, or sometimes with unlimited mileage. Adding the cost of insurance, petrol and IVA (impuesto de valor agregado, the value added tax or VAT), it becomes very pricey indeed to operate a rental vehicle without several others to share expenses. Weekend or weekly rates, with unlimited mileage, are a much better bargain. Small vehicles with unlimited mileage cost about US$340 to US$450 per week, while 4WD vehicles cost in excess of US$100 per day. Some companies will give discounts for extended rentals, say a month or more.

One-way rentals can be awkward or impossible to arrange. Some companies, most notably Hertz, will arrange this but with a substantial dropoff charge. With smaller local agencies, this is next to impossible. Smaller agencies will, however, usually arrange paperwork for taking cars into Argentina, so long as the car is returned to the original office. There may be a substantial charge, around US$90, for taking a car into Argentina; Chilean insurance may not be valid in Argentina.

When traveling in remote areas, where fuel may not be readily available, carry extra fuel. Rental agencies will often provide a spare bidón for this purpose.

Purchase

If you are spending several months in Chile, purchasing a car merits consideration, but it has both advantages and disadvantages. On the one hand, it is more flexible than public transport and likely to be cheaper than multiple rentals; reselling it at the end of your stay can make it even more economical. On the other hand, any used car can be a risk, especially on rugged back roads. Fortunately, even the smallest hamlet seems to have a competent and resourceful mechanic.

Chile no longer has a domestic automobile industry, but good imported vehicles are available at prices higher than Europe or the USA, but much more reasonable than in Argentina. Japanese and Korean vehicles like Toyota and Hyundai are especially popular, but Argentine Peugeots are also common. Parts are readily available, except for some older models. Do not expect to find a dependable used car for less than about US$3000, much more for recent models.

If you purchase a car you must change the title within 30 days; failure to do so can result in a fine of several hundred dollars. In order to buy a vehicle, you must have a RUT (Rol Unico Tributario) tax identification number, available through Impuestos Internos, the Chilean tax office; issuance of the RUT takes about 10 days. The actual title transfer is done at any notary through a compraventa for about US$10.

All vehicles must carry so-called *seguro obligatorio* (minimum insurance), which covers personal injuries up to a maximum of about US$3000 at a cost of about US$20 per year. All companies issue these policies, which run from April 1 to March 31 of the following year. Additional liability insurance is highly desirable.

Since Chilean policies are not valid in Argentina, but Argentine policies are valid in Chile and other neighboring countries, it is worth buying a reasonably priced Argentine policy across the border if you plan to visit several countries.

Note that, while many inexpensive vehicles are for sale in the free zones of Regions I and XII (Tarapacá and Magallanes), only legal permanent residents of those regions may take a vehicle outside of those regions, for a maximum of 90 days per calendar year.

Shipping a Car or Motorcycle

Given its current openness toward foreign trade and tourism, Chile is probably the best country on the continent for shipping a vehicle from overseas. After the author shipped his pickup truck from California to the port of San Antonio, southwest of Santiago, it took less than two hours of very routine paperwork to get the vehicle out of customs. If the car is more than a few days in customs, however, storage charges can add up quickly.

To find a reliable shipper, check the Yellow Pages of your local phone directory under Automobile Transporters. Most transporters are accustomed to arranging shipments between North America and Europe, rather than from North America or Europe to South America, so it may take some of them time to work out details. One reliable US shipper is A-Amak Overseas Shipping (☎ 619-562-8070, fax 562-5657; toll-free 800-530-1119), 8402 Magnolia Ave, Suite H, Santee, California 92071.

When shipping a vehicle into Chile, do not leave anything whatsoever of value in the vehicle if at all possible. Theft of tools in particular is very common.

Road Rules

While Chileans sometimes drive carelessly or a bit too fast (especially in the cities), if you have come from Argentina you will think them saints. Most Chilean drivers are courteous to pedestrians, and will rarely do anything willfully dangerous. Driving after dark is not advisable, especially in rural areas in southern Chile, where pedestrians, domestic animals and wooden carts are difficult to see on or near the highways. If you are involved in an automobile accident, consult the entry on Legal Matters in the Facts for the Visitor chapter.

Unless otherwise posted, speed limits are 50 kmh in town and 100 kmh in rural areas. In contrast to neighboring Argentina, Chile's Carabineros enforce speed limits with US$75 fines; bribing them is not an option.

BICYCLE

Bicycling is an interesting and inexpensive alternative for traveling around Chile, although camping is not a bargain for the solo cyclist, and it will probably be cheaper to stay at residenciales. Because even the best paved roads often lack adequate shoulders, a *todo terreno* (mountain bike) is a better choice than a racing bike. In areas like the increasingly popular and almost completely unpaved Camino Austral, a racing bike is almost useless.

Cycling is an increasingly popular recreational activity and there are many good routes, but the weather can be a drawback. From Temuco south, it is changeable and you must be prepared for rain; from Santiago north, especially in the Atacama, water sources are infrequent. In some areas, the wind can slow your progress to a crawl; north to south is generally easier than south to north, but some readers report strong headwinds southbound in summer. Chilean motorists are usually courteous, but on narrow, two-lane highways without shoulders, they can be a real hazard to cyclists.

LP reader Paul Arundale, who has cycled extensively through the Southern Cone, offers the following suggestions on travel in Chile:

Chile offers ideal cycling conditions on rough unsurfaced roads in the north and south of the country, but in the middle it is difficult to avoid using the Panamericana; while this is not dangerous, having a wide hard shoulder for much of the central part, it is certainly no fun with the mountains far away and the diesel fumes all too close. January and February are months best avoided as all of Santiago seems to be on the road in pickup trucks and vans heading north or south and the unsurfaced roads are usually little more than one-vehicle wide, making continual traffic in either direction a frazzling experience. For those on a longer tour, Chile has the best-stocked bike shops in South America and even the smallest town has at least one bike shop offering all the latest Japanese parts. If flying between New Zealand and Chile, LanChile carries bikes wrapped in cardboard free between Chile, Easter Island and Tahiti.

Another reader claims that spare parts are more basic and hard to come by, though easier for mountain bikes than for racing bikes; 27-inch tires are particularly hard to find. There's a cluster of shops along Calle San Diego in Santiago.

Arundale adds:

Cyclists en route from Argentina will find several unsurfaced routes crossing the Andes into Chile such as the Bajo Caracoles to Cochrane road in the south, and the Bardas Blancas to Talca and the Jáchal to Vicuña routes either side of Santiago which offer ideal traffic-free cycling for the well-prepared. There are few fences near these roads and a tent can be pitched anywhere.

Readers interested in detailed information on cycling in South America can find more material in Bruce Junek's *Cycling in Latin America*.

HITCHING

Along with Argentina, Chile is probably the best country for hitching in all of South America. The major drawback is that Chilean vehicles are often packed with families with children, but truck drivers will often help backpackers. At *servicentros* on the outskirts of Chilean cities on the Panamericana, where truckers gas up their vehicles, it is often worth soliciting a ride.

Women can and do hitchhike alone, but

should exercise caution and especially avoid getting into a car with more than one man. In Patagonia, where distances are great and vehicles few, hitchers should expect long waits and carry warm, windproof clothing. Carry some snack food and a water bottle, especially in the desert north.

Along the Panamericana, from Arica to Puerto Montt, hitching is fairly reliable, but competition may be great in the summer months, when Chilean students hit the highway with their backpacks. In the Atacama you may wait for some time, but almost every ride will be a long one. Along the Camino Austral, in Region XI (Aisén), vehicles of any kind are few except between Coihaique and Puerto Aisén, and hitching requires great patience. Readers report that increasing traffic between Chaitén and Coihaique has made that stretch of highway easier to hitch.

Because hitching is never entirely secure, Lonely Planet does not recommend the practice.

FERRY

Most bus services between Puerto Montt and Coihaique, in Region XI, pass through Argentina; if you want to explore the less easily accessible parts of the Camino Austral Longitudinal (Southern Longitudinal Highway), it's necessary to take Naviera Magallanes (Navimag) or Transportes Marítimos Chiloé Aysén (Transmarchilay) ferries from Puerto Montt, Hornopirén or Chiloé to Chaitén or Puerto Chacabuco. Navimag's enormously popular ferry service from Puerto Montt to Puerto Natales is one of the continent's great travel experiences.

The Santiago addresses of these companies appear below; for representatives in the regions, see the appropriate city entries.

Navimag
    Avenida El Bosque
    Norte 0440
    (☎ (02) 2035030, fax 2035025)
Transmarchilay
    Agustinas 715, Oficina 403
    (☎ /fax (02) 6335959)

Puerto Montt to Puerto Chacabuco

Navimag and Transmarchilay operate services from Puerto Montt to Puerto Chacabuco, with bus service continuing on to Coihaique. For details of schedules and fares, see the Puerto Montt entry in the La Araucanía & Los Lagos chapter. Transmarchilay also runs a tourist ship, the *Skorpios*, from Puerto Chacabuco to Parque Nacional Laguna San Rafael.

Puerto Montt to Puerto Natales

Navimag operates ferries from Puerto Montt to Puerto Natales. These ships depart weekly, usually Sunday, taking about three days to reach Puerto Natales, but erratic Patagonian weather can play havoc with schedules. For details of schedules and fares, see the Puerto Montt entry in the La Araucanía & Los Lagos chapter.

La Arena to Puelche

Transmarchilay's shuttle ferry, about 45 km southeast of Puerto Montt, connects two northerly segments of the Camino Austral all year.

Hornopirén to Caleta Gonzalo

The last mainland stop southbound on the Camino Austral, Hornopirén is a scenic village where, in summer, Transmarchilay ferries sail to Caleta Gonzalo, about 60 km north of Chaitén.

Chiloé to the Mainland

There are three connections between Chiloé and the mainland. The most frequent is with Transmarchilay or Cruz del Sur ferries between Chacao, at the northern tip of the Isla Grande, and Pargua, on the mainland. For details of fares and schedules, see the Chiloé chapter.

The other connections are by Transmarchilay ferries between the port of Quellón on Chiloé, and Chaitén or Puerto Chacabuco on the mainland. For details of fares and schedules, see the La Araucanía & Los Lagos, Chiloé and Aisén & the Camino Austral chapters.

Chilean Patagonia & Tierra del Fuego

Mar del Sur operates an automobile/passenger ferry between Puerto Ibáñez, on Lago General Carrera south of Coihaique, to the border town of Chile Chico. Sailings are one to four times daily.

There is a daily ferry link between Punta Arenas and Porvenir, the only town in Chilean Tierra del Fuego. For details of fares and schedules, see the Punta Arenas entry in the Magallanes chapter.

LOCAL TRANSPORT
To/From the Airport

In Santiago, inexpensive (US$1.60 to US$2) airport buses are frequent, but travelers with heavy luggage might take advantage of door-to-door airport services for US$7.50. See the Santiago chapter for more details.

In the regions, airlines often arrange bus services between downtown and the airport – either their own bus or one run by a local company. The cost of this bus is sometimes included in your air ticket, and sometimes is extra. Top-end hotels sometimes provide transportation for their clients, but in a few places you must use public transport or a taxi.

Bus

Even small towns have extensive bus systems which can seem chaotic to the novice rider. Buses, however, are clearly numbered and usually carry a placard indicating their final destination. Since many identically numbered buses serve slightly different routes, pay attention to these placards. On boarding, tell the driver your final destination and he will tell you the fare and give you a ticket. Do not lose this ticket, which may be checked en route.

Train

Both Santiago and Valparaíso have commuter rail networks. The former runs from Rancagua, capital of Region VI, to Estación Central on the Alameda in Santiago, while the latter runs from Quillota to Valparaíso and Viña del Mar. For details, see the respective city sections.

Metro

Santiago is the only Chilean city with a subway, the Metro, which is fast, efficient, clean and cheap. For details, see the Santiago chapter.

Taxi

Most Chilean cabs are metered, but fares vary. In Santiago, it costs Ch$250 (about US$0.65) to *bajar la bandera* ('lower the flag'), plus Ch$60 (US$0.15) per 200 meters. Each cab carries a placard indicating its authorized fare.

In some towns, such as Viña del Mar, cabs may cost twice as much. In others, such as Coquimbo, meters are less common, so it is wise to agree upon a fare in advance if possible. Drivers are generally polite and honest, but there are exceptions. Tipping is not necessary, but you may tell the driver to keep small change.

TOURS

Several Chilean operators arrange tours throughout the country; the ones listed here all have English-speaking staff. For more details on companies offering alternative and outdoor-oriented travel options, see also the Activities entry in the Facts for the Visitor chapter.

- Cascade Expediciones (☎ (02) 2327214, fax 2339768), Orrego Luco 054 in Providencia, Santiago, runs a variety of adventure trips throughout the country, including custom day and weekend excursions in the mountains near Santiago, horseback expeditions across the Andes into Argentina, tours of the Juan Fernández archipelago, trekking in Araucaria forests near Pucón and in Torres del Paine, explorations of the Atacama Desert and the northern altiplano, sea kayaking in the fjords of Chiloé, diving at Easter Island, and whitewater rafting and kayaking on the Biobío and Futaleufú.

Altué Expediciones (☎ (02) 2321103, fax 2336679), Encomenderos 83, Las Condes, Santiago, also arranges whitewater rafting, sea kayaking and many other adventure activities.

Santiago

Santiago is a city of contrasts, a metropolis whose shining new international air terminal greets foreign bankers and franchises rushing to invest their money in South America's most dynamic economy, where prosperous professionals pack fine restaurants, and cell phones and car alarms have become status symbols to a burgeoning middle class. At the same time, struggling street vendors board city buses to hawk everything from pins and needles to pens and ice cream to housemaids who ride for hours to scrub floors and change diapers in exclusive suburbs, where gardeners lug rakes and push-mowers on the backs of their bicycles. Santiago's skyline is unprepossessing, but its glitzy exterior reflects a decade of vigorous economic growth – though improvements have come at a price.

Chile's sprawling capital is really many cities in one – Santiago proper, the former colonial core, is surrounded by another 31 *comunas* of greater or lesser antiquity that have grown together to form the present megacity. Each comuna has its own separate municipal administration, including mayor and council, but the national government legislates and administers many urban services, such as public transportation, throughout the Región Metropolitana.

Unfortunately, most streets are too narrow for the heavy rush-hour traffic, and a blanket of smog frequently lurks above the city, as the phalanx of the Andes, rarely visible except immediately after a rain, blocks the dispersal of pollutants. However, there are many beautifully landscaped parks in which to take refuge from the pollution.

Besides growing out, the city has grown up, as ever more skyscrapers dominate the landscape, both downtown and rising toward the Andes in nearby comunas like Providencia and Las Condes, which have been usurping downtown's historical role as the city's commercial and financial center.

Most areas of interest to visitors are between downtown Santiago and the Andes, along with the surrounding central comunas of Ñuñoa, Estación Central, Quinta Normal, Recoleta and Independencia.

HISTORY

Gazing west from the rocky overlook of Cerro Santa Lucía to the skyscrapers and apartment blocks of metropolitan Santiago, it's hard to imagine that just six months after Pedro de Valdivia founded the city in 1541, Mapuche warriors nearly obliterated it. Spanish troops regrouped on the fortified summit of Santa Lucía and Valdivia made immediate plans to rebuild the precarious settlement.

Valdivia had laid out a regular grid from the present-day Plaza de Armas, but for two years 'Santiago del Nuevo Extremo' was little more than a besieged hillside camp. Its tile-roofed adobe houses resisted fire, but colonists nearly starved under Indian pressure. Two years passed before assistance arrived from Peru; after returning to Peru himself for new troops and supplies, Valdivia pushed southwards, founding Concepción in 1550 and Valdivia in 1552.

All these early settlements were merely fortified villages. In Santiago, most houses were built around central patios, enhanced with gardens and grape arbors, but open sewers ran down the middle of the streets. As the settlements became more secure, soldiers formed households with Indian women. Tradesmen like shoemakers, blacksmiths, armorers and tanners provided services for the colonists. In the beginning, the towns were administrative centers for the new colony and bases for sorties into Mapuche territory, but most of the population lived in the countryside.

By the late 16th century, Santiago was a settlement of just 200 houses, inhabited by not more than 700 Spaniards and mestizos, plus several thousand Indian laborers and servants. Occasionally flooded by the Río Mapocho, it nevertheless lacked a safe water supply, and communications between town and countryside were difficult. Despite their precarious position, wealthy encomenderos and other elite elements sought to emulate European nobility, with platoons of servants and imported products from Europe and China. The Spaniards' lack of such resources as weapons, ammunition and horses contributed to their expulsion by the Mapuche from the area south of the Biobío. Wealthy households still enjoyed luxuries like velvet and silk.

Subject to the Viceroyalty of Peru, Chile remained a backwater of imperial Spain for nearly three centuries, yielding little exportable wealth. Nevertheless, by the late 18th century, Santiago had begun to acquire the substance of a city proper, as new *tajamares* (dikes) restrained the Mapocho, improved roads handled increased commerce between the capital and its port of Valparaíso, and authorities targeted various beautification projects to please the landowning aristocracy.

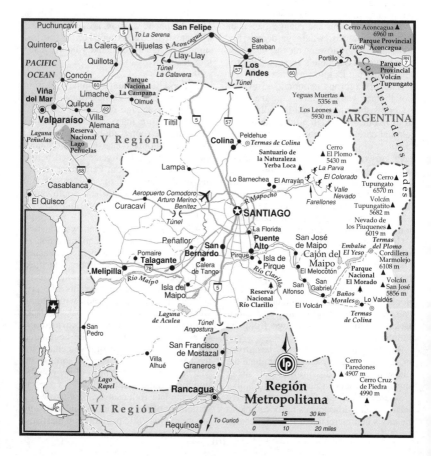

As colonial rule ended in the early 19th century, Chile's population – including the 100,000 sovereign Mapuches south of the Biobío – was perhaps half a million, 90% of whom lived in the countryside. Santiago had barely 30,000 residents, city streets remained largely unpaved and most country roads were still potholed tracks. There were few schools and libraries and, although the Universidad de San Felipe (founded in 1758 as a law school) provided intellectual spark, cultural life was bleak.

By the mid-19th century, though, the capital had more than 100,000 inhabitants, and a railway and telegraph line linked it with Valparaíso, a bustling commercial center of 60,000 people. The landed aristocracy built sumptuous houses, adorned them with imported luxuries, founded prestigious social clubs, and visited their fundos during the holidays. Social life revolved around clubs, the track, the opera and outings to exclusive Parque Cousiño. Those of the governing class fashioned themselves as ladies and gentlemen who valued civilized customs, tradition and breeding, sending their children to be educated in Europe. For the elite at least it is still true that, as British diplomat James Bryce remarked at the turn of the century:

The leading landowners spend the summers in their country houses and the winter and spring in Santiago, which has thus a pleasant society, with plenty of talent and talk among the men, a society more enlightened and abreast of the modern world than are those of the more northern republics, and with a more stimulating atmosphere.

From its inauspicious beginning, Santiago has become one of South America's largest cities – the Región Metropolitana contains well over four million inhabitants. The Museo de Santiago, in the colonial Casa Colorada off the Plaza de Armas, documents the city's phenomenal growth, in large part a function of oppression in the countryside. Poverty, lack of opportunity and paternalistic fundos drove farm laborers and tenants north to the nitrate mines,

and also into the cities – between 1865 and 1875, Santiago's population increased from 115,000 to more than 150,000, mainly due to domestic migration. This trend continued in the 20th century and, by the 1970s, more than 70% of all Chileans lived in cities, mostly in the heartland.

After WWII, rapid industrialization created urban jobs, but never enough to satisfy demand. In the 1960s, continued rural turmoil fostered urban migration, resulting in squatter settlements known as *callampas* (mushrooms, so called because they sprang up virtually overnight) around the outskirts of Santiago and other major cities. Planned decentralization has eased some of the pressure on Santiago, and regularization, including the granting of land titles, has transformed many callampas. They still contrast, however, with affluent eastern suburbs like El Golf, Vitacura, La Reina, Las Condes and Lo Curro.

ORIENTATION

Although Santiago is immense, Santiago Centro is a relatively small, roughly triangular area bounded by the Río Mapocho and woodsy Parque Forestal to the north, the Vía Norte Sur to the west, and the Avenida del Libertador General Bernardo O'Higgins (more commonly and manageably known as the Alameda, a shorthand for the earlier 'Alameda de las Delicias') to the south. The apex of the triangle is Plaza Baquedano, where the Alameda intersects two other main thoroughfares, Avenida Providencia and Avenida Vicuña Mackenna.

Within this triangle, centered on the Plaza de Armas, downtown Santiago's street plan largely conforms to the standard grid that the Spaniards imposed on all their American possessions. Surrounding the plaza are many of the most notable public buildings, including the Municipalidad (city hall), the Catedral Metropolitana, and the Correo Central (main post office). Paseo Ahumada, a pedestrian mall, leads south to the Alameda, while a block south of the Plaza de Armas it intersects with Paseo Huérfanos, another pedestrian mall. Other public buildings, including the presidential palace, dominate the Barrio Cívico around Plaza de la Constitución, west of Paseo Ahumada and just north of the Alameda.

One of Santiago's most attractive parks, Cerro Santa Lucía, overlooks the Alameda between the Plaza de Armas and Plaza Baquedano. Across the Mapocho from Plaza Baquedano, on either side of Avenida Pío Nono, Barrio Bellavista is Santiago's lively 'Paris quarter.' Overlooking Bellavista is the enormous Cerro San Cristóbal, which rises dramatically from the plain to

the north of Avenida Providencia, which leads eastward toward the comunas of Providencia, Las Condes, Vitacura and Lo Barnechea. Avenida Vicuña Mackenna leads southeast toward increasingly fashionable Ñuñoa.

West of the Via Norte Sur, Barrio Brasil is an intriguing enclave of early-20th-century architecture that is presently experiencing an urban renaissance. Farther west and south are the agreeable open spaces of Parque Quinta Normal and Parque O'Higgins, both popular weekend refuges for Santiaguinos and their families.

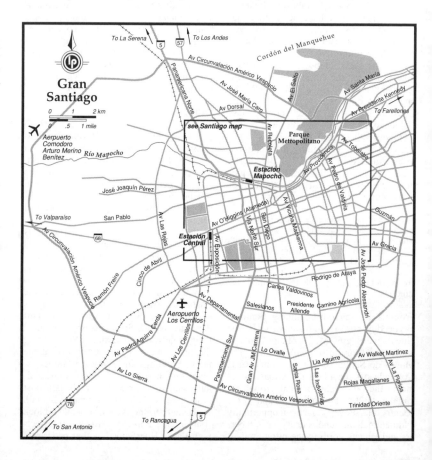

Travelers planning an extended stay in Santiago might acquire Carlos Ossandón Guzmán's *Guía de Santiago* (Editorial Universitaria), which has gone through nine editions. It has good maps and illustrations, is especially strong on architectural history, and contains a valuable summary in English.

INFORMATION
Tourist Offices
Sernatur (☎ 2361420, 2361416), Chile's national tourist service, occupies the old market building at Avenida Providencia 1550, midway between Manuel Montt and Pedro de Valdivia Metro stations. The friendly and capable staff, which always includes an English speaker, offers maps and other information, including lists of accommodations, restaurants and bars, museums and art galleries, transport out of Santiago and leaflets on other parts of the country. It's open weekdays 9 am to 5 pm, and Saturdays 9 am to 1 pm.

Sernatur also operates an information booth (☎ 6019320), open weekdays 9 am to 9 pm and weekends 9 am to 5.30 pm, on the ground floor of the international terminal at

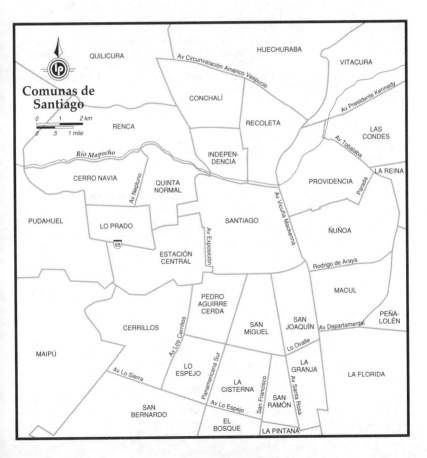

Comunas de Santiago

Aeropuerto Arturo Merino Benítez at Pudahuel. A new office recently opened at the San Borja bus terminal, alongside the train station.

The Municipalidad de Santiago maintains a tourist kiosk near the intersection of the Ahumada and Huérfanos pedestrian malls, a block from the Plaza de Armas, open 9 am to 9 pm daily. It is also very helpful but less well stocked with written information. The main municipal Oficina de Turismo (☎ 6327785) occupies part of the colonial Casa Colorada, Merced 860, near the Plaza de Armas; it's open weekdays 10 am to 6 pm only.

All these offices distribute, free of charge, the pocket-size *Plano del Centro de Santiago*; this handy map details downtown, Providencia and other inner comunas of the capital, and includes a useful diagram of the Metro system. More detailed maps are available from the Municipalidad at a reasonable price, about US$2.

Foreign Embassies & Consulates

For the addresses of diplomatic representatives of overseas and neighboring countries, see the Facts for the Visitor chapter.

Money

Ubiquitous ATMs have made exchange houses less important than they used to be, but numerous cambios on Agustinas, between Bandera and Ahumada, still change travelers' checks and foreign cash. There are also exchange facilities and ATMs in Providencia (where rates are slightly lower than downtown) and at the airport (where rates are notably lower), so change minimal amounts at the airport unless you're arriving on a weekend.

The easiest way to locate money changers is to stroll down Paseo Ahumada where, if you remotely resemble a gringo, aggressive touts will direct you to nearby exchange facilities (most of these men are trustworthy, but some travelers have had unpleasant experiences). Cambios pay slightly less for travelers' checks than for US cash, but do not usually charge any additional commission. The man who leads you there expects a small tip. On Saturdays, when most downtown cambios are closed, try Lacov Tour at Moneda 772, Oficina 315.

The American Express Bank (☎ 672-2156), Agustinas 1360, exchanges travelers' checks for US cash, which can be useful in more remote destinations. The local Thomas Cook representative is Turismo Tajamar (☎ 2329595), Orrego Luco 032, Providencia, which deals only with replacing lost or stolen checks; Cambio Andes, Agustinas 1036, changes Thomas Cook checks for US cash. Readers have also recommended Cambios Afex, Moneda 1148, to change checks for cash.

Financial Emergencies The following local representatives of major international banking institutions can deal with replacement credit cards and/or travelers' checks:

American Express
    (☎ 800-201022, 123-00202158)
Diner's Club
    (☎ 800-220220, 213213)
Visa/MasterCard
    (☎ 6386162, 2526100, 2320000)

Post & Communications

Santiago's telephone area code is ☎ 02. For long-distance overseas calls, go to Entel at Paseo Huérfanos 1133, open daily 8.30 am to 10 pm, or at Avenida 11 de Septiembre 1919 in Providencia. CTC has many long-distance offices, the most central of which is at Moneda 1151, but there are many others at downtown locations and Metro stations. Chilesat and Telex-Chile also have many long-distance offices.

For telegrams and telexes, go to Telex-Chile at Morandé 147, opposite Plaza de la Constitución. It's open weekdays 8.30 am to 8.30 pm, Saturday 9 am to 2 pm, and Sunday 9.30 am to 1.30 pm. Try also VTR Telecomunicaciones, Bandera 168.

For cellular communications, contact BellSouth Celular downtown at Agustinas 1019 (☎ 3395032), in Las Condes at Avenida El Bosque Norte 0134

(☎ 3395000; Metro: Tobalaba), or at the international airport (☎ 6019252).

The Correo Central (main post office), on the north side of the Plaza de Armas, handles poste restante services and also has a philatelic desk. It's open weekdays 8 am to 10 pm, Saturdays 8 am to 6 pm, and is closed Sundays. Kiosks at the entrance sell envelopes and postcards, and will also wrap parcels for a small fee. Correos de Chile has another large downtown post office at Moneda 1155, and a convenient Providencia branch at Avenida Providencia 1466.

For private international courier service, try Federal Express (☎ 2315250), Avenida Providencia 1951 (Metro: Pedro de Valdivia), or DHL Express at Santa Rosa 135 (☎ 6392171) or Suecia 072 (☎ 2327539) in Providencia (Metro: Los Leones).

Travel Agencies
Santiago seems to have travel agencies on nearly every corner, on downtown streets like Agustinas, Teatinos and Huérfanos, and in affluent Providencia. For good prices on air tickets, contact the Student Flight Center (☎ 2325388, 334-5166/7, fax 2333220), Avenida Providencia 2594, Oficina 426, in Providencia (Metro: Tobalaba).

The American Express representative is Turismo Cocha (☎ 2301000, fax 2035110), Avenida El Bosque Norte 0430 in Las Condes (Metro: Tobalaba). The Thomas Cook representative is Turismo Tajamar (☎ 2329595), Orrego Luco 023 in Providencia (Metro: Pedro de Valdivia).

Several agencies in Providencia and Las Condes specialize in adventure or eco-tourism excursions, arranging climbing and riding trips in the Cajón del Maipo east of Santiago, other nearby destinations like Parque Nacional La Campana, and throughout the country. For more information, see the Cajón del Maipo entry at the end of this chapter, and the activities entry in the Facts for the Visitor chapter.

Bookshops & Newsstands
Santiago's largest and best-stocked book-store is the Feria Chilena del Libro,

MICHAEL SULLIVAN
Colonial vs modern in downtown Santiago

Huérfanos 623 at Miraflores, with several other branches, including Avenida Providencia 2124. With an excellent selection of books in both Spanish and English, it's a fine place to browse. Editorial Universitaria (☎ 6994666), Agustinas 1138, is also a very good and serious store, as is Librería Manantial (☎ 6967463) at Plaza de Armas 444 (the entrance is a corridor on the south side of the Catedral). Fondo de Cultura Económica (☎ 6954843), Paseo Bulnes 152, is a Latin American institution with branches throughout the region, specializing in literature, social sciences, history and economics.

Calle San Diego, south of the Alameda, contains Santiago's largest concentration of used bookshops, although quality varies. One of the best, Librería Rivano at San Diego 119, Local 7, has a fine collection on Chilean history, not all of which is displayed to the public. In the Plaza Mulato Gil de Castro complex at Lastarria 307, Local 100, Ricardo Bravo Murúa

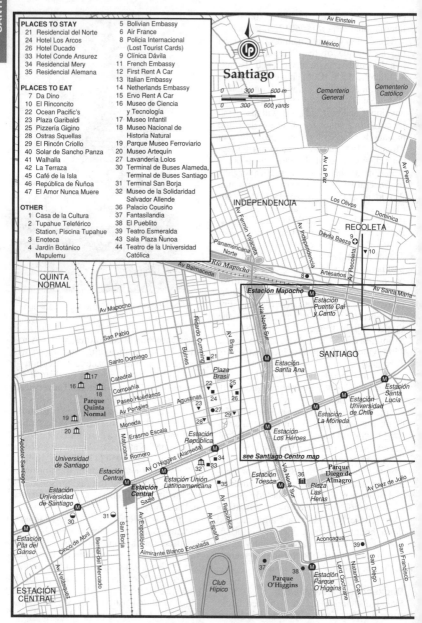

PLACES TO STAY
21 Residencial del Norte
24 Hotel Los Arcos
26 Hotel Ducado
33 Hotel Conde Ansurez
34 Residencial Mery
35 Residencial Alemana

PLACES TO EAT
7   Da Dino
10 El Rinconcito
22 Ocean Pacific's
23 Plaza Garibaldi
28 Pizzería Gigino
28 Ostras Squellas
29 El Rincón Criollo
40 Solar de Sancho Panza
41 Walhalla
42 La Terraza
45 Café de la Isla
46 República de Ñuñoa
47 El Amor Nunca Muere

OTHER
1   Casa de la Cultura
2   Tupahue Teleférico
    Station, Piscina Tupahue
3   Enoteca
4   Jardín Botánico
    Mapulemu
5   Bolivian Embassy
6   Air France
8   Policia Internacional
    (Lost Tourist Cards)
9   Clínica Dávila
11 French Embassy
12 First Rent A Car
13 Italian Embassy
14 Netherlands Embassy
15 Ervo Rent A Car
16 Museo de Ciencia
    y Tecnología
17 Museo Infantil
18 Museo Nacional de
    Historia Natural
19 Parque Museo Ferroviario
20 Museo Artequín
27 Lavandería Lolos
30 Terminal de Buses Alameda,
    Terminal de Buses Santiago
31 Terminal San Borja
32 Museo de la Solidaridad
    Salvador Allende
36 Palacio Cousiño
37 Fantasilandia
38 El Pueblito
39 Teatro Esmeralda
43 Sala Plaza Ñunoa
44 Teatro de la Universidad
    Católica

Santiago

0   300   600 m
0   300   600 yards

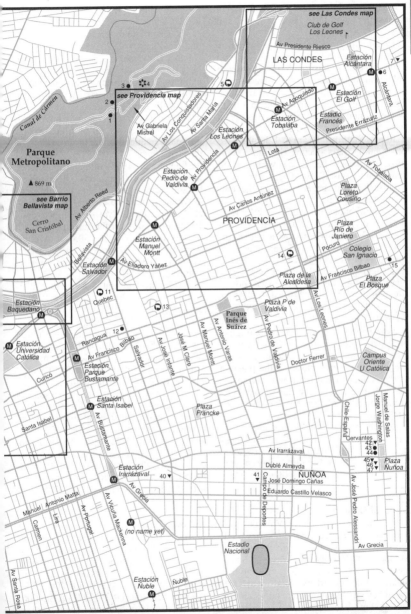

(☎ 6397141) is another good antiquarian bookseller who also stocks maps and postcards.

Behind the grape arbor at the Phone Box Pub, Avenida Providencia 1652, Librería Chile Ilustrado (☎ 2460683) has a superb selection of books on Chilean history, archaeology, anthropology and folklore. Specializing in rare materials, but with much general-interest stock, it's open weekdays 9.30 am to 1.30 pm and 4 to 7.30 pm, Saturday 10 am to 1.30 pm. Two other booksellers occupy the same complex: Books (☎ 2351205), with a good selection of used but fairly expensive English-language paperbacks, and the feminist bookshop Lila.

For new books in English, try Librería Inglesa at Huérfanos 669, Local 11, or at Pedro de Valdivia 47 in Providencia. Eurotex (☎ 2326035), Santa Magdalena 116 in Providencia (Metro: Los Leones), carries English language books as well. For magazines and newspapers, Libro's has a downtown branch (☎ 6990319) at Huérfanos 1178 and in Providencia (☎ 2328839) at Avenida Pedro de Valdivia 039.

Newspapers and magazines in English and many other European languages, as well from other Latin American countries, are available at two kiosks at the junction of the Ahumada and Huérfanos pedestrian malls. If a newspaper appears to have been around more than a few days, you can often haggle over the price.

French speakers will find reading material at the Librería Francesa, with branches downtown (☎ 6392407) at Paseo Estado 337, Local 22, and in Providencia (☎ 231-9777) at Avenida Providencia 2286, Local 104.

Cultural Centers

Where passenger trains to Viña del Mar and Valparaíso once arrived and departed, the Corporación Cultural de la Estación Mapocho (☎ 6972990) has become Santiago's premier cultural center, offering live theater, concerts, art exhibits, a café and special events like the annual book fair. It's on the south bank of the Río Mapocho at the north end of Bandera (Metro: Puente Cal y Canto).

The Centro de Extensión de la Universidad Católica (☎ 2220275), Alameda 390 (Metro: Universidad Católica), also regularly presents artistic and photographic exhibits. The Centro de Arte Violeta Parra (☎ 6352387), Carmen 340, shows films and presents live folkloric music.

Several suburban comunas have their own cultural centers, all of which change programs frequently. The Instituto Cultural de Providencia (☎ 2094341), Avenida 11 de Septiembre 1995, offers free lectures, film cycles and art exhibits. Others possibilities include the Casa de la Cultura de la Municipalidad de Ñuñoa (☎ 2253919) at Avenida Irarrázaval 4055 (open daily 10 am to 8 pm) and the Instituto Cultural de Las Condes (☎ 2128503) at Avenida Apoquindo 6570 (open daily except Monday, 10.30 am to 1.30 pm and 3.30 to 7 pm).

The Centro Cultural de España (☎ 235-1105), Avenida Providencia 927 (Metro: Salvador), is one of Santiago's most active foreign cultural representatives. The Instituto Chileno-Norteamericano de Cultura (☎ 6963215), Moneda 1467, has frequent photographic and artistic exhibits on various topics in various media. There is also a decent English-language library, which carries North American newspapers and magazines, and free films (usually in video format). Other comparable cultural centers include the Instituto Chileno-Británico (☎ 6382156) at Santa Lucía 124, with current British newspapers and periodicals, the Instituto Goethe (☎ 638-3815) at Esmeralda 650, and the Instituto Chileno-Francés (☎ 6335465) at Merced 298.

National Parks

For trekking and mountaineering information, visit the main offices of the Corporación Nacional Forestal (☎ 6966677, Anexo 123), known by its acronym Conaf, at Avenida Bulnes 259, Oficina 206. There is a regional office (☎ 2052372) at Eliodoro Yañez 1810, Providencia.

Laundry

Dry cleaners are abundant, but self-service laundries are relatively few. At most of these, 'self-service' means dropping off your clothes and picking them up later. Most inexpensive hotels will usually wash clothes for a reasonable price.

Lavandería Lolos is at the corner of Ricardo Cumming and Moneda (Metro: República). There's also Lavandería Auto-servicio (☎ 6321772) at Monjitas 507, corner of Mosqueto, and Laverap at Avenida Providencia 1645 (Metro: Pedro de Valdivia).

Camera Repair

For prompt and efficient, but not cheap, camera repair service, contact Harry Müller Thierfelder (☎ 6983596), Ahumada 312, Oficina 312. Other possibilities are Tec-Fo (☎ 6952969), Nueva York 52, Oficina 204, and Image Market (☎ 2321138), Santa Magdalena 16 in Providencia (Metro: Los Leones).

Medical Services

For medical emergencies, try the Posta Central (☎ 6341650) at Avenida Portugal 125 (Metro: Universidad Católica). Private clinics include the Clínica Universidad Católica (☎ 6334122) at Lira 40, the Clínica Dávila (☎ 7354030) at Avenida Recoleta 464 in Recoleta, or the Clínica Las Condes (☎ 2111002) at Lo Fontecilla 411, Las Condes.

Dangers & Annoyances

Santiago has a growing reputation for petty street crime, especially downtown and in areas like Cerro Santa Lucía. The US Consulate recommends that visitors take cabs everywhere after dark, and avoid buses which are said to crawl with pickpockets, but adds that a visit to Chile is usually without incident. The author's opinion is that travelers should be alert, but not obsessed with personal security. Do take special care with personal belongings when seated at sidewalk cafes in heavily traveled areas.

Every year, around the anniversary of the 1973 coup, Providencia's Avenida 11 de Septiembre becomes the site of very contentious demonstrations, and many visitors prefer to avoid the area at that time.

WALKING TOUR

An appropriate starting point for an orientation walk through downtown Santiago is the **Estación Mapocho**, at the corner of Bandera and Balmaceda on the south bank of the Río Mapocho, where rail passengers from Valparaíso and Viña del Mar used to arrive from 1912 until the mid-1980s. It is now the city's foremost cultural center. Across Balmaceda, between 21 de Mayo and Puente, the wrought-iron **Mercado Central**, designed by architect Fermín Vivaceta in 1872, is one of Santiago's most-colorful attractions; any of its numerous seafood locales is a fine choice for lunch or an early dinner.

Two blocks southeast, open to the public at Esmeralda 749, the **Posada del Corregidor** (1765) is a whitewashed, two - story adobe structure with an attractive wooden balcony. Continue down MacIver to the corner of Santo Domingo, where the **Casa Manso de Velasco** (1730) resembles the Posada del Corregidor, then head west to the **Templo de Santo Domingo** (1808), a massive stone church at Santo Domingo 961.

One block south is the **Plaza de Armas**, the city's historical center, flanked by the **Correo Central** (main post office, 1882), the Museo Histórico Nacional in the **Palacio de la Real Audiencia** (1804), the **Municipalidad de Santiago** (1785) and the **Catedral Metropolitana** (1745). Half a block east of the Plaza, the colonial **Casa Colorada** (1769) houses the city museum.

Two blocks west of the plaza, at Morandé 441, the former **Congreso Nacional** (1876) has become the Foreign Ministry since the Congreso moved to Valparaíso. Government offices also occupy the nearby **Palacio Edwards**, Catedral 1187, which formerly belonged to an elite Anglo-Chilean family. Immediately south of the ex-Congreso, fronting on Compañía, are the **Tribunales de Justicia** (Law Courts). Across the street, at Bandera and

SANTIAGO

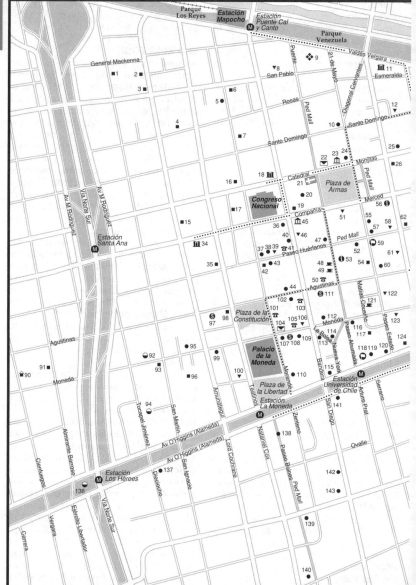

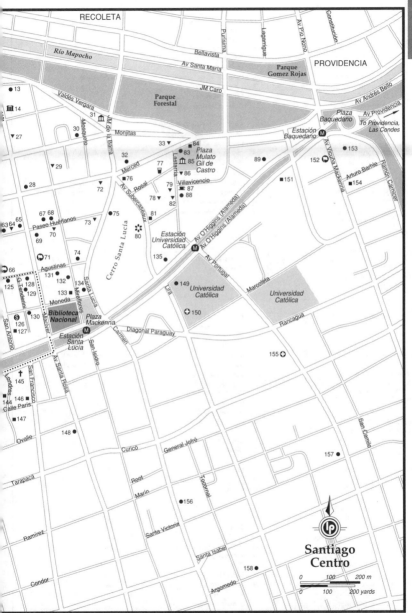

RECOLETA

PROVIDENCIA

Río Mapocho

Parque
Forestal

Parque
Gomez Rojas

Purísima

Lagarrigue

Av Pío Nono

Constitución

Bellavista

Av Santa María

JM Caro

Av Andrés Bello

Av Providencia

To Providencia,
Las Condes

Plaza
Baquedano

Estación
Baquedano

Valdés Vergara

Mosqueto

JM de la Barra

Monjitas

Merced

Av Subercaseaux

Cerro Santa Lucía

Plaza
Mulato
Gil de
Castro

Villavicencio

Lastarria

Av O'Higgins (Alameda)
Av O'Higgins (Alameda)

Av Vicuña Mackenna

Ramón Carnicer

Arturo Barhle

Estación
Universidad
Católica

Av Portugal

Lira

Universidad
Católica

Macoleta

Universidad
Católica

Rancagua

Paseo Huérfanos

Agustinas

Santa Lucía

Miraflores

Moneda

Biblioteca
Nacional

Plaza
Mackenna

Estación
Santa
Lucía

San Antonio

Mac Iver

Av Santa Rosa

Plaza
Pedro
Montt

San Isidro

Carmen

Diagonal Paraguay

San Camilo

San Francisco

Londres

Calle Paris

Ovalle

Curicó

General Jofré

Tocornal

Root

Marín

Tarapacá

Ramírez

Santa Victoria

Santa Isabel

Santiago
Centro

Condor

Argomedo

0   100   200 m
0   100   200 yards

PLACES TO STAY

1	Hotel Caribe
2	Hotel Souvenir
3	Hotel Pudahuel
4	Hotel Indiana
6	Nuevo Hotel Valparaíso
7	Hotel Cervantes
15	Hotel Europa
16	Hotel España
17	Hotel Metrópoli
19	City Hotel
26	Hotel Tupahue
35	Hotel Panamericano
42	Hotel Gran Palace
54	Hotel Ritz
62	Hotel Santa Lucía
76	Hotel Foresta
81	Hotel Montecarlo
84	Hostal del Parque
90	Hostelling International
91	Hotel Turismo Japón
93	Hotel di Maurier
96	Residencial Tabita
98	Hotel Carrera
117	Hotel Conquistador
124	Hotel El Libertador
127	Hotel Galerías
133	Hotel Riviera
144	Hotel Vega
146	Hotel París
147	Residencial Londres
151	Holiday Inn Crowne Plaza
154	Hotel Principado

PLACES TO EAT

8	Bar Central
12	Kan-Thu
27	Da Carla
29	El Puente de Bórquez
33	Les Assassins
39	Bar Nacional
46	Bar Nacional
48	Café Haiti
49	Café Caribe
51	Chez Henry
58	El Vegetariano
61	Le Due Torri
64	La Escarcha
70	San Marcos
72	Izakaya Yoko
73	Brunch & Coffee
78	Capricho Español
79	Gatopardo
82	Don Victorino
85	Pérgola de la Plaza
86	Cocoa
87	Café del Biógrafo
100	100% Natural
106	El Novillero
121	Café Cousiño
122	Pizza Napoli
123	El Naturista

OTHER

5	Sala Agustín Sire
9	Mercado Central
10	Templo de Santo Domingo
11	Posada del Corregidor
13	Instituto Goethe
14	Casa Manso de Velasco
18	Palacio Edwards
20	Librería Manantial
21	Catedral Metropolitana
22	Correo Central
23	Palacio de la Real Audiencia
	(Museo Histórico Nacional)
24	Municipalidad de Santiago
25	Cine Río
28	Feria Artesanal La Merced
30	Lavandería Autoservicio
31	Palacio de Bellas Artes
32	Teatro La Comedia
34	Palacio La Alhambra
36	Tribunales de Justicia
37	American Airlines
38	Ladeco
40	Iberia
41	Entel
42	Libro's, Cine Gran Palace
43	Huimpalay
44	Viasa
45	Real Casa de Aduana
	(Museo Chileno de Arte
	Precolombino)
47	Harry Müller Thierfelder
	(Camera Repair)
50	BellSouth Celular
52	Cine Centralm,
	Cine Huérfanos
53	Municipal Tourist Kiosk
55	Librería Francesa
56	Casa Colorada (Museo de
	Santiago), Oficina de Turismo
	(Municipal)
57	National Airlines
59	Paraguayan Embassy
60	Cine Imperio
63	Cine Huelen
65	Cine Rex
66	German Embassy
67	Librería Inglesa
68	Feria Chilena del Libro
69	Cine Lido
71	Brazilian Consulate
74	Lys Rent A Car
75	Ascensor (Elevator)
77	Bar Berri
80	Jardín Japonés
83	Instituto Chileno-Francés
85	Museo Arqueológico de
	Santiago
88	Cine El Biógrafo
89	Cine Alameda
92	Tour Express
	(Airpost Buses)

94	Terminal Los Héroes
95	Instituto Chileno-
	Norteamericano de Cultura
97	American Express Bank
99	Departamento de Extranjería
	(Tourist Card Extensions)
101	Telex-Chile
102	Editorial Universitaria
103	VTR Telecomunicaciones
104	Correos de Chile
105	CTC
107	Lloyd Aéreo Boliviano (LAB)
108	Cambios Afex
109	Avianca
110	Sala Antonio Varas
111	Cambio Andes
112	Chile Típico
113	Bolsa de Comercio
114	Tec-Fo (Camera Repair)
115	Club de La Unión
116	Líneas Aéreas Paraguayas
	(Lapsa), Lufthansa, Saeta
118	Canadian Consulate
119	ACE Turismo, Alitalia, Pluna
120	Swissair
124	Venta de Pasajes, Galería
	Libertador (train tickets)
125	Teatro Municipal
126	Lacov Tour
	(Money Exchange)
128	Transmarchilay
129	United Airlines
130	Aerolíneas Argentinas
131	LanChile
132	Varig
134	Instituto Chileno-Británico
135	Instituto Nacional de
	la Juventud
136	Centropuerto (Airport Buses)
137	Confitería Las Torres
138	Altar de la Patria
139	Fondo de Cultura Económica
140	Corporación Nacional Forestal
	(Conaf)
141	Universidad de Chile
142	Librería Rivano
143	Cine Normandie
145	Iglesia de San Francisco
	(Convento y Museo de
	San Francisco)
148	DHL Express
149	Centro de Extensión de la
	Universidad Católica
150	Clínica Universidad Católica
152	Argentine Consulate
153	Teatro Universidad de Chile
155	Posta Central
156	Centro de Arte
	Violeta Parra
157	Claustro del 900
158	Los Adobes de Argomedo

Compañía, the late colonial **Real Casa de Aduana** (royal customs house) contains the outstanding Museo Chileno de Arte Precolombino. Two blocks west, at Compañía 1340, the Moorish-style **Palacio La Alhambra** (1862) was once the home of Chañarcillo silver magnate Francisco Ignacio Ossa Mercado; it is now an art gallery and cultural center.

Running south from the Plaza de Armas, **Paseo Ahumada** is Santiago's main pedestrian thoroughfare. Municipal pressure has reduced the number of street vendors, but buskers of diverse style and quality still congregate in the evening (even though shrill Protestant evangelicals often drown out the rest). The perpendicular **Paseo Huérfanos** crosses Paseo Ahumada a block south of the plaza.

Southwest of the Plaza, between Teatinos and Morandé, **Plaza de la Constitución** offers unobstructed views of the late-colonial **Palacio de La Moneda**, which occupies an entire block. Formerly the presidential residence, La Moneda was badly damaged by air force attacks during the 1973 coup but restored in recent years. On the opposite side of La Moneda, facing the Alameda, the smaller **Plaza de la Libertad** faces in turn, across the Alameda, the **Altar de la Patria**, which crowns the subterranean tomb of Chilean liberator General Bernardo O'Higgins.

Other nearby buildings of note are the **Bolsa de Comercio** (stock exchange) at La Bolsa 64, and the **Club de La Unión** at Alameda 1091, where Santiago's stockbrokers hold their power lunches. A short walk across the Alameda (the Metro underpass is safer if not quicker) is the imposing **Universidad de Chile** (1874). A few blocks east, at Alameda 834, the striking **Iglesia de San Francisco** (1618, with later modifications) is one of Santiago's

oldest buildings, housing the **Museo de Arte Colonial**, an important collection of colonial art. Across the Alameda, at the corner of MacIver, sits the monolithic **Biblioteca Nacional**, while two blocks north at Agustinas 794, the impressive **Teatro Municipal** (1857) is Santiago's prime performing arts venue.

PALACIO DE LA MONEDA

Under the direction of Italian-born architect Joaquín Toesca, construction of a royal mint started in 1788 near the current Mercado Central on the Río Mapocho. When the flood-prone site proved inadequate, the project soon moved to its present location, a former Jesuit farm, where it was finally completed in 1805. Toesca also contributed his talents to Santiago's Catedral Metropolitana, on the Plaza de Armas.

In the mid-19th century, La Moneda became the residence of Chilean presidents, but the last to actually live there was Carlos Ibáñez del Campo, during his second term (1952-58). After the military coup of 1973, General Pinochet governed from the Edificio Diego Portales, on the Alameda near Cerro Santa Lucía. Since La Moneda's restoration in 1981, Pinochet and elected Presidents Patricio Aylwin and Eduardo Frei have had offices here.

The building itself occupies the entire block bounded by Morandé and Teatinos,

Palacio de La Moneda

between Plaza Libertad and Plaza de la Constitución; the main entrance on Moneda faces the latter. With 20 days' advance notice, it's possible to take a guided tour of the interior. Contact the Dirección Administrativa del Palacio de La Moneda (☎ 6714103).

MERCADO CENTRAL

Occupying an entire block bounded by San Pablo, Puente, 21 de Mayo and Avenida Balmaceda, across from the Río Mapocho, Santiago's central market is a distinctive wrought-iron structure dating from 1872; in its superstructure, note the Chilean star that repeats all the way around the building. Besides an appealing selection of fresh fruit, vegetables and fish, there are a number of eating places ranging from modest to the finest.

DOWNTOWN MUSEUMS

For a complete listing of museums in downtown Santiago, ask for Sernatur's leaflet *Galerías de Arte y Museos*, which also gives opening hours and transport details. Most museums are free Sundays and closed Mondays.

Museo de Santiago

Part of the colonial Casa Colorada, this museum documents the capital's growth from its modest nucleus to the current sprawl. Exhibits include maps, paintings, dioramas and colonial dress. Particularly intriguing are the diorama of the 1647 earthquake (when 10% of the population died), a model of the Iglesia de La Compañía after the fire of 1863, and the diorama of the departure of troops for the north in the War of the Pacific. There is also a life-size recreation of a *sarao*, a parlor gathering of Santiago's late-colonial elite.

At Merced 860, the museum (☎ 6330723) is open Tuesday to Saturday, 10 am to 6 pm, Sundays and holidays 10 am to 2 pm only. Admission costs US$1.25. There is also a combination bookstore-giftshop.

Museo Chileno de Arte Precolombino

In the late-colonial (1805) Real Casa de Aduana (royal customs house), this beautifully arranged museum chronicles 4500 years of pre-Columbian civilization. There are separate displays for Mesoamerica (Mexico and Central America), the central Andes (Peru and Bolivia), the northern Andes (Colombia and Ecuador), and the southern Andes (modern Chile and Argentina plus, anomalously, parts of Brazil). Most of the well-preserved items come from the personal collections of the noted Larraín family, but there are also occasional special exhibits.

At Bandera 361, the museum (☎ 695-3851) is open Tuesday to Saturday 10 am to 6 pm, Sunday 10 am to 1 pm. Admission costs about US$1.25. It also has a good bookshop and an excellent, attractive café.

Convento y Museo de San Francisco

Exhibits at Santiago's landmark church, Iglesia de San Francisco, include a wall-size painting, attributed to an 18th-century artist, detailing the genealogy of the Franciscan order and its patrons. The several rooms depicting the life of St Francis of Assisi will exhaust all but the most earnestly devout. At Londres 4, just off the Alameda, the museum (☎ 6398737) is open Tuesday to Saturday, 10 am to 1.30 pm and 3 to 6 pm, Sundays and holidays 10 am to 2 pm only. Admission costs US$1.25 for adults, US$0.40 for children.

Palacio de Bellas Artes

Santiago's turn-of-the-century fine arts museum, modeled on the Petit Palais in Paris, fronts an entire block in the Parque Forestal, on José M de La Barra near Avenida José María Caro. It has permanent collections of French, Italian, Dutch and Chilean paintings, plus occasional and sometimes very spectacular special exhibitions.

Opening hours at the museum (☎ 633-0655) are Tuesday to Saturday, 11 am to 8 pm, Sundays and holidays 11 am to 2 pm only. Admission is US$1; children pay half.

Palacio Cousiño

Originally of Portuguese descent, the prominent Chilean wine family's additional successes in coal and silver mining enabled them to build what was probably Santiago's foremost mansion, dating from 1871, embellished with Francophile artwork and featuring one of the country's first elevators. A few years back, fire destroyed the 3rd-floor interior, but the remaining floors are well-preserved reminders of elite life in the late 19th century.

The palace (☎ 6985063) is probably the most elaborate of Santiago's 19th-century mansions open to the public. Excellent guided tours, in Spanish or sometimes in English, are included in the price of admission, but interior photography is prohibited. The building's exterior and the surrounding gardens, designed by Spanish landscaper Miguel Arana Bórica, may be photographed. It's south of the Alameda at Dieciocho 438, near Parque Almagro (Metro: Los Héroes or, more conveniently, Toesca). Hours are 9.30 am to 1.30 pm, daily except Monday; admission costs US$1.25 for adults, US$0.75 for children.

Museo de la Solidaridad Salvador Allende

Having begun in 1971 with donations from artists around the world in sympathy with Chile's socialist experiment, this overly political museum literally went underground after the military coup of 1973 – the entire collection spent 17 years in the warehouses of the Museo de Arte Contemporáneo, awaiting the return of civilian rule. Supplemented by works from Chilean artists in exile, a part of the collection is now on display in this small museum (☎ 6971033) in a cul-de-sac at Virginia Opazo 38 (Metro: República). Hours are weekdays 11 am to 1 pm and 2 to 7 pm.

CERRO SANTA LUCIA

Honeycombed with gardens, footpaths and fountains, Cerro Santa Lucía (known to the Mapuche as Huelén) has been a handy hilltop sanctuary from the bustle of downtown Santiago since 1875. At its base, on the Alameda, sits a large stone engraved with the text of a letter in which Pedro de Valdivia extolled the beauty of the newly conquered territories to Spain's King Carlos V. A short distance north is a striking mural of Nobel Prize poet Gabriela Mistral.

Also fronting the Alameda is a very attractive fountain, around which staircases climb to the summit, whose parapet reveals a perfect view of the city, Cerro San Cristóbal and the Andes – smog permitting. The north side of the park, along Avenida Subercaseaux, features a pleasant **Jardín Japonés** (Japanese Garden). Santa Lucía's landscaping is a modern development – Bryce noted in 1914 that 'The buildings which had defaced it having been nearly all removed, it is now laid out as a pleasure ground, and planted with trees.'

Cerro Santa Lucía is an easy walk from downtown to the east end of Huérfanos, where a glass *ascensor* (elevator) carries passengers up the steep hillside, or a short ride on the Metro to Estación Santa Lucía. It has acquired an unfortunate reputation for night-time muggings but is generally safe during the day, although visitors should not be complacent.

Museo Arqueológico de Santiago

Featuring outstanding exhibits on Chile's indigenous peoples from colonial times to the present, this misleadingly named museum is more accurately ethnohistorical than archaeological. Its major defect is some outdated rhetoric that makes its subjects sound more like Chilean possessions than people in their own right.

At the Plaza del Mulato Gil de Castro, Lastarria 321 on the east side of Cerro Santa Lucía, the museum is part of an interesting neighborhood that includes many art galleries, excellent bookshops and varied restaurants. It's open weekdays 10 am to 2 pm and 3.30 to 6.30 pm, Saturdays 10 am to 2 pm only. Admission is free.

BARRIO BELLAVISTA

Across the Río Mapocho beneath Cerro San Cristóbal, on both sides of shady Avenida Pío Nono and many side streets, Bellavista is one of Santiago's liveliest neighborhoods on weekends, but is usually quiet the rest of the time. Overlapping the comunas of Providencia and Recoleta, its houses painted in lively pastels like those of Valparaíso's hill areas, Bellavista has countless ethnic restaurants and a very active Friday/Saturday evening crafts fair, starting at Parque Gómez Rojas across from the Universidad de Chile law school and continuing up Avenida Pío Nono.

La Chascona (Museo Neruda)

Nicknamed for the poet's widow Matilde Urrutia's unruly hair, Pablo Neruda's eclectic Bellavista house sits on a shady cul-de-sac at the foot of Cerro San Cristóbal, a short distance off Pío Nono.

The Fundación Neruda (☎ 7378712), at Márquez de La Plata 0192, conducts tours of La Chascona on a first-come, first-served basis daily except Monday, 10 am to 1 pm and 3 to 6 pm. Admission costs US$2.50 for adults, half that for children; tours last an hour and are very thorough. The Fundación also arranges one-day bus tours (lunch included), which take in the poet's

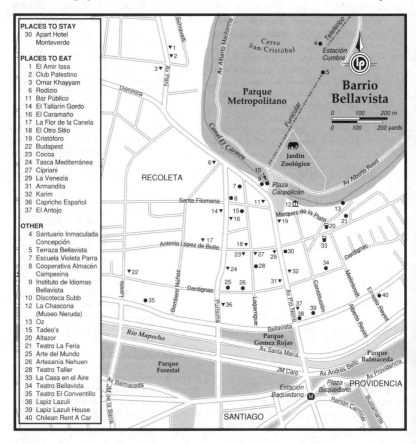

PLACES TO STAY
30 Apart Hotel Monteverde

PLACES TO EAT
1 El Amir Issa
2 Club Palestino
3 Omar Khayyam
6 Rodizio
11 Bar Público
14 El Tallarín Gordo
16 El Caramaño
17 La Flor de la Canela
18 El Otro Sitio
19 Cristóforo
22 Budapest
23 Cocoa
24 Tasca Mediterránea
27 Cipriani
29 La Venezia
31 Armandita
32 Karim
36 Capricho Español
37 El Antojo

OTHER
4 Santuario Inmaculada Concepción
5 Terraza Bellavista
7 Escuela Violeta Parra
8 Cooperativa Almacén Campesina
9 Instituto de Idiomas Bellavista
10 Discoteca Subb
12 La Chascona (Museo Neruda)
13 Oz
15 Tadeo's
20 Altazor
21 Teatro La Feria
25 Arte del Mundo
26 Artesanía Nehuen
28 Teatro Taller
33 La Casa en el Aire
34 Teatro Bellavista
35 Teatro El Conventillo
38 Lapiz Lazuli
39 Lapiz Lazuli House
40 Chilean Rent A Car

WAYNE BERNHARDSON

Protesters urge a reckoning for those 'disappeared' under the military regime,
Plaza de la Constitución

three houses: here, at Isla Negra and in Valparaíso (see the Middle Chile chapter for descriptions of the latter two).

Cementerio General

Both Chile's distant and recent history are on display here, where the tombs of figures like José Manuel Balmaceda, Salvador Allende and diplomat Orlando Letelier are reminders of political turmoil from the 19th century to the present. A recent addition, erected in 1994, is a memorial to the 'disappeared' victims of the Pinochet dictatorship.

At the north end of Avenida La Paz, north of the Río Mapocho via the Cal y Canto bridge, the Cementerio General is open every day during daylight hours.

PARQUE METROPOLITANO (CERRO SAN CRISTOBAL)

Crowned by a 36-meter white statue of the Virgin Mary, 869-meter San Cristóbal towers above downtown Santiago from the north side of the Mapocho. Reached by funicular railway, *teleférico* (aerial tramway), bus, or on foot, it dominates Parque Metropolitano, central Santiago's largest open space and a major recreational resource for residents of the capital. There are several restaurants, snack bars and coffee shops.

The easiest route to the summit of San Cristóbal is the funicular, which climbs 485 meters from Plaza Caupolicán, at the north end of Pío Nono. Built in 1925, the funicular makes an intermediate stop at the **Jardín Zoológico** (zoo), which has a modest collection of scandalously neglected exotic animals (a tiger actually escaped and roamed the area for several hours in early 1996), before continuing to the **Terraza Bellavista** where, on a rare clear day, there are extraordinary views of the city and its surroundings. At the summit proper, Pope John Paul II said mass at the **Santuario Inmaculada Concepción** during his visit to Santiago in 1984.

A short walk from the Terraza is the Estación Cumbre, the start of the 2000-meter-long **teleférico**, which goes from Cerro San Cristóbal, via Tupahue, to a station near the north end of Avenida Pedro de Valdivia Norte (about 1200 meters from the Pedro de Valdivia Metro station).

At the Tupahue teleférico station is the **Piscina Tupahue**, with large swimming pools. A short walk east from Tupahue are the **Casa de la Cultura** (an art museum), Santiago's famous **Enoteca**, (a restaurant and wine museum) and the **Jardín Botánico Mapulemu** (the botanical garden). Further east, there are also large swimming pools at **Piscina Antilén**, reachable only by bus or on foot.

In summer, from December to March, the funicular operates from 10 am to 8.30 pm weekdays, 10 am to 9 pm weekends

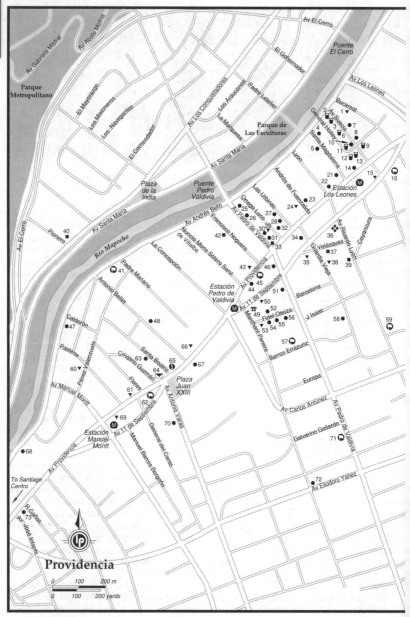

Parque
Metropolitano

Parque de
Las Esculturas

Plaza
de la
India

Puente
Pedro
Valdivia

Río Mapocho

Estación
Pedro de
Valdivia

Estación
Los Leones

Plaza Juan
XXIII

Estación
Manuel
Montt

To Santiago
Centro

Providencia

0   100   200 m

0   100   200 yards

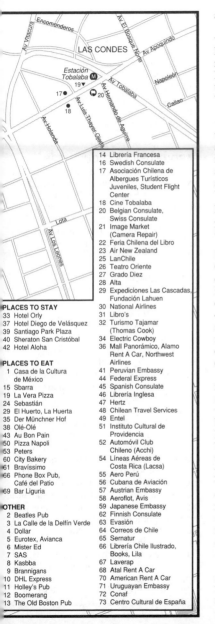

14 Librería Francesa
16 Swedish Consulate
17 Asociación Chilena de
   Albergues Turísticos
   Juveniles, Student Flight
   Center
18 Cine Tobalaba
20 Belgian Consulate,
   Swiss Consulate
21 Image Market
   (Camera Repair)
22 Feria Chilena del Libro
23 Air New Zealand
25 LanChile
26 Teatro Oriente
27 Grado Diez
28 Alta
29 Expediciones Las Cascadas,
   Fundación Lahuen
30 National Airlines
31 Libro's
32 Turismo Tajamar
   (Thomas Cook)
34 Electric Cowboy
36 Mall Panorámico, Alamo
   Rent A Car, Northwest
   Airlines
41 Peruvian Embassy
44 Federal Express
45 Spanish Consulate
46 Librería Inglesa
47 Hertz
48 Chilean Travel Services
49 Entel
51 Instituto Cultural de
   Providencia
52 Automóvil Club
   Chileno (Acchi)
54 Líneas Aéreas de
   Costa Rica (Lacsa)
55 Aero Perú
56 Cubana de Aviación
57 Austrian Embassy
58 Aeroflot, Avis
59 Japanese Embassy
62 Finnish Consulate
63 Evasión
64 Correos de Chile
65 Sernatur
66 Librería Chile Ilustrado,
   Books, Lila
67 Laverap
68 Atal Rent A Car
70 American Rent A Car
71 Uruguayan Embassy
72 Conaf
73 Centro Cultural de España

PLACES TO STAY
33 Hotel Orly
37 Hotel Diego de Velásquez
39 Santiago Park Plaza
40 Sheraton San Cristóbal
42 Hotel Aloha

PLACES TO EAT
1 Casa de la Cultura
   de México
15 Sbarra
17 La Vera Pizza
24 Sebastián
29 El Huerto, La Huerta
35 Der Münchner Hof
38 Olé-Olé
43 Au Bon Pain
50 Pizza Napoli
53 Peters
60 City Bakery
61 Bravíssimo
66 Phone Box Pub,
   Café del Patio
69 Bar Liguria

OTHER
2 Beatles Pub
3 La Calle de la Delfín Verde
4 Dollar
5 Eurotex, Avianca
6 Mister Ed
7 SAS
8 Kasbba
9 Brannigans
10 DHL Express
11 Holley's Pub
12 Boomerang
13 The Old Boston Pub

and holidays; the rest of the year hours are 10 am to 7 pm weekdays and 10 am to 8 pm weekends and holidays. The teleférico keeps slightly different hours: in summer, it runs 10.30 am to 8 pm daily except Monday, when hours are 3 to 8 pm only; the rest of the year, weekday hours are 3 to 7 pm, while weekend/holiday hours are 10.30 am to 7 pm.

From either direction, the funicular-teleférico combination (about US$4 for adults, US$2 for children), plus the Metro, is a good way to orient yourself to Santiago's complex geography. The funicular alone costs US$1.50 to Estación Cumbre, US$2.25 for a roundtrip. From Plaza Caupolicán, Buses Tortuga Tour also reaches Avenida Pedro de Valdivia Norte via Tupahue, on a winding, roundabout road.

PARQUE QUINTA NORMAL

Once an area of prestigious mansions, the comuna of Quinta Normal is now much less exclusive but of great historical interest. West of downtown, the cool, woodsy 40-hectare Parque Quinta Normal attracts strolling Santiaguinos, family picnickers, impromptu soccer games and (on Sundays) increasing numbers of parading evangelicals.

The most noteworthy of several commendable museums is the **Museo Nacional de Historia Natural** (☎ 6814095), with exhibits including the mummified body of a 12-year-old child, sacrificed at least 500 years ago and discovered in 1954 by a team from the Universidad de Chile on the icy summit of El Plomo, a 5000-meter peak near Santiago (There are reports that this mummy is a credible replica of the original, which is kept under wraps). Bone fragments of the giant Pleistocene ground sloth known as the 'milodon,' from the famous cave near Puerto Natales in southern Chile (see the Magallanes chapter), are also on display.

In the middle of the park, there's an artificial lagoon where you can rent rowboats and, for kids, the floating equivalent of bumper cars. Beyond the lagoon, visit the **Museo de Ciencia y Tecnología**

(☎ 6816022), open Tuesday to Friday 10 am to 5 pm, weekends 11 am to 5.20 pm. Specifically for children, about 50 meters to the north, is the **Museo Infantil** (☎ 6816022).

Near the southern entrance, the lovingly maintained steam locomotives at the open-air **Parque Museo Ferroviario** are a tribute to pioneers of the Chilean railroads. It's open Tuesday to Friday 10 am to 5.30 pm, weekends 11 am to 6.30 pm; admission costs US$1.25 for adults, US$0.75 for children.

Across from the southern entrance, at Avenida Portales 3530, housed in an offbeat structure designed for the Paris Exhibition of 1889 and dismantled and installed opposite the Quinta Normal after the turn of the century, the **Museo Artequín** (☎ 6818656) is an interactive museum of replica art, mostly European masters. It's open daily except Monday, 10 am to 5 pm; admission costs US$1.75.

To get to Parque Quinta Normal, take the Metro to Estación Central and then walk or catch a northbound bus up Matucana. There are park entrances on Avenida Portales, Matucana, Santo Domingo and Apostól Santiago. Public hours are 8 am to 8 pm daily.

PARQUE O'HIGGINS

In a previous incarnation as Parque Cousiño, 80-hectare Parque O'Higgins was the preserve of Santiago's elite, but it is now a more egalitarian place. Parts of the park are dilapidated, making it less appealing than Parque Quinta Normal, but it still provides an entertaining glimpse of what many working-class Chileans do on weekends.

The section known as **El Pueblito**, featuring full-size replicas of rural buildings and a gaggle of inexpensive restaurants with raucous salsa bands on Sunday afternoon, also contains the **Museo del Huaso**, honoring Chile's counterpart to the Argentine gaucho, which often features good folkloric music. El Pueblito also has a small **Acuario** (Aquarium), a **Museo de Insectas y Caracoles** (Museum of Insects and Snails) and a mini-zoo.

Fantasilandia (☎ 6893035) is an amusement park for children, open daily except Mondays in summer but weekends and holidays only the rest of the year. Admission is free for children shorter than 90 cm, while those between 91 and 140 cm pay US$7, and all others US$7.50.

To get to Parque O'Higgins, take the Línea 2 of the Metro to Parque O'Higgins station and walk west on leaving the station.

PARQUE DE LAS ESCULTURAS

At the other end of Santiago, in affluent Providencia, this open-air sculpture garden is a pleasant hangout on the banks of the Mapocho. There is also an indoor exhibition hall at Avenida Santa María 2201, a short walk across the river from the Pedro de Valdivia Metro station. It's open daily, 10 am to 2 pm and 3 to 6 pm.

PLAZA ÑUÑOA

As upscale high-rise development dissolves the community feeling of once-suburban areas like Providencia and Las Condes, Santiaguinos have gained a new appreciation of areas such as middle-class Ñuñoa, where attractive single-family houses and tree-lined streets recall what other parts of the capital have lost. It's close enough to the front range of the Andes that the mountains are usually visible despite the city's frequent smog.

Middle-class does not mean dull, however – Ñuñoa has an active cultural life centered around Plaza Ñuñoa, where the Universidad Católica has one of Santiago's most important theater venues, and a progressive municipal administration has promoted live concerts and a crafts and flea market. Restaurants and dance clubs pull visitors from downtown, especially on weekends, the Estadio Nacional hosts soccer matches and rock concerts, and foreign students from the Universidad de Chile's nearby Macul campus add a cosmopolitan element.

To get to Plaza Ñuñoa from elsewhere in the city, take bus Nos 212, 338 or 382 from Plaza Italia (the area around Plaza

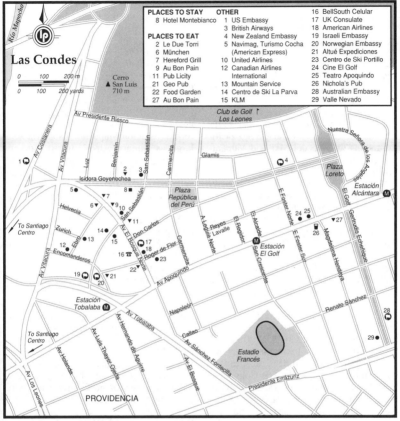

PLACES TO STAY
8 Hotel Montebianco

PLACES TO EAT
2 Le Due Torri
6 München
7 Hereford Grill
9 Au Bon Pain
11 Pub Licity
21 Geo Pub
22 Food Garden
27 Au Bon Pain

OTHER
1 US Embassy
3 British Airways
4 New Zealand Embassy
5 Navimag, Turismo Cocha
   (American Express)
10 United Airlines
12 Canadian Airlines
   International
13 Mountain Service
14 Centro de Ski La Parva
15 KLM

16 BellSouth Celular
17 UK Consulate
18 American Airlines
19 Israeli Embassy
20 Norwegian Embassy
21 Altué Expediciones
23 Centro de Ski Portillo
24 Cine El Golf
25 Teatro Apoquindo
26 Nichola's Pub
28 Australian Embassy
29 Valle Nevado

Baquedano), 433 from Alameda and Vicuña Mackenna, 606 from the Terminal de Buses Santiago, 600 from Estación Central, or 243 from Compañía. Metrobús directly connects Estación Salvador with Plaza Ñuñoa.

LANGUAGE COURSES

For intensive (but not inexpensive) language courses, try the Instituto de Idiomas Bellavista (☎ 7775933), Dominica 25 near Cerro San Cristóbal. Also in Bellavista, at Lagarrigue 362-A, the Escuela Violeta Parra (☎ 7358240, fax 2298246) has earned

praise for emphasizing the social context of language instruction, through arranging field trips to community and environmental organizations, vineyards and the like, as well as tours to nearby national parks.

The Instituto Goethe (☎ 6397371), Esmeralda 650, offers intensive Spanish language courses, consisting of four weeks of 25 class-hours per week for US$425; classes are available for beginning, intermediate and advanced students. The Instituto also offers twice-weekly conversation classes for US$90 for four weeks. Classes are no larger than 10 to 12 students.

SANTIAGO

ORGANIZED TOURS

If time is limited, consider a tour of Santiago and its surroundings. The municipal tourist kiosk on Ahumada offers thematic walking tours of the downtown area Tuesday mornings at 10.30 am and Wednesday afternoons at 3 pm, but verify these times. Tours include free admission to selected museums, and can sometimes accommodate English speakers.

Several agencies run day and night tours of the capital (around US$20 each), excursions to Viña del Mar and Valparaíso (around US$40), visits to the Cousiño Macul and Concha y Toro wineries, and ski trips to Farellones, Valle del Nevado and Portillo (see Ski Resorts under Around Santiago). Among them are ACE Turismo (☎ 6960391) at Alameda 949, 16th floor; Chilean Travel Services (☎ 2510400) at Antonio Bellet 77 in Providencia; and Turismo Cocha (☎ 2301000) at Avenida El Bosque Norte 0430 in Las Condes (Metro: Tobalaba). It may be slightly cheaper to sign up on the spot rather than to make advance reservations.

A Santiago city tour includes sights like the Iglesia de San Francisco, Cerro Santa Lucía and Cerro San Cristóbal. There are also half-day tours to major museums, including the Museo Chileno de Arte Precolombino, the Museo de Arte Colonial at the Iglesia de San Francisco and the Museo Nacional de Historia Natural in the Quinta Normal. Day tours to Valparaíso and Viña del Mar take in the waterfront, the Academia Naval, the Universidad de Santa María, the Museo de Bellas Artes at the Palacio Baburizza and the Viña del Mar casino.

For tours and activities outside the city, see the Around Santiago section.

SPECIAL EVENTS

Santiago hosts a variety of special events throughout the year. January's Festival del Barrio Brasil highlights an area currently undergoing a major renewal. Late in the month, the suburban comuna of San Bernardo hosts the Festival Nacional del Folclore.

In March, Aeropuerto Los Cerrillos is the site of the Feria Internacional del Aire y del Espacio, a major international air show attended, in part, by weapons sellers. The last Saturday of April, the Gran Premio Hipódromo Chile determines Chile's best three-year-old race horses. Over the course of the winter, several other racing events take place here and at the Club Hípico.

Santiago's annual Feria Internacional del Libro (International Book Fair) takes place the last two weeks of November in the former Estación Mapocho. Though not so large as Buenos Aires', it still attracts authors from throughout the country and the continent. Each day focuses on a single country, usually Latin American or European, but there's the occasional oddity such as Iran.

At around the same time, Chile's indigenous peoples – Mapuche, Diaguita, Atacameña, Aymara and Rapa Nui – celebrate their heritage at the Feria Indígena Cerro Huelén, held near the fountain on the south side of Cerro Santa Lucia. Musicians, dancers and others give performances daily, while crafts workers display their weavings, wood carvings, basketry and jewelry. Typical food is also available.

PLACES TO STAY

Santiago has abundant budget accommodation, but travelers should be selective – lodgings in this category differ much more in quality than in price.

Places to Stay – bottom end

Hostel Santiago has a new Hostelling International facility (☎ 6718532, fax 672-8880) conveniently located at Cienfuegos 151 in Barrio Brasil (Metro: Los Héroes). Rates for the 120 beds are US$10 per night for members, US$12.50 for non-members, but guests automatically become members after six nights. There are pleasant common areas, including a cafeteria and TV lounge, and the four- and six-bed rooms all have locking closets. Quick, inexpensive laundry service is available.

Hotels, Hospedajes & Residenciales

Santiago's main budget hotel zone is a

seedy but not really dangerous neighborhood near the former Terminal de Buses Norte, around General Mackenna, Amunátegui, San Pablo and San Martín (Metro: Puente Cal y Canto), where accommodations range from truly squalid to basically acceptable. Single women may feel uncomfortable here late at night, especially on General Mackenna, where many prostitutes hang out.

Best in the area is the labyrinthine *Hotel Caribe* (☎ 6966681), San Martín 851, which is still good value at US$7 per person with shared bath and hot showers. Although popular with travelers, it's large enough that there's usually a room, though singles may be at a premium. Rooms are spartan but some are very large, and the manager and staff are very friendly. Ask for a room at the back or upstairs, since foot traffic on the squeaky-clean floors makes the lobby and passageway a bit noisy. The doors have flimsy hasps and padlocks, but you can leave valuables in the safe; they will happily and securely store your personal belongings at no charge if you go trekking or take some other excursion. Meals, snacks and drinks are available at reasonable prices.

Now rivaling the Caribe among budget travelers is the more central, and very slightly cheaper *Nuevo Hotel Valparaíso* (☎ 6715698), with entrances at both San Pablo 1182 and Morandé 791, but the rooms are very insecure – store your valuables safely. Another ambivalent recommendation is the odd but friendly *Hotel Pudahuel* (☎ 6984169), San Pablo 1419, described by one reader as an 'old, beautiful, European-style building' with large and bright rooms, but the lobby has a distinct odor of cat and it can be noisy. Rates with shared bath are US$7.50 per person, while doubles with private bath go for US$18.

Hotel Indiana (☎ 6714251), a dilapidated mansion with dependable hot water at Rosas 1343, is Santiago's Israeli hangout; beds cost around US$5. Comparably priced *Hotel Souvenir*, Amunátegui 856, has primordial plumbing, dim lights,

sagging staircases and murky corridors, but also clean sheets and hot water.

A better neighborhood, with slightly dearer accommodations, is Barrio París Londres, south of the Alameda near Iglesia San Francisco (Metro: Universidad de Chile). Very popular *Residencial Londres* (☎ /fax 6382215), Londres 54, is outstanding value at US$11 per person with hot water, clean and secure rooms, and a pleasant and helpful staff. Arrive early, since it fills up quickly – singles are almost impossible to get. If nothing's available, try *Hotel París* (☎ 6394037), around the corner at Calle París 813, where small but clean and comfy singles/doubles with private bath cost US$15/25; some rooms lack windows, however. The París has a less expensive nearby annex.

Barrio Brasil's highly recommended *Residencial del Norte* (☎ 6951876), Catedral 2207, charges US$10 per person in a family atmosphere (Metro: Santa Ana). Also recommended is comparably priced *Residencial Alemana* (☎ 6712388), Avenida República 220 (Metro: República). Closer to the Metro, but slightly more expensive, is *Residencial Mery* (☎ 696-8883), Pasaje República 36.

On a quiet cul-de-sac near the corner of Moneda and Amunátegui, the very central *Residencial Tabita* (☎ 6715700, fax 6969492), Príncipe de Gales 81, charges US$15 per person with shared bath, US$18/32 with private bath.

Places to Stay – middle

Santiago's mid-range accommodations are sometimes better value than its budget selection. Many of these hotels have agreeable little rooms with private bath and toilet; for a few bucks more there is often telephone, TV and refrigerator.

Rates start around US$22/30 at conveniently located *Hotel España* (☎ 6985245), Morandé 510, for clean but stark rooms, some with balky plumbing. Watch the surcharge on credit cards. Opinions differ on nearby *Hotel Cervantes* (☎ 6965318), Morandé 631, where some rooms are cramped, with lumpy beds, and others are bright and spacious. Rates are US$34/37 with private bath, but there are slightly cheaper doubles with shared bath and hot water. It also has a decent restaurant.

Bright, cheerful *Hotel Vega* (☎ 6322498, fax 6325084), Londres 49, has undergone a slightly cheesy remodeling job, but its clean and spacious rooms are one of Santiago's best midrange bargains at US$32/38.

Air passengers in transit to other parts of the country might consider *Hacienda del Sol y la Luna* (☎ 6019254, fax 6019663), Cuarta Hijuela 9978 in Pudahuel, which charges US$25/45 with breakfast and provides free airports transfers. Other facilities include a restaurant (abundant meals cost around US$15), tennis courts and a swimming pool.

In Barrio Brasil, at Agustinas 2173, family-oriented *Hotel Los Arcos* (☎ 699-0988) is good value at US$28/35. In the same area, slightly more central *Hotel Turismo Japón* (☎ 6984500), Almirante Barroso 160, is excellent value at US$35/45, with spacious gardens and an English-speaking owner who will exchange books. Some rooms are small at *Hotel Ducado* (☎ 6969384, fax 6951271), Agustinas 1990, but it's a good and friendly place charging US$35/46.

Friendly but tacky *Hotel di Maurier* (☎ 6957750, fax 6966193), Moneda 1510, is convenient to the airport bus; rates are US$27/36 with shared bath, US$33/43 with private bath. *Hotel Europa* (☎ 695-2448, fax 6971378), Amunátegui 449, has small and simple but very clean rooms in excellent condition for US$33/40.

There are a number of other respectable downtown hotels in the US$35/50 range. These include *Hotel El Libertador* (☎ 6394212) at Alameda 853, *Hotel Gran Palace* (☎ 6712551) at Huérfanos 1178, and *Hotel Panamericano* (☎ 6723060) at Teatinos 320.

Well-maintained *Hotel Foresta* (☎ /fax 6396261), in an interesting neighborhood at Subercaseaux 353, is a first-rate choice for US$40/65. Recommended *Hotel Metrópoli* (☎ 6723987), Sótero del Río 465 (a cul-de-sac off Catedral between Teatinos

and Morandé), has worn but clean and comfortable rooms with private bath for US$45/58, though some have mixed opinions of it.

Accommodation of any kind is scarce in Bellavista, but *Apart Hotel Monteverde* (☎ 7773607, fax 7370341), Pío Nono 193, is the exception for US$44/50 with breakfast. Rooms have kitchenettes with microwaves, but the street is very noisy Friday and Saturday nights.

One of the best midrange places is *Hotel Montecarlo* (☎ 6381176, fax 6335577), Subercaseaux 209, opposite Cerro Santa Lucía. Rooms are small but cheery, all have private bathrooms and the staff are friendly, but beware the noise from the busy street. Rates are US$47/54. Try also *City Hotel* (☎ 6954526) at Compañía 1063 for US$44/51, or the pleasant *Hotel Riviera* (☎ 6331176), Miraflores 106, where smallish rooms cost US$48/55.

Hotel Santa Lucía (☎ 6398201, fax 6331844), Huérfanos 779, 4th floor, is also good value at about US$55/65; rooms are attractive with TV, telephone, strongbox, refrigerator and private bath. While the street below can be very noisy, double-paned windows make the rooms nearly soundproof. For about the same price, highly regarded *Hotel Conde Ansurez* (☎ 6996368, fax 6958475), Avenida República 25 (Metro: República), offers European atmosphere for US$55/65.

Hotel Ritz (☎ 6393401), Paseo Estado 248, is comfortable and central for US$55/65, but traffic noise is considerable and it has some maintenance problems. Rather quieter, for US$56/72, enthusiastically recommended *Hotel Principado* (☎ 2228142, fax 2226065) is at Arturo Buhrle 015, just off Vicuña Mackenna (Metro: Baquedano).

Places to Stay – top end

Santiago has many expensive, first-rate hotels, including well-known international chains. Most have gourmet restaurants, cafés, bars and money exchange services for their clients.

Nevertheless, some of the best values are

at the low end of the range. In a well-preserved older building at Pedro de Valdivia 027 (Metro: Pedro de Valdivia), *Hotel Orly* (☎ 2318947, fax 2520051) reflects the Providencia of more dignified, less commercial times; for US$75/85, rooms are a little small, but the hospitable staff are a big plus. Also in Providencia, the much newer *Hotel Diego de Velásquez* (☎ /fax 2344400; Metro: Pedro de Valdivia or Los Leones), Diego de Velásquez 2141, is excellent value for US$75/85, including a room-service American-style breakfast, cable TV and many other services.

In Las Condes, *Hotel Montebianco* (☎ 2330427, fax 2330420), Isidora Goyenechea 2911, is a sparkling new place that has rooms with attractive attached patios. Rates are US$81/110 for air-conditioned rooms with TV, telephone and private bath. At Plaza Mulato Gil de Castro, at Merced 294 alongside the Instituto Chileno-Francés, *Hostal del Parque* (☎ 6392694, fax 6392754) charges US$96/110.

Rates at downtown *Hotel Conquistador* (☎ /fax 6965599), Miguel Cruchaga 920 (a small street off Paseo Estado near the Alameda), start at US$116/139. *Hotel Tupahue* (☎ 6383810), San Antonio 477, charges US$118/130, including continental breakfast, but the air-conditioning is suspect and it's not really good value. Glittering *Hotel Galerías*, (☎ 6384011, fax 6330821) a block from the Alameda at San Antonio 65, has rooms for US$117/165, and features a swimming pool.

Another choice in Providencia, with an accommodating English-speaking staff, is *Hotel Aloha* (☎ 2332230, fax 2332494), Francisco Noguera 146 (Metro: Pedro de Valdivia), where rates are US$133/146.

Rates at the *Holiday Inn Crowne Plaza* (☎ 6381042, fax 6330960), Alameda 136, start at US$212/225; the hotel has offices, shops, car rentals and a post office. At venerable *Hotel Carrera* (☎ 6982011, fax 6721083), overlooking Plaza de la Constitución at Teatinos 180, rates start at US$220/230. It was from here, in 1985, that deadly serious opponents of the dictatorship aimed a time-delay bazooka at

General Pinochet's office at La Moneda – the recoil was too strong for a photo tripod and the explosion destroyed the hotel room's interior instead.

Providencia's *Santiago Park Plaza* (☎ 2336363, fax 2336668), at Ricardo Lyon 207 (Metro: Los Leones), charges US$242/254, while the *Sheraton San Cristóbal* (☎ 2335000, fax 2328000), north of the Mapocho at Avenida Santa María 1742, has rooms starting at US$271 double. The *Hyatt Regency Santiago* (☎ 2181234, fax 2182513), Avenida Kennedy 4601 in Las Condes, has rooms starting at US$280/295.

PLACES TO EAT

Downtown Santiago has an abundance of eateries from the basic to the elegant, especially around the bus terminals, the Huérfanos and Ahumada pedestrian malls, the Plaza de Armas and the Alameda. The best choice of restaurants, however, is in and around Cerro Santa Lucía, Barrio Bellavista, and the comunas of Providencia, Las Condes and Ñuñoa.

Among the varied choices are Italian pasta, Indian curry, Middle Eastern stuffed grape leaves, Mexican food (both Tex-Mex and regional cuisine), Peruvian specialties and Chilean parrillada and seafood. Sernatur's free publications offer some idea of this formidable range, but the *Centro* volume of CTC's Turistel series has the most comprehensive and systematic listings. Another possibility is the bilingual guide *Dining Out/Comiendo Fuera*, with a selection of 100 Santiago restaurants and evaluation of Chilean wines, available for US$15 by phoning ☎ 2186069.

Downtown & Vicinity

Avoid greasy McDonalds clones like *Burger Inn* or *Max Beef*. For cheap snacks, pastries and drinks there's a string of stand-up places in the Portal Fernández Concha on the south side of the Plaza de Armas, serving items like hot dogs, sandwiches and fried chicken with fries. In the same arcade, highly regarded *Chez Henry* (☎ 6721992) is no longer inexpensive, but neither is it outrageous – for about US$6 their famous pastel de choclo is the only meal you'll need all day (other dishes are dearer, but selective diners can still eat well at moderate prices). Portions are huge, but ready-made items from the takeaway deli are cheaper and no less appealing.

For lunch, one of Santiago's best and cheapest eating places is the Mercado Central on San Pablo, a few blocks north of the Plaza, with a wealth of tremendous seafood dishes – be adventurous. Its lively atmosphere makes the historic building worth visiting in its own right, while the varied food at the numerous stalls and restaurants is often a bargain. The most obviously appealing places are those like *Donde Augusto* (☎ 6722829), picturesquely set among the central fruit and vegetable stands, but those restaurants are not dramatically better than the smaller, cheaper places on the periphery.

Vegetarians can munch at moderately priced *El Naturista* (☎ 6984122), Moneda 846 and *El Vegetariano* (☎ 6397063), Huérfanos 827, Local 18. Carnivores should try *El Novillero* (☎ 6991544), Moneda 1145. Many travelers have recommended *Bar Central*, San Pablo 1063, which serves generous portions of excellent seafood and is also popular with Santiaguinos. For Chinese food, try enthusiastically recommended *Kan-Thu* (☎ 6399511), Santo Domingo 769.

Italian restaurants are good and numerous but surprisingly expensive, like *Da Carla* (☎ 6333739) at MacIver 577, *San Marcos* (☎ 6336880) at Huérfanos 618 and traditional favorite *Le Due Torri* (☎ 6333799), San Antonio 258. For Italian fast food, try *Pizza Napoli* (☎ 6330845), Paseo Estado 149.

Serving Chilean specialties like pastel de choclo, *Bar Nacional* (☎ 6953368), Bandera 317, is a lunchtime favorite with downtown office workers. There's a second branch (☎ 6965986) at Huérfanos 1151.

For onces, afternoon tea, a good central place for juices and sandwiches is *100% Natural* (☎ 6971860), directly west of La Moneda at Valentín Letelier 1319. Across

from the elevator on the west side of Cerro Santa Lucía, *Brunch & Coffee* (☎ 633-7127), Santa Lucía 298, is a small, misleadingly named but bright and cheerful juice bar with good, inexpensive sandwiches. *La Escarcha* (☎ 6332316), Huérfanos 747, has downtown's best ice cream, but there are better choices in Providencia.

For inexpensive espresso and cocoa, go to any of the several stand-up bars, such as *Café Haití* at Ahumada 140, *Café Caribe* almost next door at Ahumada 120, or *Café Cousiño* at Matías Cousiño 107, all of which have many other branches around town. Some women feel uncomfortable at these coffee bars, colloquially referred to as café con piernas (coffee with legs), since most of them attract male clientele by dressing their young female staff in tight, revealing minidresses.

Cerro Santa Lucía Just south of the Mapocho, several restaurants are clustered in and around Plaza del Mulato Gil de Castro, Lastarria 321; at *Pérgola de la Plaza* (☎ 6393604), the tasty lunch specials (about US$5) are great bargains. Renovated and used as artists' studios, the surrounding buildings house a cluster of galleries and bookshops.

Alongside its namesake cinema, *Café del Biógrafo* (☎ 6399532), Villavicencio 398, is a neighborhood hangout. Its US$5 lunches are excellent, as are the baguettes and the casual atmosphere, but service can be slow. *Don Victorino* (☎ 6395263), Lastarria 138, is one of several restaurants that offer excellent lunches at moderate prices, with an extensive but costlier dinner menu. Service is first-rate, and the atmosphere relaxed. In the same category are nearby *Gatopardo* (☎ 6336420), Lastarria 192, which serves Bolivian food, and *Capricho Español* (☎ 6339466), Rosal 346, for Mediterranean cuisine.

Santiago has a growing number of outstanding Peruvian restaurants, the best of which is probably *Cocoa* (☎ 632-1272), Lastarria 297. It's fairly expensive, but the pisco sours and desserts are large and exquisite – unquestionably the best

Street market, Valdivia
WAYNE BERNHARDSON

Fruits of the sea,
WAYNE BERNHARDSON

and fruits of the land
MICHAEL SULLIVAN

Mapuche women in Temuco market
HELEN HUGHES

Viña Cousiño Macul winery near Santiago
HELEN HUGHES

Antofagasta fish market
WAYNE BERNHARDSON

Images of Santiago

Architectural detail

Interior, Iglesia de San Francisco

Mural, Barrio Bellavista

Cerro Santa Lucía

Rafters and kayaker, Cajón del Maipo

chocolate cake the author has tasted in Chile. Closer to downtown, at Miraflores 443, *El Puente de Bórquez* (☎ 6382917) has inexpensive Peruvian lunches and a peña Fridays and Saturdays at 8.30 pm.

French cuisine is the rule at *Les Assassins* (☎ 6384280), Merced 297-B, where outstanding fixed-price lunches cost only about US$7. It's better to go early or late for lunch, because it has fewer than 20 tables; the downstairs is tobacco-free.

Japanese restaurants tend to be expensive, but the exception is the plain but very fine *Izakaya Yoko* (☎ 6321954), Merced 456, where it's possible to find excellent, filling meals for around US$5 to $6 without drinks, which are also reasonably priced. It's a small but very popular place.

Barrio Brasil Conveniently close to Santiago's youth hostel, *Pizzería Gigino* (☎ 698-2200), Agustinas 2015, keeps long hours, with pizza and pasta dishes for about US$5, but is also notable for a grossly mismatched collection of paintings covering virtually every open spot on the walls, giving it an exceptionally undisciplined and informal atmosphere.

Moderately priced *Plaza Garibaldi* (☎ 6994278), Moneda 2319 (Metro: República), has excellent Mexican dishes and beers, but a less varied menu than its more upscale counterparts in Providencia and Vitacura. Santiago's best Peruvian bargain, though the quality's not so high as its counterparts at Cerro Santa Lucía and Bellavista, is *El Rincón Criollo* (☎ 6967962), Avenida Brasil 75, with typical lunches that include an appetizer, main course, wine, dessert and a pisco sour for just US$6.

At Ricardo Cumming 221, *Ocean Pacific's* (☎ 6972413) is a reasonably priced, family-style seafood restaurant with excellent, friendly service and particularly good homemade bread, but the menu is misleading – many items listed are often not available. Not far away at Ricardo Cumming 94, slightly more expensive *Ostras Squellas* (☎ 6994883) usually has most of what appears on the menu.

Barrio Bellavista
North of the Mapocho, a short walk from the Baquedano Metro station, Pablo Neruda's old haunts are in a great dining area, especially lively on weekends. Many, but not necessarily the best, restaurants line both sides of Pío Nono between the bridge and Plaza Caupolicán.

El Antojo (☎ 7370398), Pío Nono 69, is a good Middle Eastern restaurant which is one of few places in the area to offer fixed-price lunches Saturdays. *Armandita* (☎ 7373409), Pío Nono 108, is an Argentine-style parrilla whose lomo a lo pobre (more typically Chilean) is good value for US$7 including french fries and juice or soft drink, but the service is sluggish. Across the street at Pío Nono 127, *Karim* (☎ 7378129) serves kebabs and other Middle Eastern specialties.

La Venezia (☎ 7370900), Pío Nono 200, is a moderately priced Italian restaurant. Across the street and down the block, rather than across the Aegean, *Cristóforo* (☎ 7377752), Pío Nono 281, serves Greek food and has comfortable outdoor seating. Its reasonably priced vaina doble packs a punch. *Bar Público* (☎ 7370095), Pío Nono 398, is an excellent, inexpensive dinner choice; the tiny 2nd-floor balcony offers a fine view of Bellavista street life.

The outstanding Peruvian restaurant *Cocoa* (☎ 7350634) has a branch at Antonia López de Bello 60. Another good Peruvian choice, though probably not quite so good a value, is *La Flor de la Canela* (☎ 7771007), Antonia López de Bello 125. The service is so rapid and attentive as to almost seem an affront, but there's a good tobacco-free section. Much more expensive is *El Otro Sitio* (☎ 7773059), Antonia López de Bello 53.

El Caramaño (☎ 7377043), a self-styled 'anti-restaurant' at Purísima 257, is so informal that there's no sign outside (ring the bell to get in) and visitors scribble on the interior walls. It has very fine Chilean food and friendly service. At Purísima 165, *Tasca Mediterránea* (☎ 735-3901) has excellent fixed-price lunches, good service and Bohemian atmosphere.

Another Spanish restaurant, with economical lunches, is *Capricho Español* (☎ 777-7674), one block south at Purísima 65.

At Lagarrigue 195, *Cipriani* (☎ 737-4569) has a Sunday Italian buffet for US$10, and cheap weekday lunches. Recommended *El Tallarín Gordo* (☎ 7378567), Purísima 254, also serves Italian food. *Rodizio* (☎ 7779240), Bombero Núñez 388, is a great-looking Brazilian parrilla, but even though it's an all you can eat, the US$23 price tag will deter budget watchers as well as dieters.

Budapest, at the corner of Dardignac and Loreto, serves good pizza and sandwiches. *El Rinconcito*, at the corner of Manzano and Dávila Baeza in Recoleta's Patronato district, is a very cheap Middle Eastern picada run by a Lebanese immigrant by way of Chicago – excellent for hummus, falafels and the like. More expensive Middle Eastern fare is available at *Omar Khayyam* (☎ 7774129) at Avenida Perú 570, the *Club Palestino* at Avenida Perú 659, and *El Amir Issa* (☎ 7773651) at Avenida Perú 663.

Providencia

A perennial vegetarian favorite is *Café del Patio* (☎ 2361251), at Providencia 1670, Local 8-A (Metro: Manuel Montt), but even non-vegetarians flock to *El Huerto* (☎ 2332690), Orrego Luco 054 (Metro: Pedro de Valdivia), internationally renowned for imaginative meatless meals. It's become more expensive, but the smaller menu at its adjacent café *La Huerta* offers quality food at much lower prices.

Since the resumption of official relations with the return of democracy, Mexico's cultural imprint is stronger than ever, especially in the capital's cuisine. Affiliated with the diplomatic mission, the *Casa de la Cultura de México* (☎ 3343848), Bucarest 162 (Metro: Los Leones), features outstanding regional dishes rather than Tex-Mex borderlands food; it also has superb crafts and a bookshop.

For Italian fast food, try *Pizza Napoli* (☎ 2256468) at Avenida 11 de Septiembre 1935 (Metro: Pedro de Valdivia). *La Vera*

Pizza (☎ 2321786), Providencia 2630 (Metro: Tobalaba), has good variety but is a bit pricey. *Sbarra*, Suecia 055, is part of an Italian-style chain that sells food by weight; the selection is ample and the quality's not bad.

German food is the fare at *Der Münchner Hof* (☎ 2332452), Diego de Velásquez 2105 (Metro: Los Leones). *Olé-Olé* (☎ 2333568), Guardia Vieja 156, is a highly regarded and pricey Spanish restaurant with superb service; lunches are reasonably priced (about US$10), but portions are not large. There's a well-segregated non-smoking section.

For sandwiches and onces, one of Santiago's best traditional venues is *Bar Liguria* (☎ 2357914), Providencia 1373 (Metro: Manuel Montt). The North American sandwich and baked goods chain *Au Bon Pain* (☎ 2318958) is at Providencia 1936, but fresh home-baked goods like blueberry muffins, cheesecake and pecan pie are available at *City Bakery* (☎ 2353653), Almirante Pastene 202 (Metro: Manuel Montt).

The cheapest fixed-price lunches in town are at *Peters* (☎ 2040124), Marchant Pereira 132 (Metro: Pedro de Valdivia); weekdays before 1 pm or after 3 pm, four-course meals, including a salad bar, cost only US$2.50. Homesick Brits will find Santiago's best pub lunches, for about US$7 to $8, at the *Phone Box Pub* (☎ 235-9972), Providencia 1670 (Metro: Manuel Montt). Its grape arbor patio is a pleasant sanctuary from the busy avenue outside.

For exceptional ice cream and other desserts, go to *Sebastián* (☎ 2319968), Andrés de Fuenzalida 26 (Metro: Pedro de Valdivia or Los Leones), or *Bravíssimo* (☎ 2352511) at Providencia 1406 (Metro: Manuel Montt).

Las Condes

At the corner of Avenida El Bosque Norte and Roger de Flor (Metro: Tobalaba), the *Food Garden complex* contains a number of decent, inexpensive fast food eateries, including a branch of *Sbarra*, the juice bar *Jugomanía*, and a good frozen yogurt outlet.

Although it imports nearly all its ingredients frozen from North America, the sandwich and baked goods chain *Au Bon Pain* is an exception to the rule that foreign franchises are not worth patronizing; it's also the only place in town to find bagels. There are two Las Condes branches, at Avenida El Bosque Norte 0181 (☎ 3320046) and at Avenida Apoquindo 3575 (☎ 3315080).

Although the pun deserves severe reproach, popular *Pub Licity* (☎ 2466414) at Avenida El Bosque Norte 0155 has excellent meals ranging from simple sandwiches to much more elaborate fare. The informal *Geo Pub* (☎ 2336675), Encomenderos 83, has excellent US$5 lunches and is also a popular weekend hangout.

Enormously popular with professionals on expense accounts, *München* (☎ 233-2108), Avenida El Bosque Norte 0204, serves German food. Beefeaters dine at the *Hereford Grill* (☎ 2319117), El Bosque Norte 0355, while there's a branch of downtown's *Le Due Torri* (☎ 2313427) at Isidora Goyenechea 2908 for Italian food. *Da Dino* (☎ 2081344), Avenida Apoquindo 4228 (Metro: Escuela Militar), is expensive for pizza, but quality is high.

Chang Cheng (☎ 2129718), Avenida Las Condes 7471, is an excellent upscale Chinese restaurant, serving both Mandarin and Cantonese cuisine.

Outlying Comunas
Plaza Ñuñoa is an increasingly popular dining area, given choices like *República de Ñuñoa* at Trucco 33 and *El Amor Nunca Muere* at Trucco 43 (open for dinner only). *La Terraza*, nearby at Jorge Washington 58, is more upscale. Decorated in a Cuban motif at Irarrázaval 3465, *Café de la Isla* prepares good sandwiches and excellent juices, to the accompaniment of recorded jazz.

Ñuñoa's upscale restaurant row is along José Domingo Cañas, with venues like *Solar de Sancho Panza* (☎ 2251413), Cañas 982, which specializes in Spanish cuisine. Another excellent choice is *Walhalla* (☎ 2098492), Campo de Deportes

329, corner of Cañas, with moderately priced Swiss food in attractive surroundings, with excellent service.

So wildly popular that reservations are essential even on weeknights, the distractingly noisy and Canadian-run *Santa Fe* (☎ 2151091), Avenida Las Condes 10690 in Vitacura, features well-prepared Tex-Mex specialties like fajitas, enchiladas and burritos. The salsas are milder than one would find in the North American borderlands, but given the size of the portions, the US$10 to $15 entrees are still good value.

ENTERTAINMENT
Santiago's main nightlife districts are Barrio Bellavista, Providencia's Avenida Suecia, and Plaza Ñuñoa, though other venues are scattered throughout the city.

Dance Clubs
Tadeo's, Lagarrigue 282 in Bellavista, has a spacious dance floor, with a crowd in the mid-20s range; its most notable recent event was the Fiesta del Preservativo (Condom Festival). Also in Bellavista, at Pío Nono 430, *Discoteca Subb* specializes in punk-style bands.

One of Santiago's most-fashionable discos is the techno-pop *Oz* (☎ 7377066), in a converted warehouse at Chucre Manzur 6, a cul-de-sac just off Antonia López de Bello in Bellavista, but collects a hefty cover charge. Its Providencia counterpart, though a bit cheaper, is *Kasbba* (☎ 2317419) at Suecia 081 (Metro: Los Leones).

Nightclubs
Dating from 1879, *Confitería Las Torres* (☎ 6986220) at Alameda 1570 (Metro: Los Héroes) reinforces its turn-of-the-century atmosphere, complete with spectacular woodwork, with live tango on weekends. The stage set features enormous blowups of Argentine tango legend Carlos Gardel, while the walls are lined with photographs of Chilean presidents – perhaps the only place in the world where portraits of Allende and Pinochet hang side by side.

The food is good but expensive, and the service excellent.

Los Adobes de Argomedo (☎ 2222104), Argomedo 411, is a gaudy pseudo-folkloric restaurant-nightclub with stereotypical entertainment, but the Chilean food is good and varied. Expect to pay around US$25 per person, with wine. Although it is very large, reservations are a good idea.

Music & Theater

Santiago has numerous performing arts venues for both music and drama. Most prestigious is the *Teatro Municipal* (☎ 633-2804), Agustinas 749, with offerings from classical to popular. The box office is open 10 am to 7 pm weekdays, 10 am to 2 pm weekends, but since members have priority, seats can be hard to come by.

The *Teatro Universidad de Chile* (☎ 6345295), Baquedano 043 in Providencia, presents a fall season of ballet, orchestral and chamber music. Admission prices range from US$2.50 for standing room to US$19 for the best seats; season ticket packages are also available. Another notable Providencia venue is the *Teatro Oriente* (☎ 2321360), on Pedro de Valdivia between Providencia and Andrés Bello; the ticket office is at Avenida 11 de Septiembre 2214, Oficina 66.

The well-established *Teatro La Comedia* (☎ 6391523) offers contemporary dramatic presentations at Merced 349, near Cerro Santa Lucía, Thursday through Sunday. *Teatro Esmeralda* (☎ 7774189), across the Alameda at San Diego 1035, specializes in classics like Shakespeare. Other downtown venues include the Universidad de Chile's Sala Agustín Sire (☎ 6965142) at Morandé 750; the *Teatro Casa Amarilla* (☎ 672-0347) in the Centro Cultural Mapocho at Balmaceda 1301; the *Teatro Estación Mapocho* (☎ 7356046) at the same address; and the *Sala Antonio Varas* (☎ 6961200) at Morandé 25.

More known for experimental theater, Barrio Bellavista is home to companies like *Teatro El Conventillo* (☎ 7774164) at Bellavista 173, *Teatro Taller* (☎ 235-1678) at Lagarrigue 191, *Teatro Bellavista*

(☎ 7356264) at Dardignac 0110, and *Teatro La Feria* (☎ 7377371) at Crucero Exéter 0250.

In summer, there is an inexpensive open-air theater program at *Parque Manuel Rodríguez*, south of Plaza Baquedano, in Providencia. The *Teatro de la Universidad Católica* (☎ 2055652), Jorge Washington 24, gets much of the credit for Plaza Ñuñoa's recent renaissance; nearby is the *Sala Plaza Ñuñoa* (☎ 2096094), Jorge Washington 50.

Pubs

The numerous bars clustered around Avenida Suecia and General Holley (Metro: Los Leones) in Providencia have adopted the North American custom of happy hour (two drinks for the price of one), even until midnight in some cases, and serve decent if unexceptional food. Nearly all have live music, mostly but by no means exclusively cover versions of international hits. Among them are *Brannigans* (☎ 2325172) at Suecia 035, the *Old Boston Pub* (☎ 231-5169) at General Holley 2291, Australian-run *Boomerang* (☎ 3345457) at General Holley 2285, *Holley's Pub* just across the street, *Mister Ed* (☎ 2312624) at Suecia 0152, and the nostalgic *Beatles Pub* (☎ 2770556) at Suecia 0188.

More original than its nearby rivals, *La Calle del Delfín Verde* (☎ 3345094), Suecia 0180, features live jazz, and specializes in vegetarian meals and non-beef meats such as chicken and pork. Across Avenida Providencia, waiters in bolo ties serve reasonably priced beer (including Guinness on tap) and respectable food at the *Electric Cowboy* (☎ 2317225), Guardia Vieja 35, which features live rockabilly music on weekends.

Bellavista's *La Casa en el Aire* (☎ 735-6680), Antonia López de Bello 0125, has theater, poetry and live music. Across the street at Antonia López de Bello 0124, *Altazor* also has live music.

One of Santiago's liveliest, most informal bars is *Bar Berri* (☎ 6384734), Rosal 321 near Cerro Santa Lucía; it also has good, inexpensive lunches. *Nichola's Pub*

(☎ 2460277), a neighborhood spot at Avenida Apoquindo 3371 in Las Condes, has the cheapest pisco sours in town. A nameless bar at Irrarázaval 3442, just west of Plaza Ñuñoa, features excellent live rock bands on the way up.

Cinemas

Commercial Cinemas Santiago's commercial cinema district is along Paseo Huérfanos and nearby side streets, where many former large theaters now have two or three screens showing different films. There are also venues in suburban comunas like Providencia and Vitacura. Most cinemas have half-price discounts on Wednesdays.

Teatro Apoquindo
    Apoquindo 3364, Las Condes
    (☎ 2313560)
Cine Central
    Huérfanos 930 (☎ 6333555)
Cine El Golf
    Apoquindo 3368, Las Condes
    (☎ 2313485)
Gran Palace
    Huérfanos 1176 (☎ 6960082)
Cine Huelen
    Huérfanos 779 (☎ 6331603)
Cine Huérfanos
    Huérfanos 930 (☎ 6336707)
Cine Imperio
    Estado 235 (☎ 6397960)
Las Condes
    Apoquindo & Noruega, Las Condes
    (☎ 2208816)
Cine Lido
    Huérfanos 680 (☎ 6330797)
Lo Castillo
    Candelaria Goyenechea 3820, Vitacura
    (☎ 2421342)
Teatro Oriente
    Pedro de Valdivia 099, Providencia
    (☎ 2317151)
Cine Rex
    Huérfanos 735 (☎ 6331144)
Cine Río
    Monjitas 743 (☎ 6333550)

Art Cinemas For film cycles and unconventional movies, the following cinemas are the best bets. These also usually have half-price discounts on Wednesdays.

Cine Alameda
    Alameda 139 (☎ 6392479)
Centro de Extensión de la Universidad Católica
    Alameda 390 (☎ 6351994)
Cine El Biógrafo
    Lastarria 181 (☎ 6334435)
Cine Normandie
    Tarapacá 1181 (☎ 6972979)
Cine Tobalaba
    Providencia 2563, Providencia
    (☎ 2316630)

SPECTATOR SPORTS

Soccer

Santiago has several first-division soccer teams. Major matches usually take place at the Estadio Nacional, at the corner of Avenida Grecia and Marathon in Ñuñoa. For tickets, contact the following teams.

Colo Colo
    Cienfuegos 41
    (☎ 6952251, 6951094)
Universidad Católica
    Andrés Bello 2782, Providencia
    (☎ 2312777)
Universidad de Chile
    Campo de Deportes 565, Ñuñoa
    (☎ 2392793)

Horse Racing

Santiago has two racecourses, which are usually open weekends. The Hipódromo Chile (☎ 7369276) is at Fermín Vivaceta, north of the Mapocho along Avenida Independencia in the comuna of Independencia, while the Club Hípico de Santiago (☎ 683-6535) is at Almirante Blanco Encalada 2540 (Metro: Unión Latinoamericana).

THINGS TO BUY

Popular artisanal products include lapis lazuli, black pottery and copperware, plus attractively carved wooden moai from Easter Island. The Feria Artesanal La Merced, Merced at MacIver, is a good place for an overview, but there are several well-stocked shops, including Chile Típico (☎ 6965504) at Moneda 1025, Local 149, Huimpalay (☎ 6721395) at Huérfanos 1162, and Claustro del 900 (☎ 6341800), located in an old convent at Santa Victoria 329, near Avenida Portugal.

Bellavista is a popular area for crafts, both at Pío Nono's weekend street fair and at shops like Artesanía Nehuen (☎ 777-7367), Dardignac 59, which has a wide selection of materials from throughout the country and will pick up customers at their hotels. Nearby is the Cooperativa Almacén Campesina (☎ 7372117), Purísima 303.

Several shops in the area specialize in lapis lazuli jewelry, including Lapiz Lazuli at Pío Nono 3, and Lapiz Lazuli House at Bellavista 016. For antiques, try Arte del Mundo (☎ 7352507) at Dardignac 67.

Several readers have enjoyed the artisan's village at Los Graneros del Alba (☎ 2464360), Avenida Apoquindo 9085 in Las Condes. In addition to Santiago's largest crafts selection, imported from throughout the country, the market, popularly known as 'Los Dominicos' after the nearby convent, has good food for a variety of budgets, and often has music and dancing on weekends. Among possible purchases are copperware, huaso horsegear, furniture, sculpture, jewelry and alpaca woolens. Los Dominicos is open 11 am to 7.30 pm daily all year. The quickest way to get there is to take the Metro to the end of Línea 1 at Escuela Militar and then catch a bus out Avenida Apoquindo, but it's also possible to catch bus No 327 from Avenida Providencia, No 344 from the Alameda or Avenida Providencia, No 229 from Catedral or Compañía, or No 326 from Alameda and Miraflores.

Another convenient market, open in summer only, is the daily crafts market on the north side of Avenida Providencia, at the exit from the Pedro de Valdivia Metro station.

In the suburban comuna of Lo Barnechea, the Feria San Enrique features antiques and bric-a-brac, art work and outstanding crafts with a minimum of kitsch, and also sponsors free folkloric music and dance presentations by groups like the Universidad de Chile's Ballet Folklórico – for current information, contact the Corporación Cultural de Lo Barnechea (☎ 243-4758). The crafts fair proper starts around 11.30 am Sundays, from October through December only. From San Pablo or Compañía in downtown Santiago, or from Avenida Providencia, take bus No 203, 205 or 206.

Chileans themselves flock to modern shopping centers, including the Mall Panorámico (☎ 2332244) at the corner of Avenida 11 de Septiembre and Ricardo Lyon in Providencia (Metro: Pedro de Valdivia or Los Leones); Parque Arauco (☎ 2420601) at Avenida Kennedy 5413, Las Condes; and Alto Las Condes, Avenida Kennedy 9001.

GETTING THERE & AWAY

Given Chile's 'crazy geography,' Santiago is an unavoidable reality – nearly every visitor either arrives at the capital or passes through here at one time or another.

Air

International Most major international airlines have offices or representatives in Santiago. The following list includes the most important ones:

Aeroflot
 Guardia Vieja 255
 10th floor
 Providencia
 (☎ 3310244, fax 3310248)
Aerolíneas Argentinas
 Moneda 756
 (☎ 6393922)
Aero Perú
 Fidel Oteíza 1953, 5th floor
 Providencia
 (☎ 2742023, fax 2746505)
Air France
 Alcántara 44, 6th floor, Las Condes
 (☎ 3620140, fax 3620362)
Air New Zealand
 Andrés de Fuenzalida 17, Oficina 62
 Providencia
 (☎ 6983338, fax 6994053)
Alitalia
 Alameda 949, Oficina 1001
 (☎ 6983338, fax 6994053)
American Airlines
 Huérfanos 1199
 (☎ 6790000, fax 6723214)
 Avenida El Bosque Norte 0107
 Local 11, Las Condes
 (☎ 3344746, fax 2460945)

Avianca
    Moneda 1140, 6th floor
    (☎ 6954105, fax 6731341)
    Santa Magdalena 116, Local 106
    Providencia
    (☎ 2316646, fax 2318306)
British Airways
    Isidora Goyenechea 2934, Oficina 302
    Las Condes
    (☎ 2329560, fax 2327858)
Canadian Airlines International
    Ebro 2740, Oficina 302, Las Condes
    (☎ 2327111, fax 2311811)
Cubana de Aviación
    Fidel Oteíza 1971, Oficina 201, Providencia
    (☎ 2741819, fax 2748207)
Iberia
    Bandera 206, 8th floor
    (☎ 6981716, fax 6969479)
KLM
    San Sebastián 2839, Oficina 202
    Las Condes
    (☎ 2330991, fax 2330483)
LanChile
    Agustinas 640
    (☎ 6323442, fax 6381729)
    Pedro de Valdivia Norte 0139, Providencia
    (☎ 2323448)
Líneas Aéreas de Costa Rica (Lacsa)
    Fidel Oteíza 1921, Providencia
    (☎ 2097477, fax 2096480)
Líneas Aéreas Paraguayas (Lapsa)
    Moneda 970, 16th floor
    (☎ 6301679, 6901155)
Lloyd Aéreo Boliviano (LAB)
    Moneda 1170
    (☎ 6712334, fax 6711421)
Lufthansa
    Moneda 970, 16th floor
    (☎ 6301655, fax 6301636)
Northwest
    Avenida 11 de Septiembre 2155, Torre B
    Oficina 1204, Providencia
    (☎ 2334343, fax 2334766)
Pluna
    Alameda 949, Oficina 1601
    (☎ 6968400, fax 6965179)
SAS
    Avenida Suecia 0119, Oficina 705
    Providencia
    (☎ 2333585, fax 2335283)
Saeta
    Moneda 970, 16th floor
    (☎ 6301675, fax 6989868)
Swissair
    Paseo Estado 10, 15th floor
    (☎ 6337014/5/6/7, fax 6337018)

United Airlines
    Tenderini 171
    (☎ 6320279, fax 6320189)
    El Bosque Norte 0177, 19th floor
    Las Condes
    (☎ 3320000, fax 3320299)
Varig
    Miraflores 162
    (☎ 6930999, fax 6930928)
Viasa
    Agustinas 1141, 6th floor
    (☎ 6982401)

Domestic LanChile, Ladeco and National
are the main domestic carriers. LanChile
has daily northbound flights to Antofagasta, Iquique and Arica, and southbound
flights to Puerto Montt and Punta Arenas,
plus some intermediate stops. They also fly
about six days a week to Calama, and two
or three times weekly to Easter Island.

Ladeco has daily flights to La Serena,
Antofagasta, Calama, Iquique, Arica,
Puerto Montt and Punta Arenas. They also
have less frequent flights to Temuco, Valdivia, Osorno and Balmaceda/Coihaique.
National, which also has a limited schedule
of international flights, serves the same
destinations but less frequently than the
other carriers.

Alta, flying out of Aeropuerto Los Cerrillos, generally operates smaller planes to
destinations not served by other airlines.
Lassa and Transportes Aéreos Robinson
Crusoe are air-taxi services to the Juan Fernández archipelago only.

Alta
    Las Urbinas 030, Providencia
    (☎ 2441777, fax 2441780)
Ladeco
    Huérfanos 1157
    (☎ 6395053, fax 6338343)
Lassa
    Avenida Larraín 7941
    La Reina
    (☎ 2734354/5209, fax 2734309)
National Airlines
    Huérfanos 885 (☎ 6399012)
    Pedro de Valdivia 041, Providencia
    (☎ 2520300, fax 2520164)
Transportes Aéreos Robinson Crusoe
    Monumento 2570, Maipú
    (☎ 5313772)

Sample domestic airfares are listed below; LanChile and Ladeco have comparable prices. National fares are slightly cheaper.

Antofagasta	US$192
Arica	US$225
Calama	US$215
Concepción	US$90
Copiapó	US$144
Coihaique	US$205
Iquique	US$219
La Serena	US$111
Puerto Montt	US$158
Punta Arenas	US$292
Temuco	US$128

Bus

Santiago has four main bus terminals. Since closure of the dilapidated Terminal de Buses Norte, most northbound long-distance services now use the rejuvenated Terminal San Borja (Metro: Estación Central), Alameda 3250, whose inconspicuous access is via the market alongside the main railway station. All services are likely to be in flux as companies relocate to better facilities.

Tur-Bus and Pullman Bus, however, use the Terminal de Buses Alameda at the corner of Alameda and Jotabeche (Metro: Universidad de Santiago), while buses for Valparaíso/Viña del Mar and many southbound destinations leave from the adjacent Terminal de Buses Santiago (also known as Terminal de Buses Sur), Alameda 3800 between Los Muermos and Ruiz Tagle.

Some northbound buses also leave from Terminal Los Héroes, on Tucapel Jiménez near the Alameda, where some long-distance buses from Terminal Santiago make an additional stop for passengers.

Domestic Fares can vary dramatically among companies, so explore several possibilities. Discounts are common outside the peak summer season, and bargaining may even be possible. For long journeys, especially to the desert north, consider a *salón cama* bus, which has reclining sleeperette seats with foot-rests, calf-rests and extra legroom. See the table for sample fares and journey times from Santiago.

Companies serving northern destinations from Terminal San Borja include:

Buses Evans (☎ 6985953)
  to Arica and intermediate points along
  the Panamericana
Buses Ligua (☎ 6987339)
  to La Ligua

Sample Bus Routes from Santiago

Destination	Time/hours	Pullman	Salón Cama
Antofagasta	18	US$40	
Arica	28	US$50	
Castro	19	US$27	US$45
Chillán	6	US$10	
Concepción	8	US$11	
Copiapó	11	US$25	
Iquique	26	US$45	US$63
La Serena	7	US$17	US$25
Osorno	14	US$19	US$37
Puerto Montt	16	US$21	US$40
Puerto Varas	15	US$19	
Punta Arenas	60	US$100	
Temuco	11	US$14	US$29
Valdivia	13	US$16	US$35
Valparaíso	2	US$3.50	
Villarrica	13	US$19	US$33
Viña del Mar	2	US$3.50	

Carmelita (☎ 6955230)
    to Coquimbo, La Serena, Antofagasta,
    Iquique and Arica
Combarbalá (6960313)
    to various parts of the Norte Chico
Fénix (☎ 7763253)
    to Arica and intermediate
    points
Flota Barrios (☎ 7760665)
    to Valparaíso/Viña del Mar; north
    to Arica and intermediate points
Géminis (☎ 6972132)
    to Arica and intermediate points
Lasval (☎ 6721817)
    to the Norte Chico
Los Corsarios (☎ 6963912)
    to Los Vilos and La Serena
Los Diamantes de Elqui (☎ 6724415)
    to Los Vilos, La Serena and Copiapó
Nueva Transmar (☎ 6995551)
    to beach resorts from Valparaíso north
Pullman Bus/Fichtur (☎ 6968915)
    to Arica and intermediates
Ramos Cholele (☎ 6717388)
    to Iquique and Arica
Tas Choapa (☎ 7794694)
    to Los Vilos, Copiapó and inter-
    mediate points
Vía Choapa (☎ 6980922)
    to the Norte Chico

Companies serving northern and southern
destinations from Terminal Los Héroes
include:

Cruz del Sur (☎ 6969324/5)
    to Los Lagos and Chiloé
Fénix (☎ 6969089)
    to Arica and intermediate points
Lasval (☎ 6724904)
    to the Norte Chico
Libac (☎ 6985974)
    to Coquimbo, La Serena, Vallenar
    and Calama
Los Diamantes de Elqui (☎ 6969321)
    to Los Vilos, La Serena and Copiapó
Tramaca (☎ 6969839)
    to Antofagasta, Calama, Arica and
    intermediate points

Buses serving various destinations from
the smaller Terminal de Buses Alameda,
Alameda 3750, at the southern exit from
the Universidad de Santiago Metro station,
include:

Pullman Bus (☎ 6985559)
    to Arica and intermediate points north-
    bound; south to Curicó; Valparaíso/Viña
    del Mar
Tur-Bus (☎ 7780808)
    to destinations along the Panamericana,
    from Arica to Puerto Montt; Valparaíso/
    Viña del Mar

Companies serving southern and some
northern destinations from the Terminal de
Buses Santiago (☎ 7791385) include:

Bus Norte (☎ 7795433)
    to southern Los Lagos and Punta Arenas
Buses Jac (☎ 7761582)
    to Temuco, Villarrica and Pucón
Buses Lit (☎ 7795710)
    to Los Vilos, Coquimbo and La Serena
Cruz del Sur (☎ 7790607)
    to Los Lagos and Chiloé
Fénix (☎ 7794648)
    to Los Angeles, Angol, Valdivia and inter-
    mediate points
Inter Sur (☎ 7796312)
    to many destinations in the Los Lagos
    region
Longitudinal Sur (☎ 7795856)
    to Temuco and Valdivia
Pullman Lit (☎ 5217198)
    to the southern mainland and nearly all
    coastal resorts
Tas Choapa (☎ 7794694)
    to Chillán, Concepción/Talcahuano,
    Temuco, Puerto Montt and intermediate
    stops on the Panamericana
Transbus (☎ 7798649)
    to Rancagua, Talca, Chillán and Concepción
Turibüs (☎ 7791377)
    to southern Los Lagos and Punta Arenas
Vía Tur (☎ 7793839)
    to Chillán and mainland points south
Varmontt (☎ 2313505)
    to southern Los Lagos

International Most international buses
depart from Terminal de Buses Santiago.
There are direct buses to every country on
the continent except the Guianas and
Bolivia, but only masochists are likely to
attempt the 4½- to 10-day marathons to
destinations like Quito, Ecuador (US$110),
Bogotá, Colombia (US$160) and Caracas,
Venezuela (US$200). Tepsa (☎ 7795263)

and Ormeño (☎ 7793443) cover these northern routes, with stops in Lima, Peru (US$88), about the longest trip any traveler is likely to undertake.

Argentina is the most frequent destination; the city of Mendoza has a much wider selection of buses and destinations within Argentina than is available from Santiago. Lines that cross the Andes to Mendoza (seven hours, US$25) and Buenos Aires (18 hours, US$65) include Ahumada (☎ 7795243; also at Terminal Los Héroes, ☎ 6969798), Fénix (☎ 7763253), Nueva O'Higgins San Martín (☎ 7795727), TAC (☎ 7796920) and Cata (☎ 7793660).

Chile Bus (☎ 6980412) goes to Mendoza; São Paulo, Brazil (72 hours, US$115) and intermediates, while Pluma (☎ 7796054) goes to Mendoza; Montevideo, Uruguay (US$95, 24 hours); Asunción, Paraguay (30 hours) and Brazilian destinations. Tas Choapa (☎ 7794925) serves Mendoza, Córdoba (15 hours, US$57), Buenos Aires (US$64), Montevideo (US$70, 15½ hours) and Bariloche (21 hours, US$36).

Igi Llaima (☎ 7791751) and Buses Jac (☎ 7761582) go to Junín de los Andes, San Martín de Los Andes and Neuquén via Temuco (summer only). To Córdoba, Buenos Aires and Brazil, try also Chevalier (☎ 7796054).

From Terminal Santiago, Coitram (☎ 7761891), Chi-Ar Internacional (☎ 696-5694) and Nevada (☎ 7764116) run taxi colectivos to Mendoza, which are only slightly more expensive (about US$28) and much quicker than buses – and drivers may stop on request for photo opportunities on the spectacular Andean crossing. Prices may be open to haggling outside the peak summer season.

Train
The Empresa de Ferrocarriles del Estado (EFE) runs passenger service to Concepción, Temuco, Valdivia, Osorno and Puerto Varas from the Estación Central (☎ 689-5199, 6985401), Alameda 3322 (Metro: Estación Central). Only in summer is there service south of Temuco. Station hours are daily from 7 am to 11 pm.

If the Estación Central is inconvenient, book passage at the Venta de Pasajes (☎ 6398247) in the Galería Libertador, Alameda 853, Local 21. It's open weekdays 8.30 am to 1 pm, Saturday 9 am to 1 pm. There is another office (☎ 2282983) at the Galería Comercial Sur, Local 25, at the Escuela Militar Metro station, which keeps the same hours. For details of fares and timetables, see the Getting Around chapter.

EFE also runs frequent commuter service between Santiago and Rancagua, capital of Region VI.

GETTING AROUND
To/From the Airport
Aeropuerto Internacional Arturo Merino Benítez (☎ 6019001, 6019709), which also serves as the airport for most domestic flights, is in Pudahuel, 26 km west of downtown Santiago. Note that, although Línea 1 of the Metro ends at Pudahuel, the Metro does *not* reach the airport.

The cheapest transportation to the airport, Centropuerto (☎ 6019883) buses charge only US$1.60 from Plazoleta Los Héroes, outside the Los Héroes Metro station, between 6.05 am and 10.30 pm, there are 40 departures daily. Slightly more expensive Tour Express (☎ 6717380), Moneda 1529 near San Martín, has 44 departures daily between 5.30 am and 10 pm. Buses from Pudahuel leave from the front of the international terminal, and will drop you at the city terminal or just about anywhere along the route. The fare is US$2 one way, US$3.50 roundtrip.

Minibuses belonging to Shuttle (☎ 635-3030), Navett (☎ 6956868) or Transfer (☎ 2045840) will transport passengers door-to-door between the airport and any part of Santiago for US$7.50. Departing passengers should call the day before their flight if possible, but they will sometimes pick up passengers on short notice. Due to contract complications, some of these shuttle services were in question at press time, and may or may not continue to operate.

LanChile passengers can check their bags at the airline's office at Parque Arauco shopping center, Avenida Kennedy 5413, Las Condes, up to four hours before flight time, then catch Navett to the airport.

Taxi fares are negotiable; a cab to or from downtown can cost anywhere from about US$10 (if your Spanish is good) to US$25, but may be shared.

Bus

Santiago's buses go everywhere cheaply, but it takes a while to learn the system – check the destination signs in their windows or ask other passengers waiting at the stop. Many buses now have signed, fixed stops, especially in the downtown area, but that doesn't necessarily mean they won't stop at other points. Fares vary slightly depending on the bus, but all are within a few cents of US$0.40 per trip; hang on to your ticket, since inspectors may ask for it.

Taxi Colectivo

Taxi colectivos are, in effect, five-passenger buses on fixed routes. They are quicker and more comfortable than most buses and not much more expensive – about US$0.75 within Santiago city limits, although some to outlying suburbs like Puente Alto are a bit dearer. Taxi colectivos resemble ordinary taxis, but have an illuminated roof sign indicating their destination and a placard in the window stating the fixed fare.

Taxi

Santiago has abundant metered taxis – black with yellow roofs. Fares vary, but it costs about US$0.65 to *bajar la bandera* ('drop the flag,' ie start the meter) and about US$0.15 per 200 meters. Most Santiago taxi drivers are very honest, courteous and helpful, but a few will take roundabout routes, and a handful have 'funny' meters.

There is also a system of radio taxis which can be slightly cheaper.

Car Rental

Santiago has dozens of car rental agencies, from internationally known franchises to lesser-known local companies that tend to be cheaper. For details of car rental rates,

see the Getting Around chapter. Many rental companies have airport offices at Pudahuel in addition to the city offices below:

Alamo
    Avenida 11 de Septiembre 2155, Oficina 1204, Providencia
    (☎ 2334343, fax 2334766)
American
    Antonio Varas 91, Oficina 206, Providencia
    (☎ /fax 2510704)
Atal
    Andrés Bello 1051, Providencia
    (☎ 2359222, fax 2360636)
Automóvil Club de Chile (Acchi)
    central office: Avenida Vitacura 8620, Vitacura
    (☎ 2125702, 2746261, fax 2295295)
    tourism & member services:
    Fidel Oteíza 1960
    (☎ 2253790)
Avis
    Guardia Vieja 255, Oficina 108, Providencia
    (☎ 3310121, fax 3310122)
Budget
    Francisco Bilbao 3028, Providencia
    (☎ 2049091)
Chilean
    Bellavista 0183, Providencia in Barrio Bellavista
    (☎ /fax 7376902)
Dollar
    Santa Magdalena 163, Providencia
Ervo
    Francisco Bilbao 2846, Providencia
    (☎ 2234117)
First
    Rancagua 0514, Providencia
    (☎ 2256328)
Hertz
    Andrés Bello 1469, Providencia
    (☎ 2259666, fax 2360252)
Lys
    Agustinas 535 (☎ 6337600)
Trocal
    Manquehue Norte 600, Oficina 201-C
    Las Condes
    (☎ 2203070)

Metro

Carrying up to 660,000 passengers daily, Santiago's Metro system has two functioning lines and another that should open before the next edition of this book. For destinations along these lines, it's far

SANTIAGO

quicker than city buses, which must contend with the capital's narrow, congested streets. The Metro operates Monday to Saturday 6.30 am to 10.30 pm, Sundays and holidays 8 am to 10.30 pm. Trains are clean, quiet and frequent, but at most hours it's very difficult to get a seat.

Signs on station platforms indicate the direction in which the trains are heading. On east-west Línea 1, 'Dirección Las Condes' heads toward Escuela Militar station in the wealthy eastern suburbs, while 'Dirección Pudahuel' goes to San Pablo (it does *not* reach the international airport). On the north-south Línea 2, 'Dirección Centro' reaches Puente Cal y Canto station a few blocks north of the Plaza de Armas, while 'Dirección La Cisterna' heads towards the southern comuna of Lo Ovalle. Los Héroes, beneath the Alameda, is the only transfer station between these two lines. Línea 5 (planners have apparently decided to skip Líneas 3 and 4) will use Baquedano (on Línea 1) as a transfer station, passing through Ñuñoa and Macul en route to the eastern comuna of La Florida.

Fares vary slightly depending on the time of day and the line, but range from about US$0.25 to US$0.40 Tickets can be purchased from agents at each station; a convenient *boleto inteligente* or *boleto valor* (multi-trip ticket) is also available at a slight discount. Charges are according to the following schedule; note that weekends and holidays are always middle hours.

Hora alta	Hora media	Hora baja
(peak)	(middle)	(low)
7.15-9 am	9 am-6 pm	6-7.15 am
6-7.30 pm	7.30-9 pm	9-10.30 pm

Tickets have a magnetic strip on the back. After slipping your ticket into a slot, pass through the turnstile and continue to the platform; your ticket is not returned unless it's a boleto inteligente with remaining value (several individuals may use the same boleto inteligente by simply passing it back across the turnstile). No ticket is necessary to exit the system.

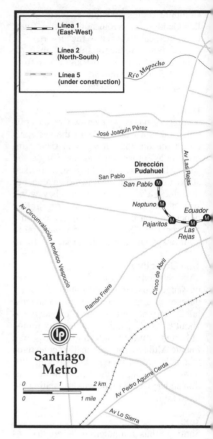

Línea 1 (East-West)

Línea 2 (North-South)

Línea 5 (under construction)

Río Mapocho

José Joaquín Pérez

Dirección Pudahuel

San Pablo

San Pablo Ⓜ

Av Las Rejas

Neptuno Ⓜ

Ecuador

Pajaritos Ⓜ ⒽⓂ

Las Rejas

Av Circunvalación Américo Vespucio

Cinco de Abril

Ramón Freire

Santiago Metro

0   1   2 km
0   .5   1 mile

Av Pedro Aguirre Cerda

Av Lo Sierra

Around Santiago

There are many worthwhile sights outside the capital proper but still within the Región Metropolitana, as well as others outside the region but near enough for reasonable day trips.

TEMPLO VOTIVO DE MAIPU

In the southwestern suburban comuna of Maipú, this monstrous manifestation of patriotic and ecclesiastical hubris is a

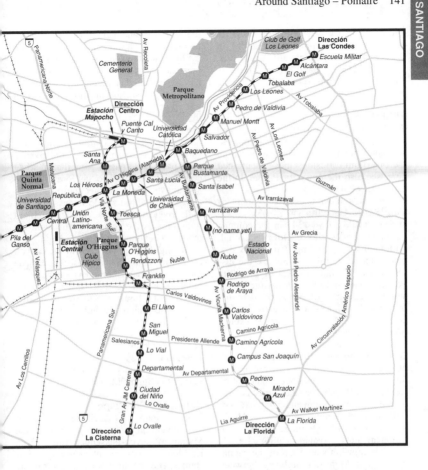

10-story concrete bunker that probably only a truly devout structural engineer could appreciate, though it achieves partial redemption through its stained glass windows. The attached **Museo del Carmen** contains exhibits on religious history and customs, while the Templo's grounds contain late colonial ruins which are fenced off because of earthquake damage.

The Templo is open to the public 8.30 am to 7.30 pm, while the Museo is open Saturday 4 to 8 pm, Sundays and holidays 11 am to 2 pm and 4 to 8 pm.

From the Alameda in Santiago, take any bus that says Templo. Taxi colectivos leave from the Alameda and Amunátegui.

POMAIRE

In this small, dusty village near Melipilla, southwest of Santiago, skilled potters spend their days at their wheels to produce unique and remarkably inexpensive ceramics – a punchbowl with half a dozen cups, for instance, costs only about US$10. Unfortunately, most items are too large and fragile for most travelers to take home, but it's still worth a day trip from the capital for a tour and a small souvenir. For lunch, try *Restaurant San Antonio* (☎ 8312168), at the corner of San Antonio and Arturo Prat.

From Santiago, take Buses Melipilla (☎ 7762060) from Terminal San Borja, Alameda 3250.

WINERIES

While Santiago's growth has displaced many of the wineries that once surrounded the capital, it has spared others, even within the city limits. Besides those mentioned here, see also the entry for Pirque, in the Cajón del Maipo.

Santiago's most accessible winery is **Viña Santa Carolina** (☎ 2380367/2855) at Rodrigo de Araya 1341 in the comuna of Macul, near the Estadio Nacional. Although the sprawling capital has displaced the vineyards themselves, the historical *casco* (main house) of the Julio Pereira estate and the *bodegas* (cellars or storehouses) are still here, open to the public with 24 hours' advance notice. Taxi colectivos out Avenida Vicuña Mackenna pass within easy walking distance.

Also within Santiago's city limits, **Viña Cousiño Macul** is in the comuna of Macul, but the grounds themselves are not open to the public. Tours of the bodegas take place weekdays at 11 am; the sales office is open weekdays 9 am to 1 pm and 2 to 6 pm, Saturdays 9 am to 1 pm only. Take bus No 39 or 391 from Santo Domingo out Américo Vespucio Sur to Avenida Quilín 7100.

Thirty-four km southwest of the capital on the old Melipilla highway between Peñaflor and Talagante, the grounds and buildings of **Viña Undurraga** (☎ 817-2308) are open to the public weekdays from 9.30 am to noon and 2 to 4 pm. Buses Peñaflor (☎ 7761025) covers this route from the Terminal San Borja, Alameda 3250; be sure to take the smaller Talagante micro rather than the larger bus to Melipilla.

CAJON DEL MAIPO

Southeast of the capital, easily accessible by public transportation, the Cajón del Maipo (canyon of the Río Maipo) is one of the main weekend recreation areas for Santiaguinos. Camping, hiking, climbing, cycling, whitewater rafting, skiing and other activities are all possible. The area has experienced a recent environmental controversy over the location of a natural gas pipeline from Argentina through the Cascada Las Animas, a private nature reserve.

Two main access routes climb the canyon: on the north side of the river, a good paved road passes from the suburban comuna of La Florida to San José de Maipo and above, while another narrower, less-traveled paved route follows the south side of the river from Puente Alto. The southern route crosses the river and joins with the other just beyond San José de Maipo.

Among the popular stops in the canyon are El Melocotón, San Alfonso, Cascada de Las Animas, San Gabriel (where the pavement ends and beyond which the main gravel road follows the Río Volcán, a tributary of the Maipo), El Volcán, Lo Valdés, Parque Nacional El Morado and rustic thermal baths at Baños Morales and Termas de Colina.

Regular buses to San José de Maipo leave about every half hour from the Parque O'Higgins Metro station.

Rafting the Río Maipo

From September to April, several adventure travel companies run descents of the Maipo in seven-passenger rafts, from El Melocotón to Guayacán/Parque Los Héroes. The one-hour-plus descent, passing through Class III and IV rapids, costs about US$35 (US$45 with lunch), including transport to and from Santiago. Trips generally do not operate from mid-December to mid-January; for operators, see the list in the Facts for the Visitor chapter.

Pirque

One of the gateways to the Cajón, Pirque is an easygoing village just beyond Puente Alto. On weekends there is a crafts fair featuring leather workers, goldsmiths and silversmiths. Cyclists will find the paved but narrow route up the south bank of the

Maipo much less crowded and more pleasant than the north bank route.

Chile's largest winery, **Viña Concha y Toro** (☎ 8503168, 8500007) has spacious grounds in Pirque. Tours of the grounds and vats take place daily except Sunday from 10 am to 1 pm and 3 to 6 pm, but call ahead to be sure of a spot. At the end of the tour you can taste three different wines for about US$1.

About three km east of Concha y Toro, on the road up the south side of the Cajón, the *Wailea Coffee Store* has good sandwiches, kuchen and coffee. There is also a string of restaurants, all very popular on weekends.

Getting There & Away Buses from the corner of Tarapacá and Avenida Santa Rosa, three blocks south of the Santa Lucía Metro station, go to Puente Alto, where the No 14 bus goes on to Pirque. From Santiago's Plaza Italia (Metro: Baquedano), taxi colectivos to Puente Alto and Pirque cost about US$1.

Reserva Nacional Río Clarillo

One of the closest nature reserves to Santiago, 10,000-hectare Río Clarillo is a scenic tributary canyon of the Cajón del Maipo, 23 km from Pirque. Its primary attractions are the river and the forest, with sclerophyllous (hard-leafed) tree species unique to the area (though similar to those in other Mediterranean climates, like California's). In addition to abundant bird life, the endangered Chilean iguana also inhabits the reserve.

From Pirque, Buses LAC has hourly departures to within two km of the reserve. Bus No 32 ('El Principal') leaves every three hours or so from Calle Gandarillas, half a block from the Pirque's Plaza de Armas.

Lagunillas

Ranging from 2250 to 2580 meters above sea level, this small resort, 84 km southeast of Santiago via San José de Maipo, is a very modest counterpart to the region's other high-powered ski resorts. Accommodation

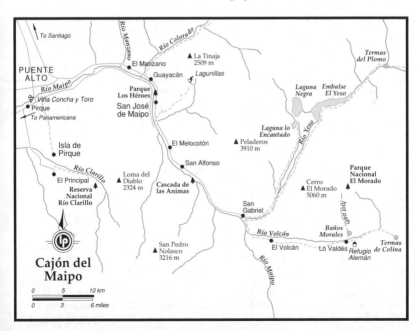

Cajón del Maipo

is available through the Club Andino de Chile (☎ 5528095), the Refugio Suizo (☎ 2055423) or in nearby San Alfonso, but it's also an easy day trip from the capital. Ask the Club Andino about transportation.

Cascada de las Animas

Near the village of San Alfonso, this private nature reserve arranges outings ranging from relaxing picnics, day trips and camping to more strenuous activities like hiking, horseback riding and rafting or kayaking. The Santiago office, Expediciones Las Cascadas (☎ 2519223, 232-7214) is at Orrego Luco 054, 2nd floor, Providencia.

Refugio Alemán

Overlooking the canyon from a southside perch above the Río Volcán, across from Baños Morales and surrounded by poplars, the Refugio Alemán (☎ 8501773 in Santiago) is a popular weekend destination throughout the year. Accommodation with full board costs US$53 per person; children to age seven pay half, while those two or younger stay free. Accommodation alone costs US$23, US$30 with breakfast, but travelers with their own sleeping bags can crash in the attic for US$11. The Refugio's restaurant also serves very fine meals separately for non-guests: US$7 for breakfast, US$10 for an elaborate onces of sandwiches, kuchen, ice cream, cookies and coffee, and US$12 for lunch or dinner.

Parque Nacional El Morado

Only 93 km from Santiago, this relatively small (3000 hectares) but very scenic park rewards visitors with views of 5060-meter Cerro El Morado from **Laguna El Morado**, a two-hour hike from the humble hot springs of **Baños Morales**. While it's a stiff climb at the beginning, the trail soon levels off; really motivated hikers can continue to the base of Glaciar El Morado, on the lower slopes of Cerro El Morado.

Conaf maintains a small Centro de Información at the park entrance, where rangers collect an admission charge of US$1.25 for adults, US$0.50 for children. Rental horses

are available for about US$5 per hour at Baños Morales, where there's also camping and simple accommodation.

Getting There & Away T-Arrpue (☎ 211-7165) runs weekend buses from Santiago's Plaza Italia directly to Baños Morales.

Termas de Colina

The road ends at this basic hot springs resort (☎ 7372844 in Santiago), 12 km above Lo Valdés. Buses Cordillera (☎ 737-6352) provides weekend transportation from Terminal San Borja, at Santa Rosa and Alameda, for US$11 roundtrip.

SKI RESORTS

Chile has acquired an international reputation among skiers, and Chile's best downhill skiing is to be found in the high cordillera of Middle Chile, primarily up the valley of the Río Mapocho beyond Farellones, and along Ruta 60 to Mendoza, Argentina. Most ski areas are above 3300 meters, and so have long runs, a long season and generally deep, dry snow. Snowboarders are increasingly welcome.

The season generally runs from June to early October. Most resorts adjust their rates from low season (mid-June to early July and mid-September to early October), to mid-season (mid-August to mid-September), to high season, the most expensive (early July to mid-August). For current conditions, check the English-language *Chip News* online; see the Online Services appendix.

El Colorado

One of the closest ski areas, only 45 km east of the capital and just beyond Farellones, El Colorado (☎ 2110426, fax 2207738) has over a dozen lifts climbing to 3333 meters above sea level, with a vertical drop of 903 meters. Daily lift tickets cost US$38, with discounts for children and seniors; season passes are also available.

For information in Santiago, contact Centro de Ski El Colorado (☎ 2463344, fax 2064078), Avenida Apoquindo 4900, Local 47/48 in Las Condes. There is lodging at

Refugio Manquimávida (☎ 2206879, fax 2295062 in season) for US$61 double with half-board.

La Parva

Only four km from Farellones, elevations on La Parva's 13 separate runs range from 2662 to 3630 meters (968 meters vertical drop). Accommodation is available at the *Hotel Condominio Nueva La Parva*; for the most current information, contact Centro de Ski La Parva (☎ 2332476, fax 2313233), San Sebastián 2874, Las Condes.

Valle Nevado

Another 14 km beyond Farellones, Valle Nevado is a well-planned, high-altitude ski area, ranging from 2805 to 3670 meters, with nine runs up to 1.7 km in length. Half-day lift tickets cost US$20 in low season; US$25 in high season, while full-day tickets run US$27 to US$31. Multi-day tickets are also available, but the savings is minimal. Rental equipment is available on site, and there's also a ski school.

At *Hotel Valle Nevado*, rates start at US$1092/1806 single/double per week in the low season and reach US$3122/4396 in the high season, including half-board and lift tickets. With full board, rates are US$1302/2226 in the low season, and US$3346/4844 in the high season. The *Hotel Puerta del Sol* is 20% to 30% cheaper, while *Hotel Tres Puntas* is another 15% to 20% cheaper, with half-board only.

Bus transport to and from the international airport at Pudahuel costs US$45 roundtrip; more expensive minibus, taxi and helicopter service are also available.

For bookings, contact Valle Nevado (☎ 2060027) at Gertrudis Echeñique 441, Las Condes.

Portillo

Known for its dry powder, Chile's most famous ski resort is the site of several downhill speed records. Altitudes range from 2590 to 3330 meters on its 11 runs, the longest of which is 1.4 km. Just a short distance from the Chilean customs post, on the trans-Andean highway to Mendoza (Argentina), Portillo is 152 km from Santiago.

Hotel Portillo is not cheap, with singles/doubles starting at US$778 per person for a week's stay in low season, rising as high as US$3780 for a suite; prices include all meals, eight days of lift tickets, with taxes (foreigners, however, are exempt from the 18% IVA. Lower-priced alternatives involve bunks and shared bath, but even those run US$626 per person in low season, US$810 in high season.

Ski facilities may or may not be open to non-guests, but lift tickets are in the US$35 daily range. Additional services include a ski school, baby sitters, sauna and massage, and the like. Meals are available in the hotel restaurant, which has superb views of Laguna del Inca. Moderately priced accommodation is available in the city of Los Andes, below the snow line, 69 km to the west.

In summer, the hotel charges around US$71/118 single/double, with breakfast. For more information contact the Centro de Ski Portillo (☎ 2313411, fax 2317164), Roger de Flor 2911, Las Condes.

Middle Chile

In addition to the Metropolitan Region of Santiago, the country's heartland consists of Regions V (Valparaíso), VI (O'Higgins), VII (Maule) and VIII (Biobío). Its most significant feature is the fertile central valley which is, at its widest, just 70 km between the Andean foothills and the coastal range. Only at the southern edge does the valley floor extend to the Pacific. Endowed with rich alluvial soils, a pleasant Mediterranean climate and Andean meltwater for irrigation, this is Chile's chief farming region, ideal for cereals, orchards and vineyards.

Middle Chile contains almost 75% of the country's population and most of its industry. Nearly a third live in the sprawling capital, but the region also includes the major port of Valparaíso and Chile's most famous resort, the 'garden city' of Viña del Mar. Copper mines dot the sierras of the Metropolitan, Valparaíso and O'Higgins regions, while just north of the Biobío, Concepción and its port of Talcahuano play an important role in the national economy. Throughout the region, the imposing Andean crest is never far out of sight, but the Los Libertadores tunnel northeast of Santiago is the only all-season crossing to Argentina.

Valparaíso & the Central Coast

Northwest of Santiago, Valparaíso and its scenic coastline play a dual role in Chile. Valparaíso is a vital port and one of South America's most distinctive urban areas, while Viña del Mar, a resort of international stature, and other coastal towns to the north are favorite summer playgrounds.

VALPARAISO

Growing spontaneously along the sea and up the surrounding coast range, Valparaíso – Valpo for short – more closely resembles a medieval European harbor than a 20th-century commercial port. Often called *La Perla del Pacífico* (Pearl of the Pacific), Chile's second-largest city occupies a narrow wave-cut terrace, overlooked by precipitous cliffs and hills covered by suburbs and shantytowns linked to the city center by meandering roads, footpaths that more closely resemble staircases and nearly vertical *ascensores* (funicular railways).

Built partly on landfill between the waterfront and the hills, the commercial center is no less distinctive, with sinuous cobbled streets, irregular intersections and landmark architecture. Parts of the city are not so clean as they might be, since many residents pay no garbage tax because their home values are so low, but other parts are improving rapidly. There is a prospect that some neglected older houses will be restored or remodeled as hotels or hostels.

History

Historians credit Juan de Saavedra, a lieutenant from Diego de Almagro's expedition whose troops met a supply ship from Peru in what is now the Bahía de Valparaíso in 1536, as the founder of the city. Despite Pedro de Valdivia's designation of the bay as the port of Santiago and the building of some churches, more than 2½ centuries passed before the Spanish crown established a *cabildo* (town council) in 1791. Not until 1802 did Valparaíso legally become a city.

Spanish mercantilism retarded Valparaíso's growth in colonial times, but after independence foreign merchants quickly established their presence. One visitor in 1822 remarked that Englishmen and North Americans so dominated the city that 'but

Middle Chile

for the mean and dirty appearance of the place, a stranger might almost fancy himself arrived at a British settlement.' Its commerce was disorderly but vigorous:

The whole space between the beach and custom-house was filled with goods and merchandise of various kinds – timber, boxes, iron-bars, barrels, bales, etc – all exposed without any method or arrangement in the open street. Interspersed among them were a number of mules, some standing with loaded, others with unloaded panniers; while the drivers, called peons, dressed in the characteristic garb of the country, made the place ring with their noisy shouts. Here and there porters were busied in carrying away packages; boatmen stood ready to importune you with incessant demands . . . .

Only a few months later, another visitor had similar impressions, noting that although 'even the governor's house and the custom-house are of poor appearance . . . all the symptoms of great increase of trade are visible in the many new erections for ware-houses.'

Valparaíso's population at independence was barely 5000, but the demand for Chilean wheat brought on by the California Gold Rush prompted such a boom that, shortly after mid-century, the city's population was about 55,000. Completion of the railroad from Santiago was a further boost and, by 1880, the population exceeded 100,000. As the first major port-of-call for ships around Cape Horn, the city had become a major commercial center for the entire Pacific coast and the hub of Chile's nascent banking industry.

The opening of the Panama Canal was a notable blow to Valparaíso's economy, as European shipping avoided the much longer and more arduous Cape Horn route. Furthermore, Chilean exports of mineral nitrates declined as Europeans found synthetic substitutes, indirectly affecting Valparaíso by further reducing maritime commerce in the region. The US Great Depression was a calamity, as demand for Chile's other mineral exports declined. Not until after WWII was there significant recovery, as the country began to industrialize.

Valparaíso remains less dependent on tourism than neighboring Viña del Mar, but many Chilean vacationers make brief excursions from nearby beach resorts. As capital of Region V, the city is an important administrative center. Its major industries are food processing and exporting the products of the mining and fruit-growing sectors. The port is presently undergoing a US$47 million expansion, but the city's congested location may still mean that some exports will be diverted north to Quintero and south to San Antonio. The navy's conspicuous presence is also an important factor in the economy.

Orientation

The city of Valparaíso, 120 km northwest of Santiago at the south end of the Bahía de Valparaíso, has an extraordinarily complicated layout that probably only a lifetime resident can completely fathom. In the congested commercial center, pinched between the port and the almost sheer hills, nearly all major streets parallel the shoreline, which curves north as it approaches Viña del Mar. Avenida Errázuriz runs the length of the waterfront, alongside the railway, before merging with Avenida España, the main road to Viña.

The focus of downtown is Plaza Sotomayor, near the port. Behind and above the downtown area, Valparaíso's many hills are a rabbit's warren of steep footpaths, zig-zag roads and blind alleys where even the best map sometimes fails the visitor. The best map currently available is Atlas de Chile's *Planos de Valparaíso, Viña del Mar, Reñaca y Concón* (1995), with a good street index, but it costs about US$6. The city map in Turistel's *Centro* volume is, however, much improved, and the municipal Departamento de Turismo's cheaper *Valparaíso: Ciudad Puerto* is suitable for short-term visitors.

Information

Tourist Offices Better tourist information is available in Viña del Mar, but Valparaíso's municipal Departamento de Turismo (☎ 251071/308), Condell 1490, is open weekdays 8.30 am to 2 pm and 3 to 5 pm. Its information kiosk on Muelle Prat (the pier), near Plaza Sotomayor, has friendly and well-informed personnel, distributes free but adequate city maps and sells slightly better ones. From mid-December to mid-March, it's open 10 am to 2 pm and 3 to 7 pm daily, but the rest of the year it's open Thursday through Sunday only. From October to March, there are also offices in the Terminal Rodoviario (the bus station; ☎ 213246) and on Plaza Victoria.

Consulates Foreign consuls may prefer to live in Viña del Mar, but they have to work in Valparaíso. The Argentine Consulate (☎ 213691) is at Blanco 1215, Oficina 1102; the Peruvian Consulate (☎ 253403) is one floor up at Oficina 1202. The British Consulate (☎ 256117) is at Blanco 725, Oficina 26.

Money Valparaíso's exchange houses include Cambios Gema at Esmeralda 940, Local 3, Inter Cambio on Plaza Sotomayor and Cambio Exprinter at Prat 895.

Post & Communications Valparaíso's area code is ☎ 32. Correos de Chile is on Prat at its junction with Plaza Sotomayor. CTC has long-distance telephone services at Esmeralda 1054, Pedro Montt 2023 and at the Terminal Rodoviario. Entel is at Condell 1495, Chilesat at Avenida Brasil 1456.

Cultural Centers The Centro Cultural Valparaíso is at Esmeralda 1083. A branch of the Instituto Chileno-Norteamericano de Cultura (☎ 256897) is nearby at Esmeralda 1061.

Medical Services Hospital Carlos van Buren (☎ 254074) is at Avenida Colón 2454, corner of San Ignacio.

Dangers & Annoyances Valparaíso's colorful hill neighborhoods have an unfortunate reputation for thieves and robbers – local people warn against any ostentatious display of wealth – but with the usual precautions these areas are safe enough, at least during daylight. Visitors to the area west of Plaza Sotomayor and even downtown have reported muggings, so be alert for suspicious characters and diversions. Exercise all reasonable caution, avoid poorly lit areas at night and if possible walk with a companion.

Valparaíso has Chile's highest rate of AIDS, associated in part with the sex industry of one of the continent's major ports.

Plaza Sotomayor

Facing the historic **Primera Zona Naval** (ex-Intendencia de Valparaíso), an impressive structure with a mansard roof, Plaza Sotomayor is the official heart of Valparaíso, its dignified statuary crowning a simple, unadorned **Monumento a los Héroes de Iquique**, a subterranean mausoleum paying tribute to Chile's naval martyrs of the War of the Pacific. In addition to Arturo Prat, there are tombs of lesser known figures whose Anglo surnames – Reynolds, Wilson and Irving – hint at the role that northern European immigrants have played in Chilean history.

Muelle Prat

This recently redeveloped pier, at the foot of Plaza Sotomayor, is a very lively place on weekends, with a good handicrafts market, the Feria de Artesanías. Several boats offer harbor tours for about US$1.50, but do not photograph any of the numerous Chilean naval vessels at anchor. For US$2, some boats take passengers all the way to Viña del Mar – a nice change of pace from the bus.

Plaza Matriz

If Plaza Sotomayor is the city's official heart, the Plaza Matriz is its historic core, directly up the hill from the Mercado Central, where the distinctive architecture of the hills starts to take shape. Its major landmark is the **Iglesia Matriz**, a national monument dating from 1842. This is the fourth church on the site since construction of the original chapel in 1559.

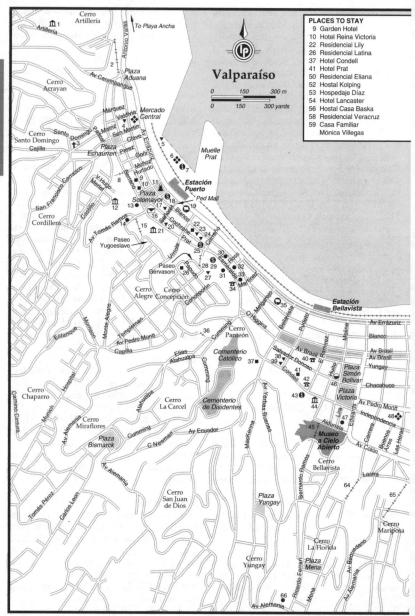

Valparaíso

0   150   300 m
0   150   300 yards

To Playa Ancha

PLACES TO STAY
9   Garden Hotel
10 Hotel Reina Victoria
22 Residencial Lily
26 Residencial Latina
37 Hotel Condell
41 Hotel Prat
50 Residencial Eliana
52 Hostal Kolping
53 Hospedaje Díaz
54 Hotel Lancaster
56 Hostal Casa Baska
58 Residencial Veracruz
59 Casa Familiar
      Mónica Villegas

MIDDLE CHILE

PLACES TO EAT
4 Los Porteños No 2
5 Bote Salvavidas
17 Valparaíso Eterno
20 La Rotonda
23 Bar Inglés
24 Mesón del Lord
27 Café Turri
38 Bambú
39 Pekín
55 Club Peruano

OTHER
1 Museo Naval y Marítimo
3 Iglesia Matriz
6 Feria de Artesanías
7 Departamento de Turismo Kiosk
11 Monumento a los Héroes de Iquique
12 Museo del Mar Lord Cochrane
13 Primera Zona Naval
14 Tribunales
16 Post Office

18 Inter Cambio
19 British Consulate
21 Palacio Baburizza (Museo de Bellas Artes)
25 Cambio Exprinter, Reloj Turri
29 Cambios Gema
30 Ladeco
31 LanChile
32 Instituto Chileno-Norteamericano
    de Cultura
33 Centro Cultural Valparaíso
34 CTC
35 Argentine & Peruvian Consulates
40 Chilesat
42 Entel
43 Municipalidad, Departamento
    de Turismo
44 Palacio Lyon (Museo de Historia Natural,
    Galería Municipal de Arte)
46 Buses La Porteña
47 Santiago Wanderers Offices
48 Mercado Artesanal Permanente
49 CTC

51 Cine Metroval
57 Terminal Rodoviario
66 La Sebastiana
    (Fundación Neruda)
69 Hospital Carlos van Buren
70 Comveq (Car Rental)

ASCENSORES
2 Ascensor Artillería
8 Ascensor Cordillera
15 Ascensor El Peral
28 Ascensor Concepción (Turri)
36 Ascensor Reina Victoria
45 Ascensor Espíritu Santo
60 Ascensor Barón
61 Ascensor Lecheros
62 Ascensor Larraín
63 Ascensor Polanco
64 Ascensor Florida
65 Ascensor Mariposa
67 Ascensor Monjas
68 Ascensor Cerro La Cruz

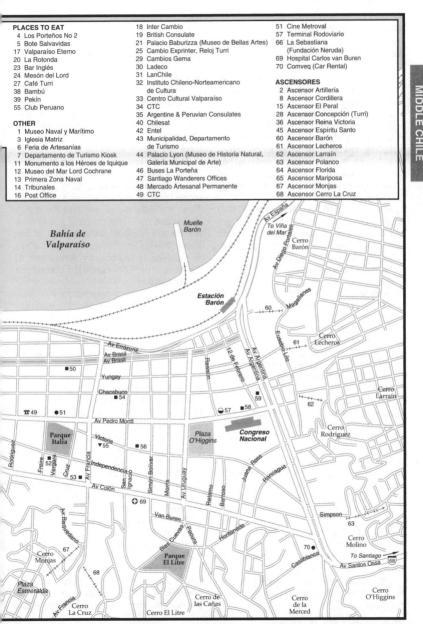

Palacio Lyon
(Museo de Historia Natural)

Once a private mansion, the neoclassical Palacio Lyon (1881) now houses Valparaíso's natural history museum, though the building merits a visit in its own right. Most of the large selection of natural history specimens are mediocre, but the upper exhibition halls compensate for this with outstanding displays on Chile's pre-Hispanic cultures and their environments, including dioramas of subsistence activities. There is also superb material on the oceans and their future, a subject of great importance to a maritime country like Chile.

At Condell 1546, the Museo (☎ 257441) is open Tuesday to Friday 10 am to 1 pm and 2 to 6 pm, Saturday 10 am to 6 pm, and Sunday and holidays 10 am to 1 pm only. Admission is about US$0.85, half that for children, but it's free Sundays.

Galería Municipal de Arte

In the basement of the Palacio Lyon, but with a separate entrance from the Museo de Historia Natural, the municipal art gallery hosts fine arts exhibitions throughout the year. At Condell 1550, the Galería (☎ 220062) is open daily except Sunday, 10 am to 7 pm; admission is free.

Congreso Nacional

Mandated by the 1980 constitution, which moved the legislature away from the Santiago-based executive branch, this imposing building has proved to be a notable inconvenience since the return to constitutional government – rapid physical communication between the two is only possible by helicopter. Talk continues of returning the Congreso to Santiago, which would leave Valparaíso with an unanticipated modern monument, but conservative elements strongly oppose the move.

When the Congreso is in session, the building is open to the public Friday 3 to 5 pm. It's at the junction of Avenida Pedro Montt and Avenida Argentina, opposite the bus terminal.

Hills of Valparaíso

Valparaíso is undoubtedly the single most distinctive city in Chile and one of the most intriguing in all of South America. On a sunny Sunday afternoon, it's possible to spend hours riding the ascensores and strolling the back alleys. There are 16 ascensores, built between 1883 and 1916, some of them remarkable feats of engineering – **Ascensor Polanco**, on the east side of Avenida Argentina, rises vertically through a tunnel, for example.

One of the best areas for urban explorers is Cerro Concepción, reached by **Ascensor Concepción** (dating from 1883, the oldest in the city). Also known as Ascensor Turri, it climbs the slopes from the corner of Prat and Almirante Carreño, across from the landmark clock tower known as the Reloj Turri. Cerro Alegre, behind Plaza Sotomayor, is reached by **Ascensor El Peral**, near the Tribunales (law courts) just off the plaza.

For a quick, inexpensive tour of Valparaíso, catch the Verde Mar 'O' micro on Serrano, near Plaza Sotomayor, all the way to Viña del Mar for about US$0.40. This is also the bus to Pablo Neruda's Valparaíso home, now a museum (see La Sebastiana, below).

Palacio Baburizza
(Museo de Bellas Artes)

Designed for an Italian nitrate baron but named for the Yugoslav who purchased it from him, this landmark Art Nouveau house (1916) is noteworthy for imaginative woodwork, forged-iron details and a steeply pitched central tower. Set among attractive gardens, it was a private residence until 1971, when the city acquired it as a fine arts museum.

The 1st floor displays the Pascual Baburizza collection of mostly derivative 19th-century French and Spanish artists, but the 2nd floor of Chilean landscapes includes excellent works like Englishman Thomas Somerscales' 'Crepúsculo sobre Aconcagua' (Dusk over Aconcagua), with superb use of light. There are also works by artists like Manuel González, the father of Chilean impressionism, the title of whose anti-war painting 'El Pago de Chile' (The Payment of Chile), depicting a mutilated soldier from the War of the Pacific, was changed to 'Capitán Dinamita' (Captain Dynamite) by glory-conscious agents of the Pinochet dictatorship. A modern sculpture entitled 'El Juicio' (The Judgment), by Mario Irarrázaval (born 1940), shows a bound prisoner at the mercy of three judges, perhaps symbolizing Chile under the rule of the armed forces.

On Cerro Alegre's Paseo Yugoeslavo, reached by Ascensor El Peral from the Plaza de Justicia, the Museo (☎ 252332) is open daily except Monday 9.30 am to 6 pm, but the building and its grounds alone justify a visit. Admission is free, but donations are accepted.

Museo del Mar Lord Cochrane

Overlooking the harbor, built in 1842 for Lord Thomas Cochrane but never occupied by him, this tile-roofed, colonial-style house above Plaza Sotomayor held Chile's first astronomical observatory – however unlikely that might seem, given Valparaíso's constant fogs. Its pleasant gardens offer excellent views, while the Museo itself displays an excellent collection of model ships in glass cases, along with acrylic paintings.

To reach the Museo (☎ 213124), take Ascensor Cordillera from the west side of Plaza Sotomayor and walk east to Calle Merlet 195. From mid-September to mid-March, it's open 10 am to 1 pm and 3 to 8 pm daily; the rest of the year hours are 10 am to 6 pm. Admission costs US$0.85.

Museo Naval y Marítimo

One of few Chilean museums with sufficient resources for acquisitions and a truly professional presentation, Chile's naval and maritime museum focuses on the War of the Pacific (specifically honoring naval and national icon Arturo Prat), but there are also major displays on Lord Cochrane (the navy's founder), Admiral Manuel Blanco

Encalada and other lesser figures. The most interesting displays, though, deal with voyages around the Horn, giving credit to sailors of every European country.

Reached by Ascensor Artillería from the triangular Plaza Aduana (also known as Plaza Wheelwright), the immaculate museum building served as Chile's naval academy from 1893 to 1967. At the top of the ascensor, Paseo 21 de Mayo offers souvenir stands, a small café with an attractive terrace and outstanding views of the port to the east. Open Tuesday to Friday 9.30 am to 12.30 pm and 2.30 to 6 pm, weekends and holidays 10.30 am to 6 pm, the Museo (☎ 281845) charges about US$1 for adults, half that for children.

Museo a Cielo Abierto

Students from the Universidad Católica's Instituto de Arte created the brightly colored abstract murals that cover numerous hillside sites on Cerro Bellavista, reached by Ascensor Espíritu Santo. Concentrated on Calle Aldunate and Paseos Guimera, Pasteur, Rudolph and Ferrari, Valparaíso's 'open sky museum' is not great art, but still adds a spot of color to some otherwise rundown areas. The tourist kiosk on Muelle Prat distributes a locator map of the area.

La Sebastiana (Fundación Neruda)

Pablo Neruda probably spent less time at La Sebastiana, his least known and least visited house, than at La Chascona or Isla Negra, but he made it a point to watch Valparaíso's annual New Year's fireworks from his lookout on Cerro Bellavista. Restored and open to the public, La Sebastiana may be the best destination for Neruda pilgrims – it's the only one of his three houses that visitors can wander around at will rather than subject themselves to regimented tours that seem out of character with the informal poet. In addition to the usual assemblage of oddball artifacts within the house, the Fundación Neruda is building a new cultural center alongside it.

To reach La Sebastiana (☎ 256606), at Ferrari 692, take Verde Mar bus 'O' or 'D' on Serrano near Plaza Sotomayor and disembark in the 6900 block of Avenida Alemania, a short walk from the house. Alternatively, take Ascensor Bellavista near Plaza Victoria and ask directions. The house is open to the public daily except Monday, 10.30 am to 2.30 pm and 3.30 to 6 pm. Admission is US$2.

Neruda's most famous house, with an extensive collection of maritime memorabilia, is at Isla Negra (see Around Valparaíso).

Special Events

Año Nuevo (New Year's) is one of Valparaíso's biggest events, thanks to the massive fireworks display that brings hundreds of thousands of spectators to the city to watch the spectacle.

April 17, marking the arrival of the authorization of the cabildo of Valparaíso in 1791, is the city's annual official day (imperial Spain's glacial bureaucracy and slow communications across the Atlantic delayed receipt of the authorization for more than three years).

Places to Stay

Viña del Mar has a better choice of accommodations in all categories, but Valparaíso has a few alternatives, the most interesting of which are hospedajes in the scenic hills. Phone ahead before visiting any of these places, which can be difficult to find and may have a limited number of beds.

Probably the cheapest passable place is *Hospedaje Díaz* (☎ 238087), Avenida Colón 2281, where singles/doubles cost only US$8/13. At Papudo 462 on Cerro Concepción, reached by Ascensor Concepción (Turri), the family-oriented *Residencial Latina* (☎ 237733) comes highly recommended at a price of US$10 per person. Reader-recommended *Hospedaje Anita* (☎ 239327), on Cerro Alegre, may be worth a look.

Near the bus terminal is quiet, comfortable *Casa Familiar Mónica Villegas* (☎ 215673), Avenida Argentina 322 near

Chacabuco. Try also appealing *Residencial Veracruz*, opposite the new Congreso Nacional at Pedro Montt 2881, or *Residencial Eliana* (☎ 250954) at Avenida Brasil 2164.

Most budget hotels are on or near Plaza Sotomayor, but standards are less than ideal at places like *Residencial Lily* (☎ 255995), Blanco 866 next to the Bar Inglés, even though it may do in a pinch. Conspicuous by its attractive mansard roof but suffering from deferred maintenance and a noisy location at Plaza Sotomayor 190, *Hotel Reina Victoria* (☎ 212203) starts around US$10 per person for 4th-floor singles with shared bath, rising to US$18/23 for 2nd-floor singles/doubles with private bath and breakfast. Around the corner at Serrano 501, the similarly priced *Garden Hotel* has spacious rooms but is the subject of mixed reports.

One of the best values in town is *Hostal Kolping* (☎ 216306), on the south side of Plaza Victoria at Francisco Valdés Vergara 622, where singles/doubles cost US$16/25 with shared bath, US$23/35 with private bath, breakfast included.

For truly upscale accommodations you'll have to go to Viña del Mar, but for slightly better digs try *Hotel Prat* (☎ 253081) at Condell 1443 for US$30/33; the comparably priced but declining *Hotel Condell* (☎ 212788) at Pirámide 557; or the rather better *Hotel Lancaster* (☎ 217391), Chacabuco 2362, for US$33/45. In the same range, at Victoria 2449, is highly recommended *Hostal Casa Baska* (☎ 234036).

Places to Eat

Traditionally, visitors dine in Viña del Mar, but a recent gastronomic revival has made Valparaíso an equally good place to eat. For the cheapest eats, try the area around the bus terminal.

Downtown, informal *Valparaíso Eterno* (☎ 255605), upstairs at Señoret 150, drips with bohemian atmosphere and is also an inexpensive lunch favorite for the city's downtown business crowd. At Valdivia 169, *Los Porteños No 2* (☎ 252511) has large portions and excellent service, but the menu is limited. Across the street, the 2nd-floor marisquerías at the Mercado Central charge less than US$3 for three-course meals, but the fish is usually fried.

Recommended *Bambú* (☎ 234216), Pudeto 450, has vegetarian lunches for as little as US$2.50, while *Pekín* (☎ 254387), nearby at Pudeto 422, serves Chinese food. The *Club Peruano* (☎ 237961), at Victoria 2324 near Parque Italia, serves moderately priced Peruvian specialties.

Try *Mesón del Lord* (☎ 231096), Cochrane 859, for good lunches (including vegetarian alternatives) in a traditional porteño atmosphere. Another traditional favorite is the *Bar Inglés* (☎ 214625), entered from either Cochrane 851 or Blanco 870, but prices have risen so that it's no longer a great bargain, even for lunch. At *La Rotonda* (☎ 217746), Prat 701, the lunch menu includes a daily special for about US$10, but consider splitting à la carte dishes from the extensive menu – portions are huge. Both seafood and service are excellent.

Bote Salvavidas (☎ 251477), on Muelle Prat, is a traditional but expensive seafood restaurant. One of the author's best meals ever in Chile was at *Café Turri* (☎ 252091), on Paseo Gervasoni at the upper exit of Ascensor Concepción (Turri), with superb seafood in an agreeable setting, attentive but unobtrusive service and panoramic views of Valparaíso and the harbor from the 3rd-floor balcony – the waiters bring binoculars while you await your meal. Although not really cheap, it is an exceptional value.

Entertainment

Most of Valparaíso's nightlife is in Viña, Reñaca and Concón, except for sleazy waterfront bars. The two-screen Cine Metroval (☎ 253029), Pedro Montt 2112, shows current films.

Spectator Sports

Santiago Wanderers (☎ 217210), Lira 575, is Valparaíso's first-division soccer team; they play at the Estadio Municipal at Playa Ancha.

Things to Buy

For an excellent selection of crafts, visit the Mercado Artesanal Permanente at the corner of Avenida Pedro Montt and Las Heras.

Getting There & Away

Air The nearest commercial airport is Aeropuerto Torquemada, north of Viña del Mar, but the number of flights is limited; see the Viña del Mar entry for details. Lan-Chile (☎ 251441, fax 233374) has a Valparaíso office at Esmeralda 1048, while Ladeco (☎ 216355) is at Esmeralda 973.

Bus – domestic Nearly all bus companies have offices at Valparaíso's Terminal Rodoviario, Avenida Pedro Montt 2800, across from the Congreso Nacional. Because services from Valparaíso and Viña del Mar are almost identical, most information (including telephones) is included here and only data which differs appears under bus transport for Viña. Note that some northbound long-distance buses, especially those at night, involve connections with buses from Santiago, which can mean waiting on the Panamericana – ask before buying your ticket.

The company with the most frequent and convenient service between Santiago and Valparaíso/Viña del Mar (1¾ hours/two hours) is Tur-Bus (☎ 212927 in Valpo, 822621 in Viña). Buses leave about every 15 minutes between 6 am and 9 pm (10.30 pm weekends). Some Viña buses go direct to Santiago, while others go via Valparaíso, but the fare is identical at about US$3.50 one way and US$6 roundtrip. Slightly cheaper, Cóndor Bus (☎ 214637 in Valpo, 882345 in Viña) leaves every half hour. Tur-Bus also runs extensive southbound routes on the Panamericana to Talca (US$8), Chillán (US$13), Concepción (US$15), Temuco (US$18), Osorno (US$23) and Puerto Montt (US$25).

Buses La Porteña (☎ 216568), Molina 366, covers coastal and interior destinations in the northern sector of Region V, including La Ligua (US$2), Pichidangui (US$3) and Los Vilos (US$3). Buses

Ligua Alfer (☎ 235277) goes to La Ligua via Viña's Aeropuerto Torquemada and Quillota.

Sol del Pacífico (☎ 288577), Galvarino 110 at Playa Ancha, serves the region's northern beaches from Quintero north as far as Papudo (US$1.50) and also goes to La Ligua (US$2); these services pass along Avenida Errázuriz. Sol del Pacífico also has offices at the bus terminals in Valparaíso (☎ 213776) and Viña (☎ 883156), offering southbound services on the Panamericana to Talca (US$9), Chillán (US$11), Concepción (US$13) and Los Angeles (US$13).

Buses Zambrano (☎ 258986 in Valpo, 883942 in Viña) follows the Panamericana north to Arica (US$50) and intermediate points like La Serena (US$16), Copiapó (US$20) and Iquique (US$45). Similar services are available from Pullman Bus/Los Corsarios (☎ 256898 in Valpo, 883489 in Viña), which also offers salón cama buses to La Serena (US$23) and Copiapó (US$35). Tramaca (☎ 250811 in Valpo, 881324 in Viña) covers similar routes, with salón cama service to Antofagasta (US$60) and Calama/Chuquicamata (US$63).

Flota Barrios (☎ 253674 in Valpo, 882-725 in Viña) and Chile Bus (☎ 256325 in Valpo, 881187 in Viña) cover the same routes. Transportes Lasval (☎ 214915 in Valpo, 684121 in Viña) serves the cities of the Norte Chico, primarily Ovalle (US$14) and La Serena/Coquimbo.

Fénix Pullman Norte (☎ 257993 in Valpo, 684636 in Viña) goes daily at 8 am to Los Andes (US$3) and serves destinations on the Panamericana from Arica in the north to Temuco, Villarrica and Valdivia (US$18) in the south. Bus Norte (☎ 258322) goes nightly to Temuco, Valdivia, Osorno and Puerto Montt, and makes connections in Santiago with Turibús for Punta Arenas (US$101).

Tas Choapa (☎ 252921 in Valpo, 882258 in Viña) goes to Santiago and intermediate destinations southbound on the Panamericana as far as Puerto Montt. Other companies serving the south include Buses Lit (☎ 253948 in Valpo, 882348 in Viña) and

Sol del Sur (☎ 252211 in Valpo, 687277 in Viña), with service to Talca, Chillán and Concepción.

Buses JM (☎ 256581 in Valpo, 883184 in Viña), has frequent buses to Los Andes (US$3), plus daily service to Concepción/Talcahuano (US$15). Buses Alfa 3 (☎ 252-173) goes from Valparaíso/Viña to San Felipe and Los Andes via Concón, every 10 minutes in summer. Buses Dhino's (☎ 221-298) also goes to Los Andes via Limache, Quillota and San Felipe.

Bus – international Valparaíso and Viña both have direct services to Argentina, bypassing Santiago. Unless otherwise noted, all these buses leave between 8 and 9 am. Buses leaving from Valparaíso also stop in Viña.

Fénix Pullman Norte leaves daily for Mendoza (US$25), Tuesday and Thursday for Buenos Aires (US$70). El Rápido (☎ 258322 in Valpo, 685474 in Viña) goes daily to Mendoza, where it makes connections for Buenos Aires; there is a direct Tuesday service to Buenos Aires, with connections to Montevideo (US$80). Chile Bus (☎ 256325 in Valpo, 881187 in Viña) departs daily at 7 am and 8.15 am for Mendoza via Santiago, with connections to São Paulo (US$113) and Rio de Janeiro (US$118).

Buses CATA (☎ 234544 in Valpo, 882-809 in Viña) has daily departures for Mendoza at 8.30 am, with connections for La Rioja (US$54), to Buenos Aires at 11 am, and again to Mendoza at 8.30 pm, with connections for Catamarca (US$61), Tucumán (US$72), and Salta or Jujuy (US$90).

Buses TAC (☎ 257587 in Valpo, 685767 in Viña) goes daily to Mendoza at 8 am, with connections to other Argentine cities, and direct to Buenos Aires at 7.30 am Tuesday and Friday. Tur-Bus goes daily to Mendoza at 7.30 am.

Tas Choapa goes daily to Mendoza at 8.15 am, with connections for Buenos Aires, daily to Córdoba (US$70) at 11 am, and daily except Saturday to Bariloche (US$45). Buses Ahumada (☎ 216663) goes daily to Mendoza (US$25) at 7.45 am, Wednesday and Saturday to Buenos Aires (US$75) at 9 am.

Getting Around
Bus & Colectivo Valparaíso and Viña del Mar are only a few km apart, connected by countless local buses (about US$0.40) and slightly more expensive taxi colectivos.

Train Valparaíso's Estación Puerto (☎ 217-108) is at Plaza Sotomayor 711, corner of Errázuriz, with an additional station at Muelle Barón. Merval operates regular commuter trains between the Valparaíso/Viña area and the towns of Quilpué, Villa Alemana and Limache. The area's endemic traffic congestion makes the frequent, inexpensive service between Valparaíso and Viña a superior alternative to either bus or taxi.

Boat From Muelle Prat, tourist launches carry passengers to Viña for US$2.

Car Rental Driving in the congested Valparaíso/Viña area makes little sense, but cars can be useful for visiting beach resorts to the north. Most agencies have offices in Viña del Mar, but try Comveq (☎ 212153) at Avenida Argentina 850.

AROUND VALPARAISO
Reserva Nacional Lago Peñuelas
Not really a lake, Lago Peñuelas is a reservoir built before the turn of the century to supply potable water to Valparaíso and Viña del Mar. Nevertheless, this 9260-hectare Conaf reserve along Ruta 68 is a popular site for weekend outings; fishing is possible, and it has a representative sample of coast range vegetation and lesser fauna and birds.

Lago Peñuelas is 30 km southeast of Valparaíso. Any of the very frequent buses linking Santiago with Valparaíso and Viña del Mar will drop passengers at the reserve.

Lo Vásquez
Every December 8, Chilean authorities close Ruta 68 as nearly half a million

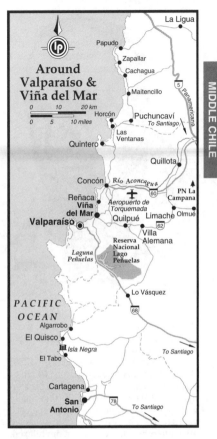

pilgrims converge on this small town's **Santuario de la Inmaculada Concepción**, 32 km southeast of Valparaíso and 68 km northwest of Santiago. Masses take place hourly from 6 pm the night before until 8 pm on the 8th.

Isla Negra (Museo Neruda)
Even more outlandish than La Chascona in Santiago, Pablo Neruda's oceanside house sits on a rocky headland between Valparaíso and Cartagena. Once vandalized and boarded up by agents of the Pinochet dictatorship, it houses the Museo Neruda, with the poet's collections of bowsprits,

Pablo Neruda

a short bus ride north of Valparaíso, it is popularly known as the Ciudad Jardín (Garden City), for reasons obvious to any visitor – from Avenida España's Reloj de Flores (Clock of Flowers), which greets visitors at the entrance to town, Viña's manicured subtropical landscape of palms and bananas contrasts dramatically with the colorful disorder of its blue-collar neighbor. Many moneyed Chileans and other wealthy Latin Americans own houses here, but while Viña is not cheap, neither is it impossibly dear.

Colonial Viña was the hacienda of the prominent Carrera family, who sold it to a Portuguese businessman named Alvarez in the mid-19th century. Alvarez's daughter and sole heir later married into the Vergara family, who have bestowed their name upon many city landmarks. Soon thereafter, Viña's history as the country's Pacific playground began as the railroad linked Valparaíso with Santiago – the porteños of Valparaíso, many of them foreigners, now had easy access to the beaches and broad green spaces to the north, and soon built grand houses and mansions away from the cramped harbor city.

With construction of hotels and subdivision of the sector north of the Estero Marga Marga, Viña became an increasingly attractive to Santiaguinos, for whom it became a popular weekend destination. Viña has recently lost popularity to competing resorts like La Serena.

Viña visitors anticipating balmy summer weather are often disappointed – like San Francisco, the city and the entire central coast are subject to cool fogs that don't burn off until early afternoon, and ocean temperatures are downright chilly. Those expecting to enjoy sun and surf often wish they had brought woolen sweaters and wet suits.

ships-in-bottles, nautical instruments, wood carvings and other memorabilia. Isla Negra is *not*, by the way, an island.

In summer, Isla Negra (☎ (035) 461284) is open for visits weekdays from 10 am to 8 pm, but advance reservations are imperative, since there are up to 40 tours daily with guides whose interest and competence vary greatly. The rest of the year, hours are 10 am to 6 pm and tours are more relaxed. Admission and tour fees are US$2.50 for adults, US$1.25 for children.

Although tours last only half an hour, visitors can hang around and photograph the grounds as long as they like. Pullman Bus (☎ 250858 in Valpo, 680424 in Viña) services to San Antonio can drop pilgrims almost at the door of Isla Negra (US$2). It's also possible to catch a bus from Santiago's Terminal Sur.

VIÑA DEL MAR

Viña del Mar (Viña for short) has long been Chile's premier beach resort, but it is also a bustling commercial center. Only

Orientation

Viña is about 10 km north of Valparaíso via the shoreline Avenida España. It consists of two distinct sectors: an established and prestigious area of traditional mansions south of the Estero Marga Marga, and a newer, more regular residential grid to its north. Several bridges, most notably Puente Libertad, connect the two sectors. North of the heavily polluted Marga Marga, most streets are identified by number and direction, either Norte (north), Oriente (east) or Poniente (west). Avenida Libertad separates Ponientes from Orientes. These streets are usually written as a number, but are sometimes spelled out, so that 1 Norte may also appear as Uno Norte.

The commercial and activity centers of Viña are south of the Marga Marga, on Plaza Vergara and Avenidas Arlegui and Valparaíso, which parallel the river. South of Alvarez is a zone of turn-of-the-century mansions that belonged to the Santiago/ Viña elite, whose centerpiece is the famous Quinta Vergara (see below). Viña's main attraction, of course, is the white-sand beaches that stretch northward from Caleta Abarca to the suburbs of Reñaca and Concón. The city's very limited industry is several km inland.

Information

Tourist Offices The municipal Central de Turismo e Informaciones (☎ 883154) is near the junction of Libertad and Arlegui, just north of Plaza Vergara. Most of the year it's open weekdays from 9 am to 2 pm and from 3 to 7 pm, Saturday 10 am to 2 pm only, but in the summer peak season it's open daily except Sunday, 9 am to 7 pm.

It distributes an adequate map and a monthly flyer entitled *Todo Viña*, which includes useful information and a calendar of events.

Sernatur's regional office (☎ 882285, fax 684117) is at Valparaíso 507, 3rd floor, but the entrance is a little difficult to find and the staff are oriented more toward businesses than individuals.

The Automóvil Club de Chile (Acchi; ☎ 689505) is just north of the Marga Marga at 1 Norte 901.

Money For US cash or travelers' checks, try Cambios Symatour at Arlegui 684/686, Cambios Afex at Arlegui 641 or Inter-Cambio at 1 Norte 655-B.

Post & Communications Viña's area code is ☎ 32, the same as Valparaíso's. Correos de Chile is at Valparaíso 846. CTC has long-distance offices at 14 Norte 1184, Valparaíso 628 and at the corner of Valparaíso and Villanelo. Entel is at Valparaíso 510, Local 10.

For cellular communications, contact BellSouth Celular (☎ 975891) at Libertad 1191.

Art Galleries Viña has many private art galleries open to visitors. Among them are Galería de Arte Modigliani (☎ 684991) at Valparaíso 363, Local 105, and Arte Gallery at Valparaíso 335.

Cultural Centers Viña has an active cultural life. There are frequent exhibitions of art and sculpture at the Centro Cultural Viña del Mar (☎ 689481), Avenida Libertad 250, which is open weekdays 9.30 am to 1 pm and 2 to 8 pm, Saturday 10 am to 1 pm only.

Similar programs take place at the Sala Viña del Mar (☎ 680633), Arlegui 683, which is open daily from 10 am to 8 pm except Sunday, when hours are from 10 am to 1 pm.

Viña has several international cultural centers, including the Instituto Chileno-Norteamericano (☎ 686191) at 3 Norte 532, the Instituto Chileno-Británico at 1 Oriente 252 (☎ 971440) and 3 Oriente 824 (☎ 971061), and the Alianza Francesa (☎ 685908) at Alvarez 314.

National Parks Conaf (☎ 970108), 3 Norte 541, has information on protected areas like Parque Nacional La Campana.

Laundry Laverap is at Libertad 902.

Medical Services Hospital Gustavo Fricke (☎ 680041) is east of downtown at Alvarez 1532, at the corner of Cancha.

Dangers & Annoyances Summer is the pickpocket season in Viña, so keep a close eye on your belongings, especially on the beach.

In-line skaters have become so ubiquitous in Viña that pedestrians must be alert to avoid collisions.

Museo de Arqueológico e Historia Francisco Fonck

Specializing in Easter Island (Rapa Nui) archaeology and Chilean natural history, this museum features an original moai from Chile's remote Pacific possession at the approach to its entrance. It is also the site of the **Biblioteca William Mulloy**, probably the best concentration of books, maps and documents on the subject of Easter Island (the founders originally intended to locate the library on the island itself, but the difficulties of building a suitable facility for the preservation of materials under conditions of high humidity and the presence of insect pests were insurmountable).

At 4 Norte 784, the Museo (☎ 686753) is open Tuesday to Friday 10 am to 6 pm, weekends 10 am to 2 pm; admission costs US$0.75.

Other Viña Museums

Between Hotel O'Higgins and the Puente Libertad, Viña's **Acuario Municipal** (Municipal Aquarium) is open Tuesday to Sunday, 10 am to 2 pm and 4.30 to 7 pm. Admission costs US$0.25 for adults, half that for children.

At Quillota 214, the **Museo Palacio Rioja** (☎ 689665) is another turn-of-the-century mansion that is now a municipal museum. Also hosting frequent musical and theater presentations, it's open daily except Monday, 10 am to 2 pm and 3 to 6 pm; admission is US$0.25.

On Avenida Marina near the outlet of the Estero Marga Marga, housed in the Castillo Wulff, the **Museo de la Cultura del Mar Salvador Reyes** (☎ 625427) is open Tuesday to Saturday 10 am to 1 pm and 2.30 to 6 pm, Sunday and holidays 10 am to 1 pm only. Admission costs US$1 for adults, half that for children.

Quinta Vergara

Once the residence of the prosperous Alvarez-Vergara family, now a public park, the magnificently landscaped Quinta Vergara contains the Venetian-style **Palacio Vergara**, which dates from 1908. The building houses the **Museo Municipal de Bellas Artes** (☎ 680618), which is open daily except Monday 10 am to 2 pm and 3 to 6 pm. Admission is about US$0.25, half that for children.

Frequent summer concerts at the Quinta's **Anfiteatro** complement the famous Festival Internacional de la Canción (see Special Events, below). The grounds, the only entrance to which is on Errázuriz at the south end of Calle Quinta, are open daily from 7 am to 7 pm.

Jardín Botánico Nacional

Chile's national botanical garden comprises 61 hectares of native and exotic plants which, since 1983, has been systematically developed as a research facility with an expanded nursery, library, educational programs and plaques for identification of individual specimens. Conaf has restricted automobiles and recreational activities like soccer and picnicking, making it a more interesting and relaxing place to spend an afternoon.

From Calle Viana in downtown Viña, take Bus No 20 east to the end of the line, then cross the bridge and walk about 10 minutes; the Jardín (☎ 672566) is on your left. Grounds are open daily except Monday 9 am to 7 pm in summer; the rest of the year it's open weekends and holidays only, 10.30 am to 6.30 pm. Admission is about US$1 for adults, US$0.25 for children.

Beaches

Many of Viña's beaches are either crowded or contaminated, but those in the northern suburbs are far better – from 2 Norte, take Pony Bus Nos 1, 10, 10-A (summer only) or 111 north to Reñaca and Concón, for example. For more details, see the Around Viña del Mar entry, below.

Organized Tours

A pleasant way of getting to know Viña del Mar is an hour's ride around town in a

WAYNE BERNHARDSON
The ironclad battleship Huascár, Talcahuano

WAYNE BERNHARDSON
Palacio Baburizza, Cerro Alegre, Valparaíso

WAYNE BERNHARDSON
Ascensor Aduana, Valparaíso

WAYNE BERNHARDSON
Reloj de Flores, Viña del Mar

WAYNE BERNHARDSON
Mural at Estación Puerto, Valparaíso

Images of Norte Grande

WAYNE BERNHARDSON
Llareta shrub, Parque Nacional Lauca

WAYNE BERNHARDSON
Desert sculpture along the Panamericana

WAYNE BERNHARDSON
Cactus flower, Parque Nacional Lauca

WAYNE BERNHARDSON
El Tatio, the world's highest geyser field

HJ VAN BROEKHUIZEN
Valle de la Luna

WAYNE BERNHARDSON
Pallachatas volcanoes and Laguna Cotacotani

horse-drawn carriage, leaving from Plaza Vergara, about US$15 for two people.

Aguitur, Viña's Asociación de Guias de Turismo (☎ 681882, fax 680294), operates out of the same building as the municipal tourist office. It can arrange tours of Viña or Valparaíso (US$23, three hours), Viña and Valparaíso (US$29, four hours), Zapallar (US$39, eight hours), Isla Negra (US$40, eight hours) or Santiago (US$45, 10 hours), as well as a three-hour night tour of Viña and Valparaíso for US$39. English-, French-, German- and Italian-speaking guides are available.

Special Events
Viña del Mar's most wildly popular attraction is the annual Festival Internacional de la Canción (International Song Festival), held every February in the amphitheater of the Quinta Vergara. This pompous competition of the kitschiest artistes from the Spanish-speaking world (for balance, there's usually at least one really insipid Anglo performer) resembles the Eurovision Song Contest; every evening for a week, everything stops as ticketless Chileans gaze transfixed at TV sets in their homes, cafés, restaurants and bars. Patient and discriminating listeners may hear some worthwhile folk music. The Latin American TV network Univisión usually broadcasts the better-known acts in the USA and elsewhere, but the contract is now up for grabs.

Places to Stay
Accommodations are so plentiful that it would be impossible to list everything, but the entries below are a good sample. Prices rise in summer, but outside the peak months of January and February supply exceeds demand and prices drop (except on major holidays like Easter). March is an especially good month, when the weather is still ideal but most Chileans have finished their holidays.

Places to Stay – bottom end
Budget travelers will find several alternatives on or near Agua Santa and Von Schroeders, as well as downtown near the bus terminal. Off-season prices run to about US$10 per person, in season twice that or more, but a weak Argentine economy can also mean negotiable prices even in summer and at mid-range hotels.

Hostel The local affiliate of Hostelling International is *Hotel Capric* (☎ 978295), Von Schroeders 39, which has dormitory accommodations for about US$10 in summer; the rest of the year, when students occupy the dormitory accommodations, it charges about the same for regular singles.

Residenciales & Hospedajes Mediocre *Residencial La Montaña* (☎ 622230), Agua Santa 153, is the cheapest in town, for about US$8 per person. *Residencial Blanchait* (☎ 974949), Valparaíso 82-A, charges US$10 per person with shared bath.

Residencial Agua Santa (☎ 901351), in an attractive blue Victorian building at Agua Santa 36, charges US$20 double in peak season. Almost next door, at Agua Santa 48, *Residencial La Nona* (☎ 663825) costs US$12.50. For the same price, family-run *Residencial Pudahuel*, a 3rd-floor walkup on Pasaje Cousiño, close to Plaza Vergara, is clean and very central, but also just upstairs from a popular disco/pub.

Hotel Capric (☎ 978295), Von Schroeders 39, charges US$15 for singles with shared bath (there's only one of them) and a skimpy breakfast, but it's not bad. Across the street at Von Schroeders 46, remodeled *Residencial Caribe* (☎ 976191) has tiny rooms with private bath for the same price.

Residencial Ona Berri (☎ 688187), upstairs at Valparaíso 618, has rooms for US$15 per person with shared bath, US$20 with private bath. Comparable *Residencial Victoria* (☎ 977370), Valparaíso 40, costs US$15 per person with shared bath, US$18 with private bath.

One of Viña's better values is *Residencial Oxarán* (☎ 882360) at Villanelo 136, a quiet but central location between Arlegui and Valparaíso, with very clean rooms, hot showers and breakfast for US$15/25

MIDDLE CHILE

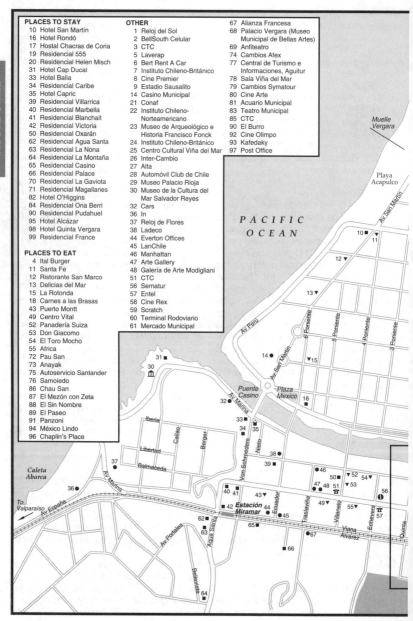

MIDDLE CHILE

PLACES TO STAY
10 Hotel San Martín
16 Hotel Rondó
17 Hostal Chacras de Coria
19 Residencial 555
20 Residencial Helen Misch
31 Hotel Cap Ducal
33 Hotel Balia
34 Residencial Caribe
35 Hotel Capric
39 Residencial Villarrica
40 Residencial Marbella
41 Residencial Blanchait
42 Residencial Victoria
50 Residencial Oxarán
62 Residencial Agua Santa
63 Residencial La Nona
64 Residencial La Montaña
65 Residencial Casino
66 Residencial Palace
70 Residencial La Gaviota
71 Residencial Magallanes
82 Hotel O'Higgins
84 Residencial Ona Berri
90 Residencial Pudahuel
95 Hotel Alcázar
98 Hotel Quinta Vergara
99 Residencial France

PLACES TO EAT
 4 Ital Burger
11 Santa Fe
12 Ristorante San Marco
13 Delicias del Mar
15 La Rotonda
18 Carnes a las Brasas
43 Puerto Montt
49 Centro Vital
52 Panadería Suiza
53 Don Giacomo
54 El Toro Mocho
55 Africa
72 Pau San
73 Anayak
75 Autoservicio Santander
76 Samoiedo
86 Chau San
87 El Mezón con Zeta
88 El Sin Nombre
89 El Paseo
91 Panzoni
94 México Lindo
96 Chaplin's Place

OTHER
 1 Reloj del Sol
 2 BellSouth Celular
 3 CTC
 5 Laverap
 6 Bert Rent A Car
 7 Instituto Chileno-Británico
 8 Cine Premier
 9 Estadio Sausalito
14 Casino Municipal
21 Conaf
22 Instituto Chileno-
      Norteamericano
23 Museo de Arqueológico e
      Historia Francisco Fonck
24 Instituto Chileno-Británico
25 Centro Cultural Viña del Mar
26 Inter-Cambio
27 Alta
28 Automóvil Club de Chile
29 Museo Palacio Rioja
30 Museo de la Cultura del
      Mar Salvador Reyes
32 Cars
36 In
37 Reloj de Flores
38 Ladeco
44 Everton Offices
45 LanChile
46 Manhattan
47 Arte Gallery
48 Galería de Arte Modigliani
51 CTC
56 Sernatur
57 Entel
58 Cine Rex
59 Scratch
60 Terminal Rodoviario
61 Mercado Municipal

67 Alianza Francesa
68 Palacio Vergara (Museo
      Municipal de Bellas Artes)
69 Anfiteatro
74 Cambios Afex
77 Central de Turismo e
      Informaciones, Aguitur
78 Sala Viña del Mar
79 Cambios Symatour
80 Cine Arte
81 Acuario Municipal
83 Teatro Municipal
85 CTC
90 El Burro
92 Cine Olimpo
93 Kafedaky
97 Post Office

PACIFIC OCEAN

Muelle Vergara

Playa Acapulco

Caleta Abarca

To Valparaíso

Puente Casino

Plaza Mexico

Estación Miramar

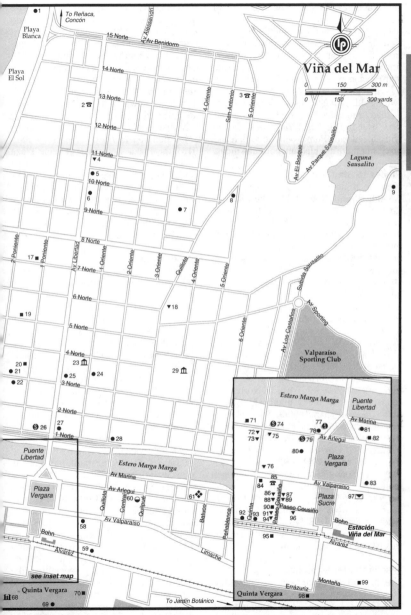

MIDDLE CHILE

single/double with shared bath, US$25/30 with private bath.

Friendly but rundown, family-run *Residencial Magallanes* (☎ 685101), set back from the street at Arlegui 555, seems overpriced at US$17.50 (US$35/44 with private bath), but may also be willing to bargain. *Residencial France* (☎ 685976), on the 'wrong side of the tracks' (in Viña, at least) at shady Montaña 743, is a bit ragged, but very friendly for US$18/30 single/double with shared bath. Some rooms are small and boxy, but there are pleasant common areas.

Places to Stay – middle

Near the grounds of the Quinta Vergara, at Alcalde Prieto Nieto 0332, *Residencial La Gaviota* (☎ 974439) is a bargain at US$20/29 with shared bath, US$25/36 with private bath. Several fine places fall into the same category, including *Residencial Villarrica* (☎ 942807) at Arlegui 172 for US$20/32 and *Residencial Casino* (☎ 662753) at Alvarez 110. *Hotel Balia* (☎ 978310), Von Schroeders 36, charges US$25/37.

In the quieter, more residential area north of the Marga Marga, *Hostal Chacras de Coria* (☎ 901419), 7 Norte 669, charges US$31/41. Rates at tranquil *Residencial Helen Misch* (☎ 971565), 1 Poniente 239, are US$28/48. Prize-winning *Residencial 555* (☎ /fax 972240), 5 Norte 555 (apparently their lucky number), charges US$32/42 with shared bath, US$38/52 with private bath. *Residencial Palace* (☎ 663134), Paseo Valle 387, charges US$34/43, while *Residencial Marbella* (☎ 978770), Valparaíso 78, costs US$40/49.

At the upper end of the range is enthusiastically recommended *Hotel Quinta Vergara* (☎ 685073, fax 691978), Errázuriz 690, with an English-speaking owner whose rates are US$50/63 with breakfast. During the annual song festival, though, this can be a noisy location.

Places to Stay – top end

Having moved from what is now the Hotel Quinta Vergara, *Hotel Rondó* (☎ 883144), 1 Norte 157, is recommended for US$57/72. Visitors with a little more money could try the oddball *Hotel Cap Ducal* (☎ 626655), an old ship set on a foundation in the surf at Avenida Marina 51, for US$60/68; the restaurant is worth a try. Several readers have complained about the size and quality of rooms at *Hotel San Martín* (☎ 689191), San Martín 667, despite its views of Playa Acapulco. Rates are US$81/94.

My personal choice would be the venerable, dignified *Hotel O'Higgins* (☎ 882-016) on Plaza Latorre (between Plaza Vergara and Puente Libertad). Rates start at US$70/94, but you can pay up to US$181 double and accumulate a huge room-service bill without even working up a sweat. It's worth mentioning, however, that this 1934 landmark could use some modern improvements.

Places to Eat

Like many other seaside resorts, Viña is sinking under the weight of its hotels and restaurants, but there are good values for diners. At the corner of Quinta and Arlegui, *Autoservicio Santander* is a deli with meals for about US$3. *Panadería Suiza*, downstairs at the corner of Arlegui and Villanelo, has good, cheap pastries and kuchen.

For sandwiches, coffee and desserts, try *Anayak* (☎ 680093) at Quinta 134 or, especially, *Samoiedo* (☎ 684610) at Valparaíso 637. *Pau San*, Quinta 122, has Chinese lunches for less than US$2, while the *Centro Vital*, Valparaíso 376, is a health club with a vegetarian café.

Pasaje Cousiño, a small passageway off Valparaíso near Plaza Vergara, has several good, moderately priced eateries. *Panzoni* (☎ 682134), Cousiño 12-B, features friendly service, excellent atmosphere and fine Italian and Middle Eastern specialties; it's especially popular for lunch. Other possibilities clustered on Cousiño include the modest, inexpensive *México Lindo* (credible Tex-Mex specialties like enchiladas and burritos, but the sauces are bland and the drinks are expensive) at No 136-140; *El Sin Nombre* (cheap lunches, tobacco-free); friendly, inexpensive *Chaplin's Place* (☎ 692955) at No 16, *Chau San* (Cantonese lunches for as little as US$2.50); *El Paseo*; and *El Mezón con Zeta* (live entertainment at night).

Despite a somewhat misleading name, *Ital Burger*, Libertad 920, has reasonably priced pasta dinners for about US$6.

Ristorante San Marco (☎ 975304), San Martín 597, and *Don Giacomo* (☎ 688889), upstairs at Villanelo 135, both serve Italian specialties.

Several correspondents have praised *Puerto Montt*, at Valparaíso 158-A but reached by a narrow off-street passageway, for large portions of well-prepared and reasonably priced fish, but they go on to say the wine is overpriced. *Delicias del Mar* (☎ 901837), San Martín 459, is a Basque seafood restaurant. There's a branch of the Valparaíso institution *La Rotonda* at 6 Poniente and 3 Norte.

Carnes a las Brasas, at the corner of Quillota and 6 Norte, serves full parrilladas with wine and an aperitif for US$10 to US$15. *El Toro Mocho*, Arlegui 484, has reasonable beef and occasional live entertainment, usually a singer-guitarist. Most notable for its outlandish facade and decor, *Africa* (☎ 882856), Valparaíso 324, serves both meat and seafood.

Santa Fe (☎ 691719), at the corner of San Martín and 8 Norte, is the Viña branch of Santiago's popular but relatively expensive Tex-Mex restaurant.

Entertainment
Viña has nightlife but can be surprisingly quiet except on weekends and in Reñaca and Concón, where transportation connections aren't so great.

Cinemas First-run movies often hit Viña even before Santiago. Try the *Cine Arte* (☎ 882798) at Plaza Vergara 142, *Cine Olimpo* (☎ 882616) at Quinta 294, *Cine Premier* (☎ 973002) at Quillota 898 or *Cine Rex* (☎ 685050) at Valparaíso 758.

Dance Clubs There's a place in Antofagasta called 'Disco Hell,' but Viña may run

away with that title thanks to a plethora of night spots such as *El Burro* on Pasaje Cousiño, *In* at Caleta Abarca, *Scratch* at Bohn 970, *Kafedaky* at the corner of Quinta and Viana, and *Manhattan* at Arlegui 302, 2nd floor. More suburban venues include Reñaca's *Cantina Cocodrilo* at Avenida Borgoño 13101 and *Baby Oh* at Santa Luisa 501, and Concón's *César* at Playa Amarilla.

It's not really a dance club per se, but Hotel Alcázar, Alvarez 646, holds a *noche de tango* every Saturday from 9 pm. There's also dancing Friday and Saturday evenings at Hotel O'Higgins, and at Restaurante Don Giacomo, Villanelo 135.

Theater Plays and concerts take place at the Teatro Municipal (☎ 681739) on Plaza Vergara.

Gambling The Casino Municipal de Viña del Mar (☎ 689200), overlooking the beach on the north side of the Marga Marga, offers opportunities to squander your savings on slot machines, bingo and card games, in between dinner and cabaret entertainment. At San Martín 199, it's open daily from 6 pm into the early morning. There's a US$6 cover charge.

Spectator Sports
Everton, Viña's second-division soccer team, plays at Estadio Sausalito (☎ 978-250). Team offices (☎ 689504) are at Viana 161.

Horse racing takes place at the Valparaíso Sporting Club (☎ 689393), Los Castaños 404.

Things to Buy
The crafts stalls along Pasaje Cousiño are a good place to search for jewelry, copperware and leather goods in particular.

Getting There & Away
Air LanChile (☎ 680560) is at Ecuador 289, while Ladeco (☎ 979089) is at Ecuador 80. Ladeco once had direct summer flights to Argentina but no longer operates international services; it is uncertain

whether LanChile, which flies only out of Santiago, will take up the slack.

Alta (☎ 692920), at Libertad 22, Local 1, flies daily northbound to La Serena (US$54), Copiapó (US$87), Antofagasta (US$115), Calama (US$130) and Iquique (US$139). Southbound, Alta flies three times daily to Concepción (US$62) except Saturday, when there are only two flights; one of these flights continues to Temuco (US$82), while another heads to Valdivia (US$92) and Osorno (US$95) except on Saturday. The Temuco flight continues to Puerto Montt (US$100), Balmaceda (US$120), Puerto Natales (US$200) and Punta Arenas (US$175).

Bus Viña's Terminal Rodoviario is at Valparaíso and Quilpué, two long blocks east of Plaza Vergara. The services included here originate in Viña; for details of companies that originate in Valparaíso and stop also in Viña, see the Getting There & Away entry for Valparaíso.

Pullman Norte (☎ 883489) runs northbound services on the Panamericana to La Serena (US$16), where it has connections to Copiapó (US$23), Caldera (US$24), Chañaral (US$28), Antofagasta (US$48), Iquique (US$57) and Arica (US$62). It also has semi-cama service to Antofagasta (US$48) and Iquique (US$59).

Nueva O'Higgins San Martín (☎ 681-585) goes to Mendoza daily at 7 and 10 am.

Getting Around

To/From the Airport Sol del Pacífico buses to Concón along Avenida Libertad pass by Viña's Aeropuerto Torquemada, about 15 km north of town on the inland road to Concón.

Navett minibuses connect with flights from Santiago's Aeropuerto Internacional Arturo Merino Benítez; make reservations with LanChile or Ladeco.

Bus Running along Arlegui, frequent local buses marked 'Puerto' or 'Aduana' link Viña with Valparaíso; from Muelle Vergara at Playa Acapulco, you can also catch a launch to Valparaíso's Muelle Prat, near Plaza Sotomayor (US$2).

Train For easier connections to Valparaíso, the Metro Regional Valparaíso (Merval) has two stations: Estación Miramar at Alvarez and Agua Santa, and Estación Viña del Mar at the southeast corner of Plaza Sucre.

Taxi Viña's taxis are twice as expensive as those in Santiago.

Car Rental For the cheapest rates, try Bert (☎ 681151) at Libertad 872. There are many others, including Mach Viña (☎ 259-429) at Las Heras 428, Cars (☎ 684994) at Avenida Marina 140 and Euro (☎ 883559) at Hotel O'Higgins.

AROUND VIÑA DEL MAR

North of Viña are several less celebrated but more attractive beach towns, along a coastline with many spectacular rock outcrops, crashing surf and blowholes, but Chile's moneyed elite are rapidly appropriating the best sites and cutting off public access in many places.

Reñaca & Concón

Among the nearby beach towns are overbuilt suburbs like Reñaca, which has its own tourist office (☎ 900499) at Avenida Borgoño 14100, plus the area's most extensive beach (also one of the cleanest). The wall-to-wall, multi-tiered apartment buildings here and at nearby Concón exemplify urban claustrophobia and mean no budget accommodations, but Reñaca's *Hotel Montecarlo* (☎ 830397, fax 833971), Avenida Vicuña Mackenna 136, has earned a reader recommendation for US$42 single. Bodyboarders frequent Concón's Playa Negra.

One local dining treat is the seafood at Concón's *La Picá Horizonte* (☎ 903665), San Pedro 120, a little hard to find but worth the effort. From the Muelle de Pescadores (Fisherman's Pier), climb the steps (behind Restaurant El Tiburón) and, at the top, walk one short block along the dirt road to San Pedro.

Quintero & Horcón

Another 23 km beyond Concón, Quintero is a peninsular beach community that was once part of Lord Cochrane's hacienda. There are reasonable accommodations at *Residencial María Alejandra* (☎ 930266), Lord Cochrane 157, where singles with shared bath cost about US$10 and those with private bath are only slightly costlier.

Across the bay to the north, the quaint working port of Horcón is also something of an artists' colony. Its short, narrow beach is nothing to speak of, but nearby Playa Cau Cau is the place for beach volleyball, body surfing and the like. Horcón's clutter of cheap seafood restaurants rank among the area's best – try *El Ancla*, which also offers accommodations. Take the Sol del Pacífico bus from Viña.

Zapallar & Papudo

At Zapallar, the Malibu of Chilean beach resorts about 80 km north of Viña, multi-million-dollar houses cover the densely wooded hillsides from the beach nearly to the ridgetops, but public access is nevertheless excellent. *Residencial La Terraza* (☎ 741026), Alcalde 142, two short blocks west of the highway but some distance from the beach, has good singles/doubles for US$45/55 in season, US$30 off-season, and has a good restaurant. On the beach, *Restaurant César* (☎ 741507) is popular with upper-income Chileans but is really a lesser value than more modest places in Horcón.

Less exclusive Papudo, 10 km farther north, has a wider range of accommodations; the dilapidated *Hotel de Turismo* (☎ 711240) at Blanco 19, from the town's early resort days, merits special inspection. The beachfront restaurant *La Cabaña* has drawn reader's praise but is not cheap.

La Ligua

Inland from Papudo, motorists passing on the Panamericana will notice white-coated vendors hawking the famous 'dulces' (sweets) of La Ligua, a modest but tidy agricultural town whose superb archaeological museum, the Museo de La Ligua

(☎ 712143) at Pedro Polanco 698, is a pleasant surprise. Once the city slaughterhouse, this professionally organized and remodeled building re-creates a Diaguita/Inca burial site, with materials uncovered in downtown La Ligua, and also displays a selection of materials from the 19th-century mining era and historical photographs of the city's early days. Admission costs US$0.65.

La Ligua also has a good artisans' market on the Plaza de Armas. Economical accommodations are available for about US$6 at *Residencial Regine I* (☎ 711196) at Condell 360, or the slightly more expensive *Residencial Regine II* (☎ 711192), Esmeralda 27. Modern, well-managed *Hotel Anchimallén* (☎ 711685), Ortiz de Rosas 694, has rooms with private bath and breakfast for US$32/45. *Restaurant Lihuén* (☎ 711143), Ortiz de Rosas 303, has good sandwiches and outstanding ice cream.

PARQUE NACIONAL LA CAMPANA

After scaling the 1828-meter peak of Cerro La Campana, which he called 'Bell Mountain,' Charles Darwin fondly recalled one of his finest experiences in South America:

The evening was fine, and the atmosphere so clear, that the masts of the vessels at anchor in the bay of Valparaíso, although no less than twenty-six geographical miles distant, could be distinguished clearly as little black streaks. A ship doubling the point under sail, appeared as a bright white speck . . . .

The setting of the sun was glorious; the valleys being black, whilst the snowy peaks of the Andes yet retained a ruby tint. When it was dark, we made a fire beneath a little arbor of bamboo, fried our *charqui* (dried strips of beef), took our *mate*, and were quite comfortable. There is an inexpressible charm in thus living in the open air . . . .

We spent the day on the summit, and I never enjoyed one more thoroughly. Chile, bounded by the Andes and the Pacific, was seen as in a map. The pleasure from the scenery, in itself beautiful, was heightened by the many reflections which arose from the mere view of the Campana range with its lesser parallel ones, and of the broad valley of Quillota directly intersecting them . . . .

Created in 1967 by private donation and managed by Conaf, La Campana occupies 8000 hectares in a nearly roadless segment of the coastal range that once belonged to the Jesuit hacienda of San Isidro. In geological structure and vegetation, its jagged scrubland resembles the mountains of Southern California and protects remaining stands of the roble de Santiago (*Nothofagus obliqua*), the northernmost species of the common South American genus, and the Chilean palm (*Jubaea chilensis*).

The Chilean palm, also known as the Palma de Coquitos for its tasty fruits (one Chilean writer called them miniature coconuts), grows up to 25 meters in height and measures up to 1½ meters in diameter. In more accessible areas, it declined greatly in the 19th century because it was exploited for its sugary sap, obtained by toppling the tree and stripping it of its foliage. According to Darwin, each palm yielded up to 90 gallons of sap, which cutters concentrated into treacle by boiling it. In some parts of the park you can see the ruins of ovens that were used for this purpose; there are also old-fashioned charcoal kilns.

Information

There are stations at each entrance, where the rangers collect the small fee and may have maps. The largest of these is the Administración at Granizo.

Geography & Climate

In the province of Quillota in Region V (Valparaíso), about 40 km east of Viña del Mar and 110 km northwest of Santiago via the Panamericana, La Campana consists of several distinct sectors administered by Conaf. Altitudes range from 400 meters above sea level to 2222 meters on the summit of Cerro Roble. The park has a Mediterranean climate strongly influenced by the ocean. Annual maximum temperatures average 19°C and minimum temperatures 9°C, but these statistics obscure dramatic variation – summer can be very hot and dry, while snow touches higher elevations in winter. Mean annual rainfall, about 800 mm, falls almost entirely

between May and September. Profuse wildflowers and a more dependable water supply make spring the best time for a visit, but the park is open all year.

Cerro La Campana

Thousands of Chileans and increasing numbers of visitors reach the summit of La Campana every year from the Administración at Granizo, most easily accessible from Viña del Mar. It's conceivable to hitch to the campground at the abandoned mine site at the end of the old but well-maintained road from the Administración, considerably shortening the hike to the summit, but it's much more interesting and rewarding to hike the trail from the park entrance. Figure at least four hours to the top, and three hours back down.

From the Administración, at 373 meters above sea level, the very steep trail to the summit climbs 1455 meters in only seven km – an average grade of nearly 21%! Fortunately, most of the hike is in shade, and there are three water sources en route: at **Primera Aguada**, at an elevation of 580 meters; at **Segunda Aguada** (backcountry camping is possible near a cold, clear spring, about two hours from the Administración); and the drive-in campground at the abandoned mine site, where the trail continues to the summit.

At the point where the trail skirts a granite wall, prior to the final steep climb, the Sociedad Científica de Valparaíso and the city's British community have placed a plaque commemorating the 101st anniversary of Darwin's climb (which took place August 17, 1834). At another point slightly beyond this, the Club Montañés de Valparaíso has placed another plaque, honoring climbers who died in 1968 when an earthquake unleashed a landslide.

On a clear day, the view from La Campana, from the Pacific to the Andes, is no less spectacular than when Darwin saw it, from the ships at anchor in the harbor to the summit of Aconcagua. Unfortunately, many Chileans feel obliged to leave a visible record of their climbing success and, consequently, carry spray paint in their backpacks.

Good, sensible footwear is essential. Chilean women in high heels have made it to the summit, but good treaded hiking boots are the best bet – parts of the trail are slippery even when dry, so that even sneakers can be awkward.

Palmas de Ocoa

Reached by a sometimes rough gravel road from the village of Hijuelas on the Panamericana, Palmas de Ocoa is the northern entrance to La Campana.

At Casino, two km beyond the park entrance, a good walking trail connects Palmas de Ocoa (Sector Ocoa) with Granizo (see Information, above), 14 km to the north. To reach the high saddle of the Portezuelo de Granizo takes about two hours of steady hiking through the palm-studded canyon of the Estero Rabuco. On clear days, which are becoming rarer, the Portezuelo offers some of the views that so impressed Darwin.

About halfway up the canyon is a good, flat campsite where wild blackberries are abundant and the fruit from abandoned grapevines ripens in late summer. Water is very limited. Farther up the canyon, just below the Portezuelo, is a conspicuous and dependable spring, but elsewhere livestock have fouled the water, so carry a water bottle. At the Portezuelo, the trail forks: the lower branch plunges into Cajón Grande, while the other follows the contour westward before dropping into Granizo.

The hike from Palmas de Ocoa to Granizo, or vice-versa, is an ideal weekend excursion across the coastal range, allowing the hiker to continue to either Santiago or Viña, depending on the starting point. It is probably better to start from Granizo, where public transport is better – at Palmas de Ocoa, Conaf rangers will help you get a lift back to the Panamericana, where it is easy to flag a bus back to Santiago.

Also at Sector Ocoa, another foot trail leads six km to Salto de la Cortadera, an attractive waterfall that is best during the spring runoff. Ask the rangers for directions to the trailhead.

Places to Stay & Eat

Camping is the only alternative in the park proper – Conaf has formal camping areas at Granizo, Cajón Grande and Ocoa. It's feasible to make day trips from Viña del Mar and even from Santiago, though a trip from Santiago would be time-consuming as there is no regular public transportation between Hijuelas and Sector Ocoa.

Conaf permits backcountry camping, but inform the rangers before attempting the routes between Palmas de Ocoa and Granizo or Cajón Grande. This is steep, rugged country, and fire is a very serious hazard, especially in summer and autumn.

In nearby villages like Olmué, there are both accommodations and good dining, the latter at places like *Hostería Aire Puro* (☎ (033) 441381), Avenida Granizo 7672. These places are very popular on weekends.

Getting There & Away

La Campana enjoys good access from both Santiago and Viña del Mar. From Valparaíso/Viña (US$1, 1¾ hours), Ciferal Express (☎ 953317) goes to within about one km of the Granizo entrance, slightly farther from Cajón Grande, every 30 minutes in season; the easiest place to catch the bus is on 1 Norte in Viña. Local transport (Agdabus) leaves every 20 minutes from Limache and Olmué.

Direct access to Sector Ocoa is more problematic. Most any northbound bus from Santiago will drop you at Hijuelas (there is a sharp and poorly marked turnoff to the park just before the bridge across the Río Aconcagua), but from there you will have to hitch or walk 12 km to the park entrance, or else hire a taxi.

From October to April, Altué Expediciones (☎ 2321103, fax 2336799), Encomenderos 83 in Santiago, runs full-day tours to La Campana for US$55, including an asado in Sector Ocoa.

LOS ANDES

Founded in 1791 by Ambrosio O'Higgins, Los Andes is a friendly foothills town on the international highway to the legendary ski resort at Portillo, near the Argentine border, and the Argentine city of Mendoza.

Los Andes' **Museo Arqueológico**, Avenida Santa Teresa de los Andes 398, is open daily except Monday, 10.30 am to 1 pm and 3 to 7.30 pm. From 1912 to 1918, Gabriela Mistral taught classes at the former **Colegio de Niñas** (Girls' School, now the Círculo Italiano), Esmeralda 246.

Information
In summer, there's a tourist information kiosk on Avenida Santa Teresa between Esmeralda and O'Higgins. Correos de Chile is at the corner of Santa Rosa and Esmeralda. Entel is at Esmeralda 463, Chilesat at Esmeralda 399. The hospital is at the corner of Avenida Argentina and Avenida Hermanos Clark.

Places to Stay & Eat
Hotel Central (☎ 421275), at Esmeralda 278, is friendly and passable, but for US$12.50 per person with shared bath, it's overpriced for what it is – some rooms do not even have windows. Rooms with private bath go for US$38 double. An alternative is *Residencial Susi*, Santa Rosa 151.

A better but more expensive choice is *Hotel Plaza* (☎ 421169, fax 426029), facing the north side of the Plaza de Armas at Esmeralda 353 (the official street address is one block north, at Rodríguez 370). Rates are US$39/43 single/double, for comfortable, heated rooms with cable TV, and its café is a good breakfast choice.

Half a block from museum, the *Centro Español*, O'Higgins 674, has a good daily fixed-price lunch. Another good choice for lunch and dinner is the historic *Círculo Italiano*, Esmeralda 246.

Getting There & Away
Los Andes' Terminal Rodoviario is on Membrillar between Esmeralda and O'Higgins, one block east of the Plaza de Armas. There are many buses to and from Santiago; buses from Santiago to Mendoza, Argentina stop here, but it's a good idea to buy tickets in advance.

Southern Heartland

RANCAGUA
Founded in 1743 on lands 'ceded' by Picunche cacique Tomás Guaglén, Rancagua played an important role in Chilean independence. In 1814, it was the site of the Desastre de Rancagua (Disaster of Rancagua), when Spanish Royalist troops vanquished Chilean patriots, many of whom were exiled to the Juan Fernández archipelago. Chilean liberator Bernardo O'Higgins went into exile in Mendoza, Argentina, but the battle was only a temporary setback for criollo self-determination.

Capital of Region VI, Rancagua is mostly an agricultural service center, but the regional economy also depends on the copper of the huge El Teniente mine, in the mountains to the east. One popular mountain attraction is Conaf's Reserva Nacional Río de los Cipreses.

Orientation
On the north bank of the Río Cachapoal, Rancagua (population about 180,000) is 86 km south of Santiago; the Panamericana passes east of the city. Like most cities of colonial origin, it has a standard grid pattern, centered on Plaza de los Héroes. Surrounded by the major public buildings, the plaza features an equestrian statue of Bernardo O'Higgins, while its northeastern corner has a carved wooden statue of Tomás Guaglén. Between Avenida San Martín and the plaza, the commercial street of Independencia is a pedestrian mall; street names change on each side of San Martín, but street numbering does not.

Information
Tourist Offices Sernatur (☎ 230413, fax 232297) is at Germán Riesco 277, 1st floor. Try also Acchi, the Automóvil Club de Chile (☎ 239930), Ibieta 09. There's a municipal Kiosco de Turismo on Paseo Independencia, opposite the Plaza de los Héroes.

MIDDLE CHILE

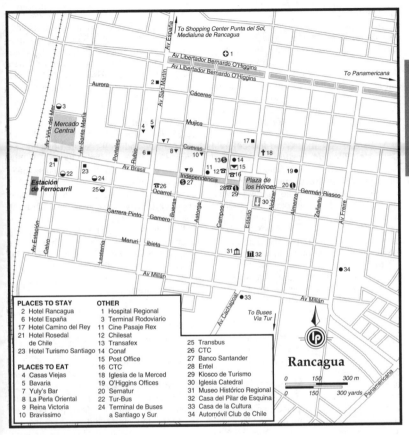

PLACES TO STAY
2 Hotel Rancagua
6 Hotel España
17 Hotel Camino del Rey
21 Hotel Rosedal
   de Chile
23 Hotel Turismo Santiago

PLACES TO EAT
4 Casas Viejas
5 Bavaria
7 Yuly's Bar
8 La Perla Oriental
9 Reina Victoria
10 Bravíssimo

OTHER
1 Hospital Regional
3 Terminal Rodoviario
11 Cine Pasaje Rex
12 Chilesat
13 Transafex
14 Conaf
15 Post Office
16 CTC
18 Iglesia de la Merced
19 O'Higgins Offices
20 Sernatur
22 Tur-Bus
24 Terminal de Buses
   a Santiago y Sur
25 Transbus
26 CTC
27 Banco Santander
28 Entel
29 Kiosco de Turismo
30 Iglesia Catedral
31 Museo Histórico Regional
32 Casa del Pilar de Esquina
33 Casa de la Cultura
34 Automóvil Club de Chile

Rancagua

0   150   300 m
0   150   300 yards

Money Transafex (☎ 235273), Campos 363, is the only place to cash travelers' checks, but Banco Santander has an ATM at Independencia 672.

Post & Communications Rancagua's area code is ☎ 72. Correos de Chile is on Campos between Cuevas and Independencia. CTC has long-distance offices at Campos 344 and San Martín 440, Entel at Independencia 468 and Chilesat at Campos 381, Local 4.

Cultural Centers At Millán and Cachapoal,

four blocks south of Plaza de los Héroes, Rancagua's Casa de la Cultura was the headquarters of royalist Colonel Mariano de Osorio during the battle for the city. Administered by the Municipalidad, it now offers regular exhibitions of paintings and photographs.

National Parks Conaf (☎ 221293) is at Cuevas 480.

Medical Services Rancagua's Hospital Regional is on O'Higgins between Astorga and Campos.

Things to See

At the corner of Estado and Cuevas, the **Iglesia de la Merced** is a national monument dating from the mid-18th century, when it served as the Convento y Templo de la Merced de Rancagua. During the battle of Rancagua, it was headquarters for O'Higgins' patriots. Another religious landmark, the **Iglesia Catedral** at the corner of Estado and Plaza de los Héroes, dates from 1861.

At Estado and Ibieta, the late-colonial **Casa del Pilar de Esquina** (☎ 221254) belonged to Fernando Errázuriz Aldunate, an important figure in the independence movement and one of the drafters of the constitution of 1833. It's open to the public weekdays except Monday, 9 am to 1 pm and 2.30 to 6.30 pm, weekends and holidays 9 am to 1 pm only. Admission costs US$1 for adults, US$0.50 for children, but it's free Tuesdays.

In another colonial house, across Estado from the Casa del Pilar de Esquina, the **Museo Histórico Regional** focuses on O'Higgins' role in Chilean independence and also contains a selection of colonial religious artwork. Hours and prices are identical to those of the Casa del Pilar de Esquina.

Special Events

In early autumn (late March), the Campeonato Nacional de Rodeo (national rodeo championship) takes place at the Medialuna de Rancagua, on Avenida España, the northward extension of Avenida San Martín. If intending to stay in Rancagua at this time, make hotel reservations early; otherwise, make it a day trip from Santiago.

Places to Stay

Easily the cheapest in town is bare-bones *Hotel Rosedal de Chile*, near the train station at Calvo 435, for about US$9 per person. Several travelers have recommended the *Hotel España* (☎ 230141), Avenida San Martín 367, which has singles/doubles for US$20/32 with shared bath, US$25/38 with private bath. *Hotel Turismo Santiago* (☎ 230855, fax 230822), Avenida Brasil 1036, charges US$40/59.

Family-oriented *Hotel Rancagua* (☎ 232-663, fax 241155), Avenida San Martín 85, is slightly dearer at US$42/60, but discounts IVA for foreign visitors. Despite its aging facade, *Hotel Camino del Rey* (☎ 239765, fax 232314), Estado 275, features a tastefully modernized interior; rates are US$50/72.

Places to Eat

Yuly's Bar, Cuevas 745, has simple but inexpensive and well-prepared lunches, as does *Casas Viejas* (☎ 230006), Rubio 216. *Reina Victoria*, Independencia 667, has good lunches for about US$4 and excellent ice cream. The Santiago ice creamery *Bravíssimo* has a branch at Astorga 307.

Bavaria (☎ 233827), part of the popular country-wide chain, is at Avenida San Martín 255. *La Perla Oriental* (☎ 235447), Cuevas 714, serves Chinese food.

Entertainment

The Cine Pasaje Rex, in the back of a gallery at the corner of Independencia and Astorga, occasionally shows good movies.

O'Higgins (☎ 225630), Almarza 331, is the perpetual cellar-dweller in Chile's first-division soccer league.

Getting There & Away

Bus Rancagua's new Terminal Rodoviario is on Avenida Viña del Mar, just north of the Mercado Central, but some companies are resisting the move because of high charges imposed on each arriving bus. Many buses that cover the Panamericana between Santiago and the Puerto Montt stop in Rancagua.

The Terminal de Buses a Santiago y Sur (☎ 230340) is at Ocarrol 1039; there is very frequent service to the capital (US$2). Tur-Bus (☎ 241117), at the corner of Calvo and Ocarrol, also has frequent service to Santiago.

Transbus (☎ 230826), Ocarrol 1034, goes to Concepción and intermediate points, while Via Tur (234502), Cachapoal 1300, goes to Los Angeles, Puerto Montt and intermediates.

Train Rancagua's Estación de Ferrocarril (☎ 225239) is on Avenida Viña del Mar between Ocarrol and Carrera Pinto. EFE's regular passenger services, which connect Santiago with Temuco and other points south, stop at Rancagua, but Metrotrén runs at least 10 commuter trains daily to the capital.

AROUND RANCAGUA
Centro de Esqui Chapa Verde
Some 50 km northeast of Rancagua via a mostly paved highway, Chapa Verde is lesser known than more prestigious ski centers like Portillo and Valle Nevado, but has four lifts and eight runs, 2870 meters above sea level. Facilities include a ski school, rental equipment, a café and a restaurant.

From Rancagua's Shopping Center Punta del Sol at the junction of Avenida Kennedy and the Panamericana, Pullman Bus (☎ 294255) runs frequent buses to Chapa Verde.

El Teniente
At Sewell, 55 km northeast of Rancagua, El Teniente belonged to Kennecott Copper Corporation until its expropriation under the Unidad Popular, and is now part of the state-owned Codelco mining enterprise. It is the world's largest subsurface mine.

Theoretically, El Teniente is closed to the public, but if you want to visit, try to convince Codelco's Rancagua office on Calle Millán, or their Santiago headquarters at Huérfanos 1270, of your specialist's interest (it may be sufficient to be a school-teacher).

Termas de Cauquenes
In the Andean foothills east of Rancagua, Cauquenes' thermal baths have received such celebrated visitors as Bernardo O'Higgins and Charles Darwin, who observed that the buildings consisted of 'a square of miserable little hovels, each with a single table and bench.' Since Darwin's day there have been sufficient improvements to allow *Hotel Termas de Cauquenes* (☎ 297226 in Rancagua, (02) 6381610 in Santiago) to now charge from US$105/186, with full board, for singles/doubles in an area that Darwin acknowledged as 'a quiet, solitary spot with a good deal of wild beauty.'

If you can't afford to stay at Cauquenes, only 28 km east of Rancagua, you can still spend the afternoon by taking a bus from Rancagua's new Terminal Rodoviario with Empresa Micro Termas de Cauquenes (US$2), weekdays at 11 am and 6.15 pm.

Reserva Nacional de los Cipreses
Set among the Andean foothills and cordillera, ranging in elevation from 900 meters to the 4900-meter summit of Volcán El Palomo in the upper drainage of the Río de los Cipreses, 37,000-hectare Los Cipreses contains a variety of volcanic landforms, hanging glacial valleys with waterfalls, and fluvial landscapes.

The reserve's flora includes extensive forests of cypress, olivillo and other native tree species, while the wildlife includes guanaco, fox, vizcacha, condor and many other birds. There are petroglyphs at several sites, and camping is possible at Ranchillos, six km from the park entrance. Several hiking trails exist, and it is possible to rent horses from local people.

Los Cipreses is 50 km southeast of Rancagua. No direct public transport exists, but visitors can take a bus as far as Termas de Cauquenes (see above) and walk another 15 km to the park entrance. With luck and persuasion, it may be possible to arrange transport with Conaf in Rancagua.

Zorro culpeo (fox)

Lago Rapel

In truth a reservoir rather than a lake, Lago Rapel was formed by the Central Hidroeléctrica Rapel, which inundated the basins of the Cachapoal and Tinguiririca Rivers in 1968. It is, however, a popular site for water sports like windsurfing, waterskiing and fishing. There are many camping areas east of El Manzano, on the south shore of the reservoir's northern arm, plus reasonable accommodations at the *Hostería y Camping Playa de Llaullauquén* (☎ 343385, (09) 7514281), on the eastern shore of its southern arm, for US$30 for a double room.

Lago Rapel is about 100 km west of Rancagua via Pelequén, on the Panamericana. It can also be reached from Santiago (147 km) with Buses Navidad from Terminal San Borja, Alameda 3250.

Pichilemu

Most easily accessible by bus from the city of San Fernando (55 km south of Rancagua), Pichilemu has been Region VI's most popular beach resort since the turn of the century. There's an Oficina de Información Turística (☎ 841017) in the Municipalidad, Angel Gaete 365.

Pichilemu gets very crowded in season, but reasonable accommodations are available – try *Residencial Las Salinas* (☎ 841-071), Aníbal Pinto 51, which has singles with shared bath for US$12, or *Residencial San Luis* (☎ 841040), Angel Gaete 237, for about US$16. Highly recommended *Hotel*

Chile España (☎ 841010), Avenida Ortúzar 255, caters specifically to surfers; rates are normally US$15 per person with breakfast, but off-season rooms sometimes go for US$10. For camping, try *Pequeño Bosque* (☎ 841601), about two km from downtown, where shady sites costs US$15 (try bargaining for a discount).

About 20 km south of Pichilemu is the smaller beach resort and fishing village of **Bucalemu**, where several residenciales on Avenida Celedonio Pastene have singles for about US$10 – try *Hotel Casablanca* (☎ 342335). From Bucalemu, it's possible to make a two- to four-day beach trek to the seaside village of **Llico**, a popular windsurfing area where there are buses to Curicó.

Surfing   In summer, the Campeonato Nacional de Surf (national surfing championship) takes place at Punta de Lobos, six km south of Pichilemu.

CURICO

Founded in 1743 by José Antonio Manso de Velasco, pleasant, attractive Curicó (population 72,000) is a service center for surrounding orchards and vineyards. While not a major attraction in its own right, it's a good base for excursions to nearby wineries, to coastal areas like Vichuquén and to parts of the Andes, such as Radal Siete Tazas, seen by relatively few foreigners.

Orientation

Beside the Río Guaiquillo, 195 km south of Santiago, Curicó lies just west of the Panamericana. Entering town from the Panamericana, broad, tree-lined Avenida Manso de Velasco skirts the eastern edge of Curicó's central quadrangle. At the north end of Manso de Velasco, Cerro Carlos Condell is a verdant, scenic overlook with a swimming pool to beat the summer heat.

Curicó's palm-studded Plaza de Armas is one of Chile's prettiest, with a wonderful, turn-of-the-century wrought-iron bandstand and cool fountains. On its south side, a local artist has sculpted a tree trunk into an image of a Mapuche warrior.

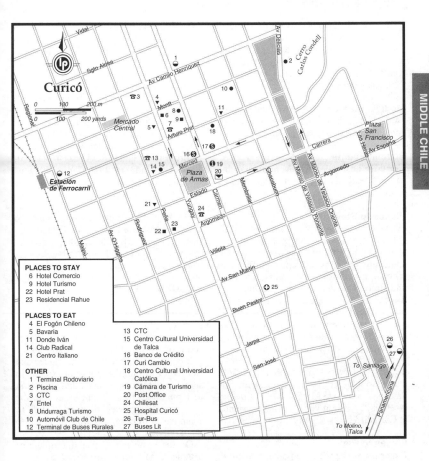

MIDDLE CHILE

PLACES TO STAY
6   Hotel Comercio
9   Hotel Turismo
22 Hotel Prat
23 Residencial Rahue

PLACES TO EAT
4   El Fogón Chileno
5   Bavaria
11 Donde Iván
14 Club Radical
21 Centro Italiano

OTHER
1   Terminal Rodoviario
2   Piscina
3   CTC
7   Entel
8   Undurraga Turismo
10 Automóvil Club de Chile
12 Terminal de Buses Rurales

13 CTC
15 Centro Cultural Universidad de Talca
16 Banco de Crédito
17 Curi Cambio
18 Centro Cultural Universidad Católica
19 Cámara de Turismo
20 Post Office
24 Chilesat
25 Hospital Curicó
26 Tur-Bus
27 Buses Lit

Information

Tourist Offices Curicó has no formal tourist office, but the private Cámara de Turismo (☎ 310086) operates out of a kiosk at the Edificio Servicios Públicos on Carmen, on the east side of the plaza. Open 9 am to 6.30 pm, it's understaffed and lacks space, but does its best. The local branch of Acchi, the Automóvil Club de Chile (☎ 311156) at Chacabuco 759, is especially helpful.

Money Curi Cambio (☎ 311985) at Merced 255, Oficina 106, is open weekdays 9.30 am to 1.30 pm and 3.30 to 6 pm. Banco de Crédito has an ATM at Merced 315.

Post & Communications Curicó's area code is ☎ 75. Correos de Chile is at Carmen 556, opposite the Plaza de Armas. CTC has long-distance offices at Peña 650 and at Camilo Henríquez 414. Entel, at Prat 377 near Yungay, is open until midnight, while Chilesat is at Yungay 430.

Travel Agencies Undurraga Turismo (☎ 310552) is at Carmen 737.

Cultural Centers The Centro Cultural Universidad de Talca, Merced 437, offers films and concerts on a regular basis and also has a small but good bookstore. The Centro Cultural Universidad Católica, Prat 220, has similar offerings.

Medical Services The Hospital de Curicó (☎ 310252) is on Chacabuco between Avenida San Martín and Buen Pastor.

Special Events
Curicó's Festival de la Vendimia (wine harvest festival) lasts four days in early March.

Places to Stay
Friendly *Hotel Prat* (☎ 311069), Peña 427, is the budget pick at US$8 per person with shared bath, although the rooms vary – some are large, bright and comfortable, with high ceilings, while others are dark and drab. The hot showers are fine, and there is a shady grape arbor over the patio, but a recent visitor reports an untended gas leak. *Residencial Rahue* (☎ 312194), across the street at Peña 410, is comparably priced and perfectly satisfactory.

At tranquil *Hotel Comercio* (☎ 310014), Yungay 730, rates start at about US$25/35 single/double, but better rooms with private bath cost US$38/52. *Hotel Turismo* (☎ 310823), set on very attractive grounds at Carmen 727, is slightly more expensive.

Places to Eat
Bavaria (☎ 319972), the popular chain, is at Yungay 715. The *Club Radical*, Merced 461, has fixed-price lunches for just US$2.50. Try also the *Centro Italiano* (☎ 310482), Estado 531.

For parrillada, the best choice is *El Fogón Chileno* (☎ 310881), Yungay 802. *Donde Iván*, at the corner of Prat and Membrillar, serves Spanish seafood.

Getting There & Away
Bus Most north-south companies have their offices at Curicó's long-distance Terminal Rodoviario on Camilo Henríquez, three blocks north of the plaza. Two exceptions are Buses Lit (☎ 315648) at Las Heras 0195 and Tur-Bus (☎ 312115) at Manso de Velasco 0106, whose buses use their own offices. Buses to Santiago (US$4) leave about every half hour.

For local and regional services, the Terminal de Buses Rurales is at the west end of Calle Prat, across from the railway station. Companies that operate from there include Buses Bravo (☎ 312193), which goes to Lago Vichuquén and the coastal resort of Iloca, and Buses Díaz (☎ 311905). Buses Hernández (☎ 491607, 491179) goes to interior destinations like Molina and Radal Siete Tazas.

Train Passenger trains between Santiago and Temuco stop at Curicó's Estación de Ferrocarril (☎ 310028) at Maipú 567, at the west end of Calle Prat, four blocks west of the Plaza de Armas.

AROUND CURICO
Wineries
One of Chile's best-known vineyards, **Bodega Miguel Torres** (☎ 310455), is on the Panamericana about eight to 10 km south of Curicó. Phone ahead and take a taxi colectivo from Camilo Henríquez and Rodríguez toward the village of Molina. In summer, the winery is open daily, 8.30 am to 1 pm and 3 to 6.30 pm; the rest of the year, it's open weekdays 8.30 am to 1 pm and 3 to 6 pm, Saturday 8.30 am to 1 pm only.

On the same route, near the village of Lontué, **Viña San Pedro** (☎ 491517) dates from the early-18th century. Hours are limited – Tuesday to Thursday, 9 am to 10.30 pm only.

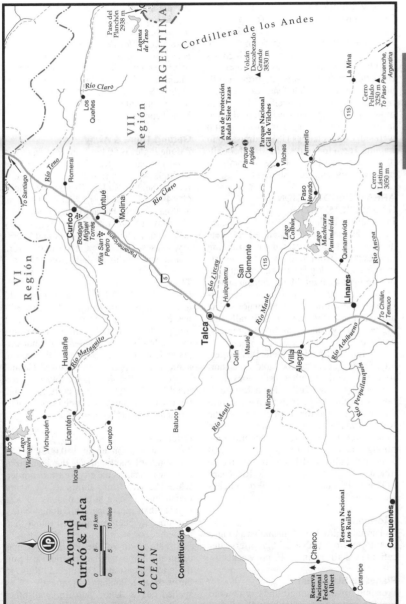

Lago Vichuquén & Reserva Nacional Laguna Torca

In the coast range only a short distance from the Pacific, 110 km from Curicó, Lago Vichuquén is a natural lake which is a popular center for water sports. Nearby is **Reserva Nacional Laguna Torca**, a 600-hectare reserve which features breeding populations of black-necked swans and other birds. In especially wet years, the two lakes join to form a single extensive coastal wetland. Conaf charges US$1 admission to Laguna Torca for adults, US$0.25 for children. There is a US$6 charge for camping in rustic sites, with cold showers.

AREA DE PROTECCION RADAL SIETE TAZAS

In the upper basin of the Río Claro southeast of Molina, 7600-hectare Radal Siete Tazas is a state-protected area ranging in elevation from 600 to 2150 meters, marking an ecological transition between the drought-tolerant Mediterranean vegetation of the north and the moist evergreen forests to the south. Its major scenic attraction is a stunning series of falls (the highest of which is about 30 meters) and pools.

The falls and pools at Siete Tazas (literally, Seven Cups) are accessible via a short footpath, while another trail goes to a viewpoint for the **Salto de la Leona**, a falls that drops more than 50 meters from a narrow gorge to the main channel of the Río Claro. The same trail continues down to the river itself. There are longer, scenic hiking trails up Cerro El Fraile and at Valle del Indio, and it's also possible to trek across the drainage of the Río Claro to exit at Parque Nacional Gil de Vilches (see below).

Information

At Parque Inglés, Conaf maintains a Centro de Información Ambiental that offers educational talks at 11 am and 7 pm weekends.

Places to Stay & Eat

Free but rustic campgrounds with cold running water are available at Radal and Parque Inglés, but the toilets at Parque Inglés are filthy and toilet paper is scattered everywhere.

Hostería Flor de la Canela (☎ 491613), near Conaf headquarters at Parque Inglés, offers accommodations from December to March for US$28 per person with shared bath, US$38 with private bath. It has a restaurant, and there is also a kiosk selling basic supplies.

Getting There & Away

Parque Inglés is 50 km from Molina over a good but narrow gravel and dirt road, but Molibüs (☎ 311065) in Curicó goes only as far as Sector Radal. Buses Hernández (☎ 491607, 491179), Maipú 1723 in Molina, goes to Parque Inglés Friday and Saturday at 5 pm, returning at 7 pm Friday and Sunday, all year. In January and February, Buses Hernández goes daily from Curicó and four times daily from Molina.

TALCA

Founded in 1690 but refounded in 1742 after a major earthquake, Talca also witnessed the signing of Chile's declaration of independence in 1818. Since its earliest days, it has been the residence of landowners and an important commercial center in a prosperous agricultural region. Capital of Region VII (Maule), the city is also a notable educational and cultural locus, thanks to its museums, universities, galleries and cultural centers.

Orientation

Talca (population about 140,000) is 257 km south of Santiago via the Panamericana, which skirts the city's eastern border, while the Río Claro limits its westward expansion. Talca's street plan is no less regular than most Spanish colonial cities, but most streets are numbered rather than named.

Streets north of the Plaza de Armas begin at 1 Norte, those to the south at 1 Sur, those to the east at 1 Oriente and those to the west at 1 Poniente. Frequently '1' is spelled out as 'Uno,' but nearly all other streets use the numeral except for 4 Norte, a divided boulevard known as Avenida Bernardo O'Higgins. O'Higgins crosses the Río Claro to the Cerro de la Virgen, which offers fine views of the city.

Information

Tourist Offices Sernatur (☎ 233669), 2 Norte 760, is open daily except Sunday 10 am to 2 pm, weekdays only 4 to 8 pm. Acchi, the Automóvil Club (☎ 232774), is at 1 Poniente 1267.

Money Marcelo Cancino Cortés, 1 Sur 898, Oficina 15, changes US, Argentine and other foreign currencies. Banco Santiago has an ATM at 1 Sur 853, one block east of the Plaza de Armas, while Banco de Crédito has one at 1 Sur 732.

Post & Communications Talca's area code is ☎ 71. Correos de Chile is opposite the plaza, on 1 Oriente. CTC has long-distance offices at 1 Sur 1156 and 1 Sur 835, Entel at 6 Oriente 1067.

Travel Agencies Bontour (☎ 234003) is at 5 Oriente 1080.

Cultural Centers The Universidad de Talca's Salón Abate Juan Ignacio Molina (Salón Molina), at 1 Poniente 1351, offers various cultural events, including films, lectures and exhibitions of artwork. The Centro Cultural de Talca, 2 Norte 1080, offers theater, concerts and art exhibits.

National Parks Conaf (☎ 233148) is at 2 Poniente 1180.

Medical Services Talca's Hospital Regional (☎ 242406) is 11 blocks east of the plaza on 1 Norte, just across the railway tracks.

Museo O'Higginiano y de Bellas Artes

In this late-colonial house, dating from 1762 and handsomely furnished in period decor, Bernardo O'Higgins officially signed Chile's declaration of independence in 1818. The house also contains archaeological and numismatic exhibits, as well as collections of Chilean and foreign painting and sculpture. Like Rancagua's Casa del Pilar de Esquina, the building has an interesting corner pillar.

At 1 Norte 874, the Museo (☎ 227330) is open Tuesday to Friday 9.15 am to 12.45 pm and 3 to 6.45 pm, Saturday 9.30 am to 12.45 pm and 3 to 5 pm, and Sunday 11 am to 1 pm. Admission costs US$1 for adults, US$0.50 for children, but it's free on Sundays.

Museo Bomberil Benito Riquelme

Travelers with incendiary tendencies can visit the firemen's museum, in the main fire station at 2 Sur 1172. Its collections of antique fire-fighting equipment, photographs and miscellanea are open to the public, so long as there's not a serious blaze raging across town.

Galleries

Several public and private art galleries occasionally host films, concerts and other events as well. In the basement of the Hotel Plaza at 1 Poniente 1141, the **Sala de Arte** is open weekdays 9.30 am to 1 pm and 3 to 7 pm, while the **Pinacoteca Universidad de Talca**, 1 Oriente 1031, is open weekdays 10 am to 1 pm and 3 to 7 pm. At the Municipalidad's **Casa del Arte/ Museo Municipal Gabriel Pando**, 1 Norte 931, opening hours are weekdays 9.30 am to 1 pm and 3 to 7 pm, Saturday 9.30 am to 1 pm only.

Places to Stay

Four blocks west of the railway station, *Hotel Alcázar*, 2 Sur 1359, is a basic but cheap alternative at about US$9 per person with shared bath; at the time of writing, it was for sale, so changes may be in the offing. Across the street at 2 Sur 1360, remodeled *Hotel Cordillera* (☎ 221817) has singles with shared bath for US$14, while single/doubles with private bath go for US$24/38.

Probably the best value in town is well-kept *Hotel Amalfi* (☎ /fax 233389), set among attractive gardens at 2 Sur 1265, for US$28/46. Upper-mid-range *Hotel*

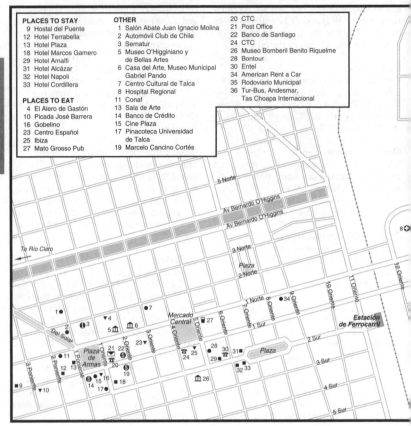

PLACES TO STAY
9 Hostal del Puente
12 Hotel Terrabella
13 Hotel Plaza
18 Hotel Marcos Gamero
29 Hotel Amalfi
31 Hotel Alcázar
32 Hotel Napoli
33 Hotel Cordillera

PLACES TO EAT
4 El Alero de Gastón
10 Picada José Barrera
16 Gobelino
23 Centro Español
25 Ibiza
27 Mato Grosso Pub

OTHER
1 Salón Abate Juan Ignacio Molina
2 Automóvil Club de Chile
3 Sernatur
5 Museo O'Higginiano y
   de Bellas Artes
6 Casa del Arte, Museo Municipal
   Gabriel Pando
7 Centro Cultural de Talca
8 Hospital Regional
11 Conaf
13 Sala de Arte
14 Banco de Crédito
15 Cine Plaza
17 Pinacoteca Universidad
   de Talca
19 Marcelo Cancino Cortés

20 CTC
21 Post Office
22 Banco de Santiago
24 CTC
26 Museo Bomberil Benito Riquelme
28 Bontour
30 Entel
34 American Rent a Car
35 Rodoviario Municipal
36 Tur-Bus, Andesmar,
   Tas Choapa Internacional

Napoli (☎ 227373), 2 Sur 1314, charges US$37/55. For US$50 double, try the new *Hostal del Puente* (☎ 220930, fax 225448), 1 Sur 407, which has an English-speaking owner.

Talca's upper-end accommodations are cheaper than in most other Chilean cities, most notably the sparkling new *Hotel Terrabella* (☎ /fax 226555), 1 Sur 641, for US$48/57. For near-luxury, try the *Hotel Plaza* (☎ 226150) at 1 Poniente 1141 for US$51/68, or the *Hotel Marcos Gamero* (☎ 223388, fax 224400) at 1 Oriente 1070, for US$53/67.

Places to Eat
One of Chile's best bargains is *Picada José Barrera* (☎ 224120), 1 Sur 530, jammed with downtown diners in search of tasty and filling three-course lunches costing less than US$2. The Mercado Central, bounded by 1 Norte, 5 Oriente, 1 Sur and 4 Oriente, has several economical cocinerías.

Other than its name, the only thing Brazilian about the *Mato Grosso Pub* (☎ 222399), 1 Norte 1198, is the music on the stereo, but the huge sandwiches and draft beer make it a good lunch choice.

Relatively expensive *El Alero de Gastón*

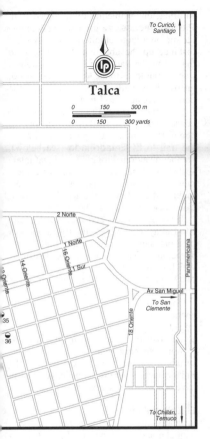

Talca

Getting There & Away

Bus Talca's main Rodoviario Municipal (☎ 243270) is at 2 Sur 1920, across the tracks but not directly accessible from the nearby railway station. There is a separate terminal, mostly for international buses, one block south at 3 Sur 1960.

Domestic companies with northbound and southbound services on the Panamericana include Buses Lit (☎ 242048), Tas Choapa (☎ 243334), Varmontt (☎ 242631), Intersur, Buses Jac as far as Temuco, and Sol del Pacífico to Valparaíso/Viña del Mar and to Concepción.

Pullman del Sur (☎ 244039) goes to the coastal resort of Constitución (US$2), while Buses Vilches (☎ 243366) goes three times daily, at 7.15 am and 1 and 4.50 pm, to the village of Vilches Alto and beyond, turning around at the entrance to Parque Nacional Vilches.

Tur-Bus (☎ 245029), at the international terminal, goes north and southbound on the Panamericana. Bonanza (☎ 242498, 245988), at the main terminal and at Avenida San Miguel 2630, crosses the Paso Pehuenche to Malargüe (US$25) and San Rafael (US$30), Argentina. From the international terminal, Andesmar (☎ 243142) goes to Bariloche (US$26), while Tas Choapa Internacional (☎ 241310) connects in Santiago for service to Mendoza.

Sample fares include Santiago or Chillán (US$6, four hours) and Temuco or Valparaíso/Viña del Mar (US$11, six hours).

Train Note the surrealistic pop-art murals at the Estación del Ferrocarril (☎ 226254) at 11 Oriente 1000, at the eastern end of 2 Sur. All trains from Santiago's Estación Central to Temuco and points south stop here en route.

In addition to long-distance service, a narrow-gauge passenger train still runs to the coastal resort of Constitución. This threatened service is well worth a detour for rail aficionados.

(☎ 233785), 2 Norte 858, has a broad menu with fine service in pleasant surroundings including a shady patio, but the food is good rather than exceptional. Other worthwhile restaurants include the *Centro Español* (☎ 224664) at 3 Oriente 1109, and *Ibiza* (which also has a takeaway rotisserie) at 1 Sur 1168. *Gobelino*, at the corner of 1 Sur and 1 Oriente, is one of the best in town.

Entertainment

The Cine Plaza, 1 Sur 770, shows current films.

Getting Around

Car Rental American Rent a Car (☎ 233-242) is at 1 Norte 1546.

AROUND TALCA
Villa Cultural Huilquilemu
Hernán Correa de la Cerda

Once an important fundo but now property of the Universidad Católica, this complex of restored 19th-century buildings, 10 km east of Talca on the highway to San Clemente, houses a variety of galleries and museums (including a fine collection of farm machinery), chapels and regional crafts. There is also a restaurant on site.

Huilquilemu (☎ 242474) is open Tuesday to Friday 3 to 6.30 pm, Saturday 4 to 6.30 pm and Sunday 11 am to 2 pm; take any San Clemente micro from Talca's Rodoviario Municipal.

PARQUE NACIONAL GIL DE VILCHES

Administered by Conaf and recently upgraded to national park status, this former 'área de protección' occupies 17,000 hectares in the Andean foothills east of Talca, between 600 and 2448 meters above sea level. Slated for expansion to about 22,000 hectares, Vilches is also the site of a puma research project with the participation of the Talca office of the private conservation organization Codeff.

Within the park, it's possible to camp in the upper basin of the Río Lircay and to make hiking excursions to the basaltic plateau of El Enladrillado, to Laguna El Alto and Laguna Tomate, and up the canyon of the Valle del Venado. Well-organized trekkers can loop across the drainage of the Río Claro to exit at Conaf's Area de Protección Radal Siete Tazas (see above).

Information

Conaf's helpful Centro de Información Ambiental, near the park entrance, has excellent displays on local natural and cultural history (there have been four sequential Indian occupations). Since Vilches has recently been declared a national park, it is likely that Conaf will begin to collect a small entrance fee.

Activities

Only 300 meters from the Centro de Información Ambiental by a signed trail, **Piedras Tacitas** is a pre-Columbian mortar site on a large granite boulder. A short distance up the abandoned logging road that forms the trail from the park entrance, a short spur leads to the **Mirador del Indio**, an overlook with splendid views of the densely forested Río Lircay valley.

From the spur to Mirador del Indio, the abandoned logging road climbs steeply for about two km to a signed junction to the trail to **El Enladrillado** (see below), another abandoned logging road that intersects a steep narrow trail to one of Chile's most extraordinary Andean views, overlooking the valley of the Río Claro, with Volcán Descabezado in the distance.

Trekkers can descend the valley of the Río Lircay, where backcountry camping is possible, and continue north to Radal Siete Tazas, in the Río Claro drainage. This trek, which ends at Parque Inglés, takes about two to three days; see the Radal Siete Tazas entry, above, for more detail.

Good but inexpensive rental horses, about US$12.50 per day, are available just outside the park entrance. These are a good alternative for visitors with little time to explore the park, but they're not really suitable for the very steep trail to El Enladrillado, where the four-legged beasts have caused serious erosion.

El Enladrillado

Probably the best single hike between Santiago and Temuco, the El Enladrillado trail offers tiring but exhilarating hiking crowned by top-of-the-world views from a unique columnar basalt plateau. About one hour's walk above the entrance station, a signed lateral follows an abandoned logging road for about half an hour to an ill-marked junction (look for an 'E' and an arrow carved in a tree at a small clearing) where the trail proper begins, just before the logging road begins to drop.

From this junction, the trail climbs steeply through dense forest, zigzagging for about an hour before leveling off and winding around various volcanic outcrops and emerging onto El Enladrillado, a site where some mad gardener appears to have set down massive hexagonal flagstones for an immense patio and planted prostrate shrubs among them. Like California's Devil's Postpile and Ireland's Giant's Causeway, this striking geological feature resulted from rapid cooling of an igneous intrusion before it reached the earth's surface; erosion of softer surrounding material has slowly exposed the resulting geometric structures to open view.

From the park entrance, figure about five hours up and 3½ hours down for this strenuous but rewarding hike, and allow at least an hour on top. There are two or three potable springs before the trail emerges above treeline, but carry as much water as possible. Close gates to keep livestock from the upper reaches of the trail.

Places to Stay & Eat
There is no formal camping within the park proper, except for backcountry sites, but there are several basic private sites, some of which sell supplies, near the entrance. Simple meals may also be available here. Choose a site as far away from the dusty highway as possible.

In Vilches Alto, six km west of the park entrance, *Hostería Rancho Los Canales* (☎ 237165 in Talca) has comfortable lodging for US$42 single and a restaurant as well.

Getting There & Away
Vilches is 65 km from Talca via paved Chile 115 and a lateral that may be the dustiest road in all of Chile (except in winter, when it's probably the muddiest). From Talca, Buses Vilches goes directly to the park entrance at 7.15 am (summer only) and 1 and 4.50 pm, returning at 9 am (summer only) and 2.30 and 6.30 pm. The fare is US$1.50.

CHILLÁN
Birthplace of Chilean liberator Bernardo O'Higgins, the market city of Chillán also marks the approximate northern border of La Frontera, that area over which Spain – and Chile – never really exercised effective

control until the state finally subdued the Mapuche in the late-19th century. Founded in 1565 as a military outpost, destroyed and refounded several more times after earthquakes and Mapuche sieges, it moved to its present site in 1835, although the old city, nearby Chillán Viejo, has never really died.

In addition to its colorful market, probably Chile's finest, Chillán has several notable museums and landmark works by the famous Mexican muralist David Alfaro Siqueiros and his colleague Xavier Guerrero. Thanks to this combination of attractions, Chillán is the best stopover of all the cities along the Panamericana between Santiago and Temuco.

Orientation
Chillán (population about 135,000), 400 km south of Santiago and 270 km north of Temuco, sits on an alluvial plain between the Río Ñuble and its smaller southern tributary, the Río Chillán. The city's focus is an area 12 blocks square, bounded by the divided, tree-lined Avenidas Ecuador, Brasil, Collín and Argentina. The center proper is the Plaza de Armas, bounded by Libertad, 18 de Septiembre, Constitución and Arauco.

Avenida O'Higgins leads north to the Panamericana (which passes northwest of the city) and south to the suburb of Chillán Viejo (the city center until the earthquake of 1835). From Chillán Viejo there is alternative access to the southbound Panamericana.

Information
Tourist Offices Sernatur (☎ 223272) is at 18 de Septiembre 455, half a block north of the plaza. From mid-December through February, it's open 8.30 am to 7.30 pm weekdays, Saturday 9.30 am to 2 pm only; the rest of the year, hours are 8.30 am to 1 pm and 3 to 6.45 pm, Saturday 9.30 am to 2 pm only. While much more helpful than in the past, the staff are still reluctant to divulge names and addresses of budget accommodations.

Chillán also has a municipal Oficina de Turismo (☎ 214117, Anexo 235) at 18 de

Septiembre 580, directly on the Plaza de Armas. In January and February, it's open 9.30 am to 7 pm, while the rest of the year opening hours are 9.30 am to 1 pm and 2.30 to 6.15 pm. There's another small information kiosk at the new bus terminal.

Acchi, the Automóvil Club de Chile (☎ 216410), is at O'Higgins 677 near El Roble.

Money For cash or travelers' checks, Schüler Cambios, Avenida Collín 585-A, is open 10 am to 1.30 pm and 3 to 8 pm weekdays, 10 am to 6 pm Saturday. More central is Banco Concepción, Constitución 550, which also has an ATM.

Post & Communications Chillán's area code is ☎ 42. Correos de Chile is at Libertad 505. CTC long-distance offices are at Arauco 625, while Entel is at 18 de Septiembre 746. Chilesat is at 18 de Septiembre 490, Local 327. Phone facilities are also available at the new bus terminal.

Travel Agencies Chillán has several travel agencies, including Centrotur (☎ 221306) at 18 de Septiembre 656, Hispanotur

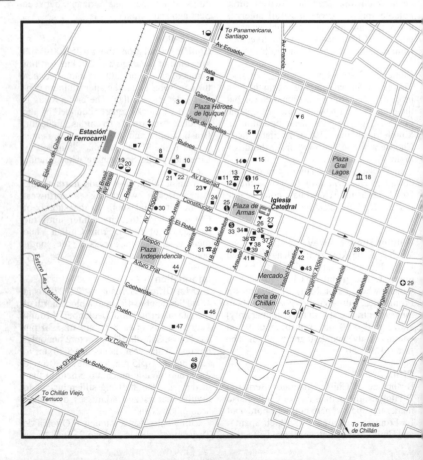

(☎ 222399) at El Roble 845 and Alto Nivel (☎ 225267) at Arauco 683, Oficina 5.

Cultural Centers The Pinacoteca Chillán Viejo (☎ 223536), in the old town, presents art exhibitions and concerts. Normal opening hours are weekdays 8 am to 8 pm.

Medical Services Chillán's Hospital Herminda Martín (☎ 212345) is six blocks east of the Plaza de Armas, at the corner of Constitución and Avenida Argentina.

PLACES TO STAY
2   Hospedaje Sonia Segui
5   Hotel Floresta
7   Hotel Libertador
8   Hotel Nevado Chillán
9   Hotel Real
10 Hostal Libertad
11 Hotel Javier Carrera
15 Claris Hotel
16 Hotel Rucamanqui
34 Gran Hotel
    Isabel Riquelme
35 Hotel Cordillera
37 Hotel Las Terrazas
41 Hotel Quinchamalí
46 Hospedaje Su Casa
47 Hospedaje Tino Rodríguez
    Sepúlveda

PLACES TO EAT
4   Pizzería Ficus
6   Planka
22 Jai Yang
23 Schwarzwald
26 Centro Español
38 Fuente Alemana
42 Friatto
44 Venecia

OTHER
1   Terminal María Teresa
3   Escuela México (Murals)
12 Ladeco
13 Chilesat
14 First Rent-a-Car
16 Sernatur
17 Post Office
18 Museo Franciscano
19 Terminal de Buses
    Inter-regionales
20 Buses Jota Be
21 Cine O'Higgins
25 Oficina de Turismo
27 Buses Loyola
28 Centro de Ski Termas
    de Chillán
29 Hospital Herminda Martín
30 Automóvil Club de Chile
31 Entel
32 Centrotur
33 Banco Concepción
36 CTC
39 Alto Nivel
40 Parador Jamón, Pan y Vino
43 Hispanotur
45 Terminal de Buses Rurales
48 Schüler Cambios

Escuela México

After a 1939 earthquake devastated Chillán, the Mexican government of President Lázaro Cárdenas donated a new school to the city. Before its completion, at the urging of Pablo Neruda, Mexican muralist David Alfaro Siqueiros decorated the library with spectacular murals honoring both indigenous and post-Columbian figures from each country's history – the northern wall devoted to Mexico and the southern wall to Chile.

Among the Mexican figures depicted on Siqueiros' murals, which bear the inflammatory title *Muerte al Invasor* (Death to the Invader), are the Aztec emperor Cuauhtémoc and his Spanish nemesis Hernán Cortés, revolutionary priest Miguel Hidalgo and his contemporary ally José María Morelos, the Zapotec Indian and President Benito Juárez, agrarian rebel Emiliano Zapata, reformist President Lázaro Cárdenas and Cárdenas' successor Manuel Avila Camacho. Chilean figures include the Mapuche resistance leaders Caupolicán, Lautaro and Galvarino, independence hero Bernardo O'Higgins, anticlerical writer Francisco Bilbao and reformist Presidents José Manuel Balmaceda and Pedro Aguirre Cerda.

Siqueiros' countryman Xavier Guerrero also participated in the project, his own simple but powerful murals, 'Hermanos Mexicanos' (Mexican brothers), flanking the staircase to the library. Unfortunately, the murals' state of preservation is declining.

While the Escuela México is a functioning school rather than a museum, the staff welcome visitors to the library at O'Higgins 250, between Gamero and Vega de Saldías. In summer, it's open 9.30 am to 12.30 pm and 3 to 6 pm daily; the rest of the year, hours are 9 am to 1 pm and 3 to 6 pm weekdays (except for Monday afternoon, when it's closed), Saturday 9.30 am to 12.30 pm only. Admission is free, but donations are welcome.

Feria de Chillán

Chillán's open-air market, one of Chile's

most colorful, is a sprawling affair with a superb selection of local crafts and mountains of fresh produce. Chilean playwright Antonio Acevedo Hernández described the scene as producing:

... the sensation of a broken rainbow fallen on the Feria, or of a fragment of the solar spectrum captured in a glorious instant, or perhaps the delirium of a mad painter projected on a massive pallet. The color is something that shouts, whirls, absorbs the light, and overwhelms the vision.

Open daily, but especially lively on Saturday, the Feria occupies the entire Plaza de la Merced, bounded by Maipón, 5 de Abril, Arturo Prat and Isabel Riquelme, but spills over into adjacent streets as well.

Museo Franciscano
Chillán's Franciscan museum displays historical materials of the order that, from 1585, proselytized among the Mapuche in 15 missions from Chillán in the north to Río Bueno in the south. On Sargento Aldea between Gamero and Vega de Saldías, it's normally open daily except Monday, 10 am to 1 pm and 3 to 7 pm, but was closed in 1996. Admission is free.

Parque Monumental Bernardo O'Higgins
In Chillán Viejo, only a short bus or cab ride from downtown, a tiled mural 60 meters long and six meters high marks O'Higgins' birthplace and illustrates scenes from his life. The associated **Centro Histórico y Cultural** displays several notable items from O'Higgins' life, but the attempt to portray the Viceroy's (illegitimate) son as a humble peasant is less than credible. The Centro compensates for these shortcomings with paintings by Chilean artists and a fine photographic natural history display.

In summer, the grounds and museum are open daily 8 am to 8 pm; the rest of the year, hours are 8 am to 6.30 pm. Admission is free.

Places to Stay – bottom end
Chillán has a good selection of budget accommodations from about US$7 per person, the cheapest of which is recommended *Hospedaje Sonia Segui* (☎ 214-879), Itata 288, whose rates include a good, generous breakfast. *Hospedaje Su Casa* (☎ 223931) at Cocharcas 555 is comparable. Try also *Hospedaje Tino Rodríguez Sepúlveda* (☎ 216181), Purén 443, which charges US$8.

Convenient *Hostal Libertad* (☎ 221263), Avenida Libertad 269, is good value for US$8 with shared bath. Comparably priced places include *Hotel Javier Carrera* (☎ 221175), Carrera 481, and the so-so *Claris Hotel* (☎ 221980), 18 de Septiembre 357.

Like most others in this category, family-run *Hotel Real* (☎ 221827), Avenida Libertad 219, needs paint, but it's clean and friendly; rooms with shared bath cost US$12/19, but try bargaining. Sometimes known as *Hotel Martín Ruiz de Gamboa* (due to a family dispute), the unimpressive *Hotel Nevado Chillán* (☎ 221013) at O'Higgins 497 charges US$15/22 with private bath.

Places to Stay – middle
The best mid-range value is recommended *Hotel Libertador* (☎ 223255), Avenida Libertad 35, where rooms with private bath cost only US$20/31. Others start around US$27/41, like *Hotel Floresta* (☎ 222253), 18 de Septiembre 278, where rooms are relatively small. Slightly dearer *Hotel Quinchamalí* (☎ 223381, fax 227365) El Roble 634, costs US$32/49, while *Hotel Rucamanqui* (☎ 222927), Herminda Martín 590 (an alleyway off Constitución), goes for US$35/55. At the upper end of the range, *Hotel Cordillera* (☎ 215211, fax 211198), Arauco 619, charges US$42/61.

Places to Stay – top end
Traditionally, Chillán's most prestigious accommodations are at *Gran Hotel Isabel Riquelme* (☎ 213663, fax 211541), Arauco 600, starting at US$78/95. A new competitor is *Hotel Las Terrazas* (☎ 227000, fax 227001) at Constitución 664, 5th floor, for US$83/92.

Places to Eat

In the newly remodeled Mercado Central, bounded by 5 de Abril, El Roble, Isabel Riquelme and Maipón, several simple but excellent and reasonably priced cocinerías prepare local specialties like pastel de choclo for as little as US$3 in season.

Schwarzwald (☎ 217703), Avenida Libertad 398, has good breakfasts and desserts but irritating music. The *Fuente Alemana* (☎ 212720), Arauco 661, is a good choice for sandwiches and kuchen.

For pizza, try *Pizzería Ficus* (☎ 212176) at Bulnes and Rosas or *Venecia* at Prat and Carrera. For Chinese food, there's *Jai Yang* (☎ 225429) at Libertad 250.

The *Centro Español* (☎ 216212), Arauco 555, has excellent food and service. Others worth a try are *Planka* (☎ 226109), Arauco 103, and *Kuranepe* (☎ 221409), O'Higgins 0420, north of the new bus terminal.

Friatto (☎ 222878), Isabel Riquelme 621, serves very good ice cream.

Entertainment

Cine O'Higgins, on Avenida Libertad near Avenida O'Higgins, shows current films.

Things to Buy

Chillán is one of central Chile's major artisan zones. Especially good are ceramics from the nearby villages of Quinchamalí, Paine and Florida. Leatherwork, basketry, horse gear and weavings are also available in the Feria (see above).

Getting There & Away

Ladeco, at the corner of Avenida Libertad and 18 de Septiembre, flies weekday afternoons to Los Angeles, Concepción (US$22) and Santiago (US$85).

Bus Chillán's new Terminal María Teresa (☎ 231119) is at Avenida O'Higgins 010, just north of Avenida Ecuador. A few companies still sell tickets and leave from the old Terminal de Buses Inter-regionales (☎ 221014) at Constitución 01, at the corner of Avenida Brasil.

Tur-Bus (☎ 212502) has 17 north-bound buses daily to Talca and Santiago;

southbound, it goes twice daily to Concepción and Los Angeles, and daily to Angol, Temuco, Valdivia, Osorno and Puerto Montt.

Línea Azul (☎ 211192) has 20 buses daily to Concepción, plus two daily to Santiago. Buses Jota Be (☎ 215862), Constitución 55, has seven daily to Salto del Laja and Los Angeles, with additional service to Angol, while Biotal (☎ 213223), Constitución 82, has three to Los Angeles, four to Concepción and seven to Talca. Cinta Azul also goes to Concepción.

Tas Choapa (☎ 223062) has regular services north and south along the Panamericana, direct services to Valparaíso/Viña del Mar, and combinations to northern Chile and Mendoza, Argentina (US$33), from Santiago. It also offers direct service to Bariloche, Argentina, daily (US$31). Igi Llaima (☎ 222991) has direct services to Neuquén, Argentina, via San Martín de los Andes and Zapala.

Sol del Sur and Sol del Pacífico also go to Santiago, Viña and Valparaíso. Buses Lit (☎ 222960) runs similar routes, also serving destinations in the coastal range behind Viña del Mar, such as Quilpué and Villa Alemana. Other companies covering the Panamericana include Buses Jac, between Temuco and Santiago; Tramaca (☎ 226922), from Santiago south to Villarrica and Pucón; Via Tur, to Santiago, Temuco and Valdivia; and Inter Sur, to Santiago.

Samples fares and approximate times include Concepción or Los Angeles (US$2.50, 1½ hours), Angol or Talca (US$5, three hours), Temuco (US$8, five hours), Valdivia (US$11, six hours), Puerto Montt (US$16, nine hours), Santiago (US$10, six hours), and Valparaíso/Viña del Mar (US$14, eight hours).

For local and regional services, the Terminal de Buses Rurales (☎ 223606) is on Sargento Aldea, south of Maipón. Buses Loyola (☎ 217838), 5 de Abril 594, runs buses to Termas de Chillán.

Train Trains between Santiago and Temuco arrive and depart from the Estación de

Ferrocarril (☎ 222424) on Avenida Brasil, at the west end of Libertad.

Getting Around

To/From the Airport Aeropuerto Bernardo O'Higgins (☎ 221655) is seven km east of town on the road to Coihueco. Ladeco runs its own minibuses, but it's close enough that taxis are not expensive.

Car Rental First Rent-a-Car (☎ 211218) is at 18 de Septiembre 380.

AROUND CHILLAN
Ninhue

Arturo Prat, the naval officer who tried to sink a Peruvian ironclad with his sword in Iquique harbor, was born in this village, 40 km northwest of Chillán via the Panamericana and another good paved road. Honoring this local hero, its **Santuario Cuna de Prat** is open Tuesday to Friday 10 am to 12.30 pm and 3 to 7 pm. Admission is free.

Buses to Ninhue leave from Chillán's Terminal de Buses Rurales on Sargento Aldea.

Termas de Chillán

Long renowned for its **thermal baths**, Termas de Chillán has more recently become celebrated for its **skiing**, on the southern slopes of 3122-meter Volcán Chillán. The runs themselves vary from 90 to 700 meters in vertical drop, and from 400 to 2500 meters in length; there are two double chairs and five surface lifts. The season ranges from mid-May to mid-October; in summer, the peak is a walk-up, with no special equipment necessary. Admission to the baths, open all year, costs US$12.50 for the day.

In peak ski season, weekly accommodations at the resort's *Nuevo Hotel Pirigallo*, including lift tickets and many other amenities, start around US$720 per person, double occupancy, in low season with half-board, rising as high as US$1140 with full board. Daily accommodations are also available starting around US$113 with half-board. There are relatively inexpensive

bunk accommodations available starting at US$515 per week with half-board or US$81 per day, including lift tickets. Reservations can be made at Centro de Ski Termas de Chillán, in Chillán (☎/fax 223-887) at Libertad 1042; in Concepción (☎/fax 234981) at O'Higgins 734; or in Santiago (☎ (02) 2512685, fax (02) 2515963) at Avenida Providencia 2237, Local P-41, Providencia.

In the summer off-season, the hotel charges US$132/203 for singles/doubles with full board. At that time, camping is possible at *Camping Termas de Chillán* (☎ 215977 in Chillán) for US$13 per site. *Parador Jamón, Pan y Vino* (☎ 222682, fax 211054), El Roble 580, 2nd floor, in Chillán, offers week-long fishing, hiking and camping excursions in the cordillera in and around the springs. Doubles normally cost US$116 with half-board.

Getting There & Away Termas de Chillán is 80 km east of the city of Chillán; all but the last nine km of the road is paved. Buses Loyola (☎ 217838), 5 de Abril 594 in the city, run buses to the springs.

CONCEPCION

Concepción's industry, convenient energy resources, port facilities and universities combine to make the capital of Region VIII Chile's second-most important city after Santiago. Vulnerable to earthquakes throughout its history, practically nothing remains of the city's colonial past, but the modern downtown has managed to integrate commerce, industry and education without sacrificing its human scale. Concepción has become a major export point for wood products from southern Chile, but the cost of extracting coal from the mines across the Biobío is making that industry economically unsustainable.

History

Founded in 1551 by Pedro de Valdivia but menaced constantly by Indians and devastated by earthquakes in 1730 and 1751, Concepción moved several times before settling at its present site in 1764. After a major Mapuche uprising in 1598, Spain did not seriously contest their control of the area south of the Biobío, and Concepción remained one of the empire's southernmost fortified outposts. The fine harbors of Talcahuano and San Vicente were major reasons for the city's location, facilitating seaborne communication with Santiago via Valparaíso.

From accounts of the late-colonial period, Concepción much resembled other Chilean cities, where the dwellings reflected clear distinctions between social classes. A British visitor in 1804 wrote:

The houses are commonly one storey high, but some are two, built of . . . *adoves*, large sun-dried bricks, and all of them are tiled. The largest have a courtyard in front, with an entrance through arched porches, and heavy folding doors . . . The windows have iron gratings, with many parts of them gilt, and inside shutters, but no glass. This article has been too dear, and it is consequently used only in the windows of the principal dwelling apartments of the richer classes. On each side of the court, or *patio*, there are rooms for domestics, the younger branches of the family, and other purposes . . .

The dwellings of lower classes are on the same plan, except that they have no courts or patios, the fronts being open to the street, but they usually have a garden at the back, where the kitchen is built separately from the house, as a precaution against fire.

This type of construction made the city especially susceptible to earthquake damage, while its low-lying site exposed it to the power of seismic seawaves. After experiencing a major quake near Valdivia in 1835, Darwin entered the Bahía de Concepción to find, as a result of the ensuing tsunami:

. . . the whole coast being strewed over with timber and furniture as if a thousand ships had been wrecked. Besides chairs, tables, bookshelves etc in great numbers, there were several roofs of cottages, which had been transported almost whole. The store-houses at Talcahuano had been burst open, and great bags of cotton, yerba, and other valuable merchandise were scattered on the shore.

After independence, Concepción's isolation from Santiago, coupled with the presence of lignite (brown coal) near Lota, enabled it to develop an autonomous industrial tradition. The export of wheat for the California Gold Rush market further spurred the area's economic growth, and secondary industries emerged later in the form of glass-blowing, timber and woolen and cotton textiles. The railway reached Concepción in 1872 and, after the Mapuche threat receded, the government bridged the Biobío to improve access to the mines and give the city a strategic role in the colonization of La Frontera, the present-day lakes region.

Mining of coal, a scarce resource in South America, now takes place in westward-sloping seams as much as three km beneath the sea, but production costs are high and the industry is moribund. Since WWII, the major industrial project to benefit Concepción has been Huachipato steel plant, built with US assistance. Inexpensive shipping and local energy have made the industry competitive despite the fact that the iron ore comes from Coquimbo, 800 km north, and limestone comes from the Madre de Diós islands, 1500 km south.

Despite Concepción's industrial importance, wages and standards of living are relatively low. This, coupled with activism at the Universidad de Concepción, made the city and its industrial hinterland the focus of a highly politicized labor movement which was a bulwark of support for Salvador Allende and the Unidad Popular. As a center of leftist opposition, the area suffered more than other regions under the military dictatorship of 1973-89. In response to a report questioning Lota's economic viability, the state coal company Enacar's dismissal of nearly 100 workers in mid-1996 occasioned a contentious strike and vigorous protests from miners, who blocked highways in southern Chile.

Orientation

Concepción sits on the north bank of the Río Biobío, Chile's only important

MIDDLE CHILE

MIDDLE CHILE

Concepción

MIDDLE CHILE

OTHER
1 Spanish Consulate
3 Automóvil Club de Chile
4 Pedro Fuentes
5 UK Consulate
6 Avis
11 Buses Cruz del Sur
12 Airport Express
13 Tur-Bus
14 Buses Tas Choapa
16 Buses Lit
17 Buses Igi Llaima
18 Sala Andes
19 Hospital Regional
20 CTC
21 Raíces (Artesanía)
22 Inter-Santiago
23 French Consulate,
   La Gruta
25 Entel
28 Turismo Ritz
30 EFE Venta de Pasajes
31 Sernatur
33 Cine Romano
34 CTC
35 Post Office, Chilesat
36 Concepción Soccer
   Club Offices
37 Casa del Arte
38 Budget
39 Italian Consulate
42 Peruvian Consulate
43 Cine Regina
44 National Airlines
45 LanChile
46 Intercam, Ladeco
50 Librería Manantial
51 Librería Paz
53 Instituto Chileno-Español
54 Argentine Consulate
55 Instituto Chileno-
   Británico
56 Instituto Chileno-
   Norteamericano
57 Laverap
58 Teatro Concepción,
   Cine Concepción, TAN
59 Cine Lido
60 Acchi Rental Cars
61 Alta
65 Brazilian Consulate
66 First Rent-a-Car
67 Turismo y Viajes Trigal
68 German Consulate
69 Instituto Chileno-Alemán,
   Sala Lessing
70 Instituto Chileno-Francés
71 Buses Los Alces
73 Conaf
75 Buses J Ewert
76 Buses Biobío
77 30 y Tanto
78 Hertz
79 Galería de Historia

PLACES TO STAY
2 Residencial Rehue
7 Casa de Huéspedes
8 Residencial Colo Colo
9 Hotel Cruz del Sur
23 Hotel El Araucano
28 Hotel Ritz
29 Residencial San Sebastián,
   Residencial Antuco
32 Hotel Tabancura
44 Hotel El Dorado
45 Hotel Alborada
47 Residencial Metro
48 Hotel San Sebastián
49 Residencial O'Higgins
62 Hotel della Cruz
64 Hotel Alonso de Ercilla
72 Hotel Cecil
74 Hotel Concepción

PLACES TO EAT
10 El Novillo Loco
11 Centro Italiano
15 China Town
23 Café Caribe
24 Dino's
26 Café Haití
27 Centro Español
40 El Naturista
41 Chung-Hwa
52 Fuente Alemana
63 Pastelería Suiza,
   Salón Inglés

navigable waterway. Cerro Caracol, a scenic overlook, blocks any eastward expansion so that Concepción and its port of Talcahuano, 15 km northwest on the sheltered Bahía de Concepción, are rapidly growing together. Concepción proper has a population of about 310,000, but combined with Talcahuano the metropolitan area has well over half a million.

Concepción's standard grid centers on Plaza Independencia, a pleasantly landscaped space with an attractive fountain. Few older buildings have survived – the drab, utilitarian buildings on the surrounding streets Aníbal Pinto, Barros Arana, Caupolicán and O'Higgins testify to the city's vulnerability to earthquakes. The bustling Plaza is often the site of impromptu performances by actors and street musicians, while Barros Arana and Aníbal Pinto are both lively pedestrian malls for two or three blocks to the north and west of the plaza.

Four blocks east of the plaza, Parque Ecuador is a pleasant refuge from the busy downtown. The park's border, Avenida Lamas, becomes Esmeralda southwest of Prat and leads to the Puente Viejo (old bridge), which continues south to the *Costa del Carbón* (Coast of Coal), where cities like Coronel and Lota supply the energy for Concepción's industry. A newer and better bridge, the Puente Nuevo, crosses the river to the west.

Information
Tourist Offices Sernatur (☎ 227976), Aníbal Pinto 460, is well stocked with maps and brochures and has a helpful and well-informed staff. In summer, when there's usually an English speaker on hand, it's open daily 8.30 am to 8 pm; the rest of the year, hours are weekdays only 8.30 am to 1 pm and 3 to 5.30 pm.

Acchi (☎ 311968), the Automóvil Club de Chile, Freire 1867, is also a good source of information.

Consulates Befitting its commercial and industrial importance, Concepción has a number of consulates:

Argentina
San Martín 472, 5th floor
(☎ 230257)
Brazil
Cochrane 754, Oficina 2
(☎ 236396)
France
Caupolicán 521 (☎ 230606)
Germany
Chacabuco 856 (☎ 242591)
Italy
Barros Arana 243, 2nd floor
(☎ 229506)
Peru
Barros Arana 348, Oficina 2
(☎ 224644)
Spain
Ejército 435 (☎ 235677)
UK
Galvarino 692 (☎ 225873)

Money Try Inter-Santiago, Caupolicán 521, Local 58, for travelers' checks, or Intercam at Barros Arana 402.

Post & Communications Concepción's area code is ☎ 41. Correos de Chile is at O'Higgins 799, corner of Colo Colo. CTC has long-distance offices at Colo Colo 487 and Caupolicán 649. Entel is at Barros Arana 541, Local 2, while Chilesat is at O'Higgins 799.

Travel Agencies Around Plaza Independencia it's hard to walk any distance in any direction without passing a travel agency. Turismo y Viajes Trigal (☎ 230-399), Chacabuco 912, has several offices throughout the region, but there are countless others.

Bookshops As a university town, Concepción has a good selection of bookshops. Try Librería Manantial (☎ 223614) at Caupolicán 481 or Librería Paz (☎ 226634) in the Galería Alessandri on the south side of Plaza Independencia.

Cultural Centers Concepción has a glut of binational cultural centers: the Instituto Chileno-Norteamericano (☎ 225506) at Caupolicán 315, the Instituto Chileno-Británico (☎ 242300) at San Martín 531,

the Instituto Chileno-Alemán (☎ 229287) at Chacabuco 840, the Instituto Chileno-Francés (☎ 226813) at Colo Colo 1 and the Instituto Chileno-Español (☎ 244573) at San Martín 450, 2nd floor.

National Parks Conaf (☎ 237272) is at Serrano 529, 3rd floor.

Laundry Laverap is at Caupolicán 334.

Medical Services Concepción's Hospital Regional (☎ 237445) is at San Martín and Avenida Roosevelt, eight blocks north of Plaza Independencia.

Galería de Historia
Vivid dioramas depicting local and regional history are the forte of this very fine museum on the edge of Parque Ecuador. Among the subjects are pre-Columbian Mapuche subsistence activities, the arrival of the Spaniards and battles between the two peoples (with fine representations of Mapuche tactics), construction of fortifications at Penco (the city's original site), treaty signings, military and literary figure Alonso de Ercilla, Chile's declaration of independence, the 1851 battle of Loncomilla, the devastating 1939 earthquake (15,000 houses destroyed) and an especially finely detailed model of a local factory.

At the corner of Victor Lamas and Lincoyán, the Galería (☎ 236555) is open Tuesday to Friday 9.30 am to 1 pm and 3 to 6.30 pm, weekends 10 am to 1 pm and 3 to 7 pm. Admission is free.

Casa del Arte
La Presencia de América Latina, a massive mural by Mexican artist Jorge González Camarena (a protégé of José Clemente Orozco) is the highlight of this university art museum, which also contains two rooms of landscapes and portraits.

In the Barrio Universitario, at Chacabuco and Larenas, the Casa del Arte (☎ 234985) is open Tuesday to Friday 10 am to 6 pm, Saturday 10 am to 4 pm and Sunday 10 am to 1 pm. Admission is free.

Special Events
Organized by the universities, commemorating the founding of the city, Concepción's Fiesta de la Primavera (Festival of Spring) lasts an entire week in early October.

Places to Stay – bottom end
Accommodations in Concepción do not vary much seasonally, since Concepción's industrial and commercial importance insulates it from such fluctuations, but many consider budget accommodations seriously overpriced.

Hostel The local Hostelling International affiliate is *Residencial San Sebastián* (☎ 242710, fax 243412), Barros Arana 741, Departamento 35, which charges US$11 per person with a hostel card.

Hospedajes & Residenciales In the summer, when university students vacate the town, there are plenty of inexpensive accommodations, but the rest of the year it can be hard to find something reasonable. Concepción's cheapest is basic *Residencial Rehue* (☎ 310600), Maipú 1859, which charges only US$7.50/10 single/double.

Focusing on university students, a standard, generic *Casa de Huéspedes* (☎ 244-152), Rengo 855, charges US$11 per person, with hot water and use of laundry and kitchen. *Residencial Metro* (☎ 225-305), Barros Arana 464, has spacious rooms with high ceilings for US$12/21; equally spacious *Residencial O'Higgins* (☎ 228303), O'Higgins 457, charges the same but includes breakfast.

Friendly, recommended *Residencial Colo Colo* (☎ 234790), Colo Colo 743, costs US$13/22 with shared bath, but it's rundown and there are only two showers for 20 rooms. *Residencial Antuco* (☎ 235-485) Barros Arana 741, Departamento 28, charges US$19/32 with breakfast.

Places to Stay – middle
As a last resort, mostly if the train's late, try *Hotel Cecil* (☎ 230677), across from the station at Barros Arana 9, where single/

doubles cost US$24/40. *Hotel San Sebastián* (☎ 243412, fax 233412), Rengo 463, is a better value at US$27/38.

At *Hotel Ritz* (☎ 226696, fax 243249), Barros Arana 721, the rates of US$32/49 seem excessive. *Residencial San Sebastián* (☎ 242710), Barros Arana 741, Departamento 35, has rooms for US$35/43 with shared bath, but rates are only slightly higher, US$40/48, with private bath.

On a quiet street but still very central at Aníbal Pinto 240, the *Hotel della Cruz* (☎ /fax 240016) is an outstanding choice for US$43/55. *Hotel Concepción* (☎ 228-851, fax 230948), Serrano 512, charges US$41/62. At *Hotel Tabancura* (☎ 238348, fax 238350), Barros Arana 786, 7th floor, rates are US$49/64.

Toward the upper end of the range is *Hotel Alonso de Ercilla* (☎ 227984, fax 230053), Colo Colo 334, at US$53/77. Try also *Hotel Cruz del Sur* (☎ 230944, fax 235655), Freire 889, which includes breakfast for US$59/83. *Hotel El Dorado* (☎ 229400, fax 231018), Barros Arana 348, is the next step up at US$63/84.

Places to Stay – top end
Concepción has two downtown luxury hotels, *Hotel Alborada* (☎ /fax 242144) at Barros Arana 457, for US$111/115, and *Hotel El Araucano* (☎ 230606, fax 230690) at Caupolicán 521, for US$134/142.

Places to Eat
Concepción's Mercado Central, occupying an entire block bounded by Caupolicán, Maipú, Rengo and Freire, has a multitude of cheap and excellent eateries, although the waitresses are more than just verbally aggressive – some literally try to drag customers into their venues. There's not much difference among these places in either price, quality or decor, but *Don José* offers a superb pastel de choclo, a regional specialty that is a meal in itself.

Pastelería Suiza, O'Higgins 780, has inexpensive fixed-price lunches, as does the next-door *Salón Inglés*. For a cheap standup cappuccino, try *Café Haití* (☎ 230755) at Caupolicán 511, Local 7, or *Café Caribe*

(☎ 241937) at Caupolicán 521, Local 34. The *Fuente Alemana* (☎ 228307), O'Higgins 513, serves good sandwiches and desserts. *El Naturista*, Barros Arana 244, offers vegetarian fare.

Dino's (☎ 243334), Barros Arana 533, is a branch of the popular southern Chilean chain, while *El Novillo Loco* (☎ 241114), Pasaje Portales 539, is for carnivores. The *Centro Español* (☎ 230685) at Barros Arana 675 and the *Centro Italiano* (☎ 230-724) at Barros Arana 935 add a bit of European flavor. For Chinese cuisine, visit *Chung-Hwa* (☎ 229539) at Barros Arana 262 or *China Town* (☎ 233218) at Barros Arana 1115.

Entertainment

Cinema Unlike many Chilean towns where video has meant the demise of the cinema, Concepción still has four decent movie theaters: the *Cine Concepción* (☎ 227193) at O'Higgins 650, the *Cine Lido* (☎ 230430) at Aníbal Pinto 343, the *Cine Regina* (☎ 225904) at Barros Arana 340 and the *Cine Romano* (☎ 227364) at Barros Arana 780. There are also frequent films at the university and at the various cultural institutes (see above).

Theater & Music Concepción has several important music and drama venues, so check the schedule for the *Teatro Concepción* (☎ 227193) at O'Higgins 650, the *Sala Andes* (☎ 227264) at Tucapel 374, the Instituto Chileno-Alemán's *Sala Lessing* (☎ 229287) at Chacabuco 840, or the *Casa del Arte* (☎ 234985) in the Barrio Universitario.

Pubs Reader's choice *30 y Tanto*, Arturo Prat 356, has good music and atmosphere, with a wide variety of empanadas.

Spectator Sports

Concepción's first-division soccer team (☎ 242684) has offices at Colo Colo 486.

Things to Buy

Local and regional crafts are on display in the Mercado Central, and also at La Gruta at Caupolicán 521, Local 64, and Raices (Artesanía) at Freire 552, Local 116. Look for woolens, basketry, ceramics, wood carvings and leather goods.

Getting There & Away

Air LanChile (☎ 240025), Barros Arana 451, has at least two flights daily to Santiago (US$90), daily flights to Temuco (US$40) and Valdivia (US$70), and Tuesday, Thursday and Sunday flights to Punta Arenas (US$249). Ladeco (☎ 480014), Barros Arana 402, averages three flights daily to Santiago, flies Sunday evenings to Temuco and Saturday afternoon to Punta Arenas.

National Airlines (☎ 246710), Barros Arana 348, Local 1, flies 15 times weekly to Santiago (US$81) and daily except Saturday to Puerto Montt (US$83), continuing Friday and Sunday to Punta Arenas (US$224).

Alta (☎ 223371), Caupolicán 246-A, flies northbound three times daily to Viña del Mar (US$62), except Saturday (two flights), and daily to La Serena (US$97), Copiapó (US$132), Antofagasta (US$148), Calama (US$185) and Iquique (US$175). Southbound, Alta flies two or three times daily to Temuco (US$35) and Puerto Montt (US$72), with morning flights continuing daily except Tuesday mornings to Balmaceda (US$120), Puerto Natales (US$185) and Punta Arenas (US$185), and weekday afternoons to Chaitén (US$86), and twice weekly to Valdivia (US$41) and Osorno (US$55).

The Argentine provincial airline TAN (☎ 238080), O'Higgins 650, Oficina 602, flies two or three times weekly over the Andes to the city of Neuquén.

Bus Concepción's Terminal de Buses Puchacay (☎ 316666) is on the outskirts of town at Tegualda 860, a side street off Avenida General Bonilla (Ruta 148), the highway to Chillán. All the buses leave from here, but because of its inconvenient location, many companies maintain a more central office as well as one at the terminal.

Tur-Bus (☎ 315555), Tucapel 530, has

13 buses daily to Santiago (two of which continue to Valparaíso and Viña del Mar) and also goes southbound to Temuco, Valdivia and Puerto Montt. Buses leave from the separate Terminal Chillancito, Camilo Henríquez 2565, the northward extension of Bulnes.

Sol del Pacífico has 10 buses daily to Santiago, six of them continuing to Valparaíso and Viña del Mar. Buses Lit (☎ 230722) at Tucapel 459 has another four to Santiago, but other companies cover the same route, including Sol del Sur (☎ 313841; eight daily), Estrella del Sur (eight), Transtur (four) and Intersur (seven).

Buses Tas Choapa (☎ 312639), Barros Arana 1081, goes twice daily to Santiago and twice to Puerto Montt, and has excellent connections to northern Chile and to Argentina. Varmontt (☎ 314010) goes nightly to Puerto Montt, while Igi Llaima (☎ 312498) at Tucapel 432 goes four times daily to Temuco and Puerto Montt, as does Cruz del Sur (☎ 314372) at Barros Arana 935, Local 9. Tur-Bus, Igi Llaima and Cruz del Sur all go to Valdivia as well.

Buses Biobío (☎ 310764), Arturo Prat 416 and at the Chillancito terminal, has very frequent service to Los Angeles, Angol and Temuco, though Jota Be (☎ 312652) also has numerous services to Los Angeles and to Salto del Laja. Línea Azul (☎ 311126) is the most frequent to Los Angeles, about every half hour from Chillancito, but Igi Llaima has another 10.

For services down the coast to Coronel, Lota, Arauco, Lebú, Cañete and Contulmo, try Buses Los Alces (☎ 240855) at Prat 699 or Buses J Ewert (☎ 229212) at Arturo Prat 535.

Charges vary considerably among companies, but typical fares from Concepción include Chillán or Los Angeles (US$3, two hours), Angol (US$2.50, 1½ hours), Talca (US$7, four hours), Temuco (US$7, four hours), Valdivia (US$10, six hours), Puerto Montt (US$12, seven hours), Santiago (US$11, seven hours) and Valparaíso/Viña del Mar (US$15, nine hours).

Train Concepción's Estación de Ferrocarril (☎ 227777) is on Arturo Prat at the end of Barros Arana, but EFE also has a Venta de Pasajes (ticket office; ☎ 225286) at Aníbal Pinto 478, Local 3. Trains leave daily at 1 and 10 pm. Fares are US$20 salón, US$29 cama alta, and US$39 cama baja.

Getting Around

To/From the Airport Aeropuerto Carriel Sur is five km northwest of downtown, on the road to Talcahuano. Turismo Ritz (☎ 237637) at Barros Arana 721, Airport Express (☎ 236444) at Tucapel 565, and Pedro Fuentes (☎ 313626) at Freire 1815, all runs airport minibuses for US$3, leaving from in front of LanChile, Ladeco and National Airlines offices.

To/From the Bus Terminal Buses and taxi colectivos connect downtown with both the Chillancito and Puchacay bus terminals.

Car Rental Concepción has several rental agencies to choose among: the Automóvil Club de Chile (Acchi; ☎ 225039) at Caupolicán 294, Hertz (☎ 230341) at Arturo Prat 248, First Rent-a-Car (☎ 233-121) at Cochrane 862, Budget (☎ 225377) at Angol 547 and Avis (☎ 241408) at Maipú 1156.

AROUND CONCEPCION
Museo Huáscar

Built in Birkenhead, England, in 1865, captured from the Peruvian navy in 1879 and now on display in Talcahuano, the *Huáscar* was one of the world's earliest ironclad battleships. Despite a nominal display of naval portraits, it's less a museum than an object, owing its remarkable state of preservation to the labor of naval conscripts whose spit-and-polish maintenance work never ends.

From Concepción, take any bus with 'Base Naval' on its placard to the Apostadero Naval, beyond the Club de Yates on Avenida Villaroel. You must leave your passport at the gate; photography is permitted, but only with the port of Talcahuano or the open sea as background – do *not* photograph other naval vessels or any part of the base itself. Opening hours are daily except Monday from 9 am to 11.30 pm and 2 to 6 pm (5 pm in winter). Admission to the Museo (☎ 545222) costs US$0.75 for adults, half that for children.

La Costa del Carbón

As an advertising slogan, the 'Coast of Coal' may sound unappealing, but beach towns south of the Río Biobío draw substantial crowds to and around Coronel (which reeks of fishmeal), Lota, Arauco and Península Lebú. The best day trip is to Lota, best known as the site of the 14-hectare **Parque Isidora Cousiño**, but the town's mid-century company-town architecture is also worth a look. Open daily 10 am to 8 pm, the park is a remarkable demonstration of the ability of cultivated beauty to survive alongside massive slag heaps. Admission costs US$1.25 for adults, half that for children.

Another unusual excursion is a tour of Enacar's undersea mine at Lota, in which you put on a hard hat, ride in a mine cart and chip off a hunk of coal with a pneumatic drill. These tours, which cost US$12.50 per person, take place daily at 10.50 am and 3 pm every day, all year. For further details, contact Parque Isidora Cousiño (☎ 249039), Carlos Cousiño 199 in Lota Alto, between 8 am and 6 pm weekdays. Reservations must be made 24 hours in advance.

Coronel, just north of Lota, has recently begun a **Muestra Cultural de Folklore** (folklore festival) in early February, during its traditional **Semanas Culturales de Coronel**.

Ruta de La Araucana

Local and regional tourist authorities are establishing a series of historical markers at famous sites from soldier-poet Alonso de Ercilla y Zuñiga's epic poem *La Araucana* in their resistance to the Spanish invasions of the 16th century. The first two markers have been placed near Punta Escuadrón, 22 km south of Concepción, and near Arauco, about two km west of the town of Carampangue.

Escuadrón is the site of the **Hito Histórico Galvarino**, commemorating the battle of Lagunillas (1557), where the Mapuche *toqui* (chief) Galvarino submitted stoically as the Spaniards severed both his hands with their swords, after which he placed his own head on the block. The Spaniards refrained from executing him, but he swore revenge and continued to resist. On being recaptured years later, he may have been executed, though some historians believe he killed himself to avoid Spanish retribution.

The **Hito Histórico Prueba y Elección de Caupolicán** marks the site where Mapuche leader Colo Colo chose Caupolicán to lead the indigenous resistance that, at Tucapel on the upper reaches of the Río Laja, routed the Spaniards and executed Pedro de Valdivia in 1553.

Beauty Among the Slag

Designed for the influential Cousiño family by an English landscape architect between 1862 and 1872, Parque Isidora Cousiño itself is an incongruous plantation of exotic trees surrounded by rose gardens and other flowers beds, ponds with black-necked swans, and loads of neoclassical statuary – a good image of Caupolicán being the only exception. Among the trees are redwoods, cypresses, acacias and the like, but very few Chilean natives. Maintenance is probably not up to the standards of the Cousiño years.

One thing the park seems to try to prove is that beauty can thrive alongside blight – the conspicuous slag heaps to the north. Some plants have even colonized the toxic tailings.

Now maintained by the state coal company Enacar, Parque Cousiño is open to the public in summer (September to March) 8 am to 8 pm Monday to Saturday, 10 am to 8 pm Sunday and holidays; the rest of the year it closes at 6 pm. Admission costs US$1.25 for adults, US$0.65 for children. ■

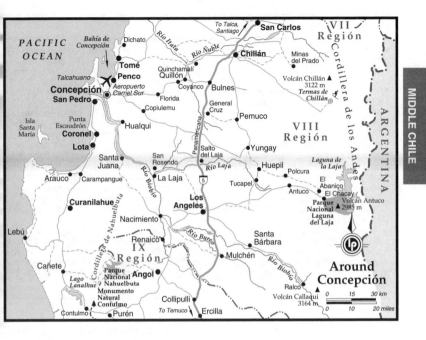

At Cañete, 135 km south of Concepción, the disappointing **Museo Araucano Juan Antonio Ríos** (☎ 611093) takes its name from a 20th-century Chilean president born nearby, rather than for any of the Mapuche people it presumably esteems. Exhibits stress historical antecedents, economic activities, funerary customs and art, particularly silverwork. It also includes a small garden of native plants and a model replica of a Spanish fortification. It's open Tuesday to Saturday 9 am to 6 pm, Sunday and holidays 8.30 am to 7 pm; the rest of the year, hours are Tuesday to Saturday 10 am to 6.30 pm, Sunday and holidays 2 to 7 pm. Admission costs US$0.75, half that for children, but it's free Sundays.

Monumento Natural Contulmo

A worthwhile stop for travelers passing through en route to Angol and Los Angeles, Monumento Natural Contulmo is a small (84-hectare) forest corridor abutting the highway. An eight-km trail leads through woods as dense and verdant as a tropical rainforest; plaques identify major tree species, but the giant ferns and climbing vines are just as intriguing. There are picnic facilities, but the nearest camping is at Lago Lanalhue, a few km to the west, where the *Camping Municipal* has 40 sites for US$9.

LOS ANGELES

Founded in 1739 as a bulwark against the Mapuche, Santa María de Los Angeles is not Hollywood, and the closest thing to a freeway is the two-lane Panamericana that skirts the town to the east. It does, however, have good access to the upper reaches of the Río Biobío and to Parque Nacional Laguna del Laja, which includes 2985-meter Volcán Antuco.

Orientation

Los Angeles (population 95,000) is an agricultural and industrial service center

Ercilla & the Araucanian Wars

In the early colonial times, armed conflict between Spaniards and Chile's Indian peoples was so bloody, protracted and pervasive that Chilean historian Alvaro Jara entitled his history of the period *Guerra y Sociedad en Chile* (War and Society in Chile). Yet, in spite of frequent brutality, the adversaries did not lack respect for each other and some even managed to see the broader picture and tragedy of the era even as they participated in it. The most prominent of these was Spanish soldier-poet Alonso de Ercilla, whose epic poem *La Araucana* is one of the classics of colonial Latin American literature.

Born into a noble Basque family in 1533 and educated in the classics, Ercilla entered the service of the Spanish royal family at the age of 15. At 21, on a visit to London, he heard of Pedro de Valdivia's death at the hands of the Araucanians and resolved to participate in the Spanish campaign against them. Spending seven years in the New World, more than 1½ years exploring Chile and fighting the Indians, he returned to Spain in 1563 and published his lengthy poem, based on personal experience, in three parts over two decades after 1569. While the epic form is itself romantic and Ercilla expresses the values of the Spanish elite, the poem is notable for its fidelity to historical events and its regard for, and analysis of, an opponent whom most Spaniards both feared and denigrated. While the Araucanians bedeviled Ercilla and his countrymen, he could still admire their courage, tactics and adaptability.

Araucanian tactics were unconventional and difficult to counter. To offset their opponents' mobility, they retreated into the forest, lured the Spaniards into swampy areas where horses were ineffective and dismounted the riders with ropes and clubs. When possible they fought in the midday heat, quickly exhausting the heavily armored Spaniards, and set traps with sharpened stakes where (in Ercilla's words) surprised soldiers would die 'impaled . . . in agony.'

---

110 km south of Chillán, but its commercial downtown is very small – within a block of the Plaza de Armas, it's almost exclusively residential. The channeled Estero Quilque, two blocks north of the plaza, flows through the city into parklands on its western edge. East of the plaza, Avenida Alemania leads to the Panamericana.

Information

Tourist Offices There's a municipal Oficina de Información Turística on Caupolicán, alongside the post office on the south side of the Plaza de Armas. Another reliable source of information is the Automóvil Club de Chile (☎ 314209), Caupolicán 201.

Money Change money elsewhere if possible, but Cultura Tours, Lautaro 164, will change US cash and perhaps travelers' checks. Banco Santander has an ATM at Colón 492.

Post & Communications Los Angeles' area code is ☎ 43. Correos de Chile is on Caupolicán, on the south side of the Plaza de Armas. CTC long-distance offices are at Paseo Quilpué, just east of Colón between Colo Colo and Rengo, and at the bus terminal. Entel is at Colo Colo 481.

Laundry The Lavandería Central del Lavado is at Villagrán 270-A.

Medical Services Los Angeles' Hospital Regional (☎ 321456) is on Avenida Ricardo Vicuña, just east of Los Carrera.

Places to Stay

Los Angeles differs from many Chilean cities in that much of the accommodations are along the Panamericana rather than in the city itself, because of the Salto del Laja, the area's biggest nearby attraction. Nevertheless, the most reasonable alternatives are in town.

Bottom-end accommodations are scarce.

Like the Plains Indians of North America, the Araucanians themselves became expert horsemen, raiding the Argentine pampas for mounts, taming them and driving them back across the Andes to aid the resistance. While Spain's commitment to dominate the region south of the Biobío was less than it might have been had the economic incentives been greater (there were no great bonanza mines to grab the Crown's attention), one of the major factors in Araucanian success was their organization – or perhaps their lack of it. Like other Europeans, the Spaniards had a hierarchical system of command which discouraged initiative and improvisation, but in the more egalitarian Indian society no single leader was indispensable.

Ercilla openly praised the intelligence and bravery of Indian leaders like Lautaro, Caupolicán and Colo Colo, some of whom distinguished themselves at a very young age. Captured by the Spaniards at age 15 and forced to serve three years as a scout, Lautaro escaped to play a leading role at the battle of Tucapel (where Colo Colo's forces killed Pedro de Valdivia), and became an important military leader until his death at the hands of the Spaniards in 1557, at age 22. Caupolicán, named *toqui* by the older Colo Colo, also helped defeat the Spaniards at Tucapel, later suffering a gruesome but stoic death when the Spaniards impaled him on a sharpened wooden pole – although legend says the disdainful cacique threw them off the platform and sat down of his own volition.

Ercilla's literary legacy still permeates all facets of Chilean society, from popular culture and tourism to revolutionary politics. The country's most popular soccer team is known, simply, as Colo Colo. A series of historical markers on the coastal highway south of Concepción marks the Ruta de La Araucana, immortalizing the bravery of caciques like Galvarino, who quietly suffered the amputation of both his hands but escaped to help lead his people against the Spanish invaders. And one of Chile's most troublesome guerrilla movements, which only recently ceased its resistance despite the return of democracy, adopted the name of Lautaro. ∎

Residencial Winser (☎ 323782, fax 320-348), Colo Colo 335, charges only US$9 per person, but it's often full. At Rengo 138, its sister *Hotel Winser* (☎ 313845) is an excellent alternative for US$12.50/30 single/double with shared bath; US$34/44 with private bath; next door to the Residencial Winser, at Colo Colo 327, it has an annex (☎ 315140) with identical prices.

Dating from 1907, the very central, distinctive *Hotel Mazzola* (☎ 321643), Lautaro 579, charges US$26/32 with private bath. *Gran Hotel Muso* (☎ 313183) at Valdivia 222 costs US$41/52, while the *Hotel Mariscal Alcázar* (☎ 311725) at Lautaro 385, starts around US$58/73.

Places to Eat

Nearly all of Los Angeles' restaurants are on or near Colón, north of the Plaza de Armas. An excellent choice for breakfast, *Café Prymos* (☎ 323731), Colón 400, also has sandwiches, outstanding ice cream, a clearly designated tobacco-free section and occasional live music. The traditional chain *Bavaria* (☎ 315531) is at Colón 357.

Julio's Pizza (☎ 314530), Colón 452, is part of a small chain with excellent food. For parrilla, the best choice is *El Alero* (☎ 312899), at Colo Colo 235, but for more varied fare try the *Centro Español* (☎ 311669) at Colón 482 or the *Club de la Unión* (☎ 322218) at Colón 261. *Chi Hwa* (☎ 313867), Colón 438, 2nd floor, serves Chinese food.

Dónde Ramón, on Colón between Janequeo and Lincoyán, is a parrilla which also has live peña entertainment.

Things to Buy

For local and regional crafts, visit the Galería Centro Español, Colón 482, Locales 7 and 8, or the Mercado Los Angeles at Villagrán and Tucapel.

Getting There & Away

Air LanChile (☎ 3223324) is at Avenida Alemania 320. Ladeco flies weekdays

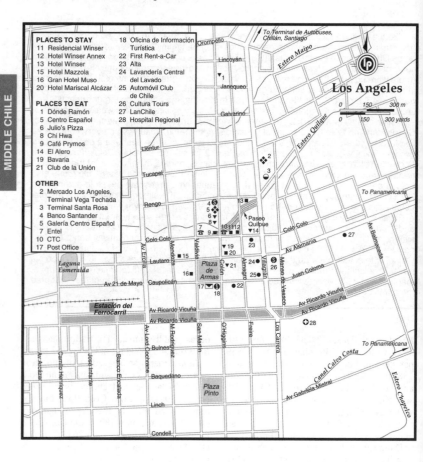

PLACES TO STAY
11 Residencial Winser
12 Hotel Winser Annex
13 Hotel Winser
15 Hotel Mazzola
16 Gran Hotel Muso
20 Hotel Mariscal Alcázar

PLACES TO EAT
1 Dónde Ramón
5 Centro Español
6 Julio's Pizza
8 Chi Hwa
9 Café Prymos
14 El Alero
19 Bavaria
21 Club de la Unión

OTHER
2 Mercado Los Angeles,
   Terminal Vega Techada
3 Terminal Santa Rosa
4 Banco Santander
5 Galería Centro Español
7 Entel
10 CTC
17 Post Office
18 Oficina de Información
   Turística
22 First Rent-a-Car
23 Alta
24 Lavandería Central
   del Lavado
25 Automóvil Club
   de Chile
26 Cultura Tours
27 LanChile
28 Hospital Regional

Los Angeles

to Concepción (US$21) and Santiago (US$92).

Alta has offices on Colo Colo between Villagrán and Almagro.

Bus Los Angeles' main terminal de autobuses has moved to Avenida Sor Vicenta 2051 on the northeastern outskirts of town, mostly easily reached via Avenida Villagrán.

There are very frequent buses between Los Angeles and Concepción with Mini Pullman, Trancyl, Biobío (☎ 314621, 320669), Igi Llaima (☎ 321666) and Los

Alces. Jota Be (☎ 317180) has 14 buses daily to Angol, the gateway to Parque Nacional Nahuelbuta, via Renaico (US$2).

Other Los Angeles bus companies, running north-south services along the Panamericana, are Biotal (☎ 317357), Cruz del Sur (☎ 317630), Fénix Pullman Norte (☎ 322502), Intersur (☎ 317327), Buses Jac (☎ 317469), Buses Laja (☎ 316729), Tas Choapa (☎ 322266), Unión del Sur (☎ 316891), Tramaca (☎ 317488), Tur-Bus (☎ 312261) and Varmontt (☎ 312647).

From Terminal Santa Rosa, at the corner of Villagrán and Rengo, ERS goes to the village of Antuco, gateway to Parque Nacional Laguna del Laja, seven times daily on weekends, three times daily on weekdays. Other rural buses leave from the Terminal Vega Techada, at the corner of Villagrán and Tucapel.

Sample fares and times include Chillán (US$2.50, 1½ hours), Concepción (US$3, two hours), Temuco (US$6, four hours), Puerto Montt (US$12, eight hours) and Santiago (US$13, eight hours).

Getting Around
First Rent-a-Car (☎ 313812) is at Caupolicán 350.

AROUND LOS ANGELES
Salto del Laja
Just east of the Panamericana, 25 km north of Los Angeles en route to Chillán, the Río Laja drops nearly 50 meters over a steep escarpment to form a miniature of Iguazú Falls before joining the Biobío at La Laja, 40 km to the west. Salto del Laja is a very popular recreation area, perhaps as much for its accessibility as its scenery.

At Km 485, camping is possible year round at *Camping Curanadú* (☎ 312686 in Los Angeles) for about US$9 per site. As well, it offers conventional accommodations at *Motel Curanadú* for US$38 double. Nearby alternatives include *Hotel Los Manantiales* (☎/fax 314275 in Los Angeles) for US$58 double, and *Hostería Salto del Laja* (☎ 321706, fax 313996 in Los Angeles) from US$66/86, both with breakfast.

German-run *Hospedaje El Rincón* (☎ (09) 4415019, fax 317168) will pick up passengers at Cruce La Mona, Km 494, or at the Los Angeles bus terminal. Rooms with breakfast cost US$15, with full board US$33. English, German and French are spoken.

Rafting the Biobío
By near unanimous consent, the Río Biobío southeast of Los Angeles is South America's premiere Class V whitewater, but massive hydroelectric development has disrupted both recreational river running

and the livelihood of the Pehuenche people who live in the region. Trips of varying length, difficulty, cost and itinerary are still available. In Concepción, contact Club South Expediciones (☎/fax (041) 232290), O'Higgins 680, Oficina 218-D, or Explorer Biobío (☎ (041) 225745, fax 232647), O'Higgins 680, Oficina 409. Both run day trips in the range of US$45, or weekend trips for US$70.

Another company is Chonos Expediciones (☎ (02) 5256256 in Santiago), Antonio Bellet 309 in Providencia, with four-day/three-night trips which start in Victoria, north of Temuco, and cost US$500 per person. Altué Expediciones (☎ (02) 2321103, fax 2336799), Encomenderos 83 in Las Condes, arranges five-day, four-night trips including a sleeper train from Santiago and an ascent of Volcán Callaquen, for US$940 per person.

To arrange the trip in the US before reaching Chile, try contacting Mountain Travel Sobek (☎ 510-527-8100, 800-227-2384 toll-free), 6420 Fairmont Avenue, El Cerrito, California 94530. Costs for 14-day trips run to about US$2725 per person, double occupancy. Another possibility is Adventure Travel International (☎ 970-353-4552, fax 353-7061), 1924 21st Avenue Court, Greeley, Colorado 80631, where five-day trips cost US$1000 (land cost only). With an optional ascent of 3164-meter Volcán Callaqui, the cost is US$1300.

Chile's Endangered Rivers

In its drive toward modernization, symbolized by more than a decade of uninterrupted growth, Chile has had to deal with limited energy resources. The country provides less than half its petroleum requirements from domestic sources, mainly from onshore and offshore fields in the southern region of Magallanes, which also yield natural gas. Coal has been nearly exhausted in the undersea mines near Concepción, though there remains some exploitable coal north of Punta Arenas. To maintain its growth, Chile requires energy, preferably clean energy to reduce the dense air pollution of Santiago, and perhaps even to encourage industrial development outside the central heartland.

To overcome these shortcomings, successive Chilean governments have made a conscious decision to encourage hydroelectricity. On the face of it, this is a wise decision: in many areas, heavy spring snowmelt in the high Andes feeds raging transverse rivers, which pass through narrow canyons that make ideal dam sites. Unfortunately, these sites also have major drawbacks – social, cultural, environmental and economic.

The most internationally notorious case is the attempt by the powerful electrical utility company Endesa (formerly a state agency) to construct a series of dams on the Río Biobío, revered by rafters and kayakers as one of the world's finest whitewater rivers. For years, Pehuenche Indian communities and environmental activists like the Grupo de Acción por el Biobío (Biobío Action Group) have protested the loss of prime community lands and scenic canyons under stagnant reservoirs like the Pangue dam site, whose rising waters have submerged the Royal Flush rapids.

The Pangue is only one of seven proposed dams on the upper Biobío, expected to provide half of Chile's hydroelectricity – but none of it to local consumers (96% of Pehuenche households lack electricity). Objections from nine Pehuenche communities, based on Endesa's inadequate environmental impact report, have stopped construction on

PARQUE NACIONAL LAGUNA DEL LAJA

In *The Voyage of the Beagle*, Darwin remarks that the inhabitants of Talcahuano believed that Concepción's great earthquake of 1835 'was caused by two Indian women, who being offended . . . stopped the volcano of Antuco.' Whether or not suppressed vulcanism triggered that quake, 2985-meter Antuco and its lava flows have dammed the Río Laja to form the laguna from which this 11,600-hectare national park takes its name. The park protects the mountain cypress *(Austrocedrus chilensis)* and the monkey-puzzle tree *(Araucaria araucana)* at the northern limit of its distribution, as well as other uncommon tree species. Mammals are rare, even though puma, foxes and vizcachas do exist. Nearly 50 bird species frequent the area, including the Andean condor.

In some ways, the lake itself belies its violent origins. From an overlook, one 19th-century American visitor described it as nearly sterile:

. . . green, calm and noiseless beneath. No ripple disturbed the surface – no bird played upon its bosom; and enveloped in morning mist, with mountains rising dark and blue on the farther shore, so gloomy, so deathlike, it seemed a fit companion for desolate Antuco, upon whose vast sides not a blade of grass, nor any other sign of life existed.

Laguna del Laja presents a less desolate scene now, as pampas grass and other pioneer species have begun to colonize the lava fields, and wildlife has returned to many sectors.

Geography & Climate

In the upper drainage of the Río Laja, 95 km east of Los Angeles, Laguna del Laja is a natural lake so modified by a variety of hydroelectric projects, including tunnels and dams, that it more closely resembles a reservoir. The park itself, however, is a mountainous area ranging from 1000 to nearly 3000 meters above sea level. Its most striking feature is Antuco's symmetrical cone, but the higher Sierra Velluda to the 570-megawatt Ralco dam, which would inundate 3395 hectares of prime alluvial bottom lands. Endesa has offered a land swap, but the governmental Consejo Nacional de Desarollo Indígena refuses to approve it, saying Endesa's proposal substitutes inferior lands. In the meantime, both Chilean and foreign adventure travel companies continue to run the river, attracting tourists and valuable foreign exchange to Chile.

The Biobío is not the only river under threat. Residents in the area of Chile's other world-class whitewater site, the Futaleufú near the Argentine border southeast of Chaitén, were recently shocked to learn that Endesa and two other hydroelectric utilities, Colbún Machicura and Chilgener, had filed claims on water rights to the river's 12,000-cubic-meter-per-second flow without any fanfare. In response, the locals have formed their own Corporación de Defensa y Desarrollo del Río Futaleufú (Codderfu), seeking to create a nationally recognized and protected river corridor. Their supporters include Codeff, Grupo de Acción por el Biobío and the California-based FutaFund, originally formed by US kayaker Chris Spelius.

Outdoor river-based recreation is making a particularly large contribution to the Futaleufú economy. In addition to the increasing number of whitewater companies operating in the area, fishing is a big money earner, as some fly fishing lodges charge up to US$3000 per guest per week.

The Aisén region's other major river, the Río Baker, carries the largest volume of any Chilean river through what is one of the country's least densely populated areas, from the outlet of Lago General Carrera to the Pacific Ocean at Caleta Tortel. There are preliminary plans to construct hydroelectric sites for a new aluminum plant – an industry noted for its high energy consumption.

Readers interested in further information can contact the Grupo de Acción por el Biobío (☎ (02) 7371420, fax 7776414) is at Lagarrigue 112, Recoleta, Santiago, or FutaFund (☎ 209-572-3882), PO Box 4536, Modesto, California 95352, USA. ∎

the southwest, beyond the park boundaries, offers a series of impressive glaciers.

Summer is fairly dry, but more than two meters of precipitation accumulate as rain and snow the rest of the year. The ski season lasts from June to October.

Trekking

Laguna del Laja has many trails suitable for either day hikes or longer excursions; the best is the circuit around Volcán Antuco, which provides views of both the Sierra Velluda and the lake. For details, consult Lonely Planet's *Trekking in the Patagonian Andes*.

If trekking or camping, buy all supplies in Los Angeles, where selection is far better and prices are much lower.

Places to Stay & Eat

There are no formal campgrounds within the park proper, but near the entrance, at Km 90 on the road from Los Angeles is *Cabañas y Camping Lagunillas* (☎ 314-275 in Los Angeles). It offers 30 sites with electricity, hot showers, fire pits and picnic tables for US$15 per site. The cabañas charge US$90 per night for up to six persons. There is a restaurant as well.

In winter, for about US$10 per person, it's possible to stay at the *Refugio Digeder* (☎ 229054), operated by Concepción's Dirección General de Deportes y Recreación, at the base of Volcán Antuco. It has beds for 50 skiers, a restaurant and ski equipment for rent; it *may* be open in summer. For reservations, contact Digeder at O'Higgins 740, Oficina 23, in Concepción.

Try also the city of Los Angeles' *Refugio Municipal* (☎ 322333 in Los Angeles) or the *Departamentos Canchas de Esquí*, belonging to the Club de Esquí de Los Angeles.

Getting There & Away

From Los Angeles' Terminal Santa Rosa at the corner of Villagrán and Rengo, ERS goes to the villages of Antuco and Abanico, gateways to Parque Nacional Laguna del

Laja, seven times daily on weekends, three times daily on weekdays. The trip takes only about 1½ hours, but it takes another several hours to walk the 11 km to Chacay, where Conaf maintains administrative offices and a small visitor center. Hitching is possible, but vehicles are few except on weekends.

ANGOL

Founded in 1553 by Pedro de Valdivia as a strategic frontier outpost – and destroyed half a dozen times over three centuries in the Mapuche wars – Angol de los Confines finally survived the Indian resistance after 1862. Easily reached by southbound travelers from Los Angeles but also from Temuco, it provides the best access into mountainous Parque Nacional Nahuelbuta, a forest reserve that protects the largest remaining coastal stands of Araucaria pines (monkey-puzzle trees).

Orientation

Angol (population 39,000), west of the Panamericana, 65 km southwest of Los Angeles and 127 km north of Temuco, is actually an outlier of Region IX (La Araucanía). It straddles the Río Vergara, an upper tributary of the Biobío formed by the confluence of the Ríos Picoiquén and Rehue. The city's older core, centered on a particularly attractive Plaza de Armas, lies west of the river. Farther west, the coastal Cordillera Nahuelbuta rises to nearly 1600 meters.

Information

Tourist Offices Angol's Oficina Municipal de Turismo (☎ 712046) is near the bridge across the Río Vergara, on the east side of the river. Open weekdays 9 am to 1 pm and 3 to 6 pm, it has few maps and brochures but a hard-working, well-informed staff.

Money Angol has no formal cambios, but Boutique Boston, on Sepúlveda between Prat and Lautaro, changes US cash weekdays, 9 am to 1 pm and 3 to 7 pm. Banco de Chile, Lautaro 2, has an ATM.

Post & Communications Angol's area code is ☎ 45. Correos de Chile is at Lautaro and Chorrillos, at the northeast corner of the Plaza de Armas. CTC has long-distance offices at O'Higgins 297, west of the river.

National Parks Conaf (☎ 711870), at Prat and Chorrillos, may be able to offer suggestions for transport to Parque Nacional Nahuelbuta.

Convento San Buenaventura

Built in 1863, this Franciscan convent is the oldest church in the region and well worth a visit. It's on Covadonga between Vergara and Dieciocho.

El Vergel (Museo Dillman S Bullock)

Developed as a plant nursery and gardens by Anglo-Chilean Manuel Bunster in the 19th century, then acquired by Methodist missionaries in 1920, the Escuela Agrícola El Vergel is an agricultural college with a national reputation for training gardeners and farmers. Its Museo Bullock, a very fine collection of natural history specimens and archaeological artifacts, is the legacy of North American Methodist Dillman S Bullock, who spent nearly 70 years in Chile, learning the Mapuche language and publishing a variety of articles on the region's biology, natural history and archaeology.

Five km east of Angol but easily reached by taxi colectivo No 2 from the Plaza de Armas, El Vergel's grounds are open daily 9 am to 10 pm, while the Museo is open 9 am to 1 pm and 3 to 7 pm. Museum admission costs US$1 for adults, US$0.60 for children.

Special Events

In the second week of January, the Municipalidad de Angol sponsors Brotes de Chile, a folk song festival with prizes ranging up to US$2500. One of Chile's most important festivals for more than a decade, it features music, dance, food and crafts.

Places to Stay

Angol has plenty of reasonable accommodations, beginning with the *Casa del*

Huésped, Dieciocho 465, for US$8 per person; *Residencial Olimpia* (☎ 711162), Caupolicán 625, charges US$11/20 single/double. Under the same management, *Hotel Olimpia* (☎ 711517), Lautaro 194, is slightly more expensive.

Hotel Millaray (☎ 711570), Prat 420, has rooms with shared bath for US$19/25, but with private bath rates are US$30/39. Comparably priced *Hostería El Vergel* (☎ 712-103), on the grounds of the agricultural college (see above), is an outstanding choice. At the top of the scale is *Hotel Chez Mayatte* (☎ 711336), Vergara 569, where rooms cost in the US$80/100 range.

Places to Eat

Café Stop, Lautaro 176, offers sandwiches and parrillada, while *Pizzería Sparlatto* at Lautaro 418 has, obviously, pizza. For a wider selection, try *Las Totoras* at Ilabaca and Covadonga, or the *Club Social*, Caupolicán 498.

Things to Buy

Angol is renowned for fine ceramics, produced at small factories open to the public. Cerámica Serra is at Bunster 153, while Cerámica Lablé is at Purén 864.

Getting There & Away

For long-distance services, Angol's Terminal Rodoviario is at Caupolicán 200, a block north of the plaza. Buses Biobío (☎ 711777) has more than a dozen buses daily to Temuco (US$3), plus another five to Concepción (US$2.50). Tur-Bus (☎ 711-655) has morning and evening departures for Santiago (US$15), while Buses Lit (☎ 711549) has a nightly departure to the capital. Igi Llaima (☎ 711920) goes to Los Angeles and Concepción (twice daily) and Santiago (nightly). Trans Tur has morning and evening buses to the capital.

The Terminal Rural, for local and regional services, is at Ilabaca and Lautaro. Buses Thiele (☎ 711854) has extensive regional services, connecting Angol to the Costa del Carbón via Contulmo, Cañete and Lebú (US$4), and to Concepción via Nacimiento and Santa Juana. Buses Jota Be has 14 buses daily to Los Angeles (US$2.50) via Renaico.

Buses Angol goes from Angol to Vegas Blancas (US$2), seven km from the entrance to Parque Nacional Nahuelbuta, Monday, Wednesday and Friday at 7 am and 4 pm, returning at 9 am and 6 pm. For details of park tours, see the following section.

PARQUE NACIONAL NAHUELBUTA

Between Angol and the Pacific, covered with Araucaria pines, the coastal range rises to nearly 1600 meters in Parque Nacional Nahuelbuta. Created in 1939 to protect one of the last non-Andean refuges of the monkey-puzzle tree, whose largest specimens reach 50 meters in height and two meters in diameter, this 6832-hectare park also features notable stands of *Nothofagus* (southern beech). Occasional sightings take place of rare mammals such as puma, the Chiloé fox and the miniature Chilean deer known as the pudú.

At Pehuenco, on the road from Angol,

Parque Nacional Nahuelbuta

Conaf maintains a **Centro de Informaciones Ecológicas**, with a small museum, where rangers offer audiovisual presentations on the local environment. Park admission costs US$2 for adults, US$0.50 for children.

Geography & Climate

In the province of Malleco in Region IX, Nahuelbuta is about 35 km west of Angol. On a mostly flat or undulating plain, some 950 meters above sea level, permanent streams have cut deep canyons, while jagged peaks rise abruptly, up to 1530 meters on the summit of Cerro Alto Nahuelbuta. Unlike the Andes, the coastal range is granitic rather than volcanic in origin.

The park enjoys warm, dry summers, but snow sometimes falls at higher elevations in winter. Mean annual precipitation is about 1000 mm, falling almost entirely between May and September. November to April is the best time for a visit.

Activities

Nahuelbuta has 30 km of roads and 15 km of footpaths, so car-touring, camping and hiking are all possible. **Piedra del Aguila**, a four-km hike from Pehuenco, is a 1379-meter overlook with views to the Andes and the Pacific. **Cerro Anay**, 1450 meters, has similar views.

Places to Stay

Conaf charges US$14 per site at campgrounds near park headquarters at Pehuenco (11 sites), and five km north at Coimallín (four sites).

Getting There & Away

Buses Angol goes to Vegas Blancas (US$2), seven km from the park entrance, Monday, Wednesday and Friday at 7 am and 4 pm, returning at 9 am and 6 pm. In summer, it also offers Sunday tours for US$13 per person, leaving Angol's Terminal Rural at 6.45 am.

Norte Grande

The Norte Grande consists of Regions I (Tarapacá) and II (Antofagasta) and the northernmost part Region III (Atacama). Prior to the arrival of the Spaniards, the oases of this desert region were more closely linked to the Andean highlands of present-day Peru and Bolivia than to coastal areas both north and south. The area's most prominent geographical features are the Pacific Ocean, the starkly desolate but unique Atacama Desert with its deeply incised canyons, and the altiplano (steppe) and high peaks of the Andes.

The region's conspicuous pre-Hispanic archaeological monuments and colonial remains complement those in Peru and Bolivia. Substantial Indian populations once lived by fishing and by irrigated agriculture in scattered oases and in the valleys which descend from the cordillera to the coast. Many Indians remain despite the influx of immigrants from central Chile to the cities of Arica, Iquique and Antofagasta.

Indian peoples left impressive fortresses, agricultural terraces and huge stylized designs (geoglyphs) made by covering the light sands of the surrounding barren slopes with darker stones – their representations of llama trains illustrate the importance of the transverse canyons as pre-Columbian transport routes. Coastal peoples exchanged products such as fish and guano for maize and *charqui* (sundried llama or alpaca meat) with their Andean kin.

The Atacama is the most 'perfect' of deserts; some coastal stations have never recorded measurable rainfall, although infrequent 'El Niño' events can bring brief but phenomenal downpours. Otherwise, the only precipitation comes from the convective fogs known as *camanchaca* or *garúa*, which sometimes condense at higher elevations and support the scattered vegetation of the *lomas* (coastal hills).

Farther inland, rainfall and vegetation increase with elevation and distance from the sea. In the precordillera, or Andean foothills, Aymara farmers still cultivate the terraces which have covered the hillsides for millennia, although alfalfa fodder for livestock has largely replaced *quinoa* (a native Andean grain) and the myriad varieties of potato. Cultivation reaches as high as 4000 meters; above this level, the Aymara pasture llamas, alpacas and a handful of sheep on the grasslands of the *puna* (highlands).

Until the late 19th century, the Norte Grande belonged to Peru and Bolivia. Treaty disputes, the presence of thousands of Chilean workers in the Bolivian mines and Bolivian attempts to increase taxation on mineral exports led to the War of the Pacific (1879-1884) against Bolivia and Peru. Within those five years, Chile overpowered its rivals and annexed the copper- and nitrate-rich lands that are now the regions of Tarapacá and Antofagasta.

Most cities in the Atacama, such as Iquique and Antofagasta, owe their existence to minerals, especially nitrates and copper. Nitrate oficinas like Humberstone flourished during the boom of the early 20th century, withered when petroleum-based fertilizers superseded mineral nitrates, and are now ghost towns. Only a handful continue to operate, as newer methods make processing lower grade ores profitable.

One of the chief beneficiaries of the War of the Pacific was British speculator John Thomas North, the single most important figure in the history of the nitrate industry. In 1875, prior to the war, Peru expropriated nitrate holdings and issued bonds to their former owners. During the war, the value of these bonds plummeted and North, using Chilean capital, bought as many as he could. When, after the war, Chile decided to restore ownership to bondholders, it was a windfall for North, who moved to gain

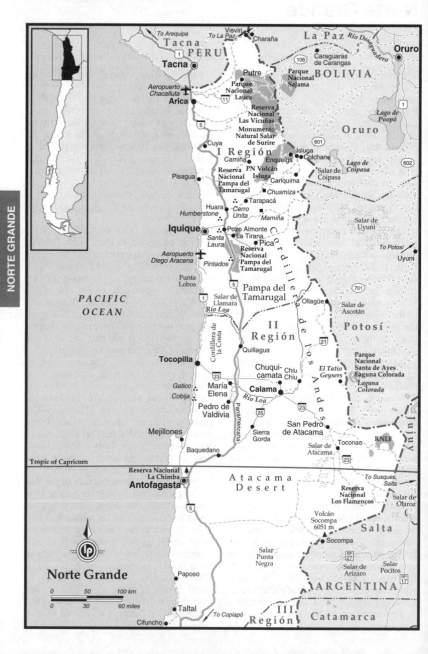

PACIFIC
OCEAN

Norte Grande

0   50   100 km
0   30   60 miles

control of all other industries on which the nitrate industry depended. Along with a handful of other entrepreneurs, he largely controlled the region's economy.

Chile's economic dependence on nitrates and copper has meant that, since the 19th century, the Atacama has played a major role in the country's political fortunes. The desert's mineral wealth meant a steady flow of revenue into the exchequer, allowing Chilean politicians to postpone dealing with major social and political issues until well into the 20th century; able to depend on mining revenue to finance government services, they failed to devise a broadly based tax system. Militant trade unions first developed in the north, introducing a new factor into Chilean politics in general.

After WWI, the nitrate industry declined as synthetic nitrates replaced mineral nitrates, but copper took up the slack. The world's largest open-pit copper mine is at Chuquicamata, near Calama, but there are many other important mines, some of them very large, dotted throughout the region.

ARICA

An early-19th-century English visitor called Arica 'one bleak, comfortless, miserable, sandy waste,' but well before Inca times it had been the terminus of an important trade route, as coastal peoples exchanged their fish, cotton and maize for the potatoes, wool and charqui of their kin in the precordillera and altiplano. With the arrival of the Spanish in the early 16th century, Arica became the port for the bonanza silver mine at Potosí in Alto Perú (present-day Bolivia). Although Arica became part of independent Peru, its 19th-century development lagged behind the frenzied activity in the nitrate mines farther south, near Pisagua, Iquique and Antofagasta. During the War of the Pacific, Arica became de facto Chilean territory, an arrangement formalized in 1929.

Where Chile and Peru once fought bloody skirmishes, wealthy Bolivians now lounge on the beach, and Quechua and Aymara Indians sell handicrafts, vegetables and trinkets. Arica is a popular year-round resort, with beach weather nearly every day; some adults have never seen rain. Despite its aridity, the city occupies an attractive site at the foot of El Morro, a spectacular headland that offers sweeping ocean and desert views.

In the 1960s, Chile made a conscious effort to industrialize the region through the automobile and electronics industries, powered by diverting the eastward-flowing Río Lauca to a hydroelectric facility in the precordillera. Industrialization failed but, by the 1970s, Arica had become a city of 120,000, a sixfold increase in less than two decades, because of international trade and active promotion of the region as a customs-free zone.

Chile has periodically proposed territorial compensation for Bolivian losses during the War of the Pacific, but offers of a narrow strip between the Lluta valley (north of the Arica-La Paz railway) and the Peruvian border for a Bolivian corridor to the sea have proved unacceptable to Peru, the area's erstwhile sovereign. Traditionally, much of landlocked Bolivia's exports pass through Arica, but Peru's grant of free port rights to Bolivia at Ilo have undercut Arica's economy.

In response, the Chilean government has proposed a number of tax and duty-free incentives to encourage investment in the provinces of Arica and Parinacota. At the same time, Arica was the site of a minor diplomatic incident in early 1996, when the mayor ordered the paving of a segment of the Panamericana belonging to the Peruvian consulate without asking the consulate's permission. This in turn gave Peru a pretext to reduce the entry of duty-free goods from the region into Peru.

Orientation

Arica (population 163,000) lies at the northeastern base of El Morro, which rises dramatically out of the Pacific. Between El Morro and the Río San José (which rarely has any surface flow), the city center is a slightly irregular grid. The main shopping street, 21 de Mayo, is a pedestrian mall running between Prat and Baquedano.

NORTE GRANDE

At the foot of El Morro are the manicured gardens of Plaza Colón, from which Avenida Comandante San Martín (do not confuse with Calle San Martín, east of downtown) snakes west and south towards the city's most popular beaches. In the other direction, Avenida Máximo Lira swerves sharply at sprawling Parque Brasil to become Avenida General Velásquez, leading to the Panamericana Norte and the Peruvian border, some 20 km to the north. To get to the Panamericana Sur, toward Iquique, take either 18 de Septiembre or 21 de Mayo eastbound.

Information
Tourist Offices Sernatur (☎ 232101, fax 254506), at Prat 305, 2nd floor, is open weekdays 8.30 am to 1 pm and 3 to 7 pm. Its friendly, helpful staff distribute a useful city map, plus a fistful of brochures on Tarapacá and other Chilean regions; if you're arriving from Peru or Bolivia, this is a good place to orient yourself. There's also a municipal tourist kiosk on the 21 de Mayo pedestrian zone near Colón, but it keeps erratic hours.

The Automóvil Club de Chile (☎ 252-678, fax 232780), Chacabuco 460, offers free information and sells maps. It's open weekdays 9 am to 1 pm and 3 to 7 pm, Saturdays 9 am to 1 pm only.

Consulates The Peruvian Consulate (☎ 231020), San Marcos 786, is open 8.30 am to 1.30 pm weekdays, while the Bolivian Consulate (☎ 231030), 21 de Mayo 575, is open 8 am to 2 pm weekdays. Several European countries have honorary consulates:

Denmark/Norway
    21 de Mayo 399 (☎ 231399)
Germany
    21 de Mayo 639, 3rd floor, Oficina 8
    (☎ 231551)
Italy
    Chacabuco & San Martín (☎ 229195)
Spain
    Avenida Santa María 2660 (☎ 224655)
UK
    Baquedano 351 (☎ 231960)

Visas To replace a lost tourist card or extend a visa, go to the Departamento de Extranjería (☎ 232411) at 7 de Junio 188, 3rd floor.

Money Arica has the best rates and least bureaucracy for changing money north of Santiago, but there are also many ATMs, including Banco Santander at 21 de Mayo 298 and Banco de Crédito at Bolognesi 221.

Reliable street changers hang out at the corner of 21 de Mayo and Colón; there are several permanent exchange houses on 21 de Mayo, where you can change US cash and travelers' checks, as well as Peruvian, Bolivian and Argentine currency. Try Yanulaque at 21 de Mayo 175, Marta Daguer at 18 de Septiembre 330, Turismo Sol y Mar at Colón 610, Oficina 4, or Daniel Concha at Chacabuco 300. The latter is open late Saturday evening, but all are closed Sundays – try the street changers or larger hotels (where rates will be less favorable).

Post & Communications Arica's area code is ☎ 58. Correos de Chile is in the same building as the tourist office at Prat 305. For long-distance phone calls, go to Entel at 21 de Mayo 345, CTC at Colón 476 or Chilesat at 21 de Mayo 372. In the alcove outside the tourist office, there is a fiber optic line with direct connection to overseas operators, but it is accessible only during regular business hours.

National Parks Conaf's regional office (☎ 241793, 222270) is at Camino Azapa 3444, Km 1, in the Azapa valley, but may soon move. For information on climbing, contact the Grupo Andino Cóndor de Arica, 18 de Septiembre 889, which meets Mondays from 8.30 to 10.30 pm. For peaks on the Bolivian border, such as Parinacota and Pomerabe, climbers should seek permission from the Primera Comisaria de Carabineros (☎ 231275), Juan Noé 721.

Bicycle Rental Residencial Caracas (☎ 253688), Sotomayor 867, rents mountain bikes by the half-day or full day.

Laundry Niko's Laundry, 18 de Septiembre 188-A, charges by the kilo. Lavandería La Moderna is on 18 de Septiembre between Colón and Baquedano.

Medical Services Arica's Hospital Dr Juan Noé (☎ 229200) is at 18 de Septiembre 1000, a short distance east of downtown.

Things to See

Overlooking the city, with outstanding views of the port and the Pacific, the 110-meter hill known as **El Morro de Arica** is also an historical monument whose open-air **Museo Histórico y de Armas** (☎ 254091) commemorates a crucial battle between Chilean and Peruvian forces on June 7, 1880, about a year into the War of the Pacific. It's accessible by car or by a footpath from the south end of Calle Colón; there's an admission charge of US$0.80.

Famous for his Parisian tower, Alexandre Gustave Eiffel designed many Latin American prefab landmarks, including Arica's **Aduana** (1874), the former customs house. Though it once fronted on the harbor, a century of landfill has left it about 200 meters inland, facing Parque General Baquedano. Recently restored as the city's Casa de la Cultura, it displays historical photographs and occasional art exhibitions on the 2nd floor, reached by a 32-step, wrought-iron spiral staircase.

Arica's other Eiffel monument is the **Iglesia San Marcos** (1875), opposite Plaza Colón. Originally intended for the bathing resort of Ancón, north of Lima, the Gothic-style building replaced a church destroyed by an earthquake in 1868.

The 1924 German locomotive that once pulled trains on the Arica-La Paz line now stands in the **Plazoleta Estación**, part of Parque General Baquedano, at the corner of 21 de Mayo and Pedro Montt. On the north side of the Plazoleta, the **Estación Ferrocarril Arica-La Paz** itself dates from 1913.

Beaches

Arica is one of Chile's best beach resorts, since the Pacific is warm enough for comfortable bathing, but note that all the beaches have strong ocean currents and may be dangerous, some more so than others.

Eiffel Beyond the Tower

Few are aware that French engineer Alexandre Gustave Eiffel, so renowned for his controversial tower in Paris, played such a significant role in the New World. New York's Statue of Liberty is his most prominent trans-Atlantic landmark (he designed the steel framework inside it), but his constructions also dot the Latin American landscape from Mexico to Chile. Arica's Iglesia San Marcos and recently restored Aduana (customs house) are but two of many examples.

In 1868, in partnership with another engineer, Théophile Seyrig, Eiffel had formed G Eiffel et Compagnie, which later became the Compagnie des Etablissements Eiffel. While the bulk of its metal construction work took place in France and its colonies, an aggressive agent in Buenos Aires obtained many contracts for South American public buildings. In addition to the Arica landmarks, his notable creations include the gasworks of La Paz, Bolivia and the railroad bridges of Oroya, Peru, but his work appears as far north as the Iglesia Santa Bárbara in Santa Rosalía, in the Mexican state of Baja California Sur. Most of these were designed and built in Eiffel's workshops in the Parisian suburb of Levallois-Perret, then shipped abroad for assembly.

What might have been his greatest Latin American monument effectively ended his career. In the late 19th century, he had argued strongly in favor of building a trans-oceanic canal across Nicaragua, but a few years later he obtained a contract to build the locks for Ferdinand de Lesseps' corruption-plagued French canal across Panama. Implicated in irregular contracts, Eiffel was sentenced to two years in prison and fined a substantial amount; though his conviction was overturned on appeal, he never returned to his career as a builder. ■

NORTE GRANDE

PLACES TO STAY
2   Hotel El Paso
5   Residencial Chillán
15 Residencial Durán
16 Residencial Las Parinas
17 Residencial Velásquez
18 Residencial Patricia
23 Hotel Aragón
25 Residencial Madrid
26 Residencial Venecia
28 Residencial Blanquita
30 Residencial Chungará
31 Hotel Lynch
32 Residencial Muñoz
33 Residencial Sur
57 King Hotel
64 Hotel Central
80 Residencial Española
85 Hotel Plaza Colón
87 Residencial Leiva
89 Hotel San Marcos
92 Residencial Sotomayor
94 Hotel Diego de Almagro
96 Hotel Tacora
97 Hostal Viña del Mar
99 Residencial Jardín del Sol
100 Residencial Rachell
106 Hotel Savona

PLACES TO EAT
11 Nuevo Mundo
19 Bavaria
20 Mercado Colón
    Caballito del Mar,
    El Rey del Marisco
24 Buen Gusto No 2
34 Shanghai
50 Govinda
51 La Fontana
52 DiMango
54 El Arriero
55 Café 21
69 Círculo Peruano
73 El Alero de 21
79 Café Café
83 La Fontana
88 Casino La Bomba
91 D'Aurelio
93 Chin Huang Tao
98 Rincón Paceño
105 Illimani

OTHER
1   Terminal de Buses
2   Hertz
3   Estación Ferrocarril
    Arica-Tacna
4   Avis
6   Cambio Daniel Concha
7   Colectivos to Tacna
8   Buses Litoral
9   Automóvil Club de Chile
10 Primera Comisaria
    de Carabineros
12 Italian Consulate
13 Transporte Humire
14 Buses Martínez
21 Turismo Lauca
22 Turismo Sol y Mar
    (Money Exchange)
27 Latinorizons
29 Parinacota Expediciones

35 Estación Ferrocarril
    Arica-La Paz
36 Niko's Laundry
37 Parinacota Expediciones
38 Ecotours
39 Lavandería La Moderna
40 CTC
41 Cambio Marta Daguer
42 American Rent-A-Car
43 Grupo Andino Cóndor de Arica
44 Hospital Dr Juan Noé
45 Plazoleta Estación
46 Vicuña Tour
47 Solari Surf Shop
48 Transtours
49 Cambio Yanulaque
53 Banco Santander
56 Municipal Tourist Kiosk
58 LanChile
59 Entel

60 Danish, Norwegian
    Consulates
61 Chilesat
62 National Airlines
63 Tropisurf
65 Ladeco
66 Huntington Surf Shop
67 Radio Taxis
    Aeropuerto Chacalluta
68 Bolivian Consulate
70 Surfing Zone
71 Budget
72 German Consulate
74 Alta
75 Viva Rent-A-Car
76 Parque General
    Baquedano
77 Ex-Aduana,
    Casa de la Cultura
78 Post Office, Sernatur

81 Turismo Payachatas
82 Jurasi Tour
84 Banco de Crédito
86 Faucett
90 UK Consulate
95 Lloyd Aéreo Boliviano
101 Residencial Caracas
    (Mountain Bike Rental)
102 Aeroperú
103 Iglesia San Marcos
104 Departamento
    de Extranjería (Visas)
107 Peruvian Consulate
108 Museo Histórico
    y de Armas
109 Club de Yates

Puerto de Arica

*PACIFIC
OCEAN*

Plaza

108 🏛

Av Comandante San Martín

El Morro de Arica

Isla de
Alacrán

• 109

To Playa El Laucho,
Playa La Lisera,
Playa Brava,
Playa Corazones

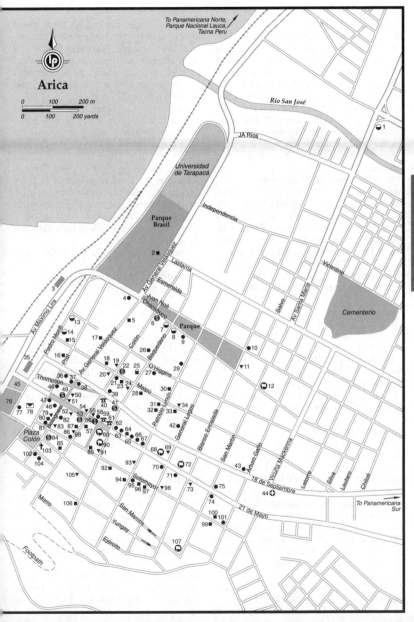

The most frequented beaches are south of town, along Avenida Comandante San Martín, where there are a number of sheltered coves and seaside restaurants. The closest site is **Playa El Laucho**, just south of the Club de Yates, followed by **Playa La Lisera** 2½ km south of downtown; both have little surf and are suitable for swimming, but nearby **Playa Brava** is only suitable for sunbathing. About 10 km south of town, **Playa Corazones** is the most southerly accessible beach. Bus No 8 from General Velásquez and Chacabuco serves this area.

Beaches along the Panamericana Norte, toward the Peruvian border, are cleaner than those to the south. **Playa Chinchorro**, two km north of downtown, is suitable for swimming and diving, while **Playa Las Machas**, a few km to the north, is too rough for swimming but ideal for surfing and fishing. Take bus No 12 from General Velásquez and Chacabuco.

Arica has several surf shops, including Huntington Surf Shop at 21 de Mayo 493, Surfing Zone on 21 de Mayo between General Lagos and Patricio Lynch, Tropisurf at 21 de Mayo 423-A and Solari Surf Shop at 21 de Mayo 160.

For fishing permits, contact the Servicio Nacional de Pesca (Sernap; ☎ 222684), Serrano 1856, just off 21 de Mayo about 10 blocks east of the hospital. It's open weekdays 8.30 am to 1 pm and 3 to 7 pm.

Poblado Artesanal

On the outskirts of Arica, this mock altiplano village, including a church and bell tower, is a good place to shop for artisanal goods like ceramics, weavings, musical instruments, carvings and similar crafts, and has an excellent restaurant, *El Tambo*.

At Hualles 2825 near the Panamericana Sur to Iquique, the Poblado Artesanal (☎ 222683) is open daily except Monday 9.30 am to 1.30 pm and 3.30 to 8 pm; there's a peña at 9.30 pm Friday and Saturday evenings. Taxi colectivos Nos 2, 7, 8, 13 and U pass near the entrance, as do buses Nos 2, 3, 5, 7, 9 and 12.

Organized Tours

Many travel agencies arrange trips around the city and to the Azapa valley, the precordillera, Parque Nacional Lauca and other altiplano destinations; some run trips themselves, while others contract their trips out. When booking a tour indirectly, find out who will be the operator.

Lauca tours cost about US$20 to US$25 with a late lunch in Putre included, but when competition is heavy in summer the price can be as low as US$15; shop around for the best deal. These tours leave around 7.30 am and return about 8.30 pm. There is presumably a legal requirement to carry oxygen for those who suffer from soroche, but there have been some complaints in this regard. This is not a minor issue, as many people become very sick at high altitudes. Avoid overeating.

Some companies which run their own trips include the well-established and recommended Transtours (☎ 253927, fax 251675) at Bolognesi 321, which has English-speaking guides and does carry oxygen; Jurasi Tour (☎ 251696) at Bolognesi 360; Parinacota Expediciones (☎ /fax 251309) at Patricio Lynch 731 and Bolognesi 475; Ecotours (☎ 231537) at Bolognesi 470; and Turismo Lauca (☎ 252322) at Maipú 346, Local 15. Belgian-run Latinorizons (☎ /fax 250007), O'Higgins 440, Departamento 37, is a recent startup; English and French are spoken.

Other agencies include Turismo Payachatas (☎ 251514), Sotomayor 199, and Vicuña Tour (☎ /fax 253773) at Prat 430, Oficina 14.

Special Events

Arica's interesting and unpretentious Carnaval Ginga draws around 15,000 spectators during a three-day weekend in late February; the Municipalidad blocks off Avenida Comandante San Martín, near El Morro, for a parade that features regional comparsas who perform traditional precordillera and altiplano dances. The music mostly consists of brass bands, so no one will confuse this with Rio de Janeiro or

Bahia, but it's worth a look for visitors who happen to be in town.

The biggest local event is June's Semana Ariqueña (Arica Week), about the same time as the Concurso Nacional de Cueca, a folkloric dance festival in the Azapa valley.

Places to Stay

Arica has abundant accommodations at reasonable prices; though many bottom-end places are cramped and smelly, and some lack hot water, others are excellent. Those in search of quiet should look south of the busy thoroughfares of Maipú and 21 de Mayo, although some places on cross-streets in the latter area are fine.

Places to Stay – bottom end

Camping There is free camping at Playa Corazones, 10 km south of Arica at the end of Avenida Comandante San Martín, but these highly frequented sites are dirty. Basic supplies are available but not fresh water, which has to be brought from town. Camping is better north of town, where the beaches are cleaner.

Camping El Refugio (☎ 227545), at Km 1.5 in the Azapa valley, charges US$15 per site. *Camping Gallinazo* (☎ 214144), 13 km north of town on the Panamericana, charges only US$4 per person, but the only public transportation is taxi colectivo No 1, which costs US$1.50 each way.

Hostel The local affiliate of Hostelling International is *Residencial Madrid* (☎ 231-479), Baquedano 685, which charges US$5. In addition, Arica usually has an inexpensive student hostel in January and February, but the location changes from year to year. Ask Sernatur for the current listing.

Residenciales Arica's cheapest residenciales charge around US$5 per person. Drab *Residencial Sur* (☎ 252457), Maipú 516, has hot water and clean sheets. Similarly priced *Residencial Muñoz*, Patricio Lynch 565, is ultra-basic and rundown, but friendly and tolerable. Other comparably priced places include *Residencial Patricia* at Maipú 269 and *Residencial Velásquez* (☎ 231989), Velásquez 669.

Frequented by many travelers, *Residencial Madrid* (☎ 231479) at Baquedano 685 has singles/doubles at US$6/11, but it's sometimes noisy and the manager can be brusque. *Residencial Rachell* (☎ 231560), in a quiet neighborhood at Sotomayor 841, is very good value for US$6 per person. Others in this price range include *Residencial Chillán* (☎ 251677) at General Velásquez 747, and *Residencial Venecia* (☎ 252877) at Baquedano 739.

Residencial Española (☎ 231703), Bolognesi 340, charges US$7/9 for singles/doubles on a quiet pedestrian walk. *Residencial Chungará* (☎ 231677), Patricio Lynch 675, is probably the pick of this category – though some rooms are small, it's clean, bright, friendly and quiet (except for the front rooms nearest the TV). Rates are US$7.50 per person.

In an excellent location at Sotomayor 442, the friendly *Residencial Sotomayor* (☎ 252336) has clean rooms with showers for US$7.50 per person, but some beds are soft and other rooms a bit close to the TV. Try also *Residencial Durán* (☎ 252975), Maipú 25, which charges US$7.50/12.50 single/double.

Residencial Blanquita (☎ 232064) at Maipú 472 is clean and has hot water; at US$9 per person, it's one of the better budget choices. French-run *Residencial Leiva* (☎ 232008), Colón 347, is quiet and well-located; rates are US$9/12 single/double with shared bath, US$16/21 with private bath.

Hostal Viña del Mar (☎ 253359, ☎ /fax 250065), Sotomayor 578, is also very good but more expensive for US$10 with shared bath. *Residencial Las Parinas* (☎ 231971), Prat 541, charges US$11/18. *Residencial Jardín del Sol* (☎ 232795), Sotomayor 848, is a step up at US$15/23 with breakfast.

Places to Stay – middle

One of Arica's traditional choices is *Hotel Lynch* (☎ /fax 231581), built around a central courtyard at Patricio Lynch 589, where simple but clean rooms with shared bath start at US$20/25; with private bath, expect about US$31/46. The staff are also helpful. Well-located *Hotel Tacora* (☎ 251240), Sotomayor 540, costs US$25/31.

Hotel Aragón (☎ 252088), Maipú 344, offers bright motel-style rooms for US$31/42, all with private bath, but the busy location makes it noisy at times. *Hotel Diego de Almagro* (☎ 224444), Sotomayor 490, has bright, clean rooms with private bath, TV, telephone and double beds for US$33/39.

Similar to the Diego de Almagro, the *King Hotel* (☎ 232094), Colón 376, is slightly cheaper at US$30/40. *Hotel Plaza Colón* (☎ 231244), San Marcos 261, costs US$33/45. Popular with tour groups, *Hotel Savona* (☎ 231000), Yungay 380, charges US$38/49. Similar, but better situated, is *Hotel San Marcos* (☎ 232149, fax 251815) at Sotomayor 367, for US$48/59. Somewhat costlier but very convenient is *Hotel Central* (☎ 252575), 21 de Mayo 425, for US$55/65.

Places to Stay – top end

On the beach at the south end of town, *Hostería Arica* (☎ 254540, fax 231133, (02) 6713165 in Santiago), at Avenida Comandante San Martín 599, has drawn some criticism for lax standards, especially with rates at US$80/98, but the management also responds well to complaints. Top of the list is *Hotel El Paso* (☎ 231222, fax 231965, (02) 2361431 in Santiago), set in pleasant gardens at General Velásquez 1109, with rooms at US$86/104.

In the restful Azapa valley, a short taxi colectivo ride from downtown, *Hotel Saint Georgette* (☎ 221914), at Diego Portales 3221, has top-end accommodation starting at US$69/87. Farther out the valley, try the *Azapa Inn* (☎ 244537), Guillermo Sánchez 660, where rates start at US$79/99.

Places to Eat

There are numerous cafés and restaurants along 21 de Mayo, 18 de Septiembre, Maipú, Bolognesi and Colón. Many foreign travelers congregate at *Café 21* (☎ 231680), at 21 de Mayo and Colón, which serves hamburgers, sandwiches, snacks, coffee and excellent lager beer. For breakfast or onces, try sandwiches and licuados at the very modest but excellent *Buen Gusto No 2*, Baquedano 559, which is also a non-smoking place. *Bavaria* (☎ 251679), Colón 613, is another decent snack bar.

Inside the fire station at Colón 357, *Casino La Bomba* (☎ 232983) is an Arica institution for its excellent, inexpensive midday meals (less than US$5) and attentive service, plus the country's hottest fresh ají. If you can't find it, listen for its deafening siren at noon. *Govinda* (☎ 231028), Bolognesi 430, has cheap vegetarian specials. *Café Café*, Bolognesi 347-A, is good for snacks and desserts.

In the Mercado Colón, at the corner of Colón and Maipú, *Caballito del Mar* (☎ 241569) has well-prepared corvina, cojinova and other tasty fish dinners for about US$5 to 6, though the service can be erratic. Upstairs in the same building, *El Rey del Marisco* (☎ 232767) is a more expensive but worthwhile alternative.

El Arriero (☎ 232636), at 21 de Mayo 385, is an outstanding parrilla with pleasant atmosphere and friendly service, but it's closed Mondays. *Illimani*, San Marcos 374, is another good parrilla.

D'Aurelio (☎ 321471), Baquedano 369, is a very good Italian restaurant with attentive service and exceptionally tasty appetizers like olives and pickled onions. The *Círculo Peruano*, General Lagos 517, serves Peruvian specialties and also has live music, while the inexpensive *Rincón Paceño*, Sotomayor 617, serves Bolivian snacks like salteñas (spicy empanadas).

For excellent typical Chilean food in agreeable surroundings, try *El Tambo* (☎ 241757) at the Poblado Artesanal, Hualles 2825 near the Panamericana Sur, or the *Club de Huasos*, open Sundays only at Km 3.5 in the Azapa valley. Visitors to the museum in the village of San Miguel de Azapa enjoy *La Picá del Muertito*, alongside the cemetery; the pork comes highly recommended. Downtown's *El Alero de 21* (☎ 252899), 21 de Mayo 736, is another possibility.

Like other coastal towns in northern Chile, Arica has several chifas of decent quality. Try *Shanghai* (☎ 231955) at Maipú 534, *Chin Huang Tao* at Patricio Lynch 317 or *Nuevo Mundo* at Blanco Encalada 810, between Chacabuco and Juan Noé.

La Fontana (☎ 254680) has very fine fruit-flavored ice cream at two locations, Bolognesi 320 and 21 de Mayo 211, Local 2. *DiMango* (☎ 224575), 21 de Mayo 244, also has good ice cream.

Things to Buy
A narrow passageway off Plaza Colón between Sotomayor and 21 de Mayo, Pasaje Bolognesi has a lively artisan's market in the evenings. There are also many permanent shops along the walkway.

See also the separate entry for the Poblado Artesanal, above.

Getting There & Away
From Arica, travelers can head north across the Peruvian border to Tacna and Lima, south toward Santiago, or east to Bolivia.

Air LanChile (☎ 252600), 21 de Mayo 345, has at least two flights daily to Santiago (US$225) via Iquique; one daily flight also stops in Antofagasta (US$87). The flight between Arica and Santiago is one of South America's most spectacular, with awesome views of the northern coastal desert and the Andes. Sit on the left side southbound and the right side northbound.

Ladeco (☎ 252021), 21 de Mayo 443, flies twice or three times daily from Arica to Iquique and Santiago; their early morning flight stops in Antofagasta, as does the midday flight on weekends. Fares are almost identical to LanChile's.

LanChile also has international services nine times daily to La Paz, Bolivia (US$92 single, US$147 roundtrip), and Tuesday, Thursday and Sunday to Santa Cruz (US$156). Lloyd Aéreo Boliviano (☎ 251919), Patricio Lynch 298, flies

Tuesday to La Paz, Thursday to La Paz with connections to Santa Cruz, Manaus and Mexico City, and Saturday to Santa Cruz.

National Airlines (☎ 250001), 21 de Mayo 417, has daily flights to Santiago (US$205) except Wednesday and Friday, when it has two; all flights stop in Iquique (US$30) and Antofagasta except for the Friday afternoon flight, which stops only in Iquique. Wednesdays, Fridays and Sundays, National flies to Arequipa, Peru (US$65 return).

Alta (☎ 250058), 21 de Mayo 804, flies weekdays only to Iquique (US$18), Calama (US$75), Antofagasta (US$78), Copiapó (US$150) and La Serena (US$175).

Two Peruvian airlines have Arica offices: Aeroperú (☎ 232852) at 7 de Junio 148, Oficina 2, and Faucett (☎ 231025) at Colón 365.

Bus – regional For the altiplano destinations of Parinacota (Parque Nacional Lauca), Visviri and Charaña (on the Bolivian border), contact Buses Martínez (☎ 232265), Pedro Montt 620, or Transportes Humire (☎ 253497), Pedro Montt 662. Both leave Tuesday at 10 am and Friday at 10 pm, while Humire departs half an hour later. Fares to Parinacota are about US$6, to Visviri US$7.50.

Buses La Paloma (☎ 222710), Germán Riesco 2071, accepts phone reservations to the precordillera villages of Socoroma and Belén (Tuesday and Friday) and to Putre (daily, US$4), departing Arica at 6.45 am. To reach the terminal, take bus No 7 to Germán Riesco, about 12 blocks east of the hospital, or arrange for their special taxibus (US$0.50) to come to your hotel. La Paloma also goes to the southern precordillera village of Codpa (US$4) Mondays and Fridays at 4 pm.

Bus Lluta serves Poconchile from the corner of Chacabuco and Vicuña Mackenna in Arica, four times daily starting at 6 am; if hitching to Parque Nacional Lauca, it is easiest to take this bus and proceed from the Carabineros checkpoint at Poconchile.

Bus & Colectivo – domestic All major bus companies have their offices at Arica's Terminal de Buses (☎ 241390), Diego Portales 948 at Avenida Santa María. Except during holiday periods, advance booking should not be necessary. Smaller regional companies usually have separate offices closer to downtown.

To Iquique, try Buses Carmelita (☎ 241-591) or Cuevas y González (☎ 241090), which have 14 departures daily between them. Taxi colectivos to Iquique, faster than buses, charge about US$12 per person. The major companies are Tamarugal (☎ 222609), Turiscargo (☎ 241052), Taxis Norte (☎ 224806) and Turistaxi (☎ 222671).

Fénix Pullman Norte (☎ 222457) goes to Antofagasta, La Serena and Santiago, with connections to the lakes region and other points in southern Chile. Buses Zambrano (☎ 241587) serves Iquique, Valparaíso and Viña del Mar. Tur-Bus (☎ 222217) goes to Calama, Antofagasta, Santiago and intermediate points.

Fichtur (☎ 241972) and Flota Barrios (☎ 223587) also go to Santiago. Tramaca (☎ 241198) goes to Calama, Antofagasta and Santiago, while Géminis (☎ 241647) also has service to Calama and Antofagasta, with international connections to Salta, Argentina (see below).

Typical fares and times include Iquique (US$6, four hours), Calama (US$19, 11 hours), Antofagasta (US$22, 12 hours) and Santiago (US$50, 26 hours).

Bus & Colectivo – international Adsubliata (☎ 241972) offers frequent bus service (US$2) to Tacna, Peru. Several companies operate taxi colectivos to Tacna for about US$4 per person; these leave from Chacabuco, between Baquedano and Colón, whenever they are full, taking about an hour including a tedious Peruvian customs inspection.

Tepsa (☎ 222817) operates services to Lima, Peru for US$35; Quito, Ecuador for US$75; Bogotá, Colombia for US$125; and Caracas, Venezuela for US$170. It's slightly cheaper to take a bus to Tacna and then buy a separate ticket to Lima or elsewhere in Peru.

Buses Litoral (☎ 254702), Chacabuco 454, run buses from Arica to La Paz, Bolivia on Tuesday and Friday at 10 pm, taking about 18 hours (longer or not at all in the rainy season) for US$23 one way. One reader reports that they are not keen about dropping passengers in Parque Nacional Lauca and will charge the full Arica-La Paz fare for this relatively short distance.

Ostensibly more comfortable than Litoral, Géminis (☎ 241647) goes to La Paz (US$35, 17 hours) and Asunción, Paraguay (US$100) Wednesday at midnight and to Salta, Argentina Tuesdays (28 hours, US$66) via Calama. These heavily booked services generally operate in summer only.

Train Arica has regular passenger trains to Tacna, Peru, but there is no conventional service to La Paz, Bolivia.

The Ferrocarril Arica-Tacna (☎ 231115) is at Máximo Lira 889. Departures are usually around noon and 5 pm (turn up about half an hour earlier for exit formalities). The 1½-hour journey costs about US$1.50, but taxi colectivos (see above) are faster and more convenient.

The Ferrocarril Arica-La Paz (☎ 231786) is opposite the Plazoleta Estación, at 21 de Mayo 51. A sort of bus on rails, the Ferrobus Arica-La Paz (☎ 232844), carries a maximum of 43 passengers to La Paz (US$52, 11 hours, meals included) Tuesday and Saturday at 9.30 am, with an additional Thursday departure in summer. Payment is in US$ only – no travelers' checks, credit cards or Chilean or Bolivian currency. This route passes through very high and cold country, so dress warmly.

Getting Around

To/From the Airport Aeropuerto Internacional Chacalluta (☎ 222831) is 18 km north of Arica, near the Peruvian border. Radio Taxis Aeropuerto Chacalluta (☎ 254-812), at Patricio Lynch and 21 de Mayo, provides door-to-door service for US$4 (shared taxi) or US$10 (single passenger).

To/From the Bus Terminal Local buses and taxi colectivos connect downtown with the main bus terminal. Taxi colectivos, only slightly more expensive than buses, are much faster and more frequent. Destinations are clearly marked on an illuminated sign on top of the cab.

Car Rental Rental cars are available from Budget (☎ 252978) at 21 de Mayo 650, Avis (☎ 232210) at Chacabuco 180, Hertz (☎ 231487), on the grounds of Hotel El Paso at General Velásquez 1109, American (☎ 252234) at General Lagos 559 and Viva (☎ 251121) at 21 de Mayo 821.

AROUND ARICA

There are varied sights and recreational opportunities in and near Arica. Most are easy day trips, especially with a car, but some of the more distant ones would be more suitable as overnighters. Closest to Arica is the irrigated Azapa valley, a prodigious producer of olives and tomatoes for export to central Chile, but also an area of major archaeological sites.

Museo Arqueológico San Miguel de Azapa

In the Azapa valley, the Museo Arqueológico displays a superb assemblage of exhibits on regional cultures from the 7th century BC to the Spanish invasion, in a building expressly designed for the purpose. The staff can point out nearby archaeological sites – ask about geoglyphs at Atoca and Alto Ramírez (Cerro Sagrado), and pre-Inca fortifications at Pukará San Lorenzo. Some local tour companies include the museum and other valley sites on their itineraries.

From January through December, the museum (☎ 224248), 12 km east of Arica, is open daily 10 am to 5.30 pm. Admission costs US$1.25 for adults, US$0.50 for children. From the corner of Maipú and Patricio Lynch in Arica, taxi colectivos charge about US$1.

NORTE GRANDE

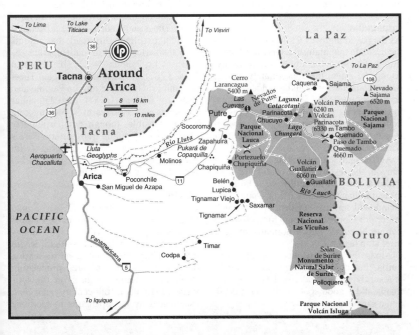

Lluta Geoglyphs

About 10 km north of Arica, the Panamericana intersects paved Chile 11, which leads east up the valley of the Río Lluta to Poconchile. A short distance inland, a series of restored pre-Columbian geoglyphs cover an otherwise barren slope on the right. These figures, made by grouping dark stones over light-colored soil, include representations of llamas, and recall the importance of pre-Columbian pack trains on the route to Tiahuanaco, a traffic which only recently disappeared with the construction of good motor roads.

Poconchile

Built in the 17th century, reconstructed in the 19th, and restored earlier this century, Poconchile's **Iglesia de San Gerónimo** is one of the oldest churches in the country. Camping is possible along the Río Lluta.

To get to Poconchile, take Bus Lluta from Chacabuco and Vicuña Mackenna in Arica to the end of the line at the Carabineros checkpoint.

Copaquilla

As the paved highway Chile 11 zigzags up the desolate mountainside, there are exceptional views of the upper Lluta valley. Along the route, the appropriately named *cactus candelabros* ('candle-holder' cactus or *Browningia candelaris)* grows just five to seven mm a year and flowers for only 24 hours. These cacti and other plants absorb moisture from the camanchaca (fog) that penetrates inland.

At Copaquilla, overlooking a spectacular canyon, the restored 12th-century fortress **Pukará de Copaquilla** was built to protect Indian farmlands below – notice the abandoned terraces, evidence of a much larger pre-Columbian population. Tours to Parque Nacional Lauca normally make a brief stop here.

Along the highway just west of Copaquilla, the eccentric *Posada Pueblo Maiko* is a surviving remainder of 1994's eclipse mania and a good spot to stop for a drink and a sandwich.

Socoroma

On the colonial pack route between Arica and Potosí, Socoroma is an Aymara farming village which features cobbled streets, the 17th-century **Iglesia de San Francisco**, and other colonial remains. Buses to Putre (see below) leave the highway and stop here briefly.

The Belén Precordillera

At Zapahuira, a gravel road leaves the paved international highway and heads south through a series of villages in an area that features numerous archaeological sites, including pre-Columbian fortresses and agricultural terraces, and colonial relics comparable to those in many parts of Peru. The highlights are the pukarás of Belén, Lupica and Saxamar, but there are also colonial churches at Belén and Tignamar Viejo.

This route makes an excellent day trip from Arica for travelers with vehicles, but only Belén has any tourist services – one simple restaurant. South of Tignamar, the road deteriorates through a narrow and dusty canyon, but improves beyond the turnoff to Timar and Codpa, where it becomes a wide, excellent dirt road that rejoins the Panamericana 21 km south of Arica.

Buses La Paloma (☎ 222710), Germán Riesco 2071 in Arica, goes to Belén Tuesday and Friday at 6.45 am. La Paloma also goes to Codpa (US\$4) and Tignamar Mondays and Fridays at 4 pm, making a loop feasible, though not particularly convenient, by public transportation. This would mean walking or hitching (with very few vehicles on the road) the 13 km between Belén and Tignamar.

PUTRE

Placed on the international travel map by the total solar eclipse of 1994, Putre is an appealing Aymara village, 3500 meters above sea level in the precordillera, where many visitors prefer to spend at least a day acclimatizing before proceeding to Parque Nacional Lauca, on the altiplano. Originally a 16th-century *reducción*, established by the Spaniards to facilitate control of the Indians, Putre retains many houses with late-colonial elements. In the surrounding hills, local farmers raise alfalfa for llamas, sheep and cattle on extensive stone-faced agricultural terraces of even greater antiquity.

Dating from 1670, the adobe **Iglesia de Putre** on the north side of the Plaza de Armas was restored two centuries later. To visit its interior, which contains valuable colonial artifacts, ask for the keys and leave a small donation.

Putre's February **Carnaval** is an informal, spontaneous affair in which visitors may be either willing or unwilling participants – fortunately, the locals fill their balloons with flour rather than water, and cover onlookers with *chaya* (multicolored paper dots) rather than fresh fruit. Two noncompetitive groups, the older *banda* and the younger *tarqueada*, provide the music; many participants are returnees from Arica. The event ends with the burning of the *momo*, a figure symbolizing the frivolity of Carnaval.

See Mauricio at the Municipalidad for short hikes to rock art sites in the vicinity of Putre.

Information Putre's area code is ☎ 58. The post office is at the corner of Carrera and Prat. Entel, on the south side of the Plaza de Armas, is open 9 am to 1 pm and 4 to 8 pm daily.

Organized Tours

Alaskan Barbara Shipton runs Birding Alto Andino (fax 222735 in the Municipalidad), Baquedano 299, which organizes specialized and more general tours of Parque Nacional Lauca and other parts of the altiplano as far as Parque Nacional Volcán Isluga. Transportation is a comfortable 4WD vehicle, with oxygen. Discounts on standard rates are available to travelers who have their own camping equipment and prefer to cook their own food; sometimes accommodation is at Conaf refugios. Unless otherwise indicated, these start and end in Putre.

Half-day-plus trips to Lago Chungará,

Parinacota and Chucuyo cost US$75 for one or two people, US$88 for three or US$100 for four. Full-day tours to Las Cuevas, Parinacota, Laguna Cotacotani and Lago Chungará costs US$150 for one or two persons, US$175 for three or US$200 for four. The very long full-day trip to the Salar de Surire costs US$288 for one or two persons, US$300 for three or US$312 for four.

The overnight trip to Lago Chungará, Parinacota and the Salar de Surire is only slightly dearer than the full-day trip to Surire, at US$325 for one or two persons, US$365 for three or US$400 for four. Prices are identical for the overnight to Parinacota, Caquena and Lago Chungará.

Three-day, two-night excursions include Lago Chungará, Parinacota, Surire and Parque Nacional Isluga, costing US$575 for one or two persons, US$625 for three or US$675 for four; the same trip ending in Pozo Almonte or Iquique costs US$650 for one or two people, US$700 for three or US$750 for four.

Places to Stay & Eat

The *Restaurant Oasis*, on Cochrane near O'Higgins, serves good plain meals and offers basic accommodations for US$4 per person, but lacks hot water. *Residencial La Paloma*, on Baquedano between Carrera and Cochrane, has hot showers and good beds for US$7 per person, but the thin walls mean it's noisy sometimes. Meals are also available.

Comparable *Restaurant Rosamel*, at the corner of Cochrane and Arturo Prat, also provides modest accommodations and serves lunch to tour groups to Parque Nacional Lauca. The slightly more expensive regular meals are also good value.

At the foot of O'Higgins, opposite the army camp, Conaf's comfortable *Refugio Putre* offers lodging when space permits for about US$10 (slightly cheaper for Chilean nationals). There are six beds, hot showers and cooking facilities.

Hostería Las Vicuñas (☎ 224997) caters to personnel from the gold mine at Choquelimpie, but has some rooms available to the

Guanacos, Vicuñas, Llamas & Alpacas

Unlike the Old World, the Western Hemisphere had few grazing mammals after the Pleistocene, when mammoths, horses and other large herbivores disappeared for reasons that are not entirely clear, but appear linked to hunting pressure by the earliest inhabitants of the plains and pampas of North and South America. For millennia, however, Andean peoples have relied on the New World camels – the wild guanaco and vicuña, the domesticated llama and alpaca – for food and fiber.

Guanacos and vicuñas are few today, but are the likely ancestors of their domesticated cousins. In fact, they were among very few potential New World domesticates – contrast them with the Old World cattle, horses, sheep, goats, donkeys and pigs which have filled so many vacant niches in the Americas. Of the major domesticated animals from across the Atlantic, only the humped camels have failed to achieve an important role here. While the New World camels have literally lost ground to sheep and cattle in some areas, they are not likely to disappear.

The guanaco *(Lama guanicoe)* ranges from the central Andes to Tierra del Fuego, at elevations from sea level up to 4000 meters or more. In the central Andes, where the human population is small and widely dispersed but domestic livestock are numerous, its numbers are small, but on the plains of Argentine Patagonia and in reserves like southern Chile's Parque Nacional Torres del Paine, herds of rust-colored guanaco are still a common sight. Native hunters ate its meat and dressed in its skins.

By contrast the vicuña *(Vicugna vicugna)* occupies a much smaller geographical range, well above 4000 meters in the puna and altiplano, from south-central Peru to northwestern Argentina. While not so numerous as the guanaco, it played a critical role in the cultural life of pre-Columbian Peru, which assured its survival – its very fine golden wool was the exclusive property of the Inca kings. Spanish chronicler Bernabé Cobo wrote that the ruler's clothing 'was made of the finest wool and the best cloth that was woven in his whole kingdom . . . most of it was made of vicuña wool, which is almost as fine as silk.'

Guanaco   Vicuña

general public from US$53/75, breakfast included. It also offers other meals.

Getting There & Away

Putre is 150 km east of Arica via paved Chile 11, the international highway to Bolivia. Buses La Paloma (☎ 222710), Germán Riesco 2071 in Arica, serves Putre daily, departing Arica at 6.45 am, and returns in the early afternoon. Buses to Parinacota, in Parque Nacional Lauca (see below), pass by the turnoff to Putre, which is five km from the main highway.

PARQUE NACIONAL LAUCA

One of Chile's most accessible parks, Parque Nacional Lauca is a World Biosphere Reserve that supports vicuña, condor, vizcacha and more than 150 species of bird, plus cultural and archaeological landmarks and Aymara herders of llamas and alpacas. Among its spectacular features is Lago Chungará, one of the world's highest lakes, at the foot of the dormant twin Pallachata volcanoes. Slightly to the south, Volcán Guallatire smokes ominously.

Lauca comprises 138,000 hectares of

Strict Inca authority protected the vicuña, but the Spanish invasion destroyed that authority and made the species vulnerable to hunting pressure over the past 500 years. By the middle of this century, poaching reduced its numbers from two million to perhaps 10,000 and caused its placement on Appendix I of the Endangered Species List, but conservation programs like those in northern Chile's Parque Nacional Lauca have achieved so impressive a recovery that economic exploitation of the species may soon benefit the communities of the puna. In Lauca and surrounding areas, vicuña numbers grew from barely a thousand in the early 1970s to more than 17,000 two decades later.

The communities of the puna and altiplano – in northern Chile, mostly Aymara Indians – still depend on llamas and alpacas for their livelihood. While the two species appear similar, they differ in several important respects. The taller, rangier and hardier llama *(Lama glama)* is a pack animal whose relatively coarse wool serves for blankets, ropes and other household goods (llama trains are rare in Chile since good roads penetrated the altiplano). It can survive or even flourish on relatively poor, dry pastures, while the smaller, more delicate alpaca *(Lama pacos)* is not a pack animal and requires well-watered, sometimes irrigated grasslands to produce a much finer wool with great commercial value. Both llama and alpaca meat are consumed by Andean households and even sold in urban markets – visit the Mercado Benedicto in Arica for 'churrasco de alpaca.'

Meager earnings from wool and meat have not been sufficient to stem the flow of population from the countryside to cities like Arica and Iquique, but, if international agreement permits it, the commercialization of vicuña wool might help do so. According to a recent Conaf study, production and sale of vicuña cloth at a price of nearly US$290 per linear meter could earn more than US$300,000 per annum for reinvestment in one of Chile's most remote and poorest regions. If, as intended, Conaf involves the area's inhabitants and respects their needs and wishes, it would set a precedent which many Latin American governments might emulate in tropical rainforests and other threatened environments. ■

Llama   Alpaca

altiplano, between 3000 and 6300 meters above sea level, 160 km northeast of Arica near the Bolivian border. Adjacent to the park, but more difficult to access, are Reserva Nacional Las Vicuñas and Monumento Natural Salar de Surire. Once part of the park, they now constitute technically separate units but are still managed by Conaf and are described below.

The park's altitude, well above 4000 meters in most parts, requires the visitor to adapt gradually. Do not exert yourself at first and eat and drink moderately; if you suffer anyway, try a cup of tea made from the common Aymara herbal remedy *chachacoma*, readily gathered around the settlements. Keep water at your bedside, as the throat desiccates rapidly in the arid climate, and wear sun block – the tropical rays can be truly brutal at this elevation.

Geography & Climate

Beyond Copaquilla, paved Chile 11 climbs steadily but gradually through the precordillera to the park entrance at Las

Cuevas, where the altiplano proper begins. Rainfall and vegetation increase with altitude and distance from the coast; it can snow during the summer rainy season, known as *invierno boliviano* (Bolivian winter).

Along the highway and at Las Cuevas, remarkably tame specimens of the vicuña *(Vicugna vicugna)*, a wild relative of the llama, are living advertisements for a major Chilean wildlife conservation success story. Pay special attention to the ground-hugging, bright green *llareta (Laretia compacta)*, a densely growing shrub with a cushion-like appearance that belies the fact that it is nearly as hard as rock – the Aymara need a pick or mattock to break open dead llareta, which they collect for fuel.

The local Aymara pasture their llamas and alpacas on verdant *bofedales* (swampy alluvial grasslands) and the lower slopes of the surrounding mountains, and sell handicrafts woven from their wool in the village of Parinacota and at Lago Chungará.

Las Cuevas

At the park's western entrance, Las Cuevas has a permanent ranger station which is a good source of information and an excellent place to view and photograph the vicuña, whose numbers have increased from barely a thousand in the early 1970s to more than 17,000 today. Over the past

WAYNE BERNHARDSON
Vizcacha

decade of protection, they have also become exceptionally tame. Don't miss a soak in the rustic thermal baths nearby, where camping may be possible.

Ciénegas de Parinacota

On the north side of Chile 11, between the tiny settlements of Chucuyo and Parinacota, *guallatas* (Andean geese) and ducks drift on the Río Lauca and nest on the shore, while the curious mountain vizcacha *(Lagidium viscacia)*, a relative of the domestic chinchilla, peeks out from numerous rockeries that rise above the swampy sediments of the largest bofedales in the park.

Most of the Aymaras' domestic livestock also graze the ciénegas (swamps), which shelter some interesting cultural relics – there is a colonial chapel just below Restaurant Matilde at Chucuyo, and another about half an hour's walk from Parinacota (see below).

Parinacota

Five km off the international highway, Parinacota is a picturesque but nearly depopulated pastoral village whose 17th-century colonial church, reconstructed in 1789, contains surrealistic interior murals, the work of artists from the Cuzco school. The murals recall Hieronymus Bosch's 'Sinners in the Hands of an Angry God,' but note also the depiction of the soldiers bearing Christ to the cross as Spaniards. According to local legend, the small table chained to the wall used to leave the church in search of spirits at night. To visit the church, ask caretaker Cipriano Morales for the key, and leave a small donation.

Conaf has a refugio at Parinacota, built originally for a high-altitude genetic research project, (see below for information on accommodation). Ask rangers for information on surrounding sights like Laguna Cotacotani and Cerro Guane Guane (see below).

Laguna Cotacotani

Laguna Cotacotani is the source of the Río Lauca, but unfortunate diversions by Endesa, the privatized national electric company, have caused fluctuations in lake levels and undermined its ecological integrity. Still, along its shores, at the foot of extensive lava flows and cinder cones, you will see extensive bird life and scattered groves of *queñoa (Polylepis tarapacana)*, one of the world's highest-elevation trees, reaching about five meters in height. Though puma are not commonly seen, tracks are not unusual, and foxes are fairly common. Follow the road along the south bank of the Río Lauca from Parinacota.

Cerro Guane Guane
Immediately north of Parinacota, Guane Guane is a 5096-meter peak with extraordinary panoramic views of the park and beyond. It is climbable along its eastern shoulder, but the last 500 meters in particular are a difficult slog through porous volcanic sand – one step forward, two steps back. The climb takes about four hours from the village. Ask advice from Conaf's rangers, and do not attempt to climb in threatening weather, since there is no shelter from lightning.

Lago Chungará
More than 4500 meters above sea level, Lago Chungará is a shallow body of water formed when a lava flow dammed the snowmelt stream from 6350-meter Volcán Parinacota, which dominates the lake to the north. About 28 km from Las Cuevas, Chungará has abundant and unusual bird life, including the Chilean flamingo *(Phoenicopterus chilensis)*, the *tagua gigante* or giant coot *(Fulica gigantea)*, and the Andean gull *(Larus serranus)*. You can reach the west end of the lake from Parinacota on foot in about two hours, but most of its wildlife is more distant, near the Conaf ranger station on Chile 11 and the Chilean customs post near the border.

Because of Arica's increasing consumption of hydroelectricity and the Azapa valley's insatiable thirst, Endesa has built an intricate system of pumps and canals that constitute a continuing menace to Lago Chungará's ecological integrity. Since the lake is so shallow, any lowering of its level would dramatically reduce its surface area and impinge on those parts where wading birds like the flamingo and giant coot feed and nest.

Feria Tambo Quemado
At the east end of Lago Chungará, the border post of Tambo Quemado is also the site of a colorful international market on alternate Fridays.

Places to Stay & Eat
While the park has no formal accommodations, there are several reasonable alternatives. In a pinch, Conaf's *Refugio Las Cuevas*, at the park entrance, may offer a bed.

In Chucuyo, directly on the highway to Bolivia near the junction to Parinacota, *Restaurant Matilde* usually has an extra bed at a very reasonable price – Matilde Morales will prepare alpaca steaks and other simple meals, and there are two other inexpensive restaurants. Limited supplies are available, but it's cheaper and more convenient to bring them from Arica.

Conaf's sparsely furnished *Refugio Parinacota*, three km from Chucuyo, offers beds for US$10 per night, slightly cheaper for Chilean nationals, but bring your own sleeping bag. Hot showers depend on the sporadic arrival of gas canisters from Arica. Two small tent campsites are available nearby for US$7.

Conaf charges US$10 per person at its lakeside *Refugio Chungará*, which has eight beds available, and US$7 per site for its nearby *Camping Chungará*, which has picnic tables and stone walls 1.2 meters high for shelter from the wind. At 4500 meters above sea level, it gets very cold at night.

Getting There & Away
Parque Nacional Lauca straddles Chile 11, the Arica-La Paz highway, which is paved all the way to the Bolivian border; the trip from Arica now takes only about three hours. From Arica, there is regular passenger service with Buses Martínez (☎ 232-265), Pedro Montt 620, or Transporte

NORTE GRANDE

Humire (☎ 253497), Pedro Montt 662. Martínez leaves Tuesday and Friday at 10 am, while Humire departs at 10 pm the same days. Fares to Parinacota are about US$6, to Visviri US$7.50.

Several travel agencies in Arica offer tours to the park – for details, see Organized Tours in the Arica entry. Although tours provide a good introduction, you spend most of the time in transit, so try to arrange a longer stay at Chucuyo, Parinacota or Chungará – one alternative is renting a car in Arica and driving to the park, providing access to more remote sites like Guallatire, Caquena and the Salar de Surire (the latter only with a high-clearance vehicle, since it involves fording several watercourses). Carry extra fuel in cans – most rental agencies will provide them – but fuel is available from ECA in Putre and perhaps from Matilde Morales in Chucuyo. Do not forget warm clothing and sleeping gear.

RESERVA NACIONAL LAS VICUÑAS

South of Lauca, Reserva Nacional Las Vicuñas consists of 210,000 sparsely inhabited hectares where the endangered vicuña has proliferated; once part of the park, it was reclassified in the mid-1980s to permit reopening of the gold mine at Choquelimpie. There is no public transport, but it may be possible to catch a lift with mining trucks.

At the base of smoking Volcán Guallatire, 60 km from Parinacota via a roundabout route, the village of Guallatire features a 17th-century church and Conaf's *Refugio Guallatire*, which provides beds for US$10 per person but is not always staffed. South of Guallatire, on the road to Surire, are the interesting ruins of a colonial silver mill.

Farther south, there are several fords of the Río Viluvio, a tributary of the Lauca, which should not be attempted with a low-clearance vehicle – or by any vehicle if the river is high in the summer rainy season. If uncertain, scout your route by wading across (the water is surprisingly warm). Take special care to avoid sandbars; should

you get stuck, there are Carabineros at Guallatire and at Chilcaya (farther south) with 4WD vehicles who *may* be able to help.

MONUMENTO NATURAL SALAR DE SURIRE

En route to Surire, 126 km from Putre and 108 km from Parinacota, flocks· of the sprinting *ñandú* (the ostrich-like rhea, *Pterocnemia pennata*) and vicuña dot the countryside. The monument itself comprises 11,300 hectares around a sprawling salt lake with breeding colonies of three species of flamingos, including the rare James flamingo *(parina chica* or *Phoenicoparrus jamesi)*. Again, there is no public transport, but it may be possible to hitch a lift with trucks from the nearby sulphur mine or with Conaf, whose *Refugio Surire* has beds for US$10. Camping is possible at Polloquere, where there are rustic thermal baths.

Although most visitors return to Putre and Arica, it's possible to make a southerly circuit through Parque Nacional Isluga and back to Arica via Camiña or Huara. Do not attempt this without consulting with Conaf and/or the Carabineros. The route is particularly iffy during the summer rainy season.

PISAGUA

Midway between Arica and Iquique, the isolated coastal village of Pisagua has a long but sometimes inglorious history. Several architectural landmarks have survived from one of Chile's largest 19th-century nitrate ports, which became a penal colony after the decline of the nitrate industry. It acquired true notoriety as a prison camp for the military dictatorship of 1973-1989; after the return to democracy, the discovery of mass graves in the local cemetery caused an international scandal.

With a small population (barely 150), Pisagua occupies a narrow shelf at the foot of the coast range, which rises almost vertically from the shore, but there are good campsites and beaches at the north end of town. Visitors not deterred by this grim history will find much of interest and, as work proceeds on a road north toward

Arica, this stretch of coastline may become as popular as the newly paved Ruta 1 south of Iquique.

Things to See

On a hillock overlooking the town, Pisagua's brightly painted **Torre Reloj** (clock tower) is a national monument dating from the nitrate glory days, when the port had a population of several thousand.

North of the palm-shaded Plaza de Armas, the surf laps at the foundations of the **Teatro Municipal**, a once-lavish theater with a broad stage, opera-style boxes, and ceiling murals of cherubim; the regional government has spent US$10,000 restoring the facade, but lacks funds for the interior. The building's northern half, which once held dressing rooms, municipal offices and a market, is also worth exploring, but be cautious – one second-story door plunges directly into the ocean. To enter the theater, ask the Carabineros for the key.

Half a block inland from the plaza, the **Colonia Penal Pisagua** was a conventional prison and not the primary site for incarceration of political prisoners after the military coup of 1973. Now the town's only hotel and restaurant, it seems to try to atone for Pisagua's grisly past by featuring portraits of leftist figures like poet Pablo Neruda and folk singer Violeta Parra.

Just beyond the police station, the abandoned **Estación de Ferrocarril** recalls the time when Pisagua was the northern terminus of El Longino, the longitudinal railway that connected the nitrate mines and ports of the Norte Grande. About two km north of town, the faded wooden crosses at Pisagua's **Cementerio** (cemetery) mark tombs from the town's historic past, but this was also the notorious site of a mass grave of victims of the Pinochet dictatorship.

Places to Stay & Eat

Pisagua's free *Camping Municipal* is basically a large parking lot at Playa Seis, a small but fine sandy beach just beyond the ruins of the former fish processing factory that once incarcerated political prisoners. It has clean toilets and de facto hot showers, since the water piped from the old rail station of Dolores, on the pampas behind Pisagua, runs through surfaces piped heated by the desert sun. It's also possible to camp north of town at Playa Blanca, beneath the Monolito Centenario, but there are no sanitary facilities.

In the former jail, *Hotel Pisagua* (☎ 731-509) charges US$34 with full board for adults, US$18 for children; B&B is also available. All the guest rooms remain labeled for their original institutional occupants – the warden, guards and other prison personnel. Visitors can dine among banana trees and gardenias in the patio; the lunch menu, usually a seafood dish, is very good and costs about US$5. In addition to superb pisco sours, there are ping pong and billiard tables for amusement.

Getting There & Away

Pisagua is 40 km west of the Panamericana by a good road from a turnoff 85 km south of the Carabineros checkpoint at Cuya and 47 km north of Huara. All but the last five km are paved, but wind often covers part of the road with a film of sand that can make the surface more slippery than it looks. There is no public transport and relatively little traffic of any kind, so hitching requires great patience.

IQUIQUE

Prior to the Spanish invasion, Iquique was a minor concentration of coastal Chango Indians who exchanged fish and guano from offshore islands for maize, potatoes and other products of the precordillera and the altiplano. During the colonial era, guano grew in importance, but the region's real wealth stemmed from the Huantajaya silver mine in the coast range, second only to the bonanza vein at Potosí.

During the 19th century, Tarapacá's minerals and nitrates were shipped by narrow-gauge railways through ports like Iquique, once little more than a collection of shanties at the base of the barren headlands. In 1835 Darwin observed that Iquique:

. . . contains about a thousand inhabitants, and stands on a little plain of sand at the foot of a great wall of rock two thousand feet in height, here forming the coast. The whole is utterly desert. A light shower of rain falls only once in very many years; and the ravines consequently are filled with detritus, and the mountain-sides covered by piles of fine white sand, even to a height of a thousand feet . . . The aspect of the place was most gloomy; the little port, with its few vessels, and small group of wretched houses, seemed overwhelmed and out of all proportion with the rest of the scene.

In a few years, Darwin would barely have recognized Iquique. As the nitrate industry grew, its population exceeded 5000 in 20 years and 40,000 by the turn of the century. Not all the nitrate ports survived, but in those that did, like Iquique, nitrate barons built opulent mansions (many of them still standing), while authorities piped in water from the distant cordillera and imported topsoil for public plazas and private gardens. Iquique reflects this 19th-century boom, its Plaza Prat complete with clock tower and theater with Corinthian columns, and many stately wooden Victorian mansions. Nearby ghost towns like Humberstone and Santa Laura, with their rusting machinery, recall the source of this wealth.

Now a city of more than 140,000, Iquique is still one of the Norte Grande's largest ports, but fishing has supplanted mining as its primary industry – Iquique ships more fishmeal than any other port in the world. Establishment of the Zona Franca (duty-free zone) in 1975 has made it one of Chile's most prosperous cities, and the recent paving of Ruta 1 to Antofagasta is bringing larger numbers of visitors.

Downtown retains the atmosphere of a 19th-century port, with ramshackle wooden houses, sailors' bars and street life, but the city is spreading south along the coast, where many houses are literally built on sand and, consequently, vulnerable to the area's frequent earthquakes. On the desert plain above Iquique, toward the Panamericana, new housing developments are making the once tiny community of Alto Hospicio an integral part of the city.

Orientation

Iquique sits on a narrow terrace at the foot of the coastal range, which abruptly rises 600 meters above the city, 1853 km north of Santiago by a combination of the Panamericana and Ruta 1, and 315 km from Arica by the roundabout Panamericana. Blocked by the mountains, Iquique has spread north and south along the coast, although the hilltop suburb of Alto Hospicio is also growing rapidly.

The city's focus is Plaza Prat. Avenida Baquedano, which runs north-south along the east side of the plaza, is the main thoroughfare, while Calle Tarapacá runs east four blocks to Plaza Condell, a secondary center of downtown activity. Most points of interest are within a roughly rectangular area marked by Sotomayor to the north, Avenida Costanera to the west, Amunátegui to the east, and Manuel Bulnes to the south. The main beaches are south of downtown, along Avenida Balmaceda and its extension Avenida 11 de Septiembre.

Information

Tourist Offices Sernatur (☎ 411523, 427686) has new quarters at Serrano 145, Oficina 303. Open weekdays 8 am to 1.30 pm and 3 to 6 pm, it's helpful and provides a free city map and brochures, but is less well stocked than its counterparts in other Chilean cities. It has a branch office at the Zona Franca (see below), north of downtown, open 10 am to 1 pm and 4.30 to 9 pm on days when the Zona Franca is open.

Another good source of information is the Automóvil Club de Chile (☎ 413-206), Serrano 154, across the street from Sernatur.

Consulates The Bolivian Consulate (☎ 421777) is at Pasaje Alessandri 429, 3rd floor (Alessandri is a block-long street between Patricio Lynch and Obispo Labbé, one block west of Plaza Prat. The Peruvian Consulate (☎ 411466) is at San Martín 385.

Money Carpinello Money Exchange, Tarapacá 376, and Cambio Sciaraffia, Tarapacá

399, change foreign currency and travelers' checks, but there are many ATMs downtown and at the Zona Franca (where there are also cambios).

Post & Communications Iquique's area code is ☎ 57. Correos de Chile, Bolívar 458, is open weekdays 8.30 am to 12.30 pm and 3 to 7 pm, Saturday 9 am to 1 pm.

Iquique has several telephone offices, including CTC at Ramírez 587 and at the Zona Franca, Módulo 212, 2nd level. Entel is at Gorostiaga 287 and Chilesat at Tarapacá 520, while Telex-Chile, San Martín 387, also offers international telephone services.

Language Courses The Swiss-run Academia de Idiomas del Norte (☎ 411827, fax 429343), Ramírez 1345, provides Spanish language instruction.

Laundry Lavarápido (☎ 425338), Obispo Labbé 1446, charges by weight. Laverap (☎ 420353) is at San Martín 490.

Medical Services Iquique's Hospital Regional Doctor Torres (☎ 422370) is at the corner of Tarapacá and Avenida Héroes de la Concepción, 10 blocks east of Plaza Condell.

Walking Tour
Because of its 19th-century heritage, derived from foreign exploitation of nitrates, Iquique's architecture resembles that of few other Latin American cities. Many city landmarks are on Plaza Prat, including the **Torre Reloj** (1877) clock tower, the **Teatro Municipal**, a neoclassical structure which has hosted opera, theater and other cultural activities since 1890, and the adjacent **Sociedad Protectora de Empleados de Tarapacá** (1913), one of the country's first labor union buildings. At the northeast corner, facing the plaza, the Moorish-style **Centro Español** (1904) is now a club and restaurant whose interior features murals and oil paintings based on themes from *Don Quijote* and from Spanish history.

South of the plaza, **Avenida Baquedano** is a preservation zone for Georgian-style buildings dating from 1880 to 1930. Among them are the former **Tribunales de Justicia** (Law Courts, now the Museo Regional) at Baquedano 951 and the **Palacio Astoreca**, a nitrate baron's mansion that is also a museum, at Baquedano and O'Higgins.

At Sotomayor and Vivar, four blocks north of Plaza Condell, the onetime **Estación de Ferrocarril** (train station) once linked Iquique with the nitrate oficinas of the interior. Built under Peruvian rule, the 19th-century **Edificio de la Aduana**, at the west end of Esmeralda, contains Iquique's Museo Naval (Naval Museum). West of the Aduana, the **Muelle de Pasajeros** (passenger pier) dates from 1901.

Museo Regional
Occupying Iquique's former courthouse, the regional museum features a mock altiplano village with adobe houses and mannequins in traditional Aymara dress, plus a large collection of pre-Columbian artifacts, including raft and canoe paddles, fish hooks and sinkers, rope, harpoons, arrows and quivers made of animal hide. There's also an exhibition of Indian ceramics and weaving, photos of Iquique's early days and a fascinating display on the nitrate industry, including a scale model of Oficina Peña Chica, east of Iquique, just north of Humberstone (see Around Iquique).

At Baquedano 951, the Museo Regional (☎ 421018) is open weekdays in summer 8.30 am to 1 pm and 3 to 8 pm, Saturday 10.30 am to 1 pm only; the rest of the year, weekday and Saturday morning hours are the same, but weekday afternoon hours are 3 to 6.30 pm only. Admission is a modest US$0.75 for adults, US$0.35 for children.

Palacio Astoreca
Built by a nitrate tycoon, this Georgian-style mansion (1904) matches the opulence of the wool barons of Punta Arenas. It has a fantastic interior of enormous rooms with elaborate woodwork and high ceilings, massive chandeliers, stained glass

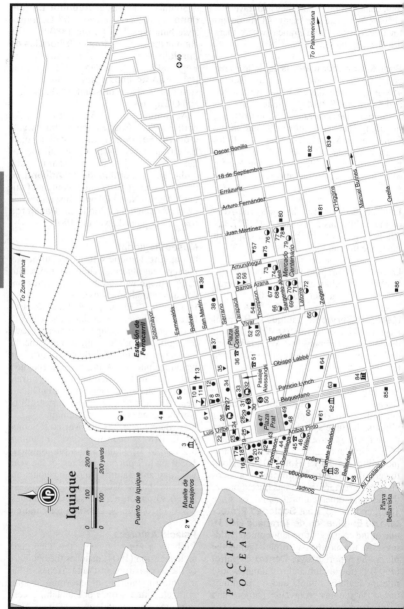

NORTE GRANDE

Iquique

To Zona Franca

Estación de Ferrocarril

PACIFIC OCEAN

Puerto de Iquique

Muelle de Pasajeros

Playa Bellavista

To Panamericana

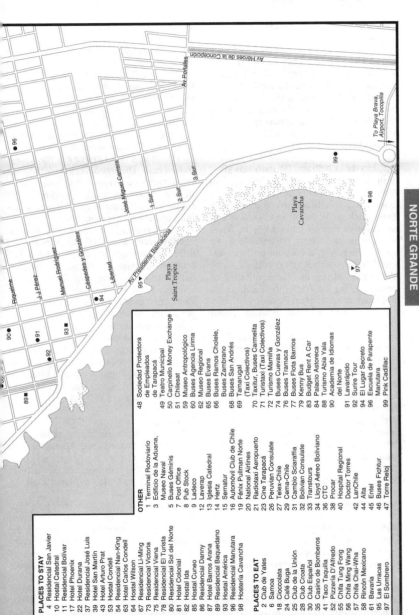

NORTE GRANDE

PLACES TO STAY
4 Residencial San Javier
10 Hostal Catedral
11 Residencial Bolívar
17 Hotel Phoenix
22 Hotel Durana
37 Residencial José Luis
39 Hotel San Martín
43 Hotel Arturo Prat
53 Hostal Condell
54 Residencial Nan-King
63 Hotel Carlos Condell
64 Hostal Wilson
67 Residencial Li-Ming
73 Residencial Victoria
75 Residencial Viena
78 Residencial El Tunista
80 Residencial Sol del Norte
81 Hotel Colonial
82 Hostal Ida
85 Hostal Cuneo
86 Residencial Danny
87 Hostal Barros Arana
89 Residencial Baquedano
93 Hostal América
96 Residencial Manutara
98 Hostería Cavancha

PLACES TO EAT
2 Club de Yates
6 Samoa
18 Cioccolata
24 Café Buga
25 Club de la Unión
28 Club Croata
30 Club Español
35 Casino de Bomberos
41 Taco Taquilla
52 Pizzería D'Alfredo
55 Chita Tung Fong
56 Chita Ming Wang
57 Chita Chai-Wha
58 Rincón Mexicano
61 Bavaria
95 Las Urracas
97 El Sombrero

OTHER
1 Terminal Rodoviario
3 Edificio de la Aduana,
   Museo Naval
5 Buses Géminis
7 Post Office
8 Pub Stock
9 Ladeco
12 Iglesia Catedral
13 Laverap
14 Hertz
15 Sernatur
16 Automóvil Club de Chile
19 Fénix Pullman Norte
20 National Airlines
21 Radiotaxi Aeropuerto
23 Cine Tarapacá
26 Peruvian Consulate
27 Telex-Chile
29 Cema-Chile
31 Cambio Sciaraffia
32 Bolivian Consulate
33 Transtours
34 Lloyd Aéreo Boliviano
36 CTC
38 Procar
40 Hospital Regional
   Doctor Torres
42 LanChile
44 Alta
45 Entel
46 Buses Fichtur
47 Torre Reloj
48 Sociedad Protectora
   de Empleados
   de Tarapacá
49 Teatro Municipal
50 Carpinello Money Exchange
51 Chilesat
59 Museo Antropológico
60 Buses Agencia Lirima
62 Museo Regional
65 Buses Evans
66 Buses Ramos Cholele,
   Buses Zambrano
68 Buses San Andrés
69 Tamarugal
   (Taxi Colectivos)
70 Taxitur, Buses Carmelita
71 Turistaxi (Taxi Colectivos)
72 Turismo Mamiña
74 Buses Cuevas y González
76 Buses Tramaca
77 Buses Flota Barrios
79 Kenny Bus
83 Budget Rent A Car
84 Palacio Astoreca
88 Turismo Abia Yala
90 Academia de Idiomas
   del Norte
91 Lavarápido
92 Surire Tour
94 El Lugar Secreto
96 Escuela de Parapente
   Manutara
99 Pink Cadillac

windows, a gigantic billiard table and balconies.

At the intersection of Patricio Lynch and O'Higgins, the Palacio (☎ 412397) is now a museum and cultural center which exhibits paintings by local artists. In summer, it's open weekdays 10 am to 2 pm and 4 to 8 pm, weekends 10 am to 1 pm only; the rest of the year, hours are Tuesday to Friday 10 am to 2 pm and 3 to 7 pm, weekends 10 am to 1 pm.

Edificio de la Aduana (Museo Naval)

Built in 1871 when Iquique belonged to Peru, the deteriorating colonial-style customs house is a two-story structure with meter-thick walls, an octagonal tower and an attractive interior patio. Only its naval museum is sufficiently presentable to be open to the public; it contains artifacts salvaged from Arturo Prat's corvette *Esmeralda*, sunk during the famous Battle of Iquique during the War of the Pacific, plus biographical material on Prat.

Fronting on Esmeralda between Aníbal Pinto and Baquedano, the Museo Naval is open Tuesday to Saturday 9.30 am to 12.30 pm and 2.30 to 6 pm, Sundays and holidays 10 am to 1 pm. Admission is free of charge.

Muelle de Pasajeros

Just west of the Edificio de la Aduana, Iquique's passenger pier dates from 1901. Harbor tours (US$2.50) leave from here, passing the buoy that marks the site of Arturo Prat's sunken corvette *Esmeralda*, from the Battle of Iquique, and approaching the colony of sea lions that covers the nearby rocks. Depending on the tide, more or fewer of the interestingly constructed steps are exposed to view.

Museo Antropológico

Iquique's small archaeological museum, run by the Universidad Arturo Prat, has good historical and environmental material, but undercuts its own credibility with the absurd speculation that Chile's indigenous peoples crossed from Australia and New Zealand via Antarctica to the southern tip of South America.

The museum's main site is at Grumete Bolados 127, but there's a small branch at the Zona Franca. The hours at the main site are weekdays 9.15 am to 1.15 pm and 3.15 to 7.15 pm, Saturdays 11 am to 1 pm; at the branch the same as the Zona Franca's (see below).

Zona Franca

Created in 1975, this monstrous monument to uncontrolled consumption is the reason most Chileans visit Iquique and many have moved here. The entire Region of Tarapacá is technically a customs-free zone, but its nucleus is this sprawling shopping center for imported electronics, clothing, automobiles and almost anything else.

The *Zofri*, as it is commonly known, employs more than 10,000 workers in 1500 different companies, which helps make Iquique's unemployment rate the lowest in the country. Also benefiting from its proximity to Peru, Bolivia and Argentina, the Zofri turns over more than US$3.2 billion per annum in merchandise.

To see this feeding frenzy of voracious consumers, and maybe replace a lost or stolen camera, take any northbound taxi colectivo from downtown. It's open Mondays 4 to 9 pm, Tuesday through Friday 10 am to 1 pm and 4.30 to 9 pm, and Saturdays 10 am to 2 pm and 5 to 9 pm.

Beaches

Playa Cavancha, beginning at the intersection of Balmaceda and Amunátegui, is Iquique's most popular beach, good for swimming and surfing but sometimes crowded. There's also a playground for kids.

Farther south, along Avenida 11 de Septiembre, crashing waves and rip currents at **Playa Brava** make it too rough to go in the water, but it's fine for sunbathing. Toward the hills, look for the massive dunes of Cerro Dragón, which looks like a set for a science fiction film. The easiest way to Playa Brava is by taxi colectivo from downtown.

Much farther south, toward and beyond the airport, the beaches are excellent and much less crowded, but the superb paved highway and improved public transport are a mixed blessing – once-pristine beaches are now so easy to reach that many of them look like dumps.

Surfing

Surfing is best in winter, when swells come from the north, but is possible at any time of year. Chilean surfers, mostly body boarders, sleep late, so there's less competition for early morning waves at Playa Cavancha. Playa Huaiquique, on the southern outskirts of town, is also a good choice, but the sea is warmer farther north near Arica.

El Lugar Secreto (☎ 427687), Vivar 1703, is Iquique's local surf shop.

Paragliding

Iquique's unique geography, with its steep coastal escarpment, rising air currents and the soft, extensive dunes of Cerro Dragón, makes it ideal for paragliding (Spanish *parapente*), an activity that involves jumping off a cliff to get airborne. It's theoretically possible to glide all the way to Tocopilla, 240 km to the south. The Franco-Argentine Escuela de Parapente Manutara (☎ /fax 418280), 18 de Septiembre 1512, offers short introductory flights for about US$25, with longer courses also available. They also offer desert tours of one, two or three days in a 4WD vehicle.

Organized Tours

Travelers have voiced considerable dissatisfaction with some Iquique tour operators in recent years, but those included here appear to be reliable. Before taking any tour, ask for a good explanation to be sure that your expectations coincide with theirs.

Turismo Abia Yala (☎ /fax 422676), Baquedano 1282, runs 12-hour tours that take in the nitrate ruins at Humberstone, geoglyph sites at Cerro Unita and Pintados, and oases at Pica and Matilla for US$25 to 30 per person. Three-hour city tours cost around US$13, 10-hour coastal excursions toward the Río Loa about US$25, the Tarapacá valley for US$30 and Pisagua (14

hours) for US$40. Most trips require a four-person minimum; English-speaking guides are available for an extra charge.

Surire Tour (☎ 445440, fax 411795), Patricio Lynch 1496, runs similar tours and trips, and will also organize excursions to more out-of-the-way places in the altiplano and the canyons of the precordillera. At Patricio Lynch 548, Local 319, Transtours (☎ /fax 428984), the Iquique branch of the highly regarded Arica operator, has comparable services.

Places to Stay – bottom end

Iquique's cheapest accommodations are a cluster of seedy residenciales on Amunátegui between Sargento Aldea and Thompson, all charging about US$5 or less per person. Among them are *Residencial Victoria* at Amunátegui 770 and the spartan *Residencial Viena* at Amunátegui 729, but these are desperation choices.

A better choice is *Hostal Sol del Norte* (☎ /fax 421546), Juan Martínez 852, for US$6 per person, but it has few singles and lacks hot water. Friendly *Residencial San Javier* (☎ 427641), Patricio Lynch 97, is cheap for US$6 per person, but the rooms are tiny cubicles with thin walls and sagging beds. It's close to the bus terminal, however.

Hospitable *Hostal Condell* (☎ 413948), Thompson 684, charges US$7 per person with shared bath, US$10 with private bath. *Hostal Ida* (☎ 411426), 18 de Septiembre 1058, charges US$7.50 per person with shared bath, US$12.50 per person with private bath.

Conveniently located *Residencial Baquedano* (☎ 422990), in the midst of an historic neighborhood at Baquedano 1315, has small but very clean singles with firm beds for US$9, but lacks hot water. Across the street from the Sol del Norte, the simple but friendly and spotless *Residencial El Turista* (☎ /fax 422245), Juan Martínez 849-857, has 55 rooms and 16 shared baths, charging US$9 per person.

The very clean and friendly *Residencial José Luis* (☎ 422844), San Martín 601, also gets short-stay trade. Singles are US$9 with shared bath, doubles US$14 with private bath; all downstairs rooms have large, comfortable double beds. Interior rooms are quieter. Rambling *Residencial Bolívar*, Bolívar 478, is a recommended choice at US$10 per person. Close to Playa Cavancha, *Hostal América* (☎ 427524), Manuel Rodríguez 550, has hot water and includes breakfast for US$11.

Franco-Argentine *Residencial Manutara* (☎ /fax 418280), 18 de Septiembre 1512, costs US$10 per person with breakfast and 24-hour hot water; lunch, dinner and laundry service are also available. Several other places also charge around US$10, including *Residencial Danny* (☎ 414161) at Vivar 1266, also easy walking distance to the beach; *Residencial Nan-King* (☎ 423311) at Thompson 752, which is quiet but often full; and *Residencial Li-Ming* (☎ 421912) at Barros Arana 705.

Hostal Cuneo (☎ 428654), Baquedano 1175, is a very fine place that charges US$12.50 per person with breakfast and shared bath, but some interior rooms lack windows; it's decorated with photos of old Iquique. Probably the best budget choice is tidy *Hostal Catedral* (☎ 412184), Obispo Labbé 233 opposite the cathedral, where singles/doubles with shared bath cost US$12.50/23, but rates with private bath have risen to US$30/35 and even then it's often full. Highly recommended, it has two levels of rooms surrounding a pleasant courtyard and garden, but it's not the value it once was.

Places to Stay – middle

Simple mid-range accommodations, usually with private bath and breakfast, start around US$20/26 at *Hotel Durana* (☎ 428-085), San Martín 294. The comparable *Hotel Colonial* (☎ 426097), Juan Martínez 1020, charges US$23/31.

Iquique's best middle-range value is the very central *Hotel Phoenix* (☎ 429933), Aníbal Pinto 451, with a friendly staff and simple but clean and bright rooms for US$28/38, including private bath and breakfast. Its ground floor offers a restaurant, but also a billiard hall, which is noisier

than some guests would prefer. Others in this range include *Hostal Wilson* (☎ 423789) at Wilson 422 for US$30/38, and *Hotel San Martín* (☎ 412260) at San Martín 823, which has drawn some criticism for small rooms, soft mattresses and mediocre breakfasts; rates are US$35/42.

In a restored historic house at Baquedano 964, with a helpful staff, *Hotel Carlos Condell* (☎ 424467) chargesUS$45/55. Prices have risen and it's less central than others in this category, but *Hotel Barros Arana* (☎ 412840) at Barros Arana 1330 near Orella, has drawn praise from many travelers. Though it's architecturally undistinguished, its clean and fresh-looking rooms with TV and private bath cost US$46/58.

Places to Stay – top end

Toward the south end of town, the new high-rise *Hotel Terrado* (☎ 437878, fax 437755), Avenida Aeropuerto 2873, is the latest entry in the luxury hotel sweepstakes for US$77/96. In the same area, the *Holiday Inn Express* (☎ 433300), Avenida 11 de Septiembre 1690, offers North American franchise conventionality for US$97 single or double.

One of Iquique's traditional favorites is *Hotel Arturo Prat* (☎ 411067), at Aníbal Pinto 695 opposite Plaza Prat, but its central location also means it can be very noisy and, for US$100/108, it's probably overpriced. Though it's less interesting architecturally, the beachfront *Hostería Cavancha* (☎ 431007), Los Rieles 250, is better value for US$100/120.

Places to Eat

Despite its unprepossessing appearance, one of Iquique's best eating places is the Mercado Centenario on Barros Arana between Sargento Aldea and Latorre, where several upstairs cocinerías offer varied seafood at reasonable prices; as of this writing, the market was undergoing remodeling to make it more attractive and hygienic.

Cioccolata (☎ 413010), Aníbal Pinto 487, is a good choice for breakfast or onces. *Café Buga* (☎ 426134), Luis Uribe 443, is another good choice for coffee.

Reader-recommended *Samoa*, Bolívar 396, has economical fixed-price lunches, as does the *Sociedad Protectora de Empleados de Tarapacá*, in an historic building at Thompson 207. The *Casino de Bomberos* (☎ 422887), Serrano 520, is also a good lunch spot.

Bavaria (☎ 427888), Aníbal Pinto 926, is the local representative of the popular nationwide chain; it also has a delicatessen with good takeout food. Also part of a chain, *Pizzería D'Alfredo* (☎ 413044), Vivar 631, has respectable pizza and firmly but politely enforces its non-smoking section.

The *Club Croata* (☎ 416222), Plaza Prat 310, has excellent four-course lunches for US$6, but the overworked waiters find it hard to maintain consistent service. Dinners are more expensive. Reasonable lunches are also available at the *Club de la Unión* (☎ 413236), Plaza Prat 278, 3rd floor.

Not to be missed are the Moorish interior and artwork at the ornate *Club Español* (☎ 423284), at the northeast corner of Plaza Prat, but it's become very expensive. If you can't afford a meal, at least peek through the windows or treat yourself to a drink inside.

El Sombrero (☎ 423655), Los Rieles 704, has excellent seafood in agreeable surroundings overlooking Playa Cavancha, but is expensive. Ditto for the *Club de Yates* (☎ 413385), just west of the Muelle de Pasajeros, where you can watch the sea lions lurking for leftovers. *Las Urracas* (☎ 421493), Balmaceda 431, is also worth a try.

Iquique has two outstanding Mexican restaurants: the Tex-Mex *Taco Taquilla* (☎ 427804) at Thompson 123 and the more genuinely Mexican *Rincón Mexicano* (☎ 422301) at Bellavista 115, which has fine food, excellent service, real corn tortillas and tasty but pricey margaritas.

Chinese restaurants are numerous – *Chifa Chai-Wha*, Thompson 917, is cheap, with a simple Chinese meal going for around US$4 per person. Others include *Chifa Tung Fong* (☎ 421548) at Tarapacá 835 and *Chifa Ming Wang* at Barros Arana 668.

Entertainment
The *Cine Tarapacá* (☎ 422329), downtown at Serrano 206, shows recent movies from around the world.

Also downtown, at the corner of Bolívar and Lynch, *Pub Stock* has live rock 'n' roll. The *Pink Cadillac* (☎ 435385), Balmaceda 2751, is a popular dance club.

Things to Buy
Most Chilean shoppers swarm to the Zona Franca (see separate entry, above), but for regional arts and crafts, Cema-Chile at Plaza Prat 570 is worth a visit.

Getting There & Away
Air LanChile (☎ 412540), Aníbal Pinto 641, has 20 flights weekly to Santiago (US$219 one way), half of which stop over in Antofagasta (US$54). Flights from Santiago to Iquique continue to Arica (US$33), daily to La Paz and Tuesday, Thursday and Sunday to Santa Cruz, Bolivia. Lloyd Aéreo Boliviano (☎ 426-750, 427058), Serrano 430, flies Tuesday to Arica and La Paz, with onward international connections.

Ladeco (☎ 413038), at San Martín 428, Local 2, flies three times daily to Santiago, mostly stopping in Antofagasta. All flights from Santiago continue to Arica. Fares are essentially identical to LanChile's.

National Airlines (☎ 428800), Aníbal Pinto 555, flies daily to Santiago (US$196), stopping in Antofagasta (US$48) except Friday and Saturday; their flights from Santiago continue to Arica (US$30) and to Arequipa, Peru, three times weekly. National also offers international services to Asunción, Paraguay on Monday, Tuesday and Thursday.

Alta (☎ 415532, fax 415533), Aníbal Pinto 791, flies nine times weekly to Arica (US$15), 14 times to Calama (US$38), usually continuing to Antofagasta (US$38), 10 times to Copiapó (US$100) and La Serena (US$127), sometimes continuing to

Viña del Mar (US$140), daily except Sunday to Santiago, and daily to Concepción (US$175).

Bus – domestic Iquique's shabby Terminal Rodoviario (☎ 426492) is at the north end of Patricio Lynch, but most companies have ticket offices near the Mercado Centenario. Buses leave from the terminal, but passengers can also board at these ticket offices. Services north (to Arica) and south are frequent, but nearly all southbound services now use Ruta 1, the coastal highway to Tocopilla (for connections to Calama) and Antofagasta (for connections on the Panamericana to Copiapó, La Serena and Santiago).

To Arica, try Buses Carmelita (☎ 412-237) at Barros Arana 841, Cuevas y González (☎ 412471) at Sargento Aldea 850 or Fénix Pullman Norte (☎ 412423) at Aníbal Pinto 531. Taxi colectivos, faster than buses, charge about US$12 per person. The major companies are Tamarugal (☎ 424-856) at Sargento Aldea 783 and Turistaxi (☎ 424428) at Barros Arana 897-A.

To Calama, Antofagasta and intermediate points, try Tramaca (☎ 412323) at Sargento Aldea 988, Kenny Bus (☎ 414159) at Latorre 944, Flota Barrios (☎ 426941) at Sargento Aldea 987 and Géminis (☎ 422-902) at Obispo Labbé 151.

Numerous companies serve Santiago, including Carmelita, Flota Barrios, Fénix Pullman Norte, Buses Evans (☎ 413462) at Vivar 955-A and Ramos Cholele (☎ 421-648), Sargento Aldea 742. Fichtur (☎ 414-304), Aníbal Pinto 865, offers costlier but more comfortable bus cama service. Ramos Cholele and Buses Zambrano (☎ 413215), Sargento Aldea 742, operate between Iquique and Valparaíso/Viña del Mar.

Buses San Andrés (☎ 413953), Sargento Aldea 798, goes daily to Pica, Arica, and Santiago. Agencia Lirima (☎ 413094), Baquedano 823, goes to interior destinations like Pica, Mamiña and Matilla, as does Turismo Mamiña (☎ 420330) at Latorre 779. Taxitur (☎ 422044), Sargento Aldea 791, has taxi colectivos to Mamiña and Pica.

Typical destinations and fares include Arica (US$6, four hours), Calama (US$15, six hours), Antofagasta (US$20, eight hours), Chañaral (US$27, 12 hours), Caldera/Copiapó (US$30, 15 hours), La Serena (US$35, 18 hours) and Santiago (US$45, 24 hours). Pullman Bus (☎ 428-749), Aníbal Pinto 865, offers semi-cama recliners to Calama (US$18), Antofagasta (US$25), Copiapó (US$44), La Serena (US$48) and Santiago or Valparaíso/Viña del Mar (US$63).

Bus – international Besides its domestic services, Géminis offers direct service to the Bolivian cities of Oruro (US$32) and La Paz (US$35, 24 hours) Tuesdays, Thursday and Saturdays. Géminis also offers Wednesday service to Jujuy and Salta, Argentina (US$55) via Calama; in summer, there's an additional Sunday bus.

Kenny Bus serves the border town of Colchane (US$8), in the altiplano of Iquique, Tuesday and Friday at 10 pm, arriving the following day at 6 am. It's also possible to find improvised transport with trucks to Colchane from the Shell station at the roundabout on the road to Alto Hospicio.

Getting Around
As in Arica, taxi colectivos are the easiest way to get around town. Destinations are clearly marked on an illuminated sign on top of the cab.

To/From the Airport Iquique's Aeropuerto Diego Aracena is 41 km south of town on Ruta 1; for about US$5, it's easy to find a taxi colectivo on Plaza Prat to connect with your flight. For door-to-door service, contact Radiotaxi Aeropuerto (☎ 415036), Aníbal Pinto 595.

Car Rental For rental vehicles, try Budget (☎ 429566) at O'Higgins 1361, Hertz (☎ 426316) at Souper 650 or Procar (☎ 413470) at Serrano 796.

AROUND IQUIQUE
Inland from Iquique are numerous geoglyphs, including the sprawling murals on

the eastern slope of the coastal range at Pintados, and the enormous human image on Cerro Unita, a hillside in the Quebrada de Tarapacá, east of Huara. Also worth seeing are the nitrate ghost towns of Humberstone and Santa Laura, the regional shrine of La Tirana, the improbable forests of Reserva Nacional Pampa del Tamarugal, the precordillera hot springs villages of Chusmiza, Pica and Mamiña, and altiplano settlements like Colchane, in Parque Nacional Volcán Isluga.

Ruta 1, the newly paved highway between Iquique and Tocopilla (in Region II), has largely superseded the older Panamericana for southbound travelers. There is spectacular coastal desert scenery, but improved access has also meant that careless campers are rapidly despoiling the area with trash.

While most of the beaches south of Iquique are too rocky for surfing, the beach near the customs post at the Río Loa, on the border between Regions I and II, is a good choice.

Humberstone & Santa Laura (Museo Arqueológico Industrial)

Once nearly deserted but for scrap metal merchants and a handful of curious tourists, the eerie pampas ghost town of Humberstone is now the center of a determined preservation effort. Around its central Plaza de Armas, nearly all the original buildings, like the theater, church and market, are still standing. Some are starting to crumble, but others such as the church are undergoing restoration.

Nitrate oficinas could be hazardous places to work. One now-faded sign reminded miners that 'One accident could destroy all your hopes.' Another warned that workers' contracts prohibited sheltering anyone not associated with the company, which provided housing, health care, food and merchandise. Goods were normally purchased only with *fichas*, tokens which took the place of cash and were worthless elsewhere. Union organizers were not welcome.

Despite its paternalistic organization,

WAYNE BERNHARDSON

Remnants of the nitrate heyday at Humberstone

Humberstone was in some ways a model company town, offering amenities like tennis and basketball courts. The most impressive recreational feature is the enormous swimming pool, built of cast iron from a shipwreck in Iquique harbor (don't be tempted to take the plunge off the diving board into the now empty pool). At the west end of town, the electrical generating plant still stands, along with the remains of the narrow gauge railway to the older Oficina Santa Laura, across the highway.

Humberstone took its name from its British manager James Humberstone, who arrived in Pisagua in 1875 under contract to the San Antonio Nitrate & Iodine Company. Perfecting the 'Shanks system' for extracting a larger proportion of nitrates from the raw *caliche* (hardpan) of the pampas, he also became an important administrator and builder of the nitrate railways. Upon his retirement in 1925, Oficina La Palma was renamed in his honor; he died in Santiago in 1939, but is buried at Hacienda Tilivilche, on the Panamericana midway between Iquique and Arica.

The most accessible of the former mining settlements, Humberstone sits just off the Panamericana, about 45 km due east of Iquique. Any eastbound bus from Iquique will drop you off there and it is easy to hitch or catch a return bus. Take food, water and a camera, since it is easy to spend many hours exploring the town, but modest supplies are now available. Early morning hours are the best time for wandering around, although afternoon breezes often moderate the midday heat.

Salitreras Nebraska (☎ 751213 in nearby Pozo Almonte, (02) 2184161 in Santiago) now administers Humberstone, Santa Laura, Peña Chica (four km north of Humberstone) and Keryma (three km northeast of Humberstone) as the Museo Arqueológico Industrial. It charges US$2.50 admission and distributes a small but informative brochure, in Spanish or English, with a map of Humberstone (note that this map does not include the outlying buildings). Every year, in early November, nostalgic former residents hold a reunion.

El Gigante de Atacama (Cerro Unita)

The Giant of the Atacama, a geoglyph 14 km east of Huara on the southern slope of Cerro Unita, is the largest archaeological representation of a human figure in the world – a massive 86 meters high.

From the figure's rectangular head, supported by a thin neck, emanate a dozen rays – four from the top and four from each side. The eyes and mouth are square, the torso long and narrow, the arms bent (one hand appears to be an arrowhead). The size of the feet suggest the figure is wearing boots, and there are odd protrusions from the knees and thighs. Alongside the giant is another odd creature with what appears to be a tail – perhaps a monkey, although a reptile seems more likely in the desert environment.

The two figures are set amidst a complex of lines and circles, and on one side of the hill (facing the Huara-Chusmiza road, visible as you approach the hill) are a number of enormous clearings. The entire Gigante is visible if you stand several hundred meters back from the base of the isolated hill, so avoid climbing it, which damages the pictures.

The Huara-Chusmiza road is paved as far as the village of Tarapacá; only the very short stretch (about one km) from the paved road to the hill itself crosses the desert. Infrequent buses leave Iquique at inconvenient hours, so the best way to visit the site is to hire a car or taxi, or take a tour – hitching is very difficult.

Tarapacá

In colonial and early republican times, San Lorenzo de Tarapacá was one of the most important settlements in Peru until the nitrate boom spurred the growth of Iquique; the Battle of Tarapacá, during the War of the Pacific, marked the town's eclipse. Today, although its 18th-century **Iglesia San Lorenzo** is being restored, other adobe buildings are crumbling, and the handful of remaining residents are nearly all frail or elderly.

About five km east of Cerro Unita, a paved lateral drops into the Quebrada de

Tarapacá to the still-irrigated but nearly depopulated valley. At the entrance to town, a monument displays a map of the battle, which took place November 27, 1879, and marks the spot where Chilean military hero Eleuterio Ramírez lost his life. On the battle's anniversary, the Chilean military holds an annual remembrance.

To visit the church, a more interesting monument, ask for the key at the store at the southeast corner of the Plaza de Armas. Tarapacá has neither accommodation nor a restaurant, so bring food from elsewhere.

Chusmiza

At 3200 meters in the Quebrada de Tarapacá, 106 km from Iquique, Chusmiza is a thermal springs resort that also bottles a popular brand of mineral water. The only formal accommodation is the relatively pricey *Hostería Chusmiza* (☎ 422179 in Iquique for reservations). Kenny Bus serves the altiplano border town of Colchane (US$8 – see below) Tuesday and Friday at 10 pm, arriving the following day at 6 am; this service passes Chusmiza.

Parque Nacional Volcán Isluga

Parque Nacional Volcán Isluga's 175,000 hectares contain natural and cultural features similar to those of Parque Nacional Lauca, but this more isolated area, with some of Chile's most traditional peoples, is much less visited than areas farther north.

Parque Nacional Volcán Isluga is 228 km from Iquique and 19 km north of the village of Isluga, the southern gateway to the park. At Colchane, 3750 meters above sea level on the Bolivian border, it is also possible to cross the border and catch a truck or bus to Oruro.

Conaf maintains a refugio at the village of Enquelga (US$10 per person) and a campground at nearby Aguas Calientes (US$7), where there are thermal baths. From Isluga, it's possible to travel north to the Salar de Surire and Parque Nacional Lauca and west to Arica, but inquire about the state of roads, especially in the summer rainy season, and do not attempt it without a high-clearance vehicle.

La Tirana

In mid-July, more than 30,000 pilgrims overrun the village of La Tirana (permanent population – 250) to pay homage to the Virgin of Carmen by dancing in the streets with spectacular masks and costumes in a Carnival-like atmosphere. One of Chile's most important religious shrines, La Tirana is 72 km from Iquique at the north end of the Salar de Pintados, in the Pampa del Tamarugal.

The **Santuario de La Tirana** consists of a broad ceremonial plaza on which sits one of Chile's most unusual, even eccentric, churches. Although there are several restaurants around the plaza, there are no hotels or residenciales – pilgrims camp in the open spaces east of town. Have a look at the **Museo del Salitre** on the north side of the plaza, which has a wild, haphazard assortment of artifacts from the nitrate oficinas. Enter through Almacén El Progreso.

MAMIÑA

Mamiña, 73 km east of Pozo Almonte at 2700 meters in the precordillera, has been a popular hot springs resort for residents of the region since the days of the nitrate boom, although it is much older than that. The **Pukará del Cerro Inca** is a preHispanic fortress on Cerro Ipla, while the **Iglesia de Nuestra Señora del Rosario** is a national historical monument dating from 1632. Its twin bell tower is unique in Andean Chile.

Places to Stay

Mamiña has no shortage of accommodation in a variety of price ranges. *Residencial Sol de Ipla*, on Ipla, is the most economical, charging US$12 per person with shared bath. *Hotel Tamarugal* (☎ (057) 412833 in Iquique), also on Ipla, costs about US$25 per person with full board; slightly more expensive is *Hotel Niña de Mis Ojos* (☎ 420451). The town's best is the historic *Hotel Refugio del Salitre* (☎ (057) 420330 in Iquique), built during the nitrate era, where rates are US$62 per person with full board. There are at least half a dozen alternatives for bathing.

Getting There & Away

From Iquique, Agencia Lirima (☎ 413094) at Baquedano 823 and Turismo Mamiña (☎ 420330) at Latorre 779 provide bus service to Mamiña. Taxitur (☎ 422044), Sargento Aldea 791, has taxi colectivos.

RESERVA NACIONAL PAMPA DEL TAMARUGAL

The desolate pampas of the Atacama seem an improbable place for an extensive forest, but the dense groves on both sides of the Panamericana, south of Pozo Almonte, are no mirage. Although not a natural forest, the trees are in fact a native species – the tamarugo *(Prosopis tamarugo)* – which covered thousands of square km of the Pampa del Tamarugal until the species nearly disappeared under the pressures of wood cutting for the nitrate mines of the Norte Grande.

Managed by Conaf, the 108,000-hectare Reserva Nacional Pampa del Tamarugal has restored much of this forest, which survives despite excessively saline soils and provides fuelwood for local people and fodder for livestock. Although there is no surface water, seedlings are planted in holes dug through the salt hardpan; after a few months' irrigation, they can reach ground water which has seeped westward from the Andean foothills.

The reserve itself consists of several discrete sectors, the most interesting of which is Pintados. Conaf's **Centro de Información Ambiental** (☎ 751055) is 24 km south of Pozo Almonte, on the east side of the Panamericana, with excellent exhibits on the biology and ecology of the tamarugo and the pampas.

Pintados

At Pintados, one of the world's most elaborate archaeological sites, more than 400 individual geoglyphs blanket a large hillside in the coast range. From close up it's difficult to discern what most of them represent, but from a distance images of people, llamas, various geometric designs and even a gigantic arrow become apparent.

Really a derelict nitrate rail yard with a number of ruined buildings and rusting rolling stock, Pintados lies seven km west of the Panamericana via a gravel road 45 km south of Pozo Almonte, nearly opposite the eastward turnoff to Pica. It's a long, dry and dusty but not impossible walk from the highway – figure about 1½ to two hours each way, with a possible detour to avoid the caretaker's junkyard dogs. Don't forget food and water. The only other way to visit the site is by car, taxi or tour from Iquique.

Places to Stay

On the west side of the Panamericana, opposite the Centro de Información Ambiental, Conaf maintains a campground (shaded sites with tables and benches cost US$7 per night). It also offers a limited number of beds in its guest house for US$11 per person. Despite the highway that bisects the reserve, it's a very pleasant and restful stopover, with extraordinary views of the southern night sky.

PICA

Spanish conquistador Diego de Almagro skirmished with local Indians near Pica on his expedition to Chile in 1535, but in later colonial times this pleasant oasis became famous for its wines and fruits, which supplied the mines at Huantajaya and beyond. In the 19th century, it supplied wheat, wine, figs, raisins and alfalfa to the nitrate mines of the pampas, then became a sort of 'hill station' for the nitrate barons. Today, limes from Pica supposedly make the best pisco sours.

Pica was so dependent on outside water that the Spaniards developed an elaborate system of more than 15 km of tunnels, like the ganats of the Middle East, to carry ground water to the village. In the 1920s, American geographer Isaiah Bowman observed:

Unlike most desert towns Pica stands in the midst of the desert without the green valley that elsewhere gives a natural basis for settlement. From its wells and springs and a reservoir in the course of a small stream descending from the piedmont the closely compacted gardens of the village are watered with scrupulous economy.

When Iquique boomed with nitrate exports, the Tarapacá Water Company piped water from Pica, 119 km to the southeast, to the coast to accommodate the city's growth. Only 42 km from La Tirana by an excellent paved road, Pica (population 1500) has become a more democratic destination, no longer a preserve of the nitrate barons, and is popular on the weekends, with several hotels and restaurants.

Things to See & Do
Most visitors take advantage of the baths at **Cocha Resbaladero**, at the upper end of General Ibáñez, where there's room to swim as well as soak. Admission costs US$0.75.

The 19th-century **Iglesia de San Andrés**, opposite the Plaza de Armas, replaced two earlier churches destroyed by earthquakes. The last two days of November, Pica celebrates the **Fiesta de San Andrés**, a religious festival that also includes traditional dances and fireworks.

In the adjacent village of Matilla, three km west, the **Iglesia de San Antonio** is a national monument dating from 1887, but built on 17th-century foundations. More interesting is the **Lagar de Matilla**, an on-site museum with a colonial wine press.

Places to Stay
Camping *Camping Miraflores* (☎ 741-333), the municipal site at Miraflores 4, charges about US$2.50 per person; it's adequate but crowded, especially on weekends, and has very little shade.

Hotels & Residenciales The simple but clean *Hotel Palermo* (☎ 741129), Arturo Prat 233, charges US$6 per person for three-bed rooms with private bath, and also has a restaurant. *Hostería O'Higgins* (☎ 741322), a modern brick construction at Balmaceda 6, charges US$9 per person. Try also *Residencial California*, Lynch 447.

The friendly, ramshackle *Hotel San Andrés* (☎ 741319), Balmaceda 197, is a non-smoking hotel that charges US$12.50 per person for large rooms with shared bath. Friendly *Hostal Los Emilios* (☎ 741126),

in a stylish older building at Lord Cochrane 213, is a very fine place that charges US$12.50 single with breakfast and shared bath.

Motel El Tambo (☎ 741320), General Ibáñez 68, has four-person cabañas for US$38, while *Motel El Resbaladero* (☎ 741316), General Ibañez 57, has six-person cabañas for US$45.

Places to Eat
There are several inexpensive restaurants near the Plaza de Armas, on Balmaceda, but nothing really special. For the best menu, the hands-down winner is *El Edén* (☎ 741196), only half a block off the Plaza de Armas at Riquelme 12, which has pleasant patio dining, but items like seafood, quinoa and juices are not always available. *Son Sang*, Esmeralda 444, serves Chinese meals, while *Los Naranjos* (☎ 741318), at Esmeralda and Barbosa, offers inexpensive three-course lunches.

Getting There & Away
Buses San Andrés runs buses and Taxitur operates taxi colectivos between Pica and Iquique; see the Iquique entry for details.

Antofagasta Region

In pre-Columbian times, the sea was the main source of subsistence for the Chango Indians, who populated the coast of the present-day Antofagasta region. A Spanish visitor to Cobija in 1581 counted more than 400 Changos, who fished from sealskin canoes and hunted guanaco in those areas where condensation from the winter camanchaca renewed pastures in the coastal range. This small population, though, could not support encomiendas and colonial Spaniards largely ignored the area. Moreover, the population could be hostile, often attacking Spanish naval parties who came ashore in search of fresh water at scattered coastal oases.

The interior of the region was different. Although the landscape was utterly barren for nearly 200 km to the east – in all the Norte Grande, the meandering Río Loa is the only river whose flow consistently reaches the Pacific – irrigated agriculture sustained relatively large sedentary populations in oases like Calama, on the Loa, and San Pedro de Atacama. At higher elevations shepherds grazed llamas, but the area was generally too dry for the more delicate alpaca. In the very high and arid Puna de Atacama, however, there was too little moisture to support any permanent human habitation – even the 5916-meter peak of Licancábur has no permanent snow cover.

In the early 18th century, the Spaniards started Cobija, 130 km north of modern Antofagasta, as a customs house; after the wars of independence, this remote outpost became Bolivia's outlet to the sea, despite its poor and scanty fresh water supply. Nearly destroyed by an earthquake and tsunami in 1877, followed by the development of mineral nitrates from the interior, it was superseded by Antofagasta.

Nitrates brought Antofagasta into the modern world. Nineteenth and 20th-century nitrate ghost towns line both sides of the Panamericana and the highway to Calama, and the oficinas of María Elena and Pedro de Valdivia still function, but copper has supplanted nitrates in the regional and national economy. Chuquicamata, the world's largest open-pit mine, dominates the mining sector, but fishing and tourism are growing in importance.

Books About the Atacama

There is a wealth of outstanding travel literature on the Atacama. Although much of it is out of print and not widely known, it is worth checking university libraries for titles like American geographer Isaiah Bowman's book *Desert Trails of Atacama* (American Geographical Society, 1924). Bowman traveled by mule over the length of the Norte Grande and across the high Andean passes between Chile and Argentina and Bolivia, recording his impressions and speculations, and photographing towns and villages off the beaten track. Decades later William Rudolph, for many years the

chief engineer at Chuquicamata, followed Bowman's footsteps in *Vanishing Trails of Atacama* (American Geographical Society, 1963), which chronicled the changing human landscape of the desert. John Aarons and Claudio Vita-Finzi published an entertaining account of a Cambridge expedition to the Atacama in *The Useless Land* (London, Robert Hale, 1960).

ANTOFAGASTA

The port of Antofagasta, the largest city in the Norte Grande, handles most of the minerals from the Atacama, especially the copper from Chuquicamata, and is still an important import-export center for Bolivia, which lost the region to Chile during the War of the Pacific. The city's distinctive architecture dates from the nitrate era.

Founded in 1870, the port of La Chimba (later renamed Antofagasta) replaced Cobija as the region's most important settlement after nitrate mining began in the Salar del Carmen, a short distance inland, and it became apparent that it provided the easiest rail route to the east. By 1877, the railroad reached halfway to Calama, but it was not completed until after the War of the Pacific, when Chile acquired the territory.

After the war, Antofagasta exported tin and silver from Bolivia, borax from the Salar de Ascotán, in addition to nitrates from the pampas. The latter commodity underwent a major expansion after the turn of the century, when Antofagasta's port proved inadequate and the nearby harbor of Mejillones took up much of the slack. Later, however, infrastructural improvements restored Antofagasta's pre-eminence and it came to handle the highest tonnage of any Pacific port in South America.

Like the rest of the Norte Grande, Antofagasta rarely receives any rainfall, but infrequent meteorological events can be catastrophic. In late 1991, a heavy storm caused a flash flood that obliterated the southern access road between the Panamericana and the city. In general, though, the city has an ideal climate, clear and dry, neither too hot nor too cold at any time of year. In the day, beach weather is the rule and at night, in the words of poet Neftalí Agrella, 'The moon hangs its lantern over Antofagasta.'

Orientation

Like Iquique, Antofagasta (population 225,000) sits on a terrace at the foot of the coastal range, some 1350 km north of Santiago and 700 km south of Arica. The north-south Panamericana passes inland, about 15 km east of the city, but there are paved northern and southern access roads.

Downtown's western boundary is north-south Avenida Balmaceda, immediately east of the modern port; Balmaceda veers northeast at Calle Uribe and eventually becomes Aníbal Pinto; to the south, it becomes Avenida Grecia. Streets run southwest to northeast in this central grid, bounded also by Bolívar and JS Ossa. Its focus is newly redesigned Plaza Colón, bounded by Washington, Sucre, San Martín and Prat.

Information

Tourist Offices Sernatur's helpful office (☎ 264044) at Maipú 240 is open weekdays 9.30 am to 1 pm and 3.30 to 7.30 pm; from December through March, it also stays open 10 am to 2 pm weekends.

In addition, there's an information kiosk (☎ 224834) on Balmaceda at Prat, in front of Hotel Antofagasta, open daily except Sunday 9.30 am to 1.30 pm and 4.30 to 7.30 pm. On Sunday, it's open 10.30 am to 2 pm.

Another good source of tourist information is the Automóvil Club de Chile (☎ 225332), Condell 2230.

Consulates The Argentine Consulate (☎ 222854), Manuel Verbal 1640, is open from 9 am to 2 pm. The Bolivian Consulate (☎ 225010), Prat 272, keeps the same hours.

Money Except for the numerous ATMs downtown, changing money can be surprisingly difficult, but try Cambio San Marcos at Baquedano 524 or Cambio Ancla Inn at Baquedano 508.

Post & Communications Antofagasta's area code is ☎ 55. Correos de Chile is at Washington 2613, opposite Plaza Colón, Telex-Chile next door at Washington 2601. CTC long-distance services are at Condell 2527, while Entel is at Baquedano 751 and Chilesat at Uribe 645.

Travel Agencies Antofagasta has a glut of travel agencies, including Tatio Travel Service (☎ 263562) at Latorre 2579, Local 20, and North Gate Tour (☎ 221565) at Baquedano 498, Oficina 14. For less conventional destinations and tours, try Chile Turismo Aventura (☎ 221835) at Sucre 379, Dept 41-C. Australian-run Intitour (☎ 266-185, fax 260882) is at Baquedano 460.

Cultural Centers For theater and other performing arts, check Teatro Pedro de la Barra (☎ 263400), Condell 2495 at Baquedano. The Teatro Municipal is at San Martín and Sucre.

National Parks For information on the region's natural attractions, contact Conaf (☎ 227804) at Avenida Argentina 2510.

Laundry Laverap is at the corner of 14 de Febrero and Aconcagua.

Medical Services Antofagasta's Hospital Regional (☎ 269009) is at Avenida Argentina 1962.

Things to See

Like Iquique, Antofagasta is a 19th-century city whose architecture is not stereotypically Latin American – the British community has left a visible imprint not just through the **Torre Reloj** replica of Big Ben and the **Plaza Colón** band shell, but also in the **Barrio Histórico** between the plaza and the old port, which features many wooden Victorian and Georgian buildings. The **Muelle Salitrero** (Nitrate Pier) at the foot of Bolívar, for instance, was the work of Melbourne Clark, an early partner in the Tarapacá Nitrate Company. At the entrance to the pier is the former **Resguardo Marítimo** (Coast Guard), built in 1910.

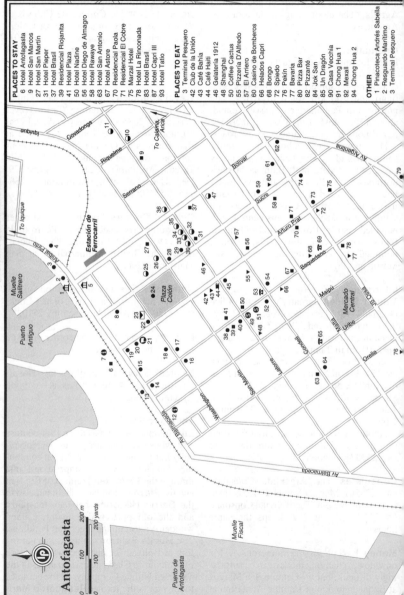

Antofagasta

PLACES TO STAY
6 Hotel Antofagasta
9 Hotel San Marcos
27 Hotel San Martín
31 Hotel Pieper
37 Hotel Brasil
39 Residencial Riojanita
41 Hotel Plaza
50 Hotel Nadine
56 Hotel Diego de Almagro
58 Hotel Rawaye
63 Hotel San Antonio
67 Hotel Astore
70 Residencial Paola
71 Residencial El Cobre
75 Marzal Hotel
78 Hotel La Rinconada
83 Hotel Brasil
87 Hotel Capri III
93 Hotel Tatio

PLACES TO EAT
3 Terminal Pesquero
42 Club de la Unión
43 Café Bahía
44 Café Haiti
46 Gelatería 1912
48 Shanghai
50 Coffee Cactus
55 Pizzería D'Alfredo
57 El Arriero
60 Casino de Bomberos
66 Helados Capri
68 Bongo
72 Spledo
76 Pekin
77 Bavaria
80 Pizza Bar
82 Pizzanté
84 Jok San
85 Un Dragón
90 Casa Vecchia
91 Chong Hua 1
92 Mexali
94 Chong Hua 2

OTHER
1 Pinacoteca Andrés Sabella
2 Resguardo Marítimo
3 Terminal Pesquero

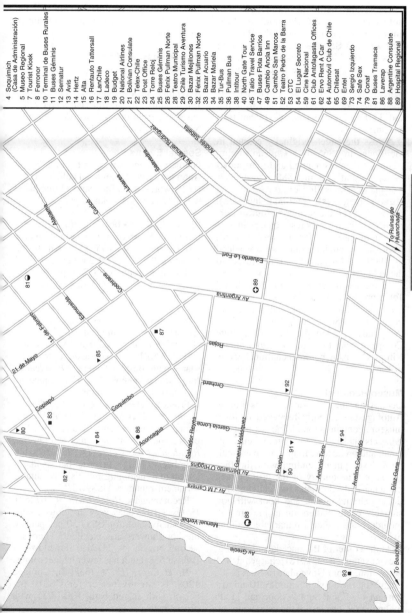

4   Soquimich
    (Casa de Administración)
5   Museo Regional
7   Tourist Kiosk
8   Ferronor
10 Terminal de Buses Rurales
11 Buses Géminis
12 Sematur
13 Avis
14 Hertz
15 Alta
16 Rentauto Tattersall
17 LanChile
18 Ladeco
19 Budget
20 National Airlines
21 Bolivian Consulate
22 Telex-Chile
23 Post Office
24 Torre Reloj
25 Buses Géminis
26 Fénix Pullman Norte
28 Teatro Municipal
29 Chile Turismo Aventura
30 Bazar Mejillones
32 Fénix Pullman Norte
33 Bazar Mariela
34 Bazar Acuario
35 Tur-Bus
36 Pullman Bus
38 Intitour
40 North Gate Tour
45 Tatio Travel Service
47 Buses Flota Barrios
49 Cambio Ancla Inn
51 Cambio San Marcos
52 Teatro Pedro de la Barra
53 CTC
54 El Lugar Secreto
59 Cine Nacional
61 Club Antofagasta Offices
62 Ervo Rent A Car
64 Automóvil Club de Chile
65 Chilesat
69 Entel
73 Sergio Izquierdo
74 Safe Sex
79 Conaf
81 Buses Tramaca
86 Laverap
88 Argentine Consulate
89 Hospital Regional

NORTE GRANDE

Across the patio, at Balmaceda and Bolívar, the former **Gobernación Marítima** (Port Authority) houses the **Pinacoteca Andrés Sabella**, a gallery honoring a local poet; it's a measure of recent political change in Chile that the gallery prominently displays Sabella's photograph with Fidel Castro. The pinacoteca is open Tuesday to Friday 10 am to 1 pm and 3.30 to 7 pm, weekends 11 am to 2 pm only.

Across the street, originally erected in Mejillones in 1866 by a Chilean mining company, then dismantled and transported to its present site in 1888, the former Aduana (Customs House) now houses the **Museo Regional** (regional museum). Across Bolívar, the former **Estación Ferrocarril** is the recently restored terminus of the Antofagasta-La Paz railway. It dates from 1887, though its 2nd story was added in 1900. Unfortunately, it is closed to the public.

To the north, across from the colorful **Terminal Pesquero** (fish market), is the Casa de Administración (administrative office) of the Sociedad Química de Chile (Soquimich), once the Lautaro Nitrate Company and then the Anglo Lautaro Nitrate Company before its nationalization in 1968.

Museo Regional

Occupying the historic customs house, Antofagasta's recently reopened regional museum contains ground floor exhibits on minerals and fossils, the regional environment, and prehistoric immigration and cultural development, ending with the Inca presence. The quality of the artifacts and particularly the dioramas is excellent; additional exhibits on the 2nd floor will presumably bring matters up to the present, including the region's remarkable mining history.

At the corner of Balmaceda and Bolívar, the museum (☎ 227018) charges US$1 admission. From November to March, it's open Monday through Saturday 10 am to 1 pm and 4 to 7 pm; Sunday hours are 11 am to 2 pm only. The rest of the year, hours are

Tuesday through Saturday 10 am to 1 pm and 3.30 to 6.30 pm, Sunday 11 am to 2 pm only.

Ruinas de Huanchaca (Minas de Plata)

Above the city, at the south end of Avenida Argentina, are the extensive remains of a 19th-century British-Bolivian silver refining plant; from downtown, take colectivo No 3 and ask for Minas de Plata.

Special Events

February 14, anniversary of the founding of Antofagasta, is a major local holiday. There are fireworks at the Balneario Municipal at the south end of Avenida Grecia.

Places to Stay – bottom end

Camping South of Antofagasta, *Camping Las Garumas* (☎ 247758) at Km 9 and *Camping Rucamóvil* (☎ 260121) at Km 11 both charge around US$12.50 per site, but may accept smaller parties for around US$4 per person.

Residenciales & Hotels Standards appear to be declining at *Hotel Rawaye* (☎ 225399), Sucre 762, but it's still cheap at US$7.50/11 for singles/doubles with shared bath. Basic but friendly *Residencial Riojanita* (☎ 268652, 281133), Baquedano 464, costs US$7 per person.

Friendly, clean and quiet *Residencial Paola* (☎ 222208), Prat 766, has rooms arranged around a central lounge for US$8 per person. Across the street at Prat 749, *Residencial El Cobre* (☎ 225162) has long been a budget favorite, but standards appear to be declining and it's only suitable for an emergency at US$9/13.

Recommended *Hotel Brasil* (☎ 267268), JS Ossa 1978, has very spacious rooms with shared bath for US$7.50 per person; the hot showers are excellent. There's a second branch (☎ 281219) downtown at Bolívar 558, but it has fewer budget rooms.

Hotel Capri III (☎ 263703), Copiapó 1208, is slightly dearer for US$10 per person with shared bath, US$18/35 with private bath.

Places to Stay – middle
Mid-range accommodations start around US$29/35 at *Hotel La Rinconada* (☎ 261-139), Baquedano 810. Boxy, bleak but tidy *Hotel San Marcos* (☎ 251763), Latorre 2946, has rooms for US$32/47 with private bath. Close to the Terminal de Buses Rurales, it's clean, with hot water and its own restaurant. *Hotel San Martín* (☎ 263-503, fax 268159), San Martín 2781, costs about US$33/47.

Hotel San Antonio (☎ 268857), Condell 2235, charges US$41/47. Well-kept but undistinguished, *Hotel Diego de Almagro* (☎ 268331), Condell 2624, costs US$41/61. Other comparable places include *Hotel Astore* (☎ 267439) at Baquedano 692 for about US$42/50 and *Hotel Pieper* (☎ 266-488), Sucre 509, for US$42/55.

Places to Stay – top end
The new *Marzal Hotel* (☎ 268063), Arturo Prat 867, charges US$54/65, while appealing *Hotel Nadine* (☎ 227008), Baquedano 519, charges US$59/74.

Having started its existence as a cluster of reconditioned tour buses, the oddball *Hotel Tatio* (☎ 244761), Avenida Grecia 1000, charges US$62/86. The more conventional *Hotel Plaza* (☎ 269046), Baquedano 461, has its own restaurant and bar and is fairly quiet; rates are US$83/112.

On the beach at Balmaceda 2575, generally acknowledged as the city's best, *Hotel Antofagasta* (☎ 268259) is also the largest in town. Rooms start around US$99/108, with an outstanding breakfast.

Places to Eat
At the unpretentious Terminal Pesquero, at the north end of the old port, a collection of inexpensive stands peddle tasty fresh shellfish. It's especially lively Saturday mornings, but even if you find sea urchins unappealing, the pelicans that crowd the pier for scraps are always amusing. Similar fare is available at the Mercado Central, on Ossa between Maipú and Uribe.

The *Casino de Bomberos*, Sucre 763, has good set lunches for about US$4. *Bavaria* (☎ 266567), Ossa 2424, is part of a reliable but uninspired chain. The always crowded, inexpensive *Spiedo*, at the corner of Prat and Ossa, specializes in grilled chicken. *Bongo* (☎ 263697), Baquedano 743, is suitable for inexpensive sandwiches and draft beer, as is *Café Bahía* (☎ 227551), Prat 470. For caffeine in a form other than soluble Nescafé, try *Café Haití* at Prat 482.

Carnivores will find *El Arriero* (☎ 264-371) at Condell 2644 a fine parrilla, with large portions, attentive service, classic decor and, unfortunately, two pianos whose crashing dinnertime duets could challenge Jerry Lee Lewis in volume if not in style. Other recommended places include *Casa Vecchia* (☎ 263167) at O'Higgins 1456 land the *Club de la Unión* (☎ 268371) at Prat 474. Possibly worth a try is *Mexall* (☎ 223672), an expensive Mexican restaurant at the corner of Orchard and Poupin.

Pizzería D'Alfredo (☎ 261643), Condell 2539, is a chain with varied pizza at reasonable prices, but Antofagasta's best pizzería is *Pizzanté* (☎ 268115), Carrera 1857, which also enforces a non-smoking section. It has large portions, reasonable prices, good service and pleasant ambience, plus a wide selection of appealing sandwiches. The popular *Pizza Bar* is at the corner of O'Higgins and Copiapó.

Like other northern Chilean cities, Antofagasta has an array of inexpensive chifas, including *Un Dragón* (☎ 221259) at Copiapó 951, *Shanghai* (☎ 262547) at Latorre 2426, *Pekín* (☎ 260833) at Ossa 2135, *Jok San* at Bernardo O'Higgins 1862, and *Chong Hua* (☎ 251430) at García Lorca 1468 and 1569.

For snacks, coffee, superb ice cream and other desserts, try *Helados Capri* at Baquedano 632, *Gelatería 1912* at Latorre 2655, and *Coffee Cactus*, in the Hotel Nadine at Baquedano 519.

Entertainment
The Cine Nacional, Sucre 731, shows recent films.

Club Antofagasta (☎ 221553), Ossa 2755, is the city's first-division soccer team.

Things to Buy
There's a good informal market for historical items like bank notes, coins, fichas from nitrate oficinas and other odds and ends at the foot of the Terminal Pesquero, on the west side of Aníbal Pinto, north of downtown.

El Lugar Secreto, Condell 2532, is Antofagasta's local surf shop. For Chile's and Antofagasta's most varied (and perhaps only) selection of condoms, Safe Sex is at Sucre 818.

Getting There & Away
Air LanChile (☎ 265151, 262526), Washington 2552, has at least two and usually three non-stops daily to Santiago (US$192); about half the northbound flights continue to Iquique (US$54) and Arica (US$87), the rest to Calama (US$26). Ladeco (☎ 269-170), Washington 2589, has similar fares and services.

National Airlines (☎ 264050), Arturo Prat 264, provides domestic services southbound to Santiago (US$175) and northbound to Iquique (US$48, with an international extension to Asunción, Paraguay) and Arica (US$78, with an international extension to Arequipa, Peru).

Alta (☎ 226089), Balmaceda 2584, flies weekdays to Arica (US$50), 19 times weekly to Iquique (US$38), 14 times weekly to Copiapó (US$75) and La Serena (US$106), daily to Viña del Mar (US$115), Monday and Saturday to Santiago (US$82) and Monday, Friday, Saturday and Sunday to Concepción (US$148).

Bus Antofagasta has no central long-distance bus terminal, but most companies operate out of their own terminals near downtown. A few long-distance and most locally based companies use the Terminal de Buses Rurales, Riquelme 513. Nearly all northbound services now use coastal Ruta 1, via Tocopilla, en route to Iquique and Arica.

Tramaca (☎ 251770), Uribe 936, has frequent buses to Calama, plus daily service to Arica, Iquique, Santiago and intermediate points. Internationally, Tramaca goes to Jujuy, Argentina (US$50), Tuesday and Friday at 7 am, and to the Bolivian destinations of Uyuni (US$17) and Oruro (US$23) Wednesdays at 11 pm.

Tramaca's regional destinations include Sierra Gorda, Baquedano, Taltal, the nitrate towns of María Elena and Pedro de Valdivia, and Tocopilla. Tramaca also handles tickets for the Calama-Oruro railway (see the entry for Calama, below), and has daily departures direct to San Pedro de Atacama at 8 am and 6.30 pm.

Géminis (☎ 251796, 263968), Latorre 3055 or Sucre 375, goes to Calama and to intermediate stops on the Panamericana between Santiago and Arica. It also crosses the Andes to Salta, Argentina (US$48, 15 hours) and Asunción, Paraguay (US$95, 36 hours). International buses fill rapidly, so purchase tickets as far in advance as possible. Fénix Pullman Norte (☎ 268896), San Martín 2717, runs nearly identical domestic routes, and also makes international connections in Santiago for Mendoza, Argentina (US$60).

Pullman Bus (☎ 262591), Latorre 2805, goes to Calama and Chuquicamata three times daily, and runs long-distance routes on the Panamericana between Arica and Santiago. Tur-Bus (☎ 264487), Latorre 2751, has nearly identical services but is more expensive.

Several companies operate from the Terminal de Buses Rurales at Riquelme 513. Local carriers include Fepstur (☎ 222982), Maravilla Bus and El Shadday (☎ 266724) to Mejillones (US$2) and Buses Tocopilla and Buses Camus (☎ 267424) to Tocopilla. Long-distance carriers include Carmelita, which covers the southbound Panamericana and continues north to Iquique and Arica; Litoral Bus (☎ 262175) to Taltal, Chañaral, Diego de Almagro and El Salvador; Buses Iquique on coastal Ruta 1 north to Iquique; Kenny Bus (☎ 262216) to Iquique, Santiago and intermediates; and Ramos Cholele (☎ 251632) to Tocopilla, Iquique and Santiago.

Flota Barrios (☎ 268559), Condell 2782, goes to Calama, María Elena and Pedro de Valdivia, and Tocopilla.

Bazar Mejillones (☎ 251332) at Latorre 2719, Bazar Acuario (☎ 224805) at Latorre 2723 and Bazar Mariela (☎ 227111) at Latorre 2727 run taxi colectivos to La Portada and Mejillones (US$1.75) all year, and to Juan López (US$2) and Hornitos (US$4) in summer only.

Typical fares and times from Antofagasta include Arica (US$25, 10 hours), Iquique (US$21, six hours), Tocopilla (US$4, 2½ hours), Calama (US$5, three hours), Chañaral (US$19, six hours), Copiapó (US$22, eight hours), La Serena (US$30, 12 hours) and Santiago (US$42, 18 hours).

Train There's no train service from Antofagasta proper, but tickets for the Calama-Oruro line are available from Tramaca (☎ 251770), Uribe 936 or Sucre 375.

Travelers hoping to cross the Andes to Salta, Argentina on the Chilean freight that connects with the famous Tren a las Nubes should contact Ferronor (☎ 224764, 227-927) at Sucre 220, 5th floor; for more detail, see the separate entry for Baquedano, below.

Getting Around
To/From the Airport Antofagasta's Aeropuerto Cerro Moreno is 25 km north of the city, at the south end of Península Mejillones. From the Terminal Pesquero, local bus No 15 goes to the airport for US$0.50, but only every two hours or so from 7.30 am to 10.30 pm.

Shared taxis leave from the stand opposite LanChile's downtown offices for US$3 per person, but Aerobus (☎ 262727) provides convenient door-to-door service for US$6.

Car Rental Rentals are available from Avis (☎ /fax 221073) at Balmaceda 2499, Hertz (☎ 269043) at Balmaceda 2492, Budget (☎ 251745) at Prat 206, Local 5, Rentauto Tattersall (☎ 2325370) at Baquedano 300, Ervo Rent A Car (☎ 261864) at Avenida Argentina 2779 and Sergio Izquierdo (☎ 263788) at Prat 801.

AROUND ANTOFAGASTA
North of Antofagasta, paved Ruta 1 leads to Mejillones and Tocopilla, then continues to Iquique as a spectacular desert coastal highway. Between Mejillones and Tocopilla are the fascinating ghost towns of Cobija and Gatico.

Reserva Nacional La Chimba
In the coastal range, northeast of Antofagasta, 2583-hectare La Chimba consists of several tributary canyons, moistened by the camanchaca. This supports a surprisingly varied flora and fauna, the latter including foxes, guanacos, reptiles and many bird species.

At the entrance to the reserve, Conaf maintains a Sede Administrativa, open 8.30 am to 1 pm and 2 to 7 pm daily. Camping is possible, but there is no formal infrastructure. Access to La Chimba is via a three-km graveled eastbound lateral off Ruta 1, 15 km north of Antofagasta; city buses Nos 14 and 29 reach the turnoff, but it's necessary to walk the rest of the way.

Monumento Natural La Portada
Probably the most photographed sight on the coast of the Norte Grande, 31-hectare La Portada's centerpiece is an offshore stack, eroded into an impressive natural arch by the stormy Pacific. About 25 km north of Antofagasta, on a short lateral off the highway south of Cerro Moreno airport, it's a pleasant spot for a relaxing beach afternoon. Take micro No 15 from Antofagasta's Terminal Pesquero.

Juan López & Bolsico
At the south end of Península Mejillones, just north of La Portada, a dirt road most suitable for 4WD leads west to the beach villages of Juan López (take the left fork at Km 11) and Bolsico (take the right fork). The latter route passes offshore Isla Santa María, a site with several impressive ocean blowholes.

Mejillones
Once an important port in its own right, 60 km north of Antofagasta, Mejillones

(permanent population about 5600) is now a weekend beach resort for residents of the regional capital. At one time the residents mined fossil guano from the hills above the town and transported it to the port by an aerial tramway.

Correos de Chile is at Las Heras 205, while CTC is at Latorre 748. The area code is ☎ 55, the same as Antofagasta's.

Places to Stay & Eat Mejillones has inexpensive accommodation at *Residencial Elizabeth* (☎ 621568), Latorre 440, for about US$6 per person, and *Residencial Marco* (☎ 621593), for about US$7.50. *Residencial Cavancha* (☎ 621566), Latorre 560, has rooms with private bath for US$15/21 single/double. Many places shut down in winter.

Tsunami (☎ 621542), Avenida San Martín 440, is an excellent but expensive seafood restaurant that also has rooms for rent.

Getting There & Away Fepstur (☎ 621-644) at Latorre 588, El Shadday (☎ 621-561) at Latorre 440, and Maravilla Bus at Latorre 549 all connect Mejillones with Antofagasta (US$1.75).

Cobija & Gatico

Stained white with guano, offshore stacks look like distant snow peaks at the desolate ghost towns of Cobija and Gatico, whose few remaining families eke out a living from fishing and collecting seaweed. In the early 19th century, though, flourishing Cobija was Bolivia's outlet to the Pacific, serving the mines of the altiplano despite a precarious water supply, whose distribution reflected the early republican hierarchy. According to Isaiah Bowman:

The best well close to the shore was reserved for the government officials and garrison. The rest of the populace was supplied with water from springs in the hills back of town, conducted in pipes and kept under lock and key, the daily quota being delivered to each family. More water might be purchased from a carrier who brought it from the interior. In those days the present of a barrel of sweet water from southern Chile or Peru was highly esteemed.

So was fresh produce. In 1851, when Cobija had a population of 1500, a North American seaman recorded the eagerness with which the settlement's residents greeted a shipment of supplies from the north:

It was a matter of no little interest to witness the avidity of the population on landing the garden-stuff brought from Arica. Probably within 10 minutes after the first boat-load of bags had been landed, all over town Indians, including soldiers, might have been seen stripping the rind from green sugar-cane . . . housekeepers bearing away piles of maize, sweet potatoes . . . an hour later the beach – which had served as the impromptu market-place – was again bare.

Today, if you visit Cobija or Gatico, about 130 km north of Antofagasta and 60 km south of Tocopilla, bring your own supplies. After an earthquake and tsunami nearly obliterated the town in 1877, Cobija's population declined rapidly; by 1907, it had only 35 inhabitants and now there are even fewer.

You may be able to purchase fish, but everything else is at a premium except for camping among the atmospheric adobe walls overlooking the sea. In only a few places are the ruins obvious, such as the plaza, the church and the cemetery (with its wooden fences and crosses, and a few crumbling adobe crypts), but for the most part visitors must guess the identity of any given building.

Baquedano

Midway between Antofagasta and Calama, Baquedano was a major rail junction where the *Longino* (Longitudinal Railway) met the Antofagasta-La Paz line. Its **Museo Ferroviario** is an open-air railroad museum with an amazing roundhouse full of antique locomotives and other ancient rail cars, but a freight line still hauls borax from the Argentine border at Socompa, where it's possible to make connections with Argentina's famous Tren a las Nubes (Train to the Clouds) to Salta. The Chilean freight is sporadic, agonizingly slow and truly filthy, but may take really persistent passengers on a rarely traveled and scenic route.

For more information on the freight to Socompa, contact Señor Lino Ardiles at Ferronor (☎ 224764, 227927) at Sucre 220, 5th floor, in Antofagasta. Ostensible departures are on Sunday, but delays are common; intending passengers must obtain a notarial certificate absolving Ferronor of legal liability for delays and/or accidents.

TOCOPILLA

The paving of Ruta 1, the coastal highway to Iquique, has made the nitrate port of Tocopilla beneficiary of a recent tourist boom, as traffic that once followed the inland Panamericana now heads directly north from Antofagasta. For travelers between Iquique and San Pedro de Atacama or Calama, Tocopilla is a far more convenient stopover than Antofagasta.

Despite its apparent isolation, Tocopilla exports the produce of the still operating oficinas of Pedro de Valdivia and María Elena. Since 1929, it has been the site of Codelco's massive thermoelectric plant, which serves the copper mining complex of Chuquicamata. Fishing is also an important industry.

Orientation & Information

Tocopilla (population 25,000) occupies a narrow coastal shelf at the base of the coastal range, 190 km north of Antofagasta, 160 km west of Calama, and 240 km south of Iquique. The main thoroughfare is north-south Arturo Prat, while the main commercial street is 21 de Mayo, one block east. Most travelers' services are a few blocks either north or south from Plaza Condell, at the corner of 21 de Mayo and Aníbal Pinto.

Tourist Office In summer, Tocopilla maintains a Caseta de Informaciones at Caleta Boy, at the southern approach to town.

Post & Communications Tocopilla's area code is ☎ 55. Correos de Chile is at the corner of 21 de Mayo and Aníbal Pinto. Entel is at 21 de Mayo 2066, CTC at Manuel Rodríguez 1337.

Medical Services Tocopilla's Hospital (☎ 821839) is at Santa Rosa and Matta, a few blocks northeast of downtown.

Things to See & Do

Like other northern coastal towns, Tocopilla's smattering of wooden buildings, mostly along Prat and 21 de Mayo, give it a turn-of-the-century atmosphere. At the corner of Prat and Baquedano, the **Torre Reloj** (clock tower) was relocated intact from the nitrate oficina of Coya, near María Elena. **Playa El Salitre**, reached by a staircase from Calle Colón, is the best spot for sunbathing, but too contaminated for swimming.

Tocopilla has a **Museo Arqueológico** (archaeological museum) in the Municipalidad, at Aníbal Pinto and 21 de Mayo, 2nd floor.

Places to Stay

Residencial Sonia (☎ 813086), Washington 1329, is the cheapest in town for about US$6 with shared bath, but friendly *Hostería Bolívar* (☎ 812783), Bolívar 1332, is a bargain for US$7.

Amiable *Residencial Alvarez* (☎ 811-578), Serrano 1234, charges US$9 for spacious, well-kept rooms with high ceilings, set around an attractive patio. Comparably priced *Residencial Royal* (☎ 811488), 21 de Mayo 1988, also has slightly more expensive rooms with private bath. *Hotel Casablanca* (☎ 813222), 21 de Mayo 2054, costs US$13/19 single/double with shared bath, slightly more with private bath.

Newish *Hotel Chungará* (☎ 812737), 21 de Mayo 1440, charges US$26/32 single/double for rooms that are clean but a little small; private bath and breakfast are included. *Hotel Vucina* (☎ 812155), 21 de Mayo 2069, costs US$28/35.

Places to Eat

Tocopilla's top restaurant is the reasonably priced *Club de la Unión* (☎ 813198), Prat 1354, which has very fine four-course Sunday lunches for US$6, including a tasty pisco sour. Service is friendly but can be erratic.

NORTE GRANDE

Chinese food is available at *Chifa Ji Kong*, 21 de Mayo 1848, and *Chifa Hoh San* (☎ 811225), 21 de Mayo 1482.

Getting There & Away

Since the paving of coastal Ruta 1, Tocopilla has become a hub for bus services both north- and southbound, and eastbound to Chuquicamata and Calama. Regional bus lines connecting Tocopilla with Iquique and Antofagasta include Buses Camus (☎ 813102) and Tocopilla Bus (☎ 811029) at 21 de Mayo 1250, while long-distance companies include Flota Barrios (☎ 811-861) at 21 de Mayo 1720, Tur-Bus (☎ 811-581) at 21 de Mayo 1495 and Tramaca (☎ 813195) at 21 de Mayo 2196.

Taxi colectivos to Chuquicamata and Calama (US$6) leave from the corner of 21 de Mayo and Manuel Rodríguez, just south of Hotel Casa Blanca. Departure times are 7 am and 3 pm.

Sample fares and times include Iquique (US$3.50, three hours), Antofagasta (US$4, 2½ hours), Arica (US$16, seven hours), Copiapó (US$27, 11 hours), La Serena (US$32, 15 hours) and Santiago (US$44, 21 hours). Tur-Bus's salón cama service to Santiago costs US$66.

TALTAL

South of Antofagasta, about 30 km beyond the La Negra truck stop, the Panamericana veers inland, while an ill-marked lateral leaves it to follow a dusty mountain road southwest to a wild desert coast comparable to the recently opened route between Tocopilla and Iquique. Passing beneath peaks that reach as high as 2664 meters, the latter route eventually ends up at the former nitrate port of Taltal, while the Panamericana passes about 25 km southeast of town.

At present, Taltal (population 9400) is a simple fishing port and modest beach town with a decaying cluster of period architecture from its nitrate heyday, but it may be in for big changes. Chile's current public works minister and probable future presidential candidate, Ricardo Lagos, plans to extend and eventually pave the coastal route all the way to Antofagasta,

opening the area to tourist traffic, while Canadian mining interests have discovered gold reserves of about 1.5 million ounces nearby.

Orientation & Information

From an intersection on the Panamericana, 210 km south of Antofagasta and 115 km north of Chañaral, a paved lateral heads northwest to Taltal, where it becomes Avenida Francisco Bilbao and then Calle O'Higgins. Trending southwest from O'Higgins, the main commercial street of Arturo Prat leads to the central Plaza Arturo Prat, while east of O'Higgins are most of the town's historic monuments.

Tourist Office In summer, Taltal maintains a helpful Oficina de Información Turística, open 9 am to 1 pm and 4 to 7.30 pm daily.

Post & Communications Taltal's area code is ☎ 55. Correos de Chile is at Prat 515. CTC is at Prat 687, Chilesat at San Martín 283.

Things to See & Do

During the nitrate era, this was the headquarters of **The Taltal Railway Company**, whose restored narrow-gauge **Locomotora No 59** (locomotive) sits on the east side of O'Higgins, between Esmeralda and Prat. Squatters and tenants now inhabit buildings like the Company's **Oficinas Generales** (general offices) and **Casa Administrador** (administrator's house). Built by Stothert & Pitt Ltd of Bath, England, the rusting crane on the **Muelle Salitrero** (nitrate pier) dates from 1903. Pick your way carefully out onto the pier, watching your step to avoid falling through the huge gaps into the sea. Taltalinos come here to fish at sunset, but nobody seems to catch anything.

Downtown monuments of the nitrate era include the wooden **Iglesia San Javier** (1897) and **Teatro Alhambra** (1921), both opposite Plaza Prat. At Prat 642, the **Museo Augusto Capdeville** is the modest municipal museum. On Esmeralda, between Torreblanca and Ramírez, Plaza

Riquelme overlooks the **Balneario Municipal**, the city beach.

Places to Stay & Eat
There's free beach camping at *Muelle de Piedra*, about two km north of town on the road to Paposo. In town, the cheapest accommodation is basic *Hotel San Martín* (☎ 611088), Martínez 279, which charges US$6 per person. *Hotel Verdy* (☎ 611105), Ramírez 345, costs US$9 per person with shared bath, but also has singles with private bath for US$35.

Taltal's best is the beachfront *Hostería del Taltal* (☎ 611173), Esmeralda 671, which has singles/doubles with shared bath for US$25/30, and more expensive rooms with private bath for US$36/41.

At the east end of Esmeralda, at the Terminal Pesquero (wholesale fish market), *Las Brisas* has moderately priced seafood fresh off the boat. All the hotels have restaurants, as does the *Club Social*, Torreblanca 162.

Getting There & Away
Several companies provide bus services north- and southbound on the Panamericana, including Tramaca (☎ 611034) at Prat 428, Litoral Bus (☎ 611015) at Prat 639, Buses Ramos (☎ 611106) at Prat 766 and Tur-Bus (☎ 611426) at Prat 631.

Typical fares from Taltal include Arica (US$33), Iquique (US$26), Calama or Tocopilla (US$11), Chañaral (US$8), Copiapó (US$13), La Serena (US$17) and Santiago (US$34).

AROUND TALTAL
Cifuncho
Midway between Taltal and the Panamericana, a graveled lateral heads southwest to Cifuncho, a tiny fishing camp that is also one of the most popular beaches in the area. En route to Cifuncho, a track suitable only for 4WD vehicles heads northwest to isolated Las Tórtolas, an even more attractive area.

Reserva Nacional Paposo
About 30 km north of Taltal, the coastal range reaches well over 2000 meters in places, dropping abruptly to the coast, where deep canyons like **Quebrada El Médano** contain rock art sites between 500 and 1000 years old and the camanchaca supports a surprisingly varied flora. Access to most of this 43,000-hectare reserve is still difficult, but may become easier as the highway improves and Conaf provides more information and assistance. There is presently a Conaf ranger at the village of Paposo, 50 km north of Taltal, but ask for details in Antofagasta before coming here.

CALAMA
In the interior of Region II, Calama is the commercial center for the world's largest open-pit copper mines at nearby Chuquicamata and claims to be the highest-altitude city in Chile. The starting point for visits to 'Chuqui' (the company town that is in fact higher than Calama), it's also convenient to historic and archaeological sites like the village of Chiu Chiu and the Pukará de Lasana, the oases of San Pedro de Atacama and Toconao, and the El Tatio geysers. Calama is now the western terminus of passenger service on the Calama-Oruro (Bolivia) railway, which formerly ran all the way to Antofagasta.

Orientation
On the north bank of the Río Loa, 220 km northeast of Antofagasta, Calama (population 105,000) sits 2250 meters above sea level. Though the city has sprawled with the influx of laborers who prefer its slightly milder climate to that of Chuquicamata, its central core is pedestrian-friendly. Named for the date of Calama's occupation by Chile in the War of the Pacific, the modest Plaza 23 de Marzo is the focus of downtown, but most visitors will find the city a brief stopover en route to the sights of the Atacama outback.

Information
Tourist Offices The municipal Oficina de Turismo (☎ 242742, Anexo 60) is at Latorre 1689, near the corner of Vicuña Mackenna. It's open weekdays 9 am to 1

pm and 3 to 7 pm (but sometimes stays open later). There's usually an English speaker on duty in summer, when it's also open Saturday mornings.

Another good source of information is Acchi, the Automóvil Club de Chile (☎ 342770), Avenida Ecuador 1901.

Consulate The Bolivian Consulate (☎ 341-976), Bañados Espinoza 2222, is open weekdays 10 am to 1.30 pm.

Money Moon Valley, Sotomayor 1818, pays good rates, with no commission for travelers' checks. Several downtown banks have ATMs, including Banco de Crédito at Sotomayor 2002 and Banco Santiago at Sotomayor 2080.

Post & Communications Calama's area code is ☎ 55, the same as Antofagasta's. Correos de Chile is at Vicuña Mackenna 2167. CTC has long-distance telephone offices at Abaroa 1756, Abaroa 1987, and Vargas 1927. Entel is at Sotomayor 2027.

Travel Agencies Calama has numerous travel agencies which arrange excursions to the more remote parts of the desert – though some of these trips can be arranged more cheaply from San Pedro de Atacama. Among them are Turismo El Sol (☎ 340-152) at Abaroa 1614, Andino Expediciones (☎ 317395) at Vivar 1963, Oficina 9, Nativa Expediciones (☎ 319834, fax 340107) at Abaroa 1796 and Moon Valley Tourist Service (☎ 317456) at Sotomayor 1814. For itineraries and costs, see the Organized Tours entry below.

Laundry Lavexpress (☎ 315361), Sotomayor 1867, is open 9 am to 9 pm daily except Sunday.

Medical Services Hospital Carlos Cisterna (☎ 342347) is at Avenida Granaderos near the corner with Cisterna, five blocks north of Plaza 23 de Marzo.

Parque El Loa

At the south end of Avenida O'Higgins (the southern extension of Abaroa), Parque El Loa features a scale model of the famous church at Chiu Chiu, with its twin bell towers, and a riverside swimming pool. It also includes Calama's **Museo Arqueológico y Etnológico** (Museum of Archaeology & Ethnology), with exhibits on the peoples of the Atacama. Museum admission costs US$1; it's open 10 am to 1 pm and 3 to 7 pm, daily except Mondays.

Organized Tours

Several popular circuits are available from or through the travel agencies listed above; the paving of the highways to San Pedro de Atacama and Chiu Chiu has made longer trips more feasible from Calama, though many travelers find San Pedro a more appealing base of operations.

Itineraries vary slightly, but the most complete goes from Calama to the geysers at El Tatio and back via traditional villages like Chiu Chiu, Caspana, Ayquina and Toconce, costing about US$90 for one exhausting full day. It is possible to take a separate tour from Calama to these villages, all of which feature traditional Andean churches.

Other tours go to San Pedro de Atacama via the Valle de la Luna (Valley of the Moon), then spend the night in San Pedro before visiting El Tatio and returning via Caspana and Chiu Chiu for about US$60, including a box lunch (but not accommodation) in San Pedro.

Special Events

Calama's major holiday is March 23, when the city celebrates the arrival of Chilean troops during the War of the Pacific with fireworks and other events.

Places to Stay – bottom end

Camping *Camping Casas del Valle* (☎ 340056), Bilbao 1507, is east of the railroad tracks and beyond the stadium.

Hostel *Hotel El Mirador* (☎ /fax 340329), Calama's affiliate of Hostelling International, is at Sotomayor 2064. Availability of hostel accommodation may be limited,

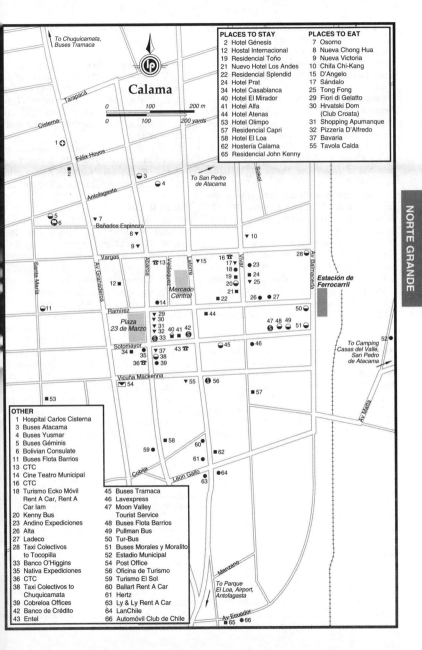

Calama

PLACES TO STAY
2 Hotel Génesis
12 Hostal Internacional
19 Residencial Toño
21 Nuevo Hotel Los Andes
22 Residencial Splendid
24 Hotel Prat
34 Hotel Casablanca
40 Hotel El Mirador
41 Hotel Alfa
44 Hotel Atenas
53 Hotel Olimpo
57 Residencial Capri
58 Hotel El Loa
62 Hostería Calama
65 Residencial John Kenny

PLACES TO EAT
7 Osorno
8 Nueva Chong Hua
9 Nueva Victoria
10 Chifa Chi-Kang
15 D'Angelo
17 Sándalo
25 Tong Fong
29 Fiori di Gelatto
30 Hrvatski Dom
   (Club Croata)
31 Shopping Apumanque
32 Pizzería D'Alfredo
37 Bavaria
55 Tavola Calda

To Chuquicamata,
Buses Tramaca

Tarapacá

Cisterna

Félix Hoyos

Antofagasta

To San Pedro
de Atacama

Bañados Espinoza

Vargas

Santa María

Av Granados

Abaroa

Velásquez

Latorre

Mercado
Central

Vivar

Av Balmaceda

*Estación de
Ferrocarril*

Ramírez

Plaza
23 de Marzo

Sotomayor

Vicuña Mackenna

To Camping
Casas del Valle,
San Pedro
de Atacama

Av Matta

Cobija

León Gallo

Manzano

To Parque
El Loa, Airport,
Antofagasta

Av Ecuador

OTHER
1 Hospital Carlos Cisterna
3 Buses Atacama
4 Buses Yusmar
5 Buses Géminis
6 Bolivian Consulate
11 Buses Flota Barrios
13 CTC
14 Cine Teatro Municipal
16 CTC
18 Turismo Ecko Móvil
   Rent A Car, Rent A
   Car Iam
20 Kenny Bus
23 Andino Expediciones
26 Alta
27 Ladeco
28 Taxi Colectivos
   to Tocopilla
33 Banco O'Higgins
35 Nativa Expediciones
36 CTC
38 Taxi Colectivos to
   Chuquicamata
39 Cobreloa Offices
42 Banco de Crédito
43 Entel
45 Buses Tramaca
46 Lavexpress
47 Moon Valley
   Tourist Service
48 Buses Flota Barrios
49 Pullman Bus
50 Tur-Bus
51 Buses Morales y Moralito
52 Estadio Municipal
54 Post Office
56 Oficina de Turismo
59 Turismo El Sol
60 Ballart Rent A Car
61 Hertz
63 Ly & Ly Rent A Car
64 LanChile
66 Automóvil Club de Chile

since it's primarily a hotel, but it's five-star all the way for US$12.50 with breakfast for a shared room with private bath and cable TV. Regular singles/doubles are still a good deal for US$30/40 with hostel card.

Residenciales & Hotels Basic *Hotel Prat*, Vivar 1957, is a perennial budget choice for US$5 per person. Tolerable by budget standards but avoided by some travelers, *Residencial Capri* (☎ 342870), Vivar 1639, charges US$6, as does clean and tidy *Nuevo Hotel Los Andes* (☎ 341073), Vivar 1920.

Long popular with foreign visitors, the fairly tranquil *Residencial Toño* (☎ 341-185), Vivar 1970, has clean sheets and provides lots of blankets for US$7.50 per person. *Residencial Splendid* (☎ 341841), Ramírez 1960, is basic but clean and secure, though some rooms are small. Singles/doubles with shared bath cost US$8/13, while rooms with private bath cost US$15/20. In the same range is *Hotel Génesis* (☎ 342841), Avenida Granaderos 2148, for US$9/13 single/double.

Friendly *Hotel El Loa* (☎ 341963), Abaroa 1617, offers spotless rooms with shared bath for US$10/18. The reader-endorsed *Hostal Internacional* (☎ 342927, fax 341553), General Velásquez 1976, is OK but a bit rundown for US$11/19.

At the very good *Residencial John Kenny* (☎ 341430), Ecuador 1991, rates start at US$12 per person, while rooms with private bath cost US$20 per person. The boxy *Hotel Atenas* (☎ 342666), at Ramírez 1961, has spacious rooms for US$15/29 with shared bath, US$20/39 with private bath.

Places to Stay – middle
A big step up is *Hotel El Mirador* (☎ /fax 340329), Sotomayor 2064, probably the best value in town for US$48/60; it's even better value as hostel accommodation (see above). Worn but appealing for its clean, spacious rooms, the Art Deco-style *Hotel Casablanca* (☎ 341938), opposite Plaza 23 de Marzo at Sotomayor 2161, charges US$42/54. Boxy, modern *Hotel Olimpo*

(☎ 342367), Avenida Santa María 1673, charges US$60/70.

Places to Stay – top end
Hotel Alfa (☎ 341565), Sotomayor 2016, charges US$70/80. Near the top of the range is the traditional favorite *Hostería Calama* (☎ 341115), Latorre 1521. At US$90/100, its rates include private bath and breakfast.

On the southern outskirts of town, near the airport, is the luxury *Park Hotel de Calama* (☎ 319900), Camino Aeropuerto 1392, which is over the top at US$140/152.

Places to Eat
At the Mercado Central, on Latorre between Ramírez and Vargas, try the typical Chilean cheese known as 'quesillo.' There are several inexpensive cocinerías. *Nueva Victoria*, Vargas 2102, is an ordinary budget restaurant, as is *Osorno* (☎ 341035), upstairs at Granaderos 2013-B, which is also a functioning peña.

The *Hrvatski Dom* (Club Croata or Croatian Club; ☎ 342126), Abaroa 1869 facing Plaza 23 de Marzo, is a slightly more up-market place but has good fixed-price lunches. Next-door *Shopping Apumanque*, Abaroa 1859, has good fixed-price meals, but the à la carte menu is much more expensive. Around the corner at Sotomayor 2093, *Bavaria* (☎ 341496) is part of a reliable but uninspired nation-wide chain.

Pizzería D'Alfredo (☎ 319440), Abaroa 1835, is the local branch of a reliable regional chain, but try also *D'Angelo* (☎ 312867), Latorre 1983. *Tavola Calda*, Vicuña Mackenna 2033, is a fine Italian restaurant but also the only place in Chile to ever charge the author for a glass of tap water. *Sándalo* (☎ 311926), Vivar 1982, specializes in meat and seafood.

For Chinese food, try *Tong Fong*, Vivar 1951, or *Chi-Kang* (☎ 341121) at Vivar 2037. *Nueva Chong Hua*, Abaroa 2006, has fixed-price Chinese meals.

For fine ice cream, other desserts, sandwiches and coffee, head to *Fiori di Gelato* (☎ 341390), Ramírez 2099 at the corner of Abaroa, on the plaza.

Entertainment

The Cine Teatro Municipal, Ramírez 2034, shows current films.

Cobreloa (☎ 341775), the local soccer team, has offices at Abaroa 1757, but plays at the Estadio Municipal on Avenida Matta, across the railroad tracks to the east.

Getting There & Away

From Calama travelers can head north to Iquique and Arica, southwest to Antofagasta, west to Tocopilla, northeast by train to Bolivia, or east by bus to San Pedro de Atacama and to Salta, in Argentina.

Air LanChile (☎ 341394), Latorre 1499, flies to Santiago (US$215) twice daily weekdays, daily on weekends; all flights stop in Antofagasta. Ladeco (☎ 312626), Ramírez 1858, has similar services and fares.

Alta (☎ 311205, fax 331211), Ramírez 1862, flies weekdays to Arica (US$50), twice daily to Iquique (US$38), twice daily to Antofagasta (US$23), daily to Copiapó (US$83) and La Serena (US$115), weekends to Viña del Mar (US$130) and Concepción (US$184) and daily except Sunday to Santiago (US$108).

Bus – domestic Calama has no central bus terminal, but most bus companies are fairly central and within a few blocks of each other.

Tramaca (☎ 312587) has its terminal at Avenida Granaderos 3048, but there's a more convenient downtown ticket office on Sotomayor between Latorre and Vivar. It has frequent buses to Antofagasta, plus several daily to Santiago, Arica and Iquique. Tur-Bus (☎ 316699), Ramírez 1802, also has services north- and southbound on the Panamericana.

Flota Barrios (☎ 341497), Ramírez 2298 and on Sotomayor between Vivar and Balmaceda, serves the same destinations along the Panamericana, as does Pullman Bus (☎ 311410), Sotomayor 1808. Géminis (☎ 341993), Antofagasta 2239, has daily buses to Santiago, Antofagasta, Arica and Iquique. Kenny Bus (☎ 342514), Vivar

1954, serves Iquique via María Elena and Pozo Almonte.

Morales y Moralito (☎ 342671), Balmaceda 1802, goes to San Pedro twice daily (US$2.50 one way, US$4.50 round-trip). Yusmar (☎ 432173), Antofagasta 2041, goes five times daily to San Pedro and daily to Toconao (US$4.50). Buses Atacama (☎ 314757), Abaroa 2105-B, goes two or three times daily to San Pedro.

Taxi colectivos to Tocopilla leave from the corner of Balmaceda and Vargas, one block north of the Tur-Bus terminal.

Sample fares and approximate times from Calama include Arica (US$22, nine hours), Antofagasta (US$5.50, three hours), Chañaral (US$21, nine hours), Copiapó (US$25, 11 hours), Vallenar (US$26, 13 hours), La Serena (US$35, 16 hours) and Santiago (US$44). Tur-Bus's salón ejecutivo service to Santiago costs US$61.

Bus – international International buses are invariably full, so make reservations as far in advance as possible.

In summer, every Wednesday at 10 am, Géminis crosses the Andes to Jujuy and Salta, Argentina, for US$40 single; the rest of the year, there's an additional Monday service. Thursday at 8 am, Géminis has direct service to Asunción, Paraguay (US$90).

Tramaca covers the same route to Jujuy and Salta, leaving Tuesday and Friday at 10 am, for US$45. Thursday morning at 2 am, it goes to Oruro and Uyuni, Bolivia (US$15).

Train Every Wednesday at 11 pm there's ordinary train service from Calama to Ollagüe, on the Bolivian border, with connections to Uyuni (US$11) and Oruro (US$18). Tickets are available either at Tramaca or at Calama's Estación de Ferrocarril (☎ 342004), Balmaceda 1777; you may also be able to purchase tickets at Tramaca offices in Antofagasta and in Santiago. Tickets must be purchased by the Saturday prior to departure.

Show your passport when buying tickets and be sure to obtain a Bolivian visa if you need one (see above for consulate information). Temperatures can drop well below freezing on this route, so bring warm clothing and sleeping gear.

Getting Around
Frequent taxi colectivos to Chuquicamata leave from Abaroa, between Vicuña Mackenna and Sotomayor. The fare is about US$0.75.

To/From the Airport Aeropuerto El Loa (☎ 312348) is only a short cab ride south of Calama, but there are reports it is difficult to get a cab from the airport to town.

Car Rental Calama rental agencies include Hertz (☎ 341380) at Latorre 1510, Budget (☎ 341076) at Avenida Granaderos 2925, and Avis (☎ 319797) at Balmaceda 2499. Turismo Ecko Móvil Rent A Car (☎ /fax 340599), Vivar 1980, Local 118, is a local agency, as is Rent A Car Iam (☎ 312412), also at Vivar 1980.

To visit the geysers at El Tatio, rent a 4WD or pickup truck – ordinary passenger cars lack sufficient clearance for the area's rugged roads. Ly & Ly Rent A Car (☎ 341-873), at the corner of Latorre and León Gallo, and Ballart (tel/fax 311515), Latorre 1518, charge in the US$100 per day range.

CHUQUICAMATA
Enormous copper reserves at Chuquicamata (or just Chuqui), 16 km north of Calama, have made Chile the world's greatest producer of that commodity. Foreign capital originally financed the exploitation of its relatively low-grade ores, with open-pit techniques originally developed in the western USA. Today, it is the world's largest open-pit copper mine and its largest single supplier of copper. Despite Chile's attempts at economic diversification, Chuqui still provides half the country's total copper output and at least 25% of annual export income. In total, copper accounts for more than 40% of Chilean exports.

Chuqui's perpetual plume of eastward-blowing dust and smoke gives away its location from a great distance in the cloudless desert, but everything here dwarfs the human scale, from massive diesel trucks that carry 200-ton loads on tires more than three meters high (and that cost US$12,000 each), to the towering mountains of *tortas* (tailings, some of which are being reprocessed) that have accumulated over eight decades. The mine complex's single most impressive feature, though, is the massive open pit, four km long, two km wide and 630 meters deep, from which the ore comes. Most of the time on two- to three-hour tours is spent simply gazing into the depths of this immense excavation. Unfortunately, the smelter plant is no longer open to the public.

Chuquicamata proper is a clean, well ordered company town whose landscape is a constant reminder of its history. The modern football stadium is the **Estadio Anaconda**, while the **Auditorio Sindical** is a huge theater, whose interior mural commemorates a 1960s strike in which several workers died. A prominent statue near Relaciones Públicas (Public Relations) honors the workers who operated equipment like the monstrous power shovel that towers nearby and created the huge excavations and the gigantic piles of tailings that surround the town.

History
Prospectors discovered the Chuquicamata deposits in 1911, but the original North American owner sold it to the Guggenheim brothers of New York City, who in turn sold it to the US Anaconda Copper Mining Company, which began excavations in 1915. Out of nothing, the company created a city (current population 13,000), with housing, schools, cinemas, shops, a hospital and clinics and many other amenities, although many accused the company of taking out much more than it put back into the country. At the same time, labor unrest added to the resentment felt toward the huge, powerful corporation.

By the 1960s, Chile's three largest mines (the others were Anaconda's El Salvador,

Copper Processing

Given Chuquicamata's low-grade ore, only large quantities make production practical. The ore is quarried by blasting and power shovels; at the mining stage, material is classified as ore or waste depending on its copper content. Sufficiently rich material is dumped into a crusher, which reduces it to fine particles. The metal is then separated from the rock by a flotation process.

This flotation process separates and concentrates the copper through chemically induced differences in surface tension, carrying it to the surface of pools of water – the large pools of blue solution at the processing works are the concentrators where this process takes place. The copper concentrate becomes a thick slurry from which smelting extracts the final product. ■

in Region III of Atacama, and Kennecott's El Teniente, in Region VI of Rancagua) accounted for more than 80% of copper production, 60% of total exports and 80% of tax revenues. Anaconda, although it paid a greater percentage of its profits in taxes than other mining companies, became the target of those who advocated nationalization of the industry.

Congressional leftists had introduced nationalization bills since the early 1950s, but support for nationalization grew even among Christian Democrats and other centrists. During the Christian Democratic government of President Eduardo Frei Montalva in the late 1960s, Chile gained a majority shareholding in the Chilean assets of Anaconda and Kennecott, partly because the companies feared expropriation under a future leftist regime.

In 1971 Congress approved nationalization of the industry by a large majority, which even included right-wing elements. After 1973, the new military junta agreed to compensate companies for loss of assets, but retained ownership through the Corporación del Cobre de Chile (Codelco), although it has encouraged the return of foreign capital. In early 1996 there was a

brief but contentious strike, revealing factionalism in the local labor movement, and some conservative legislators are urging privatization of Codelco.

Organized Tours

Chuquicamata's Oficina de Relaciones Públicas (public relations office) offers weekday tours in both English and Spanish. To go on a tour, report to the Oficina Ayuda a la Infancia, at the top of Avenida JM Carrera, by 9 am, bringing your passport for identification and making a modest donation of about US$2.50. Tours are ostensibly limited to the first 40 arrivals, but if there are at least 15 more visitors they'll add a second bus. Demand is very high in January and February, so get there early, but if demand is sufficient there may be afternoon tours as well. Children under age 12 are not permitted.

Tours begin with a 10-minute video shown in Spanish; on completion, those who understand Spanish go directly to the tour bus, while others sit through the English-language version. Visitors should wear sturdy footwear and long trousers, but the mine provides hard hats. Do not arrange the tour through agencies in Calama, which may charge considerably more than Codelco's nominal fee.

Places to Eat

Good lunches are available at the *Club de Empleados* and the *Arco Iris Center*, both across from the plaza on Avenida JM Carrera, and the *Club de Obreros*, on Mariscal Alcázar two blocks south of the stadium. Try also *Restaurant Carloncho*, on Avenida Comercial O'Higgins.

Getting There & Away

From Calama, taxi colectivos leave from Abaroa between Vicuña Mackenna and Sotomayor, just south of Plaza 23 de Marzo. From the taxi rank in Chuqui, it's a short uphill walk to the Oficina Ayuda a la Infancia. There are also public buses from Calama to Chuqui, leaving Calama from Granaderos and Ramírez, but they also go only to the Chuqui bus terminal.

AROUND CALAMA & CHUQUICAMATA
María Elena, Pedro de Valdivia & the Nitrate Ghost Towns

Just 10 km east of the point where the Panamericana crosses the Tocopilla-Chuquicamata highway is María Elena (population 7700), founded in 1926 and now one of Atacama's last operating nitrate oficinas. Built on a orderly plan that looks better on paper than in practice, its streets form a pattern like the Union Jack.

Built as a company town (though it is now a municipality), María Elena offers such amenities as a theater, supermarket, library, hospital, market and administrative offices; oddly, for a onetime British company town, it also has a baseball field. There is also a **Museo Arqueológico e Histórico** (☎ 632935), on Ignacio Carrera Pinto, open weekdays 9.30 am to 1 pm and 3.30 to 8 pm, weekends 10 am to 2 pm. Tours of the nitrate plant are possible with a week's advance notice to Soquimich's public relations office (☎ 632731) in María Elena.

Tramaca (☎ 632903 in María Elena) buses from Antofagasta continue to Calama, but Flora Barrios, Kenny Bus, Pullman

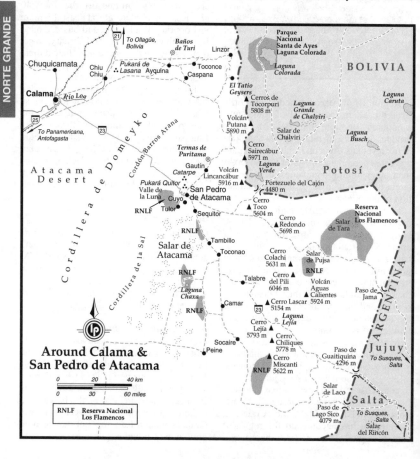

Around Calama & San Pedro de Atacama

RNLF   Reserva Nacional Los Flamencos

Bus and Camus also provide services to María Elena. *Residencial Chacance* (☎ 632749), Claudio Vicuña 437, is the only lodging in town for US$7.50 per person, but there is also camping on the Río Loa on the east side of the Panamericana. Decent food is available at *Yerco* and the *Club Social*.

Pedro de Valdivia, slightly larger than María Elena, is 40 km to the south. Founded in 1930, it is open to visits by the public; inquire at the gate. Meals are available at the *Club Pedro de Valdivia*. Tramaca (☎ 634228) and Flota Barrios (☎ 634625) connect the town with Antofagasta.

There are dozens of nitrate ghost towns in the Antofagasta region, lining both sides of the highway between Baquedano and Calama, and along the Panamericana north of the Tocopilla-Chuquicamata highway. The best-preserved is **Oficina Chacabuco**, a national monument just north of the junction between the two highways.

SAN PEDRO DE ATACAMA

Immensely popular with Chilean and foreign visitors, San Pedro de Atacama is a placid oasis of adobe houses at the northern end of the Salar de Atacama, a saline lake which has almost completely evaporated. First visited by Pedro de Valdivia in 1540, in the early 20th century it was a major stop on cattle drives from the Argentine province of Salta to the nitrate oficinas of the desert. Isaiah Bowman, in 1924, observed that:

It takes thirteen to fourteen days for cattle to be driven from Salta to San Pedro de Atacama. They wait at San Pedro one or two days, according to the need for beef at the nitrate establishments, as well as their own condition, which depends largely upon the weather they have experienced in crossing the Puna. The days of waiting are called 'la tablada.' In this time the cattle are fed liberally, and if any of them are ailing or footsore they receive the attention of a veterinary. From San Pedro it takes three days to drive them to the nitrate establishments . . .

Bowman also chronicled San Pedro's decline as railroad construction across the Andes made stock drives obsolete:

The fame that San Pedro has long enjoyed and the facilities it has for accommodating transient herds and droves attract the stockmen of Catamarca, La Rioja, San Luis, and Córdoba. For years they have sent droves of mules to be sold in the nitrate oficinas of the coastal desert farther north, but . . . completion of the Antofagasta railroad has greatly disturbed this traffic. In place of mule transport there is now railroad transport . . .

No longer on the cattle trail, San Pedro has become a popular stop on the 'gringo trail,' but many young Chileans also spend their holidays here. East of the Salar rise immense volcanoes, some active but most extinct. Symmetrical Licancábur, at 5916 meters, is one of the most conspicuous. Believe it or not, someone has dragged a mountain bike to the summit. Near San Pedro, the colorful Valle de la Luna (Valley of the Moon), one of the Atacama's most scenic areas, is part of Conaf's Reserva Nacional Los Flamencos.

The same interests who have built the massive luxury Hotel Explora in Parque Nacional Torres del Paine appear to be planning an ill-advised equivalent here, but despite increasing tourist trade, the town remains an affordable and attractive place, one which still has electricity from sunset to midnight only. Besides tourism, the other main source of local employment is irrigated farming by the indigenous communities *(ayllus)* that surround the village and the Salar.

Travelers to and from Argentina and Bolivia clear immigration with the Policía Internacional, as well as customs and agricultural inspections, just outside town to the east.

Orientation

San Pedro (permanent population 1000), 2440 meters above sea level, is some 120 km southeast of Calama via paved Chile 23. The village itself is small and compact, with almost everything of interest within easy walking distance of the Plaza de Armas.

While the streets do have names, few villagers use them, and very few buildings have numbers; consequently, directions

NORTE GRANDE

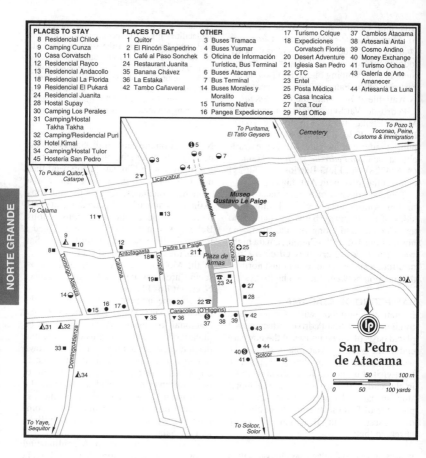

PLACES TO STAY	PLACES TO EAT	OTHER		
8 Residencial Chiloé	1 Quitor	3 Buses Tramaca	17 Turismo Colque	37 Cambios Atacama
9 Camping Cunza	2 El Rincón Sanpedrino	4 Buses Yusmar	18 Expediciones	38 Artesanía Antai
10 Casa Corvatsch	11 Café al Paso Sonchek	5 Oficina de Información	Corvatsch Florida	39 Cosmo Andino
12 Residencial Rayco	24 Restaurant Juanita	Turística, Bus Terminal	20 Desert Adventure	40 Money Exchange
13 Residencial Andacollo	35 Banana Chávez	6 Buses Atacama	21 Iglesia San Pedro	41 Turismo Ochoa
18 Residencial La Florida	36 La Estaka	7 Bus Terminal	22 CTC	43 Galería de Arte
19 Residencial El Pukará	42 Tambo Cañaveral	14 Buses Morales y	23 Entel	Amanecer
24 Residencial Juanita		Moralito	25 Posta Médica	44 Artesanía La Luna
28 Hostal Supay		15 Turismo Nativa	26 Casa Incaica	
30 Camping Los Perales		16 Pangea Expediciones	27 Inca Tour	
31 Camping/Hostal			29 Post Office	
Takha Takha				
32 Camping/Residencial Puri				
33 Hotel Kimal				
34 Camping/Hostal Tulor				
45 Hostería San Pedro				

here are given by intersections rather than street numbers. The main street Caracoles, south of the Plaza de Armas, appears as 'O'Higgins' on some maps.

Information

Tourist Office San Pedro's very helpful, knowledgeable Oficina de Información Turística (☎ 851084) is at the bus terminal, north of the museum. It's open weekdays 10.30 am to 2.30 pm and 4 to 7.30 pm, weekends 9 am to 1 pm only.

Money Cambios Atacama is on Caracoles

between Tocopilla and Toconao, Money Exchange on Toconao near Solcor, but don't expect to change travelers' checks.

Post & Communications The area code is ☎ 55. Correos de Chile is on Padre Le Paige, opposite the museum. Entel is at the southwest corner of the plaza, while CTC, on Caracoles half a block south of the plaza, is open 8.30 am to 8 pm.

Medical Services The Posta Médica (☎ 851010), on Toconao at the east side of the plaza, is the local clinic.

Warnings Local residents, especially the indigenous Atacameño peoples, can be sensitive to what they perceive to be an overwhelming presence of outsiders. Visitors should make a special effort to behave appropriately, and blend in as well as possible.

San Pedro's water has a high mineral content, and some visitors react poorly to it. If in doubt, drink bottled water.

Things to See
On the east side of the plaza stands the restored adobe **Casa Incaica**, ostensibly built in 1540 for Valdivia, but it might be safer to say that Valdivia slept here. Since it's private property, visits are not possible. On the west side stands the **Iglesia San Pedro**, a colonial church built with indigenous or artisanal materials – adobe, wood from the *cardón* cactus *(Cereus atacamensis)* and large leather straps in lieu of nails. It dates from the 17th century, though its present walls were built in 1745 and the bell tower was added in 1890.

Museo Gustavo Le Paige
If ordinary deserts are paradise for archaeologists, the Atacama is nirvana because of its nearly rainless environment, which preserves artifacts and other materials for millennia. In 1955, Belgian priest and archaeologist Gustavo Le Paige, assisted by the villagers of San Pedro and the Universidad del Norte (Antofagasta), began to organize one of South America's finest museums, offering an overview of this area's cultural evolution through an extraordinary collection of pre-Columbian artifacts. Though primarily an archaeological museum, it also includes exhibits on the Inca conquest, the Spanish invasion and even the area's social anthropology.

Some of the most interesting displays are the mummies of paleo-Indians, including a child buried in a pottery urn, and skulls that show deliberate malformation. There are also fragments of ancient weavings, pottery, tools, jewelry and paraphernalia for preparing, ingesting and smoking hallucinogenic plants.

Half a block east of the plaza, on Padre Le Paige, the museum (☎ 851002) charges an admission fee of US$2.50, but only US$1.25 with student ID. Summer hours are weekdays 9 am to noon and 2 to 6 pm, weekends 10 am to noon and 2 to 6 pm. Winter hours are daily 9 am to noon and 3 to 7 pm.

Organized Tours
San Pedro's recent tourist boom have given it the highest density of travel agencies for a town of its size in the world, but competition is fierce and there's likely to be a shakeout. Local operators organize tours to Valle de la Luna, the geysers at El Tatio, Laguna Chaxa and the Salar de Atacama, and Toconao, among other sites. Normally, without a minimum of six persons, there are surcharges. For more detailed information, see the Around San Pedro de Atacama entry below.

Special Events
In the first days of February, San Pedro celebrates the Fiesta de Nuestra Señora de la Candelaria with religious dances. Carnival takes place in February or March, depending on the date of Easter, while June 29 marks the local Fiesta de San Pedro y San Pablo.

In August, the Limpia de Canales is the resurrection of an old tradition of the cleaning of San Pedro's irrigation canals prior to the upcoming agricultural season. On August 30, the Fiesta de Santa Rosa de Lima is a traditional religious festival.

Places to Stay – bottom end
San Pedro has abundant budget accommodation of very good quality, but holiday periods, such as Chilean independence days in mid-September, tax these resources severely.

Camping *Camping Los Perales*, at the east end of Caracoles (O'Higgins), is reasonably friendly and cheap, with ample shade but cold showers only. Rates are US$2.50 per person. *Camping Cunza*, at the corner of Domingo Atienza and Antofagasta, is also very inexpensive.

NORTE GRANDE

Placid *Camping Puri* (☎ 851049), at the west end of O'Higgins, charges US$4 per person, while *Camping Takha Takha* (☎ 851038), slightly farther west, charges about US$5. Both have good sites with shade, but neither has convenient parking. The more spacious *Camping Tulor* (☎ 851027), on Domingo Atienza south of Caracoles, charges US$6 per person but lacks shade.

About three km east of San Pedro, beyond the customs post, *Camping Oasis Pozo 3* (☎ 851042) charges US$6 per person, including access to its swimming pool, and also has a restaurant. Non-guests can also use the popular swimming pool for US$1.50.

Residenciales & Hotels *Residencial El Pukará*, on Tocopilla between Antofagasta and Caracoles, is the cheapest in town for about US$7, and by no means bad. Swiss-Chilean *Casa Corvatsch* (☎ 851-101), a recent startup on Antofagasta between Domingo Atienza and Calama, has new beds and baths with hot water for US$9 per person.

At the corner of Domingo Atienza and Antofagasta, look for *Residencial Chiloé* (☎ 851017), a good value at about US$9 per person. Comparably priced *Residencial Juanita* (☎ 851039), on the south side of the plaza, is also known for its restaurant.

Residencial Rayco (☎ 851008), on Antofagasta, comes highly recommended for US$9 per person, with hot water 24 hours a day; rooms with private bath are available for US$45 double. *Residencial Andacollo* (☎ 851006), on Tocopilla between Licancábur and Padre Le Paige, costs US$10 per person, with very comfortable beds.

Standards appear to be declining at the *Residencial La Florida* (☎ 851021), on Tocopilla just a block west of the plaza, but its restaurant still serves good economical meals. Room rates are about US$10 per person. *Residencial Puri* (☎ 851049), on Caracoles west of Domingo Atienza, costs about the same, while next-door

Hostal Takha Takha (☎ 851038) charges US$12.50.

Places to Stay – middle
Hostal Tulor (☎ 851027), on Domingo Atienza south of Caracoles, offers mid-range accommodations for US$30/35 single/double. Half a block south of the plaza on Toconau, clean, agreeable *Hostal Supay* (☎ 8510076) has doubles with private bath for US$22 per person.

Places to Stay – top end
Hotel Kimal (☎ 851030), on Domingo Atienza just south of Caracoles, is a new and comfortable hotel, with attractive landscaping, at the upper end of the scale. Rates are US$48/63 single/double with private bath and breakfast.

There are mixed opinions on *Hostería San Pedro* (☎ 851011), on Solcor toward the south end of Toconao – some love it and others think it mediocre. It has recently changed hands, so changes may be in store. Room rates are US$55/70 single/double, including private bath, plus swimming pool, restaurant and solar-heated showers. Its restaurant has drawn praise for both quality and size of portions, but credit cards are no longer accepted.

Places to Eat
With outstanding fresh fruit juices and sandwiches, *Banana Chávez*, on Caracoles between Calama and Tocopilla, is probably San Pedro's best breakfast choice.

El Rincón Sanpedrino, at the corner of Tocopilla and Licancábur, has plain but inexpensive meals. *Quitor* (☎ 851056), at the corner of Licancábur and Domingo Atienza, prepares simple but nourishing meals for about US$4.

Restaurant Juanita (☎ 851039), on the Plaza de Armas, has good meals at reasonable prices. *Café al Paso Sonchek*, run by recent Eastern European immigrants, has drawn praise from visitors to San Pedro; it's on Calama between Licancábur and Antofagasta.

The excellent *Tambo Cañaveral* (☎ 851-009), at Caracoles and Toconao, doubles as

San Pedro's hottest night spot, with live Andean music Friday and Saturday nights. *La Estaka* (☎ 851038), on Caracoles near Tocopilla, has excellent food, including a nightly vegetarian special, and a lively bar.

Things to Buy
The new Paseo Artesanal, a shaded alley between the plaza and the bus station, is a good place to look for cardón carvings, llama and alpaca woolens and other souvenirs. Artesanía Antai (☎ 851080), on Caracoles between Tocopilla and Toconao, has a smaller selection.

Galería de Arte Amanecer, on Toconao near Caracoles, features local photography and artisanal goods. La Luna, 100 meters or so to the south, also sells crafts.

Getting There & Away
San Pedro doesn't really have a proper bus terminal, but rather an open area on Licancábur, across from the Paseo Artesanal, where they load and unload passengers. Buses Atacama (☎ 851057), alongside the tourist office, goes two or three times daily to Calama. Yusmar (☎ 851017), a couple doors west of the tourist office on Licancábur, runs five buses daily to Calama (US$2.50) and two to Toconao (US$2).

Morales y Moralito (☎ 851036), on Domingo Atienza between Antofagasta and Caracoles, has buses from Calama to San Pedro (US$3) three times daily. Tramaca (☎ 851034), on Tocopilla north of Licancábur, goes to Calama and Antofagasta with no change of bus.

Getting Around
Two San Pedro travel agencies rent mountain bikes: Pangea Expediciones on Caracoles between Domingo Atienza and Calama, and Turismo Nativa (☎ 851044), at the corner of Domingo Atienza and Caracoles.

AROUND SAN PEDRO DE ATACAMA
Most of San Pedro's attractions are more than walking distance from the town and public transportation is very limited, but heavy competition among numerous operators keeps tours reasonably priced. The fact that an operator is not listed below does not necessarily mean the agency is unreliable, but it's worth asking detailed questions and seeking the latest information before contracting for a tour. Some operators have drawn criticism for poor service and opportunism, particularly the agencies Ollagüe (criticized by the San Pedro tourist office for poor service, disagreeable and irresponsible guides, and even hazardous practices) and Licancábur (for poor service). Florida has drawn some reader criticism, but since its merger with Corvatsch matters seem to have improved.

Among the most popular tours are destinations Valle de la Luna (US$6), Laguna Chaxa (US$10), and the geysers at El Tatio, with a stop at the Termas de Puritama (US$19). Some agencies specialize in currently undervisited areas like Laguna Lejía (US$40), Cerro Lascar (US$40), and trekking excursions to destinations like El Tatio and the mountains and lakes toward the Argentine border for US$60 per person per day.

Among the best-established agencies are Dutch-run Cosmo Andino (☎ 851069, fax 319834), on Caracoles near Toconao, which specializes in trekking; Inca Tour (☎ 851034), on Toconao at the east side of the plaza; Turismo Ochoa (☎ 851022) on Toconao, south of Caracoles; Expediciones Corvatsch Florida (☎ 851021) in the Residencial La Florida or on Caracoles between Calama and Tocopilla; Desert Adventure (☎ 851067) at the corner of Tocopilla and Caracoles; and Turismo Nativa (☎ 851044) at the corner of Domingo Atienza and Caracoles.

Turismo Colque (☎ 851109), at the corner of Caracoles and Calama in San Pedro, is the best choice for crossing the Bolivian border at Portezuelo del Cajón and continuing to Lago Verde and Uyuni, on the Bolivian side – Chilean operators have run into problems with Bolivian authorities at this legally ambiguous border crossing, which may involve bribes to the Bolivian military in any event. Colque's three-day trip goes to Laguna Colorada, the

Salar de Uyuni and intermediate points before ending in the city of Uyuni. The price is a very reasonable US$65 per person with food; modest lodging is extra at Laguna Colorada and Hotel San Juan, near Chiguana. Travelers clear Chilean immigration at San Pedro and Bolivian immigration on arrival at the city of Uyuni.

Pukará de Quitor & Catarpe

Just three km northwest of San Pedro, on a promontory overlooking the Río San Pedro, are ruins of a 12th-century Indian pukará. From the top of the fortifications, part of the last bastion against Pedro de Valdivia and the Spanish, you can see the entire oasis. Archaeologists have reconstructed parts of its ruined walls. Three km farther north, on the east side of the river, are the ruins of Catarpe, a former Inca administrative center.

Termas de Puritama

About 30 km from San Pedro, en route to El Tatio, are the Termas de Puritama (or Baños de Puritama), a volcanic hot springs. There are no buses, so unless you have your own vehicle, a tour is probably the only alternative.

From the junction, it's a 20-minute walk along an obvious gravel track into a small canyon – if driving, leave your car at the junction. The temperature of the springs is about 33°C and there are several falls and pools. Bring food and water. Camping is possible, but there's little fuel for a fire – and it gets very cold! There are a number of ruined buildings for shelter, unfortunately dirty, but rain is unlikely.

RESERVA NACIONAL LOS FLAMENCOS

Reserva Nacional Los Flamencos consists of seven geographically distinct sectors, totaling about 74,000 hectares, mostly to the south and east of San Pedro de Atacama. Its environments range from the Valle de la Luna and the Salar de Atacama, where Laguna Chaxa is home to breeding colonies of three species of flamingos, and the high mountain lakes toward the

Argentine border. As the highway to Argentina improves in the coming years, this latter area is likely to become more easily accessible.

Information Conaf maintains a Centro de Información Ambiental at the ayllu of Solcor, about two km past San Pedro de Atacama's customs and immigration post on the road to Toconao. It's open daily, from 10 am to 1 pm and 2.30 to 4.30 pm. There's another Conaf office on the southern outskirts of Toconao, and a ranger station at Laguna Chaxa.

Valle de la Luna

Every place where flood and wind have left an array of oddly shaped polychrome desert landforms, Latin Americans call it 'Valley of the Moon' – there are others in Bolivia and Argentina – but this area west of San Pedro de Atacama, part of Reserva Nacional Los Flamencos, still deserves a visit. At the northern end of the Cordillera de la Sal, it's one of San Pedro's most popular attractions.

If driving, leave the highway to explore the dirt roads and box canyons to the north, but take care not to get stuck in the sand. You can hitch to the desert and hike around, but take plenty of water and food, and smear yourself with heavy sun block. Probably a better choice than either driving or walking is mountain bike (see the San Pedro entry for rental details), but keep to the roads and trails.

Some visitors enjoy the view and solitude at night under a full moon, in which case you should take warm clothing – at this altitude, nights are cool at any time of year, but drop well below freezing in winter. Moonlight tours from San Pedro cost only about US$5; note that in this part of Los Flamencos, Conaf no longer permits camping.

Laguna Chaxa

In the midst of the Salar de Atacama, about 25 km southwest of the village of Toconao, Laguna Chaxa is the Reserva's most easily accessible flamingo breeding site. Besides the operator's tour fees, rangers collect an admission charge of US$1.50.

EL TATIO GEYSERS

At 4300 meters above sea level, the world's highest geyser field is less breathtaking than the intermittent explosions of Yellowstone, but the visual impact of its steaming fumaroles at sunrise in the azure clarity of the altiplano is unforgettable, and the individual structures formed when the boiling water evaporates and leaves behind dissolved minerals are strikingly beautiful. Part of the proposed Parque Nacional Licancábur-Tatio (despite continued pressure for geothermal energy development), the geysers are 95 km north of San Pedro de Atacama.

Early morning, about 6 am, is the best time to see the geysers; after about 8.30 am, morning winds disperse the steam, although most tours leave by that hour and you can enjoy the large thermal pool in virtual privacy. Take special precautions to watch your step – in some places, visitors have fallen through the thin crust into underlying pools of scalding water and suffered very serious burns.

Places to Stay

Corfo, the state development agency, has a free refugio near the geysers. It's also possible to camp nearby, but nights are very cold at this elevation. Campers should bring plenty of food, since nothing is available on site.

Getting There & Away

Tours from San Pedro (see Around San Pedro de Atacama, above) usually include lunch and a hot soak at Termas de Puritama. Tours from Calama are longer and more tiring, but less so than formerly because of improved roads.

If driving, leave San Pedro no later than 4 am to reach the geysers by sunrise. The route north from San Pedro is signed, but some drivers prefer to follow the tour agencies' jeeps and minibuses in the dark (tour drivers do not appreciate this, however). Do not attempt the road, which is very rough in spots, without a high clearance pickup or jeep.

If you have rented a car in Calama, it's possible to return via the picturesque villages of Caspana, Toconce, Ayquina and Chiu Chiu (see Organized Tours under Calama, above) rather than via San Pedro, but the route is not always obvious. Some tours from Calama take this route as well.

TOCONAO

Known for finely hewn volcanic stone, the material for most of its houses, and an intricate irrigation system, the village of Toconao is about 40 km south of San Pedro. Its **Iglesia de San Lucas**, with a separate bell tower, dates from the mid-18th century.

Toconao farmers produce almonds, grapes, pomegranates, apples and herbs. Most of their orchards and fields are in the **Quebrada de Jeria**, a delightful place for a walk, rock climbing or even a swim – its water is of such high quality that, in Isaiah Bowman's time, affluent families from San Pedro sent peons with mules to Toconao to fetch casks of drinking water. In the village proper, local women sell very fine products woven of llama wool, including ponchos, pullovers, gloves and socks, as well as souvenirs cut from local stone.

Places to Stay & Eat

Toconao has several inexpensive residenciales and restaurants near the plaza – try *Casa de Pensión Lascar* for good, simple meals and lodging.

Getting There & Away

Yusmar (☎ 851017) has two buses daily to and from San Pedro.

Norte Chico

South of the Atacama proper, the Norte Chico (Little North) is a semi-arid region of transition to the Mediterranean climate of the central valley. Once known as the 'region of 10,000 mines,' this once-great silver mining zone is still important for copper and iron. Several notable rivers make irrigated agriculture productive, although the region contains only a small percentage of Chile's total arable land.

Geographically, the Norte Chico's northern boundary lies just beyond Copiapó, at about 27° S, while its approximate southern boundary is the Río Aconcagua at about 33° S. Politically, it consists of Region III of Atacama (capital Copiapó) and Region IV of Coquimbo (capital La Serena), which is the area covered in this chapter.

For most travelers, the Norte Chico's major attractions are its pleasant coastal climate, attractive beaches and colonial cities like La Serena. Off the beaten track of the Panamericana, there are intriguing villages and spectacular mountain scenery in areas where foreign travelers are still a novelty. Not far off the Panamericana are two increasingly popular national parks, Pan de Azúcar and Fray Jorge; only a handful of people visit newer and more remote reserves like Parque Nacional Llanos de Challe, on the coast north of Huasco, and Parque Nacional Nevado Tres Cruces, northeast of Copiapó, an area which seems likely to gain popularity in the coming years.

One of the Norte Chico's ephemeral attractions is the *desierto florido*, the 'flowering desert' that appears when dormant wildflower seeds sprout in years of sudden, heavy rains. Llanos de Challe is theoretically one of the best places to see this phenomenon, but the erratic geography of rainfall in the region makes it difficult to predict the best sites in any given year.

HISTORY

In pre-Columbian times the coastal Norte Chico, like the Norte Grande, was home to Chango fisherfolk, while sedentary Diaguita farmers inhabited the fertile river valleys beyond the littoral and even parts of the less fertile uplands. The Diaguita, who crossed the Andes from present-day Argentina at an undetermined date, cultivated and irrigated maize. They also raised a variety of complementary crops like potatoes, beans, squash and quinoa at different altitudes, and may have herded llamas. While their numbers were smaller and their political organization less complex than the major civilizations of Peru and Bolivia, they could mobilize sufficient labor to build agricultural terraces and military fortifications. Some decades before the European invasion, the Inca Empire began to expand its influence among the Diaguita and other southern Andean peoples, but the area remained peripheral to the Central Andean civilizations.

Europeans first saw the region in 1535, when Diego de Almagro's expedition from Cuzco crossed the Paso San Francisco from Salta. Their first impressions were less than positive. Surviving phenomenal hardship, a member of Almagro's party left a graphic, gruesome account of their miserable 800-km march over the Puna de Atacama (which took 20 days in the best of times), reporting that both men and horses froze to death and that later expeditions, finding the undecomposed horses, 'were glad to eat them.'

In the lowlands, at least food and water were available, but Almagro and his men passed quickly through the Copiapó valley and turned south to the Río Aconcagua before returning to Cuzco through Copiapó and the oases of the Norte Grande. A few years later Pedro de Valdivia's party, following Almagro's return route to establish a permanent Spanish

NORTE CHICO

settlement at Santiago, met stiff resistance from Indian warriors at Copiapó; of one party of 30 that Valdivia had ordered back to Cuzco, only the two officers survived.

In the course of his travels, Valdivia founded the city of La Serena in 1541, but Copiapó lagged well behind until its 18th-century gold boom. When gold failed, silver took its place and Copiapó really boomed, tripling its population to 12,000 after a bonanza strike at Chañarcillo in 1832, but the Norte Chico remained a frontier zone. Darwin vividly described the behavior of the region's miners:

Living for weeks together in the most desolate spots, when they descend to the villages on feast-days, there is no excess or extravagance to which they do not run. They sometimes gain a considerable sum, and then, like sailors with prize-money, they try how soon they can contrive to squander it. They drink excessively, buy quantities of clothes, and in a few days return penniless to their miserable abodes, there to work harder than beasts of burden.

Silver declined by the late 19th century but copper soon took its place, with Anaconda's huge mine at Potrerillos later supplanted by El Salvador. Recently, the area around La Serena and the northern sector around Bahía Inglesa have undergone tourist booms (La Serena has overtaken traditional holiday destinations like Viña del Mar), but mining continues to be significant.

The region is also important in Chilean cultural life – Nobel Prize-winning poet Gabriela Mistral, for instance, was a native of the Elqui valley, east of La Serena. Irrigated agriculture has always been important, but in recent years the Copiapó, Huasco and Elqui valleys have become major contributors to Chile's booming fruit exports. Their vineyards are notable for pisco, Chile's potent grape brandy.

COPIAPO

Despite much earlier encomiendas and land grants, and its founding in the mid-18th century, Copiapó is really a 19th-century city; but for Juan Godoy's discovery of silver at nearby Chañarcillo, it might have lagged

even farther behind the rest of the country. Darwin, visiting Copiapó in 1835, noted the economic distortion that the mining boom had brought to an area whose agriculture sufficed to feed it for only three months a year:

The town covers a considerable space of ground, each house possessing a garden; but it is an uncomfortable place and the dwellings are poorly furnished. Everyone seems bent on the one object of making money, and then migrating as quickly as possible. All the inhabitants are more or less directly concerned with the mines; and mines and ores are the sole subjects of conversation. Necessaries of all sorts are extremely dear; as the distance from the town to the port is eighteen leagues, and the land carriage very expensive. A fowl costs five or six shillings; meat is nearly as dear as in England; firewood, or rather sticks, are brought on donkeys from a distance of two and three days' journey within the cordillera; and pasturage for animals is a shilling a day: all this for South America is wonderfully exorbitant.

As it happened, the mining industry provided Copiapó with a number of firsts: South America's first railroad (built between 1849 and 1852 to the port of Caldera), Chile's first telegraph and telephone lines, and the country's first gasworks. In the early decades of this century, Copiapó so impressed American geographer Isaiah Bowman that he described it as:

. . . beautifully kept, with clean streets, well repaired buildings, and a thoroughly businesslike air, whether we consider the management of its mines, the appearance and administration of its famous college and its still more famous school of mines, or the excellent administration of land and water rights.

Copiapó's population (now about 98,000) has fluctuated with the mining booms, but the city retains many of the attributes Bowman described and some he did not – especially pollution from the copper smelter at nearby Paipote. Its pleasant climate and historical interest make it a worthwhile stopover on the Panamericana between La Serena and Antofagasta, and the point of departure for visits to the remote peaks near the Argentine border.

Orientation

Copiapó nestles in the narrow valley floor on the north bank of the Río Copiapó, 330 km north of La Serena, 800 km north of Santiago and 565 km south of Antofagasta. Three blocks north of Avenida Copayapu (the Panamericana), shaded by massive pepper trees, Plaza Prat marks the city's historical center.

Most areas of interest to the visitor are in or near a roughly rectangular area bounded by Calle Rodríguez to the north, the Alameda Manuel Antonio Matta to the west, Avenida Henríquez to the east, and the Río Copiapó to the south. Overlooking town from the northwest is the landmark Cerro La Cruz.

Information

Tourist Office Sernatur (☎ /fax 217248) occupies what appears to be a misplaced bomb shelter on the north side of Plaza Prat, directly in front of the Intendencia Regional at Los Carrera 691. The staff are congenial, helpful, well-informed and can provide a list of accommodations, an excellent free map and many brochures. It's open weekdays 8.30 am to 5.30 pm.

Money Banco Concepción, Chacabuco 485, changes cash dollars and travelers' checks, but also has an ATM. There are several other ATMs in the downtown area.

Post & Communications Copiapó's area code is ☎ 52. Correos de Chile is in the Intendencia Regional at Los Carrera 691, behind the Sernatur office. CTC has long-distance phone offices at the corner of Los Carrera and Chacabuco, on Plaza Prat. Entel is at Colipí 500, at the northeast corner of the plaza. Chilesat is on Chacabuco between O'Higgins and Atacama, and at the corner of Atacama and Maipú.

Travel Agencies Copiapó's main travel agencies are Turismo Atacama (☎ 212712) at Los Carrera 716, Cobretur (☎ 211072) at O'Higgins 640 and Turismo Trapiche (☎ 217546) at Vallejos 337.

Peruvian Tours (☎ 212645), O'Higgins 12, runs tours of the city, the upper Copiapó valley, Bahía Inglesa, Parque Nacional Pan de Azúcar and more remote destinations like Parque Nacional Nevado Tres Cruces and Ojos del Salado. Expediciones Puna Atacama (☎ 212684, fax 211273), Arredondo 154, runs similar trips.

National Parks For information on protected areas in Region III, including Parque Nacional Pan de Azúcar north of Chañaral, contact Conaf (☎ 213404) at Atacama 898.

Medical Services Copiapó's Hospital San José (☎ 212023, 218833) is at the intersection of Los Carrera and Vicuña, about eight blocks east of Plaza Prat.

Things to See

Around Plaza Prat, shaded by century-old pepper trees, Copiapó has a number of historic buildings from its mining heyday, including the **Iglesia Catedral** and the **Municipalidad** (a private home until 1945). On Atacama between Vallejos and Colipí, the **Asociación Minera Copiapó** is a national monument from the early mining days. A little out of the way, on Infante just east of Yerbas Buenas, the **Iglesia de Belén** is a colonial Jesuit building that was rebuilt in the mid-19th century; now functioning as the **Santuario Santa Teresa**, it's open weekdays only, 4.30 to 6.30 pm.

West of downtown, the **Alameda Matta** is an attractive, tree-lined street with a series of monuments dedicated to local figures (including Manuel Antonio Matta and prospector Juan Godoy, who discovered the Chañarcillo silver deposits) and interesting older buildings in unfortunate decline. At Atacama 98, the **Casa Matta** belonged to the influential family and now houses the regional museum.

At the corner of Juan Martínez and Batallón Atacama, the **Estación Ferrocarril** was the starting point for the first railroad on the continent. At the southern end of Batallón Atacama, mining magnate Apolinario Soto's **Palacete Viña de Cristo**, built in 1860 of European materials, was

NORTE CHICO

once the town's most elegant mansion. Now belonging to the Universidad de Atacama, it's open weekdays 8 am to 7 pm; admission is free.

A few blocks west, the historic **Escuela de Minas** (School of Mines) is now the Universidad de Atacama; on its grounds is the **Locomotora Copiapó**, the Norris Brothers locomotive that was the first to operate on the Caldera-Copiapó line.

Museo Mineralógico

Founded in 1857 and supported by the Universidad de Atacama (successor to Copiapó's famous school of mines), the mineralogical museum is very literally dazzling, a tribute to the raw materials to which the city owes its existence. Its exhibition hall displays more than 2000 samples organized according to chemical elements and structure, and a number of mineral curiosities.

At the corner of Colipí and Rodríguez, a block from Plaza Prat, the museum is open Monday to Saturday 9 am to 1 pm and weekdays only 3 to 7 pm. Admission costs US$0.75 for adults, US$0.25 for children.

Museo Histórico Regional

Built in the 1840s, the regional history museum is a national monument that belonged to the influential Matta family. At Atacama 98, the museum is open Tuesday to Thursday 9.30 am to 12.45 pm and 3 to 7.15 pm, Friday 9.30 am to 12.45 pm and 3 to 6.15 pm, Saturday 10 am to 12.45 pm and 3 to 5.45 pm, and Sundays and holidays 10 am to 12.45 pm only. Admission costs US$1 for adults, US$0.50 for children.

Museo de Ferrocarriles

South America's oldest railroad, the Copiapó-Caldera line, opened on Christmas Day 1851 to carry the produce of the silver mine at Chañarcillo. North American shipping pioneer William Wheelwright attracted investors who formed a who's who of the Chilean mining elite of the time, including Doña Candelaria Goyenechea, Agustín Edwards, Matías Cousiño, Vicente Subercaseaux and others. Though

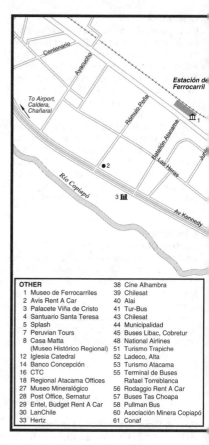

OTHER

1 Museo de Ferrocarriles	38 Cine Alhambra
2 Avis Rent A Car	39 Chilesat
3 Palacete Viña de Cristo	40 Alai
4 Santuario Santa Teresa	41 Tur-Bus
5 Splash	43 Chilesat
7 Peruvian Tours	44 Municipalidad
8 Casa Matta	45 Buses Libac, Cobretur
(Museo Histórico Regional)	48 National Airlines
12 Iglesia Catedral	51 Turismo Trapiche
14 Banco Concepción	52 Ladeco, Alta
16 CTC	53 Turismo Atacama
18 Regional Atacama Offices	55 Terminal de Buses
27 Museo Mineralógico	Rafael Torreblanca
28 Post Office, Sernatur	56 Rodaggio Rent A Car
29 Entel, Budget Rent A Car	57 Buses Tas Choapa
30 LanChile	58 Pullman Bus
33 Hertz	60 Asociación Minera Copiapó
	61 Conaf

passenger trains no longer carry Copiapinos to the beach, Wheelwright's handiwork is on display at the railroad museum, in the old station at Juan Martínez 244. There's no fixed schedule, but it's usually open around 7 pm. Admission is free.

Special Events

Copiapó and the Atacama region celebrate numerous festivals. December 8 marks the founding of the city, while February 1 is the Festival de Candelaria. Throughout the region, August 10 is Día del Minero (Miner's Day).

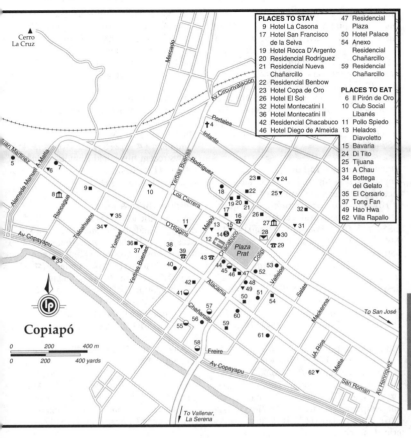

PLACES TO STAY
9 Hotel La Casona
17 Hotel San Francisco
   de la Selva
19 Hotel Rocca D'Argento
20 Residencial Rodríguez
21 Residencial Nueva
   Chañarcillo
22 Residencial Benbow
23 Hotel Copa de Oro
26 Hotel El Sol
32 Hotel Montecatini I
36 Hotel Montecatini II
42 Residencial Chacabuco
46 Hotel Diego de Almeida
47 Residencial
   Plaza
50 Hotel Palace
54 Anexo
   Residencial
   Chañarcillo
59 Residencial
   Chañarcillo

PLACES TO EAT
6 Il Pirón de Oro
10 Club Social
   Libanés
11 Pollo Spiedo
13 Helados
   Diavoletto
15 Bavaria
24 Di Tito
25 Tijuana
31 A Chau
34 Bottega
   del Gelato
35 El Corsario
37 Tong Fan
49 Hao Hwa
62 Villa Rapallo

Copiapó

NORTE CHICO

Places to Stay – bottom end

The *Residencial Benbow* (☎ 217634), at Rodríguez 541, is the cheapest in town at US$6/10 single/double. The *Residencial Rodríguez* (☎ 212861), across the street at Rodríguez 528, is equally reasonable for US$6/10 with shared bath, US$9/15 with private bath.

Residencial Chañarcillo (☎ 213281), Chañarcillo 741, has small but clean rooms for US$7/13 single/double, but avoid those too close to the noisy TV lounge. Run by the same management at O'Higgins 804, identically priced *Anexo Residencial Chañarcillo* (☎ 212284), is funky but friendly; hot water is available 7 to 11 am only.

The comparable *Residencial Chacabuco* (☎ 213428), Chacabuco 271, costs US$7.50 per person with shared bath, but twice that with private bath. Slightly more expensive are *Hotel El Sol* (☎ 215672), Rodríguez 650 and *Residencial Plaza* (☎ 212671), O'Higgins 670.

Residencial Nueva Chañarcillo (☎ 212-368), Rodríguez 540, costs US$16/24 with shared bath, US$22 per person with private bath.

Places to Stay – middle

One of Copiapó's best values is *Hotel Palace* (☎ 212852), Atacama 741, with very attractive rooms around a delightful patio for US$25/42 with private bath. At Infante 766, the very fine *Hotel Montecatini I* (☎ 211363) costs US$28/40. Under the same management, *Hotel Montecatini II* (☎ 211516, fax 214773), Atacama 374, charges US$45/60. Attractive *Hotel Copa de Oro* (☎ 216309), Infante 530, costs US$48/54.

Places to Stay – top end

Copiapó's best top-end value is the colonial-style *Hotel La Casona* (☎ 217278), O'Higgins 150, which offers accommodations in a beautiful garden setting for US$50/65. *Hotel Rocca D'Argento* (☎ 218-744, fax 211191), a new place at Maipú 580, costs US$50/66.

The spiffy *Hotel San Francisco de la Selva* (☎ 217013), Los Carrera 525, deserves a look at US$70/77 despite its noisy location. Top of the line is four-star *Hotel Diego de Almeida* (☎ 212075), O'Higgins 656, which charges US$75/82.

Places to Eat

For excellent value, try the very inexpensive grilled chicken at *Pollo Spiedo*, O'Higgins 461. The popular chain *Bavaria* (☎ 213422), Chacabuco 487, has decent but overpriced sandwiches. *Di Tito* (☎ 212-386), Chacabuco 710, is a moderately priced pizzería.

Occupying an older house at Atacama 245, *El Corsario* (☎ 215374) serves good and varied Chilean food in a patio setting. For seafood, try *Il Piron de Oro* (☎ 213416) at Atacama 1.

Other interesting alternatives include Middle Eastern food at the *Club Social Libanés* (☎ 212939), Los Carrera 350; Italian food at *Villa Rapallo* (☎ 214082), Atacama 1080; and Mexican food at *Tijuana* (☎ 219899), Infante 656.

Hao Hwa (☎ 213261), Colipí 340, is one of northern Chile's better Chinese restaurants, with good food, pleasant atmosphere and attentive service. Other chifas include

A Chau (☎ 212472) at Rodríguez 755 and *Tong Fan* (☎ 212860) at O'Higgins 390.

For ice cream, try *Helados Diavoletto* (☎ 216996), Maipú 450, whose standard and fruit flavors are both excellent. *Bottega del Gelato*, Atacama 256, is an alternative.

Entertainment

Copiapó has two downtown dance clubs: *Splash* at Juan Martínez 46 and *Alai* (☎ 217294) at Maipú 279. The *Cine Alhambra* (☎ 212187), at Atacama 455, shows recent films, and Regional Atacama (☎ 218412), Rodríguez 472, is the local first-division soccer team.

Getting There & Away

Air LanChile (☎ 213512), Colipí 526, flies daily to and from Santiago (US$144) except for Friday, when there are two flights; most flights from Santiago continue to El Salvador (US$44). Ladeco (☎ 217-285, 217406), in the Cosmocentro Plaza Real at Colipí 484, flies daily to La Serena (US$40) and Santiago.

National Airlines (☎ 218951), Colipí 350, flies daily except Saturday to La Serena (US$37) and Santiago.

Alta (☎ 217523, fax 216408), in the Cosmocentro Plaza Real at Colipí 484, flies weekdays only to Arica (US$120), 12 times weekly to Iquique (US$95), Antofagasta (US$75), Calama (US$82) and La Serena (US$32), and daily to Viña del Mar (US$87) and Concepción (US$132).

Bus – long distance Conveniently close to the Panamericana, Copiapó's main Terminal de Buses Rafael Torreblanca (☎ 212-577) is at Chacabuco 112, three blocks south of Plaza Prat and just north of the river. Virtually all north-south buses stop here, as well as many to interior destinations. Most bus companies have offices here (some of them shared) but some have downtown offices (whose addresses are listed below when appropriate), and a couple have their own separate terminals.

In the main terminal, Ramos Cholele (☎ 213113) links Copiapó with the northern Atacama destinations of Antofagasta,

Iquique and Arica; Zambrano, Evans and Carmelita share the same office and serve the same destinations. Carmelita also goes south to La Serena, Coquimbo, Ovalle and Santiago.

Tramaca (☎ 213979) covers the same Panamericana routes, along with two buses daily to Calama and half a dozen to Taltal. Andes Mar (☎ 213166) and Libac (☎ 212237), at O'Higgins 640, go to Santiago and intermediate points. Tas Choapa (☎ 213793), Chañarcillo 631, works the same routes, with connections as far as Puerto Montt in southern Chile and internationally to Argentina, Uruguay and Paraguay.

Flota Barrios (☎ 213645) has similar itineraries, plus buses to Calama, Tocopilla and Viña del Mar. Buses Fénix (☎ 214929) goes to Arica, Iquique and Santiago. Tur-Bus (☎ 213050), with its own separate terminal at Chacabuco 249, covers similar routes on the Panamericana.

Pullman Bus (☎ 211039), with its own terminal at Colipí 109, covers the Panamericana and serves Viña as well as southerly destinations off the Panamericana, including Illapel and Salamanca. They also go to northern mining towns like Diego de Almagro, El Salvador and Potrerillos. Inca Bus/Lasval (☎ 213488) runs virtually the same routes. In the same terminal, Los Corsarios serves destinations throughout the Norte Chico.

Sample destinations and fares include Arica (US$40, 16 hours), Iquique (US$35, 14 hours), Antofagasta (US$22, eight hours), Calama (US$25, 11 hours), La Serena (US$8, four hours) and Santiago (US$15, 11 hours).

Pullman Bus, Libac, Tramaca and Los Diamantes de Elqui run more expensive but more comfortable salón cama services to Santiago and Viña. Fares are about US$25.

Bus – regional Regional carriers include Recabarren (☎ 216991), Muñoz (☎ 213-166) and Casther (☎ 218889), all of which run frequently to Caldera and Bahía Inglesa for a little more than US$1. Casther and Abarán serve destinations in the upper

Copiapó valley, such as Nantoco and Pabellón, Los Loros, Viña del Cerro and Tranque Lautaro. Maximum fares are about US$2.

Getting Around
To/From the Airport Aeropuerto Chamonate (☎ 214360) is 15 km west of Copiapó, just north of the Panamericana. LanChile runs its own minibus from downtown to the airport.

Car Rental Copiapó's several car rental agencies include Hertz (☎ 213522, fax 214562) at Avenida Copayapu 173, Avis (☎ 213966) at Rómulo Peña 102 (west of the train station), Budget (☎ 218802) at Colipí 500 and Rodaggio (☎ 212153) at Colipí 127. Rodaggio has the cheapest unlimited mileage rates at US$38 per day plus 18% IVA for a small car, but pickup trucks, suitable for exploring the back country, cost at least US$80 per day.

AROUND COPIAPO
Up the valley of the Río Copiapó, southeast of the city, many worthwhile sights are accessible by public transport. Only 23 km from the city, **Nantoco** is the former hacienda of Apolinario Soto, dating from 1870. At Km 34, **Hacienda Jotabeche** belonged to the notable Chilean essayist José Joaquín Vallejo. Better known by his pseudonym, Jotabeche, Vallejo was a pioneer of Chilean literature and a keen observer of his country's customs.

Pabellón, 38 km from Copiapó, was the former rail junction to Chañarcillo; it occupies a site in the midst of a vineyard zone which also offers basic camping. **Los Loros**, 64 km from Copiapó, is a picturesque village in a rich agricultural zone that yields excellent grapes, watermelons, citrus and other fruits. **Viña del Cerro**, an archaeological monument on a spur off the main valley road, consists of the restored remains of a Diaguita-Inca copper foundry, with associated houses and other constructions, including more than 30 ovens.

Buses Casther (☎ 218889) runs buses up the valley from Copiapó's Terminal de Buses.

Chañarcillo

After Juan Godoy found silver at Chañarcillo on May 16, 1832, the town that grew up alongside the mine reached a maximum population of about 7000 before declining at the end of the 19th century, when water flooded the mines. Foxes scurry among its remaining stone and adobe ruins, which include public offices, the police station and jail, a theater, hospital and cemetery, but most of these are now difficult to distinguish. The most interesting recognizable ruin is the rustic, still-functioning well, but the cumulative impact of the site itself makes it worth a visit.

To reach Chañarcillo, take the Panamericana south to Km 59, where a dusty but excellent eastbound lateral goes toward Mina Bandurrias, a contemporary mine. The road continues east over scenic desert mountains and through deep canyons before intersecting the paved highway in the upper Río Copiapó, near Pabellón. This very interesting route is inadvisable without high clearance, and 4WD would be desirable. There's an interesting detour that dead-ends at **Mina Tres Marías**, an abandoned ridgetop mine with exceptional panoramas.

Parque Nacional Nevado Tres Cruces (Ojos del Salado)

Likely to become a major attraction for adventurous travelers, recently created Nevado Tres Cruces protects about 59,000 hectares in two separate sectors of the high Andes east of Copiapó, along Chile 31, the international highway to Argentina via Paso de San Francisco. Its major features are the high-altitude salt lakes at Laguna Santa Rosa and the Salar de Maricunga in the northern sector, and the Laguna del Negro San Francisco in the southern sector.

Though it's outside the park boundaries proper, 6893-meter Ojos del Salado might be South America's highest peak (its precise height is in dispute and Argentines claim, probably correctly, that 6962-meter Aconcagua is higher). At the 5100-meter level, the Universidad de Atacama maintains a rustic refugio that can shelter a dozen climbers; at 5750 meters, there is another with a capacity of 24.

Because Ojos del Salado straddles the border, climbers must obtain authorization from Chile's Dirección de Fronteras y Límites (Difrol; ☎ (02) 6714110, fax 6971909, 6722536) at Bandera 52, 4th floor, in Santiago, which oversees activities in the border area. It is possible to request permission prior to arriving in Chile, but climbers must also report to the Carabineros in Copiapó before proceeding to the area.

At present there is no public transport to the area, but two guides in Copiapó may be able to help with arrangements: Patricio Ríos (☎ 212714) or Marco Urbina (☎ 211-273). Or try Maximiliano Martínez at Aventurismo (☎ 316395) in Caldera.

CALDERA & BAHIA INGLESA

A minor colonial port, Caldera grew dramatically after the silver strikes east of Copiapó. The construction of the railroad in the mid-19th century provided residents of Copiapó easy access to the beach. Along with nearby Bahía Inglesa, it is still Region III's most important beach resort. Bahía Inglesa's beaches are more sheltered and attractive, but Caldera is livelier and cheaper.

Bahía Inglesa takes its name from the British privateers who took refuge here in colonial times. Now popular with visitors from central and northern Chile, it is very crowded during the January-February peak season, but the weather is just as good or better in the off-season, when it is far cheaper and more pleasant. It is also, in the words of one reader, 'suffering from condominiums – a kind of fungus, I think.'

In addition to tourism, the area's economy depends on fishing and mining. Locally cultivated scallops, oysters and seaweed are also exported, though some are consumed locally.

Orientation

On the south shore of the Bahía de Caldera, Caldera is 75 km west of Copiapó and just west of the Panamericana, which

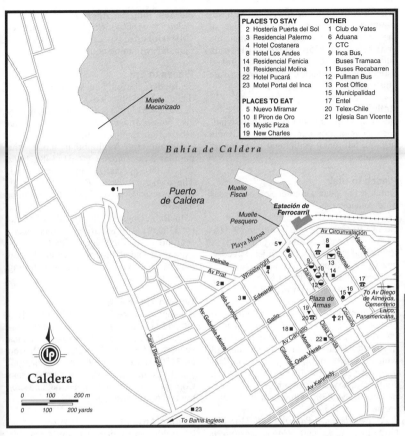

PLACES TO STAY
2 Hostería Puerta del Sol
3 Residencial Palermo
4 Hotel Costanera
8 Hotel Los Andes
14 Residencial Fenicia
18 Residencial Molina
22 Hotel Pucará
23 Motel Portal del Inca

PLACES TO EAT
5 Nuevo Miramar
10 Il Piron de Oro
16 Mystic Pizza
19 New Charles

OTHER
1 Club de Yates
6 Aduana
7 CTC
9 Inca Bus,
   Buses Tramaca
11 Buses Recabarren
12 Pullman Bus
13 Post Office
15 Municipalidad
17 Entel
20 Telex-Chile
21 Iglesia San Vicente

Caldera

Bahía de Caldera

Muelle Mecanizado

Puerto de Caldera

Muelle Fiscal

Muelle Pesquero

Estación de Ferrocarril

Playa Mansa

Av Circunvalación

Insinilla

Wheelwright

Av Prat

Edwards

Gallo

Isla Lennox

Gana

Tocornal

Vallejos

Plaza de Armas

Av Gabriela Mistral

Canal Beagle

Av Carvallo

Cifuentes

Ossa Varas

Mont

Ossa Cerda

Cousiño

Av Kennedy

To Av Diego de Almeyda, Cementerio Laico, Panamericana,

To Bahía Inglesa

0   100   200 m
0   100   200 yards

NORTE CHICO

continues north to Chañaral. Avenida Diego de Almeyda, which links Caldera with the Panamericana, continues south as Avenida Carvallo to nearby Bahía Inglesa, on the north shore of its namesake bay.

Information

Tourist Office Sernatur ostensibly maintains a summer tourist office on the Plaza de Armas, but it moves from year to year and keeps irregular hours.

Post & Communications The area code is ☎ 52, the same as Copiapó's. Correos

de Chile is at Edwards 325. CTC's long-distance telephone office is at Edwards 360, Entel is at Tocornal 383, and Telex-Chile at Ossa Cerda 370.

Things to See

At the eastern approach to town, along Avenida Diego de Almeyda, the **Cementerio Laico** was Chile's first non-Catholic cemetery; note the interesting forged ironwork. Around the plaza and towards the **Muelle Pesquero** (the colorful fishing jetty), the many distinctive 19th-century buildings include the **Iglesia San Vicente**

(1862), with its gothic tower; the **Munici-palidad**, the **Aduana** (customs house) at the corner of Gana and Wheelwright; the erstwhile **Estación Ferrocarril** (train station, 1850, for the line that linked Caldera with Copiapó); and several private houses.

Activities

Besides swimming and sunbathing, wind-surfing is a popular pastime at Bahía Inglesa, but rental equipment is no longer available.

Places to Stay

Outside the peak summer season, prices drop considerably.

Camping *Camping Bahía Inglesa* (☎ 315-424), on Playa Las Machas just south of Bahía Inglesa, has good facilities, but costs nearly US$30 per site in high season. It also has cabañas starting at US$109 for up to five persons with private bath.

Residenciales & Hotels The cheapest options are rundown *Residencial Molina* (☎ 315941) at Montt 346 and *Hotel Los Andes* (☎ 315301) at Edwards 360, both of which charge about US$9 per person. *Res-idencial Fenicia* (☎ 315594, fax 315171), Gallo 370, has singles/doubles with shared bath for US$16/30; with private bath, rates are about US$25/42.

At *Residencial Palermo* (☎ 315847), Cifuentes 150, and *Hotel Costanera* (☎ 316007), Wheelwright 543, rates are about US$30/45 with private bath. *Hotel Pucará* (☎ 315258), Ossa Cerda 460, charges US$31/36 for rooms with private bath.

At the upper end of the scale is *Hostería Puerta del Sol* (☎ 315205) at Wheelwright 750, where rates start at US$40/59. *Motel Portal del Inca* (☎ 315252) at Avenida Car-vallo 945, on the road to Bahía Inglesa, costs US$70/80.

Midway between Caldera and Bahía Inglesa, *Motel Umbral de Bahía Inglesa* (☎ 315000) charges US$100 per night for up to six persons. In Bahía Inglesa proper,

the new four-star *Apart Hotel Rocas de Bahía* (☎ 316005), El Morro s/n, charges US$90 for up to six persons. It has a restau-rant and swimming pool.

Places to Eat

Seafood is the only reasonable choice – there's a local branch of Copiapó's *Il Piron di Oro* (☎ 315109) at Cousiño 218, but try also *Nuevo Miramar* (☎ 315381) at Gana 90, overlooking the fishing pier.

Despite its Anglophone name, the popular *New Charles* (☎ 315348), Ossa Cerda 350, specializes in Chilean food. The owner of *Mystic Pizza* (☎ 315033), Carvallo 350, is in fact a Connecticut Yankee.

In Bahía Inglesa, the upscale *El Coral* (☎ 315331) at El Morro 564 offers superb seafood, including local scallops. It's expensive, but if you order carefully you may be able to eat here without shattering the budget.

Getting There & Away

For long-distance buses, see Pullman Bus (☎ 315227) at Cousiño and Gallo, Tra-maca (☎ 316235) at Edwards 415, or Inca Bus (☎ 315261) at Gana 225. Recabarren (☎ 315034), Cousiño 260, goes to Copiapó. The fares and times resemble those from Copiapó; add an hour southbound, and sub-tract an hour northbound.

Getting Around

Everything in Caldera is easily accessible on foot. Buses and taxi colectivos shuttle visitors from Caldera to Bahía Inglesa in about 10 minutes, but for some reason it can be hard to get back – plan your return carefully.

AROUND CALDERA
Santuario Naturaleza Granito Orbicular

On the scenic coastline about 12 km north of Caldera, this geological oddity consists of a number of irregularly shaped con-glomerates of various minerals. About a mile or two away, there's an offshore sea lion colony.

CHAÑARAL

On the boundary between Regions II and III, Chañaral is a dilapidated but intriguing mining and fishing port set among the rugged headlands of the Sierra de las Animas. It dates from 1833, almost a decade after Diego de Almeyda discovered the nearby Las Animas copper mine, but the area's economic powerhouse is the huge copper mine at El Salvador, in the mountains to the east.

For the people of Chañaral, El Salvador has been a mixed blessing that helps provide their economic livelihood but also pollutes the town they call home. In 1988, when they went to court to force powerful Codelco to construct a holding facility to prevent toxic runoff into the Río Salado and onto Chañaral's broad sandy beach, their successful environmental action was the first of its kind in Chile.

Just north of Chañaral, the scenic coastal Parque Nacional Pan de Azúcar (see separate entry below) straddles the regional border. This increasingly popular destination, which offers excellent camping, is the best reason for a stopover in the area.

Orientation

About 165 km northwest of Copiapó and 400 km south of Antofagasta, Chañaral (population 12,000) has two distinct sections: the industrial port that sprawls along the shoreline and the Panamericana, and a residential zone that scales the hills south of the highway. Steep sidewalks and staircases link Chañaral's streets, which respect the natural contours of the highly irregular terrain more than most other Chilean cities.

Information

Tourist Office Chañaral's tourist office is on the Panamericana, at the southern approach to town. It's open weekdays during the summer high season only.

Post & Communications The area code is ☎ 52. Correos de Chile is on Comercio, at the west end of town. CTC's long-distance offices are at Los Carrera 618, Entel at Merino Jarpa 1197.

Barquito

Barquito, two km south of Chañaral proper, contains the mechanized port facilities through which El Salvador's copper passes. In a ramshackle way, it's an interesting landscape, with a large rail yard and many antique cars among the steep headlands.

Places to Stay

Accommodation is limited. The marginal *Hotel Jiménez*, Merino Jarpa 551, is the cheapest at US$9 per person, while *Hotel Nuria*, Avenida Costanera 302, charges US$12. At *Hotel Miní* (☎ 480079), San Martín 528, rates are US$16/23 single/double. The best in town is the very appealing *Hostería Chañaral* (☎ 480055), Miller 268, where rooms start at US$37/45.

Places to Eat

For a town of its size, Chañaral has several surprisingly good, if modest, restaurants. *Restaurant Nuria*, on the plaza at Yungay 434, offers well prepared and reasonably priced seafood, salads and snacks, with friendly and attentive service. *La Playa* at Merino Jarpa 546 and *El Rincón Porteño* at Merino Jarpa 567 are also worth a visit.

There are also several basic places on the Panamericana if you're just passing through.

Getting There & Away

Chañaral's bus terminal is on Merino Jarpa between Conchuela and Los Baños, but many buses bypass town on the Panamericana (though most will stop to pick up passengers). Companies with offices in town are Tramaca (☎ 480838) at Merino Jarpa 867, Flota Barrios (☎ 480071) at Merino Jarpa 567 and Pullman Bus (☎ 480153), which also serves Diego de Almagro and El Salvador, at Freire 493.

Getting Around

For car rental, contact Rodrigo Zepeda (☎ 480015) at San Martín 407, who may also arrange excursions to Parque Nacional Pan de Azúcar for about US$100 per day with driver.

NORTE CHICO

PARQUE NACIONAL PAN DE AZUCAR

Only 30 km north of Chañaral, Pan de Azúcar comprises 44,000 hectares of coastal desert and cordillera, with sheltered coves, white sandy beaches, stony headlands, abundant wildlife and unique flora. There is excellent camping in some coastal areas, but the park is becoming an increasingly popular and crowded summer destination.

Information Conaf's Centro de Información Ambiental at Caleta Pan de Azúcar, open daily 8.30 am to 12.30 pm and 2 to 6 pm, offers slide presentations about the park's environment and also has a cactarium. At the southern entrance, rangers collect an admission charge of US$4 for foreigners (US$1.25 for children); Chileans pay half price.

Geography & Climate

Park altitudes range from sea level to 900 meters. In the coastal zone, the cold Humboldt Current supports a variety of marine life, such as otters and sea lions, and many birds, including pelicans, cormorants and the Humboldt penguin.

At higher elevations, moisture from the camanchaca nurtures a unique vegetation of more than 20 species of cacti and succulents. Farther inland, guanacos and foxes are common sights.

Isla Pan de Azúcar

About 7000 Humboldt penguins, plus other seabirds, nest in abundance on the island of Pan de Azúcar, which seems to float on the ocean as the camanchaca advances inland at twilight. With a good pair of binoculars, the birds are visible from the shore, but local fishermen also approach the 100-hectare island by boat for better views (the island proper is a restricted area). Launches charge about US$25-35 for up to 10 people from Caleta Pan de Azúcar.

Places to Stay

Under license from Conaf, concessionaire Juan Tamblay Silva (☎ 480551) operates campgrounds at Playa Piqueros (35 sites) and Caleta Pan de Azúcar (30 sites). Charges are US$10 per site; facilities include toilets, water, showers, picnic tables and welcome shade. There are also two cabañas, with kitchens, that sleep up to six people for US$80 per night.

Reservations are a good idea in January and February, especially on weekends. While the nearest supplies are at Chañaral, fish can be purchased from the families at Caleta Pan de Azúcar.

Getting There & Away

While there is no regular public transportation to the park, a decent road leads north from the Panamericana near the cemetery at the east end of Chañaral. It should be possible to arrange a taxi from Chañaral for about US$20 if you want to camp, but you'll have to pay the driver both ways – double that amount if you make arrangements to be picked up. It may be possible to hitch from Chañaral, especially on weekends.

If you're driving and approaching from the direction of Antofagasta, there is also a park entrance at Las Bombas, 45 km north of Chañaral on the Panamericana, where a good road follows Quebrada Pan de Azúcar to the coast.

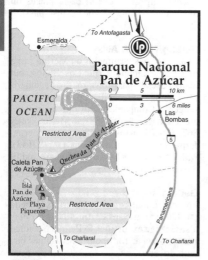

Parque Nacional Pan de Azúcar

PACIFIC OCEAN

VALLENAR

In the valley of the Río Huasco, roughly midway between Copiapó and La Serena, Vallenar dates from the late 18th century, when colonial Governor Ambrosio O'Higgins applied the transliterated name of his native Ballenagh, Ireland, to the area. Darwin later visited the area on horseback during his travels aboard the *Beagle*.

Like the rest of the Norte Chico, Vallenar developed on the basis of mining, but irrigated agriculture is also critically important; olives are the local specialty. After serious earthquake damage in 1922, Vallenar was rebuilt with wood instead of adobe, but the city's buildings still rest on unconsolidated sediments.

Orientation

Even motorists often bypass Vallenar (population 42,000), 145 km south of Copiapó and 190 km north of La Serena, because Puente Huasco (Huasco Bridge) that spans the valley does not drop down into the town, readily visible below. At the south end of the bridge, the Vallenar-Huasco highway leads east into town, crossing the river via Puente Brasil. Everything in town is within easy walking distance of the central Plaza O'Higgins, at the intersection of Prat and Vallejos.

Information

Tourist Office Vallenar's tourist office is a kiosk at the junction of the Panamericana and the Vallenar-Huasco highway, at the south end of Puente Huasco. From December to March, it's open daily 10 am to 1 pm and 4 to 8 pm.

Money Banco de Concepción has an ATM at Prat 1070.

Post & Communications Vallenar's area code is ☎ 51. Correos de Chile is at the northeast corner of Plaza O'Higgins. CTC's long-distance office is at Prat 1035, while Entel is at Colchagua 550. Chilesat is at the corner of Prat and Colchagua.

Medical Services Vallenar's hospital

(☎ 611202) is at the corner of Merced and Talca.

Museo del Huasco

Vallenar's history museum has a modest collection of local artifacts and materials, including an excellent photo collection. At Sargento Aldea 742, the museum is open Tuesday to Friday 10 am to 12.50 pm and 3.30 to 7 pm, weekends 10 am to 12.30 pm only, but the curator sometimes admits visitors even when it's technically closed. Admission costs US$0.50 for adults, US$0.25 for children.

Special Events

January 5 is a local holiday celebrating the founding of the city, while the local song festival, Festival Vallenar Canta, takes place later in the month. In the village of San Félix, 58 km up the valley of the Río Huasco, the annual grape harvest in February is occasion for the Festival de la Vendimia.

Places to Stay

The cheapest accommodations are *Residencial Oriental* (☎ 613889), Serrano 720, where singles with shared bath cost US$7.50; rooms with shared bath are US$12.50 per person. *Hotel Atacama* (☎ 611426), nearby at Serrano 873, is a little more expensive, but Vallenar's best value is *Hotel Viña del Mar* (☎ 611478), a cheerful family-run place at Serrano 611, which charges US$20 double with shared bath.

Mid-range accommodations start around US$30/35 single/double at *Hostal Vallenar* (☎ 613380), Aconcagua 455. Slightly dearer are *Hotel Real* (☎ 613963), Prat 881 and *Hotel Cecil* (☎ 614071), Prat 1059. The finest in town is the *Hostería de Vallenar* (☎ 614379), Alonso de Ercilla 848, for US$63/78; it also has a topnotch restaurant.

Places to Eat

For basic inexpensive meals, try the cocinerías in the Mercado Municipal (municipal market) at the corner of Serrano and Santiago. The popular chain *Bavaria* has two

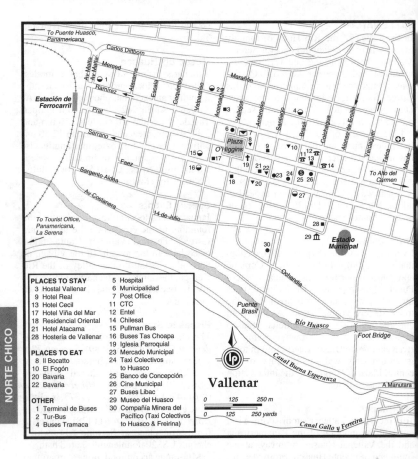

PLACES TO STAY
3 Hostal Vallenar
9 Hotel Real
13 Hotel Cecil
17 Hotel Viña del Mar
18 Residencial Oriental
21 Hotel Atacama
28 Hostería de Vallenar

PLACES TO EAT
8 Il Bocatto
10 El Fogón
20 Bavaria
22 Bavaria

OTHER
1 Terminal de Buses
2 Tur-Bus
4 Buses Tramaca

5 Hospital
6 Municipalidad
7 Post Office
11 CTC
12 Entel
14 Chilesat
15 Pullman Bus
16 Buses Tas Choapa
19 Iglesia Parroquial
23 Mercado Municipal
24 Taxi Colectivos
    to Huasco
25 Banco de Concepción
26 Cine Municipal
27 Buses Libac
29 Museo del Huasco
30 Compañía Minera del
    Pacífico (Taxi Colectivos
    to Huasco & Freirina)

Vallenar

0   125   250 m
0   125   250 yards

locales: Santiago 678 (☎ 614255) and Serrano 802 (☎ 613504).

Il Bocatto (☎ 614609), on Plaza O'Higgins, has small but good pizzas and snacks. For parrillada, try *El Fogón* (☎ 614641) at Ramírez 934.

Entertainment
The Cine Municipal (☎ 611501) is at Prat 1094.

Things to Buy
A regional specialty is the sweet wine known as *pajarete*, available in local wine shops.

Getting There & Away
Vallenar's Terminal de Buses is on Avenida Matta, at the west end of Ramírez, but many companies have more convenient offices downtown. Libac (☎ 613755) is at Brasil 715, Tramaca (☎ 612075) at Brasil 388, Pullman (☎ 612461) at Serrano 551 and Tas Choapa (☎ 613822) at Serrano 580. Flota Barrios (☎ 614295), Diamantes de Elqui (☎ 612574) and Carmelita (☎ 613037) are at the terminal. Tur-Bus (☎ 611738) is at Merced 561. It has extensive north- and southbound routes.

North-south transport schedules closely

resemble those of Copiapó, but buses and taxi colectivos also connect the town with the port of Huasco and the village of Freirina, as well as up the valley. For these regional services, contact Buses Tal (☎ 612574) at the terminal. Taxi colectivos to Huasco leave from Avenida Brasil, in front of the Compañía Minera del Pacífico, and from the corner of Brasil and Serrano.

AROUND VALLENAR
Parque Nacional Llanos de Challe
Recently designated a national park for its unique flora, most notably the endemic *Garra de León (Leontochir ovallei)*, possibly Chile's rarest and most beautiful flower, Llanos de Challe comprises 45,000 hectares of coastal desert, 50 km north of Huasco. During years of the desierto florido, it's one of the best places to see the display of wildflowers.

Llanos de Challe is accessible only by car, either by a dirt road north from Huasco Bajo, 46 km west of Vallenar, to Carrizal Bajo, or by a slightly shorter route that leaves the Panamericana 15 km north of Vallenar.

Reserva Nacional Pingüino de Humboldt
Consisting of several offshore islands on the border between Regions III and IV, this 860-hectare reserve protects nesting sites for the Humboldt penguin, but there are also dolphins, sea lions, and many seabirds. While there is no public transport, access is possible via a dirt road from Domeyko, 51 km south of Vallenar, to Carrizalillo and Caleta Chañaral, where it's possible to hire a launch to Isla Damas for about US$90. Camping is permitted on Isla Damas, but visitors must bring their own water, as well as bags to pack out trash.

LA SERENA
Well on its way to supplanting Viña del Mar as Chile's premier beach resort, La Serena is also one of Chile's oldest cities and capital of Region IV of Coquimbo. Thanks to President Gabriel González Videla's 'Plan Serena' of the late 1940s, La Serena maintains a colonial facade, but there are only a handful of genuine colonial buildings.

A recent, even more ambitious 15-year plan entitled 'Serena Norte' envisions the creation of 13,000 luxury housing units, 35 km of new roads, the planting of 20,000 trees in a 260,000-sq-meter greenbelt and 700,000-sq-meter golf and country club, with water, gas, electric and cable TV utilities. Presumably this would create 5000 permanent jobs, but water shortages remain a particularly serious concern in this semi-desert area.

Besides its beaches, La Serena has numerous attractions in the surrounding countryside, including quaint villages like Vicuña (home to Nobel Prize-winning poet Gabriela Mistral), with its nearby vineyards, and several important international astronomical observatories, which take advantage of the region's exceptional atmospheric conditions.

History
Encomendero Juan Bohón, Pedro de Valdivia's lieutenant, founded La Serena in 1544, but after Bohón died in an Indian uprising, his successor Francisco de Aguirre refounded the city in 1549. Following Chilean independence, silver and copper became the backbone of its economy, supported and supplemented by irrigated agriculture in the Elqui valley. Silver discoveries were so important that the Chilean government created an independent mint in the city.

Orientation
La Serena (population 105,000) lies on the south bank of the Río Elqui, about two km above its outlet to the Pacific Ocean, 470 km north of Santiago. The Panamericana, known as Avenida Juan Bohón, skirts the western edge of town.

Centered on the Plaza de Armas, the city plan is a regular grid, complicated by a few diagonals toward the east, but it's easy to get oriented. Most areas of interest fall within a rectangular area marked by Avenida Bohón and Parque Pedro de Valdivia to the west, the Río Elqui to the north, Calle Benavente to the east, and Avenida Francisco de Aguirre to the south.

Information

Tourist Offices Sernatur's regional office (☎ 225138, fax 213956) is on the west side of the plaza, at the corner of Prat and Matta, on the ground level of the same complex as the post office. It's open weekdays 8.30 am to 6.30 pm. The Municipalidad has an information office at the bus terminal, open Monday through Saturday 9.30 am to 1 pm and 3.30 to 9 pm, and Sundays only 9 am to 2 pm.

Hotelga, the private hotel and restaurant association, operates two information kiosks. The first (☎ 227771), in front of Iglesia La Merced, at the corner of Prat and Balmaceda, is open daily except Sunday, 10 am to 2 pm and 5 to 9 pm. The second, at Mercado La Recova at the corner of Cienfuegos and Cantournet, is open daily except Sunday 10 am to 2 pm, and weekdays only 4.30 to 8 pm.

Another good source of information is the Automóvil Club de Chile (☎ 225279) at Eduardo de la Barra 435.

Money Both US cash and travelers' checks (with a small commission), as well as Argentine pesos, are easily negotiated at any of La Serena's cambios. Try Gira Tour at Prat 689, Daire or US$100, both at Prat 645, or Intercam at Balmaceda 431. Banco Santander has an ATM at Cordovez 451.

Post & Communications La Serena's area code is ☎ 51. Correos de Chile is at the corner of Matta and Prat, opposite the Plaza de Armas. CTC has long-distance phone offices at Cordovez 446 and O'Higgins 536, while Entel is at Prat 571.

Travel Agencies La Serena's numerous travel agencies include Viajes Torremolinos (☎ 223946) at Balmaceda 431, Turismo Aerocrom (☎ 222859) at Cienfuegos 420 and Gira Tour (☎ 223535) at Prat 689.

PLACES TO STAY
1 Hotel El Escorial
2 Residencial Suiza
3 Hostal de Turismo Croata
6 Hotel Pucará
10 Hotel de Turismo Brasilia
13 Residencial El Loa
17 Hotel Francisco de Aguirre
38 Hotel Casablanca
39 Residencial La Casona de Cantournet
41 Hotel Pacífico
42 Residencial Chile
43 Residencial Lido
53 Hotel Berlín
58 Residencial Petit
60 Hotel Mediterráneo
68 Hotel Alameda
75 Residencial Norte Verde
76 Residencial Limmat (HI)
81 Hotel Los Balcones de Alcalá
85 Residencial Jofré
89 Residencial El Silo

PLACES TO EAT
4 Gelatería Mammamia
7 Boccaccio
11 El Cedro
12 El Amir
14 Muday Pub
16 Taiwan
21 Café Plaza Real
26 La Crisis
27 Café do Brasil
31 La Mía Pizza
37 Mai Lan Fan
57 Grill Bar Serena
59 Quick Biss Dos
80 Restaurant y Bar Croata

OTHER
5 Café del Patio
8 Iglesia La Merced, Hotelga Tourist Kiosk
9 National Airlines
15 Hotelga Tourist Kiosk
18 Post Office, Sernatur
19 Museo Histórico Gabriel González Videla
20 Municipalidad
22 Iglesia Catedral
23 CTC
24 Librerías Universitarias
25 Ladeco
28 Viajes Torremolinos, Intercam (Money Exchange)
29 Turismo San Bartolomé
30 Entel
32 Rally Daire (Car Rental), Daire (Money Exchange), US$100 (Money Exchange)
33 Gira Tour
34 LanChile
35 Iglesia San Agustín
36 Turismo Aerocrom
40 Iglesia Santo Domingo
44 Conaf
45 Diaguitas Tour
46 Cine Centenario
47 Alta
48 Fray Jorge Tour Service
49 Lavado Roma
50 Galería Cema-Chile
51 Banco Santander (ATM)
52 Buses Lit
54 Buses Tal, Fénix Pullman Norte
55 Buses Tas Choapa
56 CTC
61 Museo Arqueológico
62 Covalle Bus
63 Budget Rent A Car
64 Oceanic Rent A Car
65 Dollar Rent A Car
66 Buses Serenamar
67 Buses Libac
69 Automóvil Club de Chile
70 Iglesia San Francisco, Museo Colonial de Arte Religioso
71 Línea Ruta 41, Tasco Taxi Collectivos
72 Buses Flota Barrios
73 Pullman Bus
74 Lasval/Inca Bus
77 Hertz Rent A Car
78 Buses Tramaca
79 Laverap
82 Buses Frontera Elqui, Postal Bus, Buses Carlos Araya
83 Hospital Juan de Diós
84 Museo Mineralógico Ignacio Domeyko
86 Terminal de Buses
87 Buses Palacios
88 Gala Rent A Car

● 63

● 77

To Beaches, Bahía de Coquimbo

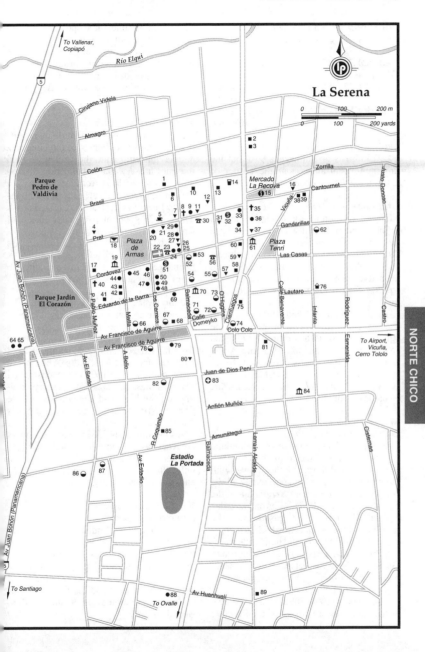

To Vallenar,
Copiapó

Río Elqui

5

La Serena

0   100   200 m
0   100   200 yards

Cirujano Videla

Almagro

Colón

Parque
Pedro de
Valdivia

Brasil

Prat

4
18

17
19

Cordovez

40
41   42
43
44   45   46
47

Parque Jardín
El Corazón

Av Juan Bohón (Panamericana)

Plaza
de
Armas

P. Pablo Muñoz

Matta

A. Bello

Eduardo de la Barra

J. Carrera

66

67   68

Av Francisco de Aguirre

78

79

80

64 65

Av El Santo

Av Estadio

R. Coquimbo

86   87

85

Estadio
La Portada

88
To Ovalle

Av Huanhuali

To Santiago

1

5
6

7
8   9   11
10   12   13   14

20   21
22   23   24
25
26   27
28
29
30
31   32   33
34

35
36
37

Mercado
La Recova
15   16

Zorrilla

Cantournet

Viciuña   38 39

Gandarillas

62

Plaza
Tenri

Las Casas

Cienfuegos

O'Higgins

49   48
50
51   52   53
54   55   56
57   58   59   60
61

70
71   72   73
69   74
75
Calle
Domeyko
Colo Colo

81

Juan de Dios Peni
83

Anfión Muñoz

Amunátegui

Balmaceda

Larraín Alcalde

82

84

89

To Airport,
Vicuña,
Cerro Tololo

Calle Benavente

Cale Lautaro

Infante

Rodríguez

Esmeralda

Castro

76

Justo Donoso

NORTE CHICO

Bookshop La Serena's best bookstore is Librerías Universitarias, Cordovez 470.

National Parks For information on Region IV's national parks and other reserves, visit Conaf (☎ 225685) at Cordovez 281.

Laundry Lavado Roma is at Los Carrera 654, Laverap at Francisco de Aguirre 447.

Medical Services Hospital Juan de Diós (☎ 225569) is at Balmaceda 916, but the emergency entrance is at the corner of Larraín Alcalde and Anfión Muñoz.

Churches
Many of La Serena's key features are on or near the beautifully landscaped Plaza de Armas. On the east side, the **Iglesia Catedral** dates from 1844. Southwest of the plaza, facing another smaller but attractively landscaped plaza, the colonial **Iglesia Santo Domingo** is a mid-18th-century relic.

At the corner of Cienfuegos and Cantournet, three blocks east of the plaza, the **Iglesia San Agustín** originally belonged to the Jesuits, then passed to the Agustinians after the Jesuits' expulsion. It has undergone considerable modification since its construction in 1755, most recently due to damage from the 1975 earthquake.

Museo Histórico Gabriel González Videla
González Videla, a native of La Serena, was president of Chile from 1946 to 1952. A controversial figure, he took power with Communist support but soon outlawed the party, driving poet Pablo Neruda out of the Senate and into exile. Exhibits on González Videla's life omit these episodes, but the museum includes other worthwhile materials on regional history and numerous paintings by Chilean artists. The adjacent **Plaza González Videla**, between the museum and the post office, is the site of the annual book fair (see below).

The museum (☎ 215082) is at Matta 495, at the southwestern corner of the Plaza de Armas. In summer, it's open Tuesday to Saturday 9 am to 1 pm and 4 to 8 pm, Sunday 9 am to 1 pm only; the rest of the year, hours are 9 am to 1 pm and 3 to 7 pm, Tuesday through Saturday only. The cost of admission varies, depending on the current exhibit.

Museo Arqueológico
La Serena's archaeological museum repeats many of the same themes of the González Videla museum, but the archaeological museum has a valuable collection of Diaguita Indian artifacts from before the Inca conquest, which truncated the autonomous cultural development of the Chilean coast. There is a good map of distribution of Chile's aboriginal population.

At the intersection of Cordovez and Cienfuegos, the museum (☎ 224492) is open weekdays 11.30 am to 1 pm and 4 to 6 pm. Admission costs US$1.25.

Museo Colonial de Arte Religioso
Occupying an annex of the colonial **Iglesia San Francisco** at Balmaceda 640, this museum features polychrome sculptures from the Cuzco School and paintings from 17th-century Quito, Ecuador. The church itself, completed in 1627 but reconstructed several times, contains 18th-century carvings on the beams of the sacristy. At the time of writing, major reconstruction was underway.

Admission costs US$1. Summer hours are weekdays 11 am to 1 pm and 6 to 8 pm, weekends and holidays 11 am to 1 pm only; the rest of the year, it's open weekends and holidays only, 11 am to pm.

Museo Mineralógico Ignacio Domeyko
La Serena's mineral museum is one of the best in a country whose economy traditionally lives or dies by mining (the mineral museum in Copiapó is probably even better). At Anfión Muñoz 870, between Benavente and Infante, the museum's opening hours are 9 am to noon, weekdays only.

Parque Jardín El Corazón

Along Avenida Juan Bohón, La Serena's new Japanese garden has come a long way in a short time, but the landscaping still needs time to mature. Between the Panamericana and the downtown area, at the foot of Cordovez, the gardens are open from 10 am to 6 pm daily. Admission costs US$1.25.

Beaches

From the west end of Avenida Aguirre, south to Coquimbo, are a multitude of beaches suitable for various activities. On a two-week vacation in La Serena, you can visit a different beach every day, but strong rip currents make some of them unsuitable for swimming. Safe beaches include Playa Canto del Agua, Playa Las Gaviotas, Playa El Pescador, Playa La Marina, Playa La Barca, Playa Mansa, Playa Los Fuertes, Playa Blanca, Playa El Faro (Sur) and Playa Peñuelas (Coquimbo). Suitable only for sunbathing and paddle-ball are Playa Cuatro Esquinas, Playa El Faro (Norte), Playa Changa (Coquimbo), Playa Punta de Teatinos, Playa Los Choros, Playa Caleta Hornos, Playa San Pedro and Playa Chungungo. All of these have regular bus and taxi colectivo service from downtown La Serena.

To reach the popular resort of Tongoy, 58 km south of La Serena, catch a taxi colectivo from Calle Domeyko, a block-long street near the corner of Aguirre and Balmaceda.

Activities

Besides swimming and sunbathing, other popular activities include sailing (if you meet a member of the yacht club) and windsurfing. Windsurfers who do not respect the rights of swimmers within 200 meters of the beach may run afoul of the Gobernación Marítima.

Organized Tours

Diaguitas Tour (☎ 214129, fax 217265), Matta 510, Oficina 6, runs a series of tours in the Limarí and Elqui valleys to sites like Valle del Encanto, Parque Nacional Fray Jorge, Termas de Socos, Vicuña, the Pichasca petrified forest, and Region IV beaches. Prices for full-day tours run about US$30; the shorter La Serena city tour costs about half that. Fray Jorge Tour Service (☎ /fax 224542), Los Carrera 594 and Turismo San Bartolomé (☎ 211670, fax 221992), Balmaceda 417, Departamento 28, have similar offerings.

Special Events

In early January, the city hosts the Jornadas Musicales de La Serena, a series of musical events with more than a decade of history.

February's Feria del Libro, the annual book fair, displays the latest work by national and foreign publishing houses. Many prominent Chilean authors visit the city and give public lectures during this time.

Places to Stay

Many families who house students from the university rent to tourists only in summer, but may also have a spare bed at other times. Seasonal price differentials in La Serena are substantial; the prices below are high-season (January and February) prices, and off-season prices may be only a fraction of these.

Places to Stay – bottom end

Hostel Serena's Hostelling International affiliate is *Residencial Limmat* (☎ 211373), Lautaro 914, charging US$10.

Residenciales & Hotels *Residencial La Casona de Cantournet* (☎ 226439), Cantournet 815, formerly *Pensión López*, has spacious singles with comfortable beds and excellent hot showers for about US$7.50 per person. The entrance is through top-end Hotel Casablanca, Vicuña 414. Close to the bus terminal, reader-recommended *Residencial Jofré* (☎ 222-335), Regimiento Coquimbo 964, charges US$9 with breakfast.

Residencial El Loa (☎ 224663), O'Higgins 362, charges US$10 per person with shared bath; some rooms are dark, but others are fine. Friendly but unimpressive *Residencial Norte Verde* (☎ 213646), Cienfuegos 672, costs US$10 per person with shared bath, US$17.50 with private bath. Others in the same range include *Residencial Petit* (☎ 212536) at Eduardo de la Barra 586 and *Residencial El Silo* (☎ 213944), some distance from downtown at Larraín Alcalde 1550.

Highly regarded *Hostal de Turismo Croata* (☎ 224997), very central at Cienfuegos 248, costs US$11 per person with shared bath, but US$25/30 with private bath. Half a block from the plaza, *Residencial Lido* (☎ 213073), Matta 547, is good value for US$11; nearby at Matta 561, recommended *Residencial Chile* (☎ 211694) has garden singles/doubles for US$12.50 per person, but also has an inconvenient 1 am curfew. Breakfast costs an additional US$1.50.

The *Hotel Pacífico* (☎ 225674), recommended as very comfortable and friendly at Eduardo de la Barra 252, has rooms for US$12/18 with shared bath, US$15/24 with private bath, but maintenance is lagging. *Residencial Limmat* (☎ 211373), Lautaro 914, charges US$14, while the newly re-done, friendly and tidy *Residencial Suiza* (☎ 216092), Cienfuegos 250, is not really Swiss, but charges US$17/20 single/double.

Places to Stay – middle

Mid-range accommodation starts around US$24/38 with private bath at *Hotel Alameda* (☎ 213052), Avenida Aguirre 452. *Hotel Berlín* (☎ 222927, fax 223975), Cordovez 535, is slightly dearer at US$25/48.

The *Hotel El Escorial* (☎ 215193, fax 221433), Brasil 476, is an older building with some newer rooms that are less charming but more functional. Rates are US$30/40. The *Hotel de Turismo Brasilia* (☎ 225248, fax 211883), Brasil 555, charges US$38/54 with breakfast. Rooms vary considerably, but it can be a bargain in off-season prices of US$13/18 with shared bath, US$20/25 with breakfast and private bath. Modern, boxy *Hotel Pucará* (☎ 211966, fax 211933), Balmaceda 319, is a full-service hotel that charges US$43/50.

Places to Stay – top end

Rates at *Hotel Casablanca* (☎ 223506), Vicuña 414, are US$57/64 with breakfast, but some otherwise comfortable rooms are dark and small. Reader-recommended *Hotel Los Balcones de Alcalá* (☎ 225999), Avenida Aguirre 781, costs US$64/75.

The very central *Hotel Mediterráneo* (☎ 225837), fax 225838), Cienfuegos 509, has rooms with private bath for US$70/86. For US$92/108, the handsome *Hotel Francisco de Aguirre* (☎ 222991, Cordovez 210, comes highly recommended, but guests who are not early risers may be disturbed by the bells at the nearby Iglesia Santo Domingo.

Places to Eat

For superb, moderately priced seafood, any of the many restaurants in the Mercado La Recova complex at the corner of Cienfuegos and Cantournet is a good choice. Competition among them is so intense that reluctant diners can often get a free pisco sour with lunch. One personal favorite is *Caleta Hornos* (☎ 221152), Local 220. Next door, *Serena*, Local 219, is also recommendable.

The best fast-food choice, with a wide selection of surprisingly good cafeteria fare at low prices, is *Quick Biss Dos* (☎ 226300), Cienfuegos 545, 2nd floor. It also has a well-segregated tobacco-free area.

Café Plaza Real, Prat 465, has decent fixed-price lunches. The *Restaurant y Bar Croata* (☎ 224663), Balmaceda 871, has decent fixed-price lunches for about US$5, but the food is hardly Balkan. Popular *Grill Bar Serena*, Eduardo de la Barra 614, serves cheap seafood. For pizza, try *La Mía Pizza* (☎ 215063), O'Higgins 460.

Coffee, ice cream and desserts are outstanding at *Boccaccio* (☎ 222296), Prat 490, but a new favorite is *Gelatería Mammamia* (☎ 216032), Prat 220. *La Crisis*, Balmaceda 487, is another popular ice cream parlor and snack bar. For coffee, snacks and sandwiches, try *Café do Brasil* at Balmaceda 465.

El Cedro (☎ 221427), Prat 568, is a recommended, though pricey, Chilean/Middle

Eastern restaurant in pleasant surroundings. Rather cheaper is *El Amir*, O'Higgins 381. *Domingo Domínguez* (☎ 242779), on the beach at Avenida del Mar 5425, is a longtime local favorite.

Taiwan (☎ 214407), Cantournet 844, serves good Chinese food, as does *Mai Lan Fan* (☎ 214828), Cordovez 740.

Entertainment
Café del Patio, Prat 470, is an excellent small café that turns into a lively jazz and blues venue Friday and Saturday nights, but keeps long hours every day of the week. In summer, some of Santiago's best play the club, but the local bands that play the rest of the year are still worth hearing. Owner Rodrigo Sugg Pierry speaks very good English despite having lived in New York.

The *Muday Pub* (☎ 221556), Brasil 659, has live music on weekends, with a cover charge of US$7.50.

The *Cine Centenario*, Cordovez 399, shows recent films.

Things to Buy
Check Mercado La Recova, at Cienfuegos and Cantournet, for musical instruments, woolens and dried fruits from the Elqui valley. Other crafts are available at the Cema-Chile artisans' gallery, Los Carrera 562.

Getting There & Away
Air LanChile (☎ 225981), Cienfuegos 463, flies daily to and from Santiago (US$111); its Monday flight from Santiago continues to and returns from Copiapó. Ladeco (☎ 225753), Cordovez 484, stops in La Serena on its daily flights between Santiago and Copiapó, but also has another flight to Santiago daily except Saturday.

National Airlines (☎ 213510)), Prat 548, flies daily except Saturday to Santiago (US$83), daily except Thursday and Saturday to Copiapó (US$35), and Saturday to Iquique (US$197) and Asunción, Paraguay.

Alta (☎ 212832, fax 215671), Los Carrera 515, flies weekdays to Arica

(US$152), 12 times weekly to Antofagasta (US$106) and Iquique (US$127), nine times weekly to Calama (US$115), seven times weekly to Copiapó (US$32) and daily to Viña del Mar (US$54) and Concepción (US$97).

Bus – regional Southwest of downtown, at Amunátegui and Avenida El Santo, La Serena's Terminal de Buses (☎ 224573) also serves nearby Coquimbo. Many companies have offices there as well; when no address appears below, assume the office is at the terminal.

Buses Serenamar (☎ 213658), Avenida Francisco de Aguirre 344, runs eight buses daily to Guanaqueros (US$1.25) and Tongoy (US$1.50).

Via Elqui (☎ 225240) has five buses daily to Vicuña. Frontera Elqui (☎ 221-664), at Juan de Dios Pení and Coquimbo, serves the upper Elqui valley destinations of Vicuña, Paihuano, Monte Grande and Pisco Elqui daily.

Los Diamantes de Elqui (☎ 225555) goes to Vicuña and Ovalle, as does Expreso Norte (☎ 224857, 225503). Tas Choapa (☎ 225959, 224915) at O'Higgins 599, Lasval/Inca Bus (☎ 225627) at Cienfuegos 698, Buses Tal (☎ 226148, 225555) at Balmaceda 594, and Buses Palacios (☎ 224-448) at Amunátegui 251 also serve Ovalle. Postal Bus and Buses Carlos Araya, operating from the offices of Frontera Elqui, both have frequent service to Andacollo. Fares to regional destinations range from US$3 to US$5.

Bus – domestic Many companies ply the Panamericana routes, from Santiago to points north. Those serving Santiago include Buses Tal (☎ 225555), with the cheapest fares, Buses AMB (☎ 211545), Géminis (☎ 224018), Lasval/Inca Bus, Tramaca (☎ 226071) at Avenida Aguirre 375, Buses Lit (☎ 224880) at Cordovez 533, Flota Barrios (☎ 213394, 226361) at Domeyko 550, Los Diamantes del Elqui, Tas Choapa, Buses Palacios, Expreso Norte, Buses Libac (☎ 226101, 225172) at Francisco de Aguirre 432, and Pullman

Bus (☎ 225284), O'Higgins 663. Los Corsarios (☎ 225157), Lasval/Inca Bus and Pullman Bus all serve Valparaíso and Viña del Mar. Inca Bus and Pullman go daily to Illapel and Salamanca in the upper Choapa valley, northeast of Los Vilos.

For Copiapó and other northern destinations as far as Iquique and Arica, try Inca Bus, Flota Barrios, Libac, Pullman, Tramaca, Carmelita (☎ 221664) or Fénix Pullman Norte (☎ 225555, 226148) at Balmaceda 594. Tur-Bus has acquired the extensive routes of Flecha Dorada and Chilebus.

Destinations and typical fares include Santiago (US$17, seven hours), Valparaíso/Viña del Mar (US$17, seven hours), Los Vilos (US$9, three hours), Illapel or Salamanca (US$10, four hours), Vallenar (US$6), Copiapó (US$8), Chañaral (US$10), Antofagasta (US$30), Calama (US$31), Iquique (US$40) and Arica (US$50). Salón cama service to Iquique or Arica costs US$62.

Bus – international In the summer months, Wednesdays and Sundays at 11 pm, Covalle Bus (☎ 213127), Infante 538, connects La Serena with the Argentine cities of Mendoza (US$35, 12 hours) and San Juan (US$45, 14 hours) via the Libertadores tunnel.

Taxi Colectivo Many regional destinations are more frequently and rapidly served by taxi colectivo. Tasco (☎ 227379), Domeyko 524, goes to Andacollo, Ovalle and Tongoy. Línea Ruta 41 (☎ 224517), also at Domeyko 524, goes to upper Elqui valley destinations like Vicuña and Paihuano.

Getting Around
To/From the Airport Cabs to La Serena's Aeropuerto La Florida, a short distance east of downtown on Chile 41 to Vicuña and the Elqui valley, cost only a couple dollars.

Car Rental For rental cars, try the Automóvil Club de Chile (☎ 225279) at Eduardo de la Barra 435, Hertz (☎ 225471) at Aguirre 0225 (west of the Panameri-

cana), Budget (☎ 225057) at Aguirre 0240, or Dollar (☎ 225714) at Aguirre 058. Lesser known local agencies include Rally Daire (☎ 226933) at Prat 645, Oceanic (☎ 214007) at Avenida Aguirre 062 and Gala (☎ 221400) at Huanhualí 435.

AROUND LA SERENA
Coquimbo
In the rocky hills of Península Coquimbo, between the Bahía de Coquimbo and the smaller Bahía Herradura de Guayacán, the bustling port of Coquimbo (population 106,000) takes its name from a Diaguita word meaning 'place of calm waters' – even Darwin remarked that it was 'remarkable for nothing but its extreme quietness.' Though now livelier, especially on a Saturday night, it's a less attractive place to stay than La Serena (even though Coquimbo no longer suffers the voracious fleas that plagued Darwin during his visit).

Half-hour boat tours of the harbor depart from the Avenida Costanera daily between 10 am and 8 pm, charging US$1 for adults and US$0.50 for children. There are very popular beaches along the Bahia Herradura de Guayacán, easily reached from either Coquimbo or La Serena.

Excellent budget accommodation is available at *Hotel Iberia* (☎ 312141), Lastra 400, for about US$11 per person with private bath and TV. For a gastronomic change of pace, try Middle Eastern fare at *Restaurant Arabe*, Alcalde 527, Chinese food at *Mai Lan Fan* (☎ 315615), Avenida Ossandón 1, or Italian at *Tavola Calda*, Bilbao 451. For seafood visit *La Picada* (☎ 311214) on the Avenida Costanera or, for parrillada, *El Brasero* at Avenida Alessandri 113.

Guanaqueros
At the south end of Bahía Guanaqueros, five km west of the Panamericana, Guanaqueros' long white sandy beach makes it one of the area's most popular resorts. *Hotel La Bahía* (☎ 391380), Avenida Costanera 274, is open all year. *El Pequeño Restaurant* (☎ 391341), Avenida Costanera 306, is worth a stopover in town.

Tongoy

On a rocky peninsula, the lively beach resort of Tongoy is Blackpool or the Jersey shore with a Latin feel, thanks to its artisans' market, family-oriented beachfront restaurants and souvenir baubles.

Hotel Plaza (☎ 391184), Fundición Norte 29, has good singles with shared bath for US$16, slightly more with private bath, and reasonably priced seafood (lunch with two huge crab empanadas, a fish entrée, salad and ice cream costs US$7). The moderately priced marisquerías along the southside Playa Grande are even more enjoyable places to spend the afternoon and watch the action. Playa Socos, on the north side of the peninsula, is more sheltered.

Observatorio Interamericano Cerro Tololo

At 2200 meters above sea level, 88 km southeast of La Serena, Cerro Tololo's four-meter telescope is the largest in the Southern Hemisphere. The Tucson-based Association of Universities for Research in Astronomy (Aura), a group of about 25 institutions including the Universidad de Chile, is responsible for its operation.

To visit Cerro Tololo, make reservations by contacting the office in La Serena (☎ 225415, fax 205212, see the Online Services appendix). There is no public transport, so car rental or hiring a taxi is pretty much the only option.

VICUÑA

In the upper Elqui valley, logos bearing the names of Capel, Control and Tres Erres piscos are as conspicuous as international soft drink billboards in the rest of the country. Vicuña (population 7700), 62 km east of La Serena, is a quiet village of adobe houses in an area that grows avocados, papayas and other fruits, but most notably provides the raw grapes that local distilleries transform into Chile's powerful brandy. Suitable either for a day trip or a few days' stay, Vicuña and its surrounding area have also acquired an oddball reputation with the arrival of several groups convinced that UFOs frequent the area.

The Starry Southern Skies

Inland from the perpetually fogbound coast, in the western foothills of the Andes, the Norte Chico hosts the most important cluster of astronomical observatories in the Southern Hemisphere, and one of the most important in the world. Within 150 km of La Serena are three major facilities: the Cerro Tololo Interamerican Observatory (CTIO) above the Elqui valley, plus the European Southern Observatory (ESO) at La Silla, and the Carnegie Institution's Observatorio Las Campanas, both east of the Panamericana on the border between Regions III and IV.

The importance of these and other observatories is likely to increase in the coming years with construction of seven major telescopes – five of them eight meters in diameter, the other two six meters in diameter. The biggest project is ESO's trapezoidal Very Large Telescope (VLT) at Cerro Paranal, 120 km south of Antofagasta, but the Carnegie Institution will also add two more at Las Campanas. At present, CTIO's four-meter instrument is the Southern Hemisphere's largest.

Chile is doing its best to encourage research, as Congress has granted customs benefits to astronomers, but the country also hopes to encourage more local participation through supervision by its Comisión Nacional de Ciencia y Tecnología (National Commission on Science and Technology). Chile's small community of 30 or so astronomers will be guaranteed a certain amount of research time on facilities that have invested US$1.5 billion. ∎

Orientation

On the north bank of the Río Elqui, across a narrow bridge from the La Serena highway, Vicuña has a very regular town plan centered on the Plaza de Armas. Avenida Gabriela Mistral, running east-west off the plaza, is the main commercial street. Every important service or feature is within easy walking distance.

WAYNE BERNHARDSON
Replica of death mask of
Gabriela Mistral, Vicuña

Information

Tourist Office The Municipalidad's information office in the Torre Bauer (see below), at the northwest corner of the Plaza de Armas, is open weekdays only, 9 am to 1 pm and 1.45 to 5.30 pm.

Money Banco del Estado, on the south side of the Plaza de Armas, offers notoriously poor rates for cash only; it's much better to change in La Serena.

Post & Communications Vicuña's area code is ☎ 51, the same as La Serena's. Correos de Chile is in the Municipalidad, at the corner of Mistral and San Martín. CTC's long-distance office is at Prat 378, half a block north of the plaza. Entel is on the west side of the plaza, on San Martín, while Chilesat is on the east side, on Prat.

Medical Services Vicuña's hospital (☎ 411263) is at the corner of Independencia and Prat, a few blocks north of the plaza.

Things to See

Built by a former German mayor, the **Torre Bauer** (1905), an eccentric clock tower on the Plaza de Armas, resembles a castle with wooden battlements. At Chacabuco 334, on the south side of the plaza, the **Museo Entomológico y de Historia Natural** (☎ 411283) specializes in insects. In summer, it's open 9.30 am to 9.30 pm daily, the rest of the year, hours are 10 am to 1 pm and 3 to 8 pm. Admission costs US$0.50.

Dating from 1875, the **Casa de los Madariaga** (☎ 411220), Gabriela Mistral 683, contains furnishings and artifacts from an influential early family. It's open daily 11 am to 1 pm and 3 to 5 pm; admission costs US$1. The **Museo Histórico de Elqui**, Prat 90, has Diaguita artifacts.

Museo Gabriela Mistral

Vicuña's landmark museum is a tangible eulogy to one of Chile's most famous literary figures, born Lucila Godoy Alcayaga in 1889, in the nearby village of Monte Grande. Despite a bust that makes her seem a particularly strict and severe schoolmarm, exhibits include a very handsomely presented photographic history of her life, plus modest personal artifacts such as her desk and a bookcase, and a replica of her adobe birthplace. Her family tree indicates Spanish, Indian and even African ancestry. Like Pablo Neruda, she served in the Chilean diplomatic corps.

The museum (☎ 411223) is on Avenida Gabriela Mistral (where else?) between Riquelme and Baquedano. Admission costs US$1. It's open Tuesday to Friday 9 am to 1 pm and 3 to 7 pm, Saturday 10 am to 1 pm and 3.30 to 6.30 pm, and Sunday 10 am to 1 pm.

Planta Capel

Capel, a cooperative with member growers throughout the Norte Chico from Copiapó to Illapel, distills part of its production at this facility, where grapes arrive in vehicles ranging from tractors and pickups to 18-wheelers. The cooperative also has its only bottling plant here. The process of distilling takes eight to 12 months, depending on the desired strength of the pisco.

Tours of the plant, across the bridge from Vicuña, are available weekdays every half hour, 9.30 am to noon and 2.30 to 6 pm, Saturdays and holidays 10 am to 12.30 am only. Mornings are best, since many Chileans are late risers and there is no minimum required – guides literally provide individual attention if only one person shows up, with free samples on conclusion. In addition to pisco, the sales room also offers pajarete, the region's delicious dessert wine.

Special Events

Vicuña holds its annual grape harvest festival, Festival de la Vendimia, in February.

Places to Stay

Vicuña has plenty of reasonable lodging. Camping is available at shady *Las Tinajas* (☎ 411731) for US$6 per site, which also includes access to the municipal swimming pool.

Residencial La Moderna (☎ 411790), Gabriela Mistral 718, is the cheapest regular accommodation for US$6 per person with shared bath, but more expensive rooms with private bath are also available. *Hostal Michel*, Gabriela Mistral 573, is also moderately priced.

Warmly recommended *Residencial La Elquina* (☎ 411317), O'Higgins 65, costs US$10/18 single/double with shared bath, US$18/30 with private bath, in an attractive house with lush gardens and fruit trees.

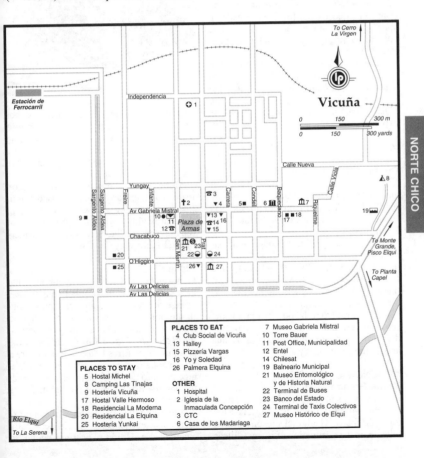

PLACES TO STAY
5   Hostal Michel
8   Camping Las Tinajas
9   Hostería Vicuña
17 Hostal Valle Hermoso
18 Residencial La Moderna
20 Residencial La Elquina
25 Hostería Yunkai

PLACES TO EAT
4   Club Social de Vicuña
13 Halley
15 Pizzería Vargas
16 Yo y Soledad
26 Palmera Elquina

OTHER
1   Hospital
2   Iglesia de la Inmaculada Concepción
3   CTC
6   Casa de los Madariaga
7   Museo Gabriela Mistral
10 Torre Bauer
11 Post Office, Municipalidad
12 Entel
14 Chilesat
19 Balneario Municipal
21 Museo Entomológico y de Historia Natural
22 Terminal de Buses
23 Banco del Estado
24 Terminal de Taxis Colectivos
27 Museo Histórico de Elqui

NORTE CHICO

Hostal Valle Hermoso (☎ 411206), Gabriela Mistral 706, charges US$18/25.

Toward the upper end of the scale, *Hostería Yunkai* (☎ 411593), O'Higgins 72, costs US$38/50. Vicuña's ritziest accommodation is *Hostería Vicuña* (☎ 411301, fax 411144) at Sargento Aldea 101, where singles/doubles cost US$72/95. It also has the town's best restaurant.

Places to Eat
There are several modest restaurants, including *Yo y Soledad* (☎ 411368) at Mistral 448 and the nearby *Halley* (☎ 411-225) at Mistral 404 (whose name is no doubt inspired by the local space cadets), specifically recommended for its pastel de choclo. *Pizzería Vargas* (☎ 411090) is at Prat 234.

Palmera Elquina, at O'Higgins 398 across from the bus terminal, is a good spot for a snack and also, apparently, the only choice for an early breakfast. The *Club Social de Vicuña*, Mistral 445, is expensive but has a good menu in an attractive setting. Consider also the hotel restaurants, especially at Hostería Vicuña.

Getting There & Away
Vicuña's new Terminal de Buses is at Prat and O'Higgins, one block south of the plaza. Elqui Mar, Frontera Elqui and Vía Elqui go to La Serena, Coquimbo and Pisco Elqui (US$2).

Pullman Bus goes to Santiago and Valparaíso/Viña del Mar, while Los Diamantes de Elqui, Buses Tal (☎ 411404) and Expreso Norte (☎ 411348) also go to Santiago. There's a wider selection of destinations, especially northbound, in La Serena.

Across Prat from the bus terminal is the separate Terminal de Taxis Colectivos, the departure point for shared taxis to Vicuña and up the Elqui valley.

AROUND VICUÑA
Monte Grande
Reached by local bus or taxi colectivo from Vicuña, Monte Grande is Gabriela Mistral's birthplace. Her burial site, on a nearby hillside, is the destination of many Chilean

Gabriela Mistral

and literary pilgrims. She received her primary schooling at the **Casa Escuela y Correo**, a modest museum open daily except Monday 9.30 am to 1 pm and 3 to 7 pm in summer; the rest of the year, hours are 10 am to 1 pm and 3 to 6 pm.

Monte Grande has no accommodation itself, but there are hotels in Pisco Elqui, just up the valley, and several cabañas in the nearby village of **Cochiguaz** (center of the universe for the New Age space cadets of the Elqui valley).

Pisco Elqui
Opportunistically renamed to publicize the area's most famous product, the former village of La Unión is a placid community in the upper drainage of the Río Claro, a tributary of the Elqui. Its main attraction, the **Solar de Pisco Elqui**, produces the premium Tres Erres brand; while they're a bit disorganized as far as tours go, it's a nice place to taste free samples and inspect the antique machinery of the old distillery and bodegas.

According to local legend, Chilean President Gabriel González Videla personally changed La Unión's original name to undermine Peruvian claims to have originated the beverage (the provincial city of Pisco, in the valley of the same name south of Lima, also produces the drink).

Places to Stay & Eat *Camping El Olivo* charges US$6 per person, including pool access and showers, and also has a simple restaurant. Congenial *Hostal Don Juan* (☎ 451087), on Arturo Prat, charges US$20 for up to three persons in a dilapidated but intriguing old building.

Hotel Elqui (☎ 451083) on O'Higgins charges US$18 per person with breakfast, including use of pool; non-guests may use the pool for US$6. Lunches are reasonable for about US$6. *Hotel Carillón* (☎ 451-086), Prat 59, has good food, but is less appealing than the Elqui; rates are US$38 double.

OVALLE

Founded as a satellite of older La Serena in the early republican era, Ovalle is the spotlessly clean capital of the prosperous agricultural province of Limarí; its beautifully landscaped Plaza de Armas has both sunny and shady areas. Although the city is half an hour east of the Panamericana, many north-south buses pass through here.

Orientation

On the north bank of the Río Limarí, Ovalle (population 51,000) sits 90 km south of La Serena and 30 km east of the Panamericana. Everything of interest is within easy walking distance of the Plaza de Armas.

Information

Tourist Offices Ovalle's ostensible tourist office is a kiosk at the southeast corner of the Plaza de Armas, but it's rarely staffed. Should the kiosk be abandoned, try the Automóvil Club de Chile (☎ 620001) at Libertad 144, whose staff are friendly, helpful and competent.

Money It's better to change elsewhere, but try Chiletur, Aguirre 373, for US cash only. There are several ATMs, including Banco de Crédito and Banco Santander, on opposite corners at Vicuña Mackenna and Victoria.

Post & Communications Ovalle's area code is ☎ 53. Correos de Chile is opposite the plaza, on Vicuña Mackenna between Victoria and Miguel Aguirre. CTC's long-distance office is at Vicuña Mackenna 499, a block west of the plaza, while Entel is at Vicuña Mackenna 115. Chilesat is on Vicuña Mackenna between Aguirre and Arauco.

Laundry Center-Lav is at Arauco 208-B.

Medical Services Ovalle's Hospital Dr Antonio Tirado (☎ 620042) is at the north end of Ariztía Poniente, between Socos and Los Pescadores.

Museo del Limarí

Ovalle's archaeological museum is a modest endeavor stressing the trans-Andean links between the Diaguita peoples of coastal Chile and northwest Argentina, although there are also pieces from the earlier Huentelauquén and Molle cultures. Some of the larger ceramics are in exceptionally fine condition.

At Independencia 329, the museum is open Monday 9 am to 1 pm and 3 to 7 pm, Tuesday through Friday 8 am to 1 pm and 3 to 7 pm, and weekends and holidays 10 am to 1 pm only. Admission costs US$1 for adults, half that for children.

Feria Modelo de Ovalle

Ovalle's lively fruit and vegetable market occupies the former repair facilities of the railroad. Also a good place to look for crafts, it's open Monday, Wednesday, Friday and Saturday from 8 am to 4 pm. Follow Vicuña Mackenna east across Ariztía, where its name changes to Avenida Benavente.

Organized Tours

For excursions to Fray Jorge, Valle del Encanto and elsewhere in the province, contact Chiletur (☎ 625281), Aguirre 373.

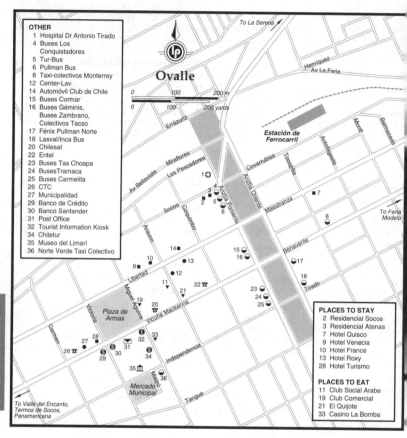

OTHER
1 Hospital Dr Antonio Tirado
4 Buses Los
   Conquistadores
5 Tur-Bus
6 Pullman Bus
8 Taxi-colectivos Monterrey
12 Center-Lav
14 Automóvil Club de Chile
15 Buses Cormar
16 Buses Géminis,
    Buses Zambrano,
    Colectivos Tacso
17 Fénix Pullman Norte
18 Lasval/Inca Bus
20 Chilesat
22 Entel
23 Buses Tas Choapa
24 BusesTramaca
25 Buses Carmelita
26 CTC
27 Municipalidad
29 Banco de Crédito
30 Banco Santander
31 Post Office
32 Tourist Information Kiosk
34 Chiletur
35 Museo del Limarí
36 Norte Verde Taxi Colectivo

Ovalle

To La Serena

Estación de
Ferrocarril

To Feria
Modelo

PLACES TO STAY
2 Residencial Socos
3 Residencial Atenas
7 Hotel Quisco
9 Hotel Venecia
10 Hotel France
13 Hotel Roxy
28 Hotel Turismo

PLACES TO EAT
11 Club Social Arabe
19 Club Comercial
21 El Quijote
33 Casino La Bomba

To Valle del Encanto,
Termos de Socos,
Panamericana

Places to Stay

Basic but passable *Hotel France* (☎ 620-828), Libertad 231, costs only US$7.50/13 single/double. *Hotel Venecia* (☎ 620968), nearby at Libertad 261, is comparable.

Hotel Roxy (☎ 620080), Libertad 155, is one of Chile's best hotel values for US$11/20 single/double with shared bath, US$16/28 with private bath. It's very friendly and clean, with a huge, attractive patio. *Hotel Quisco* (☎ 620351), Maestranza 161, has singles for US$11 with shared bath, US$20 with private bath. Also

worth a look are *Residencial Atenas*, Socos 12, which also has a restaurant, and *Residencial Socos*, Socos 22.

Ovalle's finest, the remodeled and much improved *Hotel Turismo* (☎ 623258), Victoria 295 at Vicuña Mackenna, charges US$38/50 single/double, but it's still not three times better than the Roxy.

Places to Eat

There are many reasonable places to eat along Calle Independencia, near the Mercado Municipal.

For good fixed-price lunches, try *Casino La Bomba* at Aguirre 364, the *Club Comercial* at Aguirre 244 or the *Club Social Arabe* (☎ 620015), Arauco 255, which offers Middle Eastern specialties like stuffed grape leaves. A personal favorite, however, is the unrepentantly political *El Quijote* (☎ 620501), Arauco 298, which covers its walls with images of leftist icons like Salvador Allende and Federico García Lorca, poems by Pablo Neruda, and the Universal Declaration of Human Rights, but still manages to serve excellent meals with friendly but unobsequious service.

Getting There & Away
Bus North-south bus services closely resemble those from La Serena, though some companies using the Panamericana bypass Ovalle. There is no central bus terminal, but most companies have offices on the west side of Ariztía, with others across the street or nearby.

Tur-Bus (☎ 621125), Ariztía Poniente 143, has extensive north- and southbound services. Other long-distance companies include Los Conquistadores at Ariztía Poniente 135, Pullman Bus (☎ 621476) at Ariztía Poniente 159, Tas Choapa (☎ 620-500) at Ariztía Poniente 371, Tramaca (☎ 620656) at Ariztía Poniente 379, and Carmelita (☎ 620656) at Ariztía Poniente 391. Géminis, Zambrano and Colectivos Tacso (for La Serena and Coquimbo) share an office (☎ 620430) at Ariztía Poniente 245.

Fénix Pullman Norte (☎ 621371) is at Ariztía Oriente 324, Lasval/Inca Bus (☎ 621574, 620886) at Ariztía Oriente 398; Inca Bus provides provincial services to the interior destinations like Combarbalá and Chañaral Alto. Cormar (☎ 620195), Ariztía Poniente 219, also provides regional services. Línea Las Condes, at the Mercado Municipal, goes to Punitaqui.

Taxi Colectivo Norte Verde, at the corner of Independencia and Miguel Aguirre, has frequent service to Punitaqui between 7.30 am and 8.30 pm. There are frequent colectivos to La Chimba from Tocopilla and Benavente, daily from 7 am to 9 pm. For Monte Patria, Sotaquí and Embalse La Paloma, try Taxi-colectivos Monterrey (☎ 621698), Benavente 114, daily between 6.30 am and 8 pm.

AROUND OVALLE
Monumento Arqueológico
Valle del Encanto
Valle del Encanto, a rocky tributary canyon of the Río Limarí, contains a remarkable density of Indian petroglyphs, pictographs and mortars from the El Molle culture, which inhabited the area from the 2nd to the 7th century AD. Views of the rock art are best in the early afternoon, when shadows are fewer, but it can be very hot.

Both picnicking and camping (with permission) are possible at Valle del Encanto, 19 km west of Ovalle. To get there, take any westbound bus out of Ovalle toward Termas de Socos and disembark at the highway marker; Valle del Encanto is an easy five-km walk along a clearly marked gravel road, but with luck, someone will offer a lift. Bring water for the hike, although there is potable water in the canyon itself.

Under the protection of the Municipalidad de Ovalle, the Monumento Arqueológico charges US$0.75 admission for adults, US$0.25 for children. On weekends, a concessionaire sells sandwiches and snacks.

Termas de Socos
Termas de Socos, a short distance off the Panamericana at Km 370, 100 km south of La Serena and 33 km west of Ovalle, has great thermal baths and swimming pools. Private tubs cost US$6 per person for an hour's hot soak.

Camp sites, including pool access, cost US$30 for up to five persons; a rustic cabaña with two beds costs US$37. Accommodation at *Hotel Termas de Socos* (☎ 621373) starts at US$35 per person with breakfast, rising to US$65 per person with full board. Reservations are also available in Santiago (☎ (02) 6816692).

Monumento Natural Pichasca

In the foothills 45 km northeast of Ovalle, Pichasca guards 128 hectares of petrified forest along the Río Hurtado. Local buses from Ovalle go as far as Samo Alto, 10 km to the west. Visitors with automobiles can take the gravel road north to or south from Vicuña.

Pichasca is open 9 am to 6 pm daily. Admission costs US$4 for foreigners, US$1 for children. Chileans pay US$1 for adults, US$0.25 for children.

PARQUE NACIONAL FRAY JORGE

Moistened by the camanchaca of the Pacific Ocean, Parque Nacional Fray Jorge is an ecological island of Valdivian cloud forest in an otherwise semi-arid region, 110 km south of La Serena and 82 km west of Ovalle. Where Illapel, for instance, gets only about 150 mm of rainfall per annum, Fray Jorge receives up to 10 times that to support a vegetation more closely resembling the verdant forests of southern Chile than the Mediterranean scrub that covers most of the Norte Chico. Elevations range from sea level to 600 meters.

Of Fray Jorge's 10,000 hectares, there remain only 400 hectares of this truly unique vegetation – enough, however, to make it a Unesco World Biosphere Reserve. Consequently, it is an area of great interest to scientists, but also open to the public on a limited scale. Some believe that this relict vegetation is evidence of dramatic climate change, but others argue that humans destroyed these once-extensive forests for fuel, farming and timber.

The first recorded European visitor was a Franciscan priest named Fray Jorge in 1672. Darwin, surprisingly and unfortunately, overlooked the area when he turned inland from the coastal road and passed through Illapel instead. What he missed, at elevations above 450 meters where the effect of the ocean fog is most pronounced, were stands of *olivillo (Aetoxicon punctatum), arrayán* (myrtle, *Myrceugenia correaeifolia)* and *canelo (Drimys winteri),* plus countless other shrubs and epiphytes. The few mammals include two species of

fox *(Dusicyon culpaeus* and *Dusicyon griseus),* skunks and otters. There are some 80 bird species, including the occasional Andean condor.

Information

Fray Jorge is open to the general public in summer (January 1 to March 15) Thursday to Sunday, plus holidays, 8.30 am to 6 pm; the rest of the year, it's open weekends only. Note that, because of staff limitations, the gated road may be locked outside these hours so that theoretically no one can enter or leave, but in practice, they're a bit more flexible.

Park admission is US$2 for Chilean citizens, US$4 for foreigners; children pay half. There is a Centro de Información in the process of development, with interesting photographic displays, but little progress has been made over the past several years.

Activities

In late afternoon, the rising camanchaca moistens the dense vegetation at **Sendero El Bosque,** a so-called interpretive trail that runs for one km along the ridge above the ocean (the interpretation consists of labeling common Spanish names on a few of the most conspicuous tree species). The best time to appreciate the forest's ecological characteristics, however, is early morning, when condensation from the fog leaves the plants dripping with moisture.

A short distance inland from the main forest, contrasting with the parched semi-desert of the surrounding hills, discontinuous patches of green suggest that the forest must once have been far more extensive. The trail is at the end of the road from the Panamericana, seven km from the campground at El Arrayancito. Hikers will find the last segment of the road to the trailhead very steep and dusty.

With permission from Conaf, it's possible to walk down the fire trail from the ridge to the coast. From the park Administración, an historic building that was once the casco for a local hacienda and is three km from the Centro de Información, it's possible to walk 15 km to a beach camp-site, but Conaf discourages hikers from this route because part of it goes through private property.

Places to Stay

The only option in the park itself is to camp at sheltered El Arrayancito, three km from the visitor center and seven km west of El Bosque. For US$10, each of its 13 sites has a fireplace (fuelwood is available), a picnic table, potable water, clean toilets and cold showers and plenty of annoying bugs.

Bring all supplies, since nothing is available in the park itself (except for free figs and pears in late summer).

Getting There & Away

Fray Jorge is reached by a westward lateral off the Panamericana, about 15 km north of its junction with the paved highway to Ovalle and about two km north of a Carabineros checkpoint. There is no regular public transport, but several agencies offer tours out of La Serena and Ovalle (see the respective city entries).

North-south buses can drop you at the clearly marked junction, which is 22 km from the park itself – walking it is no picnic, but hitching may be feasible. Hitching out may be easier than hitching in, so ask tour companies if you can leave the tour and perhaps even return another day.

LOS VILOS

Up to 20,000 visitors jam the working-class beach resort of Los Vilos (permanent population 8000) in the peak summer season. Midway between Santiago and La Serena, it has plenty of inexpensive accommodation, fine seafood, and is especially lively Sunday mornings when the Caleta San Pedro market offers live fresh crab, dozens of kinds of fish, a roving hurdy-gurdy man and thousands of colorful balloons.

According to local legend, the name Los

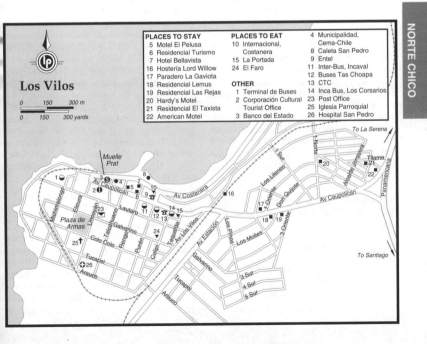

Los Vilos

0   150   300 m
0   150   300 yards

PLACES TO STAY	PLACES TO EAT	4	Municipalidad, Cema-Chile
5 Motel El Pelusa	10 Internacional,	8	Caleta San Pedro
6 Residencial Turismo	Costanera	9	Entel
7 Hotel Bellavista	15 La Portada	11	Inter-Bus, Incaval
16 Hostería Lord Willow	24 El Faro	12	Buses Tas Choapa
17 Paradero La Gaviota		13	CTC
18 Residencial Lemus	OTHER	14	Inca Bus, Los Corsarios
19 Residencial Las Rejas	1 Terminal de Buses	23	Post Office
20 Hardy's Motel	2 Corporación Cultural	25	Iglesia Parroquial
21 Residencial El Taxista	Tourist Office	26	Hospital San Pedro
22 American Motel	3 Banco del Estado		

NORTE CHICO

Vilos is a corruption of Lord Willow, a British privateer that shipwrecked nearby. A likelier alternative is that it comes from the Araucanian *vilú*, a term that means 'serpent' or 'snake,' and is common elsewhere in the region.

Orientation

Los Vilos consists of two distinct areas, an older part with a regular grid west of the railroad tracks, and a newer, less regular section between the tracks and the Panamericana. Avenida Costanera, leading to the beach, is a much more important focus of activity than the Plaza de Armas. Most hotels and restaurants are along Avenida Caupolicán, which links the town with the Panamericana.

Information

Tourist Office From December to February, Los Vilos' Corporación Cultural operates a tourist information office at Caupolicán 278, open 10 am to 10 pm daily. The staff are competent and helpful.

Money Banco del Estado is on Caupolicán near the pier, but foreign visitors are few and rates are poor, so it's better to change in Santiago or La Serena.

Post & Communications The area code in Los Vilos is ☎ 53. Correos de Chile is opposite the plaza, at the corner of Lincoyán and Galvarino. CTC's long-distance offices are on Caupolicán between Purén and Tequalda, while Entel is on Caupolicán near Purén, in front of the restaurant Internacional.

Medical Services Los Vilos' Hospital San Pedro (☎ 541061) is on Lincoyán, two blocks south of the plaza.

Things to See & Do

In addition to the usual beach activities, local launches tour the harbor daily between 10 and 2 pm, and 3 to 7 pm, leaving from Caleta San Pedro, which also has a lively fish market with several cheap restaurants.

Special Events

Early February's **Semana Vileña** (Vilos Week) is the town's biggest celebration.

Places to Stay

At Tilama 247, *Residencial El Taxista* is nearer the highway than the beach, but has comfortable singles with TV and shared bath for US$8. Although the entrance is through a bar, it is friendly and quiet, and not a bad place at all. The hospedaje *Paradero La Gaviota* (☎ 541236), Caupolicán 1259, has singles/doubles for US$7/12, as well as campsites for US$3 per person (with a four-person minimum). Inspect your room first at *Residencial Lemus*, on Caupolicán near Los Molles, where singles cost US$8, and watch for overcharging at nearby *Residencial Las Rejas* (☎ 541026), Caupolicán 1310, which should cost about US$10.

Hotel Bellavista (☎ 541196), popular and central at Rengo 020, charges US$20 per person with breakfast and shared bath, US$30 with private bath; it also has a very fine restaurant, with huge portions. There are good reports on *Residencial Turismo* (☎ 541176), Caupolicán 437, which charges US$12.50 per person.

Hostería Lord Willow (☎ 541037), Avenida Los Vilos 1444, costs US$20 per person with private bath and ocean view. In shady grounds at the junction of Caupolicán and the Panamericana, the excellent *American Motel* (☎ 541020, fax 541163), charges US$41/55, while *Hardy's Motel* (☎ 541098), Avenida 1 Norte 248, costs US$46/49. At *Motel El Pelusa* (☎ 541041), more central at Caupolicán 411, rates are US$49/65.

Places to Eat

Besides the Hotel Bellavista restaurant, *El Faro* (☎ 541190) at Colipí 224 is also highly regarded. Beachfront cafés along the costanera are cheap and good, especially *El Refugio del Pescador* at Caleta San Pedro, and *Costanera* (☎ 541010) and *Internacional*, both at Purén 80, facing the beach. *La Portada*, at the corner of Caupolicán and Tequalda, is also worth a look.

Getting There & Away

Few buses enter Los Vilos proper, but the town has refurbished the former railroad station, at the west end of Caupolicán, as its Terminal de Buses; some companies also maintain separate offices on Caupolicán. It's also possible to flag a bus either north or south from the junction of Caupolicán with the Panamericana – if you get hungry waiting, there's a good snack bar at the Copec petrol station.

Companies that do stop in town include Pullman Bus (to Santiago), Dhino's (to Santiago), Inter-Bus (to Valparaíso/Viña del Mar) and Incaval (to Santiago) on Caupolicán near Purén, Inca Bus/Los Corsarios (☎ 541578, to Santiago and La Serena) at Caupolicán 798, and Tas Choapa (☎ 541032, to Santiago, Illapel and Salamanca) at Caupolicán 712. Tur-Bus goes daily to Arica.

PICHIDANGUI

Thirty km south of Los Vilos, Pichidangui is a small, pleasant but more exclusive beach resort with many hotels and campgrounds. *Residencial Lucero* (☎ 533106), besides accommodation for US$15 per person, has an excellent seafood restaurant with reasonable prices. Conspicuously tight security probably means General Pinochet is staying at his beachfront house.

NORTE CHICO

La Araucanía & Los Lagos

Few landscapes can equal or surpass the beauty of those beyond the Río Biobío, where Fuji-like volcanic cones, blanketed by glaciers, tower above deep blue lakes, ancient forests and verdant farmland. Outside the cities, the loudest sound is the roar of waterfalls spilling over cliffs into limpid pools, but it was not always so tranquil. In the early 17th century, Mapuche resistance reduced Spanish settlements south of the Biobío to ashes and ruin.

The region's most important cities are Temuco, Valdivia, Osorno and Puerto Montt, but about half the population still lives in the countryside. Tourism plays a major role in the economy, but forest products (chain saws can drown out some waterfalls), cereals, dairy farming and livestock are also important. Local industries, such as sawmills and leather works, depend on these primary products.

Temuco, in Region IX of La Araucanía, is the starting point for exploring the area. From Temuco, travelers can visit Parque Nacional Conguillío and the upper reaches of the Biobío, head south to Lago Villarrica and Pucón, work their way to Lican Ray beside Lago Calafquén, on to Lago Panguipulli, and then to Futrono on Lago Ranco.

Farther south, east of Osorno, the Lago Puyehue route offers an easy land crossing to Argentina via Parque Nacional Puyehue, while Puerto Varas and Ensenada, on Lago Llanquihue, are stops on the route to Lago Todos Los Santos in Parque Nacional Vicente Pérez Rosales, with a ferry from Petrohué to Peulla. From Peulla, it's possible to cross to Bariloche, Argentina by a combination of boats and buses.

Puerto Montt, on the Golfo de Reloncaví, is the capital of Region X of Los Lagos and the gateway to the Chiloé archipelago and the remote, enthralling regions of Aisén and Magallanes. Despite construction and improvements on Ruta 7, the Camino Austral, the southern mainland of Region X remains accessible by road only through the Argentine province of Chubut. While the segment of this highway from Caleta Gonzalo and Chaitén south to the Río Palena is part of Region X, it is covered in the Aisén chapter.

Travelers hoping to visit the many national parks in these areas should acquire Lonely Planet's *Trekking in the Patagonian Andes*, which covers many extended walks in Conguillío, Huerquehue, Villarrica, Puyehue, Vicente Pérez Rosales and Alerce Andino national parks. It also includes several walks across the border in Argentina.

HISTORY

South of Concepción, Spanish conquistadors found small gold mines, good farmland and a large potential Indian work force; some lands were so tempting that conquistadors surrendered their central valley encomiendas for grants south of the Biobío. Despite their optimism, this area was a dangerous frontier and its settlements were constantly under the threat of Mapuche attack or natural hazards. Spanish soldier-poet Alonso de Ercilla immortalized the Mapuche resistance in his epic *La Araucana*, a classic of its genre and of Spanish literature; see the sidebar in the Middle Chile chapter.

The Mapuche constantly besieged settlements like Osorno and Valdivia, especially in the general rebellion of 1598. By the mid-17th century, the Spaniards had abandoned most of the area except for a resettled and heavily fortified Valdivia; another century passed before they reclaimed settlements south of the Biobío. In the early 19th century, foreign travelers commonly referred to 'Arauco' as a separate country, and it was not until the 1880s that treaties made the area safe for European settlement. Eventually, the Mapuche lost much of their

Common Mapuche Words & Phrases

Mapudungun, Chile's mostly widely spoken indigenous language, has great practical significance to its native speakers, who use it daily, and symbolic importance to Chileans well beyond the many Mapuche place names. Though the great majority of Mapuche also speak Spanish, the following sample of Mapudungan vocabulary may prove useful to visitors. Pronunciation is less consistently phonetic than Spanish, but still fairly straightforward. A few words have obviously been adapted from Spanish.

Pleasantries			
thank you	*caltumay*	10	*mari*
		11	*mari quiñe*
Geographical Terms		12	*mari epu*
hill	*pichi huincul*	13	*mari quila*
volcano	*pillán*	14	*mari meli*
		15	*mari quechu*
Miscellaneous		16	*mari callu*
boy	*pichi huentro*	17	*mari regle*
girl	*pichi hilcha*	18	*mari ailla*
mother	*ñuque*	19	*mari pura*
woman	*somo*	20	*epu mari*
brother	*peñi*	30	*quila mari*
sister	*sella*	40	*meli mari*
house	*ruca*	50	*quechu mari*
dog	*tre gua*	60	*callu mari*
cow	*wuaca*	70	*regle mari*
sheep	*ofisa*	80	*ailla mari*
condor	*ñancú*	90	*pura mari*
flower	*rayen*	100	*quiñe pataca*
water	*co*	110	*quiñe pataca quiñe mari*
beans	*quilli*	120	*quiñe pataca epu mari*
wine	*pulco*	130	*quiñe pataca quila mari*
white wine	*blan pulco*	140	*quiñe pataca meli mari*
		150	*quiñe pataca quechu mari*
Numbers		160	*quiñe pataca callu mari*
1	*quiñe*	170	*quiñe pataca regle mari*
2	*epu*	180	*quiñe pataca ailla mari*
3	*quila*	190	*quiñe pataca pura mari*
4	*meli*	200	*epu pataca*
5	*quechu*	210	*epu pataca quiñe mari*
6	*callu*	220	*epu pataca epu mari*
7	*regle*	230	*epu pataca quila mari*
8	*ailla*	240	*epu pataca meli mari*
9	*pura*	250	*epu pataca quechu mari*

land to large estates and were restricted to small reserves.

Today, several hundred thousand Mapuche live in the provinces between the Biobío and the Río Toltén, still commonly known as 'La Frontera.' Deprived of land by colonial Spaniards and republican Chileans, they now earn a precarious livelihood from agriculture and crafts. From 1965 to 1973, land reform improved their status, but the military coup of 1973 reversed many of these gains. Since the restoration of democracy in 1989, Mapuche peoples have been militant in seeking return of their lands and have, on several occasions, been successful.

German immigrants in the 19th century started many local industries, including breweries, tanneries, brick and furniture factories, bakeries, machine shops and

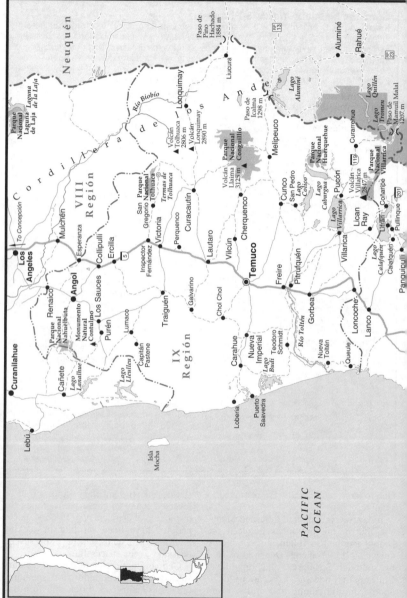

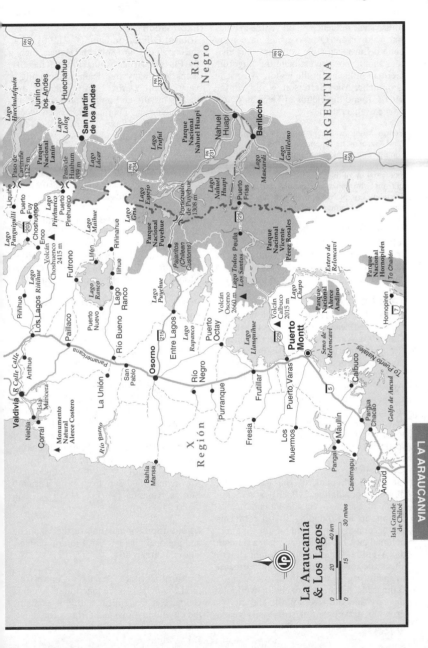

La Araucanía & Los Lagos

mills. Their influence is still visible in cities like Valdivia and Osorno, which have many central-European style buildings, but visitors should not overestimate the lingering German influence in the region. American geographer Mark Jefferson, writing in the 1920s, found the claims of German dominance exaggerated:

Puerto Montt was said to speak German and read German newspapers. I was even told I should find people there who were born in the country but could speak no Spanish. All this is exaggeration of the grossest sort . . . I found two persons who spoke no Spanish, but both were German-born. No street in the city has a German name, nor is German used on signs.

Chileans of German descent have perhaps left their greatest mark in architecture, food, and the agricultural landscape of dairy farms, but few have more than a romantic attachment to central Europe.

TEMUCO

Founded in 1881, after a famous treaty was signed on Cerro Ñielol between the Chilean government and the Mapuche, Chile's fastest-growing city is the starting point for excursions to nearby indigenous settlements and national parks in the Andes. Supporting a range of industries, including steel, textiles, food processing and wood products, it is the service center for a large hinterland, and a market town for the Mapuche and their handmade woolens.

Orientation

On the north bank of the Río Cautín, Temuco (population 210,000) is 675 km south of Santiago via the Panamericana. Despite its late founding, it still conforms to the conventional grid of the Spanish colonial city, but the Panamericana (known as Avenida Caupolicán through town) slices the town diagonally from northeast to southwest. To the north, across Avenida Balmaceda, historic Cerro Ñielol overlooks the city and the river. While the city is growing, travelers can still easily reach most sites of interest on foot.

Information

Tourist Offices Sernatur (☎ 211969) is at the corner of Claro Solar and Bulnes, facing the Plaza de Armas Aníbal Pinto. It has city maps and many free leaflets, including a very useful *Datos Utiles Temuco*, and there's usually an English speaker on duty. In January and February, it's open weekdays 8.30 am to 8 pm, Saturdays 9 am to 2 pm and 3 to 7 pm, and Sundays 10 am to 2 pm. The rest of the year, it's open weekdays only, 9 am to 12.30 pm and 3 to 6 pm.

At San Martín 0278, Acchi (☎ 215132), the Automóvil Club de Chile, is also a good source of information.

Money ATMs are abundant, but there are also several exchange houses. Change US cash and travelers' checks at Casa de Cambio Global at Bulnes 655, Local 1, Intercam at Bulnes 743 or Christopher Money Exchange at Prat 696, Oficina 419.

Post & Communications Temuco's area code is ☎ 45. Both Correos de Chile and Telex-Chile are at the corner of Diego Portales and Prat. CTC long-distance offices are at Prat 565 and on Avenida Caupolicán at Avenida Alemania. Entel is at Portales 841.

Travel Agencies Multitour (☎ 237913, fax 233536), Bulnes 307, Oficina 203, operates reasonably priced excursions ranging from city tours to visits to Mapuche villages and the national parks of the cordillera, and has English-speaking guides. Similar services are available from Turismo Ñielol (☎ 239497) at General Mackenna 450, 2nd floor, and Turismo Sur de América (☎ /fax 248505), León Gallo 0328.

Bookshops For materials on the Mapuche and regional history, visit Librería Universitaria, Portales 861.

Cultural Centers Temuco's Centro Cultural Municipal, at the junction of Avenida Balmaceda, Caupolicán and Prat, contains the city library, two auditoriums for shows and concerts and an exhibition hall.

National Parks Conaf (☎ 211912) is at Avenida Bilbao 931, 2nd floor.

Laundry Lavandería Autoservicio Marva is at Manuel Montt 415.

Medical Services Temuco's Hospital Regional (☎ 212525) is at Manuel Montt 115, six blocks west and one block north of the Plaza de Armas Aníbal Pinto.

Mercado Municipal

Dating from 1929, the municipal market building integrates practical community services (fresh food and functional clothing) with tourist appeal (seafood restaurants and quality crafts). One of central Temuco's most popular attractions, bounded by Bulnes, Portales, Aldunate and Rodríguez, it's two blocks north of Plaza de Armas Aníbal Pinto. Hours are Monday to Saturday 8 am to 7 pm, Sunday 8.30 am to 2 pm.

Monumento Natural Cerro Ñielol

Because of the presence of natural concentrations of the copihue (*Lapageria rosea*, Chile's national flower), this 85-hectare urban park merits the highest protection possible under Chilean forestry regulations. In reality, it is more a park of historical importance because Mapuche leaders, in 1881, ceded land for the founding of Temuco at the tree-shaded site known as **La Patagua**. The copihue flowers from March to July.

Administered by Conaf, Cerro Ñielol is popular for local outings, with its many picnic sites, a small lagoon, footpaths and an environmental information center. There is an admission charge of US$0.75 per pedestrian, US$0.25 for children and US$1.25 per car. At the north end of Calle Prat, it's open 8.30 am to 7 pm daily.

Museo Regional de La Araucanía

Housed in an attractive frontier-style building, the regional museum's permanent exhibits recount the history of the Araucanian peoples before, during and since the Spanish invasion. One particularly memorable presentation is a textile mural illustrating distinctions among the Pehuenches (hunter-gatherers of the cordillera), Mapuche (farmers of the plains and valleys) and Lafkenches (coastal fisher-gatherers) in terms of means of subsistence. A display on Mapuche resistance to the Spaniards illustrates native weapons, but overlooks their effective guerrilla tactics.

A regional map reveals that the present towns and cities of Curacautín, Cunco, Victoria, Lonquimay, Temuco, Villarrica and Pucón owe their origins to military outposts along the Malleco, Cautín and Toltén Rivers. After Chile stabilized the frontier in the late 19th century, immigrants from Germany, Belgium, Spain, France, Holland, Britain, Italy and Switzerland poured into the area. Catholic missionaries and construction of the railroad helped consolidate Chilean authority.

There's a good photographic display of early Temuco, including buildings destroyed in the earthquake of 1960. Besides historical materials, the museum displays a selection of paintings by regional artist Manuel Quevedo, and a sample of Mapuche crafts, including basketry from Lago Budi, and textiles, looms, silverwork and ceremonial objects. Everything is well-presented, but labeled in Spanish only.

At Avenida Alemania 084, the museum (☎ 211108) is open Monday to Saturday, 9 am to 7 pm, Sundays 10 am to 1 pm in summer; the rest of the year, hours are Tuesday to Saturday 9 am to 6 pm, Sunday 10 am to 1 pm. Bus No 9 runs from downtown to Avenida Alemania, but it's also reasonable walking distance.

Feria Libre

This fruit and vegetable market, with selections of arts and crafts goods as well, occupies several blocks along Barros Arana – from the railway station to the Terminal de Buses Rurales. Most of the vendors are Mapuche Indians who arrive in horse or bullock carts. Open daily from 9.30 am to 4 pm or whenever the last sellers pack up their wares, it's a vibrant, colorful and malodorous can't-miss. Be *very* circumspect about taking photographs, however.

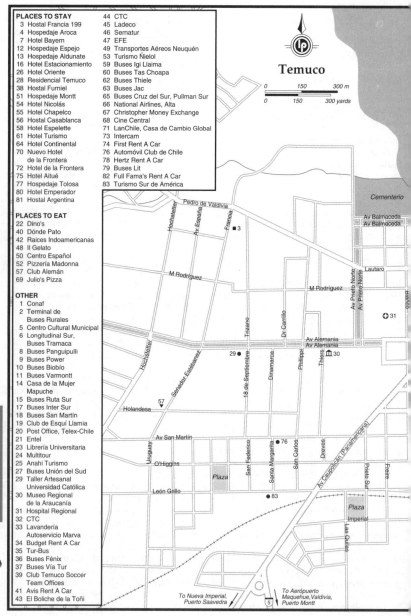

PLACES TO STAY
3   Hostal Francia 199
4   Hospedaje Aroca
7   Hotel Bayern
12 Hospedaje Espejo
13 Hospedaje Aldunate
16 Hotel Estacionamiento
26 Hotel Oriente
28 Residencial Temuco
38 Hostal Furniel
51 Hospedaje Montt
54 Hotel Nicolás
55 Hotel Chapelco
56 Hostal Casablanca
58 Hotel Espelette
61 Hotel Turismo
64 Hotel Continental
70 Nuevo Hotel
    de la Frontera
72 Hotel de la Frontera
75 Hotel Aitué
77 Hospedaje Tolosa
80 Hotel Emperador
81 Hostal Argentina

PLACES TO EAT
22 Dino's
40 Dónde Pato
42 Raices Indoamericanas
48 Il Gelato
50 Centro Español
52 Pizzería Madonna
57 Club Alemán
69 Julio's Pizza

OTHER
1   Conaf
2   Terminal de
    Buses Rurales
5   Centro Cultural Municipal
6   Longitudinal Sur,
    Buses Tramaca
8   Buses Panguipulli
9   Buses Power
10 Buses Biobío
11 Buses Varmontt
14 Casa de la Mujer
    Mapuche
15 Buses Ruta Sur
17 Buses Inter Sur
18 Buses San Martín
19 Club de Esquí Llaima
20 Post Office, Telex-Chile
21 Entel
23 Librería Universitaria
24 Multitour
25 Anahi Turismo
27 Buses Unión del Sud
29 Taller Artesanal
    Universidad Católica
30 Museo Regional
    de la Araucanía
31 Hospital Regional
32 CTC
33 Lavandería
    Autoservicio Marva
34 Budget Rent A Car
35 Tur-Bus
36 Buses Fénix
37 Buses Vía Tur
39 Club Temuco Soccer
    Team Offices
41 Avis Rent A Car
43 El Boliche de la Toñi

44 CTC
45 Ladeco
46 Sernatur
47 EFE
49 Transportes Aéreos Neuquén
53 Turismo Ñielol
59 Buses Igi Llaima
60 Buses Tas Choapa
62 Buses Thiele
63 Buses Jac
65 Buses Cruz del Sur, Pullman Sur
66 National Airlines, Alta
67 Christopher Money Exchange
68 Cine Central
71 LanChile, Casa de Cambio Global
73 Intercam
74 First Rent A Car
76 Automóvil Club de Chile
78 Hertz Rent A Car
79 Buses Lit
82 Full Fama's Rent A Car
83 Turismo Sur de América

Temuco

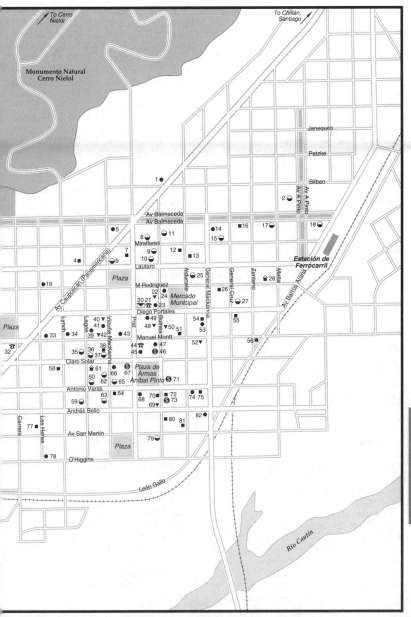

Organized Tours

Various travel agencies (see under Information, above) organize trips to attractions in and around the city of Temuco, but some of these are better arranged and more convenient in Villarrica or Pucón. A city tour of Temuco costs about US$20 per person, while full-day excursions, with lunch, include Isla Huapi (US$42), Lican Ray (US$48), Termas de Huife or Termas de Palguín (US$55), rafting on the Río Trancura (US$65) and Parque Nacional Conguillío (US$58). Discounts are usually available for groups as small as two or three.

Places to Stay

Prices for accommodation have risen dramatically in recent years, especially in the budget category, but there are still reasonable choices if you call ahead or look around. Some of the places closest to the train station and the Feria Libre are less than reputable, but some otherwise midrange places have rooms with shared bath at budget rates.

Places to Stay – bottom end

Hostel Temuco has two Hostelling International affiliates. Friendly *Residencial Temuco* (☎ 233721), Rodríguez 1341, 2nd floor, charges US$9 with breakfast, but it's small and often full in summer. *Hotel Turismo* (☎ 210583), Claro Solar 636, is very good value at US$16.

Hospedajes Clean, friendly *Hospedaje Espejo* (☎ 238408), Aldunate 124, has singles from US$6 to US$10 without breakfast. Across the street at Aldunate 187, attractive, friendly *Hospedaje Aldunate* (☎ 212976) charges US$10.

Despite short-term clientele, *Hostal Furniel* (☎ 237095), Vicuña Mackenna 570, is an OK place that charges US$7.50 per person (US$9 with breakfast). For about the same price, *Hospedaje Tolosa*, Las Heras 832, is a friendly but simple family-run place on a quiet street, though it may have to move because of lease

complications. In the US$11 range are *Hospedaje Montt* (☎ 211856) at Manuel Montt 965, Departamento 301, and amiable *Hospedaje Aroca* (☎ 234205), Lautaro 591.

Hotel Espelette (☎ 234805), Claro Solar 492, compares favorably for US$13 per person with shared bath, but rooms with private bath cost US$30/43. *Hostal Casablanca* (☎ /fax 212740), Manuel Montt 1306, has singles for US$14 with shared bath, US$17 with private bath, while *Hostal Argentina* (☎ /fax 237841), Aldunate 864, charges US$15 per person with shared bath. Rates at *Hotel Oriente* (☎ 233232), Manuel Rodríguez 1146, are US$15/25 with shared bath, US$30/45 with private bath.

Places to Stay – middle

At Varas 708 for over a century, rambling *Hotel Continental* (☎ 238973, fax 233830) has hosted guests like poet Pablo Neruda, and Presidents Pedro Aguirre Cerda and Salvador Allende. Rates begin at US$17/31 for singles/doubles with shared bath, while rooms with private bath cost US$35/44. Even if you don't stay at this one-of-a-kind hotel, you can enjoy a reasonably priced lunch in its classic dining room, or a drink at its equally classic bar.

Family-run *Hotel Turismo* (☎ 210583, fax 212932), Claro Solar 636, has spacious rooms with comfy beds from US$18 single with breakfast, but rooms with private bath are twice the price. *Hostal Francia 199* (☎ 235594), in the residential part of town at Francia 199, charges US$18 per person with shared bath, only slightly more with private bath. *Hotel Estacionamiento* (☎ 215503), Balmaceda 1246, charges US$20/25 for carpeted rooms with private bath, cable TV and jacuzzi.

Hotel Emperador (☎ 213409, fax 233-144), a good-value place with friendly staff at Bulnes 853, has pleasant rooms with private bath for US$40/49, but beware the windowless room on the ground floor. *Hotel Chapelco* (☎ 210367, fax 234331), General Cruz 401, is very comparable for US$45/58.

Places to Stay – top end

Hotel de la Frontera (☎ /fax 212638), Bulnes 733, charges US$50/62, including access to all the facilities of its newer relation across the street, but the best value of the category is *Hotel Nicolás* (☎ 210020, fax 213468), General Mackenna 420, with smallish but bright and cheery rooms with private bath and TV for US$50/70. Try also *Hotel Bayern* (☎ 213915, fax 212291), Prat 146, where rates are US$59/80.

Despite its unimpressive exterior, *Hotel Aitué* (☎ 211917, fax 212608), Varas 1048, is good value at US$66/90. Across from Hotel de la Frontera, *Nuevo Hotel de la Frontera* (☎ /fax 210718), Bulnes 726, is the largest and priciest lodgings in town. Rates are US$99/124, and it has an indoor pool.

Places to Eat

Temuco's cheapest food is available around the train station and the Terminal de Buses Rurales, but the best value is the seafood at various *puestos* (stands) in the Mercado Municipal at Portales and Aldunate – don't leave Temuco without trying it. *Restaurant Caribe*, Puesto 45 in the market, is outstanding value, but a longtime Chilean-American resident also highly recommends the slightly more formal and upscale *La Caleta* for a splurge. *Don Jeyo* (☎ 214335) at Puesto 55, *El Turista* (☎ 238056) at Puesto 32 and *El Criollito* (☎ 212583) at Puestos 38 and 39 are other good choices. Market restaurants close early, around 7 pm.

For quality fast food, try the spiffy *Dino's* (☎ 213660) at Bulnes 360, *Pizzería Madonna* (☎ 215552) at Manuel Montt 670 or the more upmarket *Julio's Pizza* (☎ 213-920) at Bulnes 778, which has excellent Italian and Argentine specialties. Another central parrilla is *Dónde Pato* (☎ 211102), Portales 680. *Raices Indoamericanas*, Manuel Montt 645, is one of few places to sample Mapuche food alongside other Chilean specialties.

For Mediterranean food, check out the *Centro Español* (☎ 238664) at Bulnes 483, but for heartier middle-European fare the *Club Alemán* (☎ 240034) is at Senador Estébanez 772. *Il Gelato*, Bulnes 420, has very fine ice cream.

Entertainment

The *Cine Central* (☎ 212897), Antonio Varas 832, shows a mix of respectable current films and occasional cheesy porn.

Club Temuco (☎ 211004), Lago 459, is the city's first-division soccer team. It plays in the Estadio Municipal, at the west end of León Gallo.

Things to Buy

The Mercado Municipal has the city's best handicrafts. Despite a lot of junk and kitsch, it's a good place for Mapuche woolen ponchos, blankets and pullovers, jewelry, pottery, polished stone mortars and musical instruments such as *zampoñas* (pan pipes) and drums. Many women also hawk these goods on the streets.

Run by a cooperative of 135 women, the Casa de la Mujer Mapuche (☎ 233886), General Mackenna 83, sells a wide selection of traditional indigenous crafts, most notably textiles and ceramics. Profits go back to the members in the form of literacy classes, crafts training and cash. The artisans are often available to discuss their work.

Other good places to look for crafts are the Galería de Arte beneath the bandstand in the Plaza de Armas, El Boliche de la Toñi at Montt 743 Interior, and the Taller Artesanal Universidad Católica at Avenida Alemania 0422.

Getting There & Away

Air LanChile (☎ 211339), Bulnes 655, has two non-stops daily to Santiago (US$128); the morning flight from Santiago continues to Valdivia (US$29), while the afternoon flight continues to Osorno (US$32). Ladeco (☎ 213180), at Prat 565, Local 2, has similar schedules.

National Airlines (☎ 239002), Claro Solar 780, Local 7, flies 12 times weekly to Santiago (US$115); Monday, Tuesday and Thursday afternoon flights to Santiago also stop in Concepción. National also has a Saturday flight to Puerto Montt (US$49) and Punta Arenas (US$212).

Alta (☎ 213161, fax 213105), Claro Solar 780, Local 5, flies two or three times daily to Concepción (US$34), two or three times daily to Puerto Montt (US$39), weekdays to Chaitén (US$70), and daily except Tuesday to Balmaceda/Coihaique (US$97), Puerto Natales (US$141) and Punta Arenas (US$168).

Transportes Aéreos Neuquén (TAN; ☎ 210500), Portales 840, connects Temuco with Neuquén, Argentina on Tuesday, Thursday, Friday and Sunday. The fare is US$70.

Bus – domestic Temuco is a major transport hub. The Terminal de Buses Rurales (☎ 210494) is at Avenida Balmaceda and Avenida Pinto; for local and regional destinations not mentioned below, check the schedules of the many companies at the terminal. Most long-distance companies have their offices in or near downtown. Times and frequencies change throughout the year, with fewer buses in winter.

Besides destinations on or near the Panamericana between Santiago and Puerto Montt, there are frequent connections to nearby national parks like Conguillío, to Curarrehue and to lakeside resorts like Villarrica and Lican Ray. There are also international services to the Argentine cities of Zapala, San Martín de los Andes, Neuquén, Mendoza, Bariloche and Buenos Aires.

Buses Biobío (☎ 210599), Lautaro 853, runs frequent services to Angol, Los Angeles and Concepción. Cruz del Sur (☎ 210701), Vicuña Mackenna 671, has daily services to Concepción, Santiago and many to Puerto Montt, including intermediate destinations like Osorno, with some continuing on to the island of Chiloé. It also offers more than a dozen daily trips to Valdivia. Pullman Sur shares offices with Cruz del Sur.

Tas Choapa (☎ 212422), Varas 609, has daily service to Valdivia and Puerto Montt, three buses to Santiago and intermediates, and also goes to La Serena. It also has a nightly direct service (11.15 pm) to Valparaíso/Viña del Mar without transfer in Santiago. Fénix (☎ 212582), Claro Solar 609, has three buses nightly to Santiago, with connections to northern Chilean destinations like Copiapó, Antofagasta, Iquique and Arica.

Tur-Bus (☎ 212613), Lagos 576, has two buses daily to Concepción, three to Chillán, five to Osorno and Valdivia, two to Puerto Montt and nine to Santiago. Buses Lit (☎ 211483), San Martín 894, goes daily to Concepción, Valdivia, Osorno and Puerto Montt, and has four buses daily to Chillán and five to Santiago.

Igi Llaima (☎ 210716), Lagos 720, goes daily to Chillán, twice daily to Santiago, and offers seven buses daily to Concepción, eight to Valdivia and four to Osorno and Puerto Montt. Varmontt (☎ 211314), Bulnes 45, goes daily to Valdivia, Concepción, Osorno, Puerto Montt and Santiago. Buses Power (☎ 236513), Bulnes 178, has three nightly buses to Santiago.

Other companies with services between Santiago and Puerto Montt include Inter Sur (☎ 234278) at Balmaceda 1378, Longitudinal Sur (☎ 213140) and Tramaca, sharing offices at Lautaro 703, and Vía Tur (☎ 213094), Vicuña Mackenna 586.

Buses Jac (☎ 210313), Vicuña Mackenna 798, offers about 29 buses daily to Villarrica and Pucón, plus four daily to Santiago, eight to Lican Ray and five to Coñaripe, and a daily service to Curarrehue. Panguisur (☎ 211560), Miraflores 871, has 11 buses daily to Panguipulli, plus three nightly to Santiago.

Buses Thiele (☎ 238682), Vicuña Mackenna 650, has three buses daily to Cañete, continuing on to Lebú, on the Costa del Carbón, and Concepción. Erbuc (☎ 212-939), at the Terminal de Buses Rurales, has three buses daily to Lonquimay, on the upper Biobío near the Argentine border.

Sample fares and times include Ancud (US$13, seven hours), Osorno (US$7, three hours), Puerto Montt (US$10, five hours), Castro (US$15, eight hours), Quellón (US$19, 11 hours), Valdivia or Los Angeles (US$4, three hours), Chillán

(US$6, four hours), Concepción (US$8, five hours), Talca (US$10, seven hours), Santiago (US$15, 11 hours) and Valparaíso/Viña del Mar (US$19, 13 hours). Salón cama buses to Santiago cost US$29.

Bus – international Fénix connects Temuco with Buenos Aires (US$75) Mondays and Wednesdays via the Libertadores tunnel, northeast of Santiago. Both Fénix and Tas Choapa have nightly services to Mendoza, with Santiago as a transfer point, for US$35.

Buses Jac, Igi Llaima and San Martín (☎ 234017), Balmaceda 1598, connect Temuco with Junín de los Andes, San Martín de los Andes (US$25), and Neuquén (US$49), usually via Paso Mamuil Malal east of Pucón but occasionally over Paso Pino Hachado, directly east of Temuco via Curacautín and Lonquimay, along the upper Biobío. Buses Ruta Sur (☎ 210079), Miraflores 1151, and Igi Llaima both go to Neuquén via Zapala (US$40). Each of these services runs about three times a week in summer only, and leaves very early, around 4 am.

Tas Choapa, Cruz del Sur and Unión del Sud (☎ 233398), General Cruz 375, have daily services to Bariloche (US$30), via Paso Puyehue east of Osorno.

Train Daily trains from Temuco go north to Santiago (all year) and south to Puerto Varas (in summer only), stopping at various stations en route. The train to Santiago takes about 11½ hours.

Buy train tickets either at the Estación de Ferrocarril (☎ 233416), on Avenida Barros Arana eight blocks east of Plaza de Armas Aníbal Pinto, or at the downtown office of Ferrocarriles del Estado (EFE; ☎ 233522), Bulnes 582. Fares to Santiago are about US$15 económica, US$26 salón, US$36 cama alta, and US$56 cama baja.

Getting Around
While Temuco has begun to sprawl, with the railway station and main bus terminal some distance from downtown, any taxi colectivo will quickly take you there. Bus

No 1 runs from downtown to the train station.

To/From the Airport Temuco's Aeropuerto Maquehue is six km south of town, just off the Panamericana. Taxis leaving from the front of Banco Osorno, on the Plaza de Armas, take passengers for US$5. Anahi Turismo (☎ 211155), Aldunate 235, runs airport minibuses in coordination with flight schedules.

Car Rental Car rental is worth considering for easy access to the surrounding national parks and Mapuche settlements. Vehicles are available from the Automóvil Club (☎ 215132) at San Martín 0278, Hertz (☎ 235385) at Las Heras 999, Avis (☎ 238-013) at Vicuña Mackenna 448 and at the airport, First (☎ 233890) at Varas 1036, and Budget (☎ 214911) at Lynch 471. Full Fama's (☎/fax 215420), Andrés Bello 1096, has probably the cheapest rates.

AROUND TEMUCO
Chol Chol
Mapuche oxcarts ply the dusty streets of Chol Chol, a village of wooden, tin-roofed bungalows with traditional Mapuche *rucas* (houses) on its outskirts. Chol Chol retains the atmosphere of a frontier town where time has stood still, or at least run slowly.

From Temuco's Terminal de Buses Rurales, Buses Epaza and Huinca Bus (☎ 210494) take about 1½ hours to Chol Chol, the former via Nueva Imperial and the latter direct, for US$1. The bus is likely to be jammed with Indians returning from the market with fruits and vegetables.

PARQUE NACIONAL TOLHUACA
Nestled in the precordillera northeast of Temuco, on the north bank of the Río Malleco, 6400-hectare Tolhuaca is one of the Chilean park system's best kept secrets, a tranquil forested getaway with excellent camping, fishing and hiking. In January and February it sometimes gets crowded, especially on weekends, but poor roads and the absence of public transport generally help keep the peace.

Laguna Malleco, the park's most conspicuously accessible feature, is a glacial relic slowly becoming a meadow as *junquillos* (reeds) colonize the shoreline sediments from the volcanic mountains that surround it. Elevations range from 850 meters around Laguna Malleco to 1830 meters on the summit of Cerro Colomahuida; 2806-meter Volcán Tolhuaca is beyond the park boundaries. Rainfall reaches 3000 mm per year, but summer is relatively dry.

Activities

Where it passes through the campground at Inalaufquén, the westward-flowing Río Malleco has several pools suitable for swimming, while shallow **Laguna Malleco** is a good spot for watching waterfowl or fishing (ask the Conaf ranger for oars to the rowboat).

Along the north shore of Laguna Malleco, a signed nature trail leads through dense forest of raulí, coigue, quila and Araucaria to its outlet, where the **Salto Malleco** (Malleco falls) tumbles 50 meters over resistant columnar basalt into a deep pool, surrounded by massive nalcas and water-loving ferns and mosses. The trail continues down to the river, through even denser vegetation.

From the north shore of Laguna Malleco, another trail climbs steeply to the **Prados de Mesacura**, then continues east to **Lagunillas** through an area of Araucaria forest with outstanding panoramas. Water is scarce on this trail, which is a full-day excursion; carry sufficient food as well.

The park's best overnight backpack trip goes to **Laguna Verde**, reached via a trailhead about five km east of Laguna Malleco, on the road to Termas de Tolhuaca. The trail crosses the Río Malleco and passes several waterfalls before reaching campsites on the north side of 1605-meter Cerro Laguna Verde.

Places to Stay

On the southeastern shore of Laguna Malleco, Conaf's *Camping Inalaufquén* has secluded woodsy sites for US$10, including running water, fire pits, picnic tables and immaculate toilets with cold showers.

Getting There & Away

From Victoria's Terminal de Buses Rurales, on the Panamericana, Buses San Gregorio goes weekdays at 4 pm to the village of San Gregorio; from there it's about a 20-km walk to the campground at Laguna Malleco. Beyond San Gregorio, the road narrows rapidly and deadfalls may be a problem after storms, but any carefully driven passenger car can pass in good weather. This would be an ideal mountain bike route, as it climbs gradually into the precordillera.

From the town of Curacautín, north of Parque Nacional Conguillío, taxi colectivos ply a rugged but passable gravel road to the modest hot springs resort of Termas de Tolhuaca (see below), but the 10-km logging road between the Termas and Laguna Malleco is impossible for ordinary passenger cars and difficult even with high clearance, making 4WD desirable.

PARQUE NACIONAL CONGUILLIO

Created primarily to preserve the distinctive Araucaria pine, or monkey-puzzle tree, Conguillío protects 60,800 hectares of alpine lakes, deep canyons and native forests surrounding 3125-meter Volcán Llaima. Since 1640, Llaima has experienced 34 violent eruptions, most recently in 1957. Some 2000 years ago, a lava flow off Llaima's northern flank dammed the Río Truful-Truful to form Laguna Conguillío.

Geography & Climate

In the Region IX province of Cautín, Conguillío is about 80 km directly east of Temuco via Vilcún and Cherquenco, but about 120 km via the northern access point of Curacautín or the southern access point of Melipeuco. Its most conspicuous feature is Llaima's smoldering, snow-covered cone, but rugged lava fields cover much of the rest of the park. The glaciated peaks of the Sierra Nevada, north of Laguna

Conguillío, consistently exceed 2500 meters, but park elevations fall as low as 700 meters.

Conguillío experiences warm summers, but up to three meters of snow can accumulate in winter. Mean annual precipitation is about 2000 mm, falling almost entirely between May and September. December to April is the best time for a visit.

Flora & Fauna

Conguillío's woodlands are more open than the denser Valdivian rainforest to the south. At lower elevations, around 1000 to 1150 meters, they consist of coigue (*Nothofagus dombeyi*) and roble (*Nothofagus obliqua*), but roble gives way to raulí (*Nothofagus alpina*) between 1200 and 1400 meters. Above 1400 meters, mixed forests of Araucaria, coigue and ñire (*Nothofagus antarctica*) predominate, while the highest elevations consist of Araucaria and lenga (*Nothofagus pumilio*).

Known to Spanish-speakers as *paragua* (the umbrella) because of its unusual shape, the Araucaria is *pehuén* to the Mapuche, who have traditionally gathered nuts from its cones as food. It is closely related to the Northern Hemisphere pines.

Activities

Conaf's **Centro de Información Ambiental** at Laguna Conguillío offers a variety of programs in January and February, including slide shows and ecology talks, hikes to the Sierra Nevada and outings for children, and boat excursions on the lake. Of course, independent travelers can undertake many of these same activities. Rowboats rent for about US$2.50 per hour.

At present, backcountry camping is not permitted within the park, but Conaf hopes to open the so-called **Ruta de los Pehuenches**, a series of Indian trails from the precordillera into the mountains. Likewise, within a few years, Conaf anticipates that the park will be open for winter use and accessible for cross-country skiing.

Formed when lava flows from **El Escorial** dammed the river, **Laguna Arco Iris** is worth a stop for travelers in the southern

part of the park; the nearby **Casa del Colono** is an early pioneer's cabin that's a minor historical monument. At **Laguna Verde**, a short trail goes to La Ensenada, a peaceful beach area; in 10 million years or so, as the weaker volcanic rock erodes, the granitic outcrops across the lake could become another Torres del Paine.

Travelers interested in vulcanism should visit the canyon of the **Río Truful-Truful**, whose colorful strata, exposed by the rushing waters, are a vivid record of Llaima's numerous eruptions.

Sierra Nevada

One of Chile's finest short hikes, the trail to the base of the Sierra Nevada leaves from the small parking lot at Playa Linda, at the east end of Laguna Conguillío. Climbing steadily northeast through dense coigue forests, the trail passes a pair of lake overlooks, the second and more scenic of which is sited where solid stands of Araucarias begin to supplant coigues on the ridgetop.

On the more exposed second half of the hike, continuing along the ridgetop, biting tábanos are a problem unless there's a breeze. Natural history lovers will take more pleasure from the abundant *lagartija (Liolaemus tenuis*, a tiny lizard) and the rosette succulent *añañisca (Rhodophiala andina)*, growing where humus formed from fallen ñire leaves has begun to mix with volcanic ash to form an incipient soil.

Conaf discourages all but the most experienced and well-prepared hikers from continuing north over the Sierra Nevada to Termas Río Blanco, an excursion detailed in *Trekking in the Patagonian Andes*, because route finding is so difficult and at least one person has died on the trip. Nevertheless, anyone can undertake the two-hour hike to the ridgetop, which provides superb views of Laguna Conguillío, expansive Araucaria forests and numerous waterfalls.

Sector Los Paraguas

Experienced climbers can tackle Volcán Llaima from Sector Los Paraguas on the west side of the park, where there is a refugio on the road from Cherquenco, or from Captrén on the north side. Before climbing, ask permission from Conaf in Temuco and from the Carabineros in Cherquenco, Melipeuco or Curacautín.

In winter, when snow may close the road to Laguna Conguillío, there is downhill skiing at Los Paraguas, whose only infrastructure is Andarivel, a single 1000-meter towbar. Contact the Club de Esquí Llaima (☎ 237923), Las Heras 299 in Temuco, which offers classes and rental equipment.

Places to Stay & Eat

At present, backcountry camping is not permitted. Conaf has taken control over campgrounds at *Los Ñirres* (44 sites), *El Estero* (10 sites), *Los Carpinteros* (12 sites), *El Hoyón* (10 sites) and *La Caseta* (12 sites), all on or near the south shore of Laguna Conguillío. In January, February and during Semana Santa (Holy Week) these are expensive at US$30 for two tents with up to five persons; the rest of the year, these sites cost US$20. Conaf reserves a limited number of backpacker sites for US$4 per person at El Estero. At *Laguna Captrén*, at the northwestern entrance to

the park, sites are available for US$15 from mid-January to the end of February, but only US$10 the rest of the year.

At the southwest end of Laguna Conguillío, *Cabañas Conguillío* (☎ 214363, 211493 in Temuco), a Conaf-authorized concessionaire, operates accommodation, a restaurant and a small store from mid-December to early March. Built around the trunks of Araucaria trees, their cabañas sleep six and cost US$90 per night. Though the price includes stove, fuel and cooking utensils, the cabañas are overpriced for what is really pretty basic, if picturesque, accommodation. A dozen new, more luxurious cabañas are projected for the near future.

At Sector Los Paraguas, the *Refugio Escuela Ski* (☎ 237923 in Temuco) has 70 beds and a restaurant. A new hotel was recently under construction.

Getting There & Away

There are several ways to approach the park. To reach Sector Los Paraguas from Temuco's Terminal de Buses Rurales, take one of Flota Erbuc buses (☎ 212939), which run a dozen times daily to the village of Cherquenco (US$1). From Cherquenco it's necessary to walk or hitch 17 km to the ski lodge in Sector Los Paraguas.

It is possible to approach Sector Conguillío from either north or south. The northern route takes the Panamericana to Victoria, then the paved highway east to Curacautín, which is 42 km from the park headquarters (an alternative to Curacautín goes via a gravel road from Lautaro). Erbuc has six buses daily via Victoria (US$2) and four via Lautaro (US$2.50). Two buses weekly, Monday and Friday at 6 am, go as far as the park entrance at Guardería Laguna Captrén in summer only; the rest of the year they go only to the junction of the rough road to Sector Los Paraguas. Otherwise, from Curacautín it may be necessary to hitch.

The southern route to Sector Conguillío passes through the villages of Cunco and Melipeuco. Narbus (☎ 211611) in Temuco has seven buses daily to Melipeuco

(US$2.50), where Hostería Huentelén can arrange a cab to park headquarters. Travelers who can afford to rent a car can combine these two routes in a loop trip from Temuco.

CURACAUTIN

Curacautín, the northern gateway to Parque Nacional Conguillío, has little to see in its own right, but is a convenient staging point for excursions into the upper Biobío drainage.

Curacautín's Oficina de Informaciones Turísticas is at the bus terminal, on the north side of the Plaza de Armas. Money can be changed at Agencia Tur Money Exchange (☎ 881272), Prat 800. Entel is at Serrano 175; the area code is ☎ 45.

Places to Stay & Eat

Hospedaje Tolosa (☎ 881752, 881650), Manuel Rodríguez 104, is a family-run place with comfortable rooms and excellent showers in a spacious shared bathroom for US$10 per person. *Residencial Rojas*, Tarapacá 249, is also inexpensive.

Hotel Turismo (☎ 811116), Tarapacá 140, charges US$11/25 single/double, while *Hotel Plaza* (☎ 881256), Yungay 175, is ordinary but passable for US$18 per person.

La Cabaña, facing the Plaza de Armas at Yungay 157, has good sandwiches.

Getting There & Away

Curacautín's Terminal de Buses is at Yungay and Rodríguez, directly on the highway to Lonquimay. Erbuc goes to Conguillío Monday and Friday at 6 am, four times daily to Lonquimay, and also connects to Temuco six times daily via Victoria, and four times via Lautaro. Buses Biobío goes six times daily to Temuco.

Fénix Pullman Norte goes to Victoria, Chillán and Santiago. Unión del Sud goes to Argentina via the Paso de Pino Hachado, but these buses usually fill up in Temuco.

AROUND CURACAUTIN

Termas de Tolhuaca

Some 35 km north of Curacautín via a rough but passable gravel road, Termas de Tolhuaca is a modest hot springs resort whose *Hotel Termas de Tolhuaca* was undergoing major remodeling at the time of this writing. Camping costs US$15 per site, while rooms cost US$62 per person with full board, but the fairly rustic baths cost only about US$5 for a long, hot soak. For information in Curacautín, contact Transporte, Turismo y Agrícola Tolhuaca (☎ 881211), Calama 240.

From Termas de Tolhuaca, a very rugged logging road, best suited to 4WD and impossible without high clearance, leads to Parque Nacional Tolhuaca (see above).

MELIPEUCO

Melipeuco, the southern gateway to Conguillío, is 90 km east of Temuco via Cunco. Good accommodation and food are available at highly praised *Hostería Huetelén* (☎ 693032), Pedro Aguirre Cerda 1, starting at US$16/25 with private bath.

From Temuco's Terminal de Buses Rurales, Narbus has seven buses daily to Melipeuco; while there's no scheduled transport from Melipeuco to Conguillío, it's possible to hire a cab or car to the visitor center for about US$15. Leonardo Barros at the Comar gas station arranges tours through the park for about US$10 per person.

VILLARRICA

Sharing its name with the smoldering, snow-capped volcano that dominates its skyline and the lake on which it lies, Villarrica is a traditional resort town that, while it remains popular, has lost ground to nearby Pucón.

Founded in 1552 by Gerónimo de Alderete, Santa María Magdalena de Villarrica failed to survive repeated Mapuche attacks during colonial times. According to one commentator of the era, the Indians were well beyond Spanish authority:

The ruins of this city are yet visible, particularly those of the walls of orchards and of a church. The town stood on the side of a lake . . . about 25 miles in circumference, and abounding with fish. The soil is very fertile, and the Indians raise maize, potatoes, quinoa, peas, beans, barley and

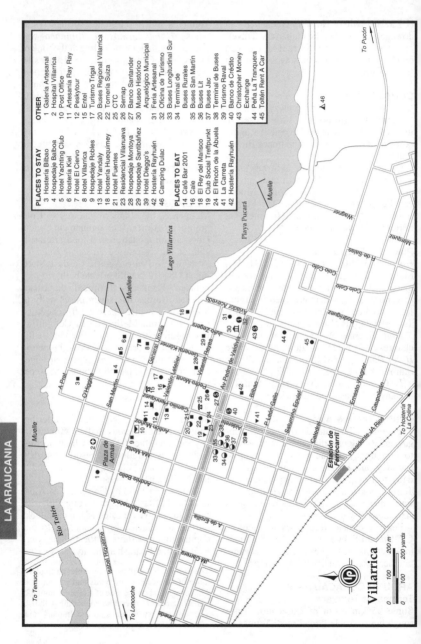

PLACES TO STAY
3   Hostería Bilbao
4   Hospedaje Balboa
5   Hotel Yachting Club
6   Hostería Kiel
7   Hotel El Ciervo
8   Hotel Villarrica
9   Hospedaje Robles
13 Hotel Yandaly
18 Hostería Huequmey
21 Hotel Fuentes
23 Residencial Villanueva
28 Hospedaje Montoya
29 Hospedaje Santibáñez
39 Hotel Diego's
42 Hostería Rayhuén
46 Camping Dulac

PLACES TO EAT
14 Café Bar 2001
16 Cale
18 El Rey del Marisco
19 Club Social Treffpunkt
24 El Rincón de la Abuela
41 La Carreta
42 Hostería Rayhuén

OTHER
1   Galería Artesanal
2   Hospital Villarrica
10 Post Office
11 Artesanía Ray Ray
12 Peskytour
15 Entel
17 Turismo Trigal
20 Buses Regional Villarrica
22 Tornería Suiza
25 CTC
26 Sernap
27 Banco Santander
30 Museo Histórico
     Arqueológico Municipal
31 Feria Artesanal
32 Oficina de Turismo
33 Buses Longitudinal Sur
34 Terminal de
     Buses Rurales
35 Buses San Martín
36 Buses Lit
37 Buses Jac
38 Terminal de Buses
39 Turismo Raval
40 Banco de Crédito
43 Christopher Money
     Exchange
44 Peña La Tranquera
45 Toltén Rent A Car

Villarrica

wheat. Apple, pear, peach and cherry-trees are seen growing where they were planted by the Spaniards before the destruction of the city. The Indians neither admit missionaries nor comisario. They have all kinds of cattle and poultry, which they exchange with other tribes for ponchos, flannels, &c being very averse to trade with the Spaniards.

Not until 1883 did the Mapuche toqui Epuléf allow the Chilean state, in the person of Colonel Gregorio Urrutia, to maintain a permanent presence in the territory. German colonists have left a visible legacy.

Orientation
On the southwest shore of Lago Villarrica, where the Río Toltén drains the lake toward the Pacific, Villarrica is 86 km southwest of Temuco. The city itself (permanent population about 20,000) displays a fairly regular grid pattern, bounded by the irregular lakeshore on the north, Avenida J M Carrera to the west, the diagonal Presidente J A Ríos on the south and Aviador Acevedo to the east. The important commercial streets are Avenida Pedro de Valdivia (the major thoroughfare) and Camilo Henríquez (which becomes Alderete south of Bilbao).

Information
Tourist Office The municipal Oficina de Turismo (☎ 411162) is at Pedro de Valdivia 1070, near Aviador Acevedo. From January 1 and March 15, it's open 8.30 am to 11 pm daily; the rest of the year, hours are 8.30 am to 1 pm and 2.30 to 6.30 pm. The staff are usually helpful and there are many leaflets, including the very useful *Datos Utiles Villarrica*, and a current list of accommodation and prices.

Money Banco de Crédito has an ATM at the corner of Pedro de Valdivia and Gerónimo de Alderete, while Banco Santander has one at Pedro de Valdivia 778. For changing US and Argentine cash, as well as US$ travelers' checks, try Christopher Money Exchange, Pedro de Valdivia 1061, but rates are notably better in Temuco.

Post & Communications Villarrica's area code is ☎ 45. Correos de Chile is on General Urrutia, near Anfión Muñoz. CTC long-distance offices are at Henríquez 544, while Entel is at the corner of Camilo Henríquez and General Urrutia.

Travel Agencies Peskytour (☎ 411385) is at Valentín Letelier 650, while Turismo Trigal (☎ 411078) is at Pedro Montt 365. Both organize climbing trips of Volcán Villarrica and other excursions to the national parks. Turismo Raval (☎ 411370), in Hotel Dieggo's at Gerónimo de Alderete 709, offers similar services.

Medical Services Hospital Villarrica (☎ 411169) is at San Martín 460.

Museo Histórico-Arqueológico Municipal
Mapuche artifacts, including jewelry, musical instruments and several roughly hewn wooden masks – powerful carvings despite their simplicity – are the focus of the municipal museum. On the grounds in front of the museum is a Mapuche ruca, oblong with thatched walls and roof, traditionally built by four men in four days under a reciprocal labor system known as *minga*. Reeds from the lake provide the thatch, so skillfully intertwined that water cannot penetrate even in this very damp climate.

Alongside the tourist office, at the corner of Pedro de Valdivia and Julio Zegers, the museum is open weekdays 9 am to 1 pm and 3 to 7.30 pm. Admission costs US$0.50.

Feria Artesanal
On Aviador Acevedo, behind the tourist office, Villarrica's artisans' market has a fine selection of local crafts and offers the chance to sample traditional Mapuche food.

Fishing
Fishing is good near Villarrica, especially on the Río Toltén, but first obtain a license from Sernap (☎ 412383), Pedro Montt

LA ARAUCANIA

541. Travelers have also recommended Gastón Balboa, San Martín 348, as a well-equipped and knowledgeable fishing guide.

Special Events

At the annual Muestra Cultural Mapuche, in January and February, local artisans display their wares to the public; there is also indigenous music and ritual dances. Late January's Jornadas Musicales de Villarrica is a music festival with nearly two decades of history.

Places to Stay – bottom end

Villarrica has substantial seasonal price differentials, with a summer peak in January and February, but prices can also rise in ski season.

Camping There are more than half a dozen campgrounds on the road between Villarrica and Pucón, but the most convenient and economical is *Camping Dulac* (☎ 412-097), just two km east of town. It can be crowded, but the shady sites provide reasonable privacy for US$15 per night. It has excellent hot showers, supplies and a restaurant.

Hospedajes, Hotels & Residenciales

Many places offer seasonal accommodation only for around US$7.50 per person (US$10 with breakfast); the tourist office provides the most current information. Among the possibilities are recommended *Hospedaje Balboa* (☎ 411098) at San Martín 734, *Hospedaje Montoya* (☎ 412-787) at Vicente Reyes 854, *Hospedaje Santibáñez* (☎ 411086) at Zegers 481 and *Hospedaje Robles* (☎ 411306) at General Urrutia 579.

Popular with some travelers but disliked by others, one of the cheapest permanent places is *Hotel Fuentes* (☎ 411595), Vicente Reyes 665, for about US$9/16 single/double with simple breakfast and shared bath. Rooms are very basic, but the downstairs bar and restaurant provide a cozy winter hearth. *Residencial Villanueva* (☎ 411392), Pedro de Valdivia 678, is comparably priced.

Places to Stay – middle

Mid-range accommodations start around US$30 double at *Hotel Yandaly* (☎ 411-452), Henríquez 401. Managed by extroverted, English-speaking Gualberto López, *Hostería Rayhuén* (☎ 411571) at Pedro Montt 668 is a charming place with hot showers, well-heated rooms and a very fine restaurant. Room rates with breakfast are US$25/35.

In part because of considerable street noise, and perhaps because it has changed hands several times, travelers have mixed opinions of *Hotel Dieggo's* (☎ 411370), Alderete 709, where rates are US$23/38. The quieter *Hostería Bilbao* (☎ 411186), Henríquez 43, charges US$25/45.

Places to Stay – top end

Hotel Villarrica (☎ /fax 411641), Körner 255, has double cabins from US$58, while *Hostería Huequimey* (☎ 411462), with excellent lake views at Letelier 1030-B, charges US$60 double with breakfast.

American-owned *Hostería de la Colina* (☎ 411503), overlooking the town from a site which is actually well above its street address of Presidente Ríos 1177, has doubles starting at US$50/70, but rooms with finer views are more expensive. There is a well stocked library and very attractive grounds with fine views of both the Llaima and Villarrica volcanoes.

At Körner 153, *Hostería Kiel* (☎/fax 411631) has rooms from US$50/75 and a good restaurant. Overlooking the lake at San Martín 802, with a good restaurant and a pool, the *Hotel Yachting Club* (☎ 411-191), costs US$64/74 with breakfast. *Hotel El Ciervo* (☎ 411215, fax 411426), Körner 241, is one of several good hotels along the same street; rooms with breakfast start at US$74/84.

Places to Eat

Most of Villarrica's restaurants are along Pedro de Valdivia and Alderete/Henríquez. *Café Bar 2001* (☎ 411470), Henríquez 379, seems typical of Villarrica's tourist cafés, with its good selection of sandwiches and kuchen. *El Rincón de la Abuela*, at the corner of Pedro de Valdivia and Camilo Henríquez, specializes in chicken and pizza.

La Carreta (☎ 412749), Alderete 768, is a good parrilla, but don't overlook the hearty fixed-price lunches at *Hostería Rayhuén* (☎ 411571), Puerto Montt 668, with its friendly but erratic service.

El Rey del Marisco (☎ 412093), Valentín Letelier 1030, is nothing fancy, but serves excellent fish and other seafood, with entrees from about US$6. Special mention goes to their pescado a la vasca, which comes spiced with garlic and garnished with red peppers, white asparagus, tasty baguettes and ají. Service can be less congenially erratic than that at Hostería Rayhuén, however.

The popular *Club Social Treffpunkt* (☎ 411081), Valdivia 640, serves German cuisine and Chilean seafood. *Cale* (☎ 412-499), Valentín Letelier 726, is a new and attractive Spanish/Mexican restaurant, run by the same owners as Pucón's Puerto Pucón y Tequila.

Entertainment

Peña La Tranquera, Acevedo 761, is a bar and folk club with live music as well as typical Chilean food.

Things to Buy

Besides the Feria Artesanal, there are several other places to look for Mapuche silverwork, baskets, woolens and carvings. Visit the Tornería Suiza at Henríquez 025, the Galería Artesanal at Andrés Bello 239, Ray-Ray at Muñoz 386 and Turismo Trigal at Pedro Montt 365.

Getting There & Away

Bus Villarrica's main Terminal de Buses is at Pedro de Valdivia 621, though a few companies have separate but nearby offices. There are frequent buses to Santiago and many regional destinations, but most southbound services on the Panamericana require a change in Temuco. Regular international services are available to the Argentine towns of Zapala, Neuquén, San Martín de los Andes, Bariloche and

Mendoza; fares are very similar to those from Temuco.

Bus – regional Buses Jac (☎ 411447), Bilbao 610, goes to Pucón (US$0.65) and Temuco (US$2) every half hour, four times daily to Valdivia (US$3), 18 times daily to Lican Ray (US$0.65) and six times to Coñaripe (US$2). It also goes twice daily to Caburgua (US$2) via Pucón, and daily to Curarrehue (US$2).

Buses Regional Villarrica (☎ 411871), on Vicente Reyes next to Hotel Fuentes, has daily buses to Pucón, Curarrehue and Puesco.

Bus – domestic Many companies have nightly service to Santiago, including Buses Jac, Tur-Bus (☎ 411534), Igi Llaima (☎ 412733), Buses Power (☎ 411121), Inter Sur (☎ 411534), Fénix Pullman Norte (☎ 411313), Buses Lit (☎ 411555) at Anfión Muñoz 640 and Longitudinal Sur (☎ 419098) at Pedro de Valdivia 599.

Fares to Santiago are around US$19, Buses Jac and Tur-Bus offer more comfortable ejecutivo service for US$28, and salón cama sleepers for US$39.

Bus – international Unión del Sud goes to Zapala (US$24) and Neuquén (US$29, 16 hours) in Argentina daily at 8 am. Igi Llaima goes Monday, Wednesday and Friday at 5 am to San Martín de los Andes (US$23) and Neuquén (US$35) via Paso Mamuil Malal. Buses San Martín (☎ 411-584), Anfión Muñoz 604, operates similar international services Tuesday, Thursday and Saturday.

Getting Around
Car Rental Turismo Trigal (☎ 411078), Pedro Montt 365, and Toltén Rent A Car (☎ 411253, fax 411330), Aviador Acevedo 893, both rent cars.

PUCON
What with growing numbers of travel agencies offering hiking, climbing, mountain biking, windsurfing, whitewater rafting and kayaking, Pucón resembles Wyoming's Jackson Hole in its youthful vitality. At least until the next major eruption of Volcán Villarrica obliterates it, this lakeside resort will remain the focus of Chile's adventure tourism industry and a locus of environmental activism.

Pucón has a wide range of accommodations in all categories, and superb food. In the days leading up to New Year's, it's a beehive of around-the-clock activity, as bars and restaurants make last minute preparations for the summer, in a boom-or-bust atmosphere of improvisation. Villarrica may be cheaper (and safer – don't buy a condo in Pucón unless it's guaranteed lava-proof), but a visit to Pucón is much livelier and more entertaining.

Orientation
Pucón (population 8000) is 25 km from Villarrica at the east end of Lago Villarrica, between the estuary of the Río Pucón to the north and Volcán Villarrica to the south. Structured along a conventional grid system, this very compact town in bounded by the lake to the north, the Costanera Roberto Geis to the west, the flanks of the volcano to the south, and Avenida Colo Colo to the east. To the northwest, a wooded peninsula juts into the lake, forming the sheltered inlet La Poza at the west end of Avenida Libertador Bernardo O'Higgins, the main commercial street and thoroughfare.

Information
Tourist Offices Pucón's municipal Oficina de Turismo (☎ 441916, Anexo 35) is at O'Higgins 669. It's open 8 am to 10 pm daily from mid-December to the end of February; the rest of the year, hours are 8.30 am to 1 pm and 3 to 6.30 pm. Annual fishing licenses are also available here for US$2.

The private Cámara de Turismo (☎ 441-671), Brasil 115, is more commercially oriented but still helpful.

Money Changing money is not difficult, but rates are better in Santiago or Temuco. Banco de Chile has an ATM in the Galería

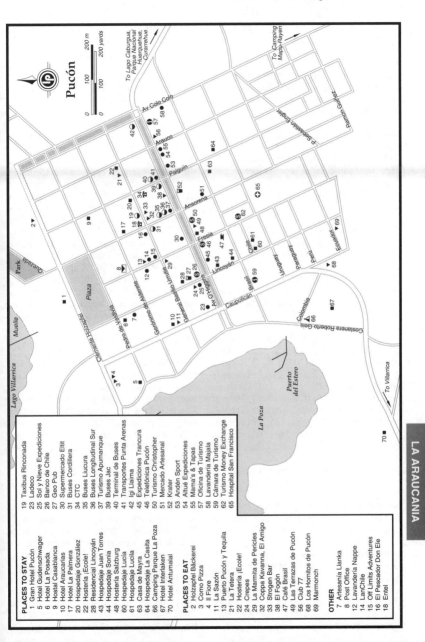

Pucón

0   100   200 m
0   100   200 yards

To Lago Caburgua,
Parque Nacional
Huerquehue,
Quaranehue

To Camping
Mapu-Rayen

To Villarrica

Lago Villarrica

Muelle

Park

Plaza

Puerto
del Estero

La Poza

PLACES TO STAY
1 Gran Hotel Pucón
5 Hotel Gudenschwager
6 Hotel La Posada
9 Hostal Casablanca
10 Hotel Araucarias
17 Hotel La Palmera
20 Hospedaje González
22 Hostería ¡Ecole!
28 Residencial Lincoyán
43 Hospedaje Juan Torres
44 Hospedaje Sonia
48 Hostería Salzburg
60 Hospedaje Lucía
61 Hospedaje Lucila
63 Casa de Mayra
64 Hospedaje La Casita
66 Camping Parque La Poza
67 Hotel Interlaken
70 Hotel Antumalal

PLACES TO EAT
2 Holzapfel Bäckerei
3 Como Pizza
4 Il Fiore
11 La Sazón
13 Puerto Pucón y Tequila
21 La Tetera
22 Hostería ¡Ecole!
24 Crepes
29 La Marmita de Pericles
32 Coppa Kavanna, El Amigo
33 Strogen Bar
38 El Fogón
47 Café Brasil
49 Las Terrazas de Pucón
56 Club 77
68 Los Hornitos de Pucón
69 Marmonch

OTHER
7 Artesanía Llanka
8 Post Office
12 Lavandería Nappe
14 LanChile
15 Off Limits Adventures
16 El Pescador Don Ele
18 Entei

19 Taxibus Rinconada
23 Ladeco
25 Sol y Nieve Expediciones
26 Banco de Chile
27 Geo Pub
30 Supermercado Eltit
31 Buses Cordillera
34 CTC
35 Buses Llucura
36 Buses Longitudinal Sur
37 Turismo Apumanque
39 Buses Jac
40 Terminal de Buses
41 Transportes Punta Arenas
42 Igi Llaima
45 Expediciones Trancura
46 Telefónica Pucón
50 Turismo Christopher
51 Mercado Artesanal
52 Krater
53 Andén Sport
54 Altué Expediciones
55 Mama's & Tapas
57 Oficina de Turismo
58 Lavandería Majala
59 Cámara de Turismo
62 Turismo Money Exchange
65 Hospital San Francisco

Alto Pucón, at the corner of O'Higgins and Lincoyán, but there are several cambios, including Turismo Money Exchange at Fresia 547, Turismo Christopher at O'Higgins 335 and Telefónica Pucón at the corner of O'Higgins and Fresia. Supermercado Eltit, O'Higgins 336, will change US and Argentine cash.

Post & Communications Pucón's area code is ☎ 45. Correos de Chile is at Fresia 183. CTC long-distance offices are at Palguín 348, while Entel is at Ansorena 299. Telefónica Pucón, at the corner of O'Higgins and Fresia, also provides long-distance and fax services.

Travel Agencies On Avenida Bernardo O'Higgins, Chile's adventure travel mecca, numerous companies arrange climbing, river rafting, mountain biking (including rentals), horseback riding, fishing and similar activities – you can watch the video replays of the day's excursions on the sidewalk. For details and prices, see the Organized Tours entry below.

Among them are reader-recommended, Colombian-American Sol y Nieve Expediciones (☎ /fax 441070) at O'Higgins and Lincoyán, Expediciones Trancura (☎ 441189) at O'Higgins 211, Turismo Apumanque (☎ 441085, fax 441361) at O'Higgins 412, Andén Sport (☎ 441048, fax 441236) at O'Higgins 535, Altué Expediciones at O'Higgins 587, Transportes Punta Arenas (☎ 449510) at O'Higgins and Palguín and Off Limits Adventures at Fresia 273. Some of these operate in summer only.

National Parks Conaf (☎ 441261) has moved east of town to Camino Internacional 1355.

Language Courses Hostería ¡Ecole!, General Urrutia 592, offers intensive Spanish language instruction in an activities-oriented context, both in summer (hiking, rafting and the like) and winter (skiing). For more detail, see the Organized Tours entry below.

Laundry Lavandería Nappe is at Fresia 224. Lavandería Majala is at Colo Colo 478, Lavandería Esperanza across the street at Colo Colo 475.

Medical Services Pucón's Hospital San Francisco (☎ 441177) is at Uruguay 325.

Organized Tours
Competition is heavy among tour companies, but prices vary less than services among them; for names and addresses, see the Travel Agencies entry above. Climbing Volcán Villarrica, a day trip if the weather holds, costs about US$35 per person. A three-hour rafting trip (only about 1½ hours on the water) down the lower Río Trancura goes for as little as US$10, but a full-day excursion (three hours on the water) on the more rugged upper Trancura costs US$40.

For climbing Volcán Villarrica, it's better to use your own boots if possible, so long as they can be fitted with crampons; bring extra high-energy snacks. Colombian-American Sol y Nieve is more expensive than most of Pucón's adventure travel agencies, but provides better equipment for climbing and rafting, and additional services (like a sumptuous barbecue at the end of the day). Transportes Punta Arenas also does tours to conventional destinations like thermal hot springs and beaches. El Pescador Don Ele, Urrutia 384, organizes fishing trips and sells gear.

In addition to its similar excursions, Hostería ¡Ecole! (☎ 441675, fax 441660) organizes hiking trips to the Fundación Lahuen's Santuario Cañi, a private nature reserve, and more remote destinations like Cochamó and the Fiordo de Cahuelmó (part of the proposed Parque Natural Pumalín, another private reserve), both in Region X. In conjunction with the Proyecto Indígena Alto Biobío, ¡Ecole! also arranges summer hiking and winter cross-country skiing on El Sendero Pehuenche, the traditional Pehuenche trail of the endangered upper Biobío drainage. For information in the USA, contact Ancient Forests International (☎ 800-447-1483; ☎ /fax 707-923-3015), Box 2453, Redway, California 95560.

Special Events
Mid-January's Jornadas Musicales de Pucón is an annual musical festival that's been going for more than a decade. A more recent event, in keeping with the growing popularity of outdoor recreation, is February's Triatlón Internacional de Pucón (Pucón International Triathlon).

Places to Stay
Pucón has abundant accommodations, including budget alternatives, but the seasonal differential is substantial, and good mid-range values are hard to find. Prices below are from the January/February high season; figure about 20% less the rest of the year.

Places to Stay – bottom
Camping Recommended *Camping Mapu-Rayen* (☎ 441378), about one km south of O'Higgins on Colo Colo, has hot showers, covered cooking areas, and is a little quieter than areas closer to the beach. Peak season rates are US$20 per site, but small parties may find it worth negotiating.

Camping Parque La Poza (☎ 441435), on shady grounds at Avenida Costanera Roberto Geis 769, charges US$20 per site.

Hospedajes Budget accommodation in Pucón starts around US$7 to 10, usually with breakfast and/or kitchen privileges, at places like *Hospedaje Lucila* at Pasaje Chile 225, *Hospedaje Juan Torres* (☎ 441-248) at Lincoyán 445, *Hospedaje Lucía* at Lincoyán 565, *Hospedaje González* (☎ 441491) at General Urrutia 484, *Hospedaje La Casita* (☎ 441712) at Palguín 555 and *Residencial Lincoyán* (☎ 441144) at Lincoyán 323.

Congenial *Hospedaje Sonia* (☎ 441269), a good place to meet people at Lincoyán 485, charges US$12.50 per person with breakfast and kitchen privileges. If there are no rooms at Sonia's, try her daughter's place at *Casa de Mayra*, Brasil 465.

In a category of its own (most fun) is *Hostería ¡Ecole!* (☎ 441675, fax 441660), formerly Hostería Don Pepe, at General Urrutia 592. At US$12 per person, though

it looks more expensive, it also has a superb vegetarian restaurant and a book exchange, holds parties and dances, and organizes informal tours to nearby attractions.

Places to Stay – middle
Mid-range accommodation starts around US$18/25 for singles/doubles with breakfast and shared bath at highly regarded *Hostería Salzburg* (☎ 441907), O'Higgins 311, whose biggest drawback is that it's on the busy main drag. Rooms with private bath cost around US$20/35.

Hostal Casablanca (☎ 441450), Palguín 136, provides reasonable accommodation for US$25/45 with breakfast, as does *Hotel La Palmera* (☎ /fax 441083), Ansorena 221, charging US$42/47. Though it's still a mid-range place by Pucón standards, *Hotel La Posada* (☎ 441088), Pedro de Valdivia 191, is no longer a bargain for US$60/75.

Places to Stay – top end
Top-end accommodation starts around US$75/90 at *Hotel Interlaken* (☎ 441276, fax 441242), on Caupolicán near Costanera Geis. Prices are about the same at *Hotel Araucarias* (☎ 441286), Caupolicán 243, but this former mid-range hotel is not the value it once was.

Germanic influence is obvious in chalet-style architecture like that of *Hotel Gudenschwager* (☎ 441156), Pedro de Valdivia 12, which has doubles with views across the lake for US$87.

Built by Ferrocarriles del Estado (the state railroad corporation) in the depths of the 1930s Great Depression, the imposing *Gran Hotel Pucón* (☎ 441001) offers lakefront luxury at Clemente Holzapfel 190. Rates start at US$95/127.

Camouflaged by lush gardens at Km 2 on the road to Villarrica, the exceptional *Hotel Antumalal* (☎ 441011/2, fax 441013) charges US$160/220 with breakfast.

Places to Eat
Most hotels have their own restaurants, but there are scores of other appealing places to eat, although some of them are only open in summer. For fast food, there are

fine empanadas at *Los Hornitos de Pucón*, Caupolicán 710. For cheap but decent eats, try *Coppa Kavanna* or *El Amigo*, both at Urrutia 407, and the *Strogen Bar* at Urrutia 417.

The inexpensive vegetarian specialties at tobacco-free *Hostería ¡Ecole!* (☎ 441675), General Urrutia 592, are one of the Pucón's special attractions. *Marmonch* (☎ 441972), Ecuador 175, has a different, inexpensive fixed-price lunch daily, while *Café Brasil*, Fresia 472, is recommended for trout and sandwiches. *La Sazón*, at the corner of Caupolicán and Urrutia, has a fixed-price lunch for about US$7.50.

Club 77, O'Higgins 635, offers traditional Chilean and regional specialties like pastel de choclo, baked empanadas and smoked trout. *Las Terrazas de Pucón* (☎ 441361), O'Higgins 323, is highly regarded for pizza, pancakes, meat and seafood, with outdoor patio dining. *El Fogón* (☎ 444904), O'Higgins 480, is a parrilla.

Puerto Pucón y Tequila (☎ 441592), Fresia 245, is a decent if overpriced Spanish/Mexican restaurant, but worth consideration. *La Marmita de Pericles*, at the corner of Fresia and Urrutia, serves crepes and fondue. Pricey *Crepes* (☎ 441-347), Lincoyán 372, is worth a look.

Il Fiore (☎ 441565), Holzapfel 83, specializes in upscale pasta, meat and seafood. *Como Pizza* (☎ 441109), next door at Holzapfel 71, serves the obvious.

For breakfast or onces, you can't do much better than Swiss-run *La Tetera* (☎ 441462), General Urrutia 580. It also has a book exchange with a good selection in English and Spanish, less so in German and French. For really exquisite sweets, try the *Holzapfel Bäckerei*, Clemente Holzapfel 524, which specializes in raspberry kuchen and other Germanic goodies; their garden seating features what may be Chile's largest *nalcas*.

Entertainment

The local branch of Santiago's *Geo Pub*, Lincoyán 361, is a popular summer hangout for Pucón's youthful adventure-oriented crowd. *Krater*, on O'Higgins near Palguín, is a pub and karaoke bar. Another possibility is *Mama's & Tapas*, at the corner of O'Higgins and Arauco.

Things to Buy

Pucón is a better place to do things than to buy things, but there's a Mercado Artesanal on Ansorena between O'Higgins and Brasil. Artesanía Llanka is at Lincoyán 140.

Getting There & Away

Air LanChile, on Fresia between Alderete and Urrutia, has occasional summer flights to and from Santiago. Ladeco maintains an office on O'Higgins near Caupolicán, but flies out of Temuco.

Bus Pucón's several bus terminals are all in the vicinity of the intersection of O'Higgins and Palguín. Long-distance services closely resemble those from Villarrica, and consequently are not mentioned in detail here.

Long-distance carriers include Tur-Bus (☎ 441965), Buses Lit (☎ 441055), Power (the cheapest but also least comfortable) and Empresa San Martín, all at the main Terminal de Buses at Palguín 383; Longitudinal Sur (☎ 442004) at Ansorena 343; Igi Llaima at the corner of O'Higgins and Colo Colo, and on Ansorena between Urrutia and O'Higgins.

Buses Jac (☎ 441923), O'Higgins 492, has countless departures from Pucón to Villarrica (1/2 hour, US$0.65), also serves Valdivia daily and adds local service to Caburgua (US$2) and Paillaco three times daily except Sunday, when it goes only twice. Buses Regionales Villarrica, alongside Tur-Bus, has four buses daily to Curarrehue and Puesco, the last stop before the border crossing to Junín de los Andes in Argentina.

Buses Cordillera (☎ 441061), Ansorena 302, goes to Paillaco on Lago Caburgua, near Parque Nacional Huerquehue, and to Termas de Huife, daily at 12.30 and 5 pm, for US$1. Buses Liucura (☎ 441061), Ansorena 309, also goes to Paillaco and Caburgua, and provides transportation to

Termas Los Pozones and Termas de Huife (US$7.50 return). Taxibus Rinconada, on Urrutia between Ansorena and Palguín, goes to Termas de Palguín.

AROUND PUCON
Casa Fuerte Santa Sylvia

In colonial times, the Villarrica region was one of the continent's southernmost encomiendas, but the general Mapuche uprising of 1599 caused the Spaniards to abandon the area and ended the forced labor system. Revealing evidence of that rebellion, excavations have found broken roofing tiles that apparently belonged to the encomendero's

residence, but there is also a chapel, houses for Mapuche servants and several graves. Small gold deposits attracted the Spaniards here, but determined Mapuche resistance soon drove them away.

Santa Sylvia is 18 km east of Pucón on the road to Termas de Huife; at the Huerquehue junction, take the road to the right. It's open daily 9 am to noon and 3 to 6 pm.

Hot Springs Resorts

La Araucanía's volcanic terrain means a multitude of hot springs, many of them in the Pucón area. **Termas de Huife**, only 30

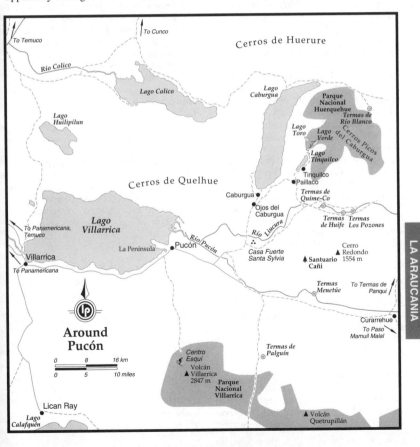

km northeast of Pucón on the Río Liucura, is an upscale location whose *Hotel Termas de Huife* (☎/fax 441222 in Pucón) is a chalet with singles/doubles for US$104/154. Day visitors, however, can use the baths all day for US$10, and meals are available in the cafeteria. More economical is the rustic **Termas Los Pozones**, a few km beyond Huife, where admission costs US$4. For transportation details, see the Getting There & Away entry for Pucón.

Termas de Palguín, 30 km southeast of Pucón on the Río Palguín, features the attractive German-built chalet *Hotel Termas de Palguín* (☎/fax 441968 in Pucón), built in the mid-1940s. Accommodation starts around US$45 per person with shared bath and full board, while rooms with private bath cost around US$85/115 for singles/doubles with full board. Day visitors can use the baths for US$10 and eat in the hotel's restaurant; camping is possible nearby. At *Rancho de Caballos* (☎ 441575), in Palguín Alto, cabaña accommodation is available for US$10 per person with hot showers and a good breakfast; rental horses are also available. For transport details, see the Getting There & Away entry for Pucón.

The unorthodox **Termas de Panqui**, 58 km east of Pucón via a 4WD road, is a North American deep ecology enclave (with Chilean participation at the business end) that offers accommodation in Sioux (Lakota) tipis and Mapuche rucas, vegetarian meals, hot pools, mud baths, yoga, tai chi, meditation and the like. Admission costs US$10, accommodation another US$10 and full board around US$20, plus IVA. Make reservations and arrange transportation through Termas de Panqui (☎ 442039, fax 442040), Ansorena 485, Oficina 5, in Pucón.

Santuario Cañi

Purchased and administered by the Fundación Lahuen to rescue it from a logging threat, Chile's first private nature reserve protects about 400 hectares of ancient Araucaria forest, 21 km east of Pucón. As part of an educational project to train local guides in natural history, the Fundación organizes overnight treks through the Cañi through its offices at Hostería ¡Ecole! (☎ 441675, fax 441660), General Urrutia 592 in Pucón.

PARQUE NACIONAL HUERQUEHUE

Mountainous Huerquehue is a compact 12,500-hectare reserve of rivers and waterfalls, alpine lakes and Araucaria and Nothofagus forests, with superb views across the Río Pucón valley to Volcán Villarrica. There are occasional sightings of the Andean condor, but woodpeckers and thrushes are far more common.

Conaf maintains a Centro de Educación e Intepretación Ambiental at the park entrance at Lago Tinquilco, where rangers collect a US$2 admission fee. The Centro is open daily 8 am to 8 pm in summer.

Geography & Climate

On the eastern shore of Lago Caburgua, 35 km northeast of Pucón, Huerquehue offers pleasant hiking and good camping. Rushing snowmelt streams have cut deep canyons whose flanks rise up to 2000 meters on Cerro Araucano.

The park enjoys warm summers, but snow accumulates at higher elevations in winter. The mean annual precipitation of 2000 mm of rain falls almost entirely between May and September, so November to April is the best time for a visit.

Lago Verde Trail

Leaving from park headquarters at Lago Tinquilco, this very fine day excursion switchbacks from 700 to 1300 meters through dense lenga forests and past several waterfalls. Frequent forest clearings reveal striking views of Volcán Villarrica in the distance. At upper elevations are solid stands of Araucaria trees.

At the outlet of Lago Chico, the first of three clustered lakes, there are fine pools for swimming on warm days. Well marked trails continue to Lago Toro and to Lago Verde, but backcountry camping is not allowed at present. The seven-km walk takes about two or three hours each way from Lago Tinquilco.

Camping
At Conaf's 18-site campground on Lago Tinquilco, rates are about US$7.50 per site.

Getting There & Away
From Pucón, Buses Jac, Buses Cordillera and Turismo Liucura provide regular transport to Paillaco, at the south end of Lago Caburgua; see the Pucón entry for details. It's another eight km on a very dusty, winding road to the park entrance at Lago Tinquilco; hitching may be feasible, but it's probably wiser to start walking and hope for a lift. Motorists may find this road difficult without 4WD.

Most Pucón adventure travel agencies have excursions to Huerquehue among their offerings.

PARQUE NACIONAL VILLARRICA
In his 16th-century epic *La Araucana*, a classic of colonial literature, Spanish poet Alonso de Ercilla paid homage to the perpetually smoldering cone of 2847-meter Volcán Villarrica, now the centerpiece of one of Chile's most accessible national parks:

Great neighbor volcano,
The forge, they say, of Vulcan,
That belches continuous fire . . .

Established in 1940 to protect its extraordinary scenery, Villarrica's 60,000 hectares also contain other, inactive volcanoes like 2360-meter Quetrupillán and, along the Argentine border, a section of 3746-meter Lanín, which has given its name to an equally impressive park across the frontier (Lanín must be climbed from the Argentine side).

Geography & Climate
Only 12 km from Pucón, this is an area of active vulcanism – a major 1971 eruption opened a four-km fracture in Volcán Villarrica that emitted 30 million cubic meters of lava and displaced several rivers. One flow, down the Río Challupén, was 14 km long, 200 meters wide, and five meters high.

Where lava flows have not penetrated, at elevations up to 1500 meters, dense forests of southern beech and Araucaria cover the mountain's flanks – Volcán Quetrupillán is the southern limit of the Araucaria's natural range. The climate resembles that of nearby Parque Nacional Huerquehue, though it tends to rain more around Villarrica.

Administratively, the park consists of three sectors. Sector Rucapillán, closest to Pucón, is most popular for its access to Volcán Villarrica, while Sector Quetrupillán and Sector Puesco are more remote but still accessible. Conaf collects a US$2 admission charge at Rucapillán.

Climbing & Trekking
Villarrica's accessibility makes it a mecca for hikers and climbers. The popular climb to the summit of Villarrica, which is physically but not technically demanding, requires equipment and either experience or a guide who knows the route; non-guided climbers require a special permit from Conaf. Do not hesitate to turn back in bad weather. For most visitors, the best bet is to arrange a full-day excursion with one of Pucón's many adventure travel companies for about US$35 per person.

The most convenient trek circles Villarrica's southern flank and leaves the park at Termas de Palguín. From Termas de Palguín there is another route to Puesco, near the Argentine border, where there is public transport back to Pucón. For trekking details, see Lonely Planet's *Trekking in the Patagonian Andes*.

Skiing
On the lower slopes of the volcano, *Refugio Villarrica* accommodates skiers in wintertime; for details, contact the Centro de Ski Volcán Villarrica (☎ 441176, 441901), in the Gran Hotel Pucón at Holzapfel 190.

Places to Stay

Pucón, Villarrica and other nearby areas are very convenient to the park, but Conaf also maintains *Camping La Llave* at Sector Rucapillán and *Camping Puesco* at Sector Puesco. Both charge about US$7.50 per site.

Getting There & Away

Although Sector Rucapillán is only a few km from Pucón, there is no scheduled public transport, but a shared taxi should cost no more than a few dollars per head. To Sector Puesco, there is regular transport from Pucón with Buses Regional Villarrica.

LICAN RAY

On the north shore of island-studded Lago Calafquén, surrounded by mountains and jammed with high-season refugees from Santiago, fashionable Lican Ray boasts one of the region's best beaches in the Playa Grande, a long strip of dark volcanic sand. After the sun sets on summer nights, most visitors promenade on its only paved street, Avenida General Urrutia, filling the restaurants, hotels and cafés.

Orientation

Lican Ray, a compact grid between the estuaries of the Río Muilpún and the Río Melilahuén, is 30 km south of Villarrica. General Urrutia, the main commercial street, is the southern extension of the paved Villarrica highway. Avenida Punulef, which runs along the Playa Grande, is the western boundary while Avenida Manquel, along the Playa Chica, is the southern limit. A rough gravel road goes west to Panguipulli, while a newly paved road follows the north shore of the lake east to Coñaripe.

Information

Tourist Office Lican Ray's municipal Oficina de Turismo (☎ 431201), directly on the plaza at General Urrutia 310, distributes maps, brochures and a list of hotels. In summer it's open 9 am to 10.30 pm daily; the rest of the year, hours are 9 am to 1 pm and 3 to 6.30 pm weekdays only.

Money Lican Ray has no exchange houses, but Supermercado Jumbito, on Urrutia between Millañanco and Huenumán, may change small amounts of US cash. In summer, Banco de Crédito operates a mobile bank with a 24-hour ATM, parked in front of the plaza Tuesdays and Wednesdays, but the nearest permanent cambio is at Villarrica.

Post & Communications Lican Ray's area code is ☎ 45. Correos de Chile is on Curiñanco between Huenumán and Marichanquín. CTC has a long-distance calling office on Huenumán near the corner of Urrutia and at Urrutia 505, while Entel is on Huenumán between Urrutia and Curiñanco.

Travel Agencies Turismo Trancura, which arranges adventure tourism activities in Pucón, has an office at the corner of General Urrutia and Marichanquín.

Medical Services There's a *posta médica* (first-aid station) on Esmeralda, behind the Plaza de Armas.

Special Events

The Gran Asado, a massive barbecue, takes place on Playa Chica the first weekend of January. In the second week of February, the town celebrates the annual Semana de Lican Ray.

Places to Stay

Residencial Temuco (☎ 431130), Gabriela Mistral 515, is fairly basic for US$9, with sagging beds and without breakfast, but it's passable and has a downstairs restaurant.

Woodsy *Residencial Catriñi* (☎ 411237), Catriñi 140, costs about US$10 per person with breakfast. While it's friendly, the eight beds in two-plus upstairs rooms take up almost all the floor space, and also sag a bit; there's one single room. The anonymous *Hospedaje* at Millañanco 145 also rents mountain bikes.

On attractive grounds at General Urrutia 860, the friendly *Hospedaje Neuquén*

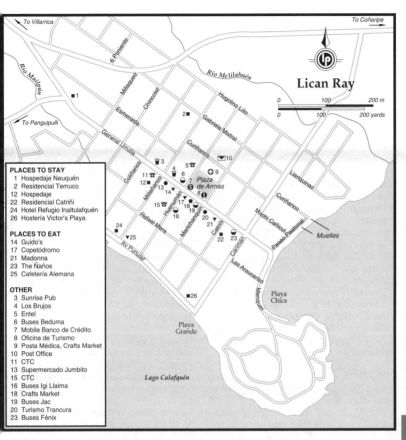

Lican Ray

To Villarrica
To Coñaripe
To Panguipulli

Río Muilinín
Río Melilahuén

0   100   200 m
0   100   200 yards

Río Melilahuén

Llandunad
Curiñanco
Machi Cañicul
Paseo Peatonal
Muelles

Playa Chica
Playa Grande

Lago Calafquén

PLACES TO STAY
1 Hospedaje Neuquén
2 Residencial Temuco
12 Hospedaje
22 Residencial Catriñi
24 Hotel Refugio Inaltulafquén
26 Hostería Victor's Playa

PLACES TO EAT
14 Guido's
17 Copetódromo
21 Madonna
23 The Ñaños
25 Cafetería Alemana

OTHER
3 Sunrise Pub
4 Los Brujos
5 Entel
6 Buses Beduma
7 Mobile Banco de Crédito
8 Oficina de Turismo
9 Posta Médica, Crafts Market
10 Post Office
11 CTC
13 Supermercado Jumbito
15 CTC
16 Buses Igi Llaima
18 Crafts Market
19 Buses Jac
20 Turismo Trancura
23 Buses Fénix

(☎ 431119), has small singles for US$10 without breakfast, US$12.50 with; there are outside tables for breakfast.

Hotel Refugio Inaltulafquén (☎ 412543), fronting on Playa Grande at Punulef 510, has rooms with shared bath for US$38 double. *Hostería Victor's Playa*, also on the beach at Punulef 120, offers rates of US$30/40 single/double.

Places to Eat
There are many cafés, restaurants and bars along General Urrutia and the Playa Grande. *The Ñaños* (☎ 431021), Urrutia 105, is one of the town's most popular establishments for its Chilean specialties. *Cafetería Alemana*, facing the beach at Punulef 440, is nothing extraordinary, but it's not bad either.

Copetódromo, on Urrutia between Huenumán and Marichanquín, is primarily a bar but also serves food. *Guido's*, Urrutia 405, specializes in meat, seafood and trout. *Madonna*, Urrutia 201, has a wider selection of toppings than most Chilean pizzerías.

LA ARAUCANIA

Entertainment

The *Sunrise Pub*, Urrutia 550, is a kara-oke bar, while *Los Brujos*, on Urrutia between Huenumán and Millañanco, offers live music.

Things to Buy

Lican Ray hosts two nightly crafts fairs in summer. The first, on Esmeralda behind the tourist office, consists of works by local artisans. The second, on Urrutia across from the tourist office, displays goods from other places in the region and around the country.

Getting There & Away

Bus Buses Jac, which has its own terminal at General Urrutia and Marichanquín, has frequent services to and from Villarrica (45 minutes), direct service to Santiago, and also goes to Coñaripe, with connections around the lake to Panguipulli. Buses Guarda goes to Panguipulli (US$2) via Calafquén daily at 7.30 am.

Several companies go to Santiago, including Tur-Bus (in season), Fénix on Urrutia between Catriñi and Carimán, Igi Llaima on Huenumán near Urrutia and Buses Beduma, at the corner of Huenumán and Urrutia.

COÑARIPE

Across the regional border, 22 km east of Lican Ray, Coñaripe is a modest resort whose black-sand beaches sprout multicolored tents during the summer holidays, but completion of the paved highway along the north shore of Lago Calafquén promises to convert it into another Lican Ray.

Pleasant but very basic *Hospedaje Antulafquén*, on the highway through town, charges US$8 per person. The very plain cafeteria opposite the hotel has fabulous humitas, but *El Mirador* is an attractive place for a more leisurely meal.

Buses Jac has several buses daily from Villarrica to Coñaripe via Lican Ray (US$2). Buses San Pedro runs three buses daily from Coñaripe to Panguipulli, while Buses Carrasco has one bus daily, at 11.30 am. Buses Interlagos also goes to

Panguipulli, as does Buses Panguipulli, six times daily from in front the supermarket. Bus Pirihueico goes to Panguipulli daily at 5 pm from in front of the CTC office. There's a minibus to Liquiñe, a nearby hot springs resort, daily at 1 pm.

PANGUIPULLI

At the northwest end of Lago Panguipulli, the town of Panguipulli (population 8300) is quieter, slower-paced and less touristy than many other lake resorts. About 115 km northeast of Valdivia by a paved highway, via Lanco on the Panamericana, it has sensational views across Lago Panguipulli to Volcán Choshuenco. The street plan is irregular, but it's small enough that getting lost is not a problem.

Information

Tourist Office Panguipulli's Oficina Municipal de Turismo (☎ 311311, Anexo 731) fronts directly on Plaza Arturo Prat. It's open daily 10 am to 9 pm from mid-December to mid-March, but keeps shorter hours the rest of the year.

Money Banco de Crédito is at the junction of Martínez de Rozas and Portales, on Plaza Arturo Prat, but has no ATM. Christopher Money Exchange, Martínez de Rozas 566, changes US cash and travelers' checks.

Post & Communications The area code is ☎ 63. Correos de Chile is on Plaza O'Higgins, a block north of Plaza Prat. Telefónica del Sur is on Portales between J M Carrera and Martínez de Rozas, while Chilesat is on O'Higgins between Pedro de Valdivia and M A Matta.

Special Events

In late January and early February, Panguipulli celebrates the town's founding during the Semana de la Rosa.

Places to Stay

Camping *Camping El Bosque* (☎ 311489), only 200 meters north of Plaza Prat, has 15 tent sites (no drive-in sites) for US$10 for two persons. Hot showers are available.

Hospedajes & Hotels Several modest hospedajes are in the US$10 range, including reader-endorsed *Hospedaje Berrocal* at J M Carrera 834, *Hospedaje Pozas* on Pedro de Valdivia between Gabriela Mistral and J M Carrera, and *Hospedaje Ormeño* on Arce near Freire. Friendly *Hotel Central* (☎ 311331), Pedro de Valdivia 115, has airy rooms and clean bathrooms with hot water (and even bathtubs) for US$20/30; upstairs rooms are quieter and larger.

At *Hostal España* (☎ 311166), O'Higgins 790, singles with private bath cost US$25/40 single/double with breakfast. *Cabañas Tío Carlos* (☎ 311215), Etchegaray 367, charges US$45 for a triple with private bath and separate kitchen.

Prices are about the same, US$25/45 with breakfast, at *Hostería Quetropillán* (☎ 311348), Etchegaray 381, a quiet location on the corner with Freire. On the road north to Lanco, 500 meters outside town, *Hotel Rayen Trai* (☎ 311292) charges US$75/88, but the service is indifferent.

Places to Eat

Try *El Chapulín* (☎ 311560) at Martínez de Rozas 639, which has meat and seafood dishes, or reader-recommended *Girasol* on Martínez de Rozas near Matta. *Café Central* (☎ 311495), Martínez de Rozas 880, serves snacks and onces. *Café Hanga Roa* (☎ 311214), O'Higgins 354, serves more elaborate lunches at reasonable prices, about US$5. *El Criollo*, on Matta between J M Carrera and Martínez de Rozas, also serves meat and seafood.

Perhaps the most interesting choice is the *Restaurant Didáctico El Gourmet*, Ramón Freire 0394, a cooking school whose graduate chefs seek jobs throughout the region and the country. It's open only during the peak summer months.

Getting There & Away

Bus Panguipulli's new Terminal de Buses is at the corner of Gabriela Mistral and Diego Portales, but Tur-Bus has its own terminal at Pedro de Valdivia and J M Carrera.

Panguisur has many buses daily to Temuco, and two daily to Santiago, at 6.30 and 8.15 pm. Tur-Bus has two early buses to Temuco and Santiago, a route also served by Intersur and Igi Llaima. Buses Pirehueico (☎ 311497), Valdivia and Chile Nuevo each have daily buses to Valdivia (2½ hours) and Puerto Montt. Buses Haedo goes to Valdivia twice daily, at 7.45 am and 2 pm.

Buses Hua Hum has several crowded buses daily to Choshuenco, Neltume and Puerto Fuy. For up-to-date information on the ferry from Puerto Fuy to Puerto Pirehueico and the Argentine border at Paso Hua Hum, ask at Hostería Quetropillán. Buses Ríos also goes to Neltume.

Ruta Andes has daily service to Coñaripe (US$1.75), with connections to Liquiñe, Lican Ray and Villarrica. Buses Panguipulli goes six times daily to Coñaripe, while Interlagos goes once daily, at 5 pm. Buses Urrutia goes to Calafquén at noon and 4 pm.

CHOSHUENCO

Choshuenco, little more than two streets at the east end of Lago Panguipulli, survives on farming, a local sawmill and visitors who enjoy its attractive black-sand beach. There are many fine walks in the nearby countryside, at the foot of 2415-meter Volcán Choshuenco.

Places to Stay & Eat

Beachfront *Hotel Rucapillán* (☎ 224402, Anexo 220), San Martín 85, is very clean, with heating, a good restaurant, hot showers and friendly staff. Rooms are about US$11 per person, with boats for hire as well. The basic but agreeable *Claris Hotel* is slightly cheaper. *Hotel Choshuenco* (☎ 224402, Anexo 214), Padre Bernabé s/n, charges US$40 double and also has a restaurant.

Hostería Pulmahue (☎ 224402), just out of town on the road to Enco at the east end of Lago Riñihue, sits among gardens above the lake. Pleasant rooms with private bath cost US$62 per person with full board.

Getting There & Away

Buses from Panguipulli to Puerto Fuy pass through Choshuenco, taking about two hours and returning to Panguipulli early the next morning. In January and February, from Puerto Fuy, the ferry *Mariela* (☎ 311348 in Panguipulli) carries passengers and vehicles to Puerto Pirehueico (two hours) daily at 9 am, returning at 5 pm. The rest of the year, it operates Tuesday and Thursday only at 7 am, returning at 10 am.

Small and medium-size autos pay US$30, while large autos, station wagons and pickup trucks pay US$40. Pedestrians pay US$2.50, cyclists US$5. The *Mariela* has a capacity of only 18 vehicles, so reservations are desirable.

VALDIVIA

After languishing throughout the colonial era, Valdivia owes much of its present character to mid-19th century German immigration. Middle-European influence has declined, but remains palpable in the city's architecture, German surnames and, in particular, the delicious regional cuisine. Though the major earthquake of 1960 destroyed many older landmarks, there are still many European-style buildings and mansions along General Lagos, near the riverfront.

On orders from Pedro de Valdivia, Juan Pastene took formal possession of this area in 1544. Valdivia himself decreed the foundation of the city of Santa María La Blanca de Valdivia in early 1552, on the site of a Mapuche settlement known as Guadalauquén. After Mapuche resistance obliterated Valdivia in 1599 and the Dutch had attempted to occupy the area, the Spaniards eventually rebuilt the city as a military encampment. There remain colonial fortifications at nearby Corral and Niebla, at the mouth of the Río Valdivia.

Orientation

Valdivia (population 95,000), 160 km southwest of Temuco and 45 km off the Panamericana, sits on the south bank of the Río Calle Calle where it becomes the Río Valdivia, near its confluence with the Río Cau Cau and the Río Cruces. Shaped in part by the meandering river, the core of the *Ciudad de los Ríos* (City of the Rivers) is a very compact, triangular area between Calle Arauco and the riverfront.

Within this core, the Avenida Costanera Arturo Prat (more conveniently known as 'Prat') is a major focus of activity, but most important public buildings are on the central Plaza de la República. From the Panamericana, Avenida Ramón Picarte is the main eastern approach. To the west, the Puente Pedro de Valdivia crosses the river to Isla Teja, a leafy suburb which is the site of the Universidad Austral.

Information

Tourist Offices Sernatur (☎ 215396, fax 218692), on the riverfront at Prat 555, is open weekdays 9 am to 8.30 pm, Saturdays 10 am to 4 pm, and Sundays 10 am to 2 pm. There is also an Oficina de Informaciones (☎ 212212) at the bus terminal, Anfión Muñoz 360, open daily 8.30 am to 10 pm.

The Automóvil Club de Chile (☎ 212-376), Caupolicán 475, is also a good source of information.

Money Valdivia has three exchange houses for both cash and travelers' checks: Cambio Global at Arauco 331, Local 24, El Libertador at Carampangue 325, and Turismo Christopher at Independencia and Arauco, Local 1. Banco Concepción, Picarte 370, has an ATM.

Post & Communications The area code is ☎ 63. Correos de Chile is at O'Higgins 575, opposite Plaza de la República. Telefónica del Sur has long-distance offices at San Carlos 107, but there are others at O'Higgins 386 and at Picarte 461, Local 2. Entel is at Arauco 601, Local 1, Chilesat at O'Higgins 575.

Travel Agencies Turismo Cochrane (☎ 212213), Arauco 436, arranges air and bus tickets and rents cars. Similar agencies include Turismo Cono Sur (☎ 212757) at Maipú 129, and Turismo Paraty (☎ 215-585) at Independencia 640.

Bookshops Libros Chiloé, Caupolicán 410, has a good selection of books by Chilean and foreign authors.

Cultural Centers The Centro Cultural El Austral (☎ 213658), Yungay 733, hosts public events in music and the arts. The Corporación Cultural de Valdivia, Prat 549, also promotes local cultural activities.

Laundry Lavamatic, Walter Schmidt 305, is open 9.30 am to 8.30 pm daily except Sunday.

Medical Services Valdivia's Hospital Regional (☎ 214066) is south of downtown at Bueras 1003, near Aníbal Pinto.

Things to See
Valdivia's **Feria Fluvial**, a riverside market north of the Sernatur office, is a great place to buy a bag of cherries and just watch the river flow. On Sundays, Valdivianos flock to the area to buy fish and fruit for the week, float downstream to Niebla and Corral, or just plain relax in the sun.

East of the bus terminal, the **Torreón del Barro** is the turret of a Spanish fort built in 1774. A 17th-century turret, the **Torreón de los Canelos**, stands at the corner of Yerbas Buenas and General Lagos, facing the Río Valdivia.

Museo Histórico y Arqueológico Mauricio van de Maele
Housed in a fine riverfront mansion on Isla Teja, one of Chile's most beautiful museums features a large, well-labeled collection from pre-Columbian times to the present, with particularly fine displays of Mapuche Indian artifacts and household items from early German settlements. Well organized tours, in Spanish only, are a bit rushed but the guides are happy to answer questions at the end.

To get to the museum (☎ 212872), which sits across the Río Valdivia from the Puerto Fluvial, take the bridge across the Río Valdivia, turn left at the first intersection and walk about 200 meters; the entrance is on the left (east) side, at Los Laureles 47.

December to March, it's open 10 am to 1 pm and 4 to 7 pm; the rest of the year, hours are 10 am to 1 pm and 2 to 6 pm. Admission is about US$1.25 for adults, US$0.50 for children.

Parque Saval
On Isla Teja, Parque Saval is a botanical garden, shady with a riverside beach. A pleasant trail follows the shoreline of Laguna de los Lotos, covered with lily pads and a good place to see birds. Admission is US$0.50, but it is also possible to camp for US$6 per night in limited facilities.

Opposite the park entrance, at the north end of Los Laureles, the Universidad Austral operates a first-rate dairy outlet which sells very fine ice cream, yogurt and cheese at bargain prices.

Special Events
Valdivia's numerous summer events are all subsets of Verano en Valdivia, a two-month long celebration that includes many minor happenings and more significant ones like late January's Festival Musical de Valdivia; February 9's Aniversario de la Ciudad, a commemoration of the city's founding; and February 17's Noche de Valdivia, with decorated river boats and fireworks.

Places to Stay
Valdivia's accommodation scene is a bit unusual, with plenty of budget choices, at least in summer, relatively few lower mid-range places, and a number of good upper-middle to top-end values. For most of the year, students from the Universidad Austral monopolize the cheapest lodging, but many of these same places vigorously court tourists in summer. Some hospedajes take their name from the street where they're located, so don't be surprised to find three or more with identical names – if someone recommends a place, be sure to get the exact street number.

Hospedajes are heavily concentrated on Avenida Ramón Picarte and Carlos Anwandter. Sernatur keeps a list of seasonal accommodation, which changes from year to year.

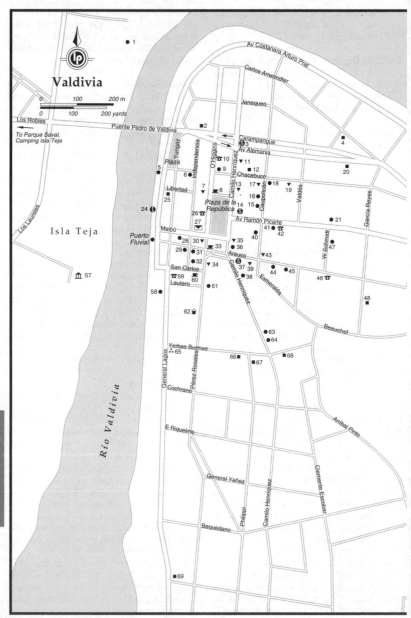

LA ARAUCANIA

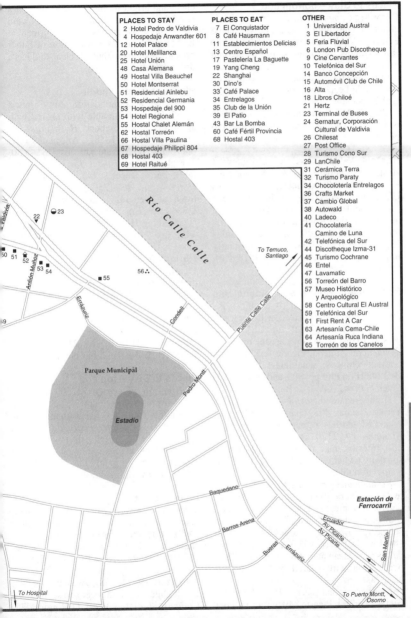

PLACES TO STAY
2 Hotel Pedro de Valdivia
4 Hospedaje Anwandter 601
12 Hotel Palace
20 Hotel Melillanca
25 Hotel Unión
48 Casa Alemana
49 Hostal Villa Beauchef
50 Hotel Montserrat
51 Residencial Ainlebu
52 Residencial Germania
53 Hospedaje del 900
54 Hotel Regional
55 Hostal Chalet Alemán
62 Hostal Torreón
66 Hostal Villa Paulina
67 Hospedaje Philippi 804
68 Hostal 403
69 Hotel Raitué

PLACES TO EAT
7 El Conquistador
8 Café Hausmann
11 Establecimientos Delicias
13 Centro Español
17 Pastelería La Baguette
19 Yang Cheng
22 Shanghai
30 Dino's
33 Café Palace
34 Entrelagos
35 Club de la Unión
39 El Patio
43 Bar La Bomba
60 Café Fértil Provincia
68 Hostal 403

OTHER
1 Universidad Austral
3 El Libertador
5 Feria Fluvial
6 London Pub Discotheque
9 Cine Cervantes
10 Telefónica del Sur
14 Banco Concepción
15 Automóvil Club de Chile
16 Alta
18 Libros Chiloé
21 Hertz
23 Terminal de Buses
24 Sernatur, Corporación Cultural de Valdivia
26 Chilesat
27 Post Office
28 Turismo Cono Sur
29 LanChile
31 Cerámica Terra
32 Turismo Paraty
34 Chocolotería Entrelagos
36 Crafts Market
37 Cambio Global
38 Autowald
40 Ladeco
41 Chocolatería Camino de Luna
42 Telefónica del Sur
44 Discotheque Izma-31
45 Turismo Cochrane
46 Entel
47 Lavamatic
56 Torreón del Barro
57 Museo Histórico y Arqueológico
58 Centro Cultural El Austral
59 Telefónica del Sur
61 First Rent A Car
63 Artesanía Cema-Chile
64 Artesanía Ruca Indiana
65 Torreón de los Canelos

Places to Stay – bottom end
Camping *Camping Isla Teja* (☎ 213584) is about half an hour's walk across Puente Pedro de Valdivia, at the end of Calle Los Robles and Los Cipreses. It's a pleasant orchard setting – free apples in late summer – with good sanitary facilities and a riverside beach, but prices have risen to US$20 per site.

Cheaper but less comfortable camping is possible at Parque Saval, for about US$6 per site.

Hostels
Valdivia has two affiliates of Hostelling International: *Residencial Germania* (☎ 212405), Picarte 873, charges US$11 with breakfast, hot showers, clean rooms and friendly German-speaking owners, while the beautifully done *Hostal Torreón* (☎ 212622), Pérez Rosales 783, whose friendly hostess is constantly improving service, charges US$18 with breakfast.

Hospedajes, Hotels & Residenciales
Friendly *Hotel Regional* (☎ 216027), Picarte 1005, is plain but clean, with hot water and a small restaurant for US$10 per person. In this same range are the marginal *Residencial Ainlebu*, Picarte 865, and two readers' choices: a nameless *Hospedaje* (☎ 224221) at Philippi 804, and *Hostal Villa Beauchef* (☎ 216044) at Beauchef 844.

Highly regarded *Hostal 403* (☎ 219389), Yerbas Buenas 403, charges US$13 with breakfast and has a good restaurant. *Casa Alemana* (☎ 212015), at García Reyes 658 Interior, has a hospitable German-speaking owner who charges US$13/25 for a single/double.

Residencial Germania (☎ 212405), Picarte 873, is a very decent place for US$15 per person with breakfast, hot showers, heated rooms, a restaurant and friendly, German-speaking owners. *Hospedaje del 900* (☎ 213055), Picarte 953 near the bus terminal, is very clean and attractive, for US$15 per person with shared bath, including breakfast.

Another popular place is *Hotel Montserrat* (☎ 215401), Picarte 849, with small but clean and bright rooms for US$15/29 for a single/double with breakfast. *Hotel Unión* (☎ 213819), Prat 514, is overpriced at US$15 per head, in part because of rather brusque ownership, but it's clean and has a downstairs bar.

Places to Stay – middle
Mid-range accommodation starts around US$25/35 single/double with shared bath at highly recommended *Hospedaje Anwandter 601* (☎ 218587), Anwandter 601, but rooms with private bath cost US$45/50. Try also homey *Hostal Torreón* (☎ 212-622), Pérez Rosales 783, for US$31/58. *Hotel Raitué* (☎ 212503), south of downtown at General Lagos 1382, charges US$40 single or double.

Charming *Hostal Villa Paulina* (☎ 212-445, fax 216372), Yerbas Buenas 389, charges US$40/57 with private bath, while *Hostal Chalet Alemán* (☎ /fax 218810), Picarte 1134, costs US$42/62. One of Valdivia's best values, across Puente Pedro de Valdivia at Las Encinas 220, *Hotel Isla Teja* (☎ 215014, fax 214911) costs US$46/54 in a tranquil but still very convenient setting. For US$50/64, the very central *Hotel Palace* (☎ 213319, fax 219133), Chacabuco 308, has small but pleasant rooms.

Places to Stay – top end
At *Hotel Melillanca* (☎ 212509, fax 222-740), Avenida Alemania 675, rates start at US$65/89, but it's questionable value for the money. *Hotel Pedro de Valdivia* (☎ /fax 212931), a pink palace with elaborate gardens at Carampangue 190, sits alone at the top of the category at US$91/109 with breakfast.

Places to Eat
Valdivia has a variety of good to excellent restaurants in all price categories. *Dino's* (☎ 213061), the popular southern Chilean chain, has a branch at Maipú 191. *Hostal 403* (☎ 219389), Yerbas Buenas 403, has a different dinner special every night.

El Patio (☎ 215238), Arauco 347, is a worthwhile choice for beef and seafood. *El Conquistador* (☎ 213129), O'Higgins 477, has a simple downstairs café and a fancier upstairs restaurant, with a balcony overlooking the plaza. *Club de la Unión* (☎ 213377), also on the plaza at Camilo Henríquez 540, offers filling, well prepared three-course meals, with tea or coffee, for about US$6. Try also the *Centro Español* (☎ 213540) at Henríquez 436, or the *Bar La Bomba* (☎ 213317), Caupolicán 594, which has good meals, reasonable prices and occasional live music.

Valdivia has two Chinese restaurants, *Yang Cheng* (☎ 224088) at Chacabuco 455 and *Shanghai* (☎ 212577) at Anwandter 898. For coffee and snacks, check out *Café Palace* (☎ 213539), Pérez Rosales 580; it's extremely popular with young people, especially Saturday mornings. For pastries and desserts, try *Establecimientos Delicias* (☎ 213566) at Henríquez 372 or *Café Hausmann* (☎ 213878) at O'Higgins 394.

There are very fine kuchen at *Pastelería La Baguette*, Caupolicán 435-B, and good ice cream at *Entrelagos* (☎ 218333), Pérez Rosales 630. Recommended by several readers, *Café Fértil Provincia*, San Carlos 169, is a hybrid bookstore-café that sometimes offers live folk music and jazz.

Entertainment

Cine Cervantes, Chacabuco 210, is the only place to see first-run movies.

Downtown pubs and discos include Discotheque Izma-31 (☎ 213737) at Arauco 425, and London Pub Discotheque (☎ 218-080) at Independencia 471.

Things to Buy

Chocolates are a regional specialty, with several different outlets including Chocolatería Entrelagos at Pérez Rosales 622 and Chocolatería Camino de Luna at Picarte 417.

There's a worthwhile, informal crafts market in the evening at the northeast corner of Arauco and Henríquez. More conventional outlets include Artesanía Cema-Chile at Henríquez 726, Ruca Indiana at Henríquez 758 and Cerámica Terra at Arauco 175, Local 4.

Getting There & Away

Air LanChile (☎ 213042), at Arauco 159, Oficina 201, has one flight daily to Santiago (US$152). Ladeco (☎ 213392), Caupolicán 579, Local 4, flies nightly to Temuco (US$25) and Santiago.

Alta (☎ 228150), Caupolicán 435, Local 1, flies twice daily weekdays and daily on weekends to Osorno (US$13), Concepción (US$41) and Viña del Mar (US$92).

Bus Valdivia's Terminal de Buses (☎ 212-212) is at Anfión Muñoz 360. Tur-Bus (☎ 212430), Tas Choapa (☎ 213124), Buses Norte (☎ 212800), Igi Llaima (☎ 213542), Buses Lit (☎ 212835) and Cruz del Sur (☎ 213840) have frequent buses to destinations on or near the Panamericana between Puerto Montt and Santiago. Typical fares are Temuco US$3.50, Puerto Montt US$6, Concepción US$10 and Santiago US$18.

Several companies serve lake district destinations. Línea Verde, Pirehueico (☎ 218609), Valdivia and Chile Nuevo go to Panguipulli, while Línea Verde has daily buses to Futrono. Buses Jac has regular service to Villarrica and Temuco. Fares to Panguipulli and Villarrica are around US$3.

Tas Choapa, Cruz del Sur, Andesmar and Buses Norte serve Bariloche (US$23).

Train Though there is talk of restoring direct rail service from Santiago, at present a bus-train combination serves Valdivia via Temuco. For tickets and information, go to the Ferrocarriles del Estado (☎ 214571), Ecuador 2000, with any east-bound bus or taxi colectivo on Arauco or Picarte.

Getting Around

From the bus terminal or train station, any bus marked 'Plaza' will take you to Plaza de la República. Buses from the plaza to the terminal go down Arauco before turning onto Picarte. There are also taxi colectivos.

To/From the Airport Valdivia's Aeropuerto Pichoy is north of the city via the Puente Calle Calle. Transfer Valdivia (☎ 225533) provides on-demand minibus service to the airport for US$5.

LA ARAUCANIA

Car Rental Rental cars are available from Hertz (☎ 218317) at Picarte 640, Autowald (☎ 212786) at Henríquez 610, and First Rent A Car (☎ 215973) at Pérez Rosales 674.

AROUND VALDIVIA
Corral, Niebla & Isla Mancera

Southwest of Valdivia, where the Río Valdivia and the Río Tornagaleones join the Pacific, there are 17th-century Spanish forts at Corral, Niebla and on the island of Mancera. Largest and most intact is the **Fuerte de Corral**, built in 1645 and restored and expanded in the 18th century. Nearby **Fuerte Castillo de Armagos**, a half-hour's walk north of Corral, sits on a crag above a small fishing village. Corral and Armagos are most easily reached by boat from Valdivia, as are the fortifications at **Isla Mancera**. **Fuerte Niebla**, on the north side of the river, is accessible by either bus or boat from Valdivia.

In 1820, a single Chilean warship under Scotsman Lord Thomas Cochrane launched an audacious but successful assault on Spanish forces at what one of his subordinates later called the 'Gibraltar of South America.' Boldly seizing a Spanish vessel in the harbor, Cochrane landed 300 musketeers who took Corral by surprise – no mean feat, since it was defended by more than 700 soldiers and 100 cannons.

Lord Cochrane himself had a colorful career. Convicted of fraud and jailed in Britain, he became one of the world's highest-ranking mercenaries, serving countries such as Chile, Brazil and Greece. Britain restored his rank in 1842 and even promoted him to Admiral in 1854.

Also a popular bathing resort for Valdivianos, Niebla has a tourist office, open daily 9 am to 1 pm and 2.30 to 7 pm in summer. One traveler has praised *Restaurant Canto del Agua*, which serves fish fresh off the boat. In Corral, which is a more tranquil place to stay, several waterfront restaurants serve huge plates of curanto; try *Restaurant Español*.

Getting There & Away The best alternative is to take a leisurely cruise on the regular launches from the Puerto Fluvial, near the Sernatur office, and return by bus in the afternoon. Departures vary according to the day and season; the trip takes about 2½ hours from Valdivia to Corral via Isla Mancera, Armagos and Niebla. Prices vary considerably, depending on the level of service, but range from about US$3 to US$10.

Among the choices are the *Neptuno* and *Ainlebu* (☎ 215889), the *Orion III* and the *Valdivia Express* (☎ 210533), the *Reina Sofía* (☎ 217364), the *Río Calle Calle* (☎ 212464) and the *Isla del Río* (☎ 225244).

Leaving daily at noon, Tour Puerta al Pacífico includes lunch and visits to Corral, Niebla and Isla Mancera for US$30. All services are less frequent outside the summer high season.

Buses to Niebla leave from the corner of Yungay and Chacabuco in Valdivia. There are 21 launches daily across the river between Niebla and Corral for US$0.75.

FUTRONO

On the north shore of Lago Ranco, Futrono is a small, quiet and dusty town (permanent population 3000), 102 km from Valdivia via Paillaco, on the Panamericana. While the lakeshore is attractive, public access is limited and difficult. The main street, Avenida Balmaceda, continues east to Llifén and Lago Maihue; although the road around the east side of Lago Ranco is very poor beyond Llifén, travelers to the town of Lago Ranco can make connections there.

Places to Stay & Eat

Modest but friendly *Hospedaje Futronhue*, on Balmaceda near Manuel Rodríguez, is clean, tidy and has hot showers for US$8 per person. *Hostería Rincón Arabe* (☎ 481-262, fax 481330), on the diagonal Manuel Montt off Balmaceda as you enter from the west, overlooks the lake, with a swimming pool and a very fine restaurant. It has recently changed ownership, but there are still excellent Middle Eastern and Chilean meals. Rooms cost about US$15 per person with breakfast.

Getting There & Away

Futrono's four bus companies have offices on Avenida Balmaceda. Buses Futrono, Buses en Directo, Buses Pirehueico and Buses Cordisur each operate several buses daily to Valdivia (US$2) via Paillaco. Cordisur continues to Llifén and Riñinahue, for connections to the town of Lago Ranco.

LLIFEN

Llifén, at the east end of Lago Ranco via a rather poor road, is a more attractive but significantly more expensive resort than Futrono. *Hostería Chollinco* (☎ 481295, fax 481205 in Valdivia), a short distance up the road to Lago Maihue, charges US$31 for campsites, not to mention US$40 per person for accommodation with breakfast. Lodging is available at *Hostería Lican* (☎ 215757, fax 213155) for US$25/45 with breakfast, or at *Hostería Huequecura* (☎ 218125 in Valdivia) for US$45/55.

RIO BUENO

On the Panamericana, 40 km north of Osorno, Río Bueno (population 13,000-plus) is a crossroads for Lago Ranco. Dating from 1778, its colonial **Fuerte San José de Alcudia** commands a bluff overlooking the river, while the **Museo Arturo Moller Sandrock**, Pedro Lago 640, contains Mapuche artifacts and documentation on German colonization in the region. The museum is open weekdays 9 am to noon and 2 to 6 pm in summer only.

Reasonable accommodation is available at the *Hotel Richmond* (☎ (064) 341363), Comercio 755, for about US$10 per person. There are several buses daily to Lago Ranco with Obando, Buses del Sur, San Martín and Buses Ruta 5.

LAGO RANCO

On the south shore of its namesake lake, the village of Lago Ranco is a modest working-class resort (permanent population about 2000) in pleasant but unspectacular country, 124 km from Valdivia via Río Bueno. The Mapuche reserve of Isla Huapi, in the middle of the lake, lends the town a strong indigenous presence.

Information

Tourist Offices Staffed by young, friendly, enthusiastic and well informed locals, Lago Ranco's municipal tourist office has free maps and leaflets on the Lake District. It's on the north side of Avenida Concepción, the main road from Río Bueno, and is open daily 8.30 am to 12.30 pm and 2.30 to 6.30 pm in summer only.

Turihott (☎ 491201), Valparaíso 111, runs auto trips around Lago Ranco and has a launch for excursions to Isla Huapi.

Special Events

Visitors are welcome to the Mapuche festival Lepun, which takes place on Isla Huapi in late January, but photography is strictly forbidden.

Places to Stay & Eat

Residencial Osorno, Temuco 103, is a spartan but tidy hotel charging about US$8 per person. *Hostería Casona Italiana* (☎ 491225), on the lakefront at Viña del Mar 145, is a clean, bright place with moderate prices, about US$20 per person. Almost next door at Viña del Mar 141, *Hostería Phoenix* (☎ 491226) is only slightly more expensive.

Camping Lago Ranco, on a crowded lakefront site with limited shade, charges US$15 per site. Hot showers are available on a limited schedule.

Getting There & Away

Weekdays at 9 am, Buses Obando goes to Río Bueno, with connections both north and south on the Panamericana. Buses San Martín also goes to Río Bueno, while Buses Ruta 5 goes to Osorno via Río Bueno.

Buses Lagos del Sur also goes to Osorno and to Riñinahue, at the east end of Lago

Ranco. Obando also has buses to Riñinahue, with connections to Futrono which include crossing the Río Calcurrupe on a barge driven by the current.

OSORNO

Founded in 1558 by García Hurtado de Mendoza, by the end of the 16th century San Mateo de Osorno had a population of more than 1000 Spaniards and mestizos, supported directly or indirectly by encomiendas of 80,000 Indians. After the great Mapuche rebellion of 1599 forced the city's inhabitants to flee to Chiloé, it was not until 1796 that the Spaniards re-established the settlement. Even after Chilean independence from Spain, growth was slow, and overland communications were difficult and dangerous because of Mapuche control over the countryside.

Since the mid-19th century, German immigrants have left their mark on the city and the region, particularly in manufacturing and dairy farming. By the turn of the 20th century, the population reached 5000, the city had its first newspapers and the railroad had arrived from Santiago. The local economy still relies on agriculture and its subsidiary industries, but tourism is increasing significantly, thanks to nearby lake resorts and the excellent communications both north and south, as well as across the Andes to Argentina. A recent construction boom has highlighted the city's increasing commercial importance.

Orientation

At the confluence of the Río Rahue and the Río Damas, Osorno (population 105,000) is 910 km south of Santiago and 110 km north of Puerto Montt via the Panamericana. The city is a key road transport hub, especially to Lago Puyehue, Lago Rupanco, Parque Nacional Puyehue and Pajaritos (the major border crossing to Argentina).

Most places of interest to the visitor are within a few blocks of the Plaza de Armas, in an area bounded by the Rahue to the west, the Damas to the north, Avenida Bilbao to the south, and Calle Angulo to the east.

Information

Tourist Offices Sernatur (☎ 237575) is on the ground floor of the Edificio Gobernación Provincial, on the west side of the Plaza de Armas. Well stocked with maps, pamphlets and information on Osorno and the entire region, it's open weekdays 8.30 am to 1 pm and 2.30 to 6.30 pm. In summer, there's usually an English speaker on duty.

From mid-December through March, the municipal Departamento de Turismo operates an information kiosk at the northwest corner of the Plaza de Armas. Its hours are 10 am to 8 pm Monday through Saturday, 10 am to 2 pm Sunday.

There is a private information office (☎ 234149), coordinated with Sernatur, at the main Terminal de Buses, Errázuriz 1400. Another good source of information is the Automóvil Club de Chile (☎ 232-269), Manuel Bulnes 463.

El Diario Austral, Osorno's daily newspaper, publishes a useful monthly *Guía de Servicios* in summer.

Money Turismo Frontera (☎ 236394) in the Galería Catedral at Ramírez 949, Local 5, and Cambiotur, Juan Mackenna 1010, change US and Argentine cash and US$ travelers' checks. Banco de Osorno has an ATM at the corner of Ramírez and Matta.

Post & Communications Osorno's area code is ☎ 64. Correos de Chile is at O'Higgins 645, opposite the Plaza de Armas. Telefónica del Sur, Mackenna 1004, is very efficient for overseas calls. CTC is at Ramírez 778, Entel at Ramírez 1107, Chilesat at O'Higgins 645 and the private Centro de Llamados at Ramírez 816.

Consulates The German Consulate (☎ 232151) is in the Edificio Paillahue at Mackenna 987, Oficina 4.

Travel Agencies In addition to Turismo Frontera (see Money, above), try Osorno Tour (☎ 238034) at Cochrane 610, 2nd floor. Lagos Austral (☎ 234137), Ramírez 949, Local 12, runs tours to Parque Nacional Puyehue.

Cultural Centers Osorno's Centro Cultural (☎ 238898), Avenida Matta 556, offers rotating exhibitions of painting, photography and other events. It's open daily 9 am to 1 pm and 3 to 7.30 pm.

The Alianza Francesa is at Los Carrera 753, while the Instituto Chileno-Norteamericano is at Los Carrera 770.

National Parks Conaf (☎ 234393) is at Martínez de Rozas 430.

Laundry Lavandería Limpec is at Prat 678.

Medical Services Osorno's Hospital Base (☎ 235572) is on Avenida Bühler, the southward extension of Arturo Prat.

Things to See
Between the Plaza de Armas and the **Estación de Ferrocarril** (railway station, 1912), new construction is threatening many deteriorating but intriguing buildings in Osorno's **Distrito Histórico** (historic district), which includes obsolete factories and weathered Victorian houses. Some, however, have been well restored, like the silos of the **Sociedad Molinera de Osorno**, an early grain mill.

West of the railway station, the bulwarks of Osorno's **Fuerte Reina Luisa**, built in 1793 on the orders of Governor Ambrosio O'Higgins (father of Bernardo O'Higgins), once guarded riverine access to Osorno. While the well restored ruins are unspectacular, they're a pleasant site for a lunchtime breather.

At Mackenna 949, the **Casa Mohr Pérez** (1876) is Osorno's oldest surviving Germanic construction, but the 1000 block of Mackenna, between Cochrane and Freire, preserves a solid row of early Germanic houses. The **Cementerio Católico** (Catholic cemetery), at Manuel Rodríguez and Eduvijes, has immense, ornate family crypts with numerous German surnames, reflecting the town's history from the 19th century to the present. There is also a larger **Cementerio Alemán** on Los Carrera, between Arturo Prat and Angulo.

Museo Histórico Municipal
Osorno's well arranged historical museum includes exhibits on Mapuche culture, the city's shaky colonial origins, German colonization and 19th-century development, local naval hero Eleuterio Ramírez and natural history displays.

The museum holds several uncommon and noteworthy objects. A very unusual collection of antique firearms includes a pistol that seems to be attached to an early Swiss army knife, while one historical photograph of Termas de Puyehue, east of Osorno, depicts the modest origins of what is now an elegant, expensive resort.

At Matta 809, the museum (☎ 233618) is open weekdays 10 am to 12.30 pm and 2.30 to 6.15 pm; additional summer hours are Saturday 11 am to 1 pm and 4 to 6 pm, Sunday 3 to 6 pm only. Admission is free.

Special Events
Osorno's Festival Regional del Folklore Campesino, for two days in mid-January, presents and promotes typical music, dance, crafts and food. Later, at the end of March, it hosts the Semana Osornina, a celebration of the city's colonial origins and Germanic heritage.

Places to Stay – bottom end
Camping *Camping Olegario Mohr*, on the south bank of the Río Damas just off the Panamericana, is a shady municipal site, with picnic tables and fire pits, but it lacks hot water and has only two toilets each for men and women. It's no longer free, and the attendants lock the front gate between 10 pm and 8 am, so it's impossible to leave or enter during those hours. Any taxi colectivo out Avenida Buschmann will drop you at the Panamericana, within a few minutes' walk of the site.

Hospedajes & Residenciales Ramshackle, basic *Hospedaje Westermeyer* (☎ 243394), at Freire 810, charges US$6 including kitchen privileges. *Hospedaje Central* (☎ 231031), at Bulnes 876, is comparable.

Close to the bus terminal, *Hospedaje de*

LA ARAUCANIA

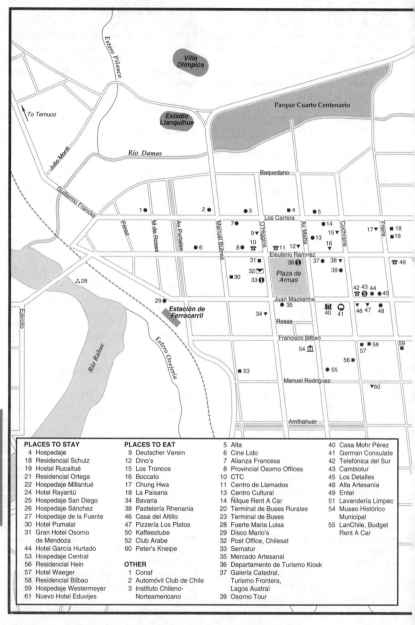

LA ARAUCANIA

PLACES TO STAY
4   Hospedaje
18 Residencial Schulz
19 Hostal Rucaitué
21 Residencial Ortega
22 Hospedaje Millantué
24 Hotel Rayantú
25 Hospedaje San Diego
26 Hospedaje Sánchez
27 Hospedaje de la Fuente
30 Hotel Pumalal
31 Gran Hotel Osorno
    de Mendoza
44 Hotel García Hurtado
53 Hospedaje Central
56 Residencial Hein
57 Hotel Waeger
58 Residencial Bilbao
59 Hospedaje Westermeyer
61 Nuevo Hotel Eduvijes

PLACES TO EAT
9   Deutscher Verein
12 Dino's
15 Los Troncos
16 Boccato
17 Chung Hwa
18 La Paisana
34 Bavaria
38 Pastelería Rhenania
46 Casa del Altillo
47 Pizzería Los Platos
50 Kaffeestube
52 Club Arabe
60 Peter's Kneipe

OTHER
1   Conaf
2   Automóvil Club de Chile
3   Instituto Chileno-
    Norteamericano

5   Alta
6   Cine Lido
7   Alianza Francesa
8   Provincial Osorno Offices
10 CTC
11 Centro de Llamados
13 Centro Cultural
14 Nílque Rent A Car
20 Terminal de Buses Rurales
23 Terminal de Buses
28 Fuerte Maria Luisa
29 Disco Mario's
32 Post Office, Chilesat
33 Sernatur
35 Mercado Artesanal
36 Departamento de Turismo Kiosk
37 Galería Catedral,
    Turismo Frontera,
    Lagos Austral
39 Osorno Tour

40 Casa Mohr Pérez
41 German Consulate
42 Telefónica del Sur
43 Cambiotur
45 Los Detalles
48 Alta Artesanía
49 Entel
51 Lavandería Limpec
54 Museo Histórico
    Municipal
55 LanChile, Budget
    Rent A Car

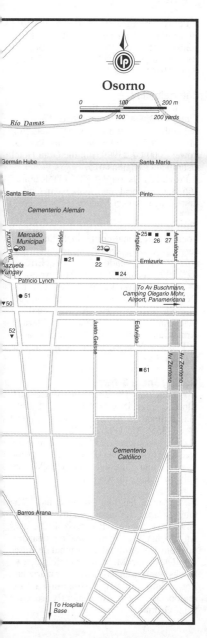

Osorno

la Fuente (☎ 239516), Los Carrera 1587, charges about US$7.50 per person after amicable haggling. It's spotlessly clean but the beds sag. *Hospedaje Sánchez* (☎ 232-560), almost next door at Los Carrera 1595, charges US$10 per person with breakfast and kitchen privileges. In the middle of the block, at Los Carrera 1551, *Hospedaje San Diego* is also worth a look.

An anonymous *Hospedaje* at Los Carrera 872, next to the Esso station, is very clean and comfortable at US$8 per person, including breakfast. At Colón 602, renovated *Residencial Ortega* (☎ 232592) is excellent value for US$10 with breakfast and shared bath; it's simple but very clean, and has pleasant common spaces.

Congenial *Residencial Hein* (☎ 234116), Cochrane 843, has small but well-maintained rooms for US$13 per person with shared bath, US$21/31 single/double with private bath.

Places to Stay – middle

Osorno's mid-range accommodation is good value, starting at appealing *Hospedaje Millantué* (☎ 242480), across from the bus terminal at Errázuriz 1339, for US$25/37. *Residencial Schulz* (☎ 237211), at Freire 530, is well recommended for US$37 double.

Upgraded *Hostal Rucaitué* (☎ 239922), Freire 546, is a very fine choice for US$33 double with breakfast, TV and private bath. Highly recommended, clean and friendly *Nuevo Hotel Eduvijes* (☎ /fax 235023), a few blocks south of the bus terminal at Eduvijes 856, is outstanding value at US$25/47 with breakfast. Highly regarded *Residencial Bilbao* (☎ 236755, fax 231-111), Francisco Bilbao 1019, charges about US$37/50.

Places to Stay – top end

Facing the Plaza de Armas at O'Higgins 615, the Art Deco *Gran Hotel Osorno* (☎ 232171, fax 239111) has provided top-end accommodation since 1930. Rates start at about US$43/70; though not really grand, the rooms are simple, clean and neat with phones and private baths. The stylish new *Hotel Pumalal* (☎ 243520, fax 242-477), Bulnes 630, charges US$45/70.

German-run *Hotel Waeger* (☎ 233721, fax 237080), Cochrane 816, gives special attention to German speakers. Perhaps Osorno's most dignified hotel, it has rooms with private bath and breakfast for US$65/91, and a very good restaurant. It's not the most expensive, though. The very fine *Hotel Rayantú* (☎ 238114, fax 238116) at Patricio Lynch 1462, charges US$73/94. *Hotel García Hurtado de Mendoza* (☎ 237111, fax 237113) at Mackenna 1040 is Osorno's priciest for US$90/120.

Places to Eat
La Naranja, Local 13 in the Mercado Municipal at Prat and Errázuriz, has very good and inexpensive food, but there are many comparable places; don't overlook the basement comedores. The *Kaffeestube* (☎ 230262), in the Supermercado Las Brisas at Mackenna 1150, serves good cafeteria food.

Dino's (☎ 233880), facing the plaza at Ramírez 898, is good for drinks, snacks, grills and ice cream. *Boccato* (☎ 238000), Ramírez 938, serves pizza, sandwiches and very good ice cream. For fine pastries and light meals, try *Pastelería Rhenania* (☎ 235457), Eleuterio Ramírez 977.

Pizzería Los Platos (☎ 233693), Mackenna 1027, has cheap lunchtime dishes for about US$4, but is perhaps most notable for not serving pizza! *Los Troncos* (☎ 231998), Cochrane 527, does serve pizza. *Chung Hwa*, Freire 543, is the local Chinese restaurant, good and reasonably priced.

The *Deutscher Verein* (German Club; ☎ 232784), O'Higgins 563, is more typically Chilean than German, but offers very good food with fine service at reasonable prices. *Bavaria* (☎ 231302), O'Higgins 743, is part of a chain that specializes in beef and seafood.

The *Club Arabe* (☎ 232779), Prat 779, has Middle Eastern lunches for US$6. *La Paisana*, alongside Residencial Schulz at Freire 530, also serves Middle Eastern food.

For a splurge, try *Casa del Altillo* (☎ 233053), in an historic house at Mackenna 1011, or the German food at *Peter's Kneipe* (☎ 232083), Manuel Rodríguez 1039.

Entertainment
Osorno's only movie theater is the Cine Lido (☎ 233890), Ramírez 650. There are a number of central discos, including Mario's (☎ 234978) at Mackenna 555 and Power 2000 (☎ 239993) in the Gran Hotel Osorno at O'Higgins 615.

Provincial Osorno (☎ 233211), Ramírez 766-B, is the local representative in Chile's first-division soccer league.

Things to Buy
Local and regional crafts, including wood carvings, ceramics and basketry, are available at the Mercado Municipal, Errázuriz 1200, Locales 2 & 3; Alta Artesanía (☎ 232446), Mackenna 1069; and Los Detalles (☎ 238462), Mackenna 1100. There's a new Mercado Artesanal on Mackenna, on the south side of the Plaza de Armas, and another small artisans' market at Plazuela Yungay, at the corner of Prat and Ramírez.

Getting There & Away
Air LanChile (☎ 236688), Matta 862, Block C, flies daily to Santiago (US$152) via Temuco (US$32), as does Ladeco (☎ 234355), Mackenna 1098.

Alta, Los Carrera 930, flies twice every weekday to Valdivia (US$13), Concepción (US$41) and Viña del Mar (US$98), but only once daily on weekends.

Bus Osorno has two bus terminals. The long-distance Terminal de Buses (☎ 234-149) is at Avenida Errázuriz 1400, near Angulo, but buses to local and regional destinations leave from the Terminal de Buses Rurales in the Mercado Municipal, two blocks west at the corner of Errázuriz and Prat. Many smaller destinations in the region are most conveniently reached from Osorno.

Bus – domestic Buses Puyehue (☎ 236-541), at the Mercado Municipal, has several buses daily to Termas de Puyehue en route to Aguas Calientes (US$2), and to Chilean customs and immigration at Pajaritos (US$3), within Parque Nacional Puyehue. Across the Río Rahue, Buses Mar (☎ 236166), Tarapacá 799, and Maicolpué (☎ 234003), Valdivia 501, connect Osorno with Bahía Mansa (two hours, US$2), the only easily accessible ocean bathing resort between Valdivia and Chiloé. Buses Ruta 5 (☎ 237020), at the main bus terminal, serves Río Bueno, with connections to Lago Ranco and Lago Rupanco. Expreso Lago Puyehue (☎ 243919) goes to Entre Lagos (US$1.25) many times daily, Sundays to Aguas Calientes (US$2.50).

Transur (☎ 234371), located in the Igi Llaima offices at the main bus terminal, goes to Las Cascadas (US$2.50), on the eastern shore of Lago Llanquihue at the foot of Volcán Osorno. Buses Via Octay (☎ 237043), also in the main terminal, serves Puerto Octay (US$1) and Frutillar on Lago Llanquihue. Mini Buses Puerto Octay, at the same office, also goes to Puerto Octay.

Many companies offer services to Puerto Montt and other regional destinations, including Tas Choapa (☎ 233933), Varmontt (☎ 232732), Tur-Bus (☎ 234170), Intersur (☎ 231325), Igi Llaima (☎ 234-371), Buses Norte (☎ 233319), Turibús (☎ 233633) and Cruz del Sur (☎ 232777).

Most of the same companies cover destinations on the Panamericana between Osorno and Santiago – typical fares include Puerto Montt (US$3, 1½ hours), Temuco (US$5, three hours), Los Angeles or Concepción (US$13, nine hours), Santiago (US$19, 14 hours), and Valparaíso/Viña del Mar (US$22, 16 hours). Many but not all of these services originate in Puerto Montt; for more details, see the Getting There & Away entry for Puerto Montt.

Bus – international Osorno has international services to Bariloche and other Argentine destinations via Puyehue pass over the Andes. Tas Choapa has connections for Mendoza and Buenos Aires via the Libertadores tunnel northeast of Santiago. Buses to destinations in Chilean Patagonia, such as Coihaique, Punta Arenas and Puerto Natales also go via Puyehue. Other principal companies are Buses Norte, Igi Llaima, Cruz del Sur and Río de La Plata (☎ 233633). Most of these services originate in Puerto Montt; see the Getting There & Away entry for the Puerto Montt section for more details.

Fares to Bariloche are about US$25, to Mendoza US$45 and to Buenos Aires, US$100.

Train Osorno's Estación de Ferrocarril (☎ 232992) is at the west end of Juan Mackenna, corner of Portales. The Santiago-Puerto Montt line has a summer service only, but it's pointless to take the train south, since buses to Puerto Montt are so frequent and convenient. Daily northbound trains to Santiago take between 17 and 20 hours.

Getting Around

To/From the Airport Osorno's Aeropuerto Carlos Hott Siebert (sometimes known as Cañal Bajo) is seven km east of downtown, across the Panamericana via Avenida Buschmann. A cab to the airport costs about US$12, but may be shared.

Car Rental For rental cars, try Hertz (☎ 230128) at Errázuriz 1720, the Automóvil Club de Chile (☎ 232269) at Bulnes 463, Ñilque (☎ 238772) at Los Carrera 951 or Budget (☎ 235303) at Matta 862, Block C.

AROUND OSORNO

Along with Puerto Montt, Osorno is one of the best centers for exploring the Chilean lakes. From Osorno, you can go east to Lago Puyehue with its thermal baths, and continue to Parque Nacional Puyehue, or south to Lago Llanquihue and the resorts of Puerto Octay and Frutillar.

LA ARAUCANIA

Entre Lagos

Entre Lagos is a modest, pleasant resort, 50 km east of Osorno on the southwest shore of Lago Puyehue. Only one km from downtown, beachfront *Hospedaje y Camping Panorama* (☎ 371398), General Lagos 687, has shady campsites for US$7.50 per tent and rooms for US$9 per person with breakfast. Eight km east of town, quiet, sheltered *Camping No Me Olvides* (☎ 238454 in Osorno) is an outstanding facility with private sites large enough for two tents, abundant firewood and excellent showers and toilets, but for US$25 it's no longer a bargain.

For hotel accommodation, try *Hostería Entre Lagos* (☎ 647225), Ramírez 65, which has singles/doubles for US$40/55, but low-season prices of US$25/35. *Pub del Campo* (☎ 371220 in Osorno), about 100 meters west of town on the road to Osorno, comes highly recommended for meals.

Termas de Puyehue

One of Chile's most famous hot springs resorts, Termas de Puyehue is 76 km east of Osorno, where paved Chile 215 forks; the north fork goes to Anticura and the Argentine border, while the southern lateral leads to Aguas Calientes and ends in Antillanca, in Parque Nacional Puyehue.

Set in elegant grounds at the junction of the two roads, the baronial *Hotel Termas de Puyehue* (☎ 232157, fax 371272 in Osorno, (02) 2313417 in Santiago) truly recalls an old world alpine resort. Singles/doubles start at US$62/90 with breakfast; half-board and full-board are also available.

PARQUE NACIONAL PUYEHUE

Created in 1941 to protect 65,000 hectares of humid evergreen forest and starkly awesome volcanic scenery, Puyehue is Chile's most popular national park in terms of numbers of visitors. It has since expanded to 107,000 hectares, but while the scenery and natural history are its most appealing features, most visitors see only a small area of what is also the country's most developed park. Most Chileans head for the hot springs at Aguas Calientes and take short walks on nearby nature trails, but outside this area there is skiing at Antillanca and hiking in truly high and wild country.

Flora & Fauna

In Puyehue's lower Valdivian forest, the dominant tree species is the multi-trunked ulmo *(Eucryphia cordifolia)*, accompanied by olivillo *(Aextoxicon punctatum)*, tineo *(Weinmannia trichosperma)* and southern beech *(Nothofagus* spp). The dense undergrowth includes the delicate, rust-barked arrayán *(Myrceugenella apiculata,* a member of the myrtle family), quila *(Chusquea* spp, a genus of solid rather than hollow bamboo which make some areas utterly impenetrable), and wild fuchsia. At higher elevations, the southern beeches lenga and coigue predominate.

In such dense forest, wildlife is scarce or hard to see. In more open areas there are occasional sightings of puma or pudú, but birds are the most common animals. On the peaks, hikers may glimpse the Andean condor; along the rivers, look for the Chilean torrent duck *(Merganetta armata, pato cortacorriente* in Spanish), which flourishes in Class V rapids.

Pudú

Geography & Climate

Mountainous Puyehue is about 75 km east of Osorno via Chile 215, the international highway to Argentina, which is paved as far as the Chilean border crossing at Pajaritos. Altitudes range from 250 meters on the delta of the Río Golgol where it enters Lago Puyehue, to 2236 meters on the summit of Volcán Puyehue.

The park has a humid temperate climate, with an annual rainfall of about 4200 mm at Aguas Calientes. The annual mean temperature is about 9°C, with a summer average of about 14°C, which falls to 5°C in winter. January and February, the driest months, are best for visiting the high country, but the park is open all year and skiing is fine in winter.

Despite Puyehue's moist climate, many areas north of the highway are no less barren than the Atacama, as plants have been slow to recolonize after a major eruption of Volcán Puyehue in 1960. On the western slopes of the volcano are many extinct fumaroles and very lively hot springs.

Aguas Calientes

One of the highlights at Aguas Calientes is the **Sendero El Pionero**, a steep 1800-meter nature trail which offers, at the end of the trail, splendid views of Lago Puyehue, the valley of the Río Golgol, and Volcán Puyehue. En route you will see the nalca *(Gunnera chilensis)*, resembling an enormous rhubarb, with edible stalks and with leaves almost large enough to serve as umbrellas. There are exceptionally fine specimens of the multi-trunked ulmo, which grows to 45 meters and is covered with white flowers in summer. Chileans greatly prize *miel de ulmo*, the honey from the pollen bees extract from these flowers.

Another easier nature trail is the **Sendero Rápidos del Chanleufú**, which follows the river for 1200 meters. For a longer excursion, take the 11-km trail to **Lago Bertín**, where there is a basic refugio. After hiking along the nature trails, or returning from a longer trek, you can soak

or swim in a heated pool filled with the therapeutic mineral waters that gave Aguas Calientes its name. This place is a more economical alternative than Termas de Puyehue.

Conaf's **Centro de Información Ambiental**, open daily 9 am to 1 pm and 2.30 to 8.30 pm, has a simple but informative display on Puyehue's natural history and geomorphology, with slide presentations daily at 5 pm. It generally has basic maps and brochures, despite occasional shortages.

Conaf rangers also lead overnight backpack trips to Lago Paraíso, Volcán Puyehue, Lago Constancia and Pampa Frutilla. For schedules and reservations on these trips, which are free of charge, make arrangements with Conaf at the park or in Osorno. Bring your own tent, food and rain gear.

Antillanca

For some of the finest views of Puyehue and the surrounding area, visit Antillanca (☎ 235114), a popular winter resort with a ski lodge, at the foot of Volcán Casablanca. The ski season runs from early June to the end of October; the ski area itself has three surface lifts, 460 meters of vertical drop and a friendly, club-like atmosphere.

At the end of the 18-km road beyond Aguas Calientes, the lodge is also open in summer, when there is good backcountry hiking and camping, but the nearest formal campground is at Aguas Calientes.

Anticura

Anticura, 17 km northwest of the Aguas Calientes turnoff, is the best base for exploring the park's wilder sectors. The international highway follows the course of the Río Golgol, but the finest scenery is the magnificently desolate plateau at the base of Volcán Puyehue, reached only by an overnight backpack from El Caulle, two km west of Anticura.

On the western slope of Puyehue, a steep morning-plus walk from El Caulle, Conaf has a well maintained refugio which is a good place to lodge or camp (ask Conaf

LA ARAUCANIA

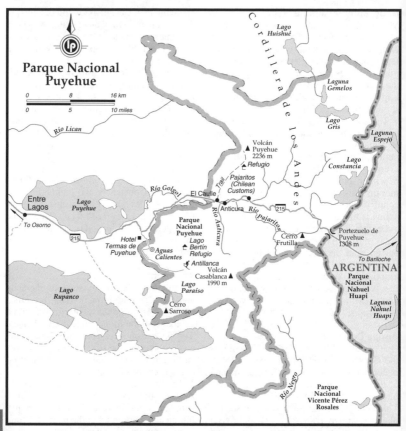

LA ARAUCANIA

rangers at Anticura about access to the refugio). From the refugio, it's another four hours or so through a moonscape of massive lava flows and extinct fumaroles to a spring with rustic thermal baths, which is a fine and private place to camp. Trekkers can continue north to Riñinahue, at the south end of Lago Ranco, or return to Anticura.

Some of Puyehue's best backcountry lies in the remote area between Chilean customs and immigration at Pajaritos and the border, which was once heavily fortified when Argentina threatened war over the Beagle Channel in 1979. Signs of these preparations have disappeared, but to visit Pampa Frutilla, the upper drainage of the Río Golgol and Lago Constancia, visitors need permission from the Carabineros and from Conaf (whose guided overnight trips into these areas simplify the process).

Another worthwhile sight, easily reached from the highway, is the **Salto del Indio**, an attractive waterfall on the Golgol where, according to legend, a lone Mapuche hid to escape encomienda service in a nearby Spanish gold mine.

Conaf has another **Centro de Información** at Anticura, but it's less elaborate than the one at Aguas Calientes.

Places to Stay & Eat

Conaf charges US$5 per site for its rustic but very attractive campground at Catrué, near Anticura, which has fresh water, picnic tables, fire pits and basic toilets. At Aguas Calientes, private concessionaires operate *Camping Chanleufú* (☎ 236988 in Osorno), which costs US$25 per site, and *Camping Los Derrumbes*, which costs US$20 for up to eight persons. Neither has hot showers, but fees entitle you to use the nearby thermal baths. In January and February, Catrué is a much better alternative to these crowded and noisy sites.

Hostería y Cabañas Aguas Calientes (☎ 236988 in Osorno) rents doubles for US$61 and four-bed cabins for US$125. Its restaurant offers reasonably priced meals, groceries and other supplies (available much cheaper, with greater variety, in Osorno).

Hotel Antillanca (☎ 235114, fax 235-672 in Osorno, (02) 2333454 in Santiago), has single/double accommodation for US$74/106, breakfast included, but lunch and dinner cost extra. Its gymnasium, sauna, disco, boutique and shops seem horribly out of place in a national park.

Getting There & Away

From Osorno's Mercado Municipal, at Errázuriz and Colón, Buses Puyehue (☎ 236541) and Expreso Lago Puyehue have several buses daily to Termas de Puyehue en route to Aguas Calientes (US$2), and to Chilean customs and immigration at Pajaritos (US$3). In winter, the Club Andino Osorno (☎ 232297, fax 238877), O'Higgins 1073, offers direct services to the ski lodge at Antillanca.

Auto traffic is heavy enough that hitching from Osorno's eastern outskirts should not be difficult if the bus schedule proves inconvenient.

PUERTO OCTAY

In the early days of German settlement, when poor roads made water transport critically important, the Lago Llanquihue harbor of Puerto Octay was a key transport link between Puerto Montt and Osorno. While modern roads have long since supplanted the lake as a freight route, the 2500 permanent residents of this peaceful, bucolic village, 50 km from Osorno at the north end of the lake, still provide a certain level of middle-European *Gemütlichkeit* for visitors to the lakes region. There are a handful of architectural landmarks and an excellent museum.

Information

Puerto Octay's Oficina Municipal de Turismo (☎ 391276, Anexo 727) is on Calle Esperanza, on the east side of the Plaza de Armas. It's open 9 am to 9 pm daily in December, January and February. Puerto Octay's area code is 64.

Museo El Colono

Puerto Octay's surprisingly professional museum includes a superb cartographic display on German colonization, relevant and well-labeled historical photographs and a rundown on local architecture. At Independencia 591, it's open daily except Monday, 9 am to 1 pm and 3 to 7 pm. Admission costs US$0.50.

Some of the museum's larger exhibits, mostly farm machinery, are displayed in a barn on Andrés Schmoelz (the road to Península Centinela) at the southern edge of town.

Special Events

Over the course of the summer, Puerto Octay hosts several festivals, which vary from year to year. Check Osorno's Sernatur office for an updated list.

Places to Stay & Eat

Several travelers have complimented the clean, comfortable and friendly *Hospedaje Tauber* (☎ 391260), upstairs at German Wulf 712, for US$10 per person with breakfast. The same folks run *Restaurant Cabañas* across the road at Pedro Montt 713.

German-run *Hotel Haase* (☎ 391213), Pedro Montt 344, is a rambling building with spacious interiors, high ceilings and three dining rooms. Soaring prices have carried it well above its former budget category – singles/doubles with shared bath cost US$25/41, while doubles with private bath are US$60.

A few km south of town, on Península Centinela, *Hostería La Baja* (☎ 391269), is a basic but agreeable place for US$11 per person with breakfast and shared bath, or US$15 with private bath. Shady *Camping La Baja* (☎ 391251) is Puerto Octay's municipal site, charging US$20 for up to eight people, but it gives backpackers and cyclists a break by charging only US$4 per person.

Further on is *Hotel Centinela* (☎ (09) 6537333, (02) 2429414 in Santiago), a massive chalet at the end of Andrés Schmoelz, the road that runs along the peninsula. Its simple but spacious rooms, commanding fine views across the lake, cost US$44/55 with private bath. It also has a large restaurant.

For empanadas, try *La Naranja* (☎ 391-219), at the corner of Independencia and Pedro Montt, which also offers simple lodging for US$9 per person.

Getting There & Away
Puerto Octay's bus stop is on Esperanza just south of Amunátegui. Via Octay (☎ 230118 in Osorno), connects Puerto Octay with Osorno's main bus terminal several times daily, while Thaebus goes to Puerto Montt. At 5 pm weekdays, Minibus Turismo Express Vergara runs from Puerto Octay south to Las Cascadas.

LAS CASCADAS
Named for nearby waterfalls, Las Cascadas is a tiny settlement fronting on a black-sand beach, on the eastern shore of Lago Llanquihue. The bus ride from Puerto Octay offers grand views of Volcán Osorno as it passes through dairy country with many small farms and tiny, shingled churches all painted yellow with red corrugated iron roofs. The road south to Ensenada is a popular bicycle route, but it's very exposed and cyclists are vulnerable to the irritating, biting flies known as tábanos.

Places to Stay & Eat
Recommended *Hostería Irma*, one km south of town on the road to Ensenada, has a bar that also serves meals. Rates are about US$15 per person. Diagonally opposite the hostería, alongside the lake, is a peaceful, quiet and free campsite with few facilities.

Camping Las Cañitas (☎ 238336 in Osorno), three km down the Ensenada road, charges US$13 per site for basic services, including cold showers. It also rents five-person cabañas for US$60.

Getting There & Away
From Puerto Octay, one late-afternoon bus each weekday goes to Las Cascadas, but there's no bus service farther south toward Ensenada, the entry point to Parque Nacional Vicente Pérez Rosales. Consequently, southbound visitors must either walk or hitch south, or return to the Panamericana and take the bus from Puerto Varas.

The bus from Puerto Octay arrives at Las Cascadas early in the evening, so unless you can continue the 22 km to Ensenada (a four-hour walk) you'll have to spend the night in Las Cascadas.

FRUTILLAR
Seemingly floating on the horizon, snow-capped Volcán Osorno dominates the landscape across Lago Llanquihue from Frutillar, one of Chile's most captivating and popular lake resorts. Noted for its meticulously preserved Germanic architecture, Frutillar consists of two distinct parts: the resort area by the lake is Frutillar Bajo (Lower Frutillar), while the bustling commercial section near the Panamericana is Frutillar Alto (Upper Frutillar), about two km west. Between them, the two have a permanent population of about 5000.

TED STEVENS
Valle de Copiapó

WAYNE BERNHARDSON
Iglesia Parroquial, Vicuña

WAYNE BERNHARDSON
Political mural, Los Vilos

Images of La Araucanía & Los Lagos

WAYNE BERNHARDSON
17th-century colonial fortifications at Corral

WAYNE BERNHARDSON
Caleta Gonzalo, ferry port on the Camino Austral

HELEN HUGHES
Volcán Villarica as seen from the streets of Pucón

HELEN HUGHES
Handicrafts at Temuco's mercado municipal

Orientation

Frutillar Bajo is about 70 km south of Osorno and 40 km north of Puerto Montt via the Panamericana. The main street, Avenida Philippi, runs north-south along the lakeshore; most hotels and other points of interest are along its west side, with fine sandy beaches on the east. Avenida Carlos Richter connects Frutillar Bajo with Frutillar Alto.

Information

Tourist Office Frutillar's Corporación de Desarrollo Turístico has moved its kiosk just south of the Municipalidad, on Avenida Philippi between San Martín and O'Higgins, but the seasonal staff, at least, are shockingly perfunctory toward visitor inquiries. As the office moves from private to municipal control, this may or may not change. Summer hours (January and February) are 10 am to 9 pm, while the rest of the year it's open 10 am to 6 pm.

Money Exchange, Avenida Philippi 883, changes cash and travelers' checks.

Post & Communications Frutillar's area code is ☎ 65. Correos de Chile is at the corner of Avenida Philippi and Manuel Rodríguez, while CTC and Entel are in Frutillar Alto.

Laundry Lavandería Frutillar (☎ 421555) is at Carlos Richter 335, in Frutillar Alto.

Showers Visitors can shower for US$0.50 at the municipal Baños Públicos (public baths) on O'Higgins, between Philippi and Pérez Rosales.

Museo de la Colonización Alemana

Built with assistance from the Federal Republic of Germany, Frutillar's museum features perfectly reconstructed buildings including a water-powered mill, a blacksmith's with a usable forge (which produces souvenir horseshoes) and a typical mansion (at least as typical as a mansion can be) set among manicured gardens with phenomenal views of Volcán Osorno.

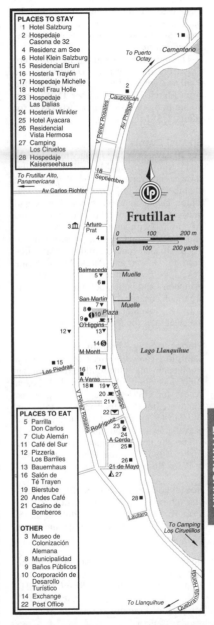

PLACES TO STAY
1 Hotel Salzburg
2 Hospedaje Casona de 32
4 Residenz am See
6 Hotel Klein Salzburg
15 Residencial Bruni
16 Hostería Trayén
17 Hospedaje Michelle
18 Hotel Frau Holle
23 Hospedaje Las Dalias
24 Hostería Winkler
25 Hotel Ayacara
26 Residencial Vista Hermosa
27 Camping Los Ciruelos
28 Hospedaje Kaiserseehaus

PLACES TO EAT
5 Parrilla Don Carlos
7 Club Alemán
11 Café del Sur
12 Pizzería Los Barriles
13 Bauernhaus
16 Salón de Té Trayen
19 Bierstube
20 Andes Café
21 Casino de Bomberos

OTHER
3 Museo de Colonización Alemana
8 Municipalidad
9 Baños Públicos
10 Corporación de Desarrollo Turístico
14 Exchange
22 Post Office

Frutillar

Lago Llanquihue

To Puerto Octay
Cementerio
To Frutillar Alto, Panamericana
To Camping Los Ciruelillos
To Llanquihue

Displayed on the grounds and within the buildings are 19th-century farming implements and household artifacts in immaculate condition.

The museum is a short walk up Arturo Prat from the lakeshore. Daily hours are 9 am to 2 pm and 3 to 7 pm in summer, but from March 15 to December 15 it's open 10 am to 6 pm. Admission costs US$2 for adults, US$1 for children.

Special Events
For 10 days, from late January to early February, the Semana Musical de Frutillar showcases a variety of musical styles from chamber music to jazz. This annual event, which began in 1968, hosts singers and musicians from throughout the country and Argentina, with informal daytime shows and more formal evening performances. There are also concerts in nearby sites like Futrono, Osorno and Puerto Montt. Some tickets are costly at about US$10-plus for symphony and ballet, but midday concerts are much cheaper.

Every November, the Semana Frutillarina celebrates the founding of the town.

Places to Stay – bottom end
Camping *Camping Los Ciruelillos*, on a small peninsula at the south end of Frutillar Bajo, has quiet, shady sites with beach access for US$18 for up to six persons. There are hot showers from 8 am to 11 am and 7 to 11 pm, and fresh homemade bread is available in the morning.

The simpler and cheaper *Camping Los Ciruelos* is in Frutillar Bajo, at the corner of Pérez Rosales and 21 de Mayo.

Hostel For US$15, there is official Hostelling International accommodation at *Hostería Winkler* (☎ 421388), Philippi 1155, though regular rooms are in the mid-range category.

Hospedajes & Residenciales On the escarpment overlooking the lake, at Las Piedras 60, *Residencial Bruni* (☎ 421-309) charges a very reasonable US$11 per person. Friendly *Hospedaje Michelle*

(☎ 421463), Antonio Varas 75, is plain but good value for US$15 with breakfast.

Places to Stay – middle
The are more mid-range accommodations than budget choices. For US$23 per person, *Hostería Winkler* (☎ 421388), Philippi 1155, is one of Frutillar's better values. *Hostería Trayén* (☎ 421346), Philippi 963, is open all year, with rooms with private bath for US$25 and a highly regarded restaurant. For the same price, with a hearty and excellent breakfast, *Hospedaje Kaiserseehaus* (☎ 421387), Philippi 1333, has earned enthusiastic recommendations.

Residenz am See (☎ 421539), directly opposite the beach at Philippi 539, charges US$35 single, while *Residencial Vista Hermosa* (☎ 421209) at Philippi 1259 costs US$35/60. Comparable *Hospedaje Las Dalias* (☎ 421393), Philippi 1095, has singles/doubles for US$38/62 with private bath and breakfast, while *Hospedaje Casona del 32* (☎ 421369, fax 421444), Caupolicán 28, costs US$40/70. *Hotel Frau Holle* (☎ 421345), Antonio Varas 54, charges US$38 per person.

Places to Stay – top end
Rates at *Hotel Ayacara* (☎ /fax 421550), in a remodeled 1910 house at Philippi 1215, start at US$89 double; it's open September to April. *Hotel Klein Salzburg* (☎ 421201, fax 421750; ☎ /fax (02) 2061419 in Santiago), Philippi 663, charges US$76/101, while its sibling *Hotel Salzburg* (☎ 421569, fax 421599), at the north end of town on the road to Puerto Octay, has luxury lodging for US$89/113.

Places to Eat
Frutillar's best value is the *Casino de Bomberos* (☎ 421588), Philippi 1065, which serves four-course lunches for about US$5 plus drinks. *Salón de Te Trayen*, part of its namesake hostería at Philippi 963, specializes in onces but also offers full lunches. *Café del Sur* (☎ 421467), Philippi 775, and the *Andes Café*, Philippi 1057, are good choices for light meals. The

Bauernhaus, just across O'Higgins from Café del Sur, has superb kuchen.

Pizzería Los Barriles (☎ 421700), upstairs at Pérez Rosales 815, has fixed-price lunches for about US$6 and slightly more expensive pizzas. The *Club Alemán* (☎ 421249), San Martín 22, has fixed-price lunches for about US$10, while the *Bierstube* (☎ 421625), Antonio Varas 24, serves an ample Germanic buffet for US$11. *Parrilla Don Carlos* (☎ (09) 6435909), on Balmaceda near Philippi, serves mixed Argentine grills.

Things to Buy
Local specialties include fresh raspberries – delicious and cheap in season – plus raspberry jam and kuchen. The Museo de Colonización Alemana sells miniature wood carvings of museum buildings.

Getting There & Away
Trains from Santiago to Puerto Montt stop at Frutillar Alto, and you can also reach Frutillar by bus from Osorno or Puerto Montt. Buses Varmontt (☎ 421367), at the corner of Alessandri and Carlos Richter in Frutillar Alto, has buses to Puerto Montt and Osorno every half hour between 7 am and 10 pm. Cruz del Sur (☎ 421552), Alessandri 360, has similar schedules. Tur-Bus (☎ 421390), Diego Portales 150, also provides long-distance services.

Getting Around
Inexpensive taxi colectivos cover the short distance between Frutillar Alto and Frutillar Bajo.

PUERTO VARAS
An important lake port during the 19th-century German colonization, Puerto Varas is the gateway to Parque Nacional Vicente Pérez Rosales and the popular boat-bus crossing, via Lago Todos Los Santos, to the Argentine lake resort of Bariloche. A popular travel destination in its own right for its access to Lago Llanquihue, Puerto Varas also contains perhaps the best-preserved concentration of Middle European architecture in the entire country.

Orientation
On the southern shore of Lago Llanquihue, Puerto Varas is only 20 km north of Puerto Montt. Unlike most Chilean cities, its hilly topography and the curving shoreline have resulted in a very irregular street plan, but most services are within a small grid bounded by Portales, San Bernardo, Del Salvador and the lakeshore. Outside this area, street numbers are disorderly to the point of chaos; on one street, three consecutive houses bear the numbers 62, 140, and 48.

The escarpment of Cerro Calvario, a steep hill southwest of downtown, has diverted Puerto Varas' growth east and west along the lakeshore. The Avenida Costanera, an eastward extension of Del Salvador, becomes paved Chile 225 to Ensenada, Petrohué, and Lago Todos Los Santos.

Information
Tourist Office Puerto Varas' municipal Oficina de Información Turística (☎ 232-437), Del Salvador 328, has a friendly, well-informed staff, and free maps and brochures about the entire area. In summer, it's open daily 9 am to 9 pm; the rest of the year, hours are 10 am to 2 pm and 4 to 6 pm.

Money There are numerous downtown ATMs, including Banco de Crédito at the corner of Del Salvador and San Pedro, but change cash and travelers' checks at Turismo Los Lagos, Local 11 in the Galería Real at Del Salvador 257.

Post & Communications The area code is ☎ 65. Correos de Chile is at the corner of San Pedro and San José. Telefónica del Sur's long-distance office, at Santa Rosa and Del Salvador, is open daily 8 am to 11 pm. Entel operates out of a converted bus at San José and San Pedro, while Chilesat is just across San José.

Travel Agencies For more conventional travel services and standard tours, like the bus-boat excursion across the Andes to

LA ARAUCANIA

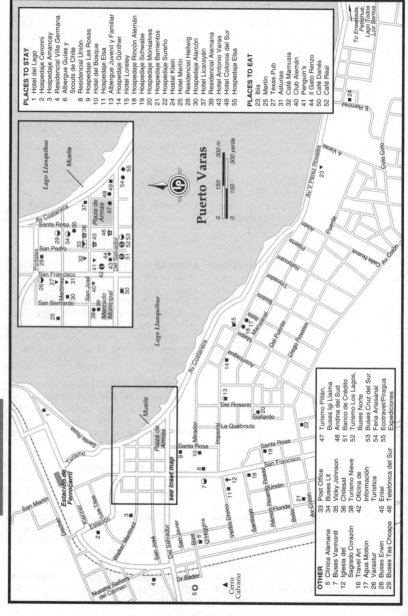

PLACES TO STAY
1   Hotel del Lago
2   Hospedaje Ceronni
3   Hospedaje Amancay
4   Residencial Villa Germana
6   Albergue Guías y
    Scouts de Chile
8   Residencial Unión
9   Hospedaje Las Rosas
10 Hotel del Bosque
11 Hospedaje Elsa
13 Albergue Juvenil y Familiar
14 Hospedaje Günther
15 Hotel Loreley
18 Hospedaje Rincón Alemán
19 Hospedaje Schwabe
20 Hospedaje Monsalves
21 Hospedaje Barrientos
22 Hospedaje Sureño
24 Hostal Klein
25 Hotel Merlín
28 Residencial Hellwig
30 Hospedaje Alarcón
37 Hotel Licarayén
39 Residencial Alemana
43 Hotel Antonio Varas
49 Hotel Colonos del Sur
55 Hospedaje Elsa

PLACES TO EAT
23 Ibis
25 Merlín
27 Texas Pub
31 Asturias
32 Café Mamusia
40 Club Alemán
41 Penguin's
44 Il Gato Renzo
50 Café Danés
52 Café Real

OTHER
5   Clínica Alemana
7   Buses Varmontt
12 Iglesia del
    Sagrado Corazón
16 Travel Art
17 Agua Motion
26 Varastur
28 Buses Erwin
29 Buses Tas Choapa
33 Post Office
34 Buses Lit
35 Vicky Johnson
36 Chilesat
38 Turismo Nieve
42 Oficina de
    Información
    Turística
45 Entel
46 Telefónica del Sur
47 Turismo Pillán,
    Buses Igi Llaima
48 Andina del Sud
51 Banco de Crédito
52 Turismo Los Lagos,
    Buses Norte
53 Buses Cruz del Sur
54 Feria Artesanal
55 Ecotravel/Piragua
    Expediciones

Puerto Varas

300 m

300 yards

Argentina, try Andina del Sud (☎ 232511), Del Salvador 72, Turismo Nieve (☎ 233-000), San Bernardo 406 or Turismo Pillán (☎ 232334), Del Salvador 100.

Puerto Varas is also one of the major regional centers for adventure tourism activities like trekking, climbing, whitewater rafting and kayaking, mountain biking and birding. Among the local operators are Ecotravel/Piragua Expediciones (☎/fax 233222) on the Costanera, Aqua Motion (☎ /fax 232747) at Imperial 0699, and Travel Art (☎/fax 232198) at Imperial 0661.

Medical Services Puerto Varas' Clínica Alemana (☎ 232336) is at Dr Bader 810, on Cerro Calvario near Del Salvador's southwestern exit from town.

Things to See & Do

Puerto Varas' architecture gives it a distinctive Middle European ambience, thanks in part to imposing landmarks like the **Iglesia del Sagrado Corazón** (1915), overlooking downtown from a promontory at the corner of San Francisco and Verbo Divino. Most other notable constructions are private houses from the early decades of this century; for a key, pick up the useful brochure *Paseo Patrimonial*, which suggests a walking tour of 28 different houses.

Lago Llanquihue and the surrounding area provide opportunities for recreational activities such as swimming, windsurfing and cycling. There are mountain bikes for rent at the Feria Artesanal, on Del Salvador between the Plaza de Armas and the Costanera, for about US$20 per day. Check adventure travel companies for rental equipment for other sports.

Organized Tours

Andina del Sud and Turismo Pillán (see Travel Agencies, above) arrange conventional excursions like city tours of Puerto Varas (US$7.50) and Frutillar (US$20), and bus trips to Saltos del Petrohué (US$12). See also the Organized Tours entry for Puerto Montt.

Several agencies offer trekking in Parque Nacional Vicente Pérez Rosales and Parque Nacional Alerce Andino, climbing Volcán Osorno, mountain biking throughout the area, birding on the Río Maullín, and rafting on the Río Petrohué. See the Travel Agencies entry above for operators; there is additional information in the individual national park entries.

Special Events

The prolonged Aniversario de Puerto Varas, comprising the last week of January and the first week of February, celebrates the city's founding in 1854. In the second week of February, the annual Concurso de Pintura El Color del Sur attracts painters from throughout the country for a contest and exhibition.

Places to Stay – bottom end

For the most current information on budget accommodations, check the Oficina de Información Turística at Del Salvador 328. Even when the office is closed, there are usually postings for hospedajes in the entryway.

Hostels In the Liceo Pedro Aguirre Cerda, a school at the corner of Rosario and Imperial, the *Albergue Juvenil y Familiar* offers beds for US$4 in January and February only. Guías y Scouts de Chile runs an *Albergue* (☎ 232774) at San Ignacio 879, charging US$5 per person; hot showers, meals and kitchen privileges are all available.

Hospedajes & Residenciales Puerto Varas' most reasonable accommodations are its many hospedajes, mostly in the US$10 range per person. Some of these are seasonal, so it's better to phone ahead unless you happen to be in the immediate vicinity.

At San Francisco 669, opposite the Varmontt bus terminal, the very basic *Residencial Unión* is clean, with hot showers and a decent restaurant, but the beds sag and it can be cold in winter. In a quiet location alongside the Iglesia del Sagrado Corazón, at Verbo Divino 427, *Hospedaje Elsa* (☎ 232803) is an excellent choice. Friendly *Hospedaje Barrientos* (☎ 233387), Florida

1361, is comparable and slightly cheaper, but a bit less central.

Other comparable and comparably priced places include *Hospedaje Schwabe* (☎ 233165) at Ramón Ricardo Rosas 361, *Hospedaje Monsalves* (☎ 232673) at Capitán Gallardo 054, and *Hospedaje Sureño* (☎ 232648) at Colón 179. *Hospedaje Alarcón* (☎ 234216), San Bernardo 313, 2nd floor, charges US$12.50 with breakfast.

Several others charge in the US$15 range, including recommended *Hospedaje Ceronni* (☎ 232016) at Estación 262, the spacious but rather gloomy *Residencial Hellwig* (☎ 232472) at San Pedro 210, and *Hospedaje Günther* (☎ 232030), Imperial 469, which also has slightly dearer rooms with private bath.

Places to Stay – middle

Mid-range accommodation starts around US$18 per person at highly recommended *Hospedaje Las Rosas* (☎ 232770), Santa Rosa 560, which has excellent views and serves an ample breakfast of kuchen, fruit and cheese. In the same category are *Hospedaje Amancay* (☎ 232201) at Walker Martínez 564, *Residencial Villa Germana* (☎ 233162) at Nuestra Señora del Carmen 873, and the very central *Residencial Alemana* (☎ 232419) at San Bernardo 416.

Attractive *Hospedaje Rincón Alemán* (☎ 232087), San Francisco 1004, charges US$25/40 single/double with breakfast. Offering sweeping views of Puerto Varas and the lake, *Hotel del Bosque* (☎ 232897, fax 233085), Santa Rosa 710, formerly Hostería La Sirena, charges US$25/40 with private bath. *Hotel Loreley* (☎ 232226), Maipú 911, has doubles for US$45.

Hostal Klein (☎ /fax 233109), Eleuterio Ramírez 1255, costs US$24 per person with breakfast, US$30 per person with half-board. *Hotel Merlín* (☎ /fax 233105), Walker Martínez 584, is an appealing place that also features one of Chile's finest restaurants; rates are US$44/62.

Places to Stay – top end

At *Hotel Antonio Varas* (☎ 232446), Del Salvador 322, formerly Hotel Asturias, rates are US$64/73. *Hotel del Lago* (☎ 232291, fax 232707), Klenner 195, starts at US$81/92, while the new *Hotel Colonos del Sur* (☎ 233369), Del Salvador 24, costs US$88/111. Overlooking the waterfront at San José 114, the chalet-style *Hotel Licarayén* (☎ 232305, fax 232955) has outstanding doubles for US$90/118.

Places to Eat

Café Real, upstairs at Del Salvador 257, has cheap fixed-price lunches, while *Asturias* (☎ 232283) at San Francisco 302 features sandwiches and desserts. The *Texas Pub*, Walker Martínez 418, Local 5, has excellent sandwiches and kuchen. *Café Danés* (☎ 232371), Del Salvador 441, is particularly good for onces. *Penguin's* (☎ 232207), San José 319, serves decent ice cream and some basic Mexican dishes.

El Gordito and *El Mercado*, both in the Mercado Municipal at Del Salvador 582, are very fine but upscale seafood restaurants. The *Club Alemán* (☎ 232246), San José 415, is another good choice, as is *Il Gato Renzo* (☎ 232214), Del Salvador 314, for Italian specialties (their pasta gets better reviews than their pizza).

President Frei is among the regular patrons of highly regarded *Merlín* (☎ 233-105), part of its namesake hotel at Walker Martínez 584. It's expensive, but worth the price by all accounts. *Café Mamusia* (☎ 233343), San José 316, serves excellent Chilean specialties in attractive surroundings. Several readers have testified that *Ibis* (☎ 232017), Pérez Rosales 1117, is worth a splurge.

Things to Buy

The local Feria Artesanal, on Del Salvador near the lakefront, has a fine selection of local handicrafts. Vicky Johnson (☎ 232-240), Santa Rosa 318, sells Puerto Varas' best coffee.

Getting There & Away

Bus Puerto Varas has no central terminal, but most bus companies have offices right downtown. Northbound buses from Puerto Montt usually pick up passengers in Puerto Varas. Fares and times closely resemble those from Puerto Montt.

Varmontt (☎ 232592), San Francisco 666, has daily buses to Santiago and more than two dozen daily to Puerto Montt. Cruz del Sur (☎ 233008), Del Salvador 237, has eight buses daily to Osorno, Valdivia and Temuco, plus frequent buses to Chiloé.

Several other companies are nearby: Buses Lit (☎ 233838) at Walker Martínez 227-B, Igi Llaima (☎ 232334) at Del Salvador 100, Tas Choapa (☎ 233831) at Walker Martínez 230, and Buses Norte, in the Galería Real at Del Salvador 257. All operate buses to Santiago, with regular services to Bariloche over the Puyehue pass.

At 11 am daily except Sunday in the summer, Buses Erwin, San Pedro 210, goes to Ensenada (US$1.25) and Petrohué (US$2.50), returning to Puerto Varas at 1 pm. The rest of the year, these buses run Tuesday, Thursday and Saturday only.

From September to March, Andina del Sud (☎ 232511), Del Salvador 72, runs daily buses to Ensenada and Petrohué, with connections for bus-boat crossing to Bariloche. These buses leave Puerto Montt at 8.30 am and return at 5 pm; from April to mid-September, they run Wednesday to Sunday, leaving Puerto Montt at 10 am and returning at 5 pm.

From November to mid-March, Varastur (☎ 232103), San Francisco 242, runs buses to Petrohué at 10 am Wednesday to Sunday, returning at 5 pm.

Train Puerto Varas is now the summer terminus for the train from Santiago, which no longer continues to Puerto Montt. The Estación del Ferrocarril (☎ 232210) is up the hill on Klenner, across from the old casino. Fares are US$21 turista, US$28 salón, US$35 for an upper bunk and US$47 for a lower bunk.

Getting Around

Travel Art (☎ /fax 232198), Imperial 0661, rents mountain bikes.

ENSENADA

At the southeastern corner of Lago Llanquihue, at the base of snow-capped, 2660-meter Volcán Osorno, Ensenada is a tranquil stopover on Chile 225 to Petrohué and Lago Todos Los Santos. To the south is the jagged crater of Volcán Calbuco, which blew its top during the Pleistocene.

Places to Stay & Eat

For US$12.50 per person, *Hostería Ruedas Viejas* (☎ 338278, Anexo 312) has cozy cabins with double beds, a private bath and small wood stoves. Meals are cheap, helpings bountiful, and the pisco sours tasty and powerful. *Hospedaje La Arena* (☎ 338-278, Anexo 332), between Ruedas Viejas and the police station, is slightly dearer.

Top of the range is the *Hotel Ensenada* (☎ 212017), the first large building on the road to Las Cascadas and Puerto Octay, beyond the turnoff to Petrohué. Resembling Puerto Octay's Hotel Centinela, it has a large restaurant decorated with odd bits of ironwork and machinery, and a raging fireplace. Room rates are US$80 double with breakfast, US$120 with half-pension.

Getting There & Away

Buses Erwin, San Pedro 210 in Puerto Varas, has daily service to Ensenada (US$1.25) and Petrohué (US$2.50), returning to Puerto Varas the same day. From Puerto Montt, Expreso JM has half a dozen buses daily to Ensenada. Andina del Sud (☎ 232511), Del Salvador 72 in Puerto Varas, also has buses to Ensenada and Petrohué, with connections for the bus-boat crossing to Bariloche.

There is no public transport between Ensenada and Las Cascadas, a distance of 22 km on the road to Puerto Octay, but hitching may be feasible. For pedestrians and cyclists, this is a hot, exposed route infested with tábanos.

PARQUE NACIONAL VICENTE PEREZ ROSALES

Beneath the flawless cone of Volcán Osorno, Lago Todos Los Santos is the centerpiece of Parque Nacional Vicente Pérez Rosales and the jewel of Chile's southern mainland lakes. A scoured glacial basin between densely forested ridges, the lake offers dramatic views of the volcano. The needle point of Volcán Puntiagudo lurks to the north while, to the east, prominent Monte Tronador marks the Argentine border.

Established in 1926 to protect this extraordinary scenery, 251,000-hectare Pérez Rosales was Chile's first national park, ironically honoring a man who, according to US geographer Mark Jefferson, 'arranging the first important settlement of Germans near Lake Llanquihue . . . hired the Indians to clear away the woods by fire.' Ecologically, the park's Valdivian rainforest and other plant communities closely resemble those of Parque Nacional Puyehue, which borders it to the north.

Pérez Rosales has a much longer history, however. In pre-Columbian times, the Camino de Vuriloche was a major trans-Andean crossing for the Mapuche. Later, Jesuit missionaries traveled from Chiloé, continuing up the Estuario de Reloncaví and crossing the pass south of Tronador to Lago Nahuel Huapi, avoiding the riskiest crossings of the region's lakes and rivers. For more than a century after the Mapuche uprising of 1599, the Indians successfully concealed this route from the Spaniards.

Geography & Climate

Parque Nacional Vicente Pérez Rosales is about 50 km east of Puerto Varas via paved Chile 225. Altitudes range from only 50 meters above sea level near the shores of Lago Llanquihue to 3491 meters on the summit of Tronador. Other high points include 2490-meter Puntiagudo and 2660-meter Osorno, a popular but difficult climb. Because lava flows from Osorno have blocked the former westward drainage into Lago Llanquihue, the Río Petrohué (the outlet from Todos Los Santos) now flows south into the Golfo de Reloncaví.

The park has a humid temperate climate, with an annual precipitation of about 2500 mm near Ensenada, rising to about 4000 mm at higher altitudes where much of it falls as winter snow. The annual mean temperature is about 11°C, with a summer average of about 16°C, falling to 6.5°C in winter. There are more than 200 days of rain annually, but January and February are the driest months.

Volcán Osorno

Adventure travel companies in Puerto Varas and Puerto Montt offer guided climbs of Volcán Osorno, which requires snow and ice-climbing gear, but experienced and well-equipped climbers should be able to handle it alone. Full-day excursions, leaving at 5.30 am, cost about US$100, but an overnight is preferable.

In winter, skiing is very popular at the **Centro de Esquí La Burbuja**, 1250 meters above sea level, reached from Ensenada. For reservations in Puerto Montt, contact Hotel Vicente Pérez Rosales (☎ 252571), Antonio Varas 447.

The *Refugio Teski Ski Club* (☎ 336490), just below snow line, has outstanding views of Lago Llanquihue. Take the Ensenada-Puerto Octay road to a signpost about three km from town and continue nine km up the lateral. The refugio is open all year, but getting there entails a long, hard uphill trek, particularly with a heavy pack. Beds are available for US$11 per night; breakfast costs US$5, while lunch or dinner costs US$9. Climbing equipment – ice axes, ropes and crampons – rent for US$20 per person.

More easily reached from Puerto Octay, **Refugio La Picada** (☎ 237589) is on the north side of Volcán Osorno, via a 20-km dirt road from Puerto Klocker. Beds are available for US$10 per person.

Petrohué

In the shadow of Volcán Osorno, Petrohué is the point of departure for the ferry excursion to Peulla, over the deep blue waters of Todos Los Santos. Ferries leave for Peulla early in the morning and return

Parque Nacional Vicente Pérez Rosales

after lunch. Daily at 3 pm in summer, Andina del Sud runs boat trips to **Isla Margarita**, a lovely island with a small interior lagoon. The roundtrip lasts about two hours and costs US$9 for adults, US$6 for children.

Conaf's **Centro de Visitantes**, opposite Hotel Petrohué, presents displays on the park's geography, geology, fauna and flora, and history. From the hotel, a dirt track leads to **Playa Larga**, a long black-sand beach much better than the one near the hotel. After passing through the military campground, look for the sign which points to the beach, which is half an hour's walk. The **Sendero Rincón del Osorno** is a five-km trail on the western shore of Lago Todos Los Santos. Six km southwest of Petrohué, the **Sendero Saltos del Petrohué** is one of a number of short recreational trails along the rapids of the river; Conaf collects a US$1.25 admission charge here.

From Cayutué, on the southern arm of Lago Todos Los Santos, it's possible to trek to Ralún, at the north end of the Estuario de Reloncaví. For this, you must hire a fisherman's launch for the 45-minute trip to

Cayutué, which is about four hours' walk from Lago Cayutué (excellent camping) and another five hours to Ralún, where there are three or four buses daily back to Puerto Varas. The track is easy to follow.

Aqua Motion, the Puerto Varas adventure travel operator, maintains an office at Petrohué, where it's possible to arrange climbs of Volcán Osorno (US$100), rafting on the Río Petrohué (US$79), and full-day 'canyoning' excursions that involve climbing (with and without ropes), hiking and swimming to explore the gorge of the Río León (US$79).

Places to Stay & Eat Other than camping, there are only two alternatives for lodging at Petrohué. Cheaper of the two is the *Casa Familiar Küscher*, across the river, for which you'll have to hire a rowboat. Rooms cost US$10 per person, but camping is possible for US$5. Rates at the distinctive *Hotel Petrohué* (☎ 258042), the other option, start at US$53/83 single/double with breakfast; other meals are also available at its restaurant, which is open to the general public. Things are quieter after March 1, the best time for a visit, but facilities are open all year.

On the lakefront a few minutes walk from Hotel Petrohué, the army campground is free and usually open to the public, but lacks sanitary services. Conaf tries to discourage people from camping here, but lacks authority over the military.

Campers should buy food and supplies in Puerto Montt or Puerto Varas rather than in Petrohué, where the only shop charges premium prices.

Getting There & Away – bus In summer, Buses Erwin (☎ 232472), San Pedro 210 in Puerto Varas, has service daily except Sunday at 11 am to Ensenada (US$1.25) and Petrohué (US$2.50), returning to Puerto Varas at 1 pm. This bus arrives at Petrohué after the ferries to Peulla have left, so plan on a night at Petrohué. The rest of the year, buses run Tuesday, Thursday and Saturday only.

From September to March, Andina del Sud (☎ /fax 257797), Varas 437 in Puerto Montt, has daily buses to Ensenada and Petrohué via Puerto Varas, with connections for its own bus-boat crossing to Bariloche. They leave Puerto Montt at 8.30 am and return at 5 pm; from April to mid-September, they run Wednesday to Sunday, leaving Puerto Montt at 10 am and returning at 5 pm.

From November to mid-March, Varastur (☎ 232103), at San Francisco 242 in Puerto Varas, has bus service to Petrohué from Wednesday to Sunday at 10 am, returning at 5 pm.

From Puerto Montt, Buses J M has five buses daily to Petrohué from December through March, but only two daily the rest of the year.

Getting There & Away – boat Andina del Sud's ferry departs Petrohué early in the morning for Peulla, a three-hour trip that is the first leg of the journey to Bariloche. Purchase tickets at the kiosk near the jetty for US$30 roundtrip for adults, US$21 for children; with lunch, the fare is US$45 for adults, US$35 for children. Tickets are also available at Andina del Sud offices in Puerto Varas and Puerto Montt.

Peulla

Approaching Peulla, the deep blue of Lago Todos Los Santos becomes an emerald green. The tiny village, which has a hotel, a school and a post office, bustles in summer as tourists pass through customs and immigration en route to Bariloche.

There is an easy walk to **Cascada de Los Novios**, a waterfall just a few minutes from the Hotel Peulla. For a longer excursion, take the eight-km **Sendero Laguna Margarita**, a rugged but rewarding climb from Peulla.

Places to Stay & Eat One km from the dock, *Hotel Peulla* (☎ 258041 in Puerto Montt, (02) 6971010 in Santiago) charges US$86/126 for singles/doubles with half-board and is worth the splurge, according to satisfied correspondents. Several readers have complained about the prices and quality at the restaurant *Tajuela*, and recommend bringing your own food in lieu of the US$20 buffet. Nearby, the more modest *Residencial Palomita* has rooms for US$15 per person with half-board. Both places are open all year.

There's a campsite opposite Conaf, and it may also be possible to get a room with a local family – several readers have recommended the home of Elmo and Ana Hernández, on the right side as you leave the jetty, for US$10.

PUERTO MONTT

Settled by German colonists in the mid-19th century, Puerto Montt still presents a middle-European façade of what Jan Morris described, in 1967, as a townscape of 'houses . . . faced with unpainted shingles, very Nordic and sensible, and here and there stand structures in the Alpine manner, all high-pitched roofs and quaint balconies.' One of southern Chile's most important cities enjoys a spectacular setting that may remind visitors from Seattle or Vancouver of Puget Sound or the Strait of Georgia. Built entirely of alerce in 1856, the Iglesia Catedral on the Plaza de Armas is the oldest building, but a commercial construction boom is transforming the downtown area.

As a gateway to the southern lakes, Chiloé and Chilean Patagonia, Puerto Montt has air, bus and train links in virtually all directions but west. Its maritime orientation is conspicuous to the most casual observer; even more conspicuous are the mountains of wood chips at the port of Angelmó, which are fast becoming a symbol of uncontrolled exploitation in southern Chile's temperate forests.

Orientation

Capital of Region X of Los Lagos, Puerto Montt (population 87,000) is 1020 km south of Santiago via the Panamericana, which skirts the northern edge of the city as it continues to Chiloé.

The city center occupies a narrow terrace, partly on landfill, behind which the hills rise very steeply. The waterfront Avenida Diego Portales turns into Avenida Angelmó as it heads west to the small fishing and ferry port of Angelmó, while to the east, Avenida Soler Manfredini continues to the bathing resort of Pelluco and connects with the rugged Camino Austral, a combination of ferries and gravel roads which ends far south, at Puerto Yungay in Region XI of Aisén.

Information

Tourist Offices Puerto Montt's Oficina Municipal de Turismo (☎ 253551, Anexo 2307) is a kiosk at Varas and O'Higgins, facing the south side of the Plaza de Armas. It's open Monday through Saturday 8.30 am to 1.30 pm and 2 to 7.30 pm, Sunday 10 am to 2 pm only. Abundantly supplied with maps and brochures, it's generally a better choice than Sernatur (☎ 252720), which inconveniently overlooks the city from the 2nd floor of the annex of the Edificio Intendencia Regional, O'Higgins 480 – a stiff climb from the waterfront. Sernatur is open weekdays 8.30 am to 1 pm and 1.30 to 5.45 pm.

Acchi (☎ 252968), the Automóvil Club, is at Esmeralda 70, east of downtown off Avenida Egaña.

Consulates The Argentine Consulate (☎ 253996) is at Cauquenes 94, 2nd floor, near Varas. Open weekdays 8 am to 1 pm, it issues visas for Argentina. European consulates include the following:

Germany
    Antonio Varas 525 (☎ 252920)
Netherlands
    Seminario 350 (☎ 253428)
Spain
    Rancagua 113 (☎ 252729)

Money There are several cambios, including Turismo Los Lagos at Varas 595, Local 3, Cambio El Libertador at Urmeneta 529-A, Local 3, Eureka Turismo at Antonio Varas 449 and La Moneda de Oro at the

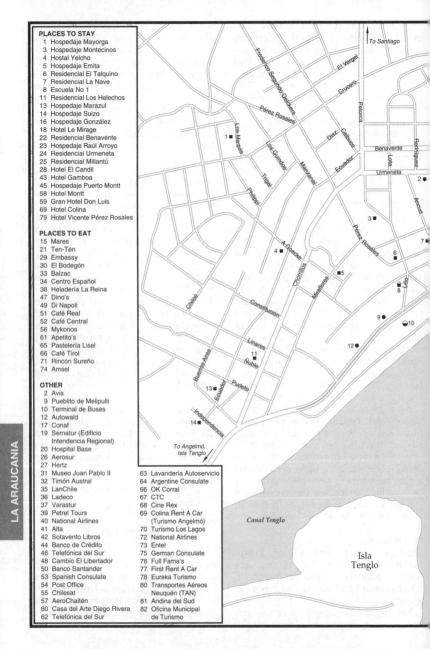

PLACES TO STAY
1 Hospedaje Mayorga
3 Hospedaje Montecinos
4 Hostal Yelcho
5 Hospedaje Emita
6 Residencial El Talquino
7 Residencial La Nave
8 Escuela No 1
11 Residencial Los Helechos
13 Hospedaje Marazul
14 Hospedaje Suizo
16 Hospedaje González
18 Hotel Le Mirage
22 Residencial Benavente
23 Hospedaje Raúl Arroyo
24 Residencial Urmeneta
25 Residencial Millantú
28 Hotel El Candil
43 Hotel Gamboa
45 Hospedaje Puerto Montt
58 Hotel Montt
59 Gran Hotel Don Luis
69 Hotel Colina
79 Hotel Vicente Pérez Rosales

PLACES TO EAT
15 Mares
21 Ten-Tén
29 Embassy
30 El Bodegón
33 Balzac
34 Centro Español
38 Heladería La Reina
47 Dino's
49 Di Napoli
51 Café Real
52 Café Central
56 Mykonos
65 Apetito's
65 Pastelería Lisel
66 Café Tirol
71 Rincón Sureño
74 Amsel

OTHER
2 Avis
9 Pueblito de Melipulli
10 Terminal de Buses
12 Autowald
17 Conaf
19 Sernatur (Edificio
    Intendencia Regional)
20 Hospital Base
26 Aerosur
27 Hertz
31 Museo Juan Pablo II
32 Timón Austral
35 LanChile
36 Ladeco
37 Varastur
39 Petrel Tours
40 National Airlines
41 Alta
42 Sotavento Libros
44 Banco de Crédito
46 Telefónica del Sur
48 Cambio El Libertador
50 Banco Santander
53 Spanish Consulate
54 Post Office
55 Chilesat
57 AeroChaitén
60 Casa del Arte Diego Rivera
62 Telefónica del Sur
63 Lavandería Autoservicio
64 Argentine Consulate
66 OK Corral
67 CTC
68 Cine Rex
69 Colina Rent A Car
    (Turismo Angelmó)
70 Turismo Los Lagos
72 National Airlines
73 Entel
75 German Consulate
76 Full Fama's
77 First Rent A Car
78 Eureka Turismo
80 Transportes Aéreos
    Neuquén (TAN)
81 Andina del Sud
82 Oficina Municipal
    de Turismo

To Santiago

El Vergel

Crúcero

Frederico Segundo Calderas

Pérez Rosales

Los Maquis

Los Guindos

Manzanal

Trigal

Philippi

Palorca

Diaz

Calbuco

Ecuador

Benavente

Lota

Rodríguez

Urmeneta

Ancud

A Gaecte

Chorrillos

Miraflores

Pérez Rosales

Lillo

Constitución

Chiloé

Linares

Buenos Aires

Ñuble

Ecuador

Pudeto

Independencia

To Angelmó,
Isla Tenglo

Canal Tenglo

Isla
Tenglo

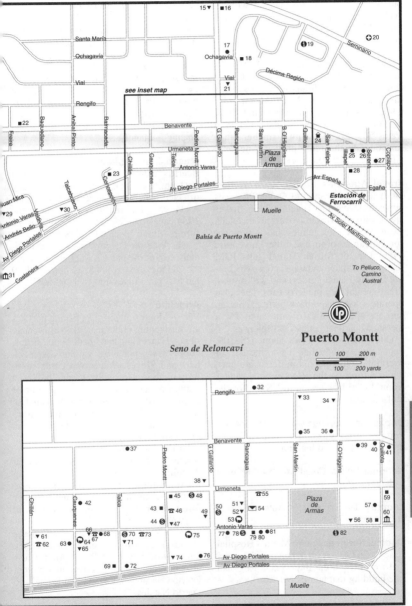

Puerto Montt

Santa María
Ochagavía
Vial
Rengifo

15 ▼   ■16
17
Ochagavía   ■ 18
Vial ▼ 21

■22
Baquedano
Aníbal Pinto
Balmaceda
Freire
Benavente
Pedro Montt
G Gallardo
Rancagua
San Martín
B. O'Higgins
Quillota

Urmeneta
Chillán
Cauquenes
Talca
Antonio Varas
Av Diego Portales

■ 23
Concepción
Talcahuano

Juan Mira
▼29
Antonio Varas
Andrés Bello
Av Diego Portales
Victoria
▼30
🏛31
Costanera

see inset map

Plaza de Armas

🛈19
✚20
Seminario
Décima Región
24
San Felipe
Maipú   ■ 25   ● 26
Osorno   ● 27
Copiapó
■ 28
Av España   Egaña
Estación de Ferrocarril
Av Soler Manfredini

Muelle

Bahía de Puerto Montt

To Pelluco,
Camino
Austral

Seno de Reloncaví

0   100   200 m
0   100   200 yards

Rengifo   ● 32
▼ 33   34 ▼
● 35   36 ●
Benavente
● 37
Pedro Montt
G Gallardo
Rancagua
San Martín
B. O'Higgins
Quillota
● 39
40 ●
● 41
38 ▼
Urmeneta
Chillán
Cauquenes
Talca
■ 45   🛈 48
● 42
43 ■   ☎ 46   49 ▼
44 🛈   ▼47
50 🛈
51 ▼
52 ▼
53 🛈
☎55
✉ 54
Plaza
de
Armas
57 ●
■ 59
60 🏛
▼ 56   58 ■
66
▼ 61
☎62   63 ●
🛈64
67
▼65
☎68
🛈 70   ☎73
▼ 71
🍴 75
Antonio Varas
77 ●   78 🛈   ■ ● ●81
79 80
🛈 82
69 ■   ● 72
▼ 74   ● 76
Av Diego Portales
Av Diego Portales

Muelle

bus terminal. There are many downtown ATMs, including Banco Santander at Gallardo 132 and Banco de Crédito at the corner of Varas and Pedro Montt.

Post & Communications Puerto Montt's area code is ☎ 65. Correos de Chile is at Rancagua 126. Telefónica del Sur has long-distance offices at Pedro Montt 114, Chillán 98 and at the bus terminal. CTC is at Antonio Varas 629, while Entel is at Varas 567, Local 2, with a smaller office just outside the ferry port at Angelmó. Chilesat is at Urmeneta 433.

Travel Agencies English-run Travellers (☎ /fax 258555, see the Online Services appendix), Avenida Angelmó 2456, makes special efforts to cater to overseas travelers. Besides arranging guides and equipment for Volcán Osorno and other adventure trips, director Adrian Turner sells IGM topographic maps and travel books (including Lonely Planet guides) and will reserve flights, rental cars and ferry trips. They also operate a used paperback book exchange, and are opening a café with cable TV, a message board and other conveniences.

Climbing Osorno costs about US$100, depending on whether it's a one-day or overnight (most people prefer overnight), while rafting on the Río Petrohué ranges from US$20 late season to US$35 for the half-day excursion.

Bookshop Sotavento Libros (☎ 256650), Portales 580, has a good selection of books on local history and literature.

National Parks Conaf (☎ 254358) is at Ochagavía 464.

Laundry The Lavandería Autoservicio is at Cauquenes 75.

Medical Services Puerto Montt's Hospital Base (☎ 253991) is on Seminario, the street that runs behind the Intendencia Regional (the building that houses Sernatur).

Casa del Arte Diego Rivera

The upstairs gallery at the Casa del Arte Diego Rivera, a joint Mexican-Chilean project finished in 1964, displays work by local artists like Jose Hugo Cárcamo, whose oils and watercolors depict regional landscapes. At Quillota 116, the gallery (☎ 253551, Anexo 2322) keeps irregular hours. Admission to exhibitions is free. The downstairs Sala de Espectáculos offers a selection of quality films that change frequently.

Museo Juan Pablo II

Puerto Montt's improving waterfront museum has begun to stress more locally oriented materials than it did a few years back, when the transitory euphoria of the 1984 papal visit led to the renaming of the former Museo Vicente Pérez Rosales.

On Avenida Diego Portales, immediately east of the bus terminal, the museum (☎ 253551, Anexo 2308) is open daily 9 am to 7 pm. Admission costs US$0.75.

Angelmó

Puerto Montt's picturesque fishing port has an outstanding crafts market, with a range of goods including handmade boots, curios, copperwork, ponchos, woolen sweaters, hats and gloves. Waterfront cafés serve tasty seafood, especially curanto, but overfishing of native species and the glut of commercially cultivated salmon has meant that tastier local specialties like sierra (sawfish) are less common on the menu than they once were.

Offshore **Isla Tenglo**, reached by inexpensive launches from the docks at Angelmó, is much quieter than bustling Puerto Montt, but recent fires have destroyed much of the island's former forest cover. For a meal, try *Restaurant Hoffman*.

Easily reached by frequent local buses and taxi colectivos, Angelmó is about three km west of downtown Puerto Montt; it is also the terminus for ferries to Chaitén, Puerto Chacabuco, Laguna San Rafael and Puerto Natales.

Organized Tours

Several agencies offer city tours of Puerto Montt (US$7.50), Puerto Varas (US$10), Frutillar (US$20), Ancud and Castro (US$32), Parque Nacional Puyehue (US$44), Petrohué and Lago Todos Los Santos (US$32) and Peulla (US$92, two days). Well-established Andina del Sud (☎ 257797), Varas 437, is very group-oriented, with fixed schedules, but reader-recommended Petrel Tours (☎ 251780), Benavente 327, has drawn praise for their individual attention. Varastur (☎ 252203), Benavente 561, Oficina 307/8, has a recommended day tour to Frutillar that includes an English-speaking guide and a sumptuous lunch.

Places to Stay – bottom end

At the northern approach to Puerto Montt, mobs of hawkers line Calle Petorca with signs offering accommodations, just as they do at the bus terminal. Indeed, Puerto Montt has such abundant budget accommodation that seasonal price differentials are relatively small, but many hospedajes are 'pirate' accommodations that do not pay taxes and some of these have dubious standards. Generally, if an hospedaje has no formal sign or does not require you to sign their register, it is probably unlicensed.

Camping *Camping Los Paredes* (☎ 258-394), six km west of town on the road to Chinquihue, charges US$16 for pleasant sites with hot showers, but it's worth haggling. There is plenty of hot water in the showers though they are a little hard to regulate. Local buses from the bus terminal will drop you at the entrance.

Farther out the road, on the shores of the Bahía de Huequillahue, *Camping Anderson* is a little remote and inconvenient, but that very inconvenience also makes it appealing. Sites cost only US$5, and fresh provisions (eggs, vegetables, cheese) are available on site. Buses Bohle makes the 20-km trip from Puerto Montt three times daily, at 7 am, 12.30 pm and 5 pm.

Hostels Summer hostel accommodation is available for US$5 at *Escuela No 1*, at the corner of Lillo and Lota, opposite the bus terminal. Cold showers, an 11.30 pm curfew and the lack of bedding (bring your own sleeping bag) may deter some travelers.

The local Hostelling International affiliate is *Residencial Urmeneta* (☎ 253262), Urmeneta 290, but the number of beds for US$10 is very limited.

Hospedajes & Residenciales *Residencial El Talquino* (☎ 253331), near the bus terminal at Pérez Rosales 114, is a bargain at only US$6 per person. Convenient to the ferry port at Angelmó, *Hospedaje Marazul* (☎ 256567), Ecuador 1558, charges US$7.50 with shared bath, US$10 with private bath.

Many travelers have expressed misgivings about standards at perennially popular *Hospedaje Raúl Arroyo*, Concepción 136, where singles are about US$8 per person, but others have no complaints. *Hospedaje Emita* (☎ 250725), Miraflores 1281, is a very reasonable alternative at US$9/11 single/double with firm beds, shared bath and hot showers.

At friendly *Hospedaje González* at Gallardo 552, spacious, sunny rooms cost US$9 with breakfast, hot water and kitchen privileges. Equally friendly but a bit noisy, *Hostal Yelcho* (☎ 262253), Ecuador 1316, charges US$9 per person, with three beds to a room.

On a cul-de-sac behind the Gimnasio Municipal at Petorca 121, *Hospedaje Montecinos* (☎ 255353) is an excellent choice for US$9 per person, though the breakfast is skimpy. *Residencial Los Helechos* (☎ 259525), Chorrillos 1500, charges US$10 per person with private bath, but some rooms lack windows. Breakfasts at recommended, comparably priced *Hospedaje Mayorga* (☎ 254493), Los Maquis 430, include delicious homemade bread.

Run by gregarious Rossy Oelckers, a Swiss-Chilean artist, *Hospedaje Suizo* (☎ 252640, 257565), Independencia 231, is one of Puerto Montt's best values for

US$11 with shared bath, plus another US$1.50 for a good and generous breakfast. It's straight up the hill from the mountain of wood chips at the entrance to the port at Angelmó.

Hospedaje Puerto Montt (☎ 252276), Pedro Montt 180, has similar facilities and prices with shared bath, but rooms with private bath cost US$30 per person. *Residencial Benavente* (☎ 253084), Benavente 948, is comparably priced with shared bath; rooms with private bath cost US$38/50.

Some rooms lack exterior windows at friendly but slightly gloomy *Residencial Urmeneta* (☎ 253262), Urmeneta 290, 2nd floor, where rates are US$14/25 with shared bath, US$25/38 with private bath.

Places to Stay – middle

Mid-range accommodation is relatively scarce, but helpful *Hotel Gamboa* (☎ 252-741), Pedro Montt 157, costs a very reasonable US$25 for spacious doubles with shared bath. Reader's choice *Residencial La Nave* (☎ 253740), Ancud 103, charges US$30 double with private bath and TV, and has a good restaurant downstairs.

Probably the best value, however, is *Residencial Millantú* (☎ 252758, fax 263550), Illapel 146, for US$25/38 with private bath and breakfast. At the upper end of the range, *Hotel El Candil* (☎ 253080), Varas 177, costs US$45/60.

Places to Stay – top end

Hotel Colina (☎ 253501, fax 259331), Talca 81, has excellent accommodation with waterfront views and private bath, and friendly and competent staff, for US$58/72. At friendly *Hotel Le Mirage* (☎ 255125, fax 256302), Rancagua 350, singles/doubles cost US$65/73 including breakfast and TV. Some travelers like *Hotel Montt* (☎ 253651, fax 253652), Varas 301, which has small but cozy rooms for US$63/75, but others think it poor value.

Hotel Vicente Pérez Rosales (☎ 252571, fax 255473), Varas 447, has long been the city's top hotel, charging US$82/95 for singles/doubles, but it has seen better days.

Overlooking downtown from its perch at Ejército 200, the northward extension of Copiapó, *Hotel Viento Sur* (☎ 258701) has drawn praise for comfort, helpful and efficient staff, and an outstanding restaurant; rooms cost US$97/112. The newer *Gran Hotel Don Luis* (☎ 259001, fax 259005), Quillota 146, has made good impressions for US$109/118.

Places to Eat

El Bodegón, Varas 931, is popular with locals and sometimes has live music at night, but some travelers have criticized its hygiene. For drinks, snacks and kuchen, try *Café Central* (☎ 254721) at Rancagua 117, opposite the post office, *Café Real* (☎ 253-750), nearby at Rancagua 137, *Café Tirol* (☎ 254275) at Varas 629, or *Apetito's* (☎ 252470) at Chillán 96. There is a fine bakery, *Pastelería Lisel*, at Cauquenes 82.

Dino's (☎ 252785), Varas 550, is the local representative of an ordinary but reliable chain. *Amsel* (☎ 253941), on the waterfront at Pedro Montt 56, is only so-so for both food and service. *Ten-Tén* (☎ 259911), Vial 467, 2nd floor, is a bright, cheerful café with an innovative lunchtime menu, perhaps the most interesting in the city. *Mykonos* (☎ 262627), Antonio Varas 326, has good, moderately priced lunches.

At Gallardo 119, Puerto Montt's best pizzería, Italian-run *Di Napoli* (☎ 254174), is a tiny venue that gets very crowded and stuffy – the ventilation is better downstairs. Prices are moderate. *Rincón Sureño* (☎ 254-597), Talca 84, has inexpensive lunches and dinners, but the food is only so-so. *Heladería La Reina* (☎ 253979), Urmeneta 508, has the best ice cream in town.

Don't leave Puerto Montt without tasting curanto or other regional seafood specialties at Angelmó's waterfront cafés – among the recommended choices are the aggressively tourist-oriented *Marfino* (☎ 259044), Avenida Angelmó 1856, and the much less pretentious *Asturias* (☎ 258496), Avenida Angelmó 2448-C. Another fine seafood place is *Embassy* (☎ 252232), Ancud 106. Downtown seafood choices include the *Centro Español* (☎ 255570) at O'Higgins

233, renowned for its paella, *Balzac* (☎ 259-495) at San Martín 244, and *Mares* (☎ 257-121) at Gallardo 548.

The bathing resort of Pelluco, east of downtown via Avenida Juan Soler, is a good hunting ground for restaurants – try the parrillada at *Fogón Las Tejuelas* (☎ 252876) or any of the other beachfront restaurants.

Entertainment
The *Cine Rex* (☎ 252836), Varas 625, shows recent films. If you can't live without country music and line dancing, the *OK Corral* (☎ 266287) is at Cauquenes 128.

Things to Buy
Timón Austral, Rengifo 430-A, sells antiques and used books. For crafts, visit the lively waterfront market Pueblito de Melipulli, opposite the bus terminal.

Getting There & Away
Air LanChile (☎ 253141), San Martín 200, flies three times daily to Santiago (US$158), with an additional flight Wednesday and Saturday. It also flies twice daily to Coihaique (US$87) and daily to Punta Arenas (US$179).

Ladeco (☎ 253002), Benavente 350, flies three times daily to Santiago except Saturday, when it has only two flights; the midday flight stops in Concepción (US$98). Ladeco also flies daily to Punta Arenas, and daily except Sunday to Balmaceda/Coihaique.

National Airlines (☎ 258277), Benavente 305, flies daily to Santiago (US$143) except Sunday (when it has two flights), Monday, Tuesday, Thursday and Sunday to Concepción (US$99), Wednesday, Saturday and Sunday to Temuco (US$54), and daily to Punta Arenas (US$165).

Alta (☎ 268646), Benavente 301, flies three times every weekday to Concepción (US$72) via Temuco (US$39), twice daily on weekends; twice daily every weekday to Chaitén (US$30), but only once on weekends; and daily except Tuesday to Balmaceda/Coihaique (US$80), Puerto Natales (US$185) and Punta Arenas (US$185).

Transportes Aéreos Neuquén (TAN; ☎ 250071), an Argentine provincial airline at Varas 445, flies Tuesday and Thursday to Bariloche (US$49) and Neuquén (US$111).

AeroChaitén (☎ 267298, fax 253219), Quillota 127, flies daily except Sunday to Chaitén (US$43). Aerosur (☎ 252523), Urmeneta 149, flies daily except Sunday to Chaitén (US$43), and Wednesday and Saturday to Futaleufú and Palena (US$62).

Bus Puerto Montt's Terminal de Buses (☎ 253143) is on the waterfront, at Avenida Portales and Lota. There are services to all regional destinations, Chiloé, Santiago, Coihaique, Punta Arenas and Argentina. Services down the Camino Austral are still limited but improving.

Bus – regional To nearby Puerto Varas (US$0.65), try Expreso Puerto Varas (the most frequent), Arguz and Varmontt (☎ 254110). Full Express and Thaebus both go to Frutillar (US$1.25); Thaebus also goes to Puerto Octay. Buses Fierro (☎ 253-022) goes to Lenca, the turnoff for the southern approach to Parque Nacional Alerce Andino, and Chaica (US$1.50) five times daily. Fierro also goes to Lago Chapo (US$1.75), the northern approach to Alerce Andino, four times daily.

Other rural destinations include the coastal town of Maullín (US$1.25), served by Buses Bohle (☎ 254526) and ETM (☎ 256253); the fishing village of Calbuco (US$1.50), served by Bohle, Buses Calbuco (☎ 252926) and Buses Aguas Azules (☎ 253835); and the villages of Ralún (US$4), Cochamó (US$4.50) and Río Puelo (popular fishing areas on the Río Petrohué and the Estuario de Reloncaví), served by Fierro, Bohle and Buses Río Frio (☎ 253258). The fare to Puelo is US$5.50. Buses Pirehueico (☎ 252926) goes to Panguipulli four times daily.

At the time of this writing, Buses Fierro (☎ 253022) has two buses daily as far as Hornopirén (US$7, three hours) on the Camino Austral, where there are summer ferry connections to Caleta Gonzalo. There

Sailing the Fjords

Almost everyone who travels to southern Chile tries, or at least entertains the idea of, sailing through the nearly uninhabited Chilean fjords, a scenic area comparable to Alaska's Inside Passage, New Zealand's Milford Sound or Norway's North Atlantic coastline, where glaciers reach the sea or sprawl within easy view during good weather.

In the recent past, before Chilean shippers grasped the tourist potential of this route, travelers begged passages in cramped bunks on rusty state-run freighters like the *Río Baker*, which carried cargo between Puerto Montt and Puerto Natales, or negotiated with truckers for a berth on ferries like the *Evangelistas* (truckers were entitled to bunks but usually slept in their own more comfortable cabs). Within the past few years, however, Naviera Magallanes (Navimag) has modernized the roll-on, roll-off ferry *Puerto Edén* for weekly four-day, three-night sailings in each direction.

Increasing numbers of visitors are taking advantage of the improved service. After waiting in Navimag's comfortable lounge at Angelmó, the port of Puerto Montt, a stream of backpackers and other passengers marches onto a ramp to board the ferry's open freight elevator to the main deck. The crew collects passports, then segregates passengers by class – those with cabin accommodations to the left, those in multi-bunk clase económica to the right.

Leaving Angelmó, the sight of Osorno's perfect cone and shattered Volcán Calbuco presage the even more impressive scenery to the south, as the ferry sails between Chiloé and the mainland. The route stays in relatively sheltered waters like the Canal Moraleda, passing the lonely lighthouse at Melinka in the Guaitecas archipelago, before entering the maze of narrower channels of Aisén. At the south end of Canal Errázuriz, the ferry heads west through the constricted Canal Chacabuco to enter the dreaded Golfo de Penas, where swells from the open Pacific can make all but the most experienced sailors queasy.

For most passengers, it's a relief to escape the Golfo de Penas and enter the Canal Messier where, after navigating the Angostura Inglesa (a passage so confined that the ship seems to graze the shoreline on both sides), the *Puerto Edén* drops anchor at its namesake settlement, a small fishing port that's the last outpost of the region's Qawashqar Indians. If schedules and conditions permit, passengers can sometimes go ashore; in any event, lighters pick up centolla (king crab) for the Punta Arenas market and a handful of Qawashqar come aboard to occupy cabins specially reserved for them under the terms of Navimag's government contract.

To the south, the route becomes increasingly scenic as the channels become narrower, the snow peaks get closer, and hundreds of waterfalls tumble from U-shaped glacial valleys. Even the second week of January, during mid-summer, the snow line on the nearest hills is probably still below 400 meters, just below the cloud banks that often cover the highest points. As Darwin remarked after navigating the fjords of Tierra del Fuego and Laguna San Rafael:

I was astonished when I first saw a range, only from 3000 to 4000 feet in height, in the latitude of Cumberland, with every valley filled with streams of ice descending to the sea coast.

The natural grandeur of Aisén and Magallanes is the reason most people make the trip, but the social experience has become a highlight in itself. While polyglot foreigners generally predominate, increasing numbers of Chileans are doing the trip, and the interaction is gratifying to almost everyone. It begins with waiting and chatting before boarding and improves as, on the first evening, the crew provides complimentary pisco sours, and the captain introduces himself, tracing the route through the southern maze. While there are separate galleys for cabin passengers and those in clase económica, the two groups mix readily outside mealtimes, enjoying the scenery and the conversation. After crossing the Golfo de Penas, the passengers delight each other with tales of how they survived the pitching and rolling.

The last evening is the most sociable of the trip, as people who were strangers a few days earlier share the wine they've purchased in Puerto Montt or Puerto Natales, and

Americans, Germans, Australians, Swiss, Chileans, Argentines, Egyptians, Danes, Brits, Irish and Brazilians dance beneath a mirror ball to incongruous medleys of salsa, technopop and oldies like 'Let's Twist Again,' 'Good Golly Miss Molly' and the theme from 'Hawaii Five-0.' Only a handful make the next morning's breakfast, but people who met on board continue to encounter other 'boat people' in Puerto Natales and Torres del Paine.

Before disembarking, the crew returns passports and, in a tacky but somehow appropriate gesture, distributes 'diplomas' to everyone who finished the voyage of 900 nautical miles – probably the longest in the world for a vessel of its kind. The only real shortcoming is the failure to provide more information about the route and its role in Chilean history and geography.

Practical Pointers Most four-passenger cabins on the *Puerto Edén* have a toilet, sink, shower and closet, plus additional storage beneath the bunks, but some have toilet and shower outside the cabin. Unless you're really claustrophobic, the porthole views in the ship's 'A' cabins do not justify the extra expense – most people prefer the views from the decks or common areas, which have much larger windows, instead. The bunks themselves are very comfortable and the beds tightly made, though the pillows are a bit small.

Some passengers have called clase económica the 'dungeon', but the bunks themselves are comfortable and have curtains for privacy, though some have low ceilings. In fact, clase económica has the atmosphere of a floating youth hostel, though it can get hot and noisy (especially in the vicinity of the engine room). The main shortcoming is the lack of space to store gear – don't leave things on the floor, as they can get wet.

Meals on board are generally well-prepared but simple; portions are ample but not large. The main courses are usually seafood, chicken, hamburgers and sausages, but vegetarian meals are available if requested in advance. Beer and wine are available, but it's cheaper to bring your own.

Neither galley has enough seats, so that clase económica dines in shifts, while cabin passengers are staggered, as the cafeteria-style service is slow-paced – you spend a lot of time standing in line. Breakfast is less crowded because of late risers. Smoking is prohibited in cabins and common areas. After meals there are videos in the main lounge, and games are also available. At certain times, passengers may visit the bridge.

Weather can be very changeable, but this means there's usually good visibility at some time during the trip; dress for cold and wind. December and January have the longest days.

Passengers prone to seasickness should refrain from eating prior to crossing the Golfo de Penas, which can be extremely rough. If the crossing is at night, you may be able to sleep through it in your bunk, but you may also feel like a human gyroscope as the boat pitches in the heavy seas, even if there is no storm – what counts is what's happening in the open ocean. The bunks are not really designed for the open sea, since they have low sides, but the stewards make the beds so tight that it's hard to fall out or even to move around much.

Fares Fares per person, which vary according to view and private or shared bath, are as follows:

Cabina Armador	High Season	Low Season
Single	US$1346	US$912
Double	US$705	US$517
Triple	US$526	US$392
Literas (Bunks)		
AA	US$346	US$235
A	US$295	US$196
B	US$233	US$175
Económica	US$130	US$120

LA ARAUCANIA

is, however, no regular public transport for the 56 km between Caleta Gonzalo and the mainland port of Chaitén, which is more easily reached by ferry both from Puerto Montt or from Quellón, on Chiloé. Since conditions and traffic on the Camino Austral are erratic, transport information changes rapidly; check details on arrival in Puerto Montt.

Bus – domestic Cruz del Sur (☎ 254731) and Transchiloé (☎ 254934) have frequent services to Ancud, Castro and other destinations on Chiloé. Varmontt (☎ 254410), Igi Llaima (☎ 254519), Buses Lit (☎ 254-011) and Etta Bus (☎ 257324) all go to Concepción and to various stops along the Panamericana as far as Santiago. Other companies that serve Santiago include Turibús (☎ 253245), Bus Norte (☎ 252-783), Tas Choapa (☎ 254828), Tur-Bus (☎ 253329), and Vía Tur (☎ 253133). Buses Lit and Tur-Bus have daily service to Valparaíso/Viña del Mar.

For the long trip to Punta Arenas (US$50), via the Atlantic coast of Argentina, contact Turibús, Ghisoni (☎ 256622) or Bus Sur (☎ 252926). Turibús also goes to Coihaique (US$33) daily via Argentina.

Sample fares and times include Ancud (US$5, two hours), Castro (US$7, three hours), Quellón (US$10, five hours), Osorno (US$2, 1½ hours), Valdivia (US$6, 3½ hours), Temuco (US$9, five hours), Concepción (US$14, nine hours), Santiago (US$21, 16 hours), and Valparaíso/Viña del Mar (US$25, 18 hours).

Bus – international Bus Norte, Cruz del Sur and Río de La Plata (☎ 253841) have daily buses to Bariloche, Argentina, via the Puyehue pass, while Tas Choapa goes to Argentina twice daily. The fare is about US$20.

Buses Andina del Sud and Varastur (☎ 252203), both at Varas 437, offer daily bus-boat combinations to Bariloche, Argentina, via Ensenada, Petrohué and Peulla. These depart Puerto Montt in the morning, arriving in Bariloche early in the evening The cost is about US$106.

Train Puerto Montt's railway station has closed and, though there is talk of building a new one on the flatter high ground north of downtown, Puerto Varas will be the southern rail terminus for the foreseeable future.

Boat The most appealing route to Chile's far south is by sea from Puerto Montt. Ferry or bus-ferry combinations connect Puerto Montt with Chiloé and Chaitén in Region X; ferries to Chiloé leave from the port of Pargua, on the Canal de Chacao, where other southbound ferries occasionally sail as well. Some continue to Puerto Chacabuco (the port of Coihaique) in Region XI (Aisén) or go to Puerto Natales in Region XII (Magallanes).

Ferries also visit truly remote spots such as Puerto Edén and Laguna San Rafael. Information about these ferry trips is included in the Aisén chapter. Travelers prone to motion sickness may consider medication prior to crossing the Golfo de Penas, which is exposed to gut-wrenching Pacific swells.

At Angelmó's Terminal de Transbordadores, Avenida Angelmó 2187, Navimag (☎ 253318, fax 258540) sails the roll-on, roll-off ferries *Evangelistas* to Puerto Chacabuco twice weekly and *Puerto Edén* weekly to Puerto Natales, a spectacular three-day cruise through the Chilean fjords. After years of neglect, new management at Navimag now actively promotes this latter excursion, comparable to Alaska's Inside Passage or New Zealand's Milford Sound.

Fares from Puerto Montt to Puerto Chacabuco range from US$50 for a basic seat, to US$175/300 per single/double for cabins, with all meals included. Bunks (US$100) and slightly cheaper cabins (US$150/250) are also available. These sailings continue to Laguna San Rafael; see the Aisén chapter for more details.

For fares from Puerto Montt to Puerto Natales, see the Puerto Natales entry in the Magallanes chapter. If possible, try to book passages between Puerto Montt and Puerto Natales at Navimag's Santiago offices (see the Getting Around chapter). In Puerto Montt, Travellers has a good record for getting its clients a berth, but last-minute arrivals at the port sometimes manage to get on.

Transmarchilay (☎ 253683, ☎ /fax 254-654), also at the Terminal de Transbordadores, sails the ferries *La Pincoya* and *Mailén* (high season only) to Chaitén (eight hours) and *El Colono* to Puerto Chacabuco (Tuesdays and Fridays, 23 hours). Fares to Chaitén range from US$20 for a fixed seat to US$25 for a recliner and US$40 and up per person for a double cabin. Comparable accommodations to Chacabuco cost slightly less than double the fares to Chaitén. Automobile fares to Chaitén are US$100, to Puerto Chacabuco US$145.

Transmarchilay and Cruz del Sur also operate auto-passenger ferries from Pargua, 60 km southwest of Puerto Montt, to Chacao, on the northern tip of the Isla Grande de Chiloé Island (see the Chiloé chapter). Fares are about US$1 for passengers or US$12 per car, no matter how many passengers. There is no extra ferry charge for passengers on buses to Chiloé.

Getting Around

To/From the Airport Local buses connect downtown Puerto Montt with Aeropuerto El Tepual (☎ 252019), 16 km west of town, for all incoming and outgoing flights.

Car Rental Regional attractions like Lago Llanquihue, Petrohué and Lago Todos Los Santos are most conveniently explored by car. Rental cars are available from the Automóvil Club (☎ 254776) at Esmeralda 70, Autowald (☎ 256355) at Portales 1330, First Rent-a-Car (☎ 252036) at Varas 447, Hertz (☎ 259585) at Varas 126, Avis (☎ 253307) at Urmeneta 1037, Full Fama's (☎ 258060, fax 259840) at Portales 506 and Colina (☎ 258328) at Talca 79.

Autowald and Full Fama's are small local agencies that will help get notarial permission for taking rental vehicles into Argentina. Daily rates range from about US$45 plus IVA and insurance for a small vehicle, to US$100-plus for a pickup truck or Jeep. Weekly rates range from about US$250 to US$500-plus.

AROUND PUERTO MONTT
Calbuco
Founded in 1604 by Spanish survivors of the destruction of Osorno, and connected to the mainland by a causeway, this island fishing village is 51 km south of Puerto Montt on a spur off the Panamericana. It has a wealth of restaurants and reasonable accommodation (US$17/30 single/double with shared bath, US$40 double with private bath) at *Residencial Aguas Azules* (☎ 461427), Avenida Oelckers 159. For seafood, try *Costa Azul* (☎ 461516), Vicuña Mackenna 202.

Calbuco's municipal Oficina de Informaciones (☎ 461349) is at Federico Errázuriz 210. Buses Bohle, ETC (☎ 252926) and Aguas Azules provide transport from Puerto Montt.

Maullín
Southwest of Puerto Montt, Maullín is a small, quiet port on the estuary of the Río Maullín, which in many ways is as much a

Around Puerto Montt

highway as the paved route to Puerto Montt – people are constantly crossing from shore to shore, and up and down the river. *Residencial Toledo* (☎ 451246), opposite the Copec petrol station at 21 de Mayo 147, has accommodation for US$8 per person. There's a very good restaurant in the bus terminal on the Costanera.

Five km west of Maullín, at the seaside resort of **Pangal**, the *Complejo Turístico Pangal* (☎ 451244) has four-bed cabañas for US$50, camping for US$12.50 per site, and a highly regarded restaurant. *Camping Punta Pangal* is slightly cheaper, but charges extra for hot showers.

At the end of a gravel road, 17 km south of Maullín, **Carelmapu** is a scenic fishing village with a couple of good restaurants, *Mi Rincón* and *La Ruca*, and modest lodging at an anonymous residencial on O'Higgins. Camping is possible at *Mar Brava*, on a cliff overlooking the Pacific. On February 2, the village celebrates the **Fiesta de la Virgen de Candelaria**.

Getting There & Away Among them, ETM, ETC and Carelmapu have about 30 buses daily from Puerto Montt (US$2) to and from Carelmapu via Maullín, between 7.30 am and 8 pm.

PARQUE NACIONAL ALERCE ANDINO

Created only in 1982, 40,000-hectare Alerce Andino protects some of the last remaining forests of alerce *(Fitzroya cupressoides)*, a conifer resembling California's giant sequoia in appearance and longevity. Its attractive and durable timber has made the species vulnerable to commercial exploitation, but alerce forest still dominates more than half the park's surface, a remarkable fact considering its proximity to populated areas.

Geography & Climate

Rising from sea level to 1558 meters on the summit of Cerro Cuadrado, mountainous Alerce Andino is only 40 km from Puerto Montt via the newly paved section of Ruta 7, the Camino Austral, that runs to La Arena, on the Estero de Reloncaví. The park consists of three main sectors: Sector Correntoso on the Río Chamiza at the northwestern end, Sector Lago Chapo only a few km to the east, and Sector Chaicas at the southwestern approach.

Exposed to Pacific frontal systems, Alerce Andino receives annual precipitation of 3300 to 4500 mm, often in the form of snow above 800 meters. The average temperature is 15°C in January and 7°C in July. The largest of several glacial lakes is Lago Chapo, on the park's northern border, which is now unfortunately exploited for hydroelectricity and pisciculture, but there are several other attractive lakes in more remote areas, generally at higher altitudes.

Flora & Fauna

Though not so tall as the sequoia, reaching only 40 meters, a 3000-year-old alerce can reach four meters in diameter. It is found primarily between 400 and 700 meters above sea level, coexisting with species like coigue, tineo, mañío and canelo. Evergreen forest, ranging from sea level to 900 meters, consists of species like coigue and ulmo, as well as ferns, climbing vines and dense thickets of quila, a solid bamboo. Coigue and lenga dominate the park's highest elevations.

The park's fauna are much less conspicuous, but there are occasional sightings of mammals like pumas, pudús, foxes and skunks, as well as birds like the condors, kingfishers and several species of waterfowl.

Hiking & Trekking

Backcountry hiking is the best reason for visiting Alerce Andino. Between the Correntoso and Río Chaica sectors, there is a good trail with several refugios along the route, but recent severe winters have covered the trail with many deadfalls that Conaf has been slow to remove. Several Puerto Montt agencies, including Travellers in Angelmó, organize trips to the park, but it is also possible to hike and trek independently.

From the campground at Río Chaica, the river has washed out part of the 4WD road, which has become a de facto trail. From Guardería Chaica, Lago Triángulo is only 9½ km, but the last part of the trail, beyond Laguna Chaiquenes, is very slow because of the deadfalls. The earlier, more open part of the trail is full of tábanos in early summer.

Places to Stay

Camping is the only option in the park proper. Conaf has a free five-site campground at Correntoso on the Río Chamiza, at the northern end of the park, and another six-site campground near the head of the Río Chaica valley. For trekkers, backcountry camping is another possibility, but Conaf also maintains rustic trailside refugios at Río Pangal, Laguna Sargazo and Laguna Fría.

Getting There & Away

From Puerto Montt, Buses Fierro has four buses daily to the village of Correntoso, only three km from the Río Chamiza entrance on the northern boundary of the park, continuing to Lago Chapo (US$1.75). Fierro also runs five buses daily to the crossroads at Lenca (US$1.50), on the Camino Austral, where a narrow lateral road climbs seven km up the valley of the Río Chaica. This offers slightly better access to a number of lakes and peaks, and is probably a better choice for the non-trekker.

At the park entrances, Conaf collects a fee of US$2 per visitor. The gate on the Río Chaica side is open 9 am to 5 pm only, so visitors out for a long day's hike should park outside the gate (which is only half an hour's walk from the end of the road) unless they're planning an overnight stay at Río Chaica campground.

HORNOPIREN

Southbound travelers on the Camino Austral often stop in this scenic village, formerly known as Río Negro, on the north shore of the sheltered Canal Hornopirén, directly opposite Isla Pelada and only a few km west of Parque Nacional Hornopirén. The village is the southern terminus of bus service on the segment of Ruta 7 from Puerto Montt, and the northern terminus of the summer ferry to Caleta Gonzalo, on Fiordo Reñihue, the point where the highway continues south.

Places to Stay & Eat

Tent camping is free at Hornopirén's shoreline park, but there are no sanitary facilities. Rambling *Hotel Hornopirén*, Carrera Pinto 388, is a family-run establishment with loads of personality, good rooms for US$10 per person with shared bath, and an excellent restaurant. The *Restaurant Central Plaza* has good, moderately priced sandwiches, but is nothing special.

Getting There & Away

While Hornopirén is directly on the Camino Austral, it's necessary to cross the Estuario de Reloncaví from La Arena to Puelche on the ferry *Tehuelche*; there are eight sailings daily in each direction between 7 am and 8.45 pm. The 30-minute trip costs US$14 for cars and pickup trucks, US$1 for pedestrians, but bus passengers pay no extra charge.

Bus Buses Fierro, on the Plaza de Armas, has two buses daily to and from Puerto Montt (US$7).

Ferry In summer, Transmarchilay's ferry *Mailén* makes the six-hour trip to Caleta Gonzalo Wednesdays at 4 pm and Thursday through Sunday at 3 pm; there is also a Monday sailing to Chaitén (nine hours) at 8 am. Most cars and pickup trucks pay US$90 to Caleta Gonzalo, US$100 to Chaitén, while passengers pay US$14 to Caleta Gonzalo, US$15 to Chaitén. Cyclists pay an additional US$9 to Caleta Gonzalo, US$10 to Chaitén, while motorcyclists pay US$16 more to Caleta Gonzalo and US$19 to Chaitén.

Chiloé

About 180 km long but only 50 km wide, the Isla Grande de Chiloé is a well watered, densely forested island of undulating hills, linked to the Chilean mainland by frequent ferries across the Canal de Chacao. Between the Isla Grande and the mainland, the Golfo de Ancud and the Golfo de Corcovado are dotted with many smaller islands of archipelagic Chiloé. Politically, the province of Chiloé belongs to Region X of Los Lagos.

Prior to the arrival of the Spaniards in the 16th century, Huilliche Indians cultivated potatoes and other crops in Chiloé's fertile volcanic soil. Spain took possession in 1567 and founded the city of Castro the following year. Jesuit missionaries were among the first settlers, but early-17th-century refugees from the Mapuche uprising on the mainland also established settlements. During the Wars of Independence, Chiloé was a Spanish stronghold, resisting criollo attacks in 1820 and 1824 from heavily fortified Ancud, until final defeat in 1826.

Distinctive shingled houses with corrugated metal roofs line the streets of Chiloé's towns and punctuate the verdant countryside. For much of the year, rain and mist obscure the sun which, when it finally breaks through the clouds, reveals majestic panoramas across the Golfo de Ancud to the snow-capped mainland volcanoes.

Ancud and Castro are the only two sizable towns. Some towns, most notably Castro, have picturesque neighborhoods of *palafitos*, rows of houses built on stilts over the water, where boats can anchor at the back door on a rising tide. Other palafitos can be found at Quemchi, Chonchi and smaller ports.

Do not miss the smaller villages, with more than 150 distinctive wooden churches up to two centuries old, nine of them national monuments. There are 18th-century churches at Achao, Chonchi, Quilquico, Isla Quinchao and Villupulli, while those at Dalcahue, Nercón and Rilán date from the 19th century. Castro's gaudy Iglesia San Francisco was built this century.

Nearly all Chiloé's 130,000 inhabitants live within sight of the sea. More than half make their living from peasant agriculture, but many others depend on fishing for food and money. The nearly roadless western shores and interior still preserve extensive forests, while the densely settled eastern littoral contributes wheat, oats, vegetables and livestock to a precarious economy. Despite great natural beauty, there are still many contemporary parallels with the 19th century, when Chiloé was one of Chile's poorest areas and Darwin commented that:

. . . the climate is not favourable to any production which requires much sunshine to ripen it. There is very little pasture . . . and in consequence, the staple articles of food are pigs,

Typical Chilote church

376

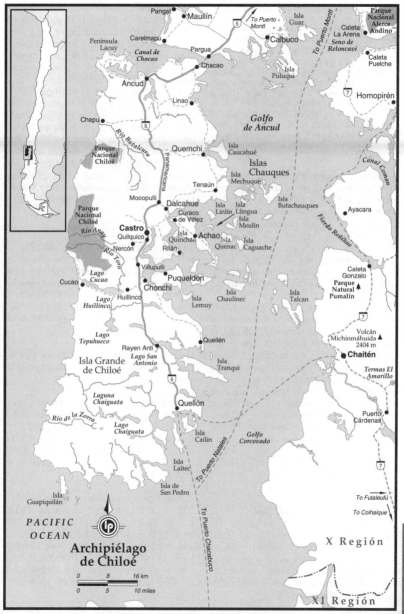

Archipiélago
de Chiloé

PACIFIC
OCEAN

potatoes and fish . . . The arts, however, are in the rudest state; – as may be seen in their strange fashion of ploughing, their method of spinning, grinding corn, and in the construction of their boats . . . Although with plenty to eat, the people are very poor: there is no demand for labour, and consequently the lower orders cannot scrape together money sufficient to purchase even the smallest luxuries. There is also a great deficiency of circulating medium. I have seen a man bringing on his back a bag of charcoal, with which to buy some trifle, and another carrying a plank to exchange for a bottle of wine.

Because of perpetual economic hardship, many Chilotes (natives of the archipelago) have reluctantly left for employment elsewhere, from the copper mines of the Norte Grande to the sheep estancias of Argentine and Chilean Patagonia. To metropolitan sophisticates, 'Chilote' is synonymous with 'bumpkin,' but the island has a rich tradition of folklore and legend that has made great contributions to Chilean literature.

In part, at least, Chiloé's reputation derives from its insularity – the waters of the Canal de Chacao were so rough that, in days of sail, settlers crossed only reluctantly to and from the mainland. Nowadays, of course, ferries sail regularly from Pargua to Chacao, but there is no prospect of a bridge that would span the channel. This isolation has encouraged self-reliance but also an unexpected courtesy and hospitality toward visitors that has changed little since Darwin remarked, more than a century and a half ago, 'I never saw anything more obliging and humble than the manners of these people.'

ANCUD

Founded in 1767 to defend Spain's Chilean coastline from foreign intrusion, the onetime fortress of Ancud (population 23,000) is now Chiloé's largest town, an attractive fishing port on a promontory overlooking the Bahía de Ancud. Its regional museum is an excellent introduction to life on the island.

Orientation

At the north end of the Isla Grande, Ancud sits on a small peninsula facing the Canal de Chacao, with the Golfo de Quetalmahue to the west. The Península de Lacuy, farther west, shelters the harbor from the swells and storms of the open Pacific.

Because of its irregular topography, Ancud has a very atypical street plan, but it's small and compact enough that directions are easy to follow. Most points of interest are within a few blocks of the north-south Avenida Costanera and the asymmetrical Plaza de Armas, on the hill above it. Calle Aníbal Pinto provides access to the Panamericana, which continues to Quellón on the island's southern tip.

Information

Tourist Office Sernatur (☎ 622665/00) is at Libertad 665, opposite the Plaza de Armas. In summer it's open 8.30 am to 8 pm weekdays, 10 am to 4 pm weekends; the rest of the year hours are 8.30 am to 1 pm and 2.30 to 6 pm weekdays. It has plenty of brochures, town maps and lists of accommodations.

Money It's better to change in Puerto Montt, but Banco de Crédito has an ATM at Ramírez 257.

Post & Communications Ancud's area code is ☎ 65. Correos de Chile is at the corner of Pudeto and Blanco Encalada. The Compañía Nacional de Teléfonos (CNT) is at Chacabuco 745 and Pudeto 298. CTC is at Chacabuco 750, while Entel is at Pudeto 219.

Travel Agencies Turismo Ancud (☎ 623-019) is at Pudeto 219, within the Hotel Lacuy. Turismo Alternativo Paralelo 42° (☎ 622458, 624013, fax 622656), at Prat 28 and Almirante Latorre 558, runs full-day tours by 4WD and foot to Duhatao and Chepu, on the west coast of the island, and to Ahui, a Spanish fortification on Península Lacuy.

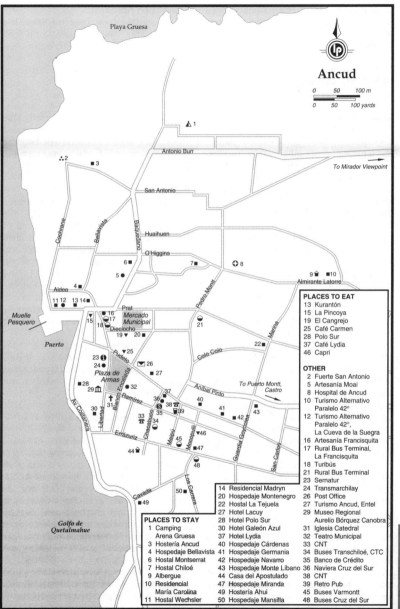

Ancud

PLACES TO EAT
13 Kurantón
15 La Pincoya
19 El Cangrejo
25 Café Carmen
28 Polo Sur
37 Café Lydia
46 Capri

OTHER
2 Fuerte San Antonio
5 Artesanía Moai
8 Hospital de Ancud
10 Turismo Alternativo
   Paralelo 42°
12 Turismo Alternativo
   Paralelo 42°,
   La Cueva de la Suegra
16 Artesanía Francisquita
17 Rural Bus Terminal,
   La Francisquita
18 Turibús
21 Rural Bus Terminal
23 Sernatur
24 Transmarchilay
26 Post Office
27 Turismo Ancud, Entel
29 Museo Regional
   Aurelio Bórquez Canobra
31 Iglesia Catedral
32 Teatro Municipal
33 CNT
34 Buses Transchiloé, CTC
35 Banco de Crédito
36 Naviera Cruz del Sur
38 CNT
39 Retro Pub
45 Buses Varmontt
48 Buses Cruz del Sur

PLACES TO STAY
1 Camping
  Arena Gruesa
3 Hostería Ancud
4 Hospedaje Bellavista
6 Hostal Montserrat
7 Hostal Chiloé
9 Albergue
10 Residencial
   María Carolina
11 Hostal Wechsler
14 Residencial Madryn
20 Hospedaje Montenegro
22 Hostal La Tejuela
27 Hotel Lacuy
28 Hotel Polo Sur
30 Hotel Galeón Azul
37 Hotel Lydia
40 Hospedaje Cárdenas
41 Hospedaje Germania
42 Hospedaje Navarro
43 Hospedaje Monte Líbano
44 Casa del Apostulado
47 Hospedaje Miranda
49 Hostería Ahui
50 Hospedaje Mansilla

CHILOE

Cultural Center The Teatro Municipal, on Blanco Encalada opposite the Plaza de Armas, hosts concerts and other cultural events.

Medical Services The Hospital de Ancud (☎ 622356) is at Almirante Latorre 405, at the corner of Pedro Montt.

Museo Regional Aurelio Bórquez Canobra

Colloquially known as the Museo Chilote, this building houses ethnographic and historical materials (including an outstanding selection of photographs) and a superb natural history display. Surrounded by towers and battlements like a small fortress, its sunny patio displays representations of figures from Chilote folklore, such as the mermaid La Pincoya (symbol of the ocean's fertility) and the troll-like Trauco.

Among the fine exhibits are watercolors by local artist Francisco Vera Cárcamo, depictions of Chilote landscapes and architecture, and scale models of several of the island's shingled wooden churches – note the variety of designs among the shingles. A very fine three-dimensional relief map of Chiloé indicates major settlements.

There's also a replica of the schooner *Ancud*, which sailed the treacherous fjords and Straits of Magellan to claim Chile's southernmost territories in the mid-19th century, along with Chile's first fire engine, sent from Europe to Valparaíso in 1852. One of Ancud's most intriguing restaurants is the thatched-roof Chilote house on the museum's patio, whose traditional kitchen, dug into the earth through an opening in the floor, serves a savory curanto on weekends.

On Libertad just south of the Plaza de Armas, the museum (☎ 622413) is open 11 am to 7 pm daily in January and February. The rest of the year, hours are 9 am to 1 pm and 2.30 to 7 pm Tuesday to Saturday, 10 am to 1 pm and 3 to 6 pm Sunday. Admission costs US$1 for adults, US$0.25 for children.

Fuerte San Antonio

At the northwestern corner of town, late colonial cannon emplacements still look down on the harbor from the early-19th-century remains of Fuerte San Antonio. During the wars of independence, this was Spain's last Chilean outpost.

Special Events

For a week in January, Ancud observes the Semana Ancuditana (Ancud Week), which includes the annual Encuentro de Folklore de Chiloé, promoting the island's music, dance and cuisine.

Places to Stay – bottom end

Camping The grassy sites at *Camping Arena Gruesa* (☎ 622975), six blocks from the Plaza de Armas at the north end of Bellavista, overlook the sea and have small cooking shelters, but they lack shade and there are many barking dogs in the neighborhood. Sites ostensibly cost US$18 including hot showers and firewood, but the friendly proprietors give a break to backpackers or small parties by charging around US$4 per person if it's not too crowded.

Camping Playa Gaviotas (☎ (09) 653-8096), five km northeast of town on Ruta 5, has similar facilities and good beach access, but little shade or shelter, for US$15 per site.

Hostels At Almirante Latorre 478, the very informal *Albergue* (☎ 622065) is better than its dilapidated exterior would suggest; floor space for sleeping bags costs US$1.25 per night, but travelers can pitch tents in the patio for less than US$1. In December, January and February, the church-sponsored *Casa del Apostulado* (☎ 623256), on Chacabuco near Errázuriz, offers floor space for US$2, mattresses for US$4, and proper beds for US$5 per night. Visitors can use the kitchen from 8 am to 10 pm.

Hospedajes Other than hostels, hospedajes provide the cheapest accommodation at about US$7.50 per person – look for signs in the windows of private houses. Many are seasonal, but some that are open all year include *Hospedaje Navarro* at Pudeto 361, *Hospedaje Bellavista* (☎ 622-384) at Bellavista 449 and *Hospedaje Miranda* at the corner of Errázuriz and Mocopulli. For clean rooms and baths, hot showers and amiable hosts, the Miranda is an especially good choice.

Hospedaje Montenegro (☎ 622239), Dieciocho 191, has singles/doubles with shared bath for around US$8/13 with private bath. Tiny but friendly *Hospedaje Cárdenas* (☎ 622535), Pudeto 331, costs US$9 and is open in summer only. Others in the same range include *Hospedaje Mansilla*, Los Carrera 971, and the very pleasant *Hospedaje Monte Líbano* (☎ 622172), Aníbal Pinto 419.

Hostal Wechsler (☎ 623970, fax 623-090), Cochrane 480, has a reputation for Germanic austerity and discipline, but is very well kept. Singles/doubles with shared bath cost US$11/20, while comfy rooms with private bath cost US$21/38, although breakfast is nothing special.

For US$12.50 per person with breakfast, *Residencial María Carolina* (☎ 622-458), Almirante Latorre 558, has many things going for it, including its quiet location, attractive common spaces and spacious gardens.

Highly recommended by many readers, *Residencial Madryn* (☎ 622128), Bellavista 491, charges around US$15 single with breakfast. At *Hospedaje Germania* (☎ 622-214), Pudeto 357, singles/doubles cost US$16/20 with shared bath, nearly double that with private bath.

Places to Stay – middle

Mid-range accommodations start around US$20/30 at *Hostal La Tejuela* (☎ 622-361), at the corner of Colo Colo and Goycolea, which also has a restaurant. Despite an unimpressive exterior, *Hotel Lydia* (☎ 622990, fax 622879), Pudeto 256, has clean, agreeable rooms from US$16/30 single/double with shared bath; rooms with private bath cost US$34/48. It also has a highly regarded restaurant.

Rates for comparable accommodation at *Hotel Polo Sur* (☎ 622200), on the waterfront at Avenida Costanera 630, are US$23/35. At *Hostería Ahuí* (☎ 622415) on the southern end of town at Costanera 906, rates are US$25/41. *Hostal Chiloé* (☎ 622869), O'Higgins 274, charges US$35 double in friendly family accommodation, with private bath and a substantial breakfast.

Hotel Lacuy (☎ 623019), Pudeto 219, comes recommended at US$31/52 for rooms with breakfast and private bath, but has thin walls and can be noisy because it's so central. Homey, well located *Hotel Montserrat* (☎ 622957), Baquedano 417, charges US$40/55.

Places to Stay – top end

Ancud's top hotel is *Hostería Ancud* (☎ 622340, (02) 6965599 in Santiago), overlooking the sea and Fuerte San Antonio at San Antonio 30, with superb views from the bar. Rooms cost US$72/92, with breakfast and private bath. It's not the most expensive, though – *Hotel Galeón Azul* (☎ 622567), Libertad 751, charges US$82/99.

Places to Eat

Visiting Chiloé without trying seafood is like going to Argentina without tasting beef. Excellent, reasonably priced local specialties are available at *El Sacho*, in the Mercado Municipal on Dieciocho between Libertad and Blanco Encalada, which has such intriguing items as 'poultry baked, brailed or bailed' and 'sauce made of seafood, butter cornstarch wine and spice spice.'

Other good seafood restaurants include *Polo Sur*, in its namesake hotel at Avenida Costanera 630, *La Pincoya* (☎ 622613), on the waterfront at Prat 61 and *Capri* at Mocopulli 710. *El Cangrejo*, Dieciocho 155, gets more notice for its decor – business cards and other scrawls on the walls make it seem that just about every visitor to Ancud has eaten here.

For good dinners, desserts and coffee, try *Café Lydia* (☎ 622990), in the Hotel

Lydia at Pudeto 256. *Café Carmen* (☎ 622-049), facing the plaza at Pudeto 169, has good local specialties and homelike service. *Kurantón* (☎ 622216), Prat 94, has a varied menu including the dish for which it's named, plus beef, fish and shellfish and pizza.

Entertainment
La Cueva de la Suegra is at Prat 28. The appropriately named *Retro Pub*, on Maipú between Ramírez and Pudeto, features a '60s ambience and music.

Things to Buy
Ancud has a plethora of outlets for artisanal goods like woolens, carvings and pottery. Besides the Museo Chilote (see above) and the Mercado Municipal, try Artesanía Moai at Baquedano 429, and Francisquita at Libertad 530. In summer, there's a small but good Feria de Artesanos on the north side of the Plaza de Armas.

Getting There & Away
Nearly all traffic reaches and leaves the island by ferry between Pargua, on the mainland 56 km southwest of Puerto Montt, and Chacao, at the northeastern corner of the island. Bus fares to and from the mainland include the half-hour ferry crossing; if you're hitching and walk on board you will have to pay US$2 for the privilege. The pier at Pargua is a good place to ask for a lift, but is very crowded in summer.

Bus Ancud's sparkling new Terminal de Buses, at Aníbal Pinto and Marcos Vera, east of downtown, has been sitting empty because bus companies don't want to pay to use it. It's likely they'll eventually concede, but at the time of this writing all were operating out of downtown offices and improvised terminals.

Cruz del Sur (☎ 622265), at the corner of Errázuriz and Los Carrera, has a dozen buses daily to Puerto Montt; some of these continue to Osorno, Valdivia, Concepción, Temuco and Santiago (US$27, 19 hours). It has a dozen buses daily to Castro and

several more to Chonchi and Quellón. Varmontt (☎ 623049), Errázuriz 330, goes to Puerto Montt, Temuco and Santiago, and south to Quellón.

Transchiloé (☎ 622876), Chacabuco 750, has several buses daily to Castro, Chonchi, Quellón and Puerto Montt. Turibús (☎ 622-289), at the corner of Dieciocho and Libertad, goes to Concepción and Santiago, Punta Arenas and Puerto Natales.

Sample fares and approximate times include Puerto Montt (US$5, two hours), Castro (US$2, one hour), Quellón (US$5, three hours), Temuco (US$14, seven hours), Concepción (US$19, 11 hours) and Santiago (US$26, 18 hours).

For buses to other destinations on Chiloé, go to one of the two rural bus terminals: on Pedro Montt opposite Prat, and at the corner of Prat and Libertad. Buses Mar Brava has three buses weekly to Chepu, at the northern end of Parque Nacional Chiloé (US$1.25). Buses Chepu also goes there.

Boat Transmarchilay (☎ 622317, fax 623-067), at Libertad 669 alongside Sernatur, sails from Quellón to Chaitén, and to Puerto Chacabuco in the Aisén Region (see the entry for Quellón below). It also runs ferries between Pargua and Chacao, as does Naviera Cruz del Sur (☎ 622506), Chacabuco 672. For automobiles, the fare between Pargua and Chacao is about US$12, including as many passengers as can fit.

DALCAHUE
Sunday's crafts market, the most important on the Isla Grande, is the primary attraction of the small fishing port of Dalcahue, which takes its name from the *dalca*, a type of open canoe in which indigenous Chilotes went to sea. The tsunami of 1960 washed away Dalcahue's palafitos, though it still features a 19th-century church, but the shipwrights at work in the harbor are worth a visit. Dalcahue is also the Isla Grande gateway to Quinchao, one of the most interesting and accessible islands of archipelagic Chiloé.

Orientation & Information

On the east coast of Chiloé, Dalcahue (population 2300) is 20 km northeast of Castro and opposite the island of Quinchao, to which there are ferry-bus connections.

Dalcahue's tourist office, a kiosk at the intersection of Freire and O'Higgins, keeps erratic hours.

Things to See

Artisans from offshore islands travel great distances for Sunday morning's casual, nonchalant **Feria Artesanal**, which has a fine variety of woolens, wooden crafts, basketry and good cheap seafood restaurants. Sellers often drop their prices without even hearing a counter offer.

The nearby **Centro Cultural Dalcahue** has replaced the former Museo Regional; its fossils, stuffed birds and antique household implements are better displayed than in the past. On the Plaza de Armas, the neo-classical **Iglesia Dalcahue**, with Doric columns, dates from 1854. It is not in especially good repair, but has a truly grisly statue of the crucified Christ, with movable arms attached with leather straps.

Special Events

Dalcahue's annual fiesta is the Semana Dalcahuina, in the second week of February.

Places to Stay & Eat

Dalcahue has remarkably good budget accommodation from about US$6 per person. Try the very friendly *Residencial Playa* (☎ 641397) at Rodríguez 009, which also has a very fine restaurant. If it's full, the comparably priced but less amiable *Pensión La Feria* is nearby at Rodríguez 011. *Residencial San Martín* (☎ 651207), at San Martín 001 opposite the plaza, has singles for US$7 and moderately priced three-course meals. *Pensión Pulemún* (☎ 651330), Freire 305, is excellent value at US$8 single.

For good inexpensive food and waterfront atmosphere, try *Brisas Marinas*, on palafitos above the Feria Artesanal. *La Dalca*, Freire 502, is also recommended.

Getting There & Away

The main bus terminal is on Freire opposite O'Higgins, but buses also load and unload at the Feria Artesanal. Expreso Dalcahue, on Freire near Eugenio, has weekday buses to and from Castro every half hour, but there are only seven on Saturdays and four on Sunday market day, at 8 and 9.30 am and 2 and 5.30 pm. However, frequent taxi colectivos from Castro charge just over US$1 for the half-hour trip.

The motor launch *Ultima Esperanza* connects Dalcahue with the outlying Islas Chauques, Tuesday and Friday at 2 pm. There are also ferries and buses across the estuary to Isla Quinchao, with connections to the village of Achao and its landmark 18th-century church. Pedestrians go free on these ferries; the roundtrip automobile fare of US$7.50 is slightly cheaper than two one-way fares.

CASTRO

Emblematically Chilote, thanks in large part to the vernacular architectural distinction of its waterfront palafitos and their crafted *tejuelas* (shingles), Castro is the capital of Chiloé province. Founded in 1567 by Martín Ruiz de Gamboa, the town languished through colonial and early republican times. When Darwin visited

Charles Darwin found Chiloé 'a most forlorn and deserted place' in 1834.

in 1834, he found it 'a most forlorn and deserted place' where:

The usual quadrangular arrangement of Spanish towns could be traced, but the streets and plaza were coated with fine green turf, on which sheep were browsing . . . The poverty of the place may be conceived from the fact, that although containing some hundred of inhabitants, one of our party was unable anywhere to purchase either a pound of sugar or an ordinary knife. No individual possessed either a watch or a clock; and an old man, who was supposed to have a good idea of time, was employed to strike the church bell by guess.

Castro overcame the economic depression of the 19th century, though its most conspicuous attraction – the bright and incongruously painted Iglesia San Francisco opposite the Plaza de Armas – dates from 1906. Like Ancud, the city is a popular summer destination, attracting many Chilean and Argentine tourists.

Orientation

On a sheltered estuary on the eastern shore of the Isla Grande de Chiloé, 90 km south of Ancud, most of the city of Castro (population 18,000) sits on a bluff above the water. Only the Costanera Avenida Pedro Montt has direct access to the shore. Nearly every point of interest is within a couple of blocks of the Plaza de Armas, bounded by Gamboa, O'Higgins, Blanco Encalada and San Martín. The Panamericana, enters town from the direction of Ancud and exits south toward Quellón, the end of the line for this branch of the longitudinal highway.

Information

Tourist Office The private Asociación Gremial Hotelera Gastronómica funds the small tourist kiosk on the north side of the Plaza de Armas, which has town maps and some information on the surrounding countryside. It's open 9 am to 9 pm daily in summer, but the rest of the year it's open weekdays from 9 am to 1 pm and 3 to 7 pm, Saturdays from 9 am to 1 pm only.

Money For the best rates, try Julio Barrientos (☎ 625079) at Chacabuco 286, or Banco de Crédito's ATM at the corner of O'Higgins and Gamboa.

Post & Communications The area code is ☎ 65. Correos de Chile is at O'Higgins 388, on the west side of the Plaza de Armas. For long-distance telephone services, go to CNT at Latorre 289, Entel at O'Higgins 480 or Telefónica del Sur at O'Higgins 667.

Travel Agencies Castro has a more vigorous tourist industry and better infrastructure than Ancud. Helpful Turismo Isla Grande (☎ 632384), Thompson 241, is a full-service travel agency that is also the representative of Transmarchilay.

Several agencies offer tours to sights like Parque Nacional Chiloé, the islands of Quinchao, Lemuy and Mechuque, and the market at Dalcahue. Contact Pehuén Expediciones (☎ 635254) at Thompson 229, which also does less conventional activities like sea kayaking; Chiloé Tours (☎ 635952) at Thompson 273; or Turismo Queilén Bus (☎ 632173) at the main bus terminal, San Martín 689.

Quelcún Turismo (☎ 632396), San Martín 581, rents mountain bikes in peak season.

Bookshop Libros Chiloé, Blanco Encalada 202, has a good selection of books on both regional and general Chilean subjects, along with a good selection of Chilean music.

Cultural Center Castro's Centro Cultural, Serrano 320, is open 11 am to 1 pm and 4 to 9 pm daily.

National Parks Conaf (☎ 632289) is at Gamboa 424. The latest information on Parque Nacional Chiloé is posted in the windows for easy access outside normal business hours.

Laundry The Clean Center is at Serrano 490.

WAYNE BERNHARDSON
Distinctive Chilote church, Cucao

WAYNE BERNHARDSON
Iglesia San Francisco, Castro

WAYNE BERNHARDSON
Fishing boats, Ancud

WAYNE BERNHARDSON
Fisherman, port of Ancud

WAYNE BERNHARDSON
Picturesque palafitos in Castro

Images of Aisén

WAYNE BERNHARDSON
Chess match, upper deck, Puerto Edén

WAYNE BERNHARDSON

WAYNE BERNHARDSON
Ferry passage through the Chilean fjords from Puerto Montt to Puerto Natales

WAYNE BERNHARDSON
Lago Riesco, near Coihaique

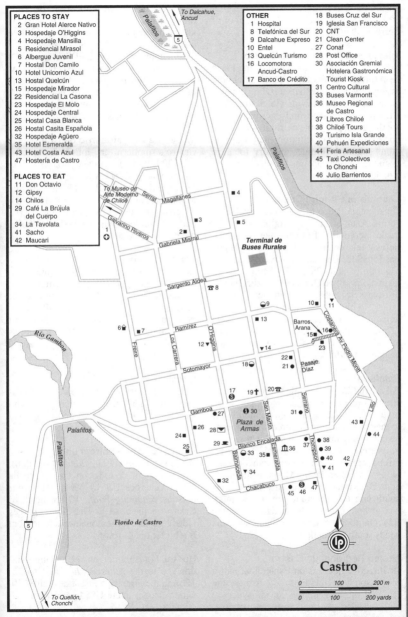

PLACES TO STAY
2 Gran Hotel Alerce Nativo
3 Hospedaje O'Higgins
4 Hospedaje Mansilla
5 Residencial Mirasol
6 Albergue Juvenil
7 Hostal Don Camilo
10 Hotel Unicornio Azul
13 Hostal Quelcún
15 Hospedaje Mirador
22 Residencial La Casona
23 Hospedaje El Molo
24 Hospedaje Central
25 Hostal Casa Blanca
26 Hostal Casita Española
32 Hospedaje Agüero
35 Hotel Esmeralda
43 Hotel Costa Azul
47 Hostería de Castro

PLACES TO EAT
11 Don Octavio
12 Gipsy
14 Chilos
29 Café La Brújula
    del Cuerpo
34 La Tavolata
41 Sacho
42 Maucari

OTHER
1 Hospital
8 Telefónica del Sur
9 Dalcahue Expreso
10 Entel
13 Quelcún Turismo
16 Locomotora
    Ancud-Castro
17 Banco de Crédito
18 Buses Cruz del Sur
19 Iglesia San Francisco
20 CNT
21 Clean Center
27 Conaf
28 Post Office
30 Asociación Gremial
    Hotelera Gastronómica
    Tourist Kiosk
31 Centro Cultural
33 Buses Varmontt
36 Museo Regional
    de Castro
37 Libros Chiloé
38 Chiloé Tours
39 Turismo Isla Grande
40 Pehuén Expediciones
44 Feria Artesanal
45 Taxi Colectivos
    to Chonchi
46 Julio Barrientos

Castro

Medical Services Castro's hospital (☎ 632445) is at Freire 852, at the foot of Cerro Millantuy.

Iglesia San Francisco de Castro

Built in 1906 at the north end of the Plaza de Armas, Castro's San Francisco church assaults the vision with its dazzling exterior paint job – salmon with violet trim. The attractive varnished-wood interior is more soothing, despite some morbidly gruesome portrayals of the crucifixion and other religious statuary. Termites and dry rot have begun to cause problems for this landmark wooden structure.

Locomotora Ancud-Castro

On Avenida Pedro Montt, near Hotel Unicornio Azul, stands the original, German-made locomotive from the narrow-gauge railway that connected Castro with Ancud via Pupelde, Coquiao, Puntra, Butalcura, Mocopulli and Pid Pid. According to legend, the only difference between 1st and 3rd-class was that the conductor would order 3rd-class passengers off the train to help push the locomotive over the crest of even gentle slopes. Service on this line ended with the massive earthquake and tsunami of 1960.

Palafitos

All around Castro, shingled houses on stilts stretch out into estuaries and lagoons; at high tide, resident fishermen tie their boats to the stilts, but from the street these houses resemble any other in town. This truly singular architecture, now the subject of determined preservation efforts, can be seen along Costanera Pedro Montt at the north end of town, at the Feria Artesanal on the south end (where some are restaurants), and at both ends of the bridge across the Río Gamboa, where the Panamericana heads south to Quellón.

Museo Regional de Castro

In attractive quarters on Esmeralda, half a block south of the Plaza de Armas, the regional museum houses an idiosyncratic but well organized collection of Huilliche relics, traditional farm implements and exhibits on the evolution of Chilote urbanism.

In summer (January and February), it's open 9 am to 8 pm daily except Sunday, when it's open 10.30 am to 1 pm. The rest of the year, it's open daily except Sunday 9 am to 1 pm and 3 to 7 pm, Sundays 10.30 am to 1 pm. Admission is free.

Museo de Arte Moderno de Chiloé

Castro's modern art museum features over 300 works by contemporary Chilean artists, many of them Chilotes, in five different exhibition halls. In the Parque Municipal, at the west end of Galvarino Riveros, the museum is open 10 am to 8 pm daily in summer, but keeps shorter hours the rest of the year.

Feria Artesanal

Castro's waterfront market has a fine selection of woolen ponchos and sweaters, caps, gloves and basketry. Note the bundles of dried seaweed and the rhubarb-like nalca, both part of the local diet, and the blocks of peat Chilotes use for fuel. The market has several excellent, inexpensive seafood restaurants.

Special Events

In mid-February, Castro celebrates the Festival Costumbrista, a week-long party with folkloric music and dance and traditional foods.

Places to Stay – bottom end

Camping *Camping Llicaldad* (☎ 635080), five km south of town on the Fiordo de Castro, charges US$14 per site for four persons. *Camping Pudú*, 10 km north of Castro on the road to Dalcahue, charges US$11 per site for reasonable facilities, but is a bit far out of town.

Hostel For summer hostel accommodation, go to the *Albergue Juvenil* (☎ 632-766), in the Gimnasia Fiscal at Freire 610, which charges about US$4 per person.

Hospedajes, Hotels & Residenciales

Castro has an abundance of inexpensive hospedajes, but some of these are only seasonal – look for handwritten signs in windows along San Martín and O'Higgins, near Sargento Aldea. Probably the cheapest is *Hospedaje Mansilla*, San Martín 879-B, which charges only US$6 with a superb breakfast and hot showers.

From an excellent location at Barros Arana 140, exceptionally friendly *Hospedaje El Molo* (☎ 635026) charges only US$9 with breakfast, an outstanding value. If it's full, try *Hospedaje Mirador*, across the street at Barros Arana 127.

At *Hospedaje Central*, on Los Carrera between Blanco Encalada and Gamboa, spotless but very small and spartan rooms with firm beds cost US$7.50 (including a *very* late breakfast). The shared baths have excellent hot showers. In the same range are *Residencial Mirasol*, San Martín 815, and *Residencial La Casona* (☎ 632246), Serrano 496.

Despite its unprepossessing appearance, *Hotel Esmeralda* (☎ 632300), formerly Hotel La Bomba, half a block south of the plaza at Esmeralda 270, now has simple but bright and airy rooms for US$10 per person with private bath. For US$10 per person with breakfast, rooms at recommended *Hospedaje Agüero* (☎ 635735), in a quiet location at Chacabuco 449, have views of the sea and Castro's southern palafitos.

Despite its attractive setting, *Hotel Costa Azul* (☎ 632440), Lillo 67, is reported 'damp and cold and a little bleak' for US$10 per person with shared bath, but don't hesitate to haggle. Rooms with private bath cost double. Rates are comparable at *Hospedaje O'Higgins* (☎ 632016), O'Higgins 831 Interior.

Places to Stay – middle

Since Hotel Plaza Beckna burned to the ground recently, mid-range accommodation is scarce, but *Hostal Casa Blanca* (☎ 632726), Los Carrera 308, has rooms with shared bath for US$15 with breakfast, while rooms with private bath and color TV cost US$23 per person. Friendly *Hostal Quelcún* (☎ 632396), San Martín 581, charges US$35/45 with private bath, but also has some bargain rooms for just US$11 per person with shared bath.

Places to Stay – top end

Top-end accommodations start around US$50/62 at recommended *Hostal Casita Española* (☎ 635186), Los Carrera 359 and *Hostal Don Camilo* (☎ 632180, fax 635-533), Ramírez 566. *Gran Hotel Alerce Nativo* (☎ 632267, fax 632309), O'Higgins 808, is good value for US$56/70 for rooms with private bath, telephone and TV.

The *Hostería de Castro* (☎ 632301, fax 635688) at Chacabuco 202, conspicuous by its exaggerated chalet design, has good harbor views. Rates are US$70/80 with private bath and breakfast. On the waterfront at Pedro Montt 228, *Hotel Unicornio Azul* (☎ 622359), Castro's most architecturally oddball accommodation, takes its name from a popular song by Cuban singer Silvio Rodríguez. Simple but attractive rooms cost US$82/99 with breakfast (in what was once a budget hotel).

Places to Eat

The palafito restaurants at the waterfront Feria Artesanal have the best food for the fewest pesos. *Brisas del Mar* and *Mariela* both have fixed-price lunches for about US$5, as well as more expensive specialties. *Maucari*, Lillo 93, has inexpensive curanto.

Don Octavio (☎ 632855), at Costanera Pedro Montt 261 across from Hotel Unicornio Azul, is no longer a budget choice but still good value for seafood. Try *Chilos* (☎ 635782), at the corner of Sotomayor and San Martín, for meat and seafood, and *Sacho* (☎ 632079), at Thompson 213, for curanto.

Café La Brújula del Cuerpo, O'Higgins 308, is an excellent choice for sandwiches, coffee and desserts. *La Tavolata* (☎ 633-882), Balmaceda 245, is a new, good and moderately priced pizzería. For Chinese food, try *Gipsy* at O'Higgins 552.

CHILOE

Getting There & Away

Bus From its central location, Castro is the major hub for bus traffic on Chiloé, both local and long distance. The Terminal de Buses Rurales (bus terminal) is on San Martín near Sargento Aldea; most but not all long-distance companies have their offices nearby.

Bus – regional Buses Arroyo (☎ 635604) has two to three buses a day to Huillinco and Cucao, the entrance to Parque Nacional Chiloé on the west coast, while Ocean Bus (☎ 635492) has two daily services on the same route. Since most of these buses leave early in the morning and return in the early evening, it's possible to visit the park on a day trip. The fare is about US$2.50 one way.

Dalcahue Expreso (☎ 635164), Ramírez 233, goes every half hour to Dalcahue weekdays, but less often weekends, while Arriagada, in the Cruz del Sur terminal at San Martín 486, goes to Dalcahue and to Achao, on Isla Quinchao. Buses Cárdenas covers the Dalcahue route less frequently, but also goes to smaller towns like Quetalco, San Juan and Calén.

Buses Lemuy serves Chonchi (US$1.50) and destinations on Isla Lemuy, including Puqueldón, as does Buses Gallardo. Buses Queilén, which also operates tours around Chiloé, has regular service to Queilén and intermediate points. Taxi colectivos to Chonchi leave from Chacabuco near Esmeralda.

Bus – long distance Cruz del Sur (☎ 632-389), San Martín 486, has a dozen buses daily to Ancud and Puerto Montt, several of which continue to Osorno, Valdivia, Temuco, Concepción and Santiago. It also has several buses daily to Chonchi and Quellón, as does Regional Sur (☎ 632071), at the bus terminal. Transchiloé (☎ 635-152), also at the terminal, has several buses daily north to Ancud and Puerto Montt, and south to Chonchi and Quellón. Varmontt (☎ 632776), Balmaceda 289, connects Castro with Ancud, Puerto Montt and Santiago.

Castro enjoys direct bus service, via Argentina, to Punta Arenas (US$70) and Puerto Natales, twice weekly with Buses Ghisoni (☎ 632358) and two to four times weekly with Bus Sur at the terminal. Turibús (☎ 635088), at the terminal, goes to Puerto Montt, Concepción and Punta Arenas (36 hours, about US$85 in summer, a bit cheaper the rest of the year). Buses Queilén also goes to Punta Arenas.

Sample fares and times include Ancud (US$3, one hour), Quellón (US$4, two hours), Puerto Montt (US$7, three hours), Puerto Varas (US$8), Valdivia (US$13), Temuco (US$15, eight hours), Concepción (US$22, 12 hours) and Santiago (US$27, 19 hours).

Boat Transmarchilay (☎ /fax 635691) has no ferries from Castro, but makes reservations at its offices at Thompson 273.

ACHAO

On the elongated offshore island of Quinchao, the village of Achao is a charming destination with a landmark church and outstanding vernacular architecture, fine food and accommodations and friendly people. Its annual folk festival, in early February, is well worth a detour from mainland Chile.

Orientation & Information

Achao is 25 km southeast of Dalcahue via a short ferry crossing and a good gravel road that follows Isla Quinchao's mountainous crest. While Achao is more than 250 years old, it does not follow the standard grid pattern of most Chilean towns, and its rectangular Plaza de Armas almost seems peripheral compared to the waterfront Calle Prat and the commercial district of Calle Serrano, which terminates in the fishing jetty.

Achao's Oficina de Información Turística is a small kiosk at the corner of Serrano and Ricardo Jara, which keeps long hours in summer and is exceptionally helpful. It also arranges excursions to offshore Isla Llingua (see Around Achao, below).

Correos de Chile is on Serrano between

Ricardo Jara and Progreso, while there's a telephone office on Pasaje Freire, south of Pedro Montt. The hospital is at the corner of Progreso and Riquelme.

Iglesia Santa María de Achao

Crowned by a 25-meter tower, sided with alerce shingles and held together by wooden pegs rather than nails, Achao's 18th-century Jesuit church is now a national monument. Currently undergoing restoration for termite damage and dry rot, it's on the south side of the Plaza de Armas.

Special Events

Early February's Encuentro Folklórico de las Islas del Archipiélago, now in its 15th year, attracts musical groups from throughout the archipelago. The quality of the groups is almost uniformly excellent, and the festival organization very professional. A simultaneous event is the Muestra Gastronómica y Artesanal, where visitors can taste traditional Chilote specialties, see and purchase local crafts and view demonstrations of antique machinery like apple presses and grain mills.

Places to Stay & Eat

In the busy summer season, there's an informal campground on Delicias between Sargento Aldea and Serrano. The cheapest regular accommodation is *Hospedaje São Paulo* (☎ 661245) at Serrano 052, which costs US$9 per person and also has a restaurant with an extensive menu. Nearby at Serrano 061, recommended *Hospedaje Achao* (☎ 661373) costs US$10 with shared bath, US$15 with private bath.

The best value in town may be friendly *Hospedaje Sol y Lluvia* (☎ 661383), Ricardo Jara 09, where comfortable, spotless rooms with shared bath and a superb breakfast cost US$12.50 per person. *Hospedaje Chilhue*, Zañartu 025, is also worth a look.

At *Hostal Plaza* (☎ 661283), Amunátegui 20, doubles with shared bath start at US$18, while those with private bath range from US$22 to US$26. *Hostería La Nave* (☎ 661219), facing the beach at the corner

of Prat and Sargento Aldea, charges US$20 double with shared bath, US$30 with private bath.

Mar y Velas (☎ 661375), Serrano 02 at the foot of the pier, has outstanding seafood, including particularly tasty oysters. Try also *Restaurant de los Amigos*, at the corner of Delicias and Sargento Aldea.

Getting There & Away

Transportes Arriagada, at the Terminal de Buses at the east end of town, runs nine buses daily to Castro via Dalcahue, between 7.15 am and 5.30 pm daily.

AROUND ACHAO
Isla Llingua

Half an hour from Achao by launch, Isla Llingua is a small island whose turn-of-the-century church is a local landmark (legend says that Chonos Indians burned the first two churches on the site to get the nails). Well-trained local guides take visitors past Chonos shell middens, into the church and its bell tower, up the local mirador for a panorama of the tiny settlement, and into the island's small but excellent artisan's market, which specializes in basketry.

For information on tours, which cost US$5 and last about two hours, contact Achao's Oficina de Información Turística at the corner of Serrano and Ricardo Jara.

Curaco de Vélez

Midway between Dalcahue and Achao, this village features a modern church (built in 1971 after the historic church burned to the ground) and a small but poorly organized museum in its Centro Cultural on the Plaza de Armas. The rest of the village, though, is a treasure of vernacular Chilote architecture, well worth a stop for visitors en route to Achao, which is a better place to stay.

CHONCHI

Known as the Ciudad de los Tres Pisos (City of Three Floors) for its abrupt topography, Chonchi's more colorful indigenous name literally means 'slippery earth.'

CHILOE

The town dates from 1767, though its landmark **Iglesia San Carlos de Chonchi**, with its three-story tower and multiple arches, dates from the mid-19th century. There is other noteworthy vernacular architecture along Calle Centenario.

Orientation & Information

Chonchi (population 3000) occupies a site above Canal Lemuy, 23 km south of Castro and three km west of the Panamericana. It is connected by launch to the port of Ichuac and by ferry to Chulchuy, both on Isla Lemuy.

Chonchi's Oficina de Información Turística (☎ 671223) is at the intersection of Sargento Candelaria and Centenario. Correos de Chile is almost next door.

Places to Stay & Eat

Hospedaje El Mirador (☎ 671351), Ciriaco Alvarez 198, is the most economical accommodation at US$7.50 per person with breakfast, and has hot showers. English and German are spoken at comparably priced, beachfront *Hospedaje La Esmeralda* (☎ 671328), Irarrázabal s/n, which also has slightly more expensive rooms with private bath and rents mountain bikes, boats and fishing gear.

In the same range are *Hospedaje Gómez* (☎ 671224) Andrade 298, *Residencial Turismo* (☎ 671257), Andrade 299 and *Hospedaje Los Tres Pisos* (☎ 671216) at Centenario 334.

Hotel Huildín (☎ 671388, fax 635030), Centenario 102, has singles with breakfast and shared bath for US$10 per person. *Hospedaje Chonchi* (☎ 671288), O'Higgins 379, has comparably priced rooms with shared bath, while those with private bath go for US$15 per person. *Hotel Remi's* (☎ 671391), Irarrázaval 57, also has a good restaurant.

Posada El Antiguo Chalet (☎ 671221), in a quiet location on Gabriela Mistral, is the best in town for US$40/60 single/double.

For Chilote seafood specialties, try *El Trébol* (☎ 671203) on the 2nd floor of the Mercado Municipal or *La Sirena* at Irarrázaval 52.

Getting There & Away

Bus & Colectivo Opposite the Plaza de Armas, Cruz del Sur (☎ 671218) and Transchiloé have several buses daily between Castro and Chonchi. Taxi colectivos (US$1) are also numerous; in Castro, these leave from Chacabuco near Esmeralda.

Boat Transmarchilay (☎ 671319) is at the foot of the pier, but no long-distance ferries leave from here at present; see the Quellón entry, below, for southern Chiloé ferry details.

There are launches to the port of Ichuac on Isla Lemuy. The ferry *El Caleuche* leaves every two hours between 8 am and 8 pm from Puerto Huichas, five km to the south, and lands at Chulchuy, with connections to Puqueldón.

PARQUE NACIONAL CHILOE

Nowhere in South America can travelers follow Darwin's footsteps more closely than in Parque Nacional Chiloé. The great naturalist left so vivid a record of his passage to the village of Cucao, now the gateway to the park, that it merits lengthy citation:

At Chonchi we struck across the island, following intricate winding paths, sometimes passing through magnificent forests, and sometimes through pretty cleared spots, abounding with corn and potato crops. This undulating woody country, partially cultivated, reminded me of the wilder parts of England, and therefore had to my eye a most fascinating aspect. At Vilinco (Huillinco), which is situated on the borders of the lake of Cucao, only a few fields were cleared . . .

The country on each side of the lake was one unbroken forest. In the same periagua (canoe) with us, a cow was embarked. To get so large an animal into a small boat appears at first a difficulty, but the Indians managed it in a minute. They brought the cow alongside the boat, which was heeled towards her; then placing two oars under her belly, with their ends resting on the gunwale, by the aid of these levers they fairly tumbled the poor beast, heels overhead into the bottom of the boat, and then lashed her down with ropes.

The village of Cucao has grown rapidly with the park's increasing popularity, and now sports several residenciales and hospedajes, several good restaurants and even a regular bus terminal. Bruce Chatwin, the late gifted travel writer and novelist, left a brief but illuminating essay on Cucao and the people of rural Chiloé in his collection *What Am I Doing Here?* (Penguin, 1989).

Indigenous Huilliche communities in and around the park are ambivalent, at best, about Conaf's management plan, which they feel has restricted their access to traditional subsistence resources. Again, there are conspicuous parallels with Darwin's time, when the great scientist wrote:

The district of Cucao is the only inhabited part on the whole west coast of Chiloé. It contains about 30 or 40 Indian families, who are scattered along four or five miles of the shore. They are very much secluded from the rest of Chiloé, and have scarcely any sort of commerce, except sometimes in a little oil, which they get from seal-blubber. They are tolerably dressed in clothes of their own manufacture, and they have

plenty to eat. They seemed, however, discontented, yet humble to a degree which it was quite painful to witness. These feelings are, I think, chiefly to be attributed to the harsh and authoritative manner in which they are treated by their rulers.

Geography & Climate
On the island's Pacific coast, Parque Nacional Chiloé is about 30 km west of Chonchi and 54 km west of Castro, via the paved Panamericana and a normally passable graveled lateral to Huillinco and Cucao. Altitudes range from sea level to 850 meters on the heights of the Cordillera de Piuchén. The annual average temperature in the temperate maritime climate is about 10°C, with a mean annual rainfall at Cucao of 2200 mm, evenly distributed throughout the year. The park is open all year, but fair weather is more likely in summer, the best time for a visit.

Flora & Fauna
Established in 1982, 43,000-hectare Parque Nacional Chiloé protects extensive

---

Lands for the Huilliche
One of the most contentious issues in the creation of national parks in so-called 'Third World' countries has been indigenous land rights – many of the properties most suitable for conservation belong, usually by custom or tradition, to native peoples who have rarely been consulted by the national and international agencies in charge of creating and managing these units. In the case of Parque Nacional Chiloé, there has been a constant struggle among various groups both official and non-governmental.

Among the interested parties are Conaf, the Comisión Nacional de Desarollo Indígena (Conadi, the National Commission on Indigenous Development), the Chilean government's Oficina de Bienes Nacionales (Land Registry), the local Junta de Vecinos (a grouping of residents), the Consejo de Caciques (council of indigenous community leaders, under recent indigenous laws), and traditional community representatives including the Lonko Mayor (headman) and the Junta de Vecinos.

Under a recent agreement, government agencies are to return 4000 hectares to the local Huilliche community, 3500 from within the park and another 500 outside its present boundaries. The proposed Parque Marino, an offshore protected area which is an issue in itself because of fishing rights, has been put aside until land issues are completely resolved.

While community involvement is overdue, not all the changes may be for the better. Local residents apparently hope to build a bridge from Cucao across the Río Chanquín, where there is now only a foot and horse bridge. A *balseo* (barge) would be a better choice for the tiny amount of auto traffic on the sandy one-lane road that runs along the park boundary, and a bridge that might increase that traffic would likely have deleterious environmental effects. ∎

stands of native coniferous and ever-green forest, plus a long and almost pristine coastline, in a nearly roadless portion of the island. The majestic alerce reaches its southern limit within the park, in pure stands at altitudes above 600 meters, while a few endemic animal subspecies can be found, most notably the Chiloé fox *Dusicyon fulvipes*. The reclusive pudú inhabits the shadowy forests of the contorted *tepú (Tepualia stimulais)*, but sightings of this miniature Chilean deer are rare in the wild. The 110 species of bird include the occasional penguin.

The northern sector of the park, including Chepu and Isla Metalqui (which has a sea lion colony) are less easily accessible without a car or, in the case of Metalqui, highly restricted because of ecological concerns. See the Ancud entry for information about tours.

Activities
Rental horses are available at Cucao for US$4 per hour or US$18 for the entire day. Be selective in choice of horses, since their quality varies considerably.

Sector Chanquín
Chanquín, across the suspension bridge from Cucao, is the starting point for almost all excursions into the park. Park admission costs US$1.50.

About one km from the bridge, Conaf's **Centro de Visitantes**, open daily from 9 am to 7.30 pm, has good displays on local flora and fauna, the indigenous Huilliche peoples, the early mining industry and island folklore. Outside are wooden carts and sleighs, used to haul heavy loads over wet ground in damp weather, a gold extractor and a chicha (apple cider) press.

Near the Chanquín campground is the **Sendero Interpretivo El Tepual**, a short nature trail built on tree trunks, which loops through dense, gloomy forest where you might expect to meet the Trauco, a troll-like creature from Chilote folklore. There are several other trails, including the **Sendero Dunas de Cucao**, which goes from the visitor center through a remnant of coastal forest to a series of dunes behind a long, white sandy beach. After the earthquake of 1960, a tsunami obliterated much of the coastal plant cover and the dunes advanced for some years, but they have since stabilized. The beach is attractive, but the cold water and dangerous currents make swimming inadvisable.

Day hikers or trekkers can follow the coast north on a three-km trail to **Lago Huelde**, where there is a Huilliche community. At Río Cole Cole, about 12 km north of Chanquín, and at Río Anay, another eight km north, there are rustic refugios in reasonably good condition, but a tent is not a bad idea in this changeable climate. Wear water-resistant footwear and woolen socks since, in Darwin's words, 'everywhere in the shade the ground soon becomes a perfect quagmire.' Biting flies make insect repellent a good idea.

Places to Stay & Eat
Local families run numerous camping sites in and around Cucao, and across the bridge between Cucao and the park entrance; rates are about US$2 per person. Within the park proper, about 200 meters beyond Conaf's visitor center, *Camping Chanquín* has very secluded sites with running water, firewood, cold showers and latrines for US$6 per site. At the refugios or along the trails, there is no charge for camping.

Travelers not wishing to camp will find several hospedajes within easy walking distance of the park entrance. *Hospedaje El Paraíso*, *Hospedaje Pacífico*, *Hospedaje y Albergue La Pincoya*, and *Albergue y Hospedaje Los Pinos* all charge US$6 per person with breakfast, while *Posada Cucao* charges around US$10. All offer reasonably priced meals.

German-run *Parador Darwin*, across the pasarela from Cucao, has an innovative menu based on local specialties, while *Doña Rosa* in the Arroyo bus station is more strictly local. At the approach to town is *Fogón Cucao*.

Limited supplies are available in Cucao, but everything except fresh fish and a few vegetables is cheaper in Castro.

Getting There & Away

Cucao is 54 km from Castro and 34 km west of Chonchi via a bumpy graveled road, passable in all but the most inclement weather. There is regular bus transport between Castro and Cucao with Ocean Bus (☎ 635492 in Castro) and Buses Arroyo (☎ 635604 in Castro). Schedules vary, but there are usually four to five buses daily, with a fare of US$2.50.

Buses Mar Brava has three buses weekly from Ancud to Chepu, at the northern end of the park (US$1.50).

QUELLÓN

Chiloé's southernmost port, the departure point for ferries to Chaitén, offers superb views of surrounding islands including Cailín, a former Jesuit estancia which, in Darwin's day, was the 'last outpost of Christianity.' Not to be confused with nearby Queilén, Quellón is 92 km south of Castro and the terminus of the Panamericana. At Rayen Anti, 22 km north of

Quellón, the Huilliche Indian community of Huequetrumao sells woolens, wood carvings and basketry.

Orientation

On the sheltered Canal Yelcho, at the southeastern corner of the Isla Grande, Quellón is 99 km from Castro. Like Chonchi, the town has an irregular terrain that does not lend itself easily to the standard Hispanic grid, but it's small enough that it's simple to find your way around. Most visitor services are concentrated in an area bounded by the Costanera Pedro Montt, Pedro Aguirre Cerda, Ladrilleros and Freire.

Information

From December to March, Quellón maintains a Caseta de Información Turística at the corner of Gómez García and Santos Vargas. It's open 9.30 am to 1 pm and 2.30 to 10.30 pm daily.

Change money before coming to Quellón, since Banco del Estado, the only

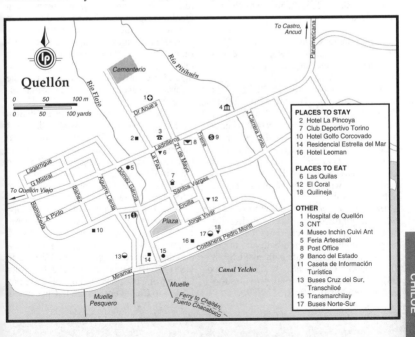

Quellón

0   50   100 m
0   50   100 yards

To Castro, Ancud

PLACES TO STAY
2 Hotel La Pincoya
7 Club Deportivo Torino
10 Hotel Golfo Corcovado
14 Residencial Estrella del Mar
16 Hotel Leoman

PLACES TO EAT
6 Las Quilas
12 El Coral
18 Quilineja

OTHER
1 Hospital de Quellón
3 CNT
4 Museo Inchin Cuivi Ant
5 Feria Artesanal
8 Post Office
9 Banco del Estado
11 Caseta de Información Turística
13 Buses Cruz del Sur, Transchiloé
15 Transmarchilay
17 Buses Norte-Sur

Canal Yelcho

Muelle
Ferry to Chaitén, Puerto Chacabuco

Muelle Pesquero

CHILOE

possibility for cash or travelers' checks, charges unreasonable commissions. Correos de Chile is on 21 de Mayo between Ladrilleros and Santos Vargas, while CNT's long-distance office is at Ladrilleros 379. The Hospital de Quellón (☎ 681-443) is at Dr Ahués 305.

Museo Inchin Cuivi Ant (Nuestro Pasado)

Admiration for Chilote technological ingenuity, in the form of uniquely local artifacts with very basic materials, is the rationale behind this new and surprisingly good museum. The outstanding explanatory panels are a bonus alongside displays of items like *cercos tejidos* (living fences, that is, woven fences of living shrubs and trees), *bongos* (local watercraft resembling dalcas), flour mills, apple presses and sledges for moving heavy loads across soggy terrain. The nascent botanical garden of native trees and shrubs will improve with time.

At Ladrilleros 225, the museum charges US$1.25 admission.

Places to Stay & Eat

The *Club Deportivo Torino*, La Paz 316, operates a summer hostel where mattress spots cost US$2 per night.

On the waterfront at Pedro Montt 427, a few doors from the Transmarchilay office, the *Hotel Leoman* (☎ 681278) is a decent place charging US$9 per person. There's hot water and a good cheap restaurant. Despite its shabby exterior, comparably priced *Residencial Estrella del Mar*, Gómez García 18, is OK inside – very spartan, but with hot water and a respectable restaurant.

Hotel La Pincoya (☎ 681285), La Paz 64, is a comfortable place with friendly staff and hot water, charging US$13/23 single/double with shared bath and breakfast; doubles with private bath cost US$38. *Hotel Golfo Corcovado* (☎ 681528, fax 681527), Santos Vargas 680, provides top-end accommodation for US$59/79.

For a small town, Quellón has fine seafood in the waterfront restaurants near the jetty and at *Las Quilas* (☎ 681206) at La Paz 385, *El Coral* (☎ 681472) at 21 de Mayo 251 and *Quilineja* (☎ 681441) at Pedro Montt 363.

Things to Buy

For Chilote crafts, visit the Feria Artesanal at the corner of Ladrilleros and Gómez García.

Getting There & Away

Bus Services to Castro are frequent with Cruz del Sur (☎ 681284) and Transchiloé, which share offices at Aguirre Cerda 52, and Buses Norte-Sur, alongside Quilineja on the Costanera Pedro Montt. The bus to Castro (1½ hours) costs about US$2.50; all three companies also go to Puerto Montt (US$5, three hours).

Boat Transmarchilay (☎ 681331) is at Pedro Montt 457, near the pier. You can reach the Aisén region by ferry from Quellón, either via Chaitén, or directly to Puerto Chacabuco (the port of Coihaique). Ferries run to a timetable but sometimes leave late, depending on how long it takes to load all the cars and trucks. Schedules also change seasonally, so verify the information given below at Transmarchilay offices.

The car ferry *La Pincoya* sails to Chaitén (five hours) Mondays and Wednesdays at 4 pm, and to Puerto Chacabuco (18 hours) Saturdays at 4 pm. Passenger fares on the Quellón-Chaitén run range from US$13 to US$20, depending on the quality of seat, while those to Chacabuco range from US$20 to US$32.

Vehicle size determines the cost of transporting a car: rates to Chaitén range from US$75 (less than four meters) to US$90 (longer than four meters), while corresponding rates to Chacabuco are US$115 to US$132. Bicycles pay US$10 to either Chaitén or Chacabuco and motorcycles pay US$18 to Chaitén or US$26 to Chacabuco.

Aisén & the Camino Austral

Beyond Chiloé and Puerto Montt, the islands, fjords and glaciers of the Region XI of Aisén (formally known as Región Aisén del General Carlos Ibáñez del Campo) mirror the landscapes of Alaska's Inside Passage, New Zealand's South Island and Norway's subarctic coastline. The still rudimentary Camino Austral Longitudinal (Southern Longitudinal Highway) awkwardly links Puerto Montt with widely separated towns and hamlets from Chaitén to Puerto Yungay, and someday may reach as far south as Villa O'Higgins, but the most convenient connections are by air or ferry from Puerto Montt, ferry from Chiloé, or overland through the Argentine province of Chubut.

For thousands of years, Chonos and Alacaluf Indians fished and hunted the intricate canals and islands of western Aisén, while their Tehuelche counterparts hunted guanaco and other game on the mainland steppes. Aisén's rugged geography deterred European settlement for centuries even after Francisco de Ulloa first set foot on the Península de Taitao in 1553. Fortune seekers believed the legendary 'City of the Caesars' to be in Trapananda, as Aisén was first known, but Jesuit missionaries from Chiloé were the first Europeans to explore the region in detail. In the late 17th century, Bartolomé Díaz Gallardo and Antonio de Vea came upon Laguna San Rafael and the Campo de Hielo Norte, the northern continental ice sheet.

Recounting his experiences in the Archipiélago Guayaneco, shipwrecked British seafarer John Byron, grandfather of the famous poet Lord Byron, made it apparent why Europeans did not flock to the inclement region. From the shore, the sailor known as 'Foulweather Jack' wrote:

. . . a scene of horror presented itself: on one side the wreck . . . together with a boisterous sea, presented us with the most dreary prospect; on the other, the land did not wear a much more favourable appearance: desolate and barren, without sign of culture, we could hope to receive little other benefit from it than the preservation it afforded from the sea . . . Exerting ourselves, however, though faint, benumbed and almost helpless, to find some wretched cover against the extreme inclemency of the weather, we discovered an Indian hut . . . within a wood, in which as many as possible, without distinction, crowded themselves, the night coming on exceedingly tempestuous and rainy.

Several expeditions (including Fitzroy's British expedition on which Darwin served as a naturalist) visited the area in the late 18th and early 19th centuries, some in search of a protected passage to the Atlantic. Argentine expeditions reached the area from the east, becoming the first non-native people to see Lago General Carrera (Lago Buenos Aires to Argentines). In the early 1870s, Chilean naval officer Enrique Simpson made the most thorough survey to that time, mapping areas as far south as the Península de Taitao.

Not until the early 20th century did Chile actively promote colonization of the region, granting the Valparaíso-based Sociedad Industrial Aisén a long-term lease for exploitation of livestock and lumber. This measure fomented a wave of spontaneous immigration from mainland Chile and the Argentine province of Chubut that threatened the Sociedad's monopoly. Small-scale colonists successfully resisted ejection from the Río Simpson valley, but the company still controlled much of the land – nearly a million hectares in and around Coihaique – and dominated the regional economy. Part of its legacy is the destruction of much of Aisén's native southern beech forest in a series of fires that raged for nearly a decade in the 1940s. Encouraged by a Chilean law that rewarded clearance with land titles, the company and colonists burned nearly three million

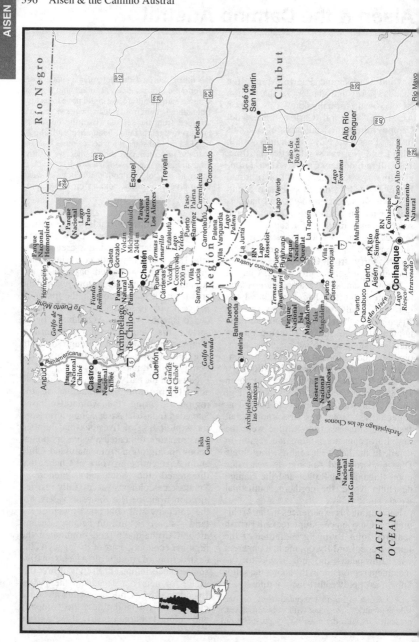

Aisén & the Camino Austral

hectares of lenga forest. While this burning was intentional, some fires escaped control and the bleached trunks of downed trees now litter hillsides from Mañihuales to Puerto Ibáñez.

Since the agrarian reform of the 1960s, the influence of the Sociedad and other large landowners has declined. Better maritime communications and the improved highway system have encouraged immigration into the area, which is still only sparsely populated. Salmon farming is becoming a major economic activity, causing ecological disruption in some coastal areas, and the region's rivers are under threat from proposed hydroelectric projects on the Río Baker and the Río Futaleufú. Part of the Campo de Hielo Sur, the continental icefield that overlaps Regions XI and XII south of Villa O'Higgins, is the subject of the last remaining border dispute between Chile and Argentina.

Recognizing that, despite improved communications, Aisén has lagged behind the rest of the country, the national government has developed a so-called *Plan Aysén* for the economic advancement of the region. It includes continuing infrastructural improvements, increasing contacts with the Argentine provinces of Chubut and Santa Cruz, promoting private investment in the agriculture, forestry, fishing and energy sectors, and decentralizing administration to give the region more autonomy in development. Some continue to have unrealistic expectations, however –

Pinochet's Folly

Near the old railroad station on Puerto Montt's waterfront, where Avenida Diego Portales becomes Avenida Juan Soler Mefredini, a fading, vandalized sign announces the beginning of Ruta 7, the Carretera Longitudinal Austral Presidente Pinochet, more popularly referred to as the Camino Austral. Only a few km east, beyond the beach suburb of Pelluco, a smooth concrete roadway becomes the spine-rattling washboard of one of the most ambitious and, to this point, least productive public works projects ever undertaken in Chile.

From Puerto Montt, paralleling the Argentine border, Chilean maps trace a solid line of Ruta 7 for more than 1100 km to the pioneer outpost of Puerto Yungay. The road is discontinuous, requiring several ferry crossings unlikely ever to be bridged or circumvented because of the phenomenal expense this would entail. It is projected to reach Villa O'Higgins, 220 km south of Cochrane at the foot of the Campo de Hielo Sur, in 1998; some politicians have fantasized about extending it through the fjords and islands of extreme southern Chile all the way to Puerto Natales, another 950 km.

Maintenance is a nightmare. In Parque Nacional Queulat, a conspicuous road sign warns motorists not to stop for any reason in one 400-meter stretch, where an ominous debris flow threatens to slither across the highway at any moment. Smaller slides are common and, in the far south, the road sits barely a meter above the banks of the flood-prone Río Baker, which carries the greatest flow of any Chilean river.

The population of the entire region, from Puerto Montt to Villa O'Higgins, is barely 80,000, and nearly half of those people live in the city of Coihaique, the only sizable population center between Puerto Montt and Punta Arenas. Why then would Chile invest US$300 million to serve so few people? While the public rationale is development, the real answer lies in geopolitics.

Like many other Southern Cone military men, General Augusto Pinochet Ugarte believes the state is an organic entity which must grow or die – that is, it must effectively occupy and develop all the territory within its formal boundaries or risk losing that territory to other states. In his textbook Geopolítica (Santiago, Editorial Andrés Bello, 1977), Pinochet asserts that the state is 'a superperson, the highest form of social evolution.' As an organic entity, it must maintain an integrated system of communications, which are 'the nerves which unite the different zones within and among themselves.' By Pinochet's logic, the longitudinal highway is the spinal cord of Chile, connecting the country's extremities to the brain in Santiago, the capital.

one local senator insists that the area could support five million people, and advocates large-scale immigration from Russia, South Africa and the former Yugoslavia.

While the present chapter focuses on Region XI, it also includes parts of Region X – on and around the Camino Austral from Caleta Gonzalo south – which are only accessible by air or sea from Puerto Montt, Chiloé or Hornopirén, or overland through Argentina.

COIHAIQUE

Founded in 1929 at the foot of the basalt massif of Cerro Macay, the regional capital of Coihaique was Aisén's first major town. Initially a service center for the properties of the Sociedad Industrial, it has outgrown its pioneer origins to become a modest but tidy city with a population of about 34,000. Despite its growth, Coihaique still has no traffic lights, and no apparent need for them.

Coihaique's most unusual feature is the pentagonal Plaza de Armas, the work of Carabineros General Marchant González, who based his confusing city plan on the shape of the national police force's emblem. Most visitors arrive by air from Puerto Montt or by ferry at Puerto Chacabuco, continuing overland to Coihaique, but increasing numbers are traveling the length of the Camino Austral.

Orientation

Situated at the confluence of the Río Simpson and the Río Coihaique, Coihaique is

---

Chilean geopoliticians, among whom Pinochet is foremost, perceive Argentina as an expansionist threat in the thinly populated lands of the far south – much as Argentine geopoliticians view Chile. For Chileans, this interpretation is not unreasonable, since the two countries barely avoided armed conflict over the Beagle Channel in 1979 and Argentina, acting on its own geopolitical principles, invaded and occupied the British-held Falkland Islands for 2½ months in 1982. Since the restoration of civilian rule, relations between the two countries have been more cordial, but the military obsession with territorial security lurks in the background. Pinochet has recently suggested that the highway bear the name Ejército de Chile (Army of Chile).

In the meantime, the near completion of the Camino Austral by the Cuerpo Militar de Trabajo (Army Corps of Engineers) has had unanticipated consequences. To some degree it has encouraged economic development in forestry, fisheries and mining, but these are extractive industries that take out more than they leave. In many areas, an abundance of cow patties symbolizes the economic marginality of a highway that carries almost no traffic.

Whether the Camino Austral will achieve Pinochet's goal of establishing an effective communications network to link the region with the Chilean heartland is doubtful without continued major improvements and expenditure. The several ferry links on the highway between Puerto Montt and Chaitén have proved inadequate for commercial traffic, which prefers the ferries from Puerto Montt and Chiloé to Chaitén and Puerto Chacabuco. Most tourists also find these routes more practical.

Meanwhile, the laterals off the Camino Austral have made communication with Argentina better than ever – in fact so much better that buses between Coihaique and Puerto Montt pass through the Argentine provinces of Chubut and Río Negro rather than use the much slower Chilean route. Argentine tourists flock across the border to Aisén and, should they ever need to, so could the Argentine military. This is probably not what General Pinochet had in mind.

For adventurous travelers, in any case, the opening of the Camino Austral has created opportunities for exploration that were previously reserved for hard-core long-distance trekkers. Remote destinations like Chaitén and Coihaique, and national parks like Queulat are now readily accessible by road, even though public transport still tends to be minimal and sporadic. Though it is hard to see the benefits to the country as a whole, visitors who want to see a rugged, remote territory can now do so in relative comfort. ■

AISEN

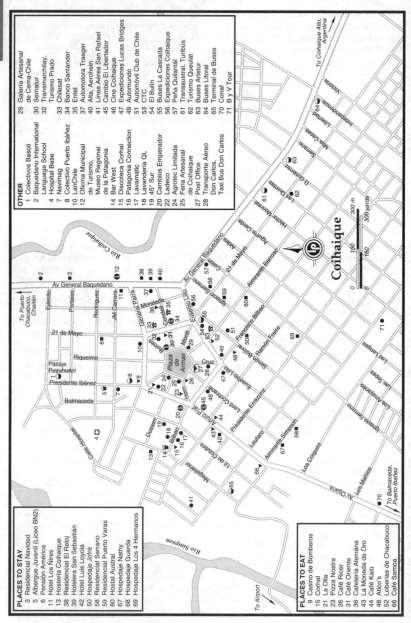

PLACES TO STAY

3　Residencial Navidad
5　Albergue Juvenil (Liceo BN2)
6　Pensión América
11　Hotel Los Ñires
13　Hostería Coihaique
38　Residencial El Reloj
39　Hotelera San Sebastián
42　Hotel Luis Loyola
50　Hospedaje Jofré
58　Residencial Serrano
59　Residencial Puerto Varas
60　Hostal Austral
67　Hospedaje Nathy
68　Hospedaje Guarda
69　Hospedaje Los 4 Hermanos

PLACES TO EAT

9　Casino de Bomberos
15　Corhal
21　La Olla
23　Pizza Nostra
26　Café Ricer
31　Café Oriente
36　Cafetería Alemána
43　La Moneda de Oro
44　Café Kalú
48　Atico's
52　Loberías de Chacabuco
64　Café Samoa

OTHER

1　Colectivos Basoli
2　Baquedano International
　　Language School
4　Hospital Base
7　Navimag
8　Colectivo Puerto Ibáñez
10　LanChile
12　Oficina Municipal
　　de Turismo,
　　Museo Regional
　　de la Patagonia
14　Bar West
15　Discoteca Corhal
16　Patagonia Connection
17　Lavamatic
18　Lavandería QL
19　45° Sur
20　Cambios Emperador
22　Ladeco
24　Agrotec Limitada
25　Feria Artesanal
　　de Coihaique
27　Post Office
28　Transporte Aéreo
　　Don Carlos,
　　Taxi Bus Don Carlos
29　Galería Artesanal
　　de Cerna-Chile
30　Sernatur
32　Transmarchilay,
　　Turismo Prado
33　Chilesat
34　Banco Santander
35　Entel
37　Automotora Traeger
40　Alta, Aerochein
41　Línea Aérea San Rafael
45　Cambio El Libertador
46　Cine Coihaique
47　Expediciones Lucas Bridges
49　Automundo
51　Automóvil Club de Chile
53　CTC
54　El Bulín
55　Buses La Cascada
56　Expediciones Coihaique
57　Peña Quilantal
61　Transaustral, Turibus
62　Turismo Queulat
63　Buses Artetur
64　Buses Litoral
65　Terminal de Buses
70　Conaf
71　B y V Tour

Coihaique

linked by road to Puerto Chacabuco to the west, Puerto Ibáñez to the south and Chaitén to the north. It's also accessible from Argentine Patagonia.

For travelers accustomed to the routine Latin American grid, Coihaique's unusual street plan can be disorienting. Its focus is the pentagonal Plaza de Armas, from which 10 streets radiate like spokes from a wheel, but within a block or two in every direction this irregularity gives way to a more conventional pattern. One way to orient yourself is to walk once around the Plaza, noting landmarks like the cathedral, then once around the outer pentangle bounded by Arturo Prat, General Parra, 21 de Mayo, Eusebio Lillo and Francisco Bilbao. This isn't foolproof, but it helps.

Avenida General Baquedano, which skirts the northeast side of town, eventually connects with the paved highway to Puerto Chacabuco and a graveled road east to the Argentine border at Coihaique Alto. Avenida Ogana heads south to Balmaceda, Puerto Ibáñez and other southerly points on the Camino Austral.

Information

Tourist Offices Sernatur (☎ 231752) is at Bulnes 35, half a block from the Plaza de Armas. Opening hours are 9 am to 1 pm and 3 to 7 pm.

Coihaique's Oficina Municipal de Turismo (☎ 232100, fax 231788) is at Baquedano 310. Another good source of information is the Automóvil Club de Chile (☎ 231706), Bolívar 254.

Money Change cash and travelers' checks at Cambio El Libertador at Prat 340, Oficina 208, Turismo Prado at 21 de Mayo 417 or Cambios Emperador at Bilbao 222. Banco Santander has an ATM at the corner of Condell and 21 de Mayo.

Post & Communications Coihaique's area code is ☎ 67. Correos de Chile is at Cochrane 202, near the Plaza de Armas. CTC is at Bolívar 191, Entel at Condell 162 and Chilesat at 21 de Mayo 472.

Travel Agencies Most of Coihaique's several travel agencies will arrange fishing holidays or visits to Laguna San Rafael, but they can be surprisingly indifferent to more unconventional alternatives. Among them are Turismo Prado (☎ /fax 231271) at 21 de Mayo 417, with English-speaking staff, and Turismo Queulat (☎ /fax 231441) at 21 de Mayo 1231.

More adventure-oriented is Expediciones Coihaique (☎ /fax 232300) at Bolívar 94, which specializes in pricey fishing holidays from Coihaique to Cochrane; Expediciones Lucas Bridges (☎ /fax 233302) at Eusebio Lillo 311; and 45° Sur (☎ 234599) at 12 de Octubre 253.

Language School The Baquedano International Language School (☎ 232520, fax 232500), Baquedano 20, offers intensive Spanish language instruction (four hours per day for two weeks). The weekly price of US$300 includes room and board with a local family.

National Parks Conaf (☎ 232599) is at Avenida Ogana 1060.

Laundry Try Lavandería QL (☎ 232266), Bilbao 160, for prompt and efficient service. Lavamatic, at the corner of Bilbao and 12 de Octubre, is also worth a try.

Medical Services Coihaique's Hospital Base (☎ 231286) is on Calle Hospital, at the west end of JM Carrera.

Museo Regional de la Patagonia

The museum, Baquedano 310, has a very fine collection of labeled historical photographs on regional history, plus miscellaneous pioneer artifacts. It's open 8.30 am to 1 pm and 2.30 to 8 pm in summer, but winter hours are more limited. Admission costs US$0.75 for adults, with children admitted free.

Activities

Outdoor activities, fishing in summer and skiing in winter, are the most popular pastimes in and around Coihaique. On most lakes and rivers, the fishing season runs from November to May, but in a few popular areas it is restricted to a shorter period. Brown and rainbow trout are the most common species.

From June to September, skiers can test the facilities at the **Centro de Ski El Fraile** (☎ 231690), only 29 km south of Coihaique. It has two lifts and five different runs, up to two km in length and ranging in difficulty from beginner to expert. Rental equipment is available, and there is also a café. Hours are 9 am to 5 pm daily.

Near Puerto Ibáñez, 81 km south of Coihaique, the **Centro de Ski Los Maillines** has steeper slopes but no formal infrastructure and is suitable only for experienced skiers.

Places to Stay – bottom end

Hostel In summer, Coihaique's cheapest accommodation is the Instituto Nacional de la Juventud's *Albergue Juvenil* (☎ 231961) in the Liceo BN2, Carrera 485, entrance on Ibáñez, for about US$3. It's open in January and February only.

Hospedajes & Residenciales Budget lodgings start around US$6 at modest places like *Pensión America*, 21 de Mayo 233, which has an inexpensive restaurant but questionable heating, and *Residencial Navidad* (☎ 235159), Baquedano 198.

Hospedaje Los 4 Hermanos (☎ 232647), a family house at Colón 495, has singles for US$7.50 per person. Friendly and comparably priced *Hospedaje Nathy* (☎ 231047), Almirante Simpson 417, is also worth checking out. The latter also permits camping in the garden.

Some travelers enjoy *Residencial Puerto Varas* (☎ 233689), Ignacio Serrano 168, but others have found the rooms cramped and occasionally noisy, and the management can be indifferent or even brusque. Rates are US$11 per person with breakfast, hot showers and a passable restaurant.

At *Residencial Serrano* (☎ 235522), Serrano 91, the proprietress keeps small, bright, comfortable singles for US$12.50 with shared bath; breakfast costs extra.

Hospedaje Guarda (☎ 232158), Simpson 471, has spacious rooms in a garden setting for US$14 per person, with an excellent breakfast.

Places to Stay – middle

Hospedaje Jofré (☎ 234150), Bilbao 649, is a very fine place that charges US$20/38 single/double, probably the best value in this category. Well-established *Residencial El Reloj* (☎ 231108), Baquedano 444, charges US$30/47, while *Hotelera San Sebastián* (☎ 233427), Baquedano 496, costs US$37/52.

There are mixed reviews of *Hotel Los Ñires* (☎ 232261), Baquedano 315, where rates are US$38/56 with breakfast and private bath – some travelers like it and others consider it poor value. *Hostal Austral* (☎ 232522), at Colón 203, is priced about the same.

Places to Stay – top end

Hotel Luis Loyola (☎ /fax 2342000), Prat 455, has most amenities, including central heating and cable TV, for US$56/77. In a class by itself is highly regarded *Hostería Coihaique* (☎ 231137), Magallanes 131, for US$98/126.

Places to Eat

Café Samoa, Prat 653, is a cozy little bar/restaurant with cheap meals and snacks. *Café Kalú* (☎ 233333), Prat 402, is a modest café with decent sandwiches and inexpensive lunches, about US$3. *Pizza Nostra*, Prat 230, is worth a try.

There are good desserts and light meals at *Café Oriente* (☎ 231622), at the corner of Condell and 21 de Mayo. Under the same ownership, the upgraded *Cafetería Alemana* (☎ 231731), at Condell and Moraleda, is a popular local hangout with similar fare.

Café Ricer (☎ 232920), at Horn 48 off the Plaza de Armas, has good fixed-price lunches with large portions and fine service; its new upstairs restaurant has a more elaborate menu. The *Casino de Bomberos* (☎ 231437), General Parra 365, has very fine meals at reasonable prices; try also *La Moneda de Oro* at Prat 431.

For seafood, there are two excellent choices: *Loberías de Chacabuco*, Almirante Barroso 553, and *Corhal*, Bilbao 123. *Atico's* (☎ 234000), Bilbao 563, specializes in beef and seafood, with a worthwhile lunch for US$8, but the mirrors and wide-screen TV detract from the food. *La Olla* (☎ 234700) is an upscale restaurant at Prat 176.

Entertainment
Cinema The Cine Coihaique, Cochrane 321, is open weekends only.

Pubs Bar West, at the corner of Magallanes and Bilbao, is self-consciously Western (in the US sense).

Music Peña Quilantál, which features live folk music, has moved to Baquedano 791, corner of Colón; shows may start considerably later than the advertised hour. El Bulín, Eusebio Lillo 134, has similar offerings.

Dance Clubs Discoteca Corhal is located at Bilbao 123.

Things to Buy
Several crafts outlets sell woolens, leather goods, wood carvings and seashells. The Feria Artesanal de Coihaique and the Galería Artesanal de Cema-Chile are both on the Plaza de Armas, while Agrotec Limitada is nearby at Dussen 360.

Getting There & Away
Air LanChile (☎ 231188), General Parra 215, flies daily to Puerto Montt (US$81) and Santiago (US$205). Ladeco (☎ 231-300), Prat 188, flies the same routes but uses larger aircraft out of Balmaceda, 50 km southeast.

Transporte Aéreo Don Carlos (☎ 231-981), Subteniente Cruz 63, flies small craft to Cochrane (US$53) Mondays and Wednesdays, to Villa O'Higgins (US$98) Wednesdays only, and to Chile Chico (US$34) daily except Sunday.

Alta (☎ 235714, fax 235712) shares offices at Baquedano 500 with the air taxi

charter Aerohein (☎ 232772), which flies to Laguna San Rafael. From Balmaceda, Alta flies daily except Wednesday to Puerto Montt (US$80), Temuco (US$97) and Concepción (US$127) northbound, and to Puerto Natales (US$75) and Punta Arenas (US$97) southbound.

Línea Aérea San Rafael (☎ 233408), another air taxi charter at 18 de Septiembre 469, flies to Laguna San Rafael on demand; for details, see the Parque Nacional Laguna San Rafael entry.

Bus & Colectivo Coihaique's Terminal de Buses is at the corner of Lautaro and Magallanes, but a number of companies have offices elsewhere in town. Regional and interregional bus services along the Camino Austral are improving in frequency and quality.

Bus – regional For frequent buses to Puerto Aisén and Puerto Chacabuco, try La Cascada (☎ 231413) at Bolívar 125, Transaustral (☎ 231333) at Baquedano 1171, or Taxi Bus Don Carlos (☎ 231981) at Cruz 63. Transaustral has Thursday and Sunday buses to Puerto Chacabuco, while La Cascada bus services connect with arriving and departing ferries. Fares to Puerto Aisén and Puerto Chacabuco are about US$2.50.

Northbound on the Camino Austral, Transportes Mañihuales, at the terminal, has buses daily to Villa Ortega and Mañihuales (US$3) at 1 pm. Transportes Fidel Pinilla (☎ 232452) goes to Mañihuales daily at the same hour.

Buses Litoral (☎ 232903), Independencia 5, has buses Tuesday and Saturday at 11 am to Puerto Cisnes, on a lateral off the Camino Austral, for US$13. Colectivos Basoli (☎ 232596), Puyuhuapi 061, is slightly cheaper, departing Mondays and Thursdays at 1 pm.

Buses Artetur (☎ 233768), Baquedano 1347, goes Tuesday and Saturday to Puyuhuapi (US$13), La Junta and Lago Verde (US$15). Transaustral goes to Puyuhuapi and La Junta (US$15) Tuesday and Saturday at 8.30 am.

Traveling through Argentine Patagonia

Without flying or sailing, the only way from Aisén to the far southern Chilean region of Magallanes is through Argentine Patagonia. For an outline of the formalities of visiting Argentina, see the Getting There & Away chapter. A brief summary of practical information on traveling in Argentina and the main routes to Magallanes follows; see also the Getting There & Away chapter. For full details, see Lonely Planet's Argentina, Uruguay & Paraguay – a travel survival kit.

Visas

There is no Argentine consulate between Puerto Montt and Punta Arenas, so if you need a visa, get one at the Argentine consulate in Santiago.

Getting Around

Air In Argentine Patagonia, distances are immense, roads can be very bad, and some travelers find the desert monotonous, so the occasional flight is sometimes a welcome relief. Argentina's three major airlines, Aerolíneas Argentinas, Austral and Líneas Aéreas del Estado (LADE), have extensive networks in southern Patagonia and Tierra del Fuego. LADE fares are very cheap, in some cases less than the bus fare for the same route, but demand is high, especially in summer. Try the airport if LADE staff insist that flights are completely booked. Other regional airlines are making inroads on the more established carriers.

Bus Argentine buses, resembling those in Chile, are modern, comfortable and fast. Most large towns have a central bus terminal, though some companies operate from their own private offices. In some more remote and less populated areas, buses are few or even nonexistent, so be patient.

Hitching Traffic in Patagonia and Tierra del Fuego is sparse and there may be long waits between lifts, since the few private vehicles are usually full with families. Paved Ruta Nacional 3, on the Atlantic coast, is the best route south, but much improved Ruta Nacional 40 is a dirt and gravel highway that still carries very little traffic south of Esquel. Whenever hitching, be sure to have warm, windproof clothes and carry snack food and a water bottle.

Routes through Southern Argentina

Coihaique to Comodoro Rivadavia One of the main routes to Argentine Patagonia is from Coihaique to Comodoro Rivadavia, an oil town on the Atlantic coast. Buses run about four times weekly (see the Coihaique entry).

Artetur's Wednesday bus to Chaitén (US$25) leaves at 10.30 am, then overnights at Residencial Patagonia in La Junta for US$6 before finishing the trip Thursday morning. B y V Tour (☎ 231-793), Simpson 1037, goes Tuesday, Thursday and Saturday at 9 am to Chaitén (US$30, 11 hours).

Southbound on the Camino Austral, Colectivo Puerto Ibáñez (☎ 233064), Presidente Ibáñez 30, goes to Puerto Ibáñez (US$7), connecting with the ferry to Chile Chico. Buses Jhonson Rossel (☎ 232452) goes to Chile Chico (US$15) Monday, Wednesday and Friday at 1 pm.

Buses Australes Pudú (☎ 231008) goes Wednesday and Saturday mornings to Villa Cerro Castillo (US$10), Bahía Murta (US$15), Puerto Tranquilo (US$16), Puerto Guadal (US$19), Puerto Bertrand (US$20) and Cochrane (US$24). Taxi Bus Don Carlos and Río Baker Taxi Bus (☎ 231052) both have slightly cheaper service; they run on Monday, Wednesday and Friday mornings, to Cochrane and intermediate points.

Comodoro (population about 100,000) is the largest city in southern Argentine Patagonia, but few foreign visitors spend more than a few hours here. The surrounding oil fields supply about a third of Argentina's crude, and travelers should not miss the **Museo del Petróleo**, one of Argentina's most impressive and professional museums. Since Comodoro is a transport hub, air and road connections are good to all parts of the country, especially southbound to Río Gallegos.

Chile Chico to Caleta Olivia From Chile Chico, there are up to three buses daily to the Argentine village of Los Antiguos, which has buses to the town of Perito Moreno (not to be confused with the rarely visited national park or the famous glacier of the same name) or to Caleta Olivia, on the coast. From Caleta Olivia, there are daily buses to Río Gallegos and frequent buses on the short hop to Comodoro Rivadavia.

Like Chile Chico, Los Antiguos has suffered from the deposition of ash from the eruption of Volcán Hudson, but its site on Lago Buenos Aires is incomparably beautiful and its mild climate a pleasure. From Perito Moreno, Wednesday LADE flights go to El Calafate (US$52), Río Gallegos (US$69) and Ushuaia (US$113).

Caleta Olivia is a miniature version of Comodoro Rivadavia, a plain but friendly oil town with frequent bus connections.

To/From Río Gallegos Río Gallegos, 800 km south of Comodoro Rivadavia, is a sizable sheep-farming town that is the starting point for trips to El Calafate, near Argentina's Parque Nacional Los Glaciares, and to Ushuaia, on the island of Tierra del Fuego. From Río Gallegos there are daily buses to Puerto Natales and Punta Arenas in Chile. Several Argentine airlines have air connections north and south, and Aerolíneas Argentinas' transpolar flight to and from Australia stops here.

Historically, every four years or so in the Parque Nacional Los Glaciares, the advance of the 60-meter high Moreno glacier, more than a km wide at its base, blocks the Brazo Rico (Rico Arm) of Lago Argentino until the weight of the water behind it bursts the dam in a spectacular natural cataclysm. It has not done so, however, since 1988. In addition to the glaciers, the nearby Fitzroy range is some of South America's finest trekking country.

There are daily buses to El Calafate from Río Gallegos. In summer, there are regular buses from Calafate to Puerto Natales, Chile, but this trip is difficult in winter, when snow sometimes cuts the road from El Calafate to Chile.

Another crossing from Argentina to Chile is by bus from Río Gallegos to Puerto Natales, via the coal town of Río Turbio. Take one of the daily buses from Río Gallegos to Río Turbio, then catch one of the frequent workers' buses from Río Turbio to Puerto Natales. LADE flies Monday to Río Gallegos (US$24) and Tuesday to El Calafate (US$17). ■

Bus – domestic Long-distance buses to Osorno and Puerto Montt (US$38) go via Argentina. Turibús (☎ 231333), Baquedano 1171, leaves Tuesday and Saturday at 4 pm, while La Cascada goes Wednesday at 10 am in summer only.

Bus – international Buses Giobbi (☎ 232-067), now at the terminal, has Tuesday and Saturday buses to Comodoro Rivadavia, Argentina (US$34), at 8.30 am. Turibús goes to Comodoro Monday and Friday at 11 am.

Boat Ferries to Chiloé, Chaitén and Puerto Montt leave from Puerto Chacabuco, two hours west of Coihaique by bus, but ferry companies have their offices in Coihaique. Schedules are subject to change. For transport to Puerto Chacabuco, see the Bus entry above.

Transmarchilay (☎ 231971), upstairs at 21 de Mayo 417, has ferries from Puerto Chacabuco to Puerto Montt Monday at 4 pm and Wednesday at 10 pm; fares range from US$20 to US$45 or more, depending on the type of seat or accommodation.

Navimag (☎ 223306, fax 233386), at Presidente Ibáñez 347, Oficina 1, also sails from Puerto Chacabuco to Puerto Montt, Wednesday at 8 pm and Friday at 7 pm. For fares, see the Puerto Montt entry in the Araucanía & Los Lagos chapter.

Getting Around

To/From the Airports From downtown, shared cabs to Aeropuerto Teniente Vidal, about five km south of town, cost only about US$4; these leave from outside the LanChile office or you can arrange to be picked up at an address of your choice. The airport has a short runway and a steep approach. Luggage retrieval is awkward and inefficient.

Ladeco's larger aircraft use the airport at Balmaceda, 50 km southeast of Coihaique. The completely paved road to Balmaceda still means nearly an extra hour's bus ride with Ruta Sur (☎ 232788) from Coihaique's downtown bus terminal.

Car Rental Because public transport in Region XI is infrequent, sometimes inconvenient and serves mostly major destinations along the Camino Austral, many travelers rent cars to see the countryside. Because the local supply is so limited, advance reservations are advisable.

Shop around because prices vary considerably, but try Automotora Traeger (☎ 231-648, fax 231264) at Baquedano 457, Automundo (☎ 231621, fax 231794) at Bilbao 510, or Turismo Prado (☎ /fax 231-271) at 21 de Mayo 417. The Automóvil Club (☎ 231649) Bolívar 254, is exceptionally friendly and helpful, meeting clients at the airport and picking up the car there as well.

RESERVA NACIONAL COIHAIQUE

Despite its proximity to the city, barely an hour's walk away, this 2150-hectare reserve is very wild country, with exhilarating panoramas of Coihaique and the enormous basalt columns of Cerro Macay behind it, and other nearby and distant peaks. Native southern beech forests of coigue and lenga, along with introduced species such as pine and larch, cover the hillsides.

There are short nature trails at Laguna Verde and Laguna Venus, but the reserve's real attractions are the extraordinary views. It is a convenient, popular retreat for the residents of Coihaique, but spacious enough so that it never feels oppressively crowded.

Geography & Climate

On the southern slopes of Cerro Cinchao, Reserve Nacional Coihaique is only five km north of town, via the paved road toward Puerto Chacabuco and a steep dirt lateral to the entrance. Altitudes range from 400 to 1000 meters above sea level. Summers are warm and relatively dry, with a mean temperature of about 12°C. Most of the 1100 mm of annual precipitation, in the form of both rain and snow, falls in winter.

Places to Stay

It's easy enough to make this a day trip from Coihaique, but with a tent you can stay at rustic Conaf campgrounds, now run by concessionaires (☎ 232718 in Coihaique) at Laguna Verde and Casa Bruja for US$3.50 per person. Facilities are very basic, but there are picnic tables, fresh water and fire pits. Bring as much food as necessary for the duration.

Getting There & Away

Local drivers can and do take ordinary vehicles up the very steep dirt road, but it's not really a good idea without a 4WD vehicle. From Coihaique, it's a snail's-pace uphill hike of about 1½ hours to the park entrance, where Conaf collects an admission fee of US$1.25, plus another hour to Laguna Verde.

MONUMENTO NATURAL DOS LAGUNAS

On the road to Coihaique Alto and the Argentine border, this 181-hectare wetland reserve has abundant bird life, including black-necked swans, coots and grebes, in an area that is ecologically transitional from southern beech forest to semi-arid steppe.

AISEN

Besides Laguna El Toro and Laguna Escondida, the bodies of water that give the monument its name, Conaf maintains nature trails, a campground (US$4 per site), a picnic area and a visitor center, open 9 am to 6 pm daily. While it lacks regular public transport, Conaf may be able to offer suggestions for getting there.

PARQUE NACIONAL RIO SIMPSON

Straddling the paved highway between Coihaique and Puerto Chacabuco, this 41,000-hectare reserve is an accessible, scenic area where streams from tributary canyons cascade over nearly vertical cliffs to join the broad valley of the Río Simpson. The native flora consist of evergreen forest, mostly southern beech species. Though it may be downgraded from national park status, it's well worth a visit for travelers to the region.

Geography & Climate

Altitudes in Parque Nacional Río Simpson range from 100 to 1900 meters above sea level. The climate is damp, with up to 2500 mm rainfall in some sectors, but summers are mild and pleasant, with mean maximum temperatures of 15°C to 17°C.

Activities

At Km 37 from Coihaique on the Puerto Chacabuco-Coihaique highway, Conaf's

Centro de Visitantes, consisting of a small natural history museum and botanical garden, is a good introduction to regional ecology and wildlife. There is a beach for swimming and many people take advantage of the river's proximity for fishing.

A short distance from the visitor center, **Cascada La Virgen** is a shimmering waterfall on the north side of the highway. Near the confluence of the Río Simpson and the Río Correntoso, 22 km from Coihaique, there is a good hike up the canyon to Laguna Catedral that requires an overnight stay.

Places to Stay

Five km east of the Centro de Visitantes, Conaf's rustic *Camping San Sebastián* charges US$4 per person, but privatization may increase prices. *Camping Río Correntoso* (☎ 232005), 24 km west of Coihaique, has 50 spacious riverside sites, plus hot showers, for US$19.

Getting There & Away

Visitors can take any of the frequent buses between Coihaique and Puerto Aisén with La Cascada, Don Carlos and Transaustral; see the Coihaique entry for details.

PUERTO CHACABUCO

At the east end of a narrow fjord, Puerto Chacabuco displaced nearby Puerto Aisén

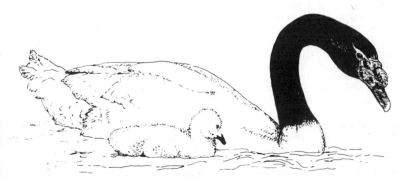

Cisne de cuello negro (black-necked swan)

AISEN

as the port of Coihaique when the latter harbor silted up. Reached by ferry from Puerto Montt or from the port of Quellón on Chiloé, and connected to Coihaique by an excellent paved highway, it is one of the most common ports of entry to Aisén.

Places to Stay & Eat
Convenient for late arrivals on the ferries, *Hotel Moraleda* (☎ 351155), at O'Higgins 82 just outside the harbor compound, charges US$9 per person. *Hotel Loberías de Aisén* (☎ 351115), JM Carrera 50, has upscale accommodation for US$59/77, plus a superb but still reasonably priced seafood restaurant with outstanding service.

Getting There & Away
Bus Buses from Coihaique, 82 km from Puerto Chacabuco by paved highway, meet arriving and departing ferries (see the Coihaique entry for details).

Boat Navimag (☎ 351111, fax 351192) and Transmarchilay (☎ /fax 351144) connect Puerto Chacabuco to Quellón at the southern tip of the Isla Grande de Chiloé, and to Puerto Montt; for details, see the previous Coihaique entry.

PARQUE NACIONAL LAGUNA SAN RAFAEL
Dense with floating icebergs calved from the Campo de Hielo Norte, the massive northern Patagonian ice sheet, Laguna San Rafael is a memorable sight even beneath the somber clouds that so often hang, like gloomy curtains, over surrounding peaks. Established in 1959, the 1.7-million-hectare park where glaciers brush the sea is the region's single most impressive and popular attraction, despite the difficulty and expense of getting there.

Geography & Climate
Laguna San Rafael proper is a nearly enclosed inlet of the sea, 225 km southwest of Puerto Chacabuco via a series of longitudinal channels between the Chonos archipelago and the Península de Taitao on the west, and the Patagonian mainland on the

east. Only the low-lying Istmo de Ofqui, linking Taitao with the mainland, impedes access to the Golfo de Penas. In the 1930s, the Chilean government began a canal to connect the two, but abandoned the project after proceeding only 300 meters.

Altitudes range from sea level to 4058 meters on the summit of Monte San Valentín, the southern Andes' highest peak. The park is damp and humid, with 3500 mm of precipitation in coastal areas.

At higher elevations, more than 5000 mm of rain and snow nourishes the 19 major glaciers that coalesce to form the Campo de Hielo Norte, which covers about 300,000 hectares. Because of the maritime influence of the Pacific Ocean, the mean annual temperature is a relatively mild 8°C.

Activities
Sightseeing around the San Rafael glacier is clearly the major attraction, but climbing and hiking are also possible for well equipped travelers in top physical condition. Visitors intending to hike should heed Darwin's caution:

The coast is so very rugged that to attempt to walk in that direction requires continued scrambling up and down over the sharp rocks of mica-slate; and as for the woods, our faces, hands and shin-bones all bore witness to the maltreatment we received, in attempting to penetrate their forbidding recesses.

Those who overcome these obstacles will see considerable wildlife, mostly birds, including flightless steamer ducks, black-browed and sooty albatross and Magellanic penguins. Otters, sea lions and elephant seals also frequent the icy waters, while pudú, pumas and foxes inhabit the surrounding forests and uplands.

Places to Stay & Eat
Laguna San Rafael has no permanent accommodations. Most visitors stay on board ship, but in cases of emergency, Conaf will permit people to stay in the unheated basement of the former hotel that serves as the park's headquarters. No food

is available at the park, so bring everything from Coihaique or Puerto Chacabuco.

Getting There & Away

The only way to gain access to and from Laguna San Rafael is by air and sea, so travel tends to be expensive and/or time-consuming. In addition to transport, Conaf charges an entrance fee of about US$6 per visitor.

Air Charter flights from Coihaique land at Laguna San Rafael's 775-meter gravel airstrip. Contact Aerohein (☎ 232772) at Baquedano 500, Transportes Aéreos San Rafael (☎ 233408) at 18 de Septiembre 469, or Transporte Aéreo Don Carlos (☎ 231981) at Cruz 63. Small planes carry five passengers for about US$550 roundtrip for the 1½-hour flight, with an hour's layover at the park.

Boat There are several alternatives for sea access to Laguna San Rafael, roughly (in more than one sense!) a 16-hour trip from Puerto Chacabuco. The cheapest is the *Calbuco*, run by the Compañía Naviera Puerto Montt (☎ 351134 in Puerto Chacabuco) which sails Fridays at 6 pm and returns Sundays at 7 am, and has reclining

Pullman seats for US$125 and berths for US$151. The Compañía Naviera also operates the 64-passenger *Yelcho*, which sails Monday, Wednesday and Friday for US$192, and the *Quellón*, which carries 28 passengers in double cabins on seven-day cruises for US$1235 per person.

Transmarchilay (☎ 231971), 21 de Mayo 417 in Coihaique, runs the 230-passenger *El Colono*, with single fares from US$210 for a reclining Pullman seat to US$263 per person for a bunk. A four-person suite costs US$560 per person.

Another relatively inexpensive alternative is the ferry *Evangelistas*, operated by Navimag (☎ 233306), Presidente Ibáñez 347 in Coihaique, which sails every four or five days in summer, less frequently the rest of the year. From Puerto Montt, the cruise takes five days and four nights. See the sidebar below for fare information.

Turismo Rucaray (☎ 332862, fax 332-725), Teniente Merino 848 in Puerto Aisén, charters the 12-passenger launch *Patagonia I* for prices ranging from US$400 per person during the off-season (March to December) to US$500 per person in January and February, based on a full complement of passengers. At the six-person minimum, prices range from US$560

Evangelistas Ferry Rates

Fares from Puerto Montt and back:

	Cabina Armador	Cabina A	Litera	Butaca A	Butaca B	Butaca
Single	US$1000	US$950	US$375	US$350	US$325	US$213
Double	US$600	US$550				
Triple		US$500				

Fares from Puerto Montt to Laguna San Rafael and back to Puerto Chacabuco:

	Cabina Armador	Cabina A	Litera	Butaca
Single	US$875	US$825	US$350	US$225
Double	US$563	US$500		
Triple		US$438		

Fares from Puerto Chacabuco to Laguna San Rafael and back to Puerto Montt:

	Cabina Armador	Cabina A	Litera A	Litera B	Butaca
Single	US$750	US$700	US$300	US$275	US$188
Double	US$475	US$425			
Triple		US$350			

off-season to US$675 in January and February.

Patagonia Connection (☎ 325103 in Puyuhuapi), Bilbao 171 in Coihaique, sails the 54-passenger catamaran *Patagonia Express* to Laguna San Rafael every Friday for US$240 per person. Their Santiago office (☎ (02) 2256489, fax 274-8111) is at Fidel Oteíza 1951, Oficina 1006, Providencia.

Northern Aisén

North of Coihaique, the Camino Austral passes through a number of pioneer villages, past Parque Nacional Queulat to Chaitén (the port for ferries from Quellón on the Isla Grande de Chiloé, and from Puerto Montt) and Caleta Gonzalo (the summer port for ferries from Hornopirén). The town of Futaleufú, on its namesake river near the Argentine border, is a magnet for rafters and kayakers from around the world, and is reached by public transport only via Chaitén.

VILLA AMENGUAL
At the southern approach to Parque Nacional Queulat, at the north end of Laguna de las Torres, Villa Amengual is a pioneer village with modest but good accommodation and food at *Hospedaje Christián*, the only place to stay and eat, for US$10 with breakfast. A few km to the north, a lateral road climbs the valley of the Río Cisnes to the Argentine border, but the road is questionable beyond Estancia La Tapera. The closest Argentine settlement is Alto Río Senguer, about 170 km from Villa Amengual.

PUERTO CISNES
Cavorting dolphins, in search of salmon dinners from floating fish farms, frolic in the waters of the Canal Puyuhuapi near the growing village of Puerto Cisnes, at the mouth of its namesake river, 35 km west of the Camino Austral via a good graveled

lateral. While the scenery is dazzling when the weather clears, the town itself may be most notable for having two gasoline stations in an area where it's possible to drive hundreds of km on the main highway without encountering any place to fill the tank.

Hotel Michay (☎ 346462), Gabriela Mistral 112, and *Residencial El Gaucho* (☎ 346483), Holmberg 140, charge around US$15 per person, but recommended *Hospedaje Bellavista*, next to the Michay, is more economical. For a meal, try reader-recommended *Guiarao*.

Getting There & Away
Buses Basoli has buses to Coihaique (US$11) Tuesday and Friday at 11 am, while Buses Litoral goes to Coihaique Wednesday and Sunday at the same hour. There are no northbound services on the Camino Austral from here, though it would be possible to connect, with good timing, at the highway junction.

PARQUE NACIONAL QUEULAT
Straddling the Camino Austral midway between Chaitén and Coihaique, 154,000-hectare Parque Nacional Queulat is a wild domain of steep-sided fjords, rushing rivers, evergreen forests, creeping glaciers and high volcanic peaks. Created in 1983, it has rapidly gained popularity since completion of the highway, but still qualifies as an off-the-beaten-track destination.

Geography & Climate
Queulat, 200 km south of Chaitén and 220 km north of Coihaique, rises from sea level on Canal Puyuhuapi to 2225 meters. Moisture-laden Pacific frontal systems drop up to 4000 mm of rain per year on the park, nurturing southern beech forests at lower altitudes, and adding snow to sizable glaciers at higher elevations. Mean annual temperatures range from 4°C to 7°C, depending on elevation. Large streams such as the Río Cisnes and the glacial fingers of Lago Rosselot, Lago Verde and Lago Risopatrón offer excellent fishing.

Information

Conaf is building a new Centro de Información Ambiental at the parking lot for the mirador toward the Ventisquero Colgante, the glacier that is the park's most popular feature. For ideas on excursions, consult rangers here, at the Administración in La Junta, or at guard stations at Pudú (the southern approach to the park), Puerto Puyuhuapi or El Pangue. Rangers collect an admission charge of US$1.50 at Sector Ventisquero.

Activities

Queulat has become a popular destination for adventure travel companies, but also presents superb hiking, camping and fishing opportunities for independent visitors, although heavy brush inhibits off-trail exploration.

From Conaf's Centro de Información, 22 km south of Puerto Puyuhuapi, a bridge crosses the Río Guillermo, where a short 600-meter trail leads to the misnamed **Laguna Témpanos** (there are no icebergs in the lake). A longer 3.2-km trail follows the crest of a moraine on the river's north bank to excellent views of the **Ventisquero Colgante**, where icefalls crash periodically onto the rocks below.

Just north of Guardería Pudú, the southern entrance to the park, a damp trail climbs the valley of the **Río de las Cascadas** through a dense forest of delicate ferns, copihue vines, tree-sized fuchsias, podocarpus and lenga, where the heavy rainfall never directly hits the ground but seems to percolate through the multistoried canopy. After about half an hour, the trail emerges at an impressive granite bowl where half a dozen waterfalls drop from hanging glaciers.

At Km 175, just north of the Portezuelo de Queulat, the view of the Queulat valley rivals anything in California's Yosemite. From the highway here, a 200-meter staircase drops to an overlook of the **Salto Río Padre García**, an especially impressive waterfall.

Places to Stay

Camping Ventisquero, convenient to the Ventisquero Colgante, has attractive sites with covered barbecues and picnic tables for US$10, but the glacial meltwater that comes out of the showers in the spotless new bathrooms will test anyone's resolve to get clean. The sites are a bit rocky.

Camping Fiordo Queulat (☎ 233302 in Coihaique), 30 km south of Puerto Puyuhuapi, charges US$20 per site. On Lago Risopatrón, 15 km north of Puerto Puyuhuapi, Conaf's *Camping Angostura* charges US$4 per site in a sopping rainforest, but the facilities are good (cold showers only, however).

Getting There & Away

Renting a car in Coihaique provides flexibility, but can be expensive without several people to share the cost. Buses connecting Chaitén and Coihaique via the Camino Austral will drop passengers at Puerto Puyuhuapi or other points along the western boundary of the park, or it's possible to take the bus from Coihaique to Puerto Cisnes. See the Chaitén and Coihaique entries for details.

PUERTO PUYUHUAPI

At the northern end of the Seno Ventisquero, a scenic fjord that's part of the larger Canal Puyuhuapi, Puerto Puyuhuapi is a modest service center that is also the northern gateway to Parque Nacional Queulat. It's also convenient to Termas de Puyuhuapi, one of Chile's most prestigious hot springs resorts.

Places to Stay & Eat

In Puyuhuapi proper, *Camping Puyuhuapi* is a free site (though it's customary to make a donation to the caretaker). Inexpensive accommodations are available at musty, drafty but friendly *Residencial El Pino* (☎ 325117) for US$9 with a good breakfast, but nearby *Hostería Elizabeth* is better and only slightly dearer at US$12.50, with good meals in a more comfortable environment.

Mid-range lodging is available at *Hostería Ludwig* (☎ 325131), at the south end of town, for US$20 per person, and at *Hostería Alemana* (☎ 325118), Uebel 450, for US$38/46 single/double. For meals and kuchen, try *Café Rossbach*.

Getting There & Away

In addition to buses that pass through between Coihaique and Chaitén, Transaustral runs buses to Coihaique (US$15) Wednesday and Sunday at 8 am. Transaustral's northbound buses continue to La Junta.

AROUND PUERTO PUYUHUAPI
Termas de Puyuhuapi

Accessible only by sea or air, on the western shore of the Seno Ventisquero, the highly regarded and very luxurious *Hotel Termas de Puyuhuapi* (☎ 325103, (02) 225-6489 in Santiago) is a hot springs resort 11 km south of Puerto Puyuhuapi at Bahía Dorita. It charges US$120/150 for singles/doubles from mid-December to mid-March, but only US$98/130 the rest of the year. Full board costs an extra US$40 per day.

Non-guests can use the thermal pools for US$10 in low season, US$15 in high season (children pay half price); transport from the mainland dock costs US$5 each way. Lunch or dinner costs US$20; children also pay half price.

LA JUNTA

At the confluence of the Río Palena and the Río Figueroa, just south of the boundary between Regions X and XI, La Junta is a modest crossroads settlement near the turnoff to Reserva Nacional Lago Rosselot and Lago Verde, a former estancia that is becoming a village. *Hostería Copihue* (☎ 314108), Varas 611, and nearby *Residencial Valderas* (☎ 314105) both charge about US$9 to 10 per person. Some northbound buses spend the night here at *Residencial Patagonia* (☎ 314115), Patricio Lynch 331, which charges only US$6 per person.

LAGO YELCHO

Surrounded by forested peaks on all sides, fed by the raging Río Futaleufú, long and narrow Lago Yelcho covers 11,000 hectares. Until the completion of the Camino Austral, the only settlements were a number of small ports like **Puerto Cárdenas**, where the Río Yelcho drains the lake. A ferry once ran the length of the lake, but there is now a graveled highway along the south shore, east to Futaleufú and Palena, continuing to the Argentine border. Puerto Cárdenas has three modest accommodations: *Hospedaje Lulu*, *Residencial Yelcho* and *Residencial Los Pinos*.

Only 15 km south of Puerto Cárdenas, the Puente Ventisquero (Glacier Bridge) is the starting point for a muddy two-hour hike to the **Ventisquero Cavi**, a large hanging glacier. The nearby *Reserva Natural de Turismo Cavi* (☎ (02) 6973000 in Santiago) has campsites for US$25; double cabañas with shared bath range from US$75 to US$168.

At Villa Santa Lucía, 78 km south of Chaitén, the south shore lateral leads eastward to **Puerto Ramírez**, at the southeast corner of the lake, before bifurcating toward Futaleufú (to the northeast) and Palena (further southeast). At the junction, *Hospedaje El Cruce* and *Hostería Veróica* offer accommodations for about US$10 per person; the Verónica also has camping.

FUTALEUFU

At the confluence of the Río Espolón and the Río Futaleufú, only a few km from the Argentine border, Futaleufú is a world-class destination for fishing, kayaking and whitewater rafting. Futaleufú is 155 km southeast of Chaitén, via an indirect route around Lago Yelcho, conveniently close to the Argentine towns of Trevelin and Esquel, and to Argentina's Parque Nacional Los Alerces.

World-class kayaker Chris Spelius, a former Olympian, runs whitewater trips on the Futaleufú through his Expediciones Chile (☎ /fax 704-488-9082), 333 Earl's

Road, Bryson, North Carolina 28713. Class IV and V descents run from December through February, last 10 days to two weeks, and cost from US$1800 to US$2400. Rafting, fishing, riding and other activities are also possible.

Places to Stay & Eat

Reasonable accommodation is available from about US$7.50 at *Residencial Carahue* (☎ 258633, Anexo 260), O'Higgins 332, *Hospedaje El Campesino* (☎ 258633, Anexo 275) at Prat 107 and *Hospedaje Cañete* (☎ 258633, Anexo 214) at Gabriela Mistral 374. *Hotel Continental* (☎ 258633, Anexo 222), Balmaceda 595, is slightly more expensive but also has good food. *Posada Campesina La Gringa* (☎ 258633, Anexo 260 (02) 2359187 in Santiago) is more upscale at US$62/100 single/double with breakfast.

Getting There & Away

Chaitur, on Manuel Rodríguez, has buses to Chaitén (US$10), leaving Monday, Wednesday, Thursday and Saturday at 4 pm, Tuesday at 1 and 4 pm.

Transporte Samuel Flores (☎ 258633, Anexo 213), Balmaceda 434, provides minivan service to Argentina.

PALENA

Palena, 43 km southeast of Puerto Ramírez, is only eight km west of the Argentine border, but there is no regular public transport across the Paso Palena Carrenleufú to the Argentine town of Corcovado, south of Trevelin. The annual **Rodeo de Palena** takes place in early February.

For inexpensive accommodation, about US$8 per person, try *Pensión Bellavista* at General Urrutia 785, or *Residencial El Paso* (☎ 258633, Anexo 226) at Pudeto 661. *Residencial Las Lengas* (☎ 741240), at Pedro Montt 977, charges US$13/20. Rather more expensive at about US$15 is *Residencial La Chilenita* (☎ 731212), Pudeto 681.

Bus Yelcho, on the Plaza de Armas, connects Palena with Chaitén.

CHAITEN

On clear days, the view from Chaitén, a pioneer port of 3600 people toward the northern end of the Camino Austral, includes 2404-meter Volcán Michinmáhuida to the northeast and 2300-meter Corcovado to the southwest. Like nearly every other Chilean town, Chaitén shudders to a midday blast from the fire station; on Sundays, it seems, it's the town's alarm clock.

While there's little to see in Chaitén proper, it's the main staging point for trips down the highway and its numerous outdoor destinations. Transmarchilay and Navimag ferries link the town to Quellón, at the south end of Chiloé, and to Hornopirén and Puerto Montt.

Orientation

Chaitén, 56 km south of Caleta Gonzalo and 45 km north of Puerto Cárdenas, consists of a few wide, puddled streets in a regular grid pattern between the Bahía de Chaitén and the Río Blanco. The Plaza de Armas, bounded by O'Higgins, Almirante Riveros, Pedro Aguirre Cerda and Libertad, is two blocks east of the bay, where the Costanera Avenida Corcovado connects the town with the ferry port, about a 10-minute walk to the north. Most other services – hotels, restaurants and shops – are between the Costanera and the plaza.

Information

Tourist Offices The municipal Caseta de Información Turística, on Todesco near the Costanera, has a handful of leaflets and a list of hospedajes. In January and February, it's open 9.30 am to 12.30 pm, 3.30 to 6.30 pm, and 8 to 11.30 pm; in March, it closes during the evening hours.

For information on Douglas Tompkins' private Parque Natural Pumalín, visit their office on Corcovado between Todesco and O'Higgins.

Money Remember to change money before coming to Chaitén. The Banco del Estado, at the corner of Libertad and O'Higgins, may change US cash but gives very poor rates, and does not exchange travelers' checks. There are no ATMs in town.

Post & Communications Chaitén's area code is ☎ 65. Correos de Chile is opposite the plaza at Riveros and O'Higgins. There are several long-distance offices, including Teléfonos del Sur on the Costanera just north of Pedro Aguirre Cerda, and Chilesat at O'Higgins 53.

Medical Services Chaitén's hospital (☎ 731244) is on Avenida Ignacio Carrera Pinto between Riveros and Portales.

Organized Tours
American-run Chaitur (☎ 731278/429, fax 731266), at the bus terminal or at Diego Portales 350, arranges trips with bilingual guides to the Yelcho glacier, Termas de Amarillo, sea lion colonies, hot springs and beaches.

Places to Stay & Eat
The nearest campground to Chaitén is *Los Arrayanes* (☎ 218202), four km north of town, where beachfront sites cost US$2.50 per person, plus US$0.75 per vehicle and per tent. There are hot showers.

For bottom-end accommodation in town, look for handwritten signs in the windows of private houses, some of which are open only in summer high season, from mid-December to late March. Several places offer beds for about US$9 with breakfast, including *Hospedaje Sebastián* (☎/fax 731225) at Avenida Padre Juan Todesco 188, and *Hospedaje Gabriel* at Todesco 141.

Friendly *Hospedaje Mahurori* (☎ 731-273), O'Higgins 141, has singles for US$7.50, doubles for US$12, with a very simple breakfast. *Residencial Astoria* (☎ 731263), Corcovado 442, costs about the same.

Hotel Schilling (☎ 731295), Corcovado 230, has singles/doubles for US$25/38

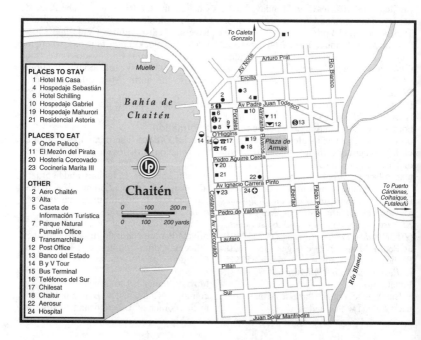

PLACES TO STAY
1 Hotel Mi Casa
4 Hospedaje Sebastián
6 Hotel Schilling
10 Hospedaje Gabriel
19 Hospedaje Mahurori
21 Residencial Astoria

PLACES TO EAT
9 Onde Pelluco
11 El Mezón del Pirata
20 Hostería Corcovado
23 Cocinería Marita III

OTHER
2 Aero Chaitén
3 Alta
5 Caseta de Información Turística
7 Parque Natural Pumalín Office
8 Transmarchilay
12 Post Office
13 Banco del Estado
14 B y V Tour
15 Bus Terminal
16 Teléfonos del Sur
17 Chilesat
18 Chaitur
22 Aerosur
24 Hospital

Chaitén

Bahía de Chaitén

Muelle

To Caleta Gonzalo

To Puerto Cárdenas, Coihaique, Futaleufú

with shared bath, and doubles with private bath for US$50. Chaitén's finest is highly recommended *Hotel Mi Casa* (☎ 731285), Avenida Norte 206, on a hill just north of town. It's a large place with its own restaurant and simple, but clean and spacious rooms costing US$33 per person with breakfast.

For seafood and other local specialties, try the simple but appealing restaurants on the Costanera Corcovado, including *Cocinería Marita III* at the corner of Carrera Pinto, and *Hostería Corcovado*, at the corner of Pedro Aguirre Cerda. *El Mezón del Pirata*, Almirante Riveros 242, has curanto, seafood empanadas and sandwiches, while *Onde Pelluco* (☎ 437460), O'Higgins 42, serves seafood, sandwiches and espresso.

Getting There & Away
Air Alta (☎/fax 731372), at Portales 154, flies every morning to Puerto Montt (US$30) and weekday afternoons only to Puerto Montt, Temuco (US$70) and Concepción (US$106). Aerosur (☎ 731228), at the corner of Carrera Pinto and Almirante Riveros, flies daily except Sunday to Puerto Montt (US$43), as does Aero Chaitén (☎ 731275), Todesco 42.

Bus Transport details for the Camino Austral change rapidly as the road undergoes improvements. The main bus station is on O'Higgins between Portales and the Costanera.

On Thursdays, Artetur, on Corcovado between Todesco and O'Higgins, takes the Camino Austral south to Coihaique (US$25, 12 hours). B y V Tour, at the corner of Corcovado and O'Higgins, goes Monday, Wednesday and Friday to Coihaique (US$30).

Chaitur (☎ 731278), at the bus terminal, goes to Futaleufú (US$10), on the Argentine border, Mondays and Fridays at 7 am and 2 pm, Tuesday, Wednesday and Thursday at 7 am only. Chaitur also goes to Caleta Gonzalo Sunday at 7 am, returning at 9 am.

Chaitur and Bus Yelcho go to Futaleufú, while Buses Alcón goes to Palena Monday,

Wednesday and Friday at 1 pm. Buses Lago Verde goes to Puerto Cárdenas, Villa Santa Lucía, Villa Vanguardia, La Junta and Lago Verde (on the Argentine border southeast of La Junta) Tuesday and Saturday at 11.30 am; return services leave Lago Verde Monday and Friday at 8.30 am.

Boat Transmarchilay (☎ 731272), Corcovado 266, sails to Puerto Montt Monday, Thursday and Friday on the *Pincoya*, and Monday on the *Mailén*. The trips takes 10 hours; for fares, see the Puerto Montt entry in the La Araucanía & Los Lagos chapter. Transmarchilay also sails Wednesday and Saturday to Quellón, at the south end of the Isla Grande de Chiloé, on the *Pincoya*. The trip lasts five hours; for fares, see the Quellón entry in the Chiloé chapter. Schedules change, so confirm them at any Transmarchilay office.

From Caleta Gonzalo, 56 km north of Chaitén, Transmarchilay sails daily except Monday to Hornopirén, where there are bus connections to Puerto Montt; see the Caleta Gonzalo entry, below, for details.

AROUND CHAITEN
Termas El Amarillo
About 25 km southeast of Chaitén, on a spur off the Camino Austral, Termas El Amarillo is a simple hot springs, with 20 walk-in campsites for US$10, and a restaurant.

CALETA GONZALO
Caleta Gonzalo, the summer ferry port to Hornopirén, is the de facto center for US entrepreneur and conservationist Douglas Tompkins' Parque Natural Pumalín. Tompkins has built a state-of-the-art walk-in campground, with a stylish shelter for cooking, on the shore of the Fiordo Reñihué. There are, however, no hot showers.

Looking as if it had been airlifted intact from Aspen, Tompkins' *Café Caleta Gonzalo* has superb four-course meals, including fresh homemade bread, for about US$5. It's the ideal place to wait for the ferry.

About 18 km south of Caleta Gonzalo, only a few minutes off the highway to

Parque Natural Pumalín

While Chile has one of Latin America's best national park systems, some observers believe the country could, and should, do much more to preserve its natural patrimony. To many conservationists, both Chileans and foreigners, the mountains of wood chips awaiting shipment from Puerto Montt to Japan are a palpable symbol of the overexploitation of Chile's woodlands. An ambitious multinational scheme to exploit southern Tierra del Fuego's lenga forests is the latest project to arouse controversy but, ironically, no single undertaking has been more conflictive than US conservationist Douglas Tompkins' attempt to create the private Parque Natural Pumalín to protect thousands of sq km of alerce and other native species in Region X.

Tompkins, an entrepreneur who made his fortune as the founder of the Esprit clothing company, became acquainted with Chile on recreational visits during the 1960s. In the early 1990s, after cashing out his interest in Esprit, he began quietly to acquire various fundos, consisting of small agricultural parcels among large blocks of native forest, in the area south of Hornopirén and north of Chaitén, between the ocean and the Argentine border. At present, his holdings total about 270,000 hectares, but the effort to finalize the project has run into several political obstacles.

First offering to donate the projected park to the state, Tompkins found that Conaf lacked the funds to administer such a large new acquisition. Alternatively, he created the non-profit Puerto Montt-based Fundación Educación, Ciencia y Ecología to hold and administer it, but needs government approval to ensure the park's legal status and transfer the property, even though there are no formal juridical obstacles.

One problem is geopolitical, as conservative politicians have questioned foreign ownership of so much land so close to an international border, even though Fundación's entire board is Chilean and the park's administration would be financed by an independent endowment. One of Tompkins' most vociferous critics is Interior Subsecretary Belisario Velasco, who has the ear of President Eduardo Frei Ruiz-Tagle and has personally obstructed Tompkins' purchase of 30,000 hectares owned by Valparaíso's Universidad Católica at Huinay, which would unite two geographically separated sectors of Pumalín.

Anti-Tompkins rhetoric, mostly but not exclusively right-wing, can be intemperate or worse. According to Christian Democrat Senator Sergio Páez, Tompkins is part of a group of foreign investors trying to depopulate the area near the Argentine border to take extraterritorial control of it: 'This is a very real threat to our national sovereignty; it is a

---

Chaitén, is a substantial grove of alerce trees where, in a few places, locals have stripped bark fiber off the trees to caulk their boats – simultaneously killing the trees, even though cheaper artificial materials are available for the purpose. If hiking here or in other southern Chilean rainforests, watch for *sanguijuelas* (leeches), which are more annoying than dangerous.

Getting There & Away

Transmarchilay's ferry *Mailén* sails to Hornopirén daily except Tuesday and Wednesday at 9 am in summer only; for fares, see the Hornopirén entry in the La Araucanía & Los Lagos chapter. Chaitur minibuses leave Chaitén at 7 am to make the Sunday ferry connection northbound.

Southern Aisén

South of Coihaique, settlements are fewer and farther apart. Part of the area was devastated by the 1991 eruption of Volcán Hudson, a relatively inconspicuous 1369-meter peak that dumped tons of ash over thousands of square km in both Chile and Argentina, ruining cropland and killing livestock by burying pasture grasses. The only substantial towns are Chile Chico, on the south shore of Lago General Carrera near the Argentine border, and Cochrane on the Camino Austral. The highway presently ends at Puerto Yungay, south of the Río Baker, but progress is proceeding, slowly, toward Villa O'Higgins.

geopolitical catastrophe. If these investors achieve their aims they will become owners of a vast tract of our southern frontiers.' Páez failed to name any of these investors, however.

Other opponents include the right-wing UDI party and the so-called Movimiento Nacionalista Chilena (Chilean Nationalist Movement), which has gone so far as to threaten (at least rhetorically) the impresario's life, replacing the slogan 'Tompkins fuera de Chile' (Tompkins out of Chile) with 'Muera Tompkins' (death to Tompkins). Some opponents have concocted wild accusations of money laundering, speculated on the presence of massive gold deposits on the property (a favorite fantasy about the area ever since the 16th century), and even hallucinated over the creation of a new Jewish state.

Another source of opposition is the Catholic Church, which distrusts Tompkins' association with the California-based Foundation for Deep Ecology, which takes a pro-choice stance on abortion rights. One measure of ecclesiastical political power is that, since the recent Irish referendum, Chile is now the only western democracy with no divorce law.

On the face of it, the most substantive criticism could be the impact of the park's creation on local land rights, since numerous small-scale colonos (agricultural colonists) occupy scattered landholdings throughout the area. Tompkins and the Fundación have pledged to respect existing land rights, even if those rights are not strictly regularized, but it's not hard to imagine that disputes could develop. In the area north of Chaitén, for example, boatwrights have secretly stripped alerce bark for caulking, a practice that, if uncontrolled, eventually kills the trees. It's not clear that, even if this could be regulated on a sustainable basis, it would be acceptable to the Fundación.

In the interim, the Fundación has prepared an elaborate management plan that foresees increased tourist visitation and has also begun to provide facilities, such as a free hostel with hot showers at the Caleta Gonzalo ferry port, for the use of local residents only. Actively courting local support, Tompkins has invited local officials to his home at Fundo Renihue, east of Caleta Gonzalo, and sponsored an annual January folk festival there. Whether this is an encouraging start or a dead end for Parque Pumalín may not be clear for some time.

For more information on Parque Pumalín, contact the Fundación Educación, Ciencia y Ecología (☎ 251910/1, fax 255145), Buin 350 in Puerto Montt, or the Foundation for Deep Ecology (☎ 415-771-1102, fax 771-1121), 1555 Pacific Avenue, San Francisco, California 94109. ∎

PUERTO INGENIERO IBÁÑEZ

Buried in ash by the eruption of Volcán Hudson, Puerto Ingeniero Ibáñez, on the north shore of emerald green Lago General Carrera, has recovered more quickly than other affected towns in the area. Surrounded by steep mountains and barren hills, the town has regular ferries to Chile Chico, where there are bus connections to the Argentine border at Los Antiguos. Across the border, Lago General Carrera is known as Lago Buenos Aires.

Livestock – cattle and sheep – are the backbone of the local economy. Local *huasos*, the Chilean equivalent of the Argentine gaucho, drive their herds along the roads. Orchard crops also do well in the low-altitude microclimate along the lake.

Long lines of poplars, planted as wind breaks, separate the fields, while black-necked swans and pink flamingos crowd the river and its shores.

The town itself is of little interest, but the surrounding countryside is very worthwhile if you can afford to rent a car. From Puerto Levicán, on the lake, there are panoramic views of the Río Ibáñez valley when dust from Volcán Hudson does not obscure the horizon.

Places to Stay & Eat

Opposite the ferry dock, the *Residencial Ibáñez* (☎ 423227), at Dickson 31, has unheated singles with plenty of extra blankets for about US$9 with breakfast; other meals are available. Next door, at Dickson

29, *Hotel Mónica* (☎ 423226) is slightly more expensive.

Getting There & Away

For ground transport from Coihaique to Puerto Ibáñez, see the Coihaique entry. Mar del Sur's car and passenger ferry *Chelenco* goes Monday, Wednesday and Saturday to Chile Chico, on the southern shore of the Lago General Carrera – check exact departure times at Mar del Sur (☎ 233466), 21 de Mayo 417, 2nd floor, in Coihaique.

Naviera Sotramin (☎ 2344240), Portales 99 in Coihaique, crosses to Chile Chico in the ferry *El Pilchero* daily except Sunday.

The passenger fare from Puerto Ibáñez to Chile Chico is US$3.50 per person, but students pay half fare. Bicycles cost US$3, while passenger vehicles pay US$34.

RESERVA NACIONAL CERRO CASTILLO

Reaching nearly 2700 meters and flanked by three major glaciers on its southern slopes, the basaltic spires of Cerro Castillo tower above southern beech forests in this sprawling 180,000-hectare reserve, 75 km south of Coihaique. This is very fine and rarely visited trekking country (not to be confused with the settlement of Cerro Castillo near Parque Nacional Torres del Paine, in Region XII of Magallanes).

Sightseeing, fishing and trekking are popular recreational options. There is an excellent four-day trek from Km 75, at the northern end of the reserve, to Villa Cerro Castillo at the southern end, which is described in Lonely Planet's *Trekking in the Patagonian Andes*.

Places to Stay

On the Camino Austral, 67 km south of Coihaique, Conaf operates a modest but sheltered and shady campground at *Laguna Chaguay* for US$3.50 per site, but tent camping is free and spectacular in the backcountry. Be sure to check in with the ranger, since trekking is potentially hazardous, even though bridges now cross rushing meltwater streams that once required fording.

At the south end of the reserve, on a short graveled lateral from the Camino Austral about 10 km west of the Puerto Ibáñez junction, Villa Cerro Castillo is a typical pioneer settlement of cement block houses with corrugated metal roofs, plus a few scattered examples of Chilote shingle houses. *Pension El Viajero* has a few rooms for US$6 per person, a bar and a cheap restaurant.

PUERTO RIO TRANQUILO

One of the larger settlements on the Camino Austral between Coihaique and Cochrane, Puerto Río Tranquilo was one of several ports linked by ferry to Puerto Ibáñez, Chile Chico and smaller lakeside outposts. Now a convenient stopover for those passing through the area, it is the junction for a new road under construction northwest to Bahía Exploradores, which will improve access to Laguna San Rafael.

Places to Stay & Eat

Residencial Los Pinos charges US$25 per room (two beds per room) with breakfast, and has a restaurant with fixed-price meals for US$6. Comparable but slightly cheaper *Hostería Carretera Austral* also has a selection of inexpensive cabañas.

Getting There & Away

Buses Don Orlando goes to Chile Chico (US$15) Tuesday and Thursday at 11.30 am. Buses between Coihaique and Cochrane also pass through town.

PUERTO GUADAL

At the west end of Lago General Carrera, 13 km east of the junction with the Camino Austral on the highway to Chile Chico, Puerto Guadal's shingled houses are palpable evidence of Chilote immigration over the past two decades. The only formal accommodation is *Hostería Guadal* (☎ 411-212), charging a very reasonable US$10 per person, but there are also acceptable free campsites along the lake. Buses Daniela goes to Chile Chico (US$10) Thursday and Sunday at 1 pm, by way of an excitingly narrow and scenic route not advisable for travelers with vertigo.

At Cruce El Maitén, the junction of the Camino Austral and the highway to Chile Chico, *Patagonia Lodge* (☎ 411323) has attractive lakeside cabañas and a restaurant. Rates are US$94 double; there is also a lakeside sauna, and horse rentals and launches for fishing.

Other nearby alternatives include *Bahía Catarina*, which has both camping and cabañas, and *Pasarela Lodge*, which has self-catering fishing cabañas for up to eight people, starting at US$90.

CHILE CHICO

Founded in 1928 by immigrant fortune seekers of several nationalities – Argentine, Brazilian, Chilean, French, German and Italian – Chile Chico derived its early prosperity from copper, the blue-tinged ore still visible in the rocky hills. The broad, recently paved Avenida O'Higgins is a tangible reminder of the optimism of the first settlers, but when miners exhausted the copper, the economy declined rapidly. It recently revived with the opening of US-based Coeur d'Alene Exploration's Fachinal gold and silver mine west of town, but there is concern that local ores may be less productive than originally thought.

Before recent developments, cultivation of high-quality fruit in Chile Chico's balmy microclimate kept the town alive if not truly prosperous; the warm, sunny weather encouraged production of apples, pears, plums and cherries equal to those from the Chilean heartland. Even many street trees are fruit-bearing apricots and peaches, rather than strictly ornamentals, but fruit is economically marginal because markets other than Coihaique are distant and transport is difficult and expensive.

Ash from the 1991 eruption of Volcán Hudson smothered local orchards, jeopardizing the town's future, and when there are high winds the skies still darken. Despite the arrival of foreign capital and improved streets, Chile Chico still has a more forlorn aspect than nearby Los Antiguos, across the border in Argentina.

Many residents have left to work in Argentina and elsewhere, and the permanent population of 2300 is only about half what it was in the 1960s. Remittances from expatriate workers, or those in other parts of Chile, are a main source of income, but some make a living catering to the Argentine tourist trade.

The mountainous road west from Chile Chico to the junction with the Camino Austral is one of the region's highlights, a borderline scary experience that several mountain bikers have enjoyed despite its steepness. If driving, proceed very slowly; there are many blind curves, and in some places the roadway is barely wide enough for a single vehicle.

Orientation

On the south shore of Lago General Carrera, Chile Chico is a compact village only a few km from the Argentine border at Los Antiguos. One block south of the lakeshore, westbound Avenida O'Higgins becomes the rugged highway to Puerto Guadal and Cruce El Maitén, on the Camino Austral just north of Cochrane.

Information

Tourist Office At the corner of O'Higgins and Lautaro, Chile Chico's Oficina de Información Turística is part of the newly opened museum.

Post & Communications The area code is ☎ 67. Correos de Chile is at the corner of Manuel Rodríguez and Balmaceda. The Compañía de Teléfonos de Coihaique is on O'Higgins between Pedro Montt and Lautaro, while Entel is directly across the street.

National Parks Conaf is at Blest Gana 121.

Organized Tours

The operators of Hostería de la Patagonia and the Hostería Austral (see Places to Stay, below) both arrange fishing excursions, horseback riding and other trips to natural attractions like Lago Jeinimeni and the Río Baker.

Places to Stay & Eat

Chile Chico's selection of accommodations has recently improved. Probably the best value in town is *Hospedaje Don Luis* (☎ 411384), Balmaceda 175, a spotlessly clean and friendly place that charges US$9 per person without breakfast. *Hospedaje Alicia* (☎ 411265), Freire 24, is also worth a look. *Residencial La Frontera*, Manuel Rodríguez 435, has secluded campsites for US$2.50 per person, plus US$2 for hot showers.

Residencial Aguas Azules (☎ 411320), Manuel Rodríguez 252, has an attitude problem and, for US$30 double, it's no real bargain. Its annex, at the corner of Balmaceda and Manuel Rodríguez, is very overpriced for US$12.50 per person – the walls are paper-thin, the beds sag like hammocks, and it even lacked matches to light the hot water heater.

Friendly *Hospedaje No Me Olvides*, about 1.2 km east of downtown on the highway to Argentina, is a popular budget choice and also serves reasonable meals. On woodsy grounds in the same area, *Hostería de la Patagonia* (☎ 411337, fax 411444) is pleasant and comfortable, but not luxurious, for US$20/32 single/double; meals cost US$9. The owners also arrange tours of the area.

The sparkling new *Hostería Austral* (☎ 411274, fax 411461), O'Higgins 501, is Chile Chico's most impressive accommodation. The room rates are US$45/58. Its restaurant is pleasant enough but fairly expensive, and nothing special unless fresh local raspberries are available for dessert. It does offer espresso, however.

For snacks and drinks, try the congenial *Café Elizabeth y Loly* (☎ 411288) at Pedro González 25, opposite the plaza, *Rapanui* at the corner of O'Higgins and Blest Gana, and *Café La Frontera*, on O'Higgins between Burgos and Lautaro.

Getting There & Away

Air Transporte Aereo Don Carlos, O'Higgins 264, flies daily except Sunday to Coihaique (US$34). The airfield is just outside town, on the road to the Argentine border.

Bus Buses Jhonson Rossel, at the corner of O'Higgins and Pedro Burgos, goes to Coihaique (US$15) Wednesday, Friday and Sunday at 1 pm via Los Antiguos, Argentina and Paso Huemules.

Eduardo Padilla, O'Higgins 424, crosses the border to Los Antiguos (US$2.50), just nine km east, four times daily Monday through Thursday, once Friday and once Saturday, but never on Sunday. From Los Antiguos, travelers can make connections to Perito Moreno, Caleta Olivia and southern Argentine Patagonia.

Buses Don Orlando, at Panadería La Espiga on O'Higgins between Pedro González and Blest Gana, goes from Chile Chico to Puerto Río Tranquilo (US$15), on the Camino Austral at the west end of Lago General Carrera, Tuesday and Friday at 4 pm. The bus also stops at Mallín Grande (US$7.50) and Puerto Guadal (US$11). Buses Daniela goes to Guadal only (US$10), connecting with Buses Pudú to Coihaique and Cochrane, Wednesday and Saturday at 1 pm.

Boat Mar del Sur's *Chelenco* crosses Lago General Carrera to Puerto Ibáñez Tuesday, Thursday and Sunday, while Naviera Sotramin's *El Pilchero* sails daily except Saturday. For fares and schedules, see the entry for Puerto Ibáñez, above.

PUERTO BERTRAND

On the southeastern shore of Lago Bertrand, 11 km south of Cruce El Maitén, Puerto Bertrand is a small but scenic village with a cluster of places to stay and eat, none of them particularly cheap. The most reasonable is *Hospedaje Quimey*, which charges US$25 per person with full board, while the *Hostería Río Baker* (☎ 411447) costs US$50 per person.

COCHRANE

Cochrane, 345 km south of Coihaique, is almost the end of the road – though the Camino Austral continues south to Puerto Yungay, public transport turns around and heads back north. Directly west are the southern outliers of the Campo de Hielo

Norte, while a few km to the east is Lago Cochrane, a popular recreational area that is known as Lago Pueyrredón across the Argentine border. There is no public transport across the border, and any traffic is scarce.

Now paving most of its streets, the small but growing town has an attractively landscaped Plaza de Armas and the last notable tourist services on the Camino Austral. In summer, its tourist information kiosk, on the plaza, is open daily 11 am to 1 pm and 3.30 to 9.30 pm Tuesday through Saturday, 10 am to 1 pm and 3.30 to 9.30 pm Sundays. Mondays, or the rest of the year, try the nearby Municipalidad for information.

For information on Reserva Nacional Lago Cochrane, north of town, visit the new Conaf office at the corner of Dr Steffens and Río Nef. Correos de Chile is at the corner of O'Higgins and Lago Brown, while there's a telephone office at the corner of San Valentín and Las Golondrinas. The hospital is on O'Higgins between Río Colonia and Lago Brown.

Places to Stay & Eat
Free, but windy and exposed campsites with no services are available at Lago Cochrane, about three km east of town. A recent reader recommendation is *Hospedaje Hilda Cruces*, Dr Steffens 451, for about US$7, with garden camping also possible.

Otherwise, Cochrane has several basic hotels, the cheapest of which is *Hospedaje Welcome*, on San Valentín between Prat and Los Ñadis, for about US$10 per person. Friendly but a little inattentive, *Residencial Sur Austral* (☎ 522150) Prat 281, charges US$12.50 per person and has a decent restaurant. A bit rundown despite its attractive gardens, *Hostería Wellmann* (☎ 522-171), Las Golondrinas 36, is still the best in town for US$28 single with breakfast.

Rogeri, Teniente Merino 502, is a good, reasonably priced restaurant.

Getting There & Away
Air Transporte Aéreo Don Carlos, alongside Residencial Sur Austral at Prat 281, flies Wednesdays and Saturdays to Coihaique (US$52). Wednesday's southbound flight from Coihaique continues to Villa O'Higgins (US$45).

Bus Buses Don Carlos goes to Coihaique (US$21) Monday, Wednesday and Friday at 8.30 am, while slightly more expensive Buses Pudú, at the corner of Teniente Merino and Río Maitén, goes Thursday and Sunday at 8.15 am. Río Baker Taxi Bus (☎ 522221), Dr Steffens 400, goes to Coihaique at 8.30 am Tuesday, Thursday and Sunday, and also has occasional service to Los Vagabundos, on the Camino Austral toward Puerto Yungay.

CALETA TORTEL
About 20 km north of Puerto Yungay, a rustic A-frame refugio (no insulation, but a wood stove) marks Río Los Vagabundos, the departure point for Caleta Tortel, a picturesque fishing village at the mouth of the Río Baker. The villagers of Caleta Tortel have petitioned for a highway extension to link them to the Camino Austral, but for the moment, the only way to get there is to be fortunate enough to arrive at Río Los Vagabundos when there's a boat, or else radio ahead from the Municipalidad or the Carabineros from Cochrane to have someone meet you in a launch.

PUERTO YUNGAY
Puerto Yungay, 1125 km from Puerto Montt, is the southern end of the Camino Austral at present, despite the solid lines that appear on some Chilean maps toward Villa O'Higgins. Before continuing south toward Puerto Yungay, it's a good idea to consult Carabineros in Cochrane about road conditions.

Magallanes & Tierra del Fuego

Chile's Region XII, the Región de Magallanes y de la Antártica Chilena, takes in all the country's territory beyond about 49° S, including the western half of the Isla Grande de Tierra del Fuego (whose eastern half is Argentine), the largely uninhabited islands of the Tierra del Fuego archipelago, and the slice of Antarctica claimed by Chile. This chapter also includes information on Argentine Tierra del Fuego, and on the southeastern corner of Argentina's Santa Cruz province, which includes the popular destinations of El Calafate and Parque Nacional Los Glaciares.

Magallanes

Battered by westerly winds and storms that drop huge amounts of rain and snow on the seaward slopes of the Andes, Magallanes is a rugged, mountainous area, geographically remote from the rest of the country. From Aisén or the Chilean mainland, Magallanes and its capital Punta Arenas are only accessible by road through Argentine Patagonia, or by air or sea.

Alacaluf and Tehuelche Indians, subsisting through fishing, hunting and gathering, were the region's original inhabitants. There remain very few individuals of identifiable Ona, Haush or Yahgan descent, while the Alacalufes and Tehuelches survive in much reduced numbers.

Magellan, in 1520 the first European to visit the region, left it his name, but early Spanish attempts at colonization failed. Tiny Puerto Hambre (Port Famine) at the southern end of the Strait of Magellan is a reminder of these efforts. Nearby, the restored wooden bulwarks of Fuerte Bulnes recall Chile's first colonization of 1843, when President Manuel Bulnes ordered the army south to the area, then only sparsely populated by indigenous peoples.

Increased maritime traffic spurred by the California Gold Rush gave birth to Punta Arenas, and its initial prosperity depended on the ships that passed through the straits between Europe and California and Australia. With the opening of the Panama Canal and the reduction of traffic around Cape Horn (Cabo de Hornos), the port's international importance diminished. Later wealth derived from the wool and mutton industry, which transformed both Argentine and Chilean Patagonia in the late 19th century.

Besides wool, Magallanes' modern economy depends on commerce, petroleum development and fisheries, which have made it Chile's most prosperous region, with the country's highest levels of employment, housing quality, school attendance and public services. Its impressive natural assets, particularly Parque Nacional Torres del Paine, have made it an increasingly popular tourist destination.

The region also, however, manifests symptoms of the global environmental crisis. The continuing deterioration of the ozone layer over Antarctica has affected far southern South America more than any other permanently inhabited area of the earth, directly affecting both the human population and the local livestock economy. Native forest conservation has become a major issue in the most remote corners of both Chilean and Argentine Tierra del Fuego.

PUNTA ARENAS

At the foot of the Andes on the western side of the Strait of Magellan, Patagonia's liveliest and most interesting city features many mansions and other imposing buildings dating from the wool boom of the late 19th and early 20th centuries. As the best and largest port for thousands of kilometers, Punta Arenas (population 105,000) attracts ships from the burgeoning South

Atlantic fish industry as well as Antarctic research and tourist vessels.

Zona Franca (free port) facilities have promoted local commerce and encouraged immigration from central Chile; luxury items like automobiles are much less expensive here, although the basic cost of living is higher. Unlike the highly successful Zofri in Iquique, however, the local free zone suffers from relative isolation and steadily declining revenues.

Punta Arenas has experienced a large influx of foreign visitors, but is utterly dead on Sundays, so that's a good time to explore some of the surrounding area or start a trip to Torres del Paine.

History

Founded in 1848, Punta Arenas was originally a military garrison and penal settlement that proved to be conveniently situated for shipping en route to California during the Gold Rush. Compared to the initial Chilean settlement at Fuerte Bulnes, 60 km south, it had a better, more protected harbor and superior access to wood and water. For many years, English maritime charts had called the site 'Sandy Point,' a phrase which, in its rough Spanish equivalent, became 'Punta Arenas.'

In Punta Arenas' early years, its economy depended on wild animal products, including sealskins, guanaco hides and feathers; mineral products, including coal, gold and guano; and firewood and timber. None of these was a truly major industry, and the economy did not take off until the last quarter of the 19th century, after the territorial governor authorized the purchase of 300 purebred sheep from the Falkland Islands. The success of this experiment encouraged others to invest in sheep and, by the turn of the century, there were nearly two million animals in the territory.

In 1875, the population of Magallanes province was barely 1000, but European immigration accelerated as the wool market boomed. Among the most notable immigrants were Portuguese businessman José Nogueira, Irish doctor Thomas Fenton, who founded one of the island's largest sheep stations, and José Menéndez, an Asturian entrepreneur who would become one of the wealthiest and most influential individuals not just in Patagonia, but in all of South America.

First engaged solely in commerce, Menéndez soon began to acquire pastoral property, founding the famous Sociedad Explotadora de Tierra del Fuego, which controlled nearly a million hectares in Magallanes alone and other properties across the border – one of Argentina's greatest estancias, near Río Grande, still bears the name of his wife María Behety. With another important family, the Brauns, the descendants of Menéndez comprised one of the wealthiest and most powerful regional elites in all of Latin America. Although few remain in Punta Arenas (having relocated to Santiago and Buenos Aires), their downtown mansions remain symbols of Punta Arenas' golden age.

Menéndez and his colleagues could not have built their commercial and pastoral empires without the labor of immigrants from many lands: English, Irish, Scots, Croats, French, Germans, Spaniards, Italians and others. On all sides of José Menéndez' opulent mausoleum, modest tombstones in the municipal cemetery reveal the origins of those whose efforts made his and other wool fortunes possible. Since expropriation of the great estancias, including those of the Sociedad Explotadora, in the 1960s, the structure of land tenure is more equitable, and energy has since eclipsed wool in the regional economy.

Orientation

Punta Arenas occupies a narrow shelf between the Andes to the west and the Strait of Magellan to the east. Consequently, the city has spread north and south from its original center between the port and the Plaza Muñoz Gamero. Street names change on either side of the plaza, but street addresses on the plaza itself bear the name Muñoz Gamero. Most landmarks and accommodations are within a few blocks of the plaza. Mirador La Cruz, at Fagnano and Señoret, four blocks west

MAGALLANES

of the plaza, provides a good view of town and the Strait.

Most city streets are one-way, though grassy medians divide Avenida Bulnes and a few other major thoroughfares. There are two main exit routes from town: Avenida Costanera leads south to Fuerte Bulnes and Avenida Bulnes heads north past the airport to become Ruta 9 to Puerto Natales, which branches off to Ruta 255 to Río Gallegos, Argentina. Travelers coming from Argentina will find Chilean traffic much less hazardous for both pedestrians and motorists.

Information

Tourist Offices Sernatur (☎ 225385) is at Waldo Seguel 689, just off Plaza Muñoz Gamero. It's open weekdays 8.15 am to 5.45 pm, with friendly, helpful and well-informed staff. It publishes an annually updated list of accommodation and transport, and provides a message board for foreign visitors.

The municipal Kiosko de Informaciones (☎ 223798) on the 700 block of Avenida Colón, between Bories and Magallanes, is open weekdays 9 am to 7 pm all year, and Saturdays 9 am to 7 pm in summer.

The Automóvil Club de Chile (☎ 243-675), O'Higgins 931, is also helpful.

Foreign Consulates The Argentine Consulate (☎ 261912), 21 de Mayo 1878, is open weekdays 10 am to 2 pm. There are also several European and other South American consulates:

Belgium
    Roca 817, Oficina 61 (☎ 241472)
Brazil
    Arauco 769 (☎ 241093)
Germany
    Avenida El Bosque 0398 (☎ 212866)
Italy
    21 de Mayo 1569 (☎ 242497)
Netherlands
    Sarmiento 780 (☎ 248100)
Norway
    Avenida Independencia 830, 2nd floor
    (☎ 241437)
Spain
    José Menéndez 910 (☎ 243566)
UK
    Roca 924 (☎ 247020)

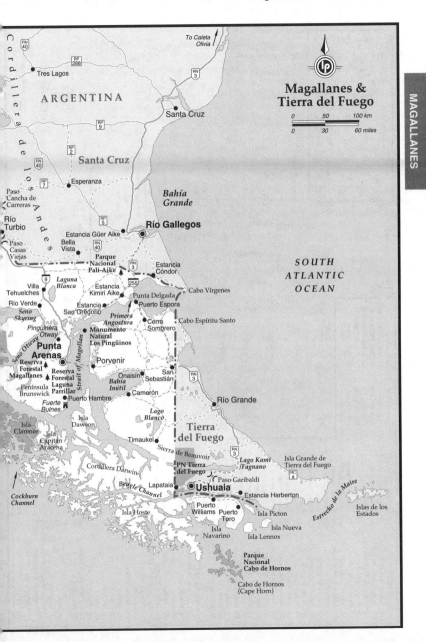

Magallanes &
Tierra del Fuego

| 0 | 50 | 100 km |
| 0 | 30 | 60 miles |

ARGENTINA

Cordillera de los Andes

RN 40

RP 288

Tres Lagos

To Caleta Olivia

RN 3

Santa Cruz

RP 9

Santa Cruz

RP 2

RN 40

RP 7

Esperanza

Bahía Grande

Paso Cancha de Carreras

Río Turbio

RP 5

Río Gallegos

Estancia Güer Aike

Bella Vista

RN 40

Paso Casas Viejas

Parque Nacional Pali-Aike

RN 3

Estancia Cóndor

SOUTH ATLANTIC OCEAN

9

Laguna Blanca

Villa Tehuelches

Estancia Kimiri Aike

255

Punta Delgada

Cabo Vírgenes

Río Verde

Estancia San Gregorio

Puerto Espora

Seno Skyring

Primera Angostura

Cabo Espíritu Santo

Pingüinera

Cerro Sombrero

Seno Otway

Punta Arenas

Monumento Natural Los Pingüinos

Reserva Forestal Magallanes

Reserva Forestal Laguna Parrillar

Porvenir

Strait of Magellan

Península Brunswick

Onaisin

San Sebastián

RN 3

Puerto Hambre

Bahía Inútil

Camerón

Río Grande

Fuerte Bulnes

Isla Clarence

Isla Dawson

Lago Blanco

Tierra del Fuego

Isla Capitán Aracena

Timaukel

Sierra de Beauvoir

RN 3

Cordillera Darwin

PN Tierra del Fuego

Lago Kami /Fagnano

Isla Grande de Tierra del Fuego

RC 8

Cockburn Channel

Beagle Channel

Lapataia

Paso Garibaldi

Ushuaia

Estancia Harberton

Estrecho de la Maire

Islas de los Estados

Isla Hoste

Puerto Williams

Puerto Toro

Isla Picton

Isla Nueva

Isla Navarino

Isla Lennox

Parque Nacional Cabo de Hornos

Cabo de Hornos (Cape Horn)

MAGALLANES

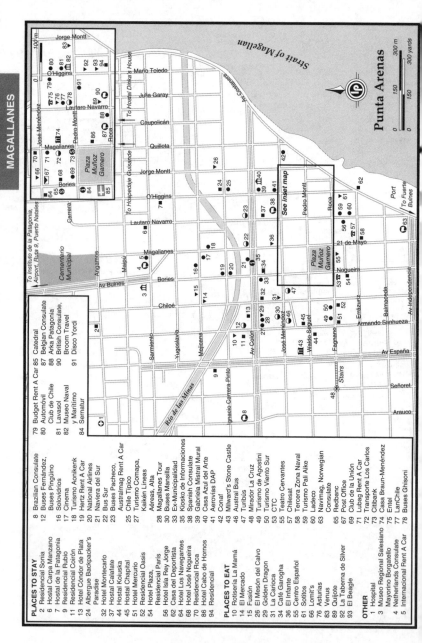

Punta Arenas

Strait of Magellan

PLACES TO STAY
2   Residencial Sonia
4   Hostal Carpa Manzano
6   Hostal Fernández,
    Buses Pingüino
7   Hostal de la Patagonia
9   Residencial Rubio
11 Residencial Coirón
13 Hotel Cóndor de Plata
19 Hotel Montecarlo
24 Albergue Backpacker's
    Paradise
32 Hotel Montecarlo
37 Hostal Calafate
44 Hostal Koluska
45 Hostal Chapital
51 Hotel Mercurio
52 Residencial Oasis
54 Hotel Plaza,
    Residencial París
56 Hotel Isla Rey Jorge
62 Casa del Deportista
64 Hotel Los Navegantes
68 Hotel José Nogueira
70 Residencial Roca
86 Hotel Cabo de Hornos
94 Residencial

PLACES TO EAT
10 Rotisería La Mamá
14 El Mercado
15 Fusión
26 El Mesón del Calvo
27 Golden Dragon
31 La Carioca
34 Café Garogha
36 El Infante
55 Centro Español
66 Lomit's
83 Asturias
89 Quijote
92 La Taberna de Silver
93 El Beagle

OTHER
1   Hospital
3   Museo Regional Salesiano
    Mayorino Borgatello
4   Netherlands Consulate
5   Internacional Rent A Car

8   Brazilian Consulate
12 Buses Fernández,
    Buses Pingüino
16 Solovidrios
17 Cinema
18 Turismo Aonikenk
20 National Airlines
21 Naviera del Sur
22 Bus Sur
23 Buses Pacheco,
    Australmag Rent A Car
25 Chile Típico
27 Turismo Comapa,
    Kaikén Líneas
    Aéreas, Alta
28 Magallanes Tour
30 Buses Mansilla
33 Ex-Municipalidad
35 Kiosko de Informaciones
38 Spanish Consulate
39 Gabriela Mistral Mural
40 Casa Azul del Arte
41 Aerovías DAP
42 Conaf
43 Milward's Stone Castle
46 Austral Bus
47 Turibús
48 Mirador La Cruz
49 Turismo de Agostini
50 Turismo Viento Sur
55 CTC
57 Teatro Cervantes
58 Tercera Zona Naval
59 Turismo Pali Aike
60 Ladeco
63 Navimag, Norwegian
    Consulate
65 Redbanc
67 Post Office
69 Club de la Unión
71 Lubag Rent A Car
72 Transporte Los Carlos
73 Citibank
74 Casa Braun-Menéndez
75 Entel
77 LanChile
78 Buses Ghisoni

79 Budget Rent A Car
80 Automóvil
    Club de Chile
81 Lavasol
82 Museo Naval
    y Marítimo
84 Sernatur
85 Catedral
87 Belgian Consulate
88 Arka Patagonia
90 British Consulate,
    Broom Travel
91 Disco Yordi

Money Money changing is easiest at cambios and travel agencies along Lautaro Navarro, which are open weekdays and Saturday mornings, but not Sundays. Travelers' checks are much easier to negotiate than in Argentina, but many hotels and restaurants also accept cash dollars, at a fair rate of exchange. Bus Sur, at Magallanes and Colón, will cash travelers' checks for Saturday afternoon arrivals.

Redbanc has an ATM at Bories 970, half a block north of the plaza, but there are several others in the area.

Post & Communications Punta Arenas' area code is ☎ 61. Correos de Chile is at Bories 911 near José Menéndez, a block north of Plaza Muñoz Gamero.

CTC has a long-distance office at Nogueira 1116, at the southwest corner of the plaza, while Chilesat has one at Errázuriz 856. Entel has an office at Lautaro Navarro 957.

Travel Agencies In addition to the agencies listed under Organized Tours below, try also Broom Travel (☎ 228312) at Roca 924 and Turismo de Agostini (☎ 221676) at Fagnano 518.

Cultural Centers The Casa Azul del Arte (☎ 223961), part of the municipal art school at Colón 1027, has exhibitions of painting and other media.

National Parks Conaf (☎ 223841) is at José Menéndez 1147.

Laundry Lavasol (☎ 243607), O'Higgins 969, isn't as cheap as it used to be, but service is still fast and efficient.

Film & Photography A good, conscientious place for film developing, including slides, is Todocolor, Chiloé 1422.

Medical Services The Hospital is at the corner of Angamos and Arauco.

Walking Tour
Punta Arenas is compact and the main sights can be seen quickly on foot. The logical starting place is the lovingly maintained **Plaza Muñoz Gamero**, landscaped with a variety of exotic conifers and an interesting Victorian kiosk (1910) that sometimes contains handicraft displays. In the plaza's center is a monument to the 400th anniversary of Magellan's voyage, donated by wool baron José Menéndez in 1920; Magellan stands on a pedestal, flanked on a lower level by a Selknam Indian symbolizing Tierra del Fuego and a Tehuelche symbolizing Patagonia. Behind the famous Portuguese navigator are a globe and a copy of his log; beneath him is a mermaid with Chilean and regional coats of arms.

Around the plaza are the **Club de la Unión** (once the Sara Braun mansion, built by a French architect and recently restored as a hotel/restaurant), the **Catedral** and other monuments to the city's turn-of-the-century splendor. At the northeast corner of the plaza, the present Citibank was the headquarters of the famous and powerful **Sociedad Explotadora del Tierra del Fuego.**

Half a block north, at Magallanes 949, is the spectacular **Casa Braun-Menéndez**, the famous family's mansion which is now a cultural center and regional history museum. Two blocks north, at the corner of Bories and Colón, the former **Municipalidad** is undergoing restoration and remodeling as a cultural center. Three blocks west of the plaza, the outlandish **stone castle** at Avenida España 959 belonged to Charly Milward, whose eccentric exploits inspired his distant relation Bruce Chatwin to write the extraordinary travelogue *In Patagonia*; it is not open to the public.

Four blocks south of the plaza, at the foot of Avenida Independencia, is the entrance to the **puerto** (port), which is open to the public. At the end of the pier, you may see ships and sailors from Spain, Poland, Japan, France, the USA and many other countries, as well as local fishing boats, the Chilean navy and countless seabirds to photograph. At the corner of Colón and O'Higgins, four blocks northwest of the plaza, is a very fine **mural** of Nobel Prize-winning poet Gabriela Mistral.

Six blocks north of the plaza, at Bories and Sarmiento, is the **Museo Salesiano**. Another four blocks north is the entrance to the **Cementerio Municipal**, an open-air historical museum in its own right.

Things to See

Most of the legacies of Punta Arenas' golden age are open to the public; those that are not museums rarely object to interested visitors taking a look around.

Casa Braun-Menéndez Also known as the Palacio Mauricio Braun, this opulent mansion testifies to the wealth and power of pioneer sheep farmers in the late 19th century. The last remaining daughter of the marriage between Mauricio Braun (brother of Sara Braun) and Josefina Menéndez Behety (daughter of José Menéndez and María Behety) is alive in her 90s in Buenos Aires, but the family has donated the house to the state. Much of it, including original furnishings, remains as it did when still occupied by the family. At present, only the main floor is open to the public, but restoration may permit access to the upper floors.

The museum also has excellent historical photographs and artifacts of early European settlement. Admission charges are modest (US$1.20), but there's an extra charge for photographing the interior. Hours are Tuesday to Sunday, 11 am to 4 pm. Access to the grounds is easiest from Magallanes, but the museum entrance is at the back of the house.

Museo Regional Salesiano Mayorino Borgatello The Salesian College Museum, at Avenida Bulnes 374 near Sarmiento, features anthropological, historical and natural history exhibits from materials collected by a missionary order which was especially influential in European settlement of the region. In summer, it is open Tuesday to Sunday 10 am to noon and from 3 to 6 pm; in winter, weekday hours are from 3 to 6 pm only, while weekend hours are identical to summer. Admission costs US$1.35.

Museo Naval y Marítimo Despite its overbearing military theme music and romantic view of Chile's presence in southern oceans, Punta Arenas' new naval and maritime museum has varied exhibits on model ships, naval history, the unprecedented visit of 27 US warships to Punta Arenas in 1908, material on the Canoe Indians of southern Patagonia, and a very fine account of the Chilean mission that rescued British explorer Sir Ernest Shackleton's crew from Antarctica (1916). The most imaginative exhibit is a ship's replica, complete with bridge, maps and charts, and radio room, that really gives the sense of being on board a naval vessel.

At Pedro Montt 981, the museum is open weekdays 9.30 am to 12.30 pm, Saturdays 10 am to 1 pm, and daily except Sunday 3 to 6 pm. Admission costs US$0.75.

Cementerio Municipal The walled municipal cemetery, at Avenida Bulnes 949, tells a great deal about the history and social structure of the region. The first families of Punta Arenas flaunted their wealth in death as in life – wool baron José Menéndez's extravagant tomb, according to Bruce Chatwin, is a scale replica of Rome's Vittorio Emmanuel monument – but the headstones among the topiary cypresses also tell the stories of Anglo, German, Scandinavian and Yugoslav immigrants who supported them with their labor. There is also a monument to the now nearly extinct Onas. Open daily, the cemetery is about a 15-minute walk from the plaza, but you can also take any taxi colectivo from the entrance of the Casa Braun-Menéndez on Magallanes.

Instituto de la Patagonia Part of the Universidad de Magallanes, the Patagonian Institute features an interesting collection of early farm and industrial machinery imported from Europe, a typical pioneer house and shearing shed (both reconstructed) and a wooden-wheeled trailer that served as shelter for shepherds. Visitors can wander among the outdoor exhibits at will, but ask the caretaker at the library for admission to the buildings.

The library also has a display of historical maps, and a series of historical and scientific publications for sale to the public. A rather overgrown botanical garden, a small zoo and experimental garden plots and greenhouses are also open to the public.

Admission costs US$1. Opening hours are weekdays, 9 am to 12.30 pm and 2.30 to 6.30 pm. Weekend visits may be possible by prior arrangement. Any taxi colectivo to the Zona Franca (the duty-free zone; see Things to Buy, below) will drop you across the street.

Organized Tours

Several agencies run trips to the important tourist sites near Punta Arenas, as well as to more distant destinations like Torres del Paine.

Turismo Pali Aike (☎/fax 223301), Lautaro Navarro 1129, goes to the Seno Otway penguin colony (US$12) daily at 3.30 pm, to Fuerte Bulnes (US$12) daily at 10 am, and to Río Verde (US$15); all their tours include sandwiches and soft drinks. Arka Patagonia (☎ 226370), Roca 886, Local 7, also runs trips for similar prices, as do Turismo Aonikenk (☎ 228332) at Magallanes 619 and Turismo Viento Sur (☎ 225167) at Fagnano 565. Most of these companies can now do both the Otway and Fuerte Bulnes trips in the same day.

From December to February, Turismo Comapa (☎ 224256, fax 225804), Colón 521, runs weekend day trips to the Isla Magdalena penguin colony on the 27-passenger launch *Antártica* for US$55. Total time on the island is less than two hours, since the crossing takes 2½ hours each way.

Naviera del Sur (☎ 220081), Avenida Colón 782, offers twice-weekly, two-day tours to the Ventisquero D'Agostini (Agostini glacier), through the fjords of Tierra del Fuego's Cordillera Darwin, for US$600 per person.

DAP Antarctica (☎ 223340), O'Higgins 891, organizes all-inclusive, four-day kayak trips to Parque Nacional Torres del Paine for US$1600.

Cruises

From November through April, Turismo Comapa (☎ 244448, fax 247514), Avenida Colón 521, runs week-long luxury cruises on the 100-passenger *Terra Australis* from Punta Arenas through the Cordillera Darwin and the Beagle Channel to Puerto Williams, Ushuaia and back. While these are expensive, starting at US$1022 per person, double occupancy, in low season (April) and reaching $3000 for a high-season single, all meals are included and they do offer a chance to visit parts of the region that are otherwise very difficult and even more expensive to reach independently. It may be possible to do just the leg between Punta Arenas and Ushuaia.

Special Events

One Lonely Planet reader endorses February's Yugoslavian folk festival, with music, dancing and 'all four food groups – fat, salt, carbos and alcohol.'

Places to Stay – bottom end

Prices for accommodations have risen recently, but there are still good values. Sernatur maintains a very complete list of accommodations and prices.

Camping *Camping Pudú*, at Km 10.5 north of town, has pleasant woodsy facilities, including barbecue pits and showers, but it's inconvenient for backpackers and expensive for single people at US$10 per site.

Hostels The cheapest accommodation in town is unquestionably the *Ejército de Salvación* (☎ 224039), Bellavista 577, six block south of Plaza Muñoz Gamero, for US$3 for foreigners only. At recommended *Casa del Deportista*, at O'Higgins 1205 near the port, rates are US$6 per person for a shared room in summer only; they occasionally have private rooms for couples. Open November through March, the *Albergue Backpacker's Paradise* (☎ 222554), Ignacio Carrera Pinto 1022, charges US$6 for dark and cramped dormitory quarters, but there are pleasant common rooms, a kitchen and cable TV.

Relocated at Bellavista 697, six blocks

south of Plaza Muñoz Gamero, after a fire destroyed its previous site, the *Colegio Pierre Fauré* (☎ 226256) is a private school that functions as a hostel in January and February; it may be able to accommodate visitors in other seasons. Singles cost US$7 with breakfast, US$6 without, but campers can also pitch a tent in the garden for US$4 per person. All bathrooms are shared, but there's plenty of hot water, and it's a good place to meet other travelers.

The regular *Albergue Juvenil* (☎ 226-705), Ovejero 265, is much less central, northeast of the cemetery; rates are US$8 per night. The local affiliate of Hostelling International, *Residencial Sonia* (☎ 248-543) at Pasaje Darwin 175, about 10 blocks northeast of the plaza, charges US$10 with hostel card.

Hospedajes Newly popular *Hostal Dinka's House* (☎ 226056, fax 244292), on a quiet street at Caupolicán 169, costs only US$7.50 with breakfast, but it's often full. There are inexpensive hospedajes in the port zone south of downtown, including the *Casa de Familia* (☎ 247687) at Paraguaya 150 for US$9 with breakfast, and *Hospedaje Nena* (☎ 242411), Boliviana 366. Homey *Hospedaje Guisande* (☎ 243295), at JM Carrera 1270 near the cemetery, has earned exuberant recommendations for US$8 with breakfast, US$13 with breakfast and dinner.

Hotels & Residenciales Perennial favorite *Residencial Roca* (☎ 243903) has moved to new quarters at Magallanes 888, 2nd floor; singles cost US$11 with breakfast and shared bath. Its former site, at Roca 1038, is now an anonymous *Residencial* (☎ 244259) in a well-heated but leaky building. A single bed in a six-bed room costs US$10 without breakfast, while a private single costs US$13 when available. Other modest and modestly priced alternatives include *Residencial Oasis* (☎ 223-240), at Fagnano 583 for about US$13, and the slightly dearer *Residencial Sonia* (☎ 248543) at Pasaje Darwin 175 (cheaper for Hostelling International members).

Across from the Fernández bus terminal, friendly *Residencial Coirón* (☎ 226449), Sanhueza 730, has spacious, sunny singles for US$13 with breakfast. Recommended *Hostal Calafate* (☎ 248415), Lautaro Navarro 850, charges US$15 per person with a substantial breakfast.

Residencial Rubio (☎ 226458), Avenida España 640, is good value at US$15/21 single/double with shared bath, US$25/40 with private bath, both with breakfast. *Residencial Par's* (☎ 223112), 4th floor, Nogueira 1116, half a block from Plaza Muñoz Gamero, costs US$18/30, while aging but spacious *Hotel Montecarlo* (☎ 223438), Avenida Colón 605, charges US$17/29 with shared bath, US$31/44 with private bath. Recommended *Hostal Koiuska* (☎ 228520, fax 228620), Waldo Seguel 480, charges US$20 per person for clean rooms with shared bath and a good breakfast.

Places to Stay – middle
Probably the best mid-range value is *Hostal Chapital* (☎ 225698), Armando Sanhueza 974, which charges US$24/31 with shared bath, US$45 double with private bath. At reader-endorsed *Hostal de la Patagonia* (☎ 241079), O'Higgins 478, rates are US$36/40 with shared bath, US$45/53 with private bath. *Hostal Carpa Manzano* (☎ 242296, fax 248864), Lautaro Navarro 336, is also worth a try for US$45/56.

Comfortably modern *Hotel Cóndor de Plata* (☎ 247987, fax 241149), Avenida Colón 556, costs US$45/57 – better value than others charging considerably more. *Hotel Mercurio* (☎ 223430), Fagnano 595, is also modern, clean and comfortable at US$49/62 with breakfast. Convenient *Hotel Plaza* (☎ 241300, fax 248613), one floor below Residencial Par's, at Nogueira 1116, charges US$49/61.

Places to Stay – top end
Once the best in town, the declining *Hotel Los Navegantes* (☎ 244677, fax 244-575), José Menéndez 647, has rooms for US$90/114. A new top-end choice is *Hotel*

Isla Rey Jorge (☎/fax 222681), 21 de Mayo 1243, for US$95/118.

The slightly more central, recently refurbished *Hotel Cabo de Hornos* (☎/fax 242134), on the east side of Plaza Muñoz Gamero, charges US$125/145. The latter has a good but costly bar, and its solarium displays a number of stuffed birds, including rockhopper and macaroni penguins, which visitors to local penguin colonies are unlikely to see.

Part of the Sara Braun mansion has become *Hotel José Nogueira* (☎ 248840, fax 248832), half a block from Plaza Muñoz Gamero at Bories 959. Rooms cost US$137/164, but selective backpackers can enjoy a drink or a meal in its conservatory/ restaurant, beneath what may well be the world's most southerly grape arbor.

Places to Eat

Fusión (☎ 224704), Mejicana 654, offers a very good fixed-price lunch for US$4, if you can tolerate the appalling music. *Quijote*, Lautaro Navarro 1087, also has reasonable lunches. *La Carioca* (☎ 224-809), José Menéndez 600, has good sandwiches and lager beer, although its pizzas are small and expensive. *Rotisería La Mamá* (☎ 225812), across from the Fernández bus terminal at Sanhueza 720, is a small family-run place with excellent, moderately priced lunches.

A good choice for breakfast, onces and people-watching is *Café Garogha* (☎ 241-782), Bories 817. Their 'selva negra' chocolate cake is a portion large enough for two, as are their sandwiches. *Lomit's* (☎ 243399), José Menéndez 722, also serves excellent sandwiches.

A local institution at Mejicana 617 (the ground-level entrance to this upstairs restaurant is inconspicuous), *El Mercado* (☎ 247415) prepares a spicy ostiones al pil pil and a delicate but filling chupe de locos (abalone stew); prices are generally moderate. It's also open 24 hours, but adds a 10% surcharge between 1 and 8 am.

The *Centro Español* (☎ 242807), above the Teatro Cervantes on the south side of Plaza Muñoz Gamero, serves delicious congrio (eel) and ostiones (scallops), among other specialties. *Golden Dragon* (☎ 241119), a Chinese restaurant at Colón 529, is also very good.

Highly regarded *Sotitos* (☎ 245365), O'Higgins 1138, serves outstanding if pricey dishes like centolla (king crab), but there are also more reasonably priced items on the menu. The same holds for nearby *El Beagle* (☎ 243057), O'Higgins 1077. Prices are moderate at *La Taberna de Silver* (☎ 225533), O'Higgins 1037, but its fish is often deep-fried. Another recommendation, specializing in lamb, is *El Mesón del Calvo* (☎ 225015) at Jorge Montt 687, but the food sometimes lags behind the atmosphere.

Asturias (☎ 243763), Lautaro Navarro 967, is worth a try at the upper end of the scale, as is *El Infante* (☎ 241331) at Magallanes 875. Recent readers' recommendations include *Venus* (☎ 241681), Pedro Montt 1046, and *Monaco* on Nogueira near the post office.

Entertainment

Since the end of the military dictatorship, which regularly enforced a curfew, Chilean nightlife is more exuberant. Café Garogha has a lively crowd late into the evening, and sometimes has live entertainment. Disco Yordi is on Pedro Montt between O'Higgins and Lautaro Navarro.

Two central cinemas often show North American and European films: Teatro Cervantes (☎ 223225) is on the south side of Plaza Muñoz Gamero, while the Cinema is at Mejicana 777.

On the outskirts of downtown, on Avenida Bulnes, are the Club Hípico (municipal racetrack) and the Estadio Fiscal (stadium), where the local entry in the Chilean soccer league plays.

Things to Buy

Punta Arenas' Zona Franca (duty-free zone) is a good place to replace a lost or stolen camera, and to buy film and other luxury items. Fujichrome slide film, 36 exposures, costs about US$5 per roll without developing, though it's increasingly difficult to find; print film is correspondingly cheap. Taxi colectivos from downtown to the Zona Franca, on Avenida Bulnes, opposite the Instituto de la Patagonia, which is open daily except Sunday, are frequent.

Chile Típico (☎ 225827), Ignacio Carrera Pinto 1015, offers artisanal items in copper, bronze, lapis lazuli and other materials.

Motorists can replace a shattered windshield – not an unusual occurrence on Patagonian roads – at Solovidrios (☎ 224-835), Mejicana 762. Prices here are a fraction of what they are in Argentina.

Getting There & Away

The Punta Arenas tourist office distributes a useful brochure with complete information on all forms of transportation and their schedules to and from Punta Arenas, Puerto Natales and Tierra del Fuego, including those that go to or through Argentina. Note that discount airfares are available from the major airlines between Punta Arenas and mainland Chile, but usually involve some restrictions.

Air From Punta Arenas, there are flights to domestic destinations, including Chilean bases in the Antarctic, and to Argentine Patagonia and the Falkland Islands.

LanChile (☎ 241232), Lautaro Navarro 999, flies daily to Puerto Montt (US$178) and Santiago (US$292) except for Sunday, when there are two flights; there are also flights Tuesday and Thursday to Concepción and Santiago. Ladeco (☎ 244544, 421100), Lautaro Navarro 1155, flies daily to Puerto Montt and Santiago, Saturdays to Concepción (US$249) and Santiago.

National Airlines (☎ 221636, fax 223-877), at Bories and Ignacio Carrera Pinto, flies Monday through Thursday to Puerto Montt (US$160) and Santiago (US$263), Friday and Sunday to Puerto Montt, Concepción (US$224) and Santiago, and Saturday to Puerto Montt, Temuco (US$212) and Santiago.

Alta (☎ 241322, fax 221362), Avenida Colón 521, flies weekdays to Puerto Natales (US$32), Balmaceda (US$97), Puerto

Montt (US$185), Temuco (US$229) and Concepción (US$255).

Aerovías DAP (☎ 223340, fax 221693), O'Higgins 891, flies to Porvenir (US$22) and back at least twice daily except Sunday. Monday, Wednesday and Friday, it flies to and from Puerto Williams, on Isla Navarino (US$66 one way). It also has Monday, Wednesday and Friday flights to Ushuaia, Argentina (US$69) and daily except Sunday to Río Grande, Argentina (US$58).

DAP's Thursday and Saturday flights between Santiago and the Falkland Islands stop in Punta Arenas; the fare from Punta Arenas to the Falklands' Mount Pleasant International Airport is US$210 one way. DAP flights to Santiago are more expensive than competing airlines. DAP also flies monthly to Chile's Teniente Marsh air base in Antarctica for US$1000 one way. The schedule permits one or two nights in Antarctica before returning to Punta Arenas.

Kaikén Líneas Aéreas (☎ 227061), Colón 521, flies daily except Sunday to Río Grande (US$69) and nine times weekly to Ushuaia (US$78).

Bus Punta Arenas has no central bus terminal; each company has its own office from which its buses depart, although most of these are clustered together, on or near Lautaro Navarro. There are direct buses to Puerto Natales, Río Grande and Río Gallegos in Argentina, and to mainland Chilean destinations via Argentina. It makes sense to purchase tickets at least a couple hours in advance.

Buses Fernández (☎ 242313), Armando Sanhueza 745, has five buses daily except Sunday to Puerto Natales (US$7), and has a reputation for excellent service. Bus Sur (☎ 244464), at Magallanes and Colón, has three buses daily to Puerto Natales except Sunday, when it has only two.

Austral Bus (☎ 241708), José Menéndez 565, has buses at 2 and 6 pm to Puerto Natales, and also goes Tuesdays to Puerto Montt (US$97). Buses Ghisoni (☎ 223-205), Lautaro Navarro 971, goes Wednesday and Saturday to Puerto Montt (US$70).

Turibús (☎ 241463), José Menéndez 647, goes Wednesday and Saturday to Puerto Montt (US$75), Castro (US$85), Concepción (US$95) and Santiago (US$100). These trips take up to two days, but the buses are very comfortable, with regular meal stops.

There are numerous services to Río Gallegos, Argentina (US$13 to US$18, five hours; note that the fare in the opposite direction exceeds US$20). The most frequent is Buses Pingüino (☎ 221812, 242313), Armando Sanhueza 745, daily at noon. Buses Ghisoni, Buses Mansilla (☎ 221516) at José Menéndez 556, and Magallanes Tour (☎ 221936) at Colón 521 also have several departures.

Buses Pacheco (☎ 242174), Avenida Colón 900, goes Monday, Wednesday and Friday at 7 am to Río Grande (US$25), in Argentine Tierra del Fuego, with connections to Ushuaia. Tuesday and Saturday at 7 am, Transporte Los Carlos (☎ 241321), Magallanes 974, goes to Río Grande (US$26) and continues directly to Ushuaia (US$46).

Boat Transbordador Austral Broom (☎ 218100), Avenida Bulnes 05075, ferries passengers (US$6) and automobiles (US$35) between Punta Arenas and Porvenir, Tierra del Fuego, in 2½ hours; the *Melinka* sails Tuesday through Saturday at 9 am, Sunday at 9.30 am from the terminal at Tres Puentes, readily accessible by taxi colectivo from the Braun-Menéndez house. The return from Porvenir is normally at 2 pm, but on Sundays and holidays, when the ferry returns at 5 pm, it's possible to do this as a day trip.

Transaustral Limitada (☎ 212836) sails monthly to Puerto Williams, on Isla Navarino, usually the second week of the month. The 30-hour trip costs US$200.

Offering ferry service from Puerto Natales to Puerto Montt via the spectacular Chilean fjords, Navimag (☎ 224256, fax 225804) has an office at Avenida Independencia 830. For schedule and fare information, see the Puerto Natales entry below.

Getting Around
To/From the Airport Aeropuerto Presidente Carlos Ibáñez del Campo is 20 km north of town. Austral Bus runs minibuses to the airport from Hotel Cabo de Hornos, on Plaza Muñoz Gamero. DAP runs its own bus to the airport, while Lan-Chile and Ladeco use local bus companies (US$1.25).

Bus & Colectivo Although most places of interest are within easy walking distance of downtown, public transportation is excellent to outlying sights like the Instituto de la Patagonia and the Zona Franca. Taxi colectivos, with numbered routes, are only slightly more expensive than buses (about US$0.30, a bit more late at night and on Sundays), much more comfortable, and much quicker.

Car Rental Hertz (☎ 248742, fax 244729) is at Ignacio Carrera Pinto 700, Budget (☎ 241696) is at O'Higgins 964, and the Automóvil Club de Chile (☎ 243675, fax 243097) is at O'Higgins 931. Other agencies include Internacional (☎ 228323, fax 248865) at Sarmiento 790-B, Australmag (☎ 242174, fax 226916) at Avenida Colón 900, and Lubag (☎ 242023, fax 214136) at Magallanes 970.

AROUND PUNTA ARENAS
Puerto Hambre & Fuerte Bulnes
Founded in 1584 by an overly optimistic Pedro Sarmiento de Gamboa, 'Ciudad del Rey don Felipe' was one of Spain's most inauspicious (and short-lived) American outposts. It still preserves ruins of an early church. Not until the mid-19th century was there a permanent European presence at suitably renamed Puerto Hambre ('Port Famine'), where a plaque commemorates the 125th anniversary of the arrival of the Pacific Steam Navigation Company's ships *Chile* and *Peru* in 1965.

Named for the Chilean president who ordered the occupation of the territory in 1843, the once-remote outpost of Fuerte Bulnes is 55 km south of Punta Arenas. Only a few years after its founding, it was

MAGALLANES

abandoned because of its exposed site, lack of potable water, poor, rocky soil and inferior pasture.

A good gravel road runs from Punta Arenas to the restored wooden fort, where a fence of sharpened stakes surrounds the blockhouse, barracks and chapel, but there is no interpretive material whatsoever. Nor is there any scheduled public transport, but several travel agencies make half-day excursions to Puerto Hambre, now a quiet fishing village, and Fuerte Bulnes; for details, see the Organized Tours entry for Punta Arenas, above. There are good picnic sites and pleasant walks along the coast.

Penguin Colonies

Also known as the jackass penguin for its characteristic braying sound, the Magellanic penguin *(Spheniscus magellanicus)* comes ashore in spring to breed and lay its eggs in sandy burrows or under shrubs a short distance inland. There are two substantial colonies near Punta Arenas. Easier to reach is the mainland pingüinera on **Seno Otway**, about an hour northwest of the city, while the larger and more interesting **Monumento Natural Los Pingüinos** is accessible only by boat to Isla Magdalena or Isla Marta in the Straits. Several cormorant and gull species are also common, along with rheas and southern sea lions.

Magellanic penguins are naturally curious and tame, though if approached too quickly they scamper into their burrows or toboggan awkwardly across the sand back into the water. If approached too closely, they will bite, and their bills can open a cut large enough to require stitches – never stick your hand or face into a burrow. The least disruptive way to observe or photograph them is to seat yourself among the burrows and wait for their curiosity to get the better of them. At Seno Otway, the grounds are fenced to prevent visitors from too close an encounter; a morning tour would be better for photography because the birds are mostly backlit in the afternoon.

Penguins are generally present from October to April, but the peak season is December through February. Visitors who have seen the larger penguin colonies in Argentina or the Falkland Islands may find Punta Arenas-based tours less worthwhile than those who have not seen penguins elsewhere.

Since there is no scheduled public transport to either site, it's necessary to rent a car or take a tour to visit them. For details, see the Organized Tours and Getting There & Away entries for Punta Arenas. Admission to the sites costs US$4 per person. There's a small snack bar at the Otway site.

Río Verde

About 50 km north of Punta Arenas, a graveled lateral leads northwest toward Seno Skyring (Skyring Sound), passing this former estancia before rejoining Ruta 9 at Villa Tehuelches. Visitors with their own car (or a rental) should consider this interesting detour to one of the best-maintained collections of Magellanic architecture in the region, which includes the impressive **Escuela Básica**, a boarding school for the surrounding area, and the shearing shed of Estancia La Mirna. The school's simple **Museo de Fauna** charges US$0.50 admission. Note the town's topiary cypresses.

Six km south of Río Verde proper, *Hostería Río Verde* (☎ 311122) is well-known for large portions of lamb, pork or seafood at its Sunday lunches, for about US$10. It's 90 km north of Punta Arenas. Despite the rustic exterior, it also offers cozy, comfortable accommodation for US$25 with private bath.

Estancia San Gregorio

Some 125 km northeast of Punta Arenas, straddling Ruta 255 to Río Gallegos, Argentina, this once enormous (90,000 hectares) estancia is now a cooperative. Since the abandonment of most of the main buildings (employee residences, warehouses, chapel and pulpería), it has the aspect of an enormous ghost town. The casco still belongs to a descendent of the famous and influential Menéndez family, but the cooperative uses the large shearing shed.

The nearest accommodation is *Hostería Tehuelche* (☎ 221270), 29 km northeast, where buses to and from Río Gallegos stop for lunch or dinner; this is also the junction for the road to the ferry that crosses the Strait of Magellan from Punta Delgada to Chilean Tierra del Fuego. Until 1968, the hostería was the casco for Estancia Kimiri Aike, pioneered by the Woods, a British immigrant family. It has clean, comfortable rooms for US$25/33 single/double, and a good restaurant and bar. Hotel staff will change US$ at fair rates, but Argentine currency is better changed before leaving Río Gallegos.

PARQUE NACIONAL PALI AIKE
Along the Argentine border, west of the Monte Aymond border crossing to Río Gallegos, this 5000-hectare park is an area of volcanic steppe where, in the 1930s, excavations at **Pali Aike Cave** yielded the first Paleo-Indian artifacts associated with extinct New World fauna like the milodon and the native horse *Onohippidium*. Junius Bird, a self-taught archaeologist affiliated with the American Museum of Natural History, spent 2½ years in research in the area. He also excavated **Fell's Cave**, just outside the park boundaries, where recent research has suggested that environmental change rather than hunting pressure led to these extinctions.

Parque Nacional Pali Aike is 196 km northeast of Punta Arenas via Chile 9, Chile 255, and a graveled secondary road from Punta Delgada, 11 km north of Estancia Kimiri Aike. There is no public transport, but Punta Arenas travel agencies can arrange tours.

PUERTO NATALES
Black-necked swans still paddle serenely around the gulls and cormorants that perch on the rotting jetties of scenic Puerto Natales, on the eastern shore of Seno Ultima Esperanza (Last Hope Sound), but the proliferation of traffic lights is an indicator of its increasing economic importance. Traditionally dependent on wool, mutton and fishing, this port of 18,000

people is the southern terminus of the scenic ferry from Puerto Montt and an essential stopover for hikers and other visitors en route to Parque Nacional Torres del Paine.

Puerto Natales also offers the best access to Parque Nacional Bernardo O'Higgins and to the famous Cueva del Milodón, and many travelers continue to Argentina's Parque Nacional Los Glaciares via the coal-mining town of Río Turbio. The visitor season starts in October and runs until April, though the peak is January and February. The rest of the year, access to attractions like Torres del Paine and the Balmaceda glacier may be much reduced.

History
The first Europeans to visit Ultima Esperanza were the 16th-century Spaniards Juan Ladrillero and Pedro Sarmiento de Gamboa, in search of a route to the Pacific, but their expeditions left no pérmanent legacy. In part because of Indian resistance, no Europeans located here until the late 19th century, when German explorer Hermann Eberhard established a sheep estancia near Puerto Prat, the area's initial settlement, later superseded by Puerto Natales.

The dominant economic enterprise was the slaughterhouse and meat packing plant at Bories, operated by the Sociedad Explotadora de Tierra del Fuego, which drew livestock from throughout southwestern Argentina as well. This factory still operates, although it has declined in importance.

Orientation
About 250 km northwest of Punta Arenas via half-paved Ruta 9, Puerto Natales itself is compact enough that walking suffices for most purposes. Although its grid is more irregular than many Chilean cities, most destinations are easily visible from the waterfront, where the Costanera Pedro Montt runs roughly north-south. The other main commercial streets are the east-west Avenida Bulnes and the north-south Avenida Baquedano. Bories and the Cueva del Milodón are north of town on the graveled highway to Torres del Paine.

Information

Tourist Office Sernatur (☎ 412125), which has maps and information about hotels, restaurants and transportation, occupies a chalet on the Costanera Pedro Montt at the intersection with the Philippi diagonal. Its hours are 8.30 am to 1 pm and 2.30 to 6.30 pm weekdays all year, 9 am to 1 pm weekends in summer (December to March) only.

Money Stop Cambios, Baquedano 380, will change US cash and travelers' checks. There are no ATMs, but Banco Santiago at Bulnes 637 will make cash advances on MasterCard.

Post & Communications Puerto Natales' area code is ☎ 61, the same as Punta Arenas'. Correos de Chile is directly on the Plaza de Armas at Eberhard 423, near Tomás Rogers; it also contains the offices of Telex Chile. CTC, Blanco Encalada 298, operates long-distance services 8 am to 10 pm daily.

Travel Agencies Turis-Ann (☎ 411141) is at Esmeralda 556; see also the Organized Tours entry below.

National Parks Conaf (☎ 411438) is at Ignacio Carrera Pinto 566.

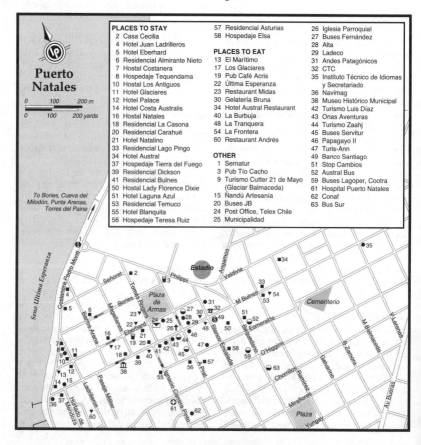

Puerto Natales

0   100   200 m
0   100   200 yards

To Bories, Cueva del Milodón, Punta Arenas, Torres del Paine

PLACES TO STAY
2 Casa Cecilia
4 Hotel Juan Ladrilleros
5 Hotel Eberhard
6 Residencial Almirante Nieto
7 Hostal Costanera
8 Hospedaje Tequendama
10 Hostal Los Antiguos
11 Hotel Glaciares
12 Hotel Palace
14 Hotel Costa Australis
16 Hostal Natales
18 Residencial La Casona
20 Residencial Carahué
21 Hotel Natalino
33 Residencial Lago Pingo
34 Hotel Austral
37 Hospedaje Tierra del Fuego
39 Residencial Dickson
41 Residencial Bulnes
50 Hostal Lady Florence Dixie
51 Hotel Laguna Azul
53 Residencial Temuco
55 Hotel Blanquita
56 Hospedaje Teresa Ruiz
57 Residencial Asturias
58 Hospedaje Elsa

PLACES TO EAT
13 El Marítimo
17 Los Glaciares
19 Pub Café Acris
22 Última Esperanza
23 Restaurant Midas
30 Gelatería Bruna
34 Hotel Austral Restaurant
40 La Burbuja
48 La Tranquera
54 La Frontera
60 Restaurant Andrés

OTHER
1 Sernatur
3 Pub Tío Cacho
9 Turismo Cutter 21 de Mayo
   (Glaciar Balmaceda)
15 Ñandú Artesanía
20 Buses JB
24 Post Office, Telex Chile
25 Municipalidad
26 Iglesia Parroquial
27 Buses Fernández
28 Alta
29 Ladeco
31 Andes Patagónicos
32 CTC
35 Instituto Técnico de Idiomas
   y Secretariado
36 Navimag
38 Museo Histórico Municipal
42 Turismo Luis Díaz
43 Onas Aventuras
44 Turismo Zaahj
45 Buses Servitur
46 Papagayo II
47 Turis-Ann
49 Banco Santiago
51 Stop Cambios
52 Austral Bus
59 Buses Lagoper, Cootra
61 Hospital Puerto Natales
62 Conaf
63 Bus Sur

Laundry Papagayo II, Bulnes 513, offers a 10% discount for loads prior to 10 am.

Medical Services Hospital Puerto Natales (☎ 411533) is at the corner of O'Higgins and Ignacio Carrera Pinto.

Museo Histórico Municipal
Puerto Natales' modest municipal museum has natural history items comprised mostly of stuffed animals, archaeological artifacts including arrowheads and spearpoints of both stone and whalebone, ethnographic materials like a Yahgan canoe and Tehuelche bolas, and historical photographs of Captain Eberhard and Puerto Natales' urban development. At Bulnes 285, it's open Tuesday to Sunday, 3 to 6.15 pm.

Language School
The Instituto Técnico de Idiomas y Secretariado, Bulnes 1231, offers intensive Spanish courses, with four hours daily instruction.

Organized Tours
Puerto Natales' many travel agencies offer visits to the main local attractions like Puerto Bories, the Cueva del Milodón and Torres del Paine. English-speaking Eduardo Scott at Hotel Austral (see below) can take eight to 10 passengers to Torres del Paine and other destinations in his minibus. Andes Patagónicos (☎ /fax 411-594), Blanco Encalada 226, has similar services and is a good place to confirm airline reservations.

Turismo Luis Díaz (☎/fax 412185), at Bulnes 433, runs one- and two-day tours to Torres del Paine, and also goes to Cueva del Milodón and to Argentina's Parque Nacional Los Glaciares.

Onas Aventuras (☎ 412707, fax 411938), Bulnes 453, rents camping equipment and also does sea kayaking and trekking trips. Both Andes Patagónicos and Turismo Díaz also rent camping equipment.

Places to Stay – bottom end
Puerto Natales is popular with budget travelers, but competition keeps prices reasonable. When your bus arrives, you may be buried in business cards or slips of paper offering bottom-end accommodations, most of which include breakfast. Quality is usually good and often excellent.

Prices start around US$6 per person with breakfast at *Residencial Asturias* (☎ 412-105), Prat 426, and *Residencial Dickson* (☎ 411218), Bulnes 307. Convenient to the ferry, *Hospedaje Tierra del Fuego* (☎ 412-138), Avenida Bulnes 29, charges US$7.50 with breakfast and shared bath, as do *Residencial Lago Pingo* (☎ 411026), Bulnes 808, and enthusiastically recommended *Hospedaje Teresa Ruiz*, Esmeralda 463.

A bit more expensive, about US$9 per person with breakfast and hot showers, is recommended *Hospedaje Elsa* (☎/fax 411807), Blanco Encalada 432. Comparably priced *Hospedaje Tequendama* (☎ 411-420), Ladrilleros 141, is very obliging and serves a good breakfast, but rooms are basic and some are very dark for US$9. For the same price, Swiss-run *Casa Cecilia* (☎ 411797), Tomás Rogers 64, has delicious breakfasts with fresh bread and sweets, though some rooms are small. It also runs a cheaper nearby annex during summer.

In the same range are recommended *Residencial Almirante Nieto* (☎ 411218) at Bories 206, attractive *Residencial La Casona* (☎ 412562) at Bulnes 280, *Residencial Temuco* (☎ 411120) at Ramírez 310, and *Residencial Carahué* (☎ 411339) at Bulnes 370. For about US$10/18, *Hostal Costanera* (☎ 411273), Ladrilleros 105, is a lesser value with music in every room – whether or not you want it.

Places to Stay – middle
Slightly dearer, around US$14 per person, is *Residencial La Bahía* (☎ 411297) at Serrano 434 (three blocks south of Yungay), which also has a superb restaurant. A traditional mid-range choice is Eduardo Scott's *Hotel Austral* (☎ 411593), Valdivia 955; rooms with shared bath cost US$15/20, while those with private bath are US$20/25. More businesslike than friendly, well-kept *Hostal Los Antiguos*

(☎ 411885), at Ladrilleros 195, charges US$16 single.

Hostal Natales (☎ 411098), Eberhard 250, charges US$19/27 with private bath. At recommended *Hotel Natalino* (☎ 411-968), Eberhard 371, rooms with shared bath cost US$18/25, while those with private bath are US$30/38. *Residencial Bulnes* (☎ 411307), Bulnes 407, charges US$19/27 with shared bath, US$25/37 with private bath. *Hotel Blanquita* (☎ 411-874), Ignacio Carrera Pinto 409, charges US$30/38 with private bath. At the upper end of the range are the *Hotel Laguna Azul* (☎/fax 411207), Baquedano 380, which costs US$45/55, and the new and attractive *Hostal Lady Florence Dixie* (☎ 411158, fax 411943), set back from the street at Bulnes 659, for US$45/60.

Places to Stay – top end
Top-end rates start around US$65/75 at the stylishly new *Hotel Glaciares* (☎ /fax 412189), Eberhard 104. Clearly showing its age is the well-worn *Hotel Palace* (☎ /fax 411134) at Ladrilleros 209, which costs US$73/88, while rooms at the comparable *Hotel Juan Ladrilleros* (☎ 411652) at Pedro Montt 161 go for US$75/87. For US$72/88, the waterfront *Hotel Eberhard* (☎ 411208, fax 411209), Costanera Pedro Montt 25 at Señoret, is now badly overpriced despite an excellent dining room with panoramic harbor views.

Unfortunately, fast-growing Puerto Natales is presently pouring raw sewage into the sound, directly across from the otherwise sparkling new and attractive *Hotel Costa Australis* (☎ 412000), at the corner of the Costanera Pedro Montt and Manuel Bulnes. Room rates start at US$100/110 with a town view, rising to US$120/130 with harbor view; suites cost US$240/250. Note that these prices do not include 20% IVA, so pay in dollars.

Places to Eat
For a small provincial town, Puerto Natales has excellent restaurants, specializing in good and reasonably priced seafood. Highly recommended *La Frontera*, Bulnes 819, has superb home-cooked meals for only US$4, but the service can be a bit absentminded. Popular *El Marítimo*, a moderately priced seafood restaurant at Costanera Pedro Montt 214, corner of Eberhard, is deservedly doing excellent business.

Equally popular *La Tranquera* (☎ 411-039), Bulnes 579, has good food, friendly service, reasonable prices and one of the continent's most hilariously mistranslated English language menus – where else can you get 'poor eel' and 'Chicken in a gas cooker'? Another good, popular and lively place is *Restaurant Midas* (☎ 411-606), on the Plaza de Armas at Tomás Rogers 169. Only a handful of foreigners patronize the excellent *Ultima Esperanza* (☎ 411391), Eberhard 354, which has huge portions (salmon is a specialty) and fine service and is less expensive than it looks.

A new addition to the scene is *Restaurant Andrés* (☎ 412380), Ladrilleros 381, whose hard-working owner literally keeps it open 24 hours. Other good choices include *La Burbuja* (☎ 411605) at Bulnes 371 and *Los Glaciares* on Eberhard between Barros Arana and Magallanes.

Hotel Austral has a good restaurant (despite serving a steady diet of salmon), while the huge dining room at unpretentious *Residencial La Bahía* (☎ 411-297), Serrano 434, can accommodate large groups for a superb curanto, with sufficient notice. It's less central than most other restaurants in town, but still reasonable walking distance.

Pub Café Acris (☎ 412710), Eberhard 351, serves excellent pizza, but the tobacco-laden atmosphere may deter some diners. Rhubarb-flavored ice cream is a local specialty at *Gelatería Bruna* (☎ 411656), Bulnes 584.

Entertainment
In addition to good food, *Pub Café Acris* (☎ 412710), Eberhard 351, offers live music on weekends. Another pub worth a visit is *Pub Tío Cacho* (☎ 411021), Philippi 553.

Things to Buy

At Manuel Bulnes 44, Ñandú Artesanía has a small but good selection of crafts, and also sells local maps and books.

Getting There & Away

Air Puerto Natales now has regular air service with Alta (☎ /fax 411847), Prat 236, which flies daily except Tuesday to Punta Arenas (US$32) southbound and to Balmaceda/Coihaique (US$75), Puerto Montt (US$140), Temuco (US$223) and Concepción (US$255) northbound. The small airfield, a few km north of town on the road to Torres del Paine, is easily reached by taxi.

As of writing, the local Ladeco office (☎ 411236) at Bulnes 530 was due to move to Tomás Rogers and Bories. Andes Patagónicos, Blanco Encalada 226, has a computerized airline information service for reservations and information on other airlines, such as LanChile and DAP. Buses from Puerto Natales will drop passengers at Punta Arenas' Aeropuerto Presidente Carlos Ibáñez del Campo.

LADE, the Argentine air force passenger service, has flights to nearby Río Turbio, just across the border.

Bus Puerto Natales has no central bus terminal, though several companies stop at the junction of Valdivia and Baquedano. To Punta Arenas (US$7), Buses Fernández (☎ 411111) at Eberhard 555 and Bus Sur (☎ 411325) at Baquedano 534 provide eight buses daily except Sunday, when there are only four. Austral Bus (☎ 411859), Baquedano 384, goes twice daily to Punta Arenas.

In summer, Bus Sur also goes daily to Parque Nacional Torres del Paine (US$7 one way; it's slightly cheaper to buy a roundtrip ticket), weekdays to Río Turbio (US$4) and Tuesday and Thursday to Río Gallegos, Argentina (US$19). El Pingüino goes Wednesday and Sunday at noon to Río Gallegos (US$18). Turismo Zaahj (☎ 412-260), Bulnes 459, runs buses to El Calafate, Argentina (5½ hours, US$30), in summer only, Monday, Wednesday and Friday at 10 am, and does a long one-day tour to the Moreno glacier (US$60). These services are increasing since the improvement of Ruta Nacional 40 on the Argentine side.

Servitur (☎ 411858), Prat 353, goes to Paine daily, as does Buses JB (☎ 411-707), Bulnes 370. Turismo Luis Díaz, Bulnes 433, operates buses to the Guardería Laguna Amarga at Torres del Paine.

Buses Lagoper (☎ 411831) and Cootra, on Baquedano between Esmeralda and O'Higgins, have frequent buses to Río Turbio (US$4), where it is possible to make connections to Río Gallegos and to Calafate.

Boat Navimag (☎ 411421, fax 411642), Costanera Pedro Montt 380, operates the car/passenger ferry *Puerto Edén* to Puerto Montt every seven to 10 days all year, though dates and times vary according to weather and tides. The four-day, three-night voyage is heavily booked in summer, so try to reserve as far ahead as possible. See the sidebar in the La Araucanía and Los Lagos chapter for detailed information on the voyage.

Getting Around

Car Rental Both Andes Patagónicos and Turis-Ann have rental vehicles, which can be a reasonable alternative to buses if expenses are shared.

AROUND PUERTO NATALES

Puerto Bories

Built in 1913 with British capital, four km north of Puerto Natales, the Sociedad Explotadora's Puerto Bories **Frigorífico** (meat freezer) once processed huge amounts of beef and mutton, and also shipped tallow, hides and wool from estancias in Chile and Argentina for export to Europe. Its operations are now much reduced, but there remain several unique metal-clad buildings and houses, classic examples of hybrid Victorian/Magellanic architecture.

Cueva del Milodón

In the 1890s, Hermann Eberhard discovered the well-preserved remains of an enormous ground sloth in a cave at this national monument, 24 km northwest of Puerto Natales. Twice the height of a human, the milodon was an herbivorous mammal that pulled down small trees and branches for their succulent leaves; like the mammoth and many other American megafauna, it became extinct near the end of the Pleistocene. A tacky full-size replica of the animal stands in the cave, which is 30 meters high, 80 meters wide, and 200 meters deep.

Bruce Chatwin's literary travelogue *In Patagonia* amusingly recounts the many fanciful stories that have grown up about the milodon, including legends that Indians kept it penned as a domestic animal and that some specimens remained alive into the last century. Paleo-Indians existed simultaneously with the milodon, occupying the cave as a shelter, and probably contributed to the animal's extinction through hunting. The best summary information on the milodon occurs in US archaeologist Junius Bird's *Travel and Archaeology in South Chile* (University of Iowa Press, 1988), edited by John Hyslop of the American Museum of Natural History.

Although the closest hotel accommodation is in Puerto Natales, camping and picnicking are possible near the site. Conaf charges US$4 for admission, less for Chilean nationals and children. Buses to Torres del Paine will drop you at the entrance, which is several km walk from the cave proper. Alternatively, take a taxi or hitch from Puerto Natales.

PARQUE NACIONAL BERNARDO O'HIGGINS

This otherwise inaccessible 3½-million-hectare park is the final destination of a spectacular four-hour boat ride from Puerto Natales through Seno Ultima Esperanza, passing Glaciar Balmaceda, to the jetty at Puerto Toro, where a footpath leads to the base of Glaciar Serrano and, on a clear day, the Torres del Paine are visible in the distance to the north. En route, passengers will glimpse the frigorífico at Bories, several small estancias whose only access

to Puerto Natales is by water, numerous glaciers and waterfalls, a large cormorant rookery, a smaller sea lion rookery and occasional Andean condors. The return trip takes the same route.

Daily in summer, weather permitting, Turismo Cutter 21 de Mayo (☎ 411176), Ladrilleros 171 in Puerto Natales, runs its namesake cutter or the motor yacht *Alberto de Agostini* to the park, and will go at other times if demand is sufficient. At US$40 per person, the trip is approaching its maximum value, and any additional increases would make the trip marginal for most travelers. Decent meals are available on board for about US$6, as are hot and cold drinks. For reservations, contact the owners, who can also arrange hiking and rafting excursions to Torres del Paine via Paso de los Toros and Río Serrano.

The 25-passenger *Motovelero Trinidad* does the same trip for US$45; make reservations through Turismo Urbina (☎ 412-735), Baquedano 256.

PARQUE NACIONAL TORRES DEL PAINE

Soaring almost vertically more than 2000 meters above the Patagonian steppe, the Torres del Paine (Towers of Paine) are spectacular granite pillars that dominate the landscape of what may be South America's finest national park, a miniature Alaska of shimmering turquoise lakes, roaring creeks, rivers and waterfalls, sprawling glaciers, dense forests and abundant wildlife. The issue is not whether to come here, but how much time to spend.

Before its creation in 1959, the park was part of a large sheep estancia, but it is recovering from nearly a century of overexploitation of its pastures, forests and wildlife. It shelters large and growing herds of guanacos, flocks of the flightless ostrich-like rhea (known locally as the ñandú), Andean condors, flamingos and many other species. Since 1978, it has been part of the United Nations' World Biosphere Reserve system.

The park's outstanding wildlife conservation success has undoubtedly been the guanaco *(Lama guanicoe)*, which grazes the open steppes where its main natural enemy, the puma, cannot approach undetected. After more than a decade of effective protection from hunters and poachers, the guanaco barely flinches when humans or vehicles approach. The elusive huemul, or Chilean deer, is much more difficult to spot.

For hikers and backpackers, this 240,000-hectare park is an unequaled destination, with a well-developed trail network as well as opportunities for backcountry travel. The weather is changeable, with the strong westerlies that typify Patagonia, but very long summer days make outdoor activities possible late into the evening. Good foul-weather gear is essential, and a warm sleeping bag and good tent are imperative for those undertaking the extremely popular Paine circuit.

Guided day trips from Puerto Natales are possible, but permit only a superficial reconnaissance. It is better to explore the several options for staying at the park, including camping at both backcountry and improved sites, or staying at the guest houses and hotels near park headquarters and at Lago Pehoé. Roads into the park are much improved, largely for the benefit of the new luxury hotels.

Orientation & Information

Parque Nacional Torres del Paine is 112 km north of Puerto Natales via a decent but sometimes bumpy gravel road that passes Villa Cerro Castillo, where there is a seasonal border crossing into Argentina at Paso Cancha de Carreras, and continues 38 km north, where there is a junction with a 27-km lateral along the south shore of Lago Sarmiento to the little-visited Laguna Verde sector of the park.

Three km north of this junction the highway forks west along the north shore of Lago Sarmiento to the Portería Lago Sarmiento, the park's main entrance; it's another 37 km to the Administración (park headquarters). About 12 km east of Portería Lago Sarmiento, another lateral forks north and, three km farther, forks again; the northern branch goes to Guardería Laguna Azul, while the western branch goes to Guardería Laguna Amarga, the starting point for the Paine Circuit, and continues to the Administración.

At the Administración, Conaf's Centro de Visitantes features a good exhibit on the park's carnivores, including the puma, two species of foxes, and Geoffroy's cat, all of which depend largely on the introduced European hare (though half the puma's diet consists of chulengos, or young guanacos).

Entry There is an entry charge of US$12.50 per person (less for Chilean nationals), collected at the Portería Lago Sarmiento, where maps and informational brochures are available, or at Guardería Laguna Amarga (where most buses now stop inbound), Guardería Laguna Verde, or Guardería Laguna Azul.

Ñandú

Huemul

Climbing Climbers headed for the Torres should know that Conaf charges a climbing fee of US$825 for up to seven persons. Before being granted permission, climbers must present current résumés, emergency contact numbers, and authorization from their consulate.

Books, Maps & Trekking Information

Both the Sociedad Turística Kaonikén in Puerto Natales and Kiosko Puma in Punta Arenas publish good topographic maps of the park at a scale of 1:100,000 with 100-meter contour intervals, which include detailed routes of the Paine circuit and other park trails. Both are widely available in Punta Arenas, Puerto Natales and the park itself; the Puma map is more current and detailed, but either is suitable for exploring the park.

For more information on trekking and camping, including detailed contour maps, consult Clem Lindenmayer's Lonely Planet

guide *Trekking in the Patagonian Andes*. Bradt Publications' *Backpacking in Chile & Argentina* and William Leitch's *South America's National Parks* both have useful chapters on Torres del Paine, but are less thorough on practical information. A well-intentioned but awkwardly translated brochure entitled *Guide, Pathway of Excursions National Park Torres del Paine* is also available.

On wildlife, Lonely Planet readers have recommended *The Fauna of Torres del Paine* (1993) by Gladys Garay N and Oscar Guineo N, available in the Museo Salesiano in Punta Arenas.

Paine Circuit

Approaching the point of gridlock, this inordinately popular trek usually begins at Guardería Laguna Amarga, where most intending hikers disembark from the bus and do the route counterclockwise. It's also possible to start at Portería Lago Sarmiento, adding two hours to the hike, or at the Administración, which means a much longer approach. For visitors hiking the circuit, it is obligatory to register with the rangers at the guarderías or at the Administración, and to give your passport number.

In some ways, the Paine circuit is less challenging than in past years, as simple but sturdy bridges have replaced log crossings and once-hazardous stream fords, and park concessionaires have built comfortable refugios with hot showers and meals at regular intervals along the trail. In theory, this makes it possible to walk from hut to hut without carrying a tent, but the changeable weather still makes a tent desirable because of the possibility of being caught in between. Camping is still possible, but only at designated sites; there is a modest charge for camping near the new refugios.

While the trek is tamer than it once was, it is not without difficulty and hikers have suffered serious injuries and even death; for this reason, Conaf no longer permits solo treks, but it is not difficult to link up with others. Allot at least five days, preferably more for bad weather; consider at least one layover day, since the route is strenuous, especially the rough segments on the east side of Lago Grey and over the 1241-meter pass to or from the Río de los Perros. The opening of a trail along the north shore of Lago Nordenskjöld, between Hostería Las Torres and the Campamento Italiano at the foot of the Río de los Franceses, has meant that it's no longer necessary to start from park headquarters, and it's possible to exit as well as enter at Laguna Amarga.

Be sure to bring food, since prices at the small grocery at Posada Río Serrano near park headquarters are at least 50% higher than in Punta Arenas or Puerto Natales, and the selection is minimal. In late summer, the abandoned garden at Refugio Dickson still produces an abundant harvest of gooseberries.

Andescape (☎ 412592), Pedro Montt 308 in Puerto Natales, has opened refugios at Lago Pehoé, Lago Grey and Lago Dickson, plus a campground at Río de los Perros. For trekkers from Guardería Laguna Amarga, this would mean roughly an 11-hour hike to the first refugio at Dickson, though there is a rustic shelter at Campamento Coirón, about three hours earlier.

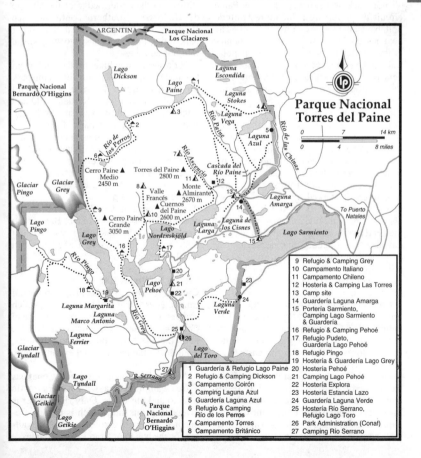

Parque Nacional Torres del Paine

1 Guardería & Refugio Lago Paine
2 Refugio & Camping Dickson
3 Campamento Coirón
4 Camping Laguna Azul
5 Guardería Laguna Azul
6 Refugio & Camping Río de los Perros
7 Campamento Torres
8 Campamento Británico
9 Refugio & Camping Grey
10 Campamento Italiano
11 Campamento Chileno
12 Hostería & Camping Las Torres
13 Camp site
14 Guardería Laguna Amarga
15 Portería Sarmiento, Camping Lago Sarmiento & Guardería
16 Refugio & Camping Pehoé
17 Refugio Pudeto, Guardería Lago Pehoé
18 Refugio Pingo
19 Hostería & Guardería Lago Grey
20 Hostería Pehoé
21 Camping Lago Pehoé
22 Hostería Explora
23 Hostería Estancia Lazo
24 Guardería Laguna Verde
25 Hostería Río Serrano, Refugio Lago Toro
26 Park Administration (Conaf)
27 Camping Río Serrano

MAGALLANES

Andescape's refugios have 32 bunks, not including sheets or sleeping bags, for US$14.50 per night, including kitchen privileges and hot showers. Breakfast is available for US$4, lunch for US$7 and dinner for US$9.50, or full board for US$19.50. A bunk plus full board costs US$33.

Campers pay US$3 per person at Andescape sites, with showers an additional US$2. Rental equipment is also available at reasonable prices.

Other Trails

Visitors lacking the time to hike the Paine circuit or preferring a bit more solitude both have alternatives within the park. The next best choice for seeing the high country is the shorter but almost equally popular trail up the **Río Ascencio** to a treeless tarn beneath the eastern face of the Torres del Paine proper. From Guardería Laguna Amarga, there's a narrow but passable road to the trailhead beyond Hostería Las Torres, where a bridge now crosses the river and avoids a sometimes hazardous ford, before the trail continues up the canyon to Campamento Chileno and Campamento Torres, the only legal campsites.

From Campamento Torres, a steep and sometimes ill-marked trail climbs through patchy beech forests to the barren tarn above, which provides dramatic views of the nearly vertical Torres. This is a feasible day hike from Laguna Amarga, and a fairly easy one from Hostería Las Torres, but it's also an exceptional area for camping despite its popularity (try to arrive early to get the best sites).

Comparable to Río Ascencio trail is the trail up the **Valle Francés**, between 3050-meter Paine Grande to the west and the lower but still spectacular Cuernos del Paine (Horns of Paine) to the east. It's a seven-hour, one-way hike from the Administración, but is also accessible by a new but still rugged trail from Hostería Las Torres along the north shore of Lago Nordenskjöld. Trekkers can pitch their tents at the Campamento Italiano at the foot of the valley, or at the Campamento Británico at its head.

Floods in the early 1980s destroyed several bridges, requiring Conaf to relocate that part of the Paine circuit that formerly crossed the Río Paine at the outlet of **Lago Paine**, whose northern shore is now accessible only from Laguna Azul. This four-hour, one-way hike, offering considerably greater solitude than the Paine circuit, leads to the rustic Refugio Lago Paine, a former outside house when the area was an estancia.

From the outlet of Lago Grey, 18 km northwest of the Administración by a passable road, a good trail leads to **Lago Pingo**, on the eastern edge of the Campo de Hielo Sur (southern continental ice field). Much less frequented than other park trails, this route has two very rustic refugios en route.

For a shorter day hike, try the walk from Guardería Lago Pehoé, on the main park highway, to **Salto Grande**, a powerful waterfall between Lago Nordenskjöld and Lago Pehoé that destroyed an iron bridge that once was a key part of the Paine circuit. From Salto Grande, an easy hour's walk leads to **Mirador Nordenskjöld**, an overlook with superb views of the lake and the cordillera.

Horseback Riding

At Río Serrano, see Brigitte Buhoffer about riding horses, or contact Baquedano Zamora (☎ 411594). Rental rates are about US$15 for two hours or US$55 per full day, lunch included.

Places to Stay & Eat

Camping The most central organized campsites are *Camping Lago Pehoé*, which charges US$14 for up to six people, and *Camping Río Serrano*, which costs US$11. Fees include firewood and hot showers, available in the morning but evenings only by request.

At Guardería Laguna Amarga, Conaf has a free camping area with a very rustic refugio and pit toilets. Only river water is available at this site, which is usually frequented by recent arrivals or people waiting for the bus to or from Puerto Natales.

On the grounds of Estancia Cerro Paine, *Camping Las Torres* charges US$4 per person and is popular with hikers taking the short trek up the Río Ascencio before doing the Paine circuit. Though covered with cow patties, the sites themselves are pleasant and scenic, but the inadequate water supply has put pressure on the modern but overburdened toilet and shower facilities.

At the more remote and recently privatized *Camping Laguna Azul*, charges are US$14 per night.

Hotels & Hosterías Despite a construction boom within park boundaries, accommodations are crowded in summer and reservations are a good idea. Low cost and even free accommodations exist, however. A short walk from the Administración, *Refugio Lago Toro* has bunks for US$5, plus US$2 for hot showers; your own sleeping bag is essential. Other refugios, such as that at Pudeto on Lago Pehoé, are free but *very* rustic.

Hostería Río Serrano (☎ 241023), a remodeled estancia house near the Administración, has rooms with shared bath for US$55/65, while those with private bath go for US$82/95. It has a reasonably priced restaurant and bar, with occasional informal, live entertainment, but several readers consider it poor value and report that the management has attitude problems. *Hostería Estancia Lazo* (☎ /fax 223771), with eight cabins and a spacious farmhouse at the Laguna Verde sector of the park, costs US$70/90 and has drawn some very favorable commentary.

Well worth considering is *Hostería Lago Grey* (☎ 248187, fax 241504 in Punta Arenas), at the outlet of its namesake lake, which costs US$96/132. *Hostería Pehoé* (☎ 411390), on a small island in Lago Pehoé and linked to the mainland by a footbridge, charges US$82/112 plus IVA for panoramic views of the Cuernos del Paine and Paine Grande, but the rooms are small and simple. It has a reasonably priced restaurant and bar, both open to the public, but service can be shoddy. The *Hostería Las Torres* (☎ 246054, fax

222641), seven km west of Guardería Laguna Amarga, charges US$95/120 and also has a restaurant/bar.

The most extravagant lodging in the park is the new *Hotel Explora* (☎ 411247 in Puerto Natales), near the Salto Chico waterfall at the outlet of Lago Pehoé, which specializes in packages ranging from four days and three nights for US$1347/2080 in the least expensive room, to eight days and seven nights for US$5398/6738 in the most expensive suite. In the off-season, accommodations may be available on a daily basis. While the building's exterior is unappealing, its relatively unobtrusive site limits the blight on the landscape; its real strength is the extraordinary view of the entire Paine massif across the lake.

Getting There & Away

For details about transportation to the park, see the Puerto Natales entry above. Bus services drop you at the Administración at Río Serrano, although you can disembark at Portería Lago Sarmiento or Guardería Laguna Amarga to begin the Paine circuit, or elsewhere upon request. Hitching from Puerto Natales is possible, but competition is heavy.

There are sometimes summer bus services between Torres del Paine and El Calafate, Argentina, the closest settlement to Parque Nacional Los Glaciares. Inquire at the Administración.

Getting Around

Hikers to Lago Grey or Valle Francés can save time and effort by taking the launch *Tzonka* from Refugio Pudeto, at the east end of Lago Pehoé, to Refugio Pehoé at the west end of the lake. The *Tzonka* runs two to four times daily (US$10), but sometimes erratically – visitors should not rely on connections.

From Hostería Grey, the 38-passenger *Tetramarán Grey I* runs twice daily to Glaciar Grey and back; the three-hour excursion costs US$30. For the latest information, contact Arka Patagonia (☎ 248167, fax 241504), Lautaro Navarro 1038-A, in Punta Arenas.

EL CALAFATE (ARGENTINA)

Neither attractive, interesting, picturesque nor welcoming, El Calafate is nevertheless an almost inescapable stopover en route to some of Argentina's most impressive sights. In reality, it's an oversized encampment of rapacious merchants fixated on making a year's income in a few short months by maintaining high prices rather than increasing sales. Lest this sound like the complaint of a dyspeptic writer, many local residents concur and, to quote one LP correspondent, 'there is no better description . . . even worse, unfriendly, expensive.' Nevertheless, increasing numbers of visitors to Chilean Patagonia find their way here.

Formally founded in 1927, this onetime stage stop takes its name from the wild barberry *(Berberis buxifolia)*, which grows abundantly in the area. In summer, El Calafate swarms with tourists from Buenos Aires, most of whom parade up and down the sidewalks of Avenida del Libertador San Martín, to the accompaniment of roaring motorcycles, before and after spending a few hours at the Moreno glacier. January and February are the most popular months so, if possible, plan your visit just before or just after peak season. From May to September, visitors are fewer and prices may drop, but days are shorter and the main attractions less accessible (though not necessarily inaccessible).

Orientation

El Calafate is 320 km northwest of Río Gallegos via paved RP 5 and RP 11, and 32 km west of RP 5's junction with northbound RN 40, which heads toward the El Chaltén sector of Parque Nacional Los Glaciares. Westbound RP 11 goes to the southern sector of Parque Nacional Los Glaciares and the Moreno glacier. RN 40 south to Río Turbio is greatly improved, permitting any vehicle to cut 100 km off the trip to Torres del Paine by avoiding the lengthy Esperanza route.

El Calafate's main thoroughfare is Avenida del Libertador General San Martín, more conveniently known as 'Avenida Libertador' or 'San Martín.' Because the town is small, most everything is within easy walking distance of San Martín.

Information

Tourist Offices The much improved Ente Municipal Calafate Turismo (Emcatur, ☎ 91090), a pseudo-chalet just before the bridge across the Arroyo Calafate at the eastern approach to town, is open 8 am to 10 pm daily. It keeps a list of hotels and prices, has maps, brochures and a message board, and there's usually an English speaker on hand.

The Automóvil Club Argentino (ACA; ☎ 91004) is at Primero de Mayo and Avenida Roca.

Money Though (or because) Calafate is a tourist destination, changing money has traditionally been problematic, but the federal government's rigid convertibility policy has at least reduced foreign exchange profiteering by local merchants.

Banco de la Provincia de Santa Cruz, Avenida Libertador 1285, will change cash dollars and travelers' checks (the latter with substantial commission), but it's open 10 am to 3 pm weekdays only. El Pingüino, Avenida Libertador 1025, also changes money, but travelers' checks carry a 5% penalty in commission.

Albergue del Glaciar (see Places to Stay, below) will change cash and travelers' checks at reasonable rates for its guests.

Post & Communications The area code is ☎ 902. Correo Argentino is at Avenida Libertador 1133, between 9 de Julio and Espora; the postal code is 9405. Calafate's Cooperativa Telefónica is at Espora 194, between Moyano and Gregores; collect calls are not possible, and discounts are available only after 10 pm.

National Parks The attractively landscaped Parques Nacionales office (☎ 910-05), at Avenida Libertador 1302 at Ezequiel Bustillo, is open weekdays 7 am to 2 pm, and has brochures including a decent map (though not adequate for trekking) of

MAGALLANES

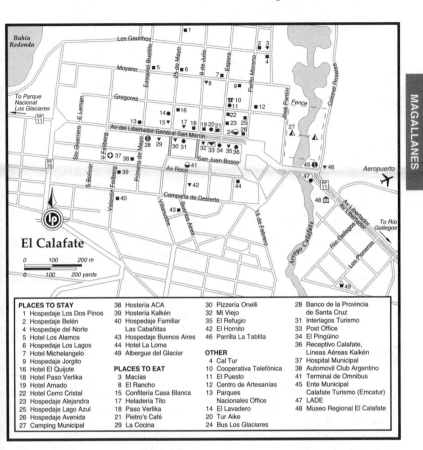

El Calafate

| Bahía Redonda | | |

To Parque Nacional Los Glaciares

Aeropuerto

To Río Gallegos

0   100   200 m
0   100   200 yards

PLACES TO STAY
1 Hospedaje Los Dos Pinos
2 Hospedaje Belén
4 Hospedaje del Norte
5 Hotel Los Alamos
6 Hospedaje Los Lagos
7 Hotel Michelangelo
9 Hospedaje Jorgito
16 Hotel El Quijote
18 Hotel Paso Verlika
19 Hotel Amado
22 Hotel Cerro Cristal
23 Hospedaje Alejandra
25 Hospedaje Lago Azul
26 Hospedaje Avenida
27 Camping Municipal

38 Hostería ACA
39 Hostería Kalkén
40 Hospedaje Familiar
   Las Cabañitas
43 Hospedaje Buenos Aires
44 Hotel La Loma
49 Albergue del Glaciar

PLACES TO EAT
3 Macías
8 El Rancho
15 Confitería Casa Blanca
17 Heladería Tito
18 Paso Verlika
21 Pietro's Café
29 La Cocina

30 Pizzería Onelli
32 Mi Viejo
35 El Refugio
42 El Hornito
46 Parrilla La Tablita

OTHER
4 Cal Tur
10 Cooperativa Telefónica
11 El Puesto
12 Centro de Artesanías
13 Parques
   Nacionales Office
14 El Lavadero
20 Tur Aike
24 Bus Los Glaciares

28 Banco de la Provincia
   de Santa Cruz
31 Interlagos Turismo
33 Post Office
34 El Pingüino
36 Receptivo Calafate,
   Líneas Aéreas Kaikén
37 Hospital Municipal
38 Automovil Club Argentino
41 Terminal de Omnibus
45 Ente Municipal
   Calafate Turismo (Emcatur)
47 LADE
48 Museo Regional El Calafate

Parque Nacional Los Glaciares. It is also in charge of remote Parque Nacional Perito Moreno, and can make contact with the ranger in charge there about visits.

Travel Agencies All of Calafate's numerous travel agencies can arrange excursions to the Moreno glacier and other attractions in the area. Among them are Tur Aike (☎ 91389) at Avenida Libertador 1080, Receptivo Calafate (☎ 91116) at Avenida Libertador 945, Interlagos Turismo (☎ 910-18) at Avenida Libertador 1175, and Cal Tur (☎ 91117) at Los Gauchos 813.

Laundry El Lavadero, 25 de Mayo 43, charges US$8 per load and is open every day, including Sunday afternoons.

Medical Services Calafate's Hospital Municipal (☎ 91001) is at Avenida Roca 1487.

Things to See
As of early 1996, the **Museo Regional El Calafate**, Avenida Libertador 557, was still closed for remodeling – a seemingly permanent state of affairs. **Laguna Nimes**, a recycled sewage pond near the lakeshore,

is remarkable for its variety of bird life – clearly the town is doing something right here.

There is aboriginal rock art at **Punta Walichu** (☎ 91059), seven km east of town near the shores of Lago Argentino, but bogus reproductions of similar sites in northern Santa Cruz have corrupted whatever limited integrity this recently privatized, grossly commercialized site might have had. Its absurd US$9 admission charge makes it one of the most flagrant tourist rip-offs in the entire country.

West and north of Calafate, **Parque Nacional Los Glaciares** offers several of the most spectacular natural attractions in South America: the **Glaciar Moreno**, the **Glaciar Upsala**, and the **Fitzroy Range** of the southern Andes. For details, see the separate entry for the park below.

Places to Stay

Prices for accommodation can vary seasonally; the peak is usually January and February, but can extend from early November to late March at some places.

Places to Stay – bottom end

Camping Now fenced, the woodsy *Camping Municipal*, straddling the creek behind the tourist office, has separate sections for auto and tent campers, good toilets, hot showers, fire pits and potable water; the entrance is on José Pantín, west of the bridge and half a block north of the YPF gas station. Easy walking distance from anyplace in town, it costs US$8 per site.

Camping Los Dos Pinos (☎ 91271), at the north end of town at 9 de Julio 218, charges US$4 per person; on those rare occasions when it rains, it can get muddy, and there are many street dogs.

Hostel El Calafate's official youth hostel is *Albergue del Glaciar* (☎ 91243), on Calle Los Pioneros, east of the arroyo. Beds cost US$13 for members and non-members alike, including kitchen privileges, laundry facilities and access to a spacious, comfortable common room. Director Mario Feldman and his family speak English, provide

visitor information, and also organize minibus excursions to local attractions. You can also make reservations in Buenos Aires (☎ (01) 312-8486).

Hotel La Loma (☎ 91016), Avenida Roca 849, also offers hostel accommodations, in addition to mid-price rooms.

Hospedajes Prices can vary considerably with the season, but the cheapest places are family inns like highly regarded *Hospedaje Alejandra* (☎ 91328), Espora 60, where rooms with shared bath cost US$10 per person. Comparably priced are *Hospedaje Los Dos Pinos* (☎ 91271) at 9 de Julio 218, the recommended *Hospedaje Buenos Aires* (☎ 91147) at Ciudad de Buenos Aires 296, *Hospedaje Lago Azul* (☎ 91419) at Perito Moreno 83, *Hospedaje Belén* (☎ 91028) at Perito Moreno and Los Gauchos, *Hospedaje Avenida* (☎ 91159) at Avenida Libertador 902, and *Hospedaje Jorgito* (☎ 91323) at Moyano 943.

Places to Stay – middle

In the low season, *Hospedaje del Norte* (☎ 91117), Los Gauchos 813 at José Pantín, charges US$15/24 for rooms with shared bath, while high season prices rise to US$20/30. Rooms with private bath cost US$20/30 in low season, US$25/36 in high season.

Several readers have praised *Cabañas del Sol* (☎ 91439), Avenida Libertador 1956, which charges US$20/26 in low season, US$31/40 in peak season. *Hospedaje Familiar Las Cabañitas* (☎ 91118), Valentín Feilberg 218, costs US$20/32 in low season, US$25/38 in peak season; an excellent breakfast costs US$6. Recommended *Hospedaje Los Lagos* (☎ 91170), 25 de Mayo 220 at Moyano, charges US$22/30 all year.

At *Hotel Paso Verlika* (☎ 91009), Avenida Libertador 1108, rates are US$30/40. Attractive *Hotel Cerro Cristal* (☎ 91088), Gregores 989, costs US$22/30 in the off-season, US$25/38 peak season, while *Hotel Amado* (☎ 91023), Avenida Libertador 1072, charges US$38/56. Members pay US$36/42 at the *Hostería ACA* (☎ 91004),

Primero de Mayo 50, while non-members are welcome for US$48/55. Like the Chilean automobile club, ACA often recognizes overseas affiliates as members.

Places to Stay – top end

Several hotels charge upwards of US$50 per night, including the stiflingly hot but otherwise pleasant enough *Hostería Kalkén* (☎ 91073) at Valentín Feilberg 119, which serves an excellent breakfast. Rates are US$50/65 in peak season, but barely half that in off-season. *Hotel La Loma* (☎ 910-16), Avenida Roca 849, costs US$51/64 in the November to March high season, but US$39/52 the rest of the year.

Hotel Michelangelo (☎ 91045), Moyano 1020, charges US$66/80 with breakfast, but is slightly cheaper in October. *Hotel El Quijote* (☎ 91017), Gregores 1191, charges US$80/95. In a class by itself is four-star *Hotel Los Alamos* (☎ 91144), Moyano 1355, where rates are US$130/160 in peak season, US$96/120 the rest of the year.

Places to Eat

In general, Calafate restaurants are poor value for money. The most reliable is *Confitería Casa Blanca* (☎ 91402) at Avenida Libertador 1202, which has good pizza and reasonable beer, but beware the expensive coffee and other hot drinks. *Pizzería Onelli* (☎ 91184), across the street at Libertador 1197, also has its adherents. *Paso Verlika* (☎ 91009), Avenida Libertador 1108, is popular and reasonably priced, especially the pizza. *Pietro's Café*, at Avenida Libertador and Espora, also serves pizza, as does *El Hornito* (☎ 91443) at Buenos Aires 155, half a block south of the bus terminal but well worth the walk up the hill.

Many hotels have restaurants, but avoid the rubber chicken at *Hotel Amado*, Avenida Libertador 1072. The kitchen at *Hotel Michelangelo* (☎ 91045), Moyano 1020, offers decent food but (unusually for Argentina) in microscopic portions, and it's not cheap. More reasonable are *Parrilla La Tablita* (☎ 91065), at Coronel Rosales 24 across from the tourist office, and *Macías*, on Los Gauchos opposite Hospedaje del Norte. The best ice cream is at *Heladería Tito*, now on Avenida Libertador between 25 de Mayo and 9 de Julio, but prices have risen sky-high – US$3 for a single-flavor cone.

Otherwise appealing *La Cocina* (☎ 912-86), a new restaurant on Avenida Libertador with an innovative Italian menu, stubbornly charged the author for two beers even though the second replaced one that had a fly in it. *Mi Viejo* (☎ 91691), Avenida Libertador 1111, is a good and popular but pricey parrilla. *El Refugio* (☎ 91318), Avenida Libertador 963, has an expensive international menu, but it's a good choice for a splurge. *El Rancho* (☎ 91644), at 9 de Julio and Gobernador Moyano, is an excellent pizzería, with good atmosphere, that also prepares superb empanadas with especially light and tasty crust. Their 'small' pizzas comprise six portions and are easily enough for two people.

Things to Buy

El Calafate's Centro de Artesanías is at Gregores and Perito Moreno. El Puesto, at Gregores and Espora, has woolen clothing and other artisanal goods. In the past few years there's been a proliferation of shops offering good but expensive homemade chocolates.

Getting There & Away

Air LADE (☎ 91262), Avenida Libertador 699, flies Monday to Río Turbio (US$17) and Río Gallegos (US$30), Tuesday to Comodoro Rivadavia (US$74), Wednesday to Río Gallegos, Río Grande (US$59) and Ushuaia (US$68), and Thursday to the town of Perito Moreno (US$31), near the Chilean border at Chile Chico, and Comodoro Rivadavia.

Receptivo Calafate (☎ 91116), Avenida Libertador 945, is the agent for Líneas Aéreas Kaikén, which flies Monday and Saturday to Puerto Madryn (US$132), Tuesday, Wednesday, Thursday and Friday to Río Gallegos (US$50) and Ushuaia (US$83), and Saturday, Sunday and Monday to Río Gallegos, Río Grande (US$69) and Ushuaia.

Bus El Calafate's new Terminal de Omnibus is on Avenida Roca, easily reached by a staircase from the corner of Avenida Libertador and 9 de Julio.

Buses Pingüino (☎ 91273) at Avenida Libertador 1025 and Interlagos (☎ 91018) at Avenida Libertador 1175 both cover the 320 km of RP 5 and RP 11, now completely paved between Calafate and Río Gallegos (US$25, six hours).

During summer there is sometimes direct service to Parque Nacional Torres del Paine Tuesday, Thursday and Saturday at 8 am (US$45, 10 hours). Buses Zaahj connects Calafate with Puerto Natales, Chile (US$28); it's cheaper to buy a roundtrip fare (US$44) in Puerto Natales.

Daily at 6 am during summer, Buses Los Glaciares (☎ 91158), Avenida Libertador 924, leaves Calafate for El Chaltén (US$25 one-way, US$50 with open return) and the Fitzroy range. The return service leaves El Chaltén at 4 pm; winter schedules may differ. Cal Tur (☎ 91117) at Los Gauchos 813 also occasionally goes to Chaltén, but Los Glaciares uses better buses. Auto traffic between El Calafate and El Chaltén is almost non-existent, so hitching is very difficult.

PARQUE NACIONAL LOS GLACIARES (ARGENTINA)

Nourished by several awesome glaciers that descend from the Andean divide, Lago Argentino and Lago Viedma in turn feed southern Patagonia's largest river, the Río Santa Cruz. Along with the Iguazú Falls, this conjunction of ice, rock and water is one of the greatest attractions in Argentina and all of South America.

Its centerpiece is the breathtaking **Moreno glacier** which, because of unusually favorable local conditions, is one of the planet's few advancing glaciers. A low gap in the Andes allows moisture-laden Pacific storms to drop their loads east of the divide, where they accumulate as snow. Over millennia, under tremendous weight, this snow has recrystallized into ice and flowed slowly eastward. The 1600 sq km trough of Lago Argentino, the country's largest

single body of water, is unmistakable evidence that glaciers were once far more extensive than today.

As the 60-meter high glacier advances, it periodically dams the **Brazo Rico** (Rico Arm) of Lago Argentino, causing the water to rise. Eventually, the melting ice below can no longer support the weight of the water behind it and the dam collapses in an explosion of ice and water. To be present when this spectacular cataclysm occurs is unforgettable; though it ruptures every four years on average, it has not done so since 1988.

Even in ordinary years, the Moreno glacier merits a visit. It is no less an auditory than visual experience, as huge icebergs on the glacier's face calve and collapse into the **Canal de los Témpanos** (Channel of Icebergs). From a series of catwalks and vantage points on the Península de Magallanes, visitors can see, hear and photograph the glacier safely as these enormous chunks crash into the water. Because of the danger of falling icebergs and their backwash, it is no longer possible to descend to the shores of the canal.

Plans for a five-star hotel at the glacier overlook, which is private property, are on hold but nevertheless constitute a threat to the park. At the same time, authorities have cleaned up the parking lot, and the site now has a good snack bar and some badly needed clean new toilets.

The Moreno glacier is 80 km west of El Calafate via RP 11. The massive but less spectacular **Upsala glacier**, on the Brazo Norte (North Arm) of Lago Argentino, is accessible by launch from Puerto Bandera, which is 45 km west of Calafate by RP 11 and RP 8. Many visitors recommend the trip for the hike to iceberg-choked **Lago Onelli**, where it is possible to camp at a refugio and return to Puerto Bandera another day.

In La Jerónima, the most southerly section of the park, **Cerro Cristal** is a rugged but rewarding hike beginning at the concrete bunker near the campground entrance. Hikers reaching the summit earn a view from Torres del Paine in the south to Cerro Fitzroy in the north.

Parque Nacional
Los Glaciares

0		15		30 km
0		10		20 miles

Places to Stay & Eat

On Península Magallanes, en route to the glacier, are two organized campsites with facilities including hot showers, fire pits and the like: *Camping Río Mitre* is 53 km west of El Calafate, while *Camping Bahía Escondida* is 72 km from El Calafate, only eight km from the Moreno glacier. Rates are US$5 per person. About midway between the two, *Camping Correntoso* is free but dirty; backpackers can also camp two nights near the Seccional de Guarda-parques, the ranger station at the glacier. Also at the glacier is a confitería that has sandwiches and fixed-price lunches and dinners ranging from US$10 to US$14.

Hostería Los Notros (☎ 91437, fax 918-16 in El Calafate) has a dozen rooms with glacier views starting at US$132/174 single/double in the off-season and rising to US$152/160 in peak season.

At *Camping Lago Roca* at La Jerónima on Brazo Sur, fishing (rental equipment is available) and horseback riding (US$10 per hour) are also possible. Camping prices are about US$5 per person; there is a con-fitería with meals for US$12, and hot showers from 7 to 11 pm.

Getting There & Away

The Moreno glacier is about 80 km from Calafate via RP 11, a rough gravel road. Bus tours are frequent and numerous in summer, and off-season transportation can be arranged as well. Calafate's numerous tour operators offer trips to all major tourist sites, but concentrate on the Moreno and Upsala glaciers; for specific operators see the entry for El Calafate or just stroll down Avenida Libertador. The roundtrip fare to Moreno glacier is about US$25 for the 1¼ hour (each way) trip, while park admission costs an additional US$5.

EL Calafate's Albergue del Glaciar runs its own minivan excursions, leaving about 8.30 am and returning about 5 pm; Hotel La Loma does similar trips. Albergue del Glaciar's trips take the slightly longer Lago Roca route to the glacier, allowing travel-ers to see more of the countryside, and approaches the glacier itself via a short hike rather than just dropping people in the parking lot. Their guides speak English competently, but make some debatable scientific statements and occasional out-right errors.

Many visitors feel that day trips give insufficient time to appreciate the glacier, especially if the inclement weather limits visibility. The changeable weather is almost sure to provide a window on the glacier at some time during your trip, but it is also worth exploring possibilities for camp-ing nearby.

Several travel agencies offer brief hikes across the glacier itself. After crossing Brazo Rico in a rubber raft, you then hike with guides through the southern beech forest and onto the glacier. This all-day 'minitrekking' excursion from El Calafate costs US$75. Full-day bus/motor launch excursions to the Upsala glacier cost about $55. Meals are extra and usually expen-sive; bring your own food.

FITZROY RANGE (ARGENTINA)

Sedentary tourists can enjoy the Moreno glacier, but the Fitzroy Range is the area's mecca for hikers, climbers and campers. The staging point for everything is the tiny, end-of-the-road settlement of **El Chaltén**, a monument to Argentina's prodigious capacity for bureaucracy. Virtually every inhabitant is a government employee here, where Chile and Argentina have recently settled one of the last of their seemingly interminable border disputes.

Foolishly sited on the exposed flood plain of the Río de las Vueltas by a planner who never visited the area, El Chaltén is a desolate collection of pseudo-chalets pum-meled by almost incessant wind, but the magnificent surroundings more than com-pensate for any squalor. Ironically, the word itself, signifying 'azure' in the Te-huelche language, was the name applied to Cerro Fitzroy. For all its faults, though, El Chaltén is a more agreeable place than El Calafate.

One of many fine hikes in the area goes to **Laguna Torre**, and continues to the base camp for climbers of the famous spire of **Cerro Torre**. There is a signed trailhead between the chalets and the rustic Madsen campground along the road to the north. After a gentle initial climb, it's a fairly level walk through pleasant beech forests and along the Río Fitzroy until a final steeper climb up the lateral moraine left by the receding Glaciar del Torre. From Laguna Torre, there are stunning views of the principal southern peaks of the Fitzroy Range. Allow at least three hours one way.

While clouds usually enshroud the summit of 3128-meter Cerro Torre, look for the 'mushroom' of snow and ice that caps the peak. This precarious formation is the final obstacle for serious climbers, who can spend weeks or months waiting for weather good enough to permit their ascent. Protected campsites are available in the beech forest above Laguna Torre, but the small climber's refugio recently burned to the ground.

Another exceptional but more strenuous hike climbs steeply from the pack station at the Madsen campground; after about an hour plus, there is a signed lateral to excellent backcountry campsites at **Laguna Capri**. The main trail continues gently to **Río Blanco**, base camp for climbers of Cerro Fitzroy, and then climbs very steeply to **Laguna de los Tres**, a high alpine tarn named in honor of the three Frenchmen who were first to scale Fitzroy. Condors glide overhead and nest in an area where, in clear weather, the views are truly extraordinary. Allow about four hours one way, and leave time for contemplation and physical recovery after the last segment, on which high winds can be a real hazard.

More ambitious hikers can make a circuit through the Fitzroy Range that is shorter than the one in Torres del Paine, but still worthwhile; another possibility is Laguna del Desierto, north of Chaltén. Recent reports suggest some restriction on hiking this loop; ask for details at the ranger station in Chaltén. There is a good private campground along the circuit, *Los Troncos*, charging about US$5, with showers, toilets and firewood.

Places to Stay & Eat

There is free camping at Parques Nacionales' *Camping Madsen* in Chaltén, with running water and abundant firewood, but no toilets – you must dig a latrine. If you don't mind walking about 10 minutes, shower at friendly *Confitería La Senyera* for about US$1; after drying off, try their enormous portions of chocolate cake. Other snacks and light meals are available, with prices, quality and ambiance superior to Calafate. *Camping Ruca Mahuida* charges US$6 per person, has meals and hot showers, and arranges local excursions. Other campsites, like *Posada Lago del Desierto*, charge about US$8 per person. *Albergue Los Ñires* is a small (eight-bed) hostel that charges US$10 per person or US$4 per person for camping; its pub-restaurant is called *The Wall*.

Posada Lago del Desierto has four-bed cabins, with outside toilets but no hot water, for US$10 per person, and very comfortable six-bed apartments, with kitchen facilities, private bath and hot water, for US$17 per person; its hotel has doubles for US$80. Meals are expensive. *Cabañas Cerro Torre* has four-bed cabins with private bath for US$25 per person.

At the *Fitzroy Inn*, accommodation with half-board costs US$53 per person, but it's possible to get a package for US$83 that includes roundtrip transportation from Calafate, one night's lodging, dinner and breakfast; two-night packages cost US$110, while three nights cost US$134. *Estancia La Quinta*, on the outskirts of Chaltén, offers lodging for US$25 per person; make arrangements at agencies in Calafate.

For cheap eats, try the kitchen in Juan Borrego's converted bus, which is also a climbers' hangout. *Chocolatería Josh Aike* has been recommended for meals, while supplies (including fresh bread) are available at *Kiosko Charito* and *El Chaltén*.

Getting There & Away

El Chaltén is 220 km from El Calafate via paved RP 11, improved but still rough RN 40, and truly rugged RP 23. See the entry on El Calafate for details on daily buses to Chaltén; buses normally return from El Chaltén at 4 pm.

Motorists should know that petrol is not available at El Chaltén except in very serious emergencies; carry a spare fuel can. The nearest gas station is at Tres Lagos, 123 km east of El Chaltén. Beyond the RP 23 junction, RN 40 is very bad, has no public transportation and carries very little traffic of any kind, so returning to Río Gallegos is almost unavoidable for north-bound travelers without vehicles. Between Tres Lagos and Bajo Caracoles, the highway is greatly improved, permitting speeds between 65 and 80 kmh en route to the small agricultural town of Perito Moreno and the junction to Los Antiguos and the border at Chile Chico.

Tierra del Fuego

Since the 16th-century voyages of Magellan, to the 19th-century explorations of Fitzroy and Darwin on the *Beagle* and even to the present, this 'uttermost part of the earth' has held an ambivalent fascination for travelers of many nationalities. For more than three centuries, its climate and terrain discouraged European settlement, yet indigenous people considered it a 'land of plenty.' Its scenery, with glaciers descending nearly to the ocean in many places, is truly enthralling.

The Yahgan Indians, now nearly extinct, built the fires that inspired Europeans to give this region its name, now famous throughout the world. It consists of one large island, Isla Grande de Tierra del Fuego, and many smaller ones, only a few of which are inhabited. The Strait of Magellan separates the archipelago from the South American mainland.

History

While Magellan passed through the Strait which bears his name in 1520, neither he nor anyone else had any immediate interest in the land and its people. In search of a passage to the spice islands of Asia, early navigators feared and detested the stiff westerlies, hazardous currents and violent seas, which impeded their progress. Consequently the Ona, Haush, Yahgan and Alacaluf peoples who populated the area faced no immediate competition for their lands and resources.

All these groups were mobile hunters and gatherers. The Ona, also known as Selknam, and Haush subsisted primarily on terrestrial resources, hunting the guanaco for its meat and its skins, while the Yahgans and Alacalufes, known collectively as 'Canoe Indians,' lived primarily on fish, shellfish and marine mammals. The Yahgans, also known as the Yamana, consumed the 'Indian bread' fungus (*Cytarria darwinii*) which parasitizes the ñire, a species of southern beech. Despite frequently inclement weather, they used little or no clothing, but constant fires (even in their bark canoes) kept them warm.

The decline of Spain's American empire slowly opened the area to European settlement and began the rapid demise of the indigenous Fuegians, whom Europeans struggled to understand. Darwin, visiting the area in 1834, wrote that the difference between the Fuegians, 'among the most abject and miserable creatures I ever saw,' and Europeans was greater than that between wild and domestic animals. On an earlier voyage, Captain Robert Fitzroy of the *Beagle* had abducted several Yahgans, whom he returned after several years of missionary education in England.

From the 1850s, there were attempts to catechize the Fuegians, the earliest of which ended with the death by starvation of British missionary Allen Gardiner. Gardiner's successors, working from a base at Keppel Island in the Falklands, were more successful despite the massacre of one party by Fuegians at Isla Navarino. Thomas Bridges, a young man at Keppel, learned to speak the Yahgan language and became one of the first settlers at Ushuaia, in what is now Argentine Tierra del Fuego. His son Lucas Bridges, born at Ushuaia in 1874, left a fascinating memoir of his experiences among the Yahgans and Onas entitled *The Uttermost Part of the Earth*.

Although the Bridges family and many of those who followed had the best motives, the increasing European presence exposed the Fuegians to diseases like typhoid and measles, to which they had had no exposure and little resistance. One measles epidemic wiped out half the native population in the district, and recurrent contagion nearly extinguished them over the next half-century. Some early sheep ranchers made things worse with their violent persecution of the Indians, who had resorted to preying on domestic flocks as guanaco populations declined.

Since no European power had any interest in settling the region until Britain occupied the Falklands in the 1770s, Spain too paid little attention to Tierra del Fuego, but the successor governments of Argentina and Chile felt differently. The Chilean presence on the Strait of Magellan, from 1843, and increasing British mission activity spurred Argentina to formalize its authority at Ushuaia in 1884, with the installation of a territorial governor the following year. International border issues in the area were only finally resolved in 1984, when an Argentine plebiscite ratified a diplomatic settlement of a dispute over three small islands in the Beagle Channel which had lingered for decades and nearly brought the two countries to open warfare in 1979.

Despite minor gold and lumbering booms, Ushuaia was for many years primarily a penal settlement for both political prisoners and common criminals. Sheep farming brought great wealth to some individuals and families and is still the island's economic backbone, although the northern area near San Sebastián has substantial petroleum and natural gas reserves. Since the 1960s, the tourist industry has become so important that flights and hotels are often heavily booked in summer. The spectacular mountain and coastal scenery in the immediate countryside of Ushuaia, including Parque Nacional Tierra del Fuego, attracts both Argentines and foreigners.

TIERRA DEL FUEGO

The Beagle exploring the Strait of Magellan

Geography & Climate

Surrounded by the South Atlantic Ocean, the Strait of Magellan and the easternmost part of the Pacific Ocean, the archipelago of Tierra del Fuego has a land area of roughly 76,000 sq km, about the size of Ireland or South Carolina. The Chilean-Argentine border runs directly south from Cape Espíritu Santo, at the eastern entrance of the Straits of Magellan, to the Beagle Channel (Canal Beagle), where it trends eastward to the channel's mouth at Isla Nueva. Most of Isla Grande belongs to Chile, but the Argentine side is more densely populated, with the substantial towns of Ushuaia and Río Grande. Porvenir is the only significant town on the Chilean side.

The plains of northern Isla Grande are a landscape of almost unrelenting wind, enormous flocks of Corriedales, and oil derricks, while the island's mountainous southern part offers scenic glaciers, lakes, rivers and seacoasts. The mostly maritime climate is surprisingly mild, even in winter, but its changeability makes warm, dry clothing important, especially when hiking or at higher elevations. The mountains of the Cordillera Darwin and the Sierra de Beauvoir, reaching as high as 2500 meters in the west, intercept Antarctic storms, leaving the plains around Río Grande much drier than areas nearer the Beagle Channel.

The higher southern rainfall supports dense forests of southern beech (*Nothofagus*), both deciduous and evergreen, while the drier north consists of extensive native grasses and low-growing shrubs. Storms batter the bogs and truncated beeches of the remote southern and western zones of the archipelago. Guanaco, rhea and condor can still be seen in the north, but marine mammals and shorebirds are the most common wildlife around tourist destinations along the Beagle Channel.

Books

Though its practical information is badly out of date, the 3rd edition of Rae Natalie Prosser Goodall's detailed, bilingual guidebook *Tierra del Fuego* (Buenos Aires, Ediciones Shanamiim, 1978) is the most informed single source on the island's history and natural history. Rumors persist of a new edition, but the old one is still for sale in local bookshops in Ushuaia.

Dangers & Annoyances

Note that collection of shellfish is not permitted because of toxic red tide conditions. Hunting is also illegal throughout the Argentine part of Tierra del Fuego.

Getting There & Around

Overland, the simplest route to Argentine Tierra del Fuego is via Porvenir, across the Strait of Magellan from Punta Arenas; for details, see the Punta Arenas entry. Transbordadora Austral Broom (☎ 218100, Anexo 21 in Punta Arenas) operates the roll-on, roll-off ferry *Bahía Azul* across the narrows at Primera Angostura, from Punta Delgada to Chilean Tierra del Fuego, but no public transportation connects with it. The ferry operates daily from 8 am to 11 pm; the half-hour crossing costs US$2 for passengers and US$13 for automobiles or pickup trucks. There are occasional breaks in service because of weather and tidal conditions.

The principal border crossing is San Sebastián, a truly desolate place about midway between Porvenir and Río Grande. Roads have improved considerably in recent years. Though they are unpaved on the Chilean side, Argentine RN 3 is smoothly paved from San Sebastián past Río Grande as far as Tolhuín on Lago Kami, and paving was due to begin on the Tolhuín-Ushuaia portion over Paso Garibaldi in 1995.

PORVENIR

Founded barely a century ago to service the new sheep estancias across the Strait of Magellan from Punta Arenas, Porvenir is the largest settlement on Chilean Tierra del Fuego. Many of its 5143 inhabitants claim Yugoslav descent, dating from the brief gold rush of the 1880s and commemorated by several monuments and a pleasant waterfront park.

Porvenir becomes visible only as the ferry from Punta Arenas approaches its sheltered, nearly hidden harbor. The waterfront road, or costanera, leads from the ferry terminal to a cluster of rusting, metalclad Victorians that ironically belie the town's optimistic name ('the future'). The beautifully manicured Plaza de Armas has a worthwhile museum, but for most travelers Porvenir is a brief stopover en route to or from Ushuaia.

Motorists will find the gravel road east, along Bahía Inútil to the Argentine border at San Sebastián, in excellent condition though a bit narrow in spots. Northbound motorists from San Sebastián should take the equally good route from Onaisín to Cerro Sombrero and the crossing of the Strait of Magellan at Punta Delgada-Puerto Espora, rather than the heavily traveled and rutted truck route directly north from San Sebastián.

Major changes are in store for Porvenir. The multi-national Trillium Corporation's controversial forestry initiative in southern Tierra del Fuego, presently under judicial scrutiny for its alleged environmental shortcomings, may result in construction of US$35 million worth of new port facilities.

Information

Tourist Offices The Oficina Municipal de Turismo (☎ 580100), on the 2nd floor at Valdivieso 402, is open 11.30 am to 1 pm and 2.30 to 4 pm weekdays. Information is also available at the kiosk on the costanera between Santos Mardones and Muñoz Gamero.

Post & Communications Porvenir's area code is ☎ 61. Correos de Chile is at the corner of Philippi and Briceño, on the Plaza de Armas. The Compañía Chilena de Teléfonos is on Damián Riobó between Valdivieso and Briceño.

Medical Services Porvenir's hospital is on Carlos Wood between Señoret and Guerrero.

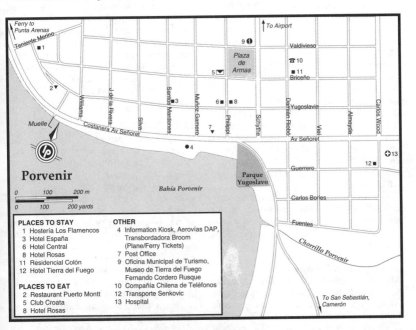

Porvenir

0   100   200 m
0   100   200 yards

PLACES TO STAY
1 Hostería Los Flamencos
3 Hotel España
6 Hotel Central
8 Hotel Rosas
11 Residencial Colón
12 Hotel Tierra del Fuego

PLACES TO EAT
2 Restaurant Puerto Montt
5 Club Croata
8 Hotel Rosas

OTHER
4 Information Kiosk, Aerovías DAP, Transbordadora Broom (Plane/Ferry Tickets)
7 Post Office
9 Oficina Municipal de Turismo, Museo de Tierra del Fuego Fernando Cordero Rusque
10 Compañía Chilena de Teléfonos
12 Transporte Senkovic
13 Hospital

Museo de Tierra del Fuego Fernando Cordero Rusque

This small but intriguing museum has some unexpected materials, including Selknam mummies and skulls, musical instruments used by mission Indians on Isla Dawson, stuffed animals from the region, a display on the evolution of police uniforms in Chile, and another on the enigmatic Julio Popper, the onetime 'dictator' of Tierra del Fuego. Probably the most improbable exhibit is one on early Chilean cinematography. On the Plaza de Armas, in the same building as the tourist office, museum hours are weekdays 8.30 am to 12.30 pm and 2.30 to 6 pm.

Places to Stay & Eat

For its size, Porvenir has good accommodation and food, but prices have recently risen. The cheapest rooms are at *Hotel España* (☎ 580160), Yugoslavia 698, which has singles for US$12.50 with shared bath, US$20 with private bath. Basic *Hotel Tierra del Fuego* (☎ 580015), Carlos Wood 489, is comparably priced. At *Residencial Colón* (☎ 580108), Damián Riobó 198, singles with shared bath cost US$13.

Hotel Central (☎ 580077), at Philippi and Yugoslavia, is good value for US$12 per person with shared bath, US$17/26 single/double with private bath. Across the street at Philippi 296, *Hotel Rosas* (☎ 580-088) charges US$26/37 for singles/doubles and has a good seafood restaurant. For upscale comfort, try *Hostería Los Flamencos* (☎ 580049), on Teniente Merino overlooking the harbor, where prices are US$48/53.

The *Club Croata* on Avenida Señoret is worth a try for lunch or dinner, along with the simple *Restaurant Puerto Montt* at Yugoslavia 1199, near Hostería Los Flamencos.

Getting There & Away

Air Aerovías DAP (☎ 580089), Avenida Señoret 542, flies across the Straits to Punta Arenas (US$22) at least twice daily except Sunday.

Bus Transporte Senkovic (☎ 580015), Carlos Wood 489, departs Wednesday and Saturday at 2 pm for Río Grande, in Argentine Tierra del Fuego (US$12.50, seven hours). From Río Grande there are connections to Ushuaia.

Boat Transbordadora Broom (☎ 580089) operates a car/passenger ferry to Punta Arenas (2½ hours; US$6 per person, US$37 per vehicle) Monday, Wednesday, Friday and Saturday at 2 pm, Sundays and holidays at 5 pm. Buy tickets at the kiosk on the costanera.

Getting Around

The bus to the ferry terminal, which departs from the waterfront kiosk about an hour before the ferry's departure, provides a farewell tour of Porvenir for a mere US$1. Taxis cost at least four times as much.

CERRO SOMBRERO

This semi-ghost town at the north end of Tierra del Fuego, 43 km south of the ferry crossing at Primera Angostura, is a former oil center that has oddball '60s architecture, cheap lodging, a restaurant open until 3 am and, of all things, an astronomical observatory. There's no public transport, but it's definitely worth a stop if you have your own car.

LAGO BLANCO

In the southern part of Chilean Tierra del Fuego, which is accessible only by private car, Lago Blanco offers excellent fishing. The nearest formal accommodation is in the village of Timaukel, just south of the large estancia at Camerón (which, despite the Spanish accent, takes its name from a Scottish pioneer sheep farming family that first settled in the Falkland Islands). The native forests in this region are presently under pressure from a controversial forestry project, which would permit the US-based Trillium Corporation to log substantial areas in return for replanting and preserving other areas.

PUERTO WILLIAMS

Captain Robert Fitzroy encountered the Yahgan Indians who accompanied the *Beagle* back to England for several years near this Chilean naval settlement on Isla Navarino, directly across the Beagle Channel from Argentine Tierra del Fuego. Missionaries in the mid-19th century and fortune-seekers during the local gold rush of the 1890s established a permanent European presence.

A few people of Yahgan descent still reside near Puerto Williams (population 1000), which is named for the founder of Fuerte Bulnes. A dispute over the three small islands of Lennox, Nueva and Picton, east of Navarino, nearly brought Argentina and Chile to war in 1978, but papal intervention defused the situation and the islands remain in Chilean possession.

Information

There is a cluster of public services, including telephone, post office, supermarket and tourist office, on Presidente Ibáñez. Money exchange is possible at the only travel agency, Turismo Navarino (☎ 621050).

Things to See & Do

The **Museo Martín Gusinde**, honoring the German priest and ethnographer who worked among the Yahgans, has exhibits on natural history and ethnography. It's open weekdays 9 am to 1 pm, and daily 3 to 6 pm.

East of town, at **Ukika**, live the few remaining Yahgan people. There is good hiking in the surrounding countryside, but the changeable weather demands warm, water-resistant clothing.

Places to Stay & Eat

Central *Hostería Camblor* (☎ 621033) is basic but clean and comfortable for US$14 single. Camping is possible near the upscale, highly recommended *Hostería Wala* (☎ 621114), which has singles/doubles at US$70/100 (winter prices may be negotiable). Both hotels serve meals.

Getting There & Away

Air Aerovías DAP flies to and from Punta Arenas Monday, Wednesday and Friday (US$67 one way). Seats are limited and advance reservations essential. DAP flights to Antarctica make a brief stopover here.

Boat Chilean naval supply vessels, which sail irregularly between Punta Arenas and Puerto Williams, sometimes take passengers. In summer, there is sporadic service across the Beagle Channel to Ushuaia; inquire at the tourist office in either place.

RIO GRANDE (ARGENTINA)

Founded in 1894 on the estuary of its namesake river, the bleak, windswept wool and petroleum service center of Río Grande is making a genuine effort to beautify and improve itself, but still has a long way to go. A recent economic boom, sparked by duty-free status, has subsided and the local economy has stagnated. Most visitors will pass through quickly en route to Ushuaia, but the surrounding countryside is not completely without interest.

Orientation

Río Grande faces the open South Atlantic on RN 3, which leads 190 km south to Ushuaia and 79 km north to the Chilean border at San Sebastián. The main street is Avenida San Martín, which runs roughly northwest-southeast and intersects Avenida Islas Malvinas/Santa Fe, as RN 3 is known through town. Most visitor services are along Avenida San Martín and along Avenida Manuel Belgrano, between San Martín and the waterfront. Do not get confused by the similarly named parallel streets 9 de Julio and 11 de Julio, which are two blocks (as well as two days) apart.

Information

Tourist Office The Instituto Fueguino de Turismo (Infuetur; ☎ 21373), in the lobby of the Hotel Yaganes at Belgrano 319, is open 10 am to 5 pm weekdays.

TIERRA DEL FUEGO

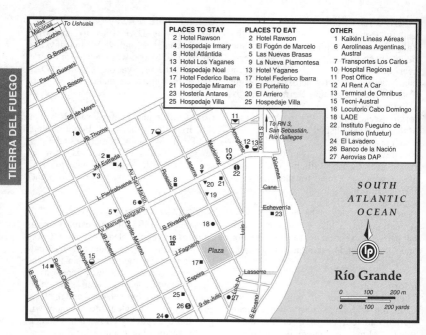

PLACES TO STAY
2 Hotel Rawson
4 Hospedaje Irmary
8 Hotel Atlántida
13 Hotel Los Yaganes
14 Hospedaje Noal
17 Hotel Federico Ibarra
21 Hospedaje Miramar
23 Hostería Antares
25 Hospedaje Villa

PLACES TO EAT
2 Hotel Rawson
3 El Fogón de Marcelo
5 Las Nuevas Brasas
9 La Nueva Piamontesa
13 Hotel Yaganes
17 Hotel Federico Ibarra
19 El Porteñito
20 El Arriero
25 Hospedaje Villa

OTHER
1 Kaikén Líneas Aéreas
6 Aerolíneas Argentinas,
   Austral
7 Transportes Los Carlos
10 Hospital Regional
11 Post Office
12 Al Rent A Car
13 Terminal de Omnibus
15 Tecni-Austral
16 Locutorio Cabo Domingo
18 LADE
22 Instituto Fueguino de
   Turismo (Infuetur)
24 El Lavadero
26 Banco de la Nación
27 Aerovías DAP

SOUTH
ATLANTIC
OCEAN

Río Grande

0   100   200 m
0   100   200 yards

Money For money exchange, try Banco de la Nación, San Martín at 9 de Julio.

Post & Communications The area code is ☎ 964. Correo Argentino is at Ameghino 712, between Piedrabuena and Estrada; the postal code is 9420. The telephone office Locutorio Cabo Domingo is at San Martín 458.

Consulate Chile has a consulate (☎ 223-23) at Beauvoir 351, the southern extension of Avenida San Martín.

Laundry El Lavadero is at Perito Moreno 221.

Medical Services Río Grande's Hospital Regional (☎ 22088) is at Avenida Belgrano 350.

Places to Stay
Because of its large number of single laborers, Río Grande is notorious for lack of quality budget accommodation. Patience and perseverance are necessary to find acceptable space, which may be a dormitory bed. Single women will probably prefer mid-range hotels.

Places to Stay – bottom end
Hospedaje Irmary (☎ 23608), Estrada 743 between San Martín and Perito Moreno, has beds for US$8 per person with shared bath, while *Hospedaje Noal* (☎ 22857), Rafael Obligado 557, charges US$13 per person with shared bath, US$15/35 single/double with private bath and breakfast. At *Hostería Antares* (☎ 21853), Echeverría 49, rates are US$15 per person.

One of Río Grande's better choices, *Hospedaje Miramar* (☎ 22462) at Mackinlay 595, has clean, well-heated singles/doubles at US$16 per person with shared bath, US$18 with private bath. Comparable *Hospedaje Villa* (☎ 22312), San Martín

277, charges US$17 single, while *Hotel Rawson* (☎ 21352), Estrada 750, is slightly more expensive at US$18/28.

Places to Stay – middle

ACA's *Hotel Los Yaganes* (☎ 30822), Belgrano 319, costs US$30/40 for members, US$42/53 for non-members. Rates at *Hotel Isla del Mar* (☎ 22883), Güemes 963, start at US$45/54.

Places to Stay – top end

Enthusiastically recommended *Posada de los Sauces* (☎ 32895), Elcano 839, charges US$55/70. *Hotel Federico Ibarra* (☎ 300-71), Rosales 357, costs US$55/65, while rates at *Hotel Atlántida* (☎ 22592), Belgrano 582, are US$60/75.

Places to Eat

Hospedaje Villa, *Hotel Federico Ibarra* and *Hotel Los Yaganes* all have restaurants. You can also try *El Porteñito*, Lasserre 566 near Belgrano. For short orders and sandwiches, there are many confiterías in and around the center, including one at *Hotel Rawson*. *La Nueva Piamontesa* (☎ 21977), Belgrano 464, is an outstanding rotisería with reasonable takeaway food.

El Arriero, Belgrano 443 between Lasserre and Mackinlay, is a parrilla, as are *Las Nuevas Brasas* (☎ 22575) at Perito Moreno 635 and *El Fogón de Marcelo* (☎ 22585) at Estrada 817.

Getting There & Away

Air Aerolíneas Argentinas and Austral share offices (☎ 22748) at San Martín 607, corner of Belgrano. Aerolíneas flies twice daily to Ushuaia (US$26) and daily to Buenos Aires (US$236), while Austral goes daily except Sunday to Río Gallegos (US$48), Comodoro Rivadavia (US$126) and Buenos Aires.

LADE (☎ 21651), Lasserre 447, flies Wednesday to Ushuaia (US$16) and Thursday to Río Gallegos (US$31), El Calafate (US$59), Perito Moreno (US$100) and Comodoro Rivadavia (US$107).

Kaikén Líneas Aéreas (☎ 30665), Perito Moreno 937, flies Tuesday, Thursday and Saturday to Punta Arenas (US$69), 20 times weekly to Ushuaia (US$33), twice daily to Río Gallegos (US$39) and less frequently to Comodoro Rivadavia (US$110). Aerovías DAP (☎ 30249), 9 de Julio 597, flies daily except Sunday to Punta Arenas (US$57).

Bus Río Grande's Terminal de Omnibus is at the foot of Avenida Belgrano, on the waterfront, but most companies have offices elsewhere in town as well. Transportes San Carlos (☎ 33871), Estrada 568, has daily buses to Ushuaia (US$20, four hours) in summer, less frequently in winter, when snow infrequently closes Paso Garibaldi. They also have service to Punta Arenas (US$30, 10 hours) Monday and Friday at 7 am, and Tuesday, Thursday and Saturday at 7.30 am. Tecni-Austral (☎ 22620), Rivadavia 996, goes to Ushuaia daily at 7.30 am.

Transporte Pacheco (☎ 23382) goes to Punta Arenas Tuesday, Thursday and Saturday at 7.30 am. Transporte Senkovic (☎ 21339) goes Wednesday and Saturday at 6.30 am to Porvenir (US$20 one way, US$36 roundtrip, seven hours) in Chilean Tierra del Fuego, meeting the ferry to Punta Arenas.

Car Rental Given the limited public transportation, fishing and other excursions outside town are much simpler with a rental car, available from AI (☎ 22657) at Ameghino 612 or Avis/Tagle (☎ 22571) at Elcano 799.

AROUND RIO GRANDE

The most interesting historic site is the **Museo Salesiano**, 10 km north of town on RN 3, established by the missionary order that converted the Indians in this part of the island. Its several distinctive buildings contain excellent geological, natural history and ethnographic artifacts, but unfortunately the order does almost nothing interpretive with them.

Estancia María Behety, 20 km west, features the world's largest shearing shed. The Río Grande **frigorífico** (freezer) can

TIERRA DEL FUEGO

process up to 2400 sheep per day. **Lago Kami/Fagnano**, the huge glacial trough on RN 3 between Río Grande and Ushuaia, merits a visit; the beautifully sited *Hostería Kaikén* (☎ (0964) 24427) offers lodging for US$10/25 single/double on the ground floor, US$15/35 on the upper floor, but it's often full. Its restaurant has good but rather costly meals, with indifferent service (at best).

Fishing

Fishing is a popular recreational activity in many nearby rivers. For information on guided trips on the Fuego, Menéndez, Candelaria, Ewan and MacLennan, contact the Club de Pesca John Goodall (☎ 24324), Ricardo Rojas 606 in Río Grande. One highly recommended place is *Hostería San Pablo* (☎ (0964) 24638), 120 km southeast of Río Grande via RN 3 and RC-a, where there is good fly fishing for trout and salmon on the Río Irigoyen. Rooms cost US$30/35 single/double with breakfast included, while lunch or dinner cost an additional US$13.

USHUAIA (ARGENTINA)

Over the past two decades, fast-growing Ushuaia has evolved from a village into a city of 42,000, sprawling and spreading from its original site on the Beagle Channel, but the setting is still one of the most dramatic in the world, with jagged glacial peaks rising from sea level to nearly 1500 meters. The surrounding countryside is Ushuaia's greatest attraction, with activities like hiking, fishing and skiing, as well as the opportunity to go as far south as roads go – RN 3 ends at Bahía Lapataia, in Parque Nacional Tierra del Fuego, 3242 km from Buenos Aires.

Argentines and Chileans may debate which is the world's southernmost city, but Ushuaia clearly overshadows modest Puerto Williams, across the Channel on Isla Navarino. Wages here are higher than in central Argentina, thanks to industrial successes in electronics assembly, fishing and food processing, but so are living expenses. The boom is subsiding, though, and growing unemployment and

the provincial government's inability to meet its payroll led to civil disturbances, in which the police killed one demonstrator and injured several others, in early 1995.

In 1870, the British-based South American Missionary Society made Ushuaia its first permanent outpost in the Fuegian region, but only artifacts, shell mounds, memories and Thomas Bridges' famous dictionary remain of the Yahgan Indians who once flourished in the area. Nearby Estancia Harberton, now open to visitors, still belongs to descendants of the Bridges family.

Between 1884 and 1947, Argentina incarcerated many of its most notorious criminals and political prisoners here and on remote Isla de Los Estados (Staten Island). Since 1950, the town has been an important naval base, supporting Argentine claims to Antarctica, and in recent years it has become an important tourist destination.

Ushuaia is supposedly a free port, but foreign visitors will find few real bargains compared to Punta Arenas. In any event, it is due to lose much of the preferential treatment it now enjoys with the imposition of IVA in 2003.

Orientation

Running along the north shore of the Beagle Channel, the recently beautified Avenida Maipú becomes Avenida Malvinas Argentinas west of the cemetery and, as RN 3, continues west to Parque Nacional Tierra del Fuego. The waterfront, its harbor protected by the nearby peninsula (site of the convenient airport), is a good place to observe shorebirds.

Unlike most Argentine cities, Ushuaia has no central plaza. Most hotels and visitor services are on or within a few blocks of Avenida San Martín, the principal commercial street, one block north of Avenida Maipú. North of Avenida San Martín, streets rise very steeply, giving good views of the Beagle Channel.

Information

Tourist Offices The municipal Dirección de Turismo (☎ 32000) has moved to

Avenida San Martín 660, between 25 de Mayo and Juana Fadul, with a branch at the airport for arriving planes and another at the port for arriving ships. They maintain a complete list of hotel accommodation and current prices, will assist in finding a room with private families, and post a list of available accommodations after closing time. They also have a message board, and the friendly, patient and helpful staff usually includes an English speaker, and less frequently a German, French or Italian speaker. Opening hours are weekdays 8.30 am to 8.30 pm, Sundays and holidays 9 am to 8 pm.

The Instituto Fueguino de Turismo (Infuetur; ☎ 23340) is on the ground floor of Hotel Albatros at Maipú and Lasserre. Automóvil Club Argentino (☎ 21121) is at Malvinas Argentinas and Onachaga.

Foreign Consulates Chile has a consulate (☎ 22177) at Malvinas Argentinas 236, corner of Jaínén, open 9 am to 1 pm weekdays. Germany maintains a consulate (☎ 22778) at Rosas 516.

TIERRA DEL FUEGO

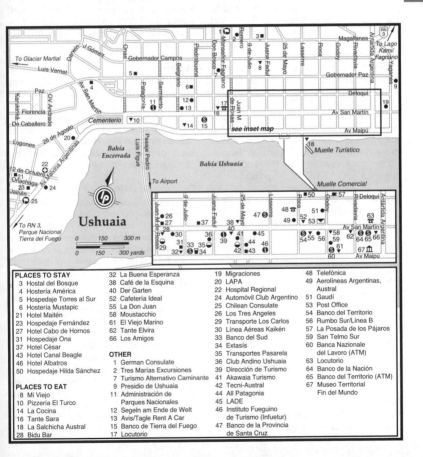

PLACES TO STAY	32 La Buena Esperanza	19 Migraciones	48 Telefónica
3 Hostal del Bosque	38 Café de la Esquina	20 LAPA	49 Aerolíneas Argentinas,
4 Hostería América	40 Der Garten	22 Hospital Regional	Austral
5 Hospedaje Torres al Sur	52 Cafetería Ideal	24 Automóvil Club Argentino	51 Gaudí
6 Hostería Mustapic	55 La Don Juan	25 Chilean Consulate	53 Post Office
21 Hotel Maitén	58 Moustacchio	26 Los Tres Angeles	54 Banco del Territorio
23 Hospedaje Fernández	61 El Viejo Marino	29 Transporte Los Carlos	56 Rumbo Sur/Línea B
27 Hotel Cabo de Hornos	62 Tante Elvira	30 Línea Aéreas Kaikén	57 La Posada de los Pájaros
31 Hospedaje Ona	66 Los Amigos	33 Banco del Sud	59 San Telmo Sur
37 Hotel César		34 Extasís	60 Banca Nazionale
43 Hotel Canal Beagle	**OTHER**	35 Transportes Pasarela	del Lavoro (ATM)
46 Hotel Albatros	1 German Consulate	36 Club Andino Ushuaia	63 Locutorio
50 Hospedaje Hilda Sánchez	2 Tres Marías Excursiones	39 Dirección de Turismo	64 Banco de la Nación
	7 Turismo Alternativo Caminante	41 Akawasia Turismo	65 Banco del Territorio (ATM)
PLACES TO EAT	9 Presidio de Ushuaia	42 Tecni-Austral	67 Museo Territorial
8 Mi Viejo	11 Administración de	44 All Patagonia	Fin del Mundo
10 Pizzería El Turco	Parques Nacionales	45 LADE	
14 La Cocina	12 Segeln am Ende del Welt	46 Instituto Fueguino	
16 Tante Sara	13 Avis/Tagle Rent A Car	de Turismo (Infuetur)	
18 La Salchicha Austral	15 Banco de Tierra del Fuego	47 Banco de la Provincia	
28 Bidu Bar	17 Locutorio	de Santa Cruz	

Immigration Migraciones is at Yaganes 120.

Money Banco de la Nación is at Avenida San Martín 190 near Rivadavia, while Banco del Sud is at Avenida Maipú 781. Banco del Territorio, at San Martín 396 at Roca, cashes travelers' checks for a 3% commission, but also has an ATM at San Martín 152. Banco de la Provincia de Santa Cruz, Lasserre 140, charges a fixed US$7 fee, no matter what the value of the check.

Banca Nazionale del Lavoro, Maipú 297 (corner of Godoy), has an ATM linked to the Cirrus system. Banco de Tierra del Fuego has one at San Martín 1052.

Post & Communications Ushuaia's area code is ☎ 901. Correo Argentino is on Avenida San Martín, at the corner of Godoy. Ushuaia's postal code is 9410.

There are convenient *locutorios* (private telephone offices) at San Martín 133 and San Martín 957. The Dirección de Turismo has a very convenient international line for collect and credit card calls to Brazil, Chile, Spain, France, Italy, Japan, Uruguay and the USA (AT&T, MCI, Sprint).

Travel Agencies Ushuaia has nearly a score of travel agencies, among them Akawaia Turismo (☎ 31371) at 25 de Mayo 64; All Patagonia (☎ 31373, fax 30707) at 25 de Mayo 31; Turismo Alternativo Caminante (☎ 32723) at Don Bosco 319, which specializes in trekking; and Rumbo Sur/Línea B (☎ 22441, fax 30699) at Avenida San Martín 342.

National Parks The Administración de Parques Nacionales (☎ 21315), San Martín 1395, is open 9 am to noon weekdays.

Laundry Los Tres Angeles (☎ 22687) is at Rosas 139.

Medical Services Ushuaia's Hospital Regional (☎ 22950, emergencies ☎ 107) is at Maipú and 12 de Octubre.

Museo Territorial Fin del Mundo
The city of Ushuaia is restoring the original facade of this unusual block construction, dating from 1903 and atypical of Magellanic architecture, that once belonged to the family of early territorial governor Manuel Fernández Valdés. An informed, enthusiastic staff oversees exhibits on Fuegian natural history, aboriginal life, the early penal colonies (complete with a photographic rogues' gallery) and replicas of an early general store and bank. There is also a bookstore and a good specialized library.

On the waterfront at Avenida Maipú and Rivadavia, the museum (☎ 21863) is well worth the US$2 admission charge (ask about student discounts). It's open Monday to Saturday, 4 to 8 pm.

Murals
Along the waterfront Avenida Maipú, note the striking mural of the Selknam/Ona 'Hain' initiation ceremony described by Lucas Bridges in his classic account of *The Uttermost Part of the Earth*. Also along Maipú, between Don Bosco and Rosas, are some overtly political anti-nuclear, pro-environment murals.

Presidio de Ushuaia
As early as 1884, Argentina's federal government established a military prison on Isla de los Estados (Staten Island), off the east coast of Tierra del Fuego, in part to support its territorial claims in a region inhabited only by hunters and gatherers with no state allegiance whatsoever. In 1902, it shifted the prison to Ushuaia and, in 1911, it merged with Ushuaia's Carcel de Reincidentes, which had incarcerated civilian recidivists since 1896.

One of Ushuaia's most famous inmates was Russian anarchist Simon Radowitzky, who assassinated Buenos Aires police chief Ramón Falcón with a bomb after a police massacre on May Day of 1909. Too young for the death penalty, Radowitzky received a life sentence at Ushuaia, briefly escaped across to Chile with the help of Argentine anarchists to whom he was a hero, was recaptured, and was later ordered released by Radical President Hipólito Yrigoyen in 1930. The military dictatorship that overthrew Yrigoyen shortly thereafter confined several Radical party figures to Ushuaia, including writer Ricardo Rojas, and diplomat and former presidential candidate Honorio Pueyrredón (along with his vice-presidential candidate Mario Guido).

Closed as a penal institution since 1947, the present building held as many as 600 inmates in 380 cells designed for one prisoner each. Incorporated into the naval base at the east end of Avenida San Martín, it's open to the public daily from 5.30 to 9 pm. Admission costs US$2; use the entrance at Yaganes and Gobernador Paz rather than the entrance to the base proper at Yaganes and San Martín.

Ferrocarril Austral Fueguino

Originally built to assist the logging industry during presidio days, Ushuaia's short-line, narrow-gauge railroad recently reopened as a tourist train under a 30-year concession, but lacks permission to enter Parque Nacional Tierra del Fuego because the concessionaire jumped the gun on an environmental impact statement. At present its only stop is at Cascada La Macarena, where there's a tourist-trap reconstruction of a Selknam/Ona camp.

From Ushuaia's Plaza Cívica, on the waterfront, Tranex (☎ 30709) operates a bus that leaves for the starting point at the Camping Municipal, eight km west of town – but the two-hour excursion would be poor value at even a small fraction of the US$28 charge. There are three departures daily, at 10 am and 3 and 5.30 pm, given a 10-passenger minimum.

Organized Tours

Local operators offer tours to the principal attractions in and around Ushuaia, including Parque Nacional Tierra del Fuego. Catamaran trips to historic Estancia Harberton, east of Ushuaia, can be arranged with sufficient notice for US$55 to US$70, but no one should arrive unannounced;

admission to the estancia costs an additional US$6 and includes the Bridges family cemetery. There are also half-day city tours (US$15 including the museum), trips to Lapataia/Parque Nacional Tierra del Fuego (US$15), and excursions over Paso Garibaldi to Lago Kami/Fagnano (US$30 full day) and Río Grande.

Boat Tours Popular boat trips, with destinations like the sea lion colony at Isla de los Lobos, leave from the Muelle Turístico (tourist jetty) on Maipú between Lasserre and Roca, and cost about US$30 for a 2½-hour excursion; with an extension to Bahía Lapataia, it costs US$45. The most common species is the southern sea lion *Otaria flavescens*, whose thick mane will make you wonder why Spanish speakers call it *lobo marino* (sea wolf). Fur seals, nearly extinct because of commercial overexploitation during the past century, survive in much smaller numbers. Isla de Pájaros, also in the Beagle Channel, has many species of birds, including extensive cormorant colonies. Trips to Estancia Harberton and its pingüinera cost US$55.

Rumbo Sur/Línea B (see Travel Agencies, above) runs the luxury catamarans *Ana B* and *Ezequiel B*. A reader recommendation is Tres Marías Excursiones (☎ 21897, ask for Héctor), Romero 514, which costs $10 per hour per person, but is smaller and can leave with fewer passengers.

Contact travel agencies like All Patagonia, Caminante or Rumbo Sur for week-long sailboat excursions around Cape Horn or the Cordillera Darwin, for about US$1200 per person. On the charter sailboat *Santa María*, German-run Segeln am Ende de Welt (☎ /fax 22771), Piedrabuena 118, crosses the channel to Puerto Williams (US$55), and also arranges longer tours, including Isla de los Estados (two weeks, US$2490) and Antarctica (four weeks, US$6500).

Activities

All travel agencies in Ushuaia arrange activities like trekking, horseback riding, canoeing, mountain biking and fishing in and around Parque Nacional Tierra del Fuego and elsewhere on the island. See the Dirección de Turismo for a listing that rates these activities from *sin dificultad* (easy) to *pesado* (very difficult).

Fishing Fishing is a popular pastime for both Argentines and foreigners; the required license is available in Ushuaia from the Asociación Caza y Pesca at Maipú and 9 de Julio, the Administración de Parques Nacionales at San Martín 1395, or Transportes Pasarela at Juana Fadul 40. Fishing licenses cost US$40 monthly, US$30 for 15 days, US$20 weekly and US$10 daily.

Spinning and fly casting are the most common means of hooking brown trout, rainbow trout, Atlantic salmon and other species. The nearest site is Río Pipo, five km west of town on RN 3. It is possible to visit the **Estación de Piscicultura**, a trout hatchery at Río Olivia, two km east of town.

Mountain Biking From October to April, local operators arrange mountain bike excursions ranging from a full day in Parque Nacional Tierra del Fuego to week-long tours over Paso Garibaldi to Lago Kami, Lago Yehuin and Río Grande. Distances range from 50 to 95 km per day and, fortunately, the wind is usually at your back.

Skiing From June to mid-September, the mountains near Ushuaia have suitable sites for both downhill and cross-country skiing, although only the period around Argentine winter holidays, in early July, is really busy. The main downhill area is **Centro de Deportes Invernales Luis Martial** (☎ 21423, 23340), seven km northwest of town, which has one 1300-meter run on a 23¡ slope, with a double-seat chairlift with a maximum capacity of 244 skiers per hour. The Club Andino Ushuaia (☎ 22335), Fadul 50, has a smaller area only three km from downtown on the same road.

East of Ushuaia, along RN 3 toward Paso Garibaldi, are cross-country ski areas at the Club Andino's Pista Francisco Jermán

five km from town, at Valle de los Huskies, 17 km from town, at Tierra Mayor, 21 km from town, at Las Cotorras, 26 km from town and at Haruwen (☎/fax 24058 in Ushuaia), 37 km from town. Rental equipment is available for around US$30 per day.

Ushuaia's biggest ski event is the annual **Marcha Blanca**, which symbolically recreates Argentine liberator José de San Martín's historic crossing of the Andes on August 17, the date of the great man's death. Attracting up to 450 skiers, it starts from Las Cotorras and climbs to Paso Garibaldi.

Places to Stay

In the summer high season, especially January and February, demand for accommodation in Ushuaia is so high that no one should arrive without reservations; if you must do so, arrive early in the day, before everything fills up. If nothing is available, the 24-hour confitería at Hotel del Glaciar is a good place to stay up drinking coffee. The tourist office does post a list of available accommodations outside the office after closing time.

Places to Stay – bottom end

Camping Ushuaia's free *Camping Municipal*, eight km west of town on RN 3 to Parque Nacional Tierra del Fuego, has minimal facilities. The *Camping del Rugby Club Ushuaia*, four km west of town, charges an extortionate US$15 per tent, but at least has reasonable facilities, including hot showers and a restaurant.

Both private and free campsites are found at Parque Nacional Tierra del Fuego, and there are also others out RN 3 toward Río Grande and Valle de los Huskies. *Camping Río Tristen*, at the Haruwen winter sports center, has a dozen sites, with shared bathrooms and showers, for US$5 per tent (two people).

Casas de Familia The tourist office regularly arranges rooms in private homes, which tend to be cheaper than hotels; because these are usually available only seasonally, and change from year to year, you should only do this through the tourist office. Prices are usually in the US$20 per person range, occasionally slightly cheaper.

Hospedajes, Pensiones & Residenciales

The cheapest permanent alternative is dilapidated *Hospedaje Ona* (☎ 24779), 9 de Julio 20 at Avenida Maipú, where dormitory-style beds cost US$15 and weekly rates are slightly lower, but it's not really good value. A better choice is *Hospedaje Torres al Sur*, Gobernador Paz 1437 between Onas and Patagonia, for $15 single. The Dirección de Turismo discourages visitors from *Hospedaje Hilda Sánchez* (☎ 23622), Deloquí 391, but many travelers have found her place congenial, if crowded and sometimes noisy. Rates are US$15 per person, and it's open all year.

Hostería América (☎ 23358), Gobernador Paz 1659, costs US$30/40. *Hostería Mustapic* (☎ 21718), at Piedrabuena 230, charges US$30/45 with shared bath, US$35/50 with private bath.

Places to Stay – middle

Mid-range accommodations start around US$45/50 at *Hotel Maitén* (☎ 22745), 12 de Octubre 140. Enthusiastically recommended *Hospedaje Fernández* (☎ 21192), Onachaga 68, has doubles for US$49, while *Hotel César* (☎ 21460), Avenida San Martín 753, costs US$45/55. On the hillside at Magallanes and Fadul, recommended *Hostal del Bosque* (☎ 21723, fax 30783) charges US$52/65 with kitchen, fridge and cable TV.

Places to Stay – top end

Waterfront hotels have the best views, but the most exclusive of them are not particularly good values; the most reasonable choice is ACA's *Hotel Canal Beagle* (☎ 21117, fax 21110), Avenida Maipú 599 at 25 de Mayo, which charges US$70/80. *Hotel Cabo de Hornos* (☎ 22187, fax 22313), Avenida San Martín at Rosas, costs US$69/79.

At *Hotel Ushuaia* (☎ 30671), Lasserre 933, rates are US$80/110, while at *Hotel*

Tolkeyén (☎ 30532), on Estancia Río Pipo five km west of town on RN 3, rooms rent for US$90/100.

Badly overpriced *Hotel Albatros* (☎ 334-46), Avenida Maipú 505 at Lasserre, charges US$132 with breakfast. For the same price, *Hotel del Glaciar* (☎ 30636), at Km 3.5 on the road west to Glaciar Martial, is a better choice, but it's still hard to call it good value at this price.

Five-star *Las Hayas Resort Hotel* (☎ 30710, fax 30719), at Km 3 on the road west to Glaciar Martial, charges US$160/170 for rooms 'surrounded by natural beauty, invaiding the hotel through its wide windows.' It sometimes lacks staff to provide all the services of a hotel in its category.

Places to Eat

Meals both cheap and good are scarce in Ushuaia. On the waterfront near the Muelle Turístico, *La Salchicha Austral* (☎ 24596) is among the most reasonable, but *La Cocina*, on Avenida Maipú between Belgrano and Piedrabuena, is a phenomenal value by current Ushuaia standards, with excellent three-course meals like lomo a la champiñon (steak with mushrooms and French fries) for US$6.50. *Der Garten*, in the gallery alongside the tourist office on San Martín, has similarly priced weekday specials, as does *Los Amigos* (☎ 22473) at San Martín 150, with a varied and interesting menu. *Pizzería El Turco* (☎ 23593), San Martín 1460, is also good and relatively inexpensive.

Café de la Esquina, at the corner of San Martín and 25 de Mayo, is Ushuaia's most popular confitería. At San Martín and Rosas, the long hours at the popular *Bidu Bar* (☎ 24605) make it a popular place to wait for the 3 am Punta Arenas bus; it has decent but not cheap meals. *Tante Sara*, at the corner of San Martín and Don Bosco, has outstanding ice cream and other desserts.

The US$12 tenedor libre (all-you-can-eat) at lively *Cafetería Ideal*, Avenida San Martín 393 at Roca, isn't really a bargain, but some travelers making it their only meal of the day find it a good choice. *Mi Viejo* (☎ 23565), Gobernador Campos 758, also has a tenedor libre special. *La Buena Esperanza*, at Maipú and 9 de Julio, has a handful of Chinese dishes.

At the pricier restaurants, reservations are essential for groups of any size. *Moustacchio* (☎ 23308), Avenida San Martín 298, has excellent food and service. *Tante Elvira* (☎ 21982, 21249), Avenida San Martín 234, also has a good reputation. *El Viejo Marino* (☎ 21911), Maipú 297, is a fairly expensive seafood restaurant. *La Don Juan* (☎ 22519), San Martín 345, is Ushuaia's only parrilla.

Entertainment
Extasís, Maipú and 9 de Julio, is a popular pub/disco. La Posada de los Pájaros (☎ 30610), at the corner of Deloqui and Godoy, is a popular café featuring live music on weekends. San Telmo Sur, Godoy 53, showcases Argentine rock and pop, while Gaudí, Godoy 136, has musical and comedy performances.

Things to Buy
Ushuaia is ostensibly a duty-free zone, but overseas visitors will find few bargains compared to Punta Arenas. Locally made chocolates are worth a taste.

Getting There & Away
Air Ushuaia has frequent air connections to other parts of Patagonia and to Buenos Aires, though its short runway, steep approach and frequent high winds have traditionally made landing here an adventure that timid flyers have preferred to avoid. A new 2700-meter runway now permits planes larger than 737s to land safely and Aerolíneas Argentinas' loss of a landing monopoly may soon permit long-distance competition from foreign airlines like Lan-Chile, Varig and Vasp.

Aerolíneas Argentinas and Austral shares offices (☎ 21091) at Roca 126. Aerolíneas flies daily to Río Gallegos (US$56) and Buenos Aires (US$252), daily except Monday and Thursday to Río Gallegos, Río Grande (US$26) and Buenos

Aires, and Monday and Thursday to Río Grande and Buenos Aires. The discount carrier LAPA (☎ 22150), Malvinas Argentinas 120, now flies from Ushuaia to Buenos Aires (US$199).

LADE (☎ 21123), in the Galería Albatros at Avenida San Martín 564, flies Thursday to Río Grande (US$16), Río Gallegos (US$43), El Calafate (US$68), Perito Moreno (US$113) and Comodoro Rivadavia (US$121).

Líneas Aéreas Kaikén (☎ 23663), San Martín 857, flies daily except Sunday to Punta Arenas, Chile (US$78); frequently to Río Grande (US$30), Río Gallegos (US$51) and El Calafate (US$83); and five times weekly to Comodoro Rivadavia (US$130).

See travel agencies for Aerovías DAP, which flies Monday, Wednesday and Friday to Punta Arenas (US$67).

Bus Transportes Los Carlos (☎ 22337), Rosas 85, crosses Paso Garibaldi via Lago Fagnano to Río Grande daily at 7 pm (US$20, four hours); Friday, Saturday, Sunday and Monday there's an additional 7 am service, while Monday and Friday at 3 am it goes directly to Punta Arenas, Chile (US$48). Tecni-Austral (☎ 23396), in the Galería del Jardín at 25 de Mayo 50, also goes to Río Grande, daily at 6 pm.

For transportation to Parque Nacional Tierra del Fuego, see the Getting There & Away entry for the park, below.

Boat At 8 am Saturdays, in theory, the *Luciano Beta* crosses from Ushuaia to Puerto Williams, Chile (US$50, 1½ hours). This is very undependable and no one should count on it.

From Puerto Williams, there are weekly sea and air connections to Punta Arenas. The *MV Tierra Australis* runs expensive cruises to Punta Arenas (3½ days, US$700) with accommodation and all meals included. See travel agents for details.

Getting Around
To/From the Airport Linked to town by a causeway, Aeropuerto Internacional

Ushuaia is on the peninsula across from the waterfront. Backpackers can walk it, but cabs are moderately priced and there's also bus service along Avenida Maipú.

Car Rental Although rural public transport is better than at Río Grande, it is still limited. Rates for a Fiat Spazio start around US$30 per day plus US$0.30 per km, plus at least US$15 insurance daily, at Avis/Tagle (☎ 22744), San Martín and Belgrano, and Localiza (☎ 30663) at Hotel Albatros, and reach up to US$120 per day plus mileage for a Toyota 4WD.

AROUND USHUAIA
Glaciar Martial
Just within the borders of Parque Nacional Tierra del Fuego, Glaciar Martial is reached via a magnificent walk that begins from the west end of Avenida San Martín, past the Parques Nacionales office, and climbs the zigzag road (there are many hiker shortcuts) to the ski run seven km northwest of town. Transportes Pasarela (☎ 21735), Fadul 40, also runs five buses daily (US$5 roundtrip) to the Aerosilla del Glaciar (chairlift), which is open 10 am to 4.30 pm daily except Monday.

From the base of the Aerosilla (which costs US$5 and saves an hour's walk), the glacier is about a two-hour walk, with awesome views of Ushuaia and the Beagle Channel. Weather is very changeable, so take warm, dry clothing and sturdy footwear.

PARQUE NACIONAL TIERRA DEL FUEGO
Its forests, bays, lakes, rivers, peaks and glaciers attract many visitors and hikers to Argentina's only coastal national park, a 63,000-hectare unit extending from the Beagle Channel in the south along the Chilean border to beyond Lago Fagnano in the north. Just 18 km west of Ushuaia via RN 3, the park lacks the integrated network of hiking trails of Chile's Torres del Paine. There are several short hiking trails, but the one major trek is now off-limits because of misguided and inexplicable policies that have declared large but lightly impacted portions of the park a *reserva estricta*, closed to all access except for scientific research, while permitting the more accessible, so-called *zona de recreación* to be trashed almost beyond belief.

Information
Parques Nacionales maintains a Centro de Información at Bahía Lapataia, at the end of RN 3. There are also rangers at the park entrance and at Lago Roca.

Flora & Fauna
Three species of the southern beech *(Nothofagus)*, known by their common names coigue, lenga and ñire, dominate the dense native forests. The evergreen coigue and deciduous lenga thrive on heavy coastal rainfall at lower elevations, but the deciduous ñire tints the Fuegian hillsides during the fall months. Other tree species are much less significant and conspicuous.

Sphagnum peat bogs in low-lying areas support ferns, colorful wildflowers, and the insectivorous plant *Drosera uniflora*; these may be seen on the self-guided nature trail, **Sendero Laguna Negra**. To avoid damage to the bog and danger to yourself, stay on the trail, part of which consists of an elevated catwalk for easier passage across the swampy terrain.

Land mammals are scarce, although guanacos and foxes exist, and marine mammals are most common on offshore islands. Visitors are most likely to see two unfortunate introductions, the European rabbit and the North American beaver, both of which have caused ecological havoc and proved impossible to eradicate. The former number up to 70 per hectare in some areas, while the handiwork of the latter is visible in the ponds and by the dead beeches along the **Sendero de los Castores** (Trail of the Beavers) to Bahía Lapataia. Originally introduced at Lago Kami/Fagnano in the 1940s, beavers quickly spread throughout the island.

Bird life is much more abundant, especially along the coastal zone, including Lapataia and Bahía Ensenada. The Andean condor and the maritime black-browed

The Frozen South

One of the unanticipated, ironic dividends of the end of the Cold War has been the increasing accessibility of Antarctica at relatively reasonable prices. About 60% of Antarctic tourists leave from Ushuaia, where it's possible to arrange visits to the frozen continent with Russian research vessels that once benefited from Soviet subsidies but must now pay their own way. To do so, they have begun to take paying passengers on 10- to 17-day Antarctic cruises on well-equipped, remodeled vessels.

Most Antarctic tours tend to the expensive, as much as US$12,000 for a month's cruise, but if space is available it's sometimes possible to get on these vessels for as little as US$1200 for a week's voyage, everything included. Several Ushuaia travel agencies, most notably All Patagonia, arrange Antarctic excursions, but it's also worth going to the port and asking around.

Overseas operators arranging Antarctic tours include Mountain Travel Sobek (☎ 510-527-8100, 800-227-2384), 6420 Fairmount Ave, El Cerrito, California 94530; Marin Expeditions (☎ 416-964-9069, 800-263-9147, fax 416-964-2366), 13 Hazelton Ave, Toronto, Ontario M5R 2E1; Nature Expeditions International (☎ 800-869-0639), PO Box 11496, 474 Willamette, Eugene, Oregon 97440; Natural Habitat Adventures (☎ 800-543-8917), 2945 Center Green Court South, Suite H, Boulder, Colorado 80301-9539; Abercrombie & Kent International (☎ 708-954-2944), 1520 Kensington Rd, Oak Brook, Illinois 60521; Forum Travel International (☎ 510-671-2993), 91 Gregory Lane, No 21, Pleasant Hill, California 94523; Zegrahm Expeditions (☎ 800-628-8747), 1414 Dexter Ave N, No 327, Seattle, Washington 98109; Ocean Voyages Inc (☎ 415-332-4681), 1709 Bridgeway, Sausalito, California 94965; and Society Expeditions (☎ 800-548-8669), 2001 Western Ave, Suite 300, Seattle, Washington 98121.

Available guidebooks to Antarctica include Diana Galimberti's Antarctica: An Introductory Guide (Buenos Aires: Zagier and Urruty Publications, 1991) and Jeff Rubin's Antarctica – a travel survival kit (Lonely Planet, 1996). ∎

albatross overlap ranges here, although neither is common. Shorebirds such as cormorants, gulls, terns, oystercatchers, grebes, steamer ducks and kelp geese are common. The large, striking upland goose (*cauquén*) is widely distributed farther inland.

Books

William Leitch's *South America's National Parks* (Seattle, The Mountaineers, 1990) has a useful chapter on Parque Nacional Tierra del Fuego, with special emphasis on natural history. Several authors have contributed to Bradt Publications' *Backpacking in Chile & Argentina* (1994), which describes treks in the area around Ushuaia but is skimpy on maps. Clem Lindenmayer's *Trekking in the Patagonian Andes* (Lonely Planet, 1997) is much more detailed.

Two useful guides for birders are Claudio Venegas Canelo's *Aves de Patagonia y Tierra del Fuego Chileno-Argentina* (Punta Arenas, 1986) and Ricardo Clark's *Aves de Tierra del Fuego y Cabo de Hornos* (Buenos Aires: Literature of Latin America, 1986).

Trekking

Most park trails are very short, and the only remaining trek permitted in the park is a mere six km along the north shore of Lago Roca to the Chilean border. The extended trek from the Río Pipo campsite, across the Montes Martial and Sierra de Valdivieso to Lago Kami/Fagnano, a rugged 30-km trip, should be simple for experienced, independent hikers, but Parques Nacionales' reclassification of the area has reduced or eliminated access. Turismo Alternativo Caminante in Ushuaia may still be able to undertake this trek. Take warm, dry clothing, good footwear, a sleeping bag, a tent and plenty of food.

Because of Argentina's perpetual fiscal

crisis and the military's proprietary attitude toward border zones, there are no official, detailed, easily available maps, but the route is fairly straightforward. Probably the best is the detailed walking map contained in Lonely Planet's *Trekking in the Patagonian Andes*.

Places to Stay

Since the *Hostería Alakush* at Lago Roca burned to the ground several years ago, camping is the only alternative for visitors wishing to stay in the park. The only organized campsite, *Camping Lago Roca*, has a confitería and hot showers for US$4 per person. Bring supplies from Ushuaia.

Camping Ensenada, *Camping Las Bandurrias*, *Camping Laguna Verde*, *Camping Los Cauquenes* and *Camping Río Pipo* are free sites which, unfortunately, are disgracefully filthy. Since they lack even pit toilets and few people bother to dig latrines, toilet paper (and worse) are scattered everywhere.

Getting There & Away

During the summer, Transporte Pasarela (☎ 21735), Fadul 40 in Ushuaia, goes to the park at 9.30 and 10 am, and 1, 5 and 7.30 pm, returning at 11 am and 2, 6 and 8.30 pm. The roundtrip fare is US$10, and you need not return the same day.

Hitching to the park is feasible, but most

Cauquén

Argentine families have little extra room in their vehicles. Park admission, payable at the ranger station on RN 3, is US$5 per person from November 1 to March 31. There are also ranger stations at Lago Roca and Lapataia.

Archipiélago Juan Fernández

Scottish maroon Alexander Selkirk left an odd legacy to the Juan Fernández archipelago. In 1966 the Chilean government, motivated explicitly by tourist concerns, renamed Isla Masatierra, the only inhabited island of the group, 'Isla Robinson Crusoe' in honor of literature's most renowned castaway. Selkirk, who spent more than four years in utter isolation on Masatierra, was the real-life model for Daniel Defoe's fictional character.

The history of the islands, though, is much more than just Alexander Selkirk, and Isla Robinson Crusoe is much more than a hermit's hideaway. Singularly tranquil, it is also a matchless national park and a Unesco World Biosphere Reserve, with much to offer the motivated traveler. Despite the government's intentions, it is not a major holiday destination and not likely to become one because of the near impossibility, and clear undesirability, of significantly expanding its tourist infrastructure.

HISTORY

Uninhabited when Spanish mariner Juan Fernández discovered them in November 1574, the islands as a group still bear his name. The modest Fernández named them the 'Islas Santa Cecilia,' but two decades passed before Spain attempted even a temporary occupation. For more than two centuries, the islands were largely a refuge for pirates and sealers who sought the pelts of the endemic Juan Fernández fur seal *(Arctocephalus phillippi)*.

According to one account, North American sealers took nearly three million sealskins off even more remote Masafuera between 1788 and 1809. Single cargoes of 100,000 pelts were not unusual, bringing the species to the point of extinction by the early 19th century. When North American sealer Benjamin Morrell visited in 1824, he speculated oddly that the absence of these seals had to do with the establishment of a Chilean penal colony:

Fur and hair-seals formerly frequented this island; but of late they have found some other place of resort, though no cause for the change has been assigned. Perhaps the moral atmosphere may have been so much affected by the introduction of three hundred felons as to become unpleasant to these sagacious animals.

Whether or not Morrell gave the fur seal too much credit for its virtue and wisdom, the Juan Fernández archipelago was most renowned for the adventures of Scotsman Alexander Selkirk, who spent more than four years marooned on Masatierra after being put ashore, at his own request, from the privateer *Cinque Ports* in 1704. This was tantamount to a death sentence for most castaways, who soon starved or shot themselves, but Selkirk survived by adapting to his new home and enduring his desperate isolation.

Ironically the Spaniards, who vigorously opposed the presence of privateers in the New World, had made his survival possible. Unlike many small islands, Masatierra had abundant water, but food could have been a problem had not the Spanish introduced goats. Disdaining fish, Selkirk tracked these feral animals and attacked them with his knife, devoured their meat and dressed himself in their skins. Sea lions, feral cats and rats – the latter two European introductions – were among his other companions.

Daily, Selkirk climbed to a lookout above Cumberland Bay (Bahía Cumberland) in hope of spotting a vessel on the horizon, but not until 1708 did his savior arrive, Commander Woodes Rogers of the privateers *Duke* and *Duchess*, with famed privateer William Dampier as his pilot. Rogers recalled first meeting with Selkirk when the ship's men returned from shore:

Immediately our Pinnace return'd from the shore, and brought abundance of Craw-fish, with a man Cloth'd in Goat-Skins, who look'd wilder than the first Owners of them.

After signing on with Rogers and returning to Scotland, Selkirk became a celebrity. Though set in the Caribbean, Defoe's fictionalized account of Selkirk's experiences became the enduring classic for which Isla Robinson Crusoe is now named.

After Selkirk's departure, privateers (*persona non grata* on the South American mainland) frequented the islands even more for rest and relaxation, of a sort, and to hunt seals. In response, Spain re-established itself at Bahía Cumberland in 1750, founding the village of San Juan Bautista. Occupation was discontinuous, though, until Chile established a permanent presence in 1877.

After the turn of the 19th century, Masatierra played a notorious role in the struggle for Chilean independence, as Spanish authorities exiled 42 Chilean patriots there after the disastrous Battle of Rancagua in 1814. The exiles, including prominent names like Juan Egaña and Manuel de Salas, neither accepted nor forgot their relegation to damp caves behind San Juan; for many years, the island remained a nearly inescapable political prison for the newly independent country. During WWI, it once again played a memorable historical role, as the British naval vessels *Glasgow* and *Orama* confronted and sank the German cruiser *Dresden* at Bahía Cumberland.

Since then, the islands have played a less conspicuous but perhaps more significant role in global history. In 1935 the Chilean government declared them a national park for preservation of their unique flora and fauna, later undertaking a program to remove the feral goats (on whose predecessors Selkirk depended so much for his subsistence) in order to preserve a priceless part of the world's natural heritage.

JUAN FERNÁNDEZ

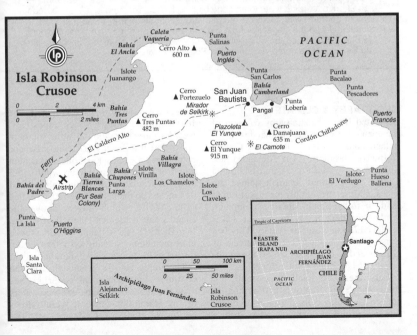

Who Was Friday?

Europeans receive credit for many achievements that other peoples accomplished first. Five hundred years after Columbus stumbled onto the Bahamas, thinking he had reached Japan, he is still known for 'discovering' a continent that Asian immigrants reached at least 12,000 years earlier. Sophisticated Polynesian navigators crossed the Pacific to South America long before Spaniards ever imagined the splendor of the Incas. And a Miskito Indian from Nicaragua spent several years' solitary exile on the Juan Fernández islands decades before Captain Stradling of the Cinque Ports put Alexander Selkirk ashore on Masatierra or Daniel Defoe made Robinson Crusoe an enduring figure in world literature.

Admittedly the young Miskito, Will, would never have seen Juan Fernández without 'help' from Europeans. Accompanying the famous English privateer William Dampier to the Pacific after meeting him in the Caribbean, Will was inadvertently left ashore when Spanish forces surprised Dampier's expedition at Cumberland Bay in 1681. For three years, he successfully evaded Spanish detection for, as Dampier wrote, 'The Moskitos are in general very kind to the English . . . but they do not love the French, and the Spaniards they hate mortally.' Even today, the Miskito of Nicaragua and Honduras prefer English to Spanish as a second language.

Will's life in the Caribbean prepared him well for his isolation in the Juan Fernández islands. Knowing the ingenuity and adaptability of the Miskito, Dampier was unsurprised to find that Will had made the most of limited resources:

He had with him his Gun and a Knife, with a small Horn of Powder and a few Shot; which being spent, he contrived a way by notching his Knife, to saw the Barrel of his Gun into small Pieces, wherewith he made Harpoons, Lances, Hooks and a long Knife, heating the pieces first in the Fire, which he struck with his Gunflint, and a piece of the Barrel of his Gun, which he hardened . . . The hot pieces of Iron he would hammer out and bend as he pleased with Stones, and saw them with his jagged Knife; or grind them to an edge by long labour, and harden them to a good Temper as there was occasion. All this may seem strange to those that are not acquainted with the Sagacity of the Indians; but it is no more than these Moskito Men are accustomed to in their own Country, where they make their own Fishing and Striking Instruments, without either Forge or Anvil . . .

GEOGRAPHY & CLIMATE

Separated from Valparaíso by 670 km of the open Pacific, the Juan Fernández archipelago consists of Isla Robinson Crusoe (formerly Masatierra), Isla Alejandro Selkirk (formerly Masafuera), and Isla Santa Clara. The original Spanish names are prosaic: Masatierra simply means 'closer to land,' ie to the South American continent, while Masafuera means 'farther out' – it is another 170 km closer to Sydney. Tiny Isla Santa Clara, known to early privateers as Goat Island, is only three km off the southern tip of Isla Robinson Crusoe.

Land areas are small, very small, but the islands' topography is extraordinarily rugged as, geologically, the entire archipelago is a group of emergent peaks from a submarine mountain range known as the Juan Fernández Ridge, which trends east-west for more than 400 km at the southern end of the Chile Basin. Isla Robinson Crusoe comprises only 93 sq km, with a maximum length of 22 km and a maximum width of 7.3 km, but reaches a maximum altitude of 915 meters on the peak of Cerro El Yunque (The Anvil), which hovers above the island's only settlement, the village of San Juan Bautista. Isla Alejandro Selkirk is even more mountainous, rising to 1650 meters on Cerro Los Inocentes, where snow has fallen.

The archipelago is far enough from the continent for subtropical water masses to moderate the chilly sub-Antarctic waters of the Humboldt Current, which flows northward along the Chilean coast. The

In Central America, the Miskito lived by hunting, fishing, gardening and gathering in the forests and on the shores of the western Caribbean. On Masatierra, without a canoe or dory (a word adapted from Miskito into English), Will could not hunt the green turtle that formed the core of Miskito subsistence, but he could fish the inshore waters of the island. There were no wild deer in Masatierra's dense forests, but he could track and kill the feral goats on which Selkirk later lived. In fact, wrote Dampier, Will was so comfortable that he could afford to be selective in his diet:

He told us that at first he was forced to eat Seal, which is very ordinary Meat, before he had made Hooks: but afterwards he never killed any Seals but to make Lines, cutting their Skins into Thongs. He had a little House or Hut half a Mile from the Sea, which was lin'd with Goats Skins; his Couch or Barbecu of Sticks lying along about two foot distant from the Ground, was spread the same, and was all his Bedding . . . He saw our Ship the Day before we came to an Anchor, and did believe we were English, and therefore kill'd three Goats in the Morning . . . and drest them with Cabbage, to treat us when we came ashore.

Dampier's return also reunited Will with a countryman named Robin ('These were names given them by the English, for they had no Names among themselves'), who 'first leap'd ashore, and running to his Brother Moskito Man, threw himself flat on his face at his feet, who helping him up, and embracing him, fell flat with his face on the Ground at Robin's feet . . . .'

This was extraordinary, but the Miskito were no strangers to remote places. It was no coincidence that Defoe placed Robinson Crusoe's fictional island in the Caribbean, where European interlopers had long depended on the Miskito for fishing, hunting and sailing skills by which 'one or two of them in a Ship, will maintain 100 Men . . .'

In reality, not just one but hundreds of Fridays helped thousands of Robinson Crusoes survive the unfamiliar and unwelcoming surroundings in the New World. Whereas the fictional Crusoe may have overshadowed the genuine Selkirk, Friday's real-life Miskito predecessor was more than just a product of Daniel Defoe's imagination. Few knew the names of Will and his countrymen except the English privateers and others 'of whom they receive a great deal of Respect.' ■

JUAN FERNÁNDEZ

climate is distinctly Mediterranean, with clearly defined warm, dry summers and cooler, wet winters. At San Juan Bautista, the maximum mean monthly temperature is 21.8°C, while the minimum mean is 10.1°C in August. Mean annual precipitation is 1000 mm, of which 70% falls between April and October; less than 10% falls in summer (December to February). Winds often exceed 25 knots.

Because of the islands' irregular topography, rainfall varies greatly over very short distances. In particular, the Cordón Chifladores (of which Cerro El Yunque is the highest point) intercepts most of the rainfall, creating a pronounced rain shadow on the southeastern portion of Isla Robinson Crusoe, which is no less barren than parts of the Atacama. By contrast, the area north of the cordón is dense rainforest, with a high concentration of the endemic species for which the islands became a national park and biosphere reserve.

The Pacific Ocean surrounds the islands, but the adjacent sea floor drops precipitously to more than 4000 meters below sea level on all sides. This leaves relatively little continental shelf to support marine fauna and flora – according to one estimate, the total area exploited for fishing is only about 325 sq km. Those maritime resources that are present, particularly the Juan Fernández lobster (*Jasus frontalis*, really a crayfish), are in great demand on the mainland and provide a substantial income for some of Isla Robinson Crusoe's residents.

FLORA

Like many oceanic islands, the Juan Fernández archipelago is a storehouse of rare plants and (to a lesser degree) animals, evolved in isolation and adapted to very specific environmental niches. The indigenous biota have suffered from the introduction of ecologically exotic species, particularly the goats which sustained Selkirk but devoured much of the original vegetation. More opportunistic plant species, resistant to grazing and to fires set by humans, colonized areas goats had degraded.

Still, a great deal remains in sectors where even an invader as agile as the goat could neither penetrate nor completely dominate the native flora. In places, the terrain is so steep that one can only proceed by grasping branches of the nearly impenetrable foliage. Once, pursuing a feral goat, Selkirk plunged over a sheer cliff and survived only because the animal's body cushioned his fall.

The vegetation of Juan Fernández presents an extraordinary mixture of geographic affinities, from the Andes and sub-Antarctic Magallanes to Hawaii and New Zealand. In their oceanic isolation, though, the flora have evolved into something very distinct from their continental and insular origins. Of 87 genera of plants on the islands, 16 are endemic, found nowhere else on earth; of 140 native plant species, 101 are endemic. These plants survive in three major communities: the evergreen rainforest, an evergreen heath and an herbaceous steppe.

The evergreen rainforest is the richest of these environments, with a wide variety of tree species such as the endemic *luma (Nothomyrcia fernandeziana)* and the *chonta (Juania australis)*, one of only two palm species native to Chile. Perhaps the most striking vegetation, though, is the dense understory of climbing vines and the towering endemic tree ferns *Dicksonia berteroana* and *Thyrsopteris elegans*. The forest was also a source of edible wild plants collected by the crews of visiting ships, as Rogers indicated:

The Cabbage Trees abound about three miles in the Woods, and the Cabbage very good; most of 'em are on the tops of the nearest and lowest mountains.

The evergreen heath replaces the rainforest on the thinner soils of the highest peaks and exceptionally steep slopes. Characteristic species are the tree fern *Blechnum cyadifolium* and various tree species of the endemic genus *Robinsonia*. The steppe, largely confined to the arid eastern sector of Isla Robinson Crusoe and to Isla Santa Clara, consists of perennial bunch grasses such as *Stipa fernandeziana*.

Exotic plant species from the mainland have provided unfortunate competition for native flora. At lower elevations, the wild blackberry *(Rubus ulmifolius)* and the shrub *maqui (Aristotelia chilensis)* have proven to be aggressive colonizers, despite efforts to control them. Lobstermen use branches from the maqui for their traps. Visiting ships, seeking fresh provisions, once collected edible wild species such as the cabbage and even planted gardens which they, and others, later harvested.

FAUNA

The only native mammal, the Juan Fernández fur seal, was nearly extinct a century ago, but has recovered to the point that about 2500 individuals now breed on the islands. The southern elephant seal *Mirounga leonina*, hunted for its blubber, no longer survives here. Of 11 endemic bird species, the most eye-catching is the Juan Fernández hummingbird *(Sephanoides fernandensis)*; the male is conspicuous because of its bright red color, while the female is a more subdued green, with a white tail. Only about 250 hummingbirds survive, feeding off the striking Juan Fernández cabbage that grows in many parts of San Juan Bautista, but the species does best in native forest.

Introduced rodents and feral cats have endangered nesting marine birds, such as Cook's petrel *(Pterodroma cookii defilippiana)*, by preying on their eggs or young. Another mammal that has proliferated since its introduction in the 1930s is the South American coatimundi (*coatí* in Spanish).

BOOKS

Available in many editions, Defoe's classic is an obvious choice, but there are many accounts of voyages that stopped at least briefly in the islands. One of the most accessible is Captain Rogers' *A Cruising Voyage Round the World*, available in a Dover Publications facsimile edition (New York, 1970). The most thorough history in English is Ralph Lee Woodward's *Robinson Crusoe's Island* (Chapel Hill, University of North Carolina Press, 1969).

If you read Spanish and have a general interest in remote oceanic islands, look for Juan Carlos Castilla's edited collection *Islas Oceánicas Chilenas* (Santiago, Ediciones Universidad Católica, 1988), which includes articles on various aspects of the natural history of Juan Fernández, Easter Island (Rapa Nui), San Félix and San Ambrosio (1000 km west of Chañaral, and inhabited only by the Chilean navy), and the uninhabited Sala y Gómez, 400 km east of Rapa Nui. There are summaries of all the articles in English.

GETTING THERE & AWAY
Air

From Santiago, two companies operate six-passenger air taxis to Juan Fernández, almost daily in summer but less frequently the rest of the year. Flights normally depart Santiago's Aeropuerto Los Cerrillos, but may be postponed when bad weather makes landing impossible on Isla Robinson Crusoe's dirt airstrip. Travel arrangements should be flexible enough to allow for an extra two or three days' stay on the island if necessary.

Lassa (☎ /fax (02) 2734309) has offices at Aeródromo Tobalaba, at Avenida Larraín 7941 in the eastern Santiago comuna of La Reina, where return flights occasionally land. The other company is Transportes Aéreos Isla Robinson Crusoe (☎ /fax (02) 5313772), whose offices are at Monumento 2570 in the southwestern comuna

of Maipú. Both companies offer charter flights for up to five passengers, but on a per person basis these are no cheaper than regularly scheduled flights.

Roundtrip fares are around US$420, but check with Lassa for discount packages that include accommodations and all meals. Another company that arranges packages is DMC Tours (☎ (02) 2341329, fax 2519528), Hernando de Aguirre 194, Oficina 22, Providencia, Santiago (Metro: Tobalaba).

San Juan Bautista is about 1½ hours from the airstrip by a combination of 4WD (down a frighteningly precipitous dirt road) to the jetty at Bahía del Padre, and motor launch (the best part of the trip, sailing more than halfway around the island's awesome volcanic coastal escarpments). Both the flight and the rest of the voyage, however, can be rough, so travelers prone to motion sickness may want to consider preventative medication. Cost of the launch, normally about US$15 return, should be included in your air ticket, but check to be certain.

Boat

Without your own boat, it's not easy to sail to Juan Fernández, but quarterly naval supply ships do carry passengers for next to nothing, barely the cost of food. Unfortunately, it's hard to learn departure dates without hiring the CIA, since even the most innocuous Chilean naval movements are top secret – but try contacting the Comando de Transporte (☎ (032) 258457) at the Primera Zona Naval, opposite Plaza Sotomayor in Valparaíso.

GETTING AROUND

Getting around Isla Robinson Crusoe presents no major problems but is not necessarily cheap, since it requires hiring a fishing boat or, perhaps more economically, accompanying the lobster catchers to their grounds. To arrange a launch, contact Polo González at Lassa's office on the plaza, or at his cabañas; rates are fixed by the Municipalidad. A launch to Puerto Inglés, for example, costs US$15 for up to

JUAN FERNÁNDEZ

eight passengers. Conaf rangers visiting outlying sites in their launch may be willing to take along passengers.

Getting to and from Isla Alejandro Selkirk, rarely visited by any foreigner, presents serious problems, but fishing boats will sometimes carry passengers. During lobster season, a Conaf ranger stays on the island. If you should manage to get there, you may have to stay for months.

SAN JUAN BAUTISTA

San Juan Bautista, the only settlement on Isla Robinson Crusoe, has a permanent population of about 500, of whom perhaps 100 are transplanted mainlanders. With only two motor vehicles (not counting launches), neither of which is ordinarily in service, San Juan Bautista is one of Chile's most tranquil places. Immigrants from the mainland soon adjust to the relaxed pace of island life. Most visitors to Juan Fernández stay here or at nearby Pangal, although it's possible to camp in parts of the national park.

The island economy depends on fishing, mostly for lobster, which are flown to Santiago by air taxi. Most of the 120 fishermen work in open boats, but a handful have cabins on their launches. Leaving early in the morning to check their 30 to 40 traps each, they return in the evening to sell their catch to individuals, hotels and the several mainland companies that purchase the lobsters for about US$20 each.

Recent competition from Peru and Australia, where production costs are lower, has undercut the local economy, but traditionally a successful lobsterman can average half a dozen per day, earning a very substantial income in a place where living costs are low except for a few imported luxuries. Some do so well in the lobster season between October and May that they can take the rest of the year off, while others spend the winter in search of *bacalao* (cod), which they salt and send to the mainland.

Links to the mainland are significant, since there is no indigenous population, but many islanders rarely or never visit the 'continent,' as they call the Chilean mainland. Children attend school locally up until the eighth grade, after which the most academically talented can obtain grants to finish their secondary education elsewhere in Chile.

Orientation

Surrounded by forests of exotic conifers and eucalyptus, planted to stem erosion on the nearby hills, San Juan Bautista occupies a protected eastward-facing site on Bahía Cumberland where, in the evening, schools of flying fish skim across the water. Away from the village, the island's vegetation is more strictly indigenous.

Launches from Bahía del Padre land at the jetty, a short walk from the main street, Larraín Alcalde, which intersects the pleasant Costanera El Palillo a few hundred meters to the south. Other streets – La Pólvora, Subida El Castillo, El Yunque and Vicente González – climb steeply from the shore. There is a bridge across Estero Lord Anson, a stream that flows into the bay. A short distance south of the jetty, there is a landing site for the Chilean navy's roll-on-roll-off cargo vessels. This serves as San Juan Bautista's de facto beach, but there is better swimming and diving off the rocks at El Palillo, at the southern end of the Costanera.

Information

Tourist Office The Municipalidad (☎ 701-045, fax 751047), on Larraín Alcalde near the plaza, has Sernatur leaflets with very decent maps and information about San Juan Bautista and Isla Robinson Crusoe.

Money There is no bank or cambio on the island, so bring all the money you need from the mainland, preferably in small bills. Hostería El Pangal and other hotels normally accept US dollars in payment for lodging, but credit card payments are impossible.

Post & Communications The area code on the island is ☎ 32. Correos de Chile is on the south side of the plaza. There are now direct telephone connections to San Juan from the mainland.

National Parks Conaf offices (☎ 751022) are at the top of Vicente González, about 500 meters above the Costanera. For information on visiting any part of the park outside the immediate environs of San Juan Bautista, it is advisable to contact Conaf in advance. Ask for a tour of its plant nursery, where both native and exotic tree species are cultivated, the latter for planting only near the town.

Medical Services The Posta Rural, a government clinic, is also on Vicente González, just below the entrance to Conaf's grounds.

Cementerio
San Juan's cemetery, at the north end of Bahía Cumberland near the lighthouse, provides a unique perspective on the island's history, with its polyglot assortment of Spanish, French and German surnames – the latter survivors of the sinking of the *Dresden*.

Cuevas de Los Patriotas
In these caverns behind San Juan Bautista, reached by a short footpath from Larraín Alcalde, Juan Egaña, Manuel de Salas and 40 other participants in Chile's independence movement spent several years after their defeat in the Battle of Rancagua in 1814.

Fuerte Santa Bárbara
In 1767 a British visitor, surprised to learn that Spain had established a permanent presence at Bahía Cumberland, reported that:

This fort, which is faced with stone, has eighteen or twenty embrasures, and within it a long house, which I supposed to be barracks for the garrison: five and twenty or thirty houses of different kinds are scattered round it . . .

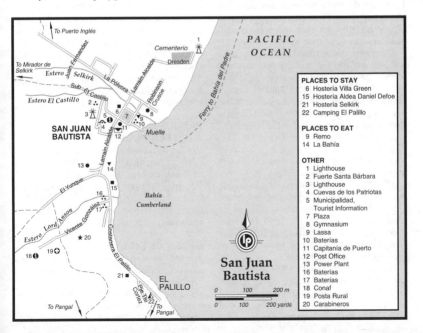

PLACES TO STAY
6 Hostería Villa Green
15 Hostería Aldea Daniel Defoe
21 Hostería Selkirk
22 Camping El Palillo

PLACES TO EAT
9 Remo
14 La Bahía

OTHER
1 Lighthouse
2 Fuerte Santa Bárbara
3 Lighthouse
4 Cuevas de los Patriotas
5 Municipalidad,
   Tourist Information
7 Plaza
8 Gymnasium
9 Lassa
10 Baterías
11 Capitanía de Puerto
12 Post Office
13 Power Plant
16 Baterías
17 Baterías
18 Conaf
19 Posta Rural
20 Carabineros

San Juan Bautista

Built in 1749 to discourage incursions by pirates, these Spanish fortifications were reconstructed in 1974. To get there, follow the path north along the Cuevas de los Patriotas, or else climb directly from the plaza via Subida El Castillo.

Special Events

June 29 is the Fiesta de San Pedro, in honor of the patron saint of fishermen. On November 22, the anniversary of the original Spanish discovery, islanders celebrate Día de la Isla.

Places to Stay & Eat

At the south end of the Costanera, Conaf's quiet and pleasant *Camping El Palillo* is free of charge, with running water and a pit latrine. There is plenty of firewood, but the nearest shower, with cold water only, is a 15-minute walk away at the jetty. There is another convenient site at *Plazoleta El Yunque* (see Parque Nacional Juan Fernández, below). Elsewhere in Parque Nacional Juan Fernández, camping is permitted just about anywhere except in the park's *zona intangible*, though in some areas you'll need to carry your own water.

Otherwise, accommodation tends towards the costly, but usually includes full board (remember that this includes lobster every day). Visitors with special dietary requirements, such as vegetarians or those who cannot eat seafood, should inform their hotel prior to arrival in the islands.

Hostería Aldea Daniel Defoe (☎ 751-075), open all year on the Costanera near Vicente González, has shoreline cabins that appear a bit ramshackle but are really very comfortable, for US$60/80 single/double with breakfast. Half-board and full board are available, and the hotel also serves meals to non-guests, although the food is dearer and no better than that at La Bahía (see below). The staff will, however, prepare lobster for one person.

Hostería Villa Green (☎ 751044), on Larraín Alcalde opposite the plaza, charges US$40/70 for a single/double including breakfast, US$65/107 with half-board, and US$77/145 with full board. On beautiful grounds on the Costanera, *Hostería Selkirk* (☎ 751107) has singles for US$50, doubles for US$90, with half-board.

Lassa runs *Hostería El Pangal* (☎ (02) 2734354, fax 2734309 in Santiago), which can be reached by launch from the jetty at San Juan Bautista, or by an hour's walk south along an interesting trail with excellent views of the village and Cerro El Yunque en route. Unfortunately, the area around Pangal is less interesting, badly eroded, and less convenient to other areas around the park. It can also be much more expensive at US$115 single or US$198 double with full board, but does have relatively economical bunks from US$31 single without meals, US$69 with full board.

If you're not staying at one of the few hotels, give restaurants several hours' notice if you wish to have lunch or dinner. Despite its modest appearance, *La Bahía* on Larraín Alcalde is one of the best-value places in Chile. Owner Jorge Angulo prepares an extraordinary ceviche, and also has succulent lobster for about US$15 per person (he does, however, require a two-person minimum so the other half of the lobster doesn't go to waste. Try also *vidriola*, an especially tasty fish that is much cheaper.

Remo, on the northeast side of the plaza, serves only sandwiches and drinks, but has longer opening hours than other places.

PARQUE NACIONAL JUAN FERNANDEZ

Parque Nacional Juan Fernández includes every square inch of the archipelago, a total of 9300 hectares, though the township of San Juan Bautista is a de facto exclusion. Park admission costs US$12.50 for adult foreigners, US$6 for children; Chilean nationals pay about half.

Mirador de Selkirk

To see what Selkirk saw, hike to his *mirador* (lookout) above San Juan Bautista. The three-km walk, gaining 565 meters in elevation, takes about 1½ hours of steady walking but rewards the climber with views of both sides of the island, although it is

WAYNE BERNHARDSON

Cuernos del Paine, Parque Nacional Torres del Paine

WAYNE BERNHARDSON

Monumento al Ovejero, Punta Arenas

WAYNE BERNHARDSON

Lago Nordenskjöld

WAYNE BERNHARDSON

Salto Grande, PN Torres del Paine

WAYNE BERNHARDSON

Cuernos del Paine, PN Torres del Paine

Images of Archipiélago Juan Fernández

Puerto Inglés, Isla Robinson Crusoe

Volcanic cliffs, Isla Robinson Crusoe

WAYNE BERNHARDSON

Kneeling moai at Rano Raraku

WAYNE BERNHARDSON

Moai at Ahu Akivi

WAYNE BERNHARDSON

Orongo ceremonial village

WAYNE BERNHARDSON

Rano Kau crater

WAYNE BERNHARDSON

Playa Ovahe

Images of the Falkland Islands

Loading wool on Weddell Island, West Falkland

King penguins

Ross Rd, Stanley

Port Howard, West Falkland

sometimes obscured by clouds. Start as early in the morning as possible and take at least a light cotton shirt since the overlook, exposed to wind and weather, can be much cooler than at sea level.

On the saddle, there are two metal plaques commemorating Selkirk's exile on the island. The first, minted by John Child & Son of Valparaíso and placed there by officials of the Royal Navy, reads:

In memory of Alexander Selkirk, Mariner, a native of Largo, in the county of Fife, Scotland, who lived on this island in complete solitude for four years and four months.

He was landed from the *Cinque Ports* galley, 96 tons, 16 guns, A D 1704 and was taken off in the *Duke*, privateer, 12th Feb, 1709.

He died lieutenant of *HMS Weymouth*, AD 1723, aged 47 years.

This tablet is erected near Selkirk's lookout, by Commodore Powell and the officers of *HMS Topaze*, AD 1868.

More than a century later, a Scottish relative added his own tribute:

Tablet placed here by Allan Jardine of Largo, Fife, Scotland, direct descendant of Alexander Selkirk's brother David. Remembrance 'Till a' the seas gang dry and the rocks melt in the sun.' January 1983.

The trail to the Mirador begins at the south end of the plaza of San Juan Bautista, climbs the Subida El Castillo, and follows the north side of Estero El Castillo before zigzagging up Cerro Portezuelo to Selkirk's lookout – fill your canteen before continuing up the hillside through dense thickets of maqui and blackberry, which gradually give way to native ferns and trees. Beyond Selkirk's overlook, the trail continues to the airstrip. If you're camping west of the pass, it's possible to walk there to catch your flight back to the mainland, but make arrangements before leaving San Juan Bautista or you could lose your reservation.

Plazoleta El Yunque & El Camote
Plazoleta El Yunque, half an hour's walk

from San Juan Bautista via a road-trail just beyond the power station at the south end of Larraín Alcalde, is a tranquil forest clearing with picnic and camping areas. A German survivor of the *Dresden* once homesteaded here; the foundations of his house are still visible.

Beyond the plazoleta is a very difficult and poorly marked trail to a saddle at El Camote, which has a splendid view of the south coast of Isla Robinson Crusoe and the offshore Islote (islet) El Verdugo. This short but exhausting hike is very rewarding but, as part of the *zona intangible*, entry is restricted without special permission. Conaf rangers may accompany motivated hikers who, in any event, will not be able to locate the trail without them. Some of the park's best-preserved flora can be found in this area.

Puerto Inglés
Only a 15-minute boat ride from San Juan Bautista, Puerto Inglés offers a reconstruction of the shelter in which Selkirk passed his years on Masatierra. There are also ruins of a cowherd's shelter and adequate water for camping, but no firewood. If you don't care to pay up to US$14 for a very short boat ride, there is a steep, tiring trail from the top of Calle La Pólvora that will take you over the ridge in about two hours.

Bahía Tierras Blancas
Isla Robinson Crusoe's only breeding colony of Juan Fernández fur seals is at Bahía Tierras Blancas, a short distance east of the landing strip above Bahía del Padre. The trail, which connects the airstrip with San Juan Bautista via Mirador Selkirk, passes close to the colony, but there is no drinking water, so you must bring your own if you plan to camp. Fishermen will also take passengers to Tierras Blancas.

If you can't visit Tierras Blancas, you can still see pods of fur seals at Bahía del Padre on your arrival, or at the north end of Bahía Cumberland, just beyond the cemetery in San Juan Bautista. Although the seals will not come up on the rocks, you can get within about 10 meters of them.

Easter Island (Rapa Nui)

How Pacific Islanders arrived at Easter Island (Rapa Nui), the world's most remote inhabited island, is no less an enigma than how their descendants could design and sculpt hundreds of colossal *moai* from hard volcanic tuff, transport these tall and heavy statues great distances from quarry to coast and erect them on great stone *ahu* (platforms).

Residents and visitors have applied various names to this small, isolated volcanic land mass. Polynesian settlers named it Rapa Nui, but the view of the seemingly infinite sea from the summit of Terevaka, the island's highest point, reveals why they also called it Te Pito o Te Henua – the Navel (Center) of the World. From here, a vessel can sail more than 1900 km in any direction without sighting inhabited land.

Dutch mariner Jacob Roggeveen, the first European to sight the island, named it Easter Island after the date of his discovery; the Spaniards first called it San Carlos (after King Carlos III). Other mariners dubbed it Davis's Land after confusing it with territory identified by the 17th-century English pirate Edward Davis. Roggeveen's legacy survived among Europeans, however: English speakers call it Easter Island, Spanish speakers refer to Isla de Pascua, Germans to Osterinsel.

HISTORY

In archaeology and antiquity, Rapa Nui raises issues totally disproportionate to its size (only 117 sq km) and population (2764 according to the 1992 census). The nearest populated land mass, 1900 km west, is even tinier Pitcairn Island of *Bounty* fame, and the next nearest inhabited 'neighbors' are the Mangarévas (Gambier) islands, 2500 km west, and the Marquesas, 3200 km northwest. The South American coast is 3700 km to the east. Yet Rapa Nui is central to some very big questions.

The most obvious ones are where the original islanders came from, how they arrived at such an unlikely destination, what inspired them to build the imposing monuments for which Rapa Nui is so famous, and how they transported these from quarry to site. Even larger questions deal with the existence and frequency of trans-Pacific contacts, and cultural exchanges between peoples for whom the world's greatest ocean would presumably have been an insurmountable barrier.

Five centuries ago, the first encounters between Europe and the Americas marked the beginning of a global transformation that no one could have anticipated when Columbus, thinking he had reached Japan, set foot in the Bahamas. Everyone knows, of course, that Europeans crossed the Atlantic long before Columbus, but their transient presence made little impact upon North America. Could trans-Pacific crossings have been more significant?

There is broad consensus that the first Americans were Asiatic peoples who crossed the Bering Strait into Alaska via a land bridge, which disappeared as sea level rose with the melting of the continental ice sheets at the end of the Pleistocene, about 12,000 years ago. Exact dates are in dispute (some argue that crossings took place during even earlier glacial epochs), although no one doubts that such migrations ceased with the rising oceans. These immigrants reached the southernmost extremes of South America and created the great civilizations of Mexico and Peru. For millennia they were isolated from their Asiatic origins.

But how isolated, and for how long? Among scholars of prehistory, there is a long-running debate between two major schools of thought: partisans of 'independent invention' assert that New World civilizations evolved in geographical isolation until the voyages of Columbus, while 'diffusionists' argue in favor of substantial

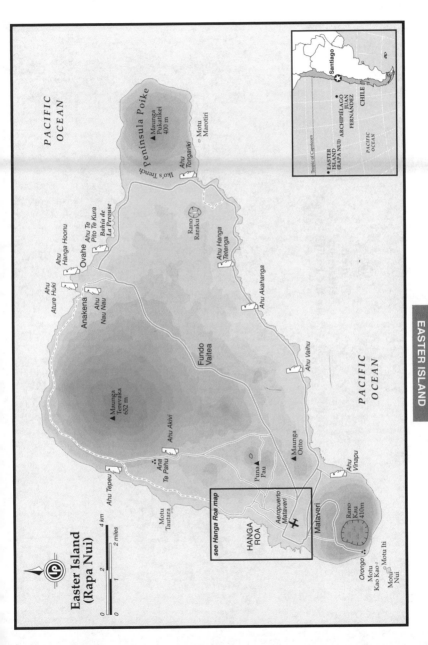

EASTER ISLAND

EASTER ISLAND

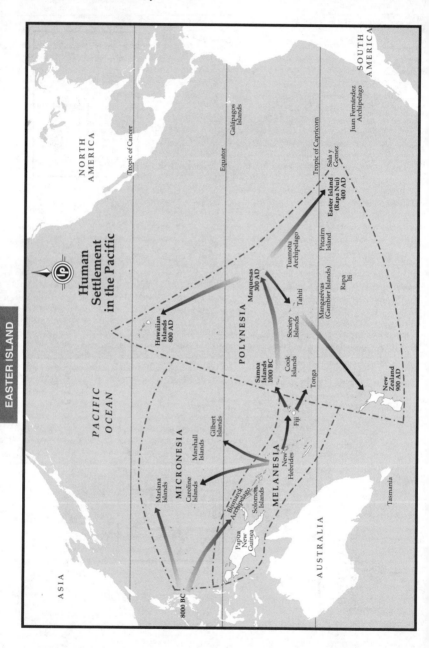

Human Settlement in the Pacific

evidence of contacts and cultural exchange across the Pacific long before 1492. Important economic plants, such as the coconut, appear to have been present in both the Eastern and Western Hemispheres when Europeans first saw the New World, while the sweet potato, a New World domesticate, was also a widely diffused Polynesian staple. Patterns of navigation and settlement in the Pacific are central to diffusionist arguments, and Rapa Nui is a key piece in a complex puzzle, the last possible stopover on eastbound voyages to South America and the first on westbound ones to Polynesia.

At the time of the Spanish invasion, the inhabitants of Peru knew of distant Pacific islands; there is evidence of long coastal voyages to Mexico and, centuries before, their ancestors may have sailed to Rapa Nui. In 1947 Norwegian explorer-archaeologist Thor Heyerdahl proved that such voyages were feasible when his balsa raft *Kon-Tiki*, built like early Pacific watercraft, sailed from South America to Raroia, in Polynesia's Tuamotu Archipelago.

After sailing past Rapa Nui on a voyage from Chile, an early-19th-century European mariner described a strong southern branch of the Humboldt (or Peru) Current that, he said, could speed vessels from northern Chile and southern Peru toward this island even with contrary winds. He strongly advised that all sailing ships follow this route to the South Sea Islands.

Under these conditions it is conceivable that South American Indians reached Rapa Nui by pre-Columbian watercraft on deliberate voyages of exploration rather than by chance drifting with the winds and currents. Given that drifters would probably not have survived a voyage for which they were unprepared, it seems unlikely they would have found Rapa Nui by chance.

It is more probable that Polynesians settled the island from the west. These peoples managed to disperse over a myriad of islands within a gigantic triangle whose apexes were at New Zealand, Hawaii and Rapa Nui, plus a handful of islands deep in Melanesia and along the southern limits of

Micronesia. Orthodox academic opinion currently favors an Asiatic origin for the Polynesian peoples who, apparently, built the Rapa Nui monuments.

Details vary, but there is general agreement that migration into the Pacific region began 50,000 years ago when ancestors of the Australian aboriginals and New Guinea highlanders first crossed the sea in search of new homelands. Papuan-speaking peoples settled the islands of New Britain, New Ireland and perhaps the Solomons, no later than 10,000 years ago – possibly much earlier.

Malay-Polynesian speakers, who had colonized the western islands of Micronesia, Fiji, Samoa and Tonga by about 1000 BC, achieved the settlement of the Pacific beyond the Solomons. A distinctive Polynesian culture may have developed on Samoa and Tonga; the final migrations probably started from Samoa and Tonga early in the first millennium AD. Large double canoes, capable of carrying the food and domestic animals required for colonization, sailed eastward to settle the Marquesas around 300 AD, or perhaps two centuries earlier. From the Marquesas, migrants settled Rapa Nui by about 400 AD, Hawaii by 800 AD or even earlier, and New Zealand by 900 AD.

Both Polynesians and South American Indians appear to have launched voyages of exploration into the Pacific, establishing the position of the islands they discovered, recording that information, and passing it on to others. Intriguingly, Rapa Nui legends describe the arrival of two different peoples – the 'Long Ears' from the east and the 'Short Ears' from the west.

Legend of Hotu Matua

By oral tradition, Rapa Nui's history falls into three distinct periods. First came the arrival of King Hotu Matua and his followers, the initial settlers. There followed a period of rivalry between the Long Ears and Short Ears, ending with the extermination of the Long Ears. Lastly, there was a more recent tribal war between the peoples of the Tuu and Hotu-iti regions.

Easter Islander in ceremonial dress

According to tradition, Hotu Matua came from the east and landed at Anakena on the island's north coast *(matua* – the 'prolific father' – is a Polynesian word for 'ancestor' and means 'father' on Rapa Nui). Some 57 generations of kings followed him – from which some estimate that he arrived around 450 AD. A second group of immigrants supposedly arrived later, from the west, led by Tuu-ko-ihu.

By the early 20th century, however, European visitors had recorded confused and contradictory versions of this legend. Hotu Matua's voyage had a number of starting points: the Galápagos Islands to the northeast, the Tuamotu Archipelago to the northwest, Rapa Iti to the west and the Marquesas to the northwest. Some versions even have Tuu-ko-ihu arriving on Hotu Matua's boats.

Trying to date events using genealogies is difficult and uncertain; researchers have collected a number of different lists of

kings descended from Hotu Matua. One, estimating 20 to 30 generations descended from Hotu Matua until the last native king died after a slave raid in 1862, concluded that Hotu Matua arrived at Rapa Nui as late as the 16th century.

Long Ears & Short Ears
In Rapa Nui oral tradition, a gap exists between the arrival of Hotu Matua and the division of islanders into Long Ear and Short Ear groups. One explanation is that Long Ear immigrants may have come from Polynesia, where some groups practiced the custom of ear lobe elongation, but it's not impossible that arrivals from pre-Columbian Peru brought the custom.

Attempting to reconcile oral tradition with migration theories, some have speculated that the Long Ears arrived with Hotu Matua from Polynesia, followed by the Short Ears under Tuu-ko-ihu from the west. Some suggest that the Long Ears built the great ahu and that the Short Ears carved the moai and placed them on the ahu, while others hold that the Long Ears carved the moai with assistance from Short Ears.

At some time, though, conflict between the two groups resulted in the near extermination of the Long Ears – perhaps a single survivor remained. Calculating from genealogies of islanders claiming descent from the last Long Ear (who had married a Short Ear woman after the end of the war), one estimate placed that survivor in the second half of the 17th century. The reasons for this warfare appear to have been demographic and ecological, resulting in damage or destruction of many of Rapa Nui's stone monuments.

Toppling of the Moai
A long peace ensued after the Short Ears' victory, but eventual dissension between different families or clans led to bloody wars in which cannibalism was practiced,

and many moai were toppled from their ahu. According to one account, tribes or clans were highly territorial and proud of their moai, while enemy groups would topple the moai to insult and anger their owners. The only moai standing today have been restored this century.

Arrival of the Dutch

Spanish vessels entered the Pacific from South America in the early 16th century, but in April 1722 a Dutch expedition under Admiral Jacob Roggeveen became the first Europeans to set foot on Rapa Nui. Roggeveen recorded his observations in the ship's log, while another crew member, Carl Behrens, published an account of the voyage. Since they landed on Easter Sunday, by common European custom Rapa Nui acquired the name Easter Island.

The Dutch found the islanders, who subsisted primarily on produce from intensively cultivated gardens and secondarily on the limited wealth of the sea, very friendly. The great moai, though, baffled them despite their obvious religious significance. According to Roggeveen:

What the form of worship of these people comprises we were not able to gather any full knowledge of, owing to the shortness of our stay among them; we noticed only that they kindle fire in front of certain remarkably tall stone figures they set up; and, thereafter squatting on their heels with heads bowed down, they bring the palms of their hands together and alternately raise and lower them.

Behrens recorded that the islanders:

. . . relied in case of need on their gods or idols which stand erected all along the sea shore in great numbers, before which they fall down and invoke them. These idols were all hewn out of stone, and in the form of a man, with long ears, adorned on the head with a crown . . .

Behrens mentioned that some islanders wore wooden blocks or discs in their elongated ear lobes – some of which were so long that, after removing the plugs, islanders hitched the lobe over the top of

the ear to keep it from flapping. He concluded that those with blocks or discs who also shaved their heads were probably priests. Those who did not cut their hair wore it long, either hanging down the back or else plaited and coiled on the top of the head.

The Spanish Expedition

Not until 1770 did Europeans again visit Rapa Nui, when a Spanish party from Peru under Don Felipe González de Haedo claimed the island for Spain and renamed it San Carlos. The Spaniards noted that male islanders generally went unclothed, wearing only plumes on their heads, while a few wore a sort of colored poncho or cloak. Women wore hats made of rushes, a short cloak around the breasts and another wrap from the waist down.

Most islanders inhabited caves, but others lived in elliptical boat-shaped houses, probably the type seen by the Dutch. Their only weapons were sharp obsidian knives. The absence of goods and metal implements suggested no commerce with the outside world, but gardens with sugar cane, sweet potatoes, taro and yams provided a healthy subsistence. An officer of the expedition recorded that the islanders' appearance:

. . . [did] not resemble that of the Indians of the Continent of Chile, Peru or New Spain in anything, these islanders being in colour between white, swarthy and reddish, not thick-lipped nor flat nosed, the hair chestnut coloured and limp, some have it black, and others tending to red or a cinnamon tint. They are tall, well built and proportioned in all their limbs; and there are no halt, maimed, bent, crooked, luxated, deformed or bow legged among them, their appearance being thoroughly pleasing, and tallying with Europeans more than with Indians.

Captain Cook

In 1774, the famous Englishman Captain James Cook led the next European expedition to land on Rapa Nui. Cook, familiar with the Society Islands, Tonga and New Zealand, concluded that the inhabitants of Rapa Nui belonged to the same

EASTER ISLAND

general lineage. Later accounts concurred on their Polynesian origins; in 1864 Eugene Eyraud, the first European missionary on the island, commented:

These savages are tall, strong, and well built. Their features resemble far more the European type than those of the other islanders of Oceania. Among all the Polynesians the Marquesans are those to which they display the greatest resemblance. Their complexion, although a little copper-coloured, does neither differ much from the hue of the European, and a great number are even completely white.

Cook believed that islanders no longer regarded the moai as idols and thought them monuments to former kings; the ahu appeared to be burial sites. His account is the first to mention that, though some moai still stood and carried their topknots, others had fallen and their ahu were damaged. Cook found the islanders poor and distressed, describing them as small, lean, timid and miserable.

It seems probable then, that war had raged since the Spanish visit in 1770, reducing the population to misery and destroying some of the moai. Another theory is that the islanders, wary of foreigners, hid in caves from Cook's crew, but this contradicts Roggeveen's account of friendly islanders. It's possible that a number of moai had been toppled even before the Spanish and Dutch visits, but that those sailors did not visit the same sites as Cook.

Only one other 18th-century European, the Frenchman La Perouse, visited Rapa Nui. After his two ships crossed from Chile in 1786, he found the population calm and prosperous, suggesting a quick recovery from any catastrophe. In 1804, a Russian visitor reported more than 20 moai still standing, including some at the southern coastal site of Vinapu. Accounts from ensuing years suggest another period of destruction, so that perhaps only a handful of moai stood a decade later.

Population, Environment & Warfare
What explains warfare on Rapa Nui and the

destruction of the moai? Recent research suggests a demographic explanation: islanders were few when Hotu Matua first landed at Anakena, but over the centuries the population grew, first slowly and then rapidly, so that sheer numbers threatened the natural resource base. Once intensively cultivated gardens yielded an agricultural surplus sufficient to support a priestly class, the artisans and laborers who produced the moai and their ahu, and even a warrior class.

There were limits to this intensification, however. Irrigation, for instance, was difficult or impossible in an environment that lacked surface streams. Forest resources, probably used for timber to move the moai to their ahu, declined greatly, a situation that worsened when warriors used fire for military purposes. Marine food resources were too poor and dispersed to provide more than a supplement to agriculture.

Conflict over land and resources erupted in warfare by the late 17th century, only shortly before Roggeveen's arrival; accounts by later European visitors, such as Cook, provide snapshots of the results of what must have been a protracted struggle in which population declined even before slave raids in the mid-19th century. Alfred Metraux estimated a population of up to 4000 for the early 19th century, while Katherine Routledge speculated on a maximum population of about 7000, but other informed guesses range up to 20,000. Colonialism, a late arrival, delivered the final blow.

Colonialism in the Pacific
Whether or not the people of Rapa Nui experienced a period of self-inflicted havoc, their discovery by the outside world almost resulted in their annihilation. The first catastrophe was the Peruvian slave raid of 1862, leading directly or indirectly to many deaths. Then followed a brief but violent period involving the transportation of many more islanders to foreign mines and plantations, the introduction of previously unknown diseases, emigration compelled by missionaries, and the near-disintegration of local culture.

The Peruvian raid happened when, after the European voyages of the late 18th century, European and North American entrepreneurs saw the Pacific as an unexploited 'resource frontier.' First came the whalers – many of them North American – who ranged the Pacific from Chile to Australia. Then came planters who set out to satisfy increasing European demand for tropical agricultural products like rubber, sugar, copra and coffee. This often resulted in indigenous peoples' becoming slaves or wage laborers on their own lands, or in the importation of foreign labor where local labor proved insufficient, inefficient or difficult to control.

Then came slavers who either kidnapped Polynesians or – to give the trade a veneer of legitimacy – compelled or induced them to sign contracts to work in lands as remote as Australia and Peru. Many died from the rigors of hard labor, poor diet, disease and maltreatment. Christian missionaries, undermining and degrading local customs, also entered the region.

Events on Rapa Nui in the 19th century closely followed this pattern. Since the 1860s, local history consists of three periods: one in which a French sea captain ruled the island; a second, from 1888 to 1952, when a Chilean-Scottish sheep-grazing concern leased nearly the entire island; and the third with the active intervention of the Chilean state.

The Peruvian Slave Raid

Violent encounters had occurred between Europeans and islanders ever since Roggeveen's landing, but the Peruvian raid of 1862 was vicious and ruthless. Slavers kidnapped about a thousand islanders (including the king and nearly all the *maori* or 'learned men') and took them to work the guano deposits on Peru's Chincha Islands. After Bishop Jaussen of Tahiti protested to the French representative at Lima, Peruvian authorities ordered the return of the islanders to their homeland, but disease and hard labor had already killed about 900 of them. On the return voyage, smallpox killed most of the rest – and the handful

who survived brought an epidemic that decimated the remaining inhabitants, leaving perhaps only a few hundred.

The first attempts at Christianizing the island occurred after this disaster. Eugene Eyraud, of the Chilean branch of the French Catholic *Société de Picpus*, initially met resistance and left in 1864, but returned in 1866. With the assistance of other missionaries, he converted the islanders within a few years.

Dutroux-Bornier Period (1870-1877)

The first attempt at commercial exploitation of the island began in 1870, when Frenchman Jean-Baptiste Dutroux-Bornier settled at Mataveri, at the foot of Rano Kau. Importing sheep, he intended to transform the entire island into a ranch and expel the islanders to the plantations of Tahiti. The missionaries, who planned to ship them to mission lands in southern Chile or the Mangarévas, opposed his claims to ultimate sovereignty over the island and its people.

Dutroux-Bornier armed local followers and raided the missionary settlements, burning houses and destroying crops, leaving many people dead or injured, and forcing the missionaries to evacuate in 1870 and 1871. Most islanders reluctantly accepted transportation to Tahiti and the Mangarévas, leaving only about a hundred people on the island. Dutroux-Bornier ruled until the remaining islanders killed him in 1877.

Annexation by Chile

Spain never pursued its interest in Rapa Nui and, in any event, lost all its South American territories early in the 19th century. On the advice of naval officer Policarpo Toro, who had visited the island as early as 1870, Chile officially annexed the island in 1888 during a period of expansion that included the acquisition of territory from Peru and Bolivia after the War of the Pacific (1879-84).

With its vigorous navy, Chile was capable of expanding into the Pacific. It valued the island partly for its agricultural potential, real or imagined, but mostly for geopolitical purposes as a naval station, to prevent its use by a hostile power, for its location on a potentially important trading route between South America and East Asia, and for the prestige of having overseas possessions – any possessions – in an age of imperialism.

Williamson, Balfour & Company

Attempts at colonization came to nothing and, with no clear government policy, by 1897 Rapa Nui fell under control of a single wool-growing company run by Enrique Merlet, a Valparaíso businessman who had bought or leased nearly all the land. Control soon passed into other hands, however.

In 1851 in Liverpool, three Scottish businessmen founded S Williamson & Company to ship British goods to the west coast of South America. Its Chilean branch, Williamson, Balfour & Company, officially came into being in 1863, when the company controlled a substantial fleet and had expanded its interests to include a wide range of products and countries. In the early 20th century, it acquired Merlet's Rapa Nui holdings, managing the island through its Compañía Explotadora de la Isla de Pascua (Cedip), under lease from the Chilean government. The company became the island's de facto government, continuing its profitable wool trade until mid-century.

How islanders fared under this system is the subject of differing accounts, but there were several uprisings against the company. One result of foreign control was the genetic transformation of the islanders, as they intermarried with immigrants of many countries and, by the 1930s, perhaps three-quarters of the population were of mixed descent, including North American, British, Chilean, Chinese, French, German, Italian, Tahitian or Tuamotuan stock.

In 1953, when Chile was seeking to consolidate its control over its far-flung and rather unwieldy territories, the government revoked Cedip's lease. The navy took charge of the island, continuing the imperial rule to which islanders had been subject for nearly a century.

Chilean Colonialism

Rapa Nui continued under military rule until the mid-1960s, followed by a brief period of civilian government, until the military coup of 1973 once again brought direct military control. There is now, however, local self-government.

By the 1960s, the island was a colony pure and simple. Islanders' grievances included unpaid labor, travel restrictions, confinement to the Hanga Roa area, suppression of the Rapa Nui language, ineligibility to vote (Chilean universal suffrage did not extend to Rapa Nui) and arbitrary naval administration. However, increased contact with the outside world soon developed after establishment of a regular commercial air link between Santiago and Tahiti in 1967, with Rapa Nui as a refueling stop.

For a variety of reasons, including islanders' dissatisfaction, increased immigration from the continent, international attention and tourist potential, and the assumption of power by President Frei Montalva – the Chilean presence soon became more benevolent. There were advances in medical care, education, potable water and electrification.

Although cattle and sheep still graze parts of the island, the chief industry is tourism – a fairly recent phenomenon that developed with regular air services from mainland Chile and from Tahiti. It has had an overwhelming impact, as nearly everyone now makes a living, directly or indirectly, from the tourist trade.

In August 1985, General Pinochet approved a plan allowing the USA to expand Mataveri airport as an emergency landing site for the space shuttle, arousing opposition both locally and on the continent, but the Rapa Nui people had no say in the decision. In 1990, however, islanders protested against fare increases by Lan-Chile (the only air carrier) and successfully occupied Mataveri airport – even preventing the landing of a jetload of Carabineros by blocking the runway with cars and rubble. The global impulse toward self-determination has reached even this remote place, as some islanders argue vocally for the return of native lands and speak hopefully of independence or at least autonomy. Their aspirations are tempered by realism though; when asked if he would like to expel the Chileans, one islander responded, 'We can't – but we'd like them to leave.'

More recently, the most contentious issue has been Unesco's proclamation of a World Heritage Site without consulting the local population. In the words of mayor Pedro Edmunds Paoa, 'I cannot accept that a group of people claiming to be experts – I don't know who they are – take decisions behind our backs.'

The current Frei administration has begun to deal with some of these matters. In late 1996, it agreed to return about 1500 hectares of land to islanders from the state development company Corfo; local elected leaders were to determine the distribution of the land among 200 applicants. The government has also expanded the airport and paved the highway around the island.

GEOGRAPHY

Just south of the Tropic of Capricorn, Rapa Nui is a small volcanic island formed where, in the distant past, lava from three separate cones of different ages coalesced in a single triangular land mass. Its total area is just 117 sq km, its maximum length 24 km and maximum width only 12 km.

All three major volcanoes are now extinct. Terevaka, the largest, rises 652 meters above sea level in the northern part of the island, while Pukatikei (about 400 meters) forms the eastern headland of the Poike peninsula; Rano Kau (about 410 meters) dominates the southwest corner. Smaller craters include Rano Raraku, from whose volcanic tuff islanders carved their giant moai, and Puna Pau, northeast of Hanga Roa, which provided the reddish scoria that forms the statues' topknots. At Orito, islanders quarried black obsidian for spear points and cutting tools. Rano Kau and Rano Raraku both contain freshwater lakes.

For the most part, Rapa Nui's volcanic

slopes are gentle and grass-covered, except where wave erosion has produced nearly vertical cliffs. In contrast, rugged lava fields cover much of the island's interior, although several areas have soil adequate for cultivation – Hanga Roa and Mataveri on the west coast, Vaihu on the south coast, the plain southwest of Rano Raraku, and inland at Vaitea.

Vulcanism has left numerous caves, many in seaside cliffs. Some, consisting of larger and smaller chambers connected by tunnels through which a person can barely squeeze, extend for considerable distances into the lava. These could be permanent shelters, refuges in wartime, or storage or burial sites.

Rapa Nui rests on a submarine platform some 50 or 60 meters below the ocean's surface, but at 15 to 30 km off the coast the platform ends and the ocean floor drops to between 1800 and 3600 meters. There are three tiny islands just off Rano Kau: Motu Nui, Motu Iti and Motu Kao Kao, of which Motu Nui is the largest. Motu Nui is a nesting ground for thousands of sooty terns.

There are no coral reefs around Rapa Nui, although some coral occurs in shallow waters. In the absence of reefs, the ocean has battered the huge cliffs, some of which rise 300 meters. Those cliffs composed of lava are usually lower but are also extremely rugged. There is no natural sheltered harbor, and Anakena on the north coast has the only broad sandy beach, although there are a few shallow bays.

Rapa Nui's rainfall supports a permanent cover of coarse grasses, but its volcanic soil is so porous that water quickly drains underground. There are no permanent streams, so water for both humans and livestock comes either from the volcanic lakes or from wells. Vegetation was once much more luxuriant – including forests with palms, conifers and other species now extinct – but islanders cut the forests long ago. Most of today's trees, like the eucalyptus, were planted only within the past century.

EASTER ISLAND

FLORA & FAUNA

Like other remote islands, Rapa Nui lacks entire families of plants and is particularly poor in native fauna; even sea birds are relatively few. Some plants are endemic, most notably the tree species toromiro *(Sophora toromiro)* and several genera of ferns. While the last native toromiro died in 1962, Conaf reintroduced 162 European-cultivated saplings into Rano Kau crater in 1995. About 30 of these of have survived, but there is concern that the genetic pool is not large enough to conserve the species; in any event, the competition from more than 60 other introduced trees and shrubs, along with a legacy of soil erosion from livestock, have made long-term viability unlikely.

Rapa Nui's original Polynesian immigrants brought small animals like chickens and rats, while the Norway (brown) rat escaped from European vessels; Europeans also brought horses and other grazing animals in the 19th century.

CLIMATE

Winds and ocean currents strongly influence Rapa Nui's subtropical climate. The hottest months are January and February, while the coolest are July and August. The average maximum summer temperature is 28°C and the average minimum 15°C, but these figures understate what can be a fierce sun and formidable heat. The average winter maximum is 22°C and the minimum 14°C, but it can seem much cooler when Antarctic winds lash the island with rain. Light showers, however, are the most frequent form of precipitation. May is the wettest month, but tropical downpours can occur during all seasons.

RAPA NUI STONEWORK

Although the giant moai are the most pervasive image of Rapa Nui, there are several other types of stonework. Other important sites include the large ahu on which the moai were erected, burial cairns (large piles of rock where bodies were entombed), and the stone foundations of the unusual *hare paenga* (boat-shaped houses). One of the most striking things about the island is the remarkable density of ruins, indicating a much larger population than at present.

Although many structures were partially demolished or rebuilt by the original inhabitants, and the moai fell during intertribal wars, Cedip's regime was also responsible for major damage. Many ahu, burial cairns, house foundations and other structures were dismantled and used to build the piers at Caleta Hanga Roa and Caleta Hanga Piko, as well as stone walls around grazing areas. Windmills were constructed over the original stone-lined wells to provide water for sheep, cattle and horses.

Collectors have pillaged other sites. Only a few moai were removed, but museums and private collections in Chile and elsewhere now feature wooden rongo-rongo tablets, painted wall tablets from houses at Orongo, small wood and stone moai, weapons, clothing, skulls and other artifacts. Islanders themselves were responsible for removing building materials from sites like Orongo.

On the other hand, archaeologists have restored a number of sites over the last 30 years. These include Ahu Tahai, Ahu Akivi, the Orongo ceremonial village, and Ahu Nau Nau. Others, such as Ahu Vinapu and Ahu Vaihu, lie in ruins but are nonetheless impressive.

Ahu

About 245 ahu form an almost unbroken line along the coast, except for headlands around Península Poike and Rano Kau. They tend to be sited at sheltered coves and areas favorable for human habitation, but only a few were built inland.

Of several varieties of ahu, built at different times for different reasons, the most impressive are the *ahu moai* that support the massive statues. Each is a mass of loose stones held together by retaining walls and paved on the upper surface with more or less flat stones, with a vertical wall on the seaward side and usually at each end. The moai on these platforms range from two to almost 10 meters in height, although even larger moai were under construction in the quarry at Rano Raraku when work suddenly ceased, probably for lack of timber to move and raise the moai.

Usually a gently sloping ramp, paved with rounded boulders or tightly placed slabs of irregular stones, comprises the landward side of the platform. Next to the ramp is a large, perhaps artificially leveled, plaza; in a few cases, these are outlined by earthworks, which form rectangular or irregular enclosures. Sometimes there are small rectangular platforms that may be altars, and large circles paved with stones, while a bit farther inland there may be foundations of boat-shaped houses. Early islanders used one- and two-person reed boats, and much larger reed boats were probably launched from *apapa* (stone ramps) leading into the sea by the side of the ahu.

Researchers have learned very little about the ceremonies connected with these ahu complexes. One theory is that the moai represented clan ancestors and that the ceremonies were part of an ancestor cult. Ahu were also burial sites: originally bodies were interred in stone-lined tombs in the ahu ramps and platforms but, after the moai had been toppled, bodies were placed around them and on other parts of ramps, then covered with stones. Other bodies were cremated at ahu sites, but whether these were bodies of deceased clan members or remains of sacrifices is unknown, though oral tradition tells of human sacrifice by burning.

Hare Paenga (Elliptical Houses)

On or near the restored plaza at Ahu Tahai are several interesting features, among them the foundations of elliptical thatched houses (hare paenga). Long and narrow, these resemble an upturned canoe; the floor shape is outlined by rectangular blocks or curb stones with small hollows on their upper surfaces, with a single narrow doorway at the middle of one side. To support walls and roof, islanders inserted poles into these hollows, then arched them across the center of the structure and, where they crossed, lashed them to a ridge pole.

As the space to be covered narrowed near the ends, the roofing poles decreased in length, lowering the roof level. A crescent-shaped stone pavement often covered the entry. These dwellings varied enormously in size; some could house more than 100 people, while others held but half a dozen.

Moai

Although all moai are similar, few are identical. The standard moai at Rano Raraku has its base at about hip level, with stiffly hanging arms and extended hands with long slender fingers, across a protruding abdomen. The heads are elongated and rectangular, with heavy brows and prominent noses, small mouths with thin lips, prominent chins and elongated earlobes, some of them carved for inserted ear ornaments. Hands, breasts, navels, and facial features are clear, while elaborately carved backs possibly represent tattoos.

It is interesting to speculate on the models for the moai, since their features – long straight noses, tight-lipped mouths, sunken eyes, and low foreheads – do not seem Polynesian. Large stone statues have also been found on the Marquesas, Raivavae, and other islands of eastern Polynesia, but also in western South America.

Since the moai at the quarry show all stages of carving, it's easy to visualize the process. Most were carved face up, in a horizontal or slightly reclining position. Workers excavated a channel, large enough for the carvers, around and under each moai, leaving it attached to the rock only along its back. Nearly all the carving, including the fine detail, occurred at this stage. The moai was then detached and somehow transported down the slope (sometimes a vertical wall), avoiding others below. At the base of the cliff, workers raised it into a standing position in trenches, where sculptors carved finer details on the back and decorated the waist with a belt surrounded by rings and symbols. When carving was finished, moai were moved to their ahu on the coast.

Moai vary greatly in size; some are as

EASTER ISLAND

short as two meters, while the longest is just under 21 meters. However, very few are shorter than three meters, and the usual length is from 5½ to seven meters. The 21-meter colossus is unique; the face alone is just over nine meters long, it measures just over four meters across the shoulders, and the body is about 1½ meters thick. Carvers completed the front and both sides, but never liberated it from the rock below.

Basalt *tokis*, thousands of which once littered the quarry site, were the carving tools. In *Aku-Aku: The Secret of Easter Island*, Heyerdahl recalls hiring a number of islanders to carve new moai at Rano Raraku; they quit after three days, but their efforts suggested that two teams working constantly in shifts would need perhaps 12 to 15 months to carve a medium-sized moai.

Many of the moai have distinctive features. One displays a three-masted sailing ship on its chest; from the bow, a line extends downward to a circular figure of what might be a head and four short legs, although the figure is so crude that it almost certainly has no connection with the carving of the moai itself. This may represent a European ship or a large *totora* reed vessel, while the figure below may be an anchor of some sort, although it could also be a turtle or tortoise held by a fishing line. Moai mostly depicted males, but several specimens have carvings that clearly represent breasts and vulva.

The most unique discovery at Rano Raraku was the kneeling Moai Tukuturi, which was almost totally buried. Slightly less than four meters high, it now sits on the southeastern slope of the mountain, where placing it upright required a jeep, tackle, poles, ropes, chains, and 20 workers. It has a fairly natural rounded head, a goatee, short ears, and a full body squatting on its heels, with forearms and hands resting on its thighs. It has a low brow with curved eyebrows, hollow and slightly oval eyes, and pupils marked by small, round cavities. Both the nose and lips are considerably damaged, but the cheeks are round and natural.

Imagine that, having carved a moai with toothpicks from hard volcanic stone, you must remove it from its cavity and lower it down the cliff face – which must have been difficult and dangerous, as broken moai suggest that ropes snapped or workers slipped. After standing it up at the base of the slope (probably by sliding it into a trench cut for the occasion) and completely carving the back, you transport it several km to the coast and stand it upright on a raised platform.

Islanders placed 300 moai on ahu or left them along the old roads in various parts of the island. There are several explanations for this feat, but any valid one must account for the transport and erection of the biggest moai ever placed on an ahu – the 10-meter giant at Ahu Te Pito Kura.

Topknots

Some archaeologists thought the reddish cylindrical topknots on many moai were hats, baskets or crowns, but there is now a consensus that these *pukao* reflect a common male hairstyle on Rapa Nui when Europeans first visited the island. Quarried from the small volcanic crater at Puna Pau, this volcanic scoria is relatively soft and easily worked. Most pukao had a clearly marked knot on the top and a partly hollow underside which allowed them to be slotted onto the moai's heads.

Since only about 60 moai had topknots, another 25 of which remain in or near the quarry, these appear to have been a late development. Carved like the moai, the topknots may have been simple embellishments, rolled to their final destination, and then, despite weighing about as much as two elephants, somehow placed on top of moai up to 10 meters in height. Early Europeans recorded that moai were still standing on their ahu with the topknots mounted.

Some believe that islanders carved the knot on top of the stone and its hollow underside only after transporting the stone to its ahu – probably to prevent its breaking in transport and to allow measurement of the head in order to carve a proper-sized hollow, but there are also hollow topknots

Moving the Moai

Just moving the moai to the site must have been an even greater problem than removing them from the rock and lowering them down the cliff. Legend says that priests moved the moai by the power of mana, an ability to make the moai walk a short distance every day until eventually it reached its destination. After suggestions that islanders could have moved the moai with a Y-shaped sledge made from a forked tree trunk, pulled with ropes made from tree bark, Heyerdahl organized 180 islanders to pull a four-meter moai across the field at Anakena, and speculated that they could have moved a much larger one with wooden runners and more labor. Another explanation is that islanders inserted round stones under the moai, which were pushed, pulled and rolled to their destinations like a block on marbles, but this fails to explain how they were moved without harming the fine details carved at the quarry.

North American archaeologist William Mulloy proposed a different method of moving the moai which, though difficult, would have been physically possible with enough labor, and is consistent with the shape and configuration of the moai. First, islanders would have fitted a wooden sledge to the moai (figure 1); the distribution of the statue's weight would have kept the relatively light and fragile head above ground when tipped over. They would then have set up a bipod astride the statue's neck, at an angle to the vertical (figures 2 & 3) and tied a cable attached to the moai's neck to the bipod's apex and pulled it forward. The head of the moai would then rise slightly and the moai would be dragged forward. When the bipod passed vertical, the statue's own weight would carry it forward along its belly. By moving the legs of the bipod forward, the entire process could be repeated.

This repetitive series of upward and forward movements recalls the islanders' legend that the moai 'walked' to their ahu. It could also explain broken moai along the old transport routes; the rope or bipod may have slipped or broken when the moai was raised, and the statue fallen to the ground. There are a few problems with Mulloy's method (for a start, it requires large trees to make the bipods) but it's theoretically possible and also a partial explanation for deforestation of the island.

Once at its ahu, the moai had to be raised onto an elevated platform. Restoration of seven moai in the 1960s by Mulloy and Gonzalo Figueroa (see the section on Ahu Akivi) suggests that leverage and support with rocks may indeed have raised the moai. ■

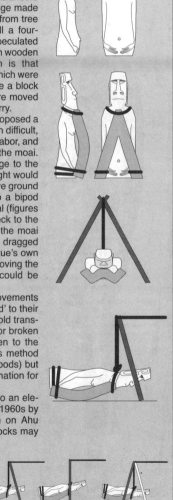

Moai kavakava, 'statue of ribs'

within the crater itself. Oral tradition says that islanders built a ramp of stones to roll the topknot to the moai's head, but Mulloy thought the most likely method of attachment was to tie it to the moai and raise the two simultaneously. This would eliminate the clumsy, time-consuming method of building a ramp and rolling the topknot up it.

Moai Kavakava

Of all the carved wooden figures that islanders produce, the most common, and at the same time the most exotic, are the moai kavakava, or the 'statues of ribs.' Each is a human figure with a large, thin and markedly aquiline nose, protruding cheekbones that accentuate hollow cheeks, extended earlobes, and a goatee that curls back on the chin. Protruding ribs in a sunken abdomen imply starvation.

According to oral tradition, at Puna Pau King Tuu-ko-ihu chanced upon two *aku aku* (sleeping ghosts) with beards, long hooked noses and pendulant earlobes reaching down to their necks, and so thin that their ribs stood out. Tuu-ko-ihu returned home and carved their portrait in wood before he forgot their appearance, and since then islanders have always carved these statues.

BOOKS

For general background on geography and environment, the most thorough source is Juan Carlos Castilla's edited collection, *Islas Oceánicas Chilenas* (Santiago, Ediciones Universidad Católica de Chile, 1987), which also deals with Chile's other insular possessions, including the Juan Fernández archipelago.

Though dated, one of the most thorough works on Rapa Nui proper is *Reports of the Norwegian Archaeological Expedition to Easter Island & the East Pacific. Volume 1: Archaeology of Easter Island* (London, Allen & Unwin, 1962). Summarizing the findings of the initial Heyerdahl expedition, it's fully illustrated, with detailed descriptions of all important sites (though none had been restored at the time). More readily accessible are Heyerdahl's popular account of his voyage in *Kon-Tiki* (Chicago, Rand McNally, 1952) and his *Aku-Aku: The Secret of Easter Island* (London, Allen & Unwin, 1958).

Englishwoman Katherine Routledge headed the first archaeological expedition, a private venture in 1914. The scientific notes of the expedition all disappeared, but she published *The Mystery of Easter Island: the Story of an Expedition* in 1919. Other pre-Heyerdahl accounts include J MacMillan Brown's *The Riddle of the Pacific* (1924) and anthropologist Alfred Metraux's *Ethnology of Easter Island* (1940, but reprinted by the Bishop Museum Press in Honolulu in 1971), based on field research conducted during a French-Belgian expedition in the 1930s.

Bavarian priest Sebastián Englert spent 35 years on Rapa Nui until his death in 1970; his *Island at the Center of the World* (New York, Scribner's, 1970) retells the island's history through oral tradition. If you read Spanish, his *La Tierra de Hotu Matua* (Editorial Universitaria, Santiago, 3rd edition 1983, but first published in 1948) is a worthwhile acquisition. Englert also analyzed indigenous speech in *Idioma Rapanui – Gramática y Diccionario del Antiguo Idioma de la Isla de Pascua* (Universidad de Chile, 1978). Another German, Thomas Barthel, offered a unique perspective on local history via obscure indigenous manuscripts in *The Eighth Land: The Polynesian Discovery and Settlement of Easter Island* (Honolulu, University Press of Hawaii, 1978).

As the 'Navel of the World,' Rapa Nui is also a focus of the debate over diffusion, independent invention and trans-Pacific contacts. Heyerdahl's *American Indians in the Pacific: The Theory Behind the Kon-Tiki Expedition* (London, Allen & Unwin, 1952) compares American Indian and Pacific cultures, legends, religion, stonework, watercraft, physical characteristics and cultivated plants.

However, there is now consensus that the initial settlers were Polynesians who arrived by way of the Marquesas. For a review of trans-Pacific migration, see Peter Bellwood's 'The Peopling of the Pacific' in *Scientific American* (Vol 243, No 5, November 1980), or his *Man's Conquest of the Pacific* (New York, Oxford University Press, 1979), which also includes a lengthy section on Rapa Nui and the Polynesian-American argument.

A very valuable but diverse collection, dealing partly with pre-Columbian contacts across the Pacific, is *Man Across the Sea* (University of Texas Press, 1971), edited by Carroll L Riley, J Charles Kelley, Campbell W Pennington and Robert L Rands. Based on meticulous research, it deals with a wide variety of related topics, particularly the diffusion of cultivated plants and domestic animals as indicators of human movement.

Some scientists have devised computer simulations of both drift and navigated voyages to try to resolve the matter of Polynesian peoples in the Pacific. One of these is *The Settlement of Polynesia: A Computer Simulation* (Canberra, ANU Press, 1973) by Michael Levison, R Gerard Ward and John Webb.

The Peruvian slave raid on Rapa Nui was no isolated incident; in the early 1860s, many Polynesian islands suffered such attacks, detailed in Henry Maude's *Slavers in Paradise: the Peruvian Labor Trade in Polynesia, 1862-1864* (published in Australia by ANU Press and in the USA by Stanford). For an account of the island from the mid-1800s almost to the present, see *The Modernization of Easter Island* (University of Victoria, British Columbia, Canada, 1981) by J Douglas Porteous. In a coffee-table format, try Michel Rougie's *Isla de Pascua*, published by Sernatur, whose superb photos record all the major sites, with text in Spanish, French and English. German speakers especially will enjoy a collection of articles entitled *1500 Jahre Kultur der Osterinsel* (Mainz, Verlag Philipp von Zabern, 1989), but anyone can appreciate its lavish illustrations, not just of moai and archaeological sites, but of other indigenous artwork as well.

EASTER ISLAND

MAPS

Most maps of Easter Island are very poor, but *Isla de Pascua-Rapa Nui: Mapa Arqueológico-Turístico* (Santiago: Ediciones del Pacífico Sur), at a scale of 1.30,000, is outstanding. Available at the tourist office and in island shops for about US$10, this foldout is a very worthwhile investment for any visitor.

GETTING THERE & AWAY

Unless you plan to make a balsa raft like the *Kon-Tiki*, the only practical way to reach Easter Island is by air. LanChile has two flights weekly (three in summer) between Santiago and Tahiti, stopping at Easter Island. The standard fare is US$812 roundtrip; travelers to and from the island pay the domestic airport tax of US$6, but westbound international passengers pay US$18.

Travelers from Australia or New Zealand can take a Melbourne/Sydney-Tahiti flight with Qantas or an Auckland-Tahiti flight with Air New Zealand and then transfer to LanChile for the onward flight to Rapa Nui and Santiago. For fare details, see the Getting There & Away chapter.

Travelers from North America may find it cheaper to purchase a LanChile Circle Pacific fare (including Easter Island and Tahiti) than a roundtrip fare to Chile plus a Santiago-Easter Island roundtrip flight.

A LanChile 21-day 'Visit Chile Pass' can include Easter Island for US$1080 – this is US$780 more than an air pass without the Easter Island option, so it's a minor saving (US$32) on the usual return fare. Because the air pass is only valid for a maximum of 21 days, using this option to visit Easter Island leaves little time for the rest of Chile. (For more details about air passes, see the Getting Around chapter).

Flights to and from Rapa Nui can be very crowded, especially in the peak summer season, so be certain to reconfirm at both ends or you may arrive at the airport to find your reservation has been canceled. The flight from Santiago takes 5½ hours, and LanChile's service is excellent and attentive; the return flight is at least an hour faster because of the prevailing westerlies and the jet stream.

GETTING AROUND

The only formal public transport on Rapa Nui is a Sunday bus to Playa Anakena, but there is no set schedule. It leaves from outside the church in Hanga Roa.

Other than that, rented horses, mountain bikes, motorcycles and cars are the main options. It's possible to walk around the island in a few days, but the summer heat, lack of shade and scattered water supply are good reasons not to do so. While distances appear small on the map, visiting numerous archaeological sites can be tiring and time-consuming. With good transport, it's possible to see all the major archaeological sites, at least superficially, in about three days, but many people take longer.

If you walk or ride a horse, mountain bike or motorbike around the island, carry a day-pack, a lightweight long-sleeved shirt, sunglasses, a large hat to shade the face and neck, plus a powerful sun-block for the sub-tropical rays. Also carry extra food and water, since neither is easily available outside Hanga Roa.

Motorbikes & Cars

Established hotels rent Suzuki jeeps for US$70 per day, but locals charge around US$40 or US$50 per 12-hour day – ask at residenciales or at Sernatur. You can ask just about anywhere, but try Easter Island Rent-a-Car (☎ 223328) on Policarpo Toro, Te Aiki (☎ 223366) at Residencial Tekena, or any of several other places that have signs in their windows. Outside high season, prices are very negotiable.

Locals rent their own motorbikes for about US$30 to US$35 a day; motorbikes are also available from Hotel Hanga Roa for US$40. Given occasional tropical downpours, a jeep is more convenient and can be more economical, especially for two or more people.

Petrol, subsidized by the Chilean government, costs about a third less than it does on the continent, so it is not a major expense for the island's relatively short distances. Outside Hanga Roa, all roads are unsurfaced, but most are in decent enough condition if you proceed with reasonable caution.

Mountain Bikes

Mountain bikes are available in Hanga Roa for about US$15 per day; they are more reliable than some horses.

Horses

Horses can be hired for about US$20 to US$30 per day, but see the beast before renting it – Rapa Nui has no glue factory and you won't want to risk being impaled by protruding ribs as your mount collapses under you. Most horse gear is very basic and potentially hazardous for inexperienced riders, but Hotel Hotu Matua or Hotel Hanga Roa may organize riding excursions and locate a horse with proper stirrups and reins.

Horses are good for visiting sites near Hanga Roa like Ahu Tepeu, Vinapu, Ahu Akivi and Orongo, but for more distant places like Rano Raraku and Anakena, motorized transport is superior.

Around the Archaeological Sites

It's possible to take in all the major sites on three loops out of Hanga Roa – the Southwest Route, the Northern Loop and the Island Circuit. These three routes involve a minimum of backtracking.

Southwest Route From Hanga Roa take the road to the top of Rano Kau crater and Orongo ceremonial village. Backtrack to Hanga Roa, then follow the road along the northern edge of the airport to Orito, site of the old obsidian quarries. From here head southward to Ahu Vinapu with its impressive, finely cut stonework.

Northern Loop Take the route from Hanga Roa to Puna Pau crater, source of the reddish volcanic scoria for the topknots of the moai. From here, continue inland to the restored Ahu Akivi, whose seven moai have been re-erected. From Ahu Akivi follow the track to Ahu Tepeu on the west

Site Distances	
Approximate road distances to important archaeological sites from Hanga Roa are:	
Ahu Tahai	1½ km
Orito	2 km
Vinapu	5 km
Orongo	6 km
Vaihu	9½ km
Ahu Akivi	10 km
Akahanga	12½ km
Puna Pau	15 km
Rano Raraku	18 km
Ahu Tongariki	20 km
Ahu Te Pito Kura	26 km
Ovahe	29 km
Anakena	30 km

coast, said to be the burial site of Tuu-ko-ihu, then head south to Hanga Roa, stopping off at Ahu Akapu, Ahu Tahai and Ahu Tautira, all of which have been restored and their moai re-erected. Because of the poorly marked trail/road between Ahu Akivi and the coast, it's probably easier to go from Hanga Roa to Ahu Akivi and then cut cross-country to Ahu Tepeu rather than the other way round.

Island Circuit From Hanga Roa, follow the southern coast, stopping at the ruins at Vaihu and Akahanga, with their massive ahu and giant toppled moai. Continue east from Akahanga and detour inland to Rano Raraku crater, source of the hard volcanic tuff for most of the island's moai, where statues in all stages of production still lie in place. Leaving Rano Raraku, follow the road east to Ahu Tongariki, a recently restored ahu whose moai and masonry were hurled some distance inland by a massive tsunami after the Chilean earthquake of 1960.

From Tongariki, follow the road to the north coast to Ahu Te Pito Kura, which boasts the largest moai ever erected on an ahu. Continue west to the beach at Ovahe and then to Anakena, the island's main beach and the site of two more restored ahu.

EASTER ISLAND

Tours

Several agencies, some of which have offices in Santiago as well as on the island, organize local tours; the addresses below include both local and Santiago information, the latter when appropriate. If you're only in transit en route to Tahiti or Santiago, Anakena Tours (☎ 223292 in Hanga Roa, (02) 6392603, fax 6394749), Estado 235, Oficina 1105 in downtown Santiago, offers a whirlwind excursion from Mataveri to Ahu Tahai and then back for your flight. This excursion can also be arranged on the spot.

Aku Aku Tour (☎ 223297), Hotel Manutara
    Badajoz 12, Oficina 301, Las Condes
    (☎ /fax (02) 2116747;
    Metro: Escuela Militar)
Archaeological Travel Service (☎ 223284)
Hahave Tour (☎ 223257)
Ile de Paque Sejours (☎ 223375)
Kia Koe Tour (☎ 223282), Hotel Hangaroa
    Napoleón 3565, Oficina 201, Las Condes
    (☎ (02) 2037209, fax 2037211;
    Metro: El Golf)
Mahinatur Services (☎ 223220)
    Residencial O Tama Te Ra'a
Manu Iti (☎ 223313)
    Residencial Sofía Gomero
Manutara Tour (☎ 223281), Hotel Chez Joseph
Martín Travel Rapa Nui (☎ 223228)
    Rapa Nui Inn
Ota'i Tour (☎ 223250), Hotel Ota'i
Rapa Nui (☎ 223331)
Rapa Nui Booking Office (☎ 223600)
Tekena Tour (☎ 223289)
    Residencial Tekena Inn
Tiki Tour (☎ 223327)
    Residencial Villa Tiki

HANGA ROA

According to the 1992 census, 2764 people live on Rapa Nui, nearly all of them in Hanga Roa. About 70% are predominantly Polynesian, considering themselves Rapa Nui rather than Chilean, while most of the remainder are immigrants from the Chilean mainland. Nearly everyone depends directly or indirectly on the tourist trade, but there is some fishing, plus livestock (mostly cattle) ranching, as well as kitchen gardens growing fruit and vegetables on the outskirts of the village. Government agencies and small general stores are the only other source of employment.

Orientation

On the western shore of Rapa Nui, Hanga Roa is a sprawling, decentralized tropical village with a highly irregular street plan. Although many of the streets bear formal names, in practice those names are rarely used, there are almost no street numbers, and most locals identify places with reference to landmarks like the harbor at Caleta Hanga Roa, the Gobernación, the market or the church. Although this section gives street directions whenever possible, it's easier to rely on the map than on street names.

Information

Tourist Office Sernatur (☎ 223255) is on Tuumaheke at Atamutekana, near Caleta Hanga Roa. The staff usually speak Rapa Nui, Spanish, English and French. The airport branch is open only for arriving and departing planes.

Money Banco del Estado, adjacent to Sernatur, changes US cash and travelers' checks, but charges a hefty 10% commission on the latter. US cash can be changed readily with local people, but often at a disadvantageous rate, so it's better to bring Chilean cash from the mainland if possible; eastbound travelers from Tahiti *must* bring US dollars. One traveler reports that the gas station offers a reasonable rate with no commission.

Some residenciales and hotels have begun to take credit cards, but this is far from universal.

Post & Communications Rapa Nui's area code is ☎ 39. Correos de Chile is on Te Pito o Te Henua, half a block from Caleta Hanga Roa. Entel, easily located by its conspicuous satellite dish, is on a cul-de-sac opposite Sernatur and Banco de Chile.

Film & Photography Take as much film as possible, since it's scarce and expensive

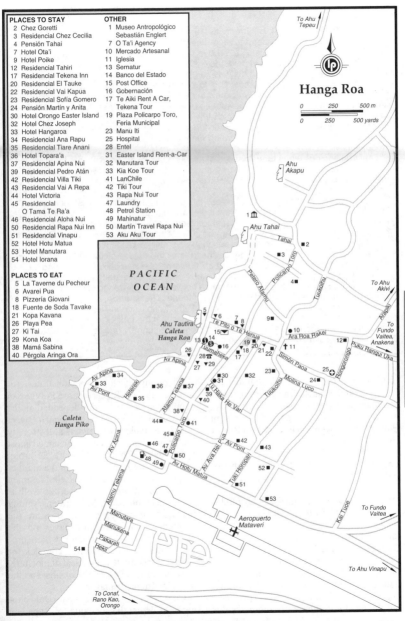

PLACES TO STAY
2 Chez Goretti
3 Residencial Chez Cecilia
4 Pensión Tahai
7 Hotel Ota'i
9 Hotel Poike
12 Residencial Tahiri
17 Residencial Tekena Inn
20 Residencial El Tauke
22 Residencial Vai Kapua
23 Residencial Sofía Gomero
24 Pensión Martín y Anita
30 Hotel Orongo Easter Island
32 Hotel Chez Joseph
33 Hotel Hangaroa
34 Residencial Ana Rapu
35 Residencial Tiare Anani
36 Hotel Topara'a
37 Residencial Apina Nui
39 Residencial Pedro Atán
42 Residencial Villa Tiki
43 Residencial Vai A Repa
44 Hotel Victoria
45 Residencial
   O Tama Te Ra'a
46 Residencial Aloha Nui
50 Residencial Rapa Nui Inn
51 Residencial Vinapu
52 Hotel Hotu Matua
53 Hotel Manutara
54 Hotel Iorana

PLACES TO EAT
5 La Taverne du Pecheur
6 Avarei Pua
8 Pizzería Giovani
18 Fuente de Soda Tavake
21 Kopa Kavana
26 Playa Pea
27 Ki Tai
29 Kona Koa
38 Mamá Sabina
40 Pérgola Aringa Ora

OTHER
1 Museo Antropológico
   Sebastián Englert
7 O Ta'i Agency
10 Mercado Artesanal
11 Iglesia
13 Sernatur
14 Banco del Estado
15 Post Office
16 Gobernación
17 Te Aiki Rent A Car,
   Tekena Tour
19 Plaza Policarpo Toro,
   Feria Municipal
23 Manu Iti
25 Hospital
28 Entel
31 Easter Island Rent-a-Car
32 Manutara Tour
33 Kia Koe Tour
41 LanChile
42 Tiki Tour
43 Rapa Nui Tour
47 Laundry
48 Petrol Station
49 Mahinatur
50 Martín Travel Rapa Nui
53 Aku Aku Tour

Hanga Roa

PACIFIC OCEAN

EASTER ISLAND

Rongo-Rongo Tablets

One Rapa Nui artifact that, until recently, resisted explanation was the Rongo-Rongo script. Eyraud, the first European to record its existence, noted that every house on the island contained wooden tablets covered in some form of writing or hieroglyphics. He could find no islander who could or would explain the meaning of these symbols.

The complete name of the tablets was ko hau motu mo rongorongo, literally meaning 'lines of script for recitation.' According to oral tradition, Hotu Matua brought these tablets, along with learned men who knew the art of writing and reciting the inscriptions. Most of the tablets are irregular, flat wooden boards with rounded edges, each about 30 to 50 cm long and covered in tidy rows of tiny symbols including birds, animals, possibly plants and celestial objects and geometric forms. The hundreds of different signs are too numerous to suggest a form of alphabet. Only a few such tablets, carved of toromiro wood, survive.

Oral tradition describes three classes of tablets. One recorded hymns in honor of the native deity Makemake or other divinities; another recorded crimes or other deeds of individuals; the third commemorated those fallen in war or other conflicts. Tablets recording genealogies may have existed.

Bishop Jaussen attempted to translate the script in 1866 with assistance from an islander said to be able to read the symbols, but this and other attempts failed; informants appeared to be either reciting memorized texts or merely describing the figures, rather than actually reading them. The last truly literate islanders had died, either as a result of the slave raid of 1862 or the subsequent smallpox epidemic.

Researchers have proposed various theories of the nature of the script. One suggested that it was not a readable script at all, but rather a series of cues for reciting memorized verse, while another claimed that the characters were ideographs like Chinese script. Another even suggested a connection between Rongo-Rongo script and a similar one from antiquity in the Indus River valley, in modern Pakistan.

Recent research by anthropologist Steven Fisher, published in New Scientist, seems to support the first of these theories. Fisher argues that the tablets were a series of religious chants, in the form of 120 different pictograms, sung by priests to elaborate their cosmological vision, based on human procreation. ∎

---

on the island. You may be able to find some Fujicolor and Ektachrome 35 mm transparencies and perhaps some Kodak 110, but little else. Check general stores in Hanga Roa, as well as Hotel Hanga Roa or Hotel Hotu Matua.

Laundry There's a laundry at the corner of Policarpo Toro and Avenida Hotu Matua.

Medical Services Hanga Roa's hospital is one long block east of the church.

Museo Antropológico Sebastián Englert

Rapa Nui is so renowned for its monuments that both researchers and visitors often ignore the islanders' traditional way of life, and their historic and modern experience, but the local museum partly redresses this shortcoming. It clearly demonstrates, for instance, that the Rapa Nui are a Polynesian people whose subsistence depended on the cultivation of crops such as *kumara* (sweet potato), a staple that islanders still strongly prefer to wheat, which is consumed most by immigrant Chileans. Kumara, taro root, *maika* (banana), *toa* (sugar cane) and other crops grew in excavated household garden enclosures known as *manavai*, as well as on terraces on Rano Kau crater. Among the most interesting garden sites are the entrances to the volcanic caves on the northwest side of the island, which provided sheltered, humid microclimates for plants that required a great deal of moisture. Garden tools, including the *okauve* and the *oka*, are also on display.

Copies of interesting historical photographs depict the encounter of Rapa Nui and European culture since the mid-19th century, although the prints are in poor condition. Legal documents reveal how, for instance, the Chilean civil register hispanicized the common local surname Te Ave into Chávez.

Other exhibits include: skulls from bodies originally entombed in ahu, basalt fish-hooks and other implements, obsidian spearheads and other weapons, sketches of elliptical houses, circular beehive-shaped huts and the ceremonial houses at Orongo, a moai head with reconstructed fragments of its eyes, moai kavakava and replicas of rongo-rongo tablets.

Just outside the museum building stands an unusual reddish moai, about 2½ meters high, found near the modern Hanga Roa cemetery and placed here by the Norwegians. With a triangular head and large sunken eyes, it appears crudely made, but may have been damaged or eroded.

This is not the only unusual moai – a kneeling figure at Rano Raraku (see below) is another. Within the museum are also several oblong-shaped stone heads, known as 'potato heads,' with eye-sockets and rudimentary features, including one with round ears. Thought to be the oldest carvings on the island, these may have preceded the Rano Raraku figures.

Named for the German priest who spent many years on the island and devoted much of his career to Rapa Nui's people and their history, Hanga Roa's museum is midway between Ahu Tahai and Ahu Akapu. Admission costs about US$1. Opening hours are Tuesday to Saturday 9 am to 12.30 pm and 2 to 5.30 pm, Sunday and holidays 9 am to noon only.

Organized Tours

A number of agencies organize tours of the island. See the earlier Getting Around entry for details.

Special Events

Every February islanders observe the Semana de Rapa Nui, a week-long celebration with music, dance and other cultural events. Much of the impetus comes from Resguardo Cultural, an islanders' organization committed to preserving local traditions.

Places to Stay

Rapa Nui is not inexpensive, but visitors can control costs by staying at one of the many residenciales or with a family. The least expensive rooms will be about US$15 per person with breakfast. Other meals may cost upwards of US$10 each, but Hanga Roa has several good, reasonably priced restaurants, or it's possible to buy food and cook for yourself.

Hosts generally meet incoming flights at the airport with a discount offer – say US$10 per person with breakfast, but most residenciales charge around US$45/75 with full board. Full board is not convenient if you spend the day at distant archaeological sites and cannot return to Hanga Roa for lunch.

Except perhaps in the summer high season, reservations are not essential. Instead, listen to offers from locals and hotel proprietors who flock to meet the incoming flights and wait outside the arrival area. Make sure you are talking to people from the hotels themselves, and not an agent who will book you into any of several places and take a commission. You will also get transport into town, helpful since Hanga Roa is so spread out that walking to some places would take an hour or more in the heat and humidity. There are no taxis.

If the place is not satisfactory, you can always move the next day; scout out the competition or ask Sernatur for help. Neither streets nor residenciales are consistently sign-posted, and buildings and houses rarely have numbers, so it is easier to locate places by referring to the map of Hanga Roa. Phone ahead before walking across town in the midday heat.

Places to Stay – bottom end

Camping Some residenciales, such as Residencial Ana Rapu (see below), offer camping in their gardens. Outside Hanga Roa, camping is officially permitted only at Playa Anakena which, unfortunately, lacks any dependable supply of potable water – you must carry your own. By the time this book appears, Conaf may have improved the facilities and water supply at Anakena.

Residenciales Residenciales still start around US$15 per person with breakfast, but there remain very few at the low end – try *Residencial Ana Rapu* (☎ 223540), where garden camping is possible for US$5 per person and good meals are available for about US$7. For US$25/35 single/double, *Residencial Tekena Inn* (☎ 223289) is OK, but a better value is the *Residencial Rapa Nui Inn* (☎ 223228), near the airport at the corner of Policarpo Toro and Avenida Hotu Matua, where rates are US$25/40 with breakfast, for a clean, spacious room with double bed and private bath. For US$25/45, *Residencial Apina Nui* (☎ 223292) is passable.

Popular, friendly *Residencial El Tauke* (☎ 223253) charges US$25 per person. Recent visitors indicate falling standards at María Hey's *Pensión Tahai* (☎ 223395), a bungalow set amidst a large, quiet and relaxing garden, a bit out of town on the road to Ahu Tahai. Rates are US$30/50 with breakfast, the same as recommended *Chez Goretti* (☎ 223459), *Residencial Tahiri* (☎ 223263) and *Residencial Pedro Atán* (☎ 223329). *Residencial Chez Cecilia* (☎ 223499) charges US$30 per person. Several readers have praised English-speaking *Pensión Martín y Anita* (☎ 223-593), across from the hospital, where plain but private rooms in a garden setting cost US$35/60.

Residencial Vinapu (☎ 223393) has been recommended for US$35/50; others in the same range include *Residencial Vai A Repa* (☎ 223331), *Residencial Tiare Anani* (☎ 223580), friendly *Residencial Vai Kapua* (☎ 223377) and *Residencial Aloha Nui* (☎ 223274). Slightly more expensive are *Hotel Chez Joseph* (☎ 223281) for US$35/56 and *Residencial Sofía Gomero* (☎ 223313) for US$35/65.

Places to Stay – middle

Most mid-range places call themselves hotels, but a few better residenciales are among them. Rates start around US$45/80 at *Hotel Orongo Easter Island* (☎ 223-294). Another recommended place is *Hotel Victoria* (☎ 223272), on a small hill to the southeast above Hanga Roa, midway between the airport and the settlement. Rates are US$50/70 with breakfast. Slightly more expensive, around US$50/80, are *Residencial Villa Tiki* (☎ 223327) and *Residencial O Tama Te Ra'a* (☎ 223220). *Hotel Poike* (☎ 223283) charges US$55/88.

Places to Stay – top end

At the bottom of the top-end places are the very good *Hotel Ota'i* (☎ 223250, fax 223482), with rooms from US$62/94 including breakfast and a swimming pool under construction as of this writing, and the equally fine *Hotel Topara'a* (☎ 223225) for US$65/90. Try also *Hotel Manutara* (☎ 223297) for US$68/105.

Hotel Hangaroa (☎ 223299), on Avenida Pont near Caleta Hanga Piko, is a lengthy walk from the middle of town, but has a swimming pool, bar and restaurant, and several souvenir shops. Rooms cost US$80/100, considerably more with full board.

For US$95/154, *Hotel Hotu Matua* (☎ 223242) is much closer to the airport than to town, so personal transport is a good idea. *Hotel Iorana* (☎ 223312) charges US$104/154 for rooms in a quiet area (except during the infrequent landings at the nearby airport) with outstanding coastal views. The restaurant has drawn criticism for small portions.

Places to Eat

Food at Hanga Roa's restaurants, which are increasing in number, is pleasantly surprising, especially the tasty seafood. Prices are mostly reasonable (except for lobster, which is very dear). Try *La Taverne du Pecheur* at Caleta Hanga Roa; *Avarei Pua* (☎ 223431), across the street; highly recommended *Mamá Sabina* (☎ 223566), across from LanChile on Policarpo Toro; or *Pérgola Aringa Ora* (☎ 223394) on Hotu Matua.

Other possibilities include *Pizzería Giovani* (☎ 223472) on Te Pito o Te Henua near Hotel Ota'i; *Kopa Kavana* (☎ 223447) at the corner of Te Pito o Te Henua and Ava Rei Pua; *Fuente de Soda Tavake* (☎ 223300) near Plaza Policarpo Toro for sandwiches; *Ki Tai* on Atamu Tekena near the south end of Caleta Hanga Roa; and *Playa Pea* (☎ 223382) at Caleta Hanga Roa. Next to Entel, upscale *Kona Koa* has drawn very favorable commentary.

Residenciales will rent a room with breakfast, half-board or full board, but you can also feed yourself with local produce – canned food may be imported from Santiago, but not fresh fruit and vegetables. On arrival from Tahiti or from Chile, bags may be checked for fresh produce.

If you intend to camp or cook your own food, there are provisions at general stores and bakeries on the main street, Policarpo Toro, where you can buy canned food, bottled drinks (soft drinks, wine, beer) as well as fresh vegetables, fruit and eggs. Fresh vegetables, fruit and fish are also available in the mornings at the Feria Municipal, the open-air market on Policarpo Toro, alongside the Gobernación.

Things to Buy
Hanga Roa has many souvenir shops, mostly on Policarpo Toro (where they tend to be dearer than elsewhere) and on the street leading up to the church. Look for small stone or carved wooden replicas of standard moai and moai kavakava, replicas of rongo-rongo tablets and cloth rubbings of them, and fragments of obsidian from Orito (sometimes made into earrings). The best selection and prices (open to haggling) are at the Mercado Artesanal (crafts market) across from the church.

For transit passengers or desperate last-minute shoppers, airport shops have a selection of crafts and souvenirs, but prices are noticeably higher.

Getting There & Around
Aeropuerto Mataveri is at the south end of Hanga Roa. LanChile (☎ 223279), the only airline that flies to Rapa Nui, has its office on Policarpo Toro near Avenida Pont.

Downtown Hanga Roa is only about a 20-minute walk from Mataveri. There is no public transport within the town, and it's very spread out, so you will probably be doing a bit of walking. To explore the rest of the island you really need independent transport – see the earlier Getting Around section.

PARQUE NACIONAL RAPA NUI
Since 1935, all of Rapa Nui's archaeological monuments have been part of the national park of the same name, administered by Conaf as an 'open-air museum.' There are admission charges to the Orongo ceremonial village of about US$10 for non-Chileans, collected by rangers at the site. These fees are valid for the length of your stay.

Although the government, in cooperation with foreign and Chilean archaeologists as well as local people, has done a remarkable job in restoring monuments and attracting visitors, it is worth mentioning that some islanders view the park as just another land grab on the part of invaders who, to them, differ little from Dutroux-Bornier or Williamson, Balfour & Company. A native-rights organization calling itself the Consejo de Ancianos (Council of Elders) wants the park, which constitutes more than a third of the island's surface, returned to its aboriginal owners. The Rapa Nui people control almost no land outside Hanga Roa proper, and have even taken their cause to the United Nations because of lack of faith in the Chilean judiciary. Many islanders, however, work for Conaf and other government agencies.

The West Coast
Lined up along the island's west coast are four large ahu complexes. Ahu Tautira is next to Hanga Roa's small pier; from here a road/track leads north to the Ahu Tahai

EASTER ISLAND

complex, connected to Ahu Akapu and Ahu Tepeu by another coastal track.

Ahu Tautira Ahu Tautira overlooks Caleta Hanga Roa, the fishing port at the foot of Te Pito o Te Henua. The torsos of two broken moai have been re-erected on the ahu.

Ahu Tahai A short walk north of Hanga Roa, this site contains three restored ahu: Ahu Tahai proper, Ahu To Ko Te Riku and Ahu Vai Uri. North American archaeologist William Mulloy directed the restoration work in 1968.

Ahu Tahai is the ahu in the middle, supporting a large, solitary moai with no topknot. To one side of Ahu Tahai is Ahu Ko Te Riku, with a large, solitary moai with its topknot in place. Despite its size, it is a relative lightweight, only about one quarter the weight of the giant moai at Ahu Te Pito Te Kura on the north coast. On the other side is Ahu Vai Uri, which supports five moai of varying sizes.

Ahu Akapu Ahu Akapu, with its solitary moai, stands on the coast north of Ahu Tahai. North of here, the road is very rough but always passable if you drive slowly.

Ahu Tepeu Large Ahu Tepeu is on the northwest coast between Ahu Akapu and Cabo Norte. To the northeast rises Maunga Terevaka, the island's highest point, while to the south is a large grassy plain over a jagged lava flow. To the west, the Pacific Ocean breaks against rugged cliffs up to 50 meters high.

The seaward side of the ahu is its most interesting feature, with a wall about three meters high near the center, composed of large, vertically placed stone slabs. A number of moai once stood on the ahu but all have fallen. Immediately east is an extensive village site with foundations of several large boat-shaped houses and the walls of several round houses, consisting of loosely piled stones.

Puna Pau
The small volcanic crater at Puna Pau has a

relatively soft, easily worked reddish scoria from which the pukao (topknots) were made. Some 60 of these were transported to sites round the island, and another 25 remain in or near the quarry.

Ahu Akivi
This inland ahu, completely restored in 1960 by a group headed by Mulloy and Chilean archaeologist Gonzalo Figueroa, sports seven moai which, unlike most others, look out to sea. In raising the moai, they used methods similar to those used at Ahu Ature Huki and steadily improved their speed and technique. Mulloy later wrote:

Clearly the prehistoric islanders with their hundreds. of years of repetition of the same task must have known many more tricks than modern imitators were able to learn.

Mulloy believed that the large number of stones in front of Ahu Akahanga on the south coast were leftovers of stones used to raise the moai, and that one moai appeared to have fallen sideways in the process. He also pointed to the tremendous numbers of stones near many ahu, including Ahu Te Pito Te Kura, as evidence that the moai may have been erected using stones for support.

Mulloy calculated that 30 men working eight hours a day for a year could have carved the moai and topknot at Ahu Te Pito Te Kura, while 90 could have transported it from the quarry over a previously prepared road in two months and could have raised it in about three months. Even if Mulloy was correct, there are complications with raising the topknots to the heads of the moai.

Ana Te Pahu
After visiting Ahu Akivi, you can follow the faint, rough but passable track to Ahu Tepeu on the west coast. On the way, stop at Ana Te Pahu, a site of former cave dwellings whose entrance is via a garden planted with sweet potatoes, taro, bananas and other plants from the Polynesian horticultural complex.

Orongo Ceremonial Village

Nearly covered in a bog of floating totora reeds, the crater lake of Rano Kau appears to be a giant witch's cauldron. Perched 400 meters above, on the edge of the crater wall, the ceremonial village of Orongo occupies one of the most dramatic sites on the island. Once the most important ceremonial site on the island, it is a much later construction than the great moai and ahu.

From the winding dirt road that climbs from Hanga Roa to Orongo, there are spectacular views of the entire island. Orongo, overlooking several small *motu* (offshore islands), was the focus of an island-wide bird cult linked to the gods Makemake and Haua in the 18th and 19th centuries.

Partly restored, Orongo ceremonial village occupies a magnificent site overlooking the ocean. Built into the side of the slope, the houses have walls of horizontally overlapping stone slabs, with an earth-covered arched roof of similar materials, giving the appearance of being partly subterranean. Since walls were thick and had to support the roof's weight, the doorway is a low narrow tunnel, barely high enough to crawl through. At the edge of the crater is a cluster of boulders carved with numerous birdman petroglyphs, with a long beak and a hand clutching an egg.

A short distance before the village, a footpath descends into the crater, where the dense vegetation includes abandoned orange trees and grapevines whose fruit local people collect in autumn. It is possible to hike around the crater, but it is slow going – give yourself a full day and take plenty to drink, since the water in the crater lakes is muddy and brackish.

Ahu Vinapu

For Ahu Vinapu, follow the road from Mataveri airport to the end of the runway, then the road south between the airstrip and some large oil tanks to an opening in a stone wall. A sign points to nearby Ahu Vinapu, where there are two major ahu.

Both once supported moai that are now overturned, mostly broken and lying face down. Accounts by 18th- and early-19th-

The Birdman Cult

Makemake, the birdman cult's supreme deity, is said to have created the earth, sun, moon, stars and people, rewarding the good and punishing the evil, and expressing his anger in thunder. In times of trouble, he required the sacrifice of a child. Makemake is also credited with bringing the birds and presumably the bird cult to Rapa Nui, although Haua aided him in this venture.

No complete record of the cult's ceremonies exists and there are conflicting accounts with respect to schedules and duration. At a given time, worshippers would move up to Orongo where they lived in stone houses, recited prayers, made offerings, held rites to appease the gods and participated in fertility dances.

The climax of the ceremonies was a competition to obtain the first egg of the sooty tern (Sterna fuscata), which bred on the tiny islets of Motu Nui, Motu Iti and Motu Kao Kao, just off Cabo Te Manga. Each contestant or his hopu (stand-in) would descend the cliff face from Orongo and, with the aid of a small reed raft, or pora, swim out to the islands. He who found the first egg became 'birdman' for the ensuing year; if a hopu found it, he called out his master's name to a man in a cave in the cliffs below Orongo. The fortunate master's head, eyebrows and eyelashes were then shaved, his face was painted red and black, and he became birdman, sequestered in a special house. The reasons for the birdman's celebrity are vague, but whoever found the first egg certainly won the favor of Makemake and great status in the community. The last ceremonies took place at Orongo in 1866 or 1867, a few years after the Peruvian slave raid. ■

century visitors suggest that the moai were not overturned simultaneously, but were all tipped over by the mid-19th century. Some had their foundations undermined, while others may have been pulled down with ropes.

One interesting find is a long brick-red stone, shaped rather like a four-sided column, standing in front of one of the ahu. Closer inspection reveals a headless moai with short legs, unlike the mostly legless moai elsewhere, and resembling pre-Inca column statues in the Andes.

Vinapu's tight-fitting stonework, especially Ahu No 1, so resembles that of Inca Cuzco and pre-Inca Tiahuanaco that some researchers have concluded South American origins. Others, however, argue that islanders could have developed such techniques independently, and that Vinapu represents the last and most advanced phase of carving on the island.

Heyerdahl's expedition challenged this theory when excavations revealed that the central wall of Ahu No 1 belonged to the oldest period. The Norwegians concluded that the ahu had twice been rebuilt and enlarged by builders unable to reproduce the finest stonework. Heyerdahl proposed three distinct periods in local history: Early, Middle and Late.

During the Early Period, islanders built ahu of large stone blocks, carved and tightly fitted, with neither burial chambers nor moai. Carbon-14 dating of the remains of fires and other materials indicates that the Early Period began sometime before 400 AD and ended around 1100 AD.

In the Middle Period, until the late 17th century, most of these structures were modified or dismantled. Islanders built paved slopes against the inland walls of the ahu, where they placed the giant moai from Rano Raraku; the platforms now often contained burial chambers. The stonework of the ahu itself was less meticulous than that of the moai.

Shortly thereafter the island experienced a period of warfare and cannibalism, perhaps occasioned by demographic pressure on limited resources, and production of the moai ceased. In this Late Period, boulders and blocks made funeral mounds as the moai, all toppled by the mid-19th century, became roofs for improvised, semi-pyramidal burial vaults with stones packed over and around the fallen moai.

Other researchers, however, dispute this chronology. One argues that Ahu No 2 at Vinapu (which lacks the same finely cut stonework as Ahu No 1) predates Ahu No 1, suggesting that Ahu No 2 derived from the *marae* platforms found on other Polynesian islands. Eventually, masonry skills improved so that descendants of the original Polynesian immigrants could produce the finely worked stones of Ahu No 1, independent of South American influence.

There is consensus that the functions of the ahu differed in each period. In the Early Period they were altars, in the Middle Period bases for the moai and in the Late Period burial sites. However, these transitions appear to have been very gradual.

Orito

The Short Ears made weapons from hard black obsidian quarried at Orito. The *mataa*, a common artifact, was a crudely shaped blade of obsidian used as a spearhead; embedded in the edges of flat wooden clubs, such blades made very deadly weapons. Non-lethal artifacts included obsidian files and drill bits that would have been attached to a wooden shaft and used to drill bone, wood or stone.

From the slopes of Rano Kau, the quarry resembles an enormous gray rectangle on Orito's southern slope, but quarrying actually took place around its whole circumference. Orito is not the only obsidian quarry – there are others on Motu Iti off Cabo Te Manga, and another on the northeastern edge of Rano Kau crater.

The South Coast

On the south coast, east of Ahu Vinapu, enormous ruined ahu and their fallen moai testify to the impact of warfare on Rapa Nui. **Ahu Vaihu** has eight large moai that have been toppled and now lie face down, their topknots scattered nearby. **Akahanga** is a large ahu with large fallen moai, while across the bay is a second ahu with several more. On the hill slopes opposite are the remains of a village, including foundations of several boat-shaped houses and ruins of several round houses.

Also on the coast, the almost completely ruined **Ahu Hanga Tetenga** has two large moai, both toppled and broken into fragments. Just beyond Hanga Tetenga, a faint track off the main road branches inland towards the crater quarry of Rano Raraku, which is readily visible.

Fundo Vaitea
Midway between Anakena and Hanga Roa, Vaitea was the center of food and livestock production under Dutroux-Bornier and Williamson, Balfour & Company, who used the island as a gigantic sheep farm – the large building on the east side of the road is the former shearing shed. The property on the west side belongs to Corfo, which raises fruit and vegetables, but may be returned to the islanders.

Anakena
Playa Anakena Anakena beach is the legendary landing place of Hotu Matua. One of several caves is said to have been Hotu Matua's dwelling as he waited for completion of his boat-shaped house, but the Norwegian expedition found no traces of very early habitation. Nearby remains of an unusually large elliptical house, about 25 meters long, are said to have been that house, but the Norwegians failed to find anything of special interest. Of much greater interest are Ahu Ature Huki and Ahu Nau Nau.

This sheltered, white-sand beach is Rapa Nui's largest, very popular for swimming and sunbathing. Anakena is a pleasant place to spend the afternoon or to overnight at Conaf's pleasant campground, but bring food and drinking water from Hanga Roa.

Ahu Ature Huki On the hillside above Playa Anakena stands Ahu Ature Huki and its lone moai, re-erected by the Norwegians and islanders. In *Aku-Aku: the Secret of Easter Island*, Heyerdahl described raising the moai onto its ahu with wooden poles:

... the men got the tips of their poles in underneath it, and while three or four men hung and heaved at the farthest end of each pole, the mayor lay flat on his stomach and pushed small stones under the huge face ... When evening came the

giant's head had been lifted a good three feet from the ground, while the space beneath was packed tight with stones.

The process continued for nine days, the giant on an angle supported by stones, and the logs being levered with ropes when the men could no longer reach them. After another nine days and the efforts of a dozen people, the moai finally stood upright and unsupported.

Ahu Nau Nau In Rapa Nui, *Mata ki te rangi* means 'eyes that look to the sky.' Some have interpreted this as a reference to the volcanic craters at the corners of the triangular island, but during the excavation and restoration of Anakena's Ahu Nau Nau in 1979 researchers learned that the moai were not 'blind' but actually had inlaid coral and rock eyes – the eyes that looked to the sky – some of which were reconstructed from fragments at the site.

Of the seven moai at Ahu Nau Nau, four have topknots, while only the torsos remain of two others. It's also thought the figures were painted and had inlaid earplugs. Fragments of torsos and heads lie in front of the ahu.

Ovahe
At Ovahe, between La Perouse and Anakena, is a small, attractive and much less frequented beach with interesting caves. Beware of sharks.

Ahu Te Pito Te Kura
On the north coast, overlooking a fishing cove at Bahía La Perouse (look for the sign by the road), is the largest moai ever moved from Rano Raraku and erected on an ahu. The name of the ahu comes from a particular stone called *te pito te kura*, meaning 'the navel of light.' Legend says that Hotu Matua himself brought this stone, symbolizing the Navel of the World, to Rapa Nui.

According to oral history, a widow erected the moai to represent her dead husband; it was perhaps the last moai to fall, although the Norwegian expedition has made that claim for the moai re-erected at Anakena. In height, proportion and general appearance it resembles the tall moai still buried up to their necks at Rano Raraku. If those standing at the quarry site are the last to have been made, the Te Pito Te Kura moai was probably the last erected on an ahu.

Nearly 10 meters long, the moai lies face down on the inland slope of the platform. Its ears alone are more than two meters long. A topknot – oval rather than round as at Vinapu – lies nearby. The sheer density of remains at sites like nearby Hanga Hoonu is even more impressive.

Rano Raraku

Known as 'the nursery,' the volcano of Rano Raraku is the quarry for the hard tuff from which the moai were cut. Moai in all stages of progress cover both its southern slopes and the crater, which contains a small lagoon. Most moai on the south slope are upright but buried up to their shoulders or necks in the earth, so that only their heads gaze across the grassy slopes. Park near the entrance gate (located in a stone wall) from which a trail leads straight up the slope to a 21-meter giant – the largest moai ever built. Follow a trail to the right to several other large moai still attached to the rock, or turn left along the trail that leads over the rim and into the crater.

Inside the crater are about 20 standing moai, a number of fallen ones and others only partly finished – about 80 in all. On the outer slope stand another 50. At the foot of the mountain and on the seaward plain lie another 30, all fallen and, with few exceptions, face down. In the quarries above are about 160 unfinished moai so that, when work stopped, some 320 moai had been completed but not yet erected on ahu, or were being worked on. The total number of moai from the Rano Raraku quarries is well over 600.

Ahu Tongariki

East of Rano Raraku, Japanese archaeologists have recently re-erected 15 moai at this site, the largest ahu ever built. A 1960 tsunami, produced by an earthquake between Rapa Nui and the South American mainland, had flattened the statues and scattered several topknots far inland. Only one of the topknots has been returned to its place atop a moai.

Several petroglyphs, cut into the flat stone outcrops among the moai, include a turtle with a human face, a tuna fish, a bird-man motif, and one that may represent a woman with her legs spread.

Península Poike

The eastern end of the island is a high plateau called Península Poike, crowned by the extinct volcano Maunga Pukatikei. Its western boundary is a narrow depression called Ko te Ava o Iko (Iko's Trench), running across the peninsula from north to south.

According to legend, the Long Ears built this trench to defend themselves from the Short Ears. In one version, Long Ear rulers decided to clear loose rock from the peninsula for purposes of cultivation; the Short Ears tired of the work and rebelled, so the Long Ears – under command of chief Iko – gathered on the peninsula and dug a trench to separate Poike from the rest of the island. They then filled the trench with branches and tree trunks, ready to be set on fire should the Short Ears try to storm across.

One of the Long Ears, though, had a Short Ear wife who allowed the Short Ears to slip into Poike and surround them. When another Short Ear force marched toward the ditch, the Long Ears lined up to face them and set the ditch on fire; the other Short Ears rushed them from behind and, in a bloody fight, the Long Ears fell and burned in their own ditch. Only three escaped: two were later killed, but the one who lived married a Short Ear and had children.

Although the ditch was once thought natural and the story a mere legend, excavations revealed thick layers of ash and charcoal, evidence of a great fire, which produced very intense heat or else burned for some time. The upper part was natural, but had been artificially enlarged to create a trench with a rectangular bottom, three to four meters deep, about five meters wide and running a couple of km across the hill-side. Not continuous, it actually comprises a number of separate trenches. Carbon dating suggested that the great fire had burnt perhaps 300 to 350 years ago, while genealogical research suggested the onset of conflict around 1680.

Although the Long Ears, suddenly forced to retreat to the Poike Peninsula, might have been able to fill the ditch with wood, they might not have had time to undertake the heavy and time-consuming labor of enlarging it. Dating of earlier fires indicates that the ditch was originally dug around 400 AD for other reasons, but was adapted for defensive purposes in the 17th century.

EASTER ISLAND

Falkland Islands (Islas Malvinas)

In the South Atlantic Ocean, 300 miles (500 km) east of Argentine Patagonia, the controversial Falklands consist of two large islands and many smaller ones. Though the Islands are officially a British colony, they are in many ways a separate country and, because they are so easily accessible from Chilean Patagonia, they appear as a separate chapter in this book.

FACTS ABOUT THE ISLANDS
History

Despite possible early Indian presence, the Islands were unpeopled when 17th-century European sailors began to frequent the area. Their Spanish name, Malvinas, derives from French navigators of St Malo.

In 1764, French colonists settled at Port Louis, East Falkland, but soon withdrew under Spanish pressure. Spain expelled a British outpost from Port Egmont, West Falkland, in 1767, but restored it under threat of war; the British later abandoned Port Egmont in ambiguous circumstances.

Spain placed a penal colony at Port Louis, then abandoned it to whalers and sealers. In the early 1820s, after the United Provinces of the River Plate (a forerunner of modern Argentina) claimed successor rights to Spain, Buenos Aires entrepreneur Louis Vernet attempted a livestock and sealing project, but Vernet's seizure of American sealers triggered reprisals that damaged Port Louis beyond recovery. Buenos Aires maintained a token force, which was expelled by the British navy in 1833.

The Falklands languished until wool became an important commodity in the mid-19th century. The Falkland Islands Company (FIC) became the Islands' largest landholder, but the population of stranded mariners and holdover gauchos grew with the arrival of English and Scottish immigrants, some of whom occupied remaining pasture lands in large holdings. Half the population resided in the port capital of Stanley, founded in 1844, while the rest worked on sheep stations. Most original landowners lived and worked locally, but their descendants often returned to Britain and ran their businesses as absentees.

From the late 1970s, local government encouraged subdivision of large landholdings to benefit family farmers. Change became even more rapid with the 1982 Falklands war, subsequent expansion of deep-sea fishing and, most recently, preliminary offshore petroleum exploration.

The Falklands War & Its Aftermath

Britain was slow to acknowledge the seriousness of Argentina's persistent claims to the Falklands, but by 1971 the Foreign & Commonwealth Office reached a communications agreement giving Argentina roles in air transport, fuel supplies, shipping and even immigration. Concerned about Argentina's chronic instability, Islanders and their UK supporters thought the agreement ominous, and suspected the FCO of secretly arranging transfer of the Islands. This process dragged on for a decade, during which Argentina's brutal 'Dirty War' gave Islanders more reason for concern.

Facing pressure from Argentines fed up with corruption, economic chaos and totalitarian ruthlessness, General Leopoldo Galtieri's disintegrating military government invaded the Islands on April 2, 1982. Seizure of the Malvinas briefly united Argentina, but British Prime Minister Margaret Thatcher, herself in shaky political circumstances, sent a naval task force to retake the Islands. Experienced British ground troops routed ill-trained, poorly supplied Argentine conscripts, and Argentina's surrender averted destruction of Stanley.

Since the end of the war, Islanders have become far more resolute in their opposition to any Argentine presence on the Islands, though many have no objection to a purely commercial relationship with their larger neighbor. Argentina, on the other hand, views with suspicion the Islanders' desire for increased autonomy as a 'free state' associated with Great Britain.

Geography & Climate

The land area of 4700 sq miles (7564 sq km) is equivalent to Northern Ireland or the state of Connecticut. Falkland Sound separates East and West Falkland; only a few smaller islands have settlements. Despite a dismal reputation, the oceanic climate is temperate (if windy). Summer temperatures rarely reach 75°F (24°C), but sustained subfreezing temperatures are unusual. Annual rainfall is only about 24 inches (600 mm).

Except for East Falkland's low-lying Lafonia peninsula, terrain is hilly to mountainous, but elevations do not exceed 2300 ft (705 meters). The most interesting geological features are 'stone runs' of quartzite boulders descending from many ridges and peaks. Bays, inlets, estuaries and beaches form an attractive coastline, with abundant wildlife.

Flora & Fauna

Grasses and prostrate shrubs dominate the flora. Native tussock grass once lined the coast but proved vulnerable to overgrazing and fire. Most pasture is rank white grass *(Cortaderia pilosa)*, supporting only about one sheep per four or five acres.

Beaches, headlands and estuaries support large concentrations of sub-Antarctic wildlife. Five penguin species breed regularly: the Magellanic or jackass, the rockhopper, the macaroni, the gentoo and the king.

One of the most beautiful breeding birds is the black-browed albatross, but there are also striated and crested caracaras,

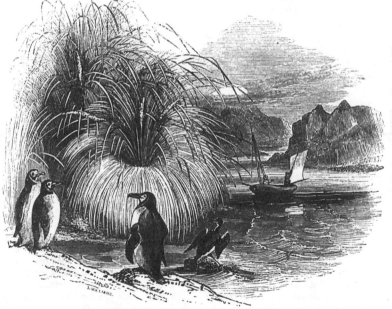

The Falkland Islands are home to a variety of penguins.

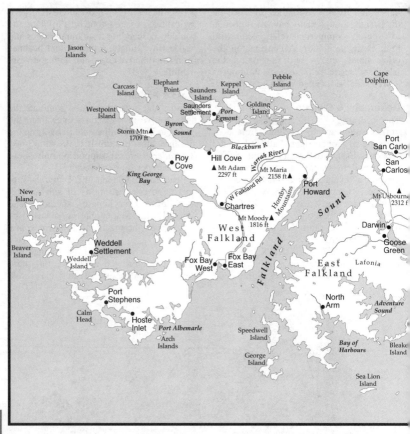

two species of cormorants, gulls, hawks, peregrine falcons, oystercatchers, snowy sheathbills, sheldgeese, steamer ducks and swans, among others. Most are present in large, impressive colonies, easy to photograph.

Elephant seals, sea lions and fur seals breed on shore, while six species of dolphins have been observed offshore. Killer whales are common, but not the larger South Atlantic whales.

Over the past decade, local government has encouraged nature-oriented tourism by constructing small lodges at outstanding sites, but there are also less-structured opportunities.

Government

A London-appointed governor administers the Falklands, but the locally elected Legislative Council (Legco) exercises significant power. Half its eight members come from Stanley; the remainder represent the countryside, or 'camp.' Selected Legco members advise the Governor as part of the Executive Council (Exco).

**Falkland Islands
(Islas Malvinas)**

Most Stanley residents work for local government (FIG) or FIC. While FIC has sold all its pastoral property, it continues to provide shipping and other commercial services. In camp, nearly everyone is involved in wool on relatively small, widely dispersed family-owned units. Tourism is economically limited, but facilities are always adequate and often excellent.

Population & People
According to the 1996 census, the population is 2564; two-thirds live in Stanley, the rest in camp. About half are native-born, some tracing their ancestry back seven generations, while most of the others are immigrants or temporary residents from the UK. Islanders' surnames indicate varied European backgrounds, but all speak English.

Thanks to their isolation and small numbers, Falklanders are versatile and adaptable. They are also hospitable, often welcoming strangers for 'smoko,' the traditional mid-morning tea or coffee break, or for a drink. This is especially true in camp, where visitors can be infrequent, but it is customary to bring a small gift – rum is a special favorite.

About 2000 British military personnel ('squaddies') reside at Mount Pleasant Airport, about 35 miles (60 km) southwest of Stanley, and at a few other scattered sites.

FACTS FOR THE VISITOR
In many ways the Falklands are a small country, with their own immigration and customs regulations, currency and other unique features.

Visas & Customs
All nationalities, including Britons, need valid passports and may need to show a return ticket or prove sufficient funds. For non-Britons, visa requirements are usually the same as for visitors to the UK. For details, consult Falkland House (☎ 0171-222-2542, fax 222-2375), 14 Broadway, Westminster, London SW1H 0BH. In Chile, contact Aerovías DAP (☎ (061) 223-340, fax 221693) at O'Higgins 891, which

Economy
Traditionally, the economy depended almost entirely on wool, but fishing has eclipsed agriculture as a revenue producer. Licensed Asian and European fleets have funded improvements in public services like schools, roads, telephones and medical care. Local government began permitting offshore seismic surveys for oil in 1993, and is considering the issuance of exploration licenses, an issue of great ambivalence for Islanders because of the potential environmental impact.

FALKLAND ISLANDS

operates flights to the Islands, or British consul John Rees (☎ 228312) at Roca 924, both in Punta Arenas.

Customs regulations are few except for limits on alcohol and tobacco, which are heavily taxed.

Money

The Falkland Islands pound (£) is at par with sterling. There are bank notes for £5, £10, £20 and £50, and coins for 1p, 2p, 5p, 10p, 20p, 50p and £1. Sterling circulates alongside local currency, which is not valid in the UK.

Credit cards are not widely used, but travelers' checks are readily accepted. Britons with guarantee cards can cash personal checks up to £50 at Standard Chartered Bank.

Costs Recent development has encouraged short-stay accommodation at prices up to £50 per day (meals included), but bed and breakfast in Stanley starts around £15. Cheaper, self-catering cabins are available in camp, plus opportunities for trekking and camping at little or no cost; some isolated families still welcome visitors without charge.

Food prices are roughly equivalent to the UK, but fresh meat (chiefly mutton) is cheap. Stanley restaurants are fairly expensive, except for short orders and snacks.

See the Getting Around section for airfare costs around the Islands.

When to Go & What to Bring

From October to March, migratory birds and mammals return to beaches and headlands. Very long daylight hours permit outdoor activities even if poor weather spoils part of the day.

Visitors should bring good waterproof clothing; a pair of Wellingtons is useful. Summer never gets truly hot and high winds can lower the ambient temperature, but the climate does not justify Antarctic preparations. Trekkers should bring a warm sleeping bag and a sturdy tent with a rainfly.

Tourist Offices

Besides their Stanley office and Falkland House (see Visas, above), the Islands have tourist representation in Europe and the Americas.

Chile
    Broom Travel, Roca 924, Punta Arenas
    (☎ (061) 228312)
Germany
    HS Travel & Consulting, PO Box 1447
    64529 Moerfelden
    (☎ /fax (61) 05-1304)
USA
    Leo Le Bon & Associates, 190 Montrose
    Ave, Berkeley, California 94707
    (☎ /fax 510-525-8846)

Useful Organizations

Based in both the UK and Stanley, Falklands Conservation is a nonprofit organization promoting wildlife conservation research as well as the preservation of wrecks and historic sites in the Islands. Membership, costing £15 per year and including its annual newsletter, is available from Falklands Conservation (☎ 0181-346-5011), 1 Princes Rd, Finchley, London N3 2DA. The Stanley representative (☎ 22247, fax 22288) is at the Beauchene Complex on John St between Philomel and Dean Sts.

The Falkland Islands Association (☎ 0171-222-0028), at 2 Greycoat Place, Westminster, London SW1P 1SD, is a political lobbying group that publishes a quarterly newsletter.

Business Hours & Holidays

Government offices are open weekdays 8 am to noon and 1.15 to 4.30 pm. Most larger businesses in Stanley stay open until 7 or 8 pm, but smaller shops may open only a few hours daily. Weekend business hours are reduced. Camp stores keep limited schedules but often open on request.

The following holidays are observed:

January 1
    New Year's Day
Late February (dates vary)
    Camp Sports

March/April (date varies)
  Good Friday
April 21
  Queen's Birthday
June 14
  Liberation Day
August 14
  Falklands Day
December 8
  Battle of the Falklands (1914)
December 25
  Christmas Day
December 26/27
  Boxing Day/Stanley Sports

Cultural Events

In a land where most people lived in physical and social isolation, the annual sports meetings provided a regular opportunity to share news, meet new people and participate in friendly competitions like horse racing, bull riding and dog trials. The rotating West Falkland sports maintains this tradition best, hosting 'two-nighters' at which Islanders party till they drop, sleep a few hours, and get up and start over again. Independent visitors are welcome, but arrange accommodations (usually floor space for your sleeping bag) in advance.

Post & Communications

Postal services are good. There are one or two airmails weekly to the UK, but parcels over one pound go by sea four or five times yearly. FIGAS delivers to outer settlements and islands. Correspondents should address letters to 'Post Office, Stanley, Falkland Islands, via London, England.'

Cable and Wireless PLC operates both local and long-distance telephones; local numbers have five digits. The international country code is 500, valid for numbers in Stanley and in camp. The British military have a separate telephone system, accessed by dialing '7' from civilian telephones.

Local calls cost 5p per minute, calls to the UK 15p for six seconds, and calls to the rest of the world 18p per six seconds. Operator-assisted calls cost the same, but with a three-minute minimum. Collect calls are possible only locally and to the UK.

Time

The Falklands are four hours behind GMT/UMT. In summer, Stanley observes daylight savings time, but camp remains on standard time.

Electricity

Electric current operates on 220/240 volts, 50 cycles. Plugs are identical to those in the UK.

Weights & Measures

The metric system is official, but people generally prefer imperial measures. There is a conversion table at the back of this book.

Books

The most readily available general account is Ian Strange's *The Falkland Islands*, 3rd edition (David & Charles, London, 1983). For a summary of the Falklands controversy, see Robert Fox's *Antarctica and the South Atlantic: Discovery, Development and Dispute* (BBC Books, London, 1985). On the war, try Max Hastings' & Simon Jenkins' *Battle for the Falklands* (Pan, London, 1983).

Robin Woods' *Guide to Birds of the Falkland Islands* (Anthony Nelson, Oswestry, Shropshire, 1988) is a detailed account of the Islands' bird life. Strange's *Field Guide to the Wildlife of the Falkland Islands and South Georgia* (Harper Collins, 1992) is also worth a look. Trekkers should acquire Julian Fisher's *Walks and Climbs in the Falkland Islands* (Bluntisham Books, Cambridge, 1992).

Maps

Directorate of Overseas Surveys topographic maps are available from the Secretariat, on Thatcher Drive in Stanley, for about £2 each. The two-sheet, 1:250,000 map of the Islands is suitable for most uses, but 1:50,000 sheets have more detail. These maps use imperial measures.

FALKLAND ISLANDS

Media

The Falkland Islands Broadcasting Service (FIBS) produces local programs and carries BBC news programs from the British Forces Broadcasting Service (BFBS). The nightly announcements, to which people listen religiously, are worth hearing.

Television, with programs taped and flown in from the UK, is available through BFBS. The only print media are the *Teaberry Express* and the weekly *Penguin News*.

Film & Photography

Color and B&W print film are readily available at reasonable prices. Color slide film is less dependably available.

Health

No special precautions are necessary, but carry adequate insurance. Flights from Britain may be diverted to yellow fever zones in Africa, so authorities recommend vaccination.

Wind and sun can combine to burn unsuspecting visitors severely. Wind can contribute to the danger of hypothermia in inclement weather. Stanley's King Edward VII Memorial Hospital has excellent medical and dental facilities.

Dangers & Annoyances

Near Stanley and in a few camp locations, there remain unexploded plastic land mines, but minefields are clearly marked and no civilian has ever been injured. *Never* enter a minefield – mines bear the weight of a penguin or even a sheep, but not of a human. Report suspicious objects to the Explosive Ordnance Disposal office (☎ 22229), near Town Hall, which has free minefield maps.

Despite its firm appearance, 'soft camp,' covered by white grass, is very boggy though not dangerous.

Activities

Wildlife is the major attraction. Penguins and other birds and marine mammals are tame and easily approached, even at developed sites like Sea Lion Island, but there are other equally interesting, undeveloped areas. Keep a respectful distance.

Fishing can be excellent; early March to late April is the best season for sea trout, which requires a license (£10) from the Stanley post office. Trekking and camping are possible, though many landowners and the tourist board discourage camping because of fire danger and disturbance to stock and wildlife. It is possible to visit the 1982 battlefields.

Accommodations

Stanley has several B&Bs and hotels, while some farms have converted surplus buildings into comfortable lodges. Others have self-catering cottages, caravans or Portakabin shelters. Reservations are essential.

In areas not often visited by tourists, some of the Islanders welcome houseguests; many farms have 'outside houses' or shanties that visitors may use with permission. Camping is possible only with permission.

Food & Drink

Mutton, the dietary staple, is very cheap. Islanders usually consume their own produce, but a hydroponic market garden now produces aubergines (eggplant), tomatoes, lettuce and other salad greens.

Stanley snack bars offer fish & chips, mutton-burgers (not that bad), pizza, sausage rolls and pasties, while the hotels have decent restaurants. At pubs, beer and hard liquor (whiskey, rum) are the favorites.

GETTING THERE & AWAY
Air

From RAF Brize Norton, Oxfordshire, there are regular flights to Mount Pleasant International Airport (16 hours, plus an hour's layover on Ascension Island). Southbound flights leave Brize Norton Mondays and Thursdays; northbound flights leave Mount Pleasant Wednesdays and Saturdays.

The roundtrip fare is £2180, but reduced APEX fares cost £1340 with 30-day advance purchase. Groups of six or more pay £1130 each. Travelers continuing to

Chile can purchase one-way tickets for half the roundtrip fare. For reservations in London, contact Carol Stewart at Falkland House (☎ 0171-222-2542), 14 Broadway, Westminster SW1H 0BH. In Stanley, contact the Falkland Islands Company (☎ 27633), on Crozier Place.

Aerovías DAP (☎ (061) 223340, fax 221693), O'Higgins 891 in Punta Arenas, connects Stanley with Chile; for details, see the Punta Arenas entry in the Magallanes chapter.

Getting Around

Outside the Stanley-Mount Pleasant area, the Government Air Service (FIGAS; ☎ 27219) serves most destinations. Sample roundtrip fares from Stanley include Salvador (£50), Darwin (£72), San Carlos (£74), Port Howard (£94), Sea Lion Island (£95), Pebble Island (£107), Fox Bay (£121), Carcass Island (£145), Weddell Island (£157) and New Island (£175).

STANLEY

Stanley's metal-clad houses, brightly painted corrugated metal roofs and large kitchen gardens are a striking contrast to the surrounding moorland. Founded in 1845, the new capital was a supply and repair port, but Cape Horn shipping began to avoid it when boats were scuttled under questionable circumstances. In the late 19th century, Stanley grew more rapidly as the trans-shipment point for wool between camp and the UK.

As the wool trade grew, so did the influence of the Falkland Islands Company, Stanley's largest employer. Its political and economic dominance were uncontested and its relatively high wages and good housing offered a paternalistic security. 'Tied houses,' however, were available only while the employee remained with FIC.

Stanley remains the service center for the wool industry, but has also become a

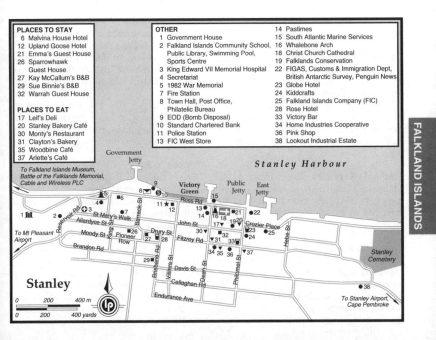

PLACES TO STAY	
6	Malvina House Hotel
12	Upland Goose Hotel
21	Emma's Guest House
26	Sparrowhawk Guest House
27	Kay McCallum's B&B
29	Sue Binnie's B&B
32	Warrah Guest House

PLACES TO EAT	
17	Leif's Deli
20	Stanley Bakery Café
30	Monty's Restaurant
31	Clayton's Bakery
35	Woodbine Café
37	Arlette's Café

OTHER	
1	Government House
2	Falkland Islands Community School, Public Library, Swimming Pool, Sports Centre
3	King Edward VII Memorial Hospital
4	Secretariat
5	1982 War Memorial
7	Fire Station
8	Town Hall, Post Office, Philatelic Bureau
9	EOD (Bomb Disposal)
10	Standard Chartered Bank
11	Police Station
13	FIC West Store
14	Pastimes
15	South Atlantic Marine Services
16	Whalebone Arch
18	Christ Church Cathedral
19	Falklands Conservation
22	FIGAS, Customs & Immigration Dept, British Antarctic Survey, Penguin News
23	Globe Hotel
24	Kiddcrafts
25	Falkland Islands Company (FIC)
28	Rose Hotel
33	Victory Bar
34	Home Industries Cooperative
36	Pink Shop
38	Lookout Industrial Estate

Stanley

To Falkland Islands Museum,
Battle of the Falklands Memorial,
Cable and Wireless PLC

To Mt Pleasant Airport

Government Jetty

Stanley Harbour

Victory Green

Public Jetty

East Jetty

Ross Rd

Reservoit Rd · St Mary's Walk · Allardyce St · Moody St · Pioneer Row · Brandon Rd

Barrack St

John St · Drury St · Fitzroy Rd

Crozier Place

Hebe St

Brisbane Rd · Villiers St · Dean St · Philomel St

Davis St · Callaghan Rd · Endurance Ave

Stanley Cemetery

To Stanley Airport,
Cape Pembroke

0   200   400 m
0   200   400 yards

FALKLAND ISLANDS

significant port for Asian and European fishing fleets.

Orientation

On a steep north-facing hillside, Stanley has sprawled east and west along Stanley Harbour. Ross Rd, the main street, runs the length of the harbor, but most government offices, businesses and houses are within a few blocks of each other.

Information

Tourist Offices The Falkland Islands Tourist Board (☎ 22215, 22281) at the Public Jetty distributes an excellent guide to Stanley and other useful brochures. Hours are 8 am to noon and 1.15 to 4.30 pm weekdays.

The Mount Pleasant Travel Office (☎ (7) 6691) is at 12 Facility Main Reception, at Mount Pleasant International Airport.

Money Standard Chartered Bank, on Ross Rd between Barrack and Villiers Sts, pays significantly better rates for travelers' checks than cash dollars, but it's even better to bring sterling than dollars. Hours are 8.30 am to noon and 1.15 to 3 pm weekdays.

Post & Communications The post office is in Town Hall, on Ross Rd at Barrack St. Cable and Wireless PLC, on Ross Rd West near Government House, operates phone, telegram, telex and fax services. Magnetic cards are cheaper than operator-assisted overseas calls. Counter hours are 8.30 am to 5 pm, but public booths are open 24 hours.

Medical Services King Edward VII Memorial Hospital (☎ 27328 for appointments, ☎ 27410 for emergencies), at the west end of St Mary's Walk, has superb facilities.

Things to See

Distinguished **Christ Church Cathedral** (1892), is a massive brick and stone construction with attractive stained-glass windows. On the small nearby plaza, the restored **Whalebone Arch** commemorates the 1933 centenary of British rule.

Since the mid-19th century, London-appointed governors have inhabited rambling **Government House**, on Ross Rd. Just beyond it, the **Battle of the Falklands Memorial** commemorates a WWI naval engagement, while **Britannia House Museum** is a recent project, with changing exhibits. Curator John Smith is especially conversant with maritime history.

Just north of the Secretariat, on Ross Rd, is the **1982 War Memorial**, designed by a Falklander living overseas, paid for by public subscription and built with volunteer labor. At the east end of Ross Road, both the Islands' tiny elite and working class rest at **Stanley Cemetery**, where surnames like Felton and Biggs are as common as Smith and Jones are in the UK.

Activities

Stanley's new swimming pool, on Reservoir Rd, has become very popular. There are also now sites for squash, badminton, basketball and the like.

Special Events

Stanley Sports, held after Christmas, features horse racing (and betting), bull riding and other events. In March, the competitive Horticultural Show displays the produce of kitchen gardens in Stanley and camp, plus a variety of baked goods, and includes a spirited auction. The July Crafts Fair presents the work of local weavers, leatherworkers, photographers and artists (there are many talented illustrators and painters).

Places to Stay

Accommodation is good, but limited and not cheap – reservations are advisable. Breakfast is always included; inquire about full board. The most economical is *Kay McCallum's B&B* (☎ 21071, fax 21148), 14 Drury St, charging £15 per person, while *Sue Binnie's B&B* (☎ 21051), 3 Brandon Rd, charges £25. *Warrah Guest House* (☎ 22649), a renovated 19th-century stone house at 46 John St, charges £25, while the popular *Emma's Guest House* (☎ 21056), 36 Ross Rd, costs £30.50/55 single/double.

With rates starting at £37.50 per person, *Malvinas House Hotel* (☎ 21355), 3 Ross Rd, has beautiful grounds and a conservatory restaurant. The venerable *Upland Goose Hotel* (☎ 21455), a mid-19th century building at 20/22 Ross Rd, starts at £39.50.

Places to Eat
Most Stanley eateries are modest snack bars with limited hours. Two bakeries serve bread, snacks and light meals: *Clayton's Bakery* on Dean St and *Stanley Bakery Café*, Waverley House, Philomel St. *Woodbine Café* (☎ 21002), 29 Fitzroy Rd, serves fish & chips, pizza, sausage rolls and similar items. *Leif's Deli* (☎ 22721), 23 John St, has specialty foods and snacks.

Most Stanley hotels have better restaurants, but meals should be booked in advance. The Malvinas House Hotel's restaurant is outstanding, the Upland Goose's passable, but both are expensive.

Entertainment
Of Stanley's several pubs, the most popular is the Globe Hotel on Crozier Place, but try also the Rose Hotel on Brisbane Rd and the Victory Bar on Philomel St. The Upland Goose Hotel has a public bar.

In winter, the pubs sponsor a darts league, with tournaments in the Town Hall, where there are also many dances with live music throughout the year. There are no cinemas, but hotels and guesthouses have video lounges.

Things to Buy
For locally spun and knitted woolens, visit the Home Industries Cooperative on Fitzroy Rd. Kiddcrafts, 2-A Philomel St, makes stuffed penguins and other soft toys with great appeal for children.

The Pink Shop, 33 Fitzroy Rd, sells gifts and souvenirs, Falklands and general interest books (including selected LP guides), and excellent wildlife prints by owner Tony Chater.

Postage stamps, available from the post office and from the Philatelic Bureau, are popular with collectors. The Bureau also sells stamps from South Georgia and British Antarctic Territory. The Treasury, in the Secretariat behind the Liberation Monument, sells commemorative coins.

Getting There & Away
Air For international flight information, see the Getting There & Away section.

From Stanley, FIGAS (☎ 27219), at the corner of Ross and Philomel Sts, serves outlying destinations in nine-passenger aircraft, arranging itineraries by demand; when you know where and when you wish to go, contact them and listen to FIBS announcements at 6.30 pm the night before departure to learn your departure time. Occasionally, usually around holidays, flights are heavily booked and seats may not be available. Some grass airstrips only accept a limited payload, so baggage is limited to 30 pounds per person.

Passages may also be arranged through the Tourist Board on the Public Jetty.

Bus Few places are accessible by road, but C&M Travel (☎ 21468) serves Stanley and Mount Pleasant airports, and will also make day trips to Darwin/Goose Green and elsewhere in summer.

Getting Around
To/From the Airport Mount Pleasant International Airport is 35 miles southwest of Stanley by road, while Stanley Airport is about three miles east of town.

C&M Travel (☎ 21468) takes passengers to Mount Pleasant for £13 single; call for reservations the day before. They also take groups to Stanley Airport or meet them there. For cabs, contact Ben's Taxi Service (☎ 21191) or Lowe's Taxis (☎ 21381).

AROUND STANLEY
Stanley Harbour Maritime History Trail
See the Tourist Board for a brochure on wrecks and condemned ships. There are informational panels near vessels like the *Jhelum* (a sinking East Indiaman deserted by her crew in 1871), the *Charles Cooper* (an American packet still used for storage) and the *Lady Elizabeth* (a three-masted freighter that struck a rock in 1913).

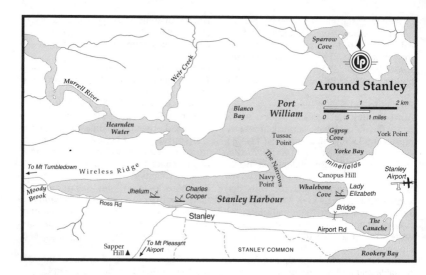

Penguin Walk & Gypsy Cove

The Falklands' most accessible penguin colonies are about 1½ hours' walk from Stanley; from the east end of Ross Rd, continue beyond the cemetery and cross the bridge over The Canache, past the *Lady Elizabeth* and Stanley Airport to Yorke Bay.

Gentoo penguins crowd the sandy beach where, unfortunately, the Argentines buried plastic mines; get your view of the penguins by walking along the minefield fence. Further on, at Gypsy Cove, are Magellanic penguins (avoid stepping on burrows) and other shore birds.

Battlefields

Tony Smith's Discovery Tours (☎ 21027, fax 22304) offers tours of 1982 battlefield sites near Stanley.

Cape Pembroke Lighthouse

Built in 1855 and rebuilt in 1906, this recently restored lighthouse is a full day's walk east of Stanley Airport.

Kidney Island

Covered with tussock grass, this small reserve north of the mouth of Port William supports a wide variety of wildlife, including rockhopper penguins and sea lions. Arrange carefully planned visits through the Agricultural Officer (☎ 27355).

CAMP

Nearly everyone in 'camp' (a term for all of the Falklands outside Stanley) is engaged in sheep ranching. Camp settlements were always company towns, hamlets near sheltered harbors where coastal shipping could collect the wool, while single shepherds lived at 'outside houses,' which still dot the countryside.

Many wildlife sites are on smaller offshore islands like Sea Lion Island and Pebble Island, whose comfortable tourist lodges are costly, but budget alternatives also exist.

East Falkland

East Falkland's road network consists of a good highway to Mount Pleasant International Airport and Goose Green. From Pony's Pass on the highway, good, all-weather roads head north to the Estancia, a farm west of Stanley, to Port Louis, and also toward Port San Carlos, but most other tracks are usable for 4WD only. FIGAS is still the most reliable means of transport to most destinations.

Port Louis Dating from the French foundation of the colony in 1764, Port Louis is the Falklands' oldest settlement. One of the colony's oldest buildings is the ivy-covered 19th-century farmhouse, still occupied by farm employees, but there are also ruins of the French governor's house and fortress and Louis Vernet's settlement scattered nearby. Visit the grave of Matthew Brisbane, Vernet's lieutenant, murdered by gauchos after the British left him in charge of the settlement in 1833.

It is possible to visit wildlife sites at Seal Bay, north of Port Louis, by arrangement with Tony Smith (☎ 21027, fax 22304).

Volunteer Beach Volunteer Beach, part of Johnson's Harbour farm east of Port Louis, has the Falklands' largest concentration of king penguins, a growing colony of about 150 breeding pairs. At Volunteer Point, several hours' walk east, is an offshore breeding colony of southern fur seals (bring binoculars). Return along Volunteer Lagoon for more birds and elephant seals.

Volunteer Beach was closed at press time due to a land dispute, but may reopen. If so, Tony Smith (☎ 21027) runs full-day excursions from Stanley, as does Montana Short's Montana Photo Tours (☎ /fax 21076) in Stanley. Mike Rendell at Stanley's Malvinas House Hotel (☎ 210-84) arranges overnight excursions for a maximum of five people. If attempting the trip on your own, contact owner George Smith of Johnson's Harbour (☎ 31399) for permission.

San Carlos In 1982, British forces came ashore at San Carlos, on Falkland Sound; in 1983, the sheep station was subdivided and sold to half a dozen local families. There is fishing on the San Carlos River, north of the settlement. Comfortable *Blue Beach Lodge* (☎ 32205) charges £49 for full board. Self-catering accommodation is available at *Waimea Fishing Lodge* (☎ 322-20) for £15 per person.

Across San Carlos Water, but four hours away by foot, is the **Ajax Bay Refrigeration Plant**, a 1950s CDC (Colonial Development Corporation) boondoggle. Gentoo penguins wander through its ruins, which served as a field hospital in 1982. Take a flashlight if you plan to explore.

Darwin & Goose Green At the narrow isthmus that separates Lafonia from northern East Falkland, Darwin was the site of an early saladero, where gauchos slaughtered feral cattle and tanned their hides; it later became the center of FIC's camp operations and, with nearby Goose Green, the largest settlement outside Stanley. The heaviest ground fighting of the Falklands War took place at Goose Green.

Sea Lion Island Off East Falkland's south coast, tiny Sea Lion is less than a mile across, but teems with wildlife, including five species of penguins, enormous cormorant colonies, giant petrels and the charmingly tame predator known as the 'Johnny Rook' (striated caracara). Hundreds of elephant seals crowd its sandy beaches, while sea lions dot the narrow

King Penguin

gravel beaches below its southern bluffs or lurk in the towering tussock.

Much of the credit for Sea Lion's wildlife has to go to Terry and Doreen Clifton, who farmed it since the mid-1970s before selling it recently. The Cliftons developed their 2300-acre (930-hectare) ranch with the idea that wildlife, habitat and livestock were compatible, and Sea Lion is one of few working farms with any substantial cover of native tussock grass. Through improved fencing and other conscientious practices, the Cliftons made it a successful sheep station and a popular tourist site, mostly for day trips from Stanley and Mount Pleasant.

Dave and Pat Grey manage the *Sea Lion Lodge* (☎ /fax 32004), which offers twin-bed rooms with full board for £51 per person. At least two full days would be desirable for seeing the island in its entirety.

West Falkland
Pioneers settled West Falkland only in the late 1860s, but within a decade new sheep stations covered the entire island and others offshore. One of the most interesting experiments was the Keppel Island mission for Indians from Tierra del Fuego.

West Falkland (nearly as large as East Falkland) and adjacent islands have fine wildlife sites. The only proper road runs from Port Howard on Falkland Sound to Chartres on King George Bay, but a system of rough tracks is also suitable for Land Rovers and motorcycles, and there is good trekking in the mountainous interior. Only a few places have formal tourist facilities.

Port Howard Scenic Port Howard, at the foot of 2158-ft (658-meter) Mount Maria, remains intact after its sale to its local managers in 1987. About 50 people live on the station, which has its own dairy, grocery, abattoir, social club and other amenities. It will be the West Falkland port for the anticipated ferry across Falkland Sound.

The immediate surroundings offer hiking, riding and fishing; wildlife sites are more remote. Visitors can view shearing and other camp activities, and there is a small war museum. Accommodation at *Port Howard Lodge* (☎ 42150), the former manager's house, costs £48 per person with full board, but make arrangements in advance to lodge at the cookhouse for a fraction of the cost.

It is possible to hike up the valley of the Warrah River, a good trout stream, and past Turkey Rocks to the Blackburn River and Hill Cove, another pioneer farm. Ask permission to cross property boundaries, and close gates; where the track is faint, look for old telephone lines. There are longer hikes south toward Chartres, Fox Bay and Port Stephens.

Pebble Island Off the north coast of West Falkland, elongated Pebble has varied topography, extensive wetlands and a good sample of wildlife. *Pebble Island Hotel* (☎ 41093) charges £48 per person with full board, but ask for self-catering cottages at the settlement and *Marble Mountain Shanty* at the west end of the island, for £15 per night.

Keppel Island In 1853, the South American Missionary Society established itself on Keppel to catechize Indians from Tierra del Fuego and teach them to grow potatoes. The settlement was controversial, because the government suspected that the Yahgans had been brought against their will, but still lasted until 1898.

Interesting ruins include the chapel, the bailiff's house, and the stone walls of Indian dwellings. Keppel is also a good place for wildlife, but visits are difficult to arrange because it has no permanent residents. If interested in visiting, contact the Agricultural Officer. FIGAS cannot land on Keppel, however, so visitors would have to arrange a boat charter.

Saunders Island Saunders was the site of the first British garrison (1765). In 1767, Spanish forces dislodged the British from Port Egmont and nearly precipitated a general war. After the British left in 1774, Spain razed the settlement, but extensive ruins still remain.

Saunders has a fine sample of wildlife and good trekking to 'The Neck,' whose sandspit beach links it to Elephant Point peninsula, about four hours from the settlement. Near The Neck is a large colony of black-browed albatrosses and rockhopper penguins, along with a few king penguins, while farther on are thousands of Magellanic penguins, kelp gulls, skuas and a colony of elephant seals.

David and Suzan Pole-Evans on Saunders (☎ 41298) rent a comfortable self-catering cottage in the settlement for £10 per person per night, as well as a six-bunk Portakabin (bedding supplied, £20 per person), with a gas stove and outside chemical toilet, at The Neck. Fresh milk, eggs and mutton are included in the price of accommodation, but you have to ask for them. Beyond that, visitors should bring their own food. Depending on the farm workload, transportation to The Neck is available for £10 per person.

Port Stephens Port Stephens' rugged headlands, near the settlement's sheltered harbor, host thousands of rockhoppers and other sea birds, while Calm Head, about two hours' walk, has excellent views of the jagged shoreline and the powerful South Atlantic. One longer trek goes to the abandoned sealing station at Albemarle and huge gentoo colonies. The Arch Islands, accessible only by boat, take their name from the huge gap the ocean has eroded in the largest of the group.

If interested in visiting Port Stephens and trekking in the vicinity, contact Peter or Anne Robertson (☎ 42307) at the settlement or Leon and Pam Berntsen (☎ 42309) at Albemarle Station.

Weddell Island Scottish pioneer John Hamilton acquired this western offshore island and others to experiment with tussock grass restoration and forest plantations, importation of Highland cattle and Shetland ponies, and exotic wildlife like guanacos, Patagonian foxes and otters. The abundant local wildlife includes gentoo and Magellanic penguins, great skuas, night herons, giant petrels and striated caracaras.

Farm owners John and Steph Ferguson (☎ 42398, fax 42399) welcome guests at *Seaview Cottage* or *Hamilton Cottage* for £10 to £25 per person, depending on the number of guests. In the newly remodeled *Mountain View House*, charges range from £12 to £45 per person, depending on the number of guests (the upper limit is the minimum for renting the house).

New Island The Falklands' most westerly inhabited island was a refuge for whalers from Britain and North America from the late-18th century well into the 19th. There remain ruins of a shore-based, turn-of-the-century Norwegian whaling factory that failed because there simply were not enough whales.

On the precipitous western coast are gigantic colonies of rockhopper penguins and black-browed albatrosses and a large rookery of southern fur seals. Potential visitors should contact Ian or María Strange (☎ 21185, fax 21186) in Stanley.

FALKLAND ISLANDS

Appendix I: Climate Charts

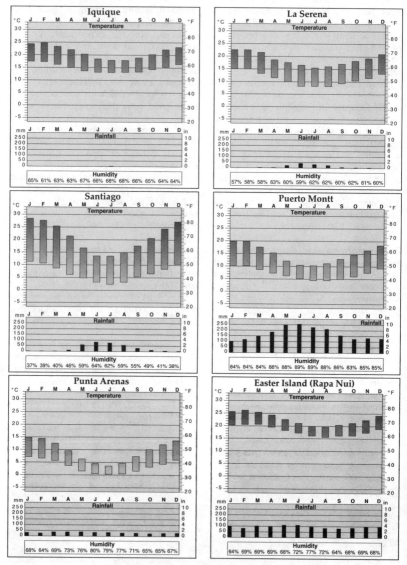

Appendix II: Online Services

Carnegie Observatories Home Page
http://www.ociw.edu/
Information on astronomical observatory at Las Campanas, between La Serena and Vallenar; in English

Cerro Tololo International Observatory
http://ctios2.ctio.noao.edu/ctio.html
Information on Cerro Tololo observatory, east of La Serena; in English

Chile Guide
http://sunsite.dcc.uchile.cl/~mvasquez/chile/index.html
Links to wide selection of Chilean websites, including travel- and tourism-oriented ones; in English and Spanish

Chilesat
http://www.chilepac.net/
Growing Chilean telecommunications enterprise, also offering Internet access; in Spanish

Chile Servidores
http://www.multi.com.uy/presenta/america/chile/
Similar in content to Chile Guide, but contains many additional links; in Spanish

Chip News
http://www.chip.cl
Weekday summary of current events and business, especially mining; in English

Compañía de Telecomunicaciones de Chile (CTC)
http://www.ctc.cl/
Information on Chile's largest telecommunications company, including Internet access; in Spanish

El Mercurio
http://hermes.mercurio.cl/
Santiago's most prestigious daily newspaper; in Spanish

Estrategia
http://www.reuna.cl/estrategia
Chile's financial daily; in Spanish

Good Hotel & Tourism Guide: Chile
http://www.chileweb.net/hallifax/
Slick but very incomplete tourism site, focusing on upscale hotels and restaurants only; in English

Kingdom of Araucanía and Patagonia
http://www.pitt.edu/~jwcst17/kap.html
Oddball site in homage to self-declared 19th-century French 'sovereign' of Mapuche territory; in English

La Epoca
http://www.reuna.cl/laepoca/
Very good Christian Democrat newspaper which began as part of 'No' campaign against Pinochet's continuation in office; in Spanish

LanChile
http://www.lanchile.com/
Global information on Chile's national airline; in English

Lonely Planet – Destination Chile
http://www.lonelyplanet.com/dest/sam/chile.htm
LP's regularly updated Chile travel site

ProChile
http://www.prochile.cl/index.en.html
Official Chilean government promotional site, including travel- and tourism-oriented material; in English

Sernatur
http://www.segegob.cl/sernatur/inicio2.html
Official Chilean government tourist agency; in English and Spanish

Travelers
email: travlers@chilepac.net
Puerto Montt-based travel agency with adventure travel tours and other services

US-BASED TOUR COMPANIES
Mountain Travel Sobek
http://www.mtsobek.com/

National Outdoor Leadership School
http://www.nols.edu
email: admissions@nols.edu

Nature Expeditions International
email: NaturExp@aol.com

USENET DISCUSSION GROUPS
Soc.culture.chil
Wide-ranging but often polemical and irritating discussion group

Rec.travel.latin-america
Regional travel discussion group with frequent though not numerous items on Chile

Appendix III: Spanish Phrasebook

Every visitor to Chile should attempt to learn some Spanish, the basic elements of which are easily acquired. If possible, take a short course before you go. Even if you can't do so, Chileans are gracious hosts and will encourage your Spanish, so there is no need to feel self-conscious about vocabulary or pronunciation. There are many common cognates, so if you're stuck try Hispanicizing an English word – it is unlikely you'll make a truly embarrassing error. Do not, however, admit to being *embarazada* (sounds like 'embarrassed') unless you are in fact pregnant!

Note that in American Spanish, the plural of the familiar 'tu' is *ustedes* rather than *vosotros*, as in Spain. Chileans and other Latin Americans readily understand Castilian Spanish, but may find it either quaint or pretentious.

Chilean Spanish
Chilean speakers relax terminal and even some internal consonants almost to the point of disappearance, so that it can be difficult to distinguish plural from singular. For example, *las islas* (the islands) may sound more like 'la ila' to an English speaker. Chileans speak rather more rapidly than other South Americans, and rather less clearly – the conventional *¿quieres?* (do you want?) sounds more like 'querí' on the tongue of a Chilean.

Other Chilean peculiarities include pronunciation of the second person familiar of 'ar' verbs as 'ai' rather than 'as,' so that, for instance, '¿Adónde vas?' (Where are you going?' will sound more like '¿Adónde vai?' Likewise, the common interjection 'pues' (well . . .) at the end of a phrase becomes 'pueh' or 'po,' as in 'sí, po.'

Vocabulary There are many differences in vocabulary between Castilian and American Spanish, and among Spanish-speaking countries in the Americas. There are also considerable regional differences within these countries not attributable to accent alone – Chilean speech, for instances, contains many words adopted from Mapuche, while the residents of Santiago sometimes use *coa*, a working-class slang. Check the glossary for some of these terms.

Chileans and other South Americans normally refer to the Spanish language as *castellano* rather than *español*.

Phrasebooks & Dictionaries
Lonely Planet's *Latin American Spanish phrasebook*, by Anna Cody, is a worthwhile addition to your backpack. Another exceptionally useful resource is the *University of Chicago Spanish-English, English-Spanish Dictionary*, whose small size, light weight and thorough entries make it ideal for travel.

Pronunciation
Spanish pronunciation is, in general, consistently phonetic. Once you are aware of the basic rules, they should cause little difficulty. Speak slowly to avoid getting tongue-tied until you become confident of your ability.

Pronunciation of the letters f, k, l, n, p, q, s and t is virtually identical with English, and y is identical when used as a consonant; ll is a separate letter, pronounced as 'y' and coming after l in the alphabet. Ch and ñ are also separate letters; in the alphabet they come after c and n respectively.

Vowels Spanish vowels are very consistent and have easy English equivalents:

a   is like 'a' in 'father'
e   is like the 'e' in 'met'; at the end of a word it's like the 'ey' in 'hey'
i   is like 'ee' in 'feet'
o   is like 'o' in 'for'
u   is like 'oo' in 'boot'; after consonants other than 'q,' it is more like English 'w'

y   is a consonant except when it stands alone or appears at the end of a word, in which case its pronunciation is identical to Spanish 'i'

Consonants Spanish consonants generally resemble their English equivalents, but there are some major exceptions:

b   resembles its English equivalent, but is undistinguished from 'v'; for clarification, refer to the former as 'b larga,' the latter as 'b corta' (the word for the letter itself is pronounced like English 'bay')

c   is like the 's' in 'see' before 'e' and 'i', otherwise like English 'k'

d   closely resembles 'th' in 'feather'

g   before 'e' and 'i' like a guttural English 'h'; otherwise like 'g' in 'go'

h   is invariably silent; if your name begins with this letter, listen carefully when immigration officials summon you to pick up your passport

j   most closely resembles English 'h,' but is slightly more guttural

ñ   is like 'ni' in 'onion'

r   is nearly identical to English except at the beginning of a word, when it is often rolled

rr   is very strongly rolled

v   resembles English, but see 'b,' above

x   is like 'x' in 'taxi' except for very few words for which it follows Spanish or Mexican usage as 'j'

z   is like 's' in 'sun'

Diphthongs Diphthongs are combinations of two vowels which form a single syllable. In Spanish, the formation of a diphthong depends on combinations of 'weak' vowels (i and u) or strong ones (a, e and o). Two weak vowels or a strong and a weak vowel make a diphthong, but two strong ones are separate syllables.

A good example of two weak vowels forming a diphthong is the word *diurno* (during the day). The final syllable of *obligatorio* (obligatory) is a combination of weak and strong vowels.

Stress Stress, often indicated by visible accents, is very important, since it can change the meaning of words. In general, words ending in vowels or the letters n or s have stress on the next-to-last syllable, while those with other endings have stress on the last syllable. Thus *vaca* (cow) and *caballos* (horses) both have accents on their next-to-last syllables.

Visible accents, which can occur anywhere in a word, dictate stress over these general rules. Thus *sótano* (basement), *América* and *porción* (portion) all have the stress on the syllable with the accented vowel. When words are written all in capitals, the accent is often not shown, but it still affects the pronunciation.

Basic Grammar

Nouns in Spanish are masculine or feminine. The definite article ('the' in English) agrees with the noun in gender and number; for example, the Spanish word for 'train' is masculine, so 'the train' is *el tren*, and the plural is *los trenes*. The word for 'house' is feminine, so 'the house' is *la casa*, and the plural is *las casas*. The indefinite articles (a, an, some) work in the same way: *un libro* (a book) is masculine singular, while *una carta* (a letter) is feminine singular. Most nouns ending in 'o' are masculine and those ending in 'a' are generally feminine. Normally, nouns ending in a vowel add 's' to form the plural – *unos libros* (some books), *las cartas* (some letters) – while those ending in a consonant add 'es': *los reyes* (the kings) is the plural of *el rey*. Gender also affects demonstrative pronouns: *este* is the masculine form of 'this,' while *esta* is the feminine form and *esto* the neuter; 'these,' 'that' and 'those' are formed by adding 's.'

Adjectives also agree with the noun in gender and number, and usually come after the noun. Possessive adjectives like *mi* (my), *tu* (your) *su* (his/her/their) agree with the thing possessed, not with the possessor. For example 'his suitcase' is *su maleta*, while 'his suitcases' is *sus maletas*. A simple way to indicate possession is to use the preposition *de* (of). 'Juan's room,' for instance, would be *la habitación de Juan*, literally, 'the room of Juan.'

Personal pronouns are usually not used with verbs, except for clarification or emphasis. There are three main categories of verbs: those which end in 'ar' such as *hablar* (to speak), those which end in 'er' such as *comer* (to eat), and those which end in 'ir' such as *reir* (to laugh); there are many irregular verbs, such as *ir* (to go) and *venir* (to come).

To form a comparative, add *más* (more) or *menos* (less) before the adjective. For example, *alto* is 'high,' *más alto* 'higher' and *lo más alto* 'the highest.'

Greetings & Civilities

In their public behavior, Chileans are exceptionally polite and expect others to reciprocate. Never, for example, approach a stranger for information without extending a greeting like *buenos días* or *buenas tardes*. Most young people use the informal 'tu' and its associated verb forms among themselves, but if in doubt you should use the more formal 'usted' and its forms.

hello	*hola*
good morning	*buenos días*
good afternoon	*buenas tardes*
good evening/night	*buenas noches*
goodbye	*adiós*, *chau*
please	*por favor*
thank you	*gracias*
you're welcome	*de nada*

Useful Words & Phrases

yes	*sí*
no	*no*
and	*y*
to/at	*a*
for	*por*, *para*
of/from	*de*, *desde*
in	*en*
with	*con*
without	*sin*
before	*antes*
after	*después*
soon	*pronto*
already	*ya*

now	*ahora*
right away	*en seguida*, *al tiro*
here	*aquí*
there	*allí*
I understand	*entiendo*
I don't understand	*no entiendo*

I don't speak much Spanish.
  No hablo mucho español.
Is there . . . ? Are there . . . ?
  ¿Hay. . . ?

Where?	*¿Dónde?*
Where is ...?	*¿Dónde está...?*
Where are. . . ?	*¿Dónde están. .?*
When?	*¿Cuando?*
How?	*¿Cómo?*
I would like. . .	*Me gustaría. . .*
coffee	*café*
tea	*té*
beer	*cerveza*
How much?	*¿Cuanto?*
How many?	*¿Cuantos?*

Getting Around

plane	*avión*
train	*tren*
bus	*ómnibus*, or just *bus*
small bus	*colectivo*, *micro*, *liebre*
ship	*barco*, *buque*
car	*auto*
taxi	*taxi*
truck	*camión*
pickup	*camioneta*
bicycle	*bicicleta*
motorcycle	*motocicleta*
hitchhike	*hacer dedo*
airport	*aeropuerto*
train station	*estación de ferrocarril*
bus terminal	*terminal de buses*

I would like a ticket to . . .
  Quiero un boleto/pasaje a . . .
What's the fare to . . . ?
  ¿Cuanto cuesta el pasaje a . . . ?
When does the next plane/train/bus leave for . . . ?
  ¿Cuando sale el próximo avión/tren/ ómnibus para . . . . ?

student/university discount
descuento estudiantil/universitario
first/last/next   *primero/último/*
   próximo
first/second class   *primera/*
   segunda clase
one way/roundtrip   *ida/ida y vuelta*
left luggage   *guardería,*
   equipaje
tourist office   *oficina de*
   turismo

Accommodations
hotel   *hotel, pensión,*
   residencial
single room   *habitación*
   single
double room   *habitación doble*
What does it cost?   *¿Cuanto cuesta?*
Can you give me a deal?
   ¿Me puede hacer precio?
per night   *por noche*
full board   *pensión*
   completa
shared bath   *baño*
   compartido
private bath   *baño privado*
too expensive   *demasiado caro*
cheaper   *mas económico*
May I see it?   *¿Puedo verlo?*
the bill   *la cuenta*

Toilets
The most common word for 'toilet' is *baño*,
but *servicios sanitarios*, or just *servicios*
(services) is a frequent alternative. Men's
toilets will usually bear a descriptive term
such as *hombres*, *caballeros* or *varones*.
Women's toilets will say *señoras* or *damas*.

Post & Communications
post office   *correo*
letter   *carta*
parcel   *paquete*
postcard   *postal*
airmail   *correo aéreo*
registered mail   *certificado*
stamps   *estampillas*
person to person   *persona a*
   persona
collect call   *cobro revertido*

Geographical Expressions
The expressions below are among the
most common you will encounter in this
book and in Spanish language maps and
guides.
bay   *bahía*
bridge   *puente*
farm   *fundo, hacienda*
glacier   *glaciar,*
   ventisquero
highway   *carretera,*
   camino, ruta
hill   *cerro*
lake   *lago*
marsh, estuary   *estero*
mount   *cerro*
mountain range   *cordillera*
national park   *parque nacional*
pass   *paso*
ranch   *estancia*
sound   *seno*
river   *río*
waterfall   *cascada, salto*

Countries
The list below includes only countries
whose spelling differs in English and
Spanish.
Canada   *Canadá*
Denmark   *Dinamarca*
England   *Inglaterra*
France   *Francia*
Germany   *Alemania*
Great Britain   *Gran Bretaña*
Ireland   *Irlanda*
Italy   *Italia*
Japan   *Japón*
Netherlands   *Holanda*
New Zealand   *Nueva Zelandia*
Peru   *Perú*
Scotland   *Escocia*
Spain   *España*
Sweden   *Suecia*
Switzerland   *Suiza*
United States   *Estados Unidos*
Wales   *Gales*
I am from   *Soy de . . .*
Where are you from?
   ¿De dónde viene?
Where do you live?   *¿Dónde vive?*

Ordinal Numbers

1st	*primero/a*
2nd	*segundo/a*
3rd	*tercero/a*
4th	*cuarto/a*
5th	*quinto/a*
6th	*sexto/a*
7th	*séptimo/a*
8th	*octavo/a*
9th	*noveno/a*
10th	*décimo/a*
11th	*undécimo/a*
12th	*duodécimo/a*

Days of the Week

Monday	*Lunes*
Tuesday	*Martes*
Wednesday	*Miércoles*
Thursday	*Jueves*
Friday	*Viernes*
Saturday	*Sábado*
Sunday	*Domingo*

Time

Eight o'clock is *las ocho*, while 8.30 is *las ocho y treinta* (literally, 'eight and thirty') or *las ocho y media* (eight and a half). However, 7.45 is *las ocho menos quince* (literally, 'eight minus fifteen') or *las ocho menos cuarto* (eight minus one quarter).

Times are modified by morning *(de la mañana)* or afternoon *(de la tarde)* instead of am or pm. It is also common to use the 24-hour clock, especially with transportation schedules.

What time is it?	*¿Qué hora es?*
It is . . .	*Es la una . . .*
	or *Son las . . .*

Numbers

1	*uno*	20	*veinte*	110	*ciento diez*
2	*dos*	21	*veintiuno*	120	*ciento veinte*
3	*tres*	22	*veintidós*	130	*ciento treinta*
4	*cuatro*	23	*veintitrés*	200	*doscientos*
5	*cinco*	24	*veinticuatro*	300	*trescientos*
6	*seis*	30	*treinta*	400	*cuatrocientos*
7	*siete*	31	*treinta y uno*	500	*quinientos*
8	*ocho*	32	*treinta y dos*	600	*seiscientos*
9	*nueve*	33	*treinta y tres*	700	*setecientos*
10	*diez*	40	*cuarenta*	800	*ochocientos*
11	*once*	41	*cuarenta y uno*	900	*novecientos*
12	*doce*	42	*cuarenta y dos*	1000	*mil*
13	*trece*	50	*cincuenta*	1100	*mil cien*
14	*catorce*	60	*sesenta*	1200	*mil doscientos*
15	*quince*	70	*setenta*	2000	*dos mil*
16	*dieciseis*	80	*ochenta*	5000	*cinco mil*
17	*diecisiete*	90	*noventa*	10,000	*diez mil*
18	*dieciocho*	100	*cien*	50,000	*cincuenta mil*
19	*diecinueve*	101	*ciento uno*	100,000	*cien mil*
		102	*ciento dos*	1,000,000	*un millón*

Appendix IV: Glossary

This list includes common geographical and biological terms as well as slang terms from everyday speech. RN indicates that a term is a Rapa Nui (Easter Island) usage, while FI means a Falklands Islands (Islas Malvinas) usage.

aerosilla – chairlift

afuerino – casual farm laborer

aguas – herbal teas

ahu (RN) – large stone platforms on which moai (statues) were erected

alameda – avenue or boulevard lined with trees, particularly poplars

albergue juvenil – youth hostel

alerce – *Fitzroya cupressoides*, large coniferous tree, resembling California redwood, for which Parque Nacional Alerce Andino is named

almuerzo – lunch

alpaca – *Lama pacos*, a wool-bearing domestic camelid of the central Andes, related to but with finer and more valuable wool than the llama

altiplano – high plains of northern Chile, Bolivia, southern Peru and northwestern Argentina, generally above 4000 meters

anexo – telephone extension

apapa (RN) – stone ramp used to launch boats

apunamiento – altitude sickness

arrayán – reddish-barked tree of the myrtle family, common in southern Chile's Valdivian forests

arroyo – watercourse

ascensores – picturesque funiculars which connect the center of Valparaíso with its hillside neighborhoods

Araucanians – major grouping of indigenous peoples, including the Mapuche, Picunche and Pehuenche Indians

ayllu – indigenous community of the Norte Grande; ayllus are more kinship-based rather than geographical, although they usually possess community lands

Aymara – indigenous inhabitants of the Andean altiplano of Peru, Bolivia and northern Chile

bahía – bay

balneario – bathing resort or beach

barrio – neighborhood or borough

bencina – petrol or gasoline

bencina blanca – white gas used for camping stoves; usually available in hardware stores or chemical supply shops

bidón – spare fuel container

bodega – cellar or storage area for wine

bofedal – swampy alluvial pasture in the altiplano, used by the Aymara to graze alpacas

boleadoras – weapon of round stones joined by a leather strap, used by Patagonian Indians for hunting guanaco and rhea; also called *bolas*

boleto inteligente – multi-trip ticket for Santiago Metro; also known as *boleto valor*

cabildo – colonial town council

cacique – Indian chieftain

calefón – hot water heater; in most inexpensive accommodations, travelers must ask to have the calefón turned on before taking a shower

caleta – small cove

caliche – hardpan of the pampas of the Norte Grande; a dry, hard layer of clay beneath the soil surface, from which mineral nitrates are extracted

callampas – shantytowns on the outskirts of Santiago, literally 'mushrooms' since they seemed to spring up overnight around the capital. Some have now become well-established neighborhoods.

camanchaca – dense convective fog on the hills of the coastal Atacama desert. The camanchaca usually dissipates in late morning and returns with the sea breeze in late afternoon.

cama – bed; also a sleeper-class seat on a bus or train

camarote – sleeper class on a ship or ferry

caracoles – winding roads, usually in a mountainous area; literally 'snails' or 'spirals'

carretera – highway

casa de cambio – money exchange house, which usually buys foreign cash and travelers' checks

casa de familia – modest family accommodation, usually in tourist centers

casco – 'big house' on a fundo or estancia

casino de bomberos – in many Chilean cities and towns, a fire station restaurant, often run by a concessionaire, offering excellent meals at reasonable prices

cerro – hill

cena – dinner

certificado – registered, as in mail

chachacoma – *Senecio graveolens*, a native Andean plant; Aymara Indians brew a tea from the leaves, which helps to relieve altitude sickness

charqui – dried llama or alpaca meat

chifa – Chinese restaurant; term most commonly used in the Norte Grande

Chilote – inhabitant of the archipelago of Chiloé; in certain contexts, the term has the connotation of 'bumpkin' despite the islands' rich cultural traditions

ciervo – deer

cine arte – art cinema (in contrast to mass commercial cinema), generally available only in Santiago and at universities

ciudad – city

coa – lower-class slang of Santiago

cobro revertido – reverse charge (collect) phone call

Codelco – Corporación del Cobre, the state-owned enterprise that oversees Chile's copper mining industry

colación – lunch

colectivo or **taxi colectivo** – shared taxi

comedor – inexpensive market restaurant; also, dining room of a hotel

comida corrida – a cheap set meal

comparsa – group of musicians or dancers

comuna – local governmental unit, largely administrative in the very centralized Chilean state

confitería – confectioner's shop

con gas – 'with gas'; carbonated mineral water

congregación – in colonial Latin America, the concentration of dispersed native populations in settlements, usually for political control and/or religious instruction; see also reducción

congrio – conger eel, a popular and delicious Chilean seafood

cordillera – chain of mountains, mountain range

costanera – coastal road; any road along a sea coast, riverside or lakeshore

criollo – in colonial times, a person of Spanish parentage born in the New World

curanto – Chilean seafood stew

desayuno – breakfast

desierto florido – in the Norte Chico, the flowering of dormant wildflower seeds in the desert during a rare year of heavy rainfall

elaboración artesanal – small-scale production, often by a family

encomendero – individual Spaniard or Spanish institution (such as the Catholic Church) exploiting Indian labor under the encomienda system

encomienda – colonial labor system, under which Indian communities were required to provide workers for encomenderos (see above), in exchange for which the encomendero was to provide religious and language instruction. In practice, the system benefited the encomendero far more than native peoples.

esquí en marcha – cross-country skiing

estero – estuary

estancia – extensive cattle or sheep grazing establishment, with a dominant owner or manager and dependent resident labor force

feria – artisans' market

FCO (FI) – British Foreign and Commonwealth Office, which appoints the Governor of the Falkland Islands

FIBS (FI) – Falkland Islands Broadcasting Service

FIC (FI) – Falkland Islands Company

ficha – token used in lieu of cash in the nitrate oficinas of the Norte Grande or the fundos of the Chilean heartland

FIGAS (FI) – Falkland Islands Government Air Service

fuerte – fort

fundo – Chilean term for hacienda, usually applied to a smaller irrigated unit in the country's central heartland

garúa – coastal desert fog; see also camanchaca

geoglyph – in the Norte Grande, pre-Colombian figures or abstract designs made by grouping dark stones over light-colored soil on hillside sites

golfo – gulf

golpe de estado – coup d'etat, a sudden, illegal seizure of government

guanaco – police water cannon, so named after the spitting wild camelid (*Lama guanicoe*).

hacendado – owner of a hacienda, who was usually resident in the city and left day-to-day management of his estate to underlings

hacienda – throughout Latin America, a large but often under-productive rural landholding, with dependent resident labor force, under a dominant owner. In Chile, the term *fundo* is more common, though it generally applies to a smaller irrigated unit.

hare paenga (RN) – elliptical (boat-shaped) house

hospedaje – budget accommodation, usually a large family home with one or two extra bedrooms for guests, and a shared bathroom

hostería – inn or guesthouse that serves meals, usually outside the main cities

hotel parejero – urban short-stay accommodation, normally patronized by young couples in search of privacy

huaso – horseman, a rough Chilean equivalent of the Argentine gaucho

ichu – bunch grass found on the altiplano

IGM – the Instituto Geográfico Militar;

mapping organization whose products are available and useful to travelers

inquilino – tenant farmer on a fundo

intendencia – Spanish colonial administrative unit

invierno boliviano – 'Bolivian winter'; summer rainy season in the Chilean altiplano, so-called because of the direction from which the storms come

IVA – *impuesto de valor agregado*, value added tax (VAT) often added to restaurant or hotel bills

isla – island

islote – small island, islet

istmo – isthmus

kumara (RN) – Polynesian word for sweet potato

kuchen – sweet, German-style pastries

La Frontera – region of pioneer settlement, between the Río Biobío and the Río Toltén, dominated by Araucanian Indians until the late 19th century

lago – lake

laguna – lagoon

latifundio – large landholding, such as a fundo, hacienda or estancia

lenga – a deciduous species of southern beech

lista de correos – poste restante

llano – plain, flat ground

llareta – *Laretia compacta*, a dense compact shrub in the Chilean altiplano, with a deceptive, cushion-like appearance, used by Aymara herders for fuel

local – a numbered addition to a street address indicating that a business occupies one of several offices at that address; for example, Maturana 227, Local 5

lomas – in the Atacama desert, coastal hills on which condensation from the camanchaca (convective fog) supports relatively dense vegetation

machista – male chauvinist (normally used as an adjective)

manavai (RN) – excavated garden enclosures

maori (RN) – learned men, reportedly able to read Rongo-Rongo tablets

Mapuche – indigenous inhabitants of the area south of the Río Biobío

marae (RN) – platforms found on Polynesian islands which resemble the ahu of Easter Island

marisquería – seafood restaurant, usually reasonably priced with excellent quality, in family-oriented beach resorts

mataa (RN) – obsidian spearhead

matua (RN) – ancestor, father; associated with Hotu Matua, leader of the first Polynesian immigrants

media pensión – half-board, in a hotel

mestizo – a person of mixed Indian and Spanish descent

micro – small bus, often traveling along the back roads

minifundio – small landholding, such as a peasant farm

minga – reciprocal Mapuche Indian labor system

mirador – lookout point, usually on a hill but sometimes in a building

moai (RN) – large anthropomorphic statues, carved from volcanic tuff

moai kavakava (RN) – carved wooden 'statues of ribs'

momios – 'mummies,' upper-class Chileans resistant to social and political change

motu (RN) – small offshore islet

municipalidad – city hall

museo – museum

música funcional – muzak

nalca – *Gunnera chilensis*, a plant resembling an enormous rhubarb, with large leaves and edible stalks; it's gathered for food on Chiloé and elsewhere in southern Chile

ñandú – large, flightless bird known in English as a rhea; similar to the ostrich

nevado – snow-capped mountain peak

Norte Chico – 'Little North,' the semiarid region between the province of Chañaral and the Río Aconcagua

Norte Grande – 'Big North,' the very arid portion of the country north of Chañaral

Nueva Canción Chilena – the 'New Chilean Song' movement, which arose in the 1960s and combined traditional folk themes with contemporary political activism

oferta – promotional fare, often seasonal, for plane or bus travel

oficina – in the Norte Grande, a 19th- and early-20th-century nitrate mining enterprise, in some cases almost a small city, with a large dependent labor force

onces – 'elevenses,' Chilean afternoon tea

palafitos – on the islands of Chiloé, rows of houses built on stilts over the water, where boats can anchor at their back doors on a rising tide

pampa – in the Norte Grande, a vast desert expanse where mineral nitrates were often mined

parada – bus stop

parque nacional – national park

parrilla – restaurant specializing in grilled meats

parrillada – grilled steak and other cuts of beef

peatonal – pedestrian mall, usually in the center of larger cities

pehuén – *Araucaria auracana*, the monkey-puzzle tree of southern Chile; its nuts are a staple of the Pehuenche Indians' traditional diet

peña – folk music and cultural club; many originated in Santiago in the 1960s as venues for the New Chilean Song movement (see Nueva Canción Chilena)

pensión – family home offering short-term budget accommodation; may also take permanent lodgers

pensión completa – full board, in a hotel

pingüinera – penguin colony

playa – beach

pora (RN) – small reed raft used for paddling to offshore islets (motus)

Porteño – a native or resident of Valparaíso

portezuelo – mountain pass

posta – clinic or first-aid station, often found in smaller towns that lack proper hospitals

postre – dessert

precordillera – the foothills of the Andes mountains

propina – a tip, for service at a restaurant or elsewhere

pukao (RN) – the topknot on the head of a moai; once a common hairstyle for Rapa Nui males

pukará – a pre-Columbian hilltop fortress in the Andes

puente – bridge

puerto – port

pulpería – company store on a fundo, estancia or nitrate oficina

puna – Andean highlands, usually above 3000 meters

punta – point

quebrada – ravine

quila – a solid bamboo found in southern Chilean rainforest, often forming impenetrable thickets; also known as *chusquea*

quinoa – native Andean grain, a dietary staple in the pre-Columbian era, still grown by Aymara farmers in the precordillera of the Norte Grande

Rapa Nui – the Polynesian name for Easter Island and its people, language and culture

reducción – the concentration of Indians in towns modeled on the Spanish grid pattern, for purposes of political control or religious instruction; the term also refers to the settlement itself

refugio – a shelter, usually rustic, in a national park or other remote area

reserva nacional – national reserve, a category of land use

residencial – budget accommodation, sometimes seasonal; in general, residenciales occupy buildings designed expressly for short-stay lodging

rhea – large, flightless bird called ñandú in Spanish, similar to the ostrich

río – river

rodeo – annual roundup of cattle on an estancia or hacienda

Rongo-Rongo (RN) – an indecipherable script on wooden tablets which some have thought to be an alphabet or other form of native writing

roto – 'ragged one,' a dependent laborer on a Chilean fundo

ruca – traditional thatched Mapuche house

ruta – route; highway

SAG – Servicio Agrícola Ganadero, the Agriculture & Livestock Service; its officials inspect baggage and vehicles for prohibited fruit and meat imports at Chilean border crossings

saladero – an establishment for salting meat and hides

salón cama – bus with reclining seats

salón de té – literally 'teahouse,' but more like an upscale cafetería

salar – salt lake, salt marsh or salt pan, usually in high Andes or Patagonia

Santiaguino – native or resident of Santiago

seno – sound, fjord

servicentro – large gasoline station with spacious parking lot, restaurants and toilet facilities, including inexpensive hot showers

sierra – mountain range

siesta – afternoon nap during the extended midday break of traditional Chilean business hours

sin gas – 'without gas,' non-carbonated mineral water

smoko (FI) – midmorning tea or coffee break, usually served with cakes and other homemade sweets

s/n – 'sin número,' indicating a street address without a number

soroche – altitude sickness

Southern Cone – in political geography, the area comprising Argentina, Chile, Uruguay and parts of Brazil and Paraguay; so called after the area's shape on the map

squaddies (FI) – British enlisted men on four-month tours of duty in the Falkland Islands

tábano – horsefly

tajamares – dikes built to control flooding of the Río Mapocho in late-colonial Santiago

tejuelas – in archipelagic Chile, especially Chiloé, shingles of varying design that typify the region's vernacular architecture

teleférico – gondola cable car

tenedor libre – all-you-can-eat fare

todo terreno – mountain bike
toki (RN) – basalt carving tool
toqui – Mapuche Indian chief
tortas – mine tailings, literally 'cakes'
totora (RN) – type of reed used for making rafts
turismo aventura – non-traditional forms of tourism, such as trekking and river rafting
two-nighter (FI) – a traditional party for visitors from distant sheep stations, who would invariably stay the weekend

Unidad Popular – 'Popular Unity,' a coalition of leftist political groups that supported Salvador Allende in the 1970 presidential election

Valle Central – 'Central Valley,' the Chilean heartland that extends south from the Río Aconcagua to near the city of Concepción; this area contains most of Chile's population and its industrial and agricultural wealth
ventisquero – glacier
vicuña – *Vicugna vicugna*, wild relative of domestic llama and alpaca, found only at high altitudes in the Norte Grande
villa – village, small town
vizcacha – *Lagidium vizcacha*, a wild Andean relative of the domestic chinchilla
volcán – volcano

Yahgans – indigenous inhabitants of the Tierra del Fuego archipelago

zampoñas – pan pipes
zona franca – at Iquique and Punta Arenas, duty-free zone where imported goods such as cameras, clothing etc are available at very low prices

Index

ABBREVIATIONS

Arg = Argentina
FI = Falkland Islands

MN = Monumento Natural
PN = Parque Nacional

RN = Reserva Nacional

MAPS

Administrative Regions
   of Chile 24-25
Aisén & the Camino Austral
   396-397
Ancud 379
Antofagasta 244-245
Archipiélago
   de Chiloé 377
Arica 212-213
Arica Around 219
Cajón del Maipo 143
Calama 255
Calama Around 260
Caldera 277
Castro 385
Chaitén 414
Chile between pages 16-17
Chillán 184-185
Coihaique 400
Concepción 190-191
Concepción Around 197
Conguillío, PN 315
Copiapó 272-273
Curicó 175
Curicó Around 177
Easter Island
   (Rapa Nui) 483
El Calafate (Arg) 447
Expansion of Chile 17
Falkland Islands (Islas
   Malvinas) 514-515
Frutillar 353
Hanga Roa 501
Human Settlement
   in the Pacific 484

Iquique 230-231
Isla Robinson Crusoe 473
La Araucanía &
   Los Lagos 304-305
La Serena 284-285
Lican Ray 331
Los Angeles 200
Los Glaciares,
   PN (Arg) 451
Los Vilos 299
Magallanes & Tierra
   del Fuego 424-425
Map Index 8-9
Middle Chile 147
Nahuelbuta, PN 205
Norte Chico 269
Norte Grande 208
Osorno 344-345
Ovalle 296
Pan de Azúcar, PN 280
Porvenir 457
Protected Areas
   of Chile 24-25
Pucón 323
Pucón Around 327
Punta Arenas 426
Puerto Montt 364-365
Puerto Montt Around 373
Puerto Natales 436
Puerto Varas 356
Puyehue, PN 350
Quellón 393
Rancagua 171
Región Metropolitana 102
Río Grande (Arg) 460

San Juan Bautista 479
San Pedro de Atacama 262
San Pedro de Atacama
   Around 260
Santiago 108-109
   Barrio Bellavista 118
   Comunas de
      Santiago 105
   Gran Santiago 104
   Las Condes 123
   Providencia 120-121
   Santiago
      Centro 112-113
   Santiago Metro 140-141
South America locator 11
Southern Patagonian
   Routes 89
Stanley (FI) 519
Stanley Around (FI) 522
Talca 180-181
Talca Around 177
Temuco 308-309
Torres del Paine, PN 443
Ushuaia (Arg) 463
Valdivia 336-337
Vallenar 282
Valparaíso 150-151
Valparaíso Around 157
Vicente Pérez
   Rosales, PN 361
Vicuña 293
Villarrica 318
Viña del Mar 162-163
Viña del Mar Around 157

TEXT

Map references are in **bold** type

accommodations 70-72
Achao 388-389
activities 67-69
adventure travel 68, 90,
   324, 429
Aguas Calientes 349
air travel 78-86, 134-136
   airlines 134-135

buying tickets 79-82
   to/from Asia
      & Africa 85
   to/from Australia &
      New Zealand 84
   to/from Canada 83
   to/from neighboring
      countries 85

   to/from the UK
      & Europe 83-84
   to/from the USA 82-83
   within Chile 93-94
Alerce Andino, PN 33,
   374-375
Allende, Salvador 19, 20,
   56, 117

539

Almagro, Diego de 13, 240, 268
alpaca 30, 222-223
Ancud 378-382, **379**
Angelmó 366
Angol 204-205
Antarctica 470
Anticura 349
Antofagasta 242-249, **244-245**
Araucanía Indians 198-199, 307
  see also Indians
Araucanian Wars 198-199
Araucaria pine 29, 314
Archipiélago de Chiloé *see* Chiloé
Archipiélago Juan Fernández 472-481
  books 477
  flora & fauna 476
  geography & climate 474
  getting around 477
  getting there & away 477
  history 472
  PN Juan Fernández 32, 480-481
  San Juan Bautista 478-480
Area de Protección Radal Siete Tazas 178
Argentina
  travel to 85, 86-90, 404-405, **89**
Arica 209-219, **212-213**
arts 40-43
astronomy 291
Atacama desert 207, 242, 268
Audiencia de Chile 16
Azapa valley 219

Bahía Inglesa 276-278
Baquedano 250
beaches
  Arica 211
  Caldera & Bahía Inglesa 276
  Guanaqueros 290
  Iquique 232
  La Serena 287
  Los Vilos 299
  Pichidangui 301
  Tongoy 291
Belén 220
Bernardo O'Higgins, PN 34, 440
bicycle travel 67, 97-98

bird watching 406, 408, 513
  Tierra del Fuego 469
  PN Lauca 221
  Puerto Varas 357
  Río Maullín 357
boat travel
  see ferry travel
Bolivia
  travel to 85, 86
Bolsico 249
books 40-42, 55-58
Bosque Fray Jorge, PN 32, 298-299
Bowman, Isaiah 240, 261
bus travel 94, 136-137
business hours 66

Cajón del Maipo 142-144, **143**
Calama 253-258, **255**
Calbuco 373
Caldera 276-278, **277**
Caleta Gonzalo 415
Caleta Tortel 421
Camino Austral 395, 398
Campo de Hielo Norte 395, 408
Campo de Hielo Sur 398
Cape Horn 422
car travel 95-97
  purchase 96
  rental 96, 139
  road rules 97
Casa Fuerte Santa Sylvia 327
Cascada de las Animas 144
Castro 383-388, **385**
Catarpe 266
Caupolicán 14, 196, 198-199
Cerro Castillo, RN 34, 418
Cerro Tololo Interamerican Observatory (CTIO) 291
Cerro Unita 238
Chaitén 413, 415, **414**
Chañaral 279
Chañarcillo 276
Chapa Verde 173
children 64
Chile Chico 419-420
Chillán 183-188, **184-185**
Chiloé 376-394, **377**
  Achao 388-389
  Ancud 378-382, **379**
  Castro 383-388, **385**
  Chonchi 389-390
  Dalcahue 382-383
  Isla Llingua 389
  PN Chiloé 33, 390-393
  Quellón 393-394, **393**
Chol Chol 313

Chonchi 389-390
Choshuenco 333
Chuquicamata 258-259
Chusmiza 239
Cifuncho 253
climate 23-27
Cobija 241-242, 250
Cochrane, Lord Thomas 16, 340
Coihaique 399-406, **400**
Coihaique, RN 33, 406
Colo Colo 196, 198
Coñaripe 332
Concepción 188-195, **190-191**
Concón 166
condor, Andean 222, 298, 328, 348, 469
Conguillío, PN 33, 314-317, **315**
consulates 49
Contulmo, MN 32, 197
Cook, Captain James 487
Copaquilla 220
Copiapó 270-275, **272-273**
copper industry 242, 258, 259, 279
Coquimbo 290
Corral 340
cruises 370-371, 429, 465, 470
Cueva del Milodón, MN 439-440
Curacautín 317
Curicó 174-176, **175**
customs 50
cycling 67, 97-98

Dalcahue 382-383
Darwin, Charles 167, 173, 189, 202, 227, 270, 370, 376, 383, 390, 408, 454
Defoe, Daniel 32, 472, 474
desierto florido 268, 283
disabled travelers 63, 78
diving 69
documents 47-50
Dos Lagunas, MN 406
drinks 74-76

Easter Island (Rapa Nui) 482-511, **483**
  Anakena 509
  books 496
  climate 492
  flora & fauna 492
  geography 491
  getting around 498-500
  getting there & away 498
  Hanga Roa 500-505, **501**
  history 482-491

PN Rapa Nui 32, 505
stonework 492
eco-tourism 90
ecology 27-28
economy 37-39
education 39
El Calafate (Arg) 446-450, **447**
El Chaltén (Arg) 452
El Colorado 144
El Enladrillado 182
El Morado, PN 32, 144
El Tatio geysers 267
El Teniente 173
electricity 59
email 54
embassies 48-49
endangered species 28-29
Ensenada 359
entertainment 76-77
Entre Lagos 348
environment 27-28
Ercilla y Zuñiga, Alonso de
196-198, 302, 329
Escuela México 185
Estancia San Gregorio 434
European Southern
Observatory (ESO) 291
Falkland Islands (Islas
Malvínas) 512-525, **514-515**
around Stanley 521-522, **522**
East Falkland 522-524
facts for the visitor 515
flora & fauna 513
geography & climate 513
getting around 519
getting there & away 518
history 512
penguin colonies 522-
523, 525
Stanley 519-521, **519**
West Falkland 524
Falklands War 512
fauna 28-30
ferry travel 98-99, 370-371, 409
film 42
fishing 401, 419
Río Toltén 319
Tierra del Fuego 458,
462, 466
Fitzroy Range (Arg) 452-454
Fitzroy, Captain Robert 459
fjords 370-371
flamingos 30, 225, 226,
266, 417
flora 28-30
food 72-74
Frei Montalva, Eduardo 19
Frei Ruiz-Tagle, Eduardo 23, 35
Frutillar 352-355, **353**

Fuerte Bulnes 433
Fuerte Niebla 340
Funcación Neruda 118, 153
fur seals 472, 476, 481
Futaleufú 412
Futrono 340

Galvarino 196
Gatico 250
gay travelers 63
geoglyphs 207
El Gigante de Atacama 238
Lluta 220
Pintados 240
geography 23-27
geopolitics 36, 57
Gil de Vilches, PN 32, 182
Glaciar Martial 469
government 34-37
guanaco 30, 222
Guanaqueros 290

Hacienda Jotabeche 275
Hanga Roa 500-505, **501**
health 59-62
insurance 60
vaccinations 60
women's health 62
hiking 68
history 13-23
hitching 98
holidays 66
Horcón 167
Hornopirén 375
horseback riding 392, 444
Easter Island 499
hot springs
Aguas Calientes 349
Around Pucón 327
Baños Morales 144
Chusmiza 239
Mamiña 239
PN Volcán Isluga 239
Termas de Cauquenes 173
Termas de Chillán 188
Termas de Colina 144
Termas de Puritama 266
Termas de Puyehue 348
Termas de Puyuhuapi 412
Termas de Socos 297
Termas de Tolhuaca 317
Termas El Amarillo 415
Huáscar, Museo 195
Huequetrumao 393
Huerquehue, PN 33,
328-329
Humberstone 237

Indians
Alacaluf 13, 395, 422, 454

Atacameño 13
Aymara 207, 220
Chango 13, 241, 268, 286
Chono 13, 395
Diaguita 13, 268
El Molle 297
Haush 422
Huilliche 13, 376, 391
Lafkenche 307
Mapuche 13, 18, 77, 101,
189, 196, 302, 307, 341, 342
Ona (Selknam) 13, 422
Pehuenche 13, 307
Pichunche 13
Puelche 13
Qawashqar, see Alacalufe
Tehuelche 395, 422
Yahgan 13, 422, 454, 459
Yamaná, see Yahgan
Iquique 227-236, **230-231**
Isla Damas 283
Isla Grande de Chiloé
see Chiloé
Isla Grande de Tierra del
Fuego
see Tierra del Fuego
Isla Huapi 341
Isla Llingua 389
Isla Mancera 340
Isla Margarita 361
Isla Navarino 459
Isla Negra 40, 157
Isla Pan de Azúcar 280
Isla Pelada 375
Isla Robinson Crusoe 472-
481, **473**
Isla Tenglo 366
Islas Malvinas
see Falkland Islands

Juan Fernández
archipelago
see Archipiélago Juan
Fernández
Juan López 249

kayaking 68
Río Futaleufú 412
Keppel Island (FI) 524

La Araucana 302, 329
La Campana, PN 32,
167-169
La Chascona 40, 118
La Chimba, RN 249
La Junta 412
La Ligua 167
La Moneda, Palacio de 115
La Parva 145
La Portada, MN 31, 249

La Sebastiana 40, 153
La Serena 283-290, **284-285**
La Tirana 239
Lago Chungará 225
Lago General Carrera 417
Lago Llanquihue 352
Lago Panguipulli 332
Lago Peñuelas, RN 157
Lago Ranco 341-342
Lago Rapel 174
Lago Todos Los Santos 362
Lago Vichuquén 178
Lago Yelcho 412
Laguna Chaxa 266
Laguna Cotacotani 224
Laguna del Laja, PN 32,
    202-204
Laguna San Rafael, PN
    34, 408-410
Laguna Torca, RN 178
Lagunillas 143
language courses 69, 123
Las Cascadas 352
Las Vicuñas, RN 226
Lauca, PN 31, 222-226
laundry 59
Lautaro 14, 198-199
legal matters 66
lesbian travelers 63
Lican Ray 330-332, **331**
literature 41-42
    see also books
llama 30, 222
Llanos de Challe, PN 31,
    283
Llifen 341
Lluta geoglyphs 220
Lo Vásquez 157
Los Andes 169-170
Los Angeles 197-201, **200**
Los Flamencos, RN 31, 266
Los Glaciares, PN (Arg)
    450-452, **451**
Los Loros 275
Los Pingüinos, MN 34, 434
Los Vilos 299-301, **299**

Magellan, Ferdinand 422, 454
Mamiña 239
Mapuche
    see Indians
María Elena 260
Maullín 373
measures 59
media 58
Mejillones 249
Melipeuco 317
Menéndez, José 423
military 35-36, 57
milodón 439

Mina Tres Marías 276
mining 272, 286
Mistral, Gabriela 40-41,
    270, 283, 292, 294
moai 486, 493-496
moai kavakava 496
money 50-52
    exchange rates 51
    tipping 52
Monte Grande 294
Montt, Jorge 18
Monumento Arqueológico
    Valle del Encanto 297
monumentos naturales
    Cerro Ñielol 33
    Contulmo 32, 197
    Cueva del Milodón 34,
        439-440
    Dos Lagunas 406
    La Portada 31, 249
    Los Pingüinos 34, 434
    Pichasca 32, 298
Moreno glacier (Arg) 450
mountain biking 67-68
    Tierra del Fuego 466
mountaineering
    see rockclimbing
music 42, 76-77

Nahuelbuta, PN 32, 205, **205**
national parks
    see parques nacionales
national reserves
    see reservas nacionales
natural monuments
    see monumentos
        naturales
Neruda, Pablo 40-41, 118,
    153, 157
Nevado Tres Cruces, PN
    31, 276
New Island (FI) 525
Ninhue 188
nitrate ghost towns 261
nitrate industry 207, 209,
    229, 237, 260

O'Higgins, Bernardo 16
Observatorio Interamericano
    Cerro Tololo 291
Observatorio
    Las Campanas 291
Ojos de Salado 276
online services 54, 527
Osorno 342-347, **344-345**
Ovalle 295-297, **296**

Paine circuit 442-444
palafitos 386
Palena 413
Pali Aike, PN 34, 435

Pampa del Tamarugal, RN 240
Pan de Azúcar, PN 31, 280, **280**
Panguipulli 332-333
Paposo, RN 253
Papudo 167
paragliding 69, 233
Parinacota 224
parques nacionales
    Alerce Andino 33, 374-375
    Archipiélago Juan Fernández
        32, 480-481
    Bernardo O'Higgins
        34, 440
    Bosque Fray Jorge 32,
        298-299
    Chiloé 33, 390-393
    Conguillío 33, 314-317, **315**
    El Morado 32, 144
    Gil de Vilches 32, 182
    Hornopirén 33, 375
    Huerquehue 33, 328-329
    La Campana 32, 167-169
    Laguna del Laja 32, 202-204
    Laguna San Rafael 34,
        408-410
    Lauca 31, 222-226
    Llanos de Challe 31, 283
    Nahuelbuta 32, 205
    Nevado de Tres Cruces
        31, 276
    Pali Aike 34, 435
    Pan de Azúcar 31, 280,
        280
    Puyehue 33, 348-351, **350**
    Queulat 33, 410-411
    Rapa Nui 32, 505
    Río Simpson 34, 407
    Tolhuaca 33, 314-315
    Torres del Paine 34, 440-445,
        443
    Vicente Pérez Rosales
        33, 360-363, **361**
    Villarrica 33, 329-330
    Volcán Isluga 31, 239
Pebble Island (FI) 524
Pedro de Valdivia (nitrate
    oficina) 261
penguins 434, 522-523, 525
    Falklands 513
    Humboldt 280, 283
    Magellanic 408
Peru
    travel to 85, 86
petroglyphs 297
Petrohué 360
Peulla 362
photography 58
Pica 240-241
Pichasca, MN 32, 298
Pichidangui 301
Pichilemu 174

pictographs 297
Pingüino de Humboldt,
  RN 31, 283
Pinochet Ugarte, General
  Augusto 22, 36, 115, 398
Pintados 240
Pirque 142
Pisagua 226-227
pisco 291, 294
Pisco Elqui 294
planning 45-46
Planta Capel 292
Poconchile 220
police 65
politics 34-37
Pomaire 141
population 39
Port Howard (FI) 524
Port Louis (FI) 523
Port Stephens (FI) 525
Portales, Diego 17
Portillo 145
Porvenir 456-458, **457**
post 52-53
Pucón 322-327, **323**
Puerto Bertrand 420
Puerto Bories 439
Puerto Cárdenas 412
Puerto Chacabuco 407
Puerto Cisnes 410
Puerto Edén ferry 370-
  371, 439
Puerto Guadal 418
Puerto Hambre 433
Puerto Ingeniero Ibáñez
  417-418
Puerto Montt 363-373, **364-365**
Puerto Natales 435-439,
  436
Puerto Octay 351-352
Puerto Puyuhuapi 411
Puerto Río Tranquilo 418
Puerto Varas 355-359, **356**
Puerto Yungay 421
Pukará de Copaquilla 220
Pukará de Quitor 266
Pumalín, Parque Natural
  415
Punta Arenas 422-433, **426**
Putre 220-221
Puyehue, PN 33, 348-351, **350**

Quellón 393-394, **393**
Queulat, PN 33, 410-411
Quintero 167

Radal Siete Tazas 178
rafting 68
  Río Futaleufú 412
  Río Maipo 142

Río Petrohué 357, 362, 366
Río Trancura 310, 324
Río Biobío 201
Rancagua 170-173, **171**
Rapa Nui
  see Easter Island
religion 43-44
Reñaca 166
reservas nacionales
  Cerro Castillo 34, 418
  Coihaique 33, 406
  La Chimba 249
  Lago Peñuelas 157
  Laguna Torca 178
  Las Vicuñas 226
  Los Flamencos 31, 266
  Magallanes 34
  Pampa del Tamarugal 240
  Paposo 253
  Pingüino de Humboldt
    31, 283
  Río Clarillo 32
  Río de los Cipreses 32,
    173
Río Biobío 201, 202
Río Bueno 341
Río de las Cascadas 411
Río Futaleufú 202
Río Grande (Arg)
  459-461, **460**
Río Simpson, PN 34, 407
Río Verde 434
rockclimbing 68
  San Rafael glacier 408
  Torres del Paine 442
  Volcán Llaima 316
  Volcán Osorno 357,
    360, 362, 366
  Volcán Villarrica 319,
    324, 329
Ruinas de Huanchaca 246

Salar de Surire, MN 226
Salto del Laja 201
San Carlos (FI) 523
San Juan Bautista 478-480, **479**
San Martín, José de 16
San Pedro de Atacama
  261-265, **262**
Santa Laura 237
Santiago 101-140, **104,
  108-109, 112-113**
  Barrio Bellavista 118,
    129, **118**
  Cerro Santa Lucia 117,
    128
  entertainment 131-133
  getting around 138
  getting there & away 134-138
  history 101

information 105-111
  museums 116-117
  organized tours 124
  orientation 103
  places to eat 127-131
  places to stay 124-127
  special events 124
  things to buy 133
  walking tour 111-115
Santuario Cañi 328
Santuario Naturaleza
  Granito Orbicular 278
Santuario de la Naturaleza
  Yerba Loca 32
Saunders Island (FI) 524
Sea Lion Island (FI) 523
sea lions 523
Selkirk, Alexander 472,
  474, 481
senior travelers 64
Seno Otway pingüinera 434
Seno Ultima Esperanza
  435, 440
silver mining 276, 283
skiing, cross country
  El Sendero Pehuenche 324
  PN Conguillío 315
skiing, downhill 67
  Antillanca 349
  Chapa Verde 173
  Coihaique 402
  PN Conguillío 316
  PN Vicente Pérez Rosales
    360
  Santiago area 143-145
  Tierra del Fuego 466
  Volcán Villarrica 329
  PN Puyehue 349
soccer 247, 257, 274, 311,
  346, 133, 155, 194, 77
Sociedad Explotadora de
  Tierra del Fuego 435,
  439
Socoroma 220
special events 66
spectator sports 77
Stanley (FI) 519-521, **519**
surfing 68
  Iquique 233

Talca 178, **180-181**
Taltal 252
Tambo Quemado 225
Tarapacá 238
taxis 100
teaching English 69
telephone 53-54
Templo Votivo de Maipú 140
Temuco 306-313, **308-309**
Termas de Colina 144

Termas de Huife 327
Termas de Palguín 328
Termas de Panqui 328
Termas de Puritama 266
Termas de Puyehue 348
Termas de Puyuhuapi 412
Termas de Socos 297
Termas de Tolhuaca 317
Termas El Amarillo 415
theater 43
Tierra del Fuego 454-471
　geography & climate 456
　getting there & around
　　456
　history 454
　Lago Blanco 458
　Porvenir 456-458, **457**
　Puerto Williams 459
　Río Grande (Arg)
　　459-461, **460**
　Ushuaia (Arg)
　　462-469, **463**
Tierra del Fuego, PN (Arg) 469
time 59
Toconau 267
Tocopilla 251
toilets 62
Tolhuaca, PN 33, 313-314

Tongoy 291
Torres del Paine, PN 34,
　440-445, **443**
tourist offices 47
tours 90-91, 100
train travel 94-95, 138
trekking 68, 453
　Paine Circuit 442
　Tierra del Fuego 470

Ushuaia (Arg) 462-469, **463**

Valdivia, Pedro de 13, 101,
　196, 268
Valdivia (town) 334-340,
　336-337
Valle de la Luna 266
Valle del Encanto 297
Valle Nevado 145
Vallenar 281-283, **282**
Valparaíso 146-157, **150-151**
Ventisquero Colgante 411
Vicente Pérez Rosales, PN
　33, 360-363, **361**
vicuña 222, 226
Vicuña 291-294, **293**
video 58
Villa Amengual 410

Villarrica 317-322, **318**
Villarrica, PN 33, 329-330
Viña del Cerro 275
Viña del Mar 158-166,
　162-163
visas 47-48
vizcacha 222
Volcán Hudson 419
Volcán Isluga, PN 31, 239
Volcán Osorno 360
Volcán Puyehue 349
Volcán Villarrica 329

War of the Pacific 18, 207,
　242, 489
Weddell Island (FI) 525
windsurfing 278, 287
wine 69, 75, 142
wineries
　Curicó area 176
　Santiago area 142-143
women travelers 62, 63
work 69

Zapallar 167
Zona Franca, Iquique 232
Zona France, Punta Arenas 423

Thanks

Thanks to all the following travelers and others who took time to write to us about their experiences in Chile.

Roger & Sheila Acraman, Michael F A'Hearn, Aurora Adelina Alemano, Luke Alexander, David W Allen, Sven Tony Andersen, Torben Andersen & Tine Pelsen, Ina Anderson, Julian & Charles Anderson, Carole M Andrews, Dominique Argenson, Sandra Arkin, Bob Aronoff, Paul Arundale, Jason Ashworth, Matías Astoreca B, Alicia Baglietto, Thierry Banos, Maureen Barden, Andrew Barnette, Don Evi Barria, Lee Barry, Luc Baudolph, Lubohir Beran, Nora Klein, Emily Benson, Jacky Benson, Armando de Berardinis, Wendy Berg, Ragnhild & Antoon Beyne-Pille, Anne Bianchi, Helene Bianchi, Elaine Birn, Erwin Bittner, Bruce B Blanch, Robert B Boardman, Astrid Bombosch, Claudia Borzutzky, Nicole Böttcher, Robert L Bradour, Sabine Brinker & Klaus Martin Wölk, Colin Broadley, Richard Browne, Lars C Brunner, Johannes Busch, Fernanda Caiuby, Catherine Campbell & Randy Butler, Leticia Cárcamo S, Glynn R Carré, Sean D Casey, Diane Caulkett, Luigi Cerri, Lisa M Choy-Zafra, Ane Line Christensen, Michel & Varinia Cinquin, Simon Clark, Dennis Clarke, Eric Clauwaert, Andy & Karen Cockburn, Alan Cohen, Jim Cohen, Linda & Larry Cohen, Alexander T Cole, Bobbi Coluni & Anne Jorgensen, Marriane Consideme, Joe Cowell, Mary & Neal Daniels, Wendeline de Beer, Hiske den Boer & Ruud Blanc, Lucy Densell, Martin Dillig, Jeri & Hugh Dingle, Carsten Dittmann, James Doyle, Hal Drakesmith, Wolfgang Drexel, Daniel Drexler, Sarah Durfee, Sue Edelstein, André Efira & Loreto Alvarez, Simon Elms, David S Erickson, James M Ethridge, Michael Falk, Natasha Fellowes, Patrick Figueroa McGinty, John & Pauline Fluerty, Eduardo Fiol Bernain, John L Franklin, Urs Frei & Roswitha Stich, Dirk Frewing, Gerry Friebe, Miguel Fuertes & Helena Centeno, Christian Gaebler,

Eric Gagnon, Francisco J García, Ricard Gavaldà, Meredith Gerson, Walter W & Ann L Glaser, Mary Glenn, Louis Glunz IV, Patrice Goutelle, Charles Grady, Eugene Graham, Catherine Geanuracos, Daniel Guerrero C, Annemo Gunnarsson, Rodrigo Guzmán P, Jennifer Haefeli, Liz Hall, Peter Hannibal, Brad Hanson, Christiane Hanstein, Bill Hart, Holger Hartmeier, Alison Harvey, Paul Hatfield & Gareth Sellors, Karsten Heck, Michelle Hecht, John T Heinzel, Lars Heitmann, Myriam Hernández, María Hey, Pat Hickey & Carol Paulson, Søren Højsgaard, Lesley Houfe, Martin Howard, David Huntzinger, Catriona Hurd, Conny Hürlimann, María Cristina Inostroza, Peter Irvine, Arjen & Marianne Jaarsma, Kate Jackson, Christopher Jessee, Alastair Jenkins & Noelle Odling, Marie Jenneteg, Don Johnston, Martin Jones, Ikki Kari, Joanne Katsanis, Kryss Katsiavariades & Talaat Qureshi, Inger Sophie Kaurin, Oliver Kempe, Paul Kempf, Daniel King, Øystein Klausen & Hans K Hystad, Eric Koehler, Lutz Kral & Ursula Wagner, Stephen Krauss, Paul D Kretkowski, Wolfgang Krones, Patricia Krueger, Sonia Kuscevic Yankovic, Steven Kusters. Oda Karen Kvaal, Fred Lager, Nicholas La Penna, Sharon Hilt Lasker, Beatrice le Mercer, Erica Linden, Julie Lomax & Nina Grinnell, Sabine Ludwig, Mari Tomine Lunden, T S Lundquist, Mark Luscombe, Hermann Luyken, Iain Mackay, Andy Mackenzie, Lachlan Mackenzie, Pete Maclean, M & Mme Marchesi, Alison Mary & Pauline Cara, Joanne F McAdam, Malcolm McCormick, Carol McDonald, Mike McDonald, Madeline McDowell, Nigel P McGrath, Don McNeill, Linda S Mendelson, Eleanore Merrill, Annette Mertens, Bill Middendorf, Andy Millard, Stephen Millard, Patrick Miller, Cathy & Dmitri Minaretzis, Henfield Molders, Nicoletta & Lionello Morganti, Kathy Morrell, Erik Muller, Linda Murray, Robert Murray, Daniel M Nebenzal, Claude Nenninger & Irene Spitzli, Barbara T Newcombe, Julie Nield

& Nick Toll, Michele Novosad, Andrzej Nowak, Jeremy Sean O'Donnell, Anne Ogburn, Brian O'Halloran, Béat Oppliger, Eugene & Mayumi Orwell, Isobel Owen, Mark Pace, James & Anne Page, Jessica Parker, Brian Passikoff, Neil Pepper, Oscar Pérez Ruiz Diaz, Bill Peterson, Deirdre C Pettitt, Alejandra Poblete Hojas, Chris Pogson, Nigel Poole, Lucy C. Porter, Louis Postruzin, Julianne Power, Phil Preston, Sue Preston, Gunter Quaißer, Diane & Michael Rabinowitz, Linda E Ramos, Joe Rathbun, Chris Read, Bob Redlinger, Dave Redmond, N J Reeve, Rufus Rieder, Judith Rhodes, Juliet Rhodes, Jerry Richmond, Vanessa Rodd, Marie Rohan, Patricia & Marvin Rosen, Deborah Rowland, Matt Rowland, Mauricio Salazar Alarcón, Paul Sanders, Rob Sangster, Jack Satkoski, Joanne Sawyer, Hilde Schepers, Arthur & Celeste Schildgen, Christian Schindler, Gudrun Schneider, Tony Schneider, Dr Dietmar Scholl, Dennis Schroeder, Paul A Scotchmer, Shelly Selin, Sarah Shay, Ru Smith, Robert Sonntag, Brent Sorensen, Raymond T Spears, Kevin Sprager, Dr Alex Starr, JEM Stevens, Volkmar Stichweh, Leigh Summersett, Caspar von Tangen-Jordan, Gavin Tanguay, Urs Teiger, Loretta Thorpe, Barbara Tily, Dominga Tolosa Riquelme, Adriana Totonelli, Daniel Turkewitz, Melvin O Turner, Carl Ulasek, John Usmar, Herve Valluy, Hendrik J van Broekhuizen, Guido van den Berg, Frederik Vandenbreuche, Emese Melinda van der Hilt, Ruud van Ginkel, Karo van Wyk, Cristina Vargas, CA Veerman, Christophe Vidal & Jens Birk, Andreas & Nadia Vogelsanger, Harald Volz, Alain Vonrufs, Jan Wagner, Claire E Watson, Carla Weemaes, PJ Whelan, Martyn Williams, Russell Willis, DM Wilson, Diarmuid Wilson, Penelope Wilton, Campbell Wood, Dan Workman, Jack Yates, Julian Yates, Dr Simon R Young, Michaela Young-Mitchell

LONELY PLANET PHRASEBOOKS

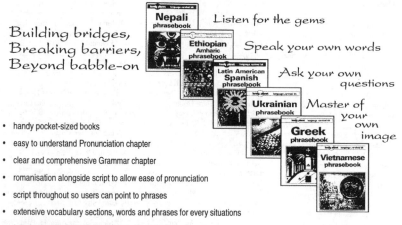

Building bridges,
Breaking barriers,
Beyond babble-on

Listen for the gems

Speak your own words

Ask your own
questions

Master of
your
own
image

- handy pocket-sized books
- easy to understand Pronunciation chapter
- clear and comprehensive Grammar chapter
- romanisation alongside script to allow ease of pronunciation
- script throughout so users can point to phrases
- extensive vocabulary sections, words and phrases for every situations
- full of cultural information and tips for the traveller

'...vital for a real DIY spirit and attitude in language learning' – Backpacker

'the phrasebooks have good cultural backgrounders and offer solid advice for challenging situations in remote locations' – San Francisco Examiner

'...they are unbeatable for their coverage of the world's more obscure languages' – The Geographical Magazine

---

Arabic (Egyptian)
Arabic (Moroccan)
Australia
  Australian English, Aboriginal and Torres Strait languages
Baltic States
  Estonian, Latvian, Lithuanian
Bengali
Burmese
Brazilian
Cantonese
Central Europe
  Czech, French, German, Hungarian, Italian and Slovak
Eastern Europe
  Bulgarian, Czech, Hungarian, Polish, Romanian and Slovak
Egyptian Arabic
Ethiopian (Amharic)
Fijian
French
German
Greek

Hindi/Urdu
Indonesian
Italian
Japanese
Korean
Lao
Latin American Spanish
Malay
Mandarin
Mediterranean Europe
  Albanian, Croatian, Greek, Italian, Macedonian, Maltese, Serbian, Slovene
Mongolian
Moroccan Arabic
Nepali
Papua New Guinea
Pilipino (Tagalog)
Quechua
Russian
Scandinavian Europe
  Danish, Finnish, Icelandic, Norwegian and Swedish

South-East Asia
  Burmese, Indonesian, Khmer, Lao, Malay, Tagalog (Pilipino), Thai and Vietnamese
Spanish
Sri Lanka
Swahili
Thai
Thai Hill Tribes
Tibetan
Turkish
Ukrainian
USA
  US English, Vernacular Talk, Native American languages and Hawaiian
Vietnamese
Western Europe
  Basque, Catalan, Dutch, French, German, Irish, Italian, Portuguese, Scottish Gaelic, Spanish (Castilian) and Welsh

---

LONELY PLANET JOURNEYS

JOURNEYS is a unique collection of travel writing – published by the company that understands travel better than anyone else. It is a series for anyone who has ever experienced – or dreamed of – the magical moment when they encountered a strange culture or saw a place for the first time. They are tales to read while you're planning a trip, while you're on the road or while you're in an armchair, in front of a fire.

JOURNEYS books catch the spirit of a place, illuminate a culture, recount a crazy adventure, or introduce a fascinating way of life. They always entertain, and always enrich the experience of travel.

'Idiosyncratic, entertainingly diverse and unexpected . . . from an international writership'
– The Australian

'Books which offer a closer look at the people and culture of a destination, and enrich travel experiences'
– American Bookseller

FULL CIRCLE
A South American Journey
Luis Sepúlveda
Translated by Chris Andrews

Full Circle invites us to accompany Chilean writer Luis Sepúlveda on 'a journey without a fixed itinerary'. Whatever his subject – brutalities suffered under Pinochet's dictatorship, sleepy tropical towns visited in exile, or the landscapes of legendary Patagonia – Sepúlveda is an unflinchingly honest yet lyrical storyteller. Extravagant characters and extraordinary situations are memorably evoked: gauchos organising a tournament of lies, a scheming heiress on the lookout for a husband, a pilot with a corpse on board his plane . . . Part autobiography, part travel memoir, *Full Circle* brings us the distinctive voice of one of South America's most compelling writers.

Luis Sepúlveda was born in Chile in 1949. Imprisoned by the Pinochet dictatorship for his socialist beliefs, he was for many years a political exile. He has written novels, short stories, plays and essays. His work has attracted many awards and has been translated into numerous languages.

'Detachment, humour and vibrant prose' – El País

'an absolute cracker' – The Bookseller

This project has been assisted by the Commonwealth Government through the Australia Council, its arts funding and advisory body.

LONELY PLANET TRAVEL ATLASES

Lonely Planet has long been famous for the number and quality of its guidebook maps. Now we've gone one step further and in conjunction with Steinhart Katzir Publishers produced a handy companion series: Lonely Planet travel atlases – maps of a country produced in book form.

Unlike other maps, which look good but lead travellers astray, our travel atlases have been researched on the road by Lonely Planet's experienced team of writers. All details are carefully checked to ensure the atlas corresponds with the equivalent Lonely Planet guidebook.

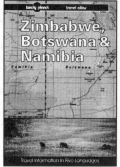

The handy atlas format means no holes, wrinkles, torn sections or constant folding and unfolding. These atlases can survive long periods on the road, unlike cumbersome fold-out maps. The comprehensive index ensures easy reference.

- full-colour throughout
- maps researched and checked by Lonely Planet authors
- place names correspond with Lonely Planet guidebooks
  – no confusing spelling differences
- legend and travelling information in English, French, German, Japanese and Spanish
- size: 230 x 160 mm

Available now:
Chile & Easter Island • Egypt • India & Bangladesh • Israel & the Palestinian Territories •Jordan, Syria & Lebanon • Kenya • Laos • Portugal • South Africa, Lesotho & Swaziland • Thailand • Turkey • Vietnam • Zimbabwe, Botswana & Namibia

---

LONELY PLANET TV SERIES & VIDEOS

Lonely Planet travel guides have been brought to life on television screens around the world. Like our guides, the programmes are based on the joy of independent travel, and look honestly at some of the most exciting, picturesque and frustrating places in the world. Each show is presented by one of three travellers from Australia, England or the USA and combines an innovative mixture of video, Super-8 film, atmospheric soundscapes and original music.

Videos of each episode – containing additional footage not shown on television – are available from good book and video shops, but the availability of individual videos varies with regional screening schedules.

Video destinations include: Alaska • American Rockies • Australia – The South-East • Baja California & the Copper Canyon • Brazil • Central Asia • Chile & Easter Island • Corsica, Sicily & Sardinia – The Mediterranean Islands • East Africa (Tanzania & Zanzibar) • Ecuador & the Galapagos Islands • Greenland & Iceland • Indonesia • Israel & the Sinai Desert • Jamaica • Japan • La Ruta Maya • Morocco • New York • North India • Pacific Islands (Fiji, Solomon Islands & Vanuatu) • South India • South West China • Turkey • Vietnam • West Africa • Zimbabwe, Botswana & Namibia

The Lonely Planet TV series is produced by:
Pilot Productions
The Old Studio
18 Middle Row
London W10 5AT UK

For video availability and ordering information contact your nearest Lonely Planet office.

Music from the TV series is available on CD & cassette.

PLANET TALK

Lonely Planet's FREE quarterly newsletter

We love hearing from you and think you'd like to hear from us.

When...is the right time to see reindeer in Finland?
Where...can you hear the best palm-wine music in Ghana?
How...do you get from Asunción to Areguá by steam train?
What...is the best way to see India?

For the answer to these and many other questions read PLANET TALK.

Every issue is packed with up-to-date travel news and advice including:

- a letter from Lonely Planet co-founders Tony and Maureen Wheeler
- go behind the scenes on the road with a Lonely Planet author
- feature article on an important and topical travel issue
- a selection of recent letters from travellers
- details on forthcoming Lonely Planet promotions
- complete list of Lonely Planet products

To join our mailing list contact any Lonely Planet office.

Also available: Lonely Planet T-shirts. 100% heavyweight cotton.

LONELY PLANET ONLINE

Get the latest travel information before you leave or while you're on the road

Whether you've just begun planning your next trip, or you're chasing down specific info on currency regulations or visa requirements, check out Lonely Planet Online for up-to-the minute travel information.

As well as travel profiles of your favourite destinations (including maps and photos), you'll find current reports from our researchers and other travellers, updates on health and visas, travel advisories, and discussion of the ecological and political issues you need to be aware of as you travel.

There's also an online travellers' forum where you can share your experience of life on the road, meet travel companions and ask other travellers for their recommendations and advice. We also have plenty of links to other online sites useful to independent travellers.

And of course we have a complete and up-to-date list of all Lonely Planet travel products including guides, phrasebooks, atlases, Journeys and videos and a simple online ordering facility if you can't find the book you want elsewhere.

**www.lonelyplanet.com
or
AOL keyword: lp**

LONELY PLANET PRODUCTS

Lonely Planet is known worldwide for publishing practical, reliable and no-nonsense trave information in our guides and on our web site. The Lonely Planet list covers just about ever accessible part of the world. Currently there are eight series: *travel guides, shoestring guides walking guides, city guides, phrasebooks, audio packs, travel atlases* and *Journeys* – a uniqu collection of travel writing.

EUROPE

Amsterdam • Austria • Baltic States phrasebook • Britain • Central Europe on a shoestring • Central Europe phrasebook Czech & Slovak Republics • Denmark • Dublin • Eastern Europe on a shoestring • Eastern Europe phrasebook • Estonia Latvia & Lithuania • Finland • France • French phrasebook • German phrasebook • Greece • Greek phrasebook • Hungar • Iceland, Greenland & the Faroe Islands • Ireland • Italian phrasebook • Italy • Mediterranean Europe on a shoestring Mediterranean Europe phrasebook • Paris • Poland • Portugal • Portugal travel atlas • Prague • Russia, Ukraine & Belaru • Russian phrasebook • Scandinavian & Baltic Europe on a shoestring • Scandinavian Europe phrasebook • Slovenia Spain • Spanish phrasebook • St Petersburg • Switzerland • Trekking in Greece • Trekking in Spain • Ukrainian phraseboo • Vienna • Walking in Britain • Walking in Switzerland • Western Europe on a shoestring • Western Europe phrasebook

Travel Literature: The Olive Grove: Travels in Greece

NORTH AMERICA

Alaska • Backpacking in Alaska • Baja California • California & Nevada • Canada • Florida • Hawaii • Honolulu • Los Angeles • Mexico • Miami • New England • New Orleans • New York City • New York, New Jersey & Pennsylvania • Pacific Northwest USA • Rocky Mountain States • San Francisco • Southwest USA • USA phrasebook • Washington, DC & the Capital Region

CENTRAL AMERICA & THE CARIBBEAN

Bermuda • Central America on a shoestring • Costa Rica • Cuba • Eastern Caribbean • Guatemala, Belize & Yucatán: La Ruta Maya • Jamaica

SOUTH AMERICA

Argentina, Uruguay & Paraguay • Bolivia • Brazil • Brazilian phrasebook • Buenos Aires • Chile & Easter Island • Chile & Easter Island travel atlas • Colombia • Ecuador & the Galápagos Islands • Latin American Spanish phrasebook • Peru • Quechua phrasebook • Rio de Janeiro • South America on a shoestring • Trekking in the Patagonian Andes • Venezuela

Travel Literature: Full Circle: A South American Journey

ANTARCTICA

Antarctica

ISLANDS OF THE INDIAN OCEAN

Madagascar & Comoros • Maldives• Mauritius, Réunion & Seychelles

AFRICA

Africa - the South • Africa on a shoestring • Arabic (Moroc can) phrasebook • Cape Town • Central Africa • Eas Africa • Egypt • Egypt travel atlas• Ethiopian (Amharic phrasebook • Kenya • Kenya travel atlas • Malawi Mozambique & Zambia • Morocco • North Africa • South Africa, Lesotho & Swaziland • South Africa, Lesotho & Swaziland travel atlas • Swahili phrasebook • Trekking in East Africa • West Africa • Zimbabwe, Botswana & Namibia • Zimbabwe, Botswana & Namibia travel atlas

Travel Literature: The Rainbird: A Central African Jour ney • Songs to an African Sunset: A Zimbabwean Story

MAIL ORDER

Lonely Planet products are distributed worldwide. They are also available by mail order from Lonely Planet, so if you have difficulty finding a title please write to us. North American and South American residents should write to Embarcadero West, 155 Filbert St, Suite 251, Oakland CA 94607, USA; European and African residents should write to 10 Barley Mow Passage, Chiswick, London W4 4PH; and residents of other countries to PO Box 617, Hawthorn, Victoria 3122, Australia.

NORTH-EAST ASIA

Beijing • Cantonese phrasebook • China • Hong Kong • Hong Kong, Macau & Guangzhou • Japan • Japanese phrasebook • Japanese audio pack • Korea • Korean phrasebook • Mandarin phrasebook • Mongolia • Mongolian phrasebook • North-East Asia on a shoestring • Seoul • Taiwan • Tibet • Tibet phrasebook • Tokyo

Travel Literature: Lost Japan

MIDDLE EAST & CENTRAL ASIA

Arab Gulf States • Arabic (Egyptian) phrasebook • Central Asia • Iran • Israel & the Palestinian Territories • Israel & the Palestinian Territories travel atlas • Istanbul • Jerusalem • Jordan & Syria • Jordan, Syria & Lebanon travel atlas • Middle East • Turkey • Turkish phrasebook • Turkey travel atlas • Yemen

Travel Literature: The Gates of Damascus • Kingdom of the Film Stars: Journey into Jordan

ALSO AVAILABLE:

Travel with Children • Traveller's Tales

INDIAN SUBCONTINENT

Bangladesh • Bengali phrasebook • Delhi • Hindi/Urdu phrasebook • India • India & Bangladesh travel atlas • Indian Himalaya • Karakoram Highway • Nepal • Nepali phrasebook • Pakistan • Rajasthan • Sri Lanka • Sri Lanka phrasebook • Trekking in the Indian Himalaya • Trekking in the Karakoram & Hindukush • Trekking in the Nepal Himalaya

Travel Literature: In Rajasthan • Shopping for Buddhas

SOUTH-EAST ASIA

Bali & Lombok • Bangkok • Burmese phrasebook • Cambodia • Ho Chi Minh City • Indonesia • Indonesian phrasebook • Indonesian audio pack • Jakarta • Java • Laos • Lao phrasebook • Laos travel atlas • Malay phrasebook • Malaysia, Singapore & Brunei • Myanmar (Burma) • Philippines • Pilipino phrasebook • Singapore • South-East Asia on a shoestring • South-East Asia phrasebook • Thailand • Thailand travel atlas • Thai phrasebook • Thai audio pack • Thai Hill Tribes phrasebook • Vietnam • Vietnamese phrasebook • Vietnam travel atlas

AUSTRALIA & THE PACIFIC

Australia • Australian phrasebook • Bushwalking in Australia • Bushwalking in Papua New Guinea • Fiji • Fijian phrasebook • Islands of Australia's Great Barrier Reef • Melbourne • Micronesia • New Caledonia • New South Wales & the ACT • New Zealand • Northern Territory • Outback Australia • Papua New Guinea • Papua New Guinea phrasebook • Queensland • Rarotonga & the Cook Islands • Samoa • Solomon Islands • South Australia • Sydney • Tahiti & French Polynesia • Tasmania • Tonga • Tramping in New Zealand • Vanuatu • Victoria • Western Australia

Travel Literature: Islands in the Clouds • Sean & David's Long Drive

THE LONELY PLANET STORY

Lonely Planet published its first book in 1973 in response to the numerous 'How did you do it?' questions Maureen and Tony Wheeler were asked after driving, bussing, hitching, sailing and railing their way from England to Australia.

Written at a kitchen table and hand collated, trimmed and stapled, *Across Asia on the Cheap* became an instant local bestseller, inspiring thoughts of another book.

Eighteen months in South-East Asia resulted in their second guide, *South-East Asia on a shoestring*, which they put together in a backstreet Chinese hotel in Singapore in 1975. The 'yellow bible', as it quickly became known to backpackers around the world, soon became *the* guide to the region. It has sold well over half a million copies and is now in its 9th edition, still retaining its familiar yellow cover.

Today there are over 240 titles, including travel guides, walking guides, language kits & phrasebooks, travel atlases and travel literature. The company is the largest independent travel publisher in the world. Although Lonely Planet initially specialised in guides to Asia, today there are few corners of the globe that have not been covered.

The emphasis continues to be on travel for independent travellers. Tony and Maureen still travel for several months of each year and play an active part in the writing, updating and quality control of Lonely Planet's guides.

They have been joined by over 70 authors and 170 staff at our offices in Melbourne (Australia), Oakland (USA), London (UK) and Paris (France). Travellers themselves also make a valuable contribution to the guides through the feedback we receive in thousands of letters each year and on our web site.

The people at Lonely Planet strongly believe that travellers can make a positive contribution to the countries they visit, both through their appreciation of the countries' culture, wildlife and natural features, and through the money they spend. In addition, the company makes a direct contribution to the countries and regions it covers. Since 1986 a percentage of the income from each book has been donated to ventures such as famine relief in Africa; aid projects in India; agricultural projects in Central America; Greenpeace's efforts to halt French nuclear testing in the Pacific; and Amnesty International.

'I hope we send people out with the right attitude about travel. You realise when you travel that there are so many different perspectives about the world, so we hope these books will make people more interested in what they see. Guidebooks can't really guide people. All you can do is point them in the right direction.'

– Tony Wheeler

LONELY PLANET PUBLICATIONS

Australia
PO Box 617, Hawthorn 3122, Victoria
tel: (03) 9819 1877 fax: (03) 9819 6459
e-mail: talk2us@lonelyplanet.com.au

USA
Embarcadero West, 155 Filbert St, Suite 251,
Oakland, CA 94607
tel: (510) 893 8555 TOLL FREE: 800 275-8555
fax: (510) 893 8563
e-mail: info@lonelyplanet.com

UK
10 Barley Mow Passage, Chiswick,
London W4 4PH
tel: (0181) 742 3161 fax: (0181) 742 2772
e-mail: lonelyplanetuk@compuserve.com

France:
71 bis rue du Cardinal Lemoine, 75005 Paris
tel: 1 44 32 06 20 fax: 1 46 34 72 55
e-mail: 100560.415@compuserve.com

World Wide Web: http://www.lonelyplanet.com
or *AOL keyword: lp*